DAVID RUBÍN'S

THE HERO

TRANSLATED BY
KATIE LaBARBERA

LETTERED BY
MICHAEL
HEISLER

BOOK TWO
(OF TWO)

ORIGINAL BOOK
DESIGN AND
LETTERING FONT
DAVID RUBÍN

SPECIAL THANKS TO LAUREANO DOMÍNGUEZ OF ASTIBERRI EDICIONES.

BOOK DESIGNER, ENGLISH-LANGUAGE EDITION
JIMMY PRESLER

DIGITAL ART TECHNICIAN, ENGLISH-LANGUAGE EDITION
CHRISTINA McKENZIE

NEIL HANKERSON EXECUTIVE VICE PRESIDENT / TOM WEDDLE CHIEF FINANCIAL OFFICER / RANDY STRADLEY VICE PRESIDENT OF PUBLISHING / MICHAEL MARTENS VICE PRESIDENT OF BOOK TRADE SALES / SCOTT ALLIE EDITOR IN CHIEF / MATT PARKINSON VICE PRESIDENT OF MARKETING / DAVID SCROGGY VICE PRESIDENT OF PRODUCT DEVELOPMENT / DALE LaFOUNTAIN VICE PRESIDENT OF INFORMATION TECHNOLOGY / DARLENE VOGEL SENIOR DIRECTOR OF PRINT, DESIGN, AND PRODUCTION / KEN LIZZI GENERAL COUNSEL / DAVEY ESTRADA EDITORIAL DIRECTOR / CHRIS WARNER SENIOR BOOKS EDITOR / DIANA SCHUTZ EXECUTIVE EDITOR / CARY GRAZZINI DIRECTOR OF PRINT AND DEVELOPMENT / LIA RIBACCHI ART DIRECTOR / CARA NIECE DIRECTOR OF SCHEDULING / MARK BERNARDI DIRECTOR OF DIGITAL PUBLISHING

PUBLISHED BY DARK HORSE BOOKS / A DIVISION OF DARK HORSE COMICS, INC.
10956 SE MAIN STREET / MILWAUKIE, OR 97222

FIRST EDITION: DECEMBER 2015
ISBN 978-1-61655-791-1

10 9 8 7 6 5 4 3 2 1

PRINTED IN CHINA

INTERNATIONAL LICENSING: (503) 905-2377 / COMIC SHOP LOCATOR SERVICE: (888) 266-4226

THIS VOLUME REPRINTS EL HÉROE LIBRO DOS, ORIGINALLY PUBLISHED IN SPANISH BY ASTIBERRI EDICIONES.

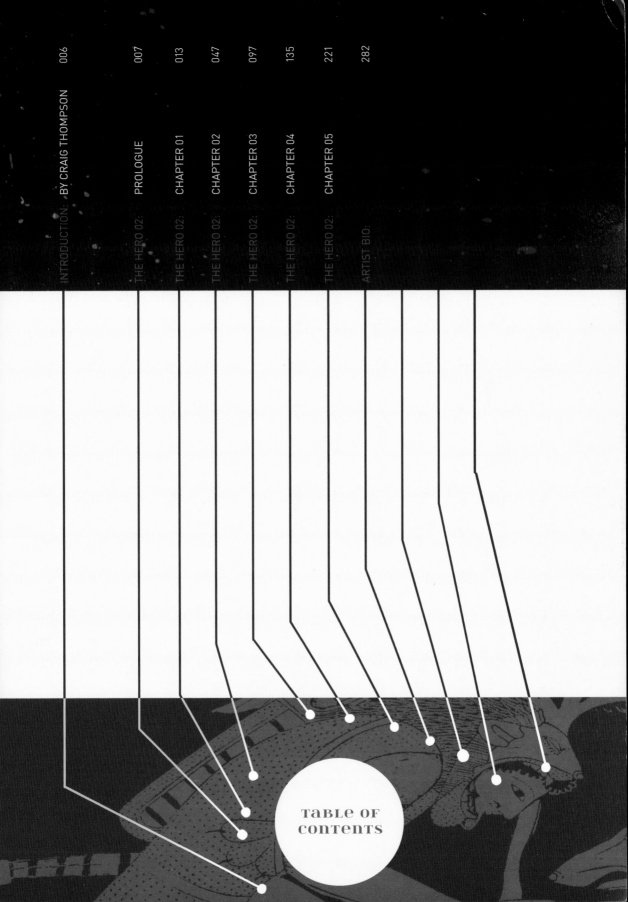

table of contents

David Rubín is my new favorite cartoonist in the Milky Way.

As Heracles was the bastard son of Zeus, comics are the bastard fusion of word and picture. And from such illegitimacy, a hero is forged.

Rubín repackages Greek mythology, churning in influences from modern design, animation, and superheroes. But he sheds all the insular, nerdy elements of superheroes that once stunted the comics medium to reveal superheroes at their most raw and primal. The aging sixty-year-old Heracles, surrounded by video monitors, self-consciously echoes Miller's Dark Knight. And how wildly appropriate that this epic opens with Heracles rising from a heap of slain Supermen.

Like Paul Pope and Rafael Grampá, Rubín infuses his comics with pure rock-and-roll virility. These pages—rather than claustrophobic, confining, and static—feel vast, expanding, and kinetic. They pulsate and glow.

While I'm name-dropping cartoonists, I'll mention that Rubín's work also shares elements with the skateboarding and graffiti culture of Brandon Graham, the edgy design of underground master Max, and the striking power of Picasso's Guernica.

Rubín brings new breath to the medium of comics, but also to these ancient Greek myths. Within his brush lines, the classic cast of Hera, Megara, Iolae, Eurystheus, and Hades are given new voices—noisy and dangerous and sexy and immediate and relevant.

These comics are a form of art restoration through playful demolition. Rubín's compositions start with the graphic precision of classic Greek vase paintings, then take that precious pottery and shatter it into pieces. The shards are dynamic comics panels, disjecta membra, Persian debris . . .

The Persian poet Rumi instructs his reader to keep breaking their heart until it opens. By shattering the container, David Rubín carves through scales and sloughs off the dust to unveil the visceral heart of the story.

Craig Thompson

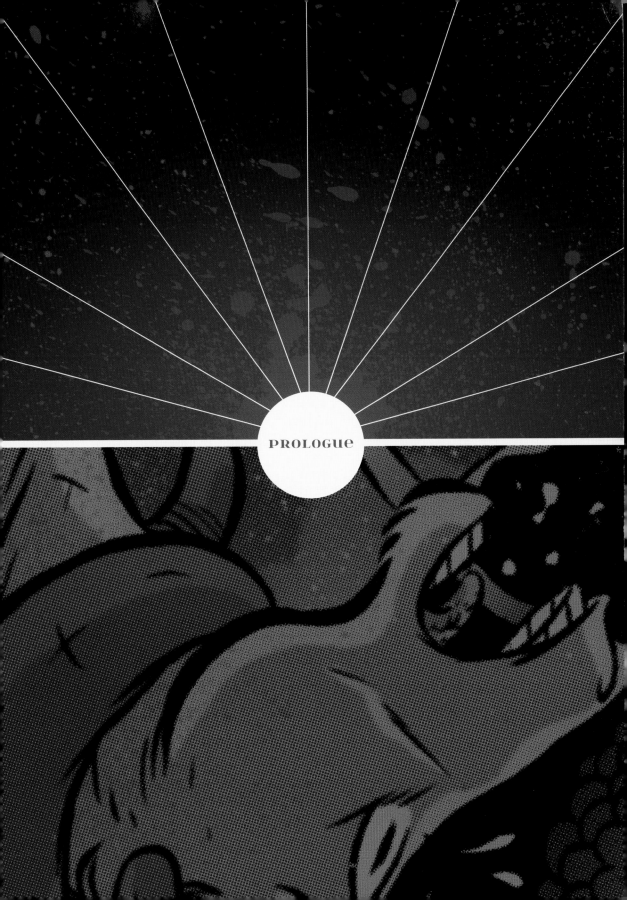

PROLOGUE

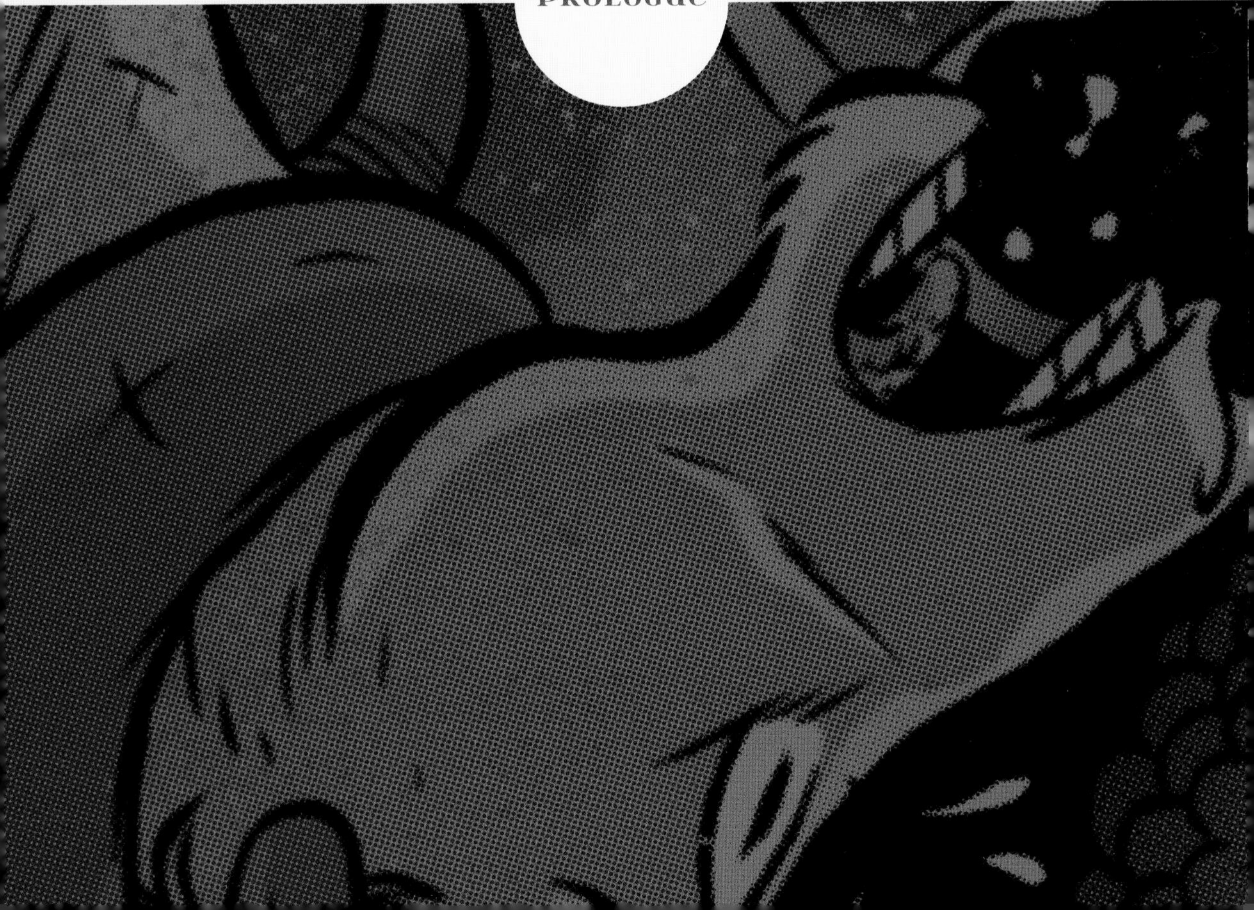

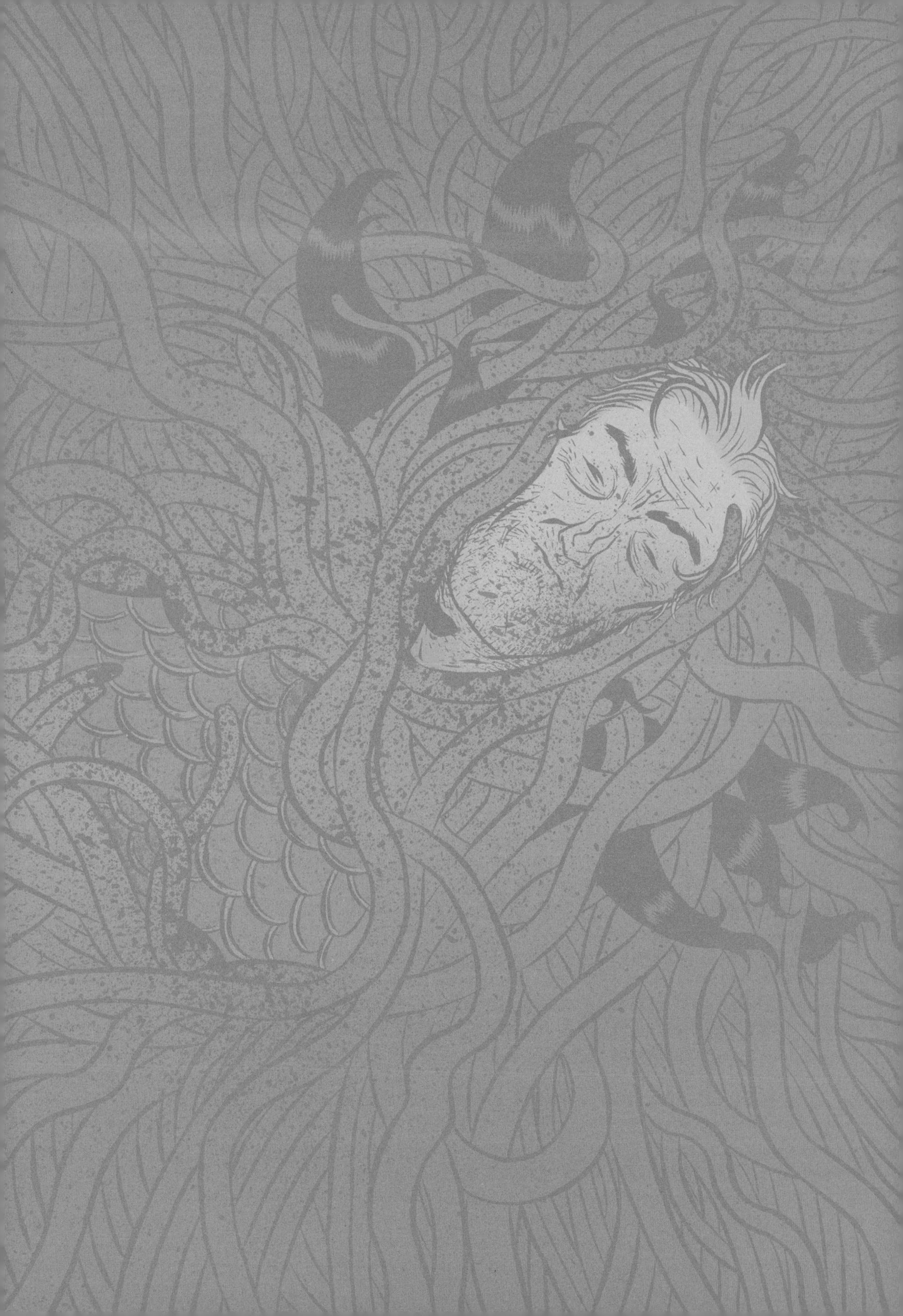

THE HERO™

BOOK TWO

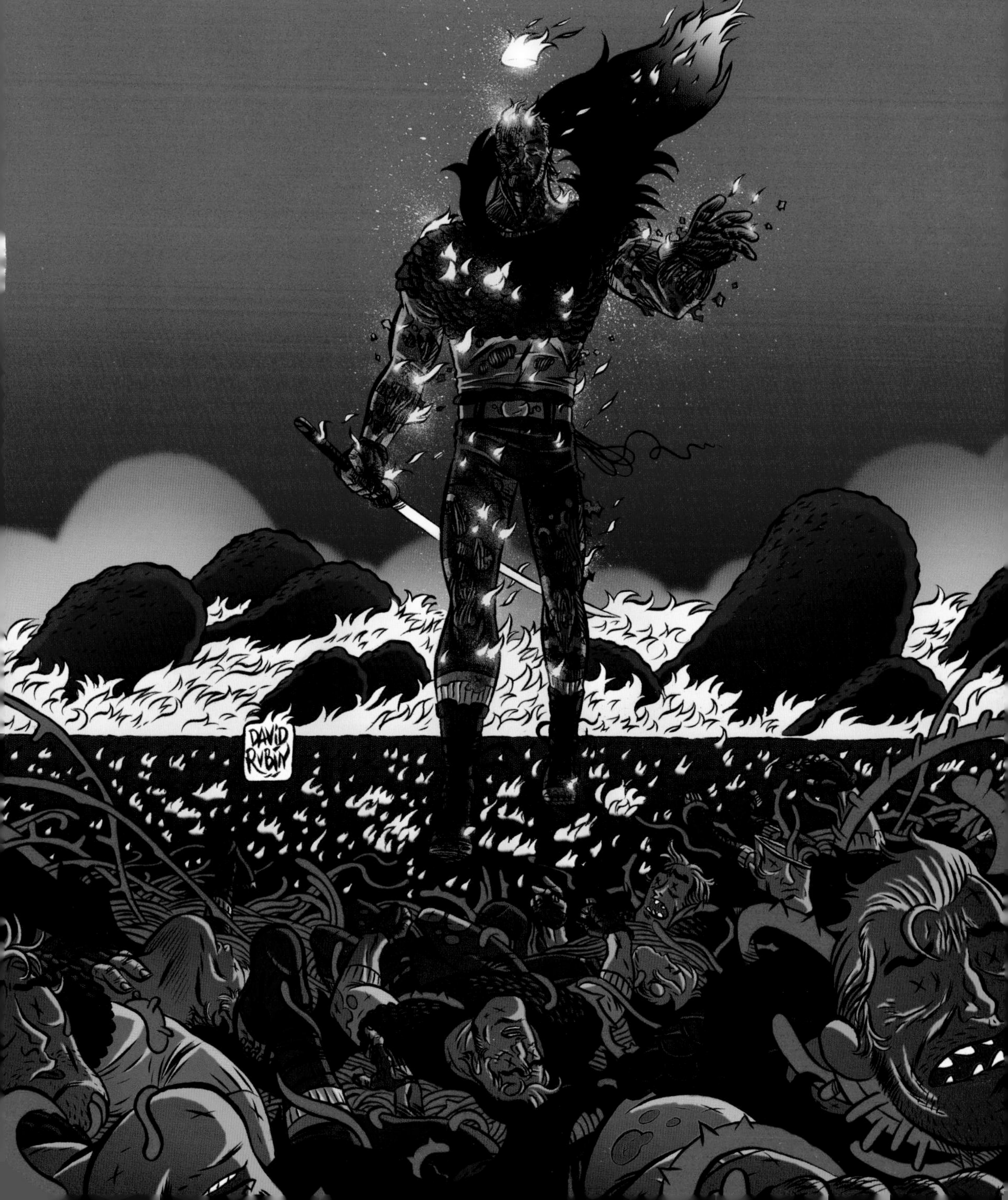
DAVID RUBIN

DARK HORSE
BOOKS
MILWAUKIE, OREGON

FIRST
PUBLISHED BY
ASTIBERRI
EDICIONES

PRESIDENT
& PUBLISHER
MIKE
RICHARDSON

EDITOR, ENGLISH-
LANGUAGE EDITION
SIERRA HAHN

ASSISTANT
EDITOR, ENGLISH-
LANGUAGE EDITION
SPENCER
CUSHING

THE STORY CONTINUES.

GOES ON.

THE SHADOW GAINS GROUND.

THE CARNIVAL OF HORROR BEGINS.

AND THE WORST PART IS...

...THERE'S NO ESCAPE.

TERROR REIGNS.

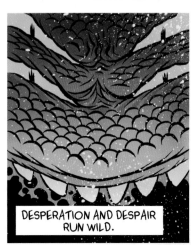

DESPERATION AND DESPAIR RUN WILD.

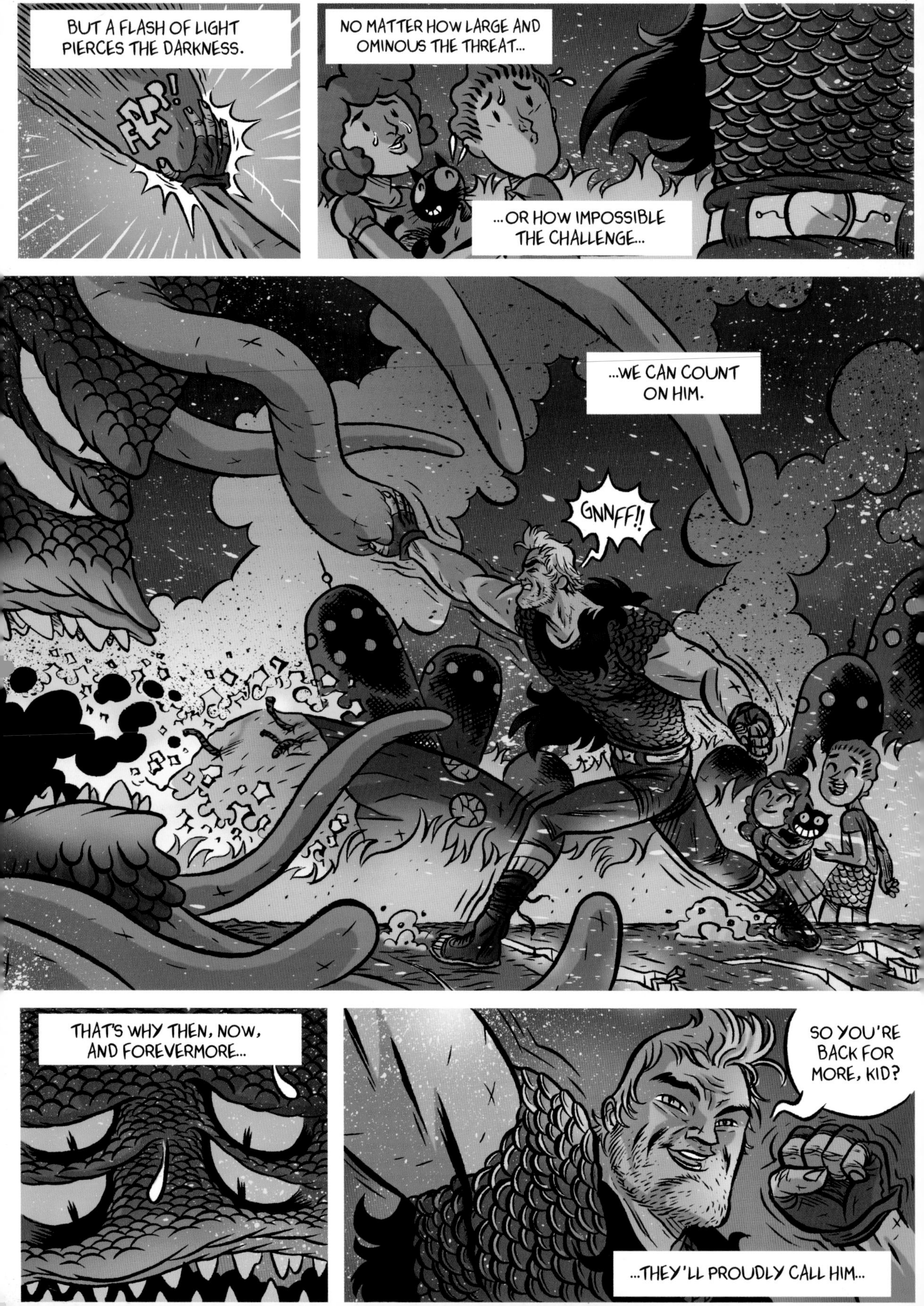
BUT A FLASH OF LIGHT PIERCES THE DARKNESS.
FPP!
NO MATTER HOW LARGE AND OMINOUS THE THREAT...
...OR HOW IMPOSSIBLE THE CHALLENGE...
...WE CAN COUNT ON HIM.
GNNFF!!
THAT'S WHY THEN, NOW, AND FOREVERMORE...
SO YOU'RE BACK FOR MORE, KID?
...THEY'LL PROUDLY CALL HIM...

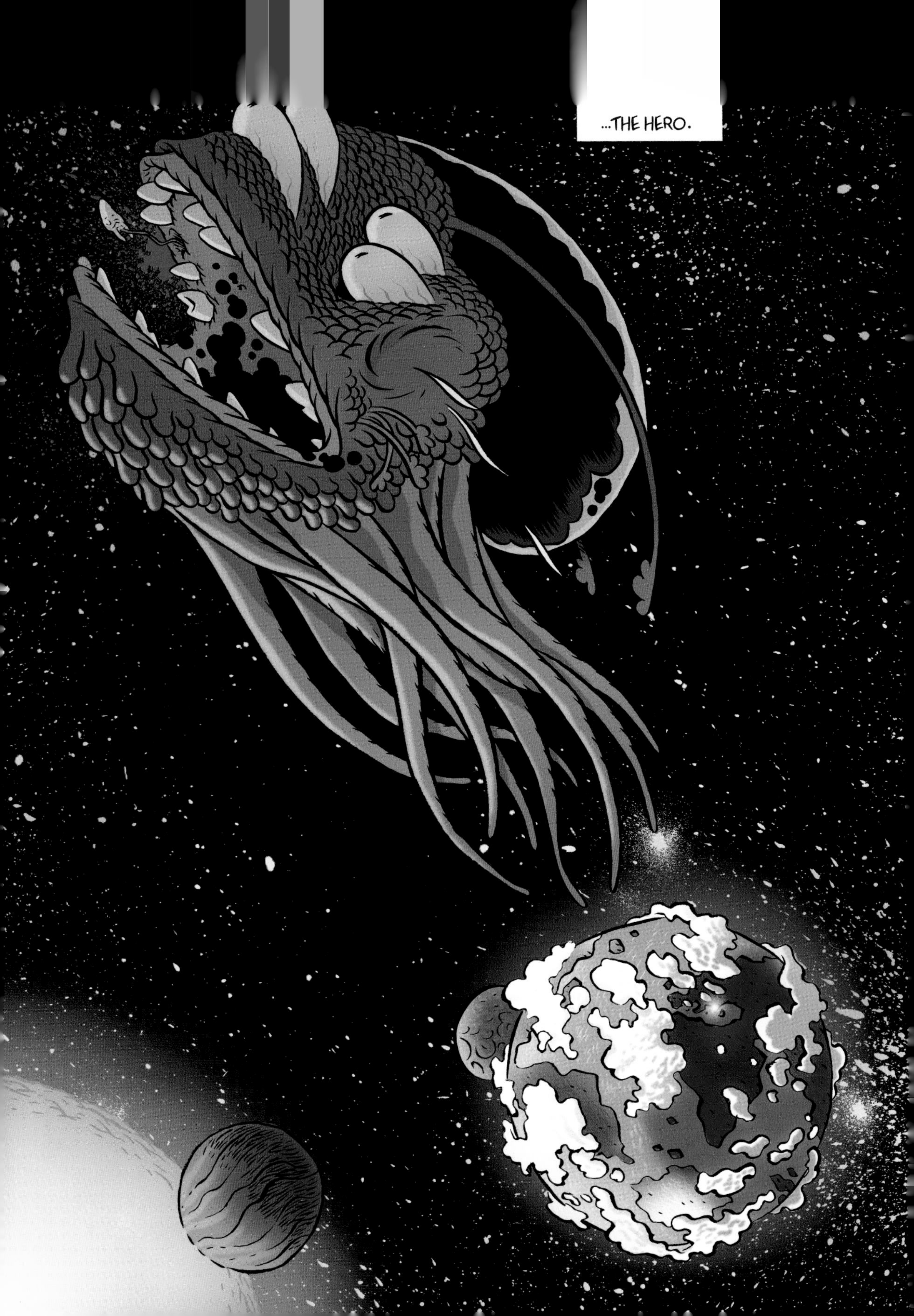
...THE HERO.

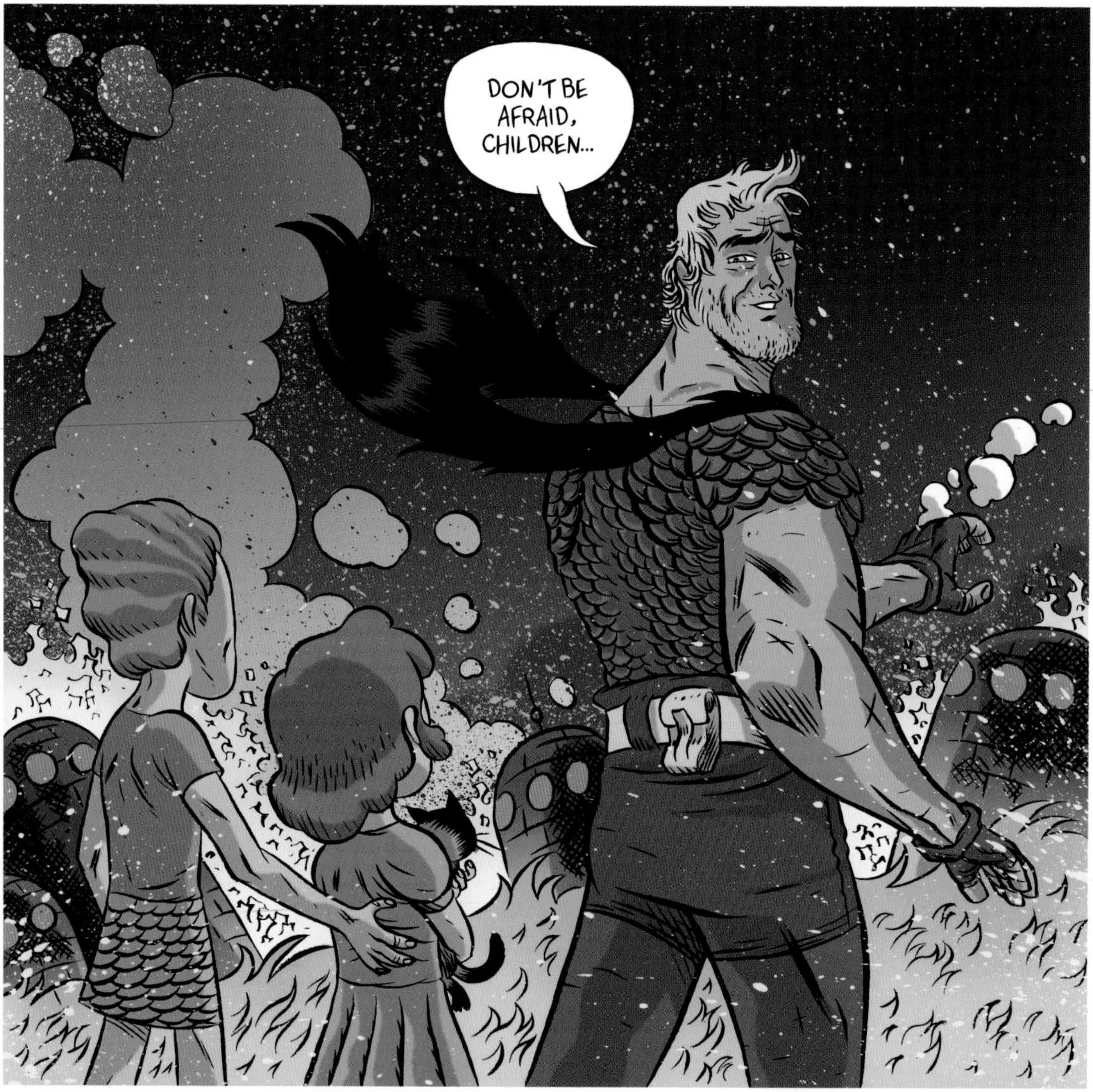
DON'T BE AFRAID, CHILDREN...

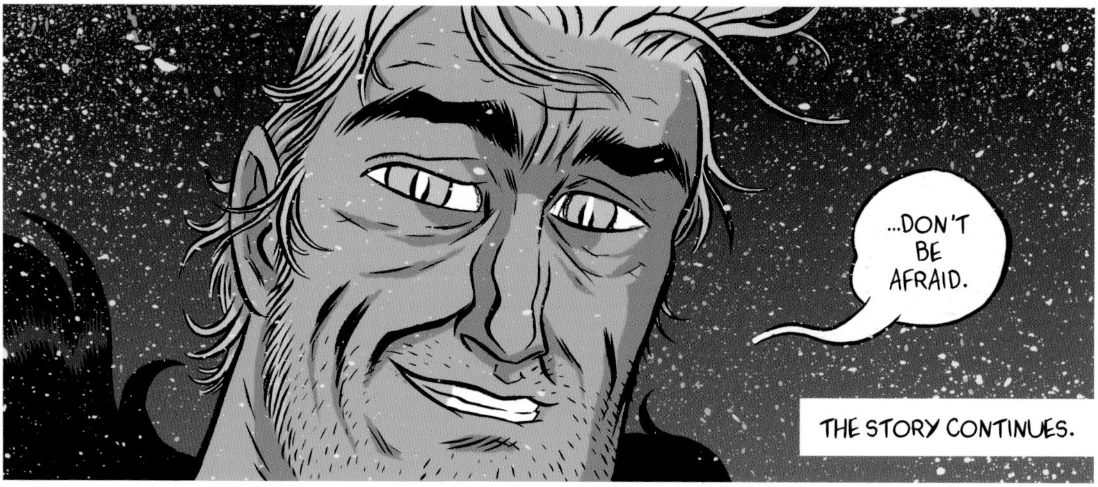
...DON'T BE AFRAID.
THE STORY CONTINUES.

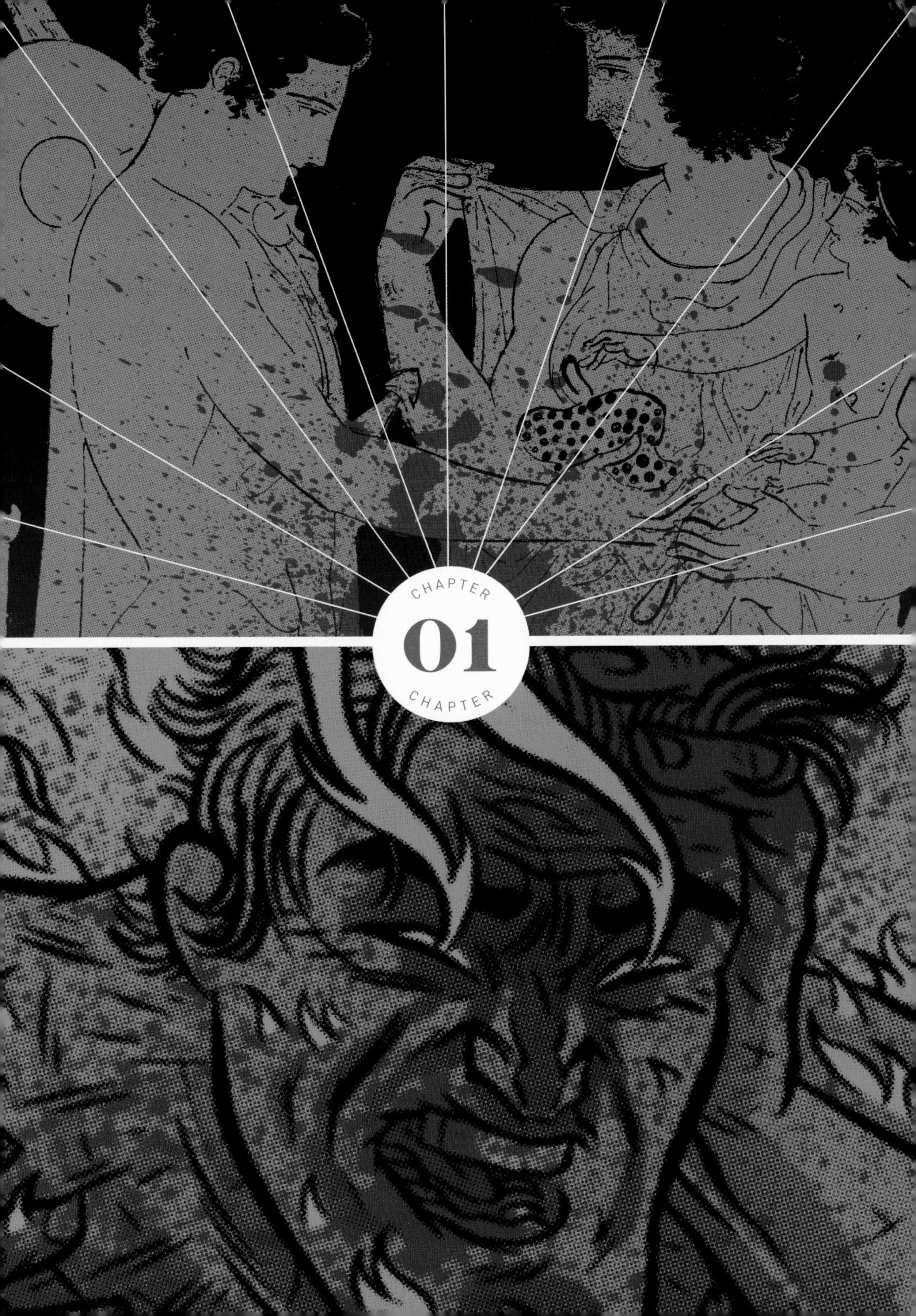
CHAPTER
01
CHAPTER

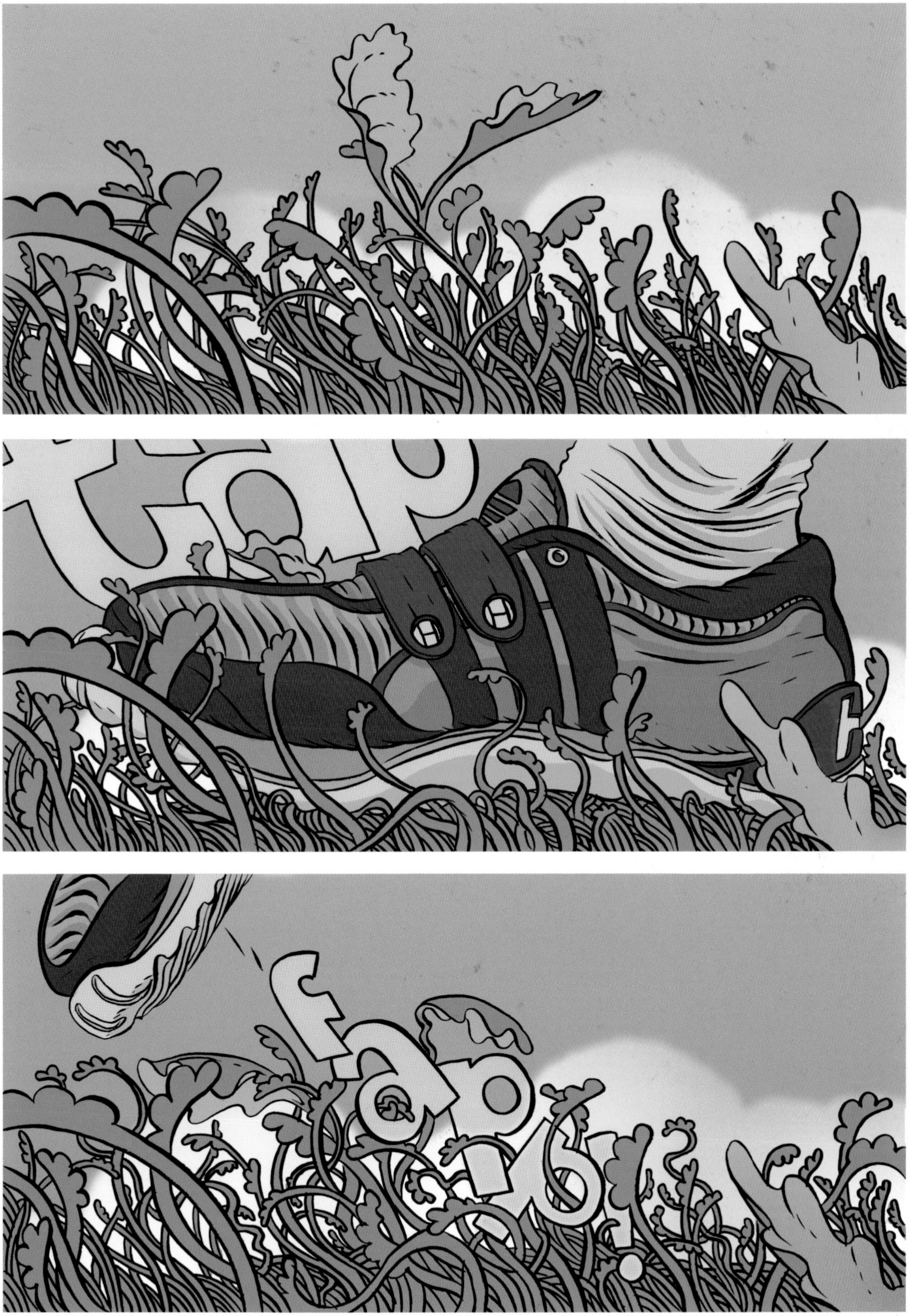
tap

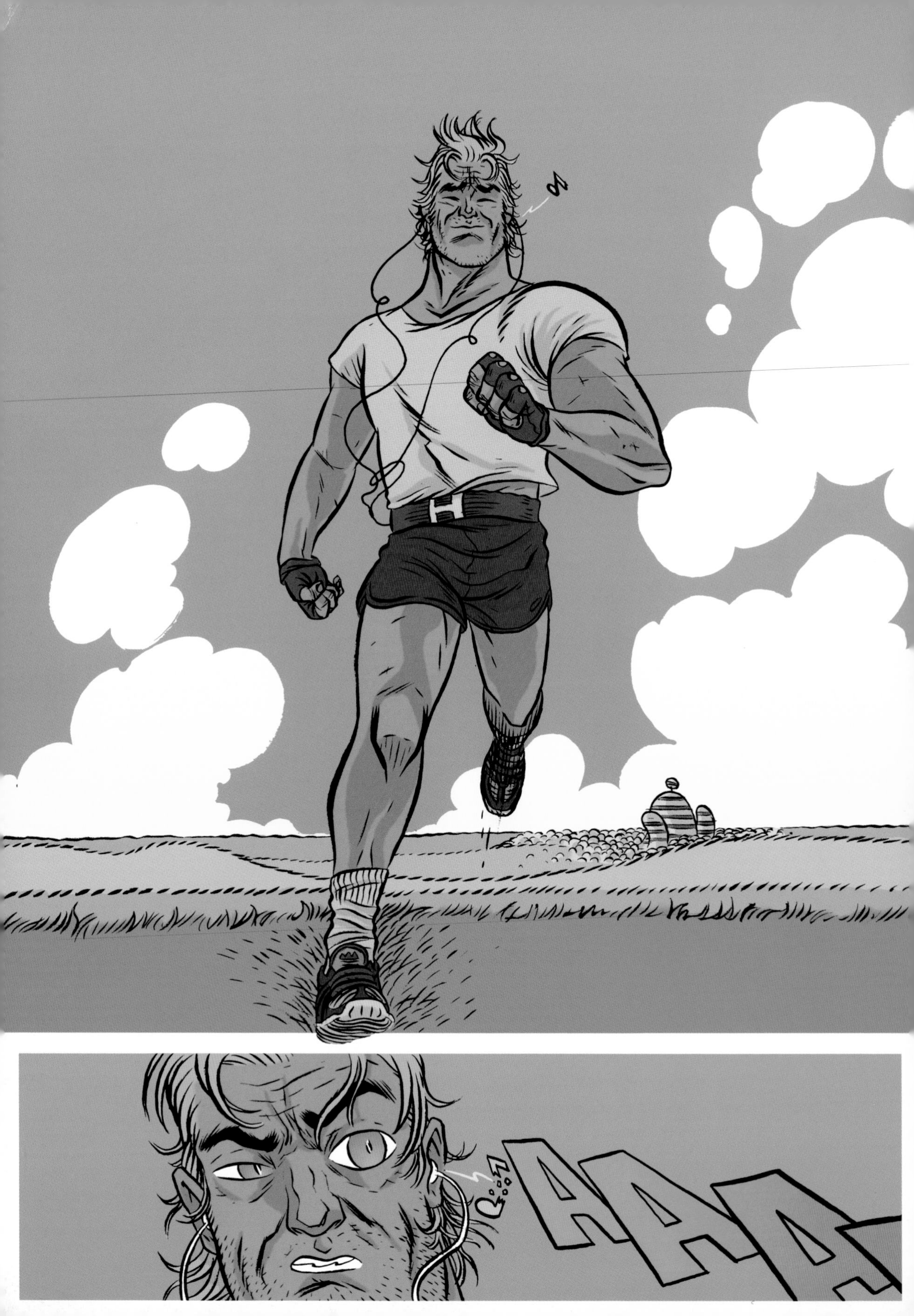
AAAA

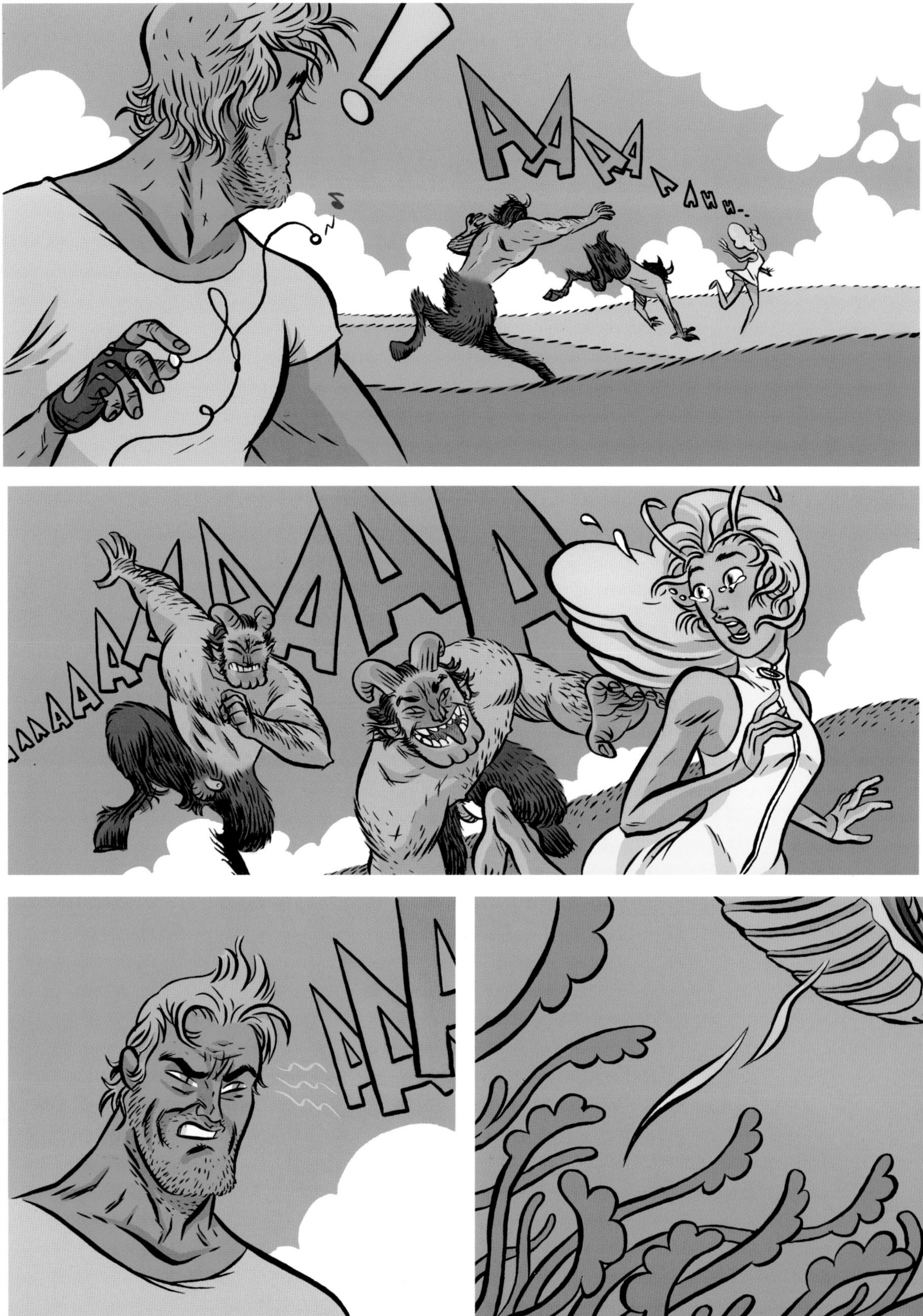
!
AAAAAAAHH..
AAAAAAAAAAAAA
AAAA

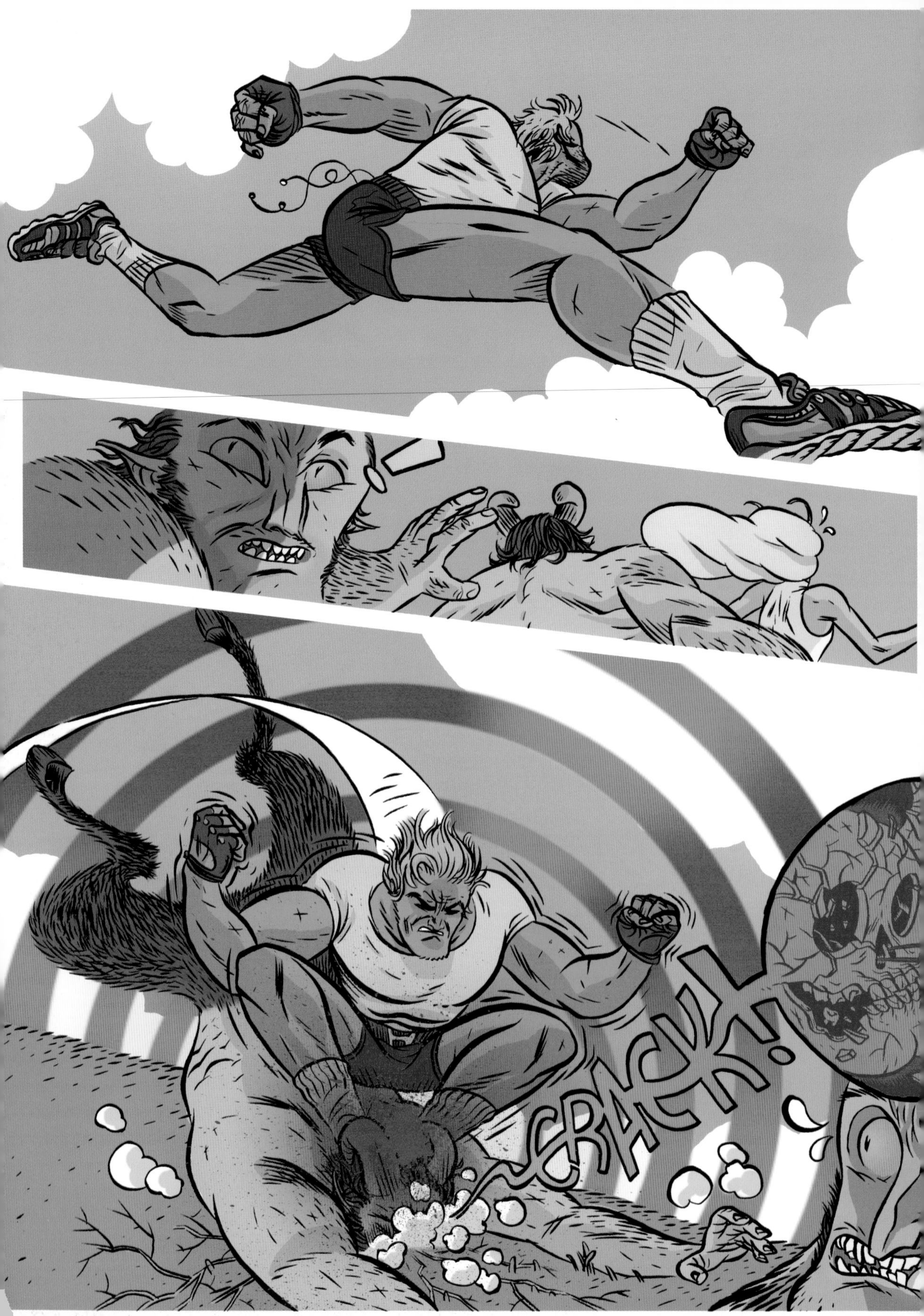
CRACK!

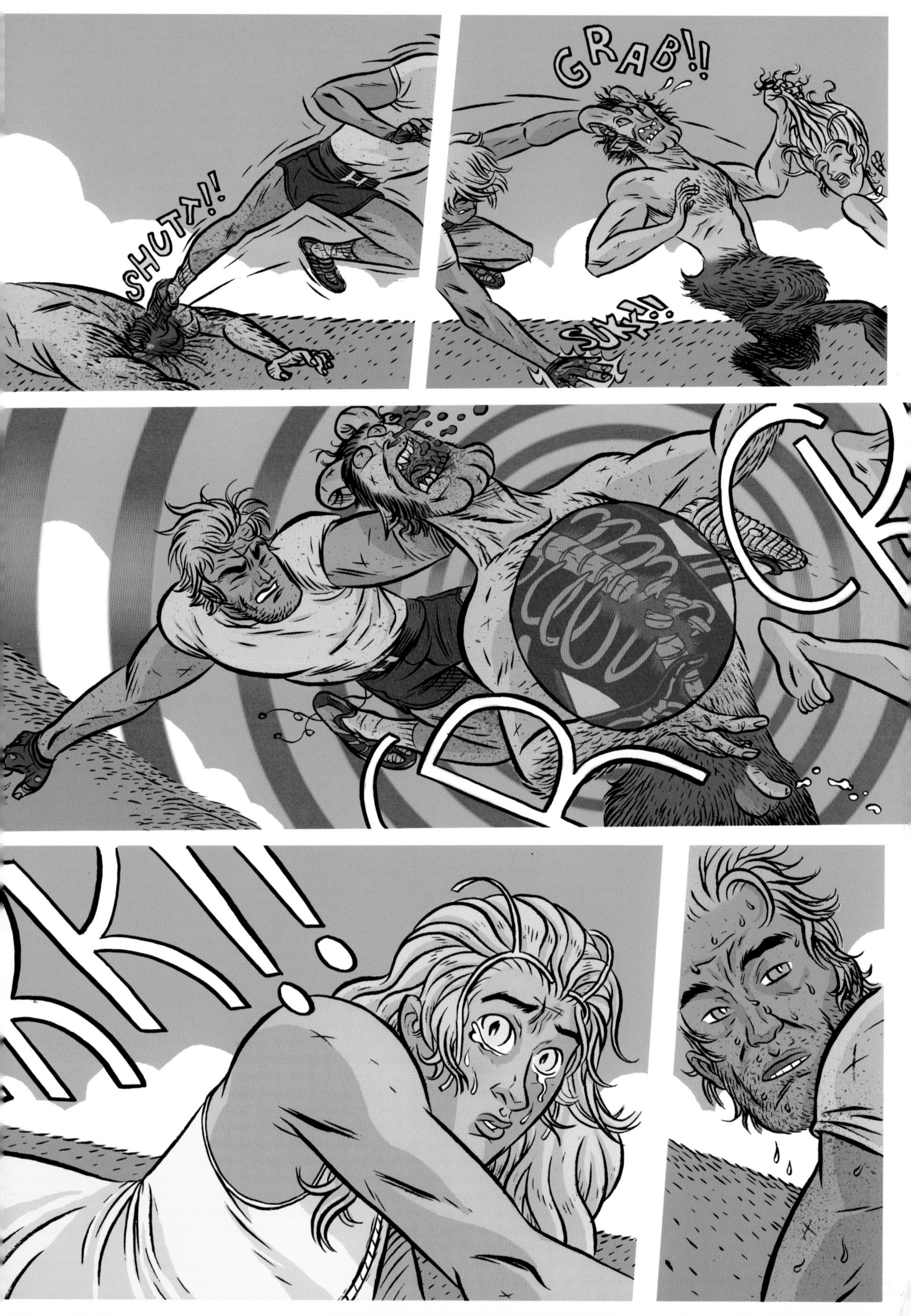
SHUTT!!
GRAB!!
SUKK!!
K!!

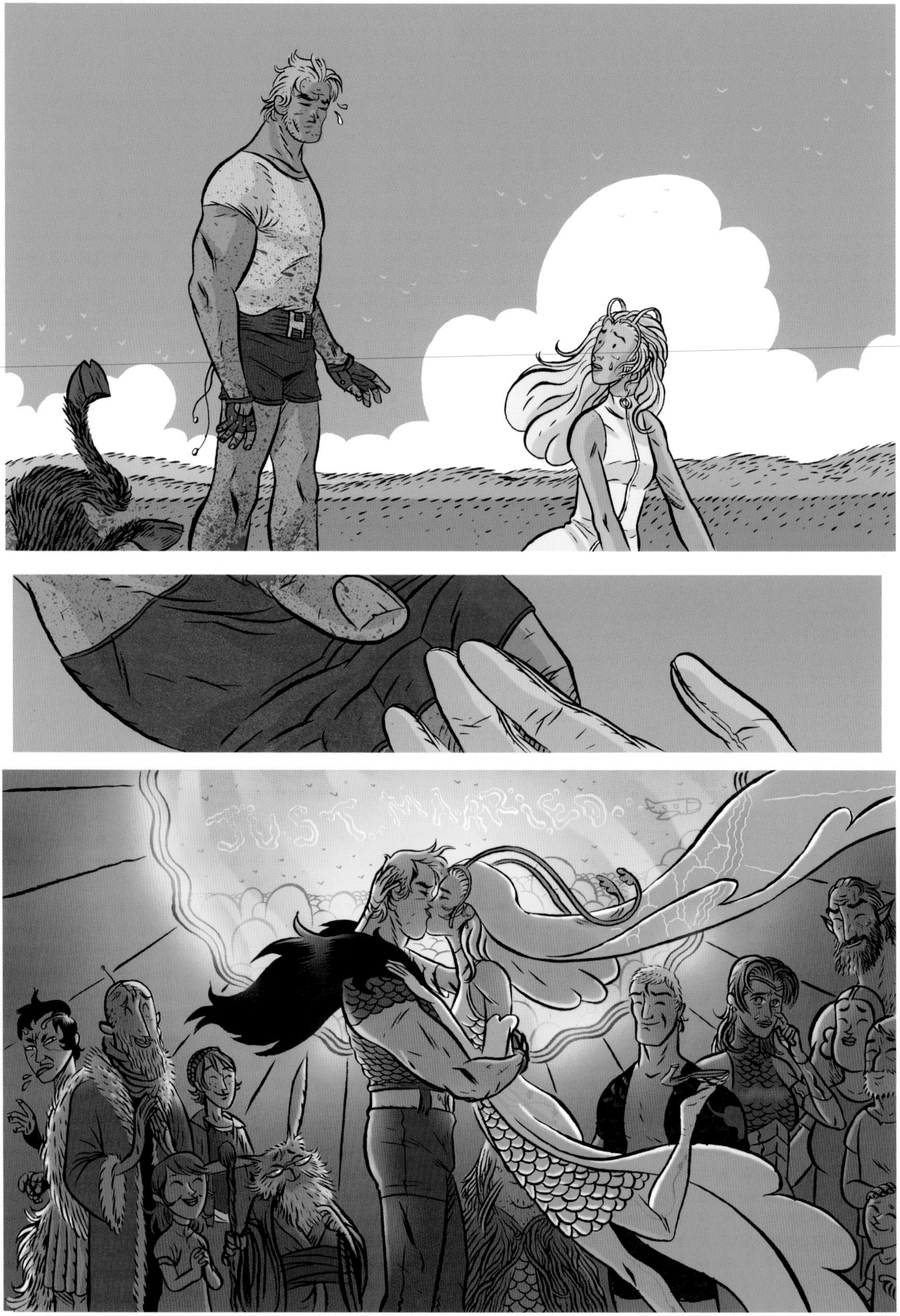
JUST MARRIED

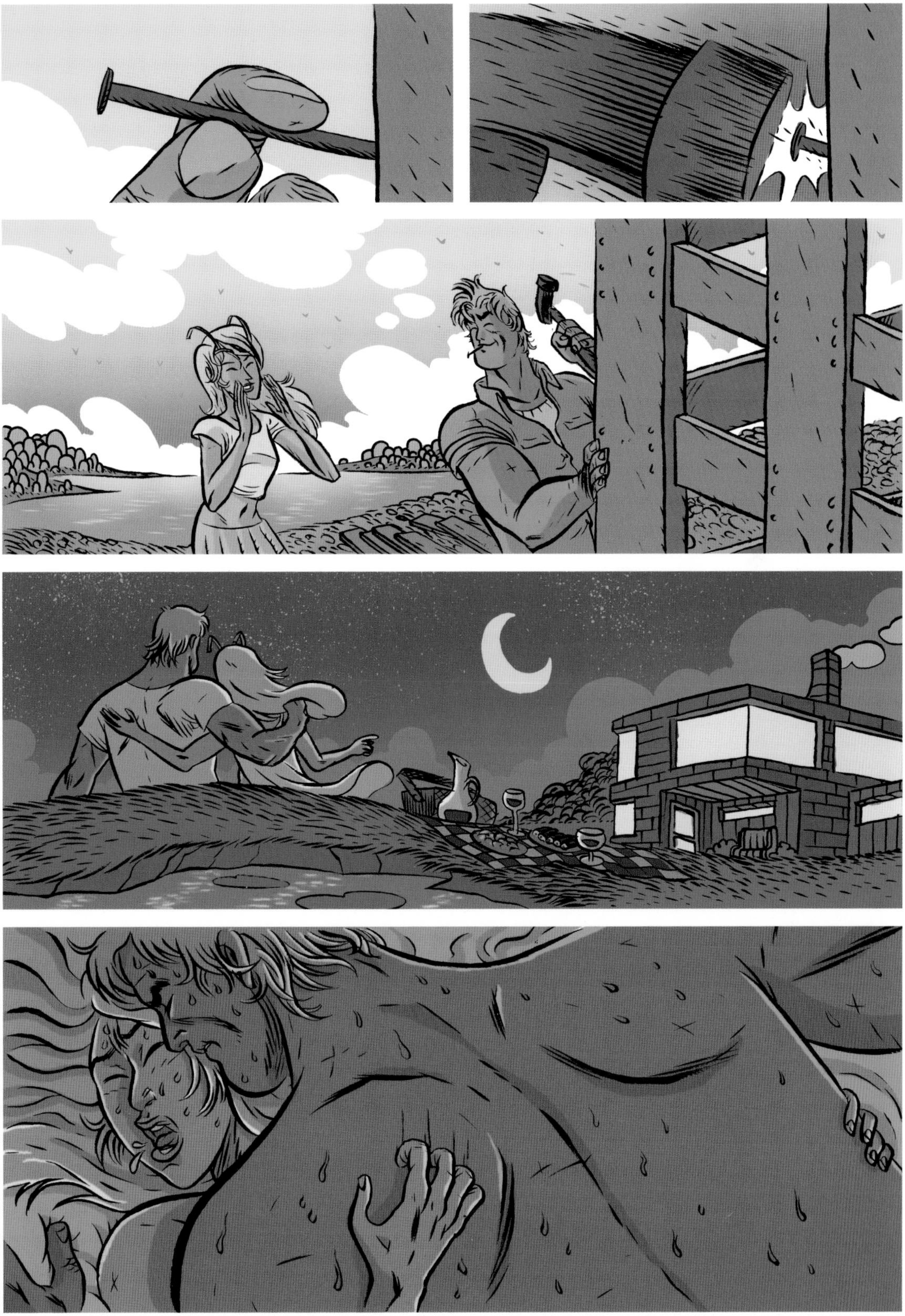

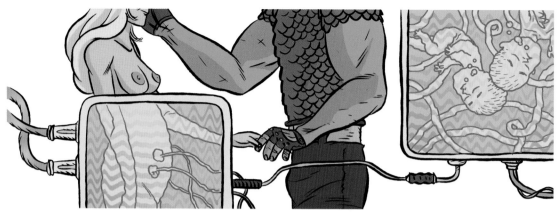

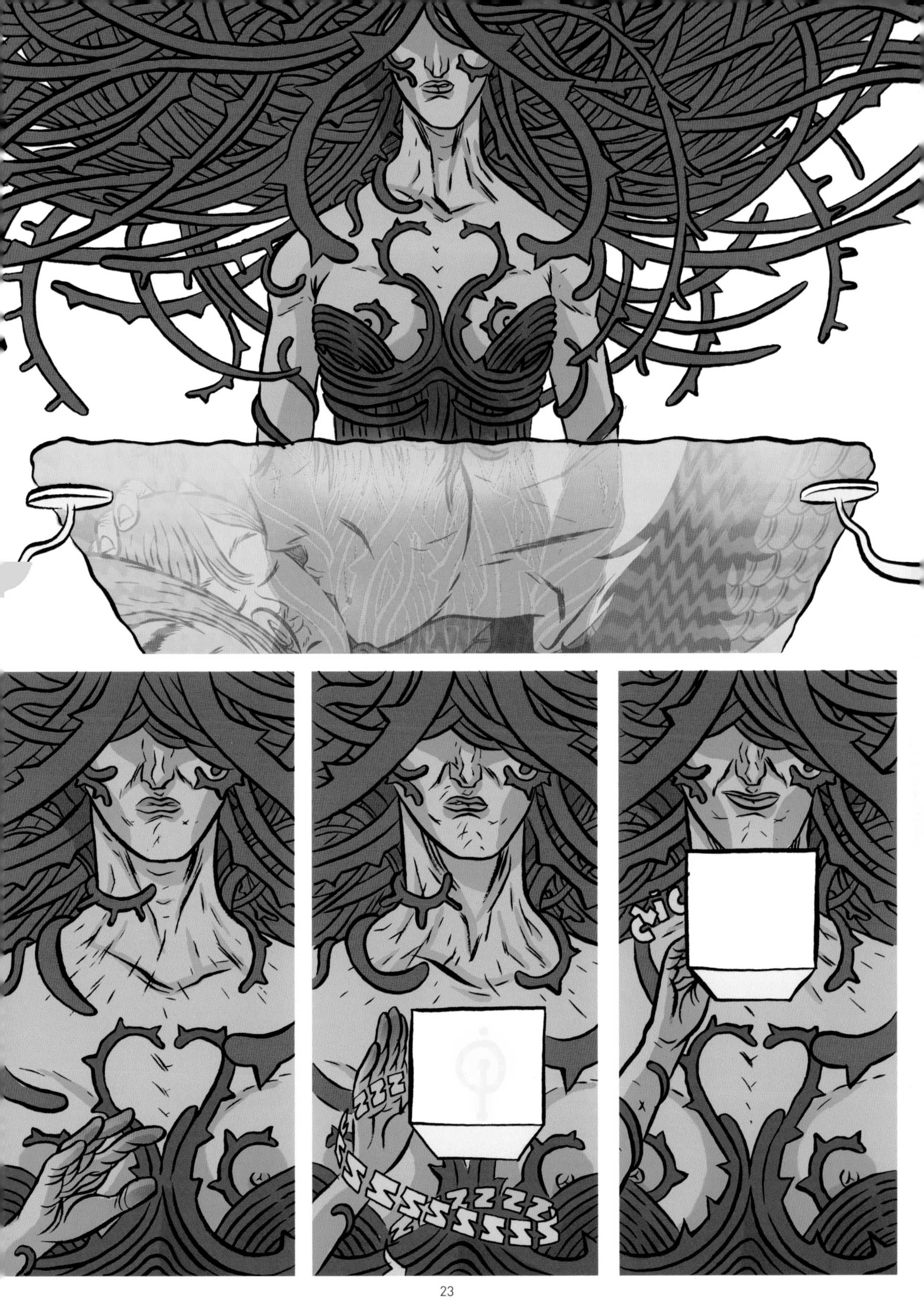
CLIC

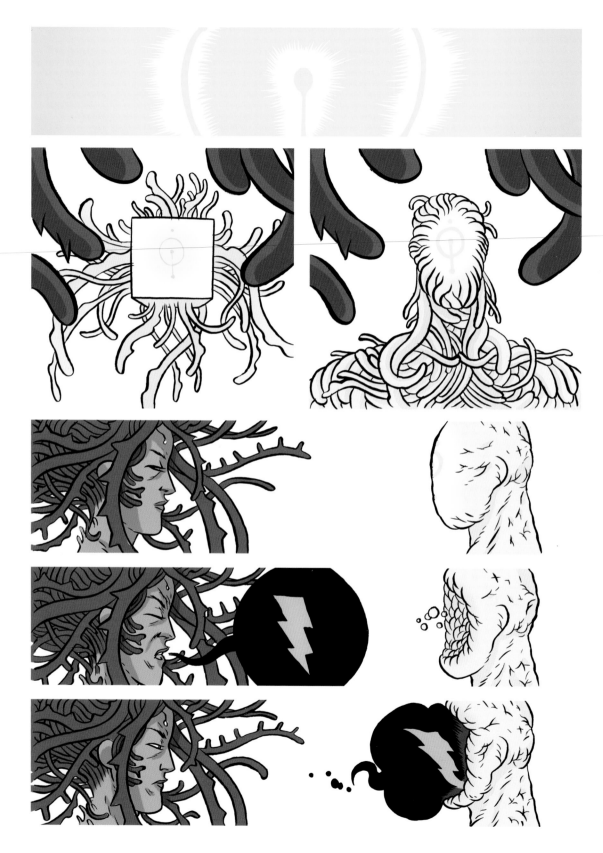

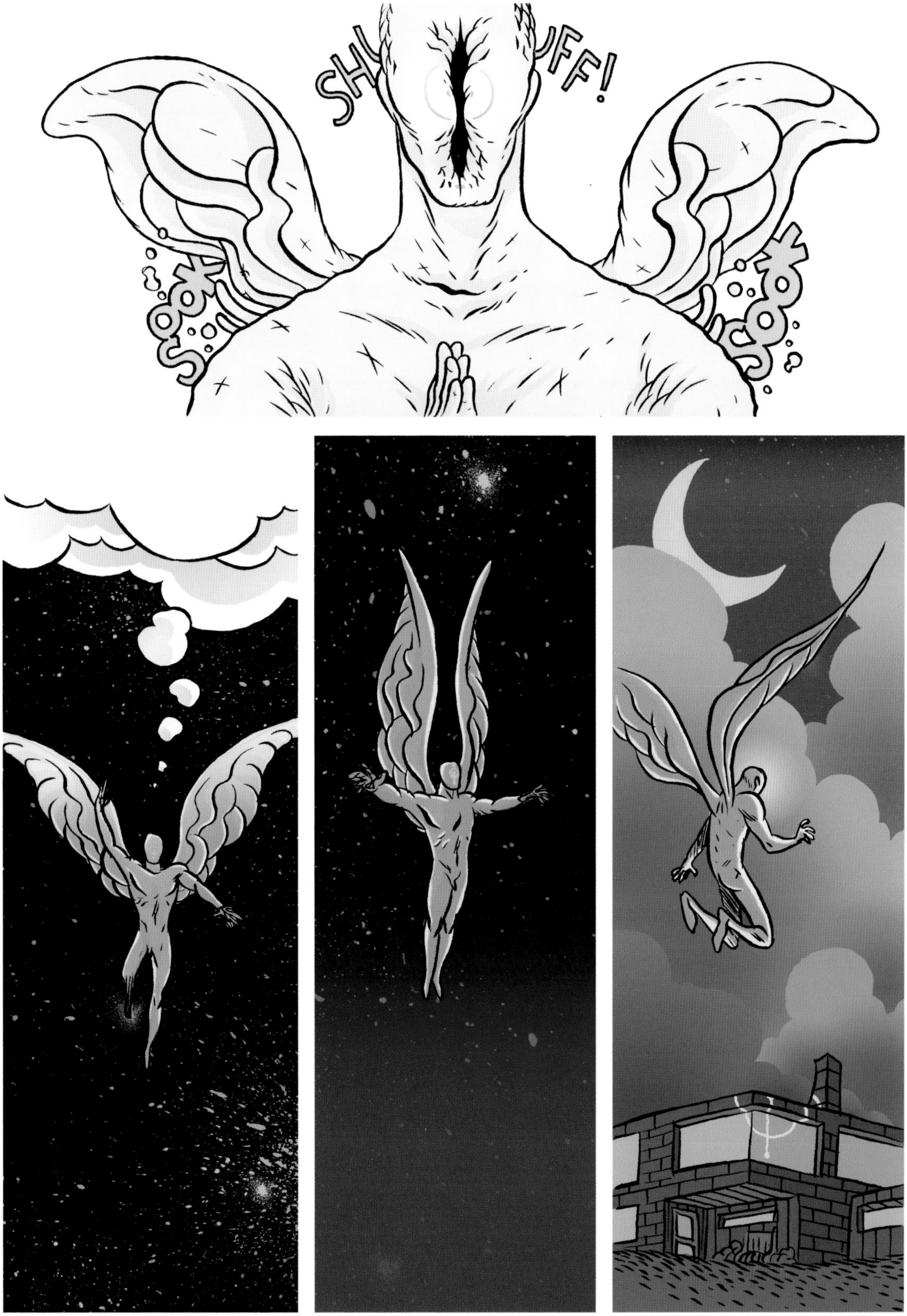
SH UFF!
SOOK
SOOK

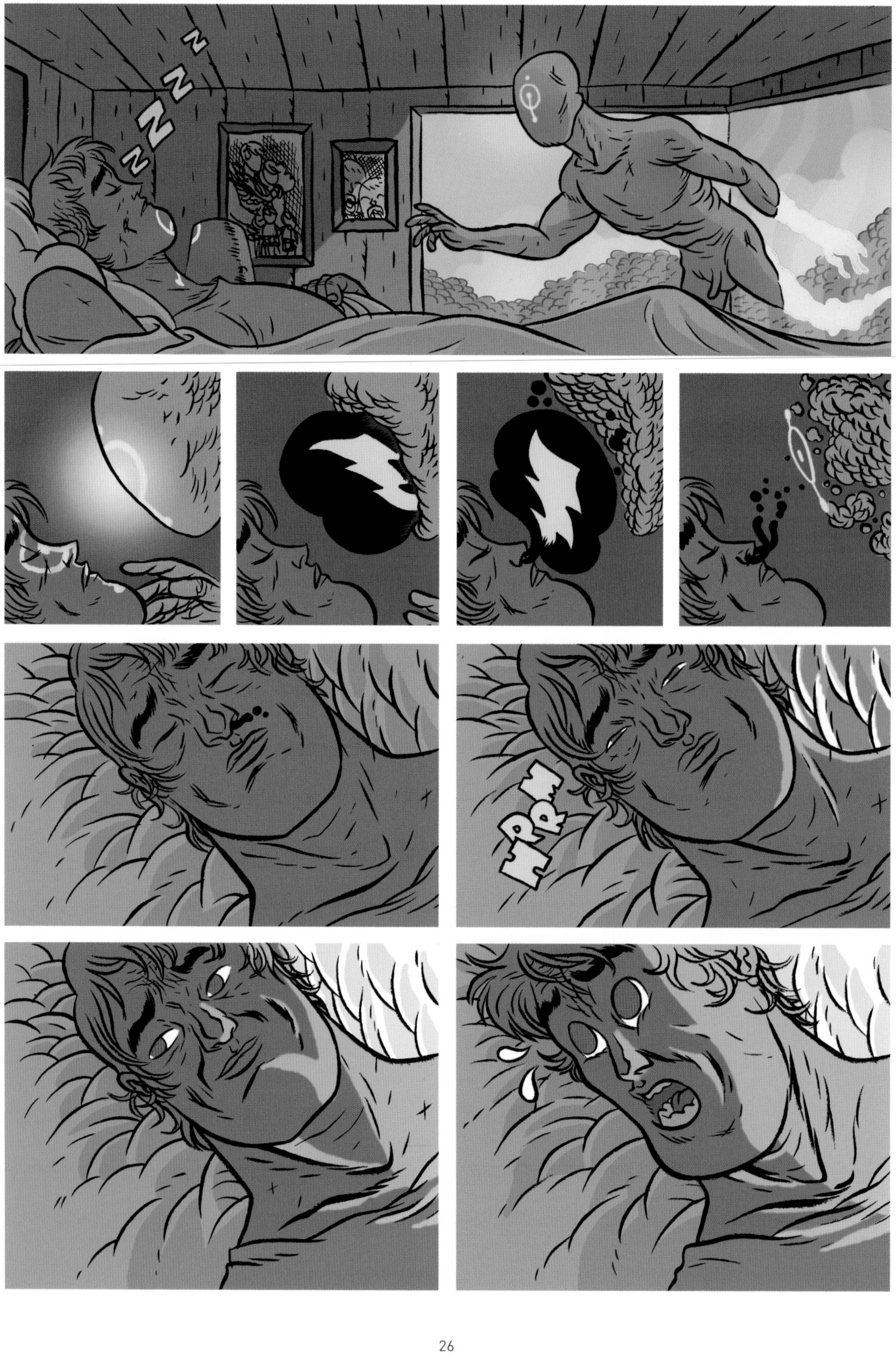
ZZZZ
MRRM

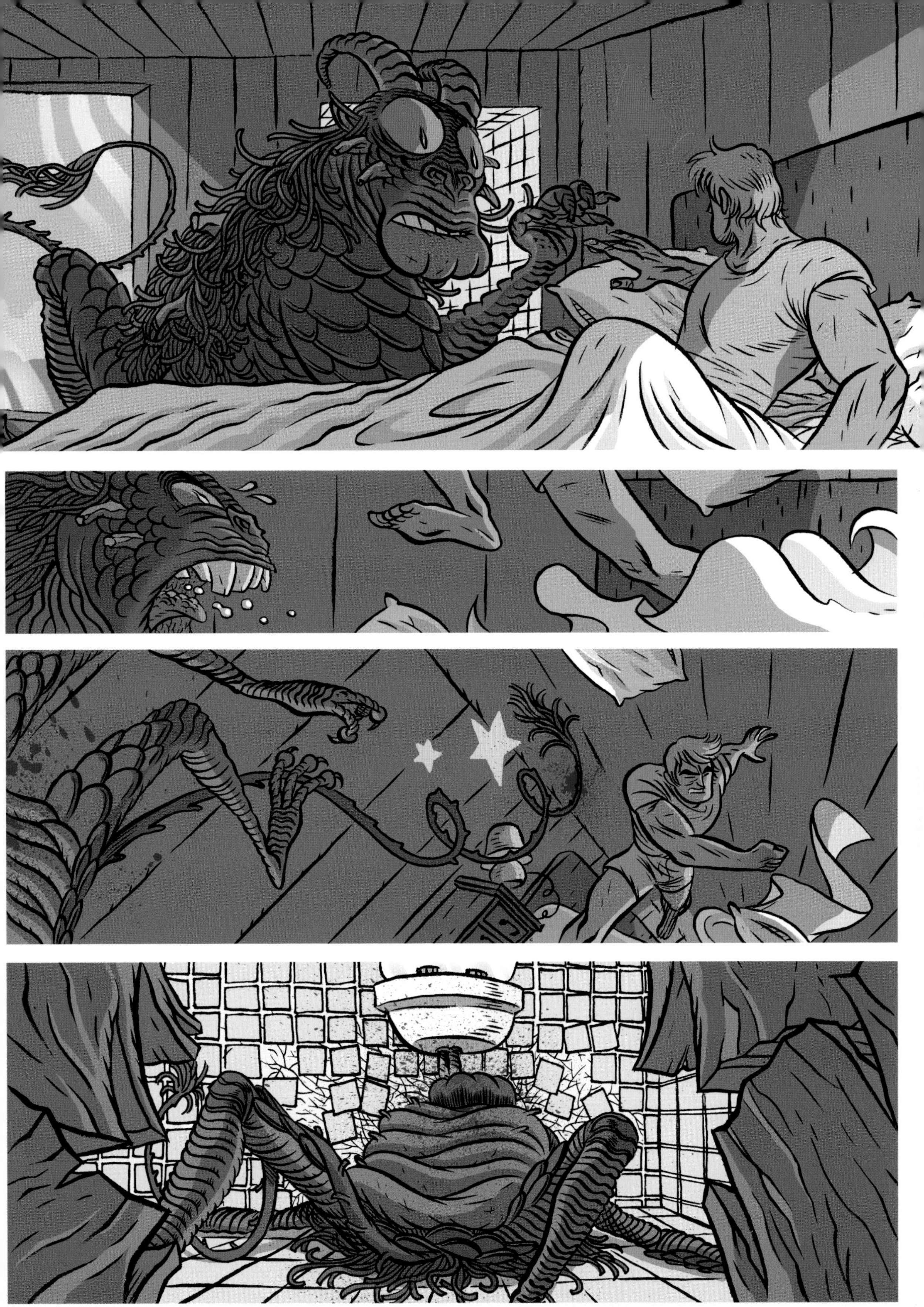

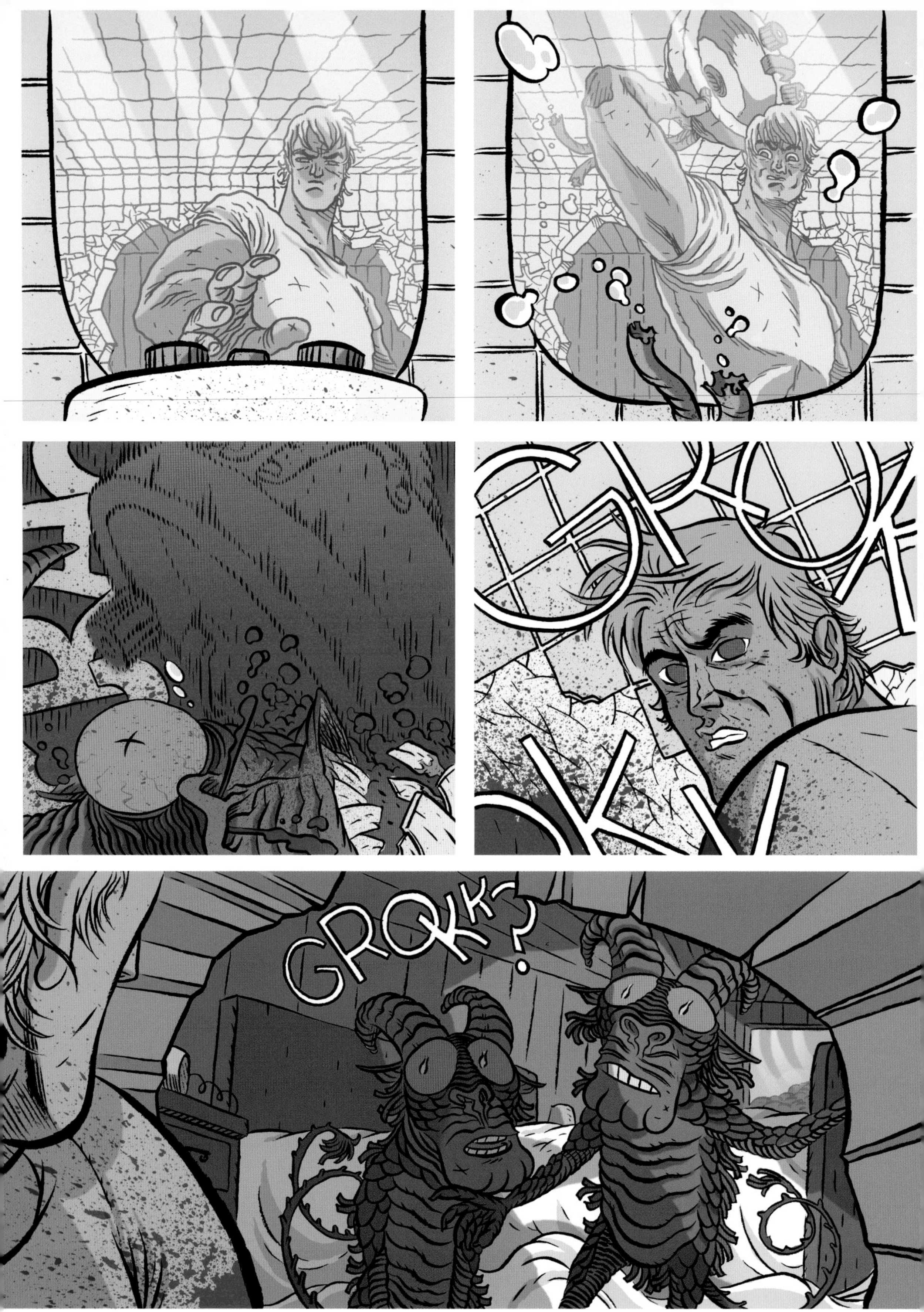

GROK
GROKK?

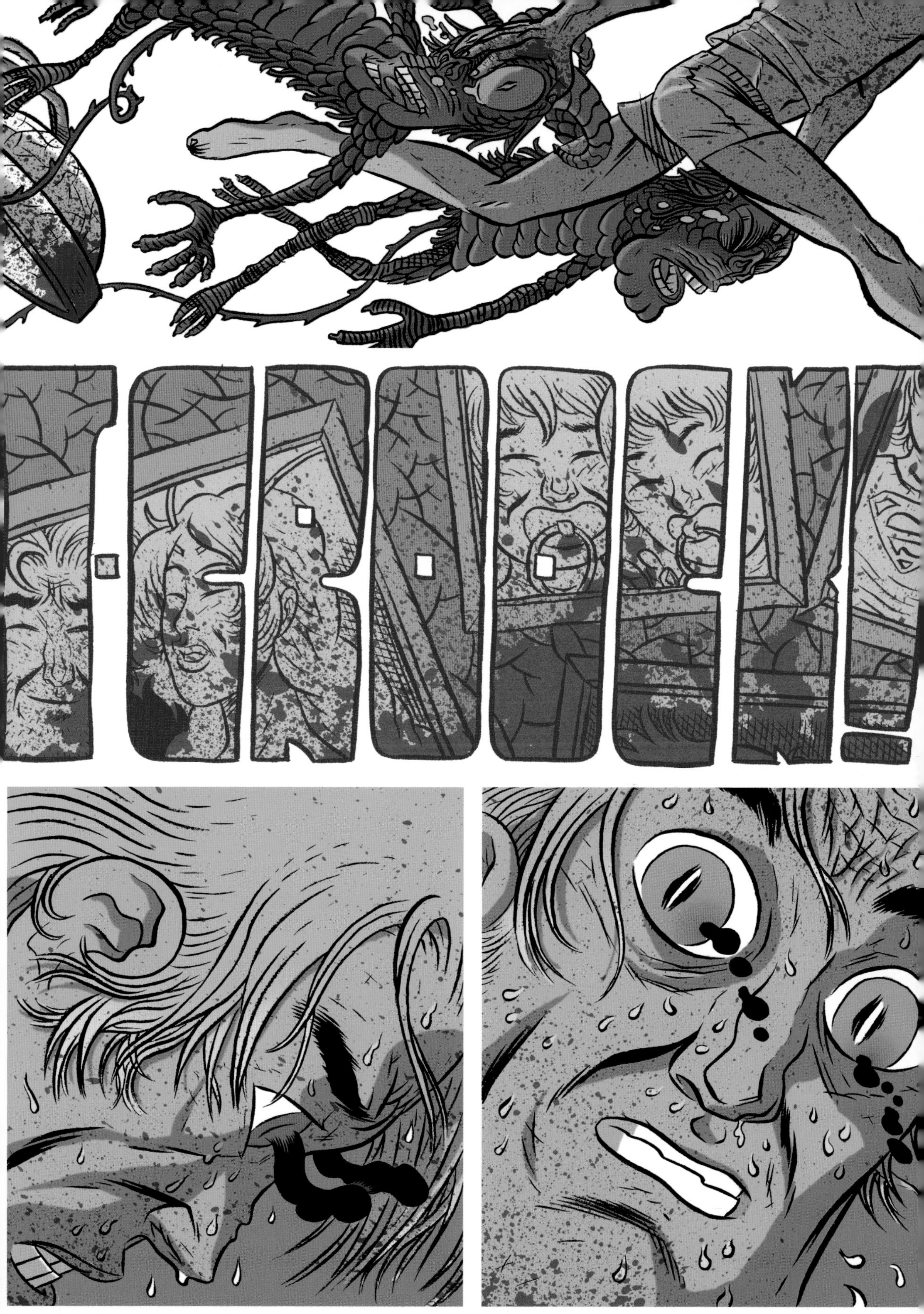
T-CROOCK!!

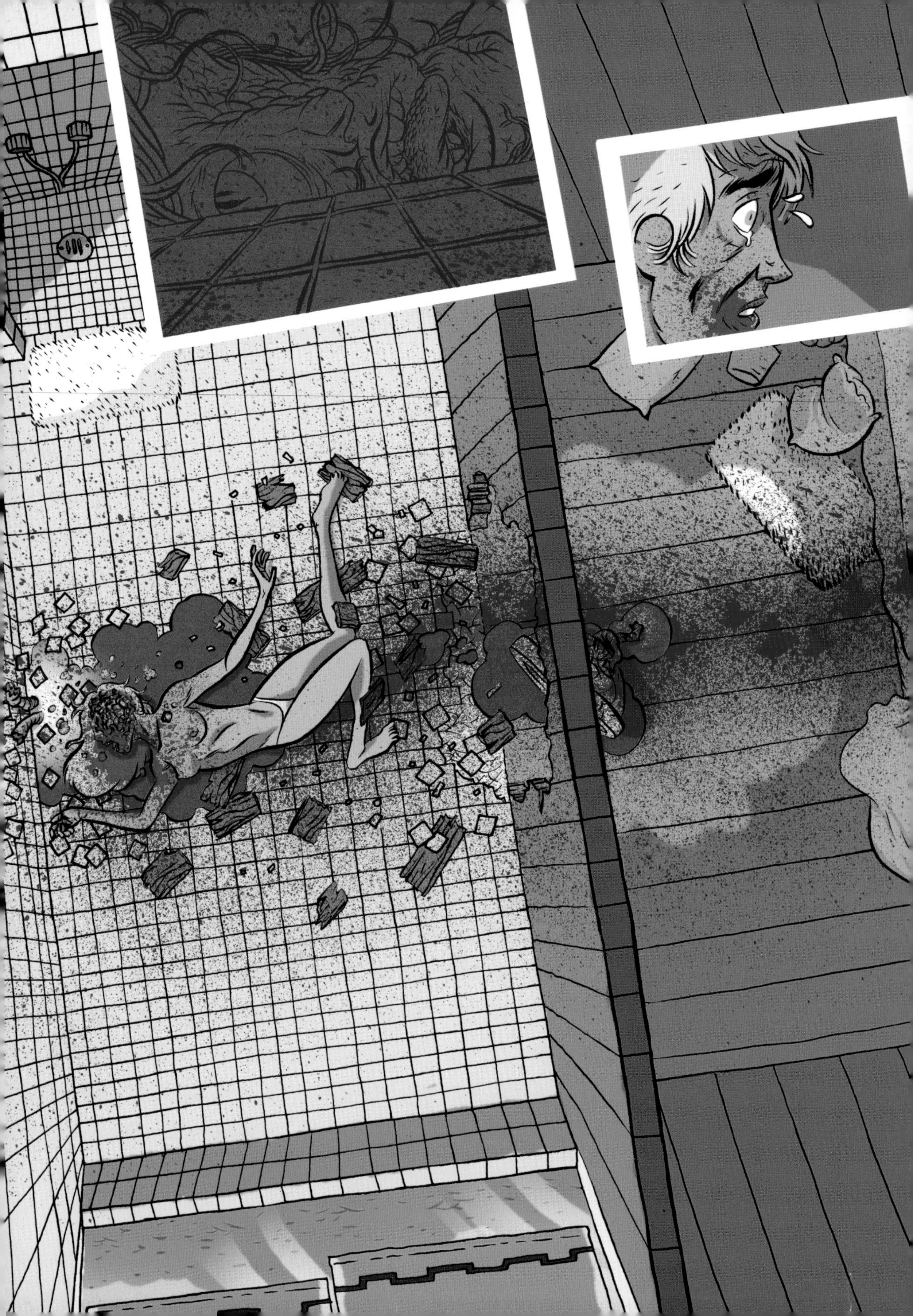

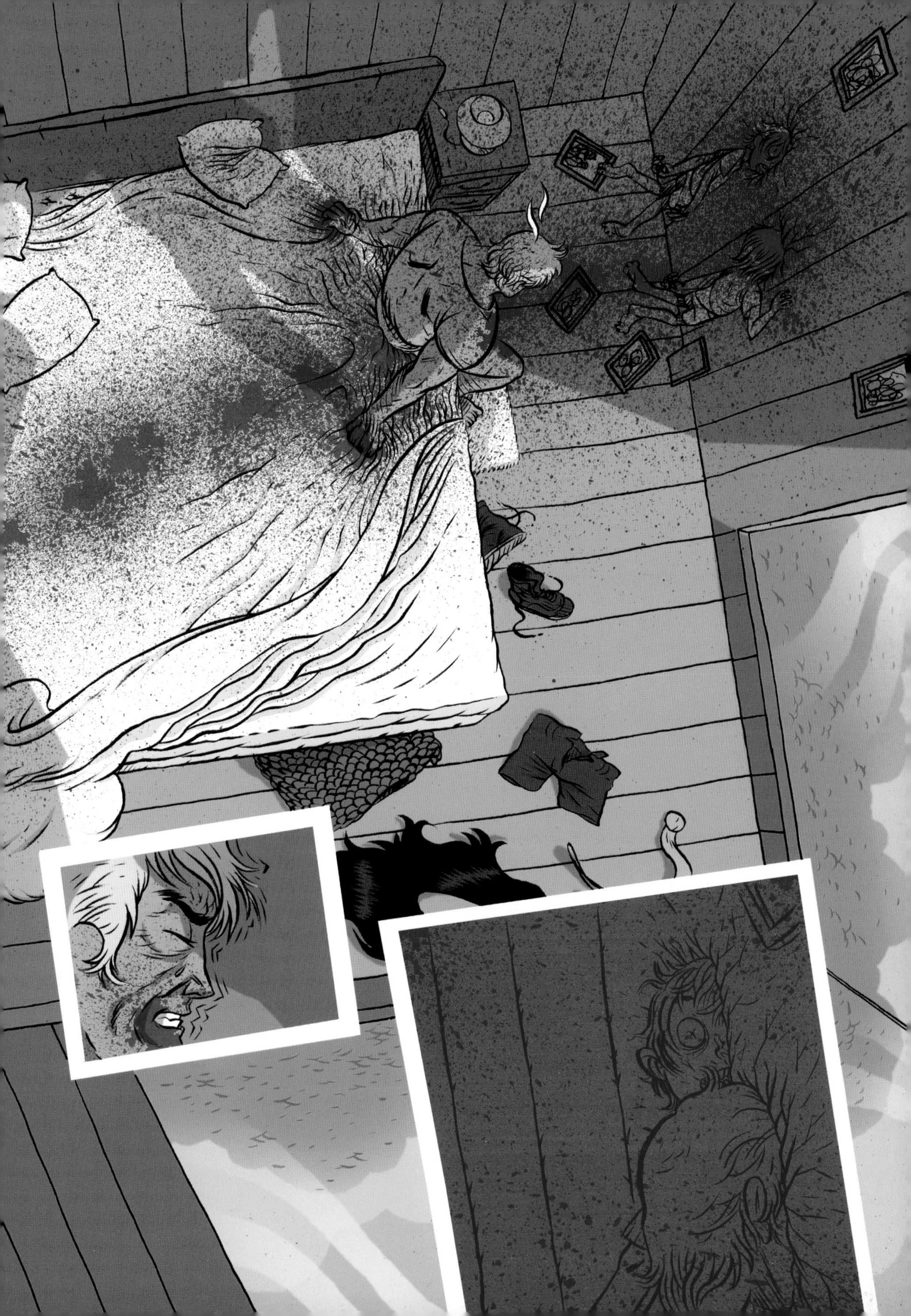

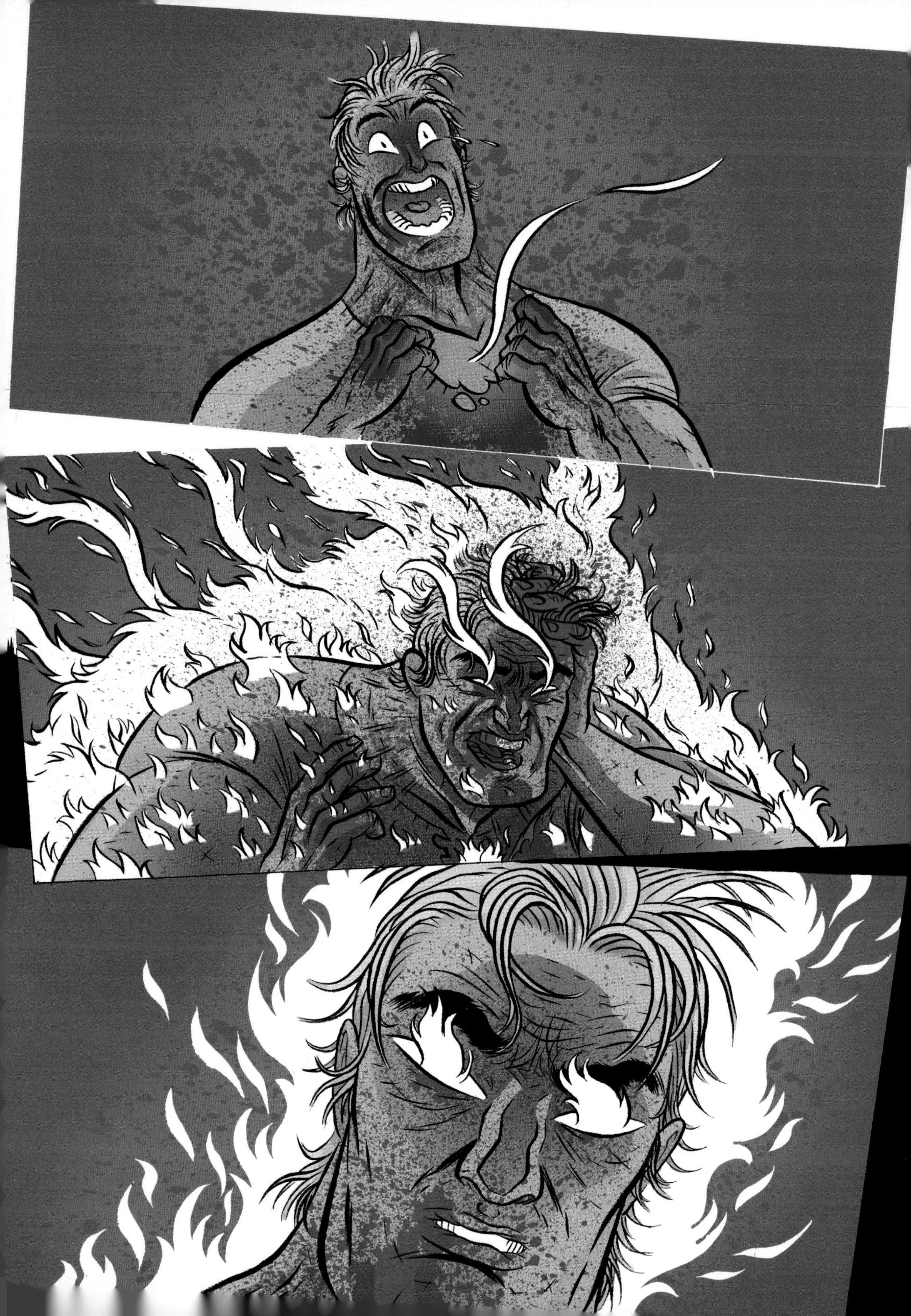

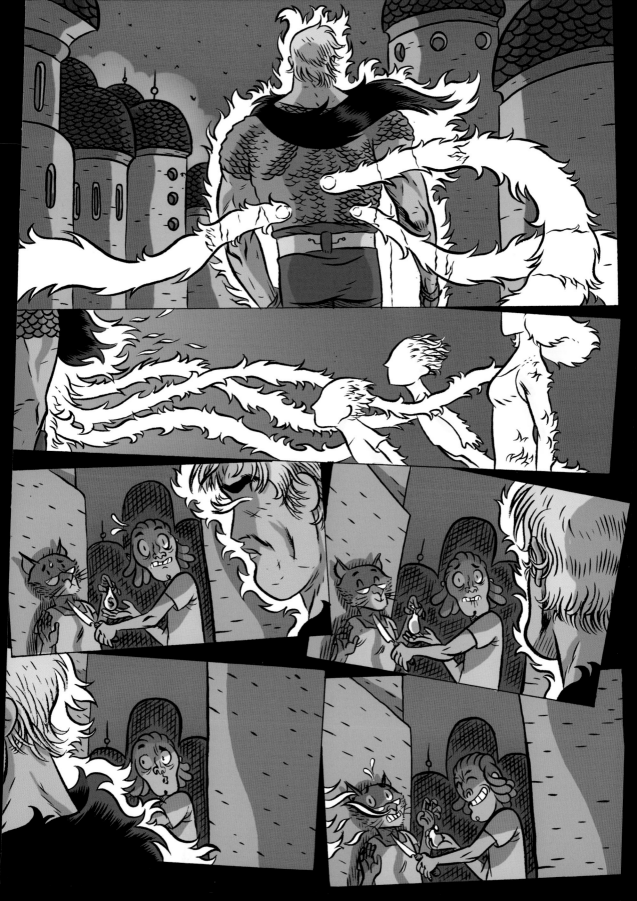

HERACLES TURNS HIS BACK ON GREECE!!
CRIME RATE THROUGH THE ROOF

Robberies, murders, rapes...An endless string of calamities has plagued the country since the disappearance of Nafplio's champion, Heracles.

The army of King Eurystheus finds itself overwhelmed by the hordes of monsters that are running rampant and taking over our city. But the disaster extends far beyond mere robberies, violent attacks, and the dramatic rise in the crime rate: the stock market has crashed, and every day, businesses large and small are closing their doors. Children can no longer play outside in the streets...Children...The effect on future generations...What future awaits them without Heracles as a role model? Our fractured society will fall apart without the Hero to light the way, and our fate is uncertain without him to save

WHERE IS
THE HERO?

?

HERACLES, WHY HAVE YO̸ ABANDONED US? —— by Robin Div

Five months have passed since the world-famous he par excellence of Nafplio threw in the towel, leaving t world submerged in the depths of darkness and despair.

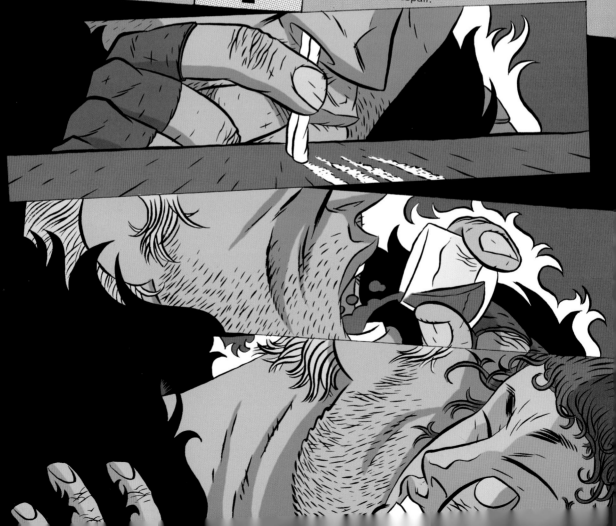

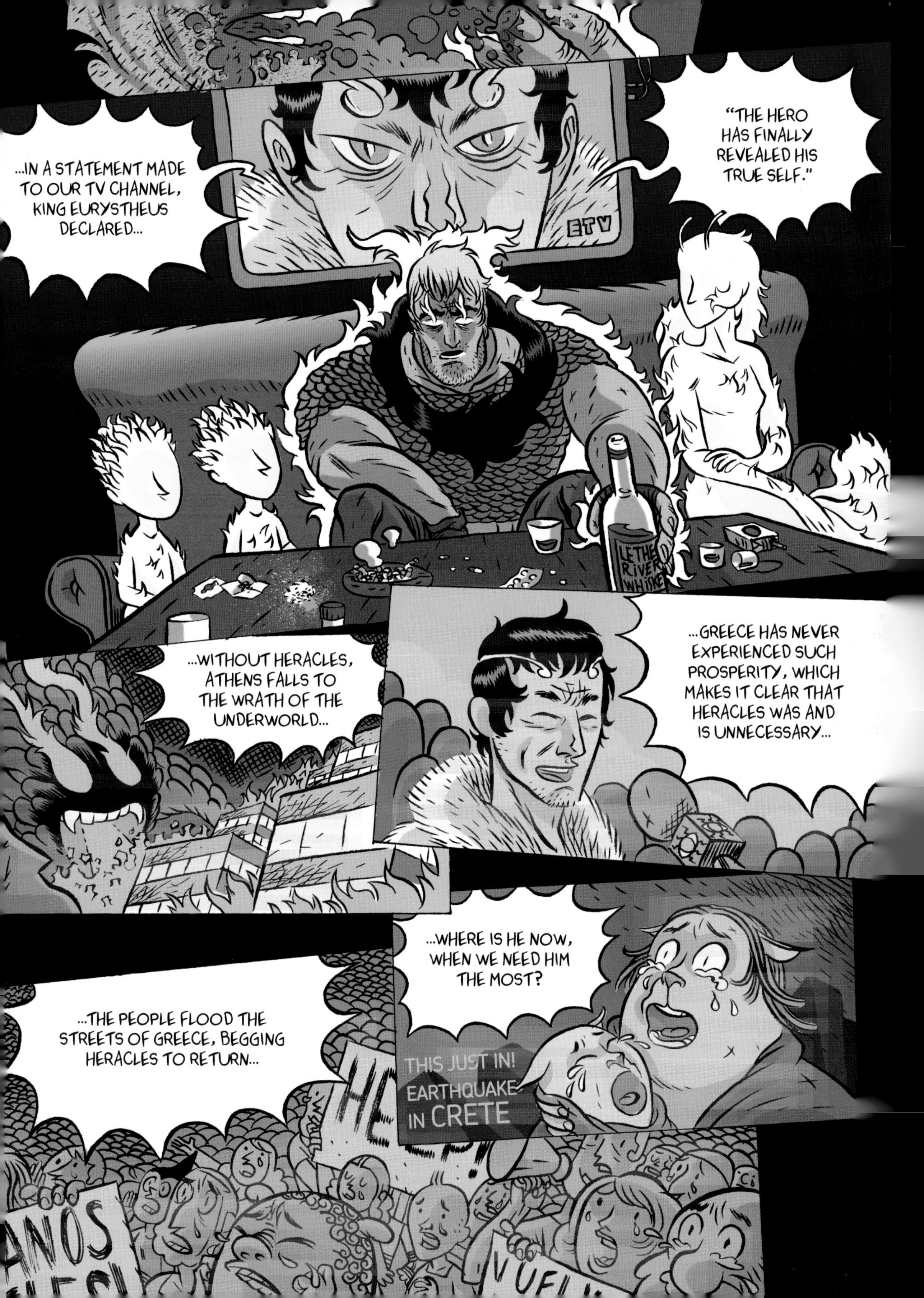
...IN A STATEMENT MADE TO OUR TV CHANNEL, KING EURYSTHEUS DECLARED...
"THE HERO HAS FINALLY REVEALED HIS TRUE SELF."
ETV
LETHE RIVER WHISKEY
...WITHOUT HERACLES, ATHENS FALLS TO THE WRATH OF THE UNDERWORLD...
...GREECE HAS NEVER EXPERIENCED SUCH PROSPERITY, WHICH MAKES IT CLEAR THAT HERACLES WAS AND IS UNNECESSARY...
...THE PEOPLE FLOOD THE STREETS OF GREECE, BEGGING HERACLES TO RETURN...
...WHERE IS HE NOW, WHEN WE NEED HIM THE MOST?
THIS JUST IN! EARTHQUAKE IN CRETE

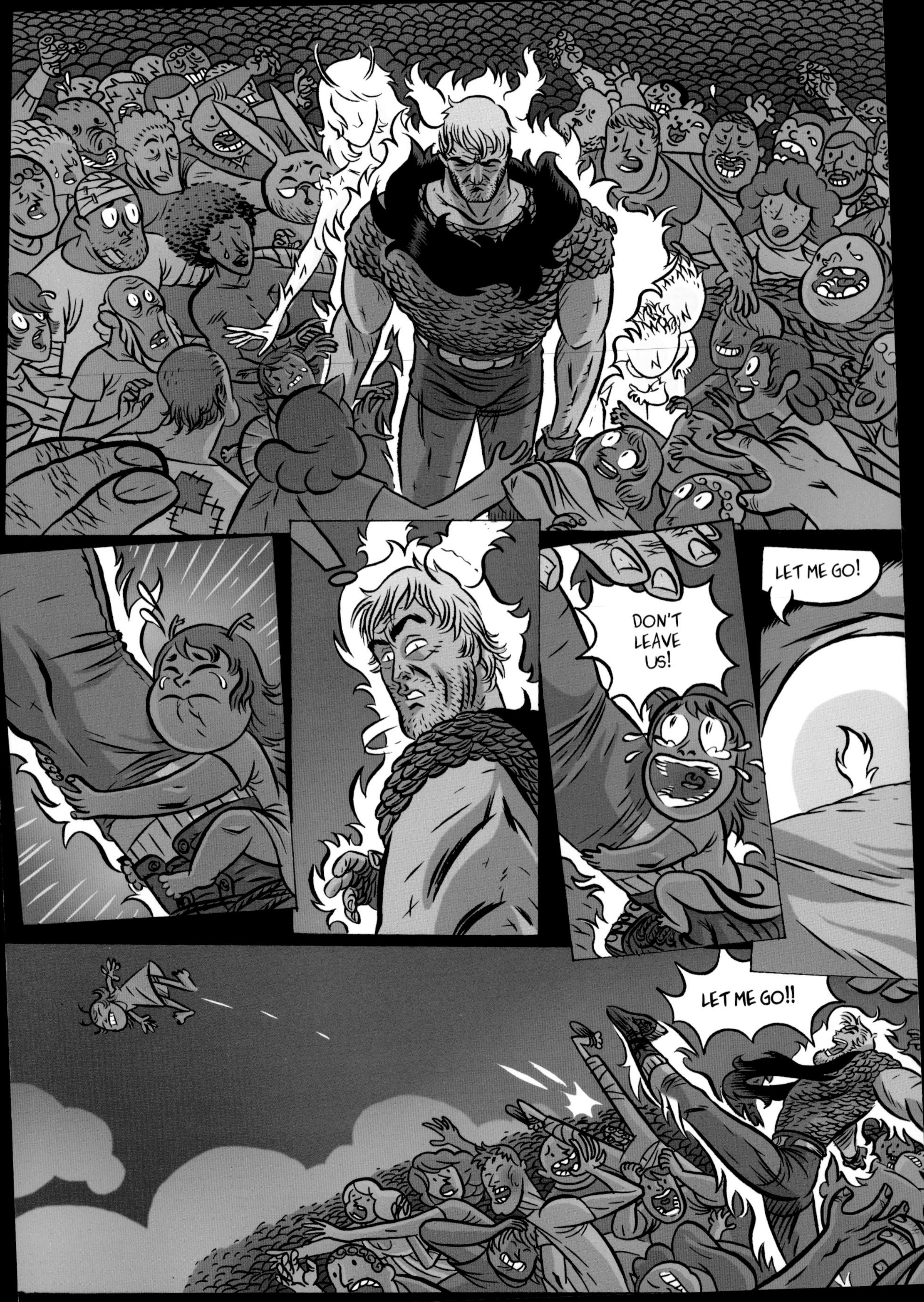
DON'T LEAVE US!
LET ME GO!
LET ME GO!!

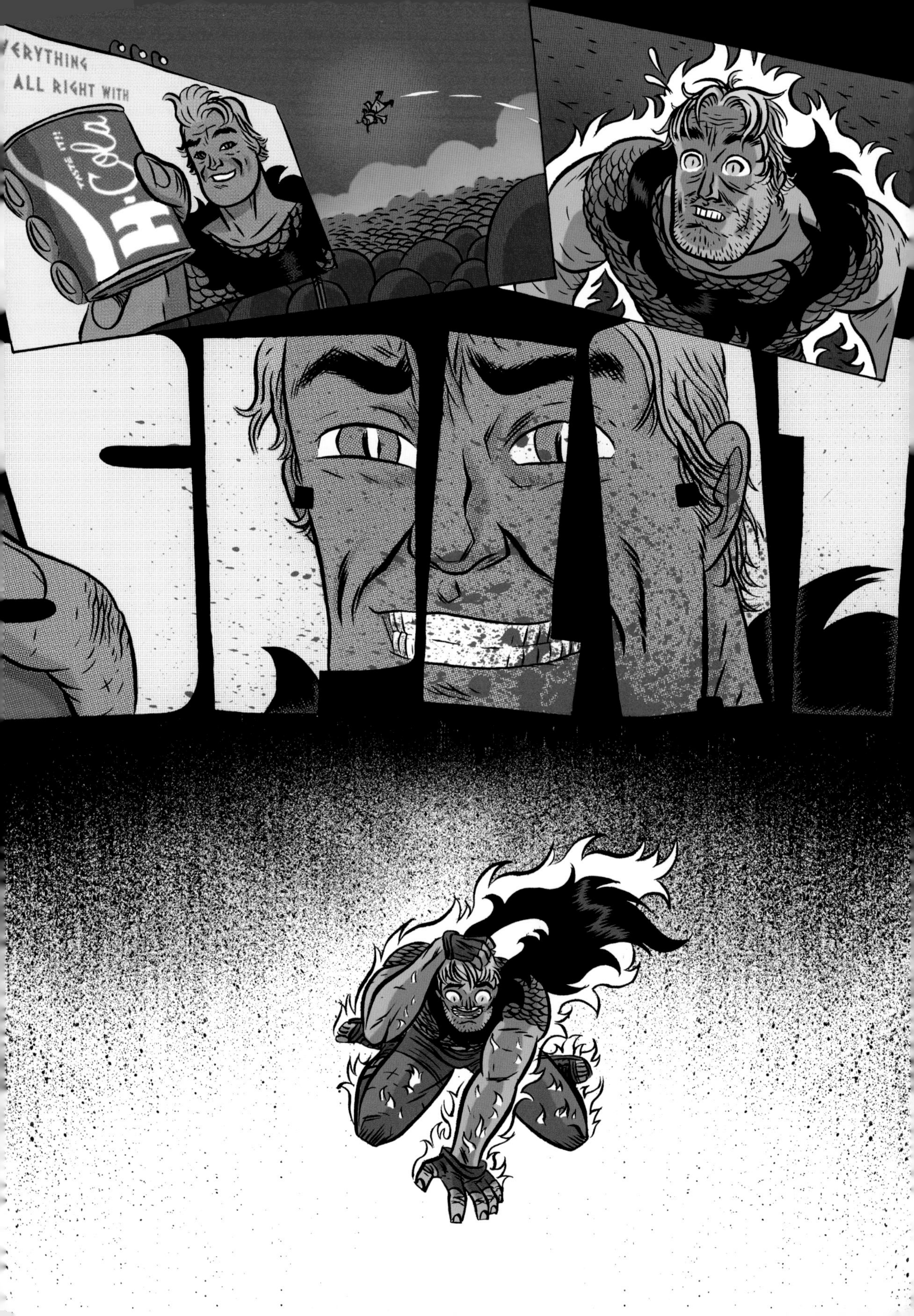
ERYTHING
ALL RIGHT WITH

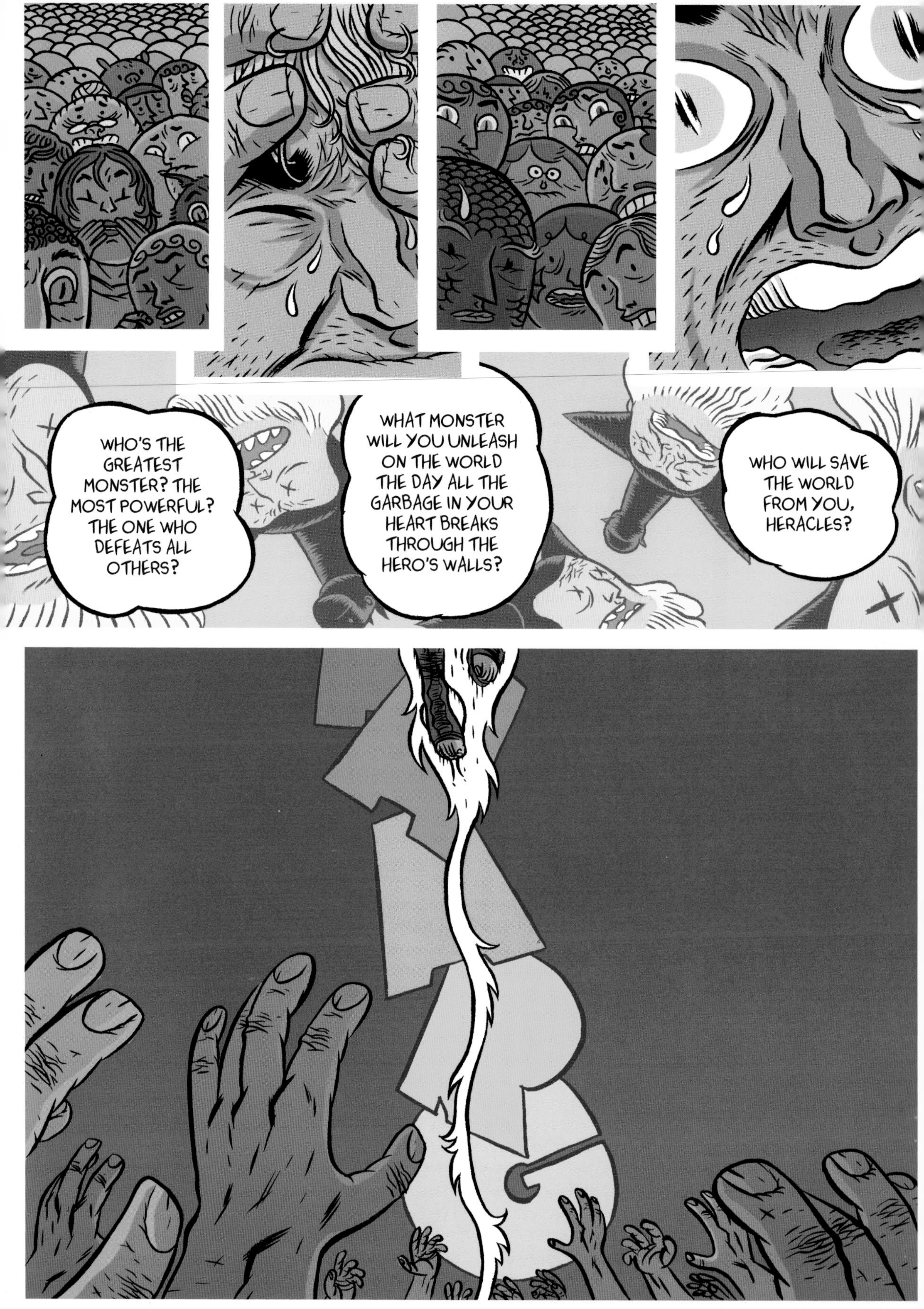

WHO'S THE GREATEST MONSTER? THE MOST POWERFUL? THE ONE WHO DEFEATS ALL OTHERS?
WHAT MONSTER WILL YOU UNLEASH ON THE WORLD THE DAY ALL THE GARBAGE IN YOUR HEART BREAKS THROUGH THE HERO'S WALLS?
WHO WILL SAVE THE WORLD FROM YOU, HERACLES?

AT THE EDGE OF THE KNOWN WORLD, TEN MINUTES LATER.

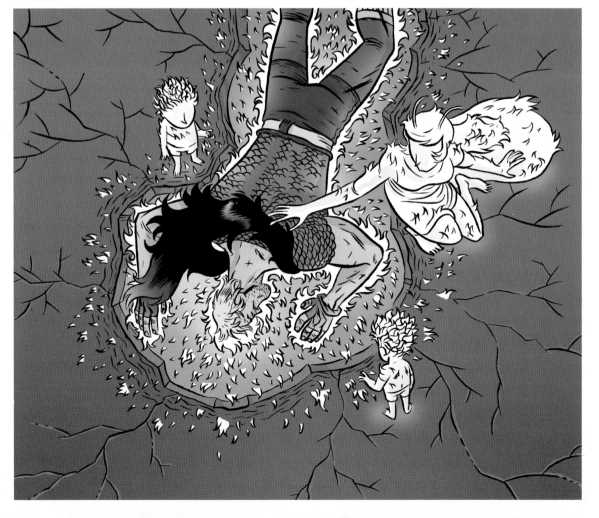

GRAB

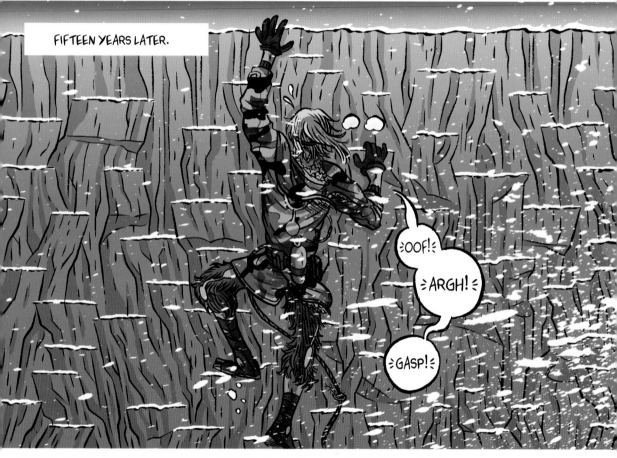

FIFTEEN YEARS LATER.

≶OOF!≷

≶ARGH!≷

≶GASP!≷

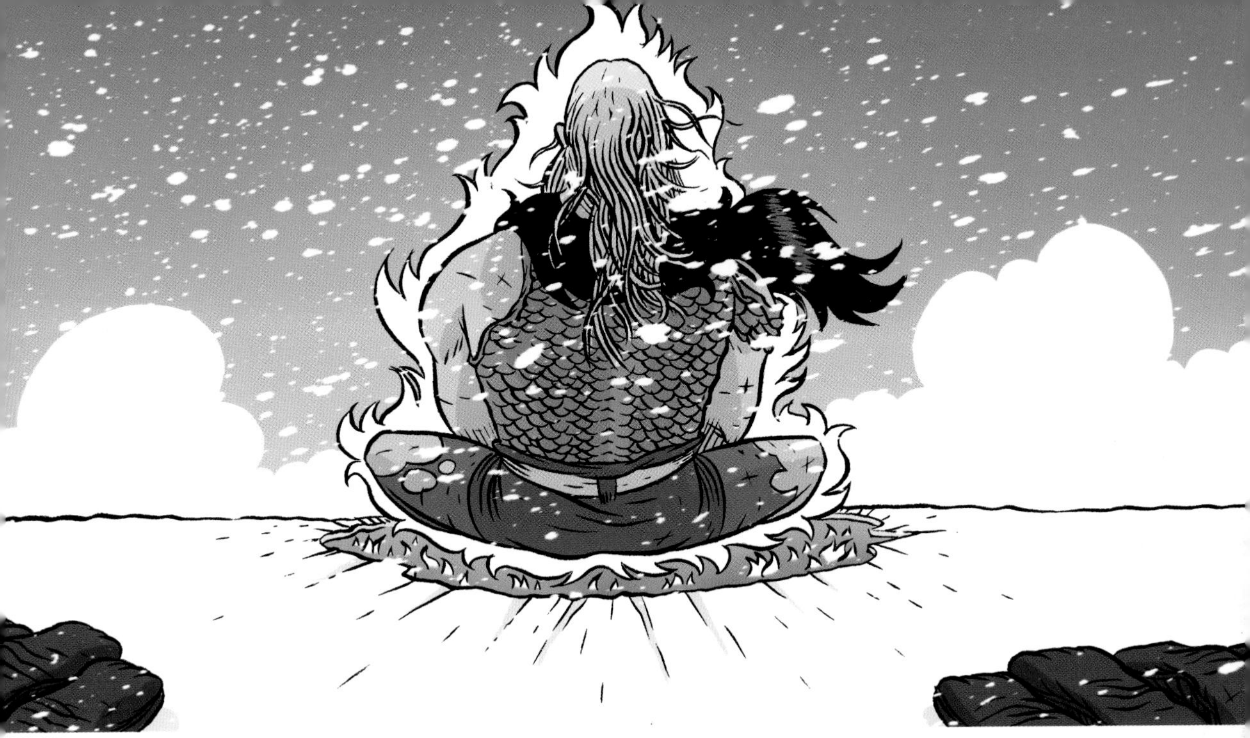
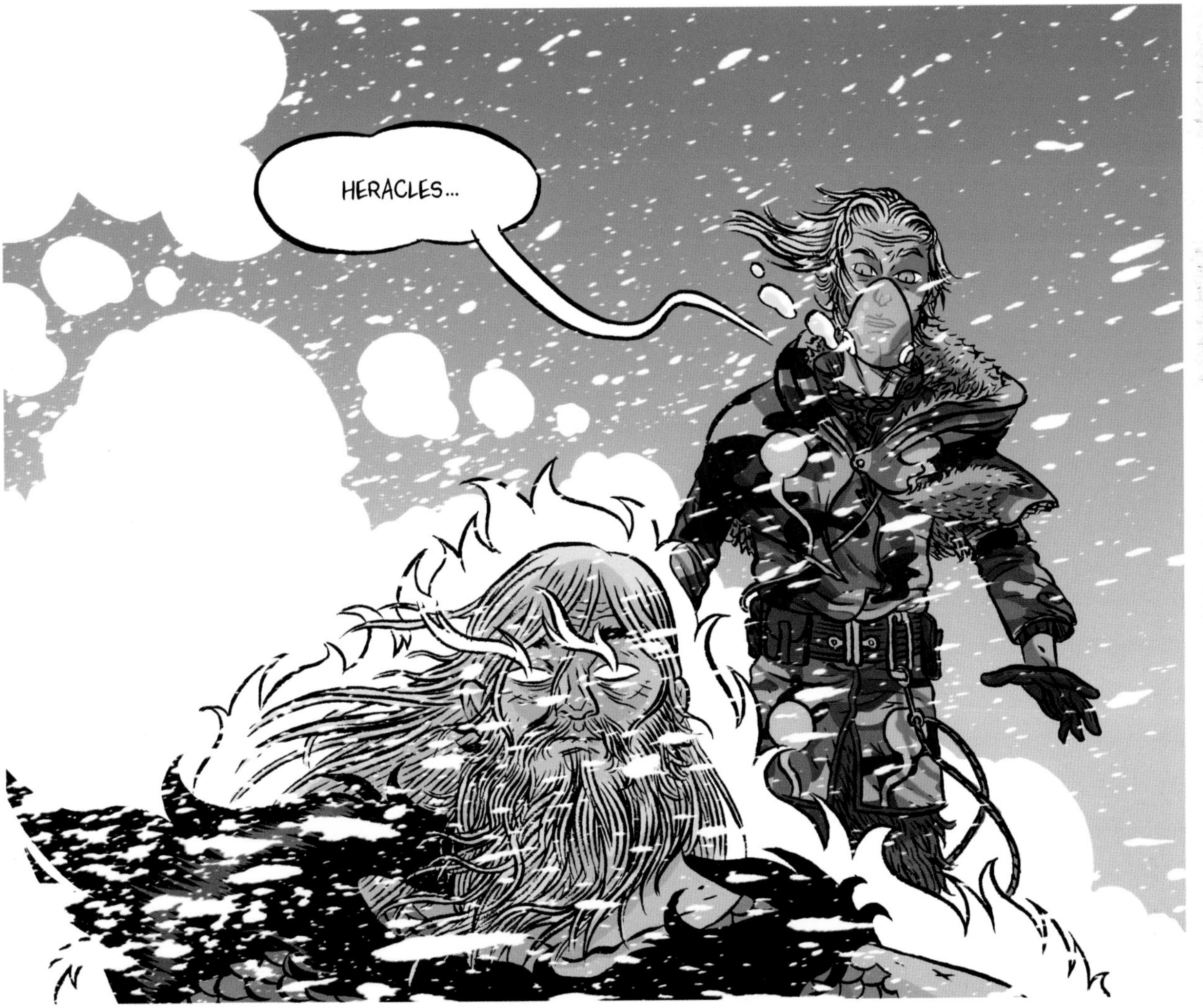
HERACLES...

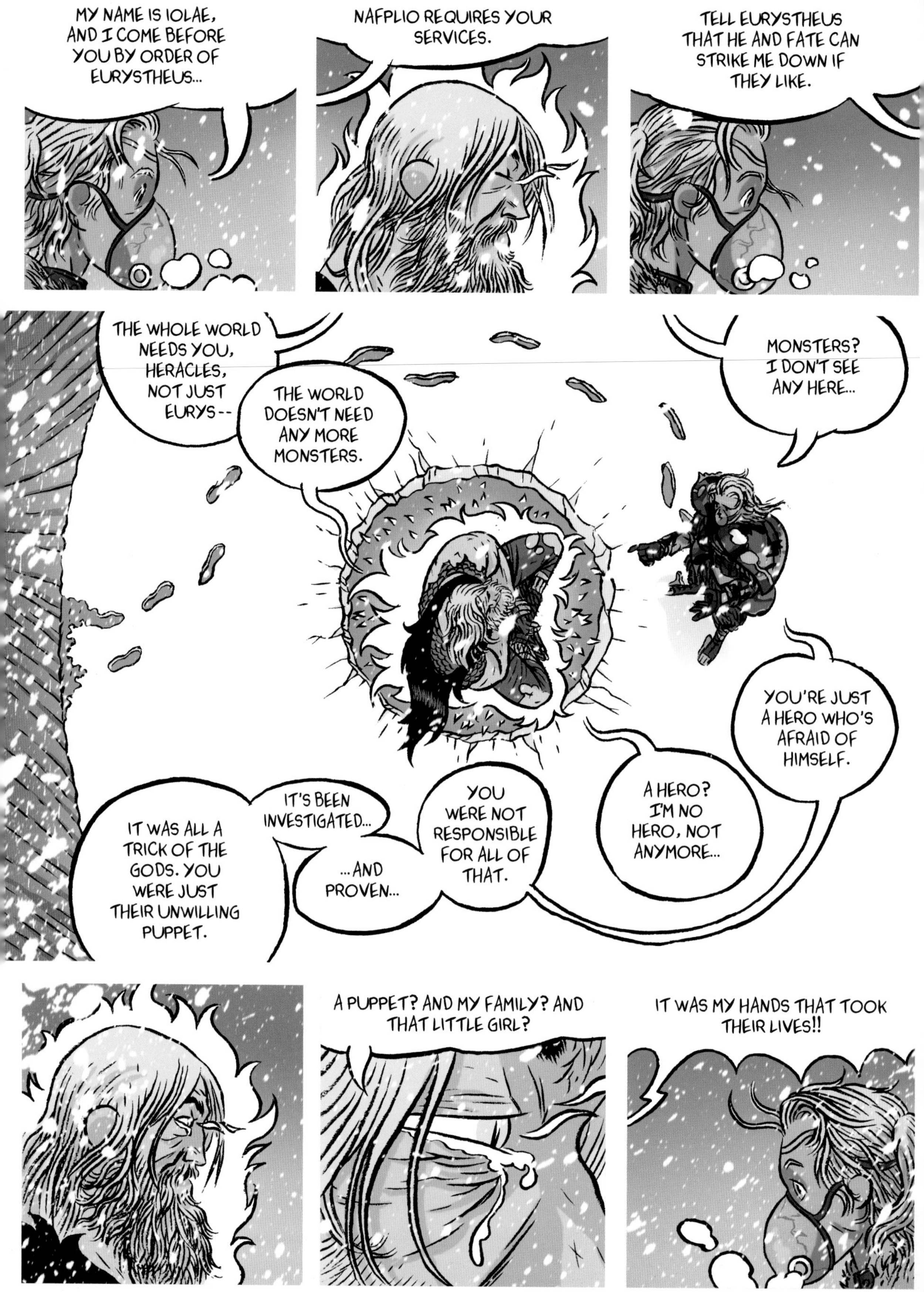
MY NAME IS IOLAE, AND I COME BEFORE YOU BY ORDER OF EURYSTHEUS...
NAFPLIO REQUIRES YOUR SERVICES.
TELL EURYSTHEUS THAT HE AND FATE CAN STRIKE ME DOWN IF THEY LIKE.
THE WHOLE WORLD NEEDS YOU, HERACLES, NOT JUST EURYS--
THE WORLD DOESN'T NEED ANY MORE MONSTERS.
MONSTERS? I DON'T SEE ANY HERE...
YOU'RE JUST A HERO WHO'S AFRAID OF HIMSELF.
A HERO? I'M NO HERO, NOT ANYMORE...
YOU WERE NOT RESPONSIBLE FOR ALL OF THAT.
IT'S BEEN INVESTIGATED...
...AND PROVEN...
IT WAS ALL A TRICK OF THE GODS. YOU WERE JUST THEIR UNWILLING PUPPET.
A PUPPET? AND MY FAMILY? AND THAT LITTLE GIRL?
IT WAS MY HANDS THAT TOOK THEIR LIVES!!

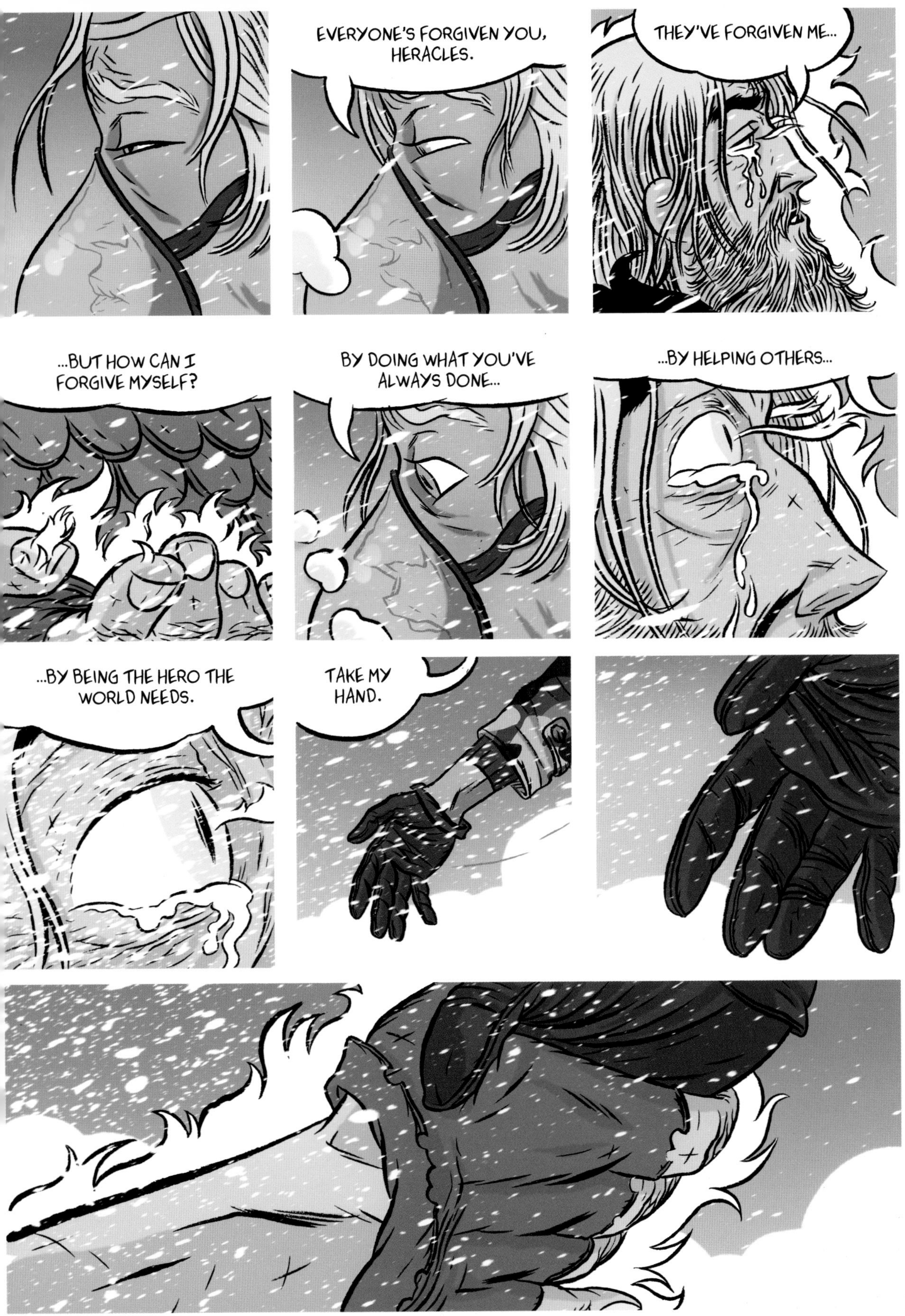
EVERYONE'S FORGIVEN YOU, HERACLES.
THEY'VE FORGIVEN ME...
...BUT HOW CAN I FORGIVE MYSELF?
BY DOING WHAT YOU'VE ALWAYS DONE...
...BY HELPING OTHERS...
...BY BEING THE HERO THE WORLD NEEDS.
TAKE MY HAND.

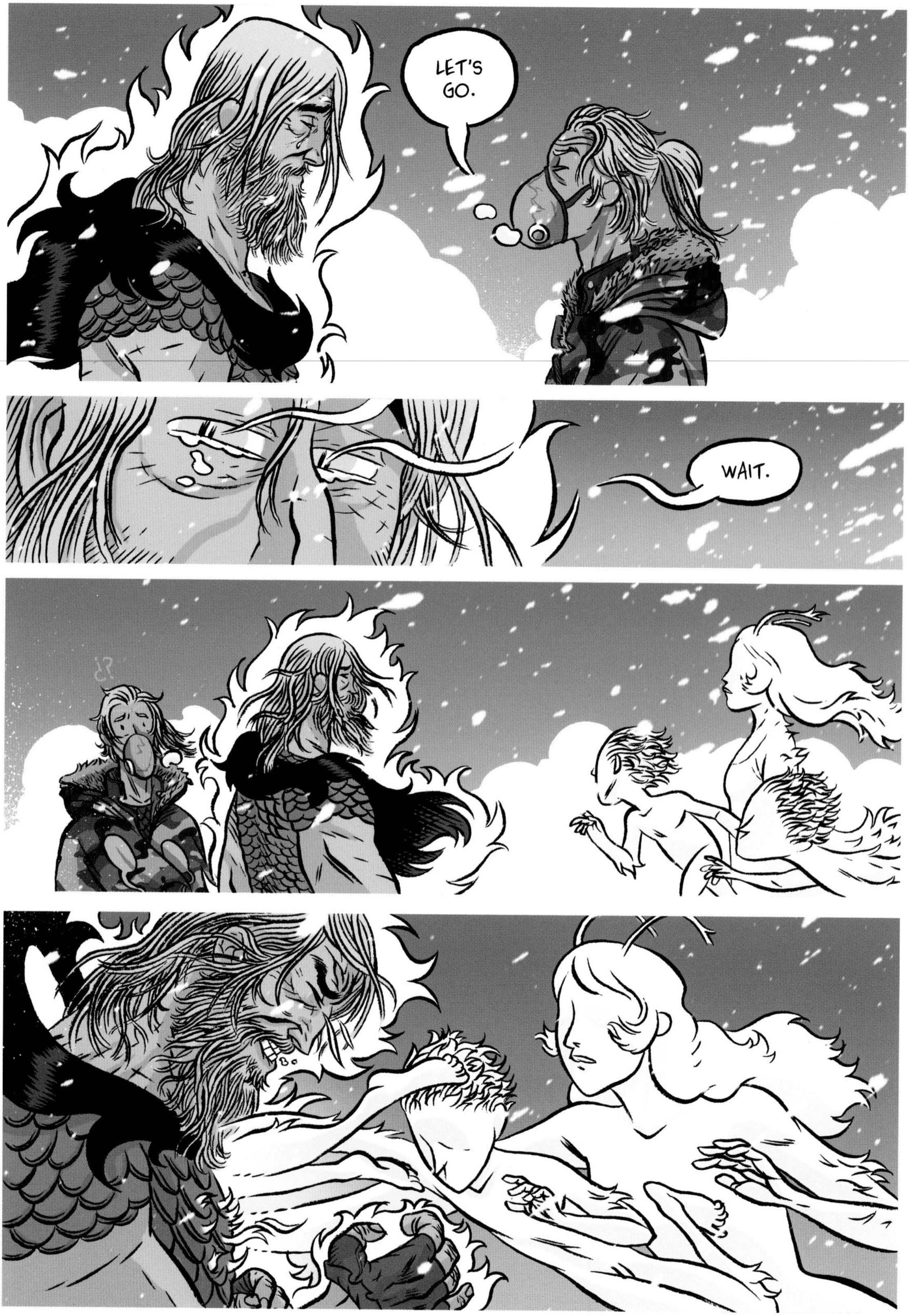
LET'S GO.
WAIT.

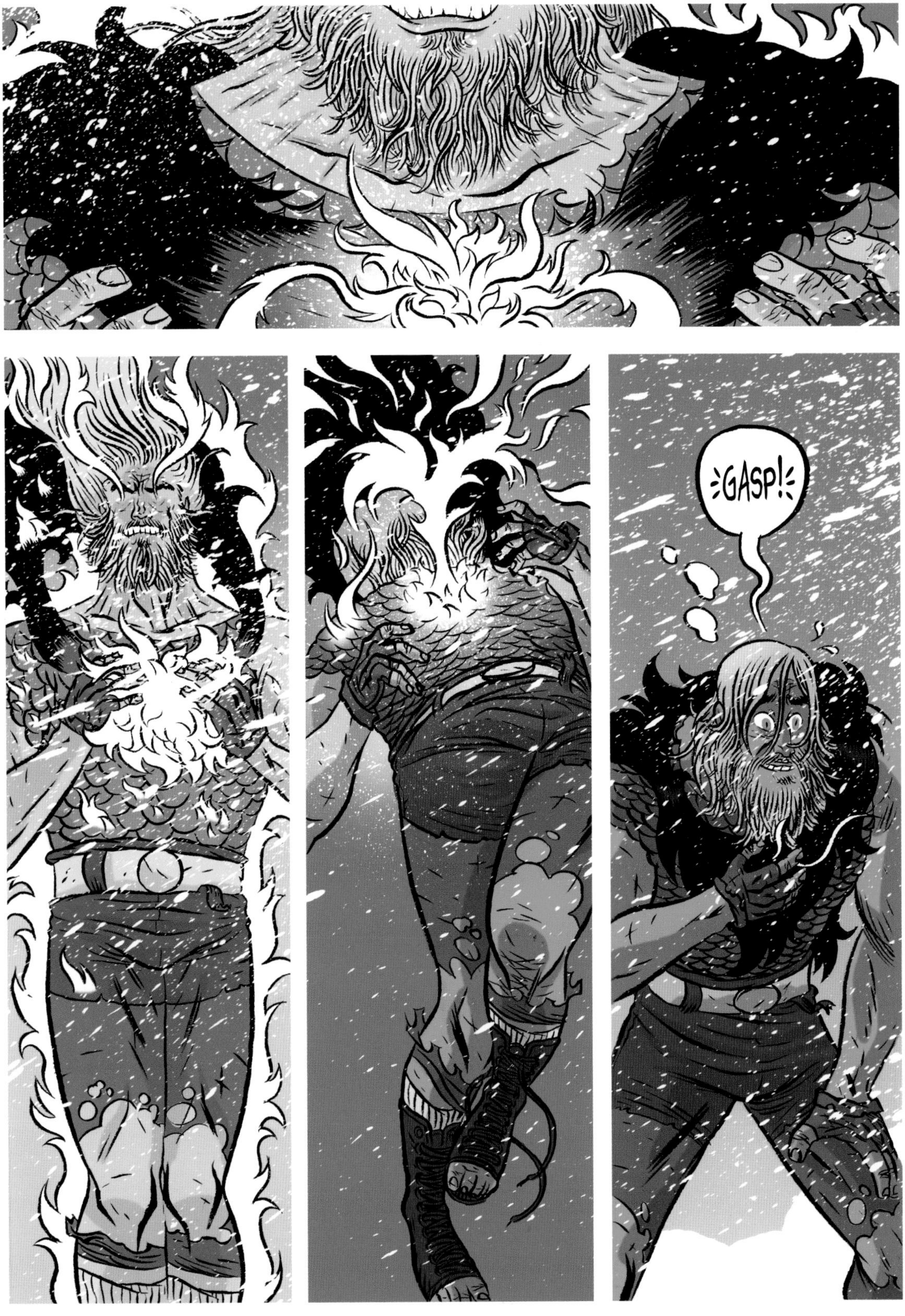
GASP!

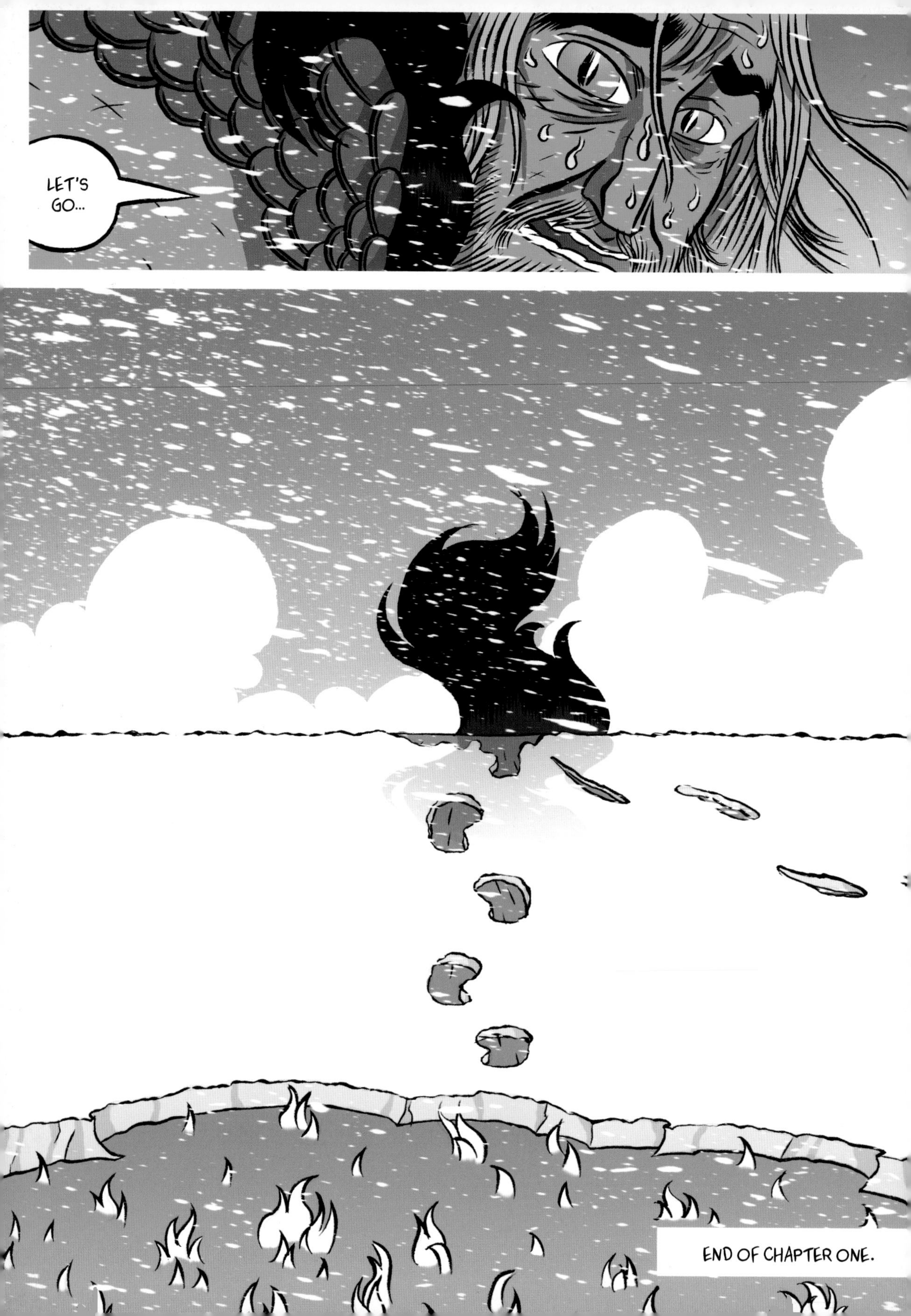
LET'S GO...
END OF CHAPTER ONE.

CHAPTER

02

CHAPTER

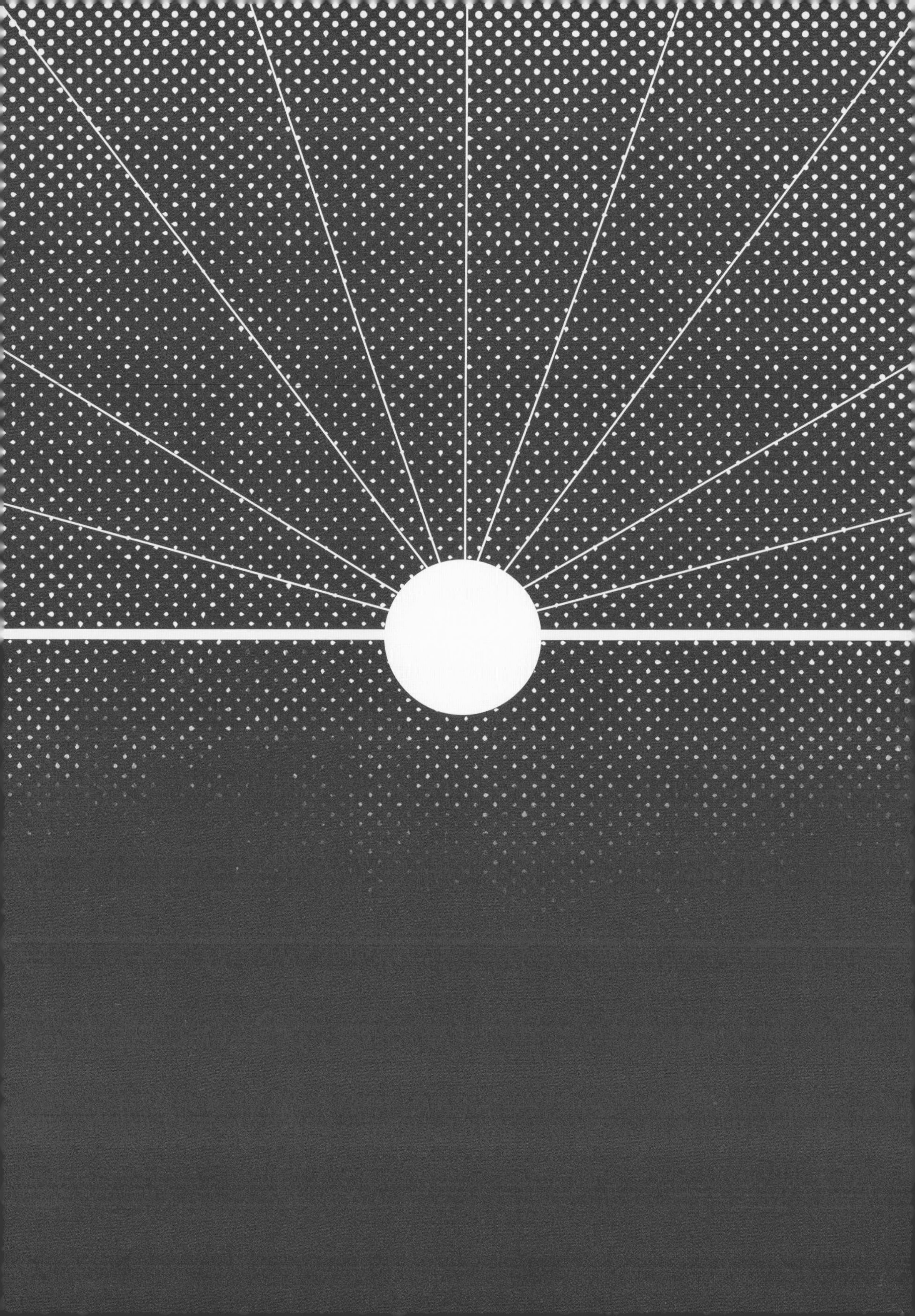

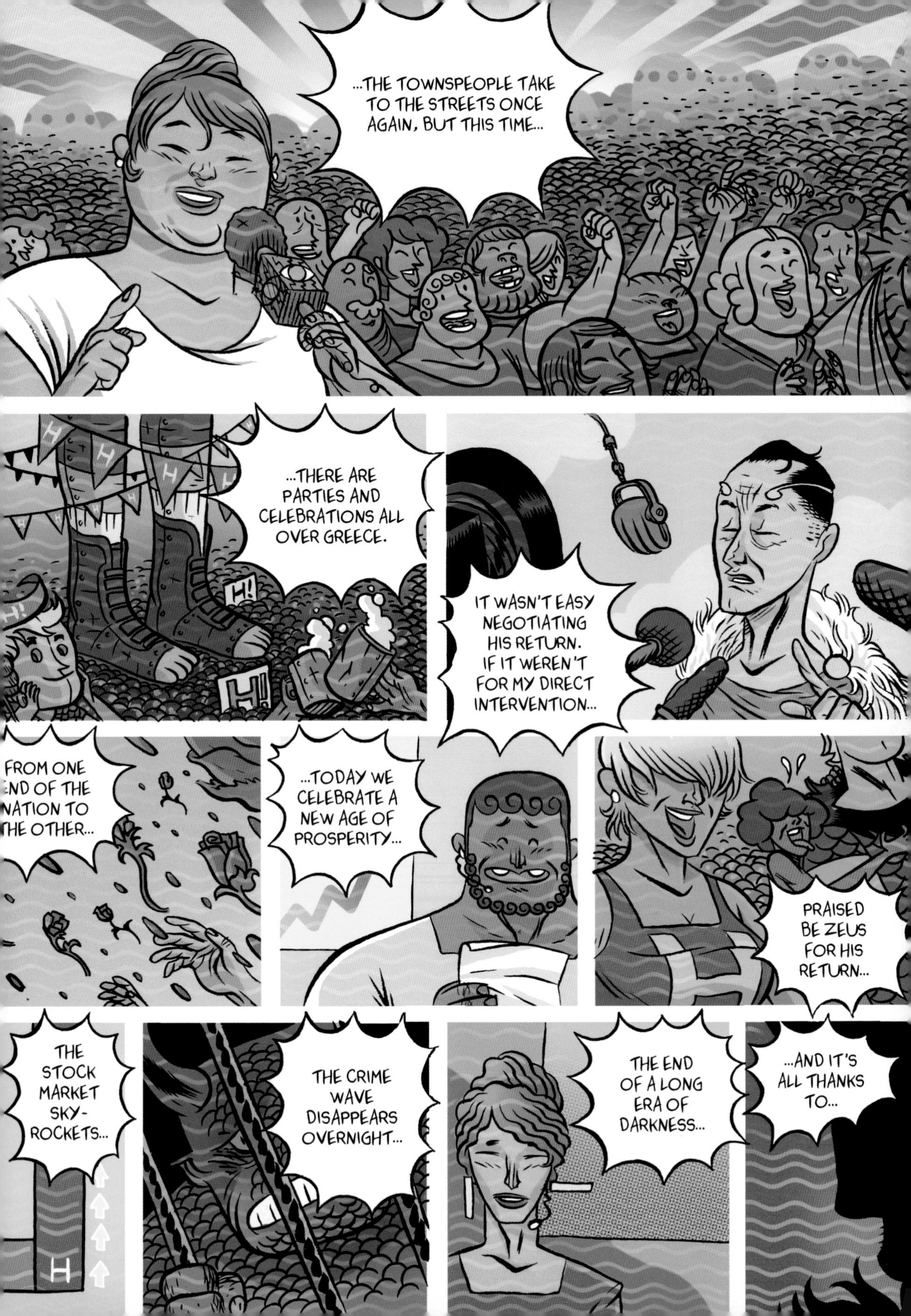
...THE TOWNSPEOPLE TAKE TO THE STREETS ONCE AGAIN, BUT THIS TIME...
...THERE ARE PARTIES AND CELEBRATIONS ALL OVER GREECE.
H!
H!
IT WASN'T EASY NEGOTIATING HIS RETURN. IF IT WEREN'T FOR MY DIRECT INTERVENTION...
FROM ONE END OF THE NATION TO THE OTHER...
...TODAY WE CELEBRATE A NEW AGE OF PROSPERITY...
PRAISED BE ZEUS FOR HIS RETURN...
THE STOCK MARKET SKY-ROCKETS...
THE CRIME WAVE DISAPPEARS OVERNIGHT...
THE END OF A LONG ERA OF DARKNESS...
...AND IT'S ALL THANKS TO...

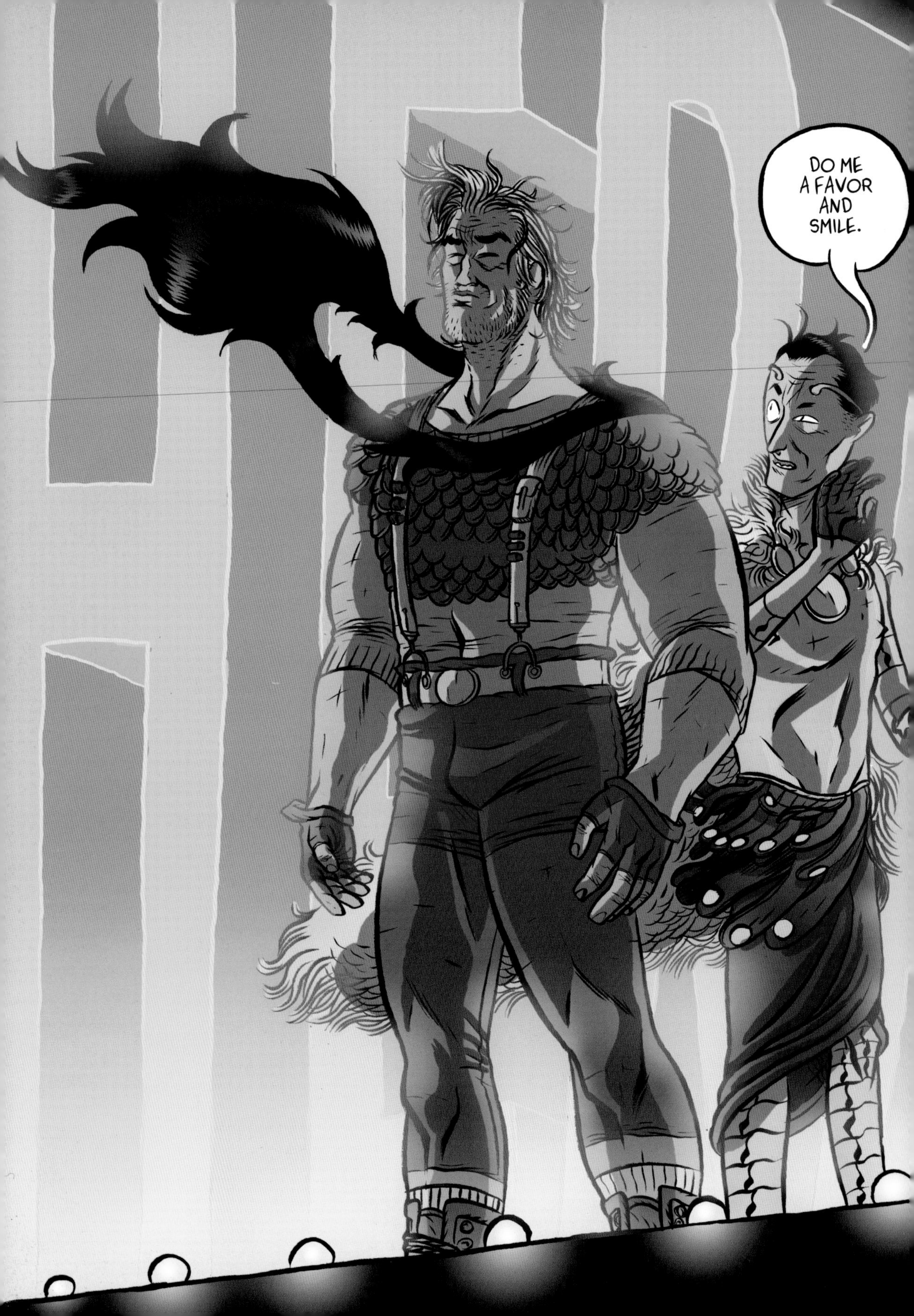
DO ME A FAVOR AND SMILE.

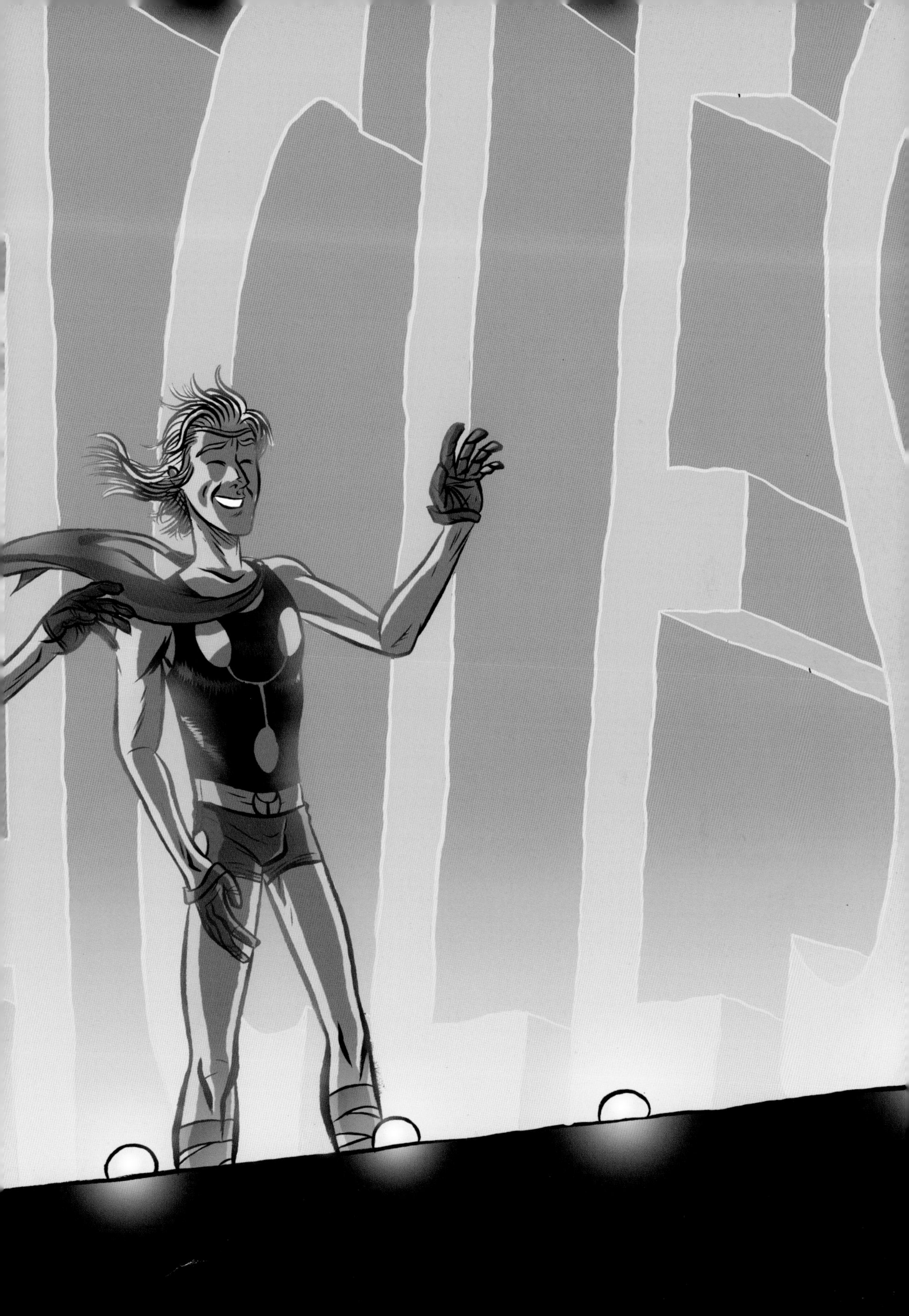

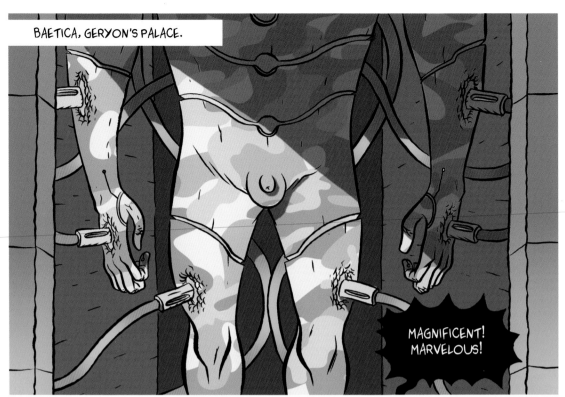

BAETICA, GERYON'S PALACE.

MAGNIFICENT! MARVELOUS!

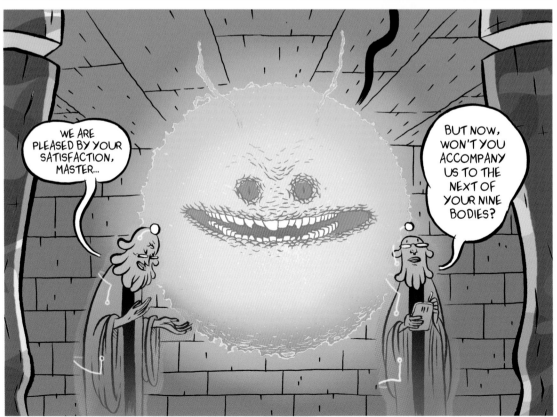

WE ARE PLEASED BY YOUR SATISFACTION, MASTER...

BUT NOW, WON'T YOU ACCOMPANY US TO THE NEXT OF YOUR NINE BODIES?

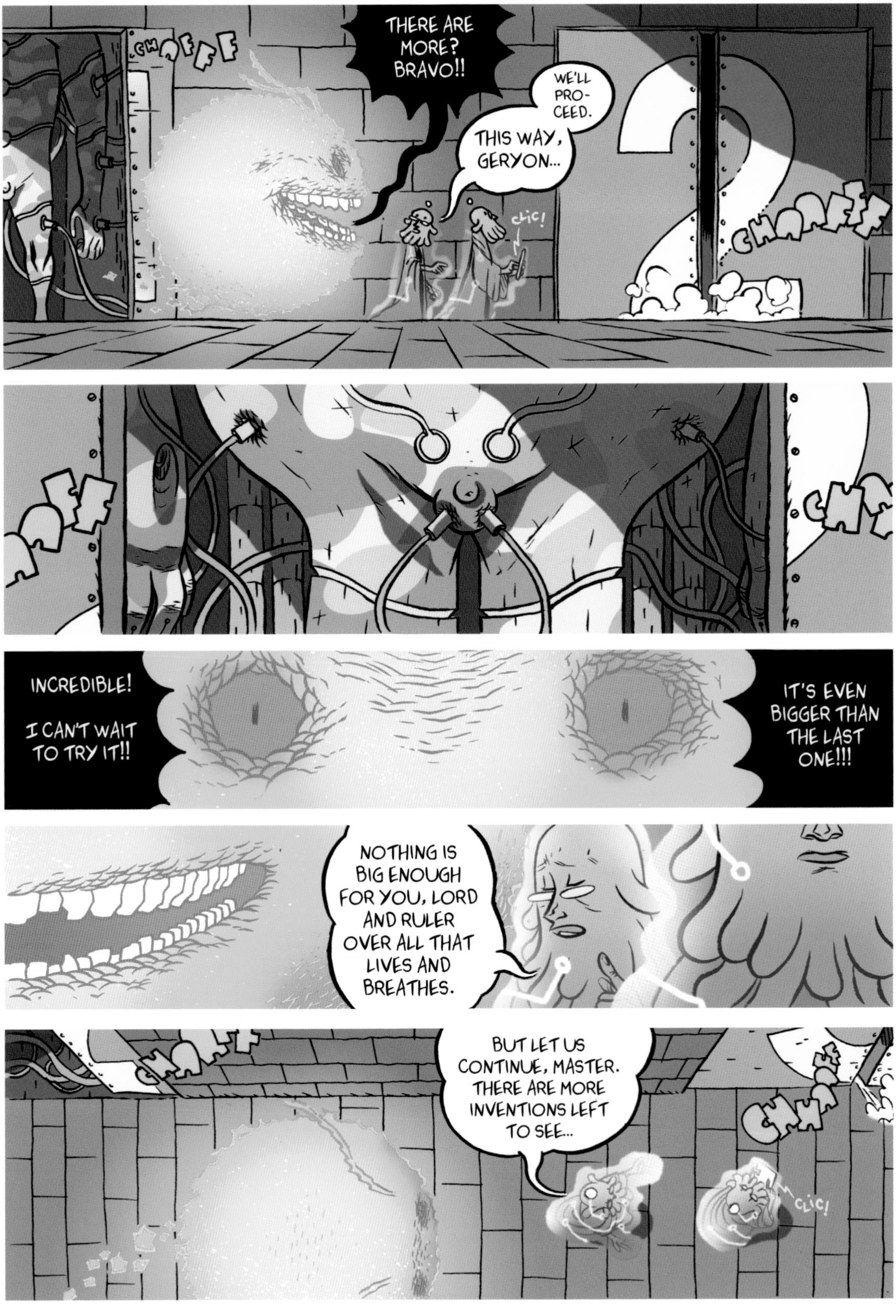
CHAFFF
THERE ARE MORE? BRAVO!!
WE'LL PRO-CEED.
THIS WAY, GERYON...
CLIC!
CHAFFF
INCREDIBLE!
I CAN'T WAIT TO TRY IT!!
IT'S EVEN BIGGER THAN THE LAST ONE!!!
NOTHING IS BIG ENOUGH FOR YOU, LORD AND RULER OVER ALL THAT LIVES AND BREATHES.
BUT LET US CONTINUE, MASTER. THERE ARE MORE INVENTIONS LEFT TO SEE...
CLIC!

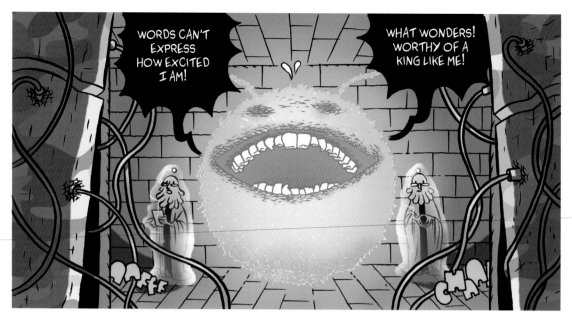

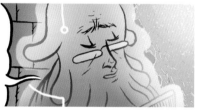

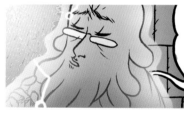

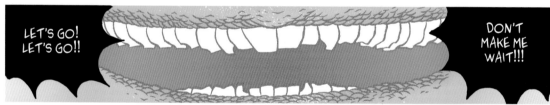

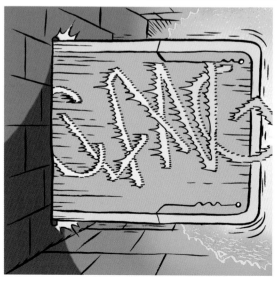

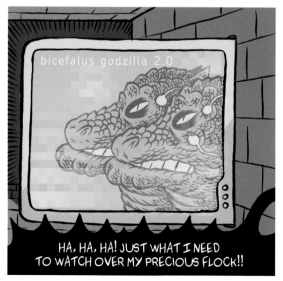

WORDS CAN'T EXPRESS HOW EXCITED I AM!
WHAT WONDERS! WORTHY OF A KING LIKE ME!
THEY ARE BUT HUMBLE TOKENS OF OUR DEVOTION, GREAT MASTER...
BUT PERMIT US ONE FINAL OFFERING, OH MAGNANIMOUS ONE...
LET'S GO! LET'S GO!!
DON'T MAKE ME WAIT!!!
bicefalus godzilla 2.0
HA, HA, HA! JUST WHAT I NEED TO WATCH OVER MY PRECIOUS FLOCK!!

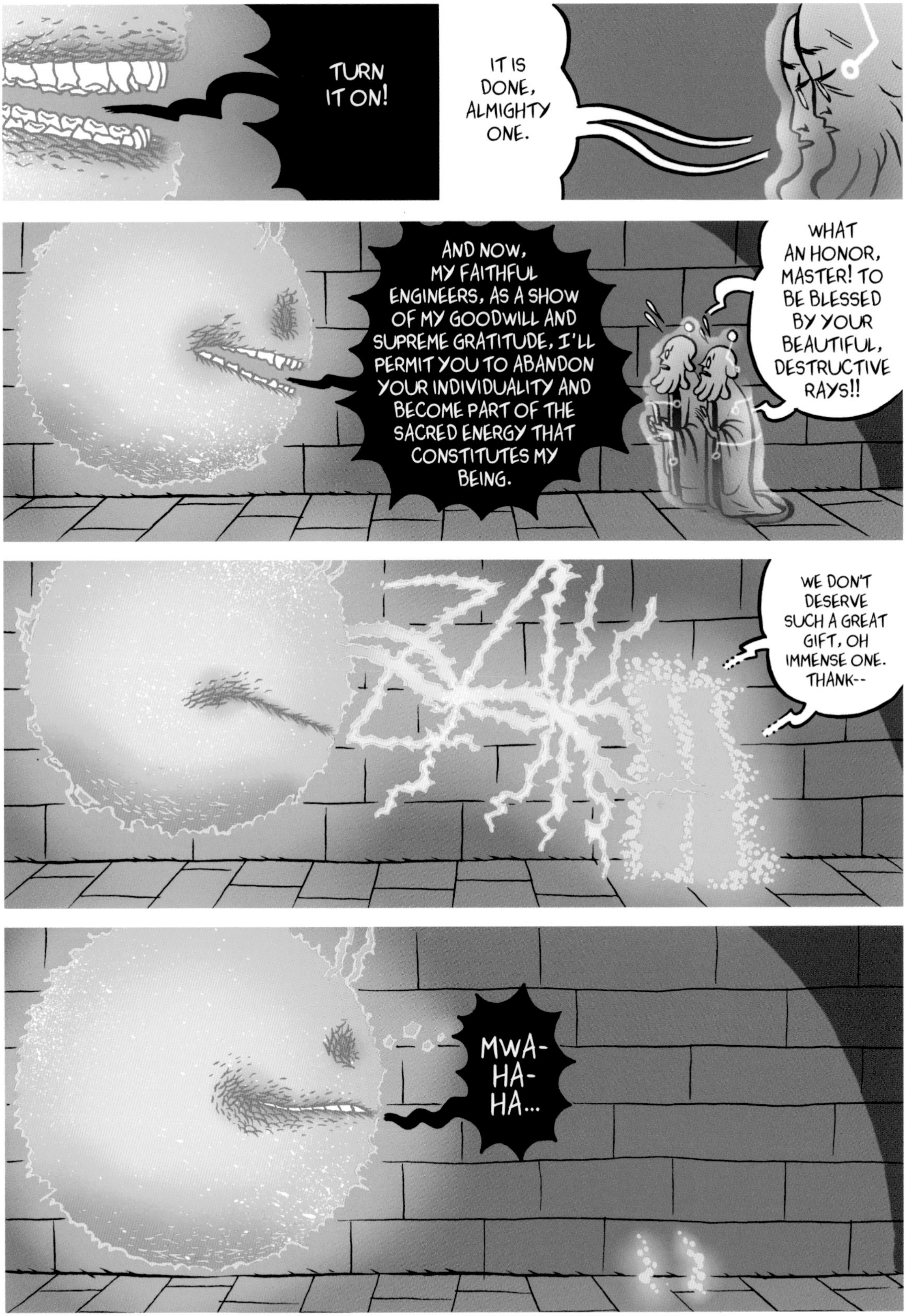
TURN IT ON!
IT IS DONE, ALMIGHTY ONE.
AND NOW, MY FAITHFUL ENGINEERS, AS A SHOW OF MY GOODWILL AND SUPREME GRATITUDE, I'LL PERMIT YOU TO ABANDON YOUR INDIVIDUALITY AND BECOME PART OF THE SACRED ENERGY THAT CONSTITUTES MY BEING.
WHAT AN HONOR, MASTER! TO BE BLESSED BY YOUR BEAUTIFUL, DESTRUCTIVE RAYS!!
WE DON'T DESERVE SUCH A GREAT GIFT, OH IMMENSE ONE. THANK--
MWA-HA-HA...

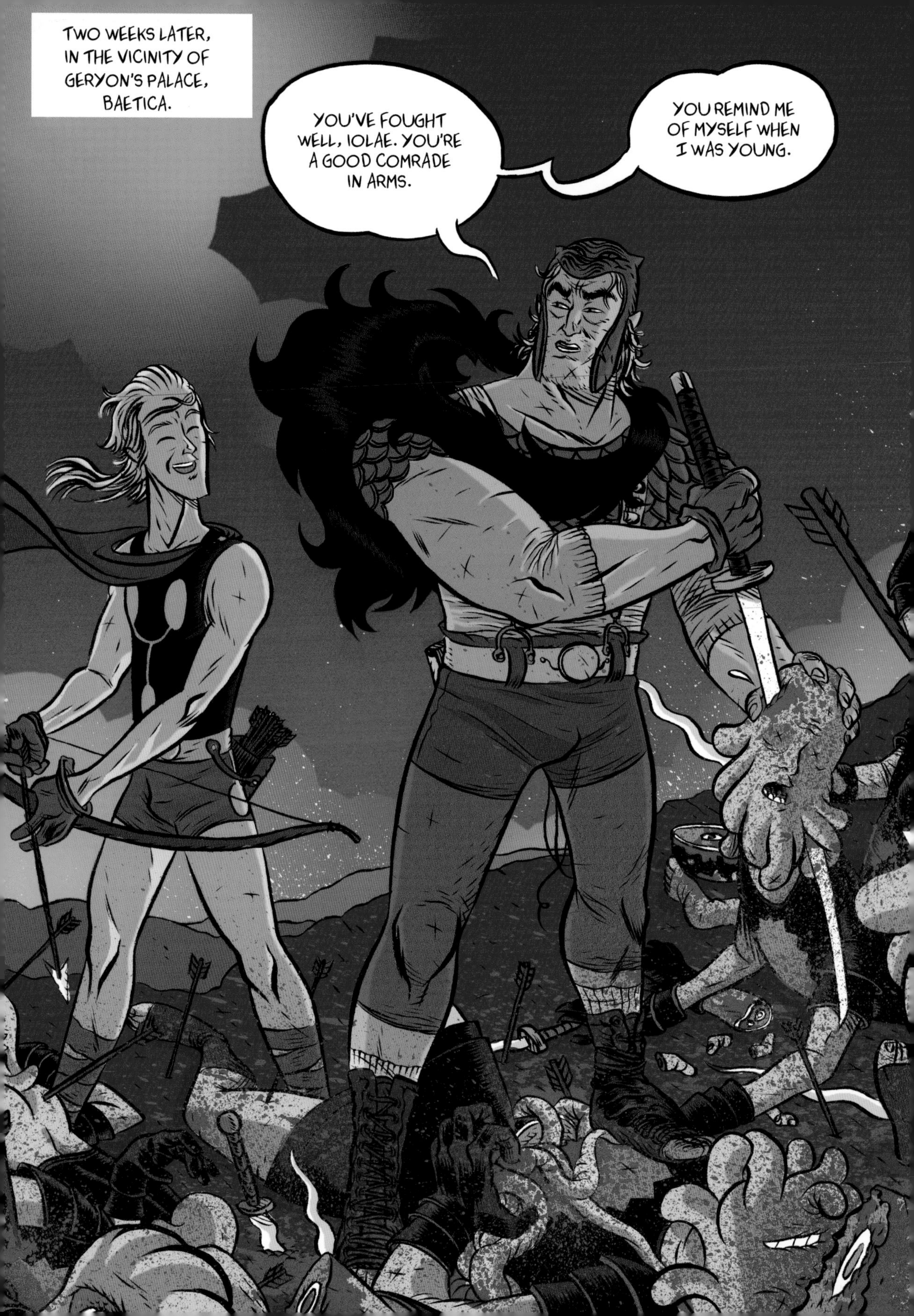
TWO WEEKS LATER, IN THE VICINITY OF GERYON'S PALACE, BAETICA.
YOU'VE FOUGHT WELL, IOLAE. YOU'RE A GOOD COMRADE IN ARMS.
YOU REMIND ME OF MYSELF WHEN I WAS YOUNG.

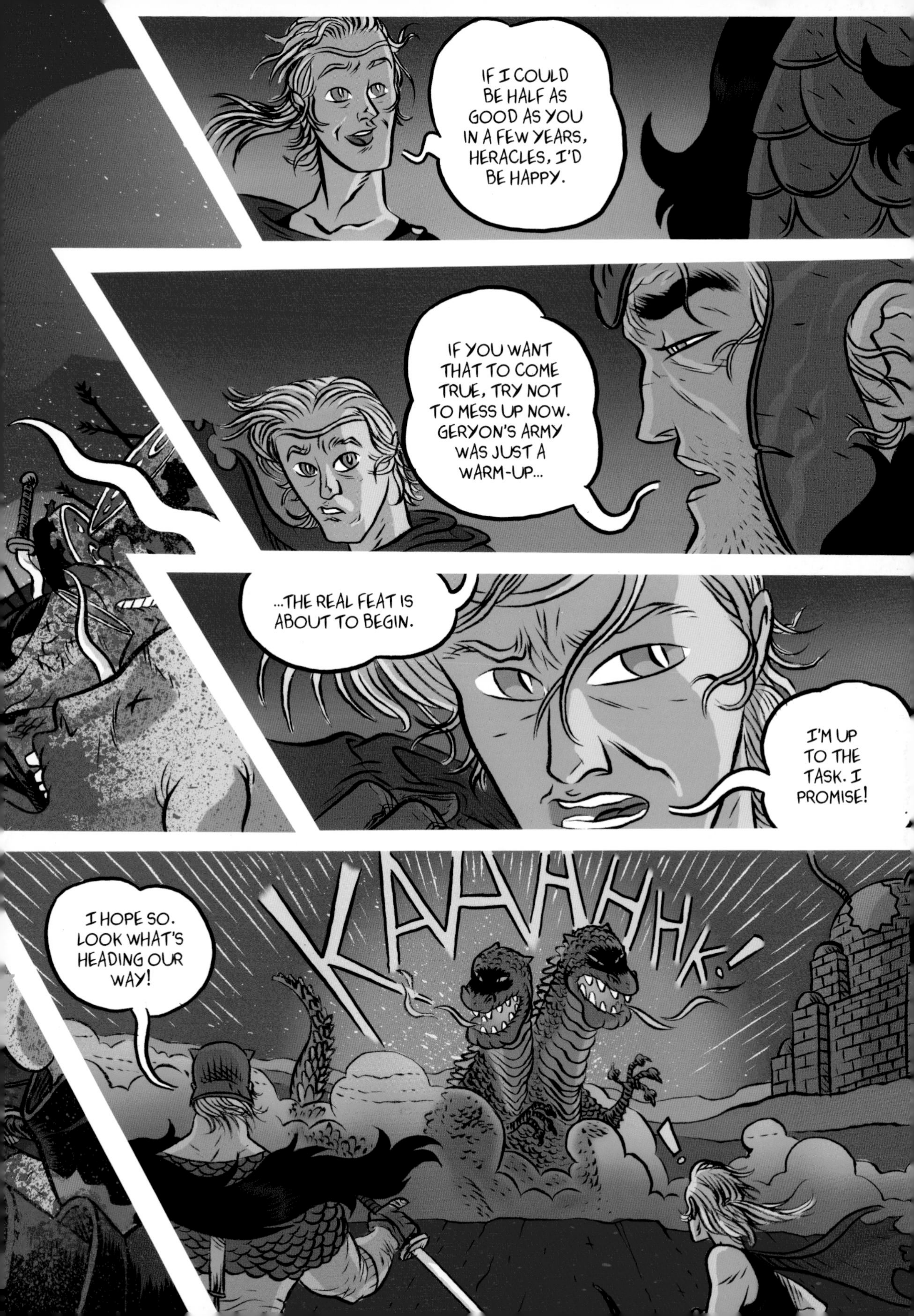
IF I COULD BE HALF AS GOOD AS YOU IN A FEW YEARS, HERACLES, I'D BE HAPPY.
IF YOU WANT THAT TO COME TRUE, TRY NOT TO MESS UP NOW. GERYON'S ARMY WAS JUST A WARM-UP...
...THE REAL FEAT IS ABOUT TO BEGIN.
I'M UP TO THE TASK. I PROMISE!
KAAAHHK!
I HOPE SO. LOOK WHAT'S HEADING OUR WAY!
!

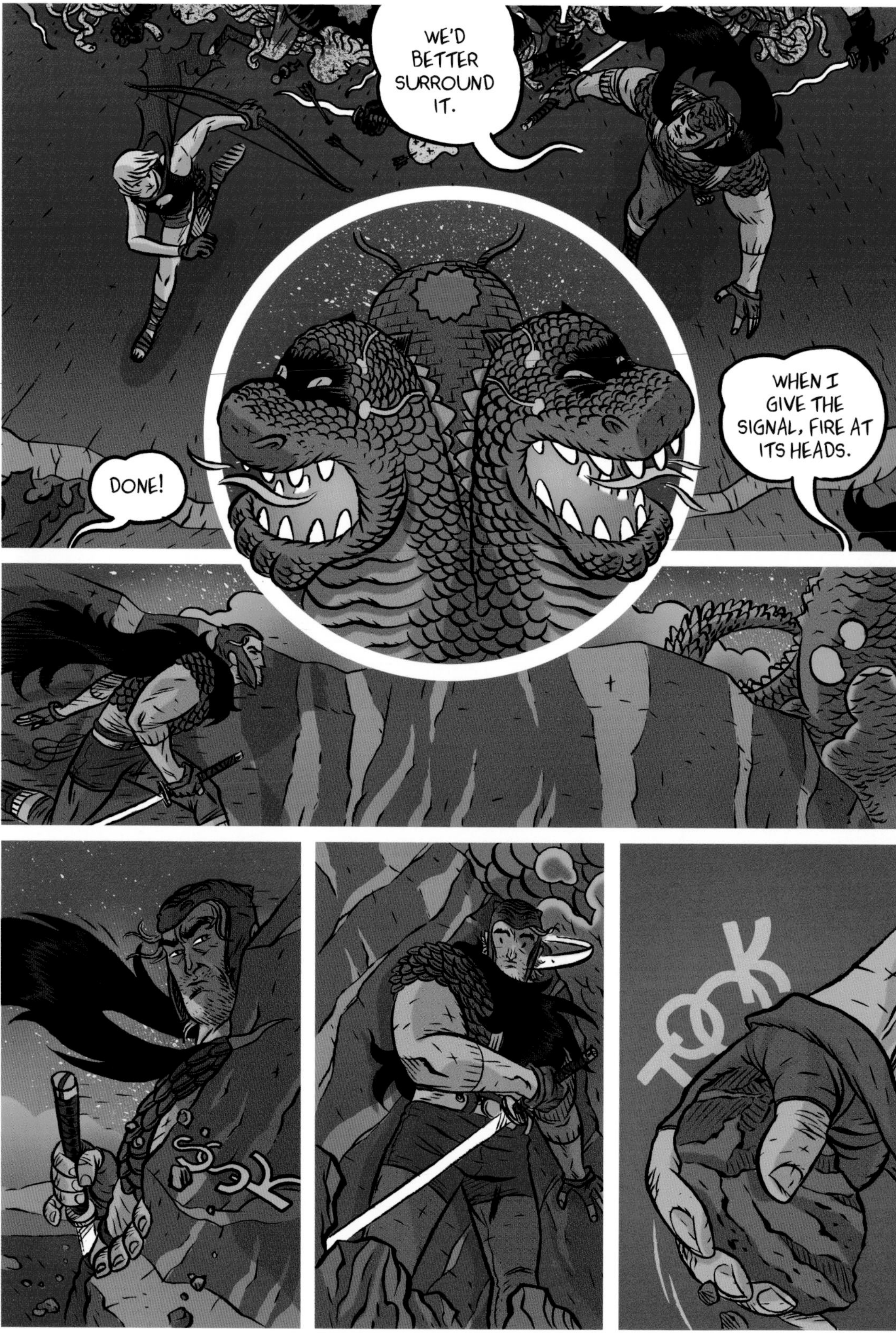
WE'D BETTER SURROUND IT.
WHEN I GIVE THE SIGNAL, FIRE AT ITS HEADS.
DONE!
TOOK

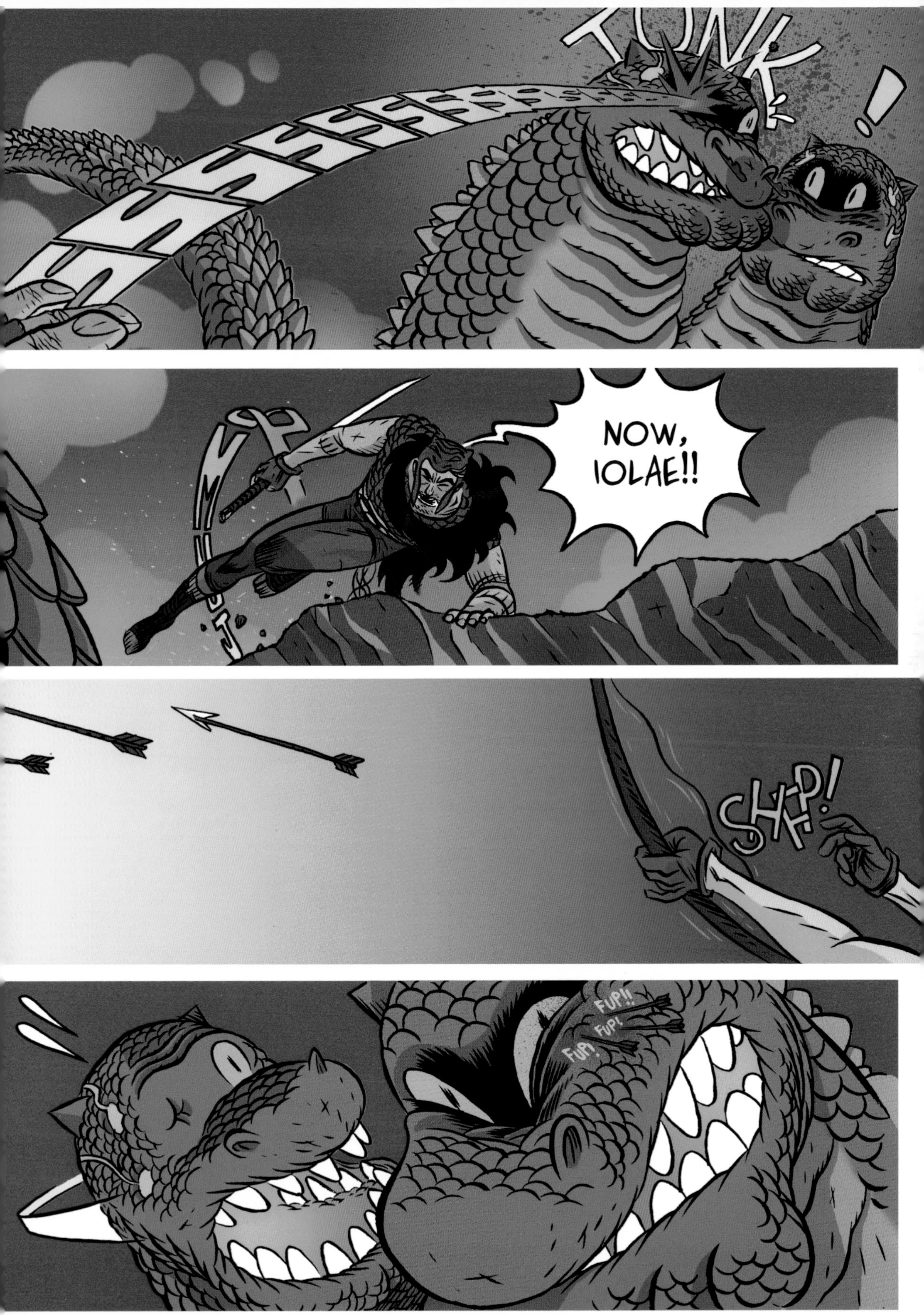
TONK
!
HSSSSSSSSSSSSS
NOW, IOLAE!!
SHTAP!
FUP!!
FUP!
FUP!

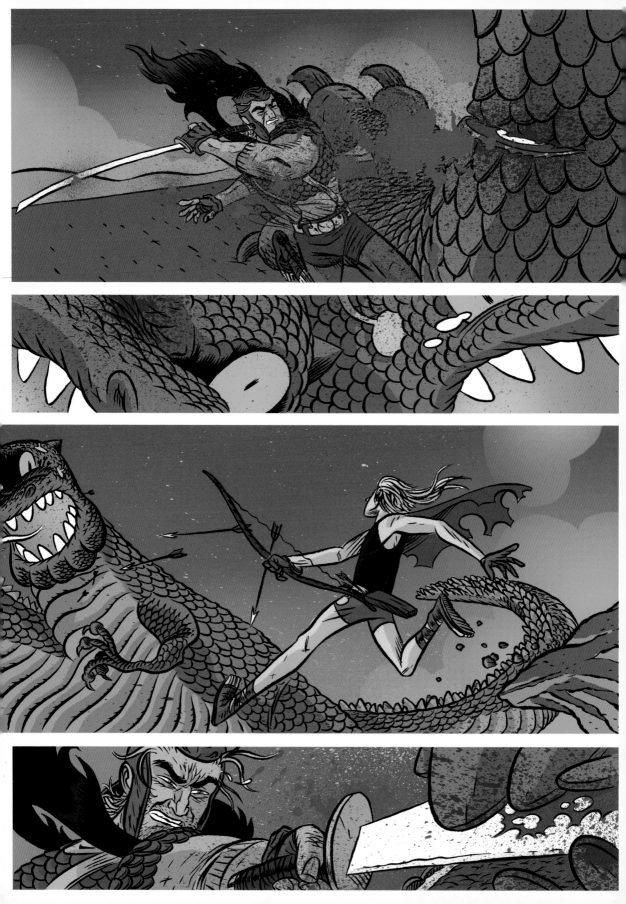

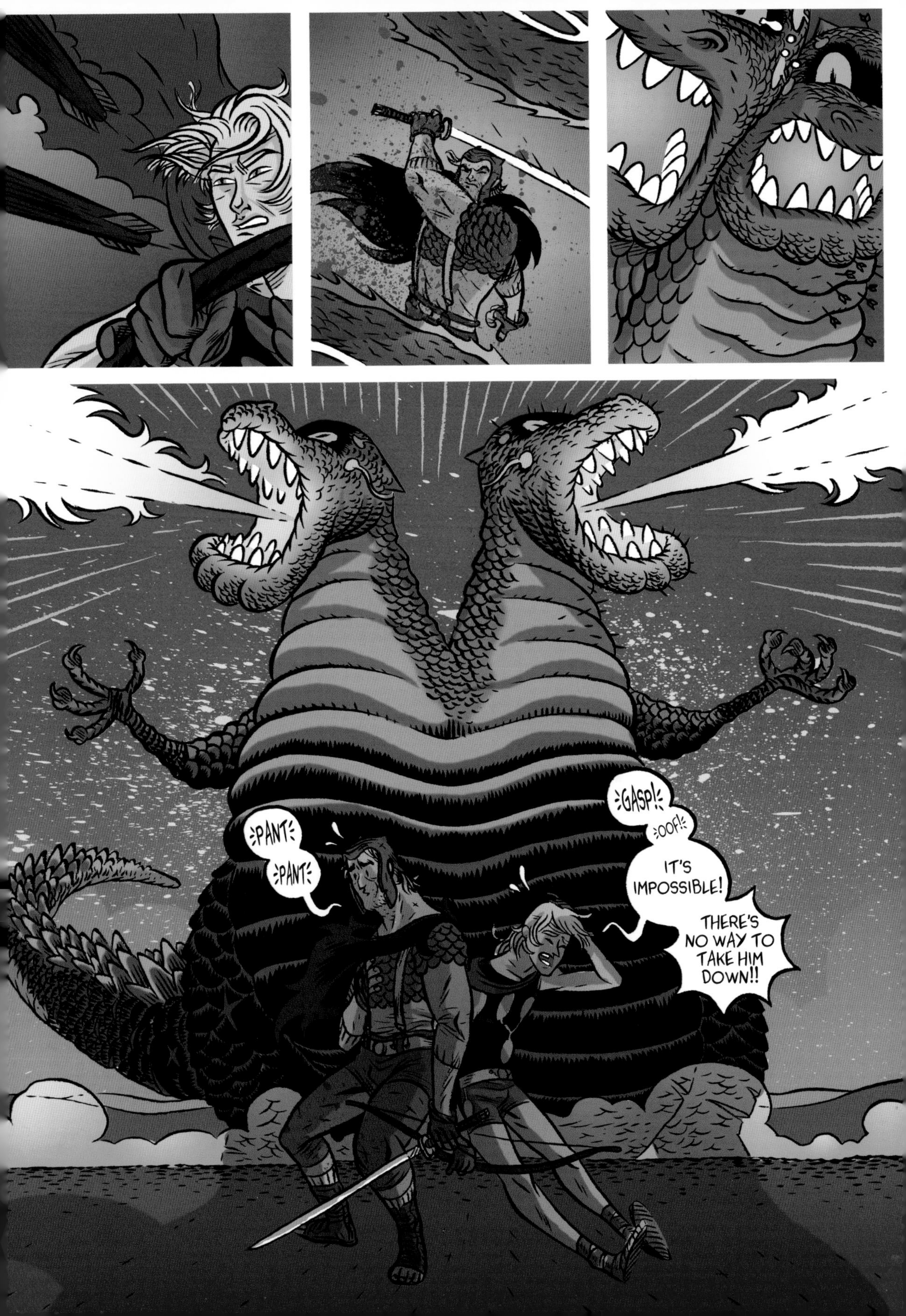
PANT
PANT
GASP!
OOF!
IT'S IMPOSSIBLE!
THERE'S NO WAY TO TAKE HIM DOWN!!

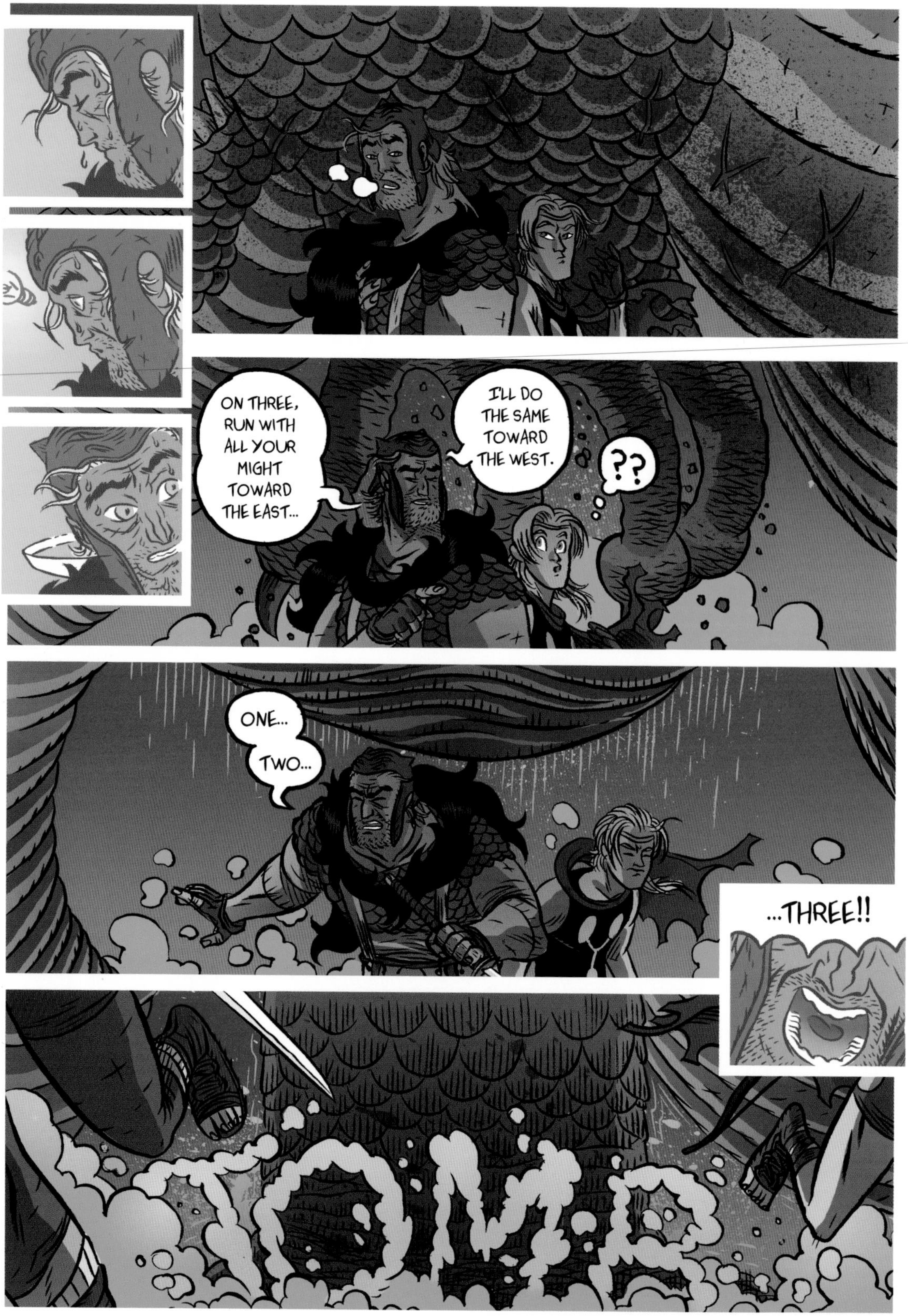
ON THREE, RUN WITH ALL YOUR MIGHT TOWARD THE EAST...
I'LL DO THE SAME TOWARD THE WEST.
??
ONE...
TWO...
...THREE!!
TOMP

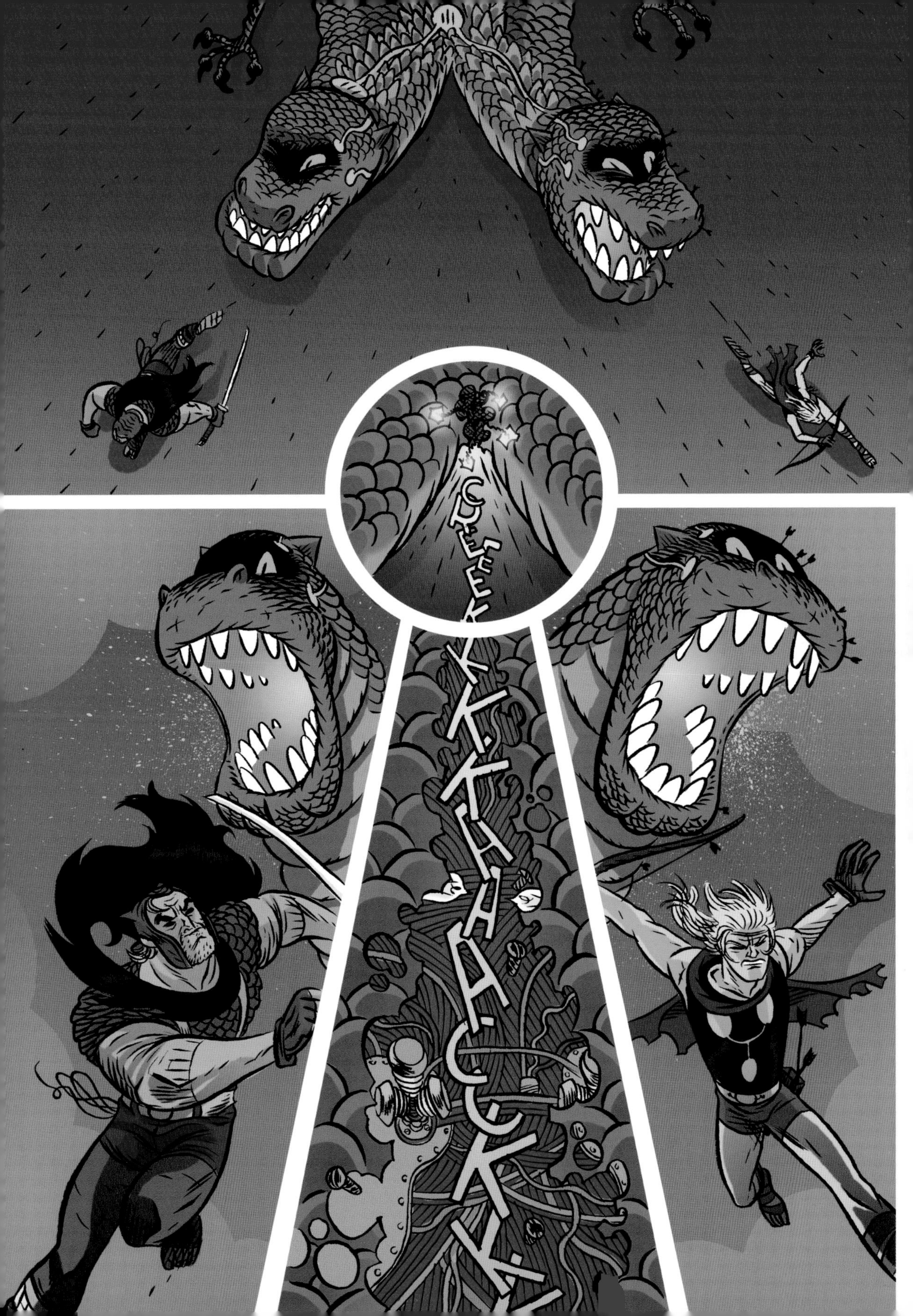
CREEKKKAAACCKK!

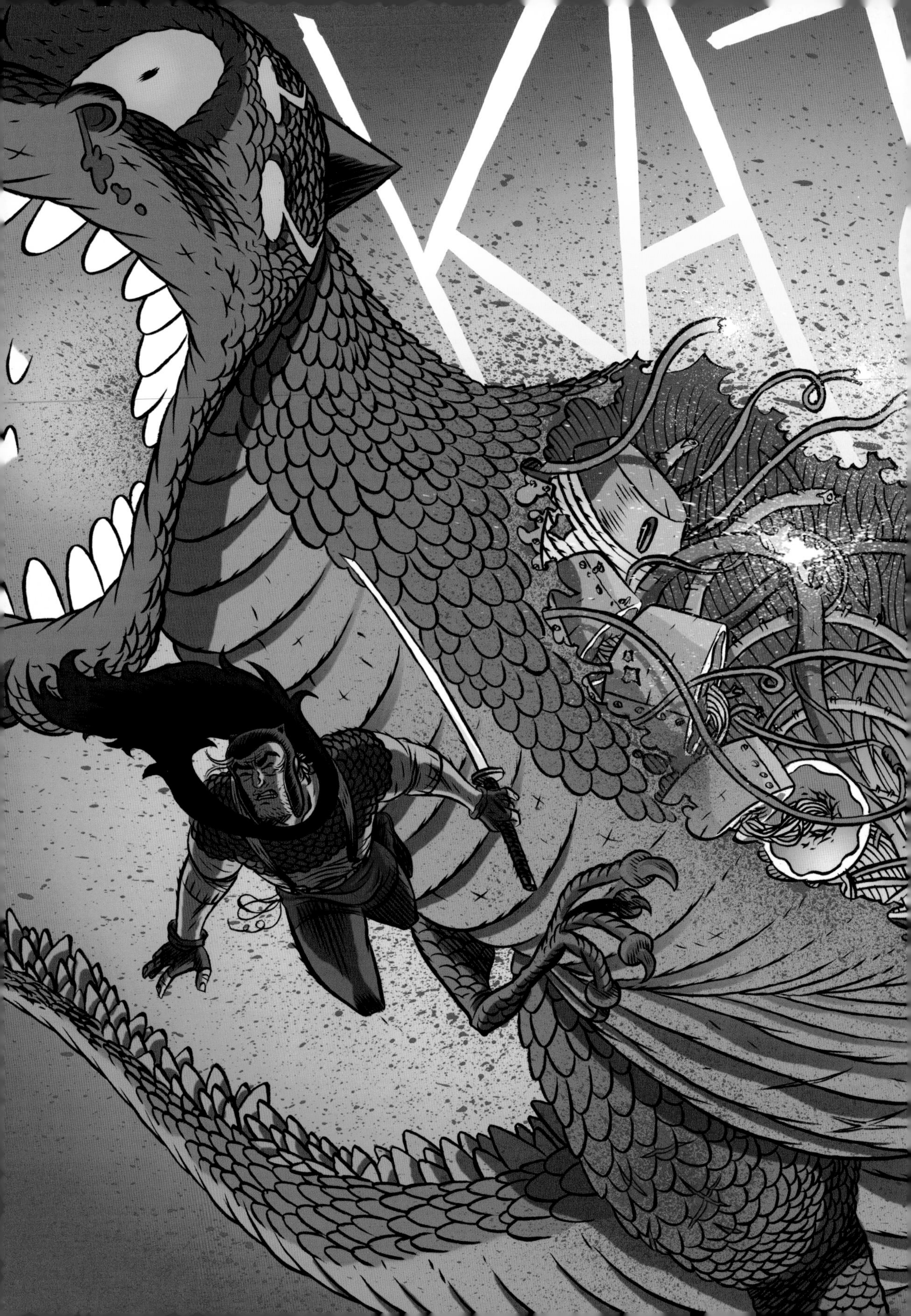

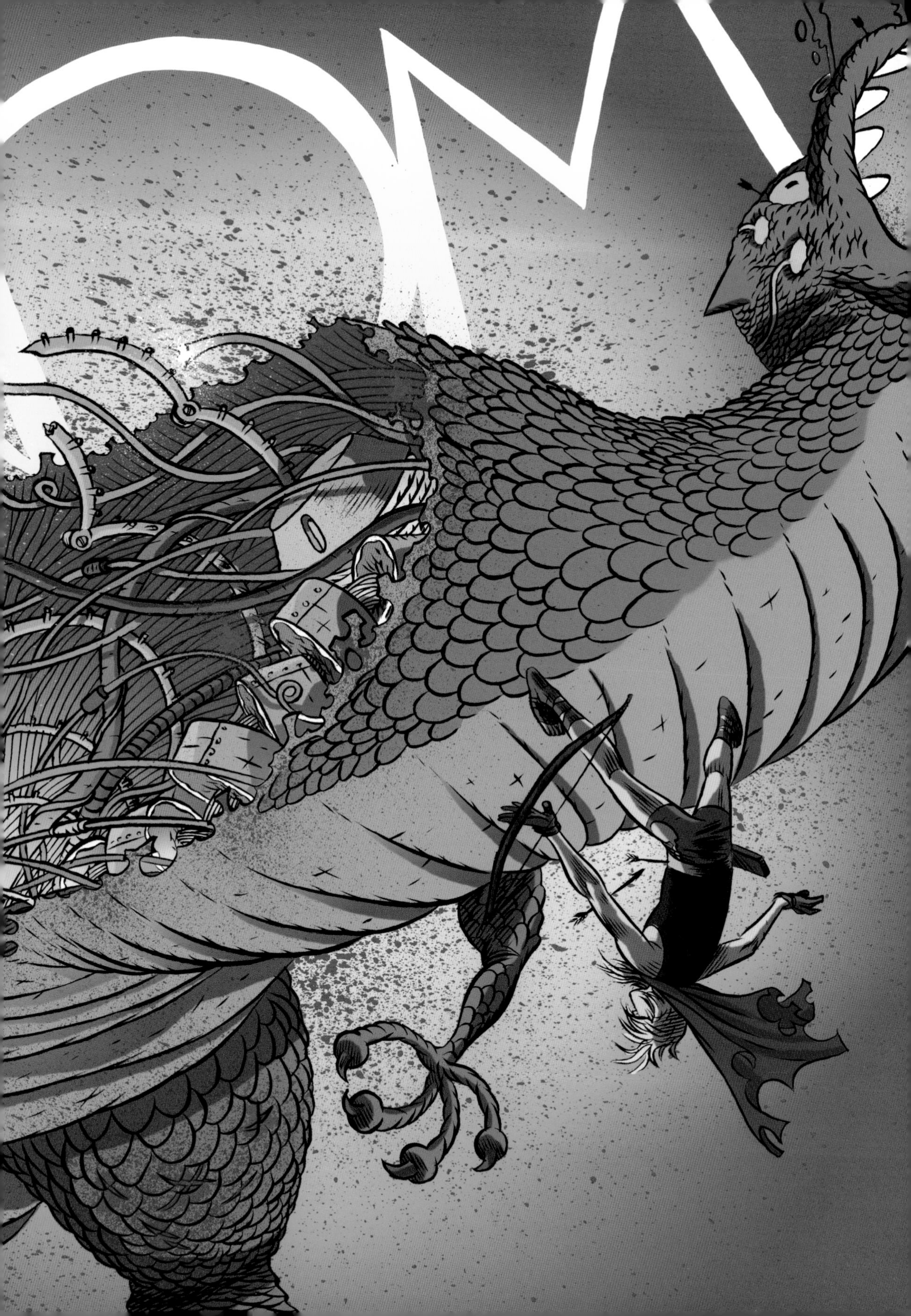

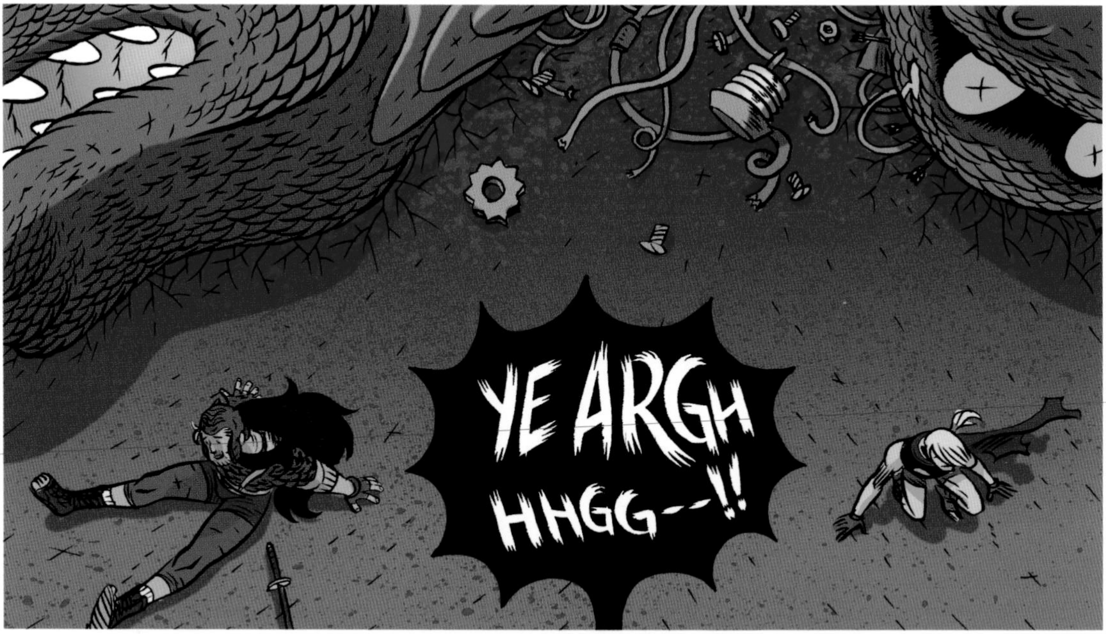
YE ARGH HHGG--!!

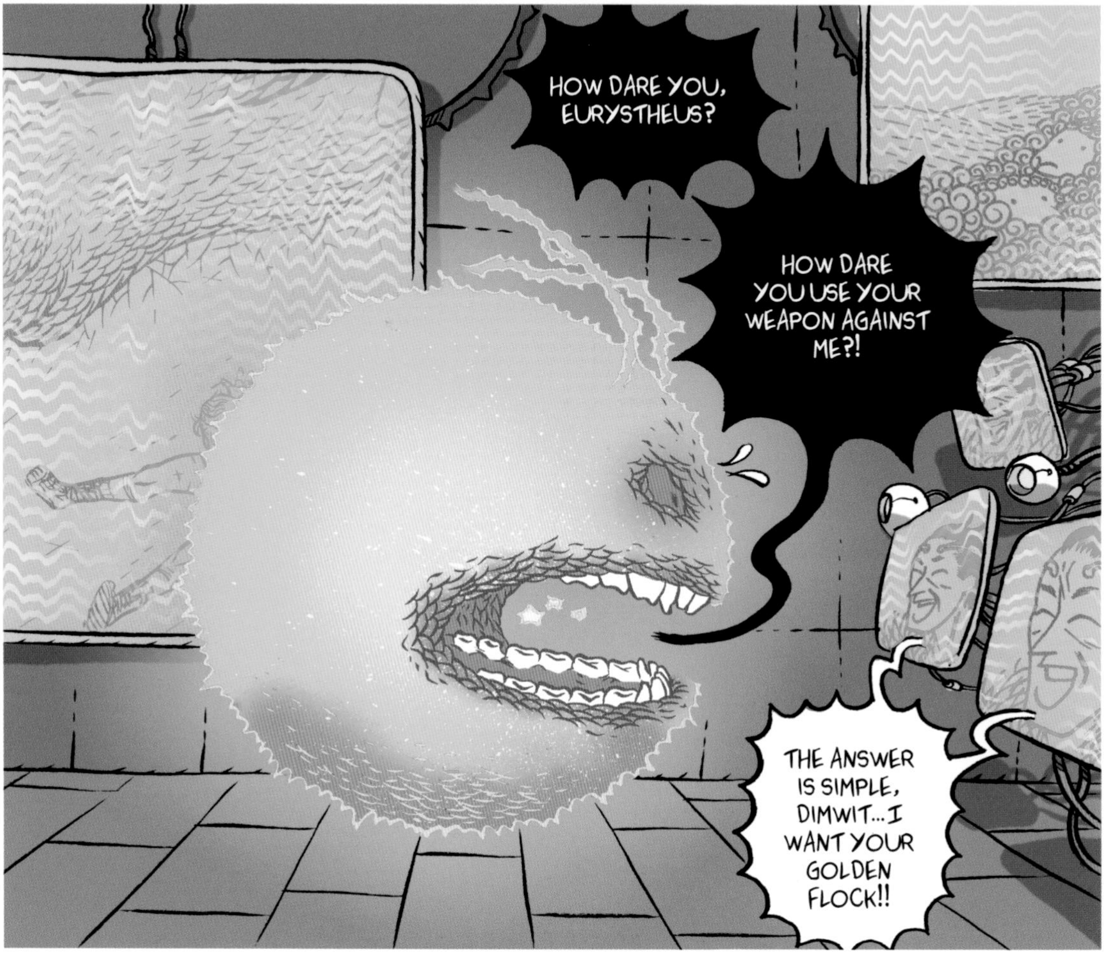
HOW DARE YOU, EURYSTHEUS?
HOW DARE YOU USE YOUR WEAPON AGAINST ME?!
THE ANSWER IS SIMPLE, DIMWIT... I WANT YOUR GOLDEN FLOCK!!

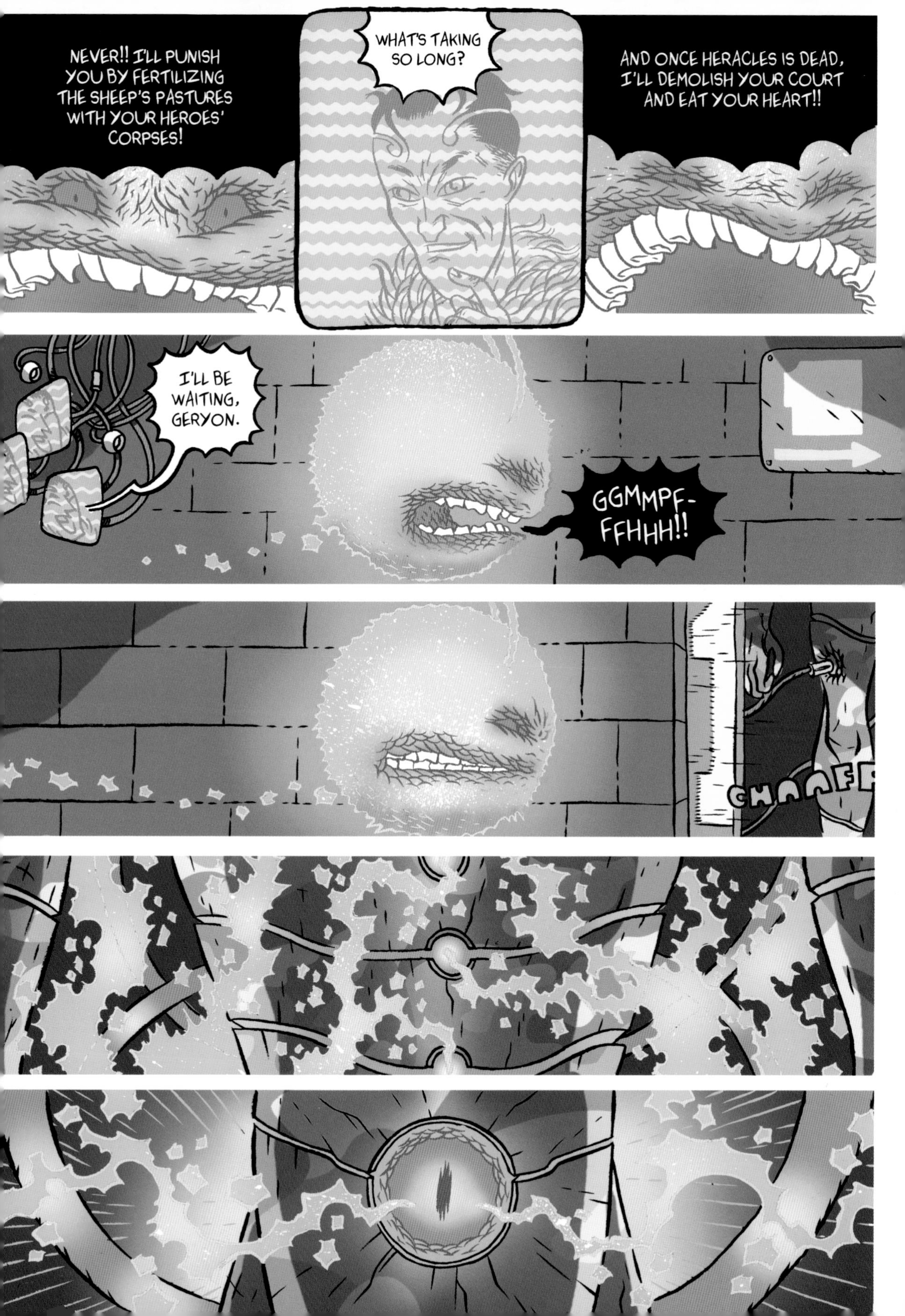
NEVER!! I'LL PUNISH YOU BY FERTILIZING THE SHEEP'S PASTURES WITH YOUR HEROES' CORPSES!
WHAT'S TAKING SO LONG?
AND ONCE HERACLES IS DEAD, I'LL DEMOLISH YOUR COURT AND EAT YOUR HEART!!
I'LL BE WAITING, GERYON.
GGMMPF-FFHHH!!

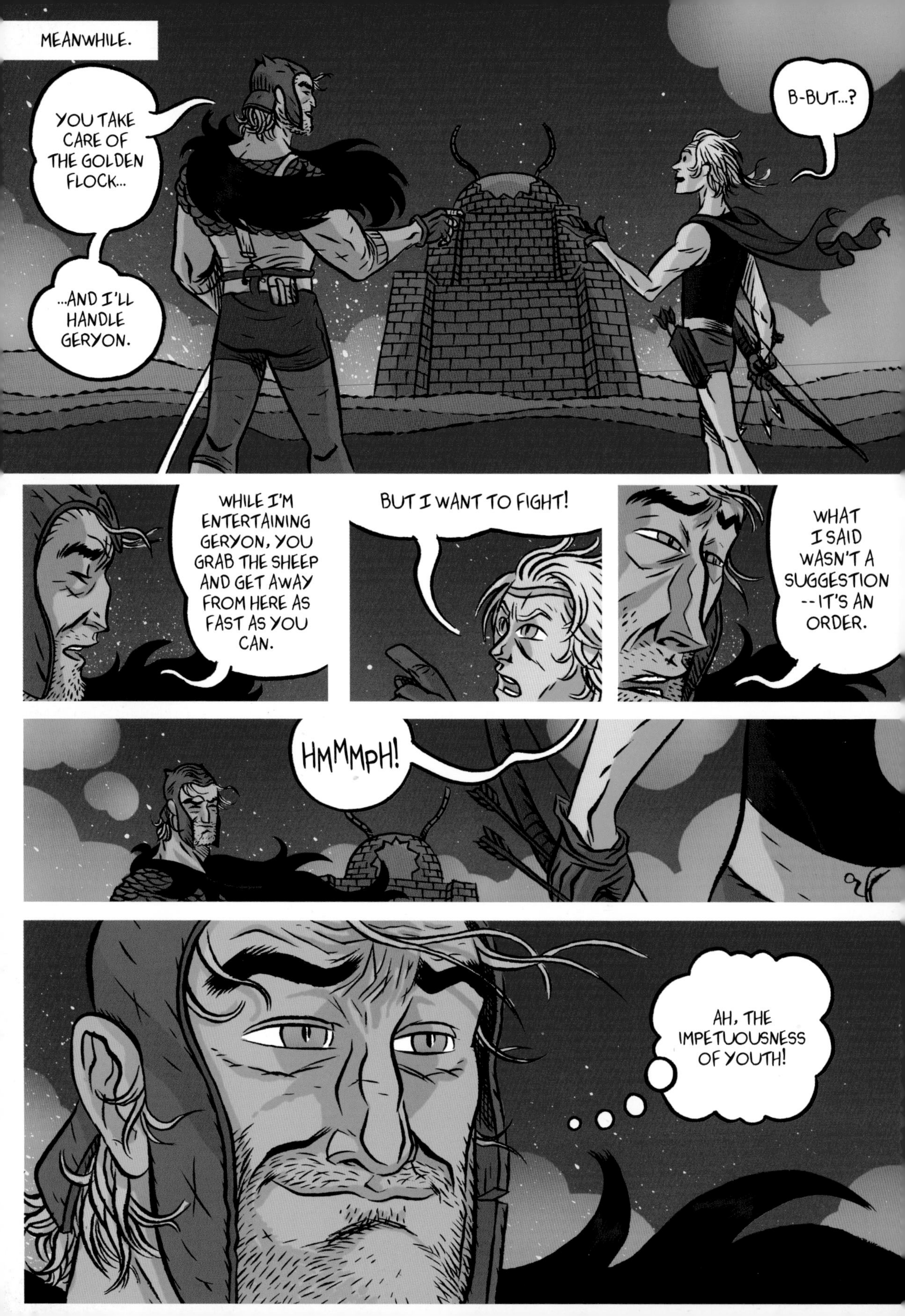
MEANWHILE.
YOU TAKE CARE OF THE GOLDEN FLOCK...
...AND I'LL HANDLE GERYON.
B-BUT...?
WHILE I'M ENTERTAINING GERYON, YOU GRAB THE SHEEP AND GET AWAY FROM HERE AS FAST AS YOU CAN.
BUT I WANT TO FIGHT!
WHAT I SAID WASN'T A SUGGESTION -- IT'S AN ORDER.
HMMMPH!
AH, THE IMPETUOUSNESS OF YOUTH!

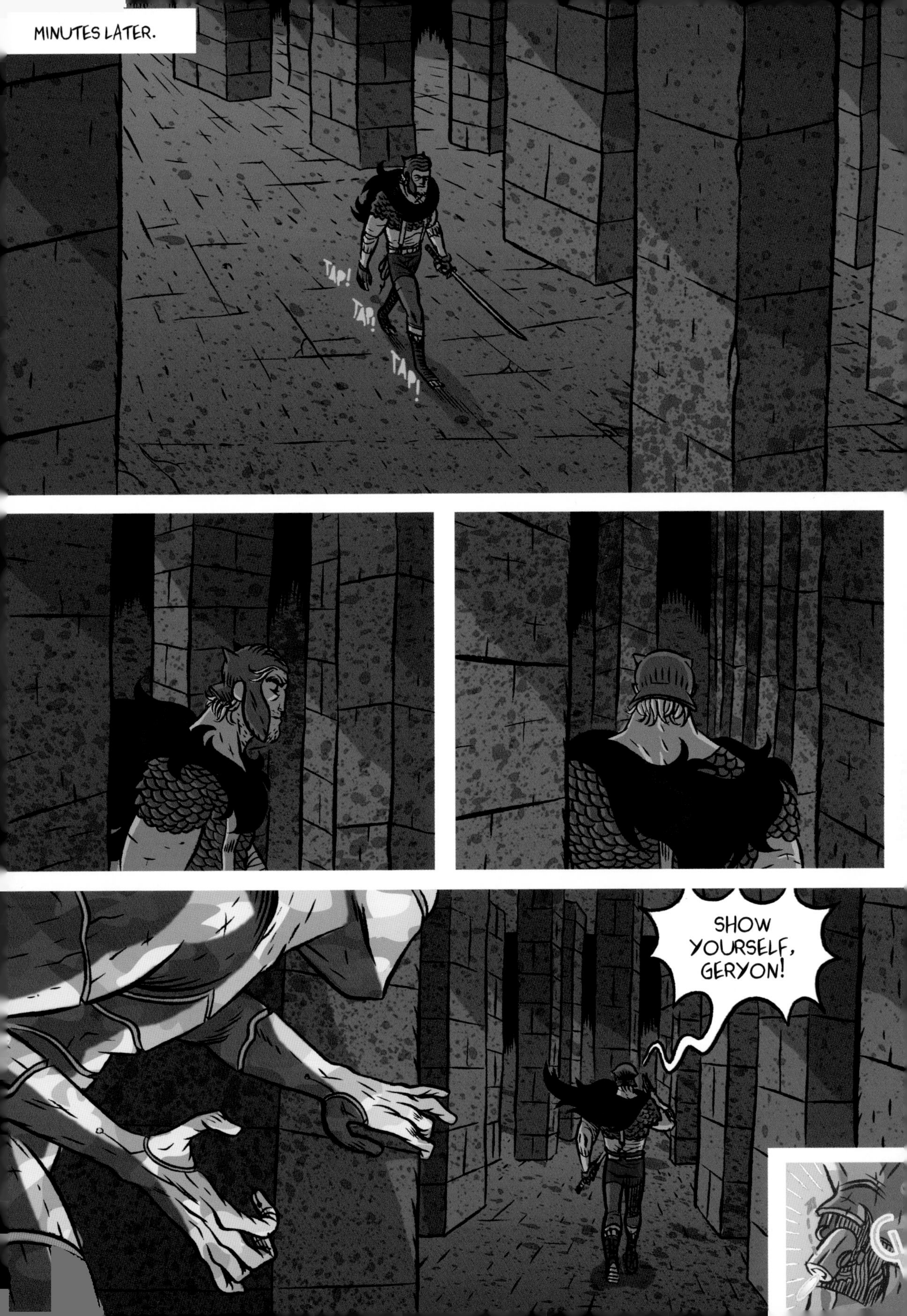
MINUTES LATER.
TAP!
TAP!
TAP!
SHOW YOURSELF, GERYON!

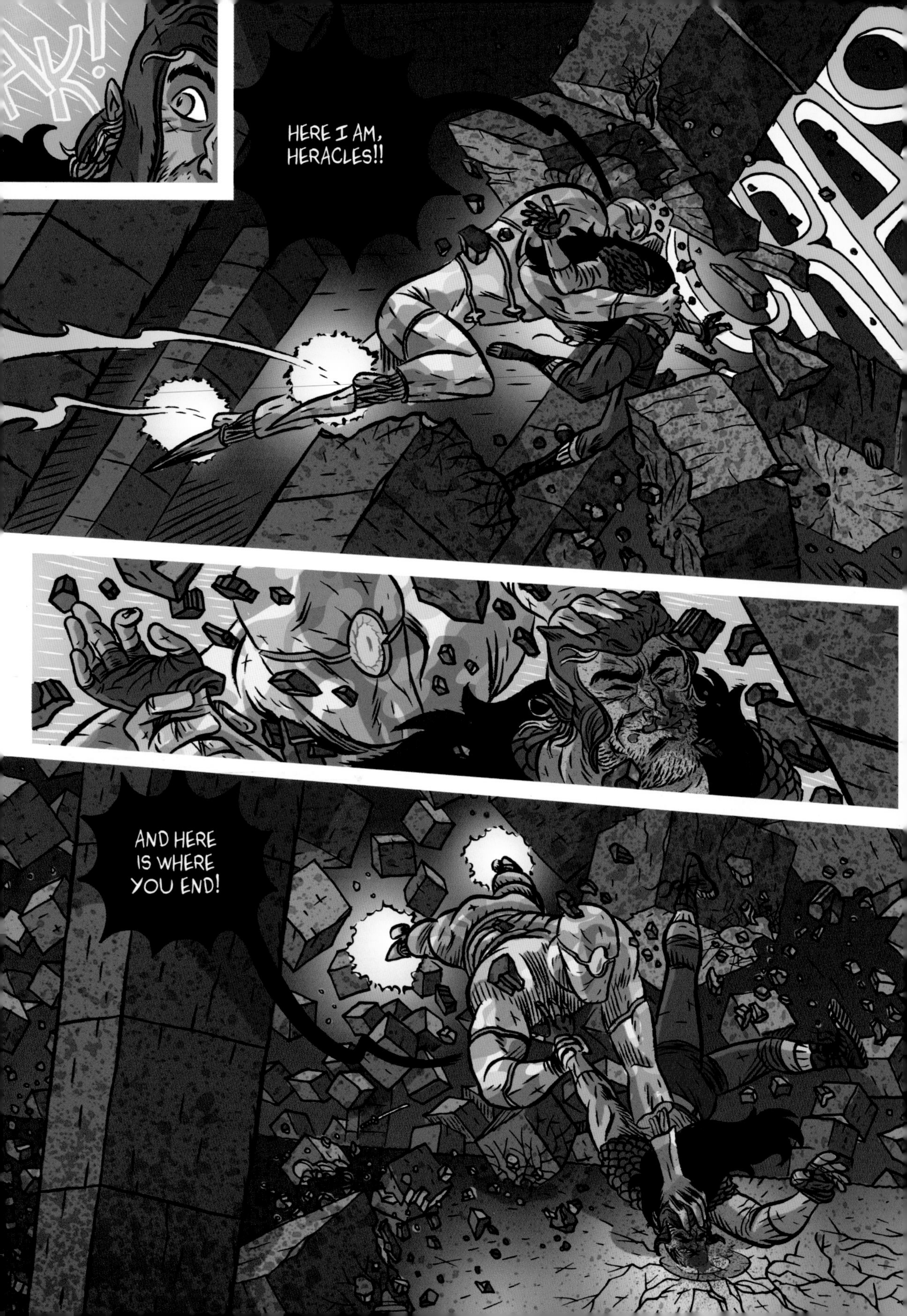
HERE I AM, HERACLES!!
AND HERE IS WHERE YOU END!

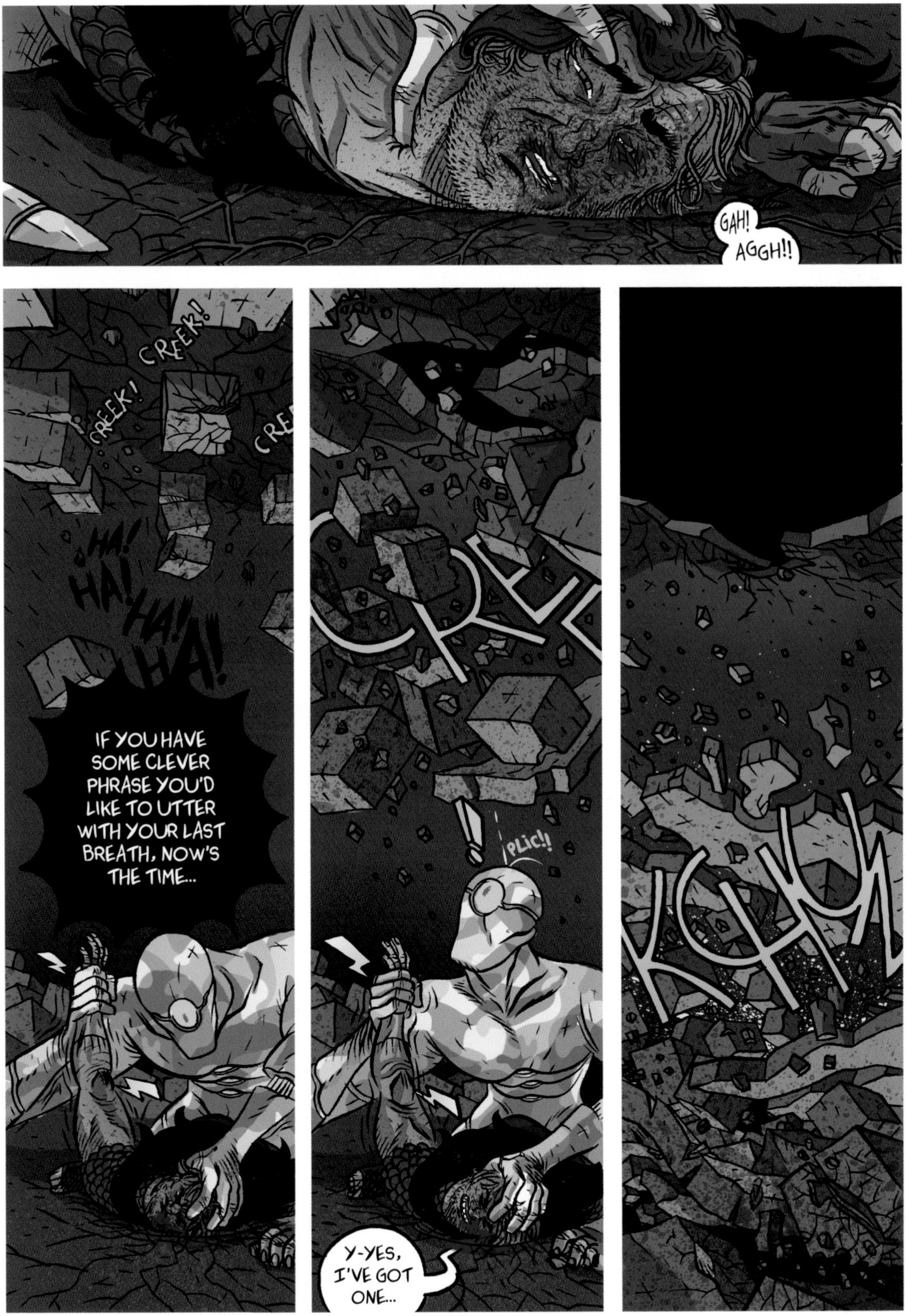

GAH! AGGH!!
CREEK! CREEK! CREE
HA! HA! HA! HA!
IF YOU HAVE SOME CLEVER PHRASE YOU'D LIKE TO UTTER WITH YOUR LAST BREATH, NOW'S THE TIME...
CREE
PLIC!!
Y-YES, I'VE GOT ONE...

RRRRRRRUMP

I'M NOT DYING AT THE HANDS OF SOME THIRD-RATE VILLAIN LIKE YOU!

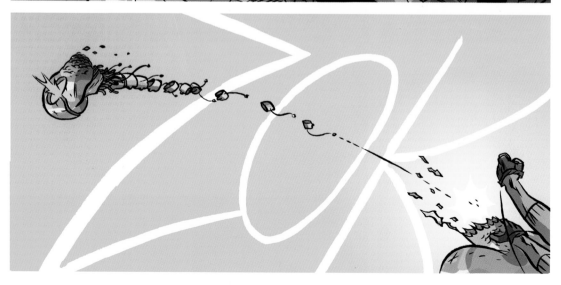

ZOK

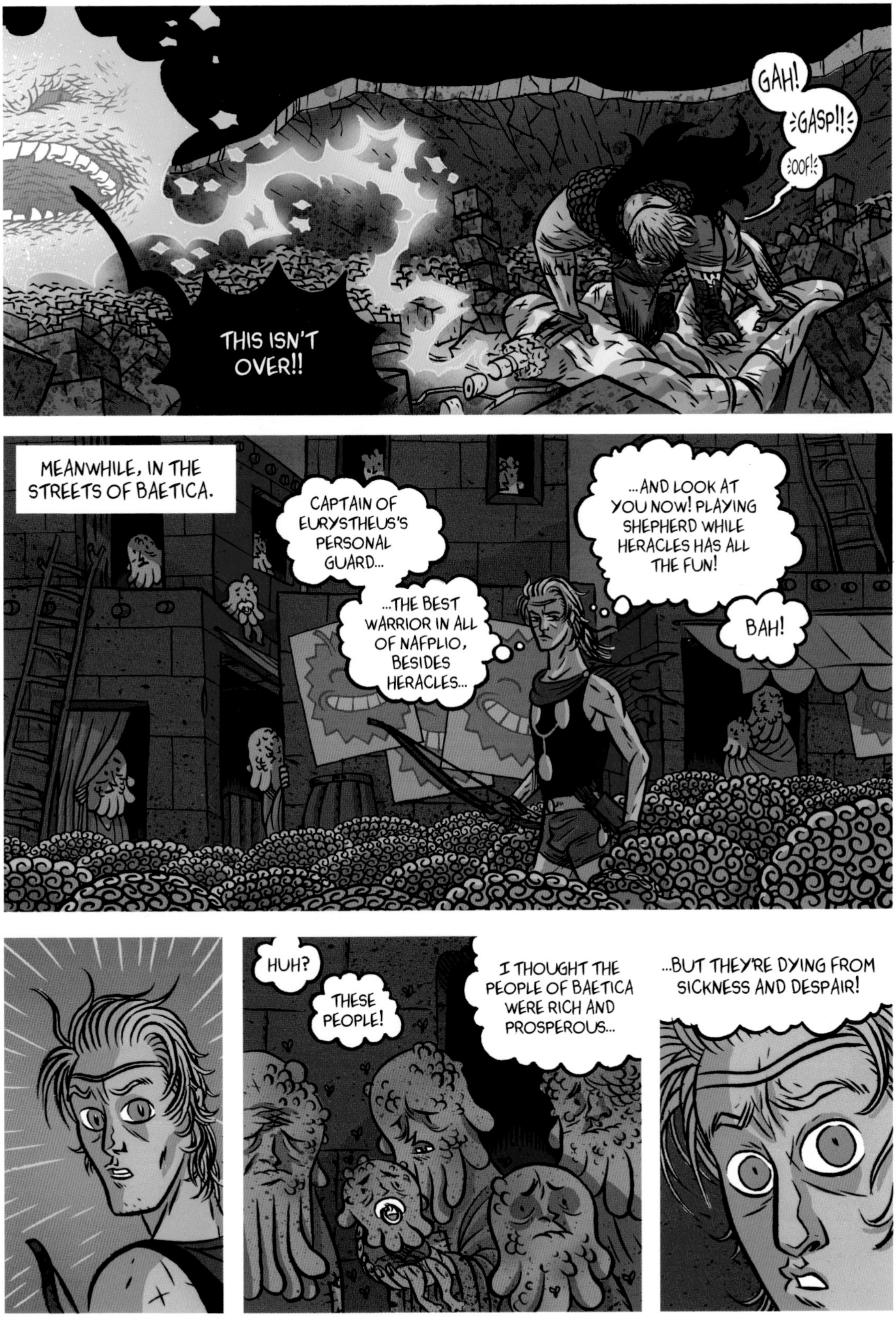
GAH!
GASP!!
OOF!
THIS ISN'T OVER!!
MEANWHILE, IN THE STREETS OF BAETICA.
CAPTAIN OF EURYSTHEUS'S PERSONAL GUARD...
...THE BEST WARRIOR IN ALL OF NAFPLIO, BESIDES HERACLES...
...AND LOOK AT YOU NOW! PLAYING SHEPHERD WHILE HERACLES HAS ALL THE FUN!
BAH!
HUH?
THESE PEOPLE!
I THOUGHT THE PEOPLE OF BAETICA WERE RICH AND PROSPEROUS...
...BUT THEY'RE DYING FROM SICKNESS AND DESPAIR!

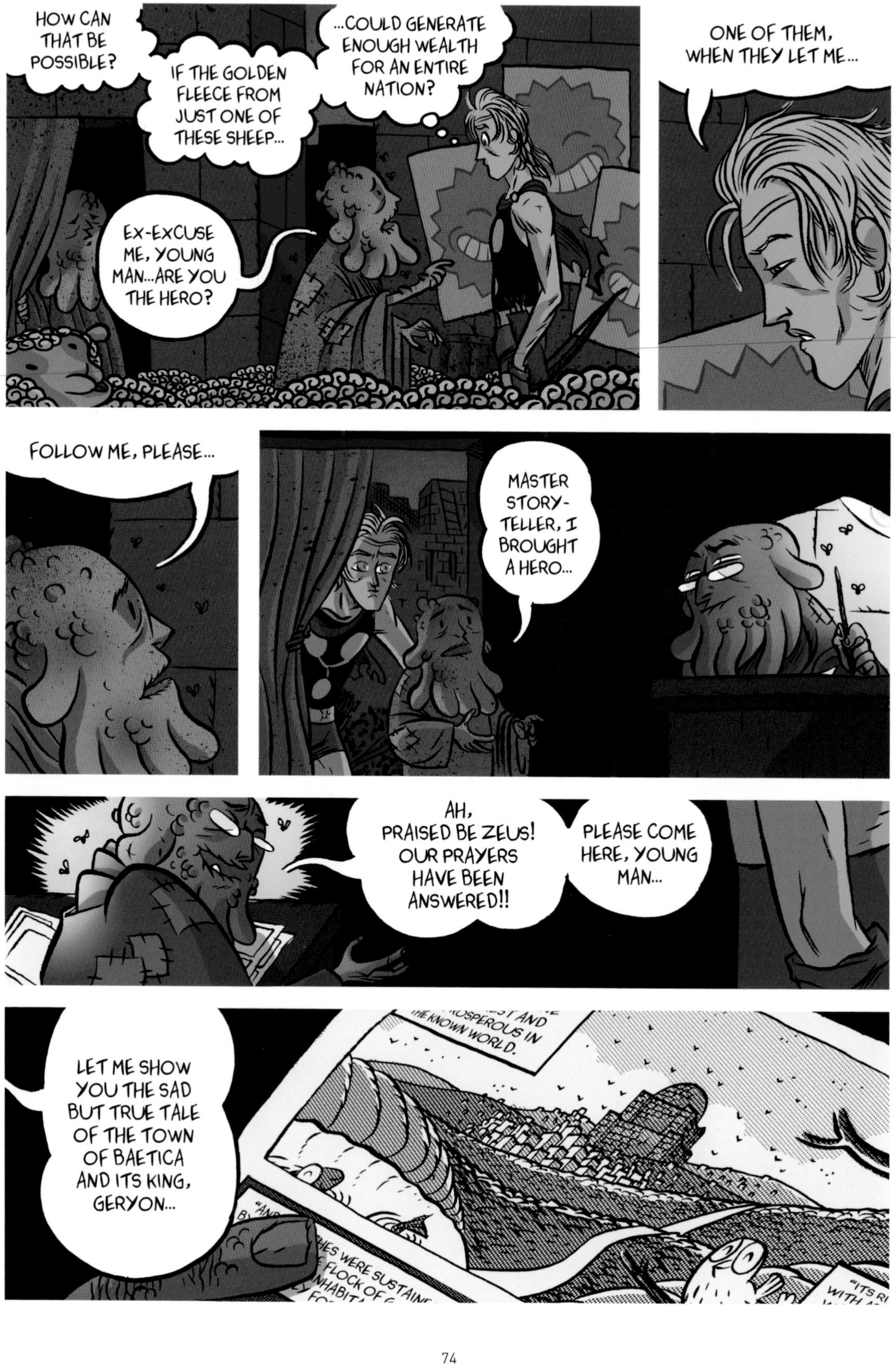
HOW CAN THAT BE POSSIBLE?
IF THE GOLDEN FLEECE FROM JUST ONE OF THESE SHEEP...
...COULD GENERATE ENOUGH WEALTH FOR AN ENTIRE NATION?
EX-EXCUSE ME, YOUNG MAN...ARE YOU THE HERO?
ONE OF THEM, WHEN THEY LET ME...
FOLLOW ME, PLEASE...
MASTER STORY-TELLER, I BROUGHT A HERO...
AH, PRAISED BE ZEUS! OUR PRAYERS HAVE BEEN ANSWERED!!
PLEASE COME HERE, YOUNG MAN...
LET ME SHOW YOU THE SAD BUT TRUE TALE OF THE TOWN OF BAETICA AND ITS KING, GERYON...
THE KNOWN WORLD.

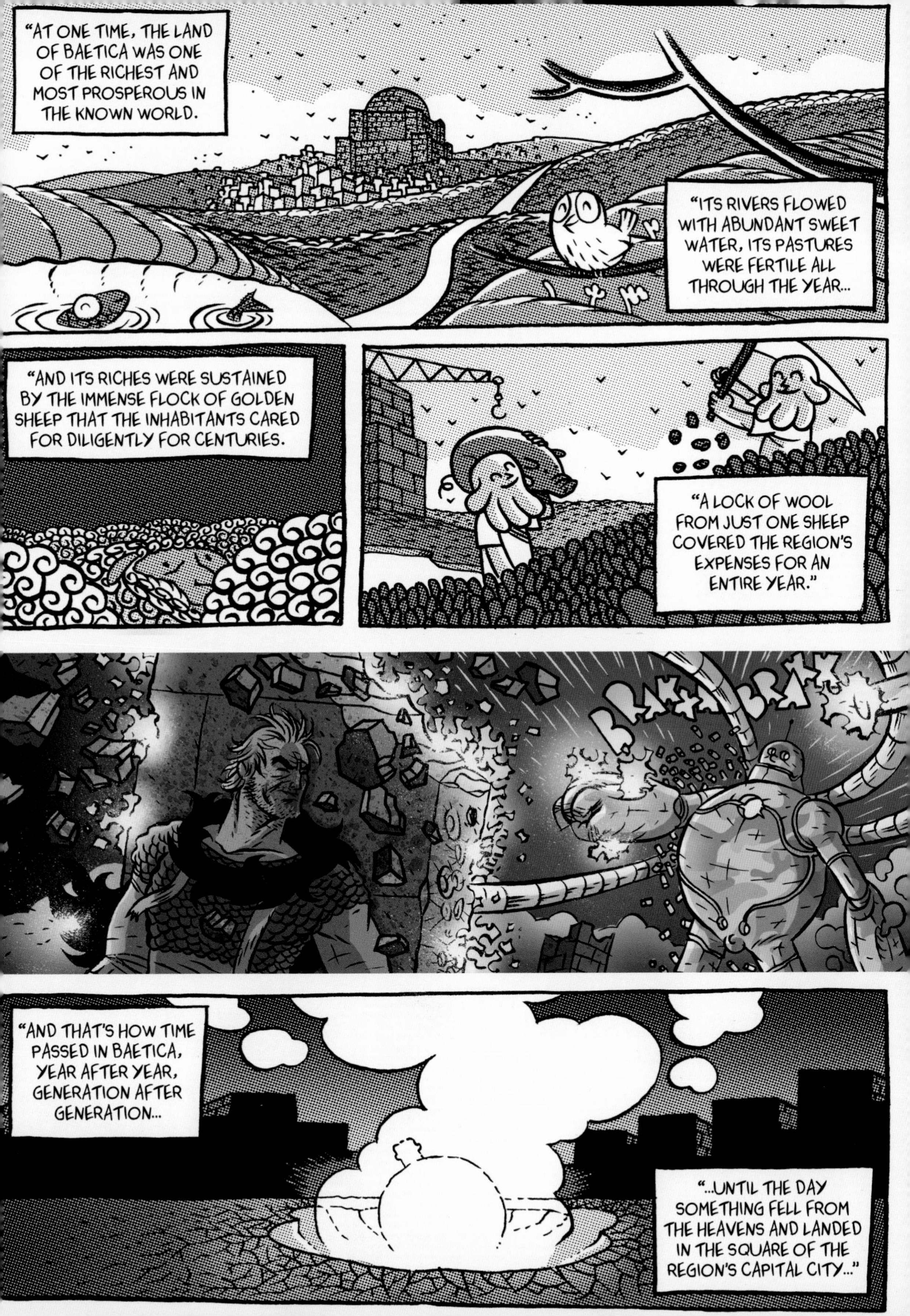
"AT ONE TIME, THE LAND OF BAETICA WAS ONE OF THE RICHEST AND MOST PROSPEROUS IN THE KNOWN WORLD.
"ITS RIVERS FLOWED WITH ABUNDANT SWEET WATER, ITS PASTURES WERE FERTILE ALL THROUGH THE YEAR...
"AND ITS RICHES WERE SUSTAINED BY THE IMMENSE FLOCK OF GOLDEN SHEEP THAT THE INHABITANTS CARED FOR DILIGENTLY FOR CENTURIES.
"A LOCK OF WOOL FROM JUST ONE SHEEP COVERED THE REGION'S EXPENSES FOR AN ENTIRE YEAR."
BRAKKA BRAKK
"AND THAT'S HOW TIME PASSED IN BAETICA, YEAR AFTER YEAR, GENERATION AFTER GENERATION...
"...UNTIL THE DAY SOMETHING FELL FROM THE HEAVENS AND LANDED IN THE SQUARE OF THE REGION'S CAPITAL CITY..."

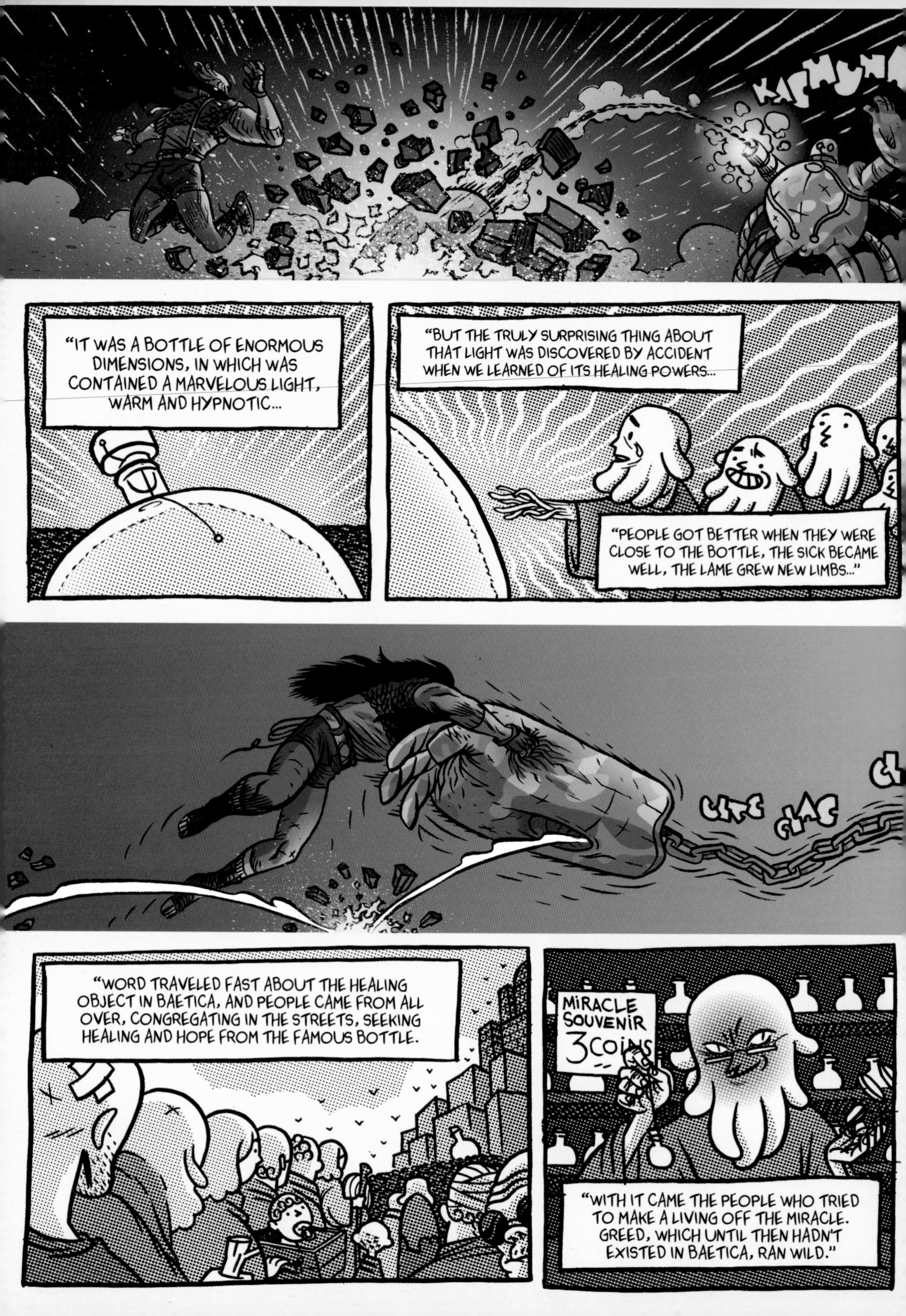

"IT WAS A BOTTLE OF ENORMOUS DIMENSIONS, IN WHICH WAS CONTAINED A MARVELOUS LIGHT, WARM AND HYPNOTIC...
"BUT THE TRULY SURPRISING THING ABOUT THAT LIGHT WAS DISCOVERED BY ACCIDENT WHEN WE LEARNED OF ITS HEALING POWERS...
"PEOPLE GOT BETTER WHEN THEY WERE CLOSE TO THE BOTTLE, THE SICK BECAME WELL, THE LAME GREW NEW LIMBS..."
"WORD TRAVELED FAST ABOUT THE HEALING OBJECT IN BAETICA, AND PEOPLE CAME FROM ALL OVER, CONGREGATING IN THE STREETS, SEEKING HEALING AND HOPE FROM THE FAMOUS BOTTLE.
MIRACLE SOUVENIR
3 COINS
"WITH IT CAME THE PEOPLE WHO TRIED TO MAKE A LIVING OFF THE MIRACLE. GREED, WHICH UNTIL THEN HADN'T EXISTED IN BAETICA, RAN WILD."

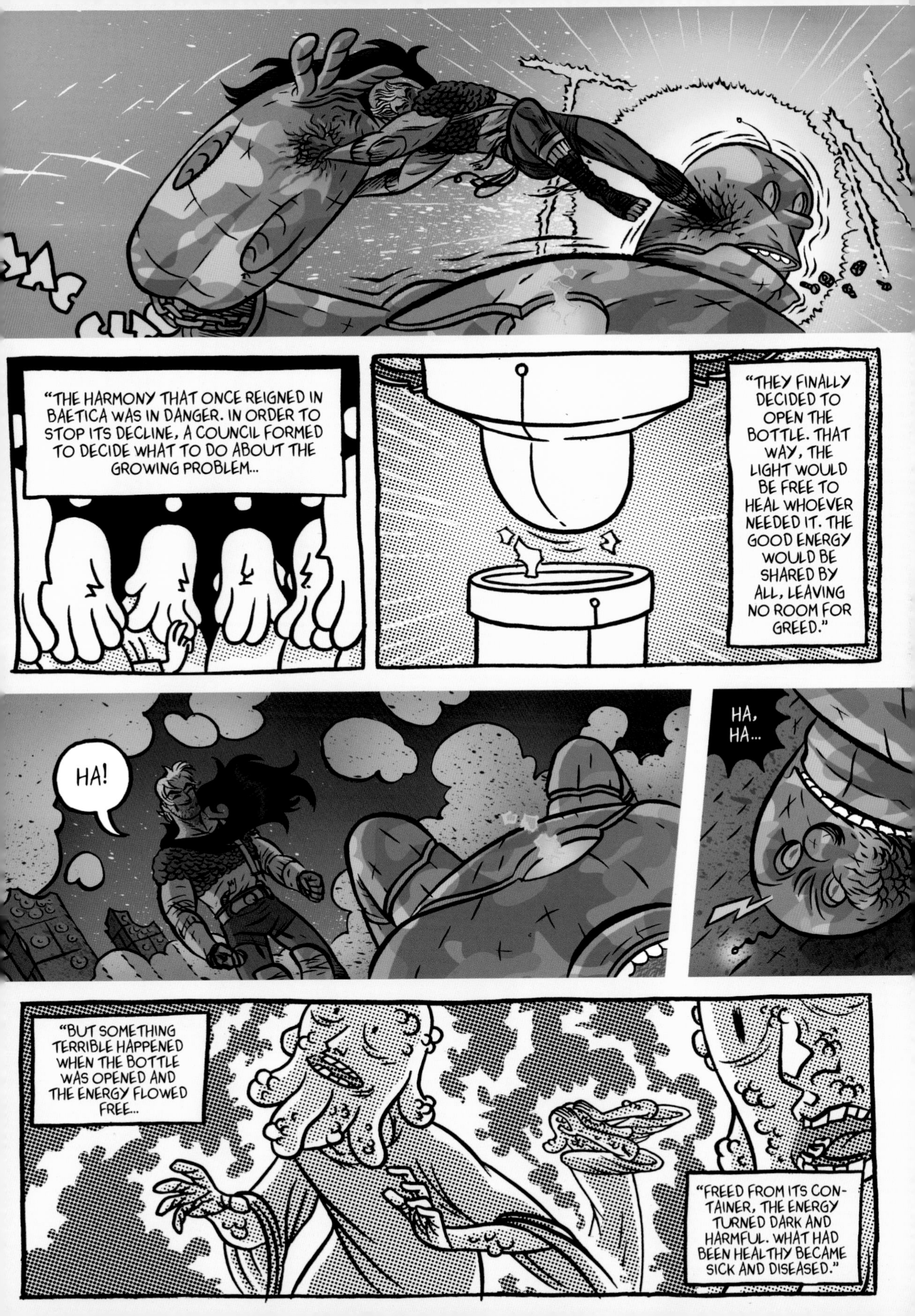
"THE HARMONY THAT ONCE REIGNED IN BAETICA WAS IN DANGER. IN ORDER TO STOP ITS DECLINE, A COUNCIL FORMED TO DECIDE WHAT TO DO ABOUT THE GROWING PROBLEM...
"THEY FINALLY DECIDED TO OPEN THE BOTTLE. THAT WAY, THE LIGHT WOULD BE FREE TO HEAL WHOEVER NEEDED IT. THE GOOD ENERGY WOULD BE SHARED BY ALL, LEAVING NO ROOM FOR GREED."
HA!
HA, HA...
"BUT SOMETHING TERRIBLE HAPPENED WHEN THE BOTTLE WAS OPENED AND THE ENERGY FLOWED FREE...
"FREED FROM ITS CONTAINER, THE ENERGY TURNED DARK AND HARMFUL. WHAT HAD BEEN HEALTHY BECAME SICK AND DISEASED."

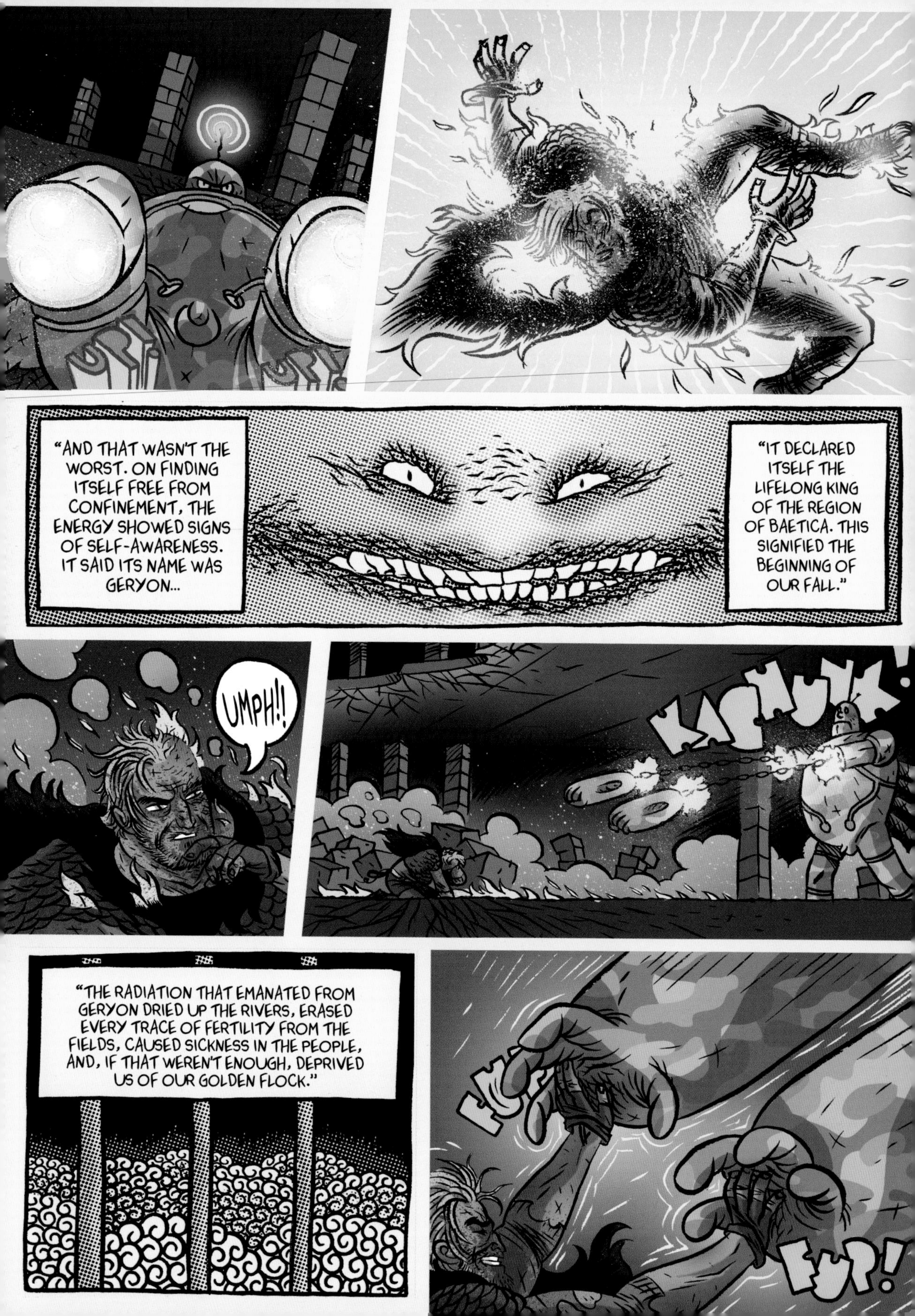
UP!
UP
"AND THAT WASN'T THE WORST. ON FINDING ITSELF FREE FROM CONFINEMENT, THE ENERGY SHOWED SIGNS OF SELF-AWARENESS. IT SAID ITS NAME WAS GERYON...
"IT DECLARED ITSELF THE LIFELONG KING OF THE REGION OF BAETICA. THIS SIGNIFIED THE BEGINNING OF OUR FALL."
UMPH!!
KACHUK!
"THE RADIATION THAT EMANATED FROM GERYON DRIED UP THE RIVERS, ERASED EVERY TRACE OF FERTILITY FROM THE FIELDS, CAUSED SICKNESS IN THE PEOPLE, AND, IF THAT WEREN'T ENOUGH, DEPRIVED US OF OUR GOLDEN FLOCK."
FUP!

WOW! I HAD NO IDEA THIS WAS GOING ON IN BAETICA.

WE MUST COME UP WITH A SOLUTION, QUICKLY!

FOLLOW US, PLEASE.

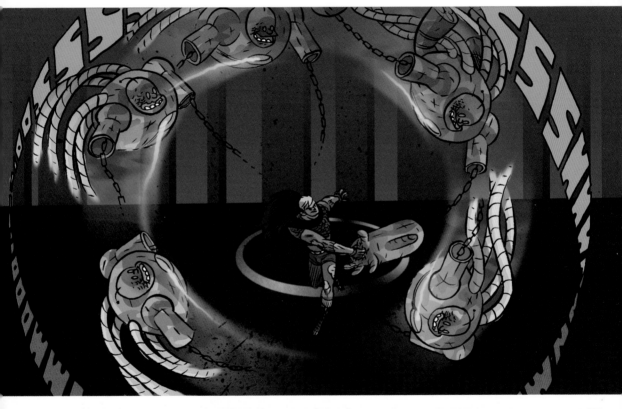

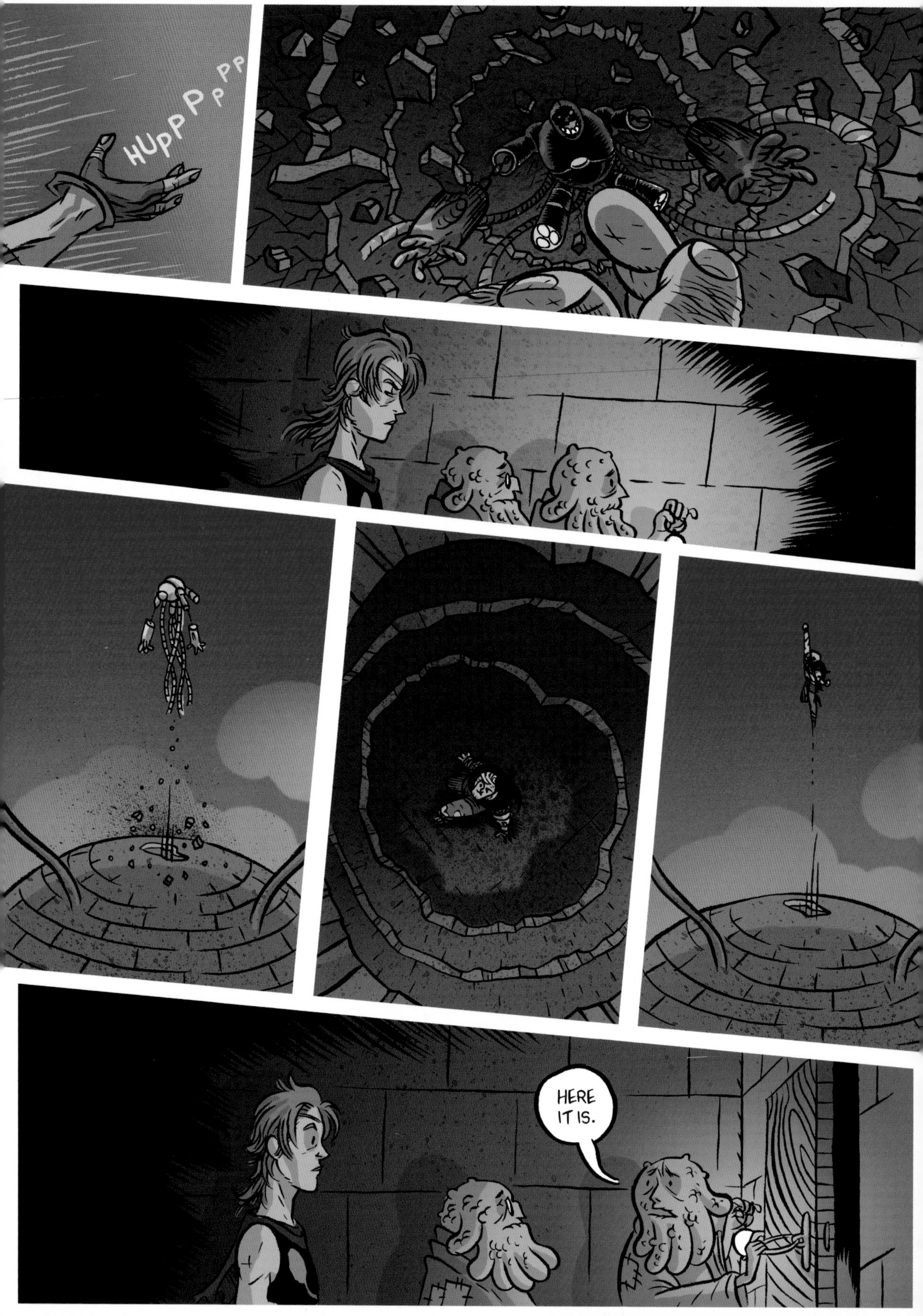
HUPPPPP
HERE IT IS.

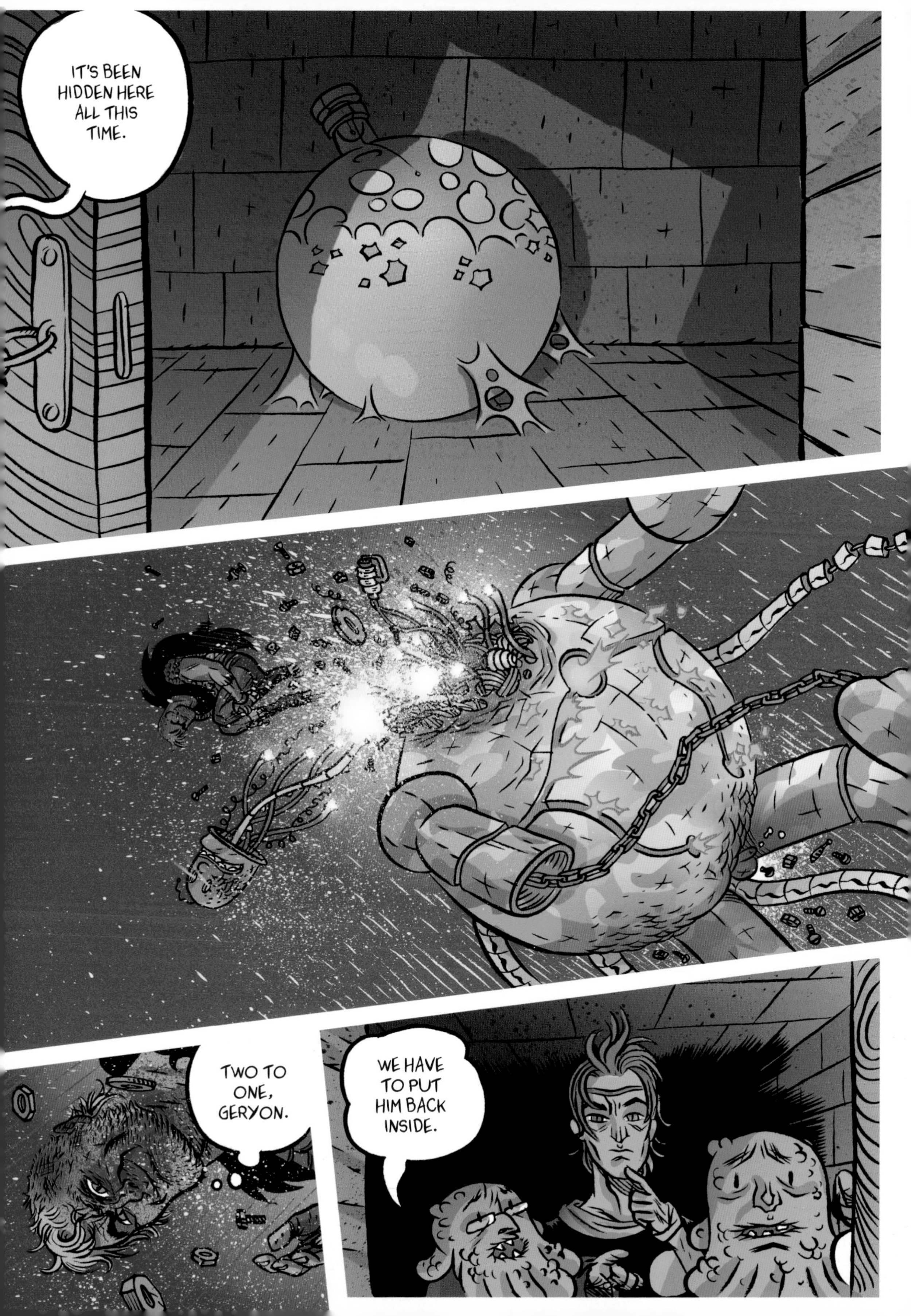
IT'S BEEN HIDDEN HERE ALL THIS TIME.
TWO TO ONE, GERYON.
WE HAVE TO PUT HIM BACK INSIDE.

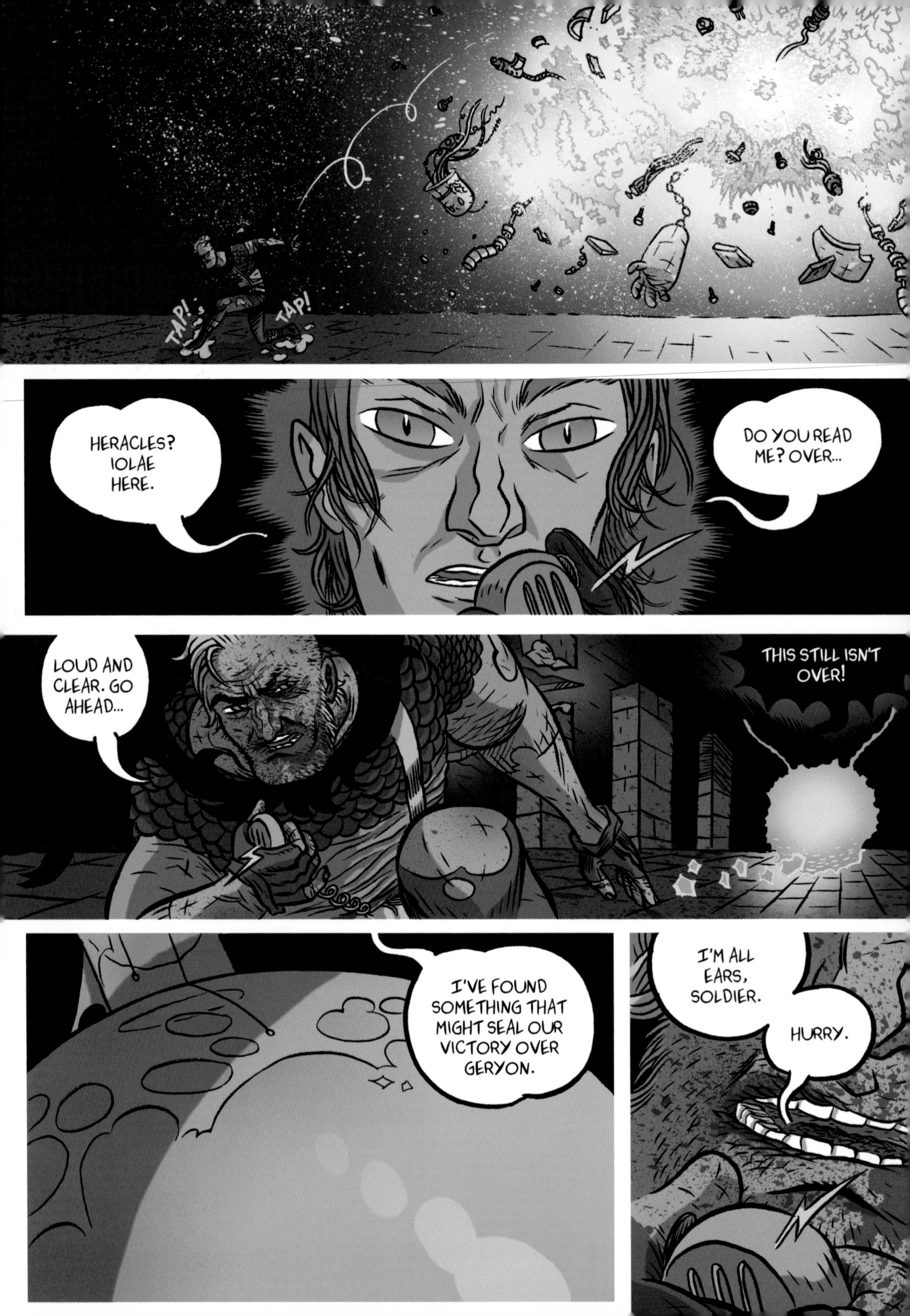
TAP!
TAP!
HERACLES? IOLAE HERE.
DO YOU READ ME? OVER...
LOUD AND CLEAR. GO AHEAD...
THIS STILL ISN'T OVER!
I'VE FOUND SOMETHING THAT MIGHT SEAL OUR VICTORY OVER GERYON.
I'M ALL EARS, SOLDIER.
HURRY.

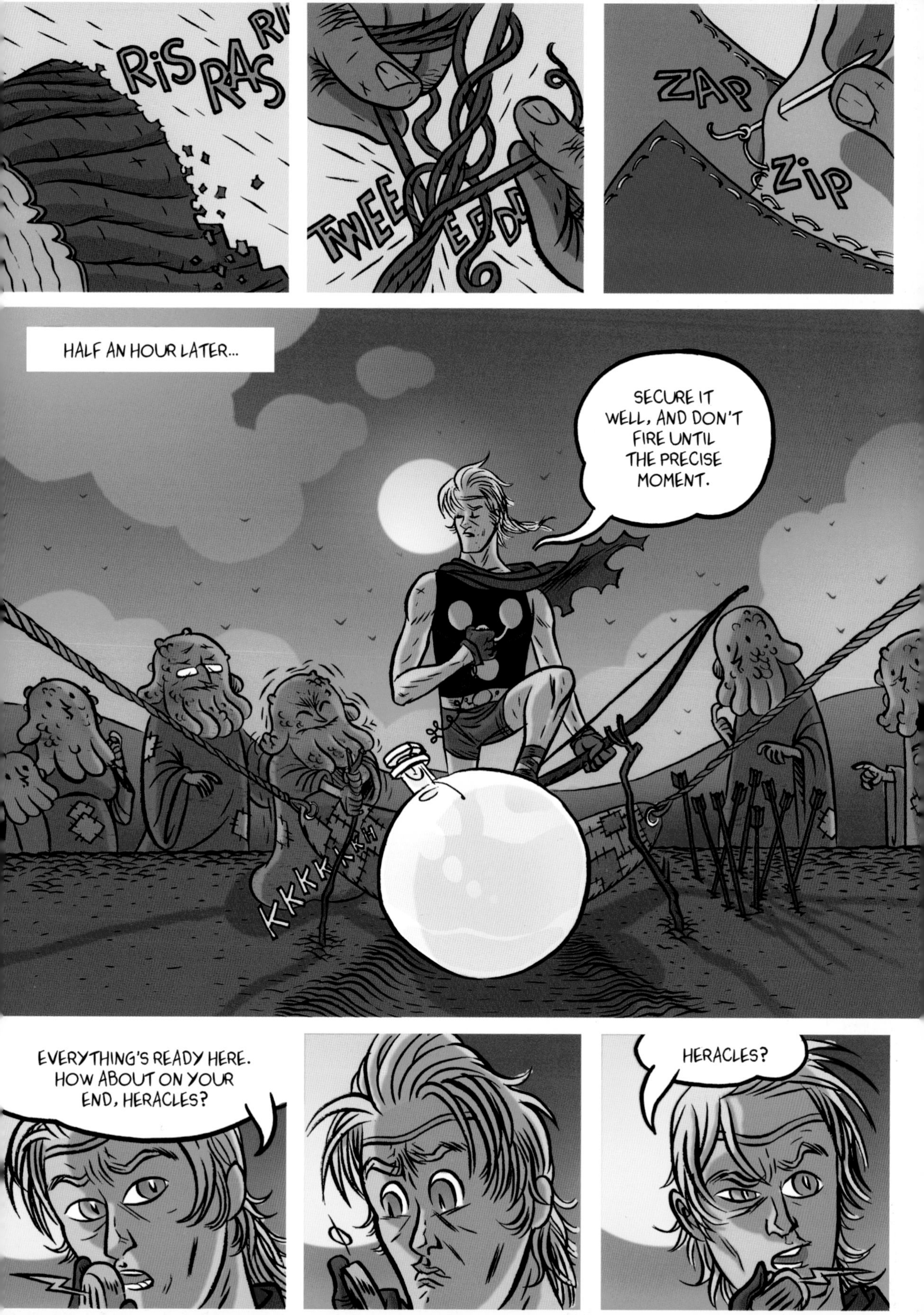
RIS RAS RI
TWEEEEED
ZAP
ZIP
HALF AN HOUR LATER...
SECURE IT WELL, AND DON'T FIRE UNTIL THE PRECISE MOMENT.
KKKKKKRH
EVERYTHING'S READY HERE. HOW ABOUT ON YOUR END, HERACLES?
HERACLES?

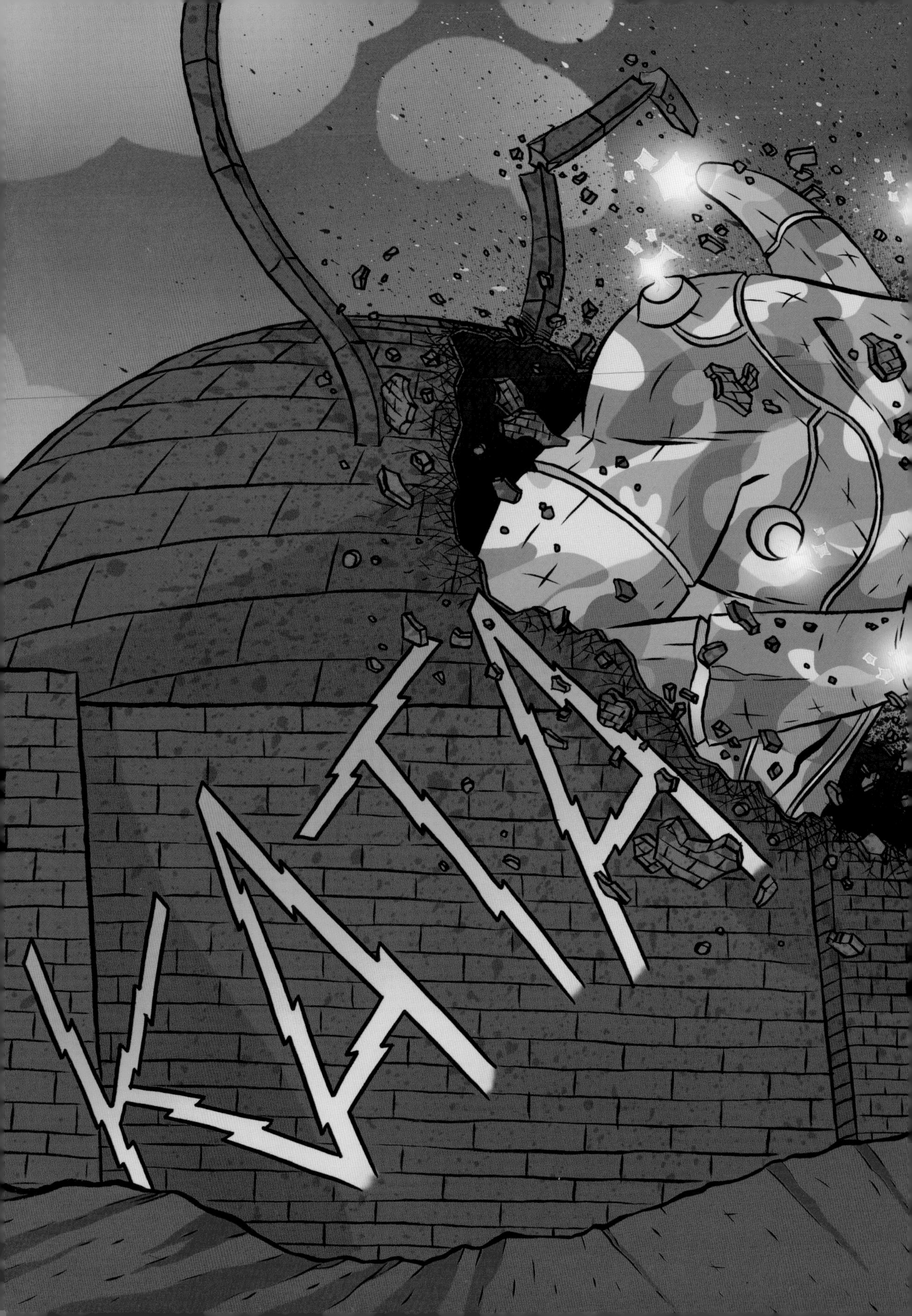

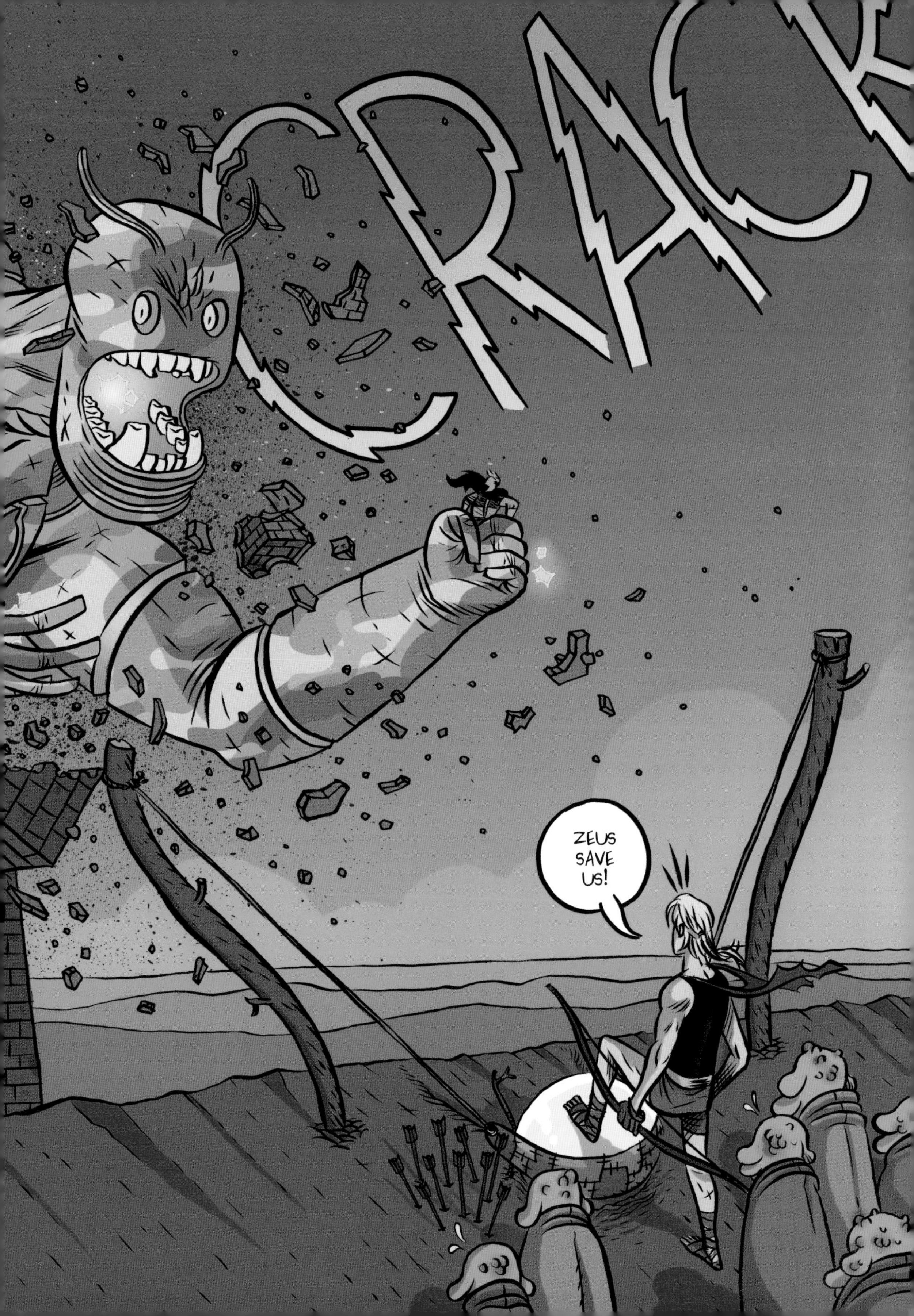
CRACK
ZEUS SAVE US!

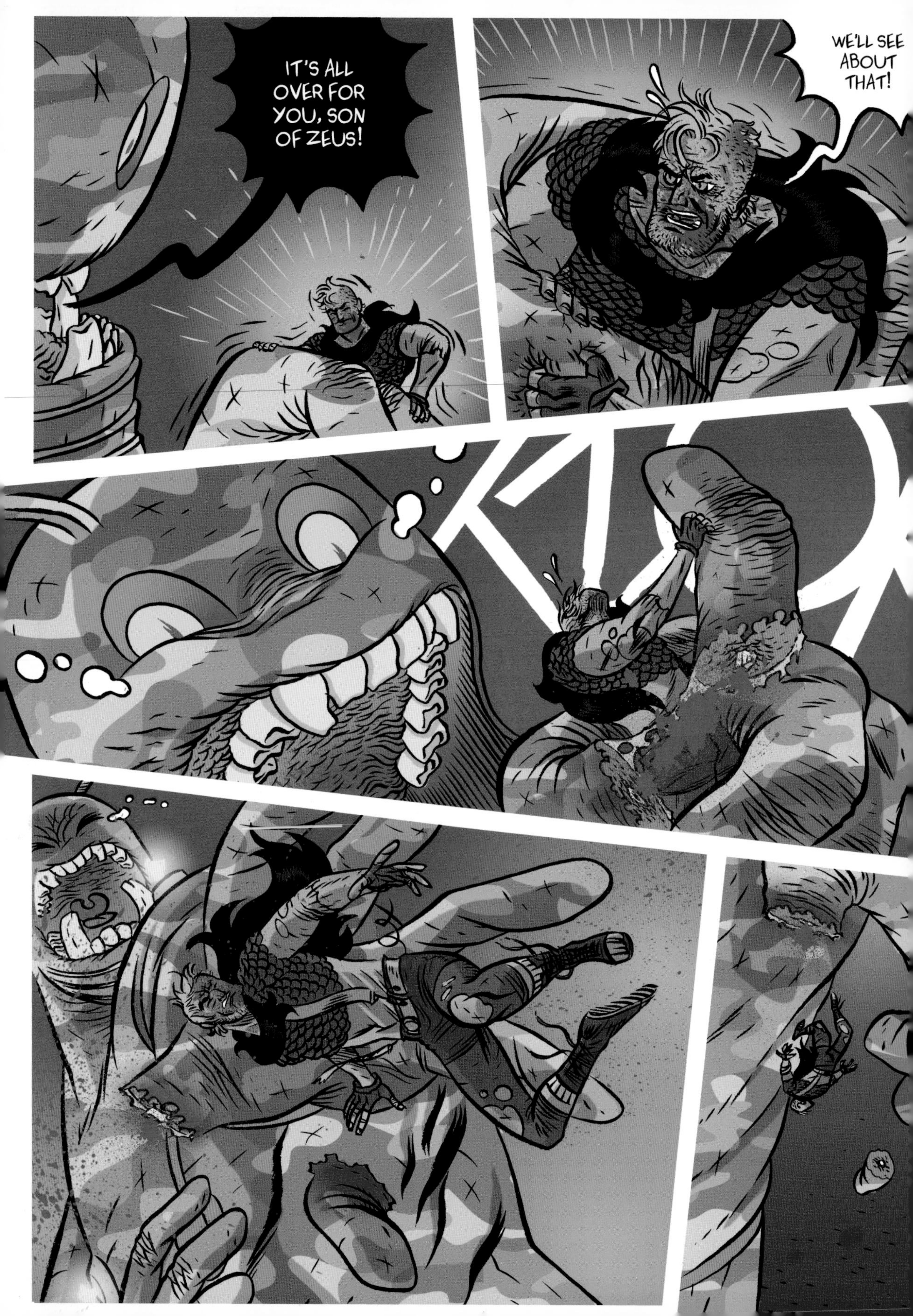
IT'S ALL OVER FOR YOU, SON OF ZEUS!
WE'LL SEE ABOUT THAT!

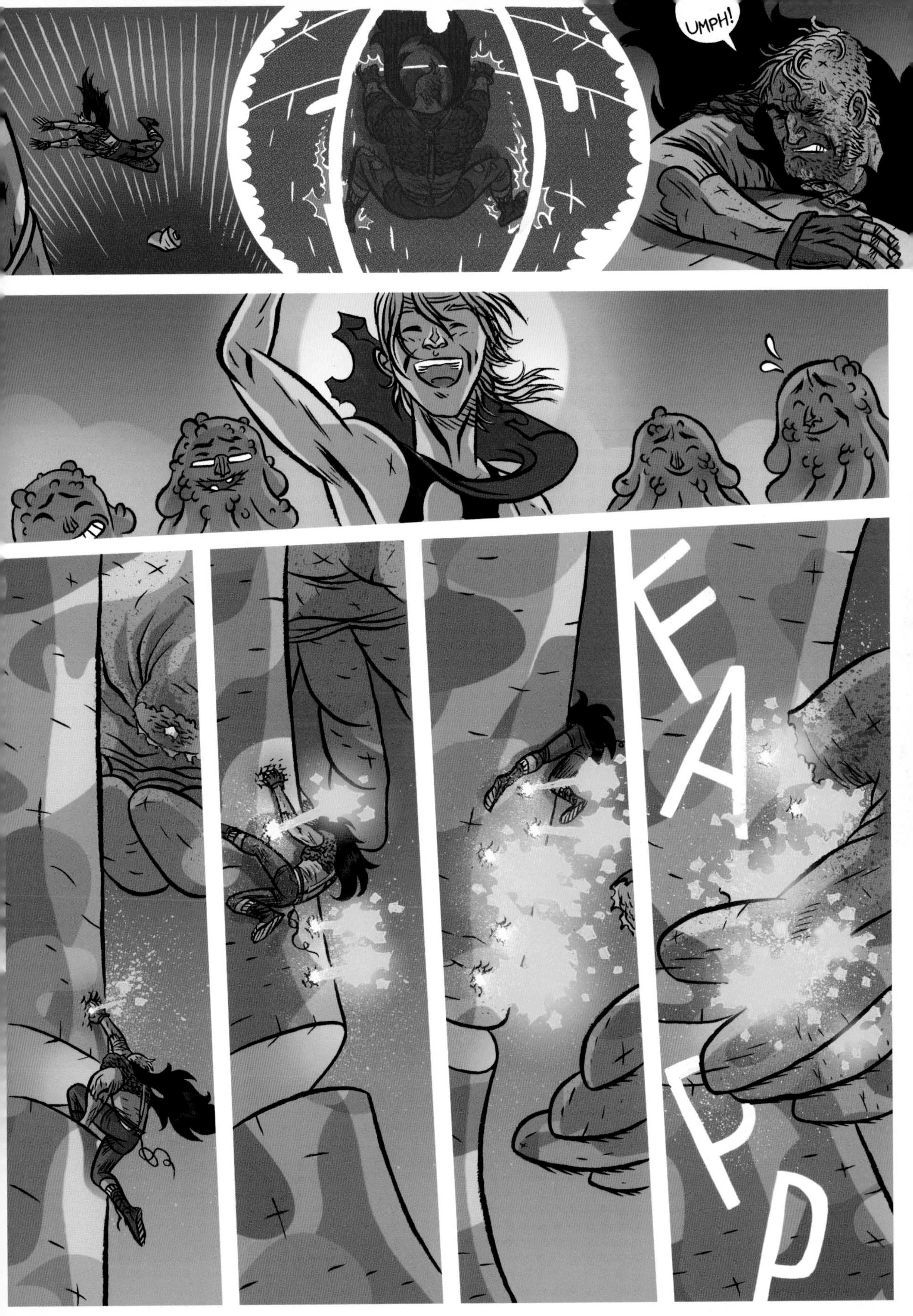
UMPH!
FAPP

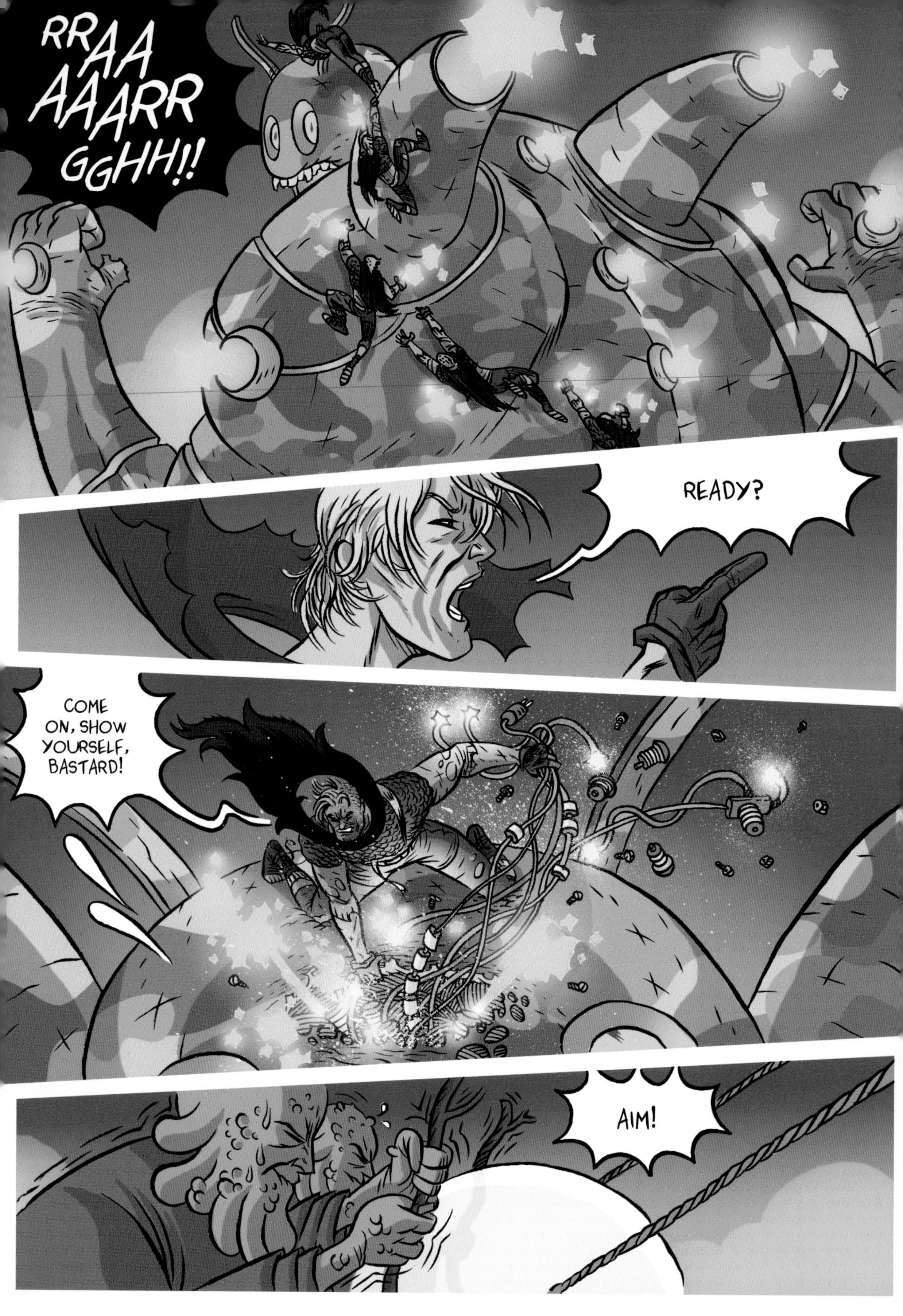
RRAA AAAARR GGHH!!
READY?
COME ON, SHOW YOURSELF, BASTARD!
AIM!

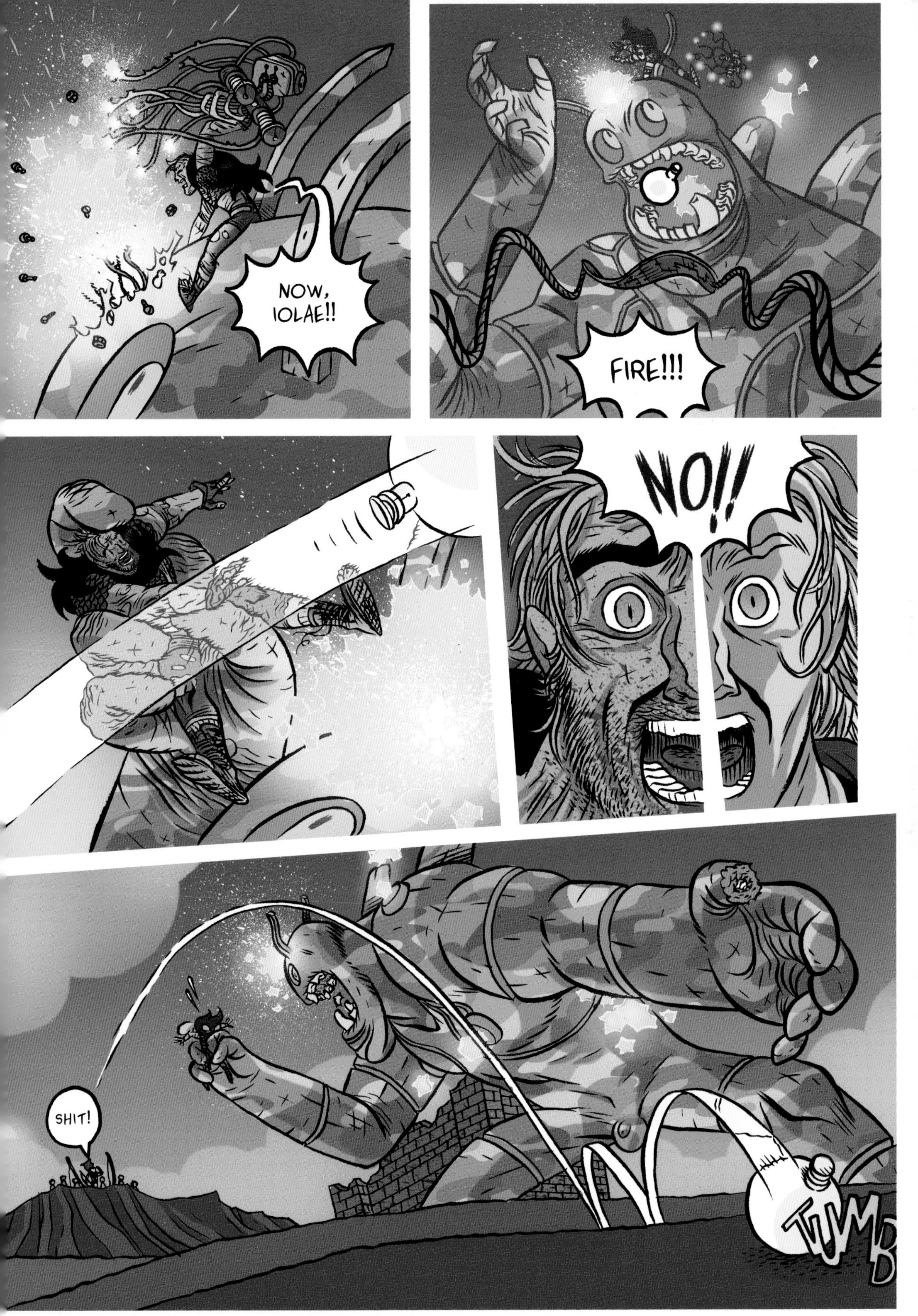
NOW, IOLAE!!
FIRE!!!
NO!!
SHIT!
TUMB

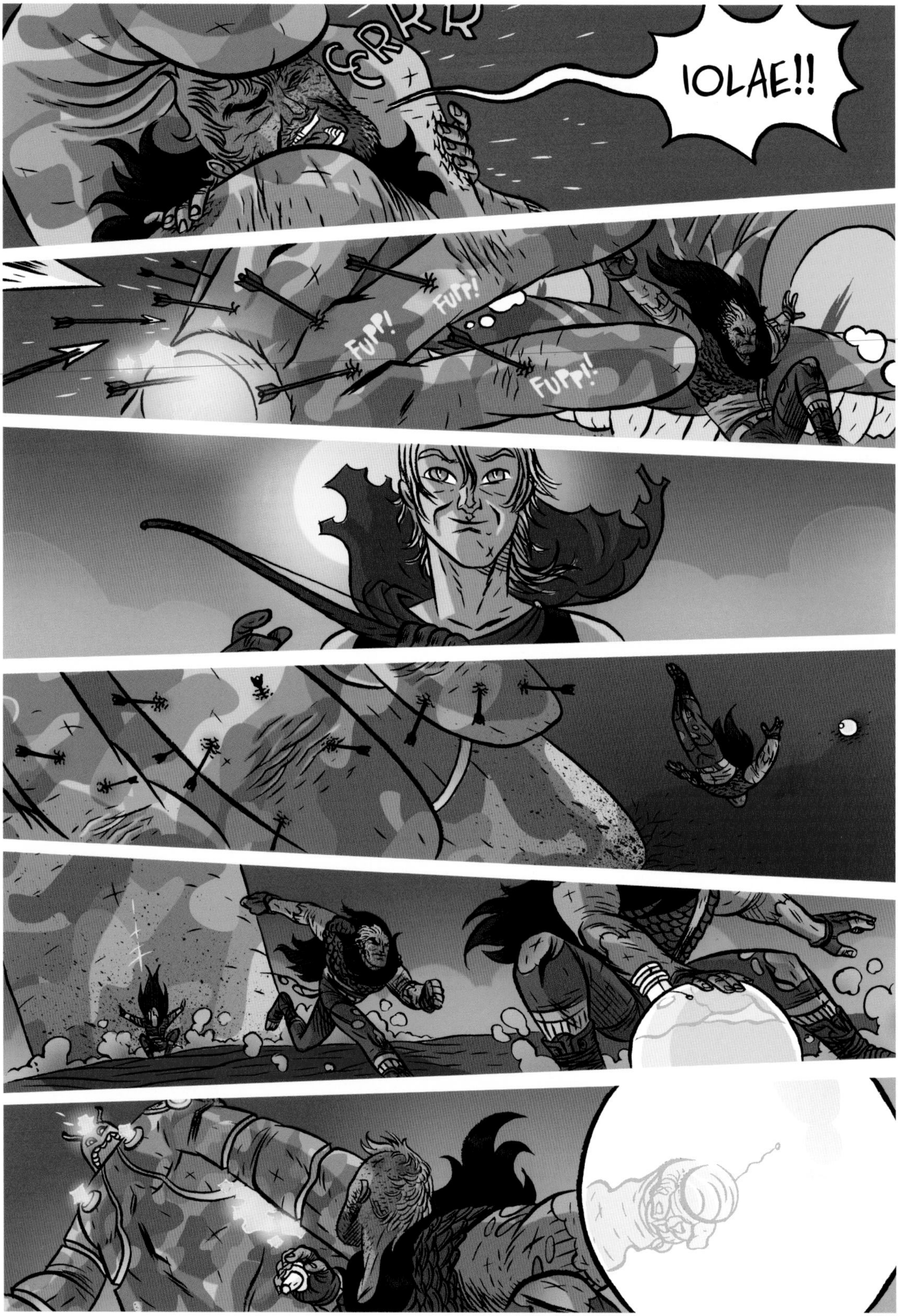
CRRR
IOLAE!!
FUPP!
FUPP!
FUPP!
FUPP!

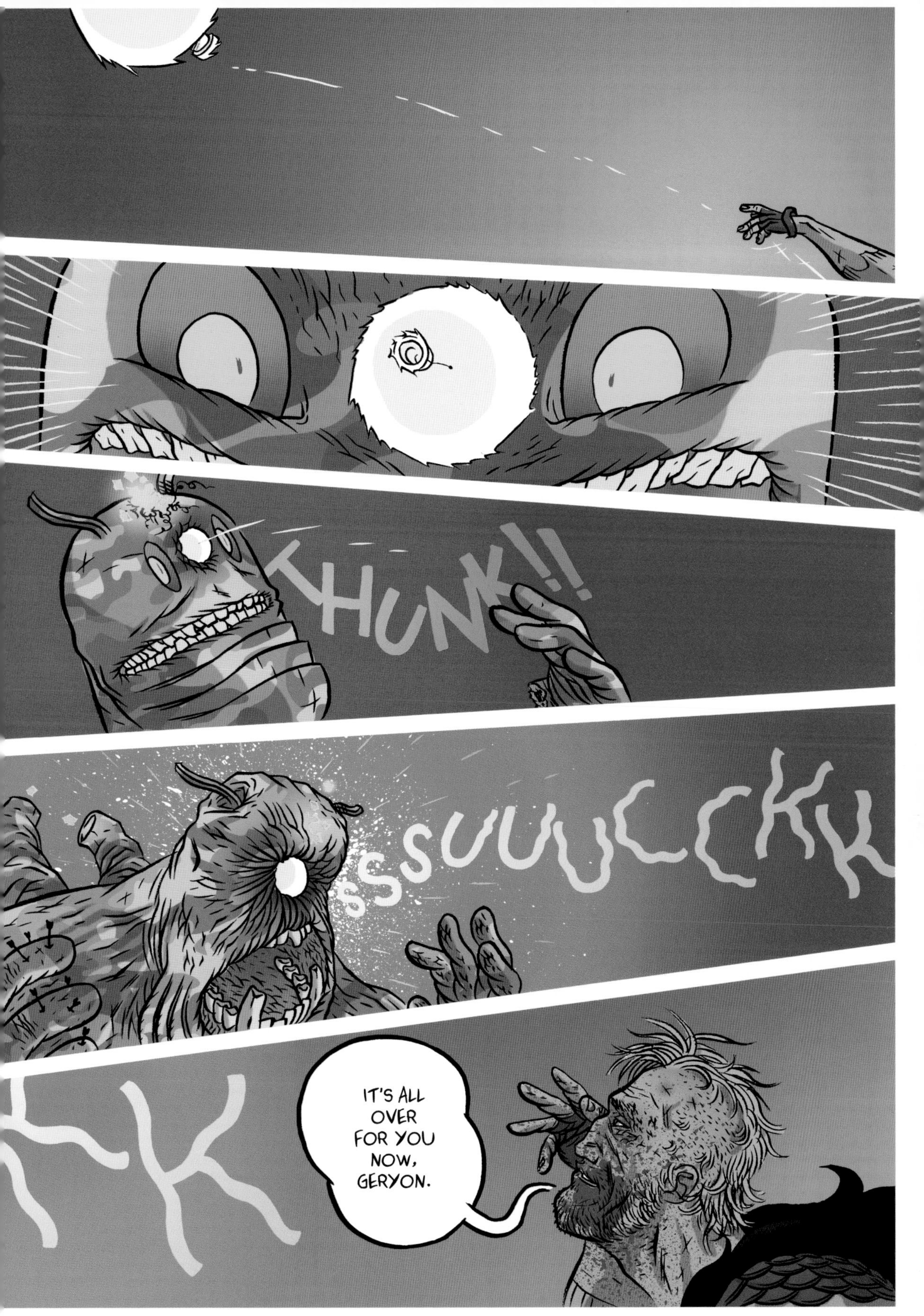
THUNK!!
SSSUUUCCKK
IT'S ALL OVER FOR YOU NOW, GERYON.

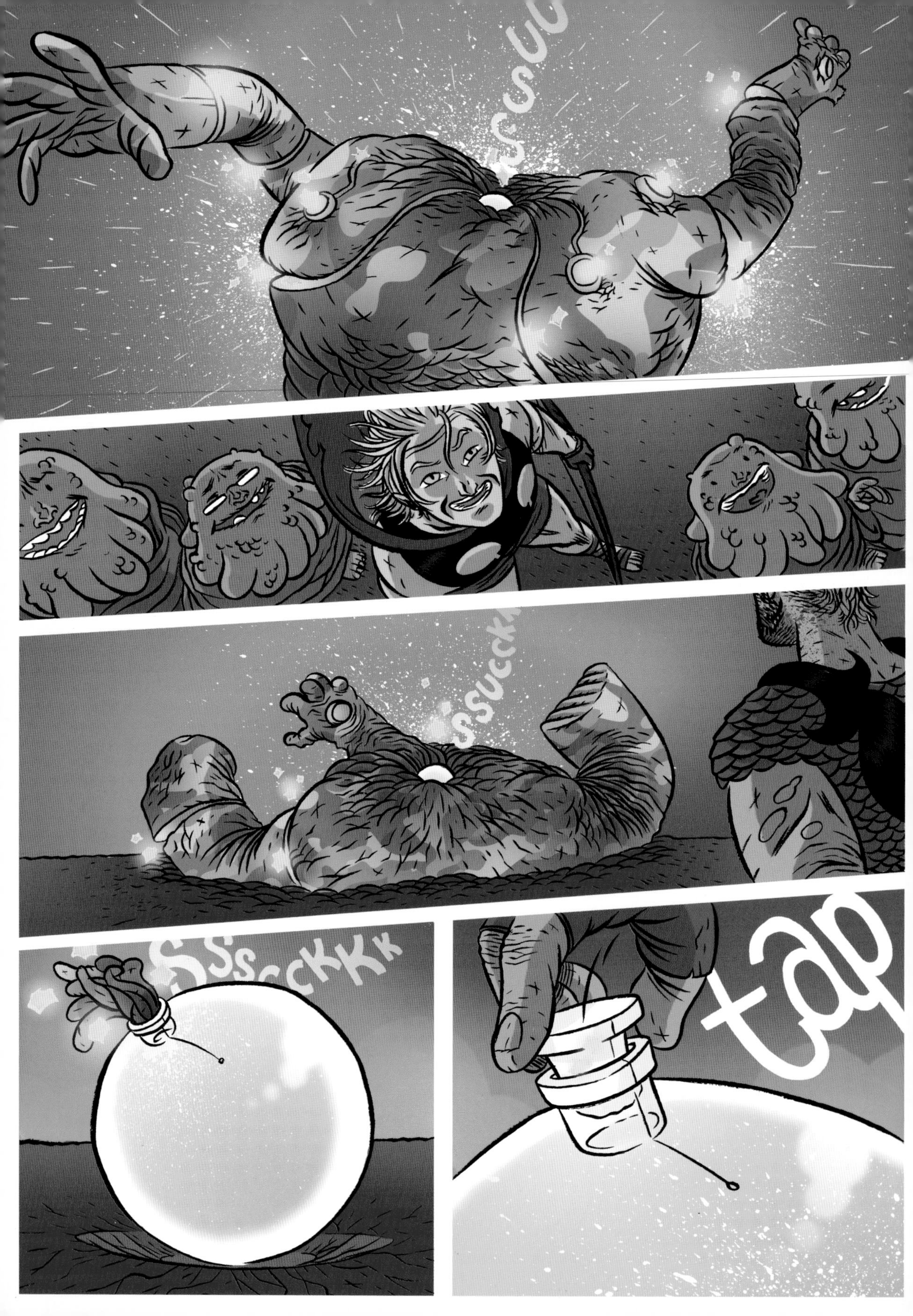
SSSUU
SSUCCK
SSSCCKKK
tap

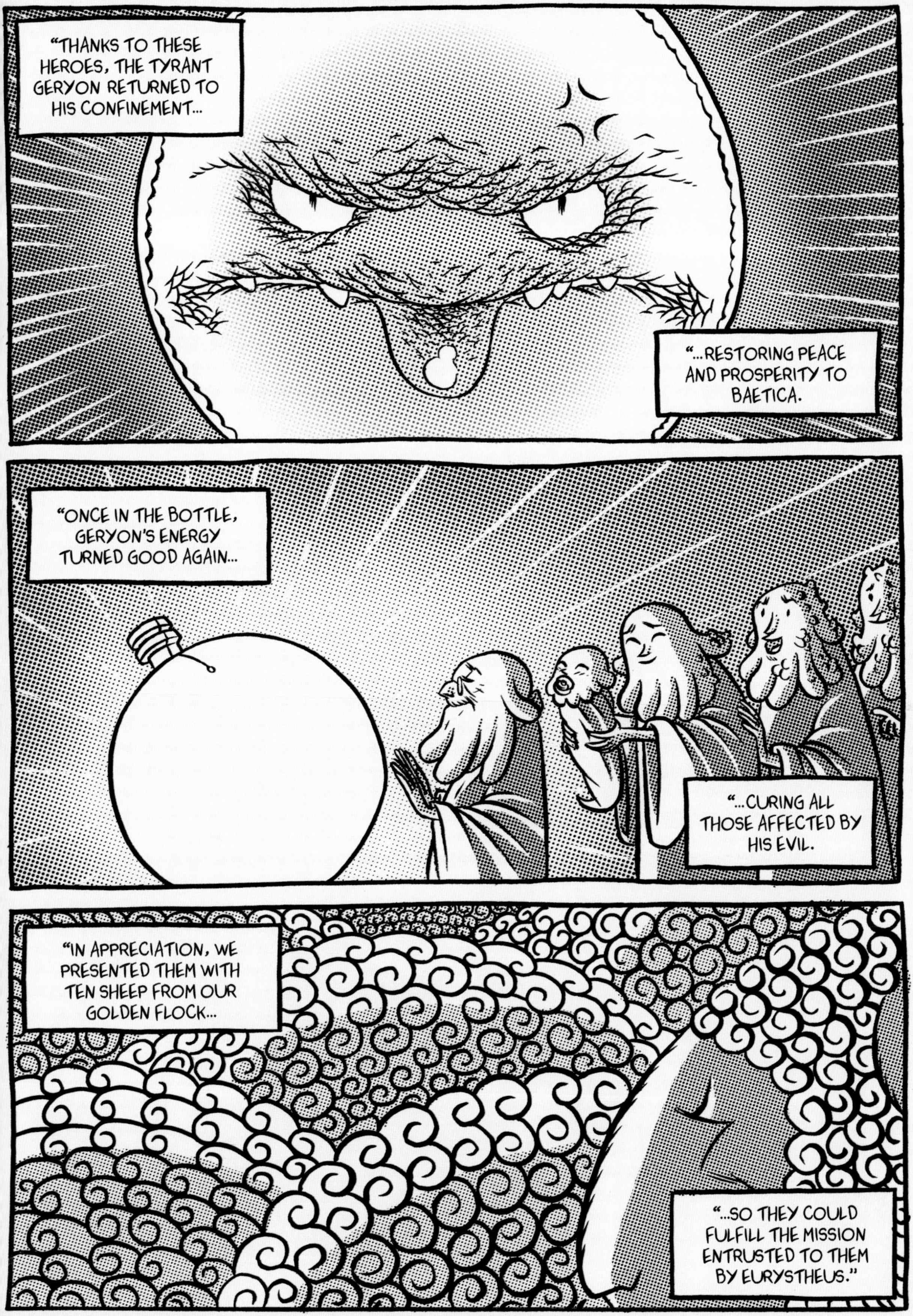
"THANKS TO THESE HEROES, THE TYRANT GERYON RETURNED TO HIS CONFINEMENT...
"...RESTORING PEACE AND PROSPERITY TO BAETICA.
"ONCE IN THE BOTTLE, GERYON'S ENERGY TURNED GOOD AGAIN...
"...CURING ALL THOSE AFFECTED BY HIS EVIL.
"IN APPRECIATION, WE PRESENTED THEM WITH TEN SHEEP FROM OUR GOLDEN FLOCK...
"...SO THEY COULD FULFILL THE MISSION ENTRUSTED TO THEM BY EURYSTHEUS."

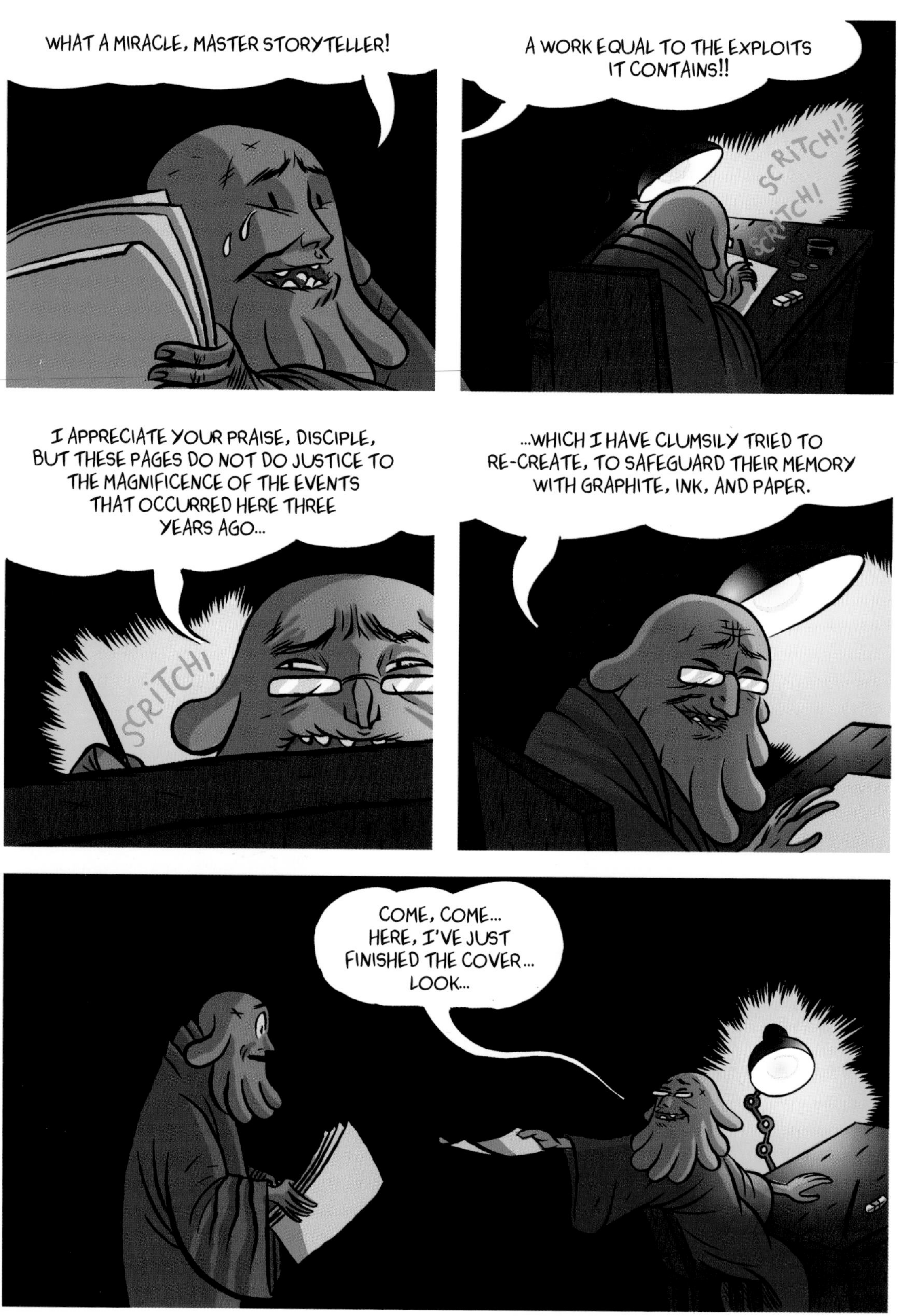
WHAT A MIRACLE, MASTER STORYTELLER!
A WORK EQUAL TO THE EXPLOITS IT CONTAINS!!
SCRITCH!!
SCRITCH!
I APPRECIATE YOUR PRAISE, DISCIPLE, BUT THESE PAGES DO NOT DO JUSTICE TO THE MAGNIFICENCE OF THE EVENTS THAT OCCURRED HERE THREE YEARS AGO...
SCRITCH!
...WHICH I HAVE CLUMSILY TRIED TO RE-CREATE, TO SAFEGUARD THEIR MEMORY WITH GRAPHITE, INK, AND PAPER.
COME, COME... HERE, I'VE JUST FINISHED THE COVER... LOOK...

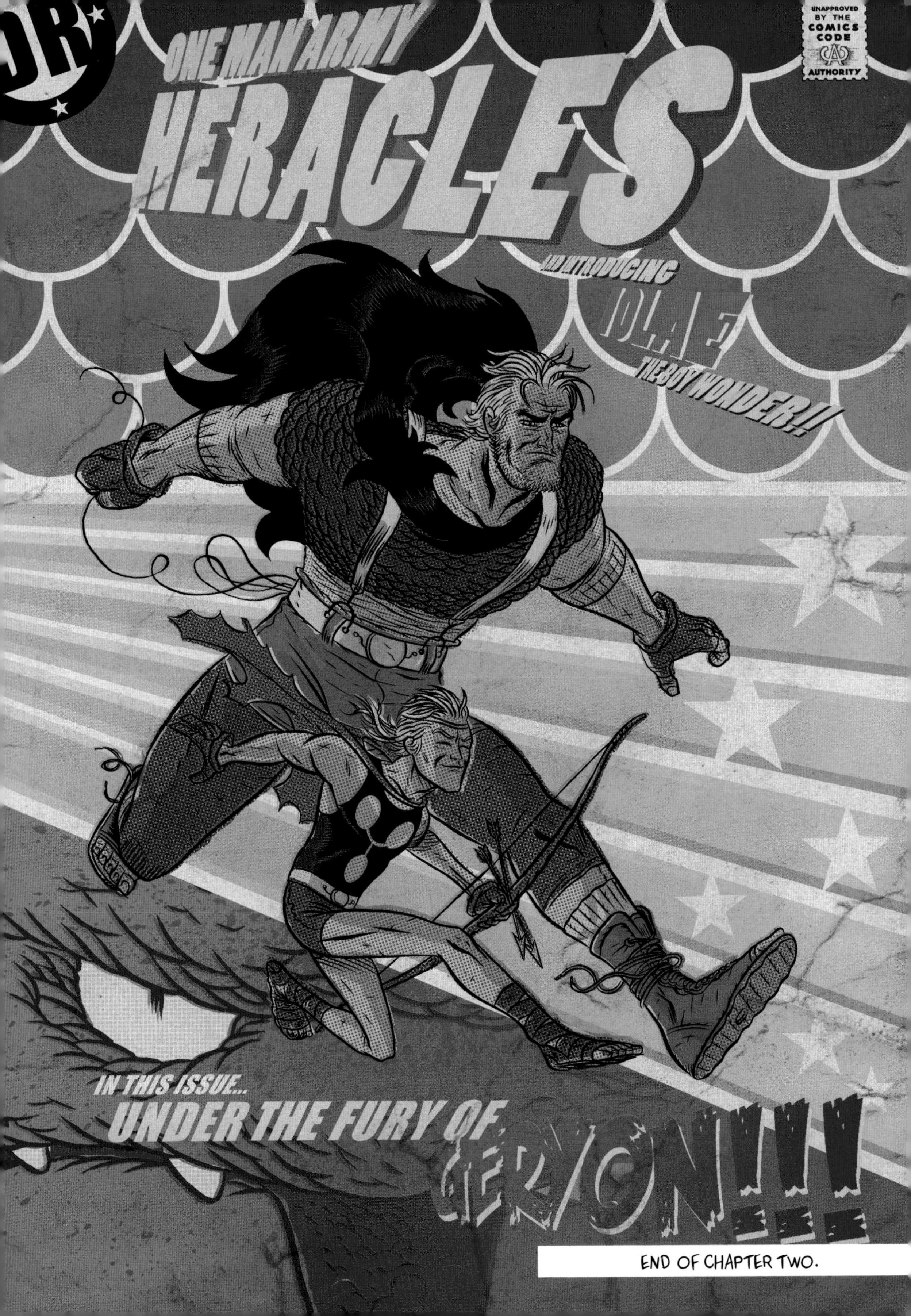
DR
UNAPPROVED BY THE COMICS CODE AUTHORITY
ONE MAN ARMY
HERACLES
AND INTRODUCING
THE BOY WONDER!!
IN THIS ISSUE...
UNDER THE FURY OF GERYON!!!
END OF CHAPTER TWO.

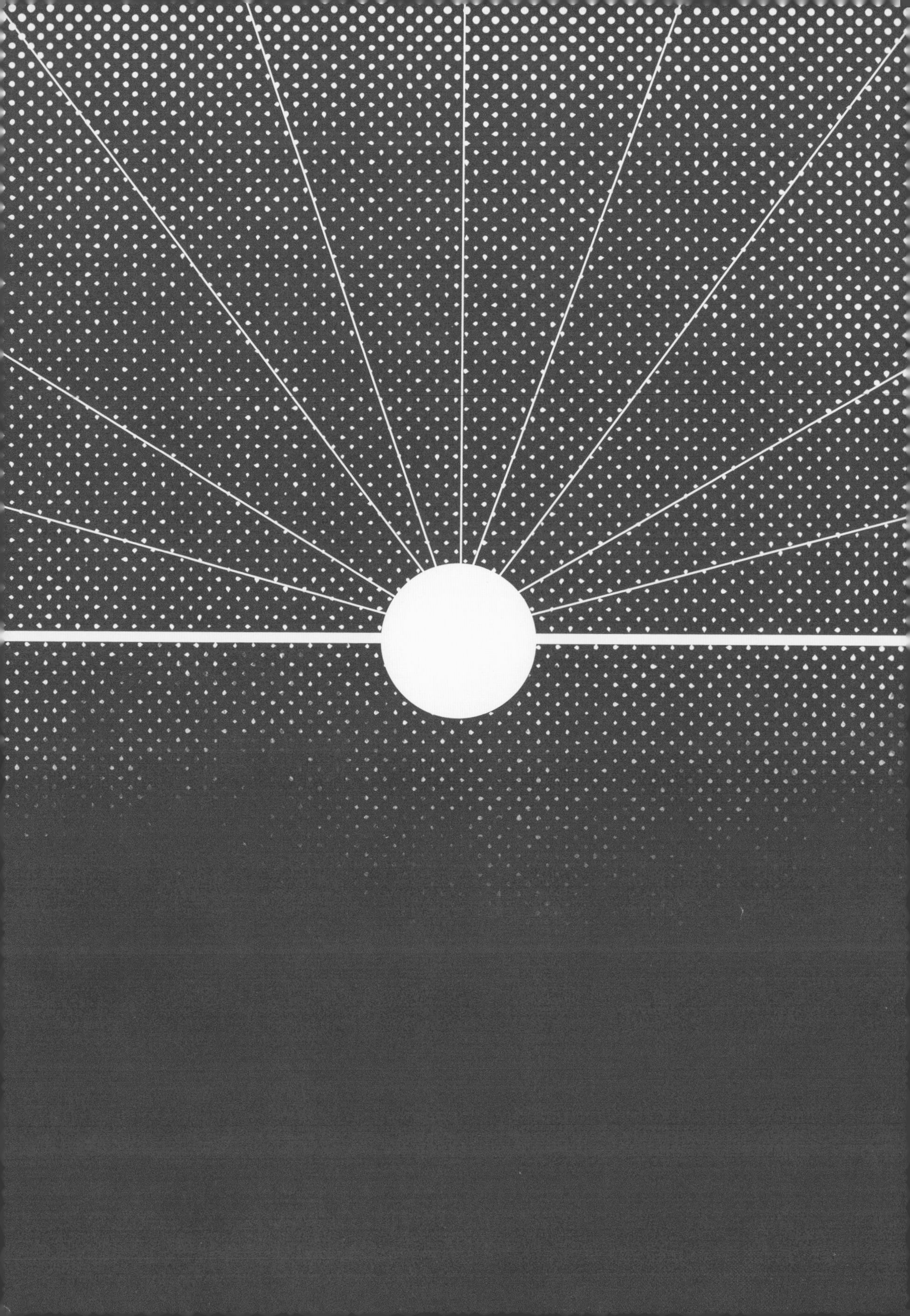

CHAPTER 03

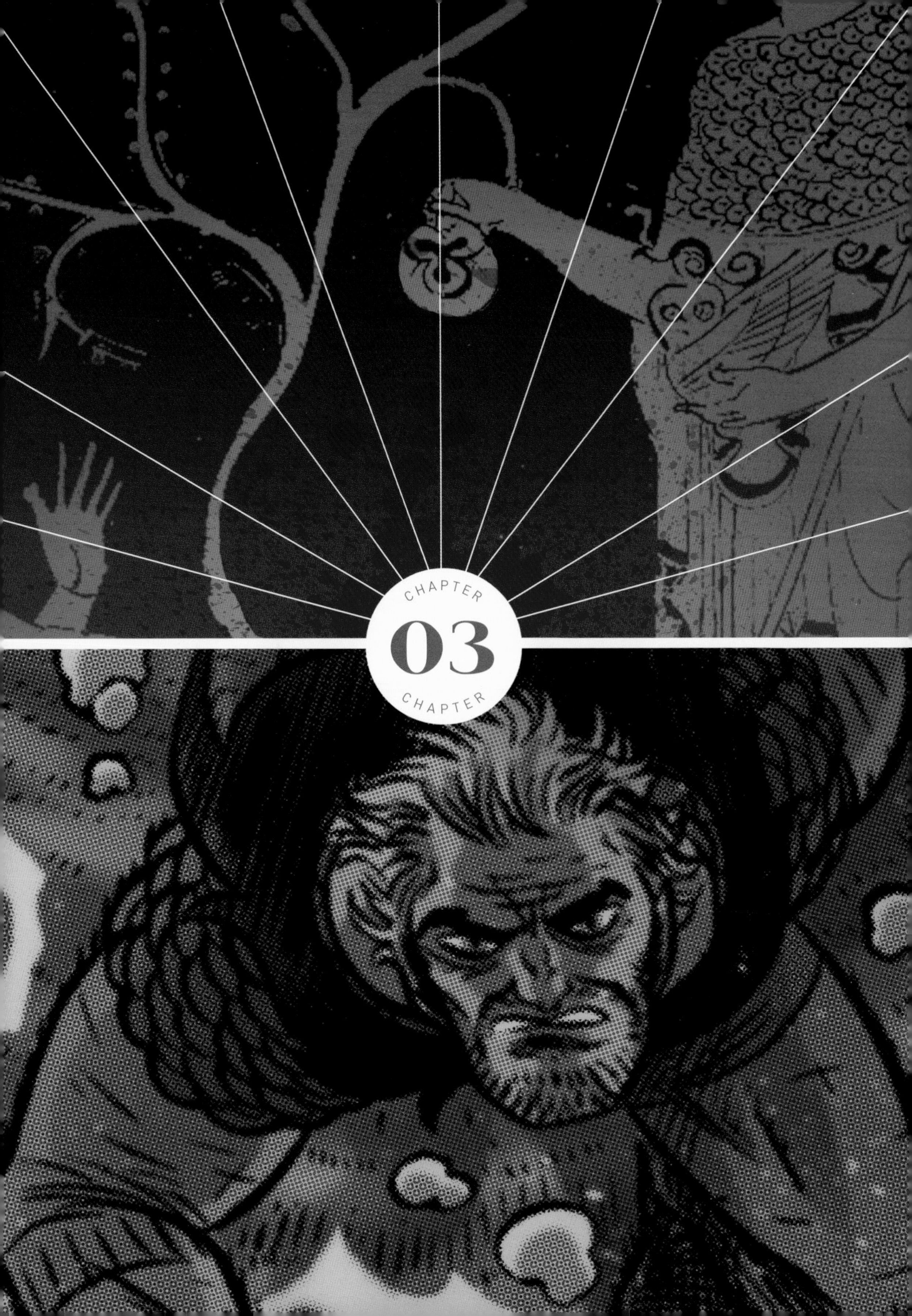
CHAPTER

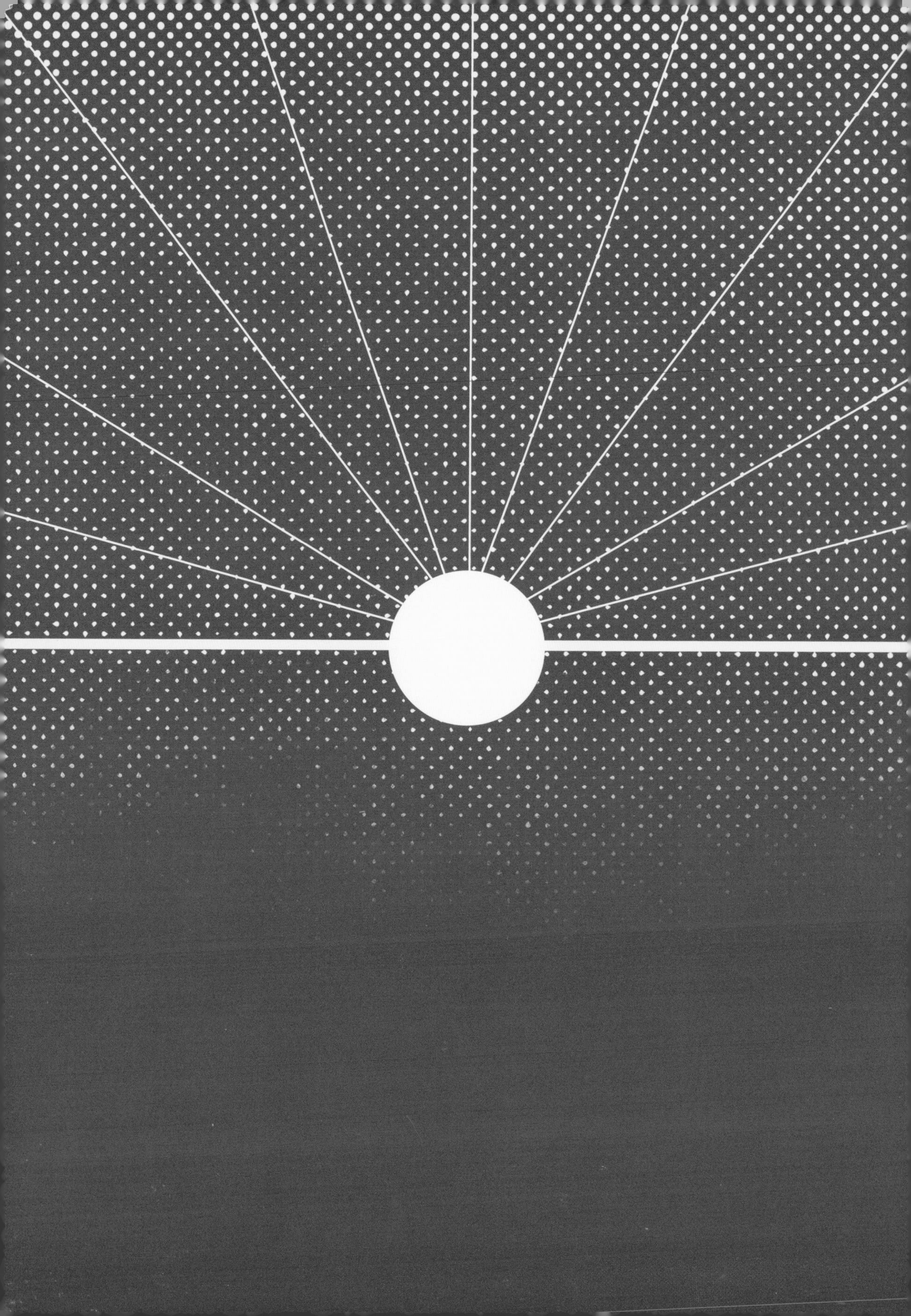

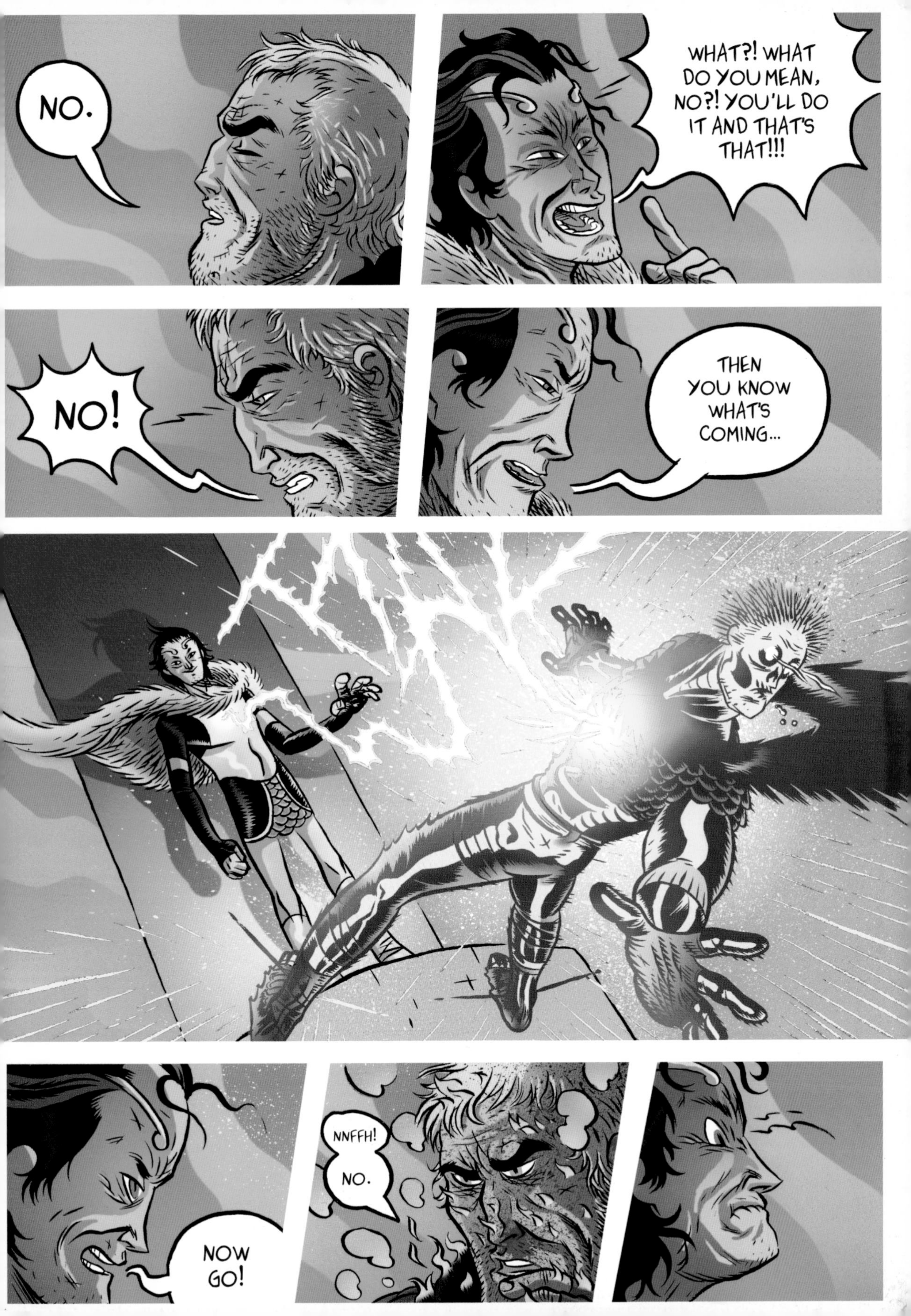
NO.
WHAT?! WHAT DO YOU MEAN, NO?! YOU'LL DO IT AND THAT'S THAT!!!
NO!
THEN YOU KNOW WHAT'S COMING...
NOW GO!
NNFFH!
NO.

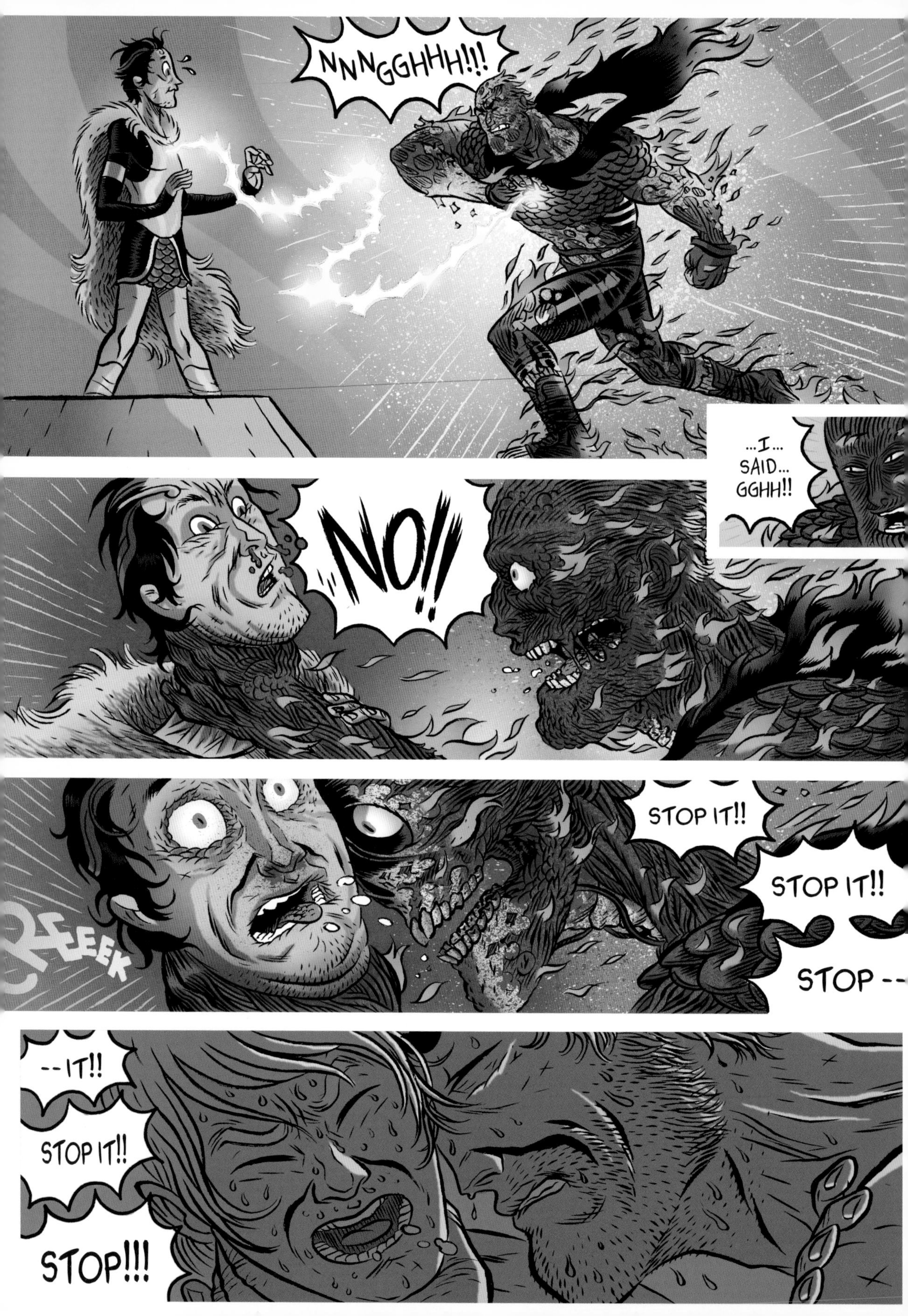
NNNGGHHH!!!
...I... SAID... GGHH!!
NO!!
STOP IT!!
STOP IT!!
STOP --
REEEK
-- IT!!
STOP IT!!
STOP!!!

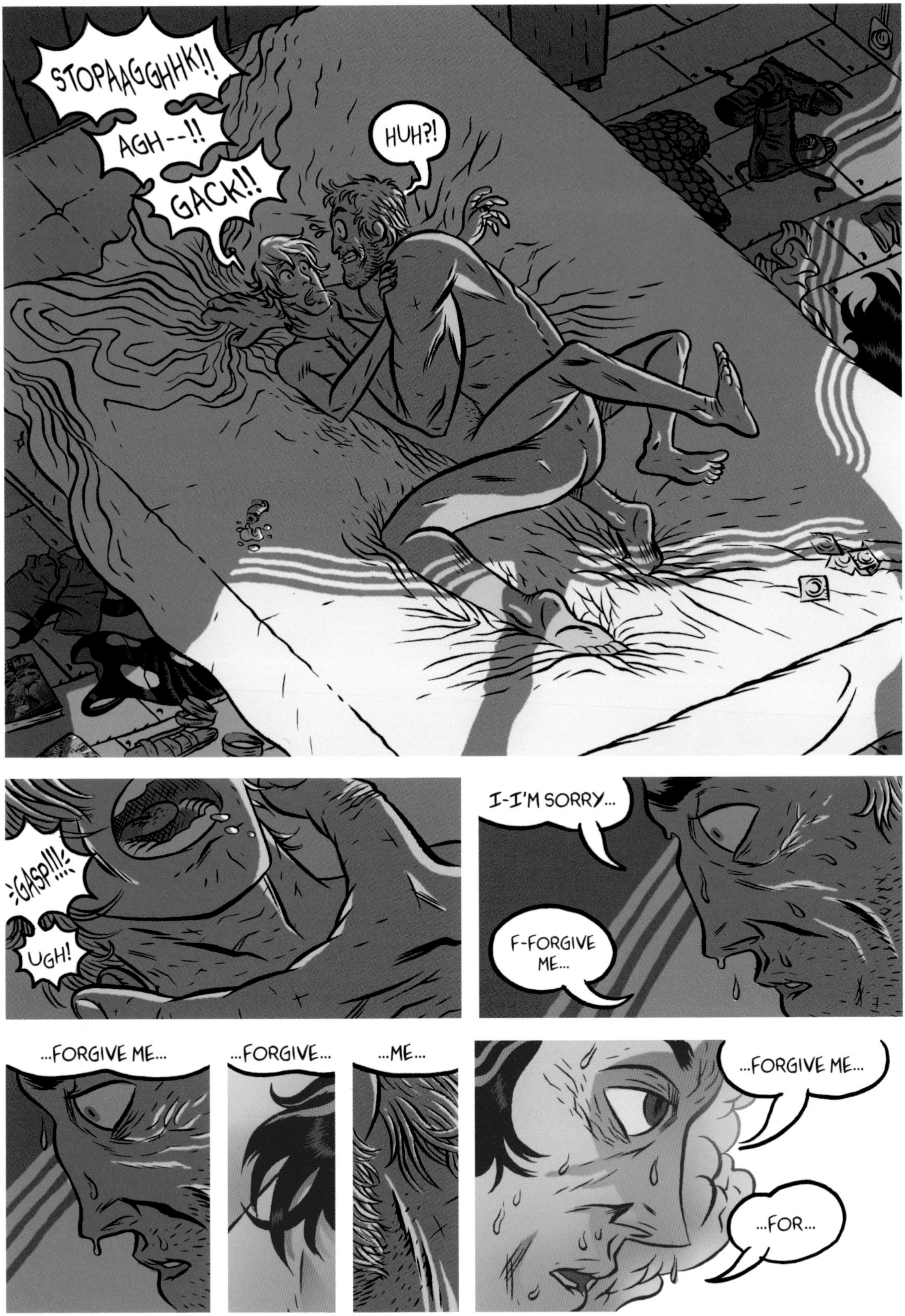

STOPAAGGHHK!!
AGH--!!
GACK!!
HUH?!
GASP!!!
UGH!
I-I'M SORRY...
F-FORGIVE ME...
...FORGIVE ME...
...FORGIVE...
...ME...
...FORGIVE ME...
...FOR...

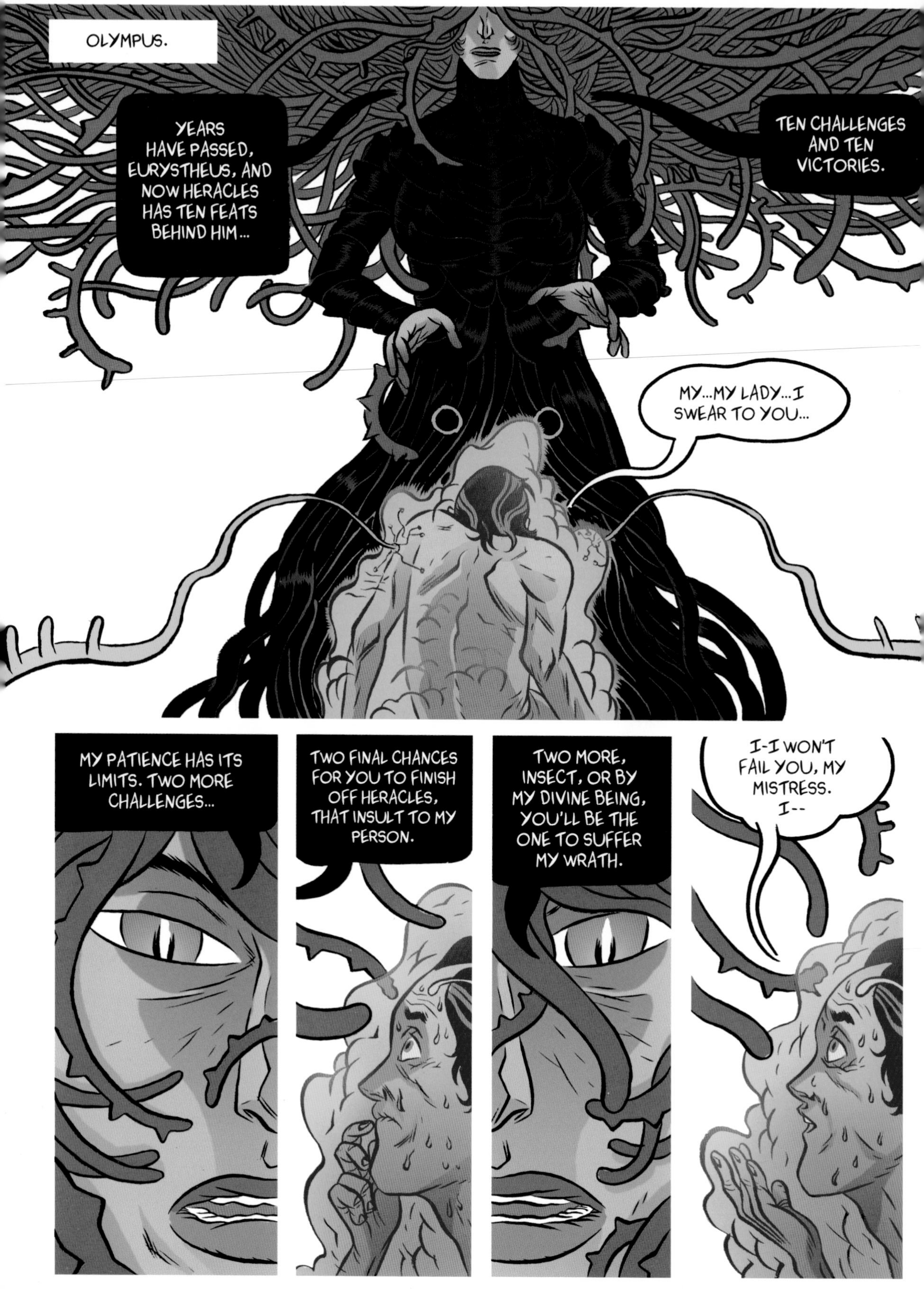
OLYMPUS.
YEARS HAVE PASSED, EURYSTHEUS, AND NOW HERACLES HAS TEN FEATS BEHIND HIM...
TEN CHALLENGES AND TEN VICTORIES.
MY...MY LADY...I SWEAR TO YOU...
MY PATIENCE HAS ITS LIMITS. TWO MORE CHALLENGES...
TWO FINAL CHANCES FOR YOU TO FINISH OFF HERACLES, THAT INSULT TO MY PERSON.
TWO MORE, INSECT, OR BY MY DIVINE BEING, YOU'LL BE THE ONE TO SUFFER MY WRATH.
I-I WON'T FAIL YOU, MY MISTRESS. I--

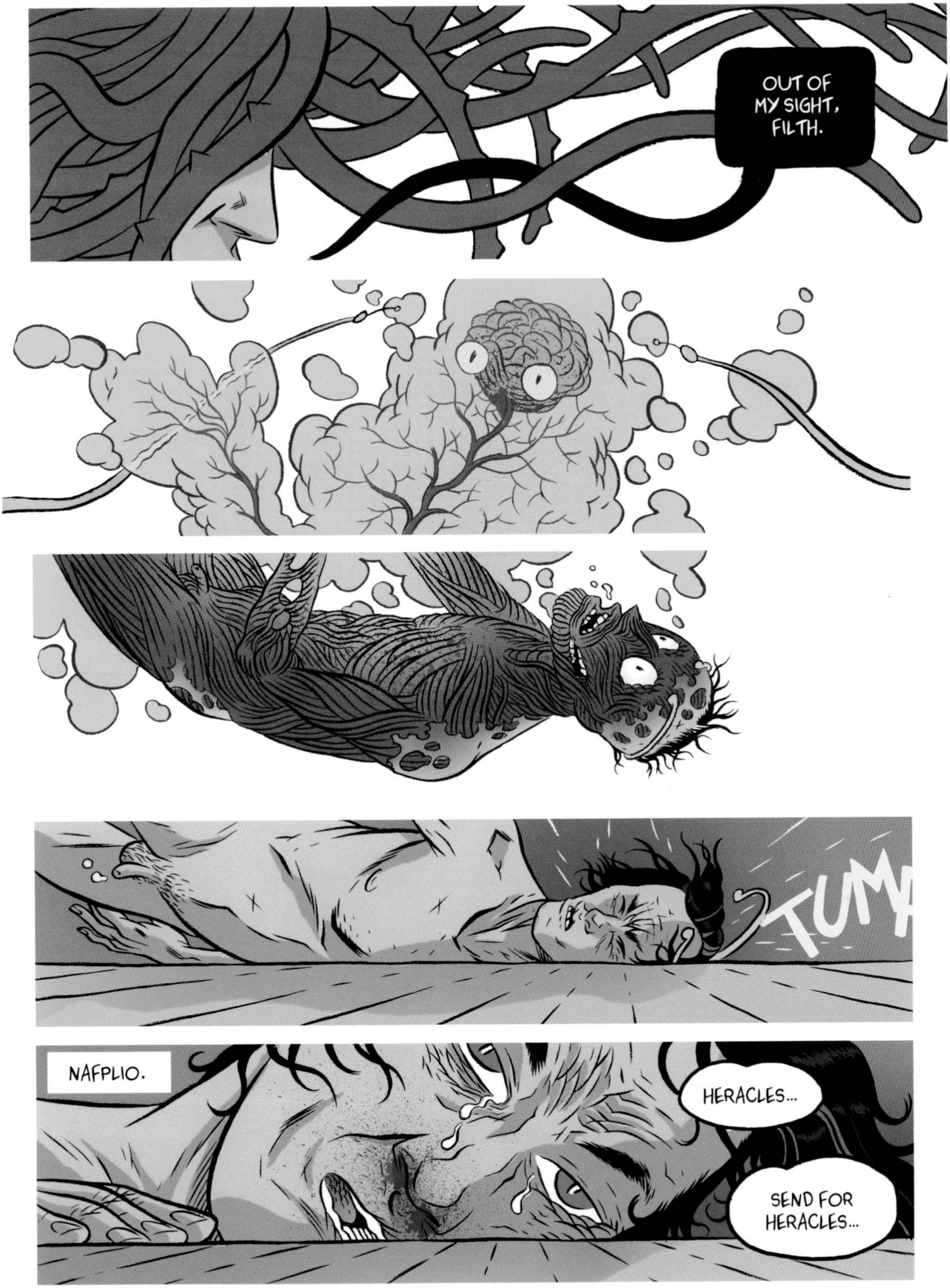
OUT OF MY SIGHT, FILTH.
TUM
NAFPLIO.
HERACLES...
SEND FOR HERACLES...

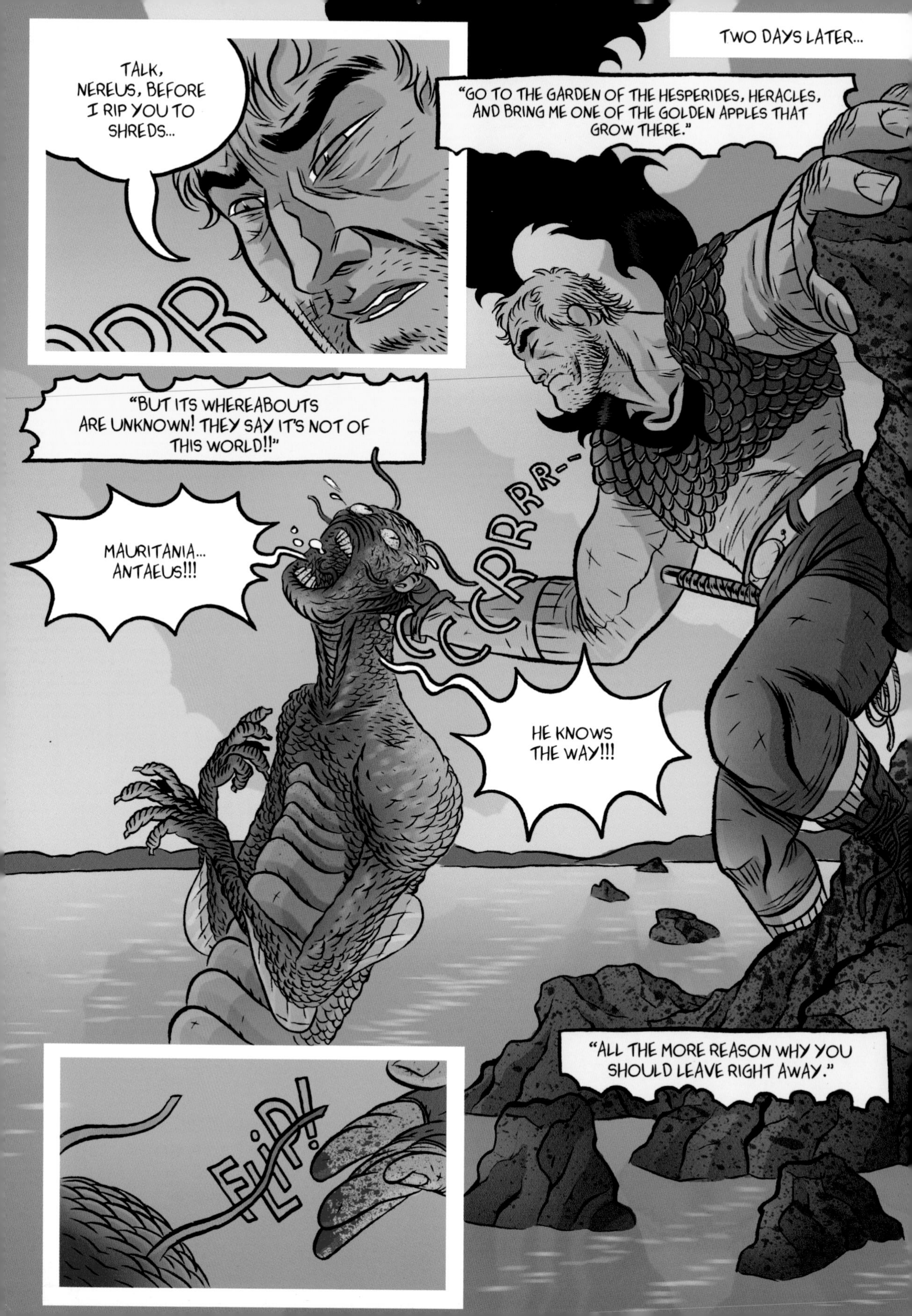
TWO DAYS LATER...
TALK, NEREUS, BEFORE I RIP YOU TO SHREDS...
"GO TO THE GARDEN OF THE HESPERIDES, HERACLES, AND BRING ME ONE OF THE GOLDEN APPLES THAT GROW THERE."
"BUT ITS WHEREABOUTS ARE UNKNOWN! THEY SAY IT'S NOT OF THIS WORLD!!"
CCRRRR--
MAURITANIA... ANTAEUS!!!
HE KNOWS THE WAY!!!
"ALL THE MORE REASON WHY YOU SHOULD LEAVE RIGHT AWAY."
FLIP!

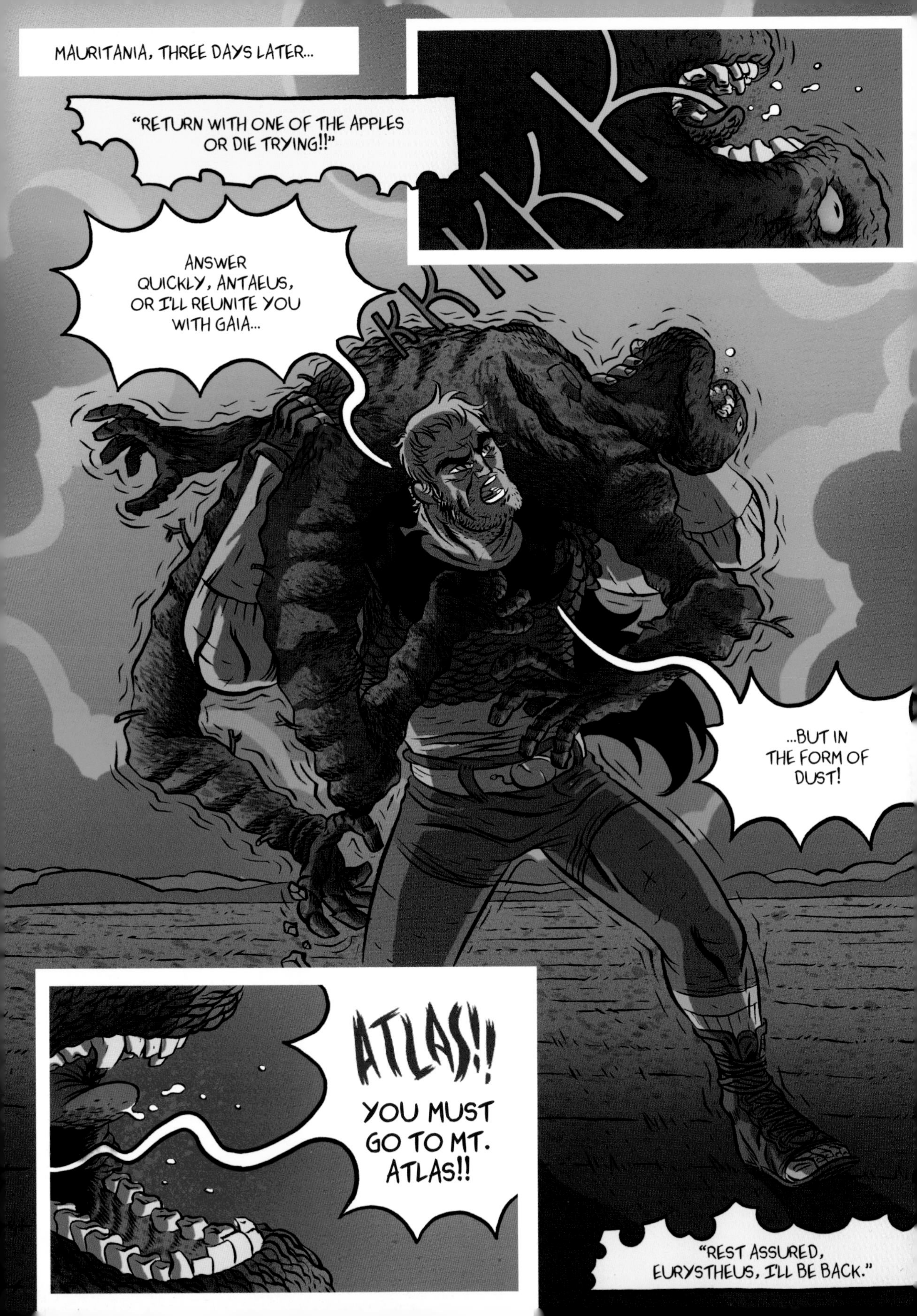

MAURITANIA, THREE DAYS LATER...
"RETURN WITH ONE OF THE APPLES OR DIE TRYING!!"
KKKKK
ANSWER QUICKLY, ANTAEUS, OR I'LL REUNITE YOU WITH GAIA...
...BUT IN THE FORM OF DUST!
ATLAS!!
YOU MUST GO TO MT. ATLAS!!
"REST ASSURED, EURYSTHEUS, I'LL BE BACK."

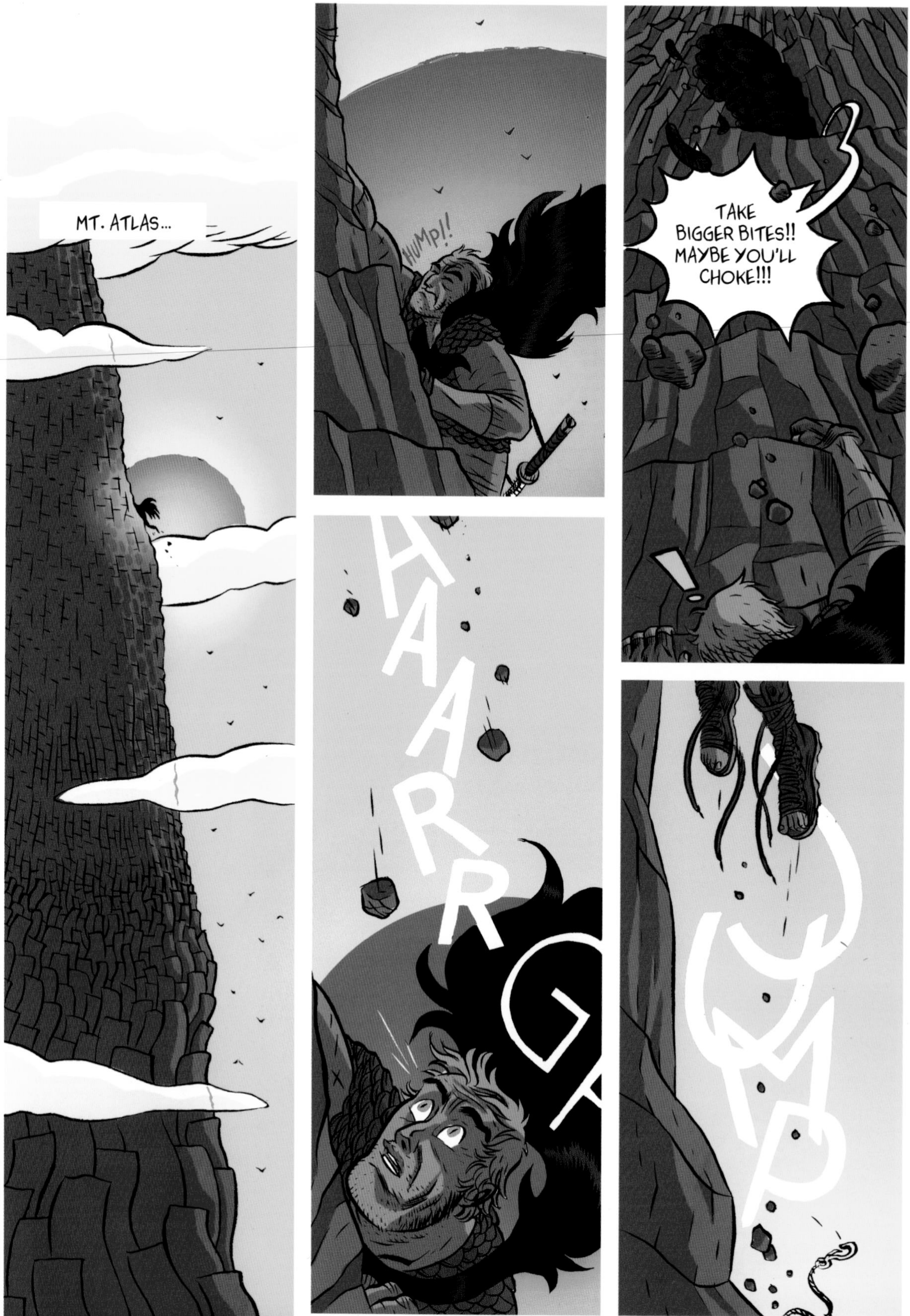
MT. ATLAS...
HUMP!!
TAKE BIGGER BITES!! MAYBE YOU'LL CHOKE!!!
!
AAARRGT
WUMP

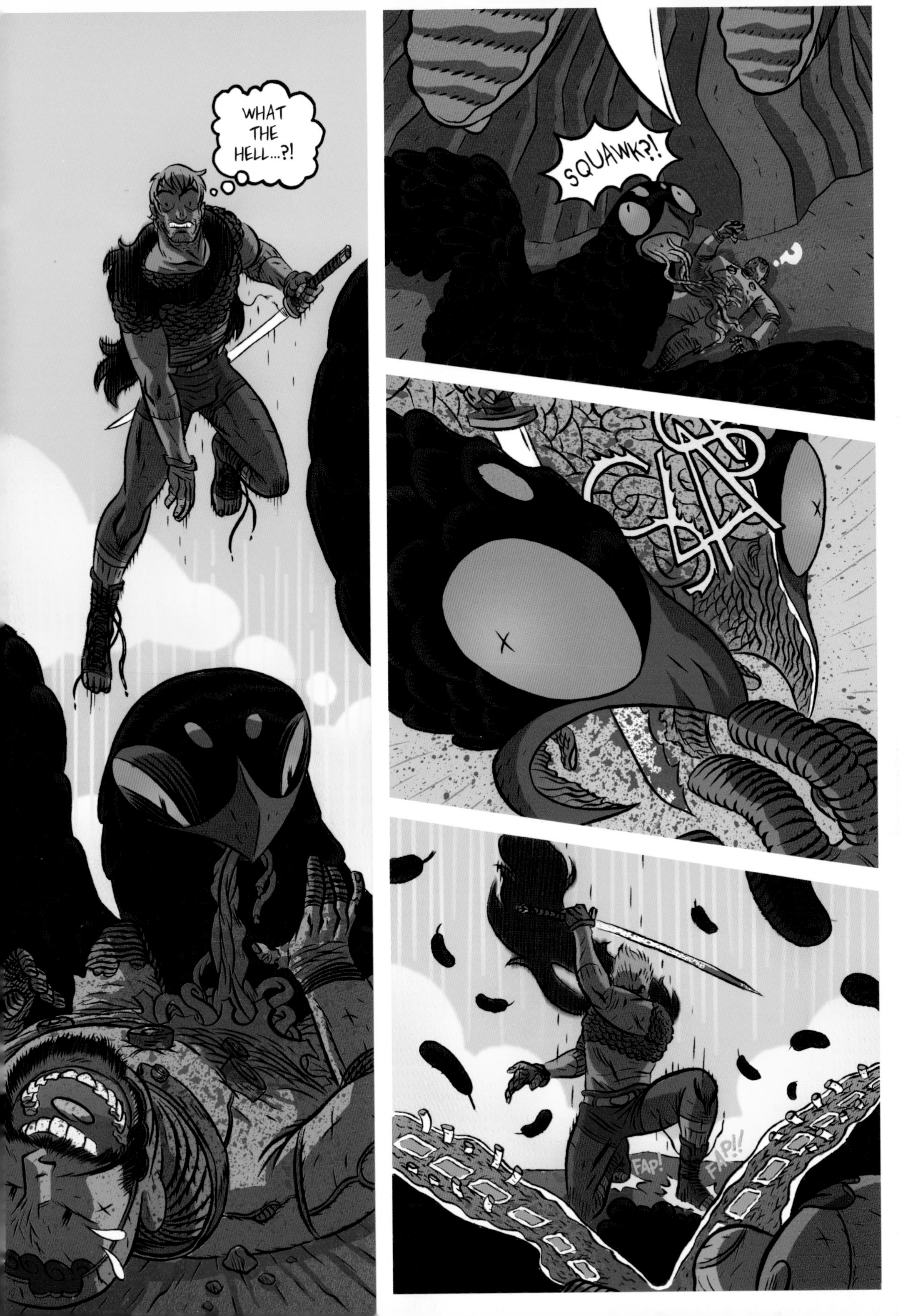
WHAT THE HELL...?!
SQUAWK?!
FAP!
FAP!!

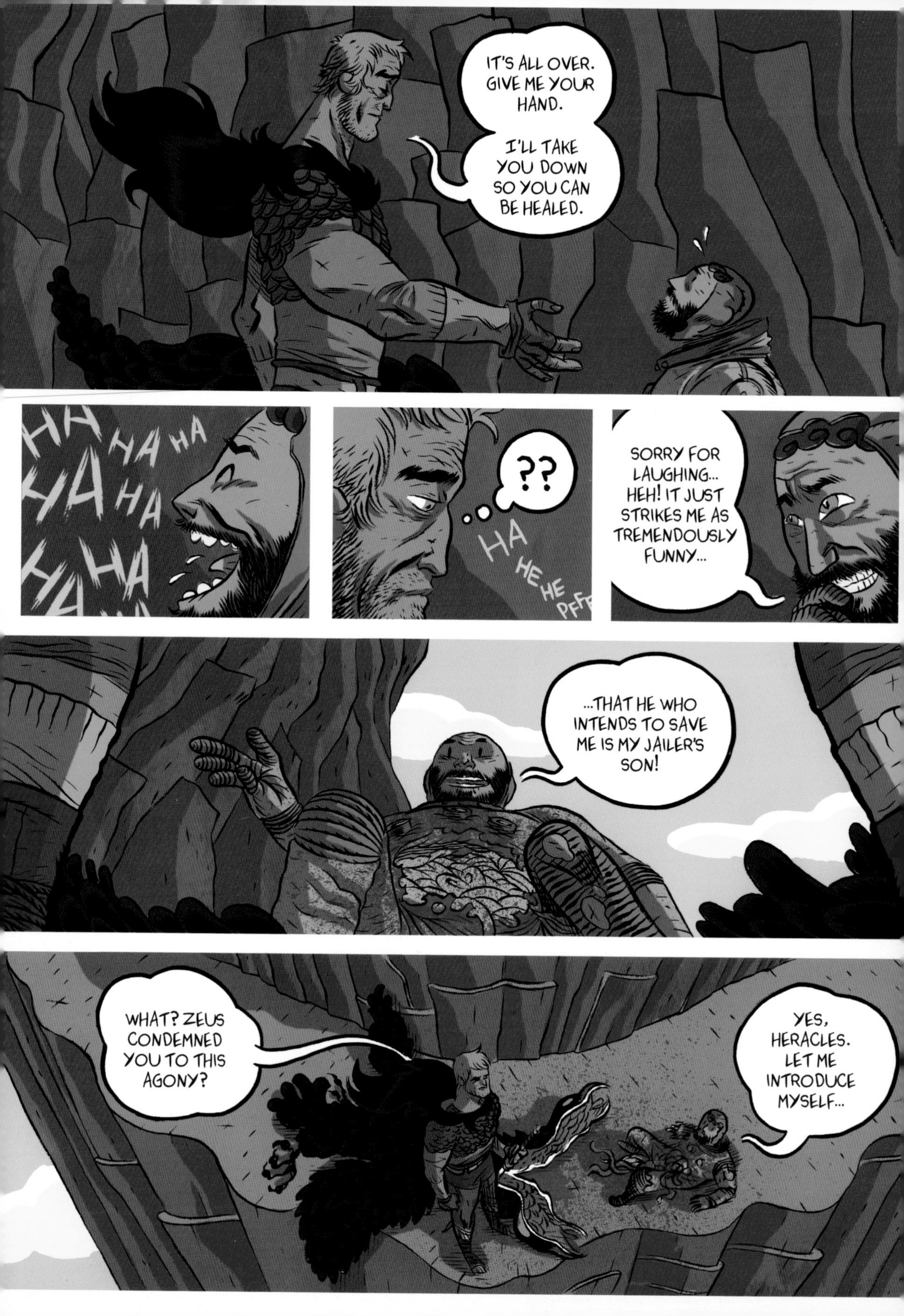
IT'S ALL OVER. GIVE ME YOUR HAND.
I'LL TAKE YOU DOWN SO YOU CAN BE HEALED.
HA HA HA HA HA HA HA HA HA HA
??
HA HE HE PFFF
SORRY FOR LAUGHING... HEH! IT JUST STRIKES ME AS TREMENDOUSLY FUNNY...
...THAT HE WHO INTENDS TO SAVE ME IS MY JAILER'S SON!
WHAT? ZEUS CONDEMNED YOU TO THIS AGONY?
YES, HERACLES. LET ME INTRODUCE MYSELF...

 MY NAME IS PROMETHEUS, AND THIS IS MY STORY...

"IT'S THE STORY OF A SCIENTIST WHOSE WORK WAS ALWAYS FOCUSED ON BENEFITING OTHERS, IMPROVING PEOPLE'S LIVES...

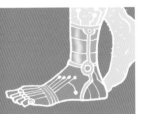  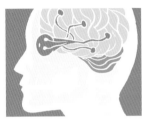 

"I COULD FIX ANY BLEMISH, CURE THE MOST TERRIBLE DISEASES...I DID IT ALL!...EXCEPT ONE THING, WHICH BECAME AN OBSESSION THAT TOOK UP ONE HUNDRED PERCENT OF MY RESEARCH..."

WHAT WAS IT?

DEATH.

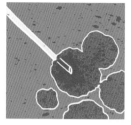

"DEATH IS NOTHING MORE THAN AN ILLNESS, AND AS SUCH IT MUST HAVE A CURE.

"THIS BECAME MY GOAL WHEN A BEAST ATTACKED MY WIFE, ENDING HER BRIEF LIFE BEFORE HER TIME, AND NONE OF MY WISDOM AND INVENTIONS COULD BRING HER BACK TO ME.

"I RELOCATED MY LABORATORY TO OUTER SPACE, WITH THE FIRM INTENTION OF NOT RETURNING TO THE WORLD OF MEN UNTIL I'D FOUND THE ANTIDOTE TO DEATH.

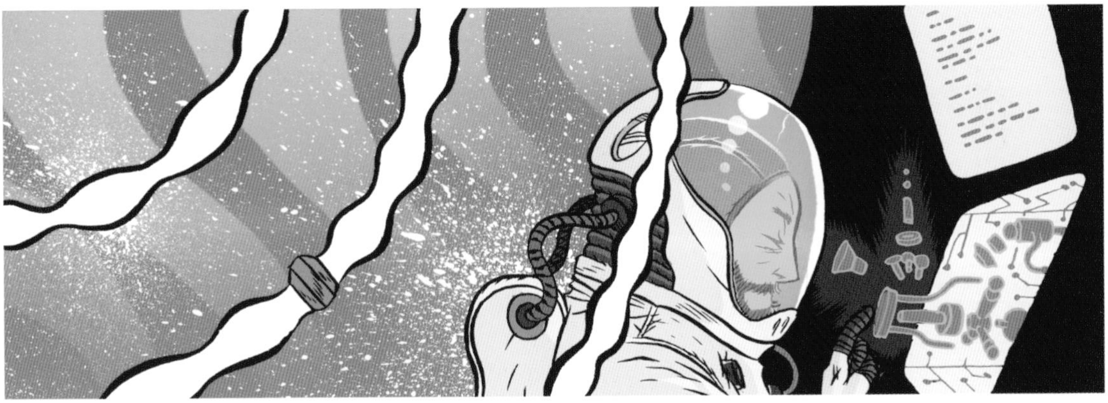

"BUT EVERY ATTEMPT WAS FUTILE, FOR EACH TEST I CARRIED OUT, EVERY NEW METHOD, EVERY NEW THEORY, TOOK ME FURTHER AWAY FROM MY OBJECTIVE.

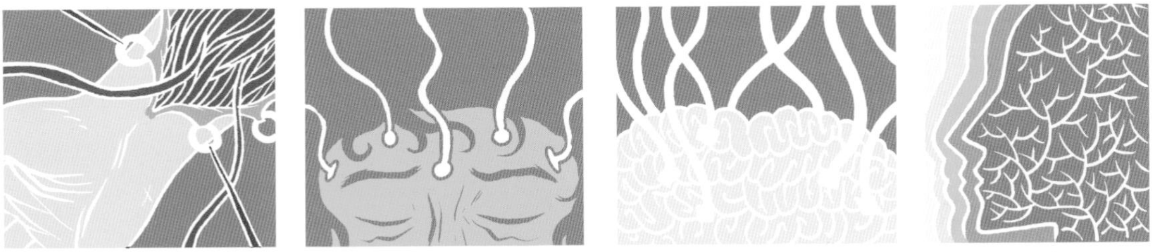

"EVERYTHING CONSPIRED AGAINST ME.

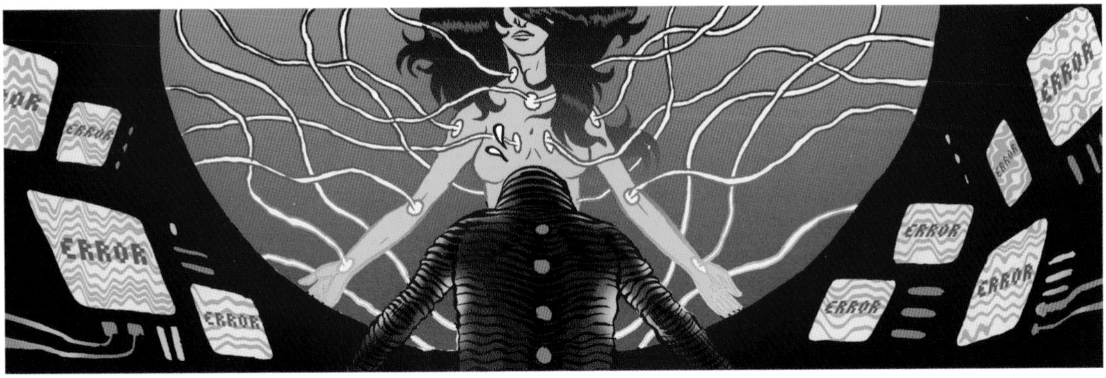
ERROR
ERROR
ERROR
ERROR
ERROR
ERROR
ERROR
ERROR

"EVEN OLYMPUS ITSELF...

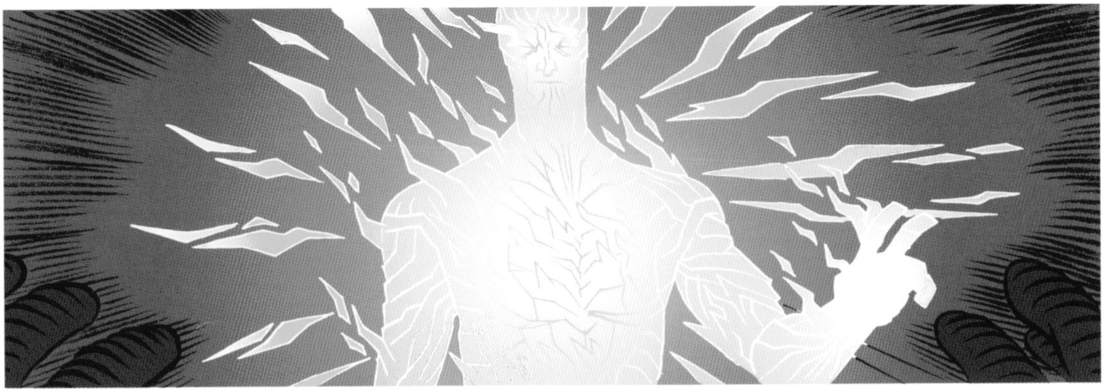

"APOLLO APPEARED BEFORE ME AT ZEUS'S COMMAND TO INFORM ME THAT THE MERE IDEA OF WHAT I WAS TRYING TO ACHIEVE WITH MY RESEARCH POSED A CHALLENGE TO THE GODS..."

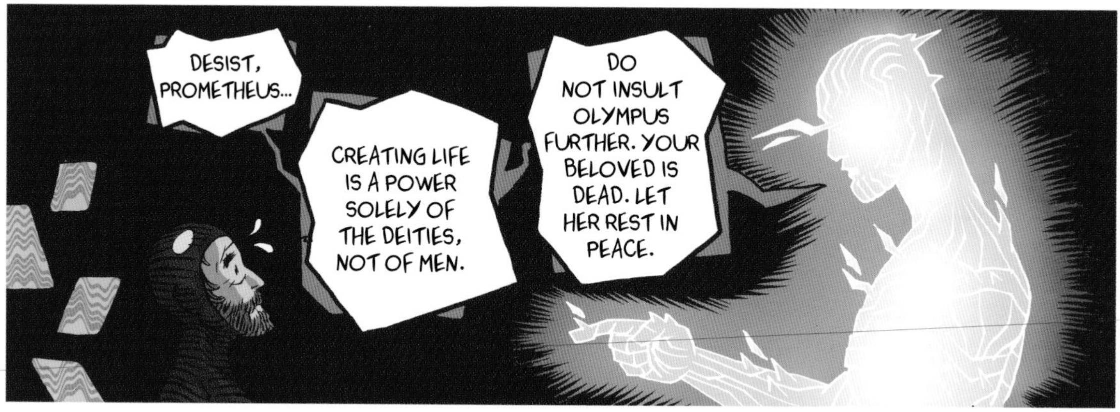
DESIST, PROMETHEUS...
CREATING LIFE IS A POWER SOLELY OF THE DEITIES, NOT OF MEN.
DO NOT INSULT OLYMPUS FURTHER. YOUR BELOVED IS DEAD. LET HER REST IN PEACE.

"INSTEAD OF DISCOURAGING ME, THE FACT THAT ZEUS HIMSELF ASKED ME TO STOP MY SEARCH BREATHED NEW LIFE INTO ME. IF OLYMPUS WAS WORRIED BY MY ADVANCES, THAT MEANT I WAS CLOSE TO REACHING MY GOAL.

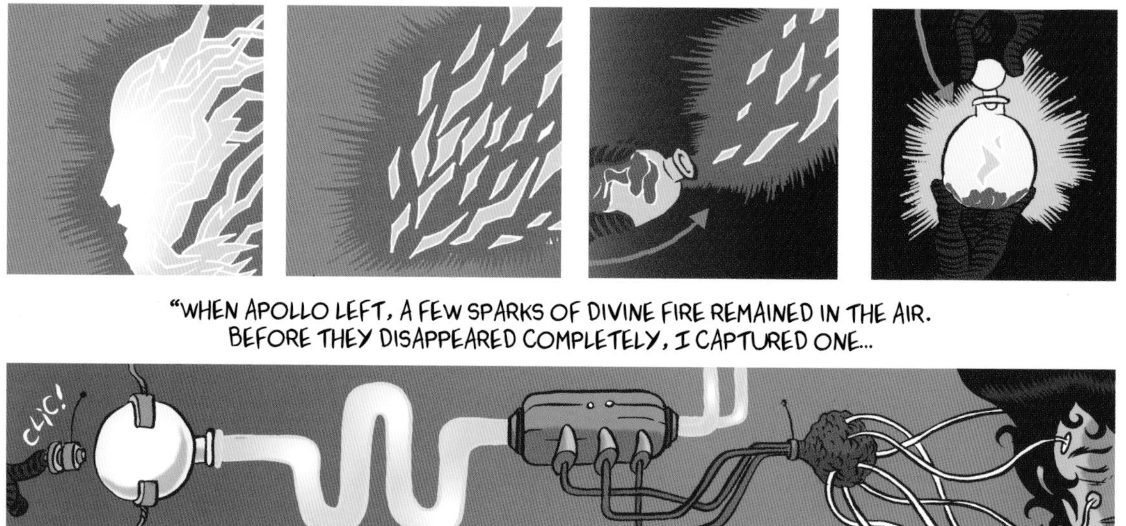

"WHEN APOLLO LEFT, A FEW SPARKS OF DIVINE FIRE REMAINED IN THE AIR. BEFORE THEY DISAPPEARED COMPLETELY, I CAPTURED ONE...

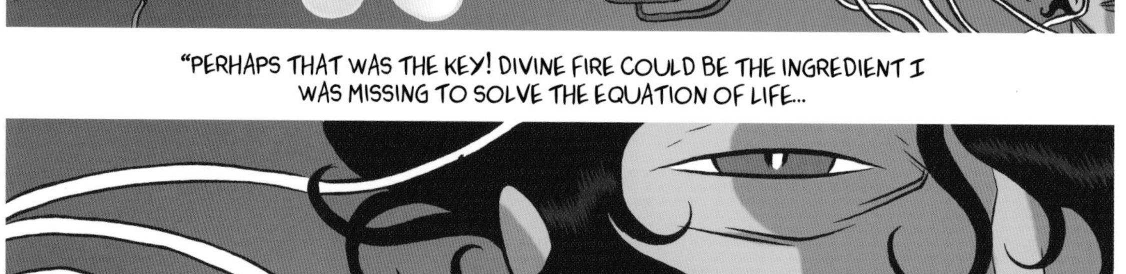
CLIC!

"PERHAPS THAT WAS THE KEY! DIVINE FIRE COULD BE THE INGREDIENT I WAS MISSING TO SOLVE THE EQUATION OF LIFE...

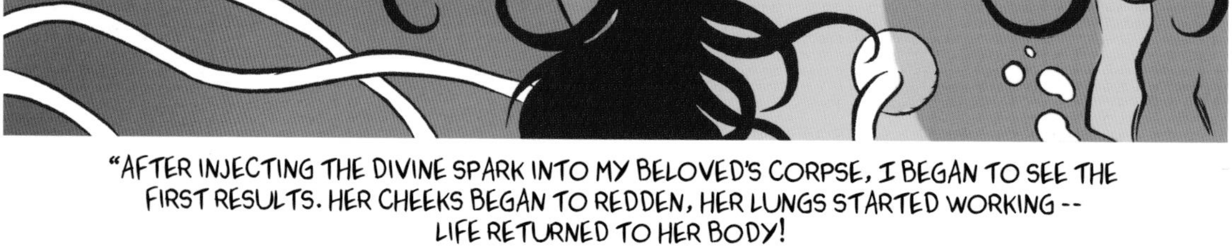

"AFTER INJECTING THE DIVINE SPARK INTO MY BELOVED'S CORPSE, I BEGAN TO SEE THE FIRST RESULTS. HER CHEEKS BEGAN TO REDDEN, HER LUNGS STARTED WORKING -- LIFE RETURNED TO HER BODY!

"BUT THE RESULT WASN'T WHAT I'D HOPED FOR...

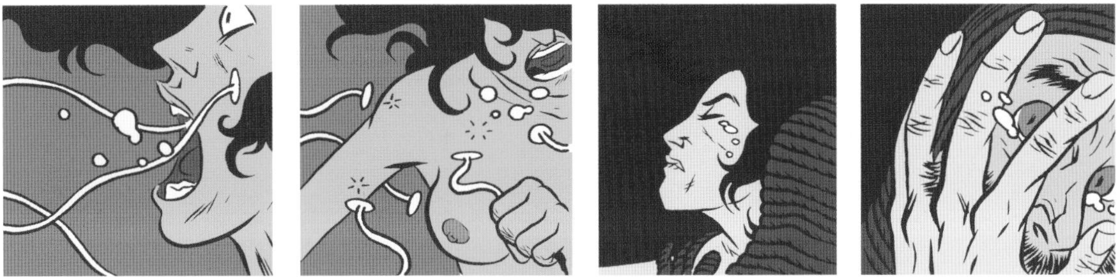

"HER BODY REJECTED THE NEW LIFE AS IF IT WERE A FOREIGN AGENT, SOMETHING HARMFUL. ALL OF HER BEING FOUGHT TO RETURN TO DEATH...

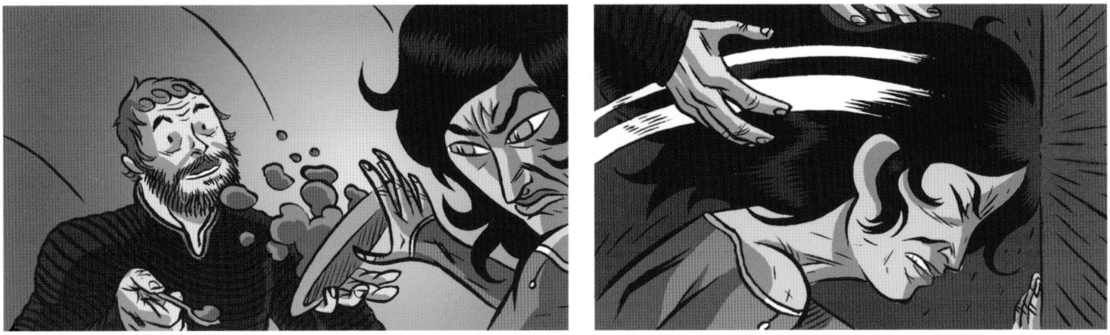

"...UNTIL FINALLY, I HAD TO GIVE UP. I LET HER GO...AND OFF SHE FLEW INTO THE ARMS OF THE GRIM REAPER...

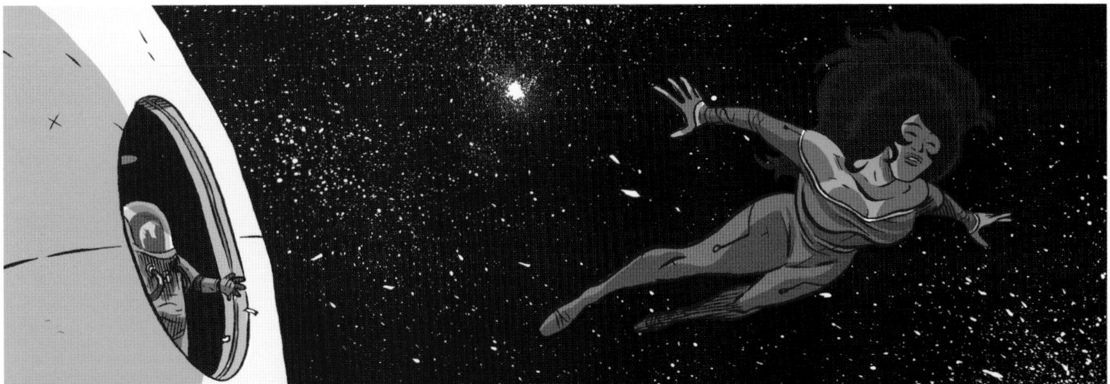

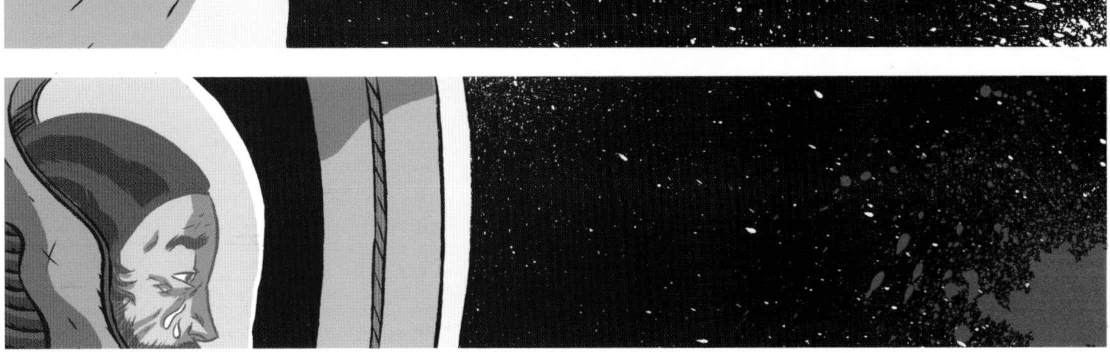

"THAT WAS ONLY THE BEGINNING OF MY AGONY...

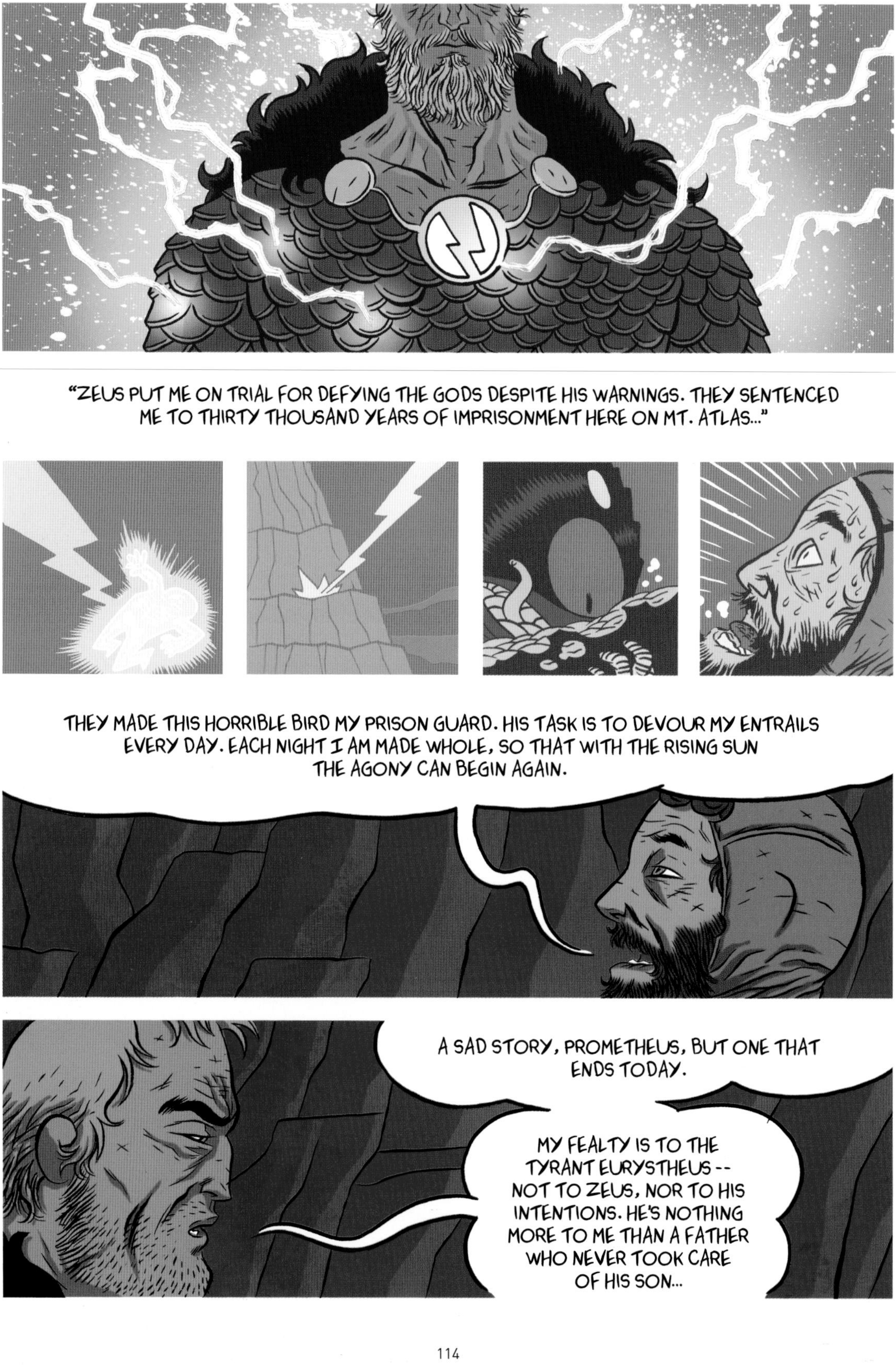
"ZEUS PUT ME ON TRIAL FOR DEFYING THE GODS DESPITE HIS WARNINGS. THEY SENTENCED ME TO THIRTY THOUSAND YEARS OF IMPRISONMENT HERE ON MT. ATLAS..."
THEY MADE THIS HORRIBLE BIRD MY PRISON GUARD. HIS TASK IS TO DEVOUR MY ENTRAILS EVERY DAY. EACH NIGHT I AM MADE WHOLE, SO THAT WITH THE RISING SUN THE AGONY CAN BEGIN AGAIN.
A SAD STORY, PROMETHEUS, BUT ONE THAT ENDS TODAY.
MY FEALTY IS TO THE TYRANT EURYSTHEUS -- NOT TO ZEUS, NOR TO HIS INTENTIONS. HE'S NOTHING MORE TO ME THAN A FATHER WHO NEVER TOOK CARE OF HIS SON...

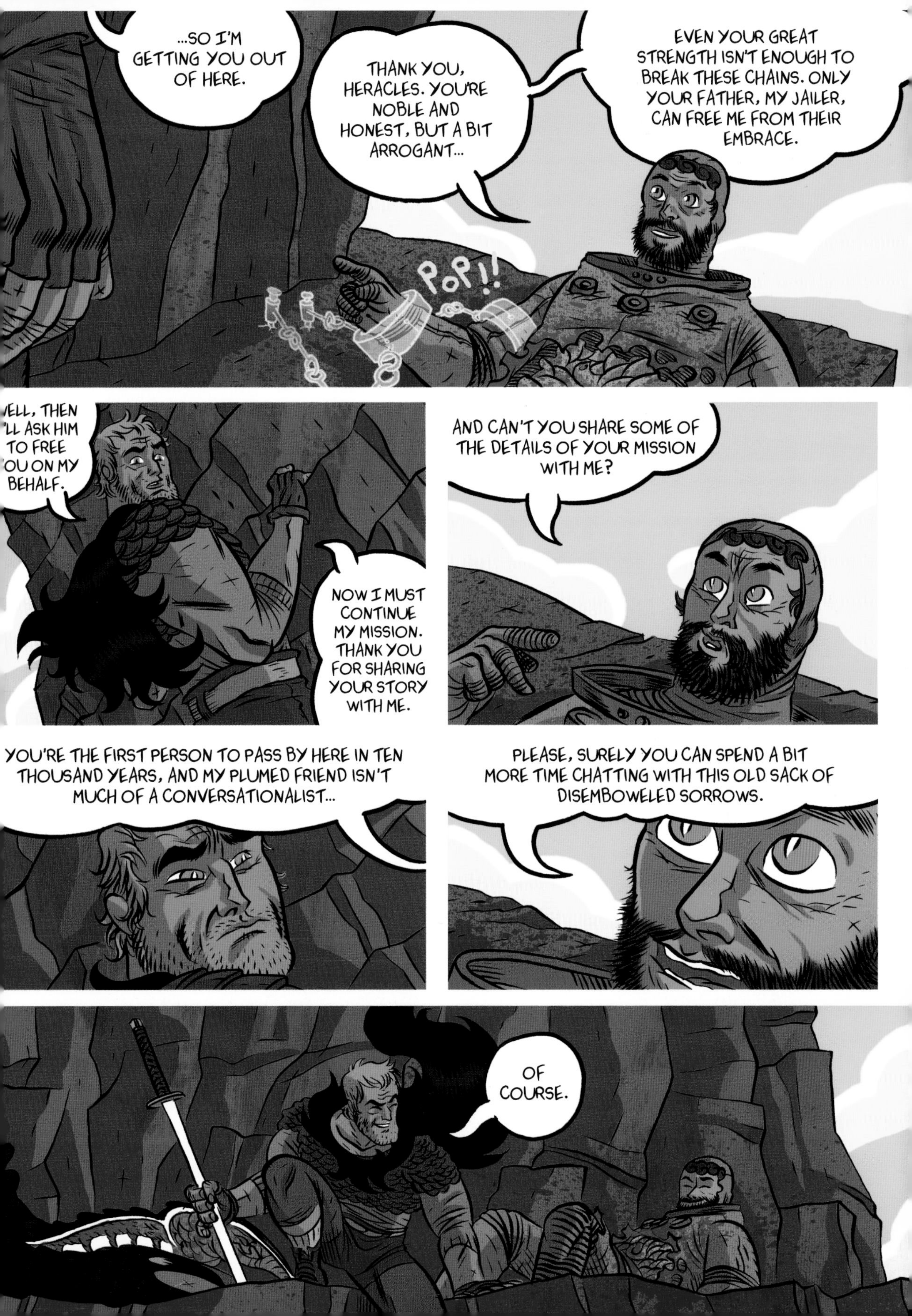
...SO I'M GETTING YOU OUT OF HERE.
THANK YOU, HERACLES. YOU'RE NOBLE AND HONEST, BUT A BIT ARROGANT...
EVEN YOUR GREAT STRENGTH ISN'T ENOUGH TO BREAK THESE CHAINS. ONLY YOUR FATHER, MY JAILER, CAN FREE ME FROM THEIR EMBRACE.
POP!!
ELL, THEN 'LL ASK HIM TO FREE OU ON MY BEHALF.
NOW I MUST CONTINUE MY MISSION. THANK YOU FOR SHARING YOUR STORY WITH ME.
AND CAN'T YOU SHARE SOME OF THE DETAILS OF YOUR MISSION WITH ME?
YOU'RE THE FIRST PERSON TO PASS BY HERE IN TEN THOUSAND YEARS, AND MY PLUMED FRIEND ISN'T MUCH OF A CONVERSATIONALIST...
PLEASE, SURELY YOU CAN SPEND A BIT MORE TIME CHATTING WITH THIS OLD SACK OF DISEMBOWELED SORROWS.
OF COURSE.

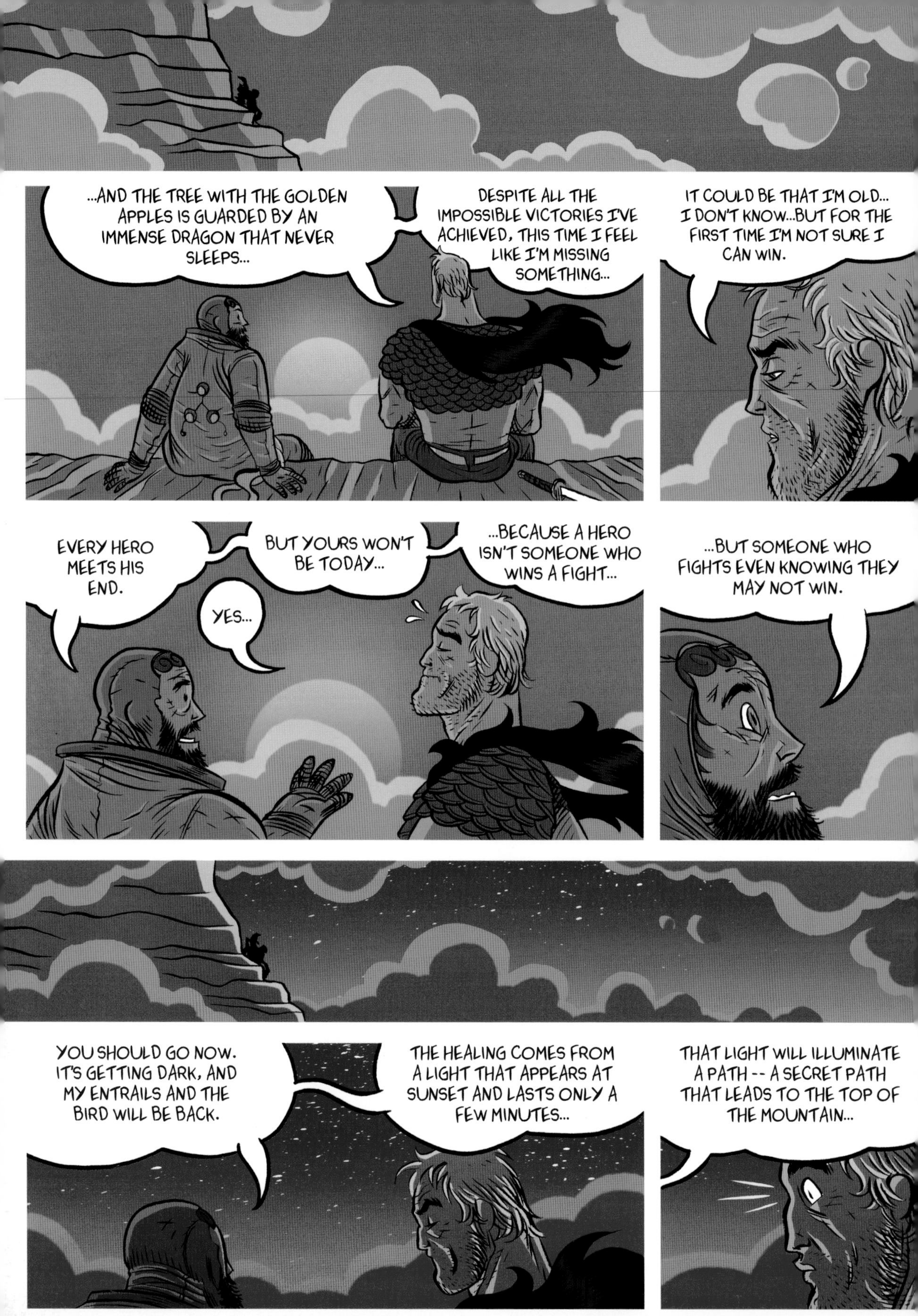
...AND THE TREE WITH THE GOLDEN APPLES IS GUARDED BY AN IMMENSE DRAGON THAT NEVER SLEEPS...
DESPITE ALL THE IMPOSSIBLE VICTORIES I'VE ACHIEVED, THIS TIME I FEEL LIKE I'M MISSING SOMETHING...
IT COULD BE THAT I'M OLD... I DON'T KNOW...BUT FOR THE FIRST TIME I'M NOT SURE I CAN WIN.
EVERY HERO MEETS HIS END.
YES...
BUT YOURS WON'T BE TODAY...
...BECAUSE A HERO ISN'T SOMEONE WHO WINS A FIGHT...
...BUT SOMEONE WHO FIGHTS EVEN KNOWING THEY MAY NOT WIN.
YOU SHOULD GO NOW. IT'S GETTING DARK, AND MY ENTRAILS AND THE BIRD WILL BE BACK.
THE HEALING COMES FROM A LIGHT THAT APPEARS AT SUNSET AND LASTS ONLY A FEW MINUTES...
THAT LIGHT WILL ILLUMINATE A PATH -- A SECRET PATH THAT LEADS TO THE TOP OF THE MOUNTAIN...

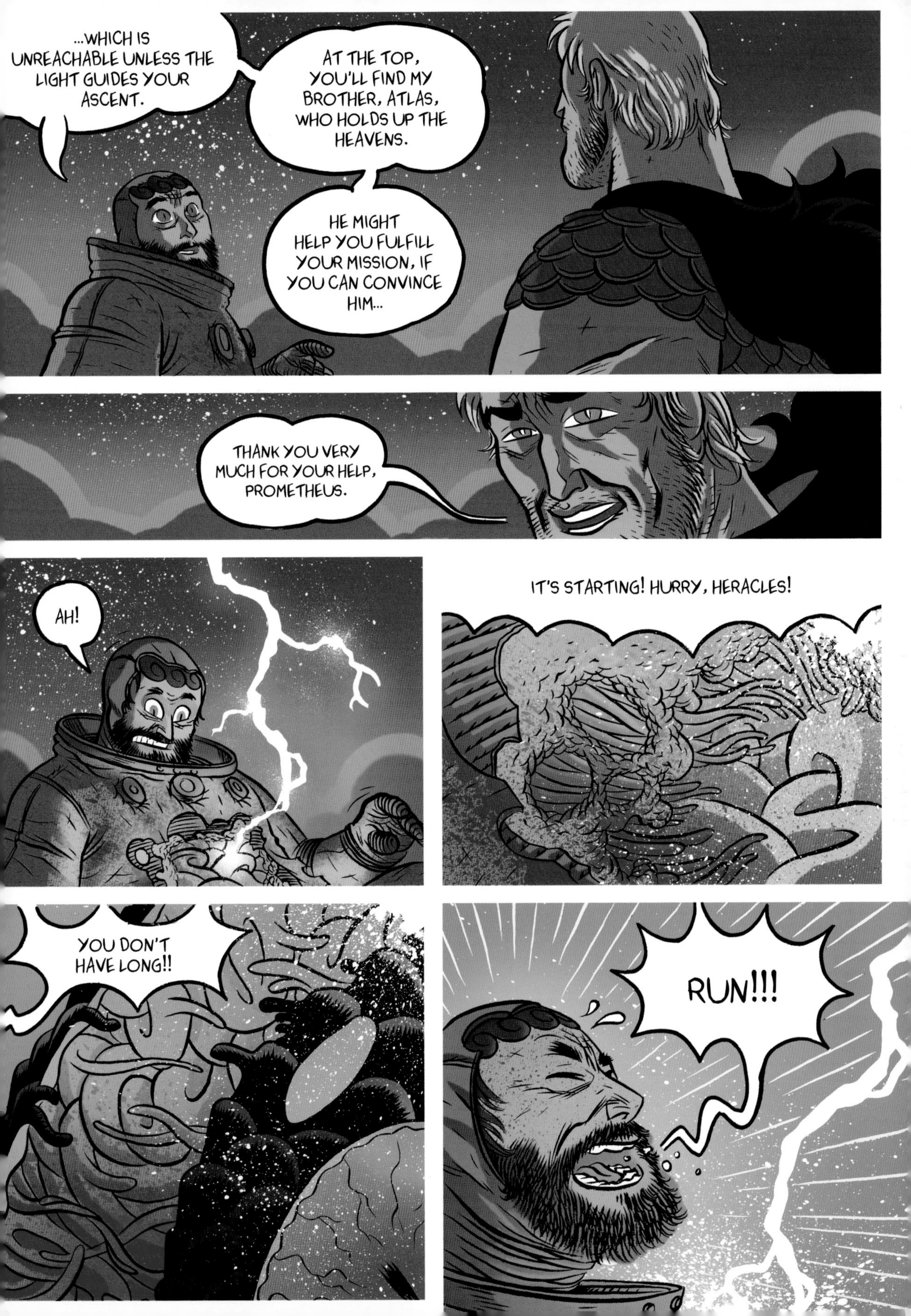
...WHICH IS UNREACHABLE UNLESS THE LIGHT GUIDES YOUR ASCENT.
AT THE TOP, YOU'LL FIND MY BROTHER, ATLAS, WHO HOLDS UP THE HEAVENS.
HE MIGHT HELP YOU FULFILL YOUR MISSION, IF YOU CAN CONVINCE HIM...
THANK YOU VERY MUCH FOR YOUR HELP, PROMETHEUS.
AH!
IT'S STARTING! HURRY, HERACLES!
YOU DON'T HAVE LONG!!
RUN!!!

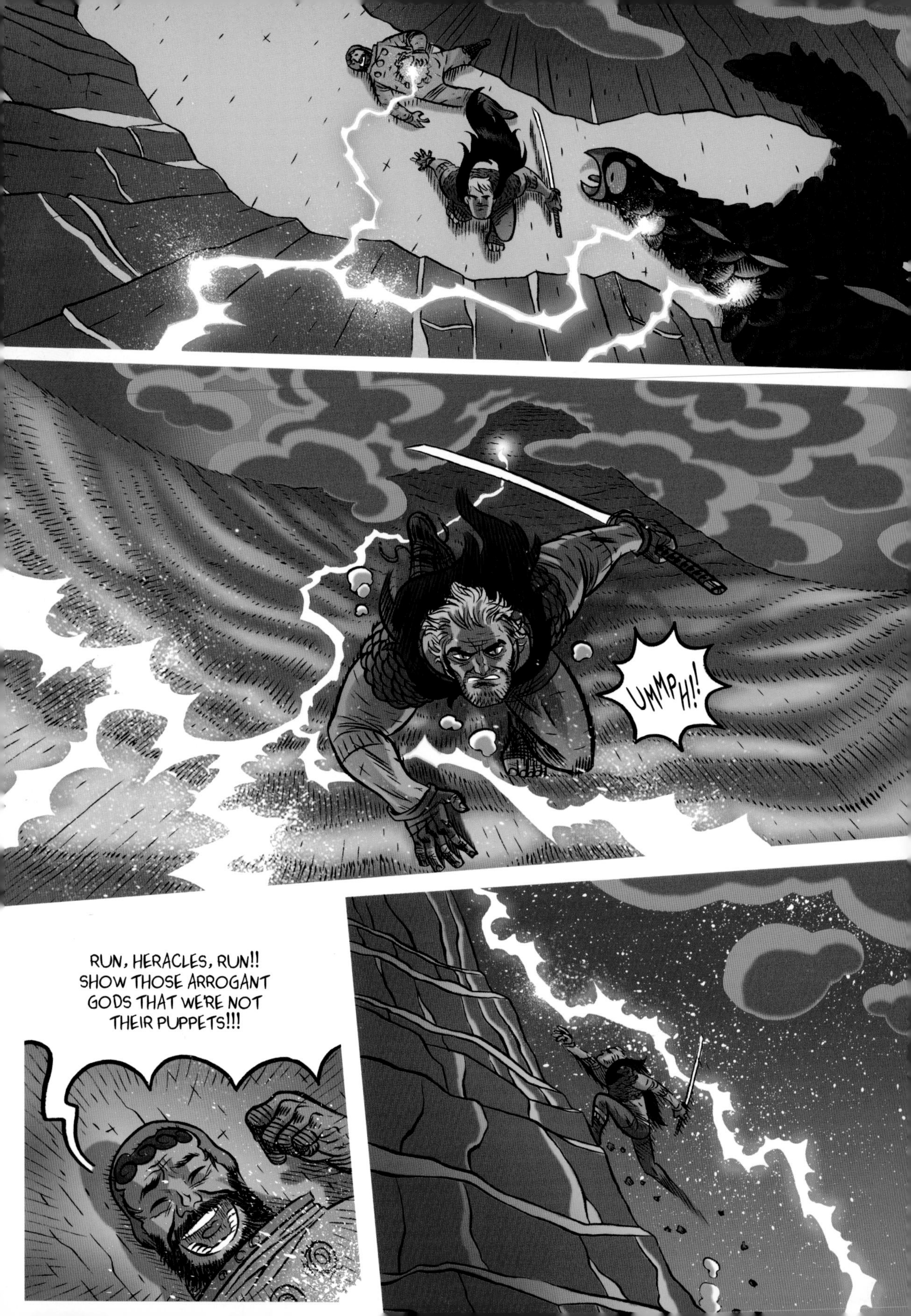
UMMPH!!
RUN, HERACLES, RUN!! SHOW THOSE ARROGANT GODS THAT WE'RE NOT THEIR PUPPETS!!!

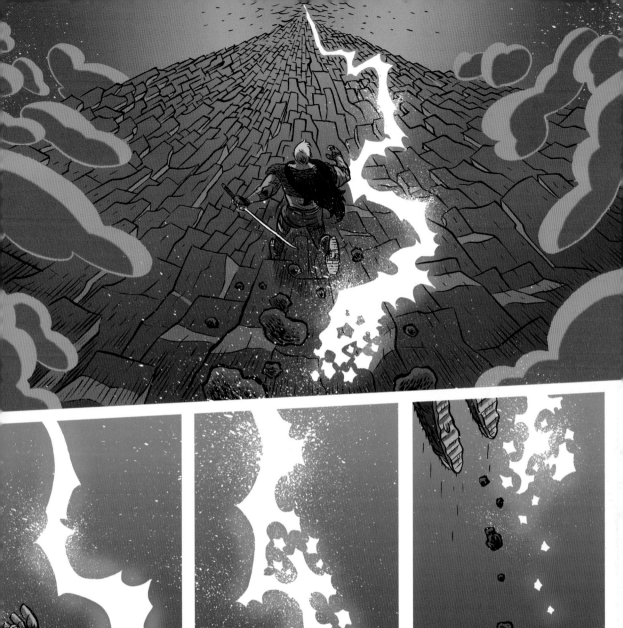

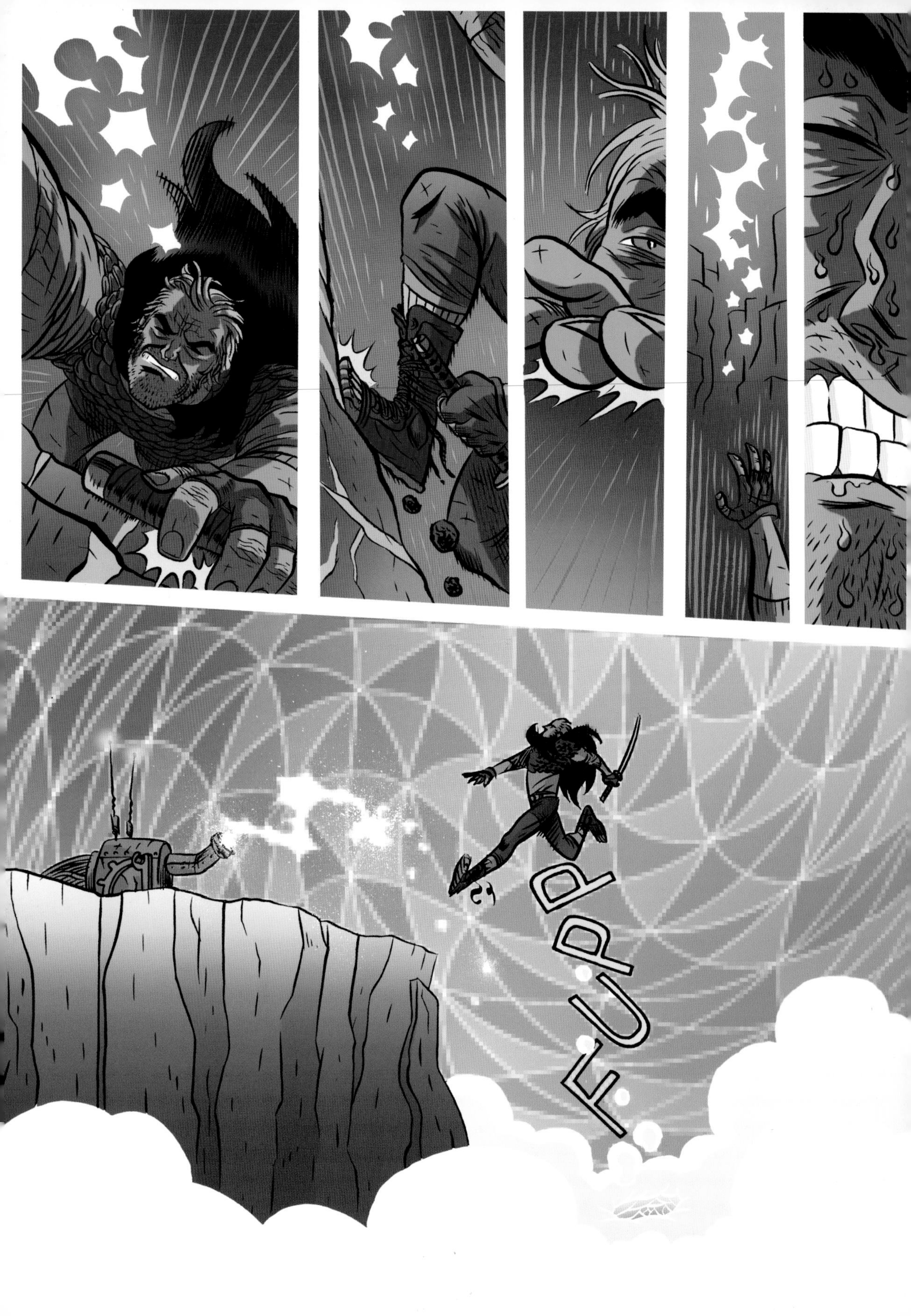
FUPR

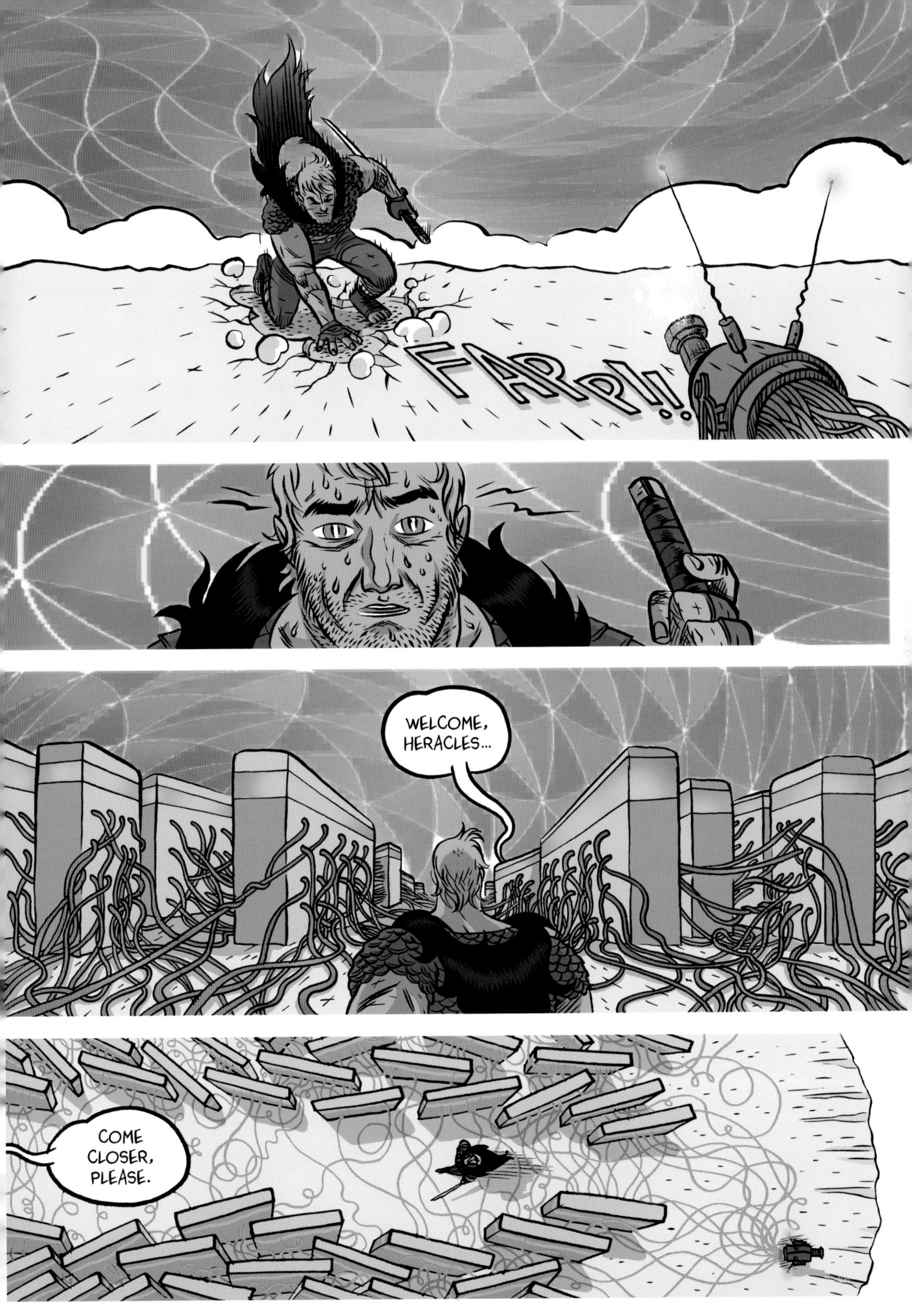
FARP!!
WELCOME, HERACLES...
COME CLOSER, PLEASE.

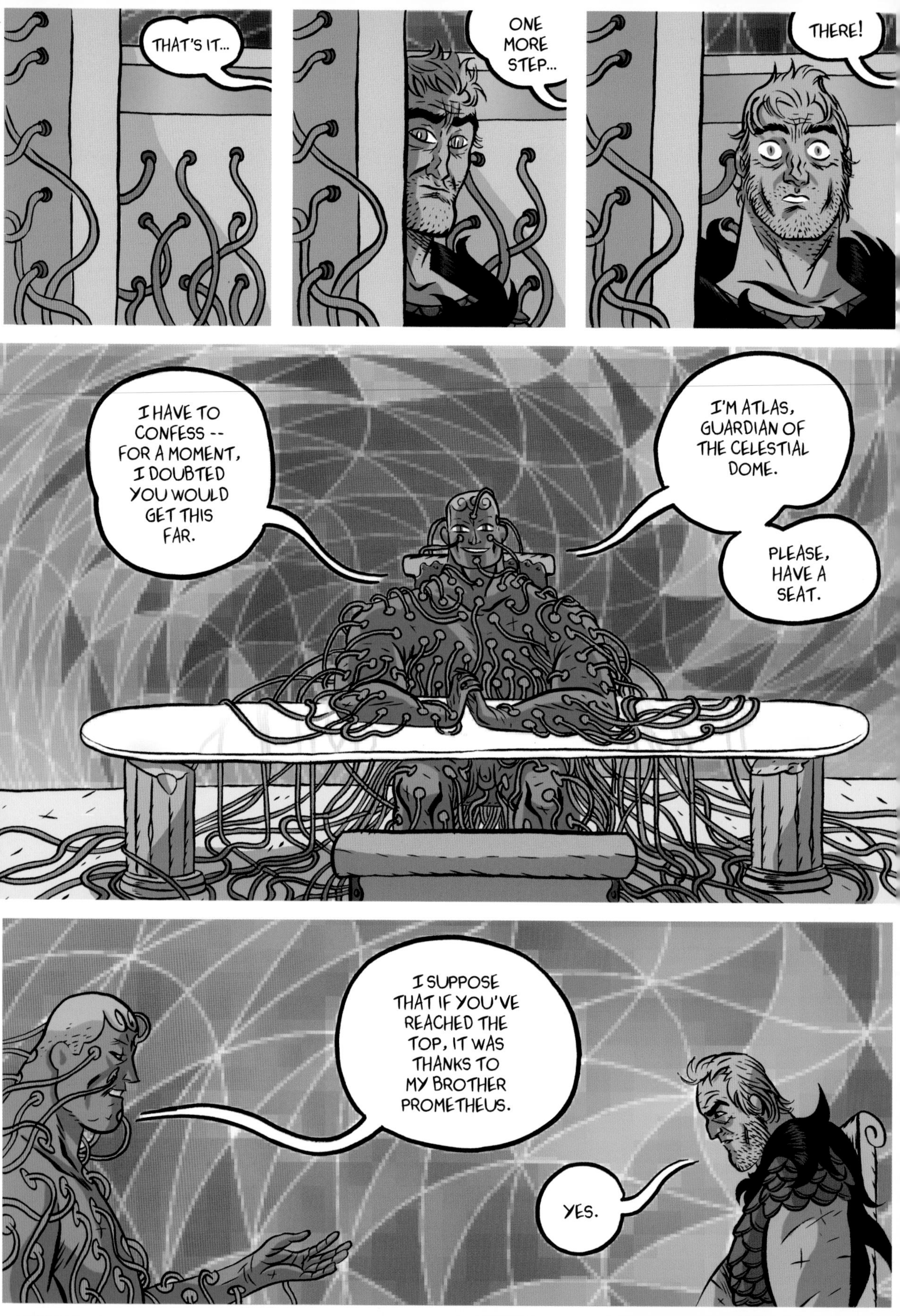
THAT'S IT...
ONE MORE STEP...
THERE!
I HAVE TO CONFESS -- FOR A MOMENT, I DOUBTED YOU WOULD GET THIS FAR.
I'M ATLAS, GUARDIAN OF THE CELESTIAL DOME.
PLEASE, HAVE A SEAT.
I SUPPOSE THAT IF YOU'VE REACHED THE TOP, IT WAS THANKS TO MY BROTHER PROMETHEUS.
YES.

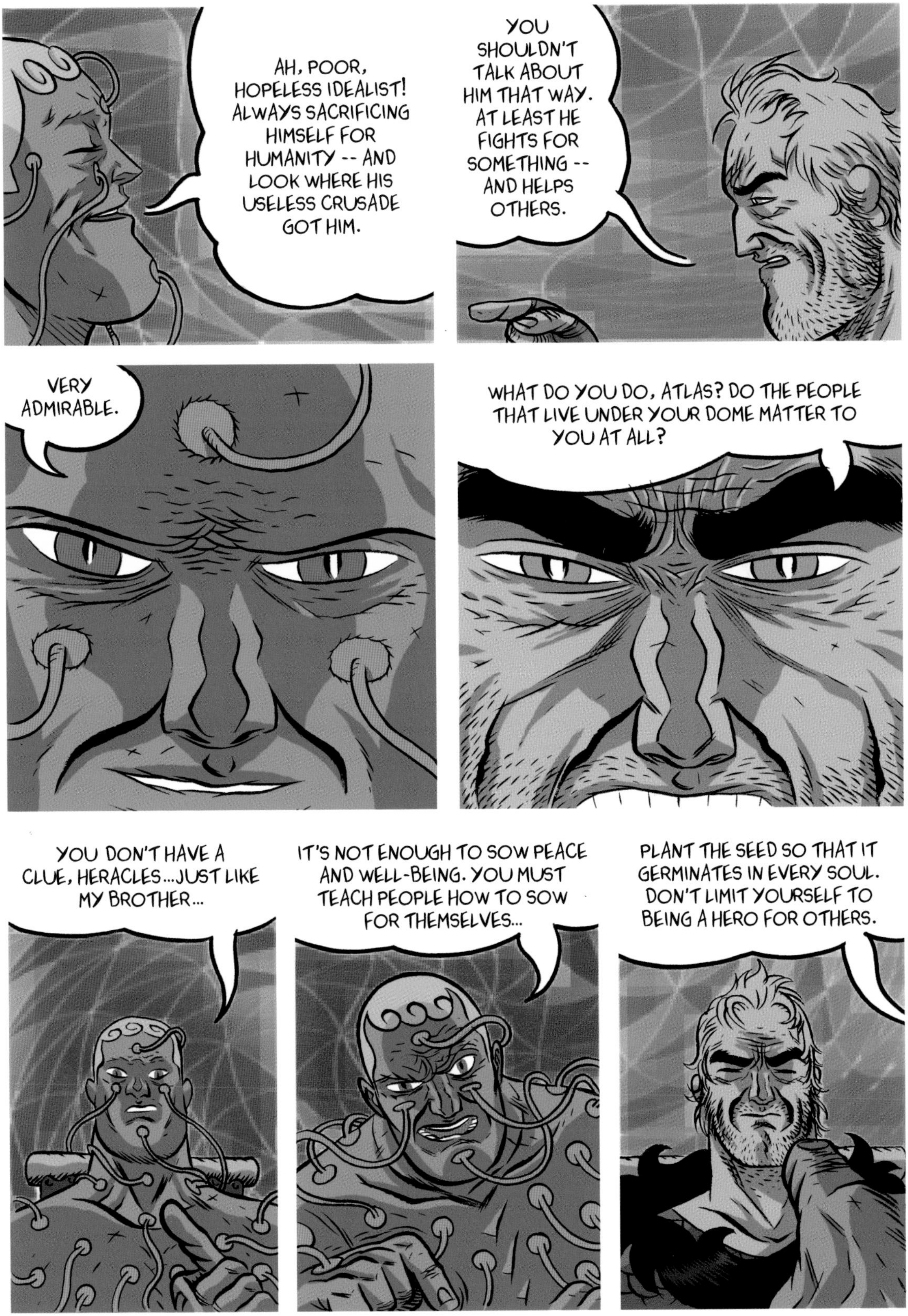
AH, POOR, HOPELESS IDEALIST! ALWAYS SACRIFICING HIMSELF FOR HUMANITY -- AND LOOK WHERE HIS USELESS CRUSADE GOT HIM.
YOU SHOULDN'T TALK ABOUT HIM THAT WAY. AT LEAST HE FIGHTS FOR SOMETHING -- AND HELPS OTHERS.
VERY ADMIRABLE.
WHAT DO YOU DO, ATLAS? DO THE PEOPLE THAT LIVE UNDER YOUR DOME MATTER TO YOU AT ALL?
YOU DON'T HAVE A CLUE, HERACLES... JUST LIKE MY BROTHER...
IT'S NOT ENOUGH TO SOW PEACE AND WELL-BEING. YOU MUST TEACH PEOPLE HOW TO SOW FOR THEMSELVES...
PLANT THE SEED SO THAT IT GERMINATES IN EVERY SOUL. DON'T LIMIT YOURSELF TO BEING A HERO FOR OTHERS.

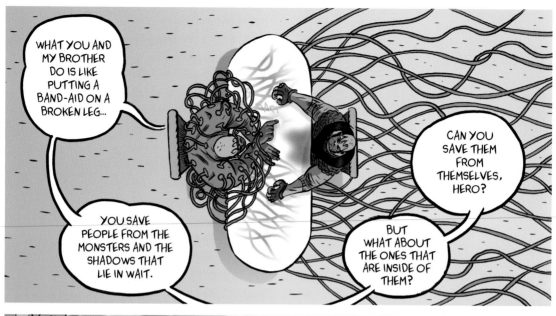

WHAT YOU AND MY BROTHER DO IS LIKE PUTTING A BAND-AID ON A BROKEN LEG...

CAN YOU SAVE THEM FROM THEMSELVES, HERO?

YOU SAVE PEOPLE FROM THE MONSTERS AND THE SHADOWS THAT LIE IN WAIT.

BUT WHAT ABOUT THE ONES THAT ARE INSIDE OF THEM?

YOU CAN'T EVEN SAVE **YOU** FROM YOURSELF... YOUR HEART IS FULL OF PAIN AND GUILT. YOUR FEATS ARE ONLY A VEIL TO HIDE YOUR SORROWS.

WHAT COULD YOU KNOW OF MY PAIN?! WHAT COULD YOU KNOW OF THE BURDEN I BEAR?!

AH...CHILD... NO ONE KNOWS MORE ABOUT SORROW THAN I.

SEE ALL THESE WIRES? EACH ONE IS CONNECTED TO A MAN'S SOUL.

I ENDURE EVERY JOY, EVERY DEFEAT, EVERY PAIN THAT AFFLICTS EACH OF YOU.

AS LONG AS I'VE EXISTED, I'VE BORNE THE WEIGHT OF A CONSTELLATION OF EMOTIONS ON MY SHOULDERS...

LET ME SHOW YOU...

TIP!

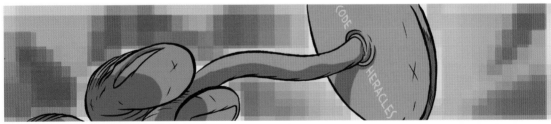

TAP!

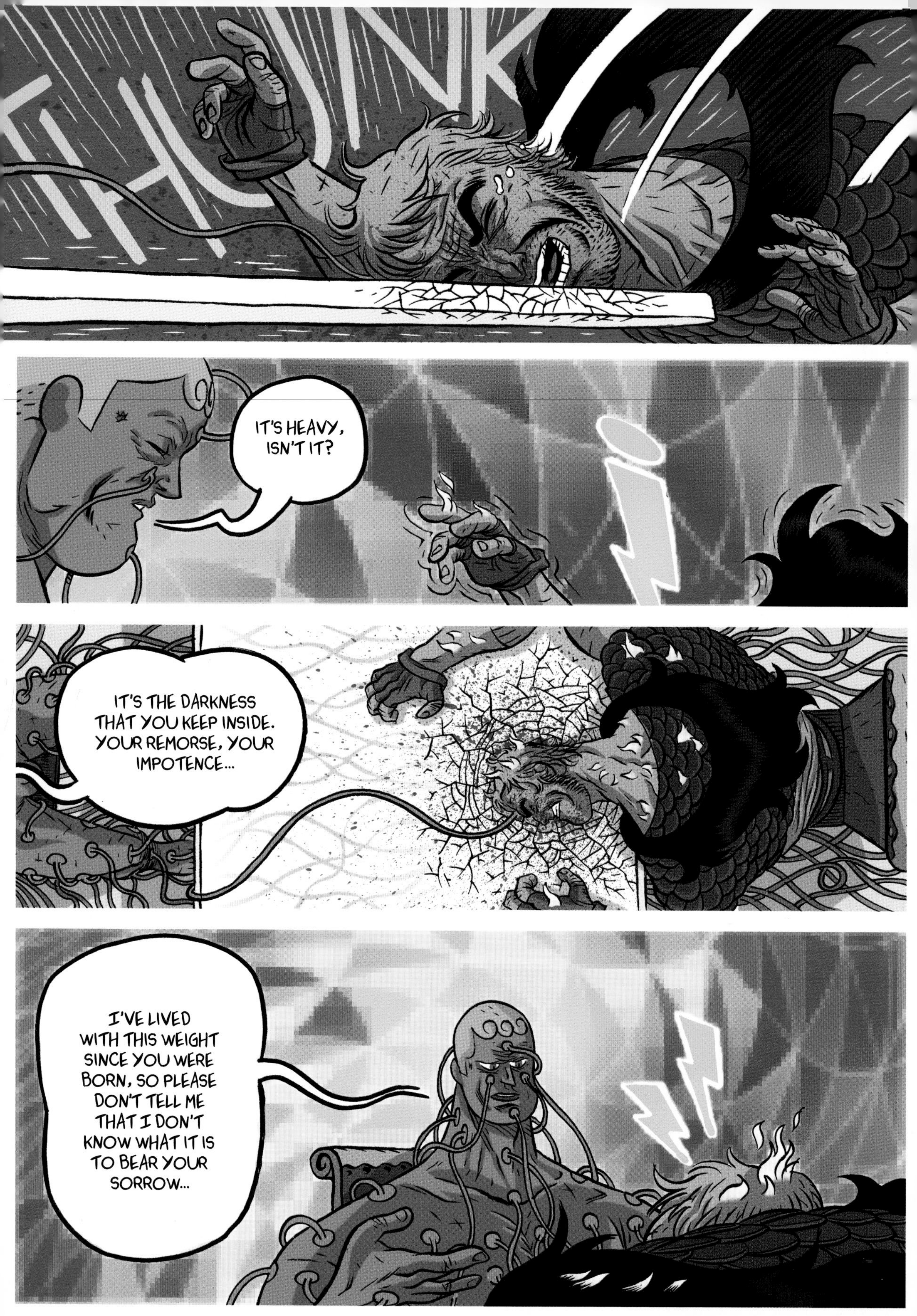
THUNK
IT'S HEAVY, ISN'T IT?
IT'S THE DARKNESS THAT YOU KEEP INSIDE. YOUR REMORSE, YOUR IMPOTENCE...
I'VE LIVED WITH THIS WEIGHT SINCE YOU WERE BORN, SO PLEASE DON'T TELL ME THAT I DON'T KNOW WHAT IT IS TO BEAR YOUR SORROW...

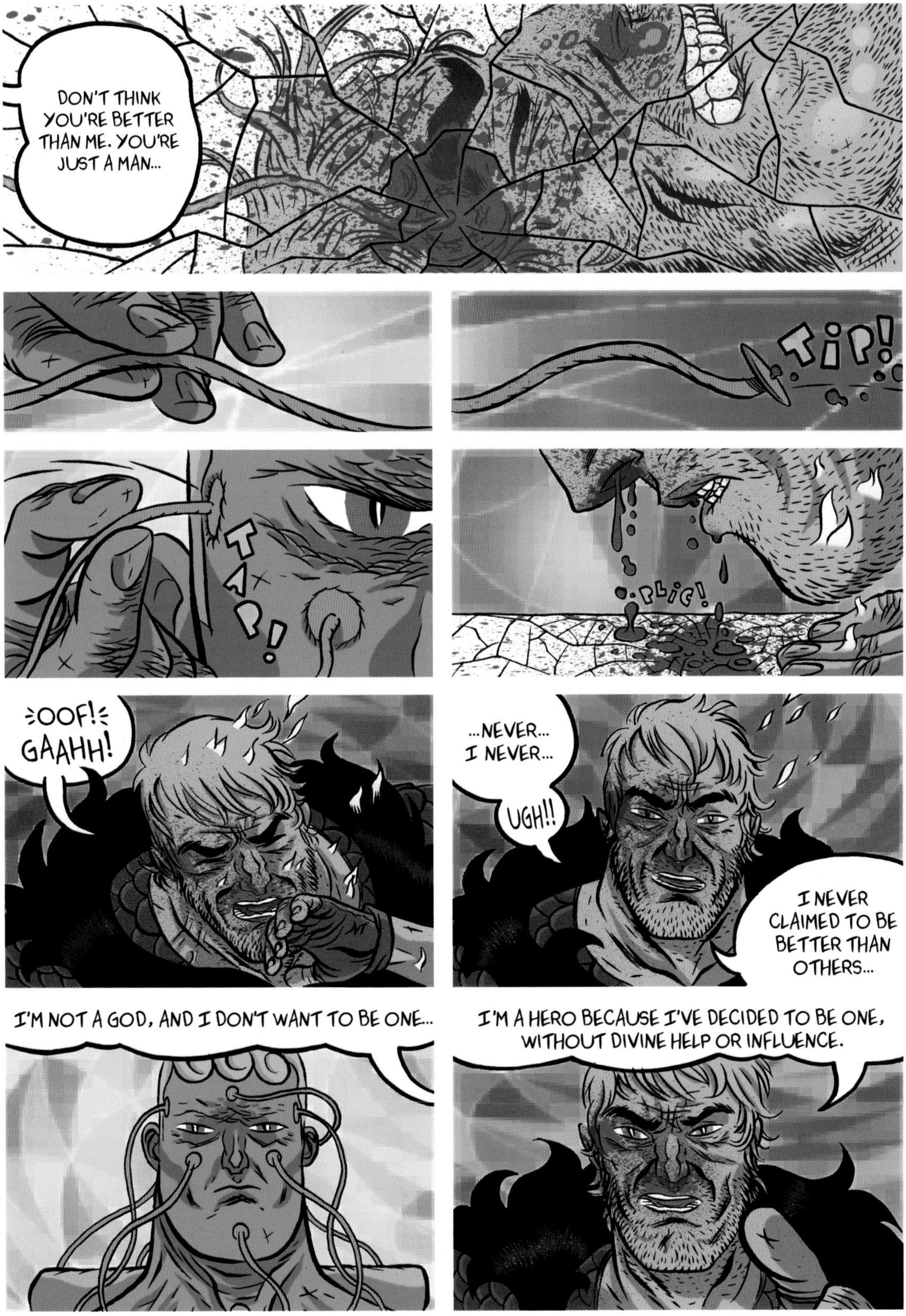
DON'T THINK YOU'RE BETTER THAN ME. YOU'RE JUST A MAN...
TIP!
TAP!
PLIC!
OOF! GAAHH!
...NEVER... I NEVER...
UGH!!
I NEVER CLAIMED TO BE BETTER THAN OTHERS...
I'M NOT A GOD, AND I DON'T WANT TO BE ONE...
I'M A HERO BECAUSE I'VE DECIDED TO BE ONE, WITHOUT DIVINE HELP OR INFLUENCE.

I'M A HERO BECAUSE I FALL DOWN AND GET BACK UP AGAIN...

TOC!

...BECAUSE I LEARN FROM EACH ONE OF MY CHALLENGES.

WHEN I WAS YOUNG, I THOUGHT I WAS WHAT I WAS BECAUSE I WAS THE SON OF ZEUS...

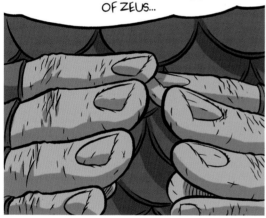

...BUT WITH EACH TEST I PASS, THAT THOUGHT GROWS FAINTER...

I HATE MY FATHER, I HATE THE GODS, BECAUSE DESPITE ALL THEY COULD DO, THEY JUST SIT THERE AND WATCH...

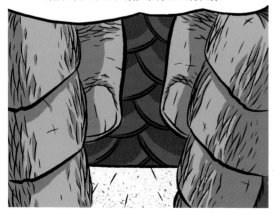

BECAUSE THEY'VE TURNED THIS WORLD INTO A GAME BOARD FOR THEIR WHIMS.

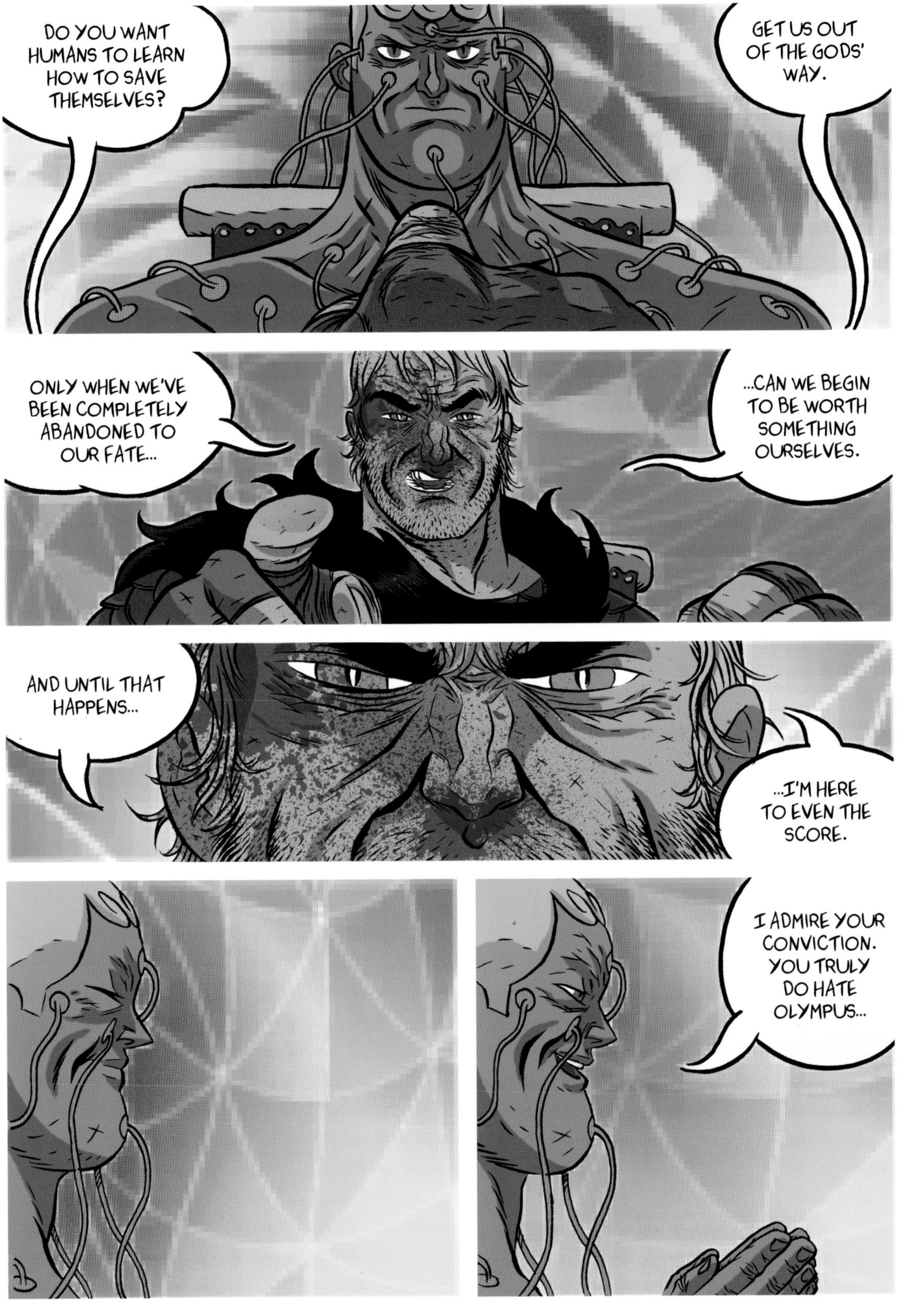
DO YOU WANT HUMANS TO LEARN HOW TO SAVE THEMSELVES?
GET US OUT OF THE GODS' WAY.
ONLY WHEN WE'VE BEEN COMPLETELY ABANDONED TO OUR FATE...
...CAN WE BEGIN TO BE WORTH SOMETHING OURSELVES.
AND UNTIL THAT HAPPENS...
...I'M HERE TO EVEN THE SCORE.
I ADMIRE YOUR CONVICTION. YOU TRULY DO HATE OLYMPUS...

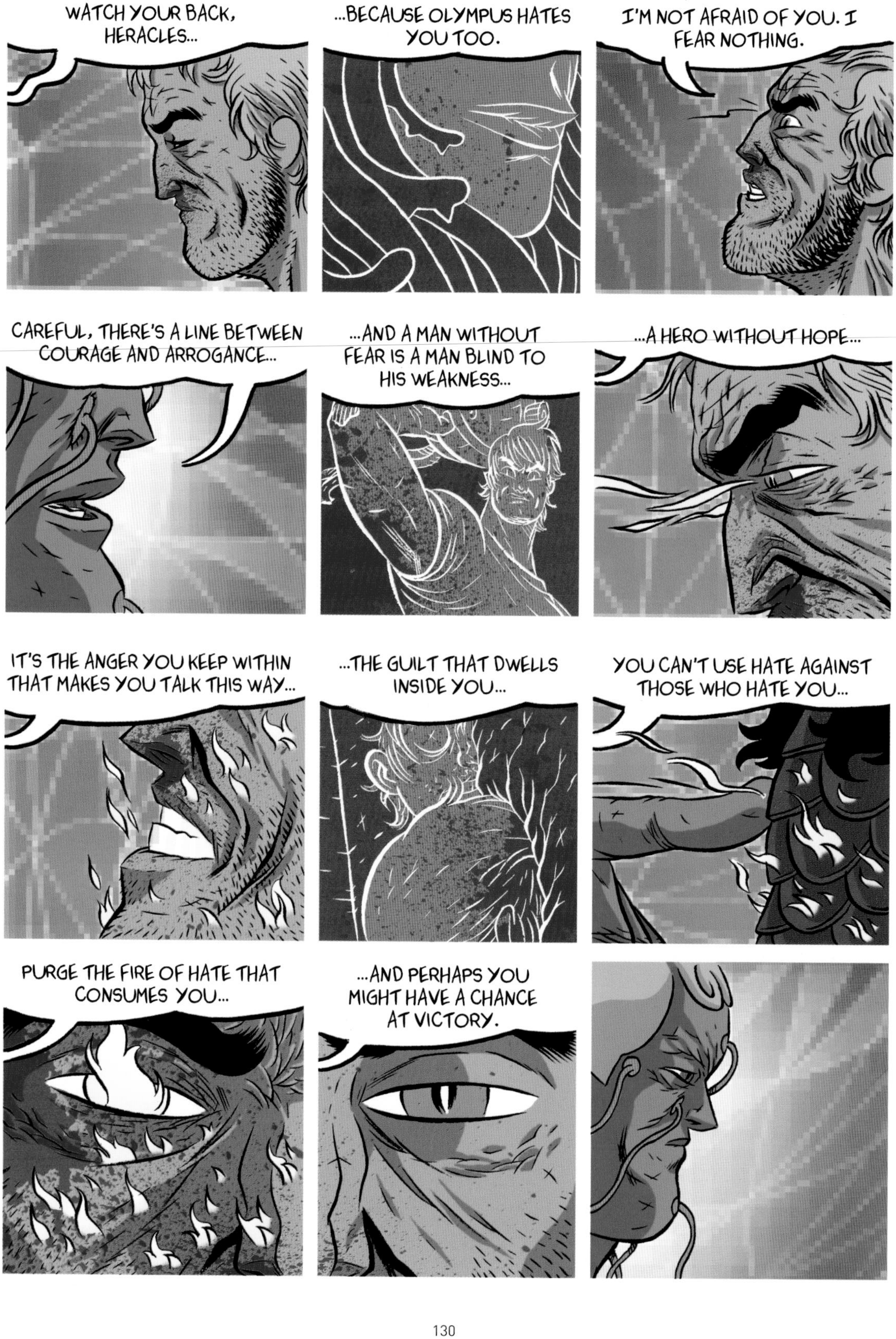
WATCH YOUR BACK, HERACLES...
...BECAUSE OLYMPUS HATES YOU TOO.
I'M NOT AFRAID OF YOU. I FEAR NOTHING.
CAREFUL, THERE'S A LINE BETWEEN COURAGE AND ARROGANCE...
...AND A MAN WITHOUT FEAR IS A MAN BLIND TO HIS WEAKNESS...
...A HERO WITHOUT HOPE...
IT'S THE ANGER YOU KEEP WITHIN THAT MAKES YOU TALK THIS WAY...
...THE GUILT THAT DWELLS INSIDE YOU...
YOU CAN'T USE HATE AGAINST THOSE WHO HATE YOU...
PURGE THE FIRE OF HATE THAT CONSUMES YOU...
...AND PERHAPS YOU MIGHT HAVE A CHANCE AT VICTORY.

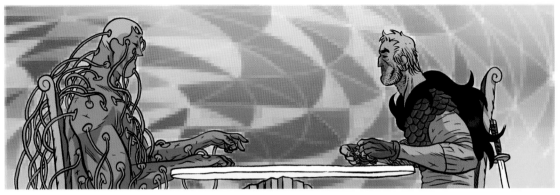

TAKE WHAT YOU CAME HERE FOR AND GO.

THAT'S ALL THERE IS TO IT?

AND THE GARDEN OF THE HESPERIDES? AND THE DRAGON?!

THEY'RE JUST STORIES, TALES TO MAKE HEROES FIGHT TO REACH THEIR GOAL...

...AN IMPOSSIBLE, NONEXISTENT CHALLENGE THAT MAKES THEM DREAM OF REACHING NEW HEIGHTS.

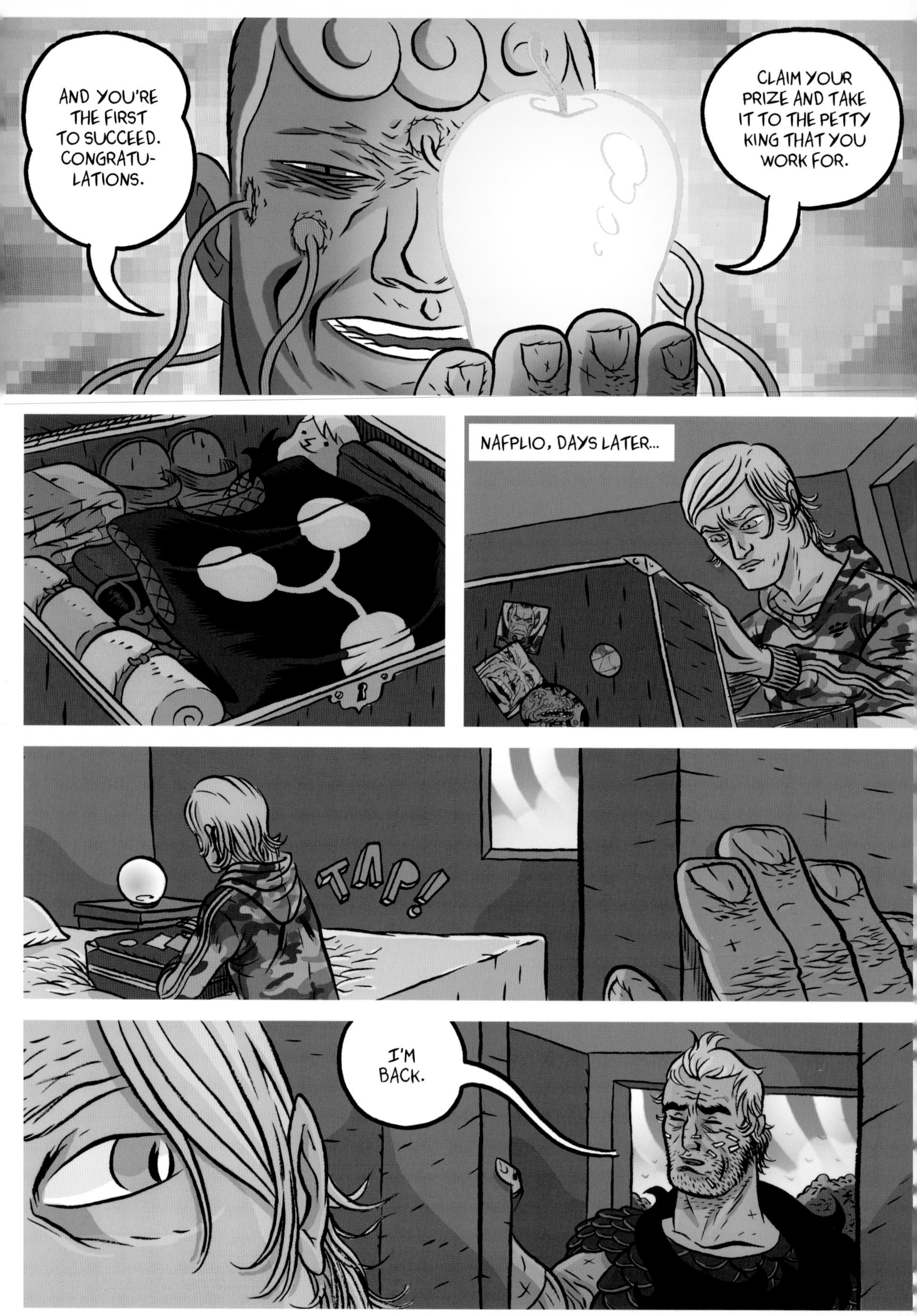
AND YOU'RE THE FIRST TO SUCCEED. CONGRATU-LATIONS.
CLAIM YOUR PRIZE AND TAKE IT TO THE PETTY KING THAT YOU WORK FOR.
NAFPLIO, DAYS LATER...
TAP!
I'M BACK.

ANOTHER TALLY MARK FOR YOUR LIST OF VICTORIES.

WHAT ARE YOU DOING?

I'M LEAVING.

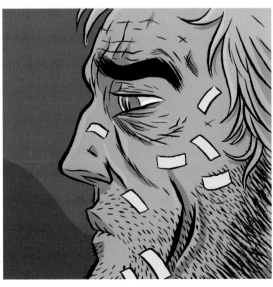

DON'T GO, PLEASE...

END OF CHAPTER THREE.

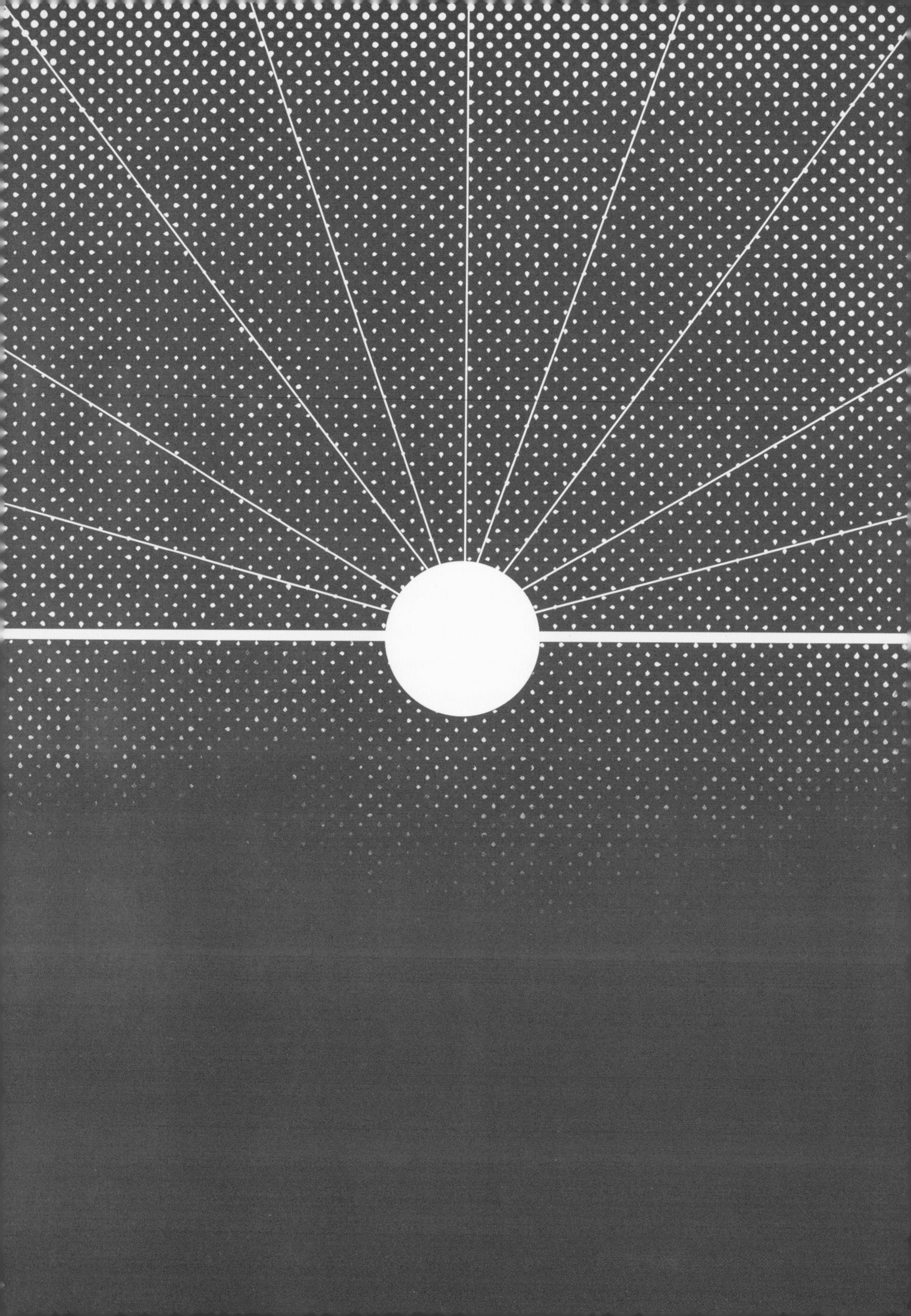

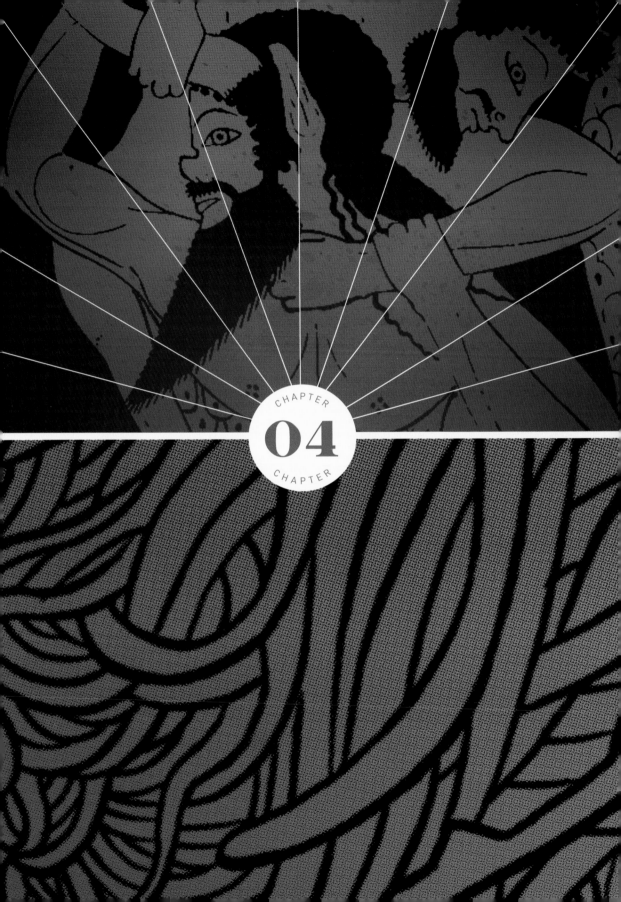

CHAPTER

04

CHAPTER

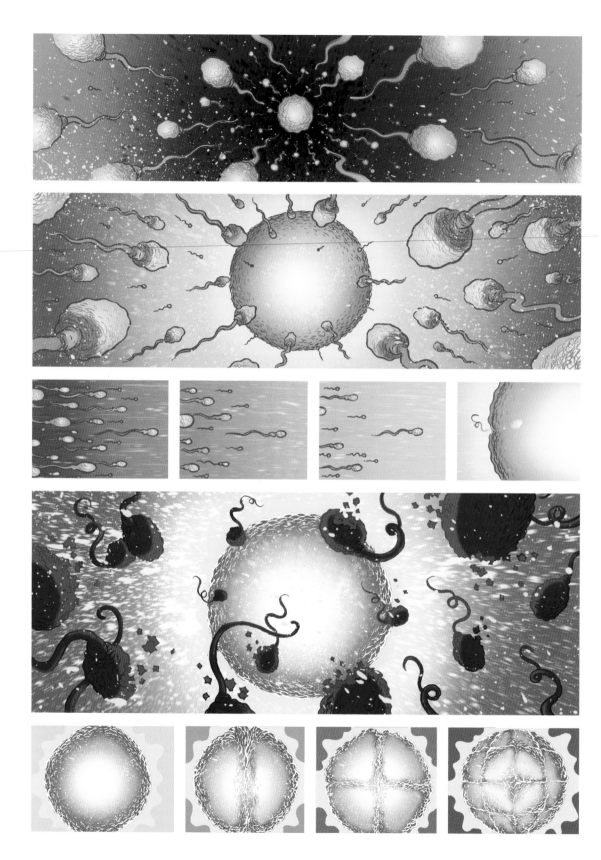

136

I'LL CALL YOU...
...HERACLES.

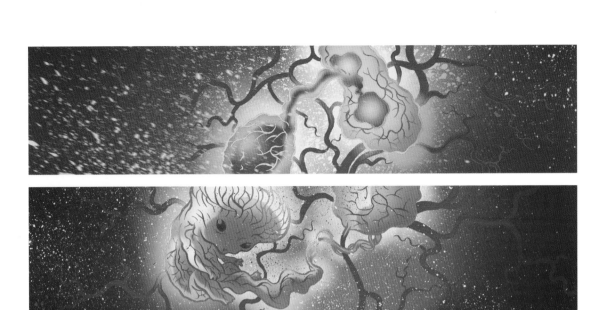

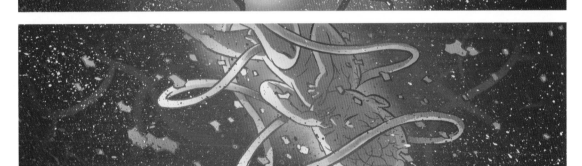

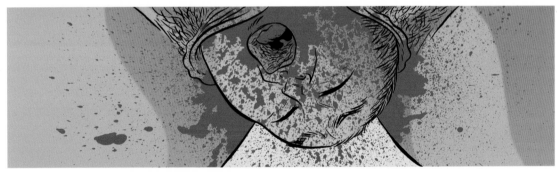

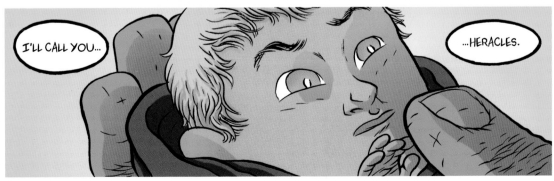

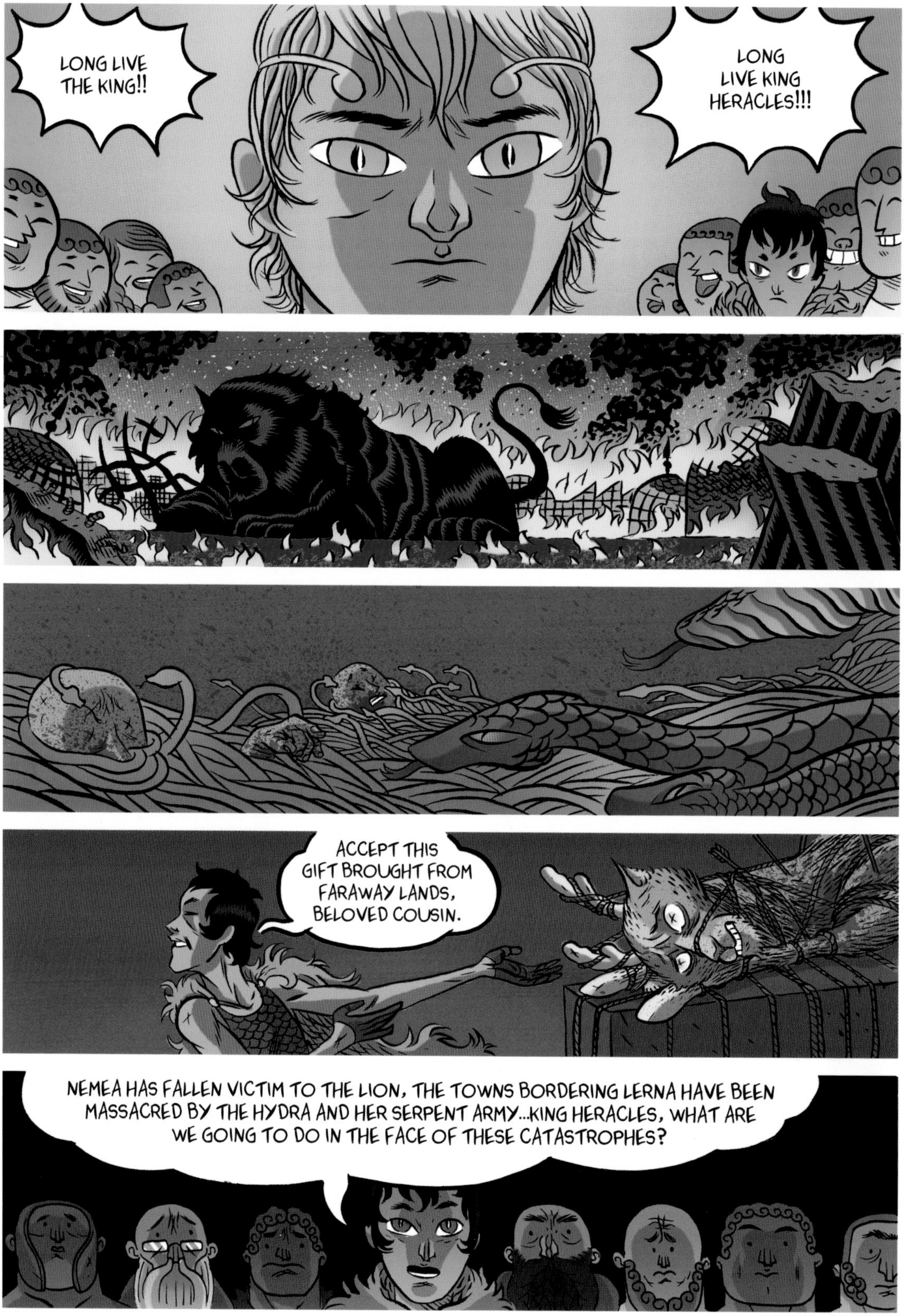

LONG LIVE THE KING!!
LONG LIVE KING HERACLES!!!
ACCEPT THIS GIFT BROUGHT FROM FARAWAY LANDS, BELOVED COUSIN.
NEMEA HAS FALLEN VICTIM TO THE LION, THE TOWNS BORDERING LERNA HAVE BEEN MASSACRED BY THE HYDRA AND HER SERPENT ARMY...KING HERACLES, WHAT ARE WE GOING TO DO IN THE FACE OF THESE CATASTROPHES?

A WALL.

WE'LL BUILD THE BIGGEST WALL IN THE WORLD AROUND NAFPLIO.

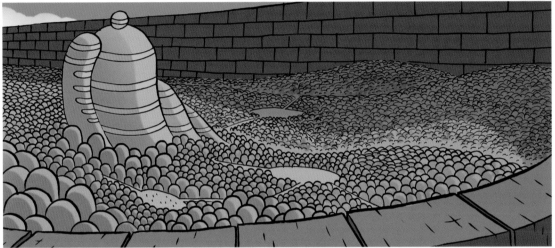

I CAN'T RISK SHELTERING YOU BEHIND MY WALLS. IF THE WILD BOAR WERE TO FOLLOW YOU HERE, MY KINGDOM WOULD BE IN DANGER.

YOU'RE GOING TO LEAVE ME ON MY OWN WITH THAT MONSTER?

NO.

WE'LL BOMBARD YOUR FOREST. REDUCE IT ALL TO ASHES -- AND THE MONSTER WITH IT.

IT'S THE LESSER EVIL. THE END JUSTIFIES THE MEANS... YOU WANT TO SAVE ARCADIA, RIGHT?

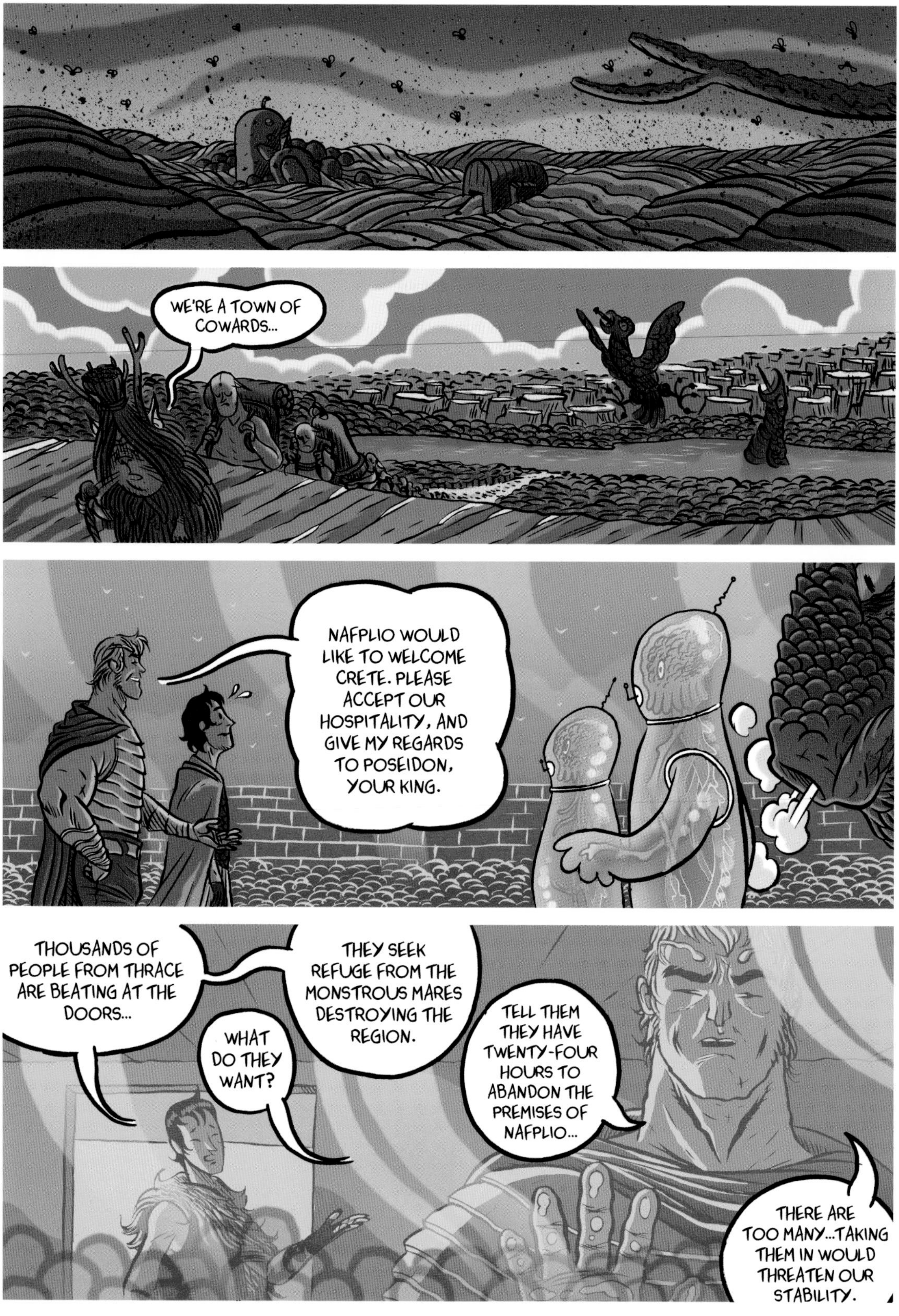
WE'RE A TOWN OF COWARDS...
NAFPLIO WOULD LIKE TO WELCOME CRETE. PLEASE ACCEPT OUR HOSPITALITY, AND GIVE MY REGARDS TO POSEIDON, YOUR KING.
THOUSANDS OF PEOPLE FROM THRACE ARE BEATING AT THE DOORS...
WHAT DO THEY WANT?
THEY SEEK REFUGE FROM THE MONSTROUS MARES DESTROYING THE REGION.
TELL THEM THEY HAVE TWENTY-FOUR HOURS TO ABANDON THE PREMISES OF NAFPLIO...
THERE ARE TOO MANY...TAKING THEM IN WOULD THREATEN OUR STABILITY.

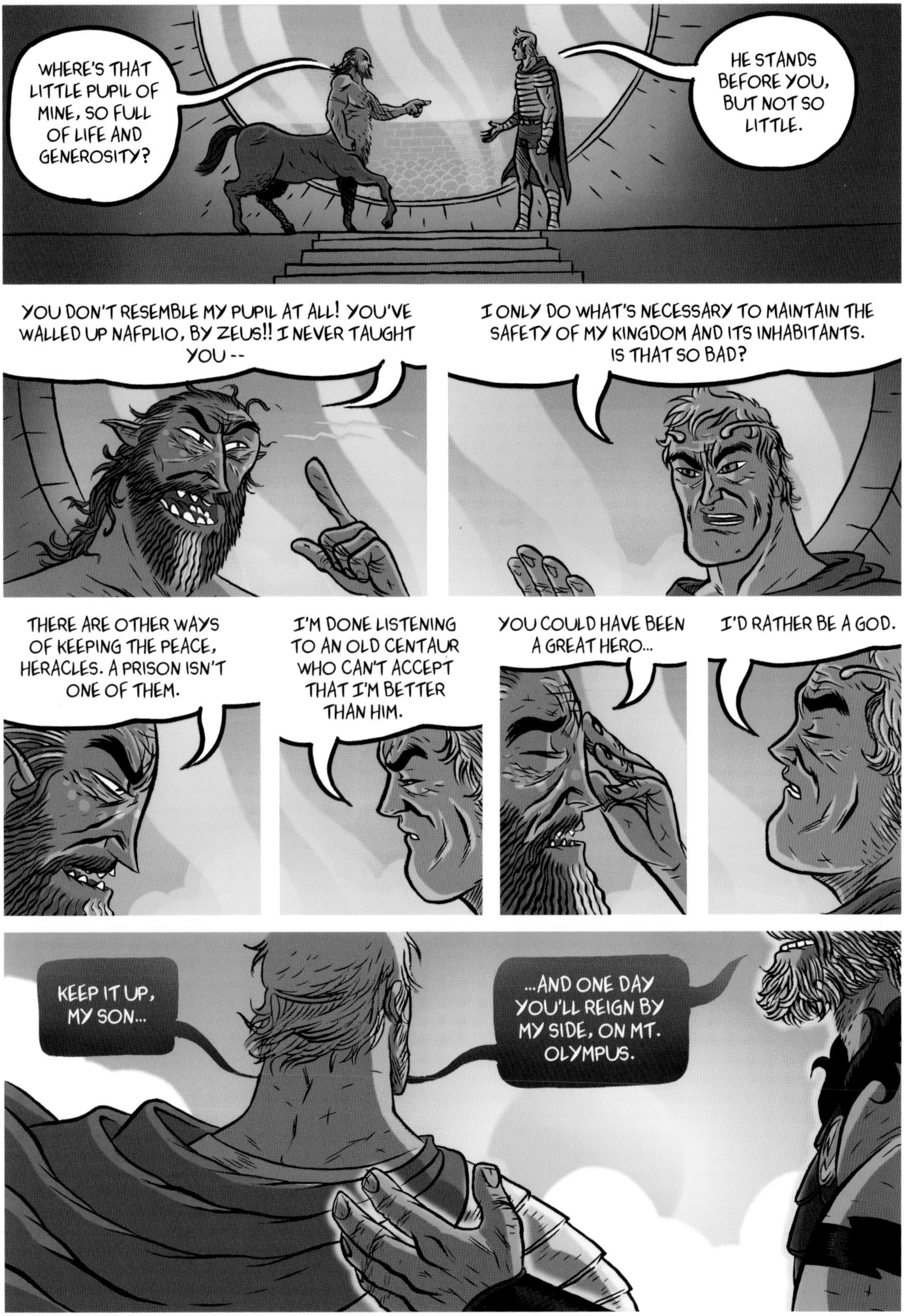
WHERE'S THAT LITTLE PUPIL OF MINE, SO FULL OF LIFE AND GENEROSITY?
HE STANDS BEFORE YOU, BUT NOT SO LITTLE.
YOU DON'T RESEMBLE MY PUPIL AT ALL! YOU'VE WALLED UP NAFPLIO, BY ZEUS!! I NEVER TAUGHT YOU --
I ONLY DO WHAT'S NECESSARY TO MAINTAIN THE SAFETY OF MY KINGDOM AND ITS INHABITANTS. IS THAT SO BAD?
THERE ARE OTHER WAYS OF KEEPING THE PEACE, HERACLES. A PRISON ISN'T ONE OF THEM.
I'M DONE LISTENING TO AN OLD CENTAUR WHO CAN'T ACCEPT THAT I'M BETTER THAN HIM.
YOU COULD HAVE BEEN A GREAT HERO...
I'D RATHER BE A GOD.
KEEP IT UP, MY SON...
...AND ONE DAY YOU'LL REIGN BY MY SIDE, ON MT. OLYMPUS.

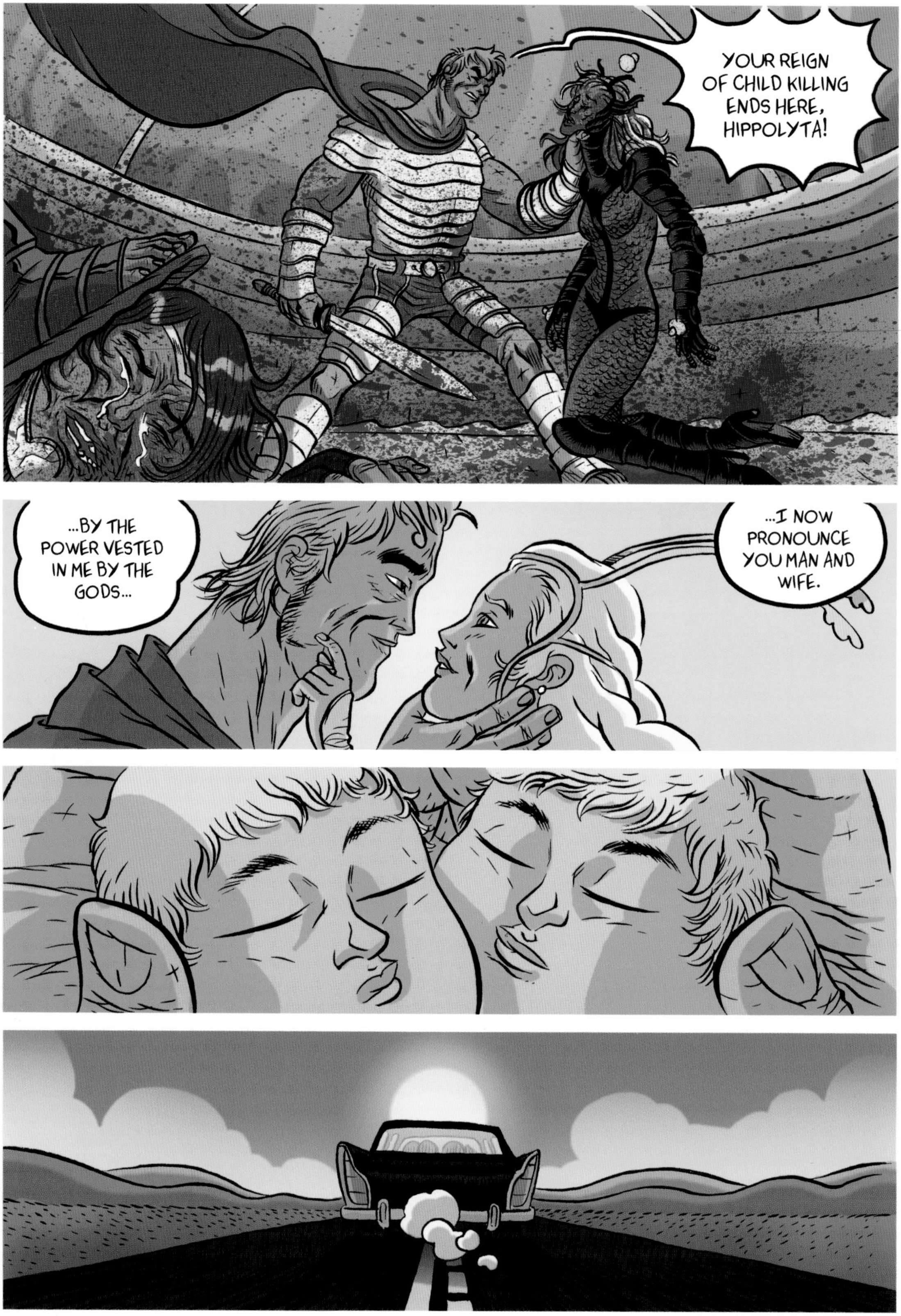
YOUR REIGN OF CHILD KILLING ENDS HERE, HIPPOLYTA!
...BY THE POWER VESTED IN ME BY THE GODS...
...I NOW PRONOUNCE YOU MAN AND WIFE.

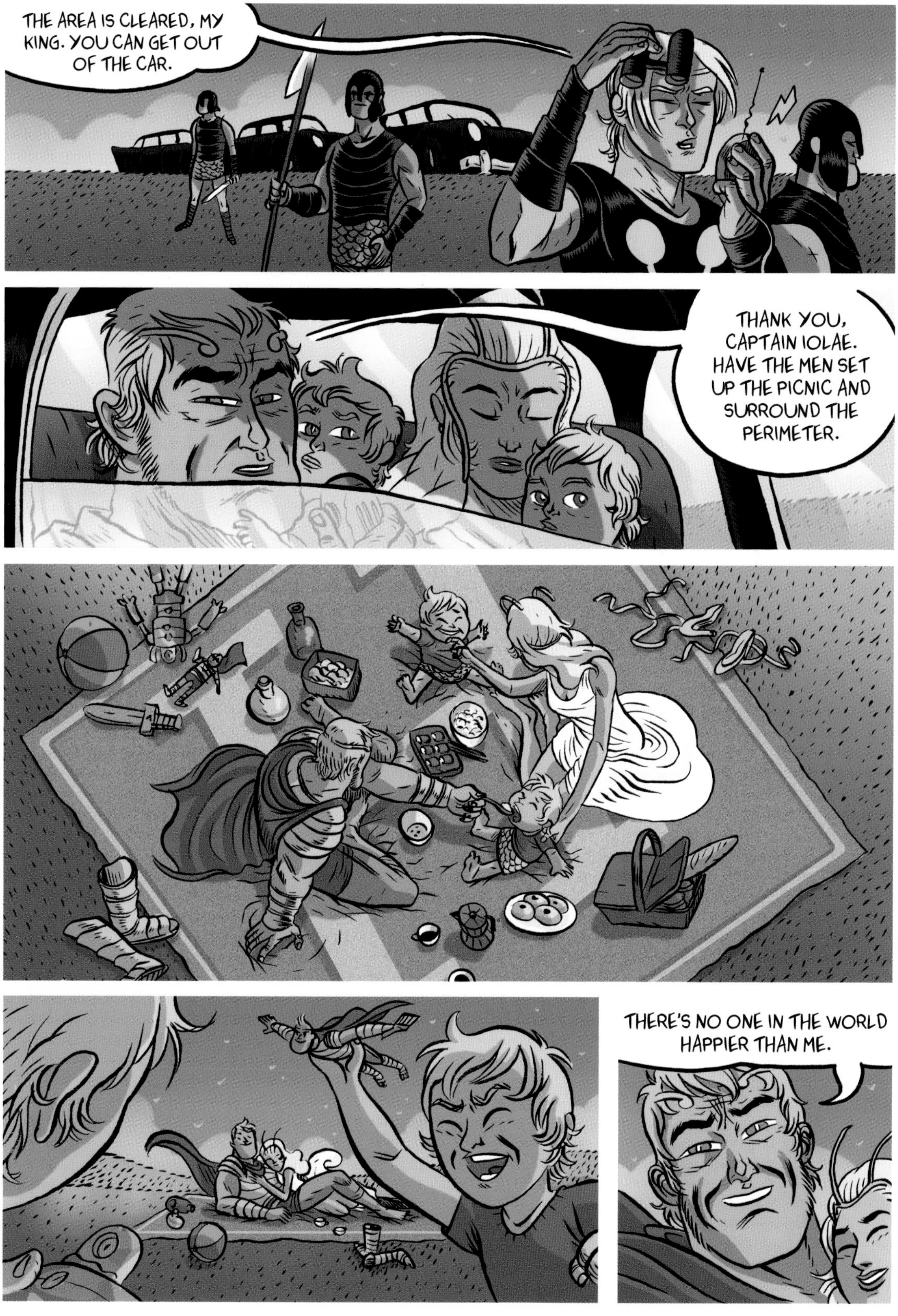
THE AREA IS CLEARED, MY KING. YOU CAN GET OUT OF THE CAR.
THANK YOU, CAPTAIN IOLAE. HAVE THE MEN SET UP THE PICNIC AND SURROUND THE PERIMETER.
THERE'S NO ONE IN THE WORLD HAPPIER THAN ME.

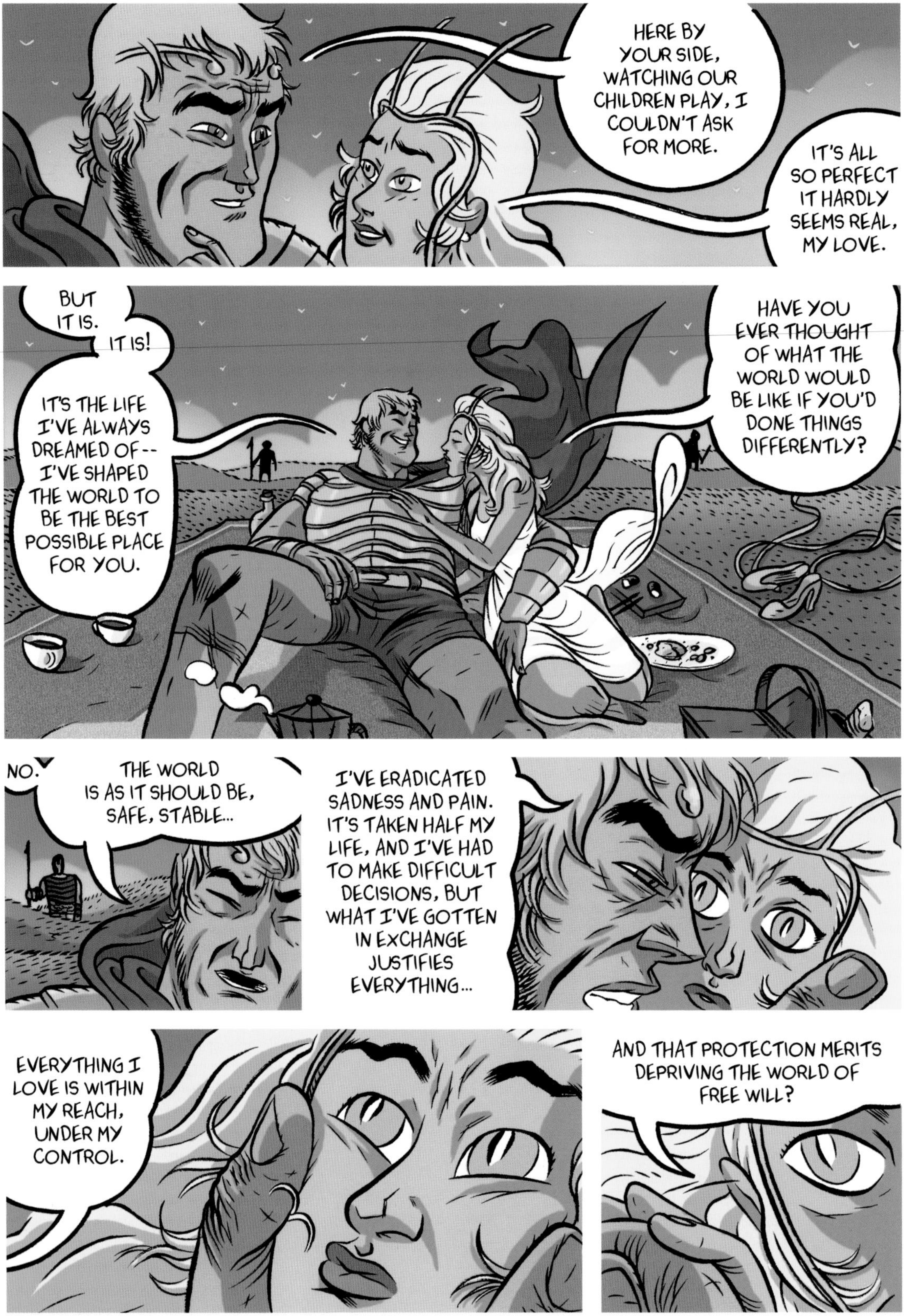
HERE BY YOUR SIDE, WATCHING OUR CHILDREN PLAY, I COULDN'T ASK FOR MORE.
IT'S ALL SO PERFECT IT HARDLY SEEMS REAL, MY LOVE.
BUT IT IS.
IT IS!
IT'S THE LIFE I'VE ALWAYS DREAMED OF-- I'VE SHAPED THE WORLD TO BE THE BEST POSSIBLE PLACE FOR YOU.
HAVE YOU EVER THOUGHT OF WHAT THE WORLD WOULD BE LIKE IF YOU'D DONE THINGS DIFFERENTLY?
NO.
THE WORLD IS AS IT SHOULD BE, SAFE, STABLE...
I'VE ERADICATED SADNESS AND PAIN. IT'S TAKEN HALF MY LIFE, AND I'VE HAD TO MAKE DIFFICULT DECISIONS, BUT WHAT I'VE GOTTEN IN EXCHANGE JUSTIFIES EVERYTHING...
EVERYTHING I LOVE IS WITHIN MY REACH, UNDER MY CONTROL.
AND THAT PROTECTION MERITS DEPRIVING THE WORLD OF FREE WILL?

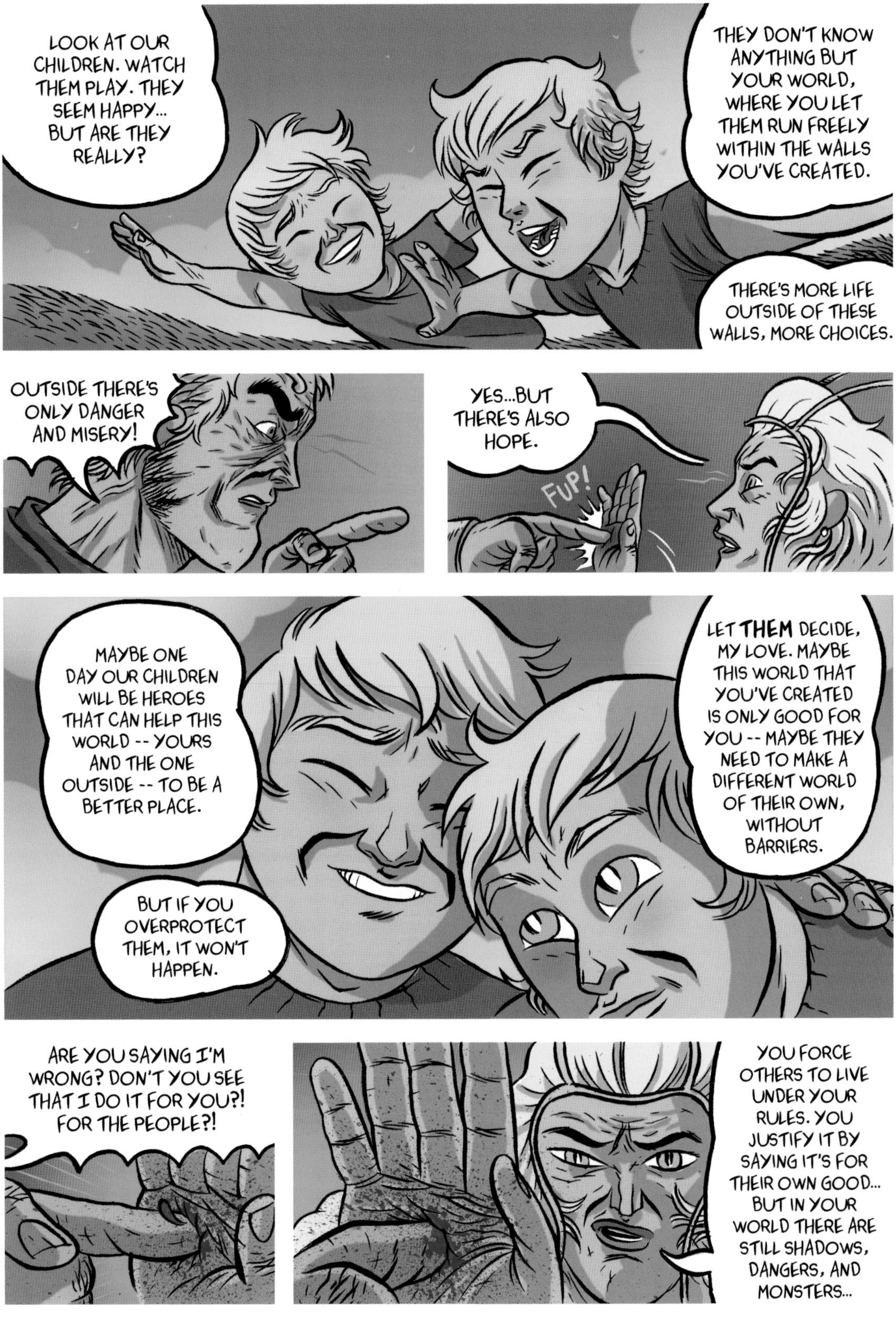
LOOK AT OUR CHILDREN. WATCH THEM PLAY. THEY SEEM HAPPY... BUT ARE THEY REALLY?
THEY DON'T KNOW ANYTHING BUT YOUR WORLD, WHERE YOU LET THEM RUN FREELY WITHIN THE WALLS YOU'VE CREATED.
THERE'S MORE LIFE OUTSIDE OF THESE WALLS, MORE CHOICES.
OUTSIDE THERE'S ONLY DANGER AND MISERY!
YES...BUT THERE'S ALSO HOPE.
FUP!
MAYBE ONE DAY OUR CHILDREN WILL BE HEROES THAT CAN HELP THIS WORLD -- YOURS AND THE ONE OUTSIDE -- TO BE A BETTER PLACE.
BUT IF YOU OVERPROTECT THEM, IT WON'T HAPPEN.
LET THEM DECIDE, MY LOVE. MAYBE THIS WORLD THAT YOU'VE CREATED IS ONLY GOOD FOR YOU -- MAYBE THEY NEED TO MAKE A DIFFERENT WORLD OF THEIR OWN, WITHOUT BARRIERS.
ARE YOU SAYING I'M WRONG? DON'T YOU SEE THAT I DO IT FOR YOU?! FOR THE PEOPLE?!
YOU FORCE OTHERS TO LIVE UNDER YOUR RULES. YOU JUSTIFY IT BY SAYING IT'S FOR THEIR OWN GOOD... BUT IN YOUR WORLD THERE ARE STILL SHADOWS, DANGERS, AND MONSTERS...

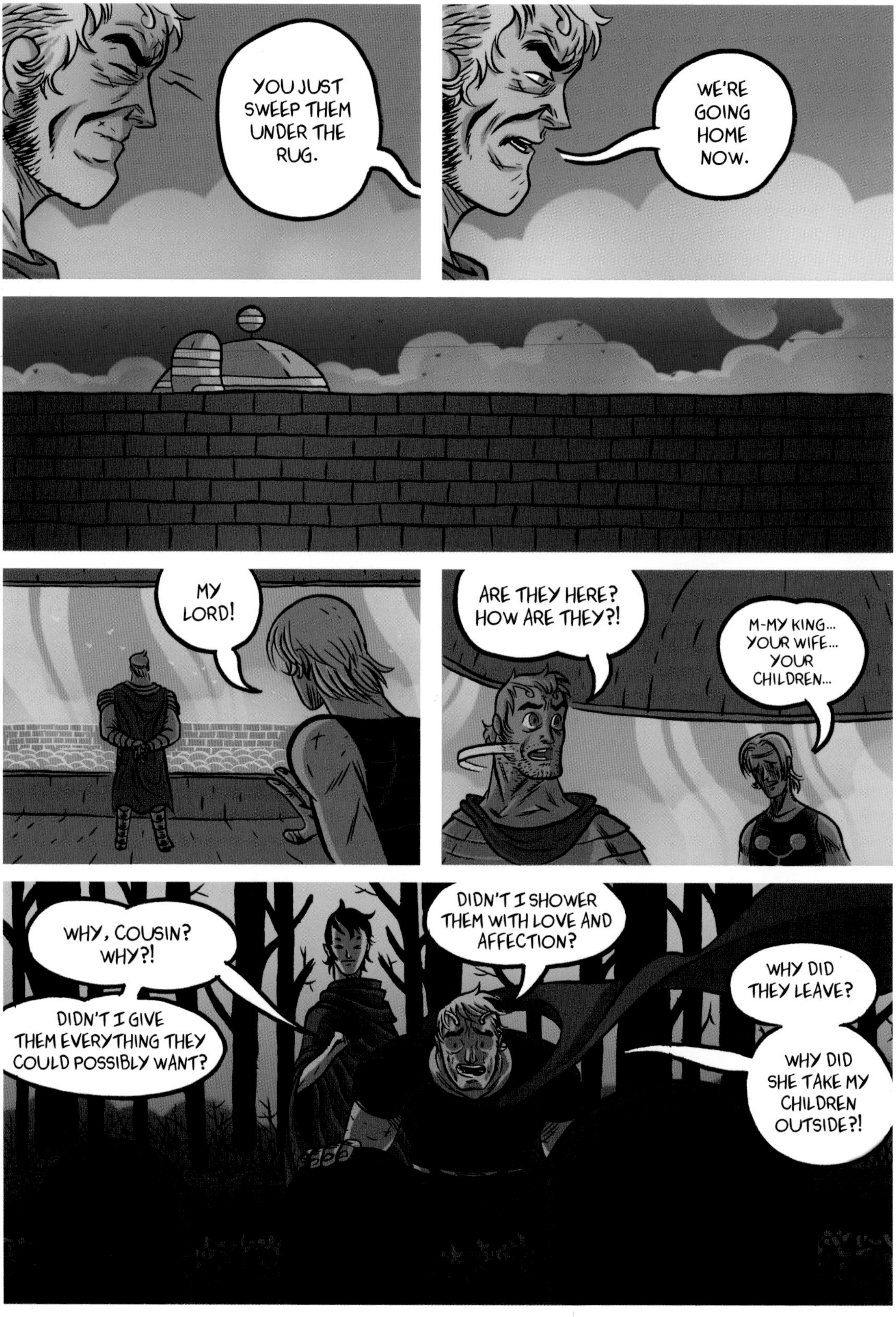
YOU JUST SWEEP THEM UNDER THE RUG.
WE'RE GOING HOME NOW.
MY LORD!
ARE THEY HERE? HOW ARE THEY?!
M-MY KING... YOUR WIFE... YOUR CHILDREN...
WHY, COUSIN? WHY?!
DIDN'T I GIVE THEM EVERYTHING THEY COULD POSSIBLY WANT?
DIDN'T I SHOWER THEM WITH LOVE AND AFFECTION?
WHY DID THEY LEAVE?
WHY DID SHE TAKE MY CHILDREN OUTSIDE?!

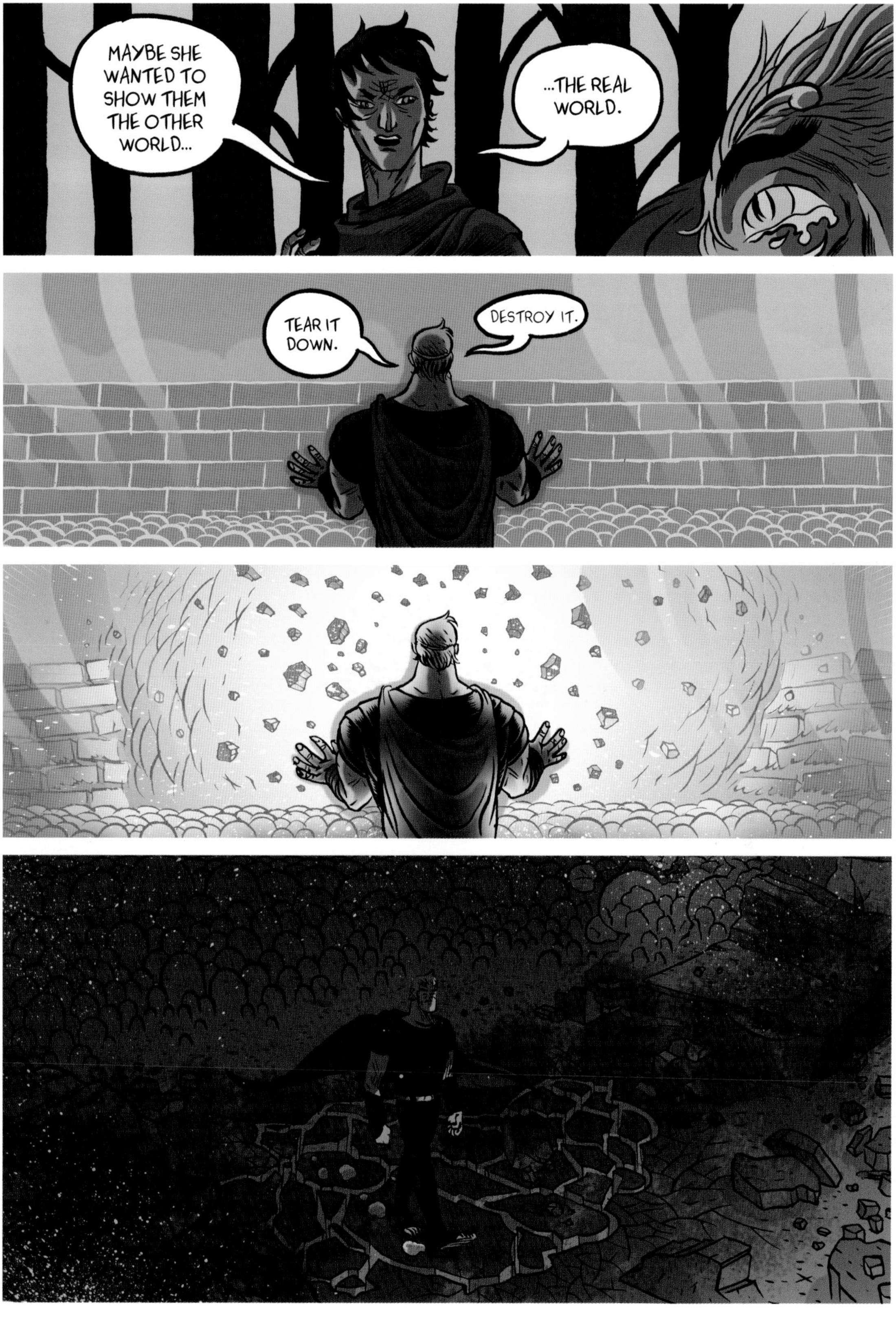
MAYBE SHE WANTED TO SHOW THEM THE OTHER WORLD...
...THE REAL WORLD.
TEAR IT DOWN.
DESTROY IT.

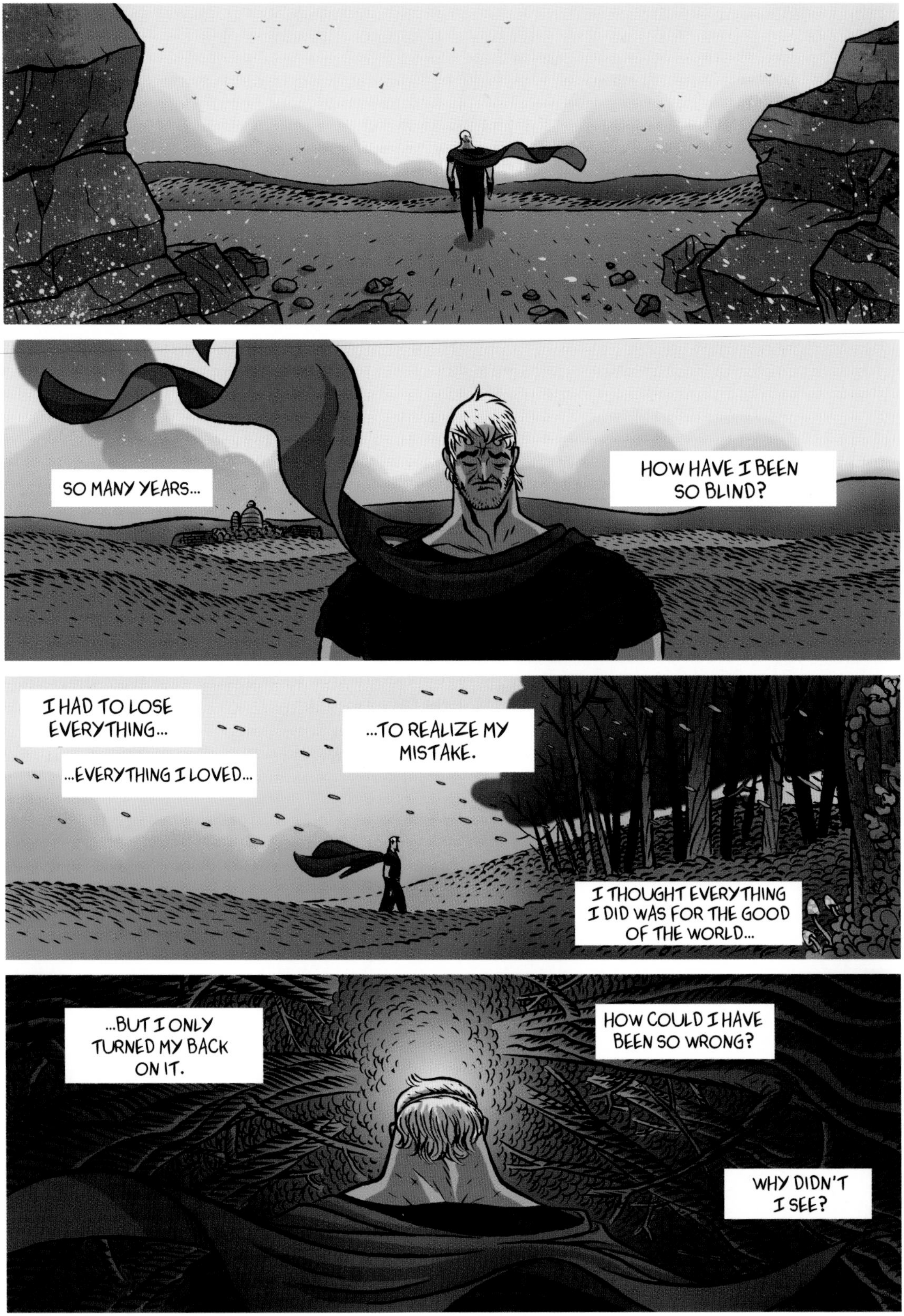
SO MANY YEARS...
HOW HAVE I BEEN SO BLIND?
I HAD TO LOSE EVERYTHING...
...EVERYTHING I LOVED...
...TO REALIZE MY MISTAKE.
I THOUGHT EVERYTHING I DID WAS FOR THE GOOD OF THE WORLD...
...BUT I ONLY TURNED MY BACK ON IT.
HOW COULD I HAVE BEEN SO WRONG?
WHY DIDN'T I SEE?

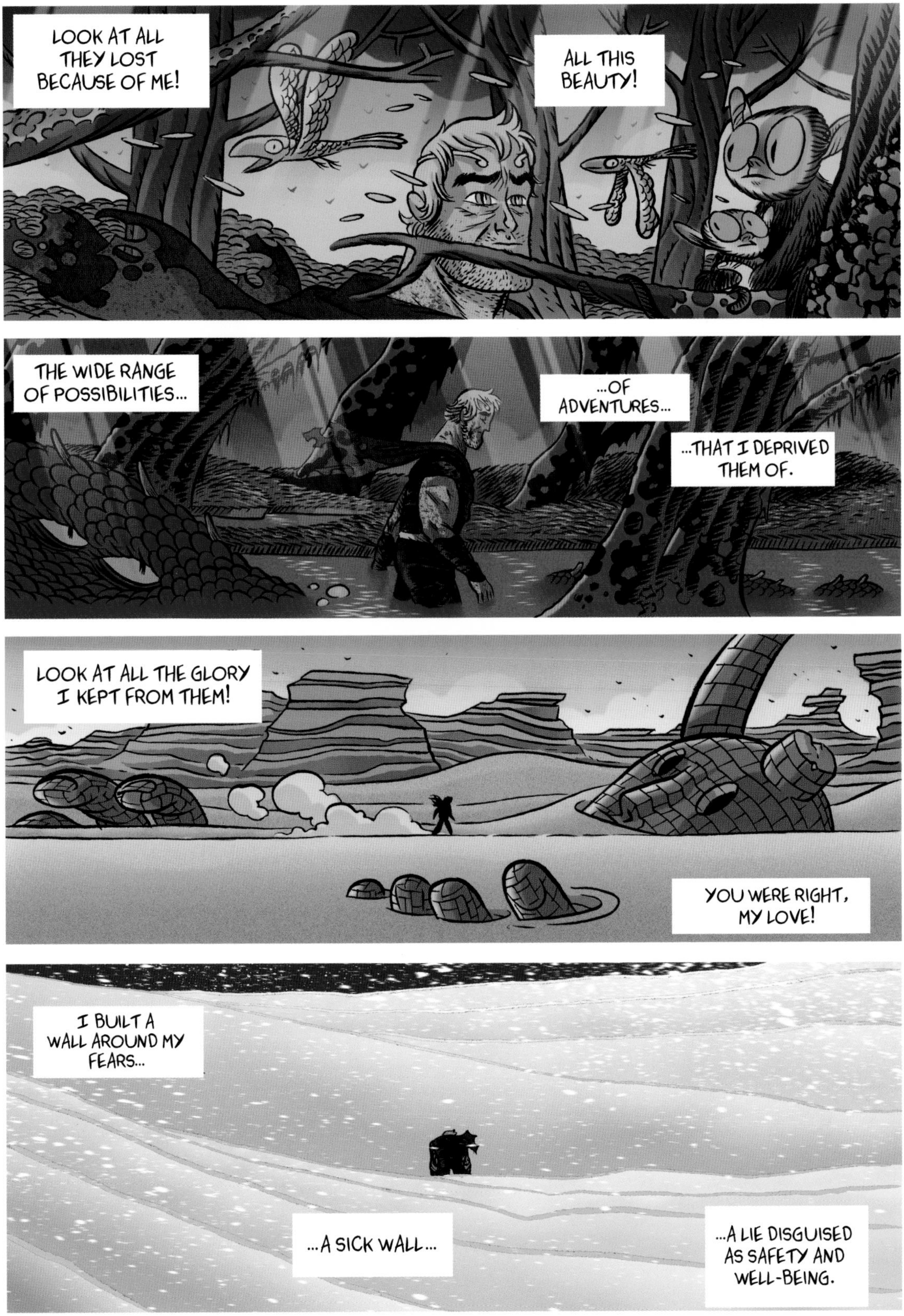
LOOK AT ALL THEY LOST BECAUSE OF ME!
ALL THIS BEAUTY!
THE WIDE RANGE OF POSSIBILITIES...
...OF ADVENTURES...
...THAT I DEPRIVED THEM OF.
LOOK AT ALL THE GLORY I KEPT FROM THEM!
YOU WERE RIGHT, MY LOVE!
I BUILT A WALL AROUND MY FEARS...
...A SICK WALL...
...A LIE DISGUISED AS SAFETY AND WELL-BEING.

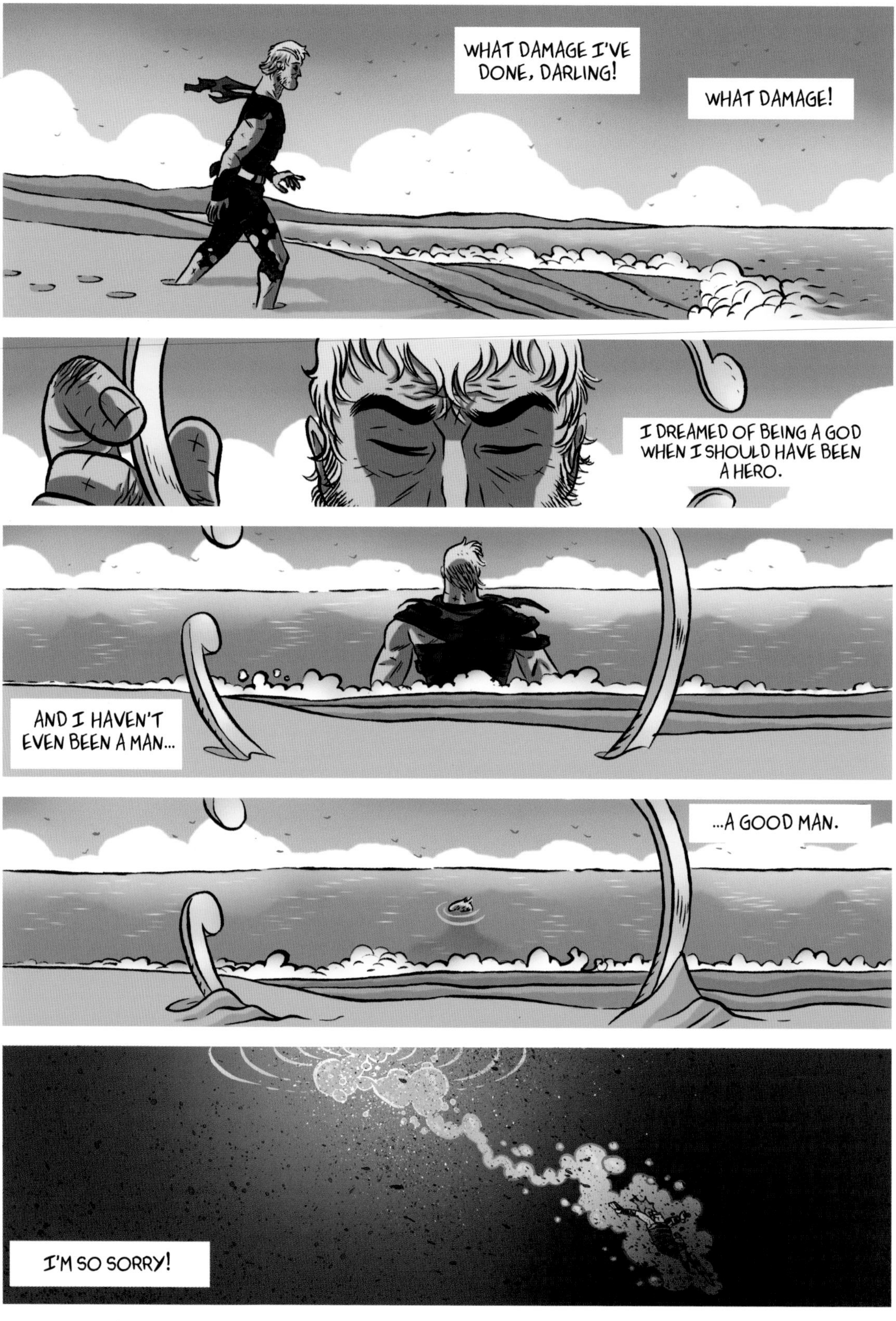
WHAT DAMAGE I'VE DONE, DARLING!
WHAT DAMAGE!
I DREAMED OF BEING A GOD WHEN I SHOULD HAVE BEEN A HERO.
AND I HAVEN'T EVEN BEEN A MAN...
...A GOOD MAN.
I'M SO SORRY!

I'M SO SORRY!!

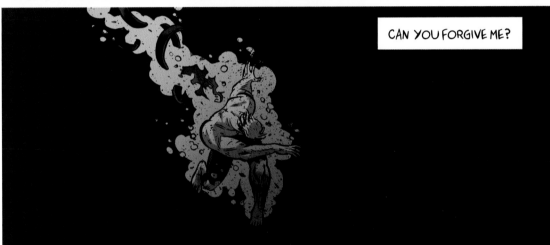

CAN YOU FORGIVE ME?

SOMEDAY, CAN YOU FORGIVE ME FOR THIS IMMENSE LIE?

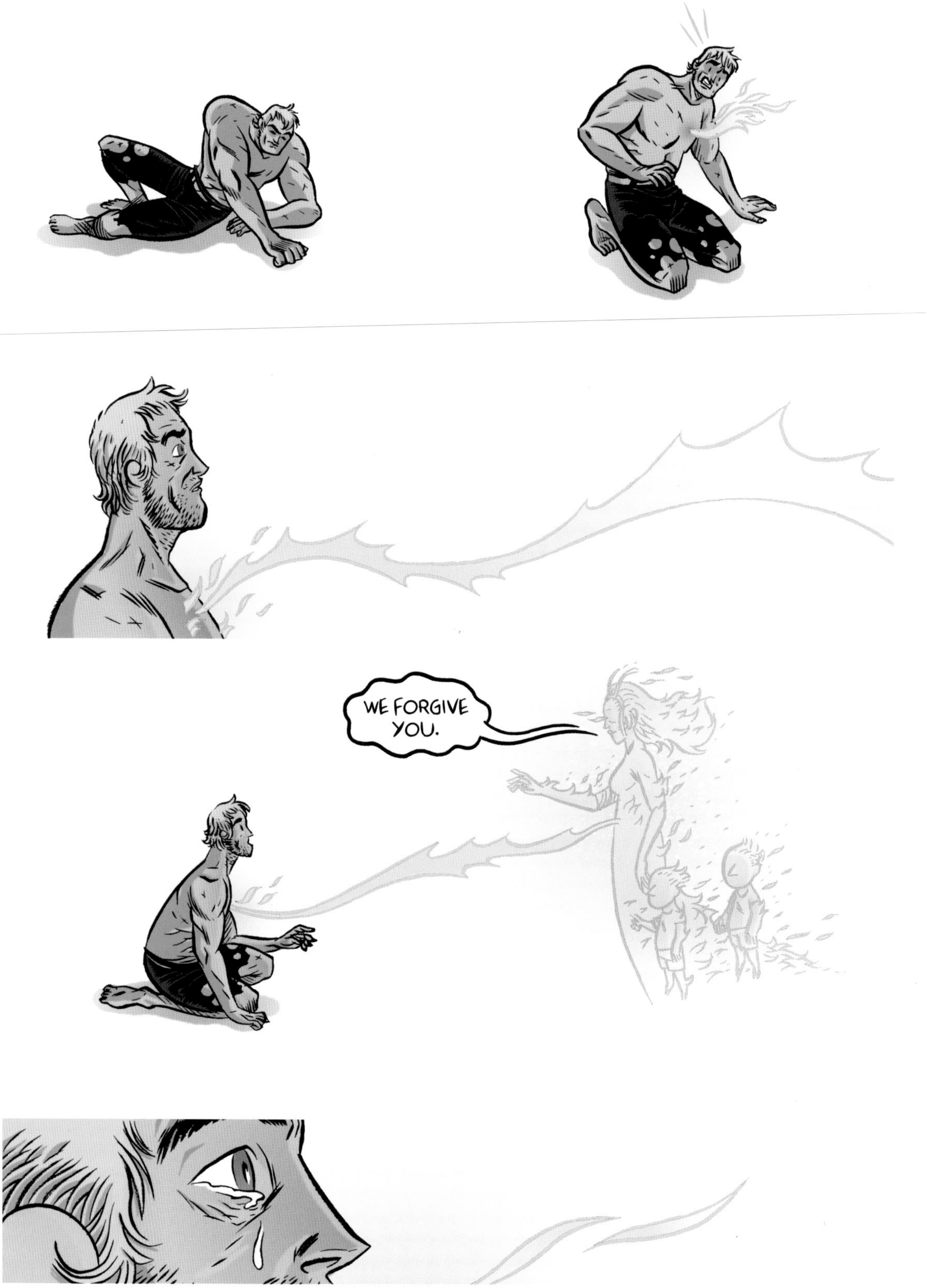
WE FORGIVE YOU.

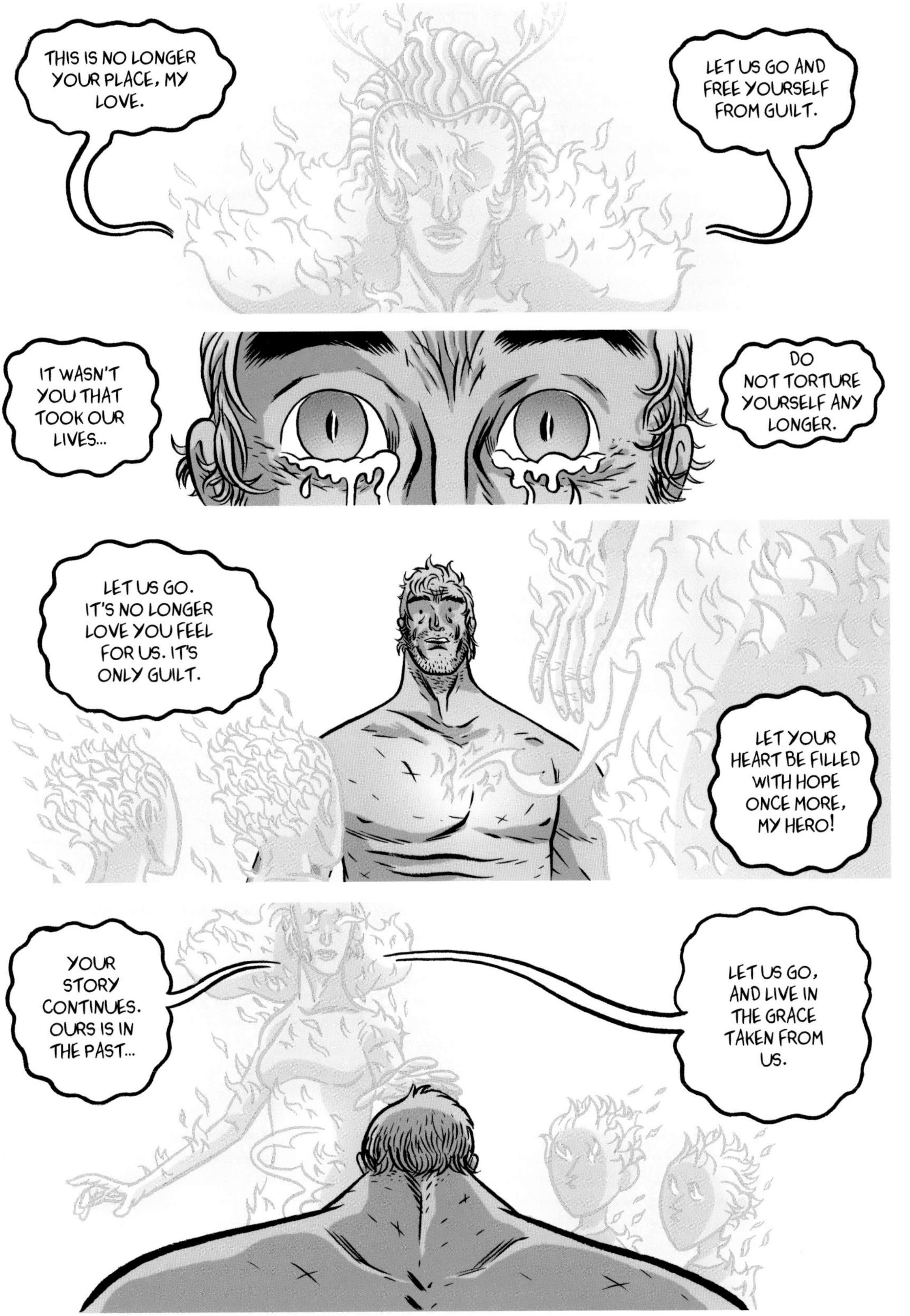
THIS IS NO LONGER YOUR PLACE, MY LOVE.
LET US GO AND FREE YOURSELF FROM GUILT.
IT WASN'T YOU THAT TOOK OUR LIVES...
DO NOT TORTURE YOURSELF ANY LONGER.
LET US GO. IT'S NO LONGER LOVE YOU FEEL FOR US. IT'S ONLY GUILT.
LET YOUR HEART BE FILLED WITH HOPE ONCE MORE, MY HERO!
YOUR STORY CONTINUES. OURS IS IN THE PAST...
LET US GO, AND LIVE IN THE GRACE TAKEN FROM US.

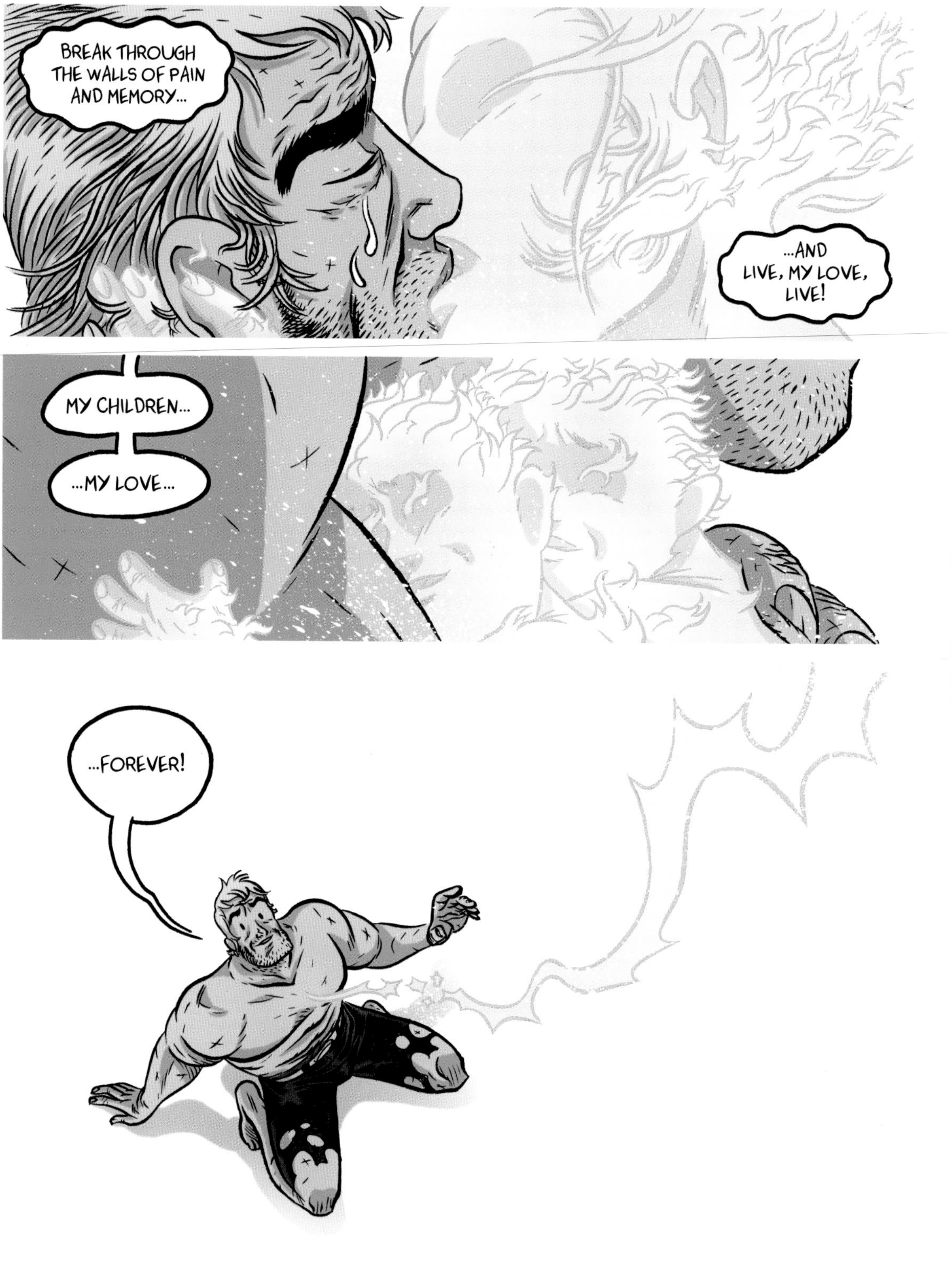
BREAK THROUGH THE WALLS OF PAIN AND MEMORY...
...AND LIVE, MY LOVE, LIVE!
MY CHILDREN...
...MY LOVE...
...FOREVER!

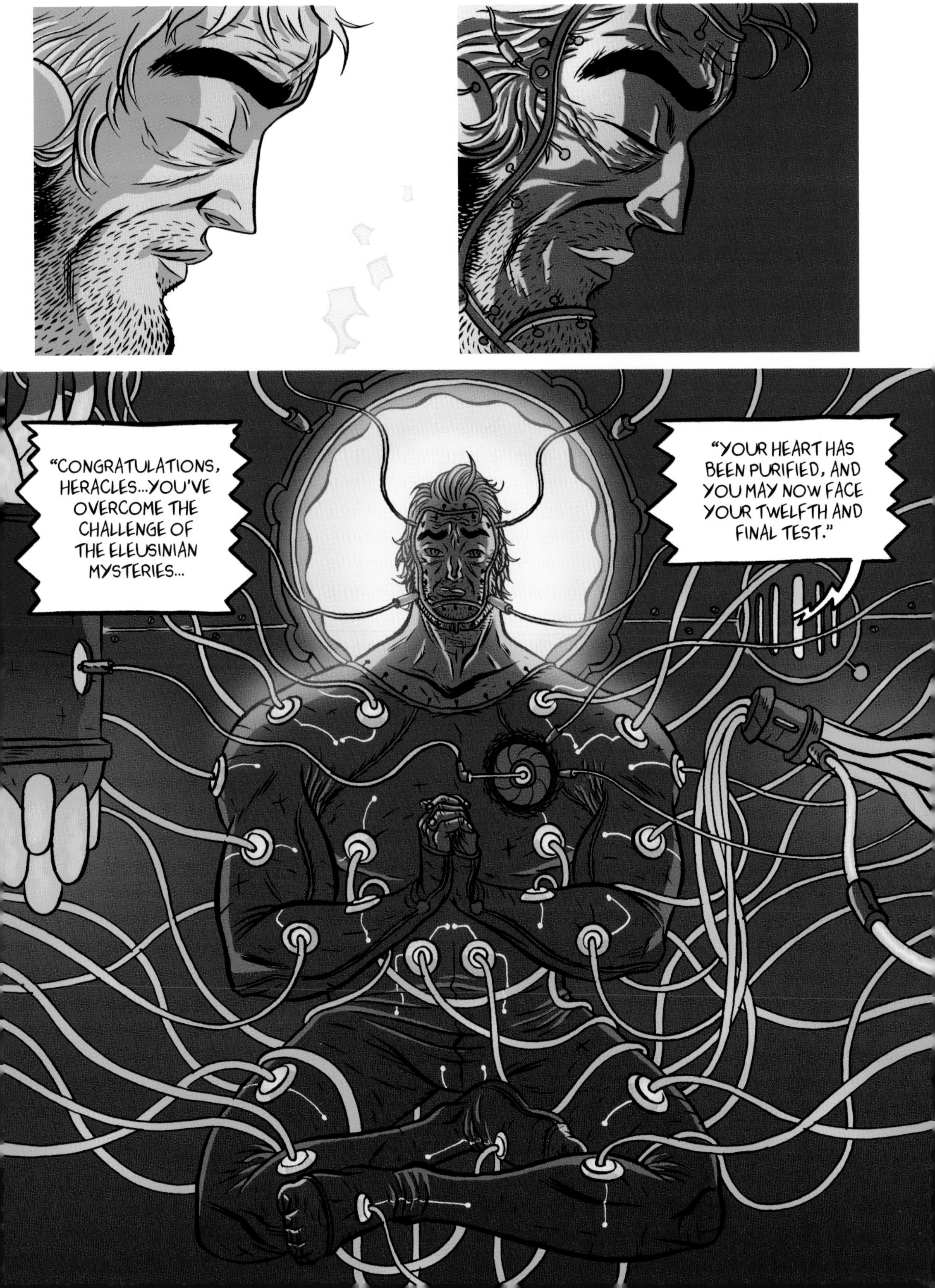
"CONGRATULATIONS, HERACLES...YOU'VE OVERCOME THE CHALLENGE OF THE ELEUSINIAN MYSTERIES...
"YOUR HEART HAS BEEN PURIFIED, AND YOU MAY NOW FACE YOUR TWELFTH AND FINAL TEST."

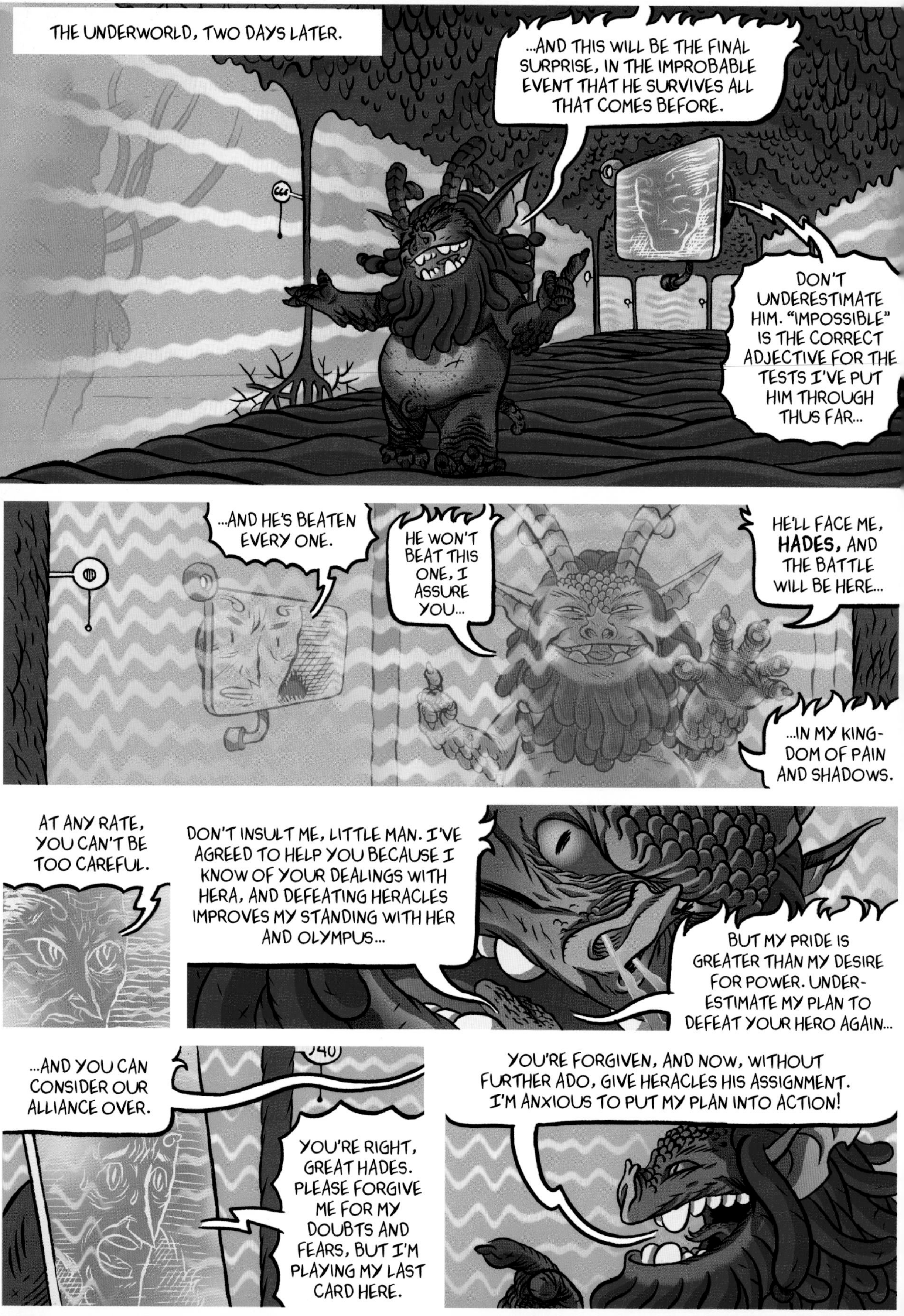
THE UNDERWORLD, TWO DAYS LATER.
...AND THIS WILL BE THE FINAL SURPRISE, IN THE IMPROBABLE EVENT THAT HE SURVIVES ALL THAT COMES BEFORE.
DON'T UNDERESTIMATE HIM. "IMPOSSIBLE" IS THE CORRECT ADJECTIVE FOR THE TESTS I'VE PUT HIM THROUGH THUS FAR...
...AND HE'S BEATEN EVERY ONE.
HE WON'T BEAT THIS ONE, I ASSURE YOU...
HE'LL FACE ME, **HADES,** AND THE BATTLE WILL BE HERE...
...IN MY KING-DOM OF PAIN AND SHADOWS.
AT ANY RATE, YOU CAN'T BE TOO CAREFUL.
DON'T INSULT ME, LITTLE MAN. I'VE AGREED TO HELP YOU BECAUSE I KNOW OF YOUR DEALINGS WITH HERA, AND DEFEATING HERACLES IMPROVES MY STANDING WITH HER AND OLYMPUS...
BUT MY PRIDE IS GREATER THAN MY DESIRE FOR POWER. UNDER-ESTIMATE MY PLAN TO DEFEAT YOUR HERO AGAIN...
...AND YOU CAN CONSIDER OUR ALLIANCE OVER.
YOU'RE RIGHT, GREAT HADES. PLEASE FORGIVE ME FOR MY DOUBTS AND FEARS, BUT I'M PLAYING MY LAST CARD HERE.
YOU'RE FORGIVEN, AND NOW, WITHOUT FURTHER ADO, GIVE HERACLES HIS ASSIGNMENT. I'M ANXIOUS TO PUT MY PLAN INTO ACTION!

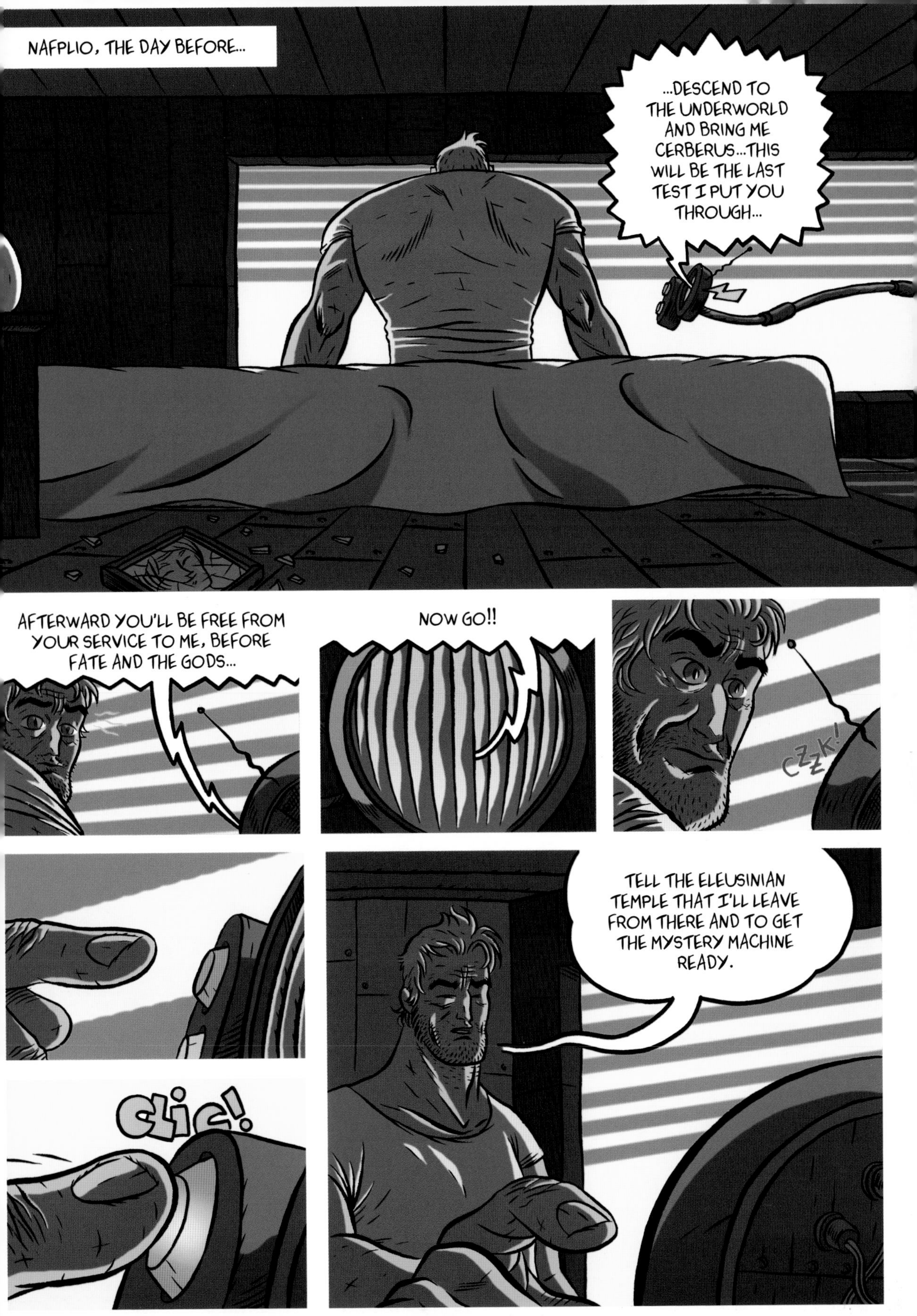

NAFPLIO, THE DAY BEFORE...
...DESCEND TO THE UNDERWORLD AND BRING ME CERBERUS...THIS WILL BE THE LAST TEST I PUT YOU THROUGH...
AFTERWARD YOU'LL BE FREE FROM YOUR SERVICE TO ME, BEFORE FATE AND THE GODS...
NOW GO!!
CZZK!
CLIC!
TELL THE ELEUSINIAN TEMPLE THAT I'LL LEAVE FROM THERE AND TO GET THE MYSTERY MACHINE READY.

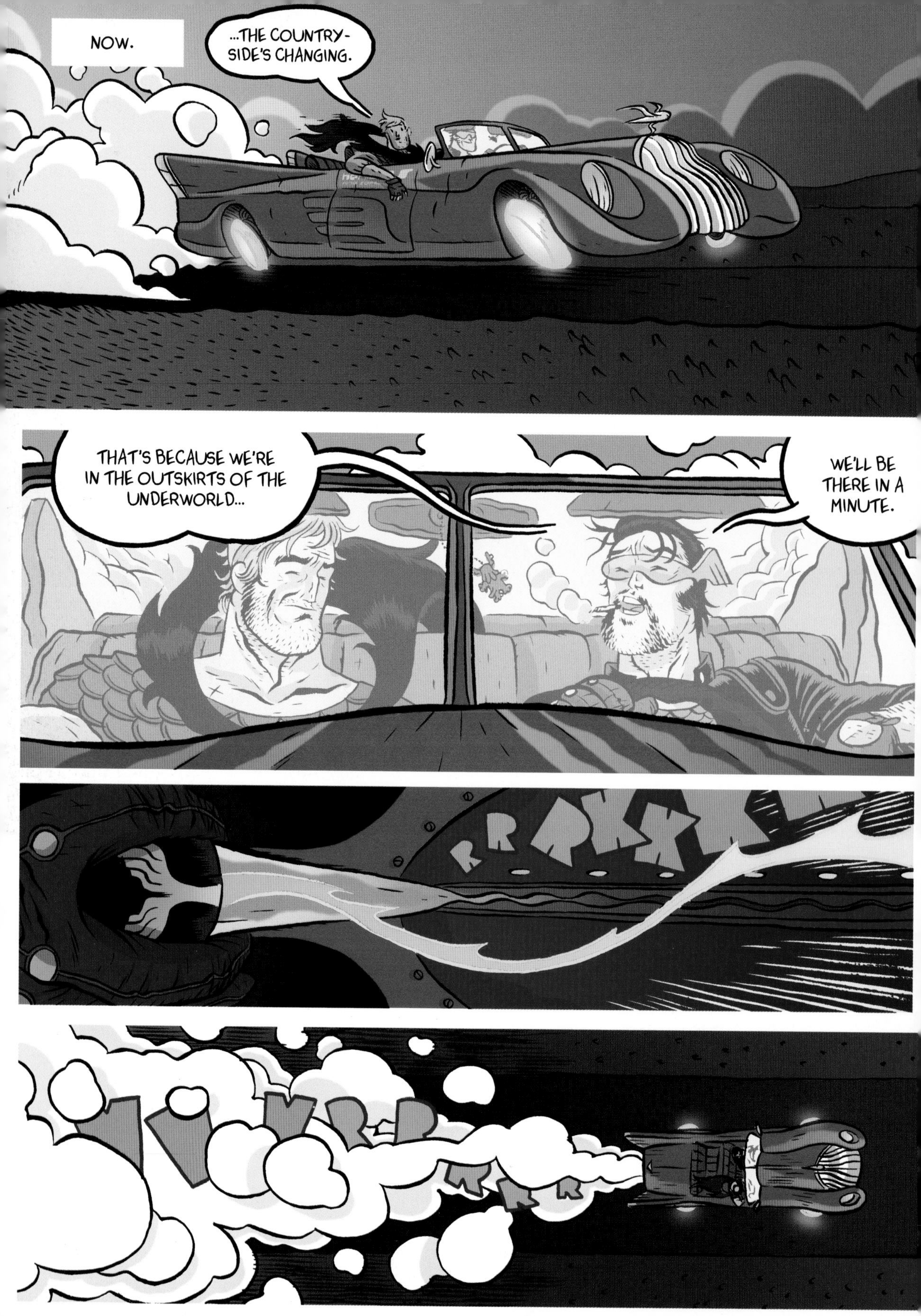
NOW.
...THE COUNTRY-SIDE'S CHANGING.
THAT'S BECAUSE WE'RE IN THE OUTSKIRTS OF THE UNDERWORLD...
WE'LL BE THERE IN A MINUTE.

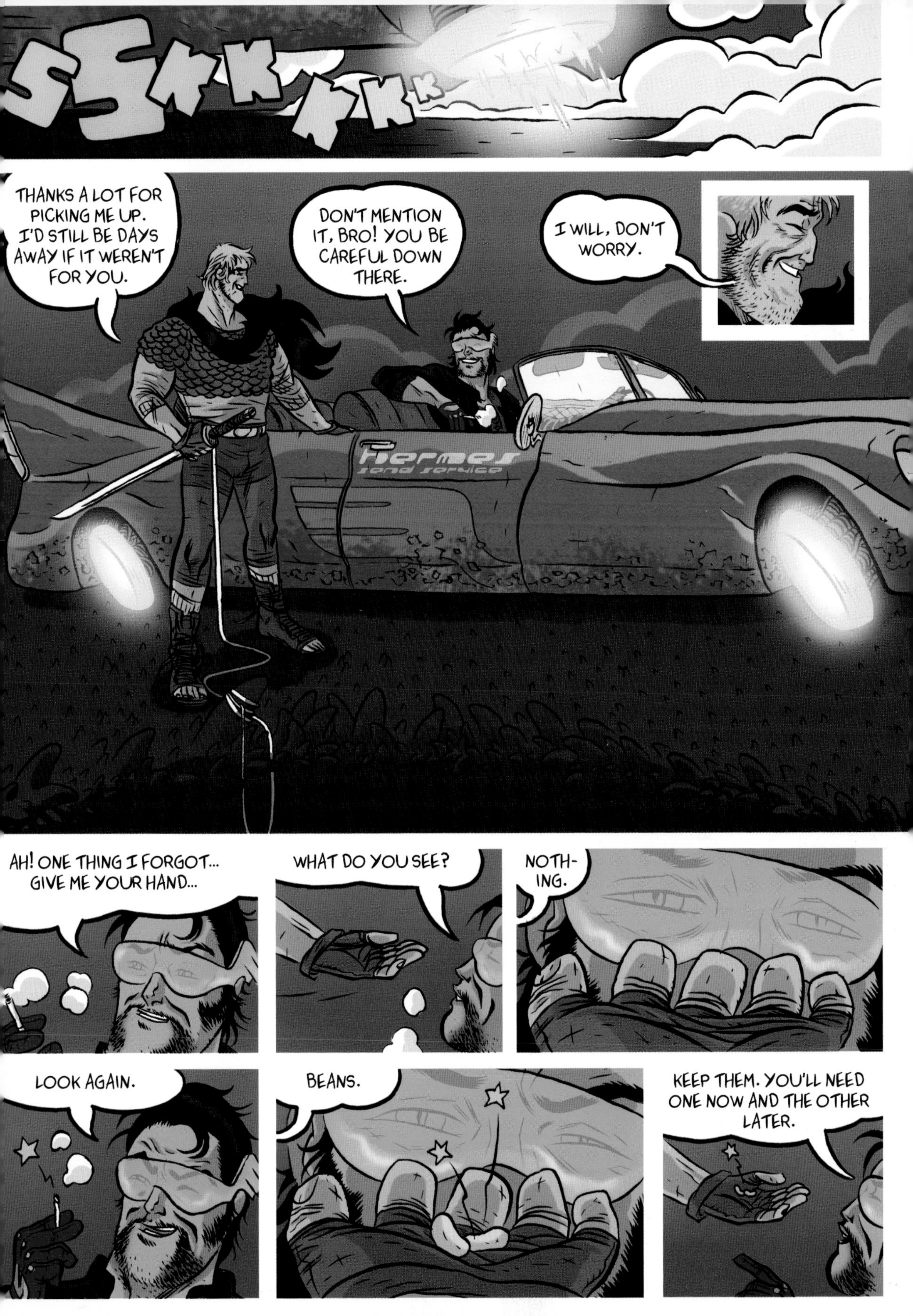
SSHKKKKKK
THANKS A LOT FOR PICKING ME UP. I'D STILL BE DAYS AWAY IF IT WEREN'T FOR YOU.
DON'T MENTION IT, BRO! YOU BE CAREFUL DOWN THERE.
I WILL, DON'T WORRY.
Hermes
send service
AH! ONE THING I FORGOT... GIVE ME YOUR HAND...
WHAT DO YOU SEE?
NOTH-ING.
LOOK AGAIN.
BEANS.
KEEP THEM. YOU'LL NEED ONE NOW AND THE OTHER LATER.

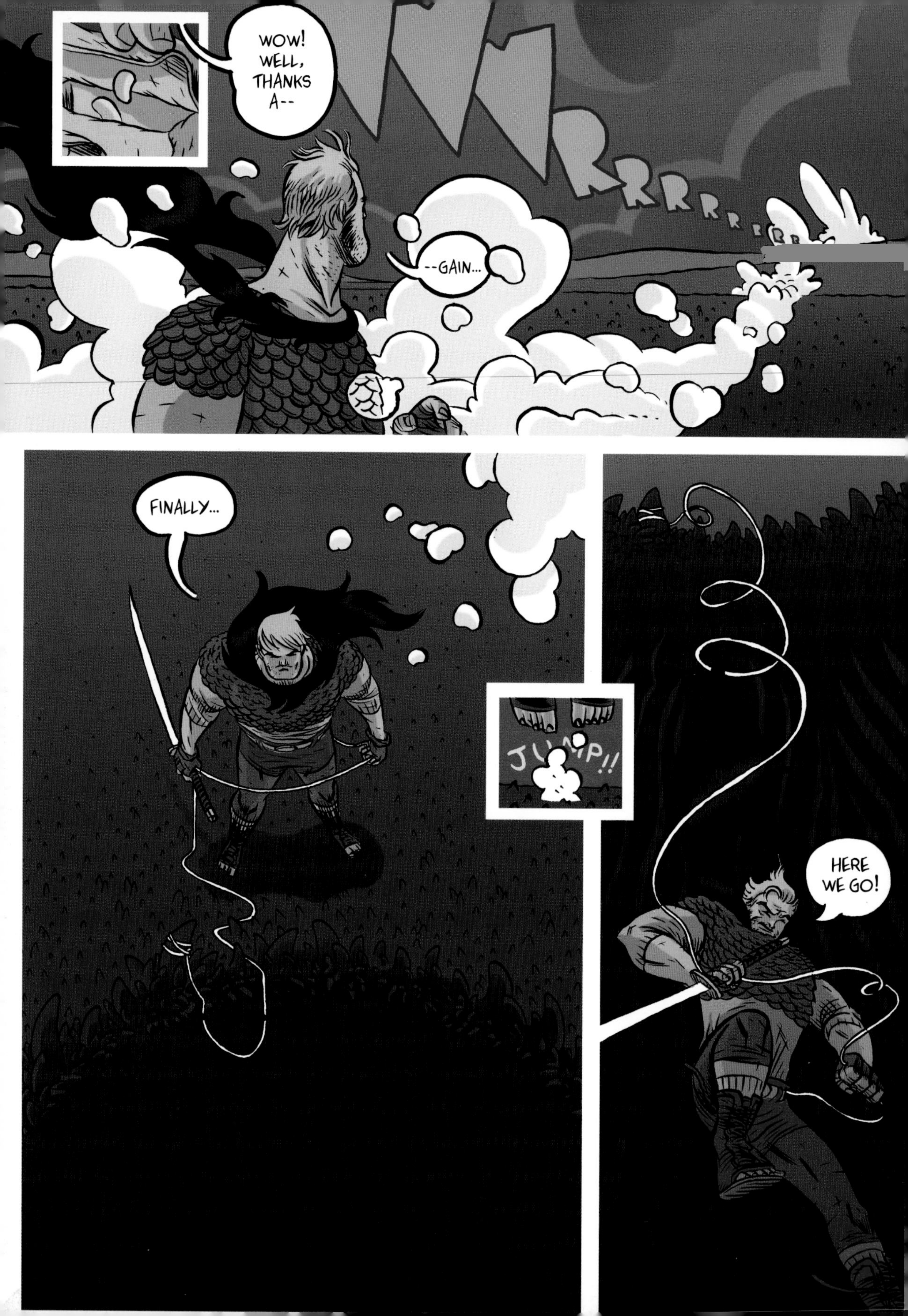
WOW! WELL, THANKS A--
WHRRRRRRR
--GAIN...
FINALLY...
JUMP!!
HERE WE GO!

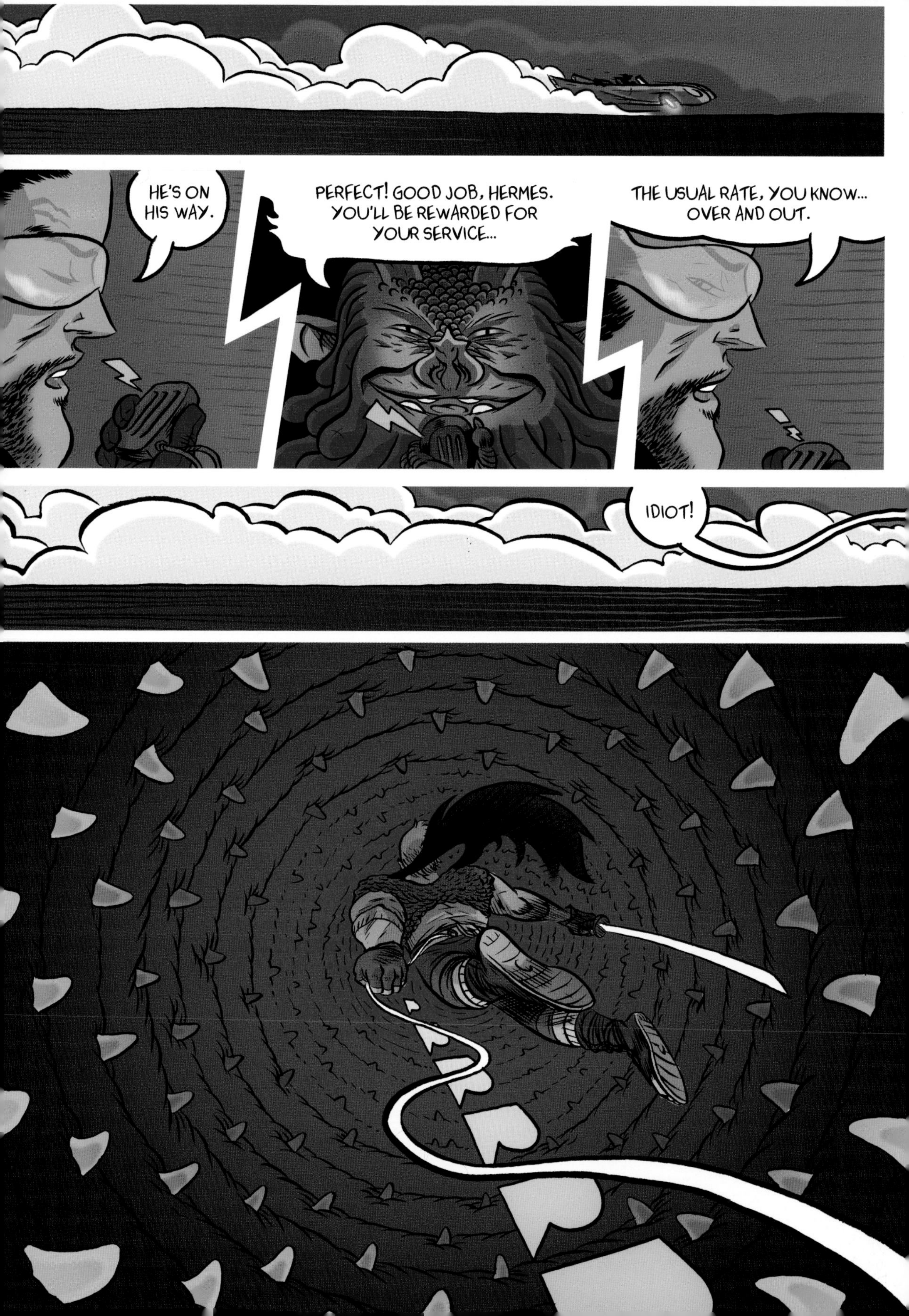
HE'S ON HIS WAY.
PERFECT! GOOD JOB, HERMES. YOU'LL BE REWARDED FOR YOUR SERVICE...
THE USUAL RATE, YOU KNOW... OVER AND OUT.
IDIOT!

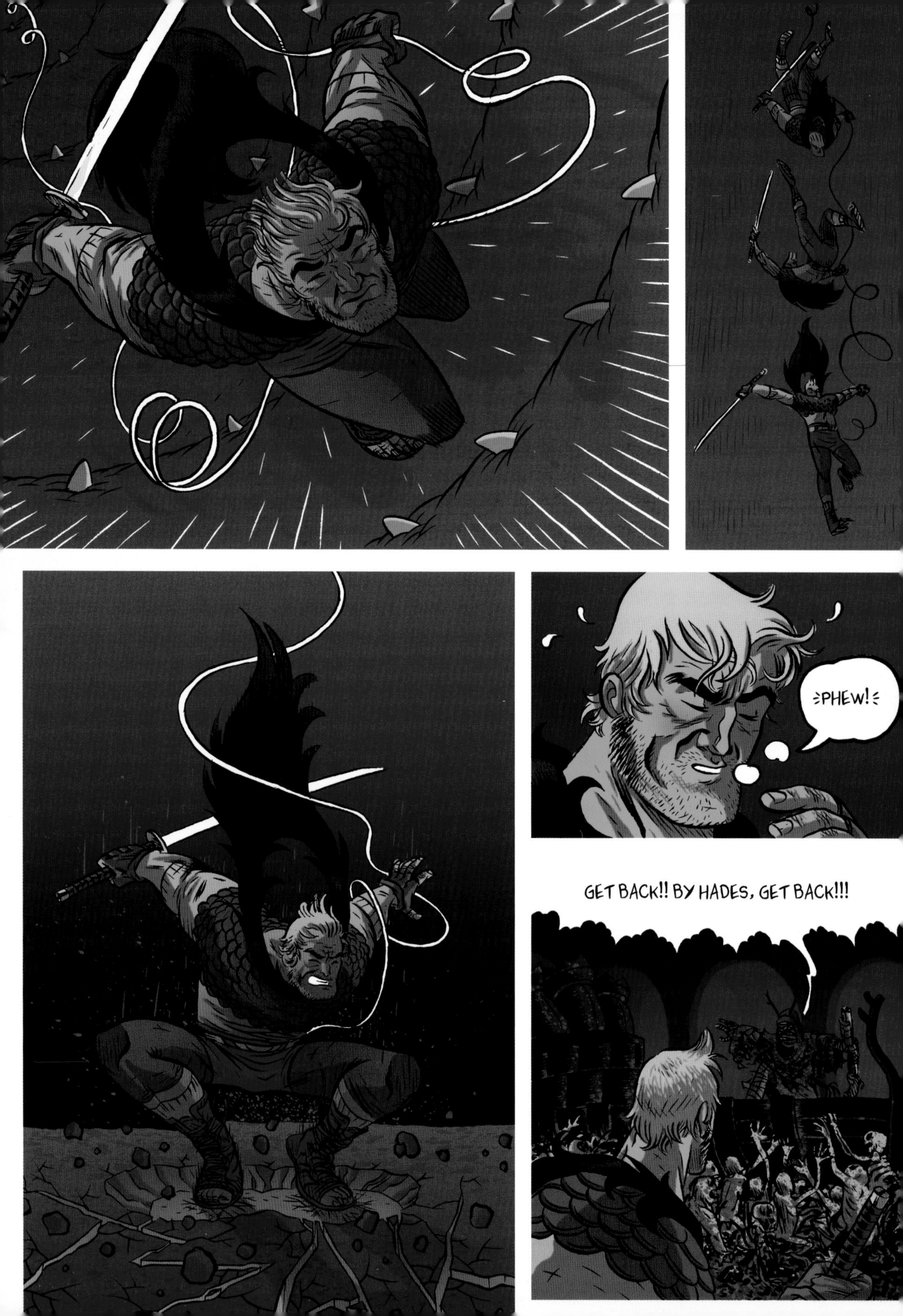
PHEW!
GET BACK!! BY HADES, GET BACK!!!

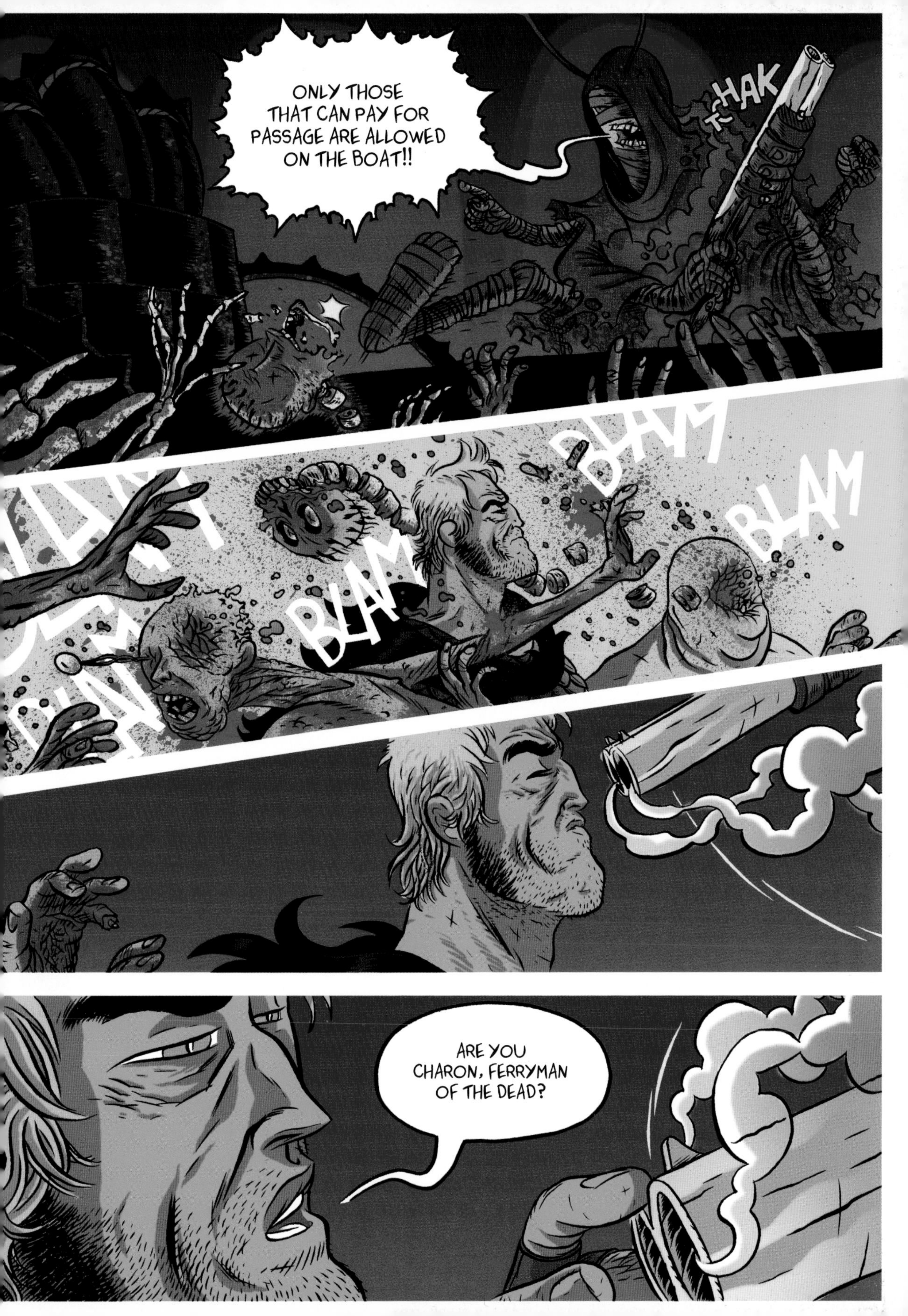
ONLY THOSE THAT CAN PAY FOR PASSAGE ARE ALLOWED ON THE BOAT!!
THAK
BLAM
BLAM
BLAM
BLAM
ARE YOU CHARON, FERRYMAN OF THE DEAD?

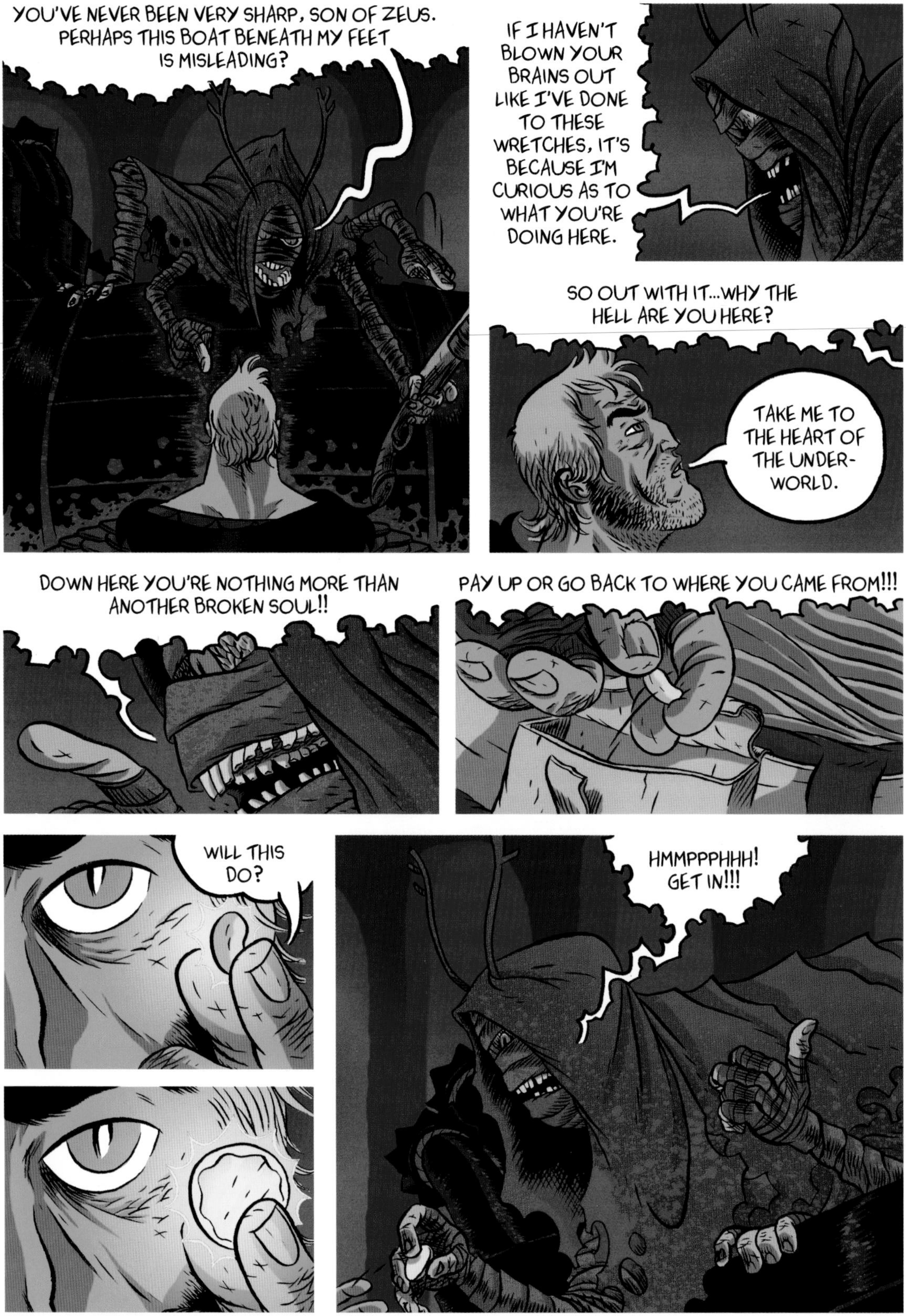
YOU'VE NEVER BEEN VERY SHARP, SON OF ZEUS. PERHAPS THIS BOAT BENEATH MY FEET IS MISLEADING?
IF I HAVEN'T BLOWN YOUR BRAINS OUT LIKE I'VE DONE TO THESE WRETCHES, IT'S BECAUSE I'M CURIOUS AS TO WHAT YOU'RE DOING HERE.
SO OUT WITH IT...WHY THE HELL ARE YOU HERE?
TAKE ME TO THE HEART OF THE UNDER-WORLD.
DOWN HERE YOU'RE NOTHING MORE THAN ANOTHER BROKEN SOUL!!
PAY UP OR GO BACK TO WHERE YOU CAME FROM!!!
WILL THIS DO?
HMMPPPHHH! GET IN!!!

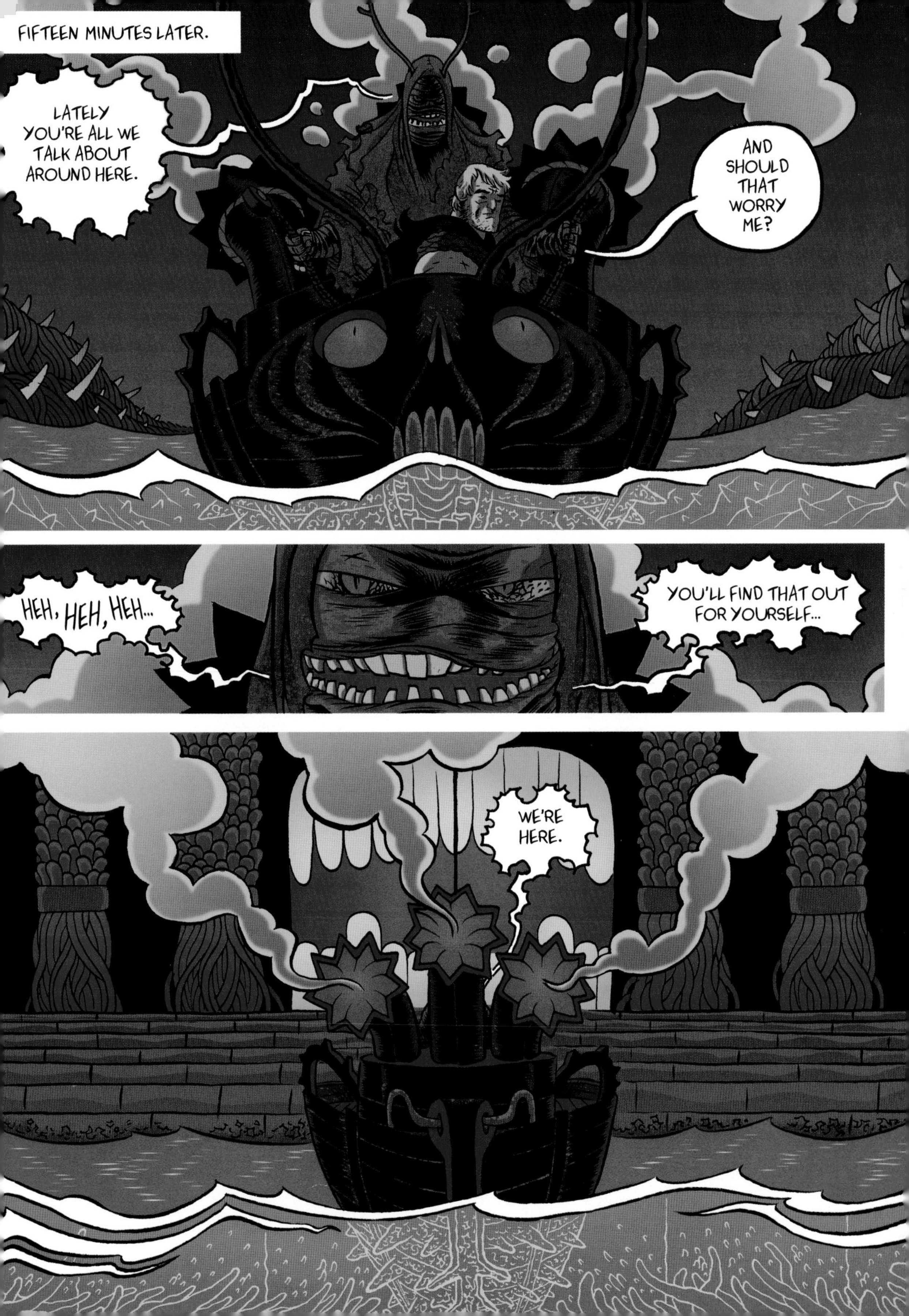
FIFTEEN MINUTES LATER.
LATELY YOU'RE ALL WE TALK ABOUT AROUND HERE.
AND SHOULD THAT WORRY ME?
HEH, HEH, HEH...
YOU'LL FIND THAT OUT FOR YOURSELF...
WE'RE HERE.

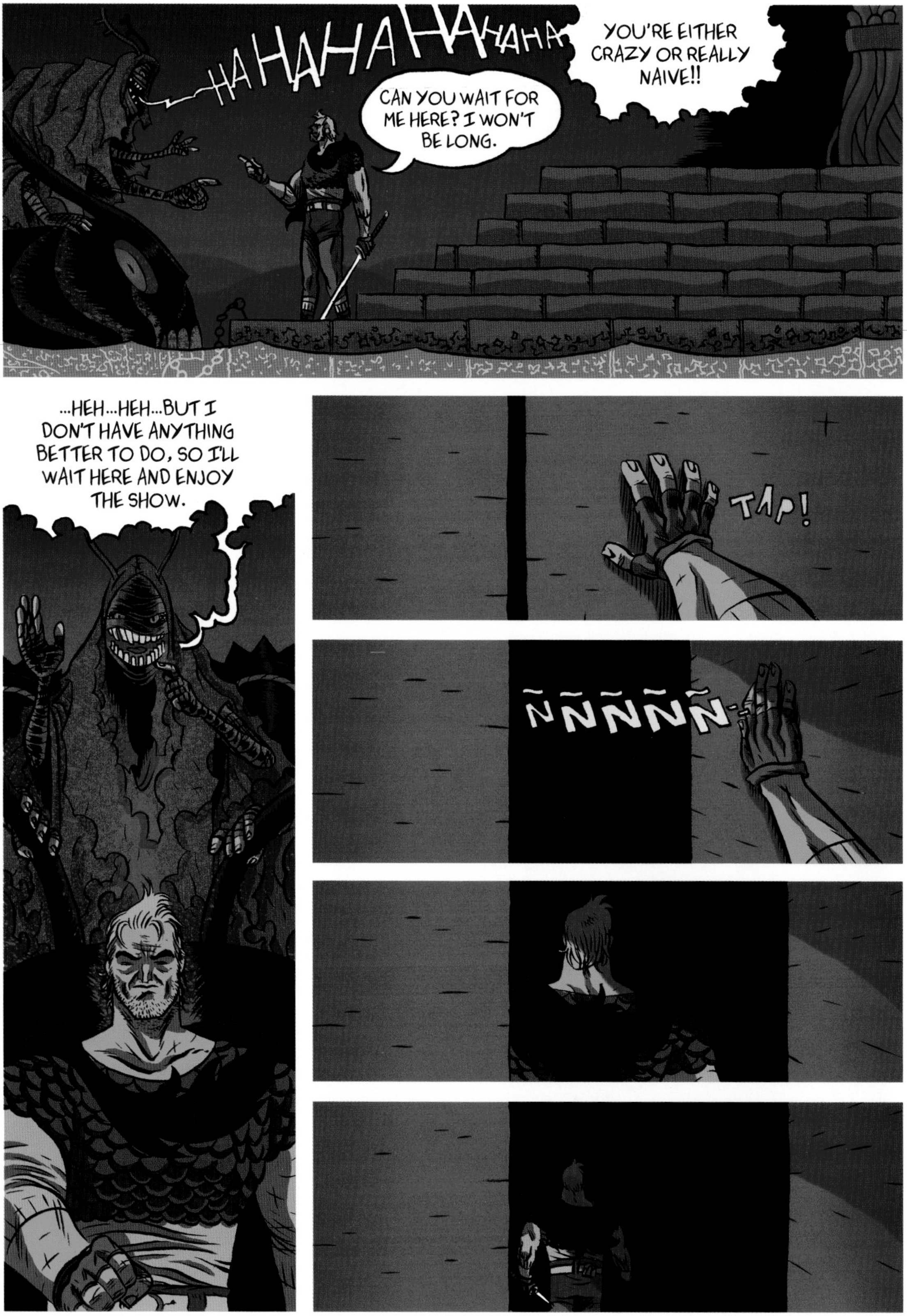
HAHAHAHAHAHAHA
CAN YOU WAIT FOR ME HERE? I WON'T BE LONG.
YOU'RE EITHER CRAZY OR REALLY NAIVE!!
...HEH...HEH...BUT I DON'T HAVE ANYTHING BETTER TO DO, SO I'LL WAIT HERE AND ENJOY THE SHOW.
TAP!
ÑÑÑÑÑ-

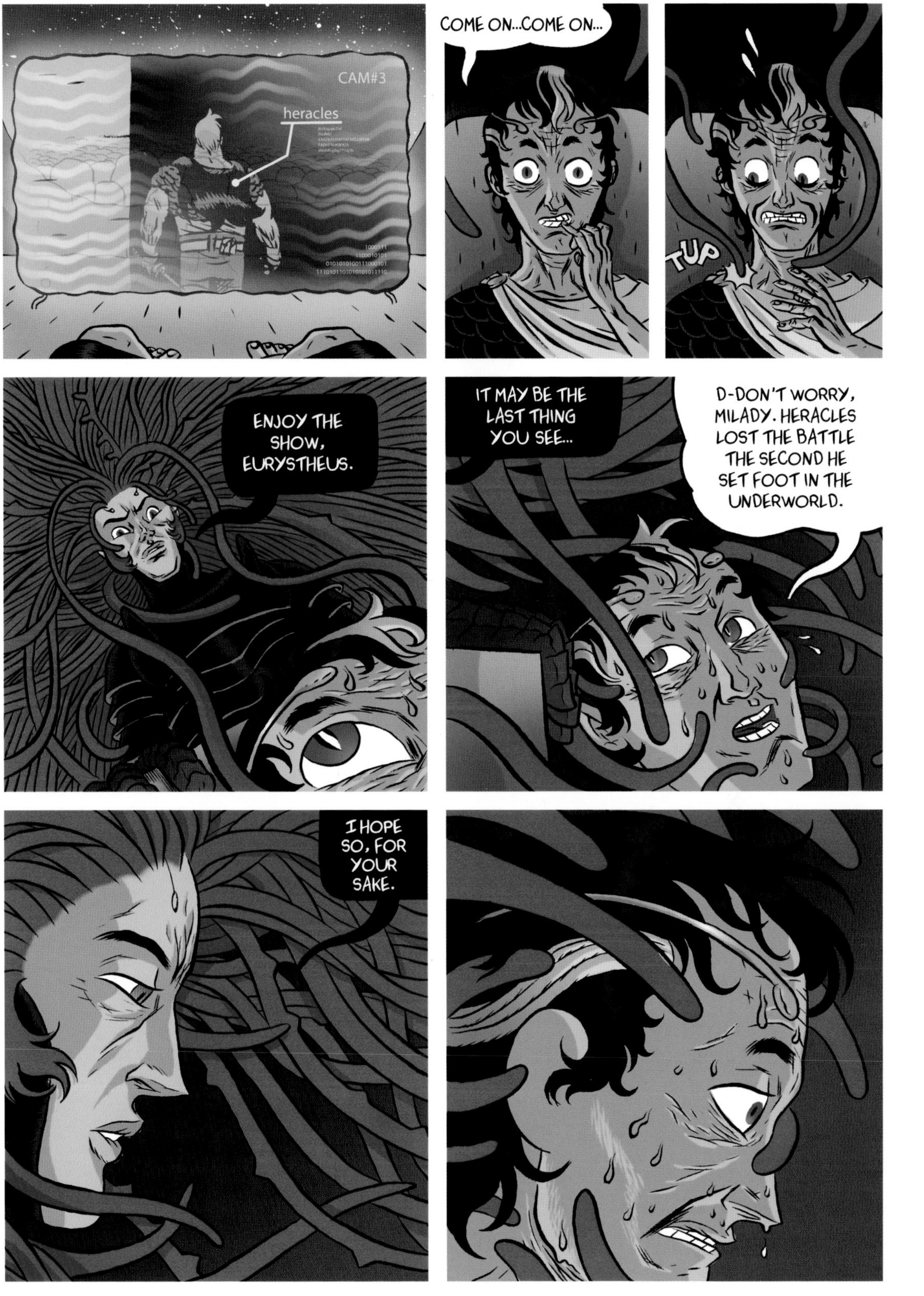
CAM#3
heracles
COME ON...COME ON...
TUP
ENJOY THE SHOW, EURYSTHEUS.
IT MAY BE THE LAST THING YOU SEE...
D-DON'T WORRY, MILADY. HERACLES LOST THE BATTLE THE SECOND HE SET FOOT IN THE UNDERWORLD.
I HOPE SO, FOR YOUR SAKE.

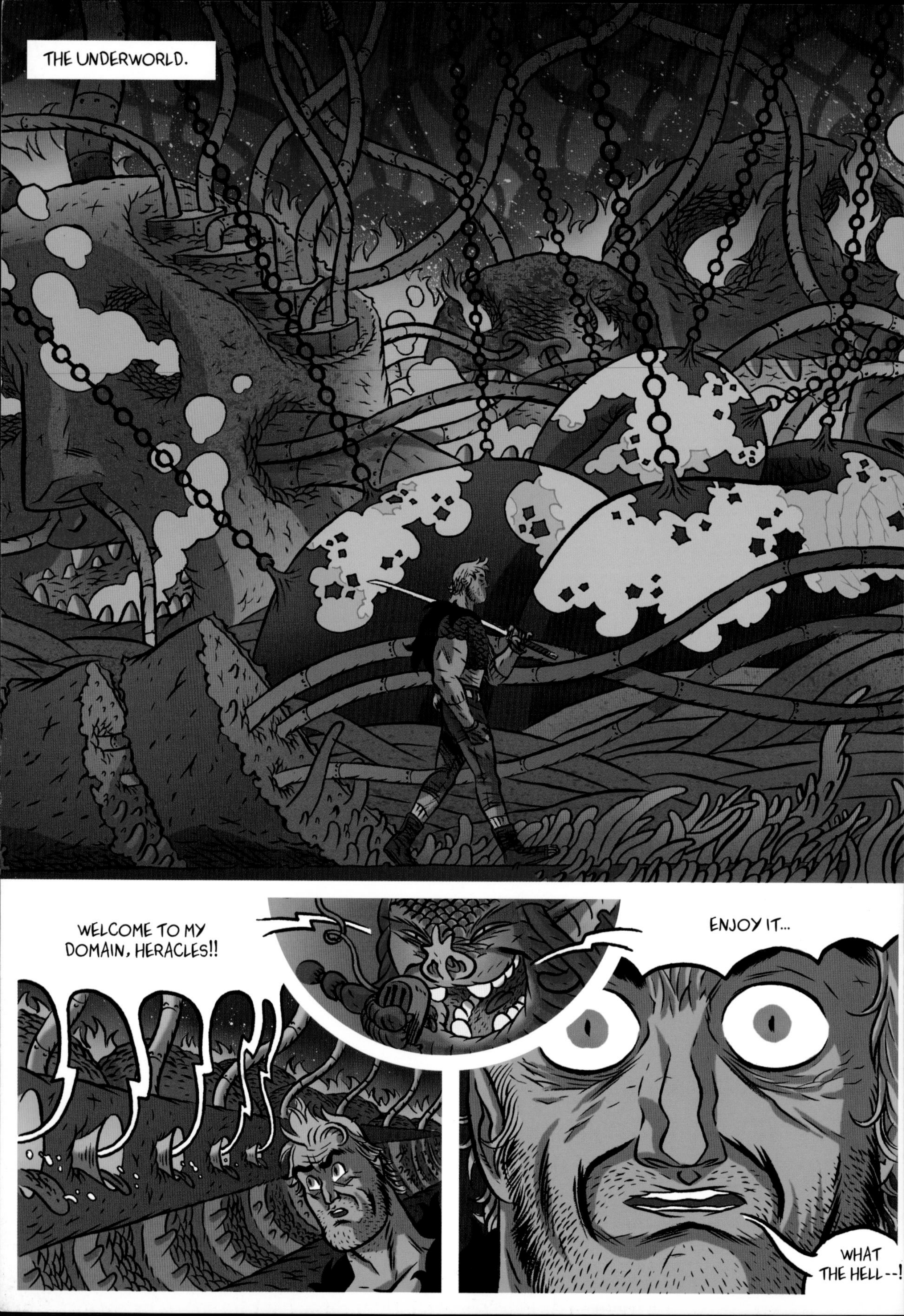
THE UNDERWORLD.
WELCOME TO MY DOMAIN, HERACLES!!
ENJOY IT...
WHAT THE HELL--!

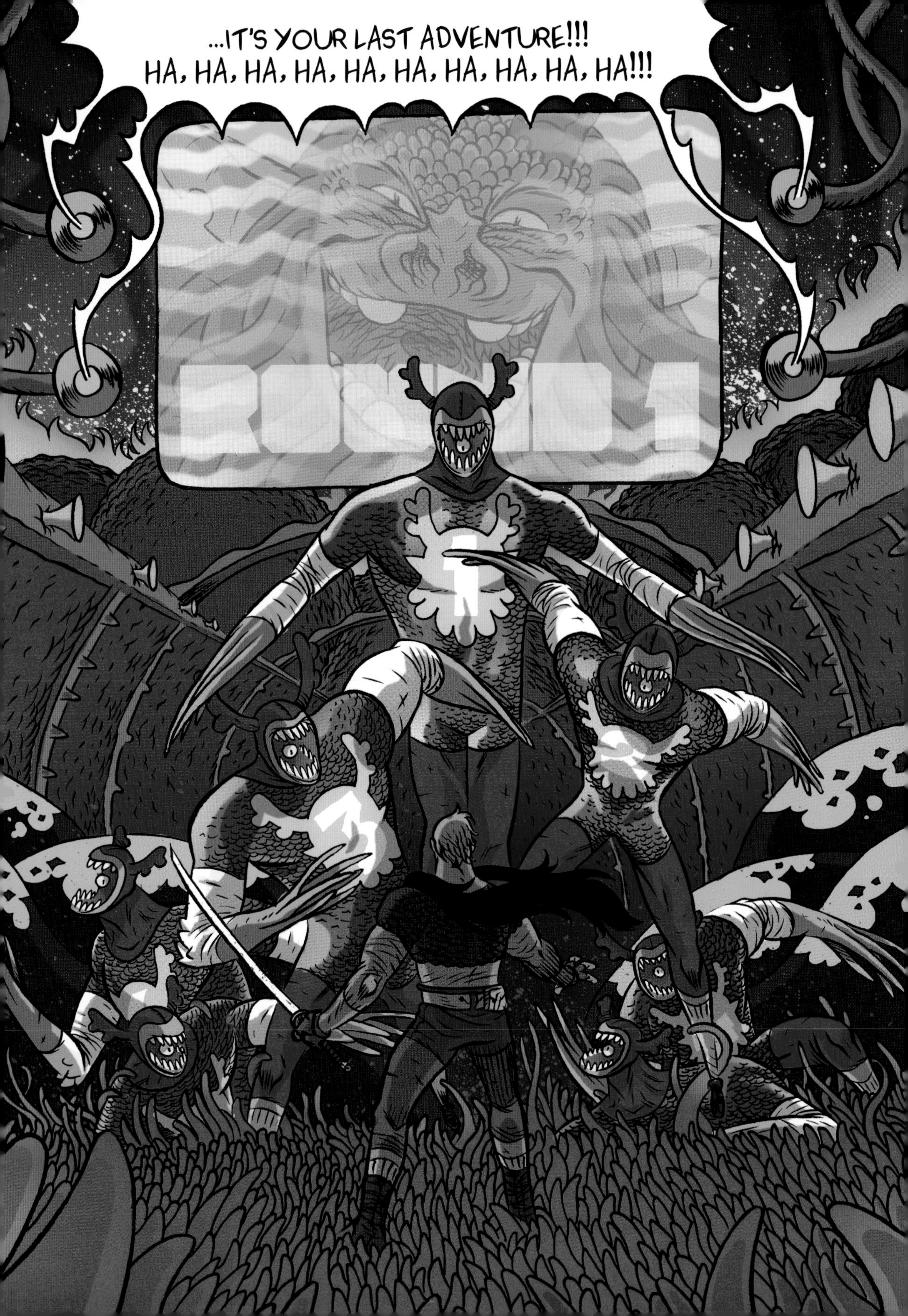
...IT'S YOUR LAST ADVENTURE!!! HA, HA, HA, HA, HA, HA, HA, HA, HA, HA!!!

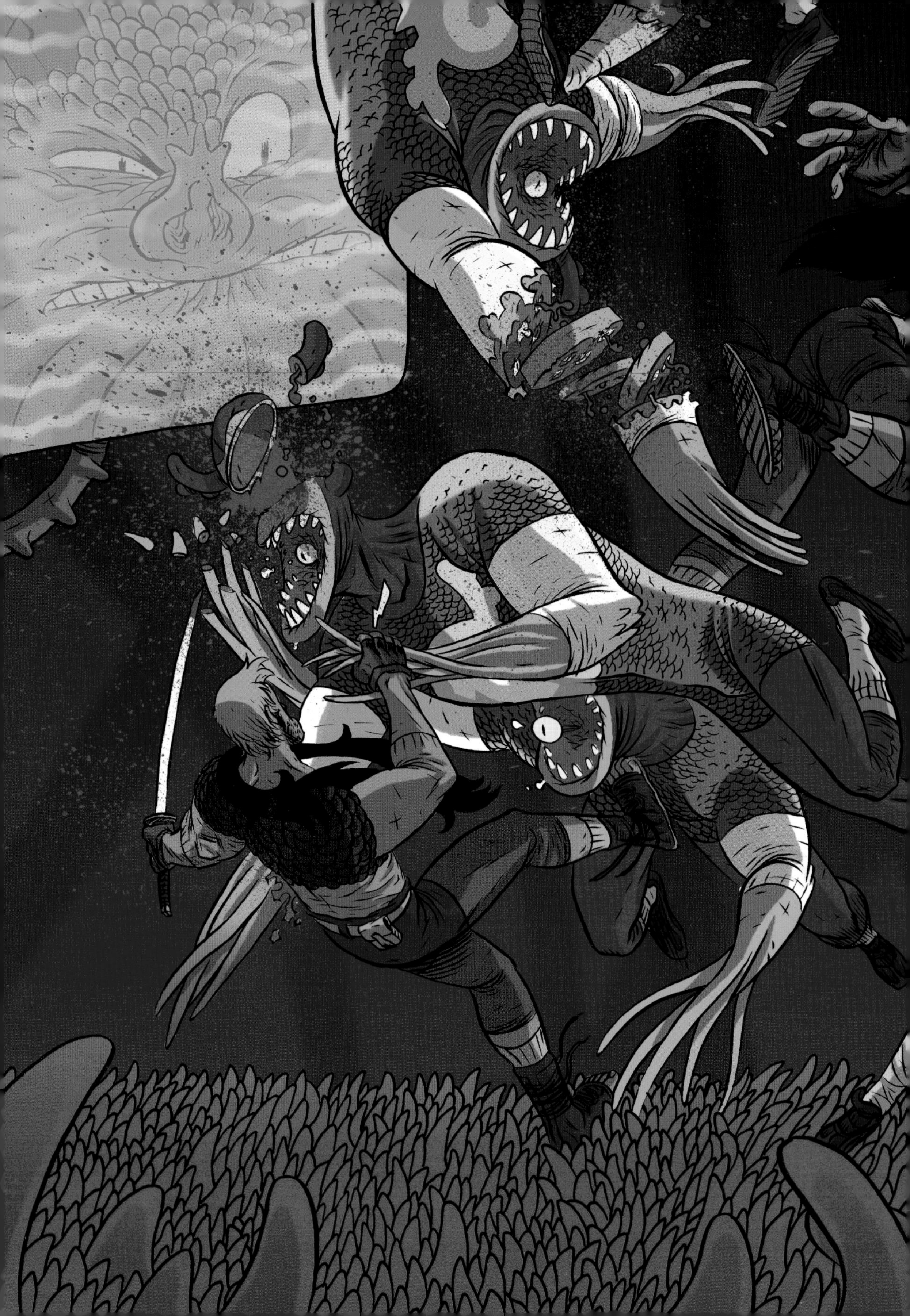

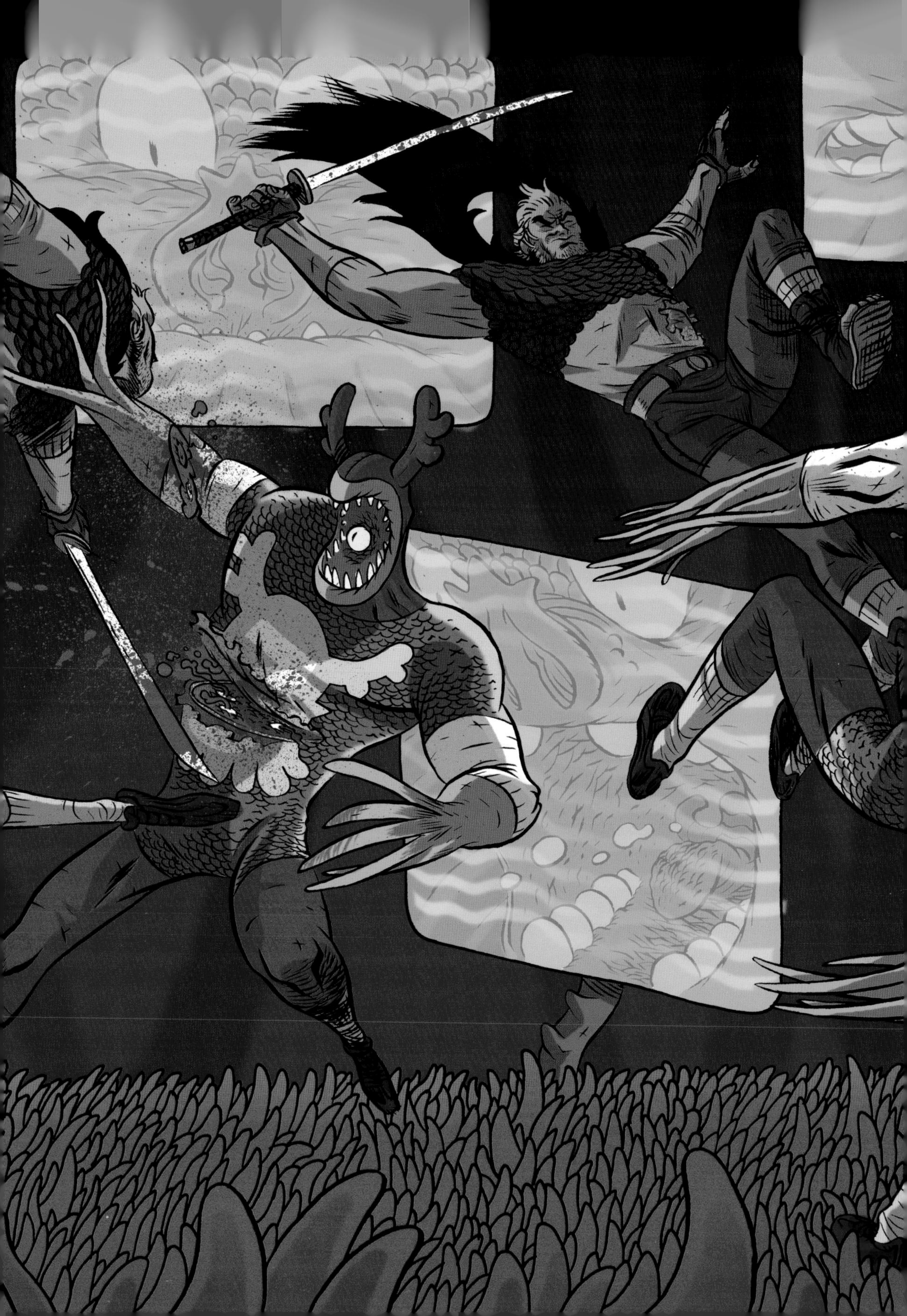

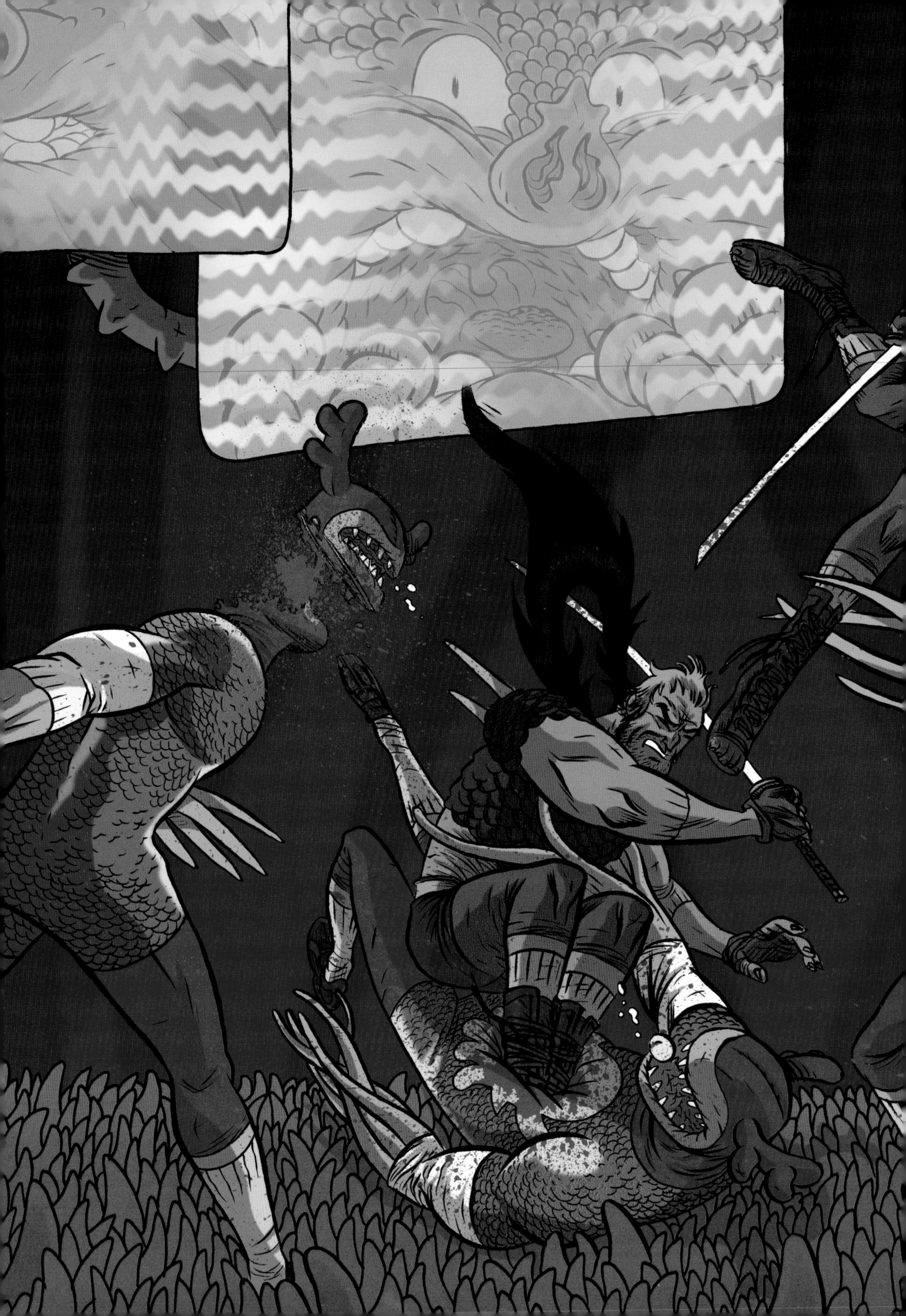

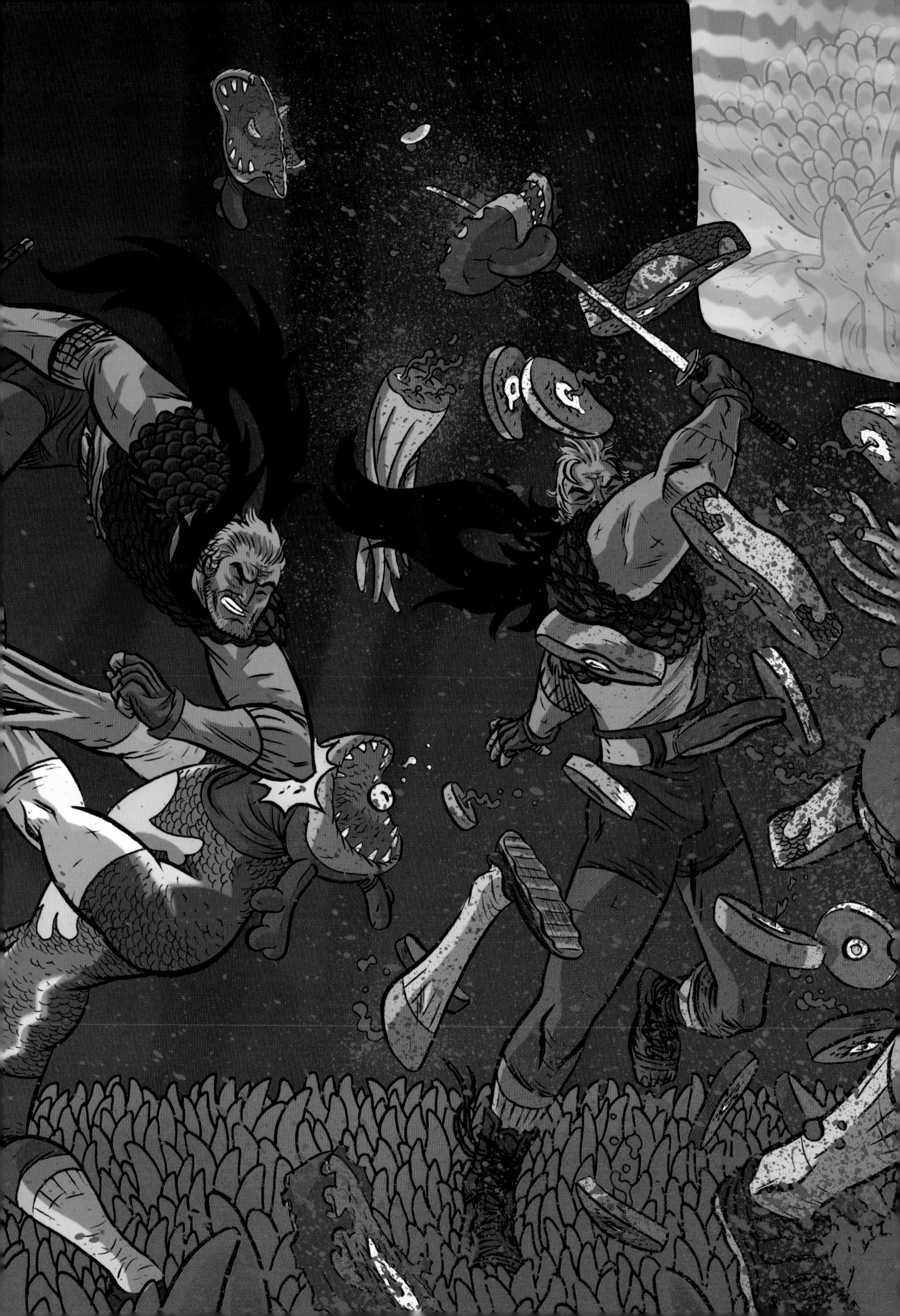

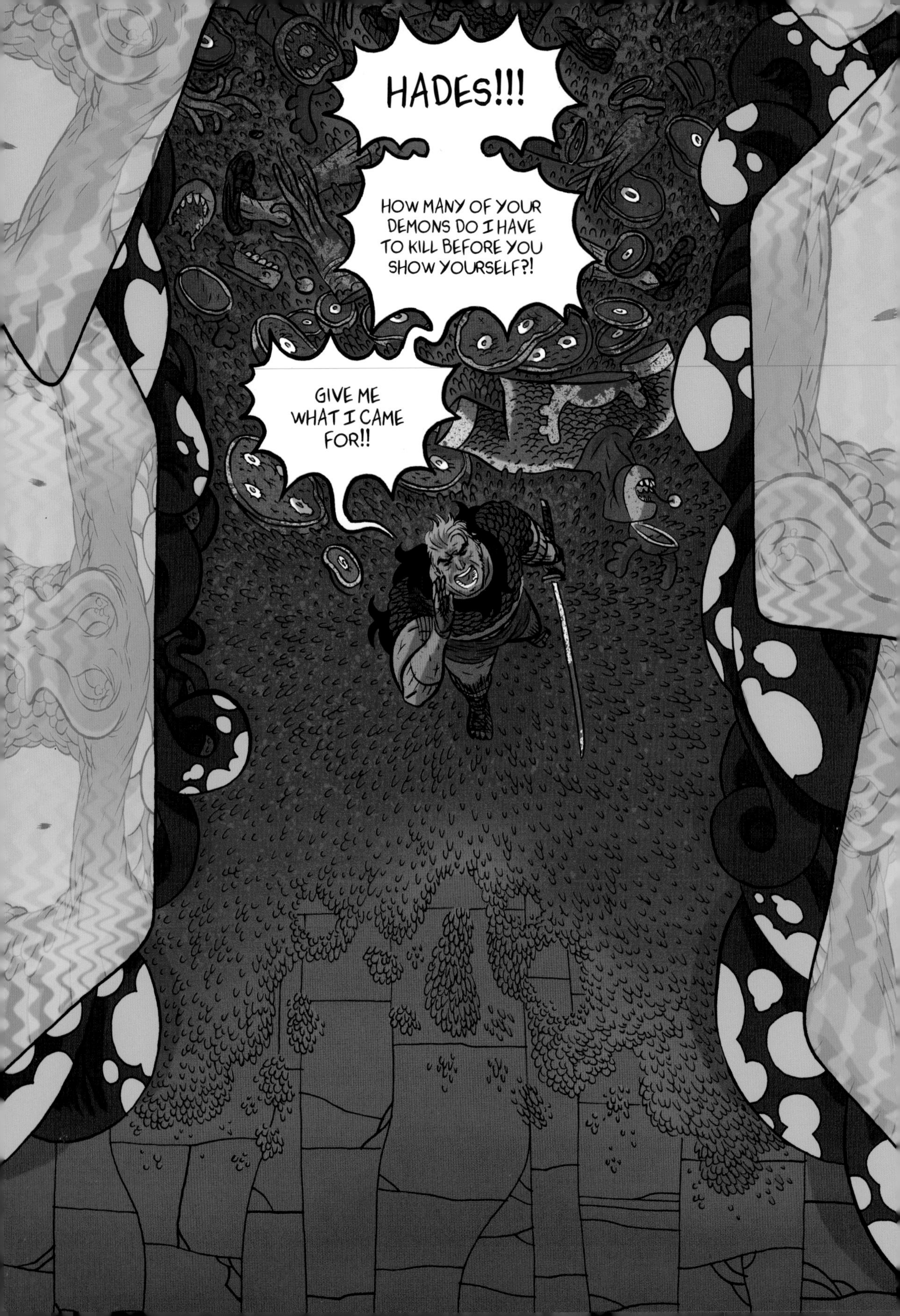
HADES!!!
HOW MANY OF YOUR DEMONS DO I HAVE TO KILL BEFORE YOU SHOW YOURSELF?!
GIVE ME WHAT I CAME FOR!!

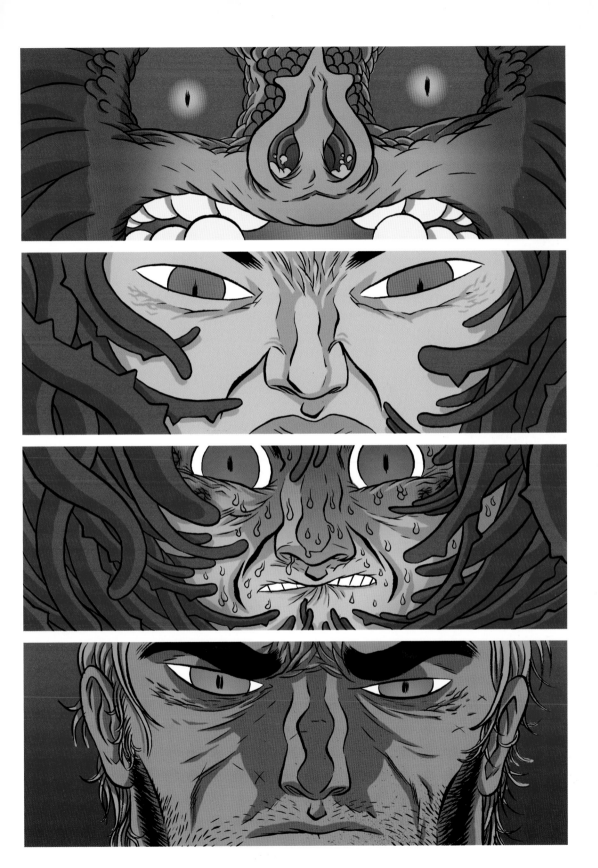

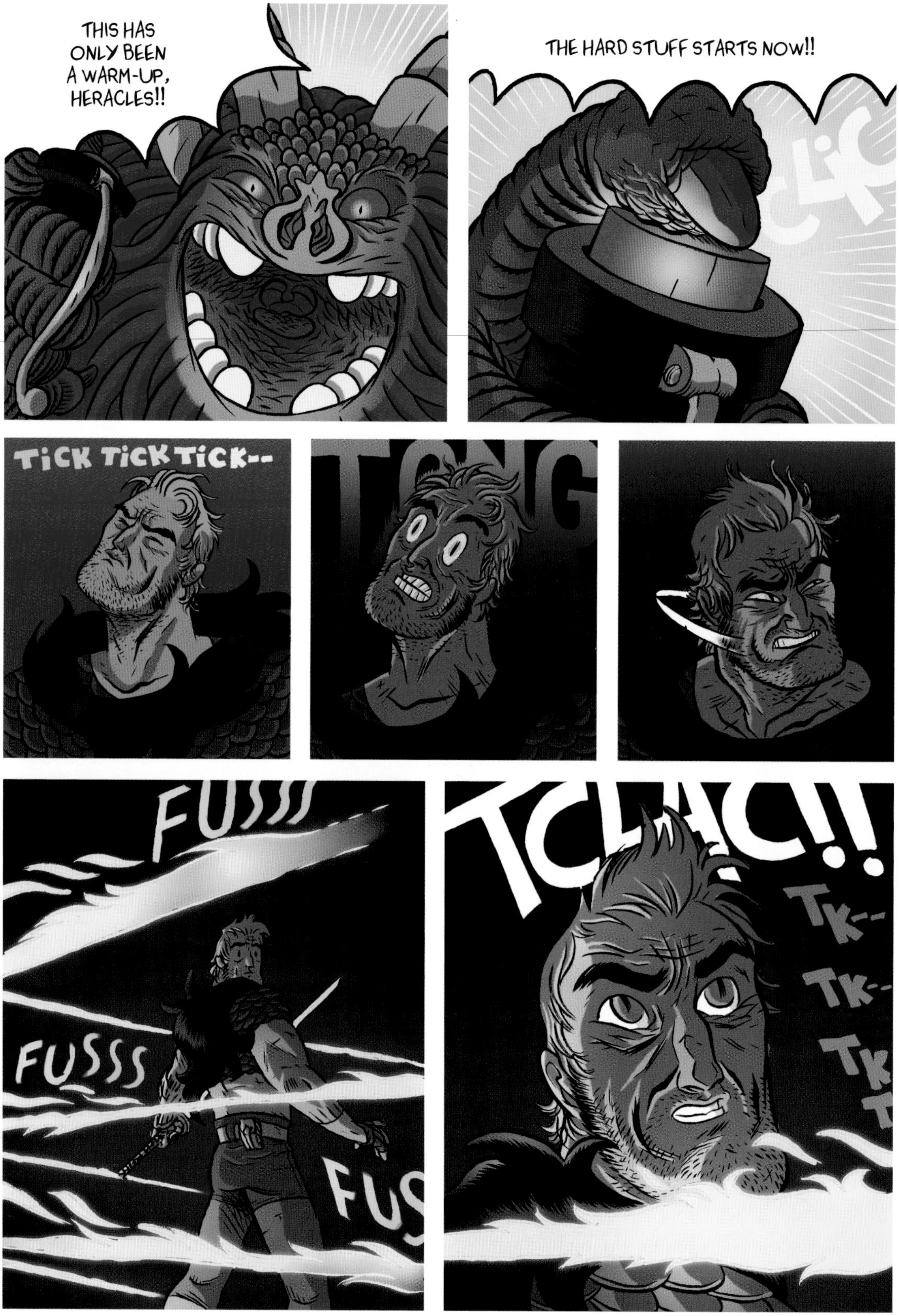
THIS HAS ONLY BEEN A WARM-UP, HERACLES!!
THE HARD STUFF STARTS NOW!!
CLIC
TICK TICK TICK--
TONG
FUSSS
FUSSS
FUS
TCLAC!!
TK--
TK--
TK

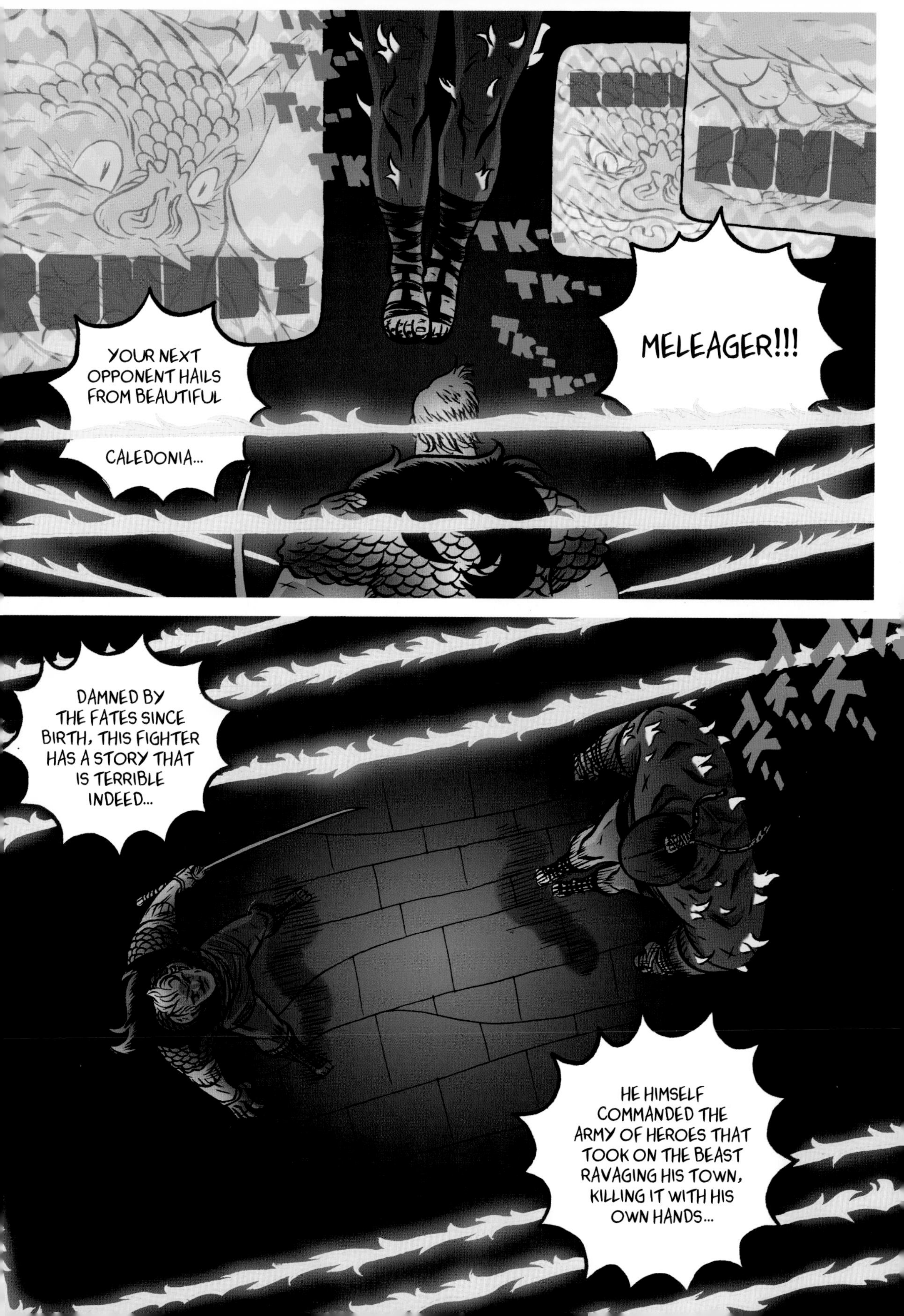
TK..
TK..
TK..
RUMMBLE
RUMMBL
RUMM
YOUR NEXT OPPONENT HAILS FROM BEAUTIFUL
CALEDONIA...
TK..
TK..
TK..
TK..
MELEAGER!!!
DAMNED BY THE FATES SINCE BIRTH, THIS FIGHTER HAS A STORY THAT IS TERRIBLE INDEED...
TK..TK..TK..
HE HIMSELF COMMANDED THE ARMY OF HEROES THAT TOOK ON THE BEAST RAVAGING HIS TOWN, KILLING IT WITH HIS OWN HANDS...

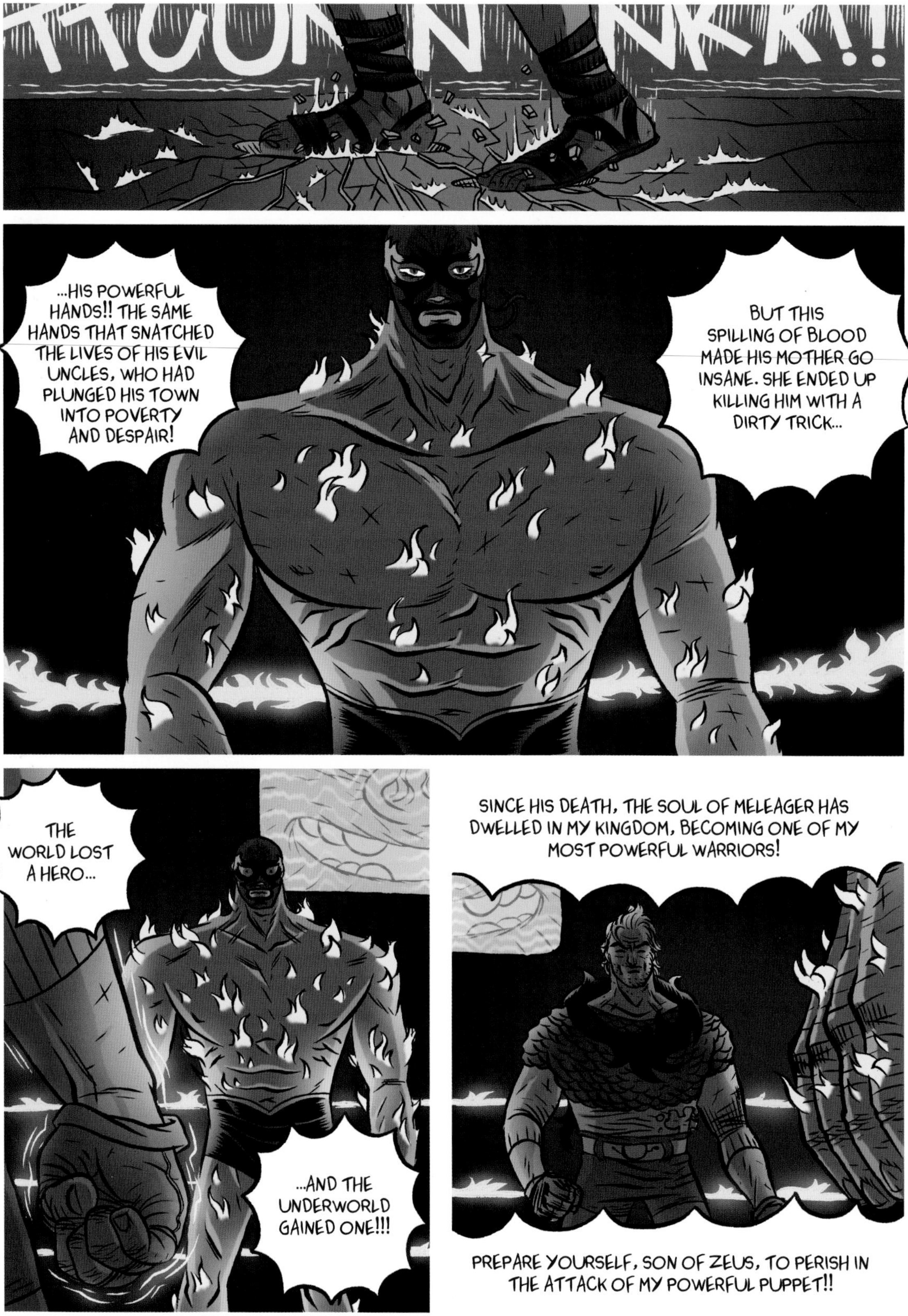
...HIS POWERFUL HANDS!! THE SAME HANDS THAT SNATCHED THE LIVES OF HIS EVIL UNCLES, WHO HAD PLUNGED HIS TOWN INTO POVERTY AND DESPAIR!
BUT THIS SPILLING OF BLOOD MADE HIS MOTHER GO INSANE. SHE ENDED UP KILLING HIM WITH A DIRTY TRICK...
THE WORLD LOST A HERO...
...AND THE UNDERWORLD GAINED ONE!!!
SINCE HIS DEATH, THE SOUL OF MELEAGER HAS DWELLED IN MY KINGDOM, BECOMING ONE OF MY MOST POWERFUL WARRIORS!
PREPARE YOURSELF, SON OF ZEUS, TO PERISH IN THE ATTACK OF MY POWERFUL PUPPET!!

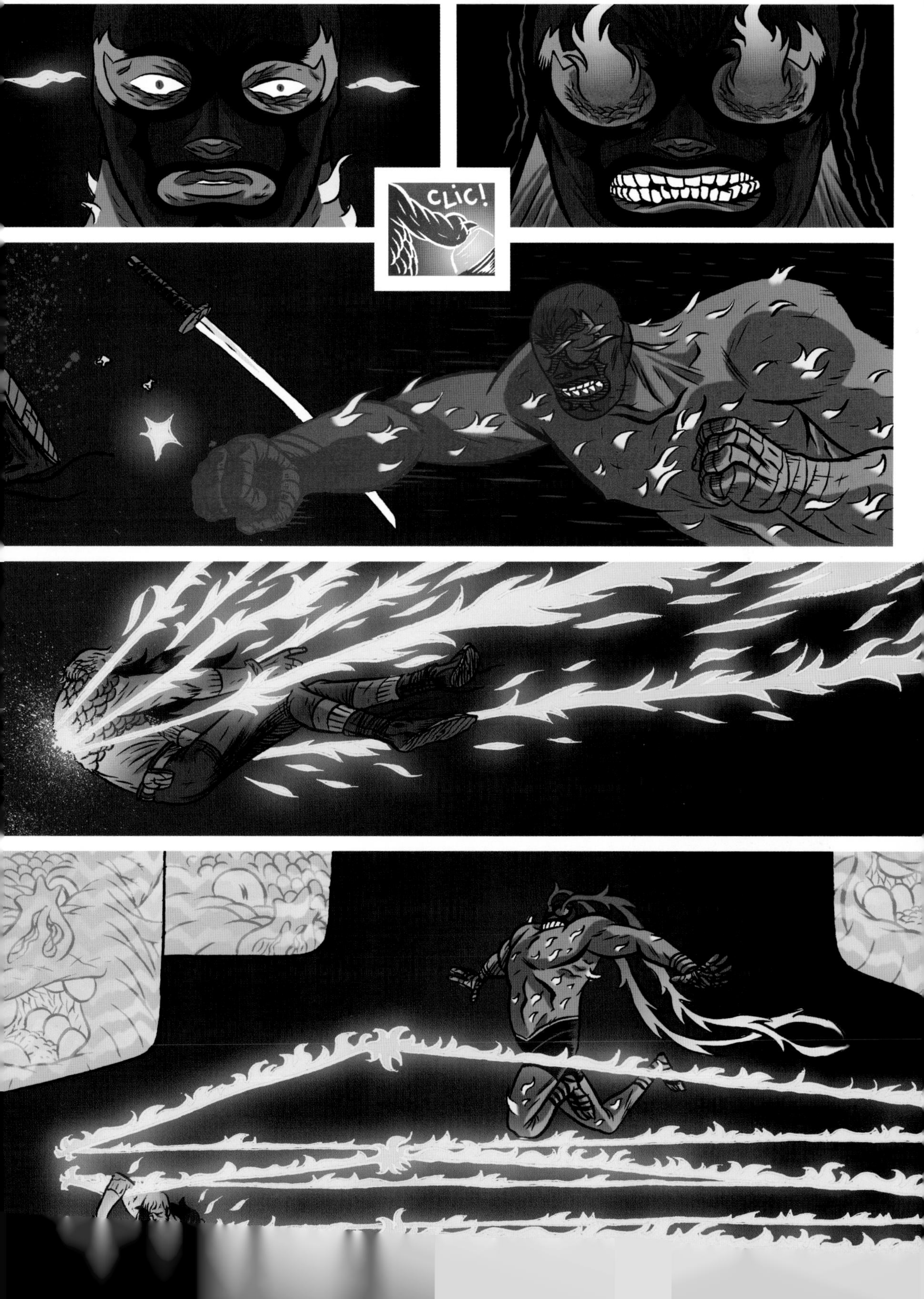
CLIC!

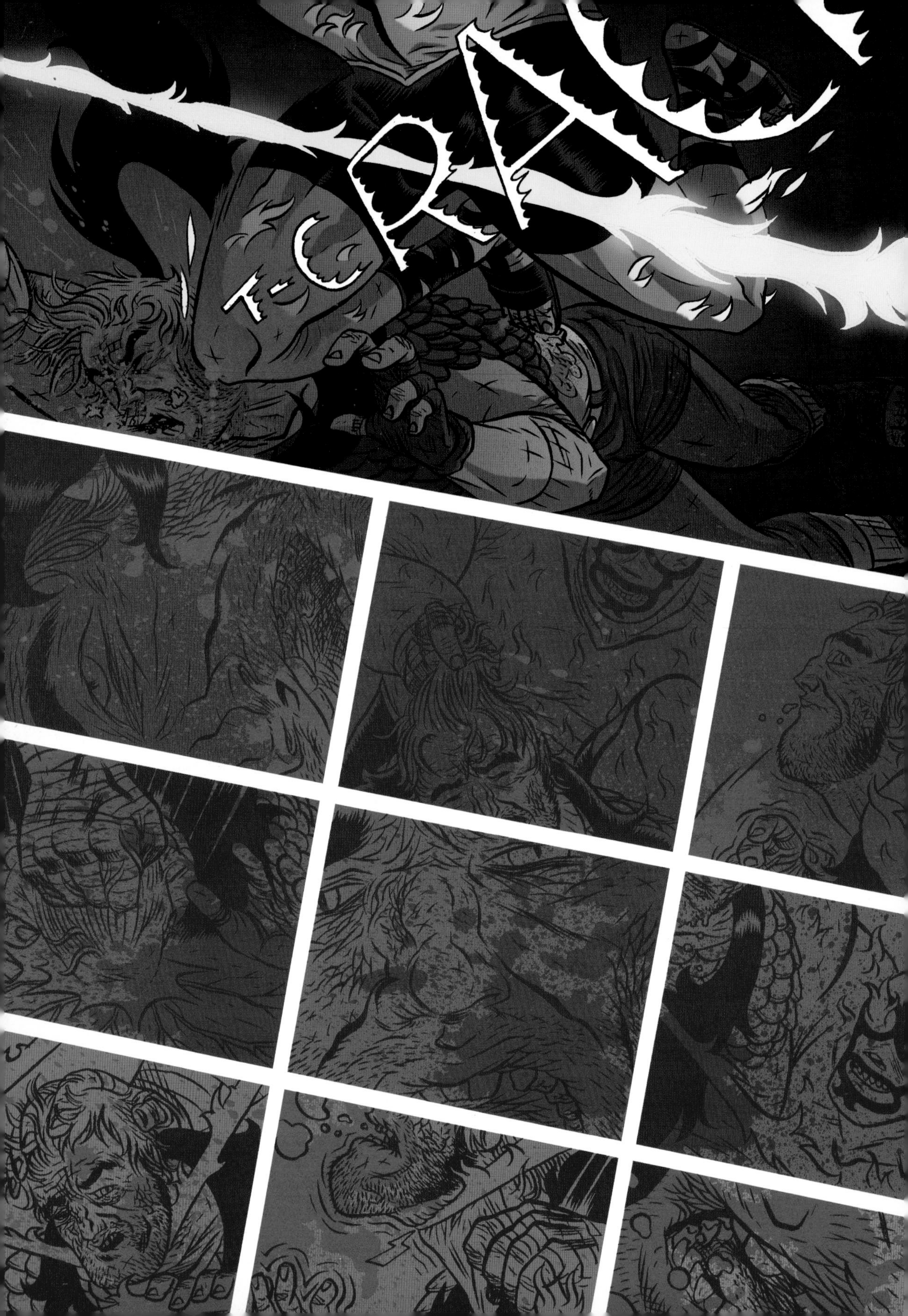
T-CRA

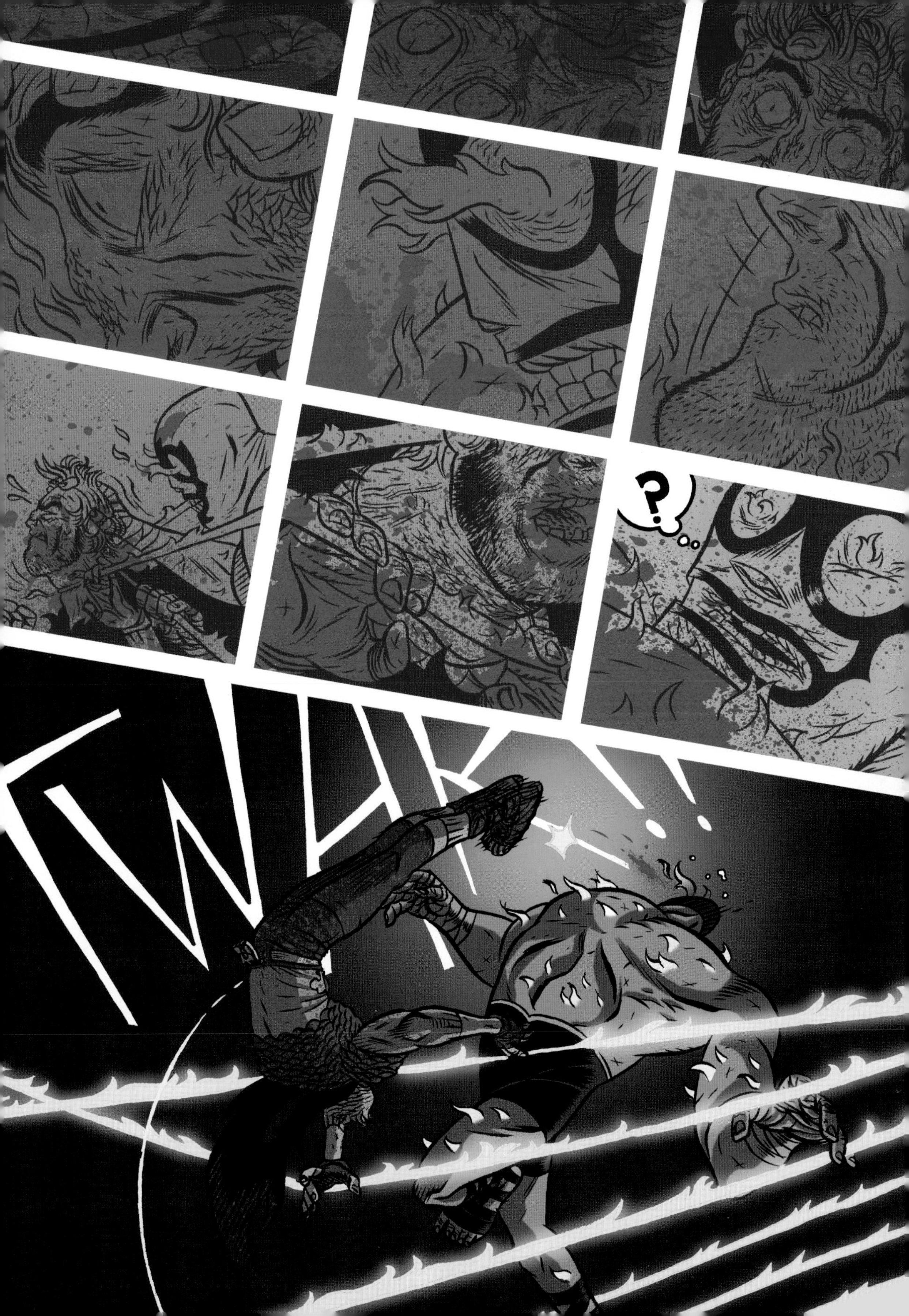
?

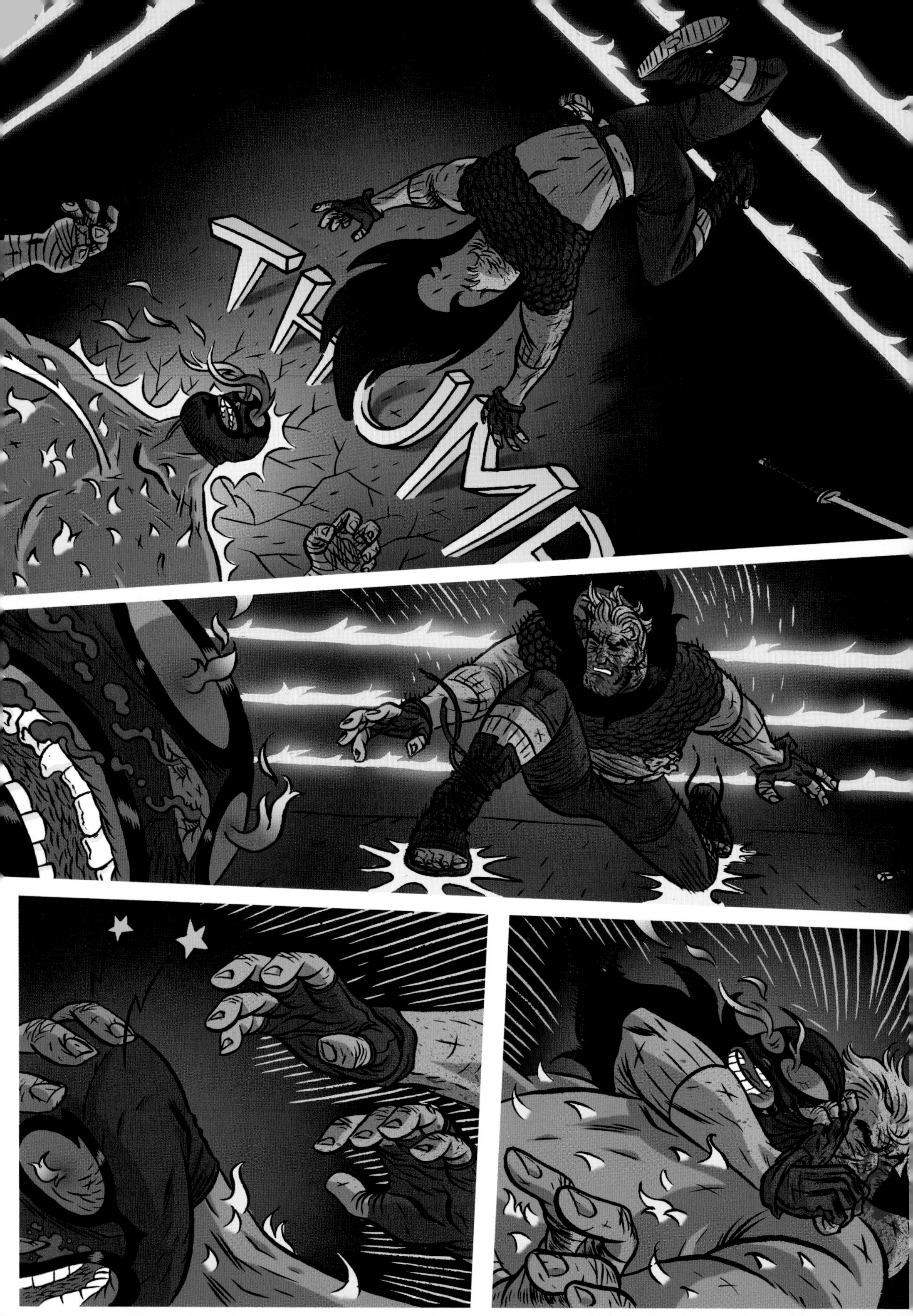
THUMP

NO...

NO!!

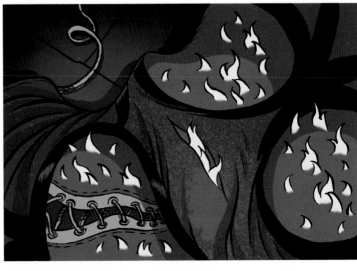

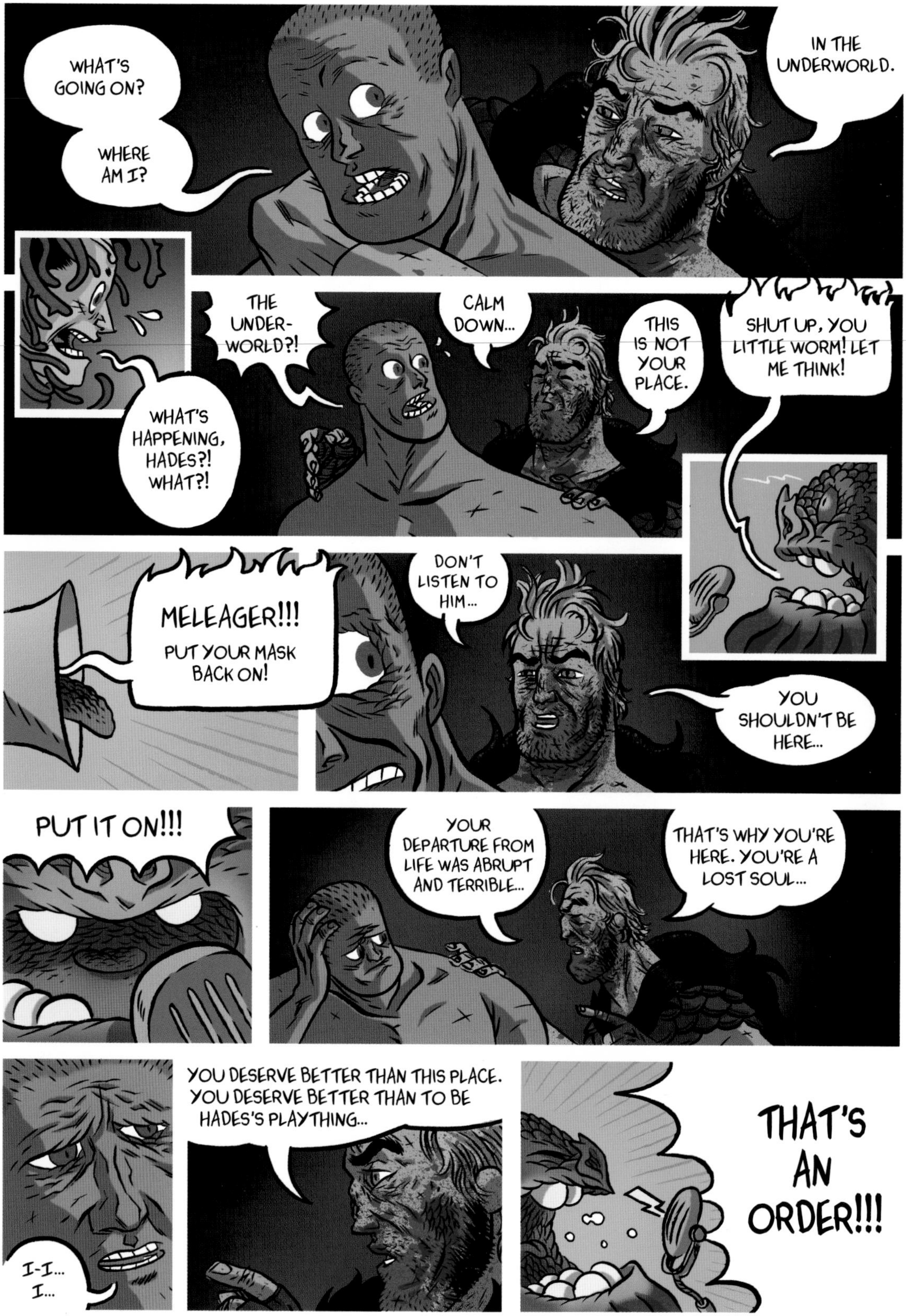
WHAT'S GOING ON?
WHERE AM I?
IN THE UNDERWORLD.
THE UNDER-WORLD?!
WHAT'S HAPPENING, HADES?! WHAT?!
CALM DOWN...
THIS IS NOT YOUR PLACE.
SHUT UP, YOU LITTLE WORM! LET ME THINK!
MELEAGER!!! PUT YOUR MASK BACK ON!
DON'T LISTEN TO HIM...
YOU SHOULDN'T BE HERE...
PUT IT ON!!!
YOUR DEPARTURE FROM LIFE WAS ABRUPT AND TERRIBLE...
THAT'S WHY YOU'RE HERE. YOU'RE A LOST SOUL...
I-I... I...
YOU DESERVE BETTER THAN THIS PLACE. YOU DESERVE BETTER THAN TO BE HADES'S PLAYTHING...
THAT'S AN ORDER!!!

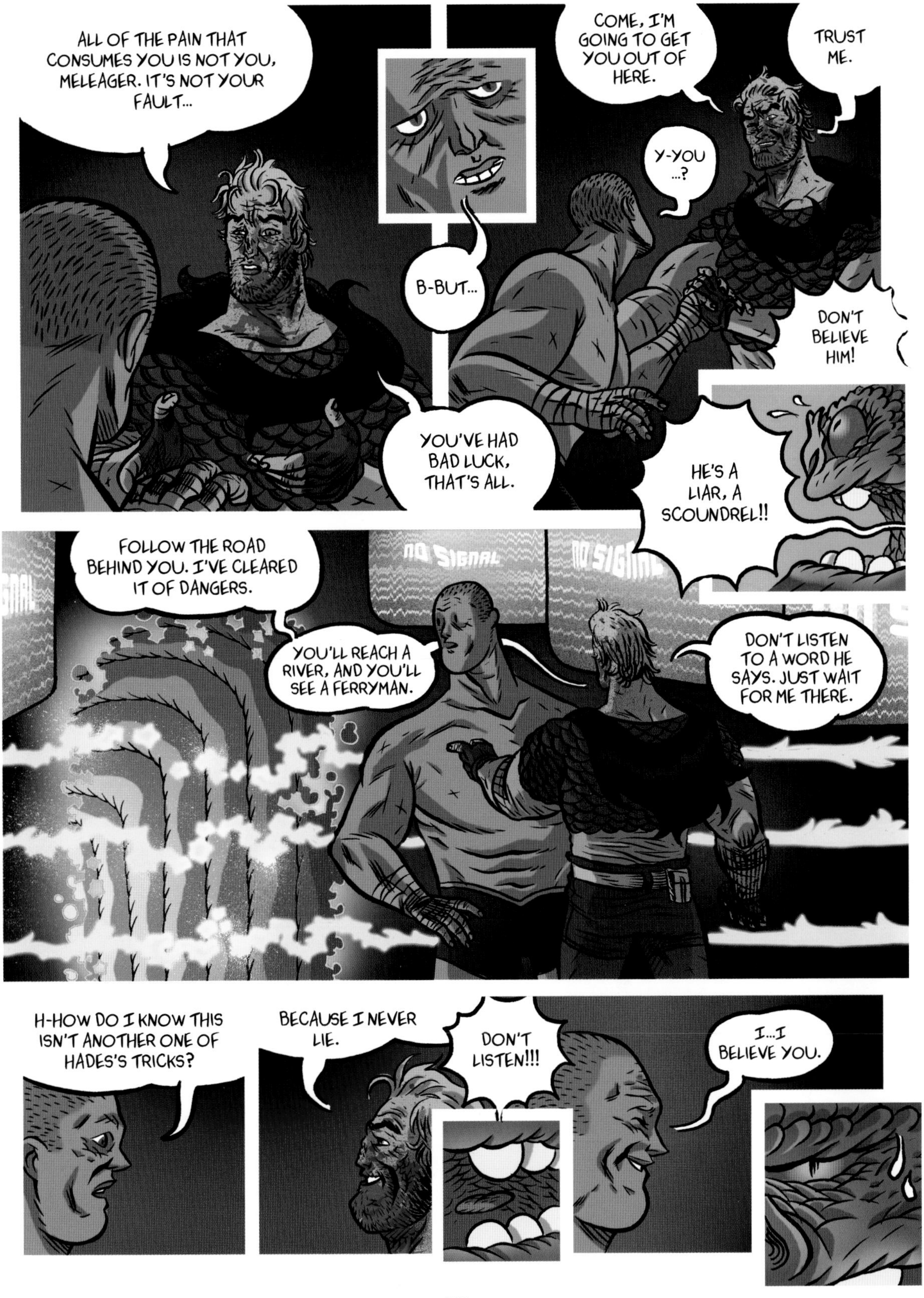

ALL OF THE PAIN THAT CONSUMES YOU IS NOT YOU, MELEAGER. IT'S NOT YOUR FAULT...
YOU'VE HAD BAD LUCK, THAT'S ALL.
B-BUT...
COME, I'M GOING TO GET YOU OUT OF HERE.
Y-YOU ...?
TRUST ME.
DON'T BELIEVE HIM!
HE'S A LIAR, A SCOUNDREL!!
FOLLOW THE ROAD BEHIND YOU. I'VE CLEARED IT OF DANGERS.
NO SIGNAL
NO SIGNAL
YOU'LL REACH A RIVER, AND YOU'LL SEE A FERRYMAN.
DON'T LISTEN TO A WORD HE SAYS. JUST WAIT FOR ME THERE.
H-HOW DO I KNOW THIS ISN'T ANOTHER ONE OF HADES'S TRICKS?
BECAUSE I NEVER LIE.
DON'T LISTEN!!!
I...I BELIEVE YOU.

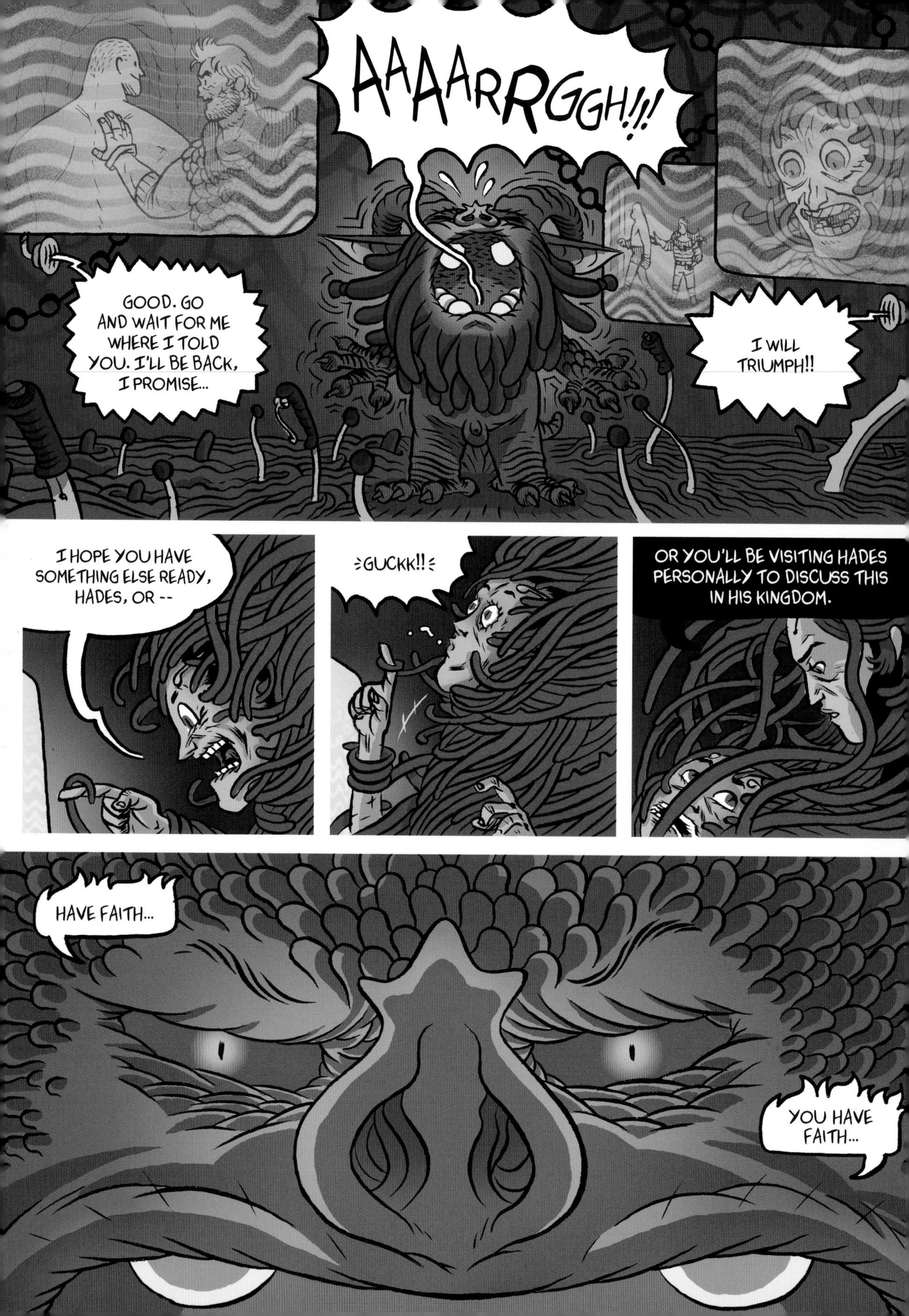
AAAARRGGH!!!
GOOD. GO AND WAIT FOR ME WHERE I TOLD YOU. I'LL BE BACK, I PROMISE...
I WILL TRIUMPH!!
I HOPE YOU HAVE SOMETHING ELSE READY, HADES, OR --
GUCKK!!
OR YOU'LL BE VISITING HADES PERSONALLY TO DISCUSS THIS IN HIS KINGDOM.
HAVE FAITH...
YOU HAVE FAITH...

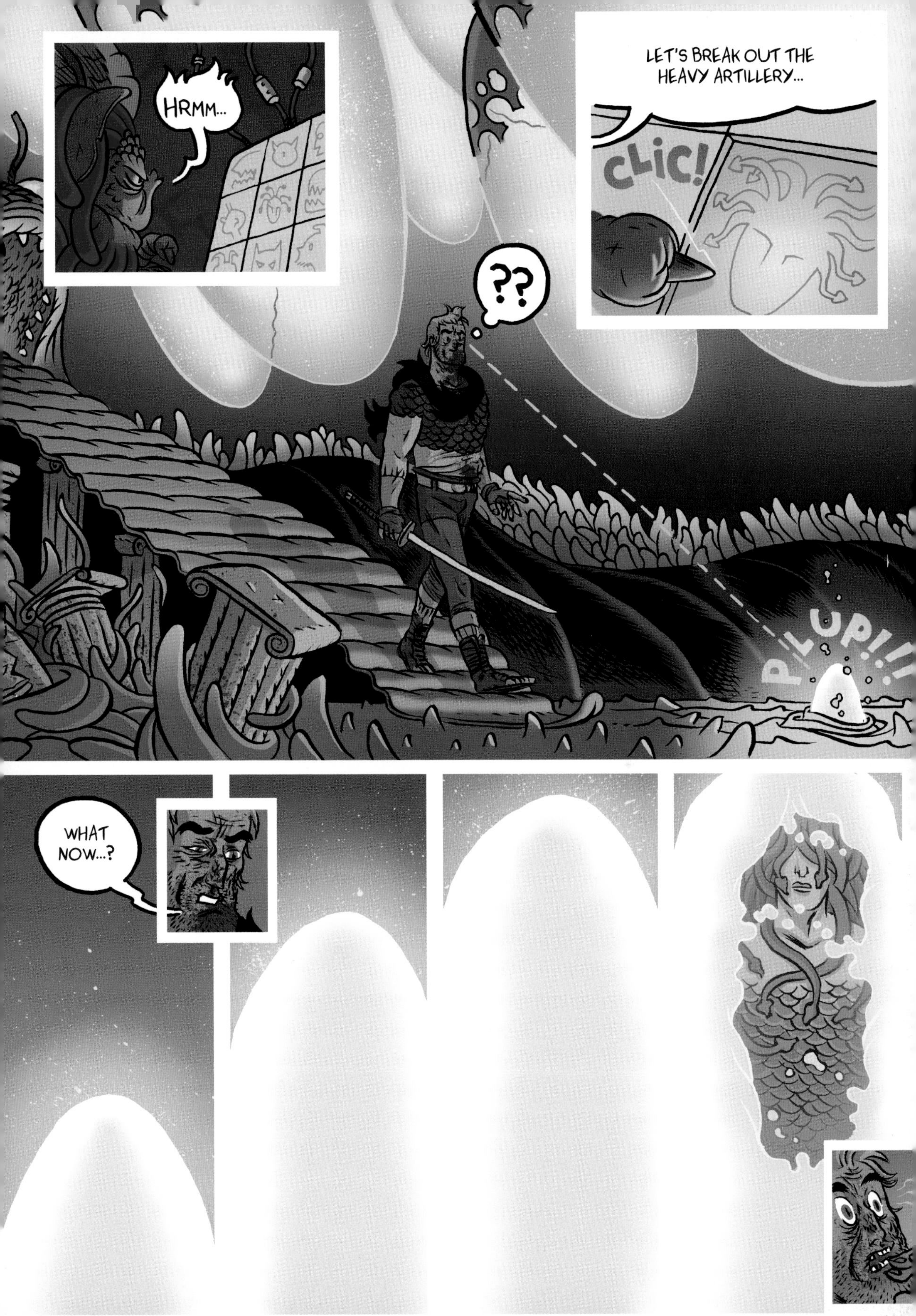
HRMM...
LET'S BREAK OUT THE HEAVY ARTILLERY...
CLIC!
??
PLUP!!!!
WHAT NOW...?

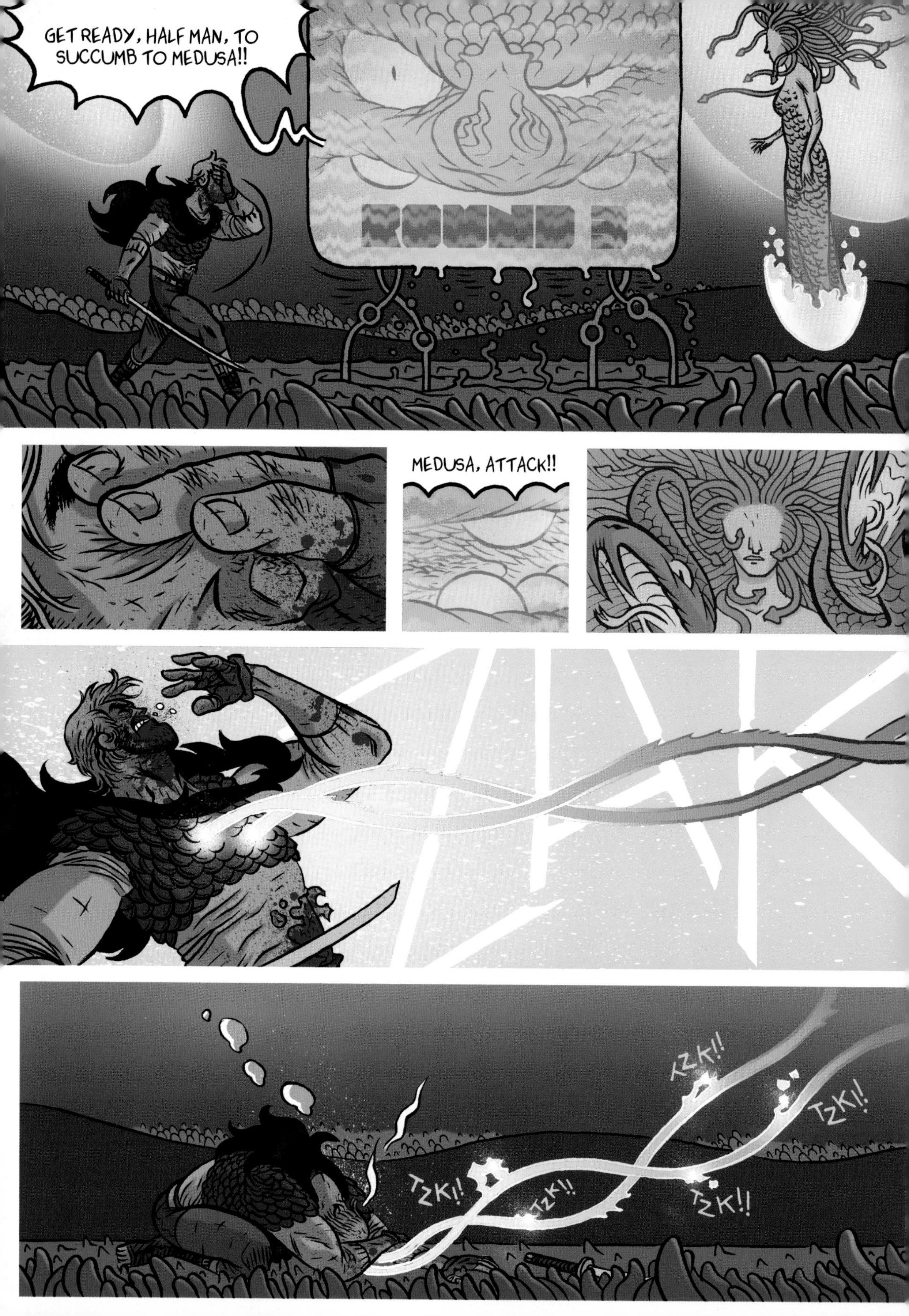

GET READY, HALF MAN, TO SUCCUMB TO MEDUSA!!
ROUND 3
MEDUSA, ATTACK!!
TZK!!
TZK!!
TZK!!
TZK!!
TZK!!

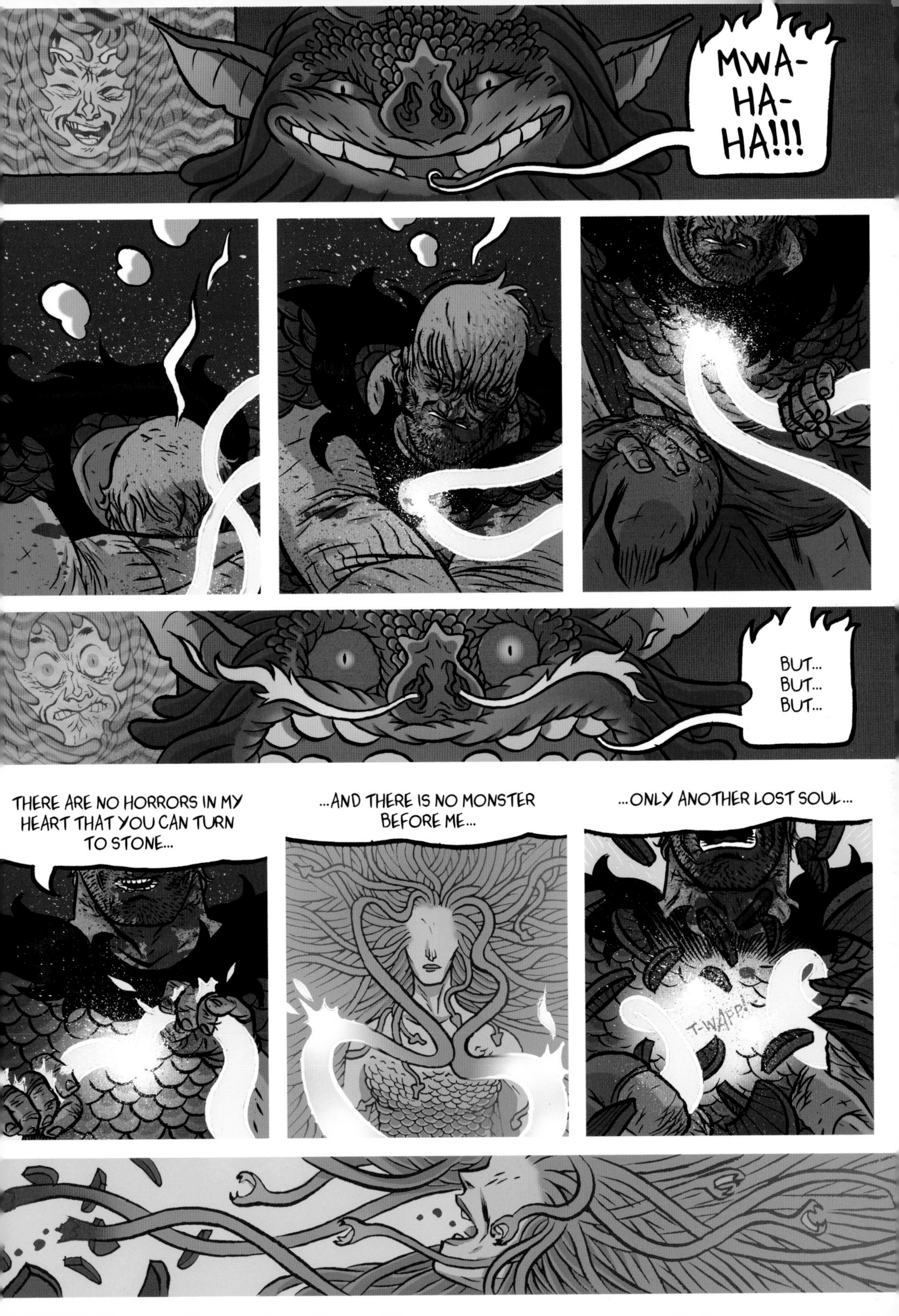
MWA-
HA-
HA!!!
BUT...
BUT...
BUT...
THERE ARE NO HORRORS IN MY HEART THAT YOU CAN TURN TO STONE...
...AND THERE IS NO MONSTER BEFORE ME...
...ONLY ANOTHER LOST SOUL...
T-WAPP!

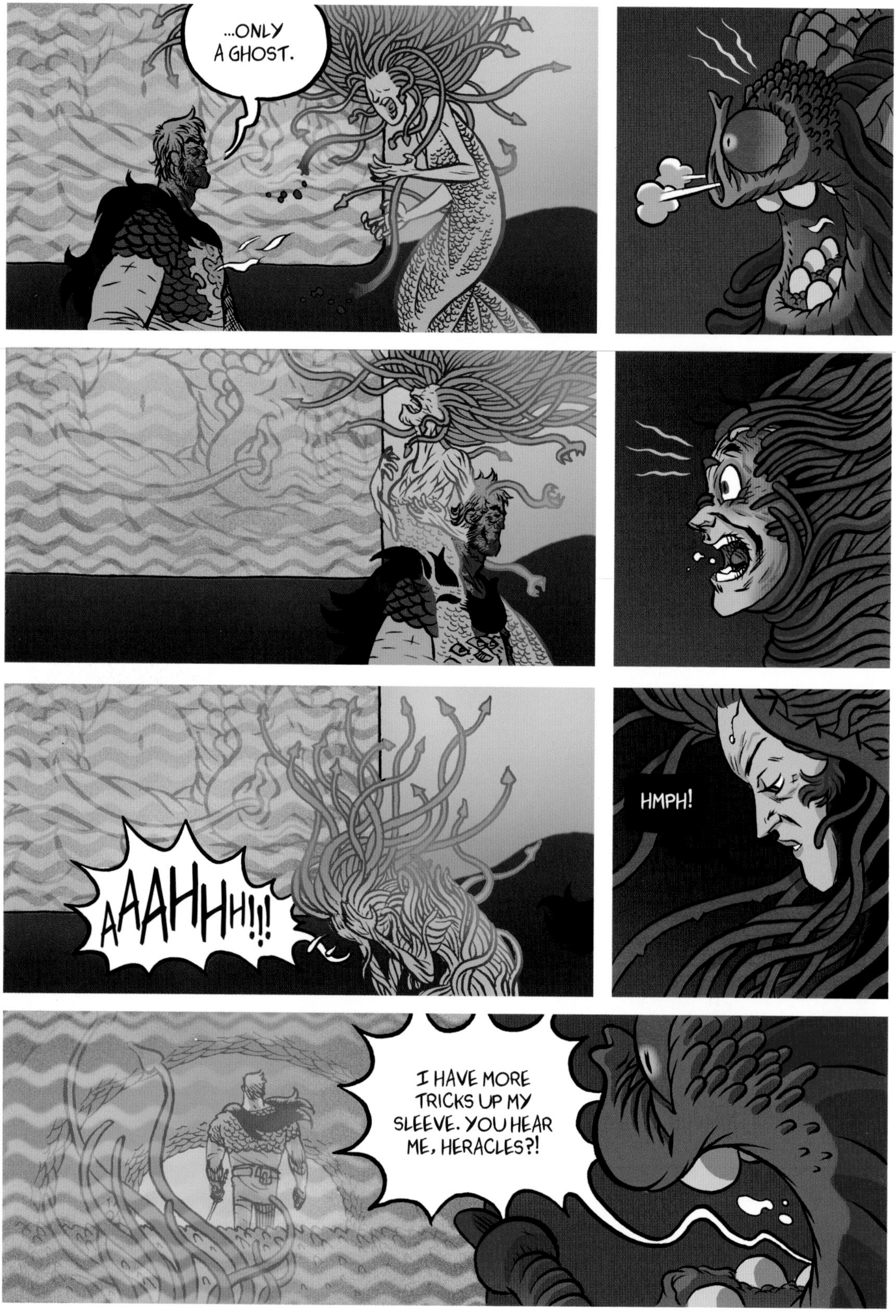
...ONLY A GHOST.
AAAHHH!!!
HMPH!
I HAVE MORE TRICKS UP MY SLEEVE. YOU HEAR ME, HERACLES?!

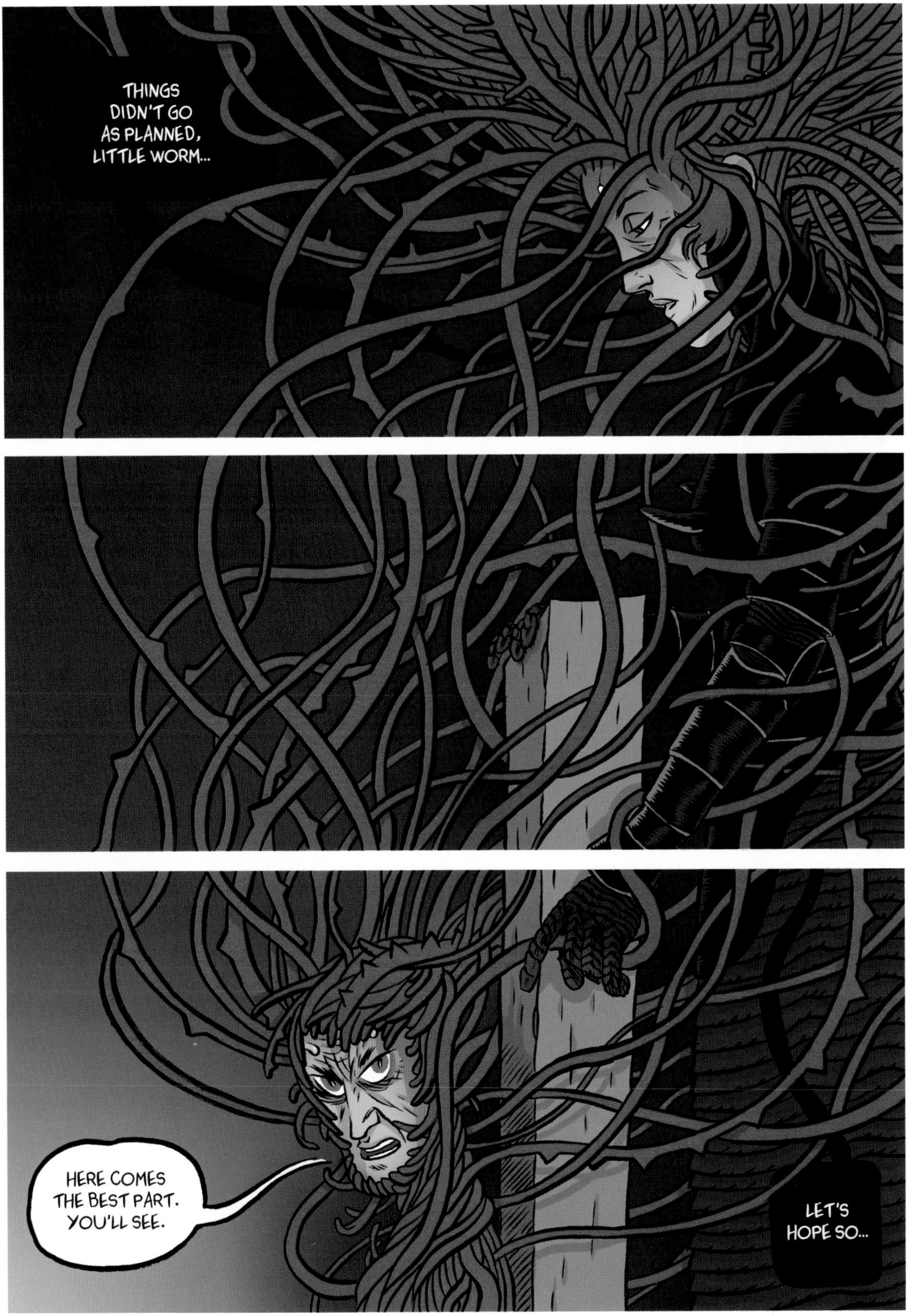
THINGS DIDN'T GO AS PLANNED, LITTLE WORM...
HERE COMES THE BEST PART. YOU'LL SEE.
LET'S HOPE SO...

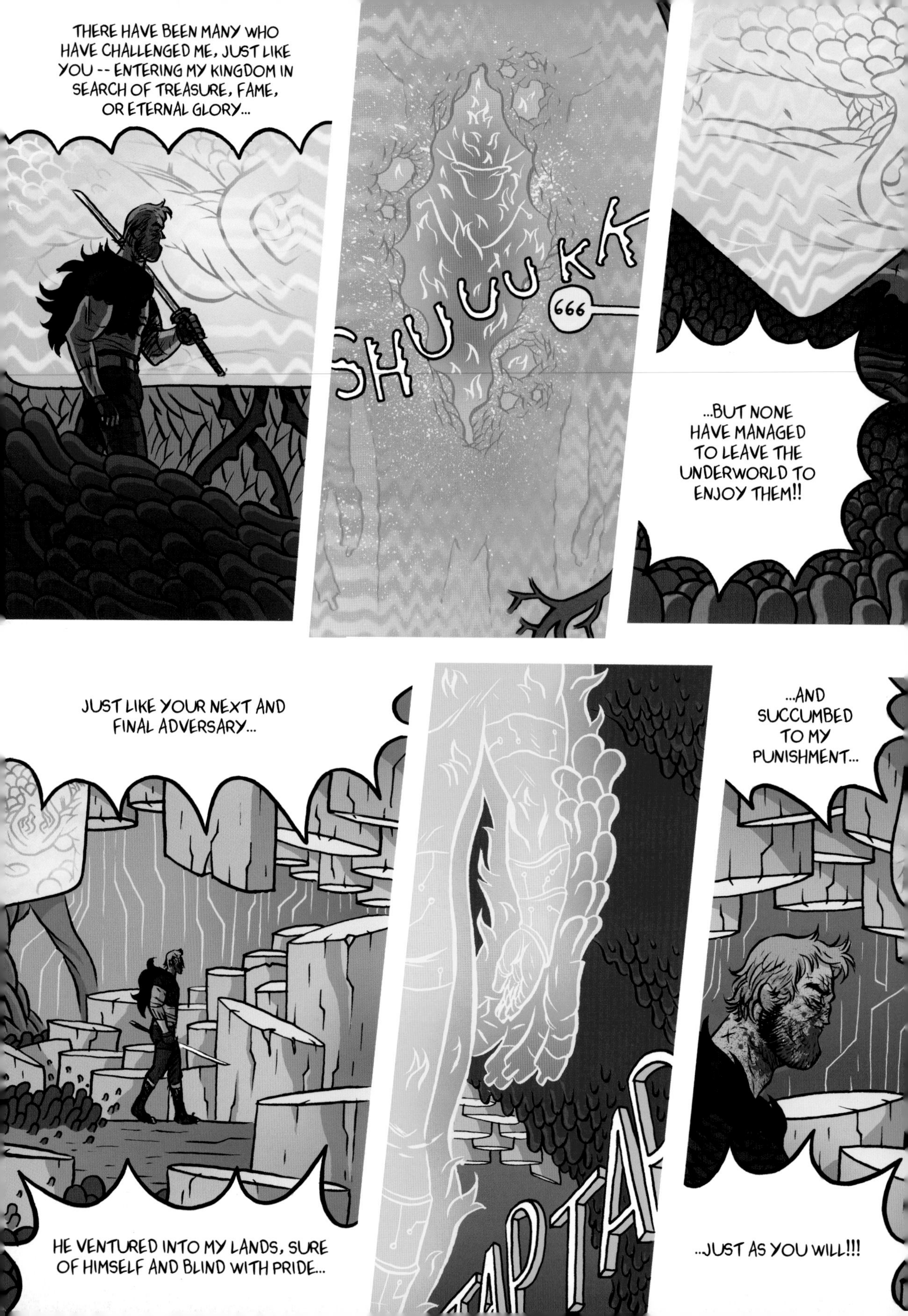

THERE HAVE BEEN MANY WHO HAVE CHALLENGED ME, JUST LIKE YOU -- ENTERING MY KINGDOM IN SEARCH OF TREASURE, FAME, OR ETERNAL GLORY...
SHUUUKK
666
...BUT NONE HAVE MANAGED TO LEAVE THE UNDERWORLD TO ENJOY THEM!!
JUST LIKE YOUR NEXT AND FINAL ADVERSARY...
HE VENTURED INTO MY LANDS, SURE OF HIMSELF AND BLIND WITH PRIDE...
TAP TAP
...AND SUCCUMBED TO MY PUNISHMENT...
...JUST AS YOU WILL!!!

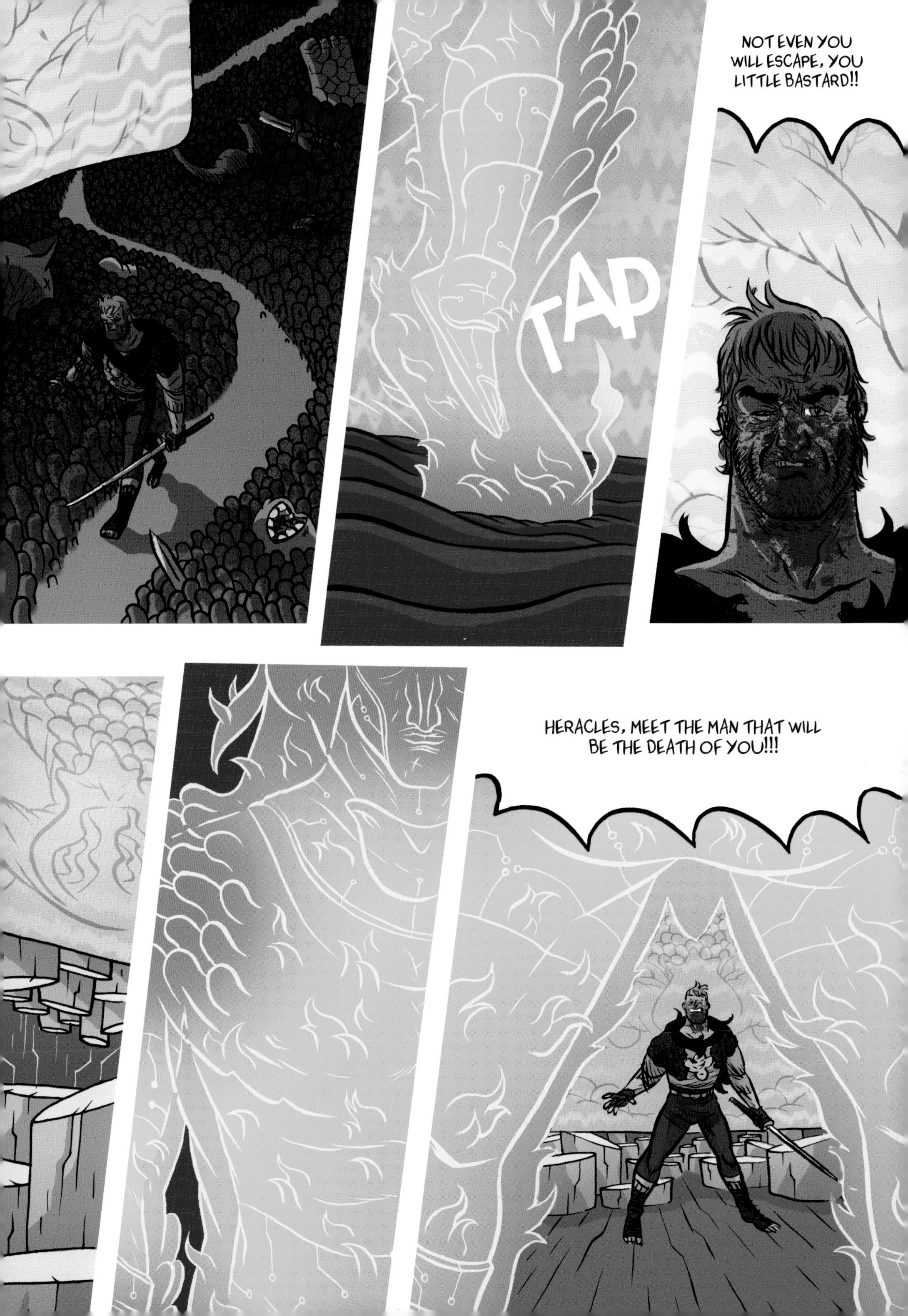
TAP
NOT EVEN YOU WILL ESCAPE, YOU LITTLE BASTARD!!
HERACLES, MEET THE MAN THAT WILL BE THE DEATH OF YOU!!!

THESEUS!!!

H-H- HELP... ME...

THESEUS!

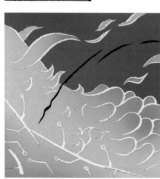

PLOFF!

CA...

WHAT?

CA- CARE...

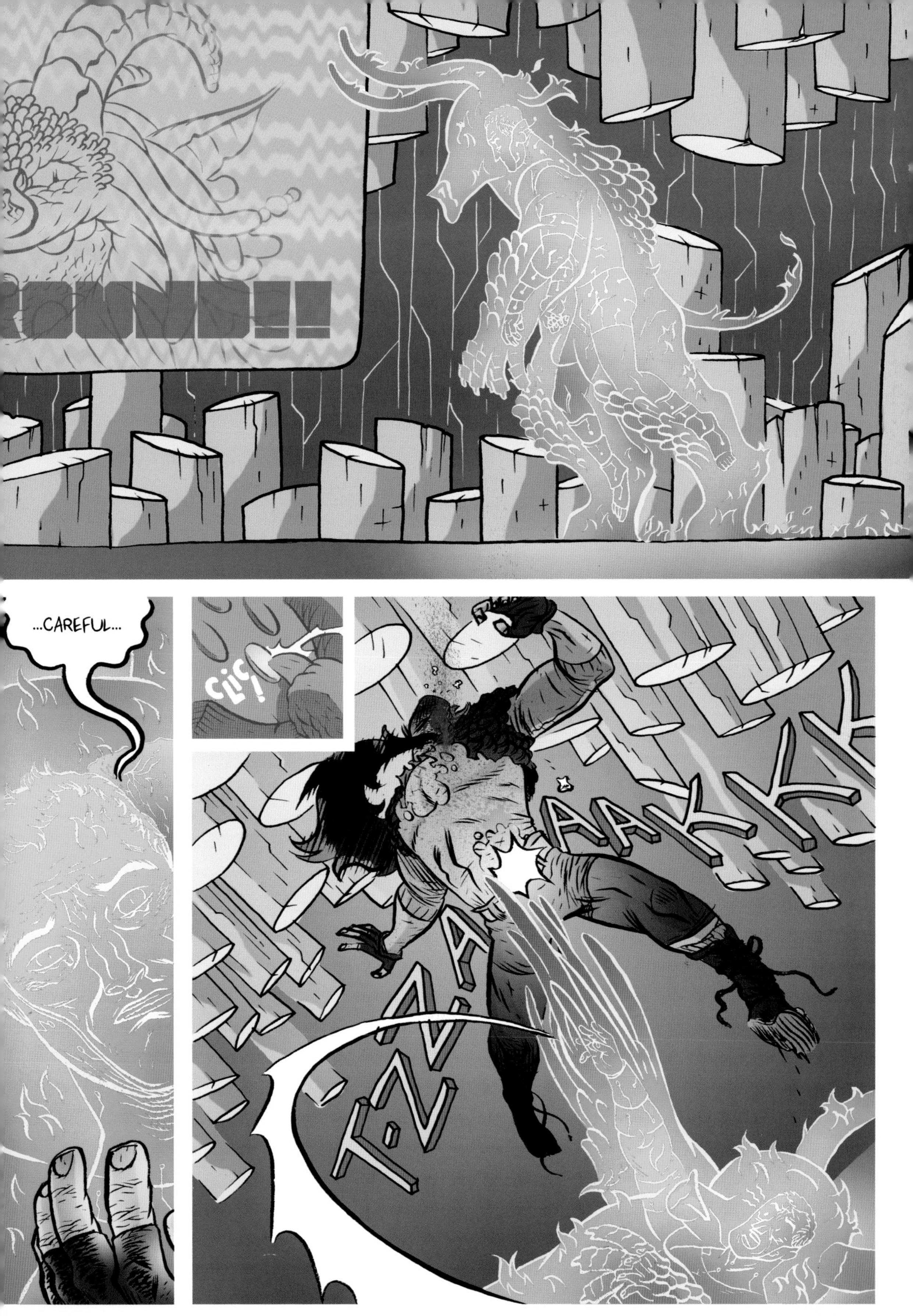

ROUND!!
...CAREFUL...
CLIC!
TZNAAAKKK

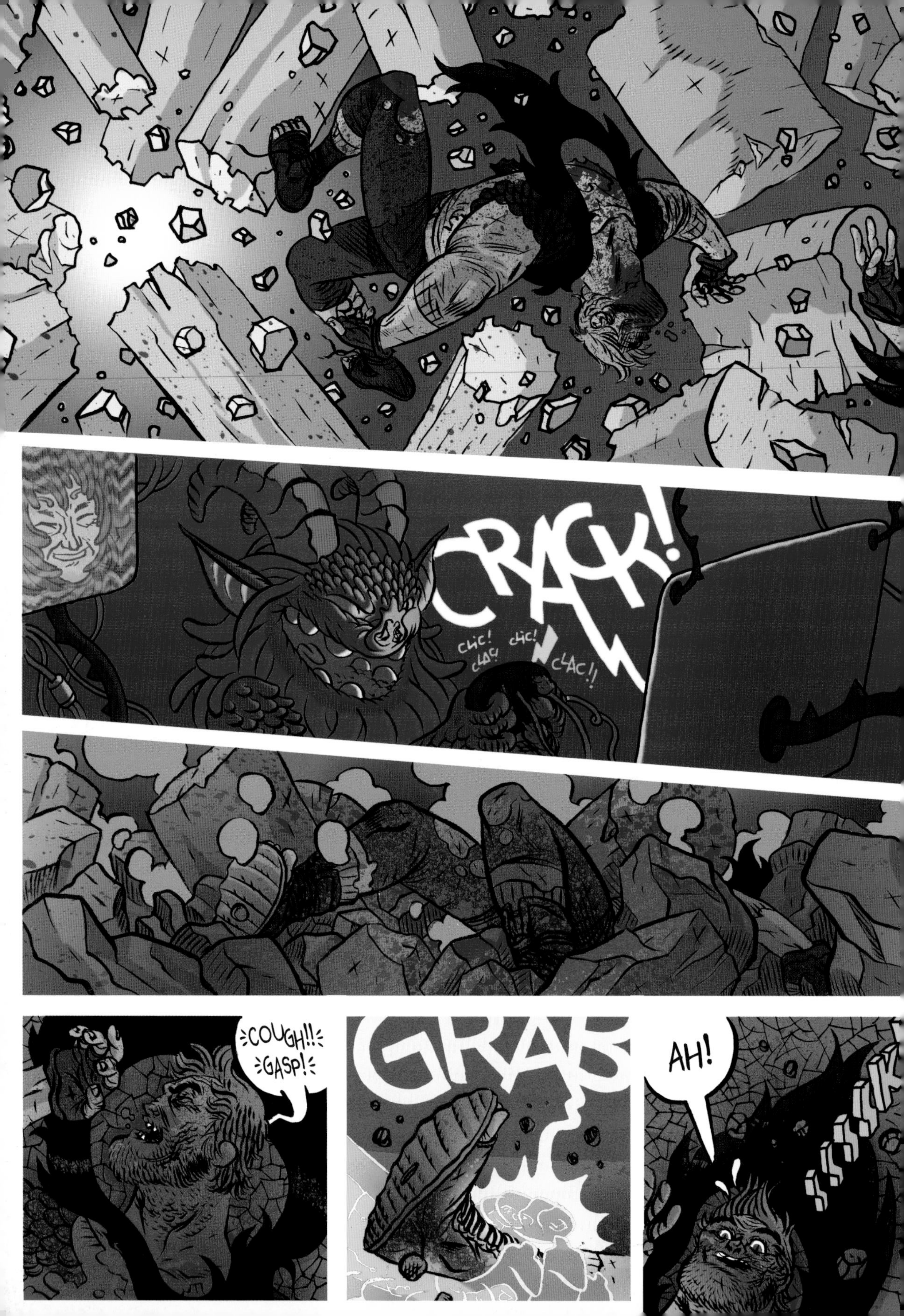
CRACK!
chic! clac! chic! CLAC!!
COUGH!! GASP!
GRAB
AH!

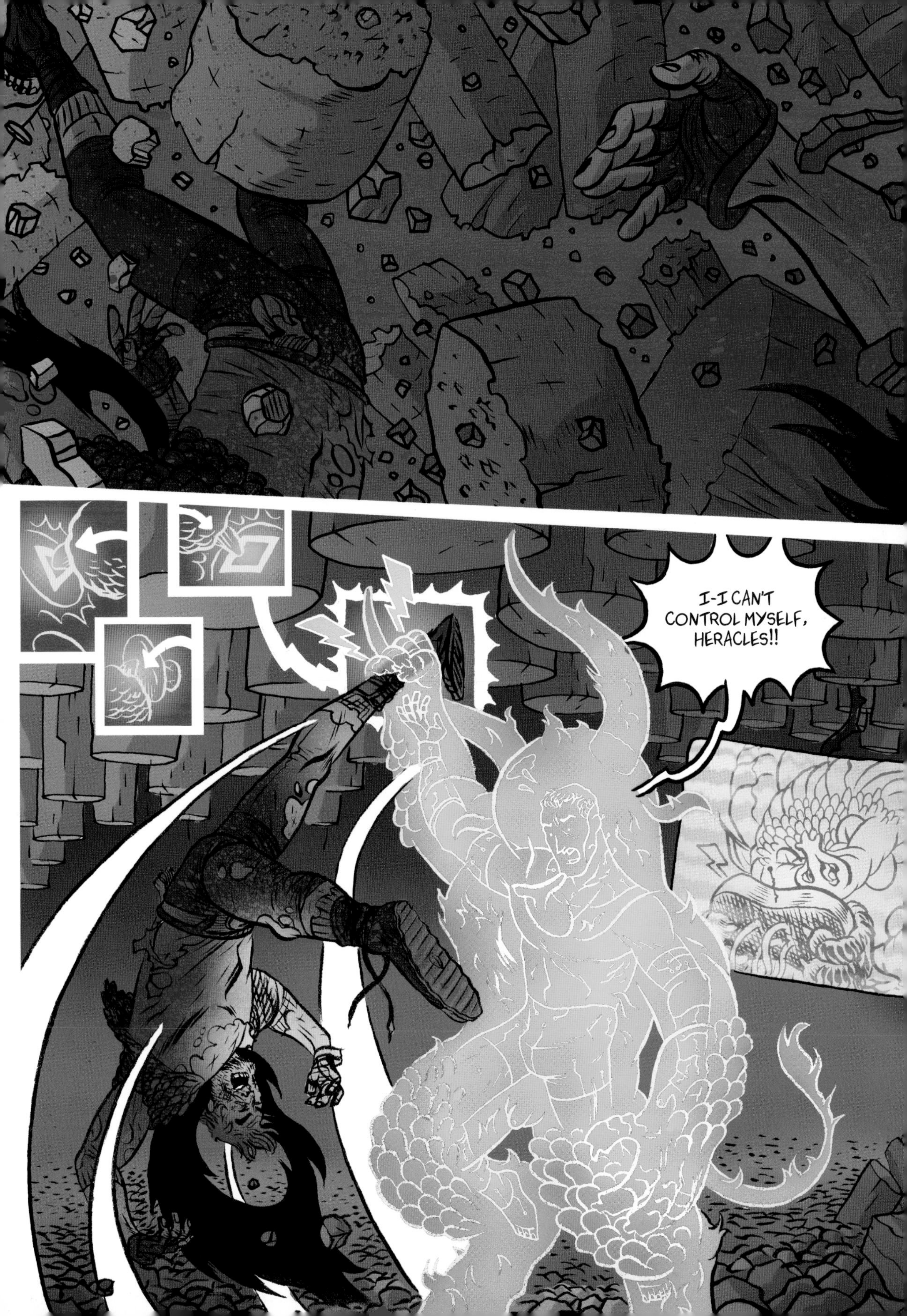
I-I CAN'T CONTROL MYSELF, HERACLES!!

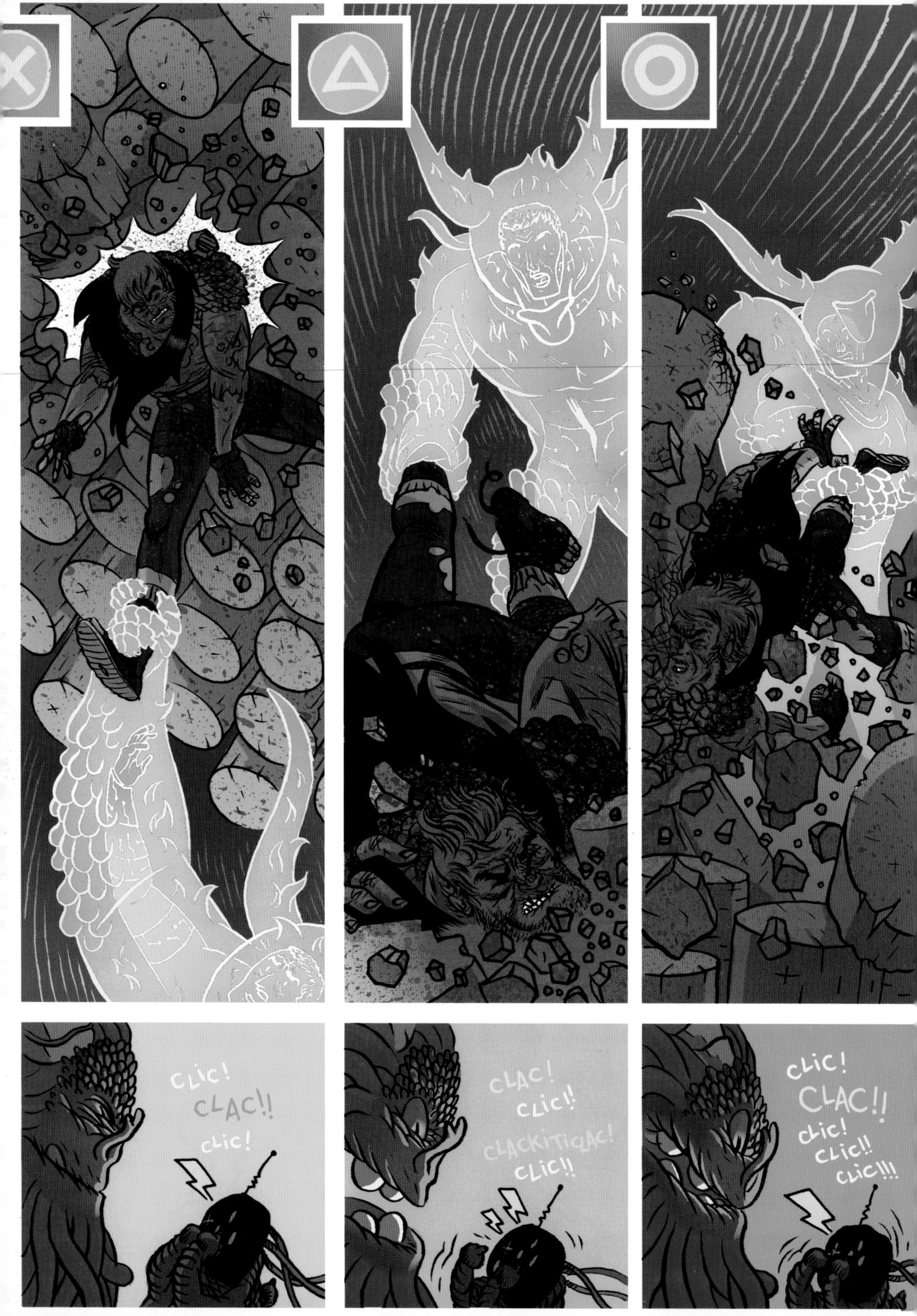
CLIC!
CLAC!!
CLIC!
CLAC!
CLIC!!
CLACKITICLAC!
CLIC!!
CLIC!
CLAC!!
CLIC!
CLIC!!
CLIC!!!

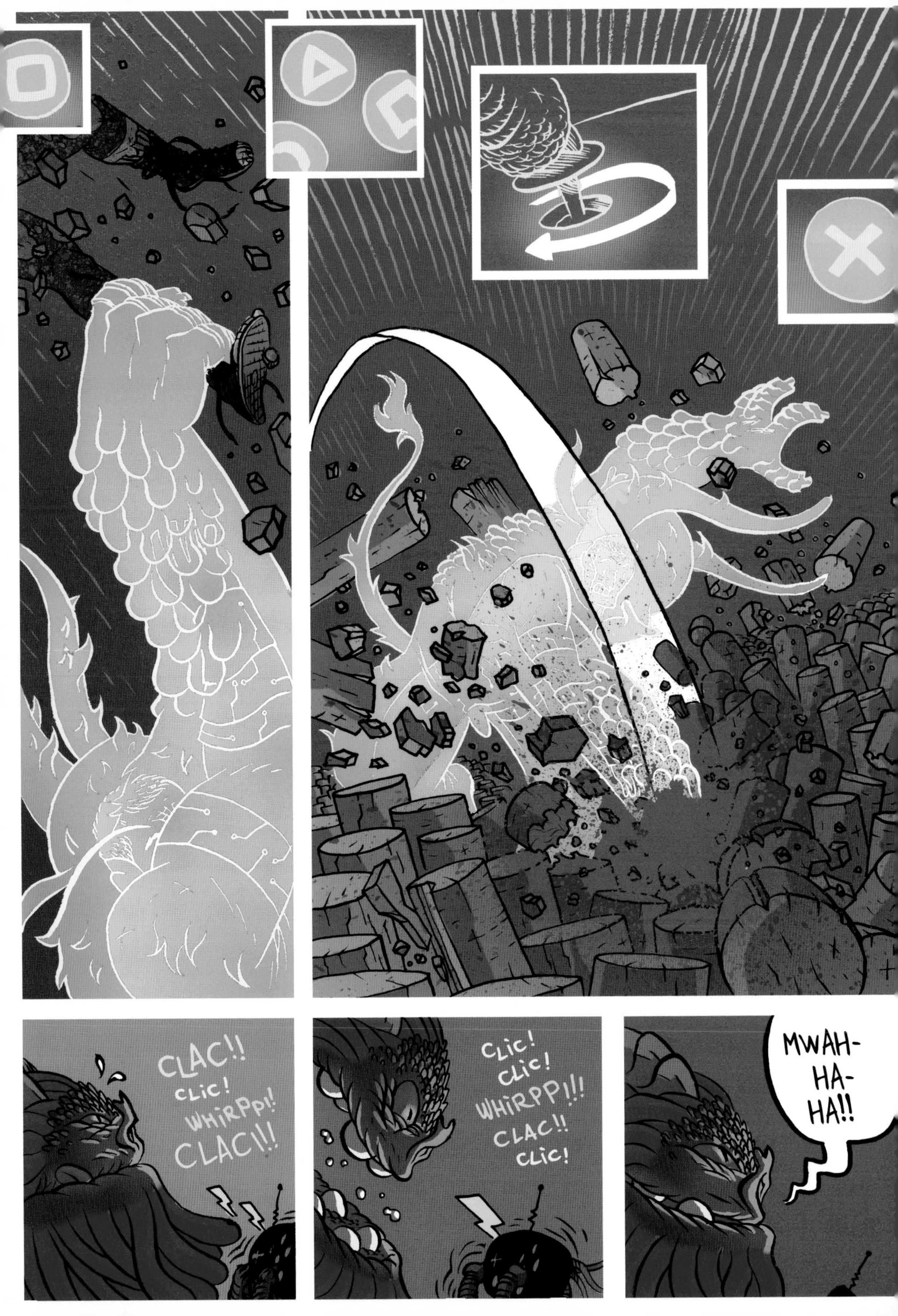

CLAC!!
CLIC!
WHIRPP!!
CLAC!!!
CLIC!
CLIC!
WHIRPP!!!
CLAC!!
CLIC!
MWAH-HA-HA!!

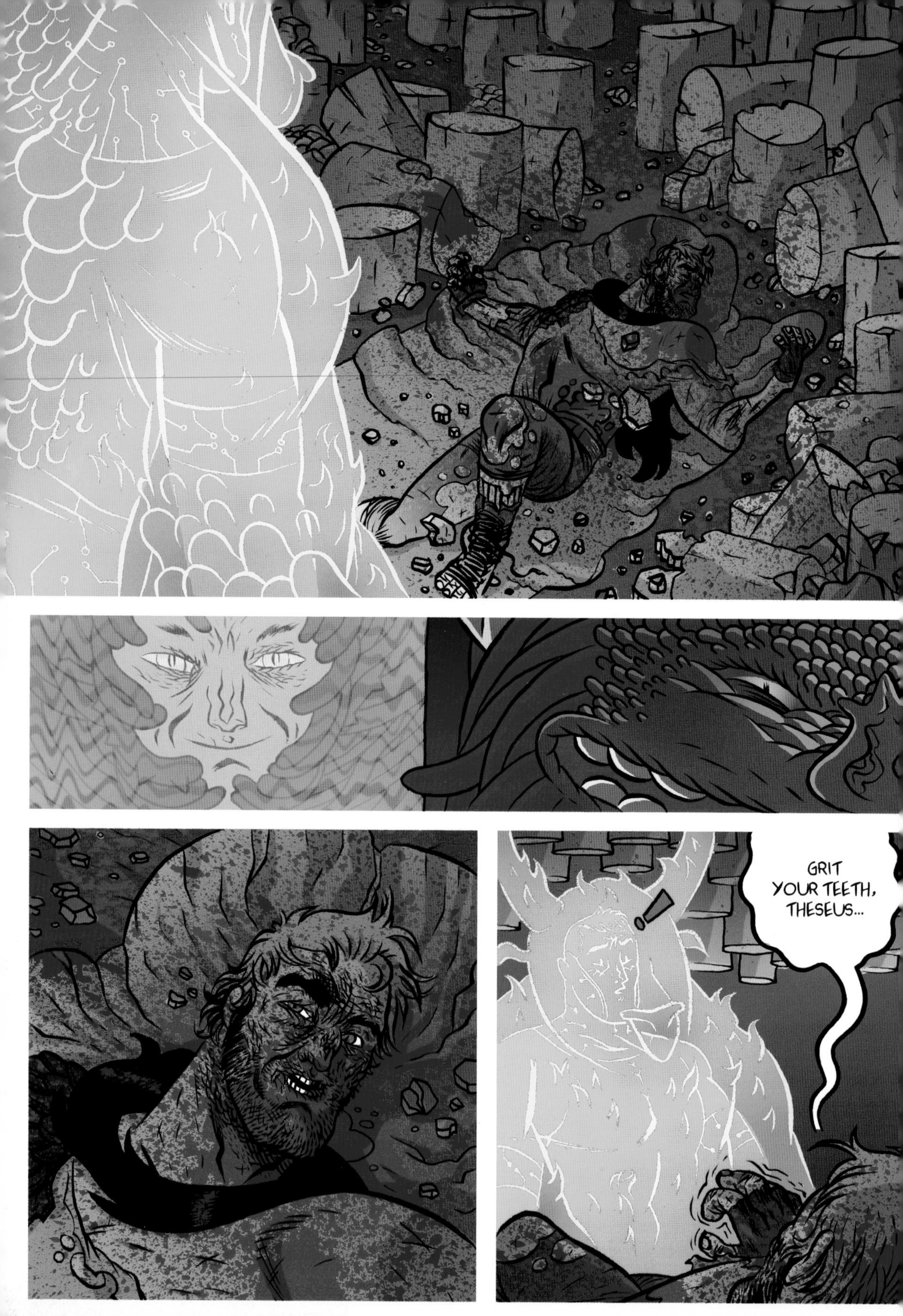
!
GRIT YOUR TEETH, THESEUS...

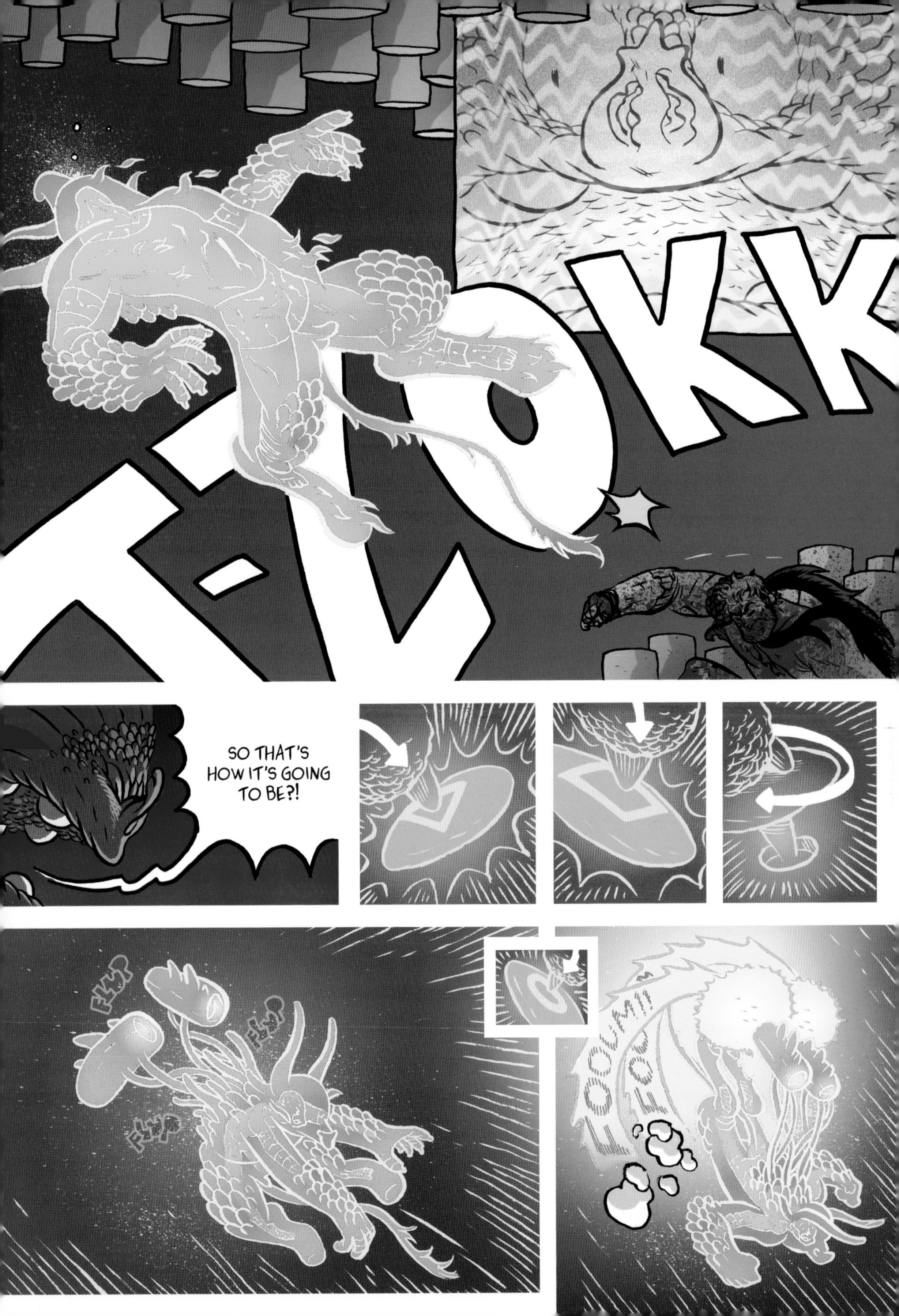
T-TOKK
SO THAT'S HOW IT'S GOING TO BE?!
FLUP
FLUP
FLUP

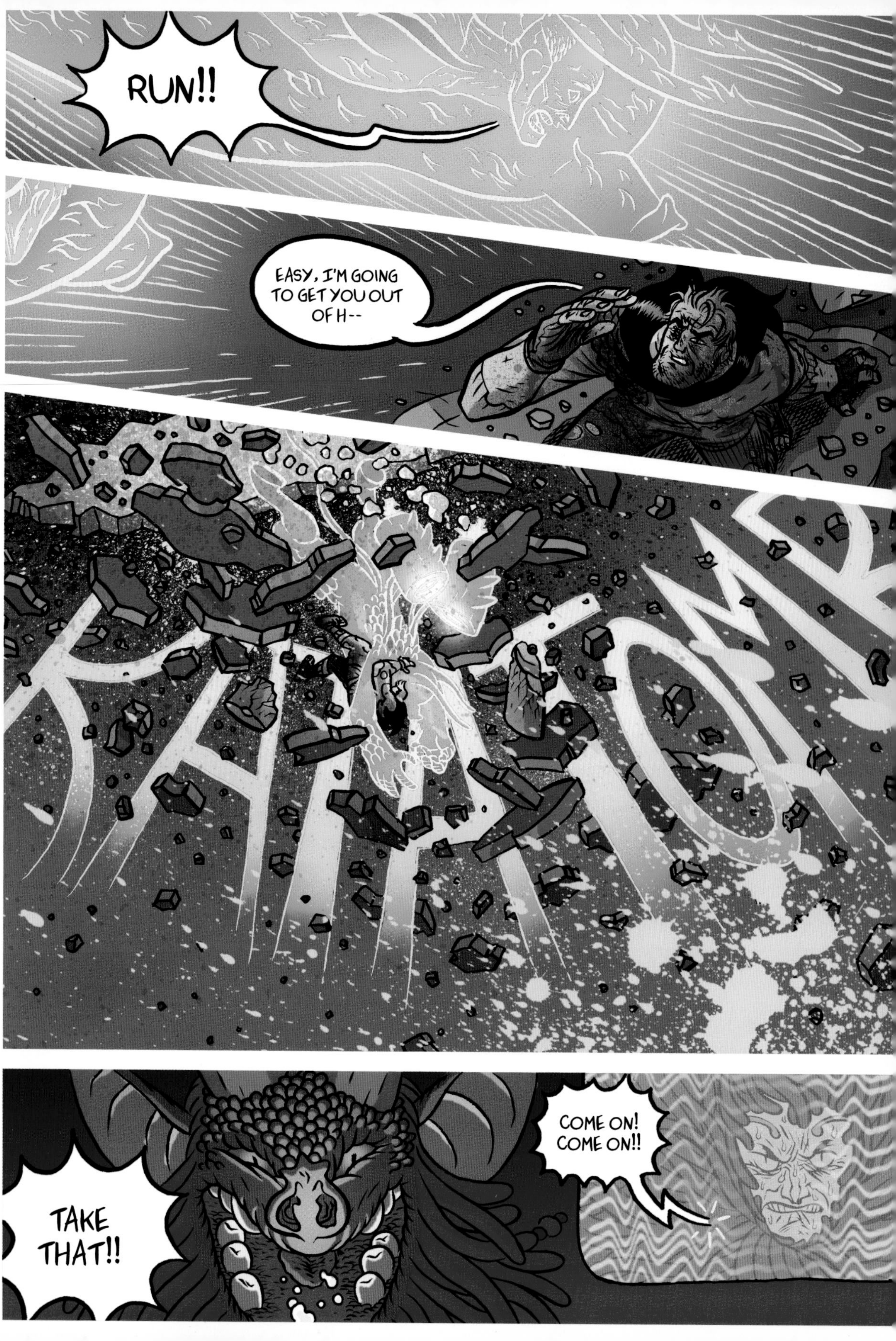
RUN!!
EASY, I'M GOING TO GET YOU OUT OF H--
COME ON! COME ON!!
TAKE THAT!!

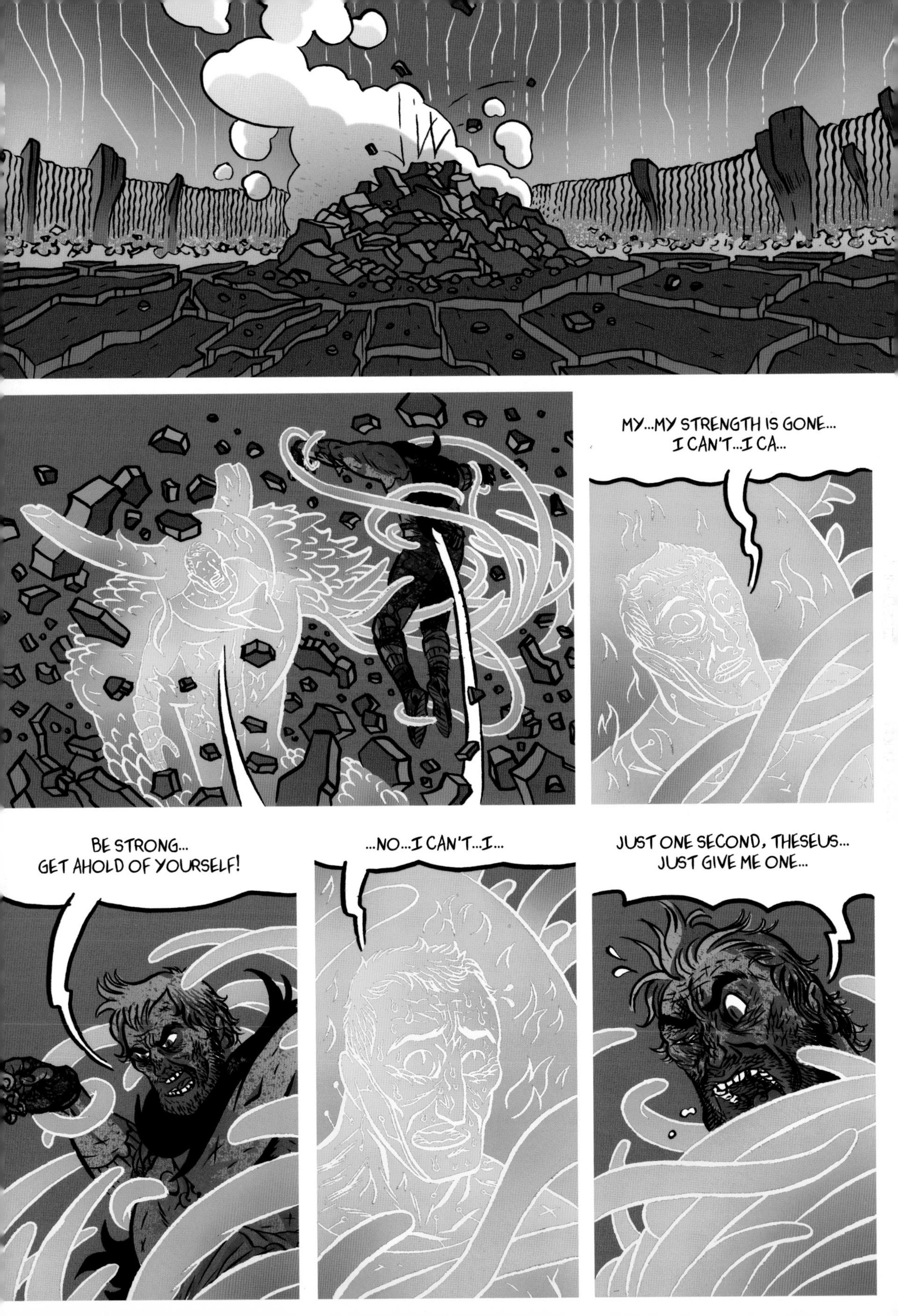
MY...MY STRENGTH IS GONE...
I CAN'T...I CA...
BE STRONG...
GET AHOLD OF YOURSELF!
...NO...I CAN'T...I...
JUST ONE SECOND, THESEUS...
JUST GIVE ME ONE...

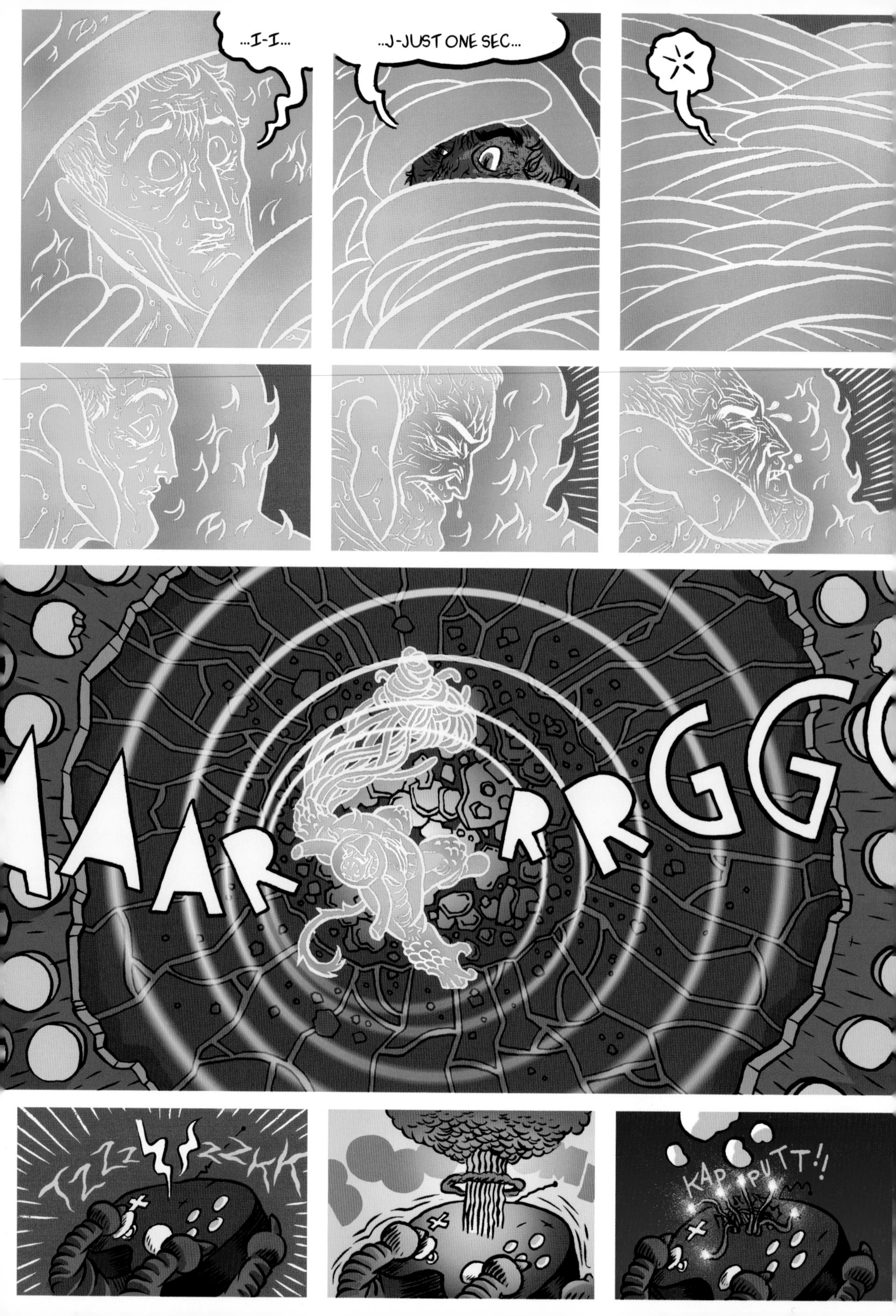
...I-I...
...J-JUST ONE SEC...
AAARRRGG
TZZZZZZZKK
KAPUTT!!

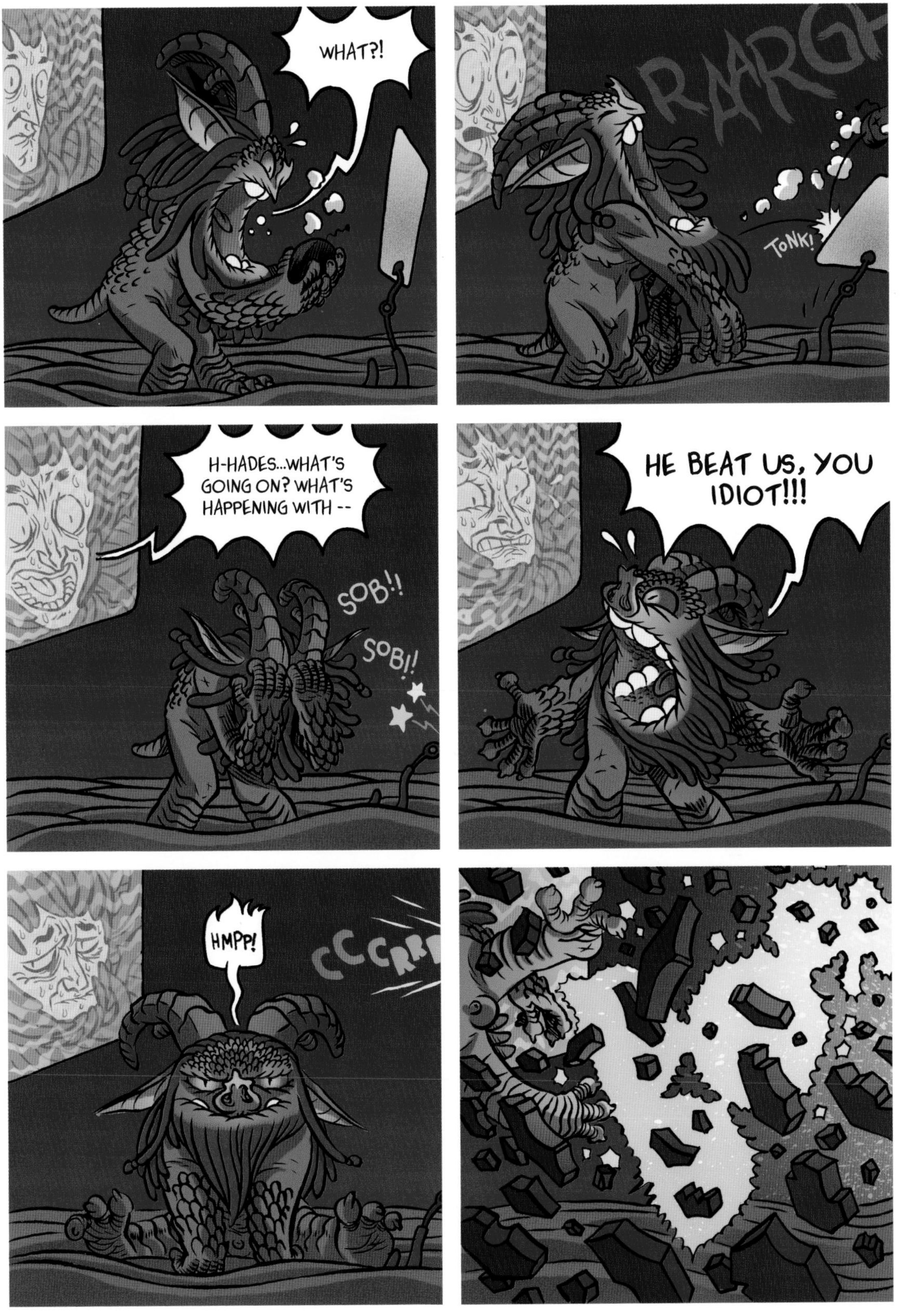
WHAT?!
RAARGH
TONK!
H-HADES...WHAT'S GOING ON? WHAT'S HAPPENING WITH --
SOB!!
SOB!!
HE BEAT US, YOU IDIOT!!!
HMPP!
CCCRR

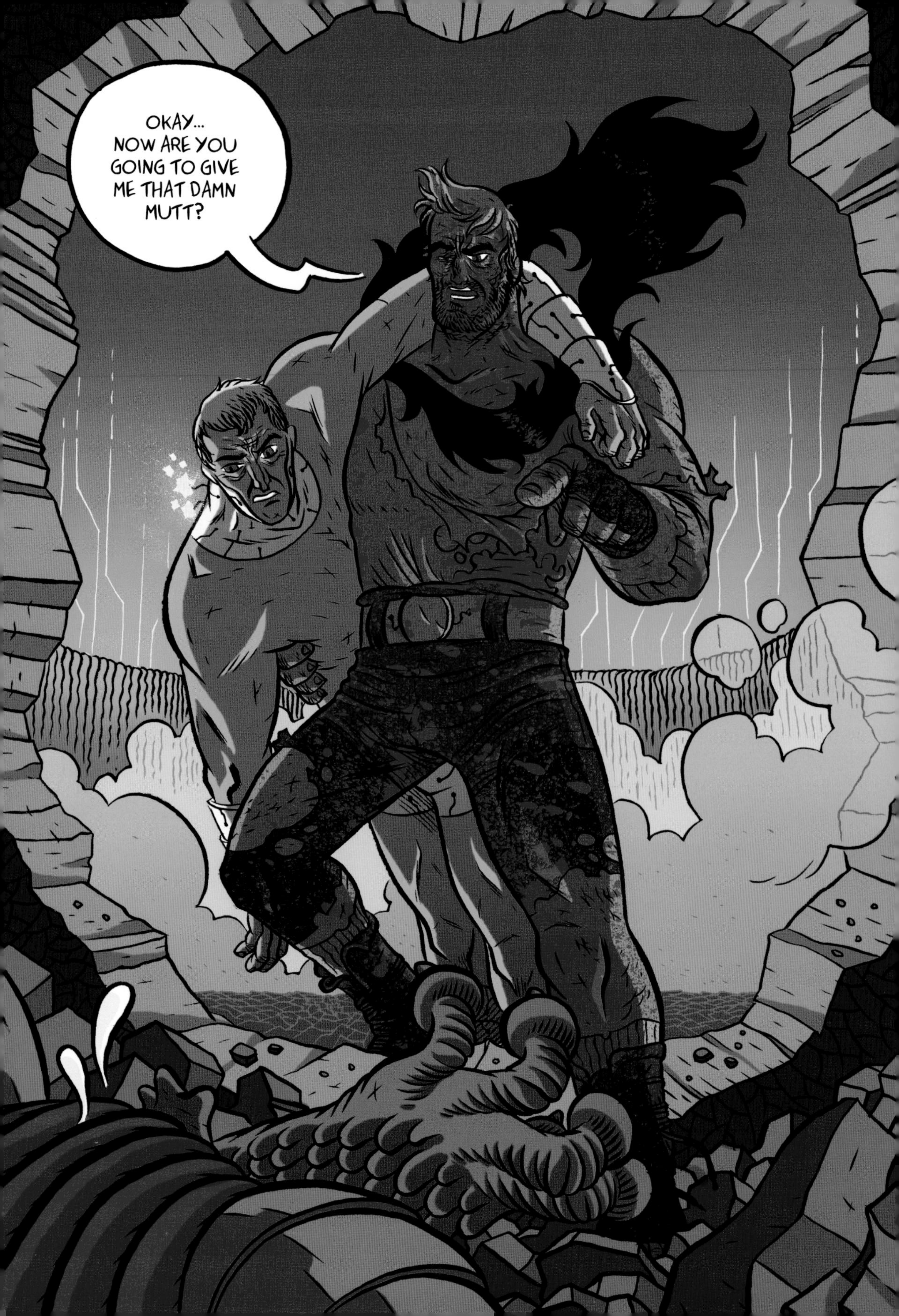
OKAY... NOW ARE YOU GOING TO GIVE ME THAT DAMN MUTT?

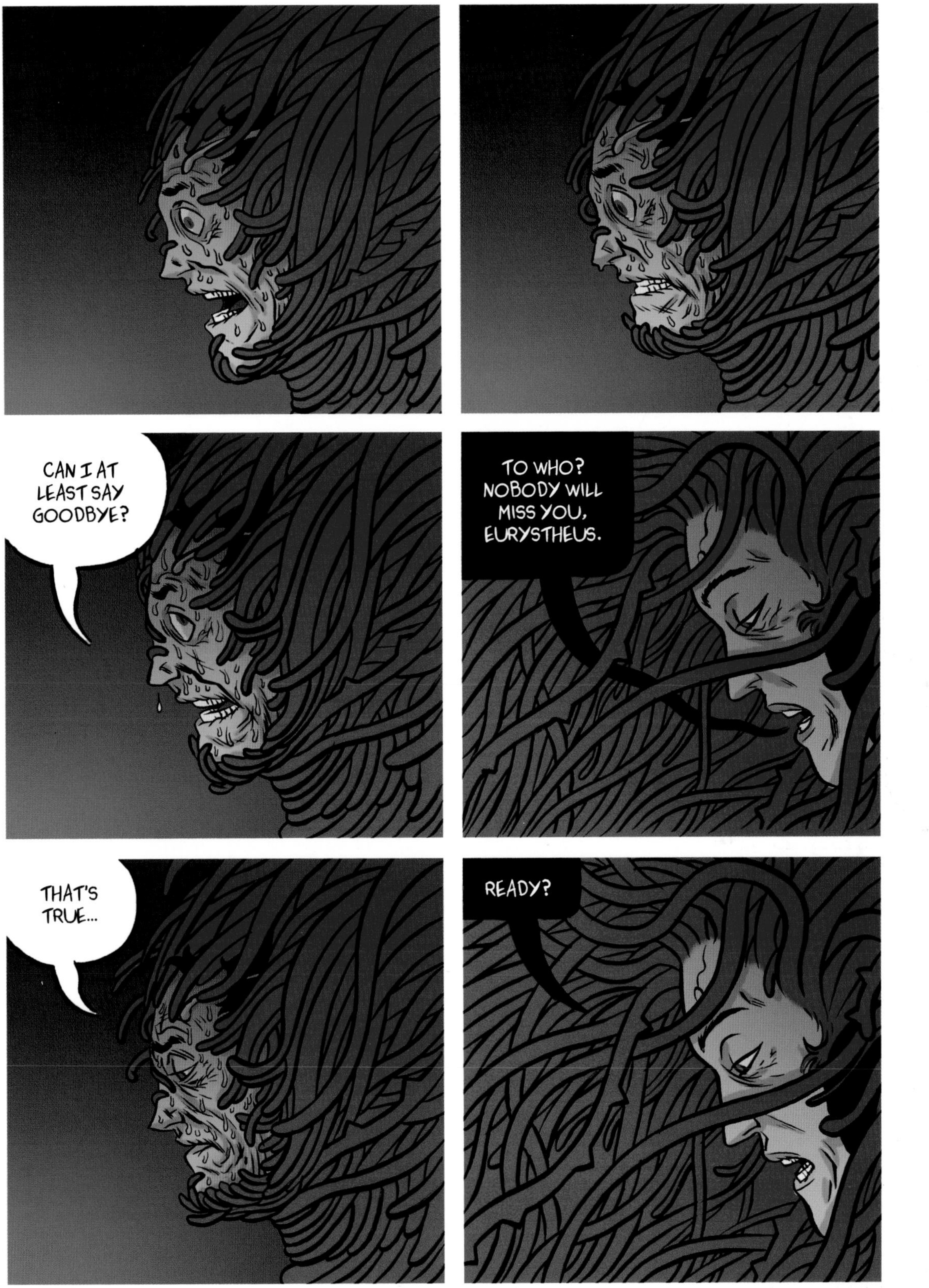
CAN I AT LEAST SAY GOODBYE?
TO WHO? NOBODY WILL MISS YOU, EURYSTHEUS.
THAT'S TRUE...
READY?

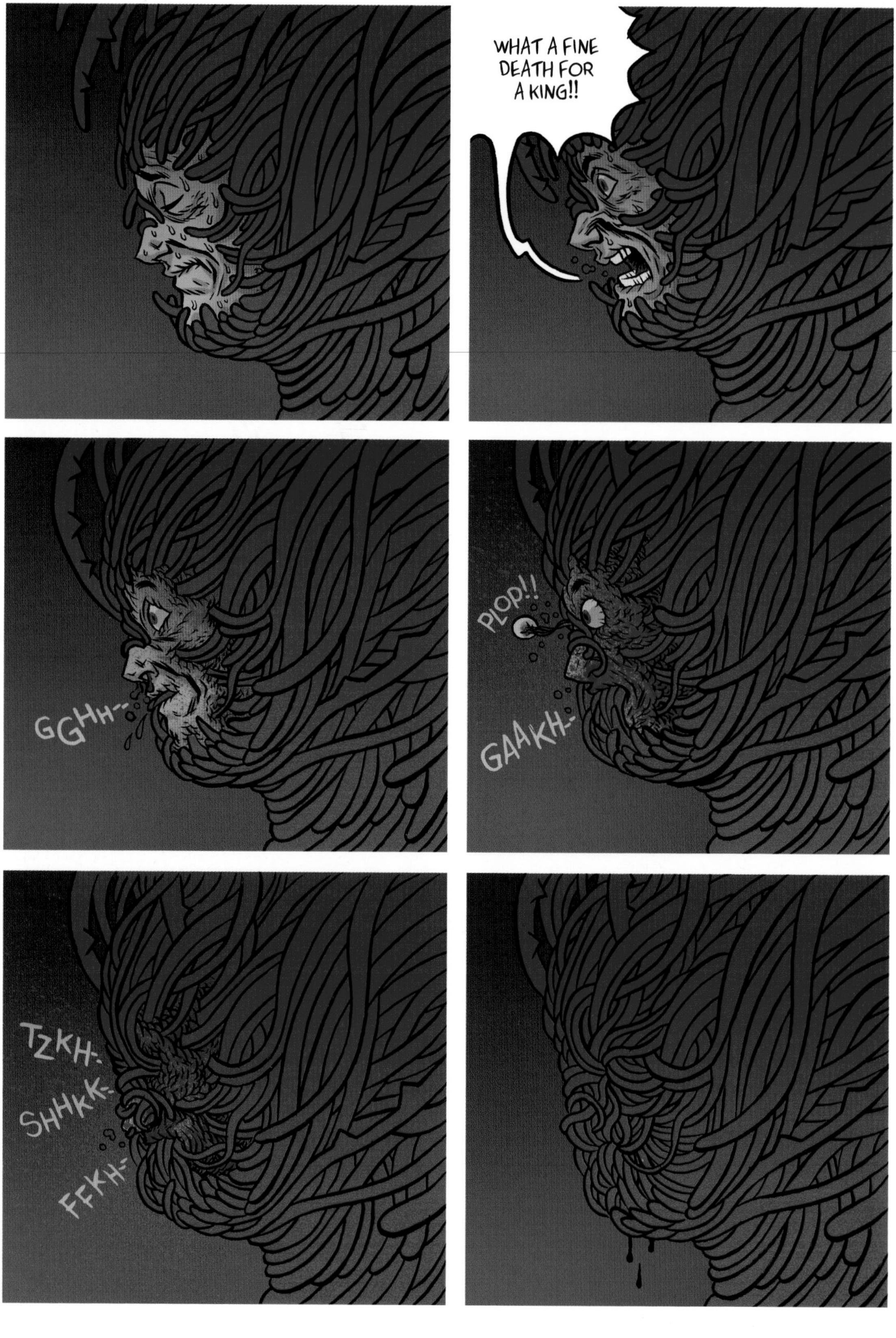
WHAT A FINE DEATH FOR A KING!!
GGHH-
PLOP!!
GAAKH-
TZKH-
SHHKK-
FFKH-

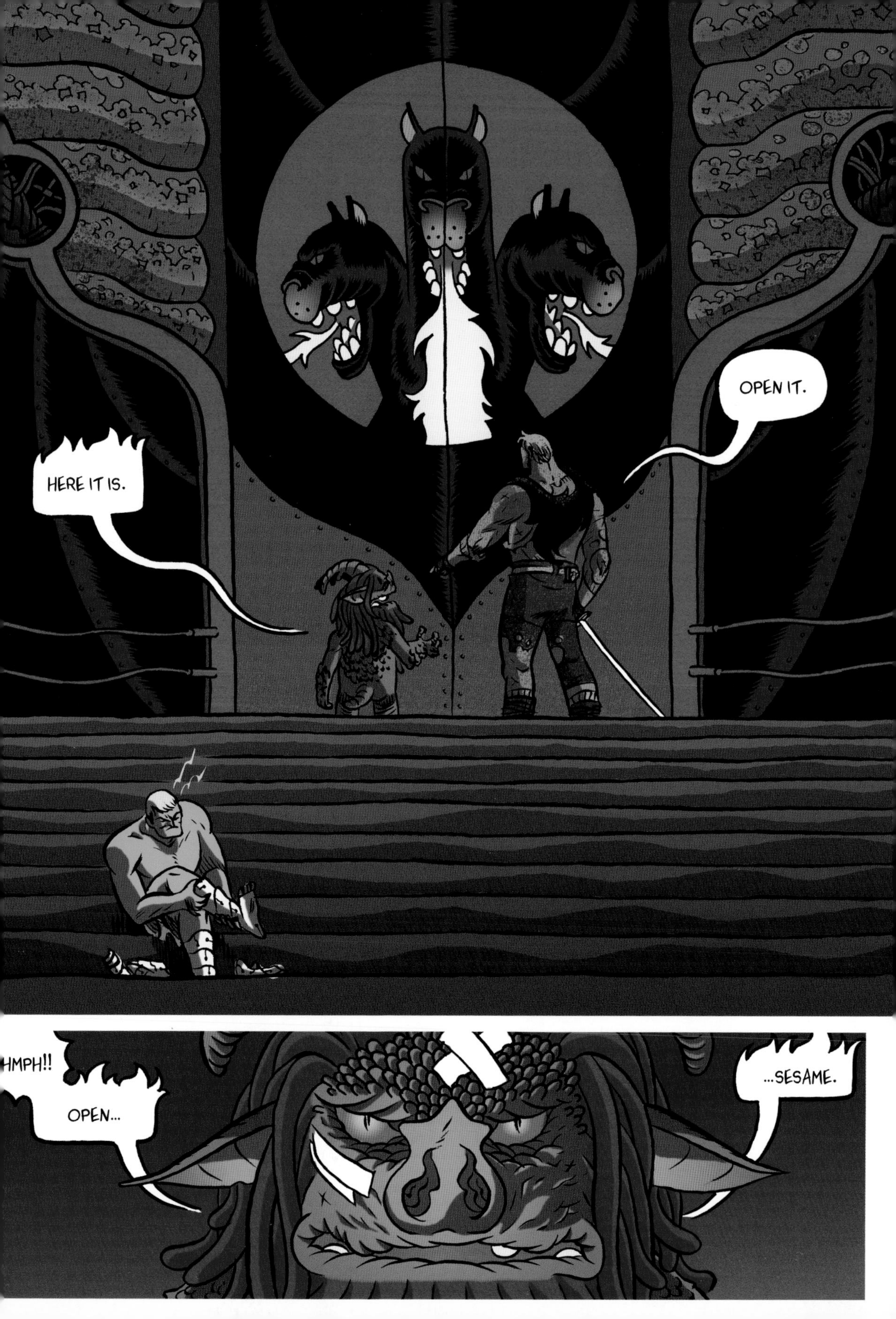

HERE IT IS.
OPEN IT.
HMPH!!
OPEN...
...SESAME.

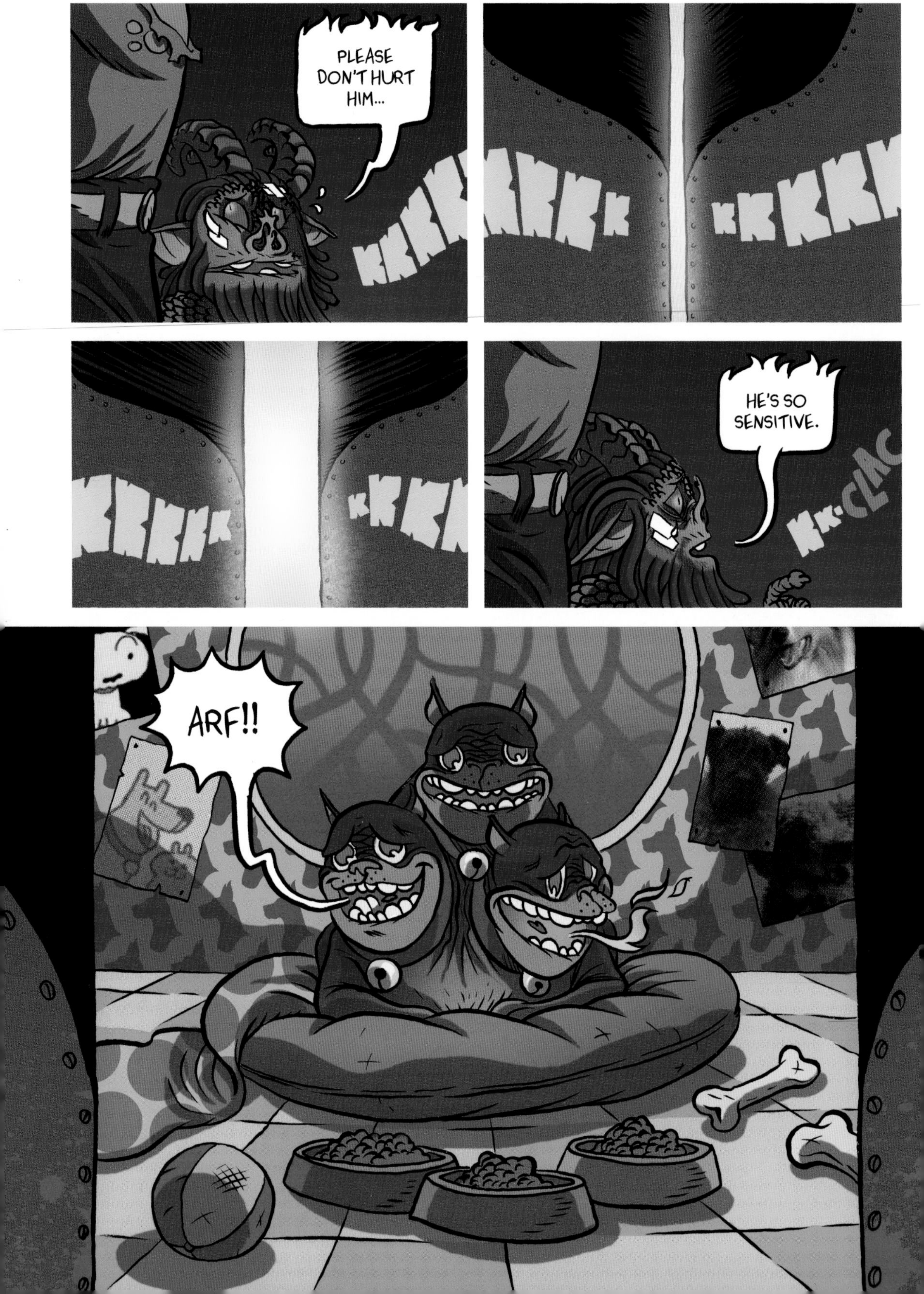
PLEASE DON'T HURT HIM...
HE'S SO SENSITIVE.
KK-CLAC
ARF!!

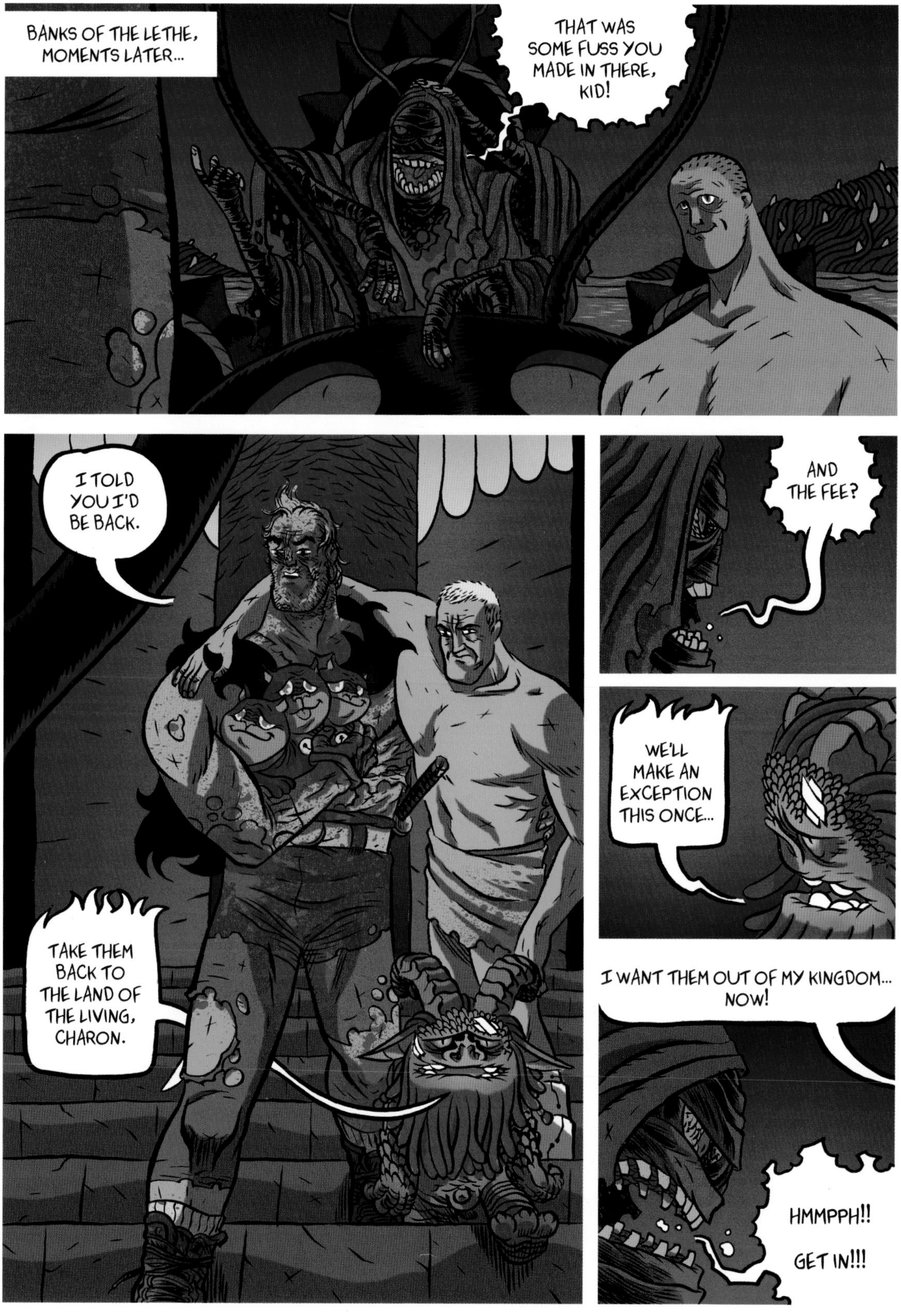
BANKS OF THE LETHE, MOMENTS LATER...
THAT WAS SOME FUSS YOU MADE IN THERE, KID!
I TOLD YOU I'D BE BACK.
TAKE THEM BACK TO THE LAND OF THE LIVING, CHARON.
AND THE FEE?
WE'LL MAKE AN EXCEPTION THIS ONCE...
I WANT THEM OUT OF MY KINGDOM... NOW!
HMMPPH!!
GET IN!!!

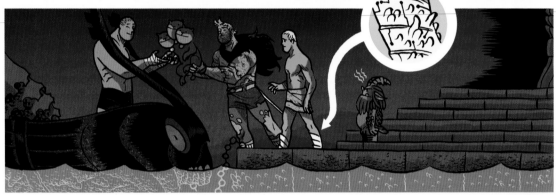

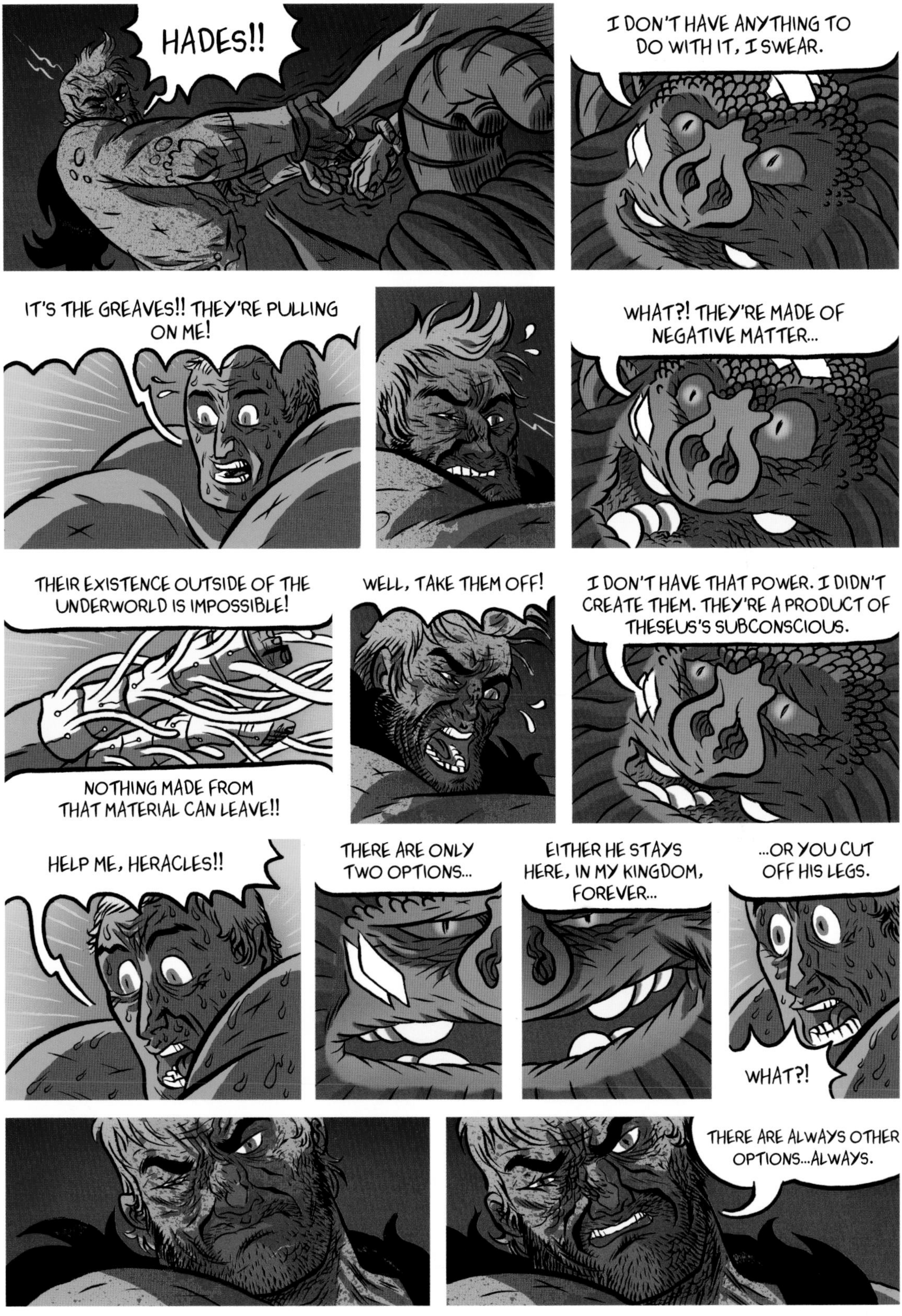
HADES!!
I DON'T HAVE ANYTHING TO DO WITH IT, I SWEAR.
IT'S THE GREAVES!! THEY'RE PULLING ON ME!
WHAT?! THEY'RE MADE OF NEGATIVE MATTER...
THEIR EXISTENCE OUTSIDE OF THE UNDERWORLD IS IMPOSSIBLE!
NOTHING MADE FROM THAT MATERIAL CAN LEAVE!!
WELL, TAKE THEM OFF!
I DON'T HAVE THAT POWER. I DIDN'T CREATE THEM. THEY'RE A PRODUCT OF THESEUS'S SUBCONSCIOUS.
HELP ME, HERACLES!!
THERE ARE ONLY TWO OPTIONS...
EITHER HE STAYS HERE, IN MY KINGDOM, FOREVER...
...OR YOU CUT OFF HIS LEGS.
WHAT?!
THERE ARE ALWAYS OTHER OPTIONS...ALWAYS.

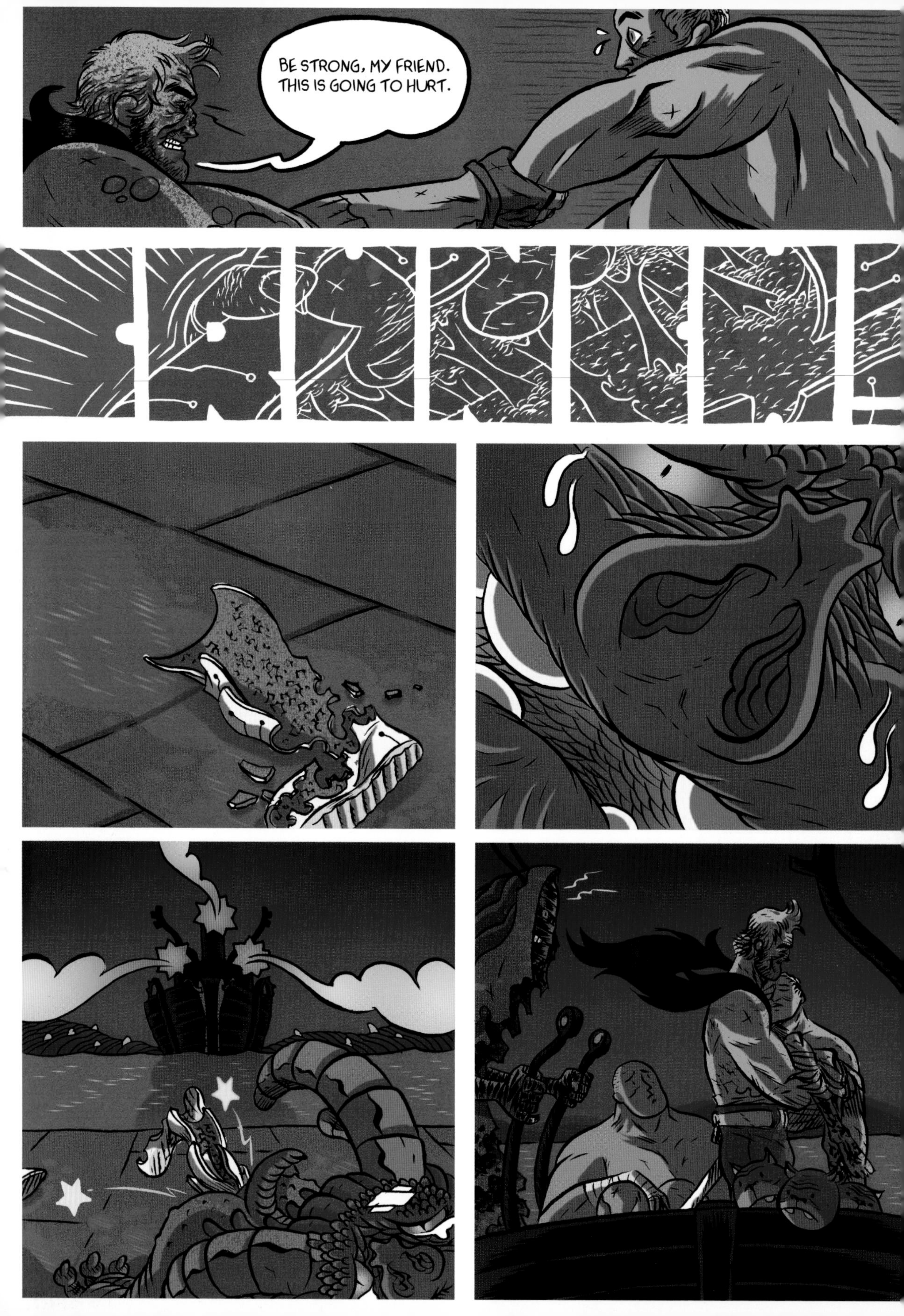
BE STRONG, MY FRIEND. THIS IS GOING TO HURT.

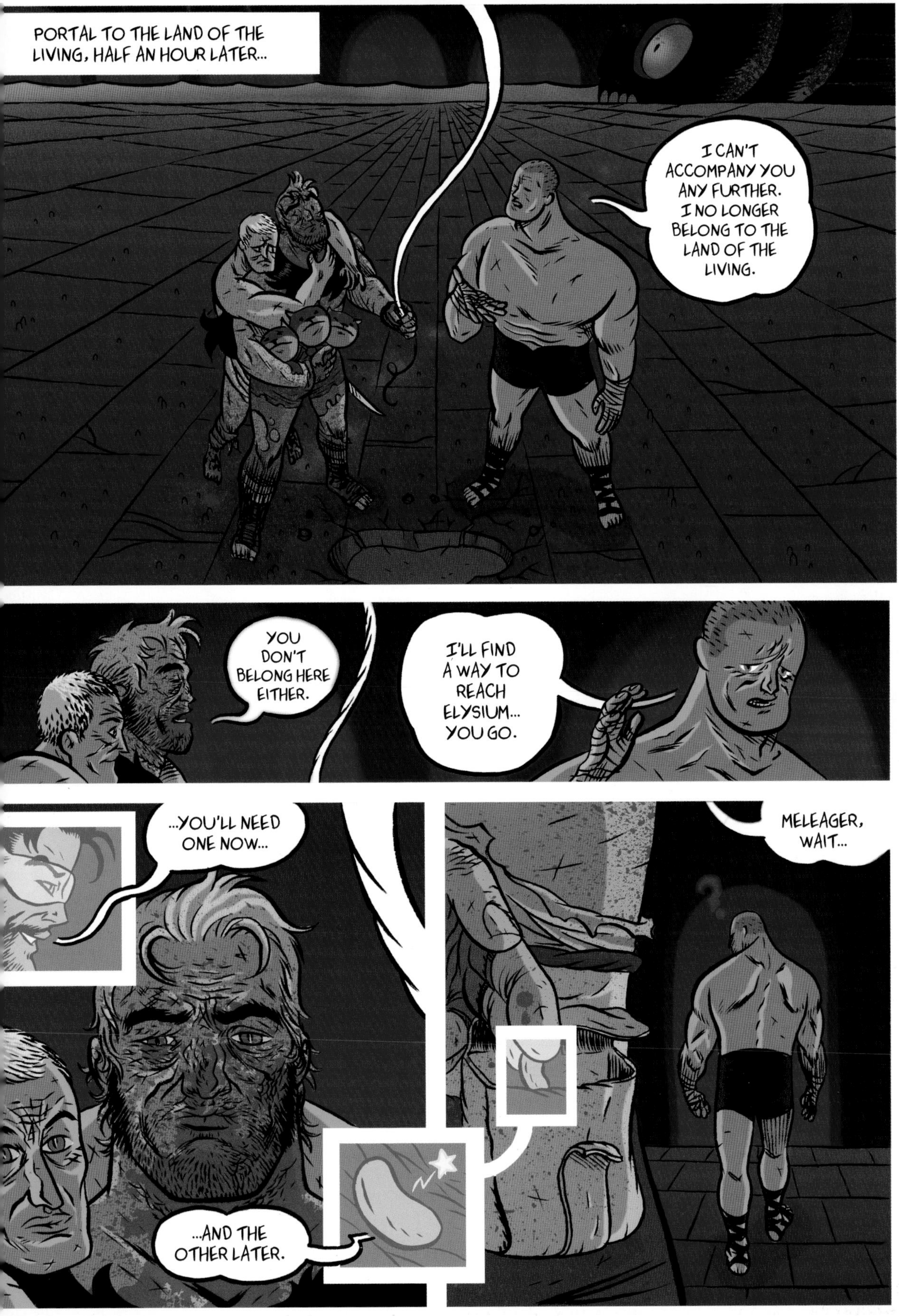
PORTAL TO THE LAND OF THE LIVING, HALF AN HOUR LATER...
I CAN'T ACCOMPANY YOU ANY FURTHER. I NO LONGER BELONG TO THE LAND OF THE LIVING.
YOU DON'T BELONG HERE EITHER.
I'LL FIND A WAY TO REACH ELYSIUM... YOU GO.
...YOU'LL NEED ONE NOW...
...AND THE OTHER LATER.
MELEAGER, WAIT...

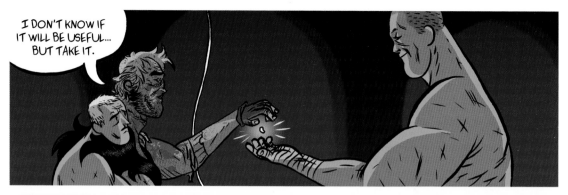

I DON'T KNOW IF IT WILL BE USEFUL... BUT TAKE IT.

THANK YOU FOR EVERY-THING.

HMMPP!!

BBBBBBBBBBZZZZZZ!!!

BBBBBBZZZZZ!!

BBBZZZ

INCOMING CALL

BBB

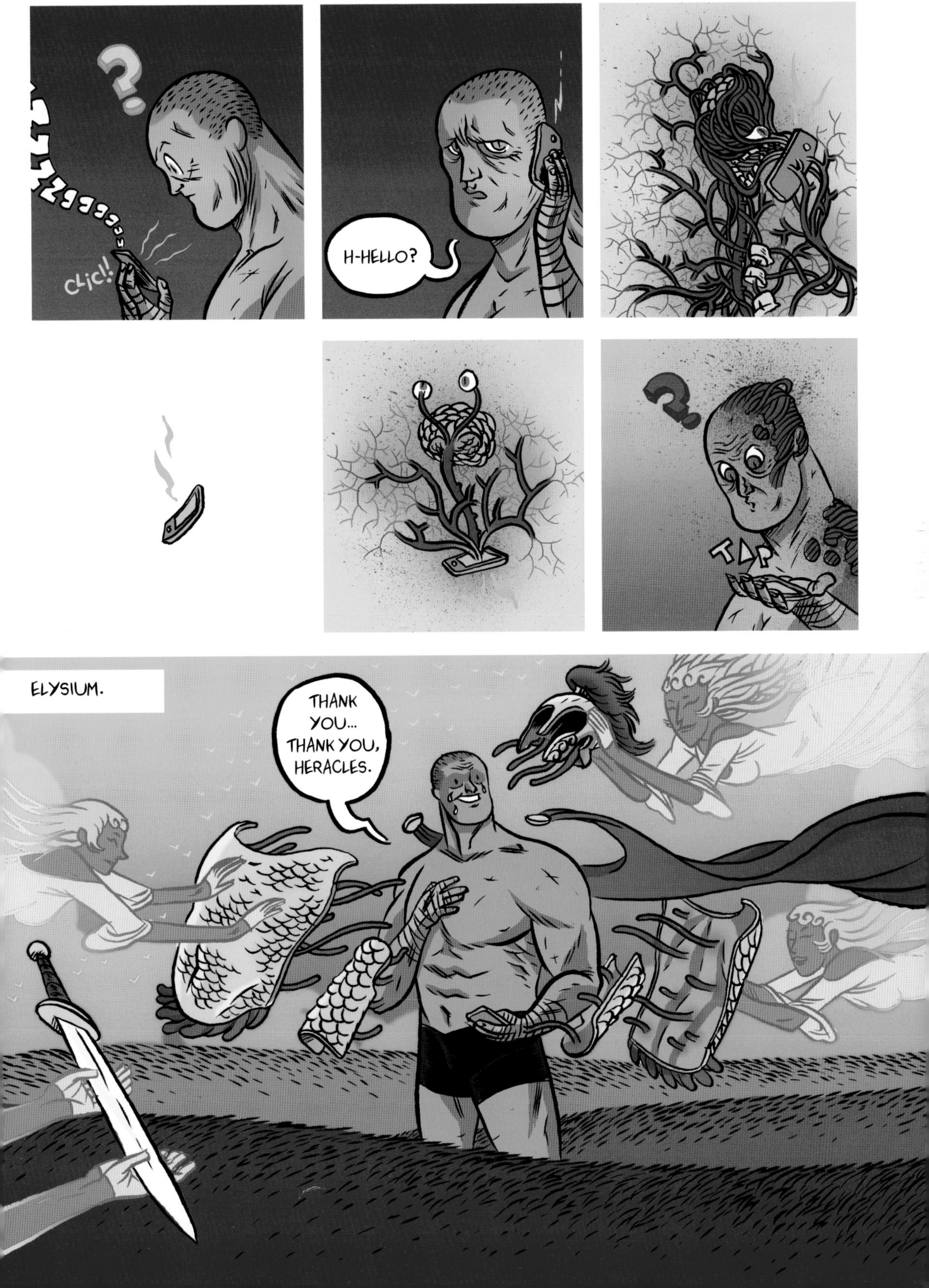
CLIC!!
H-HELLO?
TAP
ELYSIUM.
THANK YOU... THANK YOU, HERACLES.

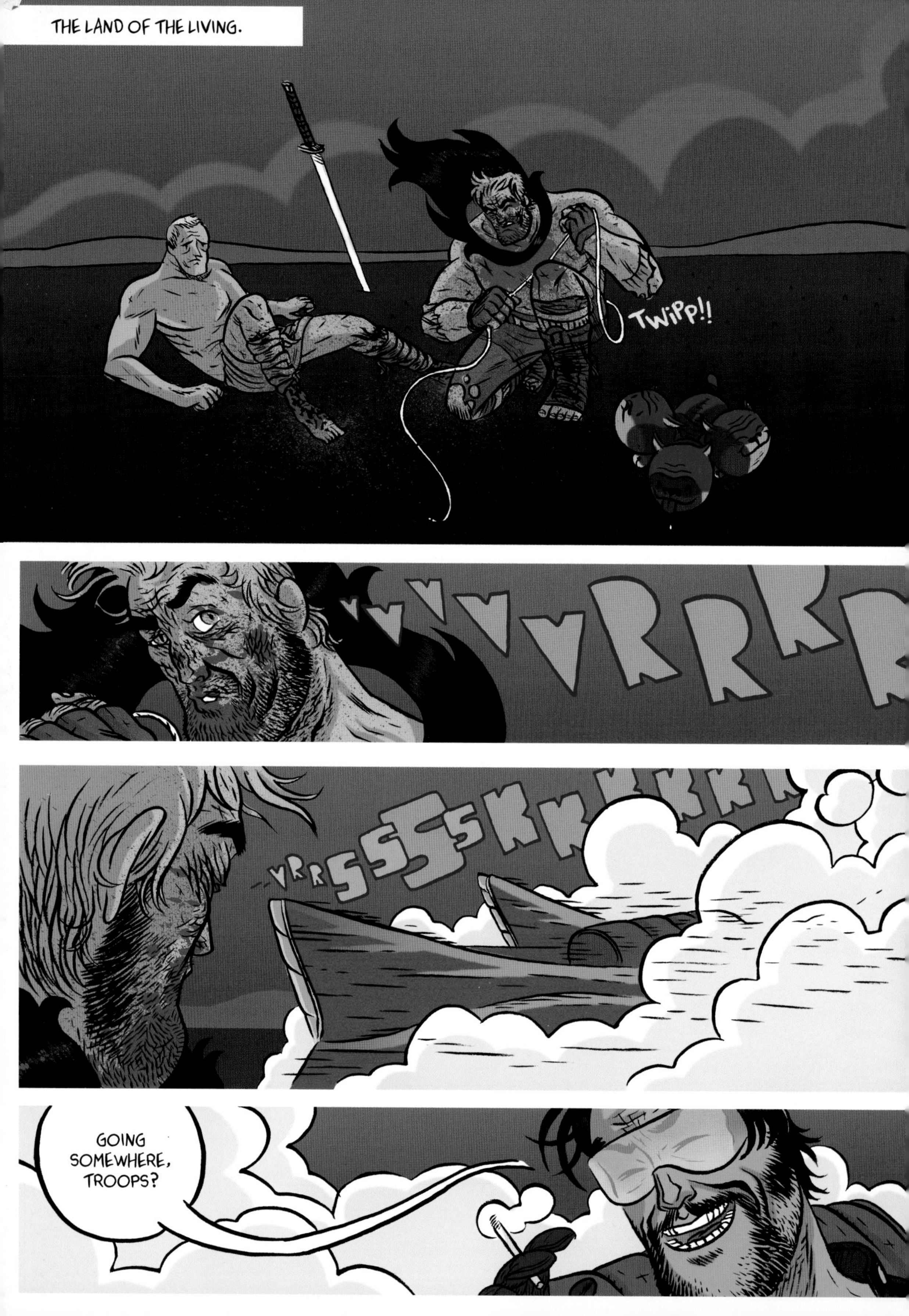
THE LAND OF THE LIVING.
TWIPP!!
VVVVVVRRRR
VRRSSSSKKRRRRR
GOING SOMEWHERE, TROOPS?

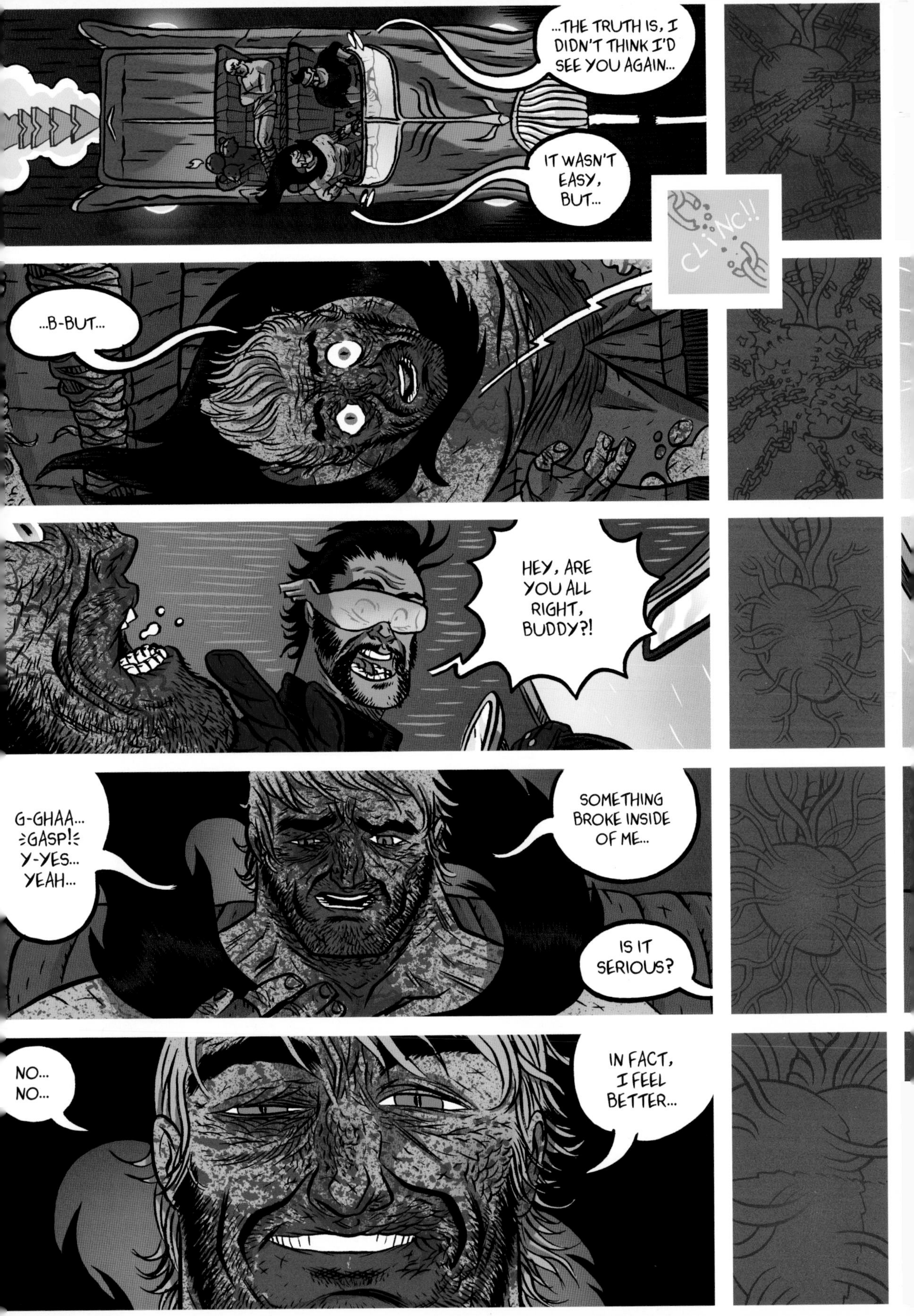
...THE TRUTH IS, I DIDN'T THINK I'D SEE YOU AGAIN...
IT WASN'T EASY, BUT...
CLINC!!
...B-BUT...
HEY, ARE YOU ALL RIGHT, BUDDY?!
G-GHAA... GASP! Y-YES... YEAH...
SOMETHING BROKE INSIDE OF ME...
IS IT SERIOUS?
NO... NO...
IN FACT, I FEEL BETTER...

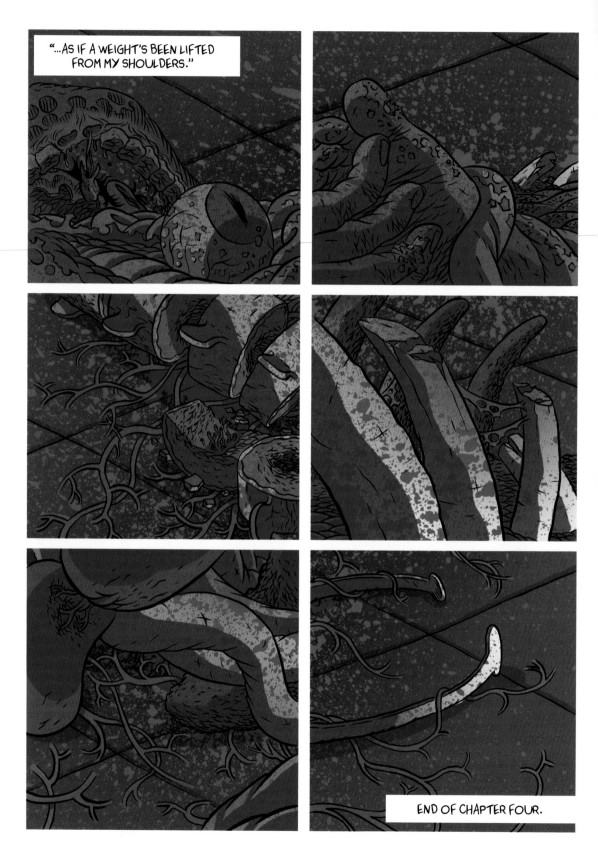

"...AS IF A WEIGHT'S BEEN LIFTED FROM MY SHOULDERS."

END OF CHAPTER FOUR.

CHAPTER

05

CHAPTER

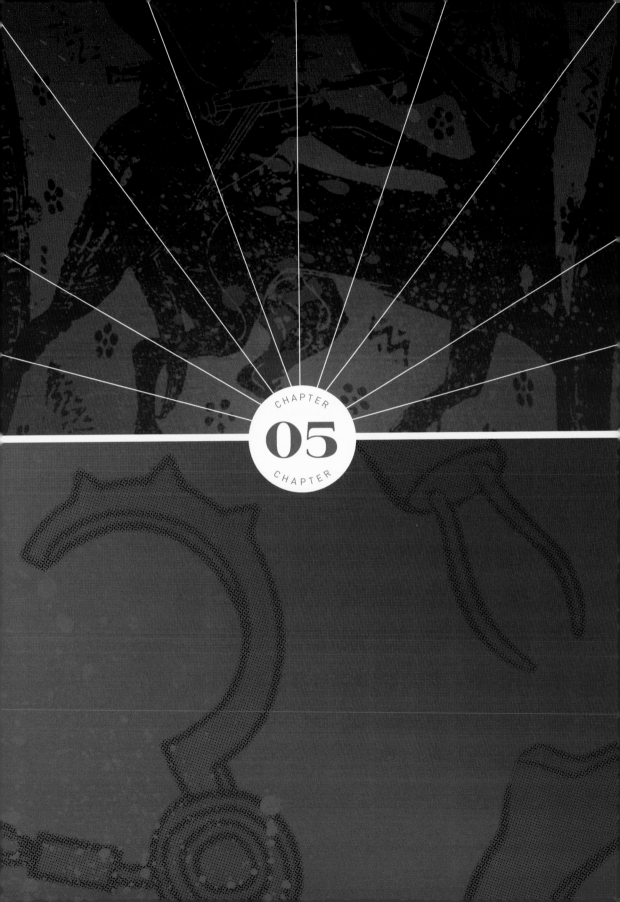

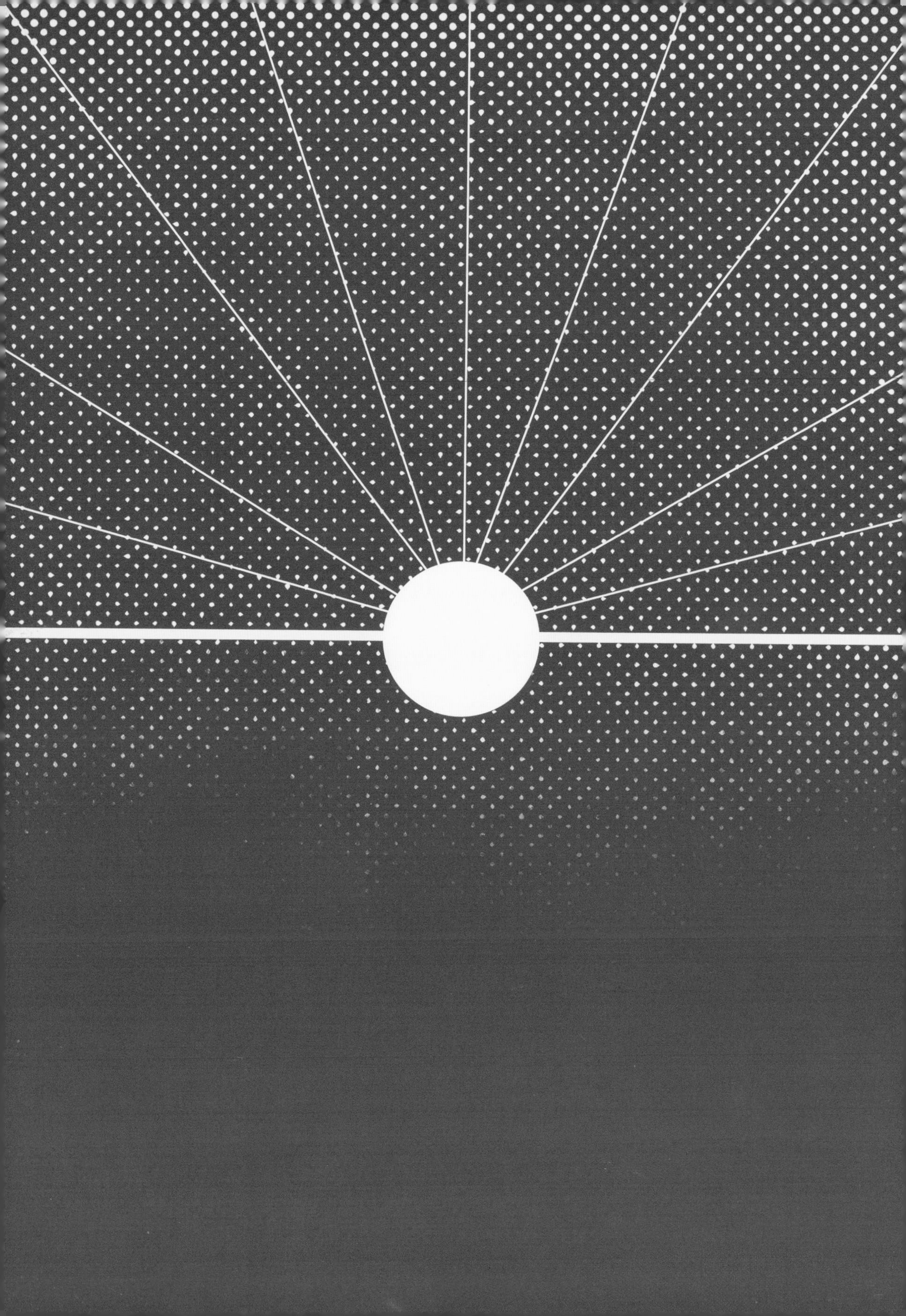

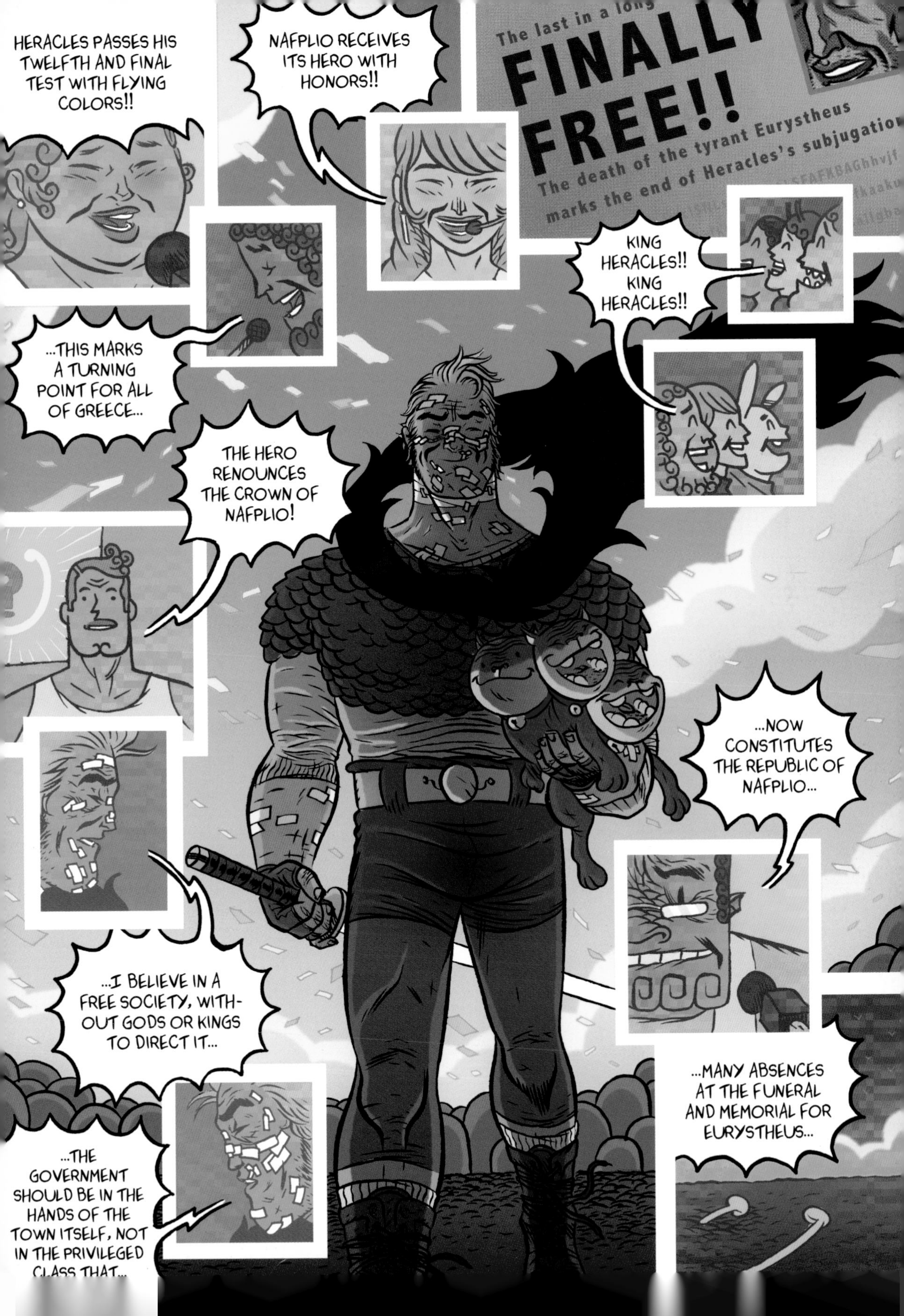
HERACLES PASSES HIS TWELFTH AND FINAL TEST WITH FLYING COLORS!!
NAFPLIO RECEIVES ITS HERO WITH HONORS!!
The last in a long
FINALLY FREE!!
The death of the tyrant Eurystheus marks the end of Heracles's subjugation
...THIS MARKS A TURNING POINT FOR ALL OF GREECE...
KING HERACLES!! KING HERACLES!!
THE HERO RENOUNCES THE CROWN OF NAFPLIO!
...I BELIEVE IN A FREE SOCIETY, WITHOUT GODS OR KINGS TO DIRECT IT...
...THE GOVERNMENT SHOULD BE IN THE HANDS OF THE TOWN ITSELF, NOT IN THE PRIVILEGED CLASS THAT...
...NOW CONSTITUTES THE REPUBLIC OF NAFPLIO...
...MANY ABSENCES AT THE FUNERAL AND MEMORIAL FOR EURYSTHEUS...

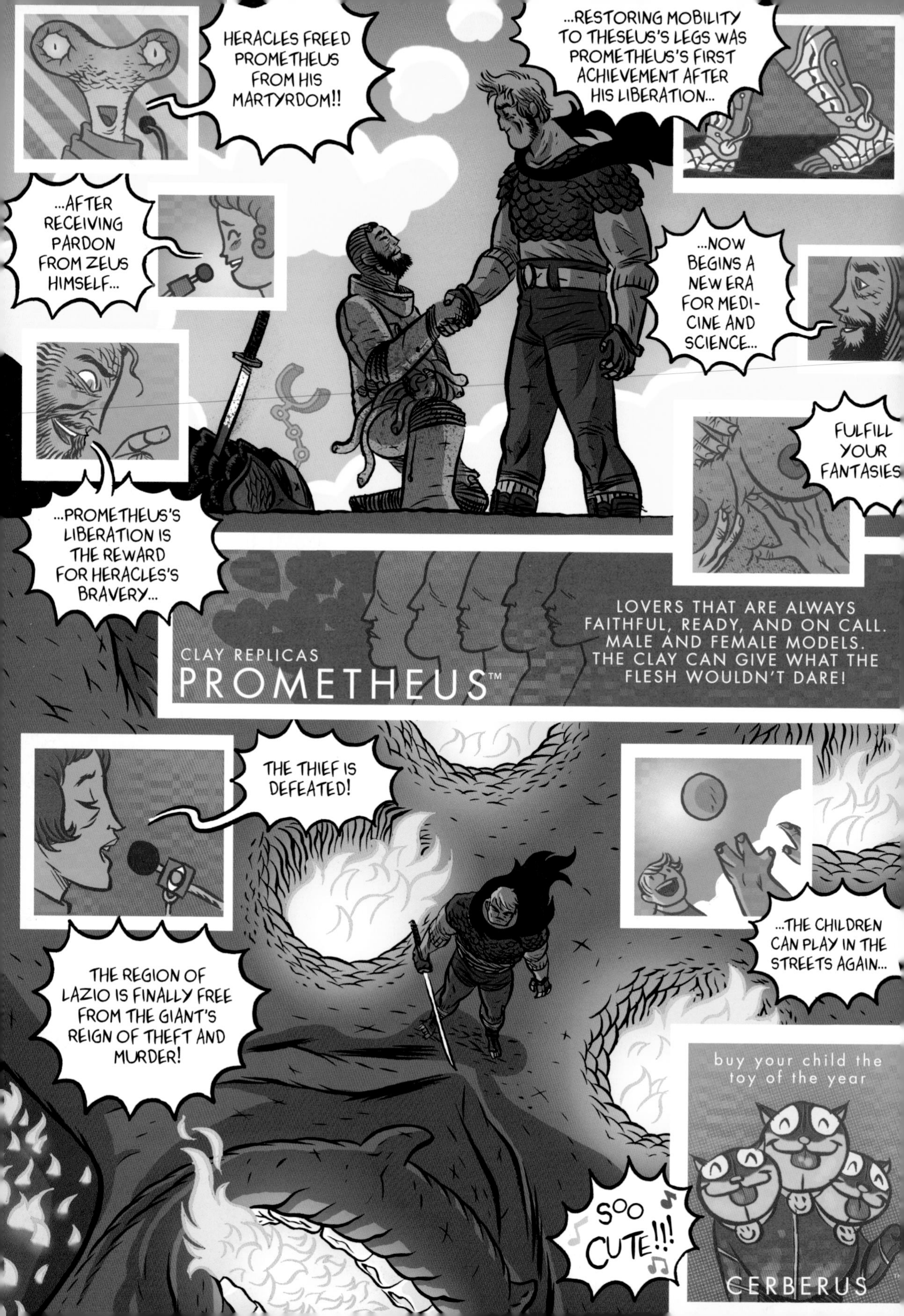
HERACLES FREED PROMETHEUS FROM HIS MARTYRDOM!!
...RESTORING MOBILITY TO THESEUS'S LEGS WAS PROMETHEUS'S FIRST ACHIEVEMENT AFTER HIS LIBERATION...
...AFTER RECEIVING PARDON FROM ZEUS HIMSELF...
...NOW BEGINS A NEW ERA FOR MEDI-CINE AND SCIENCE...
FULFILL YOUR FANTASIES
...PROMETHEUS'S LIBERATION IS THE REWARD FOR HERACLES'S BRAVERY...
CLAY REPLICAS
PROMETHEUS™
LOVERS THAT ARE ALWAYS FAITHFUL, READY, AND ON CALL. MALE AND FEMALE MODELS. THE CLAY CAN GIVE WHAT THE FLESH WOULDN'T DARE!
THE THIEF IS DEFEATED!
THE REGION OF LAZIO IS FINALLY FREE FROM THE GIANT'S REIGN OF THEFT AND MURDER!
...THE CHILDREN CAN PLAY IN THE STREETS AGAIN...
buy your child the toy of the year
SOO CUTE!!!
CERBERUS

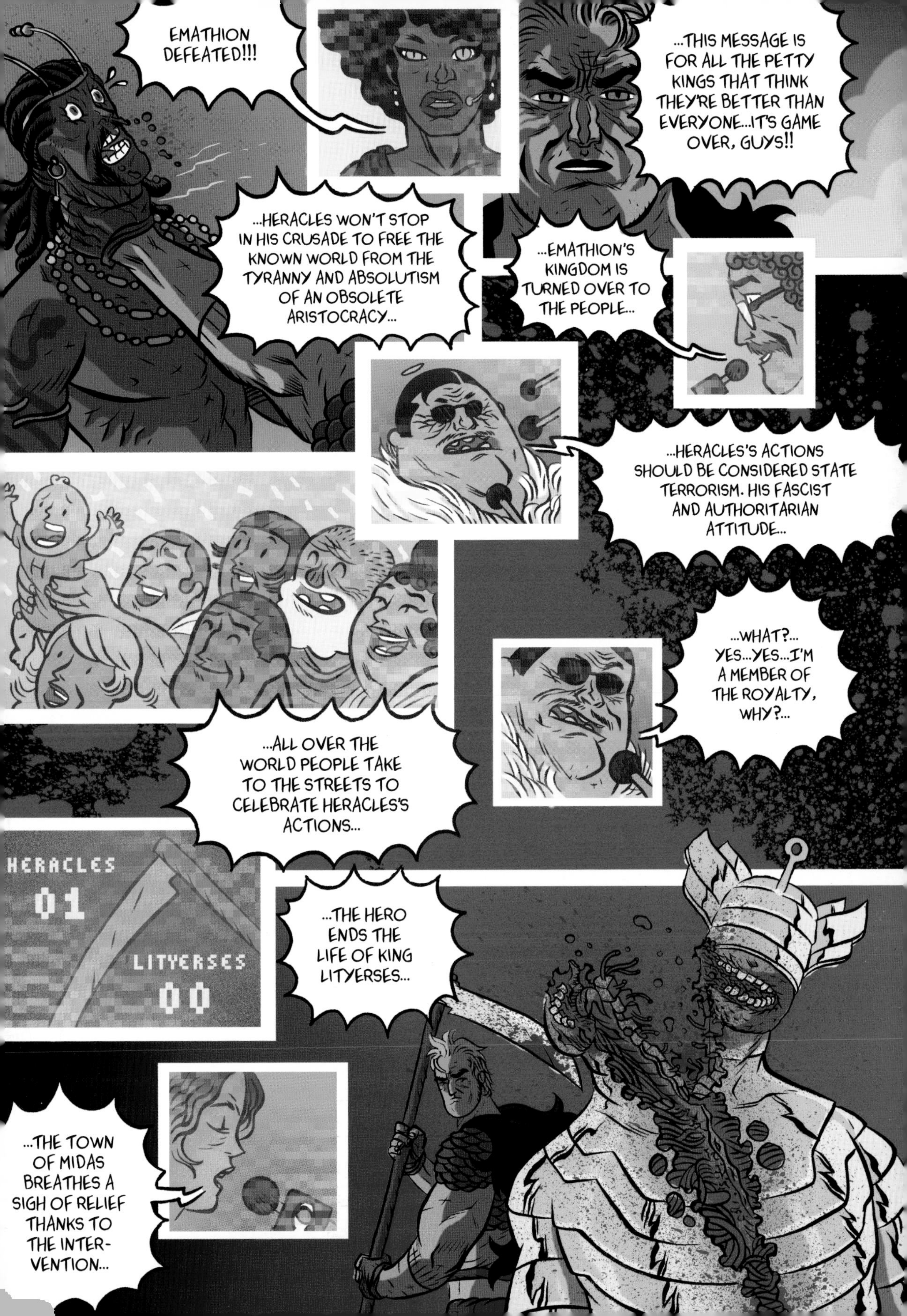
EMATHION DEFEATED!!!
...THIS MESSAGE IS FOR ALL THE PETTY KINGS THAT THINK THEY'RE BETTER THAN EVERYONE...IT'S GAME OVER, GUYS!!
...HERACLES WON'T STOP IN HIS CRUSADE TO FREE THE KNOWN WORLD FROM THE TYRANNY AND ABSOLUTISM OF AN OBSOLETE ARISTOCRACY...
...EMATHION'S KINGDOM IS TURNED OVER TO THE PEOPLE...
...HERACLES'S ACTIONS SHOULD BE CONSIDERED STATE TERRORISM. HIS FASCIST AND AUTHORITARIAN ATTITUDE...
...WHAT?... YES...YES...I'M A MEMBER OF THE ROYALTY, WHY?...
...ALL OVER THE WORLD PEOPLE TAKE TO THE STREETS TO CELEBRATE HERACLES'S ACTIONS...
HERACLES
01
LITYERSES
00
...THE HERO ENDS THE LIFE OF KING LITYERSES...
...THE TOWN OF MIDAS BREATHES A SIGH OF RELIEF THANKS TO THE INTER-VENTION...

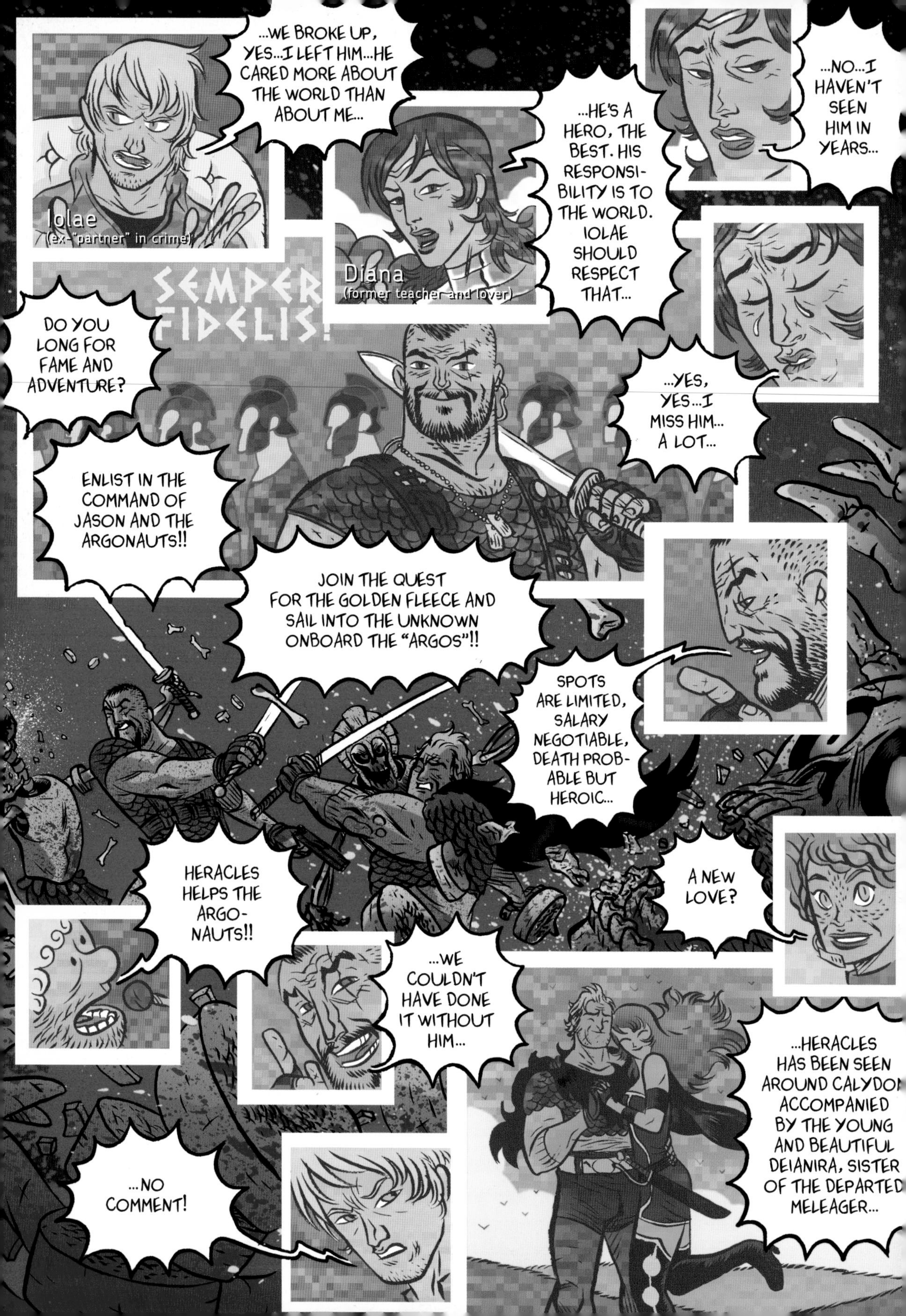

Iolae
(ex-"partner" in crime)
...WE BROKE UP, YES...I LEFT HIM...HE CARED MORE ABOUT THE WORLD THAN ABOUT ME...
Diana
(former teacher and lover)
...HE'S A HERO, THE BEST. HIS RESPONSI-BILITY IS TO THE WORLD. IOLAE SHOULD RESPECT THAT...
...NO...I HAVEN'T SEEN HIM IN YEARS...
...YES, YES...I MISS HIM... A LOT...
SEMPER FIDELIS!
DO YOU LONG FOR FAME AND ADVENTURE?
ENLIST IN THE COMMAND OF JASON AND THE ARGONAUTS!!
JOIN THE QUEST FOR THE GOLDEN FLEECE AND SAIL INTO THE UNKNOWN ONBOARD THE "ARGOS"!!
SPOTS ARE LIMITED, SALARY NEGOTIABLE, DEATH PROB-ABLE BUT HEROIC...
HERACLES HELPS THE ARGO-NAUTS!!
...WE COULDN'T HAVE DONE IT WITHOUT HIM...
...NO COMMENT!
A NEW LOVE?
...HERACLES HAS BEEN SEEN AROUND CALYDON ACCOMPANIED BY THE YOUNG AND BEAUTIFUL DEIANIRA, SISTER OF THE DEPARTED MELEAGER...

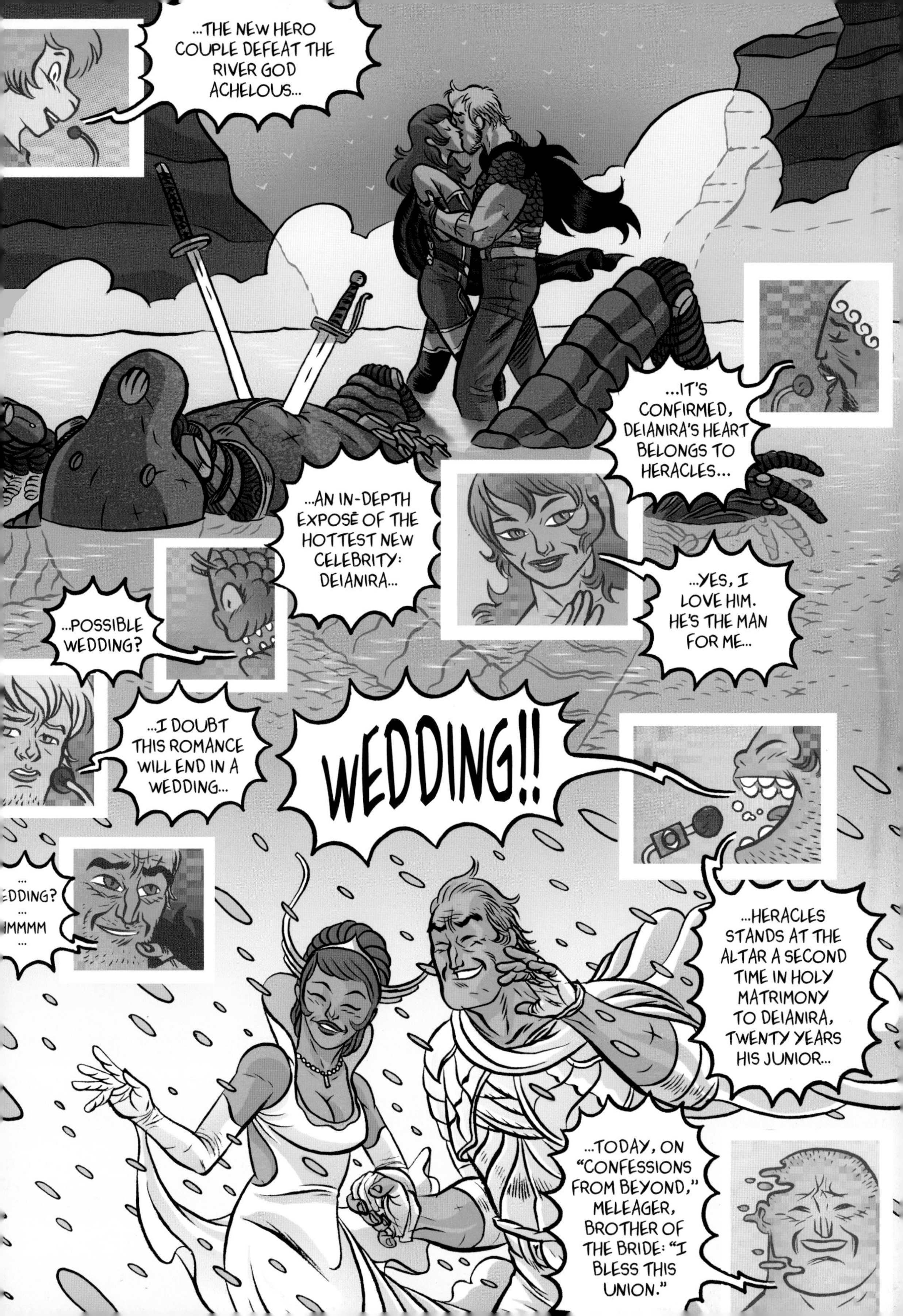
...THE NEW HERO COUPLE DEFEAT THE RIVER GOD ACHELOUS...
...IT'S CONFIRMED, DEIANIRA'S HEART BELONGS TO HERACLES...
...AN IN-DEPTH EXPOSÉ OF THE HOTTEST NEW CELEBRITY: DEIANIRA...
...YES, I LOVE HIM. HE'S THE MAN FOR ME...
...POSSIBLE WEDDING?
...I DOUBT THIS ROMANCE WILL END IN A WEDDING...
WEDDING!!
... EDDING? ... IMMMM ...
...HERACLES STANDS AT THE ALTAR A SECOND TIME IN HOLY MATRIMONY TO DEIANIRA, TWENTY YEARS HIS JUNIOR...
...TODAY, ON "CONFESSIONS FROM BEYOND," MELEAGER, BROTHER OF THE BRIDE: "I BLESS THIS UNION."

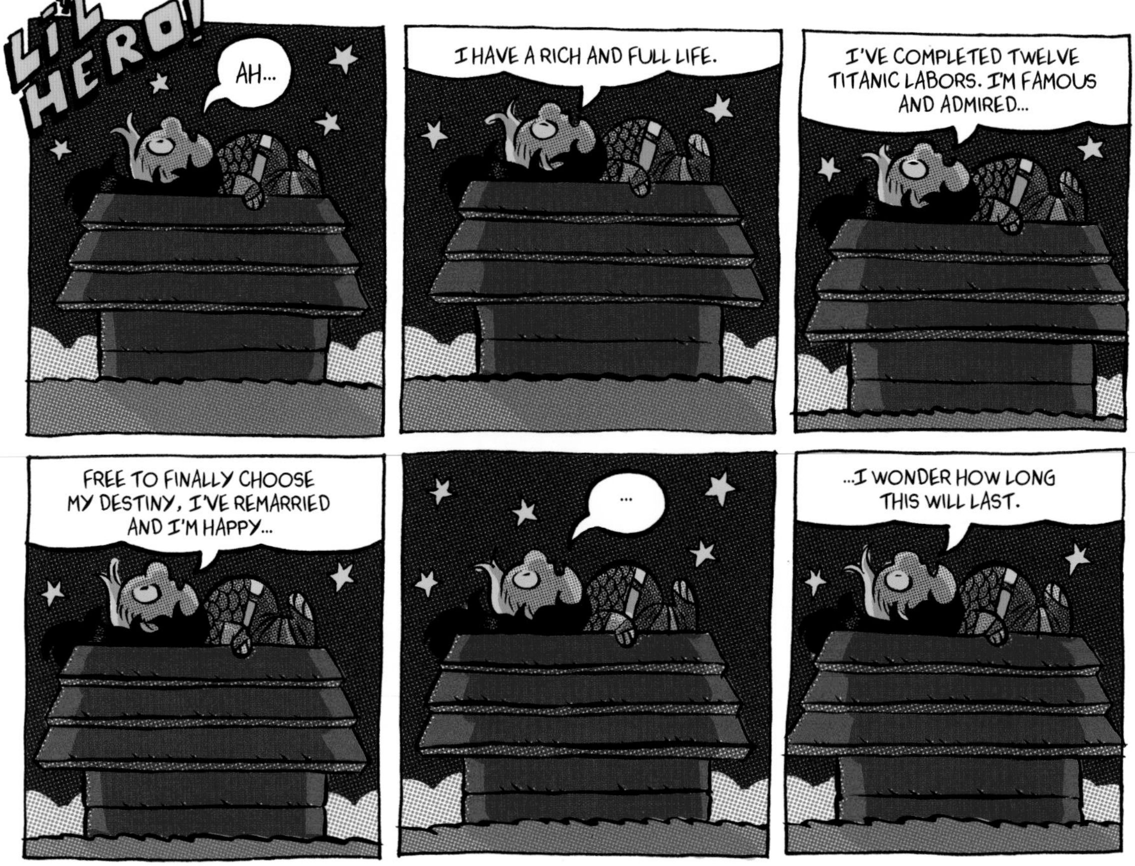
LI'L HERO!
AH...
I HAVE A RICH AND FULL LIFE.
I'VE COMPLETED TWELVE TITANIC LABORS. I'M FAMOUS AND ADMIRED...
FREE TO FINALLY CHOOSE MY DESTINY, I'VE REMARRIED AND I'M HAPPY...
...
...I WONDER HOW LONG THIS WILL LAST.

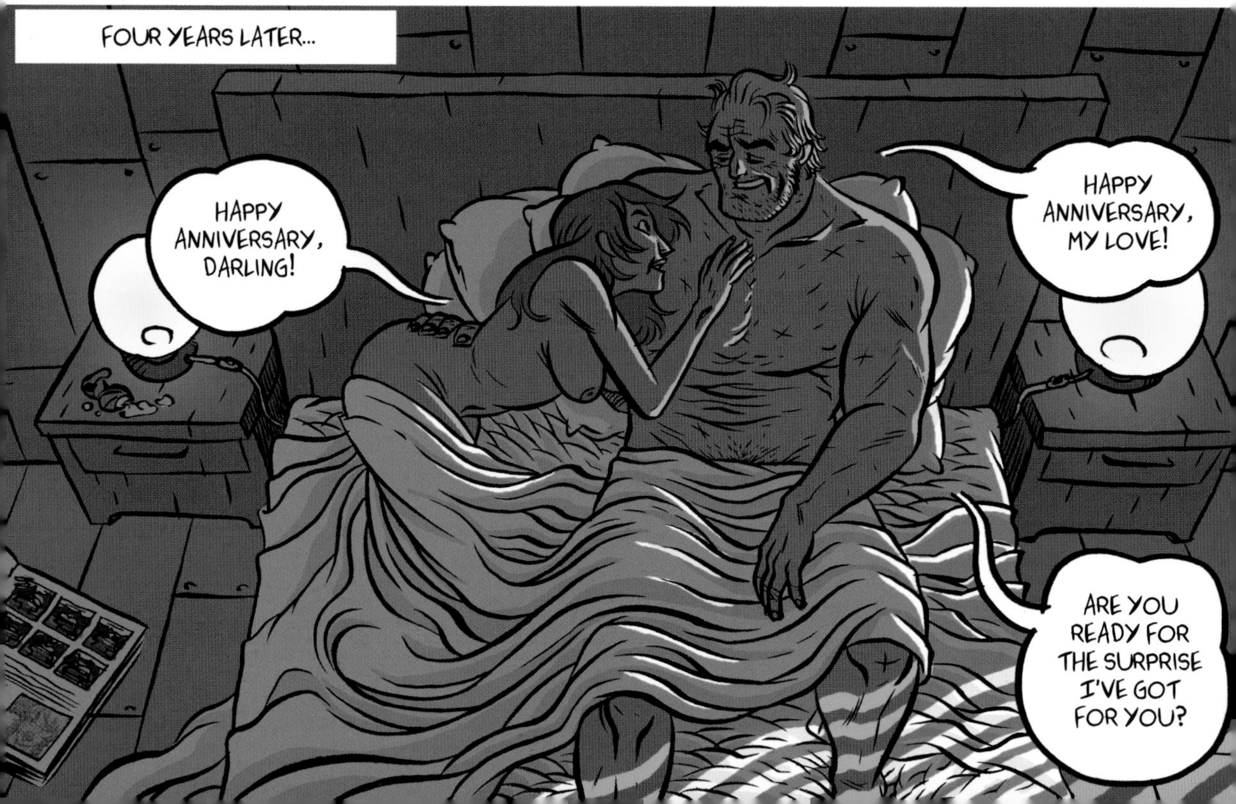
FOUR YEARS LATER...
HAPPY ANNIVERSARY, DARLING!
HAPPY ANNIVERSARY, MY LOVE!
ARE YOU READY FOR THE SURPRISE I'VE GOT FOR YOU?

OLYMPUS.

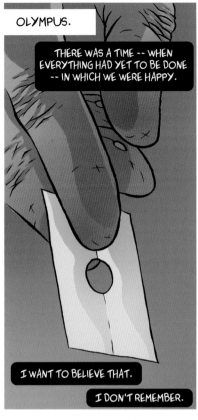

THERE WAS A TIME -- WHEN EVERYTHING HAD YET TO BE DONE -- IN WHICH WE WERE HAPPY.

I WANT TO BELIEVE THAT.

I DON'T REMEMBER.

THE SHADOW OF YOUR INDIFFERENCE ECLIPSED EVERYTHING.

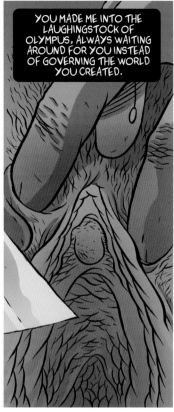

YOU MADE ME INTO THE LAUGHINGSTOCK OF OLYMPUS, ALWAYS WAITING AROUND FOR YOU INSTEAD OF GOVERNING THE WORLD YOU CREATED.

YOU HAD THE MOST POWERFUL GODDESSES, BUT YOU PREFERRED THE VULGAR PASSION OF HUMANS.

AND EVEN THEN I SUPPORTED YOU.

I DREAMED THAT EVEN THOUGH I DIDN'T HAVE EXCLUSIVE RIGHTS TO YOUR BODY, AT LEAST I HAD YOUR HEART.

BUT I DIDN'T.

YOU NEVER GAVE ME THE CHILD I WANTED, SOMEONE WORTHY OF HIS MOTHER'S DIVINE LOVE, OF HIS FATHER'S POWERFUL THRONE.

NO.

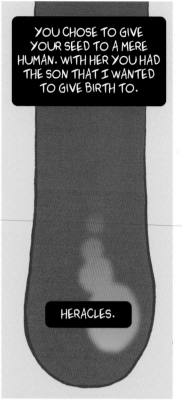

YOU CHOSE TO GIVE YOUR SEED TO A MERE HUMAN. WITH HER YOU HAD THE SON THAT I WANTED TO GIVE BIRTH TO.

HERACLES.

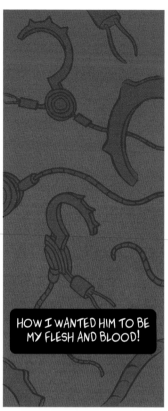

HOW I WANTED HIM TO BE MY FLESH AND BLOOD!

BUT HE'S ONLY A SOURCE OF EMBARRASSMENT FOR ME.

EVERY BEAT OF HIS HEART, EVERY BREATH HE TAKES, AND EVERY VICTORY HE WINS IS AN INSULT TO MY PERSON.

A REMINDER OF WHAT SHOULD HAVE BEEN MINE BY DIVINE RIGHT BUT WAS DENIED ME.

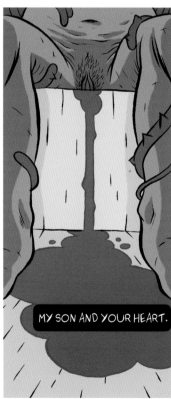

MY SON AND YOUR HEART.

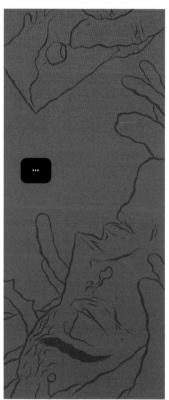

...

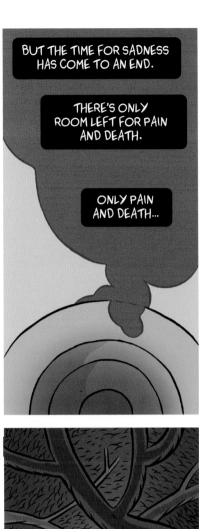

BUT THE TIME FOR SADNESS HAS COME TO AN END.

THERE'S ONLY ROOM LEFT FOR PAIN AND DEATH.

ONLY PAIN AND DEATH...

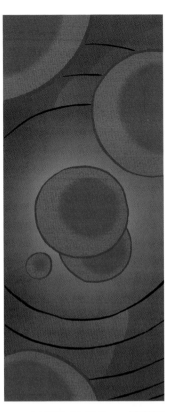

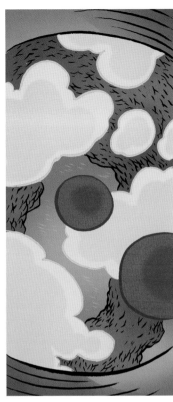

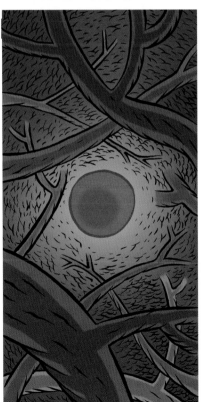

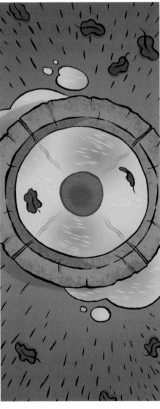

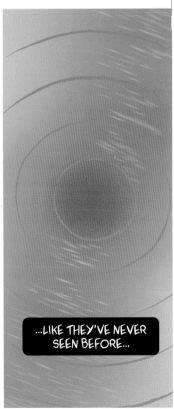

...LIKE THEY'VE NEVER SEEN BEFORE...

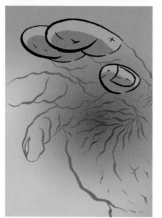

AH!

SLURP!

NAFPLIO. CHIRON'S GARDEN.

IT'S THE BEST ANNIVERSARY GIFT YOU COULD HAVE GIVEN ME!

THANK CHIRON. HE'S THE ONE THAT DECIDED TO GIVE US HIS LAND...

THANK YOU, CHIRON, THANK YOU! IT'S THE MOST BEAUTIFUL PLACE I'VE EVER BEEN!!

YOU'RE WELCOME, CHILD...

IT'S HARDLY ENOUGH FOR THE WOMAN THAT HAS BROUGHT HAPPINESS BACK TO MY MOST BELOVED PUPIL!

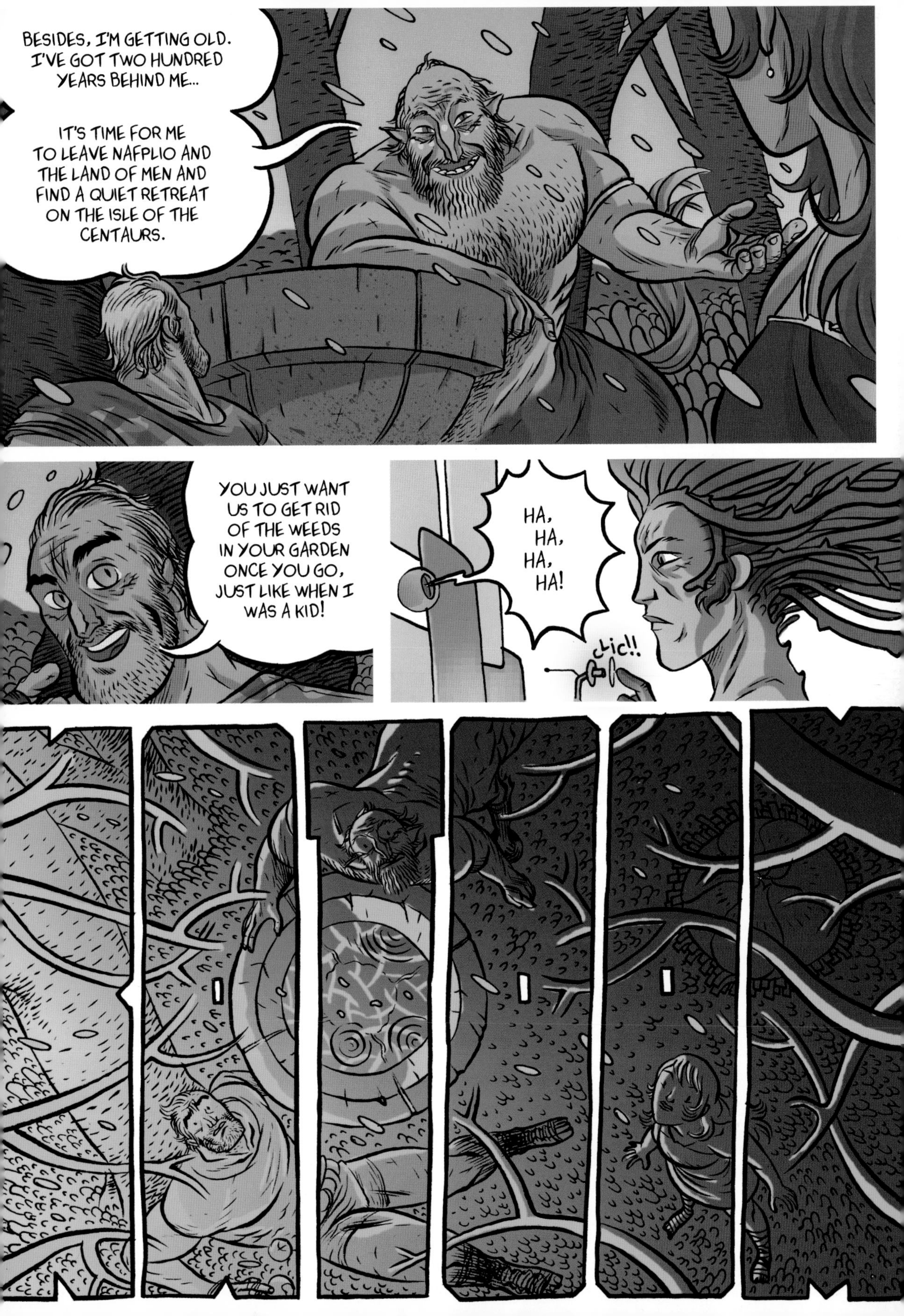
BESIDES, I'M GETTING OLD. I'VE GOT TWO HUNDRED YEARS BEHIND ME...
IT'S TIME FOR ME TO LEAVE NAFPLIO AND THE LAND OF MEN AND FIND A QUIET RETREAT ON THE ISLE OF THE CENTAURS.
YOU JUST WANT US TO GET RID OF THE WEEDS IN YOUR GARDEN ONCE YOU GO, JUST LIKE WHEN I WAS A KID!
HA, HA, HA, HA!
CLIC!!

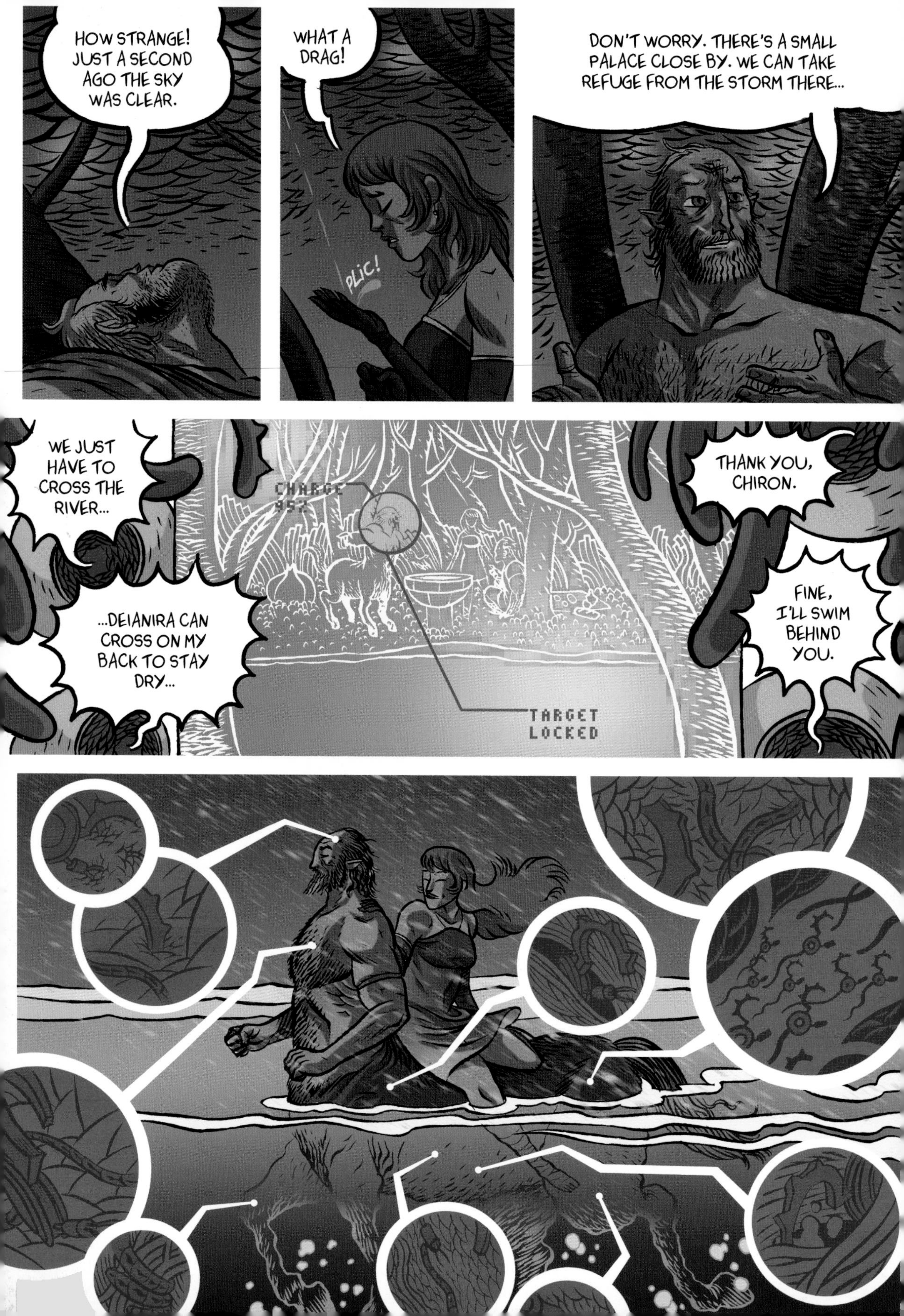
HOW STRANGE! JUST A SECOND AGO THE SKY WAS CLEAR.
WHAT A DRAG!
PLIC!
DON'T WORRY. THERE'S A SMALL PALACE CLOSE BY. WE CAN TAKE REFUGE FROM THE STORM THERE...
WE JUST HAVE TO CROSS THE RIVER...
...DEIANIRA CAN CROSS ON MY BACK TO STAY DRY...
CHARGE 95%
TARGET LOCKED
THANK YOU, CHIRON.
FINE, I'LL SWIM BEHIND YOU.

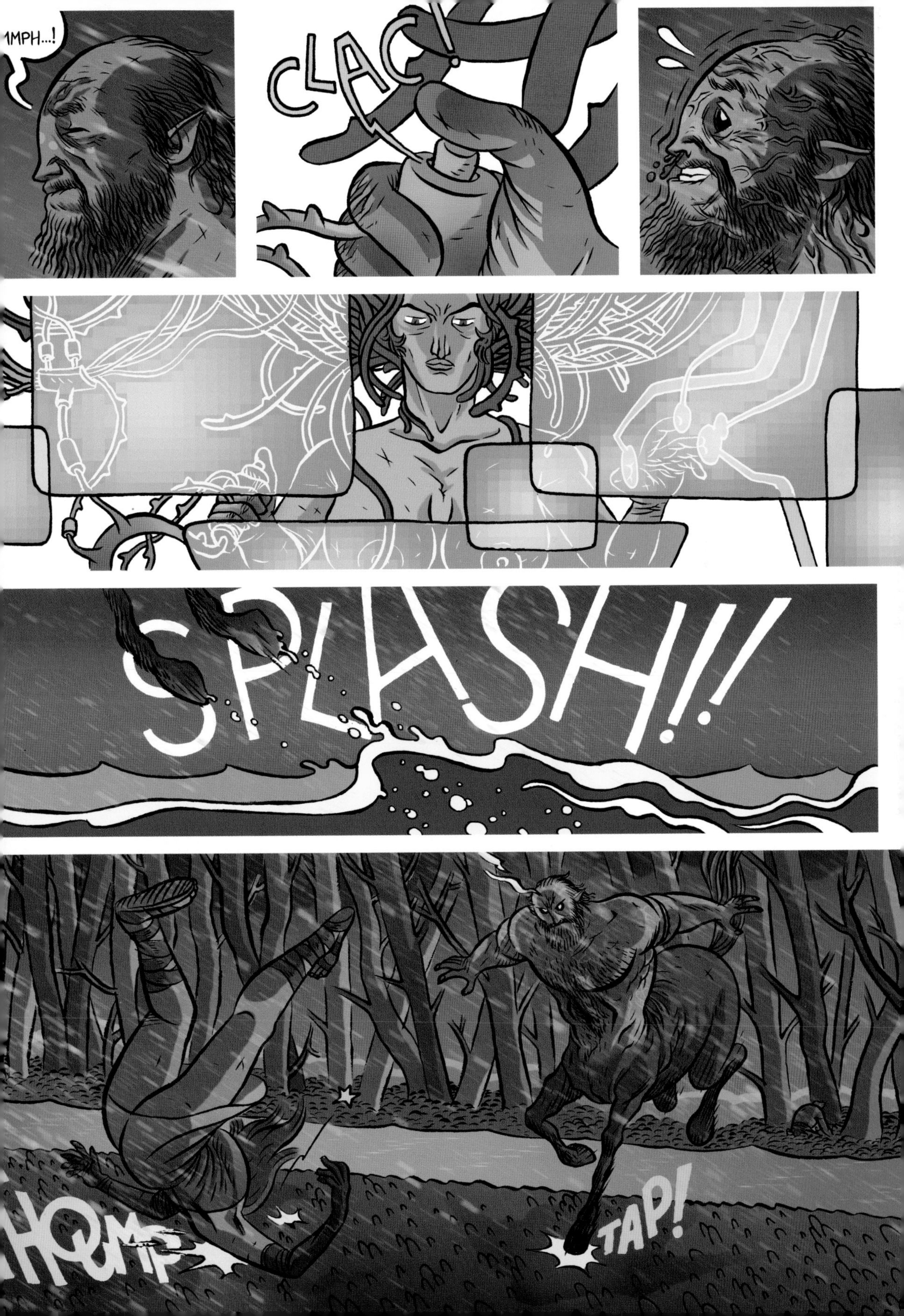
MPH...!
CLAC!
SPLASH!!
HOMP
TAP!

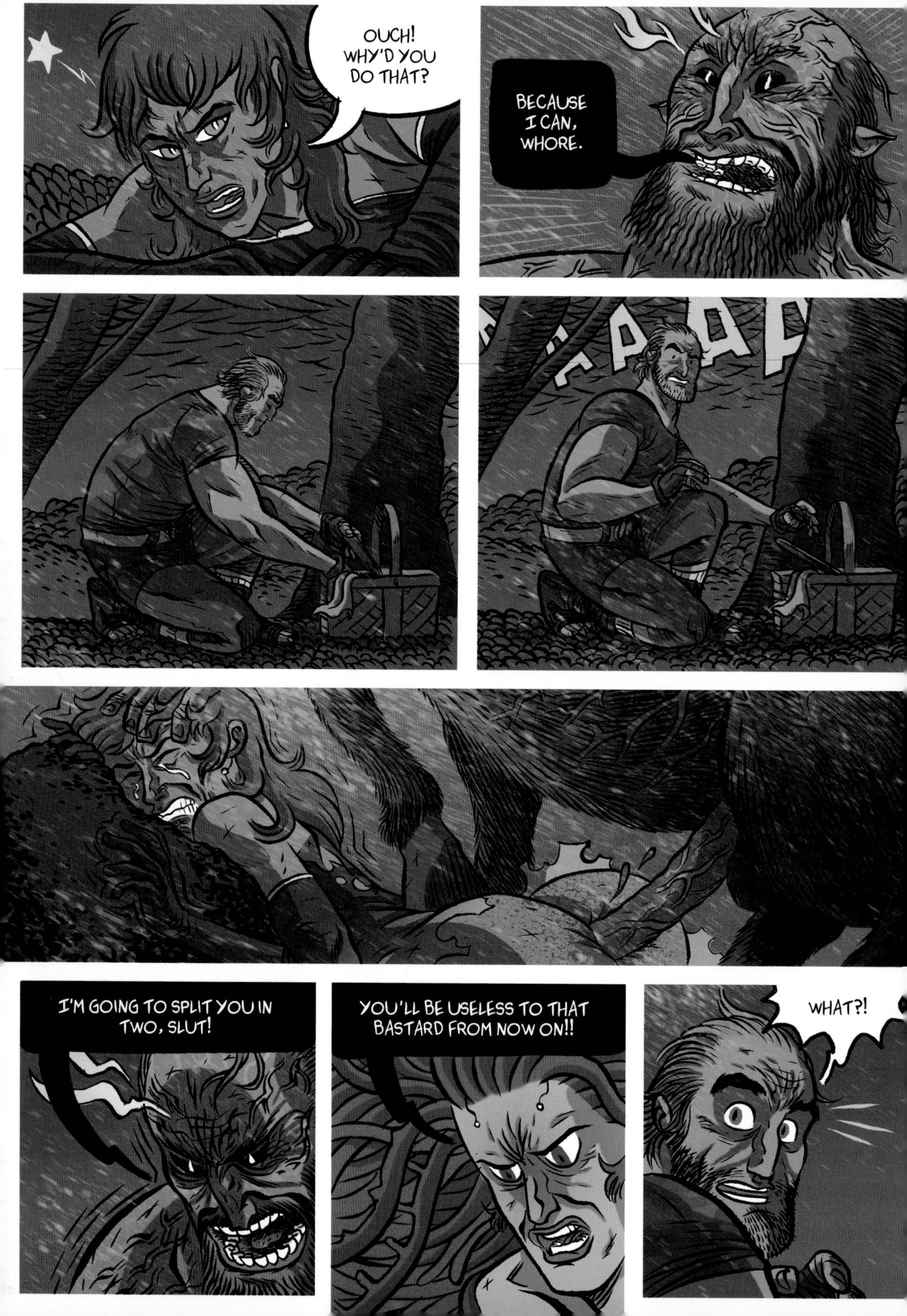
OUCH! WHY'D YOU DO THAT?
BECAUSE I CAN, WHORE.
I'M GOING TO SPLIT YOU IN TWO, SLUT!
YOU'LL BE USELESS TO THAT BASTARD FROM NOW ON!!
WHAT?!

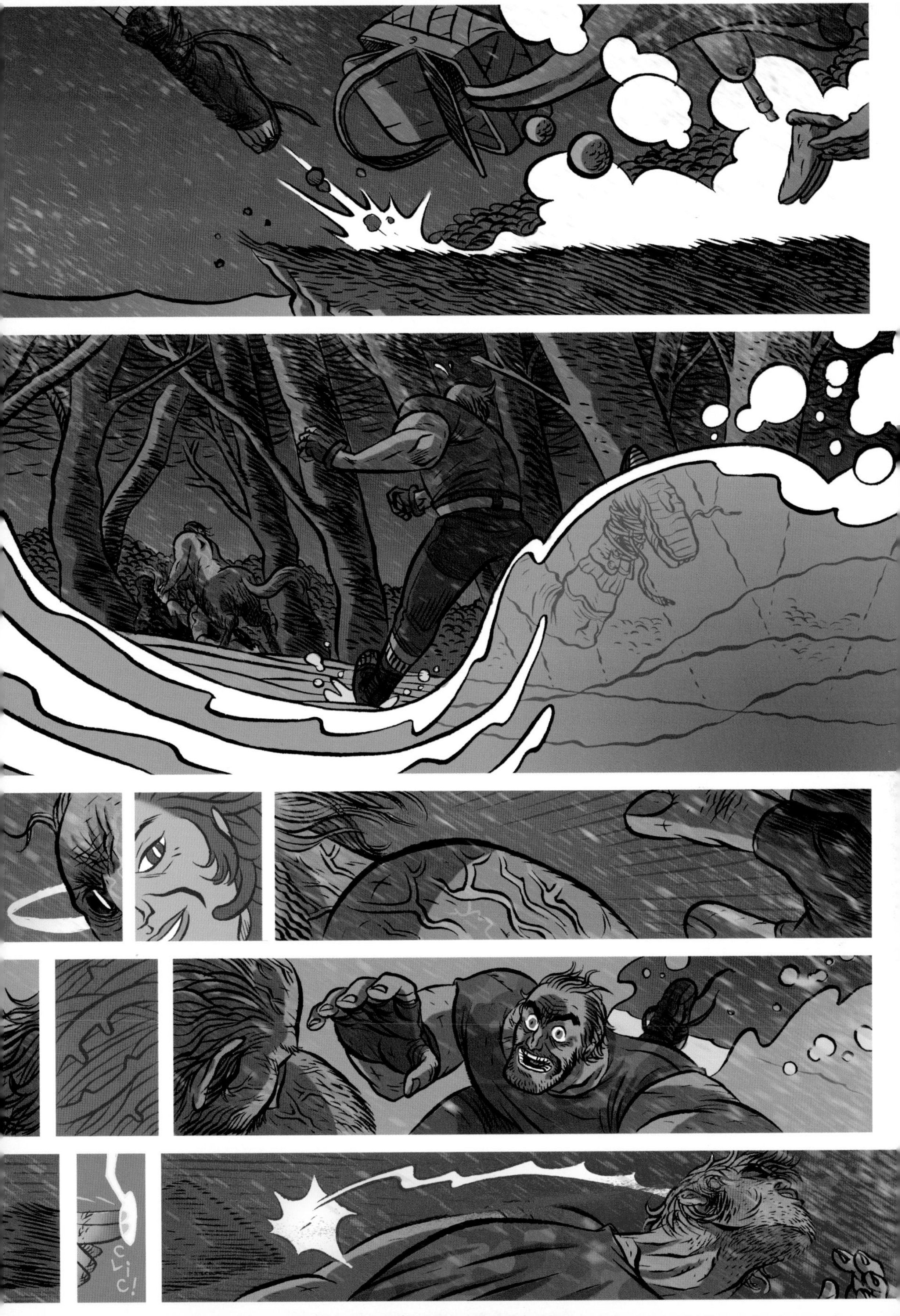
CLIC!

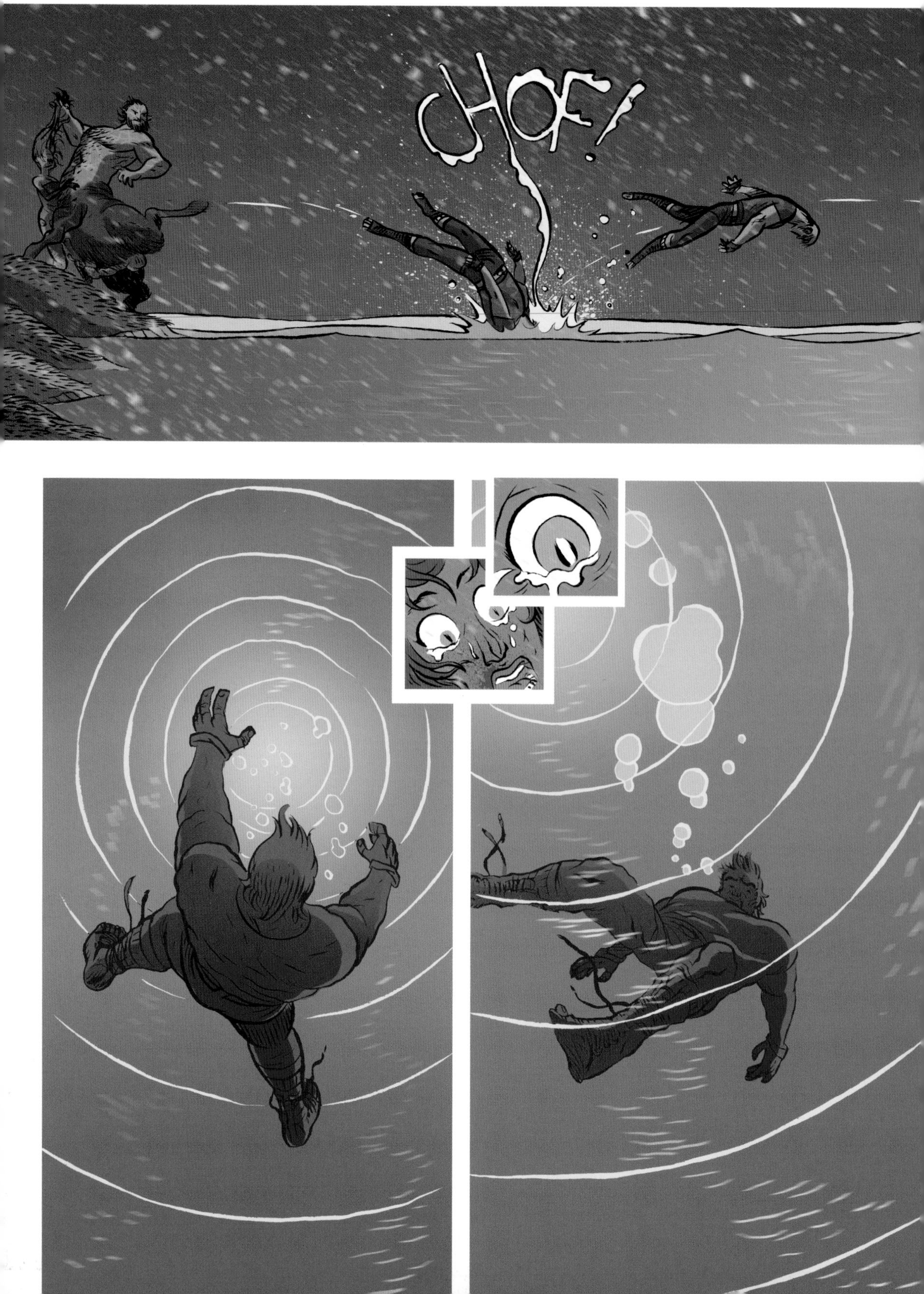
CHOF!

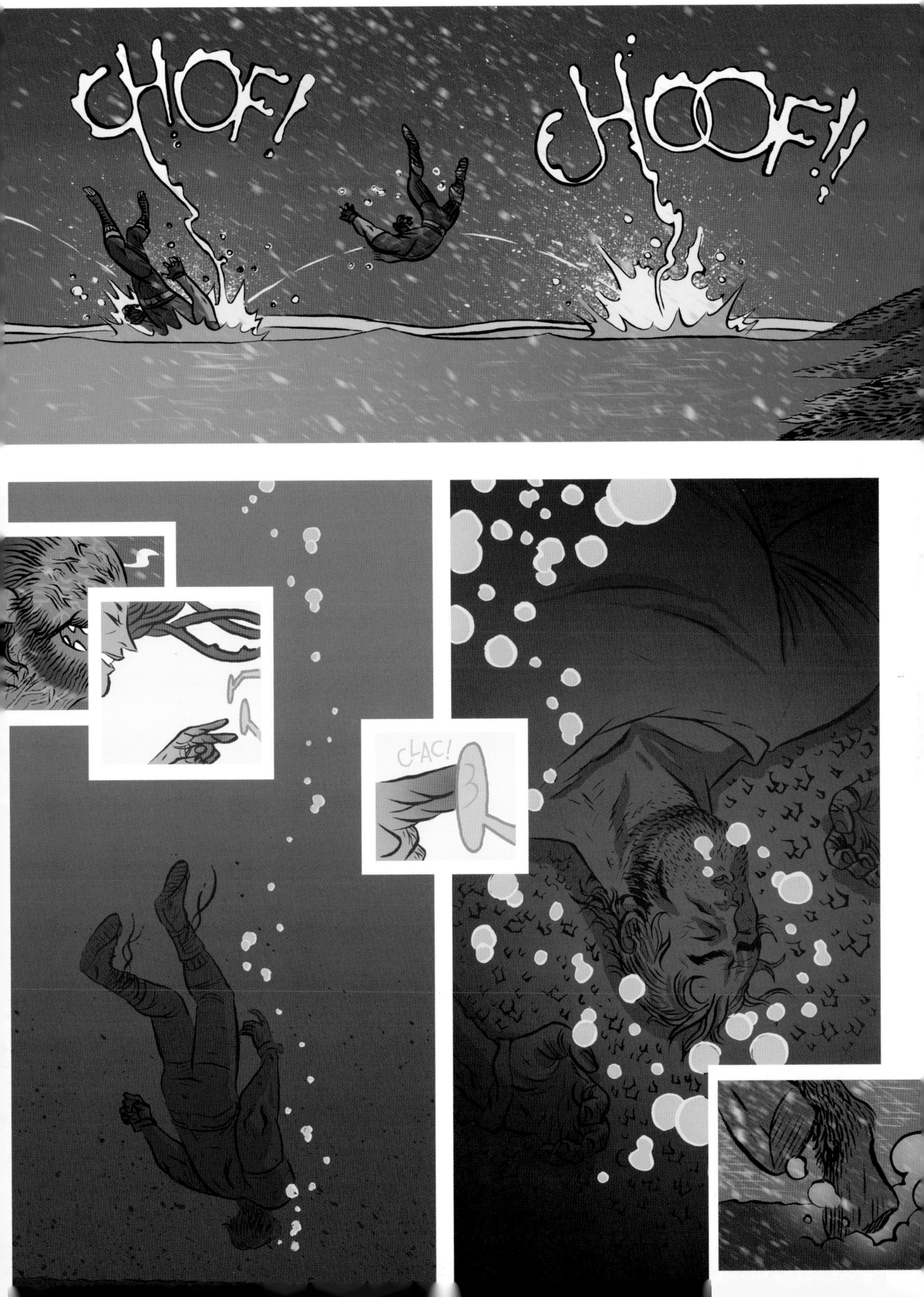
CHOF!
CHOOF!!
CLAC!

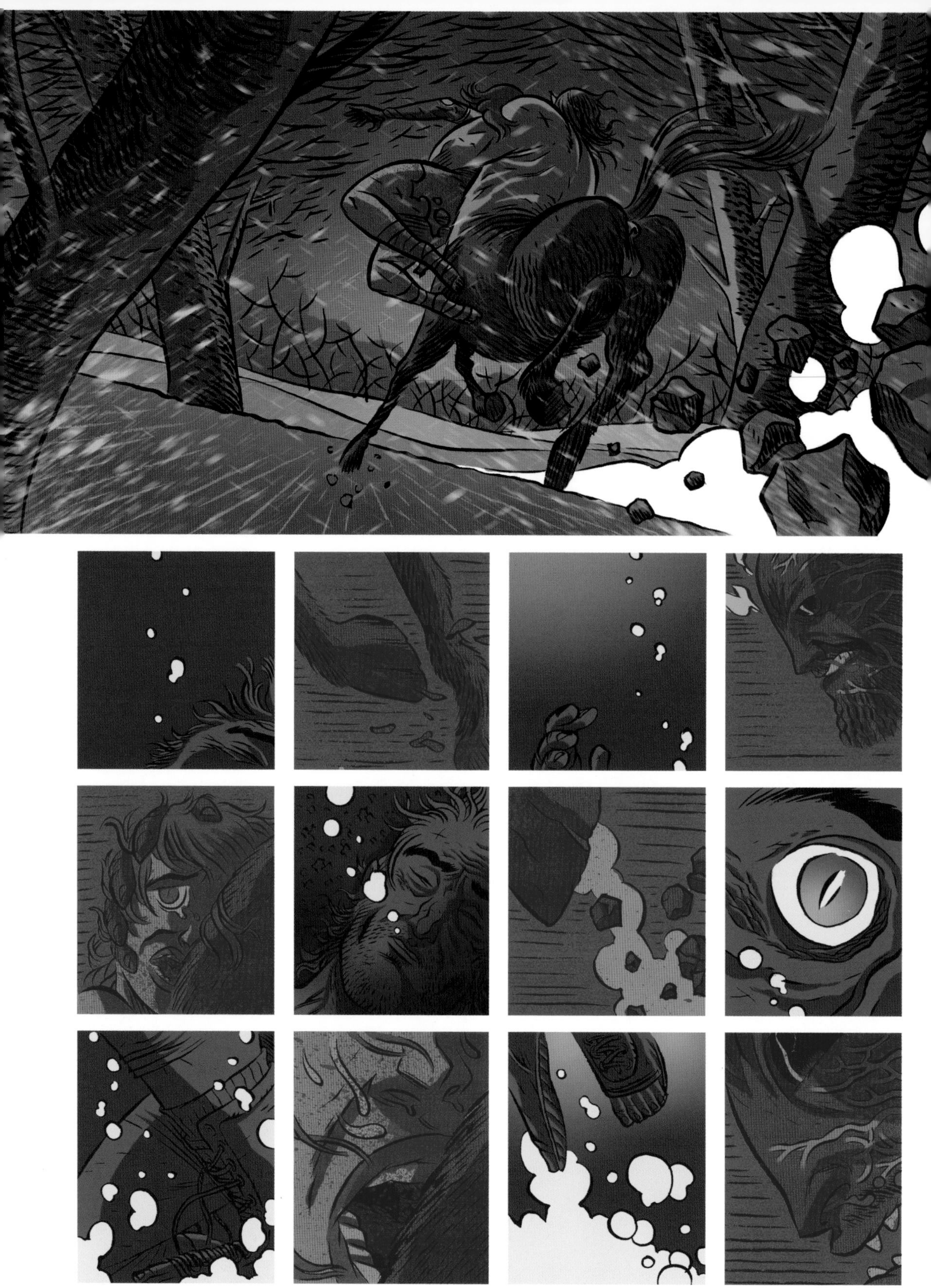

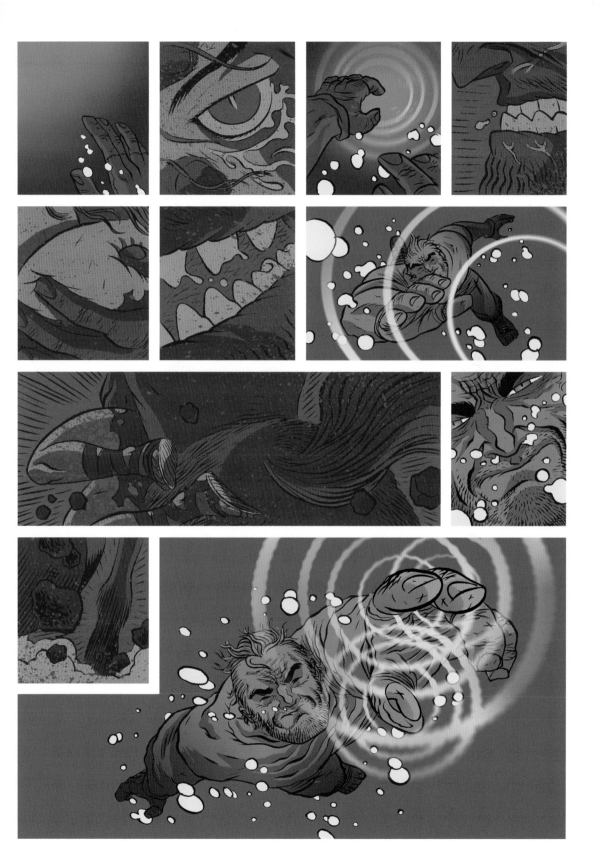

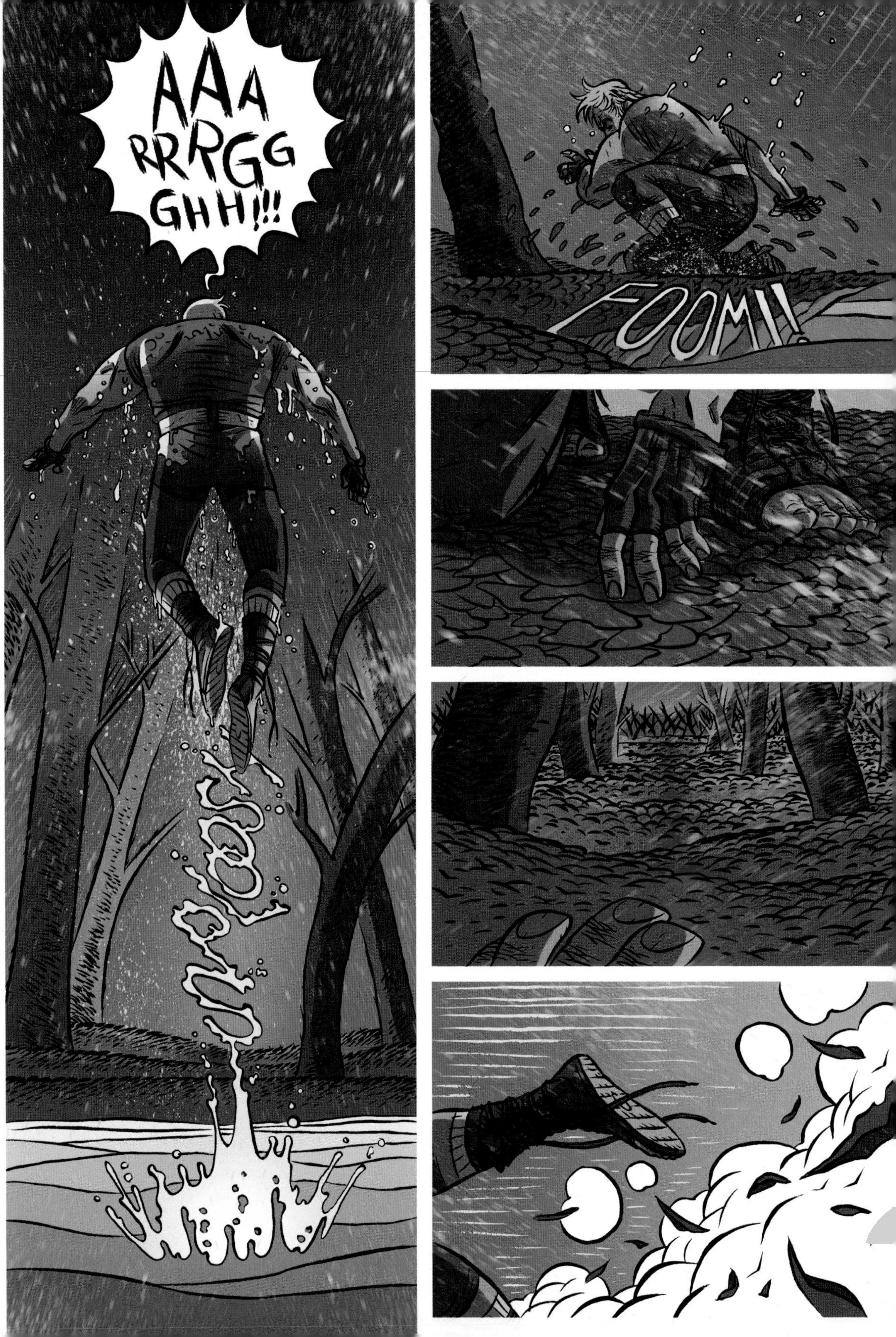
AAARRRGGGHH!!!
SPLOOSH
FOOM!!

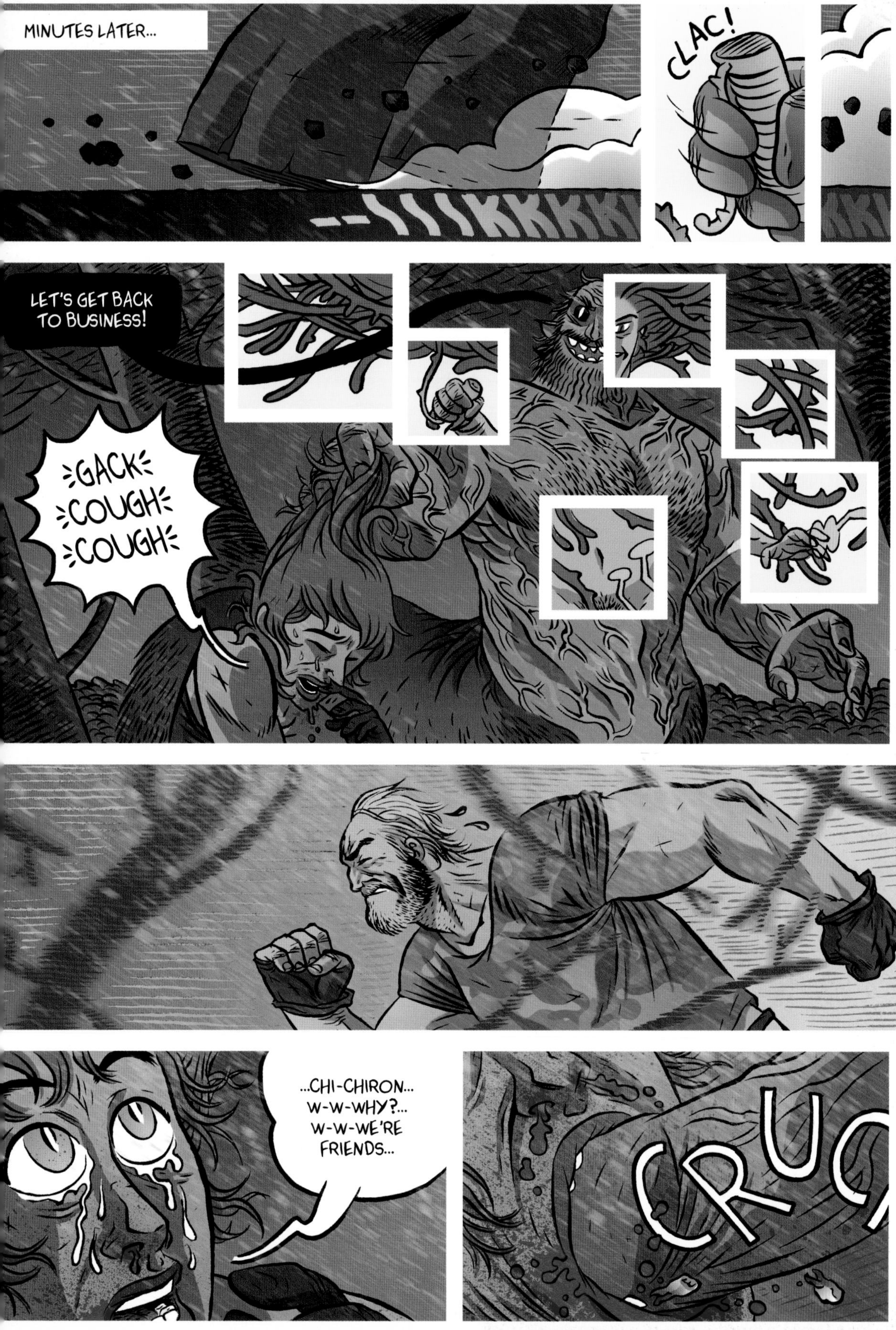
MINUTES LATER...
--IIIKKKK
CLAC!
LET'S GET BACK TO BUSINESS!
GACK COUGH COUGH
...CHI-CHIRON... W-W-WHY?... W-W-WE'RE FRIENDS...
CRUC

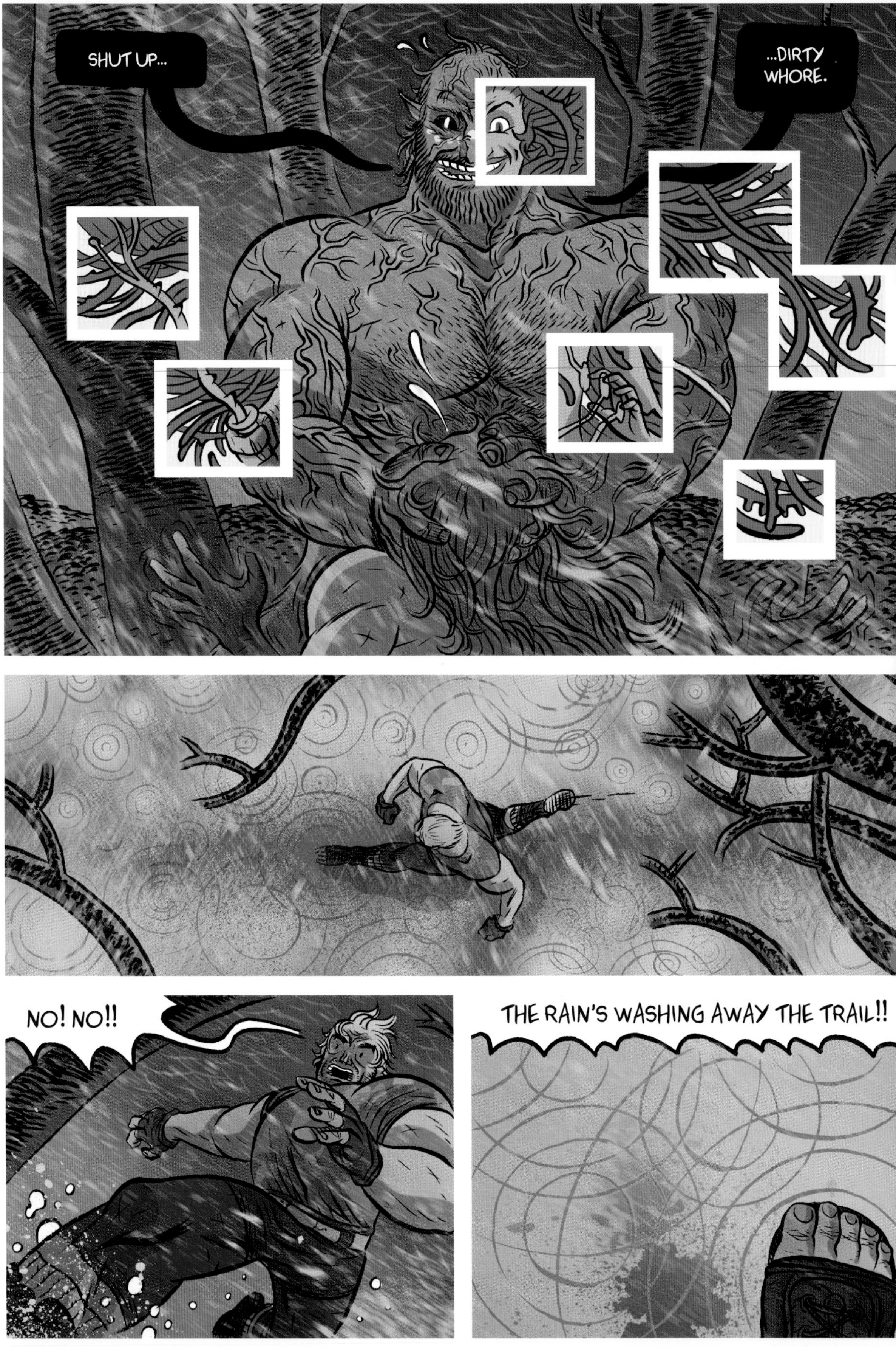
SHUT UP...
...DIRTY WHORE.
NO! NO!!
THE RAIN'S WASHING AWAY THE TRAIL!!

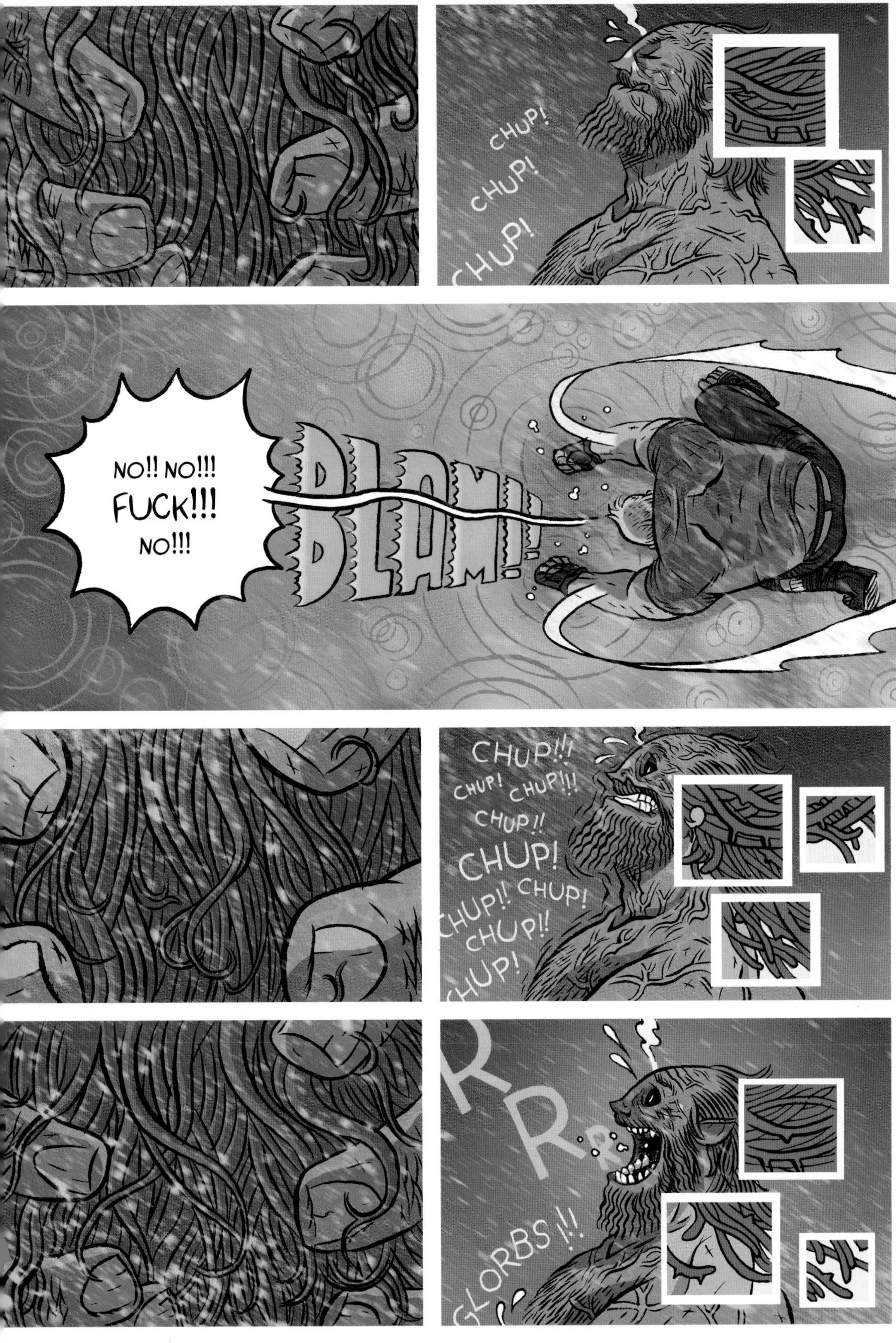
CHUP!
CHUP!
CHUP!
NO!! NO!!! FUCK!!! NO!!!
BLAM!!
CHUP!!!
CHUP! CHUP!!!
CHUP!!
CHUP!
CHUP!! CHUP!
CHUP!!
CHUP!
GLORBS!!

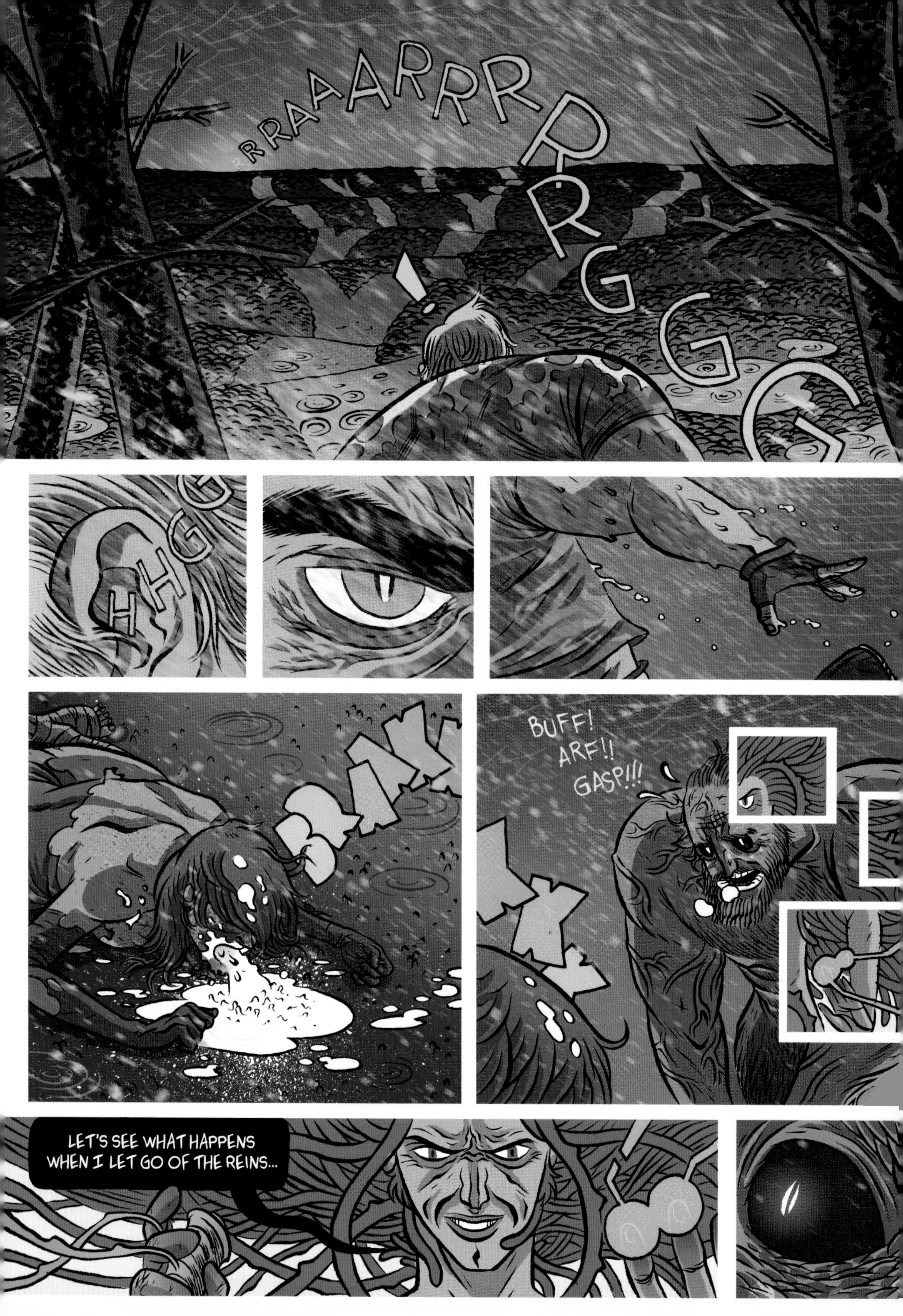

RRAAARRRRRGGG
HHGG
BRAKK
BUFF!
ARF!!
GASP!!!
LET'S SEE WHAT HAPPENS WHEN I LET GO OF THE REINS...

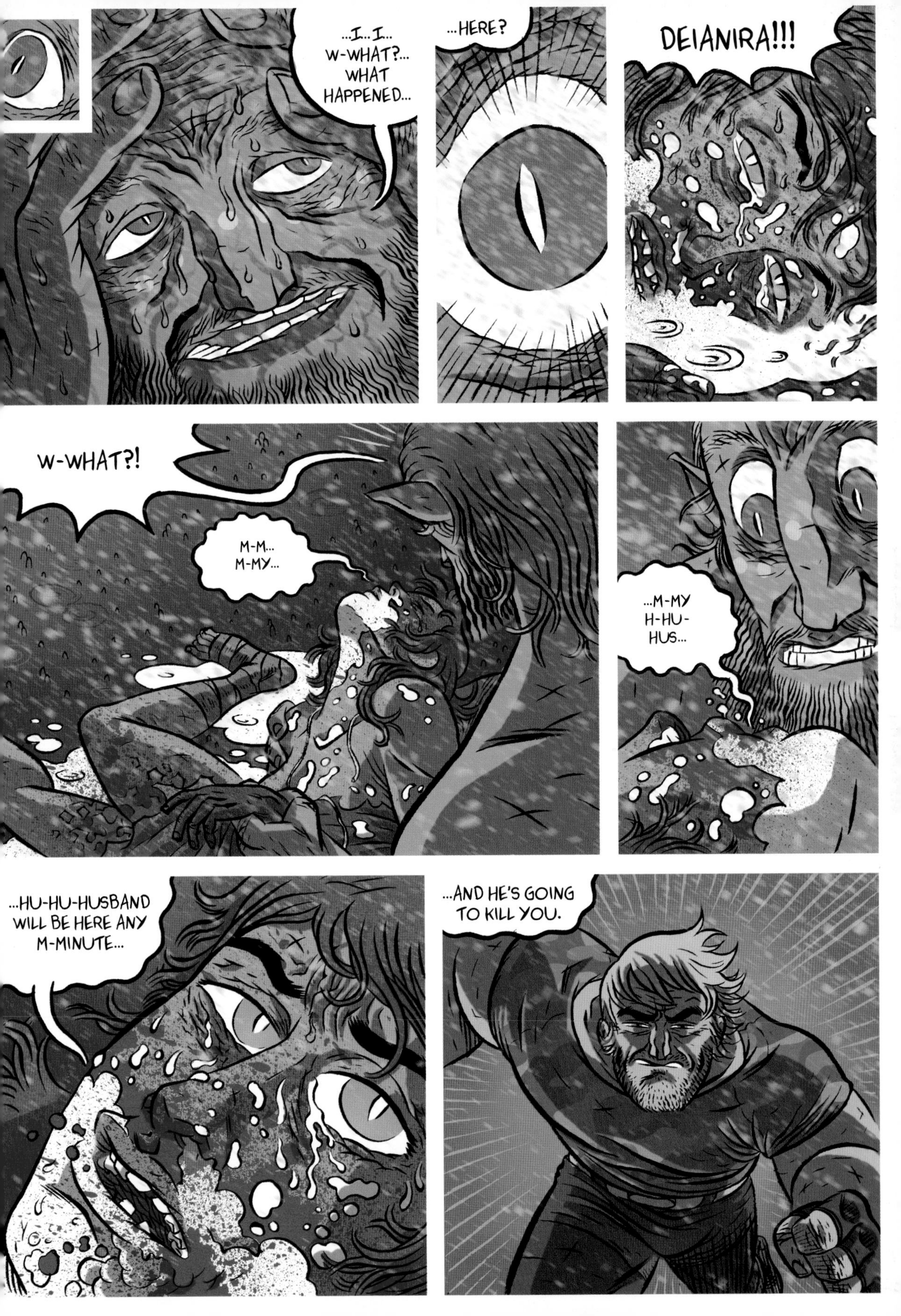
...I... I... W-WHAT?... WHAT HAPPENED...
...HERE?
DEIANIRA!!!
W-WHAT?!
M-M... M-MY...
...M-MY H-HU-HUS...
...HU-HU-HUSBAND WILL BE HERE ANY M-MINUTE...
...AND HE'S GOING TO KILL YOU.

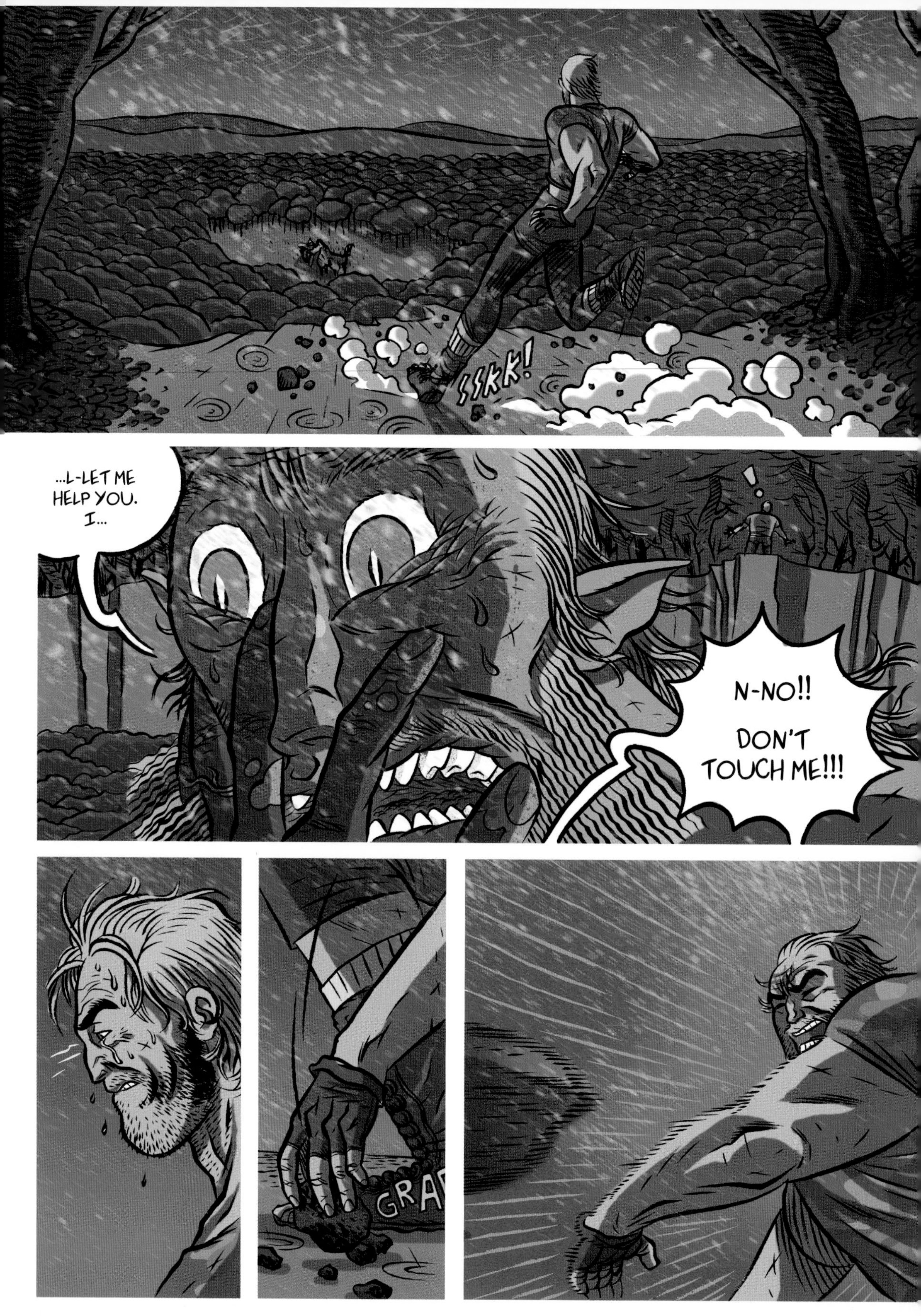
SSKK!
...L-LET ME HELP YOU. I...
N-NO!!
DON'T TOUCH ME!!!
GRA

ET'S TAKE BACK CONTROL...

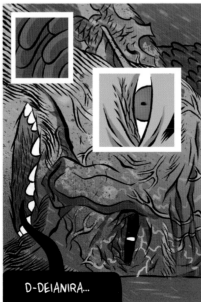

D-DEIANIRA...

I-I'VE DONE SOME-THING TERRIBLE...

I-I KNOW YOU CAN NEVER FORGIVE ME...

TOO

OMPP!!

L-LET...

LET ME DO SOMETHING FOR YOU...

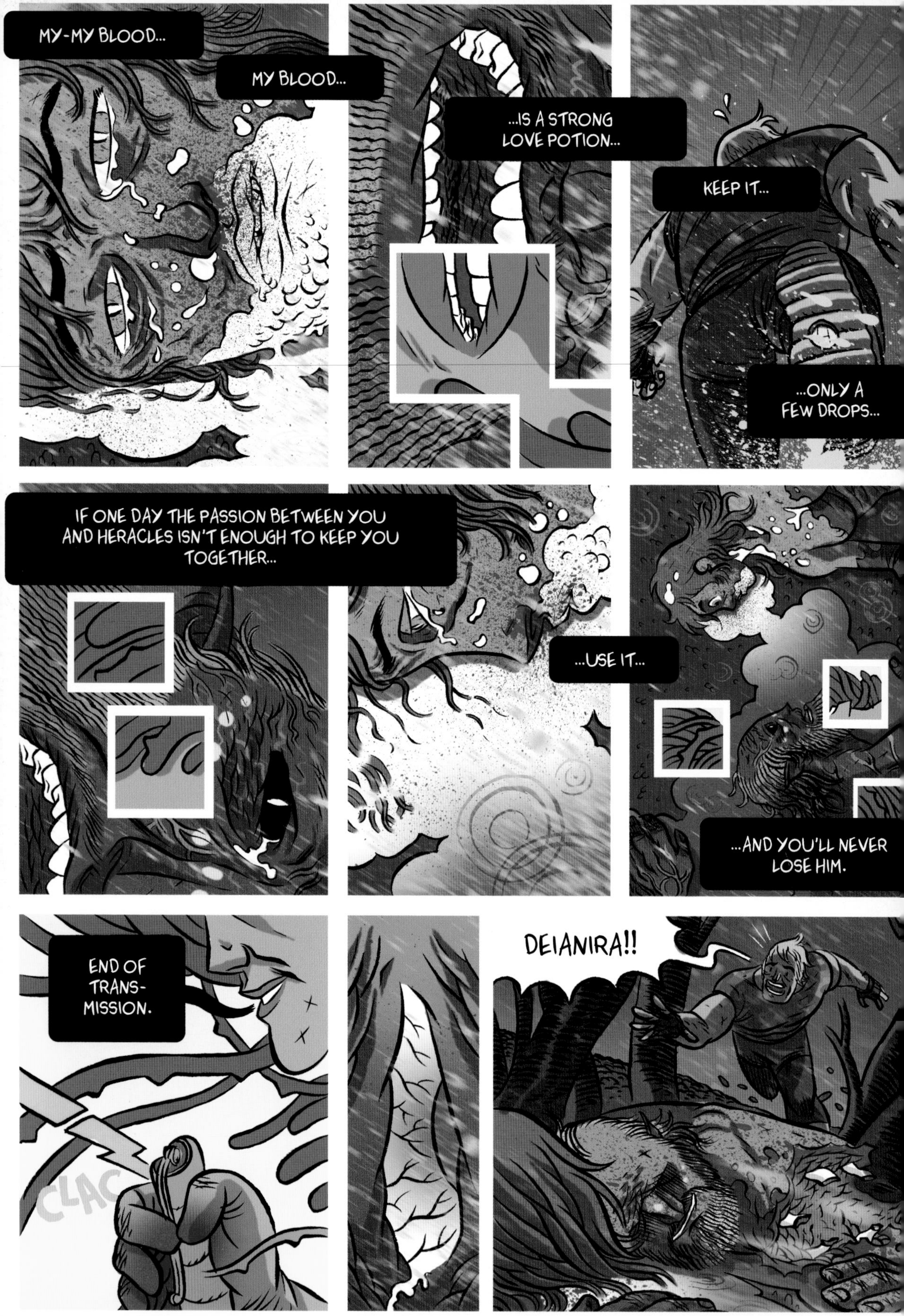
MY-MY BLOOD...
MY BLOOD...
...IS A STRONG LOVE POTION...
KEEP IT...
...ONLY A FEW DROPS...
IF ONE DAY THE PASSION BETWEEN YOU AND HERACLES ISN'T ENOUGH TO KEEP YOU TOGETHER...
...USE IT...
...AND YOU'LL NEVER LOSE HIM.
END OF TRANS-MISSION.
CLAC
DEIANIRA!!

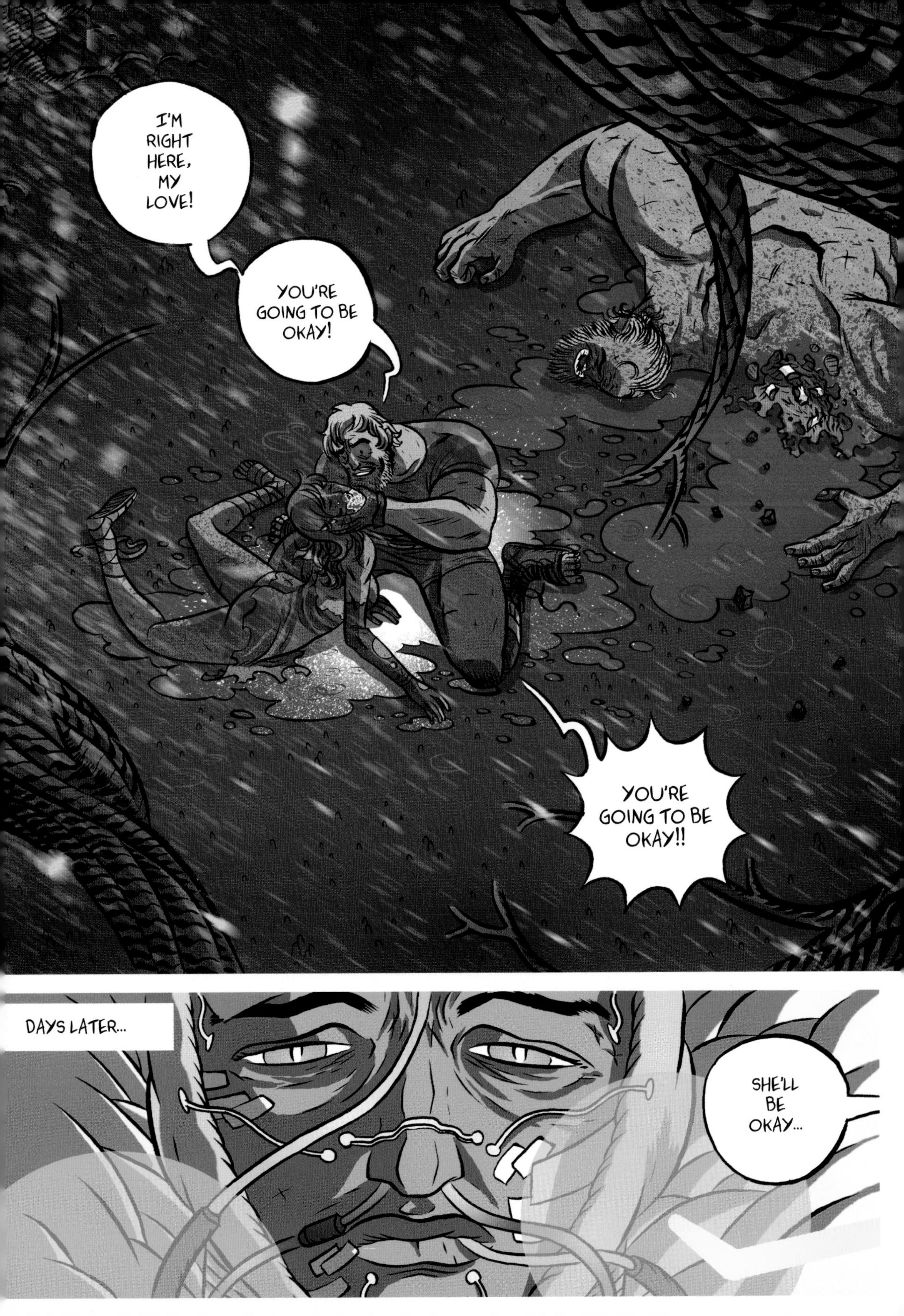
I'M RIGHT HERE, MY LOVE!
YOU'RE GOING TO BE OKAY!
YOU'RE GOING TO BE OKAY!!
DAYS LATER...
SHE'LL BE OKAY...

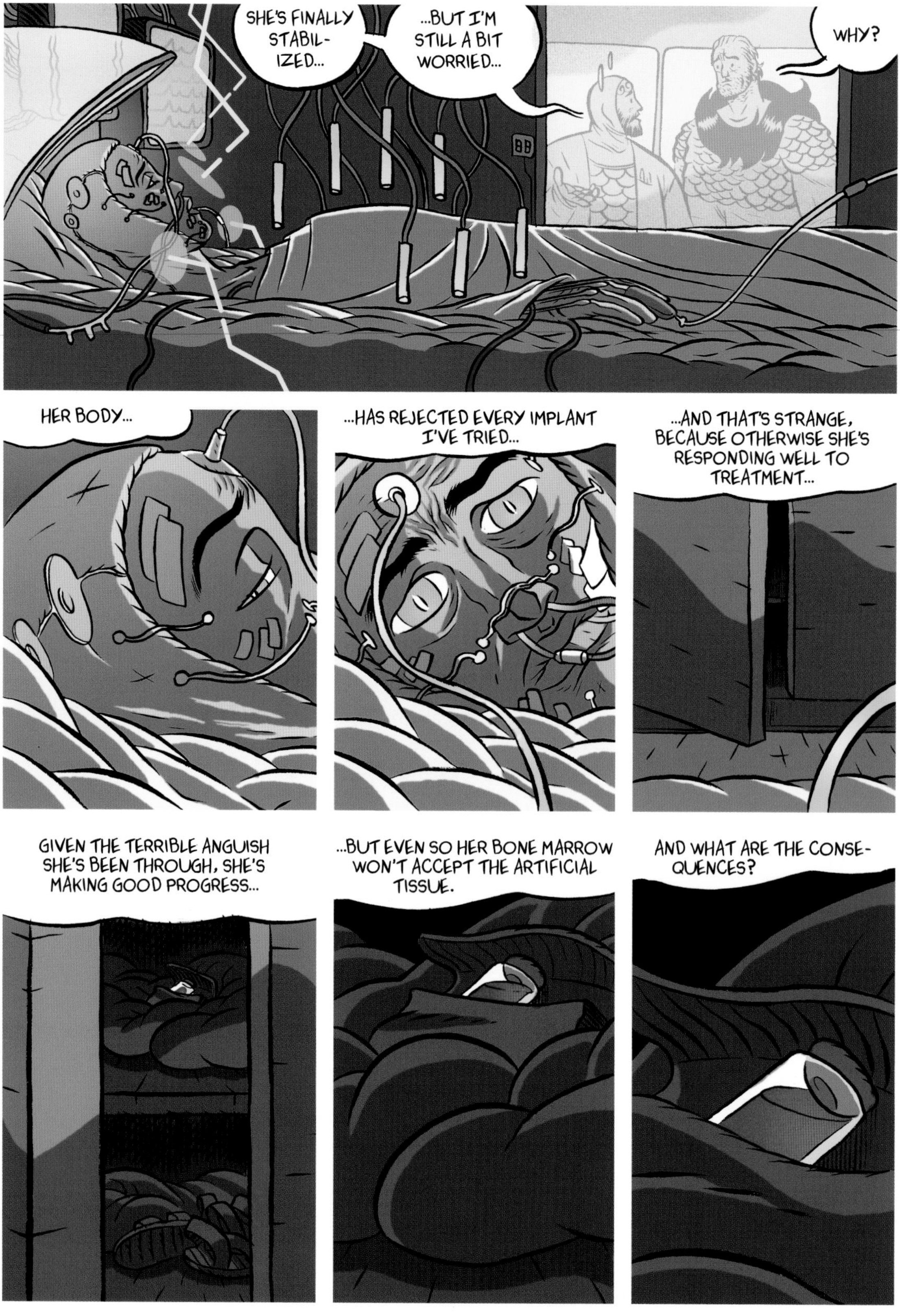
SHE'S FINALLY STABIL-IZED...
...BUT I'M STILL A BIT WORRIED...
WHY?
HER BODY...
...HAS REJECTED EVERY IMPLANT I'VE TRIED...
...AND THAT'S STRANGE, BECAUSE OTHERWISE SHE'S RESPONDING WELL TO TREATMENT...
GIVEN THE TERRIBLE ANGUISH SHE'S BEEN THROUGH, SHE'S MAKING GOOD PROGRESS...
...BUT EVEN SO HER BONE MARROW WON'T ACCEPT THE ARTIFICIAL TISSUE.
AND WHAT ARE THE CONSE-QUENCES?

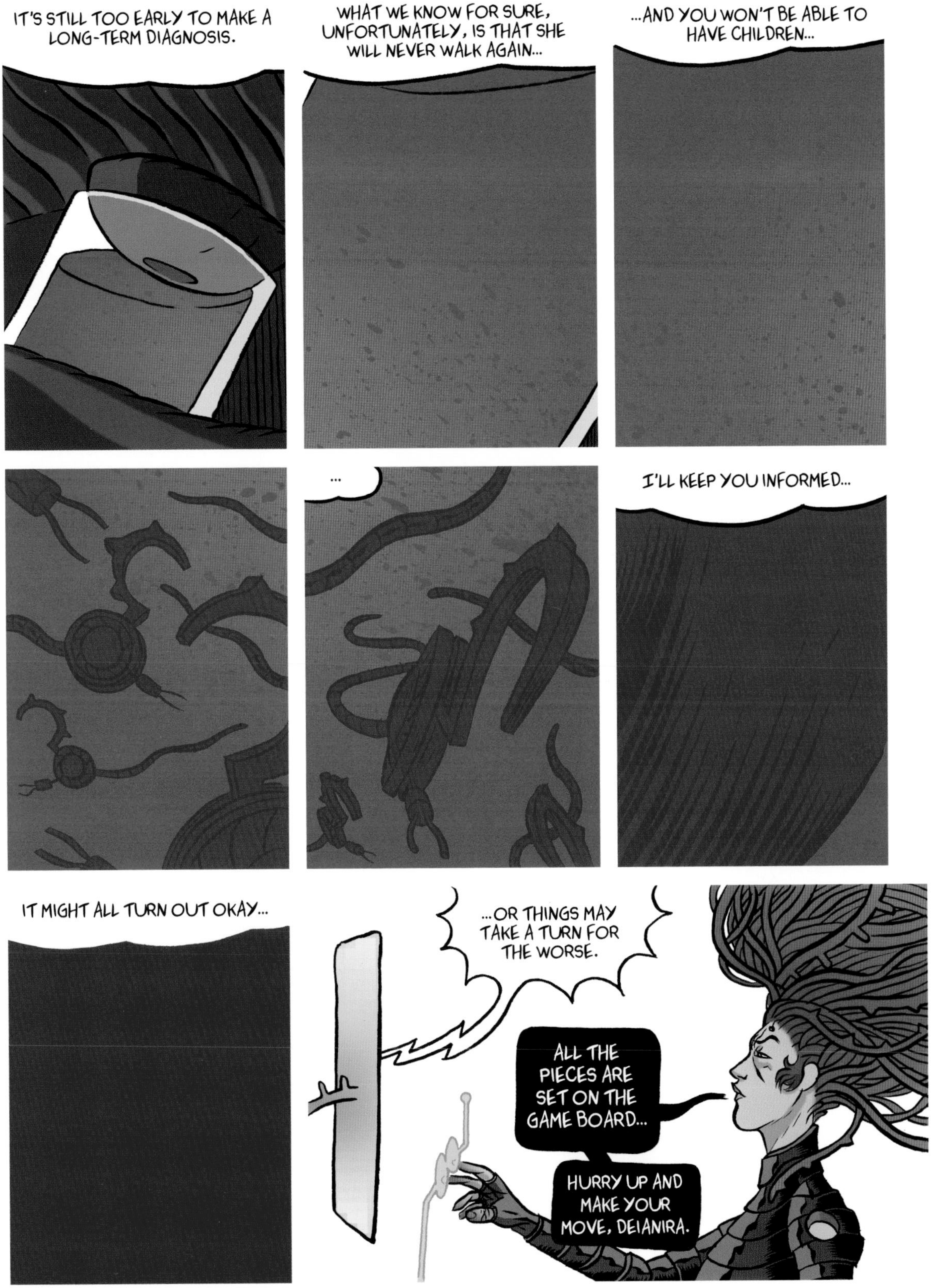

IT'S STILL TOO EARLY TO MAKE A LONG-TERM DIAGNOSIS.
WHAT WE KNOW FOR SURE, UNFORTUNATELY, IS THAT SHE WILL NEVER WALK AGAIN...
...AND YOU WON'T BE ABLE TO HAVE CHILDREN...
...
I'LL KEEP YOU INFORMED...
IT MIGHT ALL TURN OUT OKAY...
...OR THINGS MAY TAKE A TURN FOR THE WORSE.
ALL THE PIECES ARE SET ON THE GAME BOARD...
HURRY UP AND MAKE YOUR MOVE, DEIANIRA.

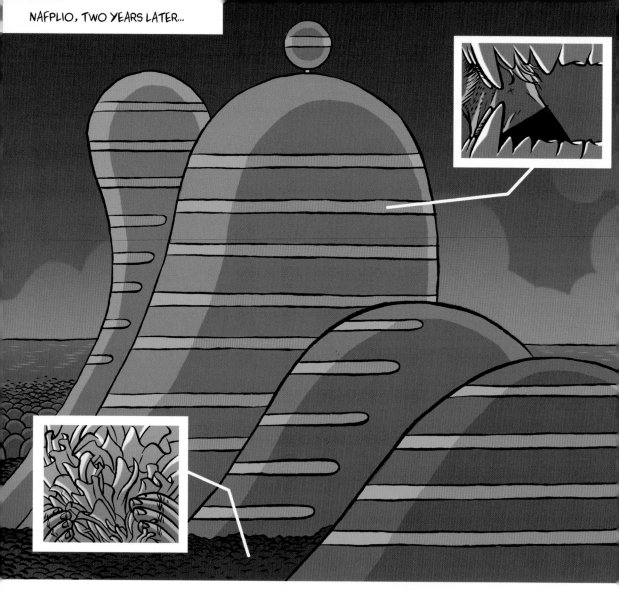

NAFPLIO, TWO YEARS LATER...

WE'RE WITHERING, MY LOVE, LIKE THE FLOWERS IN WINTER...

SO MANY VICTORIES, MY DARLING, SO MANY CHALLENGES OVERCOME...

...FOR WHAT?

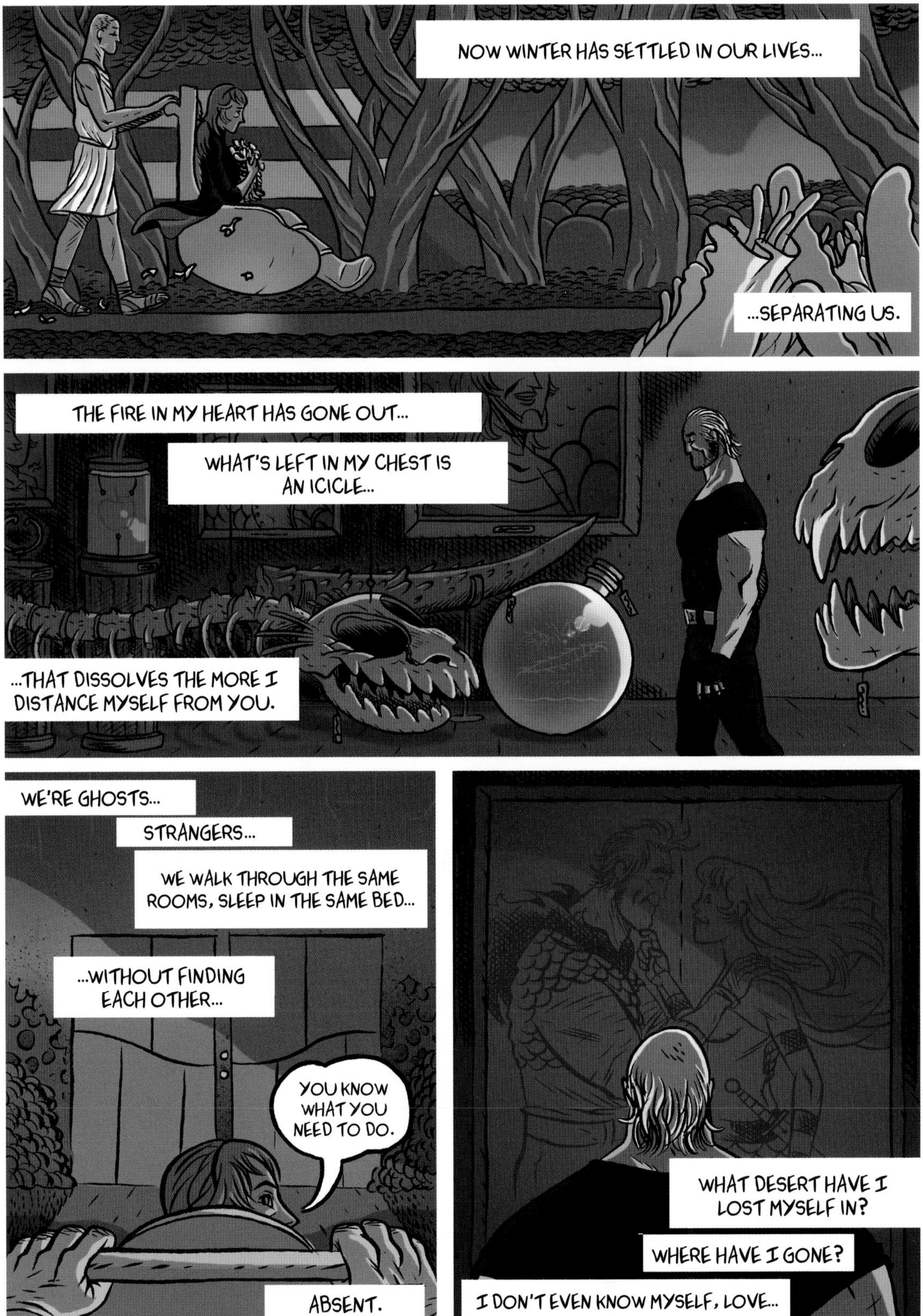
NOW WINTER HAS SETTLED IN OUR LIVES...
...SEPARATING US.
THE FIRE IN MY HEART HAS GONE OUT...
WHAT'S LEFT IN MY CHEST IS AN ICICLE...
...THAT DISSOLVES THE MORE I DISTANCE MYSELF FROM YOU.
WE'RE GHOSTS...
STRANGERS...
WE WALK THROUGH THE SAME ROOMS, SLEEP IN THE SAME BED...
...WITHOUT FINDING EACH OTHER...
YOU KNOW WHAT YOU NEED TO DO.
ABSENT.
WHAT DESERT HAVE I LOST MYSELF IN?
WHERE HAVE I GONE?
I DON'T EVEN KNOW MYSELF, LOVE...

WHERE ARE YOU, MY LOVE?

WHERE HAVE YOU HIDDEN AWAY YOUR HEART?

I, WHO WORRY ABOUT EVERY ONE OF THE SOULS THAT WALK ON THIS EARTH...

I HAVE TURNED MY BACK ON YOU, THE ONE I LOVE THE MOST.

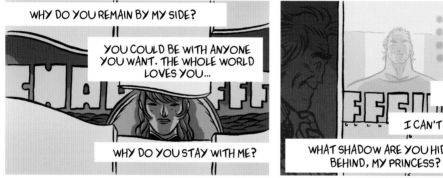

WHY DO YOU REMAIN BY MY SIDE?

YOU COULD BE WITH ANYONE YOU WANT. THE WHOLE WORLD LOVES YOU...

WHY DO YOU STAY WITH ME?

NOT LIKE BEFORE...

I CAN'T EVEN SEE YOU...

WHAT SHADOW ARE YOU HIDING BEHIND, MY PRINCESS?

IT STARTED WITH THE INCIDENT WITH THE CENTAUR...

SINCE THEN YOU DON'T EVEN LOOK AT ME.

WHAT HAVE I BECOME?

I ONLY FEEL LIKE MYSELF ON THE BATTLEFIELD...

MY HEARTBEAT ONLY QUICKENS WHEN I BRANDISH MY SWORD.

I'M NO LONGER THE WARRIOR PRINCESS, THE PROUD, STRONG WOMAN YOU FELL IN LOVE WITH.

MY PRIDE COVERS EVERY- THING...

MY ACHIEVE- MENTS...

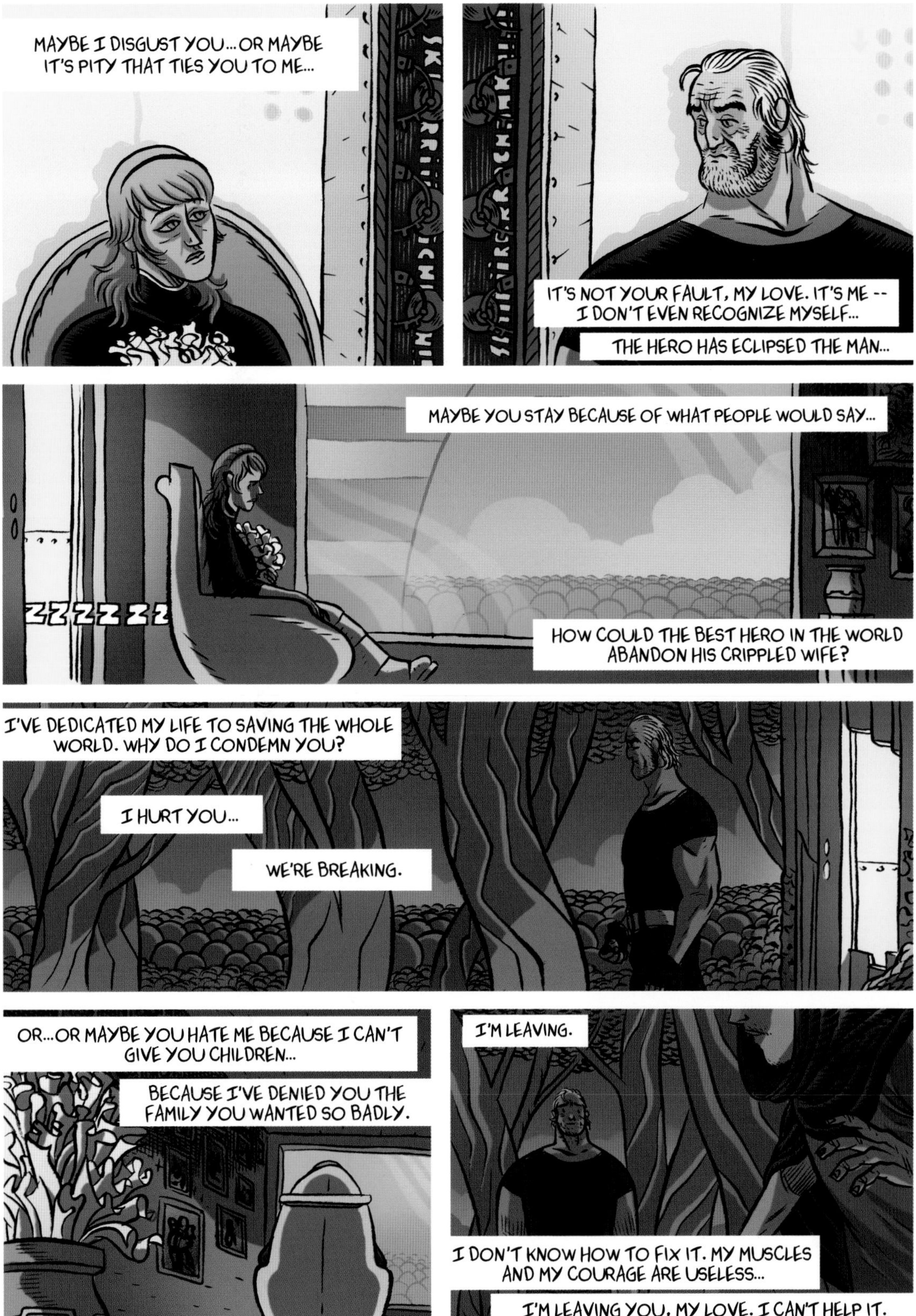
MAYBE I DISGUST YOU... OR MAYBE IT'S PITY THAT TIES YOU TO ME...
IT'S NOT YOUR FAULT, MY LOVE. IT'S ME -- I DON'T EVEN RECOGNIZE MYSELF...
THE HERO HAS ECLIPSED THE MAN...
MAYBE YOU STAY BECAUSE OF WHAT PEOPLE WOULD SAY...
ZZZZZZ
HOW COULD THE BEST HERO IN THE WORLD ABANDON HIS CRIPPLED WIFE?
I'VE DEDICATED MY LIFE TO SAVING THE WHOLE WORLD. WHY DO I CONDEMN YOU?
I HURT YOU...
WE'RE BREAKING.
OR... OR MAYBE YOU HATE ME BECAUSE I CAN'T GIVE YOU CHILDREN...
BECAUSE I'VE DENIED YOU THE FAMILY YOU WANTED SO BADLY.
I'M LEAVING.
I DON'T KNOW HOW TO FIX IT. MY MUSCLES AND MY COURAGE ARE USELESS...
I'M LEAVING YOU, MY LOVE. I CAN'T HELP IT.

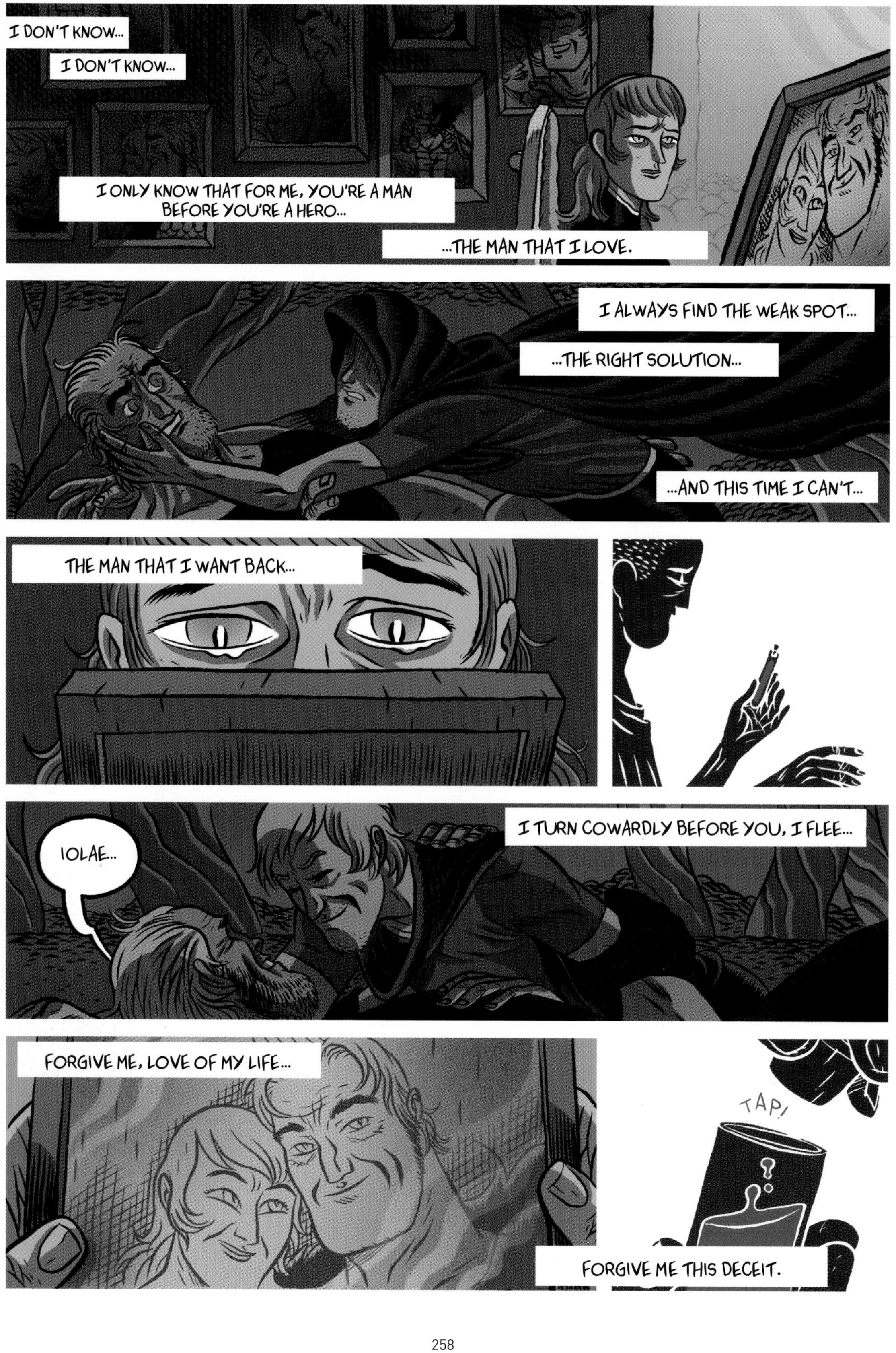
I DON'T KNOW...
I DON'T KNOW...
I ONLY KNOW THAT FOR ME, YOU'RE A MAN BEFORE YOU'RE A HERO...
...THE MAN THAT I LOVE.
I ALWAYS FIND THE WEAK SPOT...
...THE RIGHT SOLUTION...
...AND THIS TIME I CAN'T...
THE MAN THAT I WANT BACK...
I TURN COWARDLY BEFORE YOU, I FLEE...
IOLAE...
FORGIVE ME, LOVE OF MY LIFE...
TAP!
FORGIVE ME THIS DECEIT.

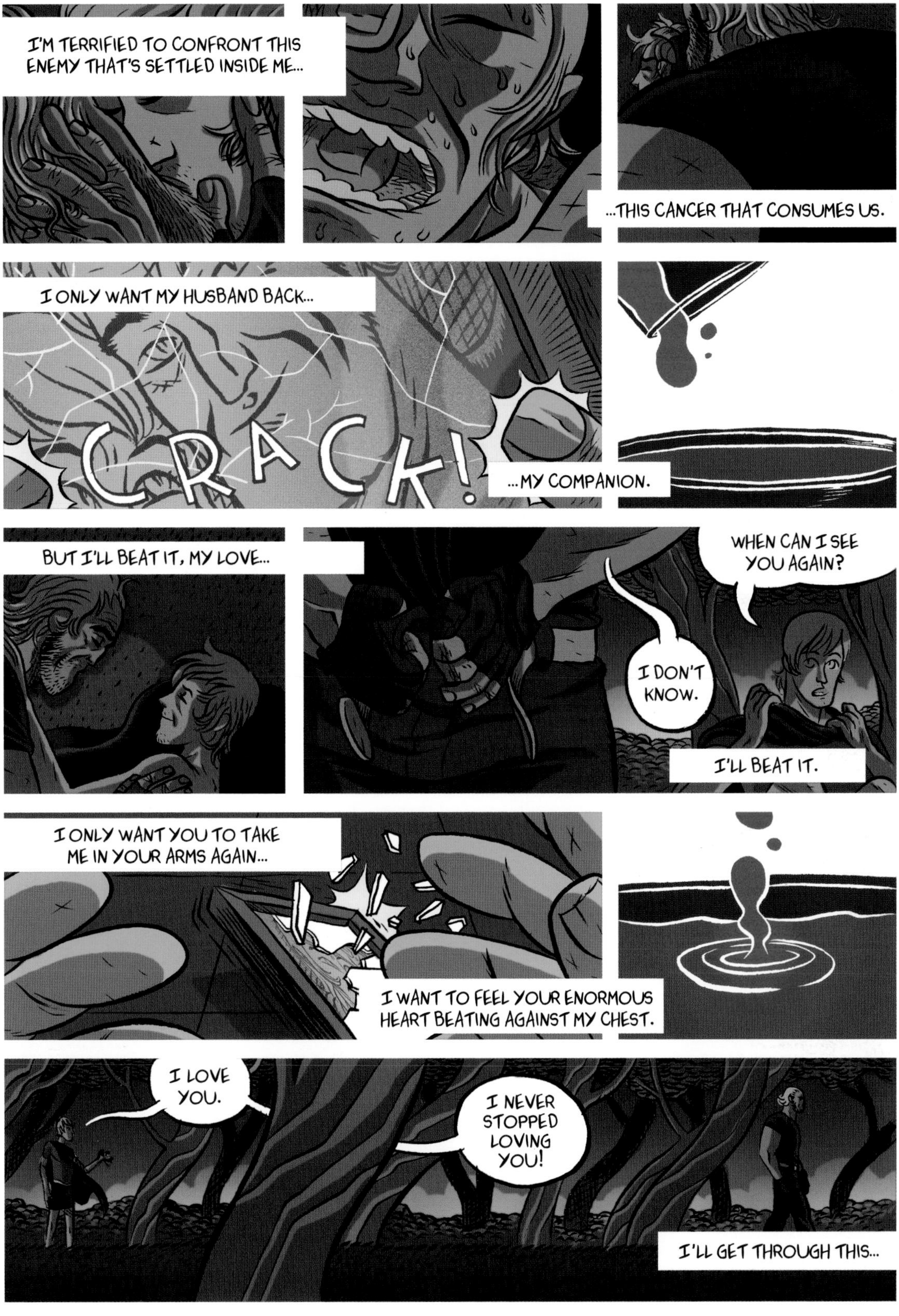
I'M TERRIFIED TO CONFRONT THIS ENEMY THAT'S SETTLED INSIDE ME...
...THIS CANCER THAT CONSUMES US.
I ONLY WANT MY HUSBAND BACK...
CRACK!
...MY COMPANION.
BUT I'LL BEAT IT, MY LOVE...
WHEN CAN I SEE YOU AGAIN?
I DON'T KNOW.
I'LL BEAT IT.
I ONLY WANT YOU TO TAKE ME IN YOUR ARMS AGAIN...
I WANT TO FEEL YOUR ENORMOUS HEART BEATING AGAINST MY CHEST.
I LOVE YOU.
I NEVER STOPPED LOVING YOU!
I'LL GET THROUGH THIS...

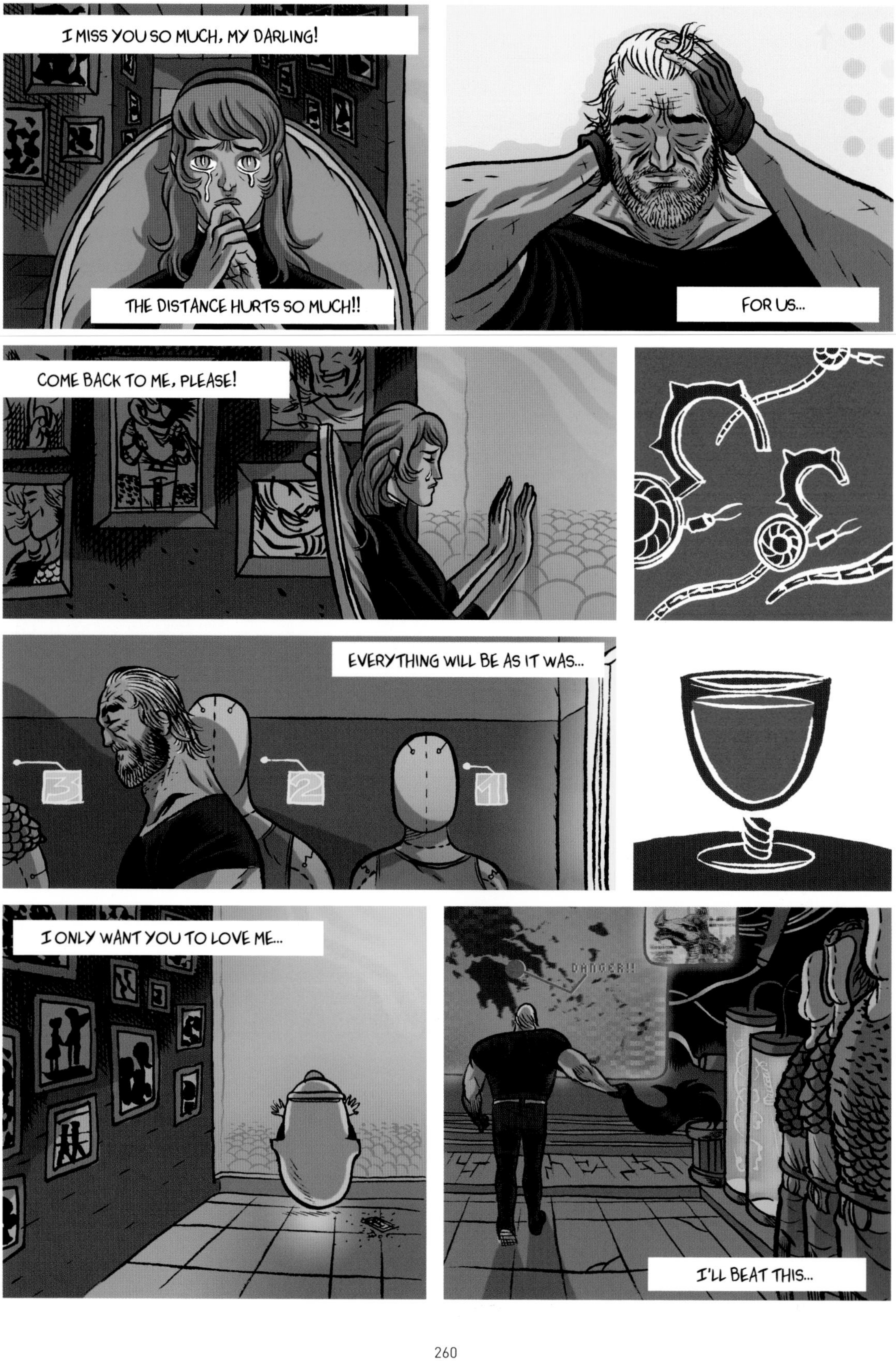
I MISS YOU SO MUCH, MY DARLING!
THE DISTANCE HURTS SO MUCH!!
FOR US...
COME BACK TO ME, PLEASE!
EVERYTHING WILL BE AS IT WAS...
3
2
1
I ONLY WANT YOU TO LOVE ME...
DANGER!!
I'LL BEAT THIS...

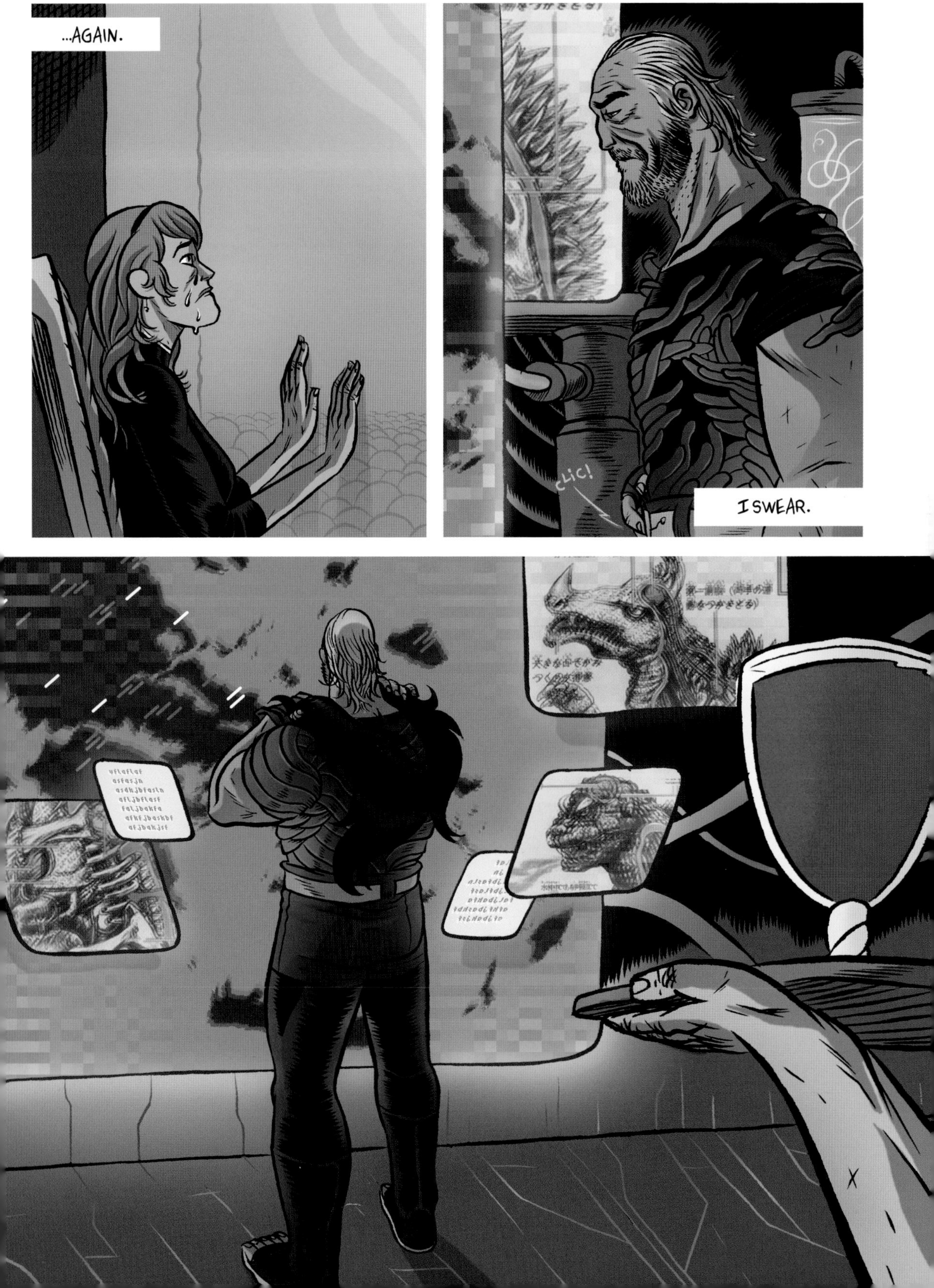
...AGAIN.
CLIC!
I SWEAR.

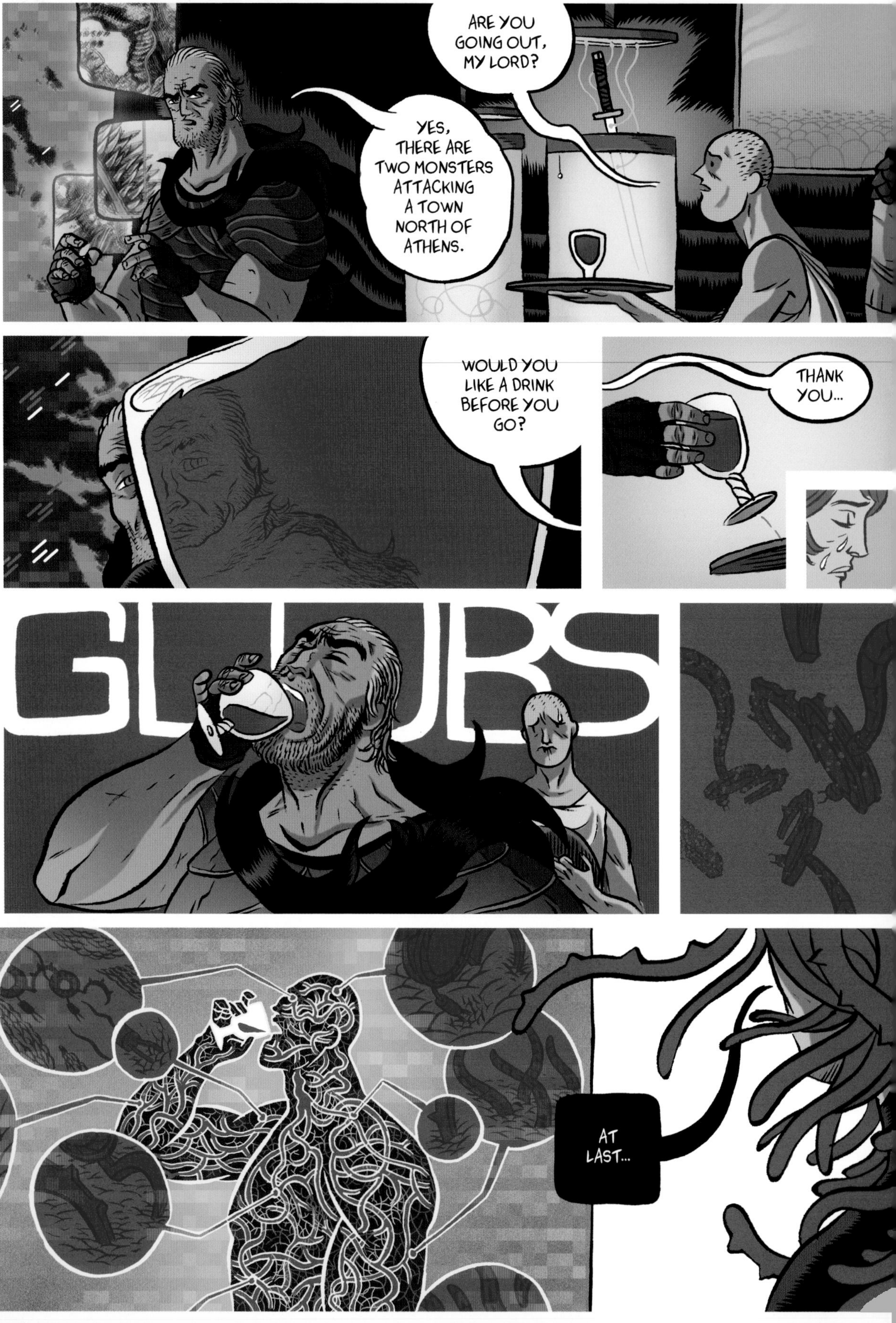

ARE YOU GOING OUT, MY LORD?
YES, THERE ARE TWO MONSTERS ATTACKING A TOWN NORTH OF ATHENS.
WOULD YOU LIKE A DRINK BEFORE YOU GO?
THANK YOU...
AT LAST...

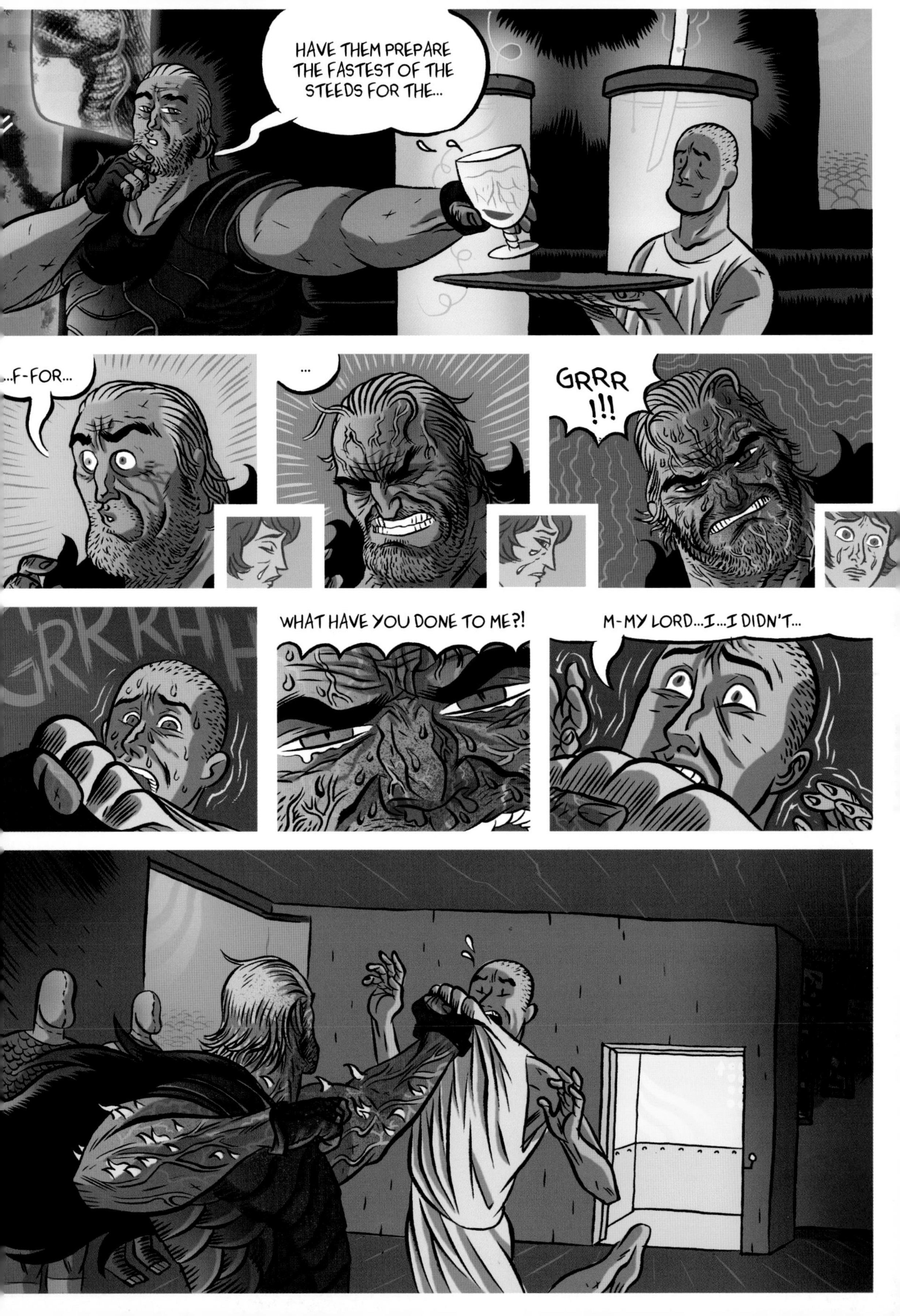

HAVE THEM PREPARE THE FASTEST OF THE STEEDS FOR THE...
...F-FOR...
...
GRRR !!!
GRKRAH
WHAT HAVE YOU DONE TO ME?!
M-MY LORD...I...I DIDN'T...

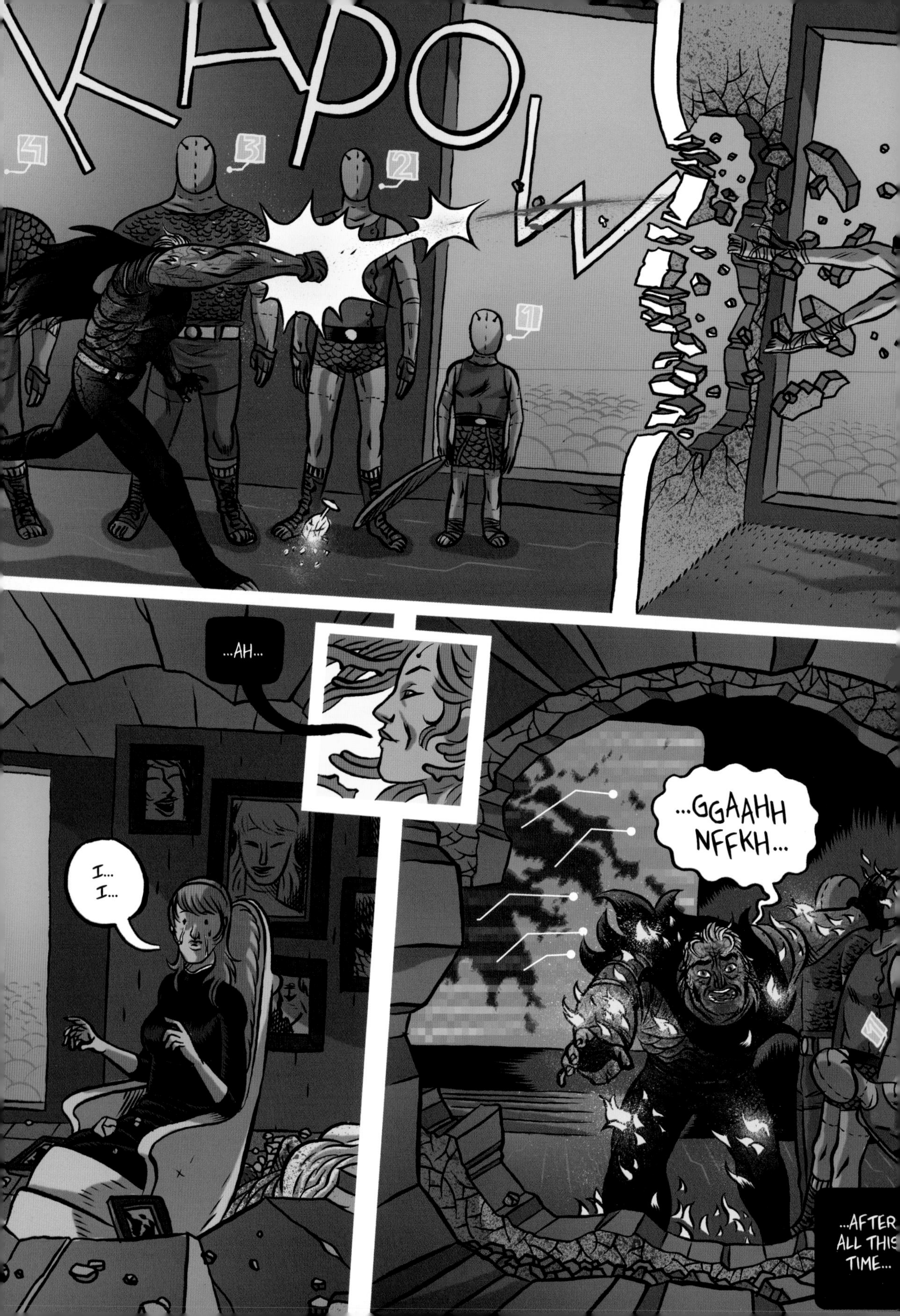
KAPOW
1
2
3
4
...AH...
I...
I...
...GGAAHH
NFFKH...
...AFTER
ALL THIS
TIME...

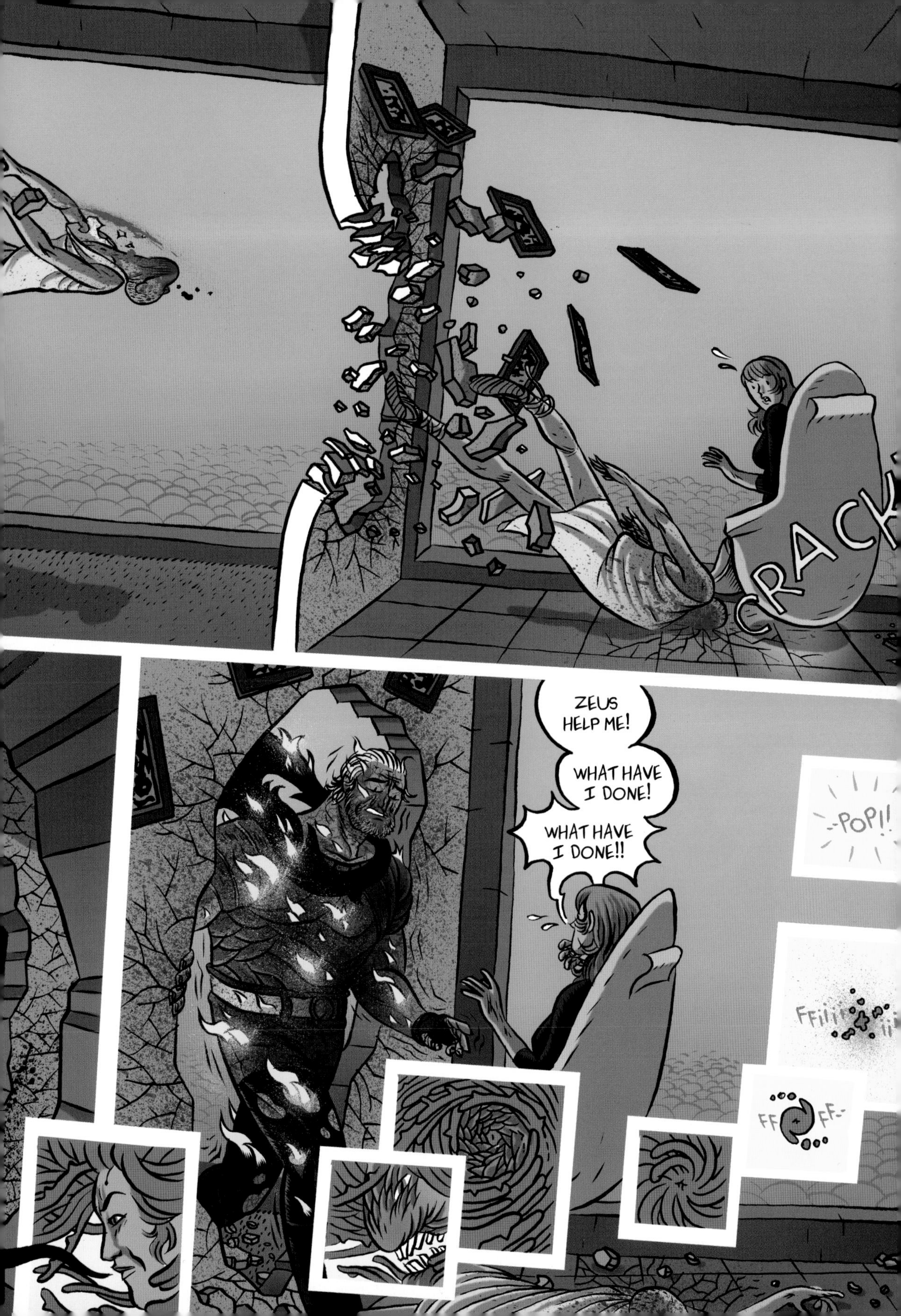
CRACK!
ZEUS HELP ME!
WHAT HAVE I DONE!
WHAT HAVE I DONE!!
-POP!!
FFiii
FF- FF-

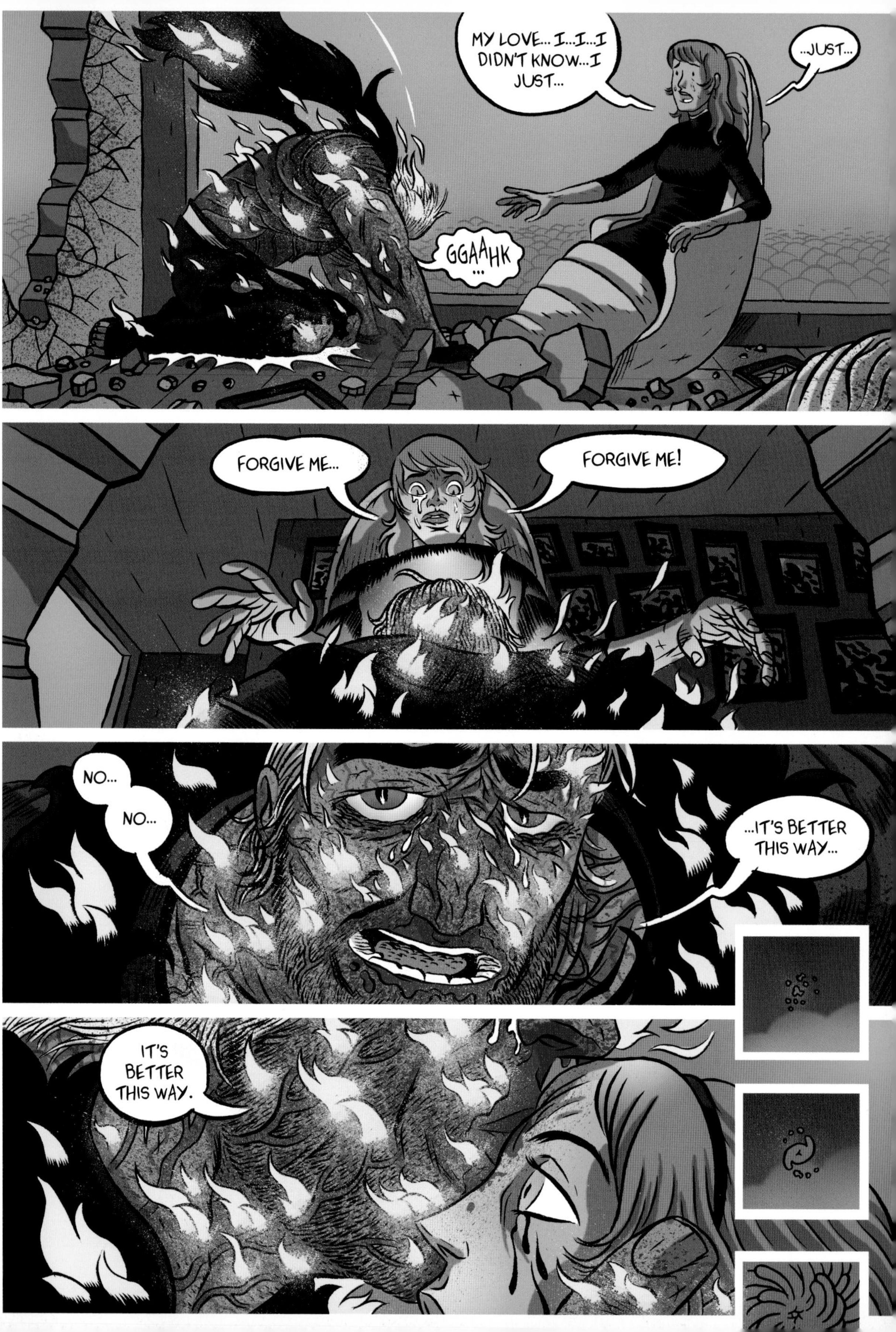
MY LOVE... I...I...I DIDN'T KNOW...I JUST...
...JUST...
GGAAHK ...
FORGIVE ME...
FORGIVE ME!
NO...
NO...
...IT'S BETTER THIS WAY...
IT'S BETTER THIS WAY.

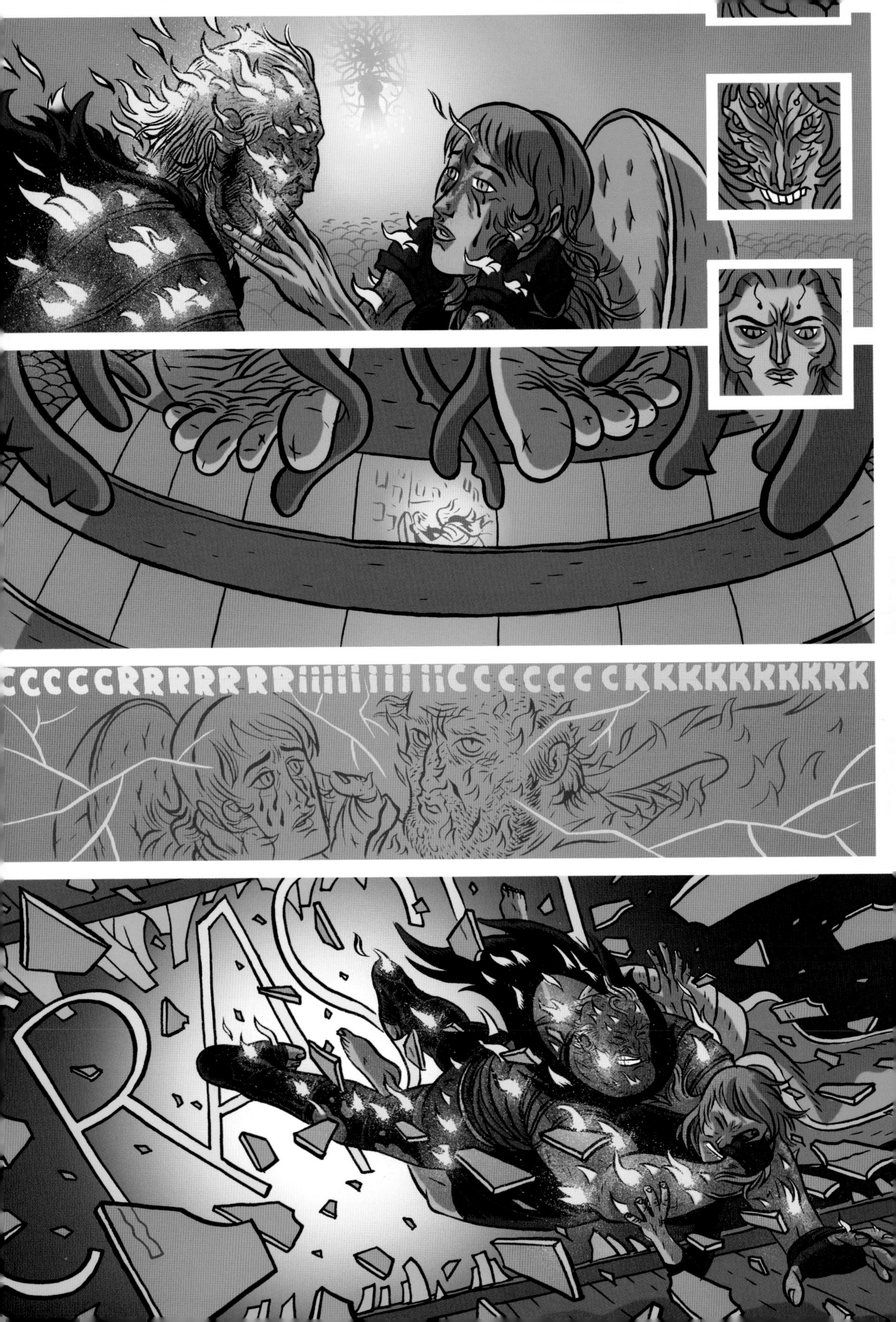
CCCCCRRRRRRRRiiiiiiiii iiCCCCCCCKKKKKKKKKK

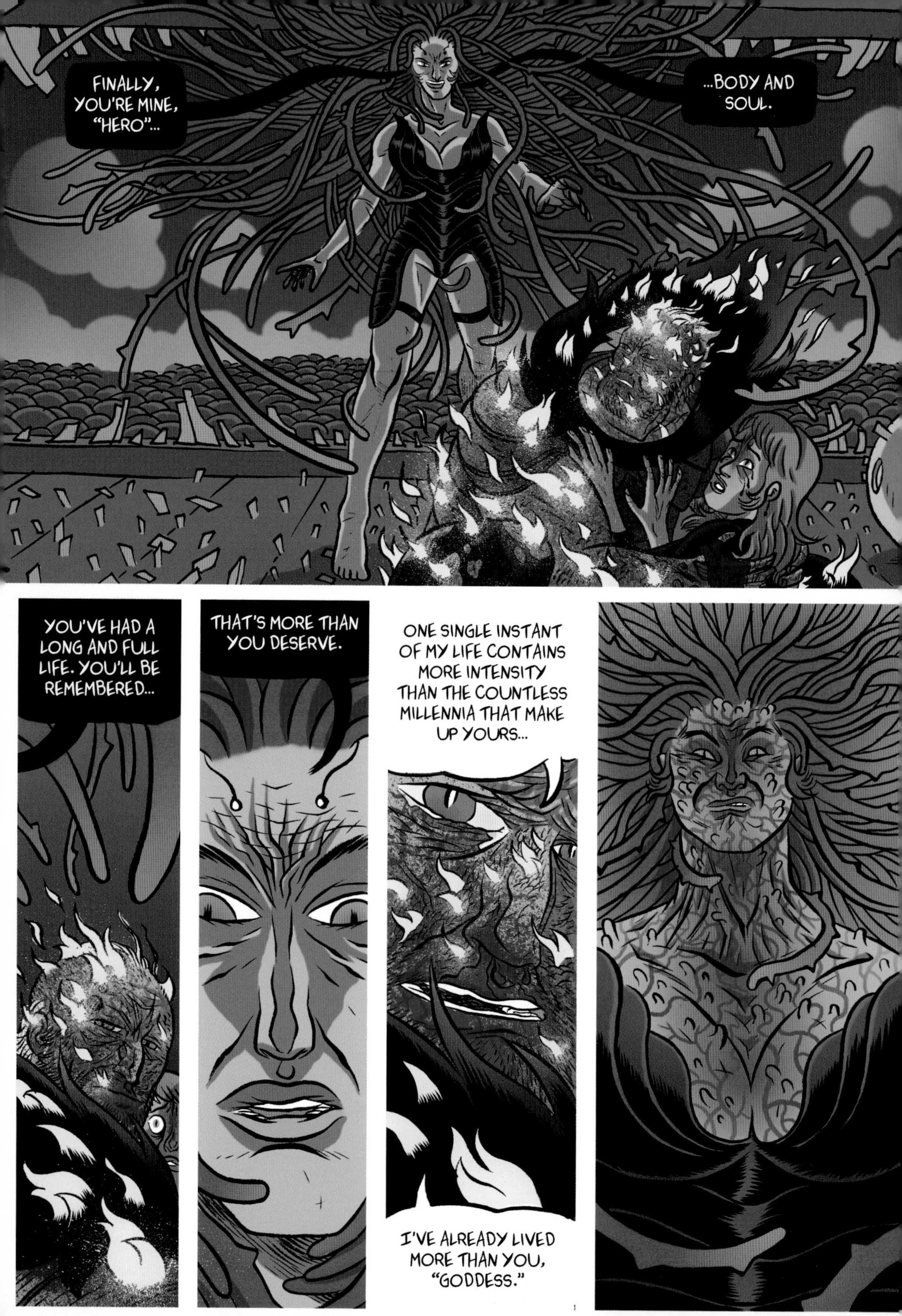

FINALLY, YOU'RE MINE, "HERO"...
...BODY AND SOUL.
YOU'VE HAD A LONG AND FULL LIFE. YOU'LL BE REMEMBERED...
THAT'S MORE THAN YOU DESERVE.
ONE SINGLE INSTANT OF MY LIFE CONTAINS MORE INTENSITY THAN THE COUNTLESS MILLENNIA THAT MAKE UP YOURS...
I'VE ALREADY LIVED MORE THAN YOU, "GODDESS."

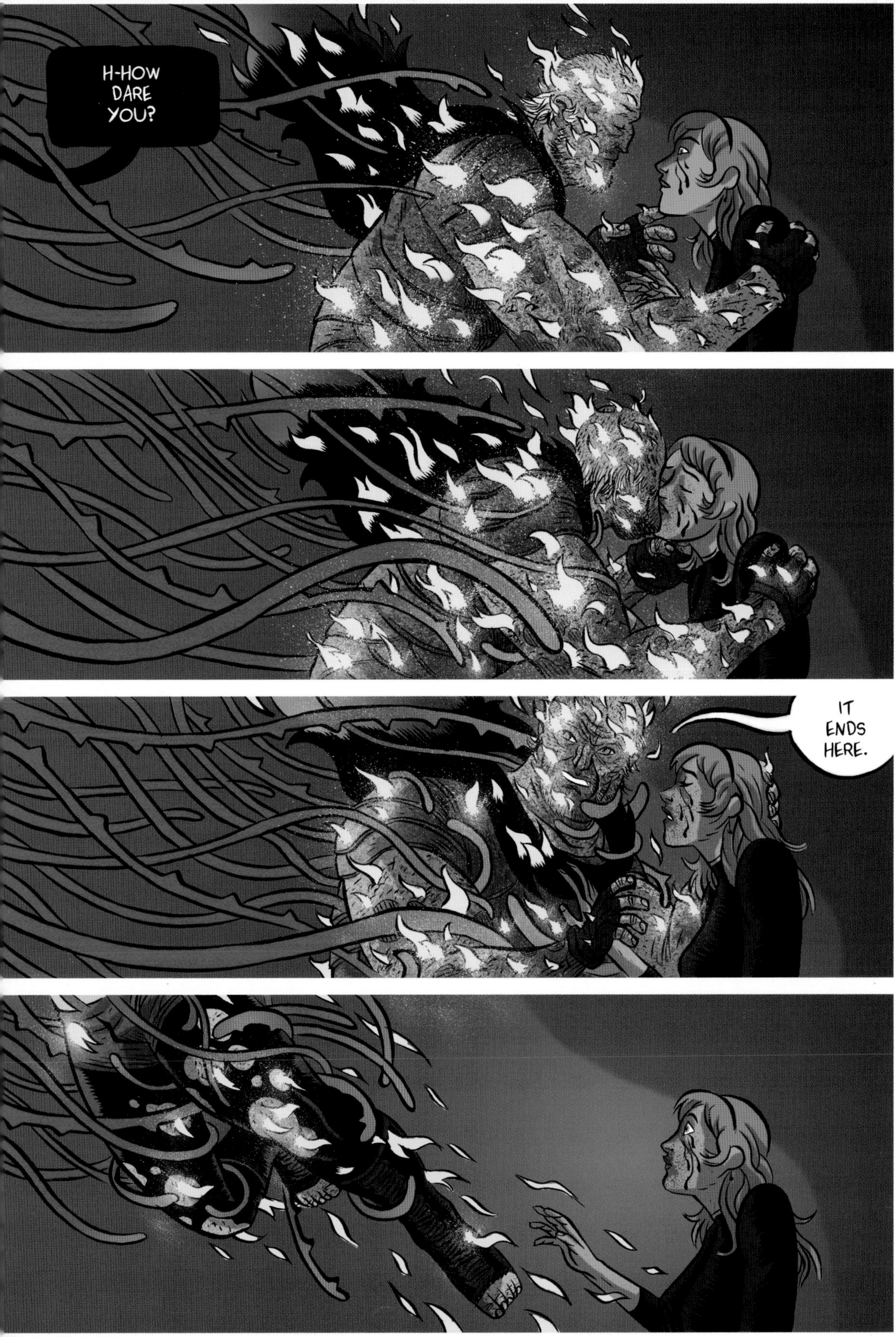
H-HOW DARE YOU?
IT ENDS HERE.

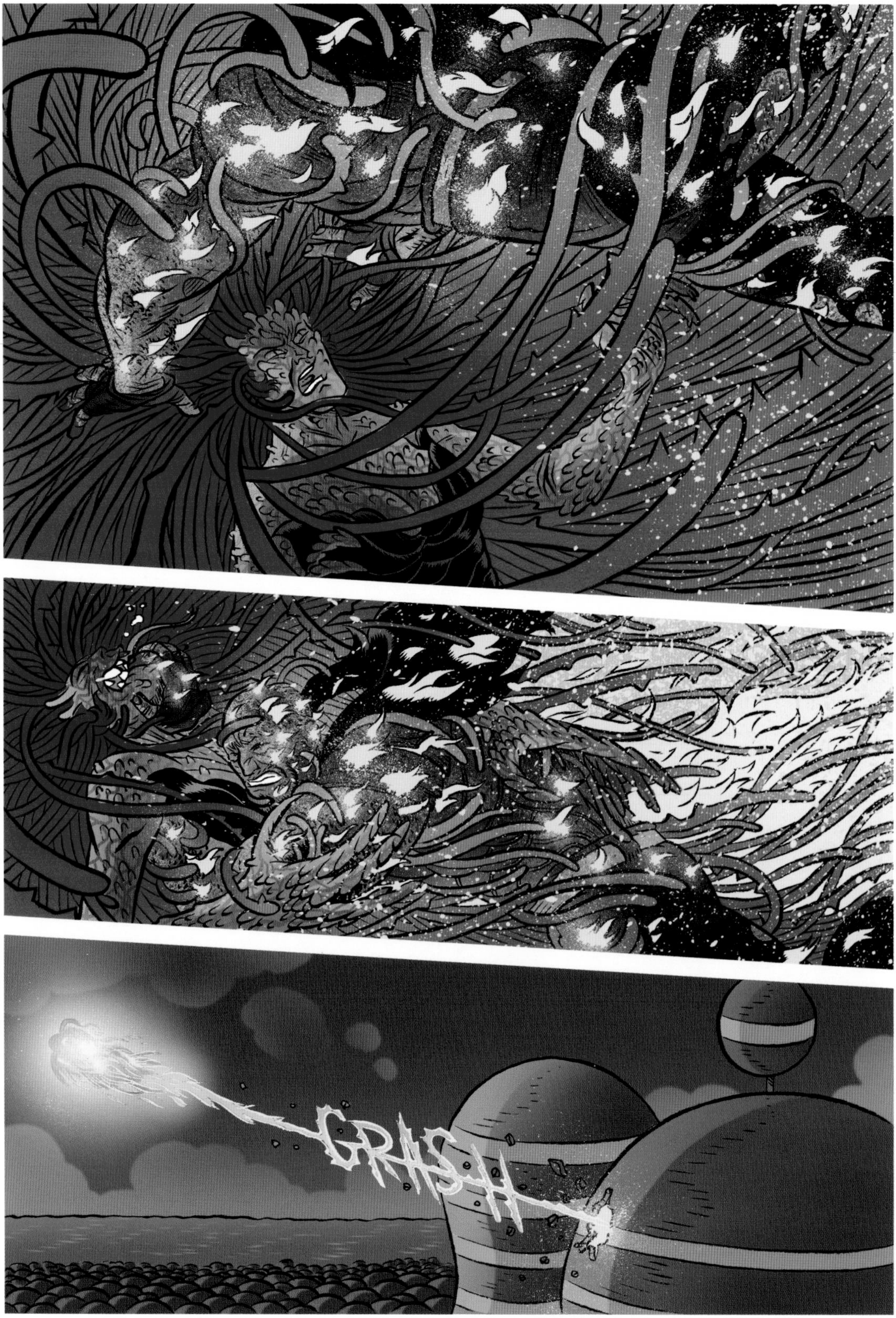
CRASH

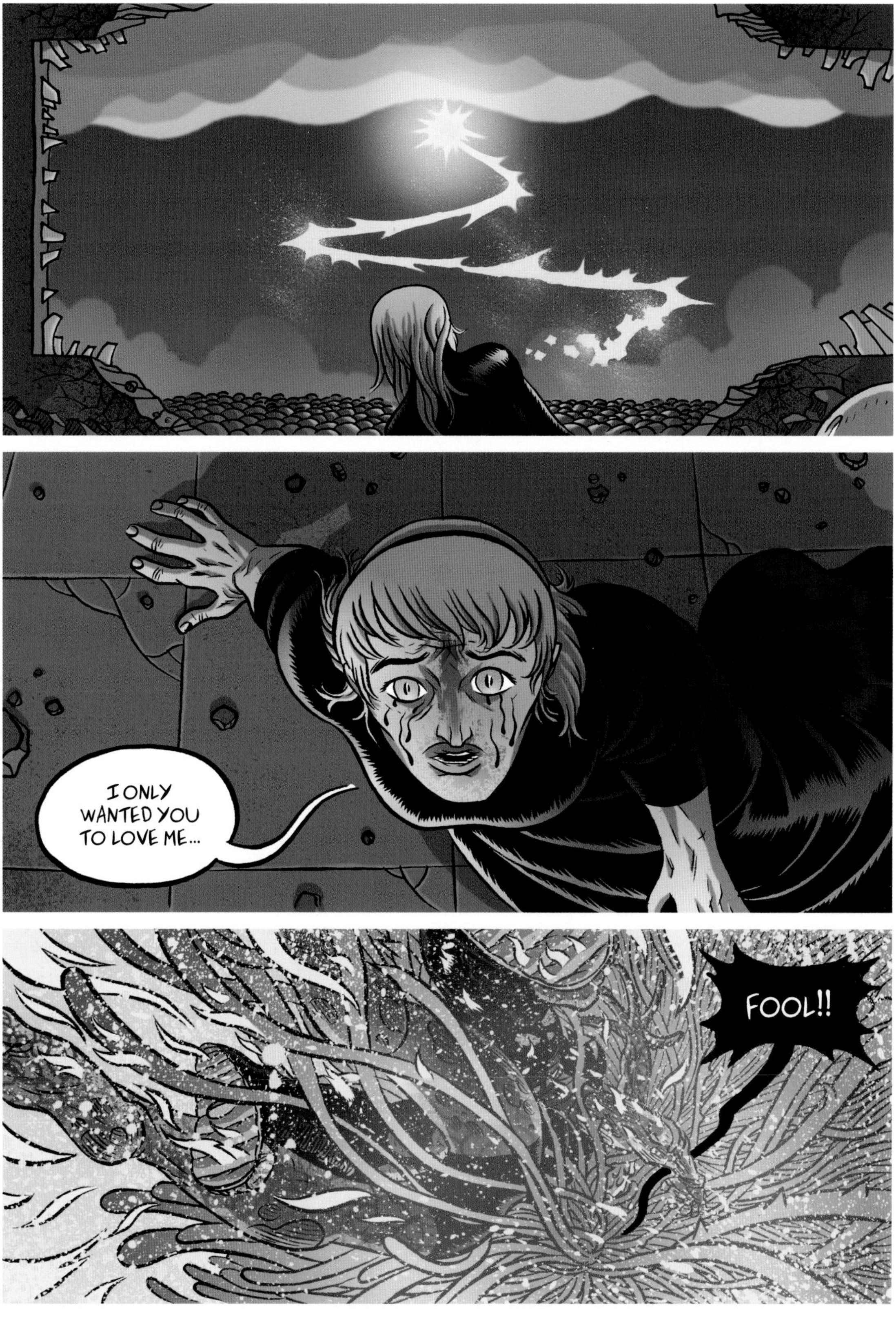
I ONLY WANTED YOU TO LOVE ME...
FOOL!!

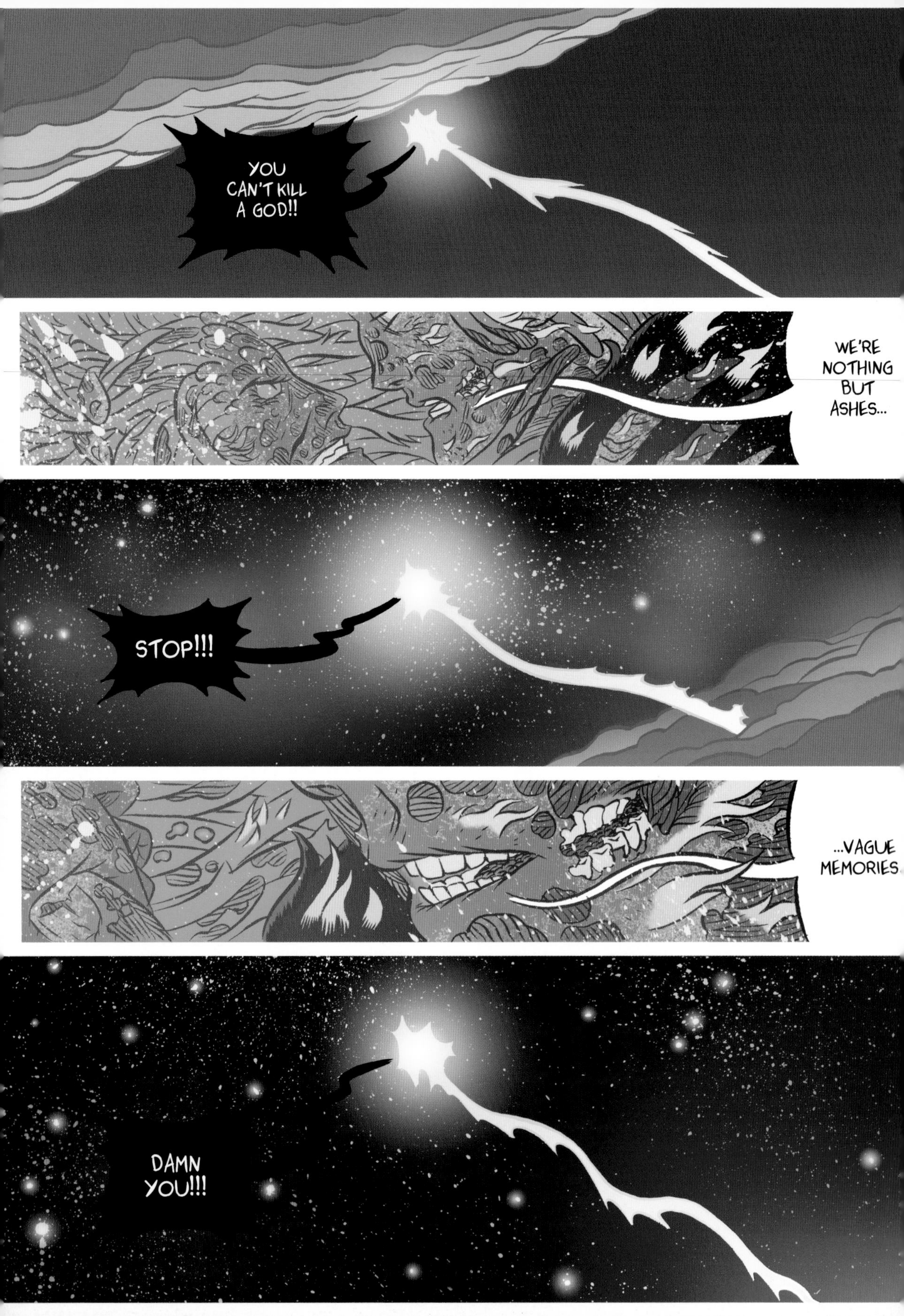

YOU CAN'T KILL A GOD!!
WE'RE NOTHING BUT ASHES...
STOP!!!
...VAGUE MEMORIES
DAMN YOU!!!

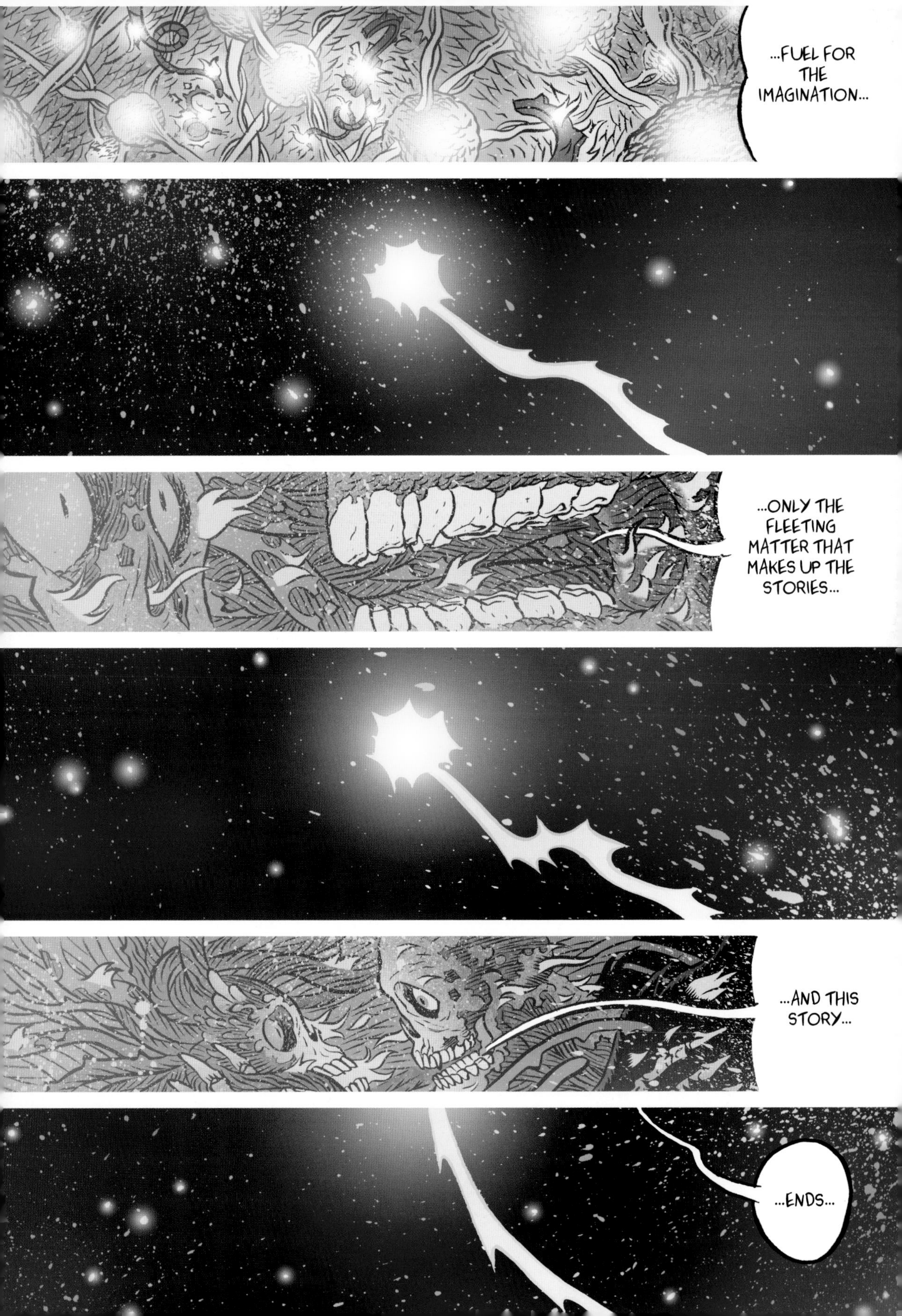
...FUEL FOR THE IMAGINATION...
...ONLY THE FLEETING MATTER THAT MAKES UP THE STORIES...
...AND THIS STORY...
...ENDS...

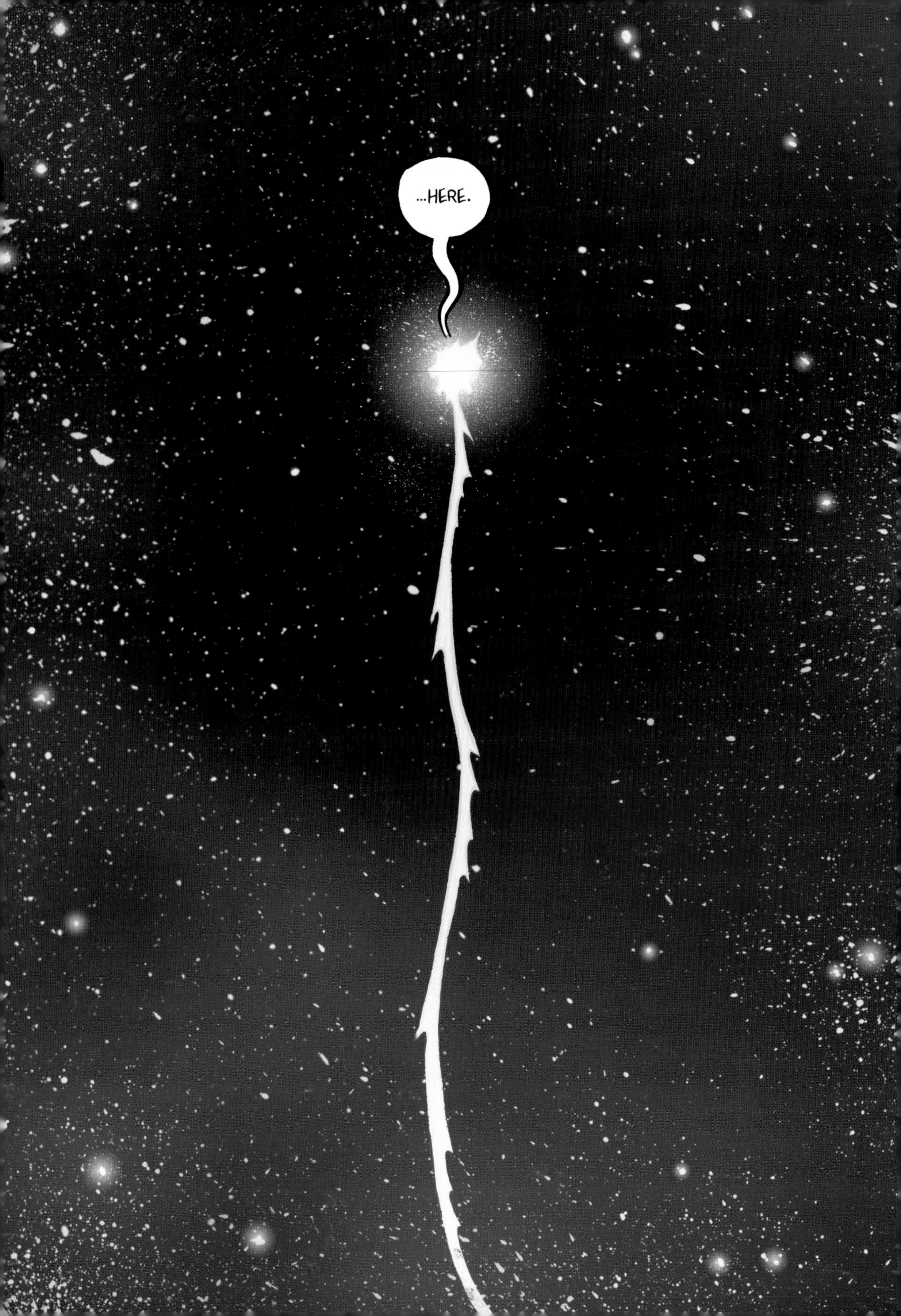

...HERE.

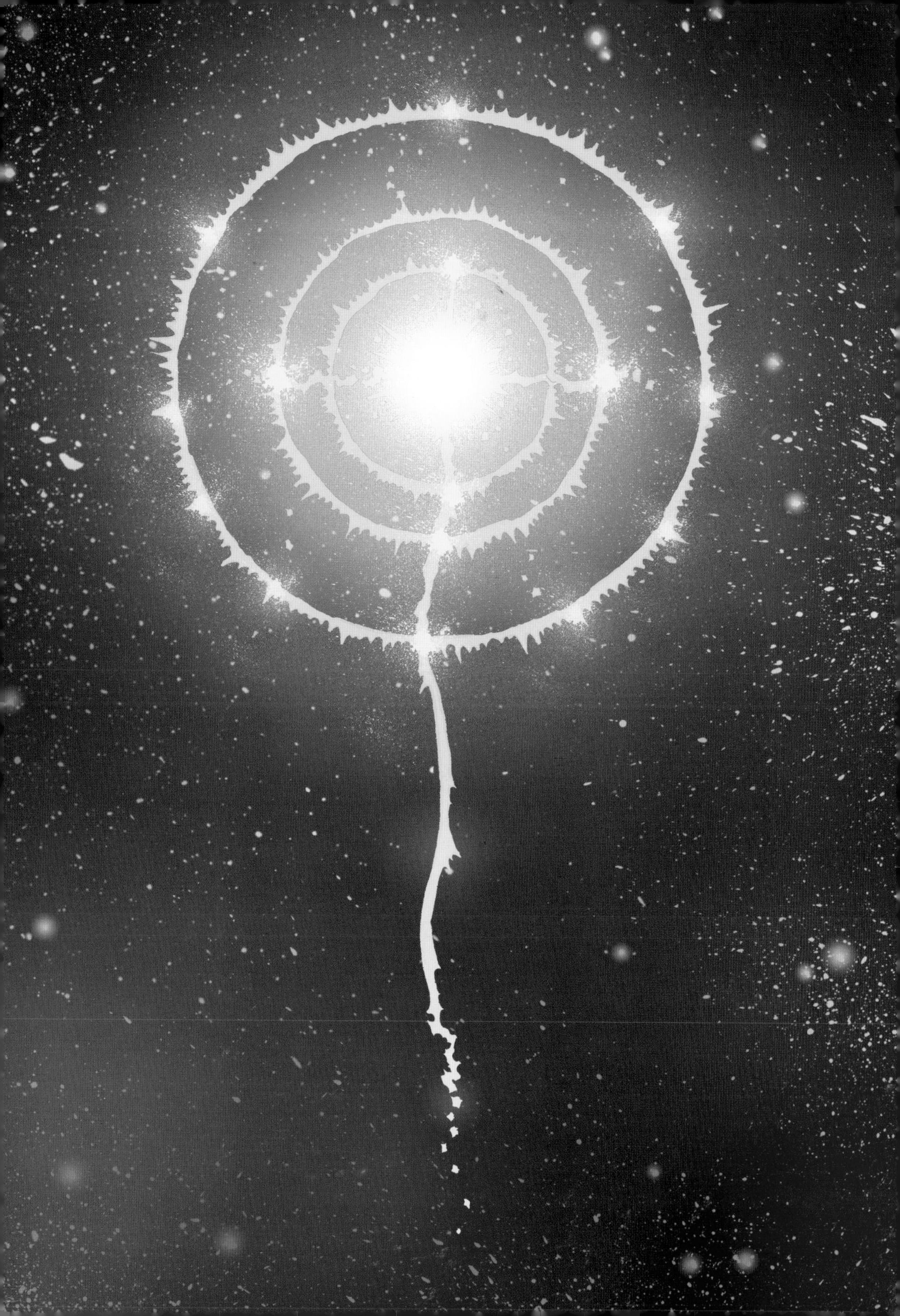

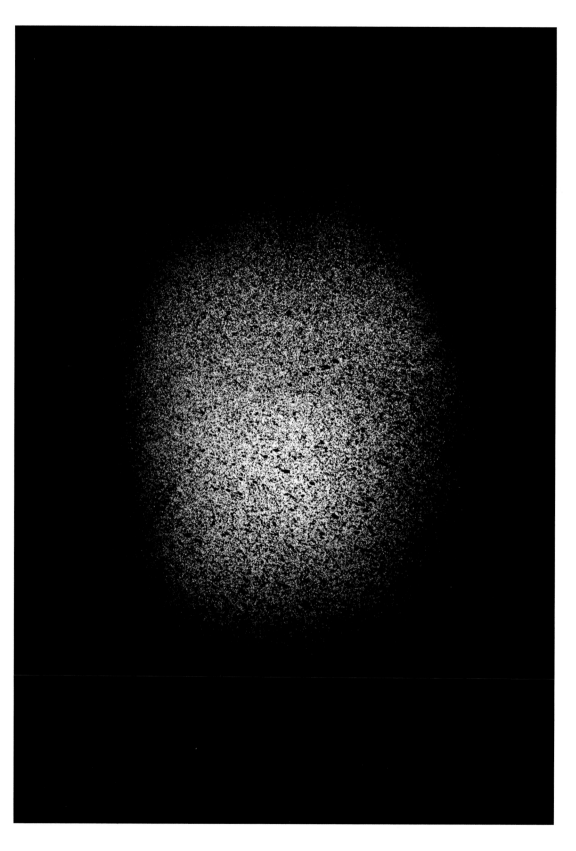

THE
END

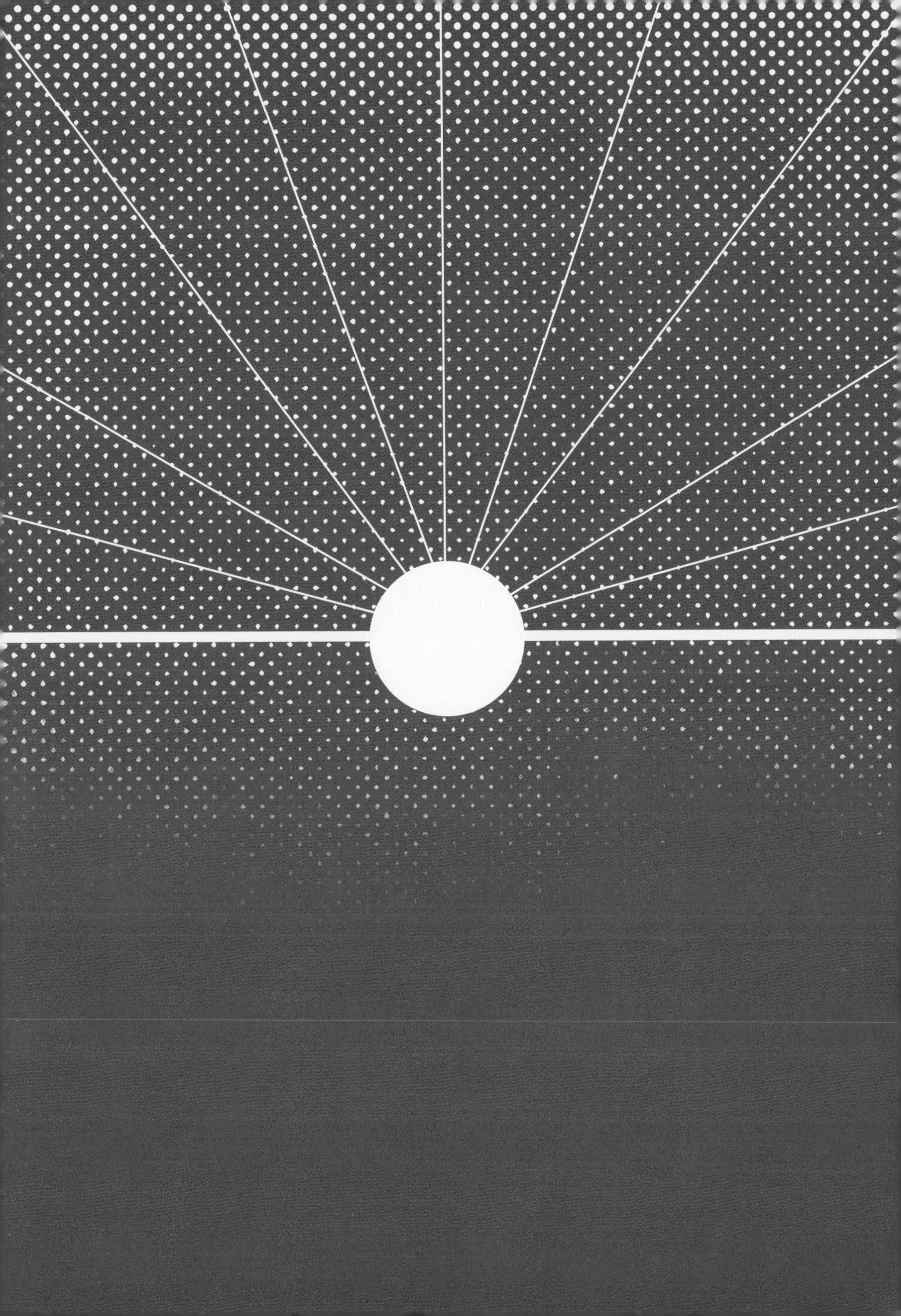

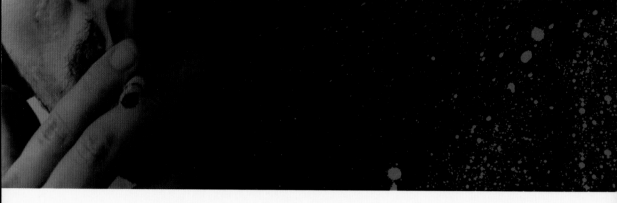

David Rubín was born in Ourense, Spain, in 1977. He studied graphic design and has ventured into the worlds of comics, animation, and illustration—all difficult and murky dealings.

His first long work, El circo del desaliento (The despondency circus), earned him the nomination for Best New Talent at the 2006 Barcelona International Comics Convention. It also won the Castelao Prize and was published in Galician, Spanish, Italian, and French.

His next graphic novel, La tetería del oso malayo (The sun bear's teahouse), was published in France, Italy, and the Czech Republic. It received four nominations at the 2007 Barcelona International Comics Convention, winning the award for Best New Talent, and was a finalist for Spain's National Comics Prize. Its international awards include the prize for Best Foreign Work at Prague's Komiksfest in 2009 and the prize for Best Foreign Author at the festival in Sarzana, Italy.

Subsequently, Rubín was nominated as Best New Artist for Cuaderno de tormentas (Storm notebook) at the Barcelona International Comics Convention.

Book one of The Hero earned him the nomination for Best Work at the Barcelona International Comics Convention in 2012; the award for Best National Work at the comics convention in Zaragoza, Spain, in 2011; the Critics' Award for Best Artist in 2011; the Entrecomics prize for Best National Work; and the Ignotus prize for Best Comic in 2012. It has been published in French and Italian.

Rubín codirected Espíritu del bosque (Spirit of the Forest), an animated feature film in 3-D. He has also adapted William Shakespeare's Romeo and Juliet to comic form, as well as El monte de las ánimas (Haunted mountain) by Gustavo Adolfo Bécquer.

His restless creative energy led him to illustrate a collection of Solomon Kane stories by Robert E. Howard and to star in Marcos Ninwe's documentary Radiografía de un autor de tebeos (X-ray of a comic book author).

He lives in A Coruña, Spain, although his greatest desire is to live on a planet that has not yet been colonized by human misery. Or at least, to try to.

SELECT BIBLIOGRAPHY
El circo del desaliento (The despondency circus) (Astiberri, 2005)
La tetería del oso malayo (The sun bear's teahouse) (Astiberri, 2006)
Corazón de tormentas (Heart of storms) (Polaqia, 2006)
Cuaderno de tormentas (Storm notebook) (Planeta DeAgostini, 2008)
Romeo y Julieta (Romeo and Juliet) (SM, 2008), adaptation of a work by William Shakespeare
El monte de las ánimas (Haunted mountain) (SM, 2009), adaptation of a work by Gustavo Adolfo Bécquer
Uxío Novoneyra: A voz herdada (Uxío Novoneyra: An inherited voice) (Xunta de Galicia, 2010), script by Kike Benlloch
Solomon Kane (Astiberri, 2010), illustrations of stories by Robert E. Howard
El héroe (The Hero) Book One (Astiberri, 2011)
El héroe (The Hero) Book Two (Astiberri, 2012)
Beowulf (Astiberri, 2013)
The Rise of Aurora West (First Second, 2014)
The Fiction (Boom! Studios, 2015)

This work is dedicated to Sara Solano for her constant support and unconditional love, and for being an extraordinary woman who, even though she knows I'm not a hero, loves me even more than if I were—because I love her more than anything in this disgusting world.

And also to a number of people without whom you wouldn't be holding this book in your hands:

At Astiberri, to Javi, Laureano, Fernando, Héloïse, Manuel, and Soraya, for trusting in me and in my work, for supporting me with dedication and enthusiasm ever since I gave them this crazy project in 2009, and for helping to steer me in the right direction.

To Tunué and Rackham, for being the first publishers to commit to foreign editions of The Hero.

To my parents, for filling my childhood with superhero comics, and for never telling me, "You're getting too old for those things."

To my sister Alba, for always greeting me with a smile, no matter what, in the best of times, and in the worst of times.

To José Domingo, Alberto Guitián, Santiago García, Pepo Pérez, David Aja, John Arcudi, and Xurxo G. Penalta, for their critiques, comments, and encouragement during the tough process of writing book two.

To Craig Thompson, for giving me a beautiful and exciting introduction, the perfect finishing touch for this work—for being not only a great author, but an excellent person and colleague as well.

To Jack Kirby, Frank Miller, Jim Steranko, Osamu Tezuka, and Akira Toriyama, for paving the way and then proving that you don't need to follow it—you only need to know it, so that through it you can make your own path—and that's the path I've taken.

To Benito Losada, for always supporting me (and many other authors), and for his immense contribution to the fields of comics and culture—because he was a great and necessary person who is greatly missed.

And to you, for reading my work, for constantly asking when book two would come out, for wanting it. You have been the fuel that's kept me going. You're directly responsible for bringing about this work, and without you it would not have been possible.

You are all the real heroes of this story. Thank you for being here, in one way or another, always.

Here The Hero ends, but the adventure continues.

CREATIVE GIANTS!

GET YOUR FIX OF DARK HORSE BOOKS FROM THESE INSPIRED CREATORS!

MESMO DELIVERY SECOND EDITION - Rafael Grampá

Eisner Award–winning artist Rafael Grampá (*5, Hellblazer*) makes his full-length comics debut with the critically acclaimed graphic novel *Mesmo Delivery*—a kinetic, bloody romp starring Rufo, an ex-boxer; Sangrecco, an Elvis impersonator; and a ragtag crew of overly confident drunks who pick the wrong delivery men to mess with.

ISBN 978-1-61655-457-6 | $14.99

SIN TITULO - Cameron Stewart

Following the death of his grandfather, Alex Mackay discovers a mysterious photograph in the old man's belongings that sets him on an adventure like no other—where dreams and reality merge, family secrets are laid bare, and lives are irrevocably altered.

ISBN 978-1-61655-248-0 | $19.99

DE:TALES - Fábio Moon and Gabriel Bá

Brazilian twins Fábio Moon and Gabriel Bá's (*Daytripper, Pixu*) most personal work to date. Brimming with all the details of human life, their charming tales move from the urban reality of their home in São Paulo to the magical realism of their Latin American background.

ISBN 978-1-59582-557-5 | $19.99

THE TRUE LIVES OF THE FABULOUS KILLJOYS - Gerard Way, Shaun Simon, and Becky Cloonan

Years ago, the Killjoys fought against the tyrannical megacorporation Better Living Industries. Today, the followers of the original Killjoys languish in the desert and the fight for freedom fades. It's left to the Girl to take down BLI!

ISBN 978-1-59582-462-2 | $19.99

DEMO - Brian Wood and Becky Cloonan

It's hard enough being a teenager. Now try being a teenager with *powers*. A chronicle of the lives of young people on separate journeys to self-discovery in a world—just like our own—where being different is feared.

ISBN 978-1-61655-682-2 | $24.99

SABERTOOTH SWORDSMAN - Damon Gentry and Aaron Conley

When his village is enslaved and his wife kidnapped by the malevolent Mastodon Mathematician, a simple farmer must find his inner warrior—the Sabertooth Swordsman!

ISBN 978-1-61655-176-6 | $17.99

JAYBIRD - Jaakko and Lauri Ahonen

Disney meets Kafka in this beautiful, intense, original tale! A very small, very scared little bird lives an isolated life in a great big house with his infirm mother. He's never been outside the house, and he never will if his mother has anything to say about it.

ISBN 978-1-61655-469-9 | $19.99

MONSTERS! & OTHER STORIES - Gustavo Duarte

Newcomer Gustavo Duarte spins wordless tales inspired by Godzilla, King Kong, and Pixar, brimming with humor, charm, and delightfully twisted horror!

ISBN 978-1-61655-309-8 | $12.99

SACRIFICE - Sam Humphries and Dalton Rose

What happens when a troubled youth is plucked from modern society and thrust though time and space into the heart of the Aztec civilization—one of the most bloodthirsty times in human history?

ISBN 978-1-59582-985-6 | $19.99

AVAILABLE AT YOUR LOCAL COMICS SHOP OR BOOKSTORE
To find a comics shop in your area, call 1-888-266-4226. For more information or to order direct: ON THE WEB: DarkHorse.com
E-MAIL: mailorder@darkhorse.com / PHONE: 1-800-862-0052 Mon.–Fri. 9 a.m. to 5 p.m. Pacific Time.

Mesmo Delivery™ © Rafael Grampá. Sin Titulo™ © Cameron Stewart. De:Tales™ © Fábio Moon & Gabriel Bá. The True Lives of the Fabulous Killjoys™ ©
Gerard Way & Shaun Simon. DEMO™ © Brian Wood & Becky Cloonan. Sabertooth Swordsman™ © Damon Gentry and Aaron Conley. Jaybird™ © Strip Art
Features, www.safcomics.com. Monsters!™ © Gustavo Duarte. Sacrifice™ © Sam Humphries & Dalton Rose. Dark Horse Books® and the Dark Horse logo
are registered trademarks of Dark Horse Comics, Inc. All rights reserved. (BL 5018)

GABRIEL BÁ AND FÁBIO MOON!

"Twin Brazilian artists Fábio Moon and Gabriel Bá have made a huge mark on comics." —*Publisher's Weekly*

TWO BROTHERS
Fábio Moon Gabriel Bá

Gerard Way • Gabriel Bá
THE UMBRELLA ACADEMY
APOCALYPSE SUITE

FÁBIO MOON
GABRIEL BÁ
De:
TALES

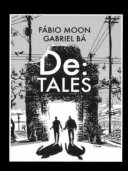

TWO BROTHERS
Story and art by Gabriel Bá
and Fábio Moon
ISBN 978-1-61655-856-7 | $24.99

DE:TALES
Story and art by Gabriel Bá and Fábio Moon
ISBN 978-1-59582-557-5 | $19.99

THE UMBRELLA ACADEMY: APOCALYPSE SUITE
Story by Gerard Way
Art by Gabriel Bá
TPB ISBN: 978-1-59307-978-9 | $17.99
Ltd. Ed. HC ISBN: 978-1-59582-163-8 | $79.95

THE UMBRELLA ACADEMY: DALLAS
Story by Gerard Way
Art by Gabriel Bá
TPB ISBN: 978-1-59582-345-8 | $17.99
Ltd. Ed. HC ISBN: 978-1-59582-344-1 | $79.95

PIXU: THE MARK OF EVIL
Story and art by Gabriel Bá, Becky Cloonan,
Vasilis Lolos, and Fábio Moon
ISBN 978-1-61655-813-0 | $14.99

B.P.R.D.: VAMPIRE
Story by Mike Mignola, Fábio Moon, and Gabriel Bá
Art by Fábio Moon and Gabriel Bá
ISBN 978-1-61655-196-4 | $19.99

B.P.R.D.: 1946–1948
Story by Mike Mignola, Joshua Dysart, and John Arcudi
Art by Fábio Moon, Gabriel Bá, Paul Azaceta, and Max Fiumara
ISBN 978-1-61655-646-4 | $34.99

AVAILABLE AT YOUR LOCAL COMICS SHOP OR BOOKSTORE!
To find a comics shop in your area, call 1-888-266-4226. For more information
or to order direct visit DarkHorse.com or call 1-800-862-0052 Mon.–Fri. 9 AM to 5 PM Pacific Time.

DARK HORSE BOOKS

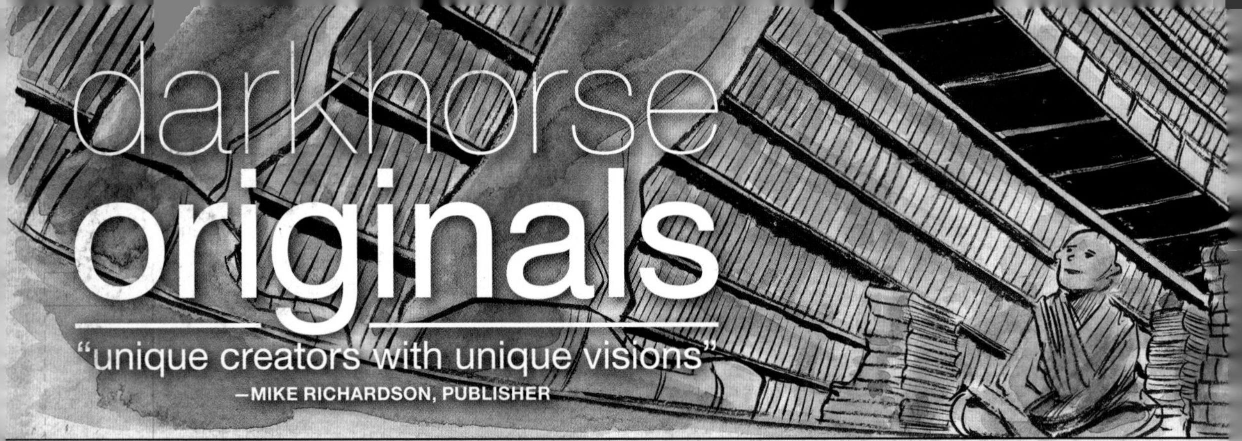
dark horse
originals
"unique creators with unique visions"
—MIKE RICHARDSON, PUBLISHER

3 STORY: THE SECRET HISTORY OF THE GIANT MAN
978-1-59582-356-4 | $19.99

365 SAMURAI AND A FEW BOWLS OF RICE
978-1-59582-412-7 | $16.99

THE ADVENTURES OF BLANCHE
978-1-59582-258-1 | $15.99

APOCALYPTIGIRL: AN ARIA FOR THE END TIMES
978-1-61655-566-5 | $9.99

BEANWORLD
Volume 1: Wahoolazuma!
978-1-59582-240-6 | $19.99
Volume 2: A Gift Comes!
978-1-59582-299-4 | $19.99
Volume 3: Remember Here When You Are There!
978-1-59582-355-7 | $19.99
Volume 3.5: Tales of the Beanworld
978-1-59582-897-2 | $14.99

BLACKSAD
978-1-59582-393-9 | $29.99

BLACKSAD: A SILENT HELL
978-1-59582-931-3 | $19.99

BLOOD SONG: A SILENT BALLAD
978-1-59582-389-2 | $19.99

THE BOOK OF GRICKLE
978-1-59582-430-1 | $17.99

BRODY'S GHOST
Book 1: 978-1-59582-521-6 | $6.99
Book 2: 978-1-59582-665-7 | $6.99
Book 3: 978-1-59582-862-0 | $6.99
Book 4: 978-1-61655-129-2 | $6.99

BUCKO
978-1-59582-973-3 | $19.99

CHANNEL ZERO
978-1-59582-936-8 | $19.99

CHERUBS
978-1-59582-984-9 | $19.99

CHIMICHANGA
978-1-59582-755-5 | $14.99

CITIZEN REX
978-1-59582-556-8 | $19.99

THE COMPLETE PISTOLWHIP
978-1-61655-720-1 | $27.99

CROSSING THE EMPTY QUARTER AND OTHER STORIES
978-1-59582-388-5 | $24.99

DE:TALES
HC: 978-1-59582-557-5 | $19.99
TPB: 978-1-59307-485-2 | $14.99

EVERYBODY GETS IT WRONG! AND OTHER STORIES: DAVID CHELSEA'S 24-HOUR COMICS
978-1-61655-155-1 | $19.99

EXURBIA
978-1-59582-339-7 | $9.99

FLUFFY
978-1-59307-972-7 | $19.99

GREEN RIVER KILLER
978-1-61655-812-3 | $19.99

HEART IN A BOX
978-1-61655-694-5 | $14.99

INSOMNIA CAFÉ
978-1-59582-357-1 | $14.99

THE MIGHTY SKULLBOY ARMY
Volume 2
978-1-59582-872-9 | $14.99

MILK AND CHEESE: DAIRY PRODUCTS GONE BAD
978-1-59582-805-7 | $19.99

MIND MGMT
Volume 1: The Manager
978-1-59582-797-5 | $19.99
Volume 2: The Futurist
978-1-61655-198-8 | $19.99

MOTEL ART IMPROVEMENT SERVICE
978-1-59582-550-6 | $19.99

THE NIGHT OF YOUR LIFE
978-1-59582-183-6 | $15.99

NINGEN'S NIGHTMARES
978-1-59582-859-0 | $12.99

NOIR
978-1-59582-358-8 | $12.99

PIXU: THE MARK OF EVIL
978-1-61655-813-0 | $14.99

RESET
978-1-61655-003-5 | $15.99

SACRIFICE
978-1-59582-985-6 | $19.99

SINFEST: VIVA LA RESISTANCE
978-1-59582-424-0 | $14.99

SPEAK OF THE DEVIL
978-1-59582-193-5 | $19.99

UNCLE SILAS
978-1-59582-566-7 | $9.99

DARK HORSE BOOKS

AVAILABLE AT YOUR LOCAL COMICS SHOP OR BOOKSTORE!
To find a comics shop in your area, call 1-888-266-4226

For more information or to order direct:
On the web: DarkHorse.com
E-mail: mailorder@darkhorse.com
Phone: 1-800-862-0052 Mon.–Fri. 9 AM to 5 PM Pacific Time.

More great

NOIR AND ESPIONAGE

from Dark Horse Books

BLACKSAD

BLACKSAD

JUAN DÍAZ CANALES AND JUANJO GUARNIDO

The *Blacksad* books first took Europe by storm in 2000 and sold over 200,000 copies in France alone. Now Dark Horse presents the beautifully painted stories of private investigator John Blacksad, up to his feline ears in mystery, digging into the backstories behind murders, child abductions, and nuclear secrets.

ISBN 978-1-59582-393-9
$29.99

MIND MGMT
matt kindt
VOLUME ONE: THE MANAGER
FOREWORD BY DAMON LINDELOF

MIND MGMT VOLUME 1

MATT KINDT

A young journalist stumbles onto a big story—the top-secret Mind Management program. Her ensuing journey involves weaponized psychics, hypnotic advertising, talking dolphins, and seemingly immortal pursuers. But in a world where people can rewrite reality itself, can she trust anything she sees?

ISBN 978-1-59582-797-5
$19.99

THE BLACK BEETLE
IN
"NO WAY OUT"
A Mystery Tale by FRANCESCO FRANCAVILLA

THE BLACK BEETLE VOLUME 1: NO WAY OUT

FRANCESCO FRANCAVILLA

Follow Francesco Francavilla's critically acclaimed pulp hero the Black Beetle—Colt City's sleuthing sentinel—as he searches island prisons, dank sewers, and swanky nightclubs for the mysterious man known as Labyrinto.

ISBN 978-1-61655-202-2
$19.99

GREEN RIVER KILLER
A TRUE DETECTIVE STORY
JEFF JENSEN | JONATHAN CASE

GREEN RIVER KILLER: A TRUE DETECTIVE STORY

JEFF JENSEN AND JONATHAN CASE

The story of one of America's most notorious killers is revealed in this true-crime comic unlike any other! Written by case detective Tom Jensen's own son, acclaimed entertainment writer Jeff Jensen, this is the ultimate insider's account of America's most prolific serial killer.

ISBN 978-1-59582-560-5
$24.99

AVAILABLE AT YOUR LOCAL COMICS SHOP OR BOOKSTORE • TO FIND A COMICS SHOP IN YOUR AREA, CALL 1-888-266-4226

For more information or to order direct: • On the web: DarkHorse.com • E-mail: mailorder@darkhorse.com • Phone: 1-800-862-0052 Mon.–Fri. 9 AM to 5 PM Pacific Time.

DarkHorse.com

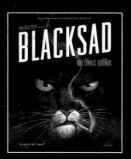

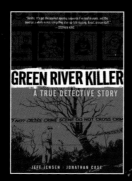

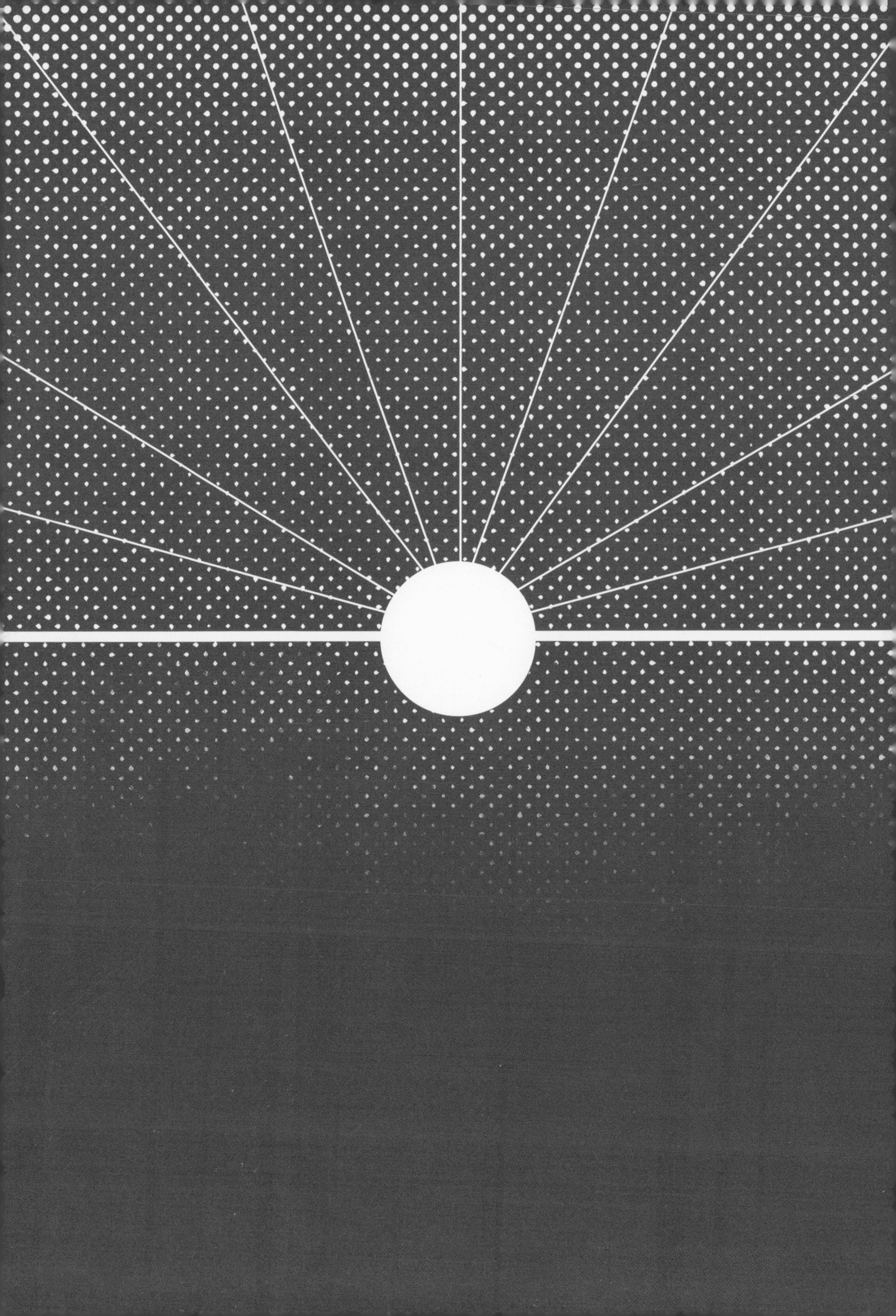

REFERENCE

THE ENCYCLOPEDIA OF
JEWISH LIFE
Before and During the Holocaust

THE ENCYCLOPEDIA OF
JEWISH LIFE

Before and During the Holocaust

Editor in Chief **Shmuel Spector**

Consulting Editor **Geoffrey Wigoder**

Foreword by **Elie Wiesel**

Volume I
A – J

Yad Vashem
Jerusalem

NEW YORK UNIVERSITY PRESS

Washington Square, New York

These three volumes are an abridgment of the multi-volume Encyclopedia of Jewish Communities published in Hebrew by Yad Vashem.

The publication was supported by a grant of the Memorial Foundation for Jewish Culture.

Foreword by Elie Wiesel translated from the French by Fred Skolnik

First pubished in the U.S.A. in 2001 by
NEW YORK UNIVERSITY PRESS

Washington Square
New York, NY 10003
www.nyupress.nyu.edu

Library of Congress Cataloging-in-Publication Data
The Encyclopedia of Jewish life before and during the Holocaust / edited by Shmuel Spector,
consulting editor: Geoffrey Wigoder; foreword by Elie Wiesel
p.cm.
Three-volume set: ISBN 0-8147-9356-8 (cloth)
Volume I: ISBN 0-8147-9376-2 (cloth)
Volume II: ISBN 0-8147-9377-0 (cloth)
Volume III: ISBN 0-8147-9378-9 (cloth)
1. Jews – Europe – History – Encyclopedias. 2. Jews – Africa, North – Encyclopedias.
3. Holocaust, Jewish (1939–1945) – Encyclopedias. 4. Europe – History, Local.
5. Africa, North – History, Local. I. Spector, Shmuel. II. Wigoder, Geoffrey, 1922–1999
DS135.E8 E45 2001
940'.04924 – dc21 2001030071

Prepared, edited and produced by The Jerusalem Publishing House,
39 Tchernichovski Street, Jerusalem, Israel.

Printed in China

Foreword

A paper universe – that is more or less how the great Yiddish novelist and poet Chaim Grade described the sorrow-stricken world of East European Jewry as it emerged from the blood-soaked and heinous tragedy known as the Holocaust.

The tempest of fire and ashes that had descended on the Jewish communities of German-occupied Europe left in its wake not cemeteries but books, nothing more than books: documents, albums, testimony, chronicles, intimate journals, and memoirs. That was all that remained – reams and reams of paper – of a rich and glorious past peopled by long lines of erudite and humble rabbis, solitary thinkers, seekers after truth and the dream, wealthy merchants and anonymous beggars shrouded in mystery.

But the enemy did not only annihilate individuals; his aim was also to destroy our social structures, our economic foundations, religious and secular, our schools, our institutions, our libraries, our workshops, our synagogues, our cultural centers – in a word: our communities.

Some had existed for centuries. My own, Sighet, dates back to 1770. Frankfurt's is more ancient; already at the beginning of the millennium Jews organized in a *kehilla* were living there. The Warsaw community, today all but moribund, existed from the 13th century and that of Tunis, tragically crippled by the antisemitic decrees of the Vichy government, since the destruction of the Second Temple. In the Jewish world one knew a town by its Jewish life. Belz and Munkacs, Bialystok and Amsterdam, Kiev and Lille and Zablotow – offering families and individuals a sense of security and countless opportunities for fulfillment, each community had its own particular characteristics and problems, its roots, its challenges, and its ambitions; in a word, its *raison d'etre*. It is in the nature of the Jew that he cannot live alone; he must be part of a collective. Alone, he runs the risk of sinking into depression or of being cut off from his roots. Hillel the Elder was right: *"Al tifrosh min ha-tzibbur"* is a piece of useful if not indispensable advice. All ethical engagement implies the Other; hence the attitude toward the community.

Big and small, flourishing and forlorn, spiritual centers and impoverished villages, how did these communities survive the Crusades, the pogroms, the endless persecution, the epidemics, the maledictions wrought by History or by men? Was it their faith in God which enabled them to survive? Or was it their sense of mission? All were condemned to be extinguished by the long arm of Berlin, the world capital of hatred for everything Jewish. To understand the extent of the unprecedented crimes committed against the Jewish people in Europe is not enough; one must also seek to understand the life of this people before the catastrophe.

In this sense, the Encyclopedia of Jewish Life, rich and rewarding, is of inestimable value and answers a real need.

It is true that the reader will again encounter here a paper landscape. But, like the burning Torah scroll enveloping Rabbi Hanina ben Teradyon at his death, this paper cries out to everything that gives meaning to life.

Elie Wiesel

Contents

Contributors
(Hebrew Edition)

Poland — Lodz and the Lodz area
Editors: Danuta Dombrovska & Abraham Wein

Poland — Eastern Galicia
Editors: Danuta Dombrovska, Abraham Wein, Aharon Weiss
Contributors: Zvi Avital, Aharon Jakubowicz

Poland — Western Galicia & Silesia
Editors: Abraham Wein & Aharon Weiss
Contibutors: Zvi Avital, Danuta Dombrovska, Shmuel Levin, Yitzchak Mais, Wila Orbach

Poland — Warsaw and the Warsaw area
Editor: Abraham Wein
Contributors: Irit Abramski-Bligh, Israel Gutman,
Abraham Klevan, Shmuel Levin, Wila Orbach

Poland — Volhynia and Polesie
Editor: Shmuel Spector
Contributors: Ester Hagar, Dan Charuv, Abraham Klevan, Mordechai Nadav

Poland — Poznan & Pomerania–Gdansk Districts
Editor: Abraham Wein (Assistant Editor: Rachel Grossbaum-Pasternak)
Contributors: Bracha Freundlich (Language Editor)

Poland — Lublin–Kielce Districts
Editor: Abraham Wein (Co-Editors: Bracha Freundlich, Wila Orbach)
Contributors: Daniel Blatman, Rachel Grossbaum-Pasternak, Abraham Klevan, Shmuel Levin

Poland — Northeast
Editors: Shmuel Spector, Rachel Grossbaum-Pasternak

Germany — Bavaria
Editor: Dr. Baruch Zvi Ophir
Contributors: Shlomo Schmiedt, Chasia Turtel-Aberzhanska

Germany — Wuerttemberg, Hohenzollern, Baden
Editor: Joseph Walk (Assistant Editor: Bracha Freundlich)
Contributors: Henry Wasserman, Ester Ramon

Germany — Hesse, Hesse–Nassau, Frankfurt
Editor: Henry Wasserman (Assistant Editor: Bracha Freundlich)
Contributors: Asher Ariav, Benjamin Armon, Jacob Borut, Abraham Frank, Ester Hagar,
Hillel Hellmann, Menachem Kaufmann, Yaacov Lozowick, Kirsten Maas, Tamar Nave,
Vera Prausnitz, Ester Ramon, Abraham Seligmann, Joseph Stern

Germany — Northwest
Editors: Daniel Frenkel, Tamar Abraham
Contributors: Peter Aufgebauer, Marlis Buchholz, Eliezer Domke, Anne E. Dunzelmann,
Hans-Heinrich Ebeling, Bernhard Gelderblom, Uwe Hager, Almuth Lessing,
Jan Lokers, Werner Meiners, Hartmut Muller, Antje Naujoks, Sibylle Obenaus,
Rainer Sabelleck, Peter Schulze, and others

Germany — Rhineland–Westphalia–Saar–Palatinate
Editors: Daniel Frenkel, Tamar Abraham
Contributors: Jacob Borut, Ester Hagar, Gad Sobol, Bracha Freundlich, Menachem Kaufmann

Germany — East
Editor: Daniel Frenkel

Hungary
Editors: Nathaniel Katzburg, Yehuda Komlosh, Livia Rothkirchen

Rumania — The Regat, South Transylvania, Transnistria
Editors: Dr. Ancel Jean, Dr. Theodore Lavi, Aviva Broshi, Zvi Shal

Rumania — North Transylvania, Bessarabia, Bukovina
Editors: Dr. Ancel Jean, Dr. Theodore Lavi

Lithuania
Editor: Dov Levin
Assistant Editor: Joseph Rosin

Latvia & Estonia
Editor: Dov Levin
Contributors: Mordechai Neustadt, Ester Hagar, Chaya Lifschitz

The Netherlands

Authors: Joseph Michman, Hartog Beem, Dan Michman

Yugoslavia

Editor: Zvi Loker

Contributors: Michael Agmon, Hans Bramer, Avraham Epstein, Moshe Etz-Hayyim, Dr. Branko Grossmann, Dr. Dusan Keckemet, Prof. Dr. Theodor Kovac, Dr. Joseph Lador-Lederer, Jenny Loebl, Mordekhai Lonyi, Joseph Loewinger, Ya'akov Maestro, Dr. Joseph Milhofer, Mordekhai Moses, Dr. Giora Schick, Magda Simin, Miriam Steiner-Aviezer, Dr. Bernard Stulli

Greece

Editor: Bracha Rivlin

Contributors: Yitzchak Kerem, Lea Bornstein-Makovetsky

Introduction: Adina Drechsler, Bracha Freundlich (with the assistance of Hanna Vardi-Stern)

Libya & Tunisia

Editor: Irit Abramski Bligh

Slovakia

Editor: Yehoshua Bichler

Czechoslovakia & Carpatho-Russia

Editors: Yehoshua Bichler, Shelomo Schmiedt
Contributor: Sylvia Null

Austria

Editor: Sylvia Null

Ukraine

Editor: Shmuel Spector

Contributors: Yitzchak Len, Ilana Guri, Rachel Grossbaum-Pasternak, Shimon Shweibish, Aharon Weis

Belorussia & Occupied Russia

Editor: Shmuel Spector

Contributors: Yitzchak Len, Ilana Guri, Rachel Grossbaum-Pasternak, Shimon Shweibish

Western Europe

Editor: Bracha Rivlin

Contributor: Emma Lopresti

Introduction

Six million Jews perished in the Holocaust. In their efforts to destroy the Jewish people and obliterate its memory the Nazis attempted to destroy the material culture created by the Jews in the Diaspora in the course of generations (synagogues, cemeteries, public buildings) as well as to destroy or plunder every work of art. Doomed to extinction were the nation's spiritual legacy, libraries, private collections. This culture was born of an inner need after the destruction of the spiritual and religious center of Jewish life – the Jerusalem Temple – and the exile of the Jewish people for a period of two thousand years. To preserve their Jewish identity, primarily religious, the Jews created new social and political frameworks in conformity with the time and place. One such framework contributing to the existence of the Jewish people in the Diaspora was the Jewish community.

Thus the Jewish community became a mainstay of Jewish life for generations. The exile which cost the Jewish people their political independence and dispersed the nation in various countries in Asia and Europe and subsequently throughout the whole world did not result in assimilation or full integration. The Jews remained apart from the societies that surrounded them – in their own special quarters and with their own public and religious institutions – and thus became a kind of separate and recognized class or group within the political and social orders of the various host countries. The community became the expression of the group existence of the Jews, or in the words of Leo Baeck, "the Jewish vehicle of settlement and adaptation."

As a special religious, social, and economic group the Jews were granted charters of rights by local rulers. The charters specified in detail or in general terms the organizational frameworks and fields of activity of the Jews. They expressed the desire of the rulers of kingdoms, of municipal councils, and of proprietors of towns to create frameworks setting forth the rights and obligations of the Jews as a tolerated class among the other classes in the state. The strength of the community and the extent of its rights depended on the good will of its benefactors. Sometimes they were generous and sometimes (for a variety of reasons) they set limits, to the extent even of abrogating these rights altogether and expelling the Jews from their borders.

Community organization among the Jews began to crystallize in the Second Temple period, not least of all under the influence of the Greek cities, which enjoyed autonomy also in the Land of Israel. Having gained autonomy the Jewish municipalities administered public property, supplied water, took care of town fortifications, maintained the synagogue, which served both for prayer and public meetings, and the public baths, kept records, etc.

During the Mishnaic and Talmudic periods full-fledged community organizations already existed. A general assembly would choose a governing body, consisting of three to seven *parnasim* (aldermen). The community would be responsible for collecting taxes on behalf of the rulers. Its other responsibilities included maintenance of public buildings (synagogues, ritual baths), health, education, and care of the poor. Officers elected or chosen from among the wealthy members of the community or its scholars oversaw the work, which was done by officials like the market inspector, cantor, scribe, preacher, judge.

Communal autonomy reached broad proportions in Babylonia. Jewish courts serving coreligionists in every facet of life had already existed under the Parthians and later the Persians. In the course of time the institution of the Exilarch (*resh galuta*) came into being, supposedly based on Davidic ancestry. The authorities recognized the Exilarch as ruling over the Jews of Babylonia on their behalf. Alongside the Exilarch there operated halakhic authorities – *geonim* heading the great yeshivas at Sura, Nahardea, Pumbedita, etc. Their expertise in interpreting the Bible, Mishna, and Talmud enabled them to carry on their activities after the Talmud received its final form around 500 C.E., their decisions being accepted in the entire Jewish world.

Jewish autonomy in Babylonia had a community structure. The community was headed by seven "best men." Its activities had two aspects, internal and general. Internally, it maintained public property, supervised weights and measures, and took care of the needy (education, food, etc.). Vis-a-vis the municipality, the community did its share in maintaining fortifications, purchasing and maintaining weapons, hiring watchmen, digging wells.

These expenses were covered by levying taxes on all members of the community, including scholars and even orphans.

Under the tolerant rule of the Fatimids in the 11th–13th centuries Jewish autonomy was strengthened in Egypt, the Land of Israel, and Syria. Under Mameluk rule in the Late Middle Ages Jewish authority in these communities was circumscribed.

Jewish communities in these countries were sometimes divided according to place of origin. Authority was broad and extended over dietary law (*kashrut*) for meat and cheese, the morals of ritual slaughterers, and welfare and education for the needy, among other things. The community also concerned itself with the care of Jewish convicts and the ransoming of Jewish prisoners. Its income was derived from renting buildings and lots left to the community in the absence of heirs. A council of seven to ten members headed the community under a chairman. The aldermen dealt with financial matters on behalf of the community. In Egypt, from the 10th to the 16th centuries, the head of the entire Jewish population was the *nagid*. In the last 200 years the *negidim* also held sway over the Jews of Syria and the Land of Israel through deputies.

In both Muslim and Christian Spain the Jews enjoyed broad autonomy until the end of the 15th century, when they were expelled from the country. In the Muslim kingdoms a number of Jewish community heads became quite prominent, like Hisdai ibn Shaprut (known as *ha-Nasi*, the Prince) in the Kingdom of Cordoba in the 10th century or R. Shemuel ha-Nagid in the Kingdom of Granada in the first half of the 11th century. In the Christian kingdoms there were no nationwide communal organizations. There was a principal community to which Jews from the towns and villages were attached. This was headed by seven "best men." The heads of the community published halakhic directives (*takkanot*) governing the responsibilities of the individual toward the community and relations between individuals. The community's courts tried criminal cases under government authorization. The community also ran aid services like Bikkur Holim.

Jewish autonomy in Christian Europe became possible because of the corporate-feudal nature of society there. Jews could not belong to any of the classes and were therefore recognized by the rulers as a separate and tolerated class. They were thus permitted to organize themselves as a class, i.e. within the framework of communities.

In the 10th–14th centuries Jewish settlement expanded in Western Europe – in France and Germany. Community organization developed commensurately. The community embraced all Jews living within its bounds and exercised authority in every area of public and private life – in religious matters, in protecting the individual and his property, and in mutual aid. To perform its services it organized a broad range of facilities: synagogues and ritual baths, cemeteries, charity funds, judicial and educational institutions, and agencies for the enforcement of enactments in the public interest. The members of the community saw in these activities an essential condition for preserving the distinct character of the Jewish nation. Throughout the responsa of the 11th–15th centuries there are numerous discussions of relations between the community and the individual or the authorities.

The many directives published with regard to community activities were produced by well-known scholars of the time: R. Gershom ben Yehuda Me'or ha-Golah, R. Yosef Tov Elem, R. Shelomo ben Yitzhak (Rashi), R. Yaakov Tam, R. Meir of Rothenburg.

A second thread running through these directives concerned resistance to the attempts of large communities to swallow up the smaller ones in their neighborhoods. From the 12th century there was a tendency to establish a centralized, national leadership for the communities. This can be seen in the Troyes synod under R. Tam and the Rashbam (R. Shemuel ben Meir) and the "Shum" synod (the Hebrew acronym of Speyer, Worms, and Mainz) as well as in the *takkanot* of R. Meir of Rothenburg.

Beginning in the 14th century the situation of the Jews in Germany and France deteriorated. The Crusades and the Black Death, blood libels, and expulsions led to the decline of the communities. Local rulers intervened in community affairs and the selection of community heads, judicial authority was limited, and rabbis were appointed by the authorities. Many of these rabbis worked to strengthen the hand of community leaders in those difficult times, such as R. Yisrael Isserlein, R. Natan of Igra, and the Maharal.

The expulsion of the Jews from France and Germany brought about mass migration to Austria, Bohemia and Moravia, and the Kingdom of Poland. Wherever they went the Jews brought with them the forms of their communal organization. Prominent leaders even tried to establish centralized leadership.

It was in the Kingdom of Poland–Lithuania that Jewish autonomy reached its peak. The Jews of Poland, who had emigrated from the West to the East from the beginning of the Middle Ages, from Germany and Bohemia–Moravia, took with them examples of charters of rights and these were granted by the Polish and Lithuanian rulers. The Jews elaborated the organization of the community on the basis of these charters and their experience in the West. At the head of the communities stood the elected aldermen (*parnasim*), under a rotation scheme ("elder of the month"). The aldermen dealt with day-to-day affairs, represented the community before the authorities, prepared the annual budget, collected taxes, and preserved public order. They appointed community workers and supervised their activities. Two elected advisory bodies served alongside them: selectmen and "best men" (*meliores*). An important function was that of community rabbi. He confirmed the directives issued by the *parnasim* and the tax register prepared by the community's tax assessors. The rabbi headed the community's election committee and accorded honorary titles in the community (*haver* and *morenu*). Community income was derived from direct and indirect taxes, the latter on commodities like meat, salt, and wax. Payments were also required for the right to live and work in the community. Since most communities operated at a deficit, they had to borrow large sums, mainly from priests and from monasteries.

The 16th century saw the development of community roof organizations in the form of provincial councils. Here the principal communities were represented by their *parnasim* and rabbis. When they convened, one of them was chosen as "provincial *parnas*."

In the second half of the 16th century the rulers of Poland–Lithuania became convinced that it would be more effective if the Jews themselves collected state taxes, principally the head tax. To this end the government authorized the existence of countrywide representation. As a consequence, there emerged from within the provincial councils the Council of the Four Lands in the Kingdom of Poland and the Council of the Land of Lithuania in the Grand Duchy of Lithuania, the latter quickly detaching itself from the former and becoming independent. The councils were comprised only of principal communities. The Council of the Four Lands included the principal communities of Great Poland, Lesser Poland, Galicia, and Volhynia while the Lithuanian Council included at first only Brest-Litovsk, Grodno, and Pinsk and later also Vilna and Slutsk. The Council of the Four Lands generally convened during the big fairs at Lublin and Yaroslav. The principal communities were each represented by two or more of their *parnasim* and rabbis. Scribes, tax collectors and bailiffs, and government lobbyists (*shtadlanim*) also participated.

The records of council meetings indicate that no area of Jewish life went untouched. If required, directives were issued. In the economic sphere the councils dealt with taxes, residence and work rights, trade restrictions (to eliminate foreign competition), promissory notes, bankruptcies, etc. An important subject was education, especially for needy children. The councils obliged the larger communities to underwrite education for the poor and to maintain yeshivas. They took a strong stand against luxurious living, issuing directives to tone down family celebrations and women's dress. Another significant item on their agenda was the division of the financial burden created by blood and Host desecration libels and by the activities of proselytes. As the libeled community was incapable of meeting the resulting costs, the councils divided them among the communities of the particular land. The Councils of the Lands continued to exist officially until they were dissolved by the Sejm (Parliament) and the king in 1764. Unofficially the provincial councils and even the Councils of the Lands continued to meet until the First Partition of Poland in 1772.

The civic equality that resulted from the French Revolution did away with the Jewish community as an autonomous entity, restricting its activities to religious affairs alone. The assimilation that resulted from the Haskala (Jewish Enlightenment) weakened the link with the community even more. All this held true in Western Europe. In the East the community was abolished in Poland in 1822 and in Russia in 1844, but most of its functions remained in the hands of the existing bodies. In addition to religion they dealt with health, welfare, and education and in the time of Czar Nicholas I even with military conscription (the cantonists).

Following the February 1917 Revolution a democratically elected federation of communities was created in Russia for the first time. It was abolished after the October 1917 Revolution. The Bolsheviks waged incessant war against the Jewish religion and Jewish national life. As alternatives they set up in the 1920s a Jewish ministry in the Soviet government and the Yevsektsiya (Jewish Section) in the Communist Party whose function was to inculcate

Communism among the Jews. These too were abolished at the end of the Twenties. Jewish life remained circumscribed within Jewish state institutions for culture and education, which toed the Soviet line. However, it should also be noted that improvised prayer houses and charitable organizations continued to exist into the early 1930s.

In Poland, between the two world wars, the Jewish community was recognized as a legal corporate body and even authorized to collect taxes from its members. Its activities centered mainly around religious and welfare services while other organizations dealt with health, education, and economic affairs. At the local level these organizations were supported financially by the communities. The awakening of Jewish political life and the consequent proliferation of Jewish political parties led to hard-fought elections for community leadership positions. Economic organizations and trade unions also ran in these elections. Some communities were dominated by Zionist or ultra-Orthodox parties, some by the Bund. In countries like Rumania and Hungary (with a chain of Orthodox and Reform communities) the situation was similar. In Germany the community assumed greater importance after the Nazis came to power. The elimination of Jews from every area of economic and cultural life forced the community to take up these functions and expand its activities, even establishing nationwide organizations. This was the situation until 1938, when the communities were abolished as entities and state-appointed representatives took their place, acting on government instructions.

As mentioned, the Nazi Occupation in World War II put an end to community organizations. Together with the millions of Jews, the Nazis destroyed numerous synagogues, some of them magnificent and of great architectural value, and Jewish institutions like schools, hospitals, orphanages and old age homes, libraries and theaters. Tombstones in Jewish cemeteries, some of them quite ancient, were used by the Nazis to pave streets and roads. The aim was to remove all traces of Jewish life going back numerous generations.

Jewish communities were reestablished in Poland after World War II, though restricted to religious affairs. Jewish committees operated alongside them and after their liquidation in 1950 a Communist-controlled Cultural-Social Association was established which published a newspaper, ran schools, and founded social clubs, all in a Yiddish-language milieu. Sometimes it also did charity work, among widows and orphans, and set up children's camps.

In 1953 the Israeli Parliament passed the Yad Vashem Remembrance Authority Law to perpetuate the memory of "the communities, synagogues, movements and organization, public, cultural, educational, religious, and welfare institutions destroyed and obliterated for the evil purpose of eradicating the name of Israel and its culture from the face of the earth." To perpetuate the memory of the lost communities Yad Vashem created a Vale of Communities where the names of the thousands of communities destroyed in the Holocaust are carved on huge stone walls. From the outset Yad Vashem also wished to commemorate these communities through written records, embarking on a project of publishing *Pinkasei Kehillot*, a multivolume encyclopedia of Jewish communities with entries on each and every one of them. Each article follows the history of the community from its beginnings until its destruction by the Nazis. Emphasis is placed on the two final periods: the years between the world wars and the years of the Nazi Occupation. Each country has its own volume, or in the case where a large Jewish population inhabited numerous settlements, a few volumes, with each embracing a geographic-administrative area.

The three volumes presented here in the English language embrace about 6,500 communities, appearing in alphabetical order. Most of the entries are condensations containing a tenth of the material in the 22 Hebrew volumes either already published or in print. The rest, for the remaining nine volumes of the series, were written directly in condensed form. Limits of space forced us to choose which parts of the articles would be condensed more and which less. After much thought it was decided to abridge more thoroughly material on the period up to World War I, leaving in the main events, and include more about the interwar period and most of all about the Holocaust period. The main reason for this was that the description of community life in the last two periods contains much new material. For reasons of space, we were obliged to eliminate statistical tables and source references.

Names of communities have been transcribed as in the language of the country in question. However, because of printing limitations, we did not reproduce diacritical marks (as in the Polish, French, Czech, and other languages). For the names of Russian settlements in the Cyrillic script we used the accepted system of English transliteration.

The Index of Communities at the end of the third volume includes, in addition to main entries, communities mentioned in the text but without a main entry and variant spellings and additional names of communities with a main entry. A second index is of persons mentioned in the text. Also included for the convenience of the reader is a glossary of terms, a selected bibliography, and a chronological table.

In preparing the Hebrew edition we debated how to specify the countries to which the various communities were attached, since borders and political alignments underwent changes over time, particularly in Eastern Europe. It was decided to give the country to which the community belonged on the eve of World War II, that is to say in September 1939 for most and around that date for a few others (Czechoslovakia, Rumania). Thus Vilna was shown as belonging to Poland whereas today it is in fact the capital of Lithuania, while Lwow, also part of Poland then, is today in the Ukraine. Likewise, Slovakia is today an independent country and Carpatho-Russia is a district in the Ukraine, whereas in 1938 they were part of Czechoslovakia. For the English edition we decided to add the current national status of the settlement as well. Thus, for the former Czechoslovakian Slovakia we have added "today Republic of Slovakia" and for the relevant parts of Poland, "today Belarus" or "today Ukraine" as the case may be. However, we thought it redundant to characterize Belorussia or the Ukraine, when they are given as such historically, as "today Republic of Belarus" or "today Republic of Ukraine." In the case of areas of Germany annexed by Poland after the war, the current Polish name of the settlement is given in parentheses. The same principle is followed in the case of the Koenigsberg region of East Prussia, where we have added the Russian name (Kaliningrad for the city of Koenigsberg and so on). We have also denoted the former parts of Yugoslavia as today the separate republics of Croatia, Bosnia, or Slovenia, and the Soviet Autonomous Republic of Moldavia, which merged in 1940 with the Bessarabian part of Rumania, as "today Republic of Moldova."

In transcribing Hebrew given names we have departed somewhat from the convention of anglicization (Isaac for Yitzhak, etc.), using instead the Hebrew form when it seemed appropriate by virtue of the cultural and social milieu in which the individual was active (for example, Eliyahu ben Shelomo rather than Elijah ben Solomon for the Vilna Gaon).

In illustrating the text of the Encyclopedia we have endeavored to depict what was both ordinary and vital in the life of the Jews and their communities, for the history of these communities, as mentioned, was much more than their tragic end. However, that end did come, and to remember it we have thought it fitting to append a pictorial supplement to the final volume of the Encyclopedia that will bring home the meaning of the Holocaust in all its unimaginable reality.

Many people participated in this project, writing and abridging the articles for both the Hebrew and English editions. Their names are given in the list of contributors.

Shmuel Spector
Editor in Chief

Abbreviations

b.	born
B.C.E.	Before Common Era (= B.C.)
c.	circa
C.	Central
C.E.	Common Era (= A.D.)
cent.	century
d.	died
dist.	district
E.	East, Eastern
Flem.	Flemish
Fr.	French
Ger.	German
Gr.	Greek
Heb.	Hebrew
Hung.	Hungarian
Ital.	Italian
J.	Jewish
Lat.	Latin
Lith.	Lithuanian
Mt(s).	Mount, Mountain(s)
N.	North, Northern
Pol.	Polish
pop.	population
prov.	province
R.	Rabbi
Rum.	Rumanian
Rus.	Russian
S.	South, Southern
Serb.	Serbian
Turk.	Turkish
Ukr.	Ukraine
W.	West, Western
WWI	World War I
WWII	World War II
Yid.	Yiddish

For organizations, see Glossary

A

AACH Rhineland, Germany. Jews arrived in 1589, reaching a peak pop. of 77 (total 310) in 1843, which steadily declined due to emigration to 38 in 1933. A synagogue was consecrated in 1859. Most Jews were fairly prosperous cattle traders. Their businesses were destroyed in the Nazi era. By 1938, five of the village's eight J. families had emigrated to the U.S. The synagogue was wrecked on *Kristallnacht* (9–10 Nov. 1938) along with J. homes. The last Jews were deported in 1942–43; at least ten perished in the camps.

AACHEN Rhineland, Germany. Jews were present during the reign of Charlemagne and were granted the right of free trade in his Jew Edict of 800. A Jew named Yitzhak was the only one of his representatives to return from a mission to the caliph Harun al-Rashid in 802. In 1241, J. residence was restricted to a Street of the Jews (*Judengasse*). Persecution and expulsion followed, with J. residence subsequently permitted only under the protection of local rulers. In 1629, the Jews were again expelled, some returning ten years later and again taking up their occupation as moneylenders. In 1794, under French rule, the Jews were accorded full civil rights. By 1806 their number had grown to 60 and by 1812 a number of Jews owned factories and workshops as well as retail and wholesale establishments. Most J. commerce and industry revolved around the textile trade. The J. pop. proceeded to grow from 96 in 1820 to 1,334 (total 103,470) in 1890. Throughout the latter part of the 19th cent., about two-thirds of the Jews engaged in commerce and the economic situation of the Jews remained far superior to that of the local, overwhelmingly Catholic pop. In 1874, Jews owned 26 factories, 23 of them manufacturing textiles; in 1890, the number of J. industrialists and merchants was equal to those in the rest of the

pop. Jews were well integrated into public life. A Jew owned the local newspaper, the *Aachener Stadt-zeitung*, and another opened the first German bookstore in 1852. From 1851, Jews were regularly elected to the municipal council and wealthy Jews were residing in the new and exclusive section of the city. Personal social relations with non-Jews was practically nonexistent. Overt antisemitism was rare but began to develop in the 1890s. The community was officially recognized in 1836, with a number of satellite communities coming under its jurisdiction. Its first cemetery was opened in 1822 and a new one in 1852. A synagogue was consecrated in 1839. In 1850, the Liberal congregation introduced an organ and appointed its first full-time rabbi, Dr. David Rothschild, who served until 1859. A Reform prayer book was used and the use of Hebrew in prayer was reduced. The J. bar mitzva service was replaced by confirmation exercises on the Protestant model. A new and larger synagogue was completed in 1862. In 1876, Dr. Theodor Julius became rabbi, serving the community until 1925 and helping publish the famous journal *Monatsschrift fuer Geschichte und Wissenschaft des Judentums* successively edited by Zacharias Frankel and Heinrich Graetz. Most Jews were nonobservant and Zionist consciousness was minimal but Jews did not deny their identity and intermarriage and conversion were rare. Orthodox circles started their own *minyanim* in 1895. The first (private) J. elementary school, opened in 1826 with 24 pupils, became a J. public school in 1845. By 1888, 97 boys and girls in separate classrooms were in attendance. Though the Bible was not studied and Hebrew instruction was limited, R. Julius conducted supplementary religious classes. The Jews of A. operated a wide range of welfare and charity services. The Zionist Organization and the Central Union (C.V.) opened offices in 1907 and 1910, respec-

tively. In 1905, the J. pop. reached a peak of 1,665, dropping to 1,420 in 1925 and 1,345 (total 162,774) in 1933, to make the community the ninth largest in the Rhineland. At the same time, J. births dropped dramatically, from 31 in 1922 to just five in 1933. By 1925, 27.5% of the J. pop. was over 50 years of age (as opposed to 19.8% in the general pop.). About 10% of the J. pop. was of East European origin. Jews continued to play a leading economic role in the Weimar Republic. J. mills were responsible for over half the textile production in the city and 50 J. firms marketed their products throughout Germany. Retail outlets like Tietz, Ehape, and the Kaufmann Co. employed hundreds of workers. The community continued to be overwhelmingly Liberal in outlook, giving the local faction 80–85% of the vote in elections to the community council. Zionist support was still limited in scope.

Support for the Nazis was negligible until 1930 and even in 1933 the 27% Nazi vote in the Reichstag elections was the lowest in Germany. When the Nazis vandalized the popular Mimetz hotel and other J. businesses in 1932, the acts were widely condemned. The public made little effort to defy the 1 April economic boycott which the Nazis instituted, but there was also little violence. In March–April 1933, Jews were expelled from trade unions and the local chamber of commerce and banned from using municipal sports facilities. In April 1934, J. parents were prevented from enrolling their children in secondary schools. Nearly all legal personnel in the civil service as well as university faculty members were dismissed. J. workers in a number of "Aryan" stores were also fired. Most of the local pop. opposed Nazi policy and a rare demonstration against the persecution of the Jews was held a week after the general boycott. However, Nazi pressure eroded support and sympathy for the Jews. In Dec. 1934, an explosive charge was set off in the synagogue, causing extensive damage. During this initial period (1933–35), 172 Jews emigrated, including 58 to Holland and 37 to Palestine, while another 107 left for other localities in Germany. However, at the same time, other Jews from nearby towns and villages were arriving. J. welfare services were united under a single roof organization and enrollment in the community J. school increased to 110 in 1934–35 as opposed to 70 in 1932–33. Under the auspices of the Juedischer Kulturbund, lectures, concerts, and theater performances were organized. Zionist activity also intensified. Fur-

ther anti-J. measures were enacted in 1936: Jews were banned from municipal bathing facilities, real estate transactions between Jews and non-Jews were prohibited, and J. children continued to be expelled from schools. Jews still occupied key economic positions with 28 manufacturers (mainly in the textile industry) and 61 merchants operating, but the process of "Aryanization" continued unabated and in 1936 a third of the city's Jews were unemployed. In 1938, the community was stripped of its autonomous legal status and placed under the jurisdiction of the municipality. At the same time, Jews were banned from "Aryan" hotels. By 1938, 160 children were in the community's J. school and 100 in its kindergarten. On *Kristallnacht* (9–10 Nov. 1938), the synagogue was burned down; J. homes and stores were vandalized; Jews were run half-naked through the streets and abused; and 70 men were arrested, mostly community leaders. Sixty were sent to the Buchenwald concentration camp and ten to Sachsenhausen. In the aftermath of *Kristallnacht*, 91 of the remaining 112 J. businesses in the city were closed down or "Aryanized" and the last J. children removed from public schools. In May 1939, 782 Jews were still living in A. Many managed to leave Germany illegally, taking advantage of organized bus tours to Holland and Belgium to escape. In April 1941 the remaining Jews were confined to a few special houses, most of them in a camp (*Judenlager*) near the railroad junction. From the beginning of the year, they were also subjected to a regime of forced labor and in Sept. they were ordered to wear the yellow badge. Deportations commenced on 25 March 1942, when 16 Jews were sent east. A second transport from Duesseldorf to Izbica in the Lublin dist. (Poland) included 144 Jews from A. above the age of 55. Another 278 Jews were deported to Theresienstadt on 25 July 1942, including residents of the old age home. Another transport left for the Theresienstadt ghetto on 11 Sept. The last Jews of A. were deported to Theresienstadt between Dec. 1943 and Sept. 1944. After the war, 62 Jews were present in the city, and the J. pop. grew from 165 in 1960 to 522 in 1993.

AALTEN Gelderland dist., Holland. J. presence in A. began in the 1620s. There were 85 Jews in 1860 (total 6,031). In WWII deportations began comparatively late and in early 1943, 81 Jews still lived there. Thirty-five survived in hiding. The entire region, particularly A., sheltered many Jews from western Holland, especially from Amsterdam. At one time 2,500

Jews and non-Jews were hidden in A. and the local Reform Protestants collected money to support those in hiding and those who were hiding them. After the war, the synagogue was rehabilitated and a small community reestablished.

ABA   Fejer dist., Hungary. Jews are mentioned in 1778 sources. Their pop. was 131 in 1880 and 59 in 1930. A school was established in 1878. In 1941, they were subjected to forced labor and on 18 June 1944 deported to Auschwitz via the Szekesfehervar ghetto.

ABADSZALOK   Jasz-Nagykun-Szolnok dist., Hungary. Jews settled in the first half of the 19th cent. and numbered 112 in 1880. In 1919, White Terror members mounted a pogrom here. On 26-29 June 1940, there were 18 J. families. In 1944, they were dispatched via the Szolnok ghetto to Auschwitz and to Austria.

ABAUJSZANTO   Abauj dist., Hungary. Jews were present in the first half of the 18th cent. and by 1765 maintained a synagogue and cemetery. In 1840, they numbered 1,212 but subsequently started leaving for the big cities. Many Jews were linked to the area's wine industry with one J. grower exporting wine to neighboring countries. Serving the community's educational needs were a school, a *talmud torah*, and a *heder*. R. Aryeh Leibish Lipschitz served the community in 1873-96 and was later rabbi of Budapest and head of the Hungarian Federation of Orthodox Communities. In 1941, the J. pop. was 681. In 1944, with the German occupation, the Jews were subjected to forced labor. On 12-15 June they were deported to Auschwitz via the Kassa ghetto.

ABONY   Pest-Pilis-Solt-Kiskun dist., Hungary. Jews are first mentioned in 1756 and in 1788 opened a J. school. In 1880, they numbered 834. Many were peddlers, with 20-25 families engaged in farming. In 1941, the J. pop. was 315. A ghetto for all the Jews in the province was established after the German occupation of 1944. On 25-27 June 1944, all were deported to Auschwitz via Kecskemet.

ABRAMOWO   Polesie dist., Poland, today Belarus. Initially only Jews lived in this farm settlement, numbering 97 in 1921. They were deported to the Treblinka death camp in Nov. 1942 via the Kamieniec Litewski ghetto.

ABRENE   (Jaunlatgale) Latgale dist., Latvia. The J. pop. in 1935 was 61 (total 1,242). All but a few fled to Soviet territory with the approach of the Germans in June 1941.

ABTERODE   Hesse, Germany. Jews lived there from the mid-17th cent. and established the largest rural community in the duchy of Hesse, numbering 39 families (23% of the total) in 1744 and 234 individuals in 1835. Many of the duchy's Hebrew teachers were first educated at the local J. elementary school (1840-1934). Affiliated with the Kassel rabbinate, the community dedicated a new synagogue (1871), which was vandalized together with other J. property on *Kristallnacht* (9-10 Nov. 1938). Most of the 97 Jews registered there during the Nazi period left before 1940; at least 17 perished in the Holocaust.

ACAS   (Hung. Akos) N. Transylvania dist., Rumania. Jews first settled in the late 18th cent. The J. pop. in 1920 was 118 (7% of the total). In May 1944 the J. community was transferred to the Simleul Silvaniei ghetto and in June deported to Auschwitz.

ACHIM   Hanover, Germany. Affiliated with Stade's rabbinate (1844), the community built a synagogue in 1864 and maintained a state-recognized J. elementary school (1878-1924). The J. pop. numbered 73 (2% of the total) in 1907 but then declined. In 1928, the smaller community of Ottersberg was attached to A. The synagogue was set on fire on *Kristallnacht* (9-10 Nov. 1938). By 1939, 18 Jews had emigrated. Thirty perished in the Holocaust.

ACS   Komarom dist., Hungary. Jews settled in the mid-18th cent., numbering 275 in 1840 and declining to 119 by 1930 after steady emigration to the cities. On 13-16 June 1944, they were deported to Auschwitz via Kisber.

ADA   Vojvodina dist., Yugoslavia. The J. community was established in 1790 and in 1868-69, at the time of the religious division of Hungarian Jewry, it adhered to Orthodoxy. It turned to Zionism between the World Wars. In 1921 the Jews numbered 370 (total 13,106). Little antisemitism was experienced until the Holo-

caust, when – under Hungarian rule – 290 of the 350 Jews perished.

ADAMOW Lublin dist., Poland. J. settlement commenced in the 19th cent. The J. pop. reached 494 in 1897 and 664 in 1921 (total 1,934). Between the World Wars the Zionists and their youth movements were active. The Germans arrived on 20 Sept. 1939, setting up a *Judenrat* and a ghetto whose pop. swelled to 1,724 by July 1942 with the arrival of refugees. A small group escaped to nearby forests and joined with a group of J. partisans in attacking the jail at A. and freeing several Jews. Nearly all were deported to the Treblinka death camp via Lukow in Oct. 1942.

ADELEBSEN Hanover, Germany. Jews arrived in the late 17th cent. and maintained a synagogue from about 1715 and apparently also a cemetery by the early 18th cent. Twelve families were present in 1752 and by the first half of the 19th cent. the community was one of the largest in the region, numbering 192 in 1848. Subsequently the J. pop. declined steadily, to 46 in 1925. In the late 19th cent., several Jews were active in public life and a few served on the municipal council. In June 1933, under Nazi rule, the J. pop. was 30, a process of emigration now setting in. The Nazis desecrated the synagogue in summer 1938 and on *Kristallnacht* (9–10 Nov. 1938), the building was burned. Twenty Jews remained in May 1939, a few still managing to leave. From Oct. 1941, the men were subjected to forced labor and on 25 March 1942, six Jews were sent to the Warsaw ghetto. The seven who remained behind were dispatched to the Theresienstadt ghetto in July. Some who had fled to Holland or France were also apprehended by the Nazis and sent to the death camps of the east.

ADELSBERG (in J. sources, Alts Berg) Lower Franconia, Germany. Jews were present from at least the early 19th cent., many engaged in farming and crafts. A synagogue was built in 1860–62. The J. pop. dropped from 63 in 1880 to 21 in 1933 (total 369). Most left after the *Kristallnacht* disturbances (9–10 Nov. 1938), when the synagogue and J. homes were vandalized.

ADELSDORF Upper Franconia, Germany. The community is first mentioned in 1669 as a victim of

peasant riots. Few Jews lived there in the 18th cent. Subsequently the Jews reached a peak pop. of 265 in 1837 (total 870) before steadily declining through emigration to the larger cities of Bavaria; in 1933, 60 remained. All 12 J. homes were vandalized on *Kristallnacht* (9–10 Nov. 1938) and the interior of the synagogue was destroyed. Jews were again attacked after an attempt on Hitler's life in Munich (9 Nov. 1939). Nine Jews under the definition of Germany's racial laws remained in A. after 25 April 1942.

ADELSHEIM Baden, Germany. A few protected J. families are known from 1338 and 1690. In the 18th cent. the Jews lived in a special quarter, were forced to wear distinctive clothes, and were confined to their homes on Sundays and Christian holidays. Straitened economic circumstances kept the J. pop. from growing beyond a peak of 64 in 1880 (total 1,602), though from the 1860s their position improved and they participated fully in the town's public life. The process of urbanization reduced the J. pop. to 35 in 1933. In the Nazi era, 20 left by Nov. 1938 (including seven to Palestine and six to the U.S.). Another six left after *Kristallnacht* (9–10 Nov. 1938), when the synagogue was vandalized, and eight were deported to the Gurs concentration camp in 1940. All died in the camps.

ADJUD Moldavia dist., Rumania. Jews first settled in the late 18th cent. They suffered when the city was ransacked by insurgents in 1821. In 1891, R. Avraham Friedman set up a court of the Ruzhin Hasidim. The J. pop. in 1899 was 827 (30% of the total). In the 1920s, the local pop. was incited to kill Jews and to plunder their shops and property. The J. pop. in 1940 was 655. During the war against the USSR (from June 1941), males aged 18–60 were sent to forced labor in Focsani and from there to Marasesti, Doaga, or Sarata. The community continued to function after the war.

ADONY Fejer dist., Hungary. Jews settled in the first half of the 19th cent. and founded a Neologist (Reform) congregation in 1868. The community numbered 75 in 1880 and 40 in 1930. In 1942, some Jews were subjected to forced labor. The remainder, about 20, were deported to Auschwitz via the Szekesfehervar ghetto on 5 June 1944.

ADORF Hesse, Germany. Numbering 45 in 1826, the Jews established a community around 1840 but

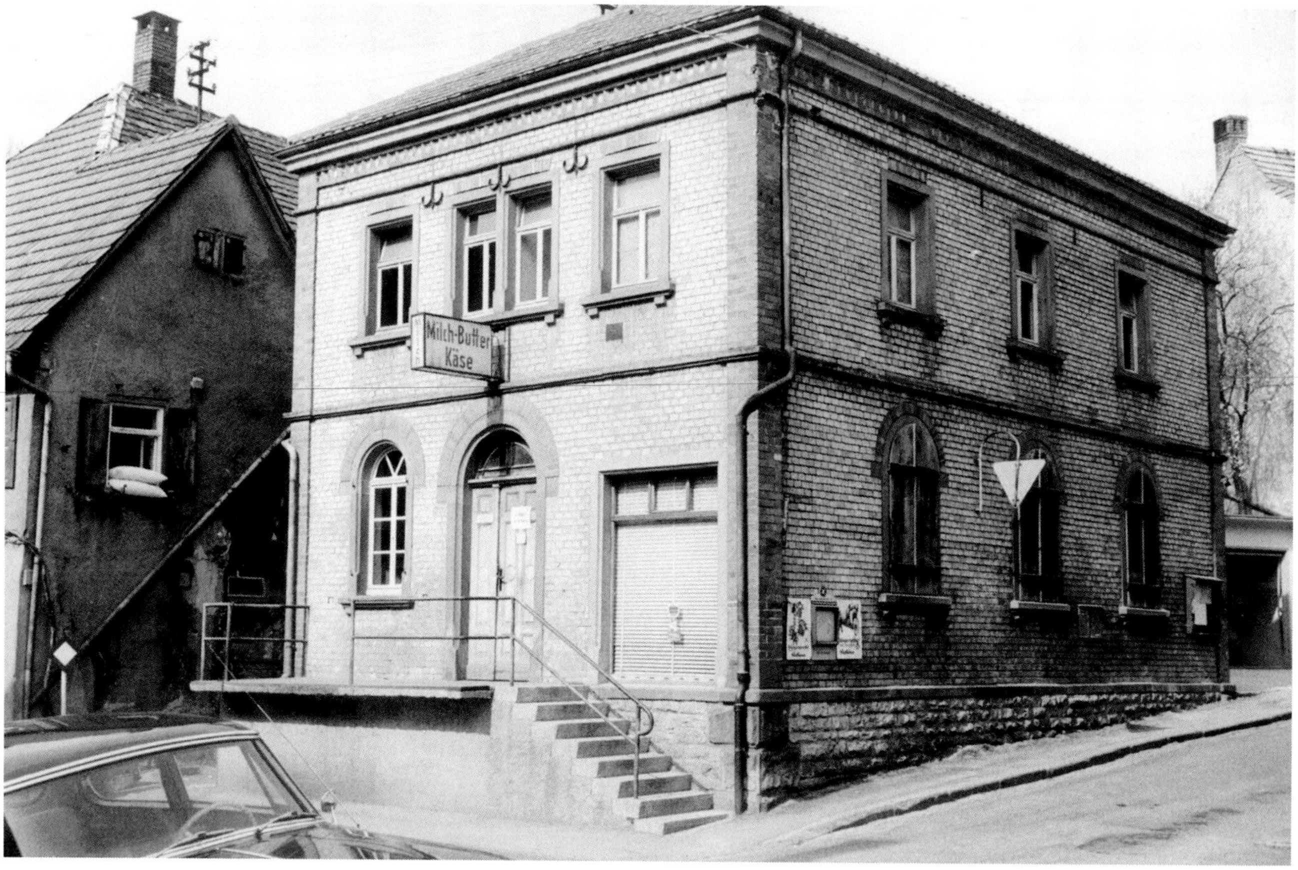
Milch-Butter
Käse

Building of former synagogue in Adelsheim, Germany

their number dwindled to 14 in 1925. After the community disbanded (1938), only three Jews remained.

AFFALTRACH Wuerttemberg, Germany. Jews first settled in 1660 under the protection of the ruling Order of St. John and engaged in moneylending and money-changing as well as limited trade in hides and cattle, peddling, and land dealings. In 1854 their pop. reached a peak of 190, thereafter declining sharply. A synagogue was built in 1851 and a J. elementary school was started in 1849. Relations with the local. pop. were satisfactory until the Nazi era. On *Kristallnacht* (9–10 Nov. 1938) the synagogue was vandalized but was not burned down. J. stores and homes were looted and impounded and Jews beaten. Of the 19 Jews there in 1933, four managed to emigrate by 1941. Four died in A., seven were deported and five of them perished. The fate of the others is unknown. In 1984 the building of the former synagogue was converted into a J. museum.

AGRINION (Agrinio, Vrachori, Vrakhori) Karilli dist., Greece. There were 200 J. families in A. prior to the Greek revolt (1821), when all were massacred. In 1943, there were between six and ten families, or 40 Jews, but no organized community. At the time of the German occupation in Sept. 1943 all the Jews fled to the hills. The Greek underground ordered the villagers to assist the Jews and all were saved from Nazi persecution. Following the war, in 1946, there were 30 Jews in A.

AHAUS Westphalia, Germany. Jews under letters of protection are first mentioned in 1667 but they were also present before that time. Their pop. comprised just a few families until the mid-19th cent. and reached a peak of 110 (total 3,100) in 1895. A synagogue was erected in 1818 and a J. school was also in operation at around that time. In mid-century, A. served as a regional congregation with four attached communities: Schoeppingen, Stadtlohn, Gronau, and Vreden. A new synagogue was built in 1863, with the congregation preserving an Orthodox character. In 1933, the J.

The Levi family in front of its sukkah, *Affaltrach, Germany*

pop. was 72. In 1934 and 1935, the synagogue was vandalized and on *Kristallnacht* (9–10 Nov. 1938), it was set on fire while J. homes and stores were seriously damaged. By late 1941, 46 Jews had left the town, including 17 for Holland and 16 for other localities in Germany. Subsequently 18 Jews were deported to the Riga ghetto and six to the Theresienstadt ghettto, most perishing in the Auschwitz and Sobibor death camps, as did some of those who reached Holland or the other German cities. The names of 47 Jews who perished in the Holocaust are known.

AHLEN Westphalia, Germany. Jews were permitted to settle in the mid-16th cent. under the protection of Bishop Franz von Waldeck and from 1678 maintained a continuous presence. In the 18th cent., the community grew steadily, reaching a pop. of around 100 in the second half of the 19th cent. (2–3% of the total). In 1847, the municipality officially recognized the J. pub-lic school which was attended by 21 children in 1893. The Rosenberg family was the most prominent in the community, owning enamelware factories and trading in grain and textiles. Until the Nazi era, family members chaired the community council. After WWI, about a third of J. breadwinners were merchants and many women were employed in sales and as maids. In the Nazi period, J. businesses declined and many Jews left the city, which reduced the J. pop. from 132 in 1933 to 52 in 1939. Of those who left, 17 reached Palestine and 17 North and South America. On *Kristallnacht* (9–10 Nov. 1938), the synagogue was set on fire and J. homes and stores were destroyed. The last 49 Jews were ordered out of the city on 6 Oct. 1939. Most left for other German cities. In all, 98 Jews who did not succeed in escaping from Germany were sent to the camps, where they perished.

AHRENSBURG   Schleswig-Holstein, Germany.

Synagogue in Ahaus, Germany, which was destroyed on Kristnallnacht

There is evidence of the presence of Jews from the last third of the 18th cent. In 1822, the small community (39 members in 1811) established a synagogue and a cemetery. In June 1933, only 16 Jews were still living in A. Ten managed to emigrate; one died; a woman married to a non-Jew committed suicide; another one living in a mixed marriage survived in the town; and one J. was deported in 1941. The fate of the two remaining Jews is unknown. The cemetery was desecrated on *Kristallnacht* (9–10 Nov. 1938).

AHRWEILER   Rhineland, Germany. Jews were already present in the 13th cent. and continued to live in A. under the protection of the Archbishop of Cologne. The J. pop. never exceeded a few dozen, reaching a peak of 82 (total 4,346) in 1885. A cemetery was opened in 1867 and a synagogue was completed in 1894. The ten families (31 Jews) in the town in 1933 earned their livelihoods as cattle traders and shopkeep-

ers (textiles and leather goods). On *Kristallnacht* (9–10 Nov. 1938), the synagogue was partially burned, J. stores were vandalized, and J. men were sent to concentration camps. By 1941, 18 Jews had left the town, 11 emigrating and seven moving to other places in Germany. Six Jews were deported to the east on 28 April 1942 and six more on 26–27 July. Thirteen Jews are known to have perished in the Holocaust.

AIDHAUSEN   Lower Franconia, Germany. The J. community numbered 82 (total 697) in 1867 with a synagogue erected in 1869. In 1933, 23 Jews remained. The synagogue and J. homes were vandalized in Oct. 1938. Ten Jews emigrated in 1935–39 and the rest were deported to Izbica in the Lublin dist. (Poland) and the Theresienstadt ghetto in 1942.

AIUD   (Hung. Nagyenyed) S. Transylvania dist., Rumania. An Orthodox J. community was established in

1880, but in 1912 it reorganized and joined the Neologist association. From the beginning of the cent. until the end of WWI, Jews dominated the wine trade and fruit exports. The community established a J. school which operated from 1920 to 1936. The J. pop. was 475 in 1930 (5% of the total). Zionist activity increased between the World Wars. In 1940, Iron Gurard Legionnaires persecuted the J. pop. In summer 1941, the J. pop. of Uioara was brought to A. and ten days later all were expelled to Alba-Iulia. Most men aged 18–60 were drafted into labor battalions while the women were sent to work in the municipality and government factories. In Feb. 1942, the Jews of A. were permitted to return. Their numbers dwindled following emigration to major towns and to Palestine.

AIX-EN-PROVENCE (locally called Aix) Bouches-du-Rhone dist., France. The first reference to Jews dates from about 1283 and mention is made of a Street of the Jews. By 1341, the Jews numbered 1,205, about 10% of the total pop. In 1430, anti-J. riots took place and subsequently Jews were forced to wear the special J. badge. There were other restrictions as well, such as a prohibition against practicing brokerage. In 1481, Provence passed to France, and in 1486 the A. municipality asked Charles VIII to expel the Jews. The general decree of expulsion, issued in 1498, became effective in 1501. Shortly after 1789, nine J. families from Avignon settled in A. By 1808, 168 Jews (53 families) were listed in the renewed community. In 1806, they were granted a cemetery. The local synagogue was inaugurated in 1840. Among the founders and heads of the J. community was the great-grandfather of the composer Darius Milhaud. The J. pop. was 228 in 1861 and 358 in 1872. By 1900, the community had dwindled to 214. Famous natives of A. were Moses Cremieux and Darius Milhaud (1892–1974). The novelist Armand Lunel (b. 1892) was also a native of A. During the 19th cent. there were three J. mayors in A. The census conducted by the Vichy government in May 1941 recorded 33 families living in A. Fifteen local Jews who failed to declare that they were Jews were tried and fined in May 1942. After the Germans entered the unoccupied zone in Nov. 1942, 2,000 J. refugees from Germany and Eastern Europe arrived in A. Most were quartered in the nearby camp of Milles. In May 1943, the Germans arrested almost all the Jews of A. They were interned in Drancy, and subsequently transported to

Auschwitz. Few survived. The J. community of A. practically disappeared during the years following WWII, and its synagogue was sold in 1952 to a Protestant church. In 1956, with the arrival of Jews from North Africa, a new community was created, numbering 1,200 Jews in 1964.

AIZPUTE (Yid. Hosenpoth) Courland dist., Latvia. Jews arrived in the 16th cent., mostly from the commercial towns of E. Prussia (Hamburg, Danzig, etc.). In 1751, the Polish parliament or Sejm authorized the construction of a synagogue and the establishment of a community, making it the first in Courland to be officially recognized. It occupied a central position in the Piltene region. The J. pop. grew rapidly in the first half of the 19th cent. owing to an influx of Lithuanian Jews, reaching 1,599 in 1835. But 618 left for the Kharkov area in the 1840s as part of the Russian resettlement program. A cholera epidemic in 1848 further reduced the J. pop., which stood at 1,170 in 1897 (total 3,340). The economic stability of the community and the dominance of German culture served to attract proponents of Haskala to A. The depredations of WWI led to a further reduction of the pop., which fell to 586 in 1920 and 534 in 1935. Those remaining mostly ran small businesses, with only around 10% defined as needy. Zionist activity commenced during WWI and exercised a decisive cultural and political influence, but fell off in the late 1930s as Zionist activists left for Palestine. A J. elementary school had an enrollment of 100. Antisemitism intensified in the 1930s with J. students at the Latvian high school attacked and efforts made to undermine the J. economy. With the arrival of the Soviets in 1940, most J. businesses were nationalized and J. public life was phased out. The Germans captured the town toward the end of June 1941. On 24 July, 39 Jews were executed at the Faduras cemetery. On 27 Oct. 1941, the remaining Jews were taken outside the town and executed by a 20-man Latvian firing squad. In all, 386 Jews were murdered.

AJAK Szabolcs dist., Hungary. Jews settled in the late 18th cent. and numbered 74 in 1880. In May 1944, the 50 remaining Jews who had not been subjected to forced labor were expelled to Kisvarda and from there deported to Auschwitz on 25–27 June.

AJDABIYA Cyrenaica dist., Libya. First settling in A. in the eighth cent., the Jews left in the 11th cent.

with the city's decline. Under Italian rule, a small community was established, numbering 54 in 1935. In WWII, A.'s Jews shared the fate of all Cyrenaican Jewry.

AKHTYRKA   Sumy dist., Ukraine. The J. pop. was 168 (total 23,399) in 1897 and 277 in 1939. A. was captured by the Germans on 18 Oct. 1941. By the end of the year, about 60 Jews were murdered in two *Aktions.*

AKMENE   (Yid. Akmian) Mazeikiai dist., Lithuania. J. settlement began in the mid-18th cent. By the first half of the 19th cent, Jews comprised two-thirds of the total pop. The 1897 J. pop. was 543, 36% of the total. Prior to WWII there were 100 Jews in A. The Germans arrived at the end of June 1941. On 4 Aug. 1941 all Jews were brought near Mazeikiai and were murdered, together with other Jews, on 9 Aug. 1941 by Lithuanian nationalists.

AKNISTE   Zemgale (Courland) dist., Latvia. The J. settlement was founded in the mid-19th cent. and numbered 199 (total pop. 473) in 1935. Nearly all were murdered by the Germans in July 1941.

ALBA-IULIA   (Hung. Gyulafehervar; Ger. Karlsburg) S. Transylvania dist., Rumania. This first and most important J. community in Transylvania was founded in the mid-16th cent.; in the 17th cent. a Sephardi community was organized. The community expanded during the 18th cent. with an influx of Ashkenazi Jews from Hungary and Walachia, as well as Sephardi Jews. During 1754–1868, the rabbi of A.-I. served as chief rabbi of Transylvania. A synagogue was built in 1840 and the Sephardim built their own in 1874. During the 19th cent., the majority of the Jews engaged in viniculture and bought land for vine-growing; in the 20th cent., most of the Jews earned their living as artisans. The J. pop. numbered 1,558 in 1930 (13% of the total). In Oct. 1940, the Iron Guard terrorized the Jews and in 1941 J. property was confiscated and the men sent to forced labor. After the war, the community was reestablished but soon dwindled as Jews left.

Typical Jewish home in Akmene, Lithuania

Shemuel Rav-On selling cigarettes and chocolate in Albania, 1943–44

ALBANIA Balkan republic. Jews lived in the port town of Durres (Ital. Durazzo) from the 13th cent. Most dealt in the salt trade. After the Ottomans conquered Durres in 1501, J. settlement in A. increased significantly, and included communities in Lezkha, Berat, and Elbasan. In 1417 Valona (Vlore) came under Ottoman rule and J. settlement there began by 1426. In the following decades the Valona community comprised Jews from France, Corfu and other Venetian settlements, the Iberian peninsula, and Naples. By 1519–20, there were 528 J. households in Valona. The Jews became active in Valona's social and economic development, primarily in the textile trade. Towards the end of the 16th cent., the J. pop. of Valona decreased and Durres attracted Jews to settle there. By 1904, only 50 Jews lived in Valona. Berat had 25 J. families in 1519–20. In 1596, the Jews of Berat and Valona were active in redeeming J. captives who

had been brought to Durres. In the 17th cent., the community gained importance. In the mid-17th cent. Nathan of Gaza passed through Berat and a number of Shabbetai Zvi followers lived there. (Shabbetai Zvi himself spent his final years in A.) By the 18th cent., many Jews in A. had converted to Christianity or Islam, while others had emigrated. In the mid-19th cent., Jews from Janina (Greece) renewed J. settlement in Gjirokaster, Delvine, Valona, Berat, Elbasan, Kavaje, Korce, Himara, and Shkoder. The financial slump in Greece in the 20th cent. led many Jews to settle in A. (Valona, Tirane, Shkoder, Gjirokaster) in the 1930s and 1940s. In 1927, Korce had five J. families. In 1930 there were 204 J. families in A. The Jews were not organized in communities and as a result communal organizations, such as J. schools, to educate the children did not exist. The J. community in A. was formally recognized in 1938 when the pop. numbered about 150, half of whom lived in Valona and the rest in Durres, Tirane, Gjirokaster, Sarande, Balish, Delvine, Fier, Shkoder, and Kavaje. The Jews of A. themselves did not suffer anti-J. prejudices or restrictions.

With the outbreak of WWII, A. was occupied by the Italians and became a transit point for Jews escaping Germany and a safe haven (primarily in Tirane and Durres) for some 400 refugees of the Nazi regime, who were assisted and hidden by the Albanians. In July 1940, all the Jews in Durres were ordered to transfer to Berat, Lushnje, and Fier. In April 1941, during the battles between Greece and Italy, and when part of Yugoslavia had been annexed to A., 120 J. refugees from Serbia, Croatia, and Macedonia arrived there. In 1941, the Italians brought 350 J. prisoners of war from Montenegro to A. In Kavaje (1941–42) the local community assisted some 200 J. refugees concentrated under harsh conditions in a camp there. Early in 1942, refugees from Pristina were transferred to Berat. Berat residents protected all the 100 or so J. refugees from Yugoslavia there. A number of J. refugees found shelter in Elbasan, Valona, Diber, Shkoder (where they were joined by refugees from Poland, Czechoslovakia, and Germany), and Tirane (disguised as Muslims). When danger approached, many went into hiding in villages in surrounding hills. A number of J. youths escaped from Yugoslavia in March 1943 and found shelter in A. That summer the Germans took over A. The Jews in Kavaje then moved to Tirane to find safer hiding places. However, Tirane was no longer safe and

some moved north to Kruje. Likewise, the Jews of Berat were forced to disperse and find shelter in other areas. In spring 1944, the governors of A. refused to cooperate in submitting lists of all the Jews in A. The Jews were promised they would be protected and the Christian and Muslim inhabitants made every effort to defend them. In Sept. 1943 and Sept. 1944, some refugees escaped to find safety in liberated Italy. As a result of the behavior and attitude of the Albanians, some 600 Jews (inhabitants and refugees) were saved from the Holocaust. Only six from Shkoder were arrested and sent to a camp in Pristina. Jews continued to live in A. after the war. There were 180 at most in the 1950s, primarily in Berat. In 1991, all but 4–5 Jews were brought to Israel.

ALBERSWEILER Palatinate, Germany. Jews are first mentioned in 1529. An organized community existed by the 18th cent., reaching a peak pop. of 271 in 1848 with over two-thirds engaged in trade. A J. public school was opened in 1855 and a synagogue was consecrated in 1868. The J. pop. declined steadily to a figure of 32 in 1933 and 15 in 1938. Four were deported by the Nazis in 1940 and perished.

ALBERT-IRSA Pest–Pilis–Solt–Kiskun dist., Hungary. Jews settled in 1746, paying heavy taxes to the proprietor of the village for protection and the right to sell alcoholic beverages and other goods. In 1869, they reached a peak pop. of 540, which subsequently declined as Jews were permitted to settle in the cities. In 1881, the community defined itself as Neologist. In 1941, the J. pop. was 145, its situation deteriorating under Hungary's racial laws. Few of the family heads sent to the Russian front for forced labor survived. The rest were subjected to a reign of terror even before the Germans arrived in spring 1944. The Jews were then expelled to the Monor ghetto (4 April) and on 8 July deported to Auschwitz.

ALBERTFALVA Pest dist., Hungary. Jews settled in the late 19th cent. and numbered 89 in 1930. They were deported to Auschwitz via Budafok on 29 June 1944.

ALEKSANDRIA Volhynia dist., Poland, today Ukraine. A few Jews remained after the destruction of A. in the Chmielnicki disturbances of 1648–49. The community grew to 2,154 (total 3,189) in 1897 with the development of light industry and the building of a railroad line and harbor. Jews from A. were among the first in Volhynia to join the Zionist movement. The instability and disturbances of WWI led to the closure of factories as the wealthy class emigrated, the J. pop. dropping to 1,293 in 1921 (total 1,781). From 1917, a Hebrew Tarbut school existed, founded by the well-known educator and Hebrew school supervisor Shemuel Rosenhak. Many of the young fled with the withdrawal of the Red Army in June 1941. Forced labor and periodic killing (85 Jews on 2 Sept. 1941) were the lot of the community under German rule. A *Judenrat* was appointed. The ghetto was liquidated on 23 Sept. 1943 when 1,000 Jews were murdered outside the town.

ALEKSANDROBOLIS (Yid. Alaksandrabal) Rokiskis dist., Lithuania. Ten J. families lived here in 1918. In WWII all Jews were killed by Lithuanian nationalists.

ALEKSANDROW (Aleksander) Lodz dist., Poland. Jews were among the first settlers in 1818, and after a few years a community was organized. Most were artisans and tradesmen who had incurred heavy debts, and it was only in 1909 that the synagogue was built. A. became a main center for the manufacture of stockings in Poland, mostly produced in home workshops. 1,673 Jews (28% of the total) lived there in 1897. From the mid-19th cent. A. became an important center of Hasidism, first of Gur led by R. Hanokh Henikh Levin and later with an independent court led by R. Yehiel Danziger. During WWI and after, the Bund and Po'alei Zion were active and established their own unions (the largest being the J. Stocking Workers Union). All the Zionist parties had pioneering groups and their own clubs. The community was led by Hasidim and Mizrachi. On 5 Sept. 1939, Jews fled the city, mainly to Lodz, and the local Poles and Germans looted their shops and houses. The Great Synagogue was burned down, the Torah scrolls destroyed, and later the Hasidim were forced to demolish the rabbi's court. The rabbi, Menahem Mendel Danziger, fled to Lodz and Warsaw, but was later sent to his death in the Treblinka death camp. On 27 Dec. 1939, the city's 3,000 Jews were expelled to Glowno. Many succeeded in finding refuge in surrounding villages and towns, only to be sent to their death with the local Jews.

ALEKSANDROW-KUJAWSKI   Warsaw dist., Poland. Jews settled in the late 19th cent., numbering 286 in 1897. By 1939 there were about 1,200 Jews (10% of the total). After the Germans occupied the town (Sept. 1939), the Jews were expelled in two waves (Sept.–Nov. 1939), many of them to Warsaw and small towns near Siedlce. They were later sent on to their death.

ALEKSIN   Tula dist., Russia. J. settlement probably commenced in the early 20th cent. In 1926, the J. pop. was 68 (total 3,942). The few remaining Jews, who had neither fled nor been evacuated, were murdered during the short German occupation of the town (29 Nov.–17 Dec. 1941).

ALESSANDRIA   Piedmont, Italy. The J. presence in A. dates from 1490, with the coming of Abraham Vitale de Sacerdoti (Cohen), who opened a bank and was granted residence rights for his family. The family dominated communal life in the next centuries, producing bankers and diplomats. The first local J. cemetery was purchased in 1595. In 1597, all Jews were expelled from the Duchy of Milan. However, by 1684 the community numbered 230 Jews After 1707, A. passed from Spanish rule to the House of Savoy, new horizons opened for the Jews, and the banker Aharon Pontremoli was commissioned as military supplier. In 1723, Piedmont Jews were officially segregated in a ghetto. In 1761, 60 families lived in A. In 1796–1814, the period of French influence in Italy, the local Jews enjoyed temporary civil emancipation. With the House of Savoy again ruling, the Jews were again restricted to the ghetto in 1837. During a wedding ceremony in 1835, the overcrowded house where the ceremony took place collapsed, killing 42 people, among them R. Matassia ben Moses Zacut Levi de Veali. In 1869, the community numbered 630. A new synagogue was inaugurated in 1871. Following emancipation in 1848 local Jews distinguished themselves in manufacturing silk and textiles, but also culturally and politically. The community dwindled, due to migration to larger cities, mainly to Turin. In 1888, the J. pop. was 400; 370 in 1900; and then 365 in 1910. In the mid-1920s, Dr. Aldo Lattes was its religious leader. Royal decree merged A. with the community of Nizza Monferrato. According to the 1930 law reforming the J. communities in Italy, the district of A. included Acqui, Asti, Nizza Monferrato, and Novi Lig-

ure. According to the 1936 census, the community numbered 260 Jews, led by R. C. Carlo Rocca. Police records from 1938 indicate the presence of 357 Jews in the town. During WWII, the area was under Nazi rule. In Feb. 1944, the local police chief sent 24 local Jews to the concentration camp in Carpi. Of the 267 local citizens who were deported to the death camps, 101 were Jews. In Dec. 1943, local Fascists looted the synagogue, the community archive, and two libraries. By Feb. 1944, the district governor dissolved the community with its communal and welfare institutions. After the war, the local police chief ordered that J. property held unlawfully must be restored at once. The community numbered 168 in 1945, dropping to 109 in 1948 and to 36 in 1965. The community was officially absorbed into the Turin community.

ALEXANDRENI   Bessarabia, Rumania, today Republic of Moldova. Jews first settled in mid-19th cent. By 1897, 1,190 Jews constituted 95% of the total pop. of this J. agricultural settlement. Jews grew corn and later tobacco. A J. school opened early in the 20th cent. The J. pop. in 1930 was 1,018 (67% of the total). There is no data on the fate of the Jews during WWII.

ALEXANDRIA   (Betcha) Kirovograd dist., Ukraine. Jews apparently settled in the late 18th cent. and numbered 3,735 (total 14,007) in 1897. Jews mainly traded in farm produce (including grain) and worked as tailors. They were victimized by pogroms in 1882; in 1904, when 20 died; in 1907, during national Duma elections; and in 1919. Until the late 1920s, a Habad synagogue and *beit midrash* were illegally maintained and until the late 1930s a J. elementary school was operating with an enrollment of 200 in the early 1930s. In the Soviet period, most Jews belonged to artisan cooperatives. The J. pop. dropped to 1,420 in 1939. The Germans entered the city on 6 Aug. 1941 and soon murdered 2,572 Jews from A. and its environs.

ALEXANDROPOULIS   (Alexandropole, Dedeagatch, Alexandropoli) Evrou dist., Greece. There was a small J. community in the early 20th cent. It operated a school and numbered 48 families in 1912. The community dwindled in the 1920s and became financially distressed in the 1930s. The J. pop. in 1940 was 165 (total 15,472). The Germans placed A. under Bulgarian rule in April 1941, when the Jews numbered 197 (total

14,000). J. movement was restricted and severe anti-J. measures were introduced. In early 1942, youths were taken to forced labor. On 3–4 March 1943, the Jews were rounded up and taken to a camp in Bulgaria. On 19 March, they were transported to the Treblinka death camp via Vienna. None survived the death camp. Of the 15 Jews from A. who survived the war, none remained there after 1960.

ALEXANDROVKA Kirovograd dist., Ukraine. Jews apparently arrived in the late 18th cent. and increased in number from 356 in 1847 to 3,213 (total 4,366) in 1897. In a Dec. 1919 pogrom, Anton Denikin's White Army murdered 48 Jews. In the Soviet period, the J. pop. dropped to 565 in 1939. Within two or three months of the German occupation of early Aug. 1941, about 600 Jews from A. and its environs were murdered. Another 300 were murdered in March 1942.

ALKMAAR Noord-Holland dist., Holland. A short-lived Sephardi community was established in 1604, under the protection of the authorities. This was the first time Jews in Holland received full equality. From the end of the 17th cent. an Ashkenazi community developed which received permission to pray publicly in 1744. The J. pop. was 358 in 1879 and 188 in 1938 (total 30,000). In March 1942 the Jews were transferred to Amsterdam and then deported to Poland; three survived the camps while 40 survived in hiding. A small community was established after the war.

ALLENDORF (now part of Stadt-Allendorf) Hesse-Nassau, Germany. Jews lived there in the 17th cent. Together with J. villagers in neighboring Hatzbach, Erksdorf, and Speckswinkel, they established a unified community (1842) and numbered over 120 in 1861. The last 29 Jews mostly emigrated after 1933. Housed in a special concentration camp, 1,000 Hungarian J. women transferred from Auschwitz were among the slave laborers at a munitions factory in A. (1944–45).

ALLENDORF AN DER LUMDA Hesse, Germany. Established around 1838, the community numbered 91 (8% of the total) in 1895. On *Kristallnacht* (9–10 Nov. 1938) J. property was destroyed and by 1939 the Jews had mostly emigrated or settled elsewhere. The remaining 20 were deported in 1942.

ALLENSTEIN (Pol. Olsztyn) East Prussia, Germany, today Poland. First evidence of a J. presence dates from 1819. With 56 members in 1820, the community grew steadily and there were 212 Jews in 1871; 471 in 1905; and 612 in 1925. In the beginning of the 19th cent. a cemetery was established, followed by a synagogue (1877) and a school. In the early 20th

Synagogue in Allenstein, Germany

cent., the Association of East Prussian Communities established an old age home and office for the care of needy J. emigrants from Eastern Europe. The famous architect Erich Mendelsohn (1887–1953) was born in A. Hugo Haase (1863–1919), chairman of the Social Democratic Party, was also born here. A year after becoming a member of Germany's first republican government in 1918, he was murdered. Antisemitism increased in the Weimar years, from hate campaigns in the early 1920s to economic boycott in the late 1920s, which threatened the existence of several J. businesses. In 1932, SA stormtroopers threw hand-

grenades into a J.-owned department store. In June 1933, about four months after the Nazi rise to power, the J. pop. was 448. The B'nei B'rith lodge was dissolved in 1933–34 and in 1935, Jews were banned from using the public baths. In summer 1933, Nazi stormtroopers severely injured two J. merchants. On *Kristallnacht* (9–10 Nov. 1938), the synagogue was burned down. By May 1939, only 135 Jews were still living in A. Those who failed to leave were moved to special houses from the beginning of 1940. In 1941, they were joined by the remaining Jews of the region. The main deportation, to the Minsk ghetto, took place on 24 June 1942. The inmates of the old age home were deported on 2 Aug. to the Theresienstadt ghetto. On 15 March 1943, the remaining Jews of A. were sent there.

ALLERSHEIM (in J. sources, Alirshi, Alersha) Lower Franconia, Germany. Jews are known from the mid-17th cent. The cemetery, consecrated in 1729, served numerous communities in the region. In 1816, the J. pop. was 90 (total 331), declining steadily to four in 1933, including the caretaker of the cemetery, who was deported with his wife to Izbica in the Lublin dist. of Poland on 24 March 1942.

ALMAZNAYA Voroshilovgrad dist., Ukraine. The J. pop. in 1939 was 165 (total 8,898). After their arrival on 12 July 1942, the Germans murdered the Jews who failed to escaped or were not evacuated.

ALMELO Overijssel dist., Holland. The J. presence dates back to the mid-17th cent. By 1901 there were 562 Jews, many active in the textile industry. In 1941, there were 403 Jews (total 36,812) and the community was well organized. In early 1942, J. youths were taken to forced labor and then deported to the east. From Nov. 265 Jews were taken to death camps, six of whom survived. 160 survived in hiding. A community was reestablished after the war.

ALMOSD Bihar dist., Hungary. The J. community was founded in the 18th cent. and grew to a peak pop. of 227 in 1830 before Jews started leaving for

Young Jewish girls in a theater performance, Almelo, Holland, 1928

the cities. In 1941, 80 remained. Between 20 May and 3 June 1944, they were deported to Auschwitz via Nagyvarad.

ALOVE (Yid. Alave) Alytus dist., Lithuania. In 1923, A. had 78 Jews. In WWII all of A's. Jews were killed.

ALPEN Rhineland, Germany. Jews began settling under letters of protection in 1714. In the 19th cent., they maintained a synagogue, cemetery, and J. school with a pop. of 60–70 (up to 8% of the total). Most engaged in trade. In 1933, 35 remained. Of these, 17 left before *Kristallnacht* (9–10 Nov. 1938) when the synagogue was set on fire and J. homes were wrecked. Another nine left soon afterwards. The last Jews were deported to the ghettoes in Riga, and Minsk in 1941 and 1942. Sixteen perished; six reached Palestine, five Brazil, and three South Africa.

ALPHEN AAN DE RIJN Zuid-Holland dist., Holland. Jews settled there in the 18th cent. The J. pop. was 70 (total 19,471) prior to the Holocaust, when all were deported; none returned.

ALSBACH Hesse, Germany. Some Jews lived there from the 15th cent., opening a burial ground (1616) before a community was established in the late 18th cent. It numbered 58 (5% of the total) in 1910 and had declined to 21 (seven families) by 1933. These mostly emigrated to the U.S. before *Kristallnacht* (9–10 Nov. 1938) when the synagogue and the cemetery were vandalized and the two remaining J. homes were looted. In 1940, A. was declared "free of Jews" (*judenfrei*).

ALSEDZIAI (Yid. Alshad) Telsiai dist., Lithuania. Jews were living here in 1662. The 1897 J. pop. was 295 (27%). In 1940 there were about 30 families. With the outbreak of WWII, Lithuanians harassed the Jews but were stopped from killing them by the local priest, Dambrauskas. In revenge, the Lithuanians shot and buried 30 women and children from the Telsiai ghetto outside the priest's home. In July 1941 all Jews were brought to the Rainiai camp. From there they were transferred to various locations and killed.

ALSENZ Palatinate, Germany. Two protected J. families were present in 1650. In 1731 there were 22

Jewish class photo, Alsedziai, Lithuania, 1937

families, trading in cattle and grain and engaged in moneylending. In 1807, the J. pop. comprised 13 families and in 1846, 22 (102 Jews), including 17 merchants and five artisans. The number of Jews dropped to 80 in 1875, 41 in 1910, and 23 in 1932. In 1861, a Jew was elected to the village council. A cemetery was opened in 1710 and expanded in 1868. A synagogue was erected in 1765 and renovated in 1911 following a fire. A J. elementary school operated between 1830 and 1916, attendance ranging from three to 24 children. The synagogue was sold in 1933. On *Kristallnacht* (9–10 Nov. 1938) the two J. homes remaining in the village were vandalized. Five Jews remained in 1939. Two perished in the Gurs concentration camp and two in Auschwitz.

ALSFELD Hesse, Germany. A community established in medieval times fell victim to the Black Death persecutions of 1348–49. Jews returned in the late 18th cent. and helped develop local industries. The modern community—numbering 252 (5% of the

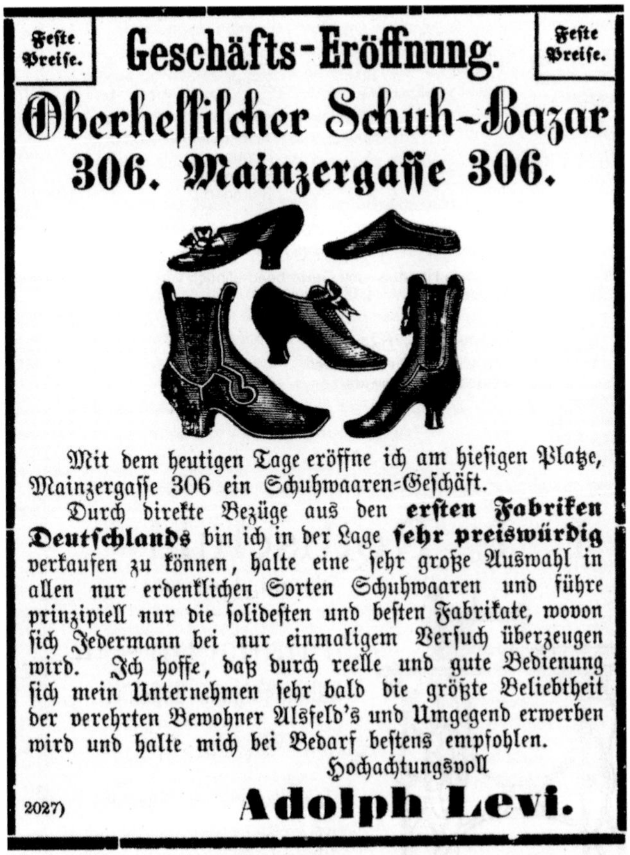
Feste Preise.
Geschäfts-Eröffnung.
Feste Preise.
Oberhessischer Schuh-Bazar
306. Mainzergasse 306.
Mit dem heutigen Tage eröffne ich am hiesigen Platze, Mainzergasse 306 ein Schuhwaaren-Geschäft.
Durch direkte Bezüge aus den ersten Fabriken Deutschlands bin ich in der Lage sehr preiswürdig verkaufen zu können, halte eine sehr große Auswahl in allen nur erdenklichen Sorten Schuhwaaren und führe prinzipiell nur die solidesten und besten Fabrikate, wovon sich Jedermann bei nur einmaligem Versuch überzeugen wird. Ich hoffe, daß durch reelle und gute Bedienung sich mein Unternehmen sehr bald die größte Beliebtheit der verehrten Bewohner Alsfeld's und Umgegend erwerben wird und halte mich bei Bedarf bestens empfohlen.
Hochachtungsvoll
2027)
Adolph Levi.

Announcement of shoe store opening, Alsfeld, Germany, 1886

total) in 1910 – became known for its strict Orthodoxy and philanthropic work. Antisemitic violence mounted even before the Nazis came to power and in 1933 Jews began emigrating to Palestine. The anti-J. boycott and *Kristallnacht* (9–10 Nov. 1938) hastened their departure by 1940. At the request of 15 Israelis born in A., the former congregation's surviving ark and appurtenances were transferred to a Haifa synagogue, Adat Yeshurun, in 1954.

ALSHEIM Hesse, Germany. The community, established in 1750, numbered 73 (5% of the total) in 1861. Religiously Liberal, it was celebrated for its choir. All 20 Jews living there in 1933 had emigrated or moved elsewhere by WWII.

ALSODABAS Pest–Pilis–Solt–Kiskun dist., Hungary. Jews settled in the late 18th cent., numbering 145 in 1880 and 44 in 1930. On 6 July 1944, they were deported to Auschwitz via Monor. After the war about 30 survivors renewed the community.

ALSOSAG Vas dist., Hungary. A J. family settled in 1746, but the community developed only in the second half of the 19th cent. Seven Jews in the area were murdered in the White Terror attacks of 1919 and many fled A. In 1930, the J. pop. was 109. In 1944, the Jews were sent to Janoshaza and Sarvar before final deportation to Auschwitz on 29 June 1944.

ALSOZSOLCA Borsod dist., Hungary. The J. pop. was 75 in 1930. On 10 June 1944, the Jews were deported to Auschwitz.

ALTDAMM (Pol. Dombie), today part of Stettin, Pomerania, Germany, today Poland. Letters of protection (*Schutzbriefe*) for nine Jews in 1481 constitute the first evidence of J. settlement here. Between 1491–93, the local Jews, together with the Jews of Pomerania, were expelled, following accusations of desecrating the Host. Resettlement occurred only in the 19th cent. In 1849, the J. pop. was 77. The small community had a prayer room and a cemetery, which was desecrated in 1926. When the Nazis came to power, there were 34 Jews living in A. On *Kristallnacht* (9–10 Nov. 1938), rioting was directed especially against the community's president and his fur store. By May 1939, there were 22 Jews and five individuals of partial J. origin (*Mischlinge*) in A. The remaining Jews were deported to the Lublin dist. of Poland on the night of 11–12 Feb. 1940 together with Jews from Stettin.

ALTDORF Baden, Germany. Jews are first mentioned in the 1570s. A permanent settlement was established by J. refugees from Ettenheim in 1716. Jews reached a peak pop. of 313 in 1855 (about 20% of the total), which declined to 51 in 1933. Fifteen emigrated in 1937–39 while 20 left for other German cities. On *Kristallnacht* (9–10 Nov. 1938) the synagogue and J. homes were vandalized and eight J. men detained in the Dachau concentration camp. The last 12 Jews were deported to the Gurs concentration camp on 22 Oct. 1940, eight of them perishing in the Holocaust, as did 15 of the Jews who had previously left the town and were subsequently deported from their places of refuge.

ALTENA Westphalia, Germany. A few J. families, numbering 15–25 people, were present in the mid-18th cent. The J. pop. reached a peak of 126 in 1821. The community built three synagogues (in

1808, 1828, and 1915) and maintained a cemetery from at least 1829. A J. elementary school operated from the late 19th cent. until WWI. The J. pop. declined to 100 in 1871, 67 (total 13,743) in 1905, and 22 in 1933. On *Kristallnacht* (9–10 Nov. 1938) Torah scrolls were burned. Seventeen Jews left the city in 1937–41, eight emigrating from Germany. The last eight Jews were deported in April and July 1942. Sixteen perished in the Holocaust.

ALTENBURG   Thuringia, Germany. Jews first settled in A. in 1364, but were expelled in the 15th cent. It is unclear when they were allowed to settle again, but in the 19th cent. there is evidence of a thriving J. community which was well integrated into the non-J. environment. Jews were active as bankers and industrialists and were members of local sports clubs. Certain individuals reached prominence in the cultural life of the town as singers or theater performers. In religious matters, the A. Jews were dependent on Leipzig, where they prayed and buried their dead. Between 1890 and 1910 and again in 1918–20, there were influxes of Jews from Galicia, the overall J. pop. reaching its peak in 1925 with 170 Jews. The newcomers founded an independent community in 1927 with its own prayer hall and religious instruction. According to the Nazi census of June 1933, there were 134 Jews living in A. (less than 0.3% of the total). Some 41% emigrated in time, making it to safe havens in the U.S., Palestine, Great Britain, and other countries. Others, who had left for other destinations in Germany or in Europe, were, in many instances, subsequently rounded up and deported as the Nazis spread out over the continent. On 28 Oct. 1938, 44 Jews of Polish origin were arrested and deported overnight to no man's land near the Polish border. On *Kristallnacht* (9–10 Nov. 1938), J. shops and the synagogue were vandalized. Two Jews were injured; others were arrested and later deported. Fifty-eight were deported to death camps in the east in 1942. At least 43% of the Jews living in A. in 1933 did not survive the Holocaust. There were 79 Jews from various concentration camps who were forced to work in a local metal plant and a nearby SS labor camp where they perished. They were buried in the municipal cemetery in A.

ALTEN-BUSECK   Hesse, Germany. The nobles of B. took so many Jews into their eight villages that the area became known as "Little Palestine" (1776). Numbering over 60 in 1831, the community dwindled to five (0.4% of the total) in 1939. The last three Jews were deported in 1942.

ALTENGRONAU   Hesse, Germany. Jews from Steinau took refuge there during the Black Death persecutions of 1348–49. The later community, numbering 51 (5% of the total) in 1905, owned one of the oldest (17th cent.) and largest J. cemeteries in Hesse, where 11 communities buried their dead. All the Jews left by 1939.

ALTENKIRCHEN IM WESTERWALD   Rhineland, Germany. Ten J. families were present in the 16th cent. In 1648, they were forced to convert or leave. In 1843, the community numbered 83, reaching a peak of 260 in 1908, but subsequently the J. pop. declined steadily as the young left for the big cities to study or pursue careers. In 1824, a J. elementary school was operating and in 1884, a new synagogue in the Moorish style with 120 seats was consecrated. In the Weimar period, Jews were active in public and social life though antisemitism remained rife. In the Nazi period, the Jews were soon ostracized socially and economically and abused in the streets. Nonetheless, community life was maintained, with the local Zionist organization numbering 15 members in 1936. In 1937, seven J. cattle traders and four J. butchers were still active. On *Kristallnacht* (9–10 Nov. 1938) the synagogue was burned and extensive damage was caused to J. homes and stores. J. men were sent to the Dachau concentration camp. At least 27 J. families are believed to have lived in the town in the Nazi era. Some emigrated to Palestine or other countries. At least 11 Jews perished in the camps.

ALTENKUNSTADT   Upper Franconia, Germany. Jews were present from the 15th cent. Their houses were destroyed during the peasant riots of 1699. A synagogue was built in 1726 (replaced in 1822) and a J. public school was opened in 1869. The J. pop. declined sharply from 400 in 1837 to 112 (total 1,288) in 1880 and subsequently to 28 in 1933. The interior of the synagogue was destroyed on *Kristallnacht* (9–10 Nov. 1938). In 1937–39, 12 Jews left the town, nine to other German cities and three to the U.S. Thirteen were expelled to Izbica in the Lublin dist. of Poland on 25 April 1942.

ALTENLOTHEIM Hesse, Germany. The J. community numbered 47 (over 9% of the total) in 1871. By 1935, eight of the remaining 24 Jews had emigrated and 12 had moved to other German towns; four were deported in 1941.

ALTENMUHR Middle Franconia, Germany. A J. community was present in the first half of the 18th cent., reaching a pop. of 250 in 1837 (total 720). A synagogue was built in 1815. In 1933 the J. pop. was 29. In the face of the Nazi economic boycott the Jews were forced to buy their food and coal outside the village. By 1937, 25 had left. On *Kristallnacht* (9–10 Nov. 1938) the synagogue was vandalized and the last three Jews soon emigrated to the U.S.

ALTENSCHOENBACH Lower Franconia, Germany. Jews are mentioned in the early 18th cent., with an organized community in the late 18th cent. and a J. school enrolling 27 children in 1850. The J. pop. declined steadily from 141 in 1814 (total 499) to 15 in 1933. On *Kristallnacht* (9–10 Nov. 1938) the synagogue was vandalized. Four Jews left the village in 1939–40 and six were deported to Izbica in the Lublin dist. of Poland and the Theresienstadt ghetto in 1942.

ALTENSTADT Hesse, Germany. Jews first settled there in 1650 and by 1834 they numbered 403 (about 50% of the total), declining to 91 (9.4%) within 60 years. Many Jews had emigrated even before the 136-year-old synagogue was destroyed on *Kristallnacht* (9–10 Nov. 1938). At least 15 perished in the Holocaust.

ALTINOVKA Sumy dist., Ukraine. The J. pop. in 1897 was 450 (1% of the total). After their arrival on 15 Sept. 1941, the Germans murdered the few remaining Jews who had neither fled nor been evacuated.

ALTKIRCH Haut-Rhine dist., France. A J. community was established in the 19th cent. A synagogue was inaugurated in 1834. It was damaged during anti-J. riots in 1848 in the area. In 1865, there were 320 Jews listed as residing in A., dropping to 309 in 1926. By 1931, only 236 Jews remained in A. During WWII, between July–Oct. 1940, the local Jews were expelled from their homes, with the rest of the Jews of Alsace-Lorraine, to the south of France.

Synagogue in Altenstadt, Germany, winter 1927

ALTLANDSBERG Brandenburg, Germany. Jews settled in A. at the end of 18th cent. In 1801, there were three J. families. The town was the center of a district community covering the Niederbarnim area which included 14 affiliated communities, numbering about 450–500 Jews in 1880. Regular prayer services and religious instruction were probably never instituted. A J. cemetery was established in 1817 and a new one probably in the last years of the Weimar period. When the Nazis came to power in 1933, there were 15 Jews in A. and about 200 living in the district community. By Feb. 1938, there were 140 Jews, half in need of financial help. No further information on their fate under Nazi rule is available.

ALTONA Schleswig–Holstein (now part of Hamburg), Germany. Although Jews were excluded from Hamburg in the late 16th century, they were welcomed in the neighboring township of A. In 1612, the count of Schauenburg granted Jews the privilege of living in A. and the freedom to practice their religion. By 1615, 15 J. families maintained a synagogue and a cemetery (opened in 1611). In 1671, the three communities of A., Hamburg, and Wandsbek established the unified

Dreigemeinde AHW. A. was the leading component, serving as the seat of the chief rabbinate and the rabbinical court (*beit din*), which had jurisdiction over the J. communities in Schleswig-Holstein, with the exception of Glueckstadt. The Great Synagogue of A. (built in 1684; burned down in 1711; rebuilt in 1715–16) was said to be one of the most imposing in Germany. With the setting up of the Klaus yeshiva (1690), headed by Tzevi Hirsch Ashkenazi ("Hakham Tzevi"; 1690–1709), A. became a famous religious and spiritual center. In 1704, 14 families originating from the Portuguese J. community of Hamburg, lived in A. and formed their own *minyan* at the local synagogue, attaining in 1719 the status of citizens. In 1771, they dedicated their own Portuguese synagogue. In 1748, the growing A. community numbered 712 families, although many of them were actually residing in Hamburg. In 1750, Yonatan Eybeschuetz (1690–1764), a Moravian scholar and kabbalist, was elected chief rabbi. His election was hotly contested by Yaakov Emden (1697–1776), the son of "Hakham Tzevi" and himself an unsuccessful candidate for the post. He accused Eybeschuetz of being a crypto–Shabbatean. The so-called "amulets dispute" was finally settled in the incumbent's favor when Frederick V of Denmark confirmed him in his office (1756). By the end of the century, the Jews of A. constituted 15% of the city's 23,099 inhabitants. The AHW union was abolished in 1812, when Hamburg came under French rule. Jacob Ettlinger (1798–1871), a leading exponent of J. Neo-Orthodoxy and the teacher of Shimshon Rafael Hirsch and Azriel Hildesheimer, became chief rabbi of A. in 1836, transforming the community into a Neo-Orthodox stronghold. Ettlinger preached in German, modernized J. education, and published a newspaper (*Der treue Zionswaechter*). In 1842, the Ashkenazi Jews finally attained the status of citizens. Frederick VII of Denmark emancipated the Jews of Holstein (1863), but four years later A. came under Prussian rule. In the same year (1867), the J. pop. of A. had reached 2,359 individuals (3.5% of the total), dwindling by 1905 to 1,773 (1%). The community maintained an elementary school for boys and girls, an orphanage, a hospital, and charitable institutions. In 1887, the Portuguese congregation disbanded and its synagogue was taken over by the main Ashkenazi community. Most Jews earned a livelihood from commerce, several entered politics, and for two decades Moritz Warburg represented A. in the Landtag. During

the first decades of the 20th cent., Jews from Eastern Europe, fleeing antisemitic persecution and economic deprivation, flocked to A. As a result, new synagogues were opened and the J. pop. grew to its highest number (2,650) in 1927. In 1920, the A. community joined the "Alliance of Torah-True J. Communities in Germany." Mayer Lerner, who served as chief rabbi (1894–1925), founded the anti-Zionist Moriah organization, which merged with Agudat Israel in 1913. The religious Zionist movement, World Mizrachi, transferred its central office to A. following the Tenth Zionist Congress (1911). The Central Union (C.V.) branch numbered 200 members in 1903. The objections of Chief Rabbi Lerner to votes for women antagonized members of the community and he was forced to resign. Joseph Carlebach (1882–1942), his successor, labored to preserve J. life in isolated regions through what became known as the Federation of J. Communities in Schleswig–Holstein and the Hansa Towns (1929).

In June 1933, the J. pop. in A. numbered 2,006. Once Hitler came to power in 1933 the boycott of J. firms and dismissal of J. officials foreshadowed a more systematic Nazi campaign, with lawyers and physicians as the next target. Jews left A. in increasing numbers, the community dwindling in 1935 to 1,570. Membership in the local Zionist groups increased and youngsters joined training farms in the countryside, in Blankenese and in Rissen, with a view to settling in Palestine. In 1936, Joseph Carlebach left A. to become the chief rabbi of Hamburg. On 1 Jan. 1938, A., together with Hamburg, Wandsbek, and Harburg-Wilhelmsburg, joined to form the "Jewish Religious Association of Hamburg." More than 1,000 J. residents of Polish origin were deported from the A. railroad station on 28 Oct, 1938. Less than a fortnight later, during the *Kristallnacht* pogrom (9–10 Nov. 1938), Nazis smashed the windows of J. stores and dispatched Jews to concentration camps. The Great Synagogue (which had celebrated its 250th anniversary in 1934) was not burned down, out of Gestapo concern for adjoining property, but hired workers later dismantled the interior and the community was presented with the bill. Most of the remaining Jews emigrated and the last transport of children, the *Kindertransport*, reached Britain in 1939. In May 1939, only 708 Jews remained in A. Very few of them survived the Holocaust. R. Carlebach, his wife, and three younger daughters were among those who were deported and murdered. "Operation Gomorrah," the fire storm created by RAF bombers

which obliterated central Hamburg in July 1943, destroyed all traces of the A. community apart from two burial grounds. One is now a historic monument, the other lies under a department store.

ALTWIEDERMUS Hesse, Germany. Many Jews of Spanish-Portuguese and Bohemian origin lived in nearby Ronneburg until about 1850. The smaller A. community, with a maximum pop. of 29 in 1910, had vanished by Dec. 1938.

ALUKSNE Vidzeme (Livonia) dist., Latvia. Jews began settling in the 1890s and reached a pop. of 233 (total 1,976) in 1920. Though economic conditions were favorable between the wars, with Jews owning eight of the town's 31 small factories and 21 of its 101 stores, many left for Riga. Under the Germans, the community's 182 Jews were murdered on 12 Aug. 1941 with the active participation of Latvian security forces.

ALUNTA (also Avanta) Utena dist., Lithuania. A.'s J. community began in the 19th cent. The J. pop. in 1923 was 222 (48% of the total). In 1939, a blood libel provoked attacks on Jews and their homes. With the Soviet occupation in fall 1940, Zionist and Hebrew activities were stopped. When the Russians retreated in June 1941, the Lithuanians ransacked and destroyed the J. homes. The Jews were brought to prepared mass graves in the Rase forest on 29 Aug. 1941, and shot.

ALUPKA Crimea, Russia, today Ukraine. Though present long before, Jews received formal residence rights in this resort town in 1903. In 1939, they numbered 242 (total 7,787) The Germans occupied A. on 8 Nov. 1941 and in Dec. murdered the few remaining Jews who had neither fled nor been evacuated.

ALUSHTA Crimea, Russia, today Ukraine. Jews were given formal residence rights only in 1903. In 1910, they numbered 544 (total 4,096). The Zionists won the elections to the community council in 1918. In 1939, the J. pop. was 277. The Germans occupied the town on 4 Nov. 1941, murdering 30 Jews on 24 Nov. and 250 from A. and the surrounding area in Dec.

ALYTUS (Yid. Alita) Alytus dist., Lithuania. A. occupies both banks of the Niemen River and at times was considered two cities. The J. community in eastern A. began in the 16th cent. In 1897, western A. had 481 Jews (33 % of the total) and eastern A. had 753 (37%). The united city's J. pop. in 1923 was 1,715 (27%). The two halves of the city had separate J. communities, with their own religious and social institutions. In the 1930s, 3–4 Jews served on the city council. There were Hebrew elementary and junior high schools and an ORT trade school. The Germans bombed A. on 22 June 1941, killing many Jews. Several hundred Jews were taken by Lithuanian nationalists to Suwalki and murdered. Scores of Jews were brought to a synagogue, which was then set alight. SS troops forced the remaining Jews into a ghetto, where they were maltreated. Many were murdered. In Aug. 1941, the remaining Jews were taken to prepared mass graves in the Vidzgiris forest and murdered.

ALZENAU Lower Franconia, Germany. The community was probably founded in the 17th cent. Jews played an important role in the town's economic development, opening tobacco factories and controlling the cattle trade. A synagogue was built in 1826 and the J. pop. grew to 112 in 1910 (total 2,135). In 1933, the J. pop. was 89. In the first years of Nazi rule the economic boycott was barely felt and Jews continued to employ 2,100 workers in 20 tobacco factories. The situation began to deteriorate in 1937 as local antisemitism intensified. Of the 52 Jews who emigrated under the Nazis, including 21 to the U.S. and 11 to Palestine, 44 left in 1937–39. A total of 24 moved to other German cities. On *Kristallnacht* (9–10 Nov. 1938), the synagogue was damaged along with J. homes and business establishments. The last 11 Jews were deported to Izbica in the Lublin dist. of Poland and the Theresienstadt ghetto in 1942.

ALZEY Hesse, Germany. The medieval community, established before 1260, was shattered by the Black Death persecutions of 1348–49 and expelled in 1391. Jews returned about 300 years later and their number grew to over 350 (7% of the total) in 1861. Mostly successful businessmen, they played an active role in the town's social and cultural life. The modern community, which embraced religious Reform, built a Moorish-style temple (1854) and its rabbi, Dr. Samuel Adler (1842–57), went on to serve Congregation Emanuel in New York. His son, Felix Adler (born in A.; 1851–1931), founded the Society for Ethical Culture.

Street in Jewish quarter of Alytus, Lithuania

Owing to the growth of antisemitism, the J. pop. declined from 320 (3.8%) in 1910 to 197 (2%) in Jan. 1933. From 1924 a branch of the German Zionist Organization gained support. After the Nazis came to power, a boycott campaign forced many Jews to emigrate and less than 100 remained on *Kristallnacht* (9–10 Nov. 1938), when their synagogue was burned down. The last 41 Jews were deported in 1942–43.

AMBERG Upper Palatinate, Germany. Jews were present in the 13th cent. In the Rindfleisch massacres of 1298, 13 were murdered and in 1403 all were expelled. The community was renewed in the 1850s and 1860s and numbered 101 in 1900 (total 22,039). The independent community dates from 1896 and a synagogue was dedicated in 1898. Also attached to it were the communities of Schwandorf, Schnaittenbach, and Nabburg. In 1933 there were 64 Jews in A. By 1941, 17 had emigrated and 23 moved to other cities in Germany. On *Kristallnacht* (9–10 Nov. 1938) the interior of the synagogue was destroyed and Jews were sent to the Dachau concentration camp. Of the 12 remaining Jews, seven were sent to Piaski in the Lublin

dist. (Poland) on 2 April 1942 and three to the Theresienstadt ghetto via Regensburg on 23 Sept.

AMERSFOORT Utrecht dist., Holland. The first Portuguese Jews to settle arrived in 1655. An Ashkenazi community developed in the 18th cent. The fine synagogue built in 1727 still stands. The local council strongly defended the rights of its Jews, who were particularly active in the tobacco industry. A noteworthy member of the community was Benjamin Cohen, an influential businessman; during the upheavals of 1787 William V and his wife found shelter in his magnificent home, which is today the home of the city council. The J. pop. in 1860 was 446 (total 12,663). In 1814–1917 A. was the seat of the Utrecht region chief rabbi. In 1940 there were 650 Jews in A. and in 1941 about 70 foreign Jews were transferred there from the coastal regions. In Aug. 1942 all the Jews were deported to the Westerbork transit camp, except for a group of children taken into hiding. A community was reestablished after the war.

AMIENS Somme dist., France. Jews settled in A. in

the beginning of the 19th cent., but its synagogue was inaugurated only in 1935. According to the German census of 1941, only 41 Jews were listed in A. After WWII, with the influx of North African Jews, the pop. stood at 440 in 1964.

AMRUS (also Suq, al-Jama, al-Sahal) Tripolitania dist., Libya. J. settlement commenced in about the 16th cent. when Jews arrived from Gharian. In the 18th cent., they were joined by J. refugees from Tunis. During the Arab Revolt of Mahdi Yehi ben Yehi in 1589, the Jews suffered extensively. They were once again attacked by Arabs after the Ottoman reforms in the 19th cent. In 1879, looters murdered a Jew in his home and in 1901 widespread anti-J. rioting broke out against the background of army conscription. Moslems also forced Jews off their land, putting an end to the auxiliary farming that had supplemented their traditional means of livelihood. The J. pop. was about 500 in 1888 and 1,000 in 1903. In the early 20th cent., about 40 J. blacksmiths occupied a row of workshops in the market and a J. quarter consisting of narrow alleyways sprang up where three synagogues were located, the last of which was completed in 1904. The Italian occupation of 1911 was accompanied by more anti-J. rioting. All 95 of the houses occupied by Jews were seriously damaged and all but 40 of the 200 J. families in A. fled to Tripoli. Many worked there as porters for awhile, returning to A. in 1912 but again fleeing when the Arab Revolt broke out in 1915. This time they remained in Tripoli until 1924. Jews opened stores on the main street of the market and J. women worked at home embroidering head coverings for Moslem women. The J. pop. rose steadily, reaching a peak of 1,502 in 1944, as many Jews arrived seeking a haven from Arab disturbances and other events. Relations with the Italians were satisfactory until the outbreak of WWII, with a sheikh as community head acting as an intermediary with the Italian authorities and the Moslem pop. In WWII, many Jews from Tripoli arrived, fleeing the Allied bombardments. From 1941, Italy's racial laws were applied with greater strictness and in 1942, as the Italian war effort collapsed, high prices and food shortages became prevalent. The British occupation brought modernization and, under the guidance of J. soldiers in the British army, the beginnings of Zionist activity, with a branch of the Ben-Yehuda Association founded in 1943. In the riots of 5 Nov. 1945, 38 Jews were massacred, including entire families and 11 children. In the 1948 distrubances, rioters confined themselves to looting. Some Jews left for Palestine in the framework of illegal immigration. The rest left through organized *aliya* in 1949–52.

AMSTERDAM capital of Holland. A Street of the Jews is mentioned in the 14th cent. but the medieval community was destroyed in the Black Death persecutions (1348–49). A new community was established only with the consolidation of Dutch independence in the late 16th cent. when forced converts (*anusim*) from Spain and Portugal began to arrive. These were permitted to return openly to the fold of Judaism in the early 17th cent., forming the first J. congregation in the city, Beth Jaacob, in 1602. The Neve Shalom synagogue was erected in 1608 and a second one, Beth Jisrael, in 1618. After the Chmielnicki massacres of 1648–49, Jews from Eastern Europe arrived. A separate German congregation was established in 1639 and afterwards a Polish congregation. The two united in 1673 as a single Ashkenazi congregation. In the 17th and 18th cents., A. was a center of J. spiritual life. Among its outstanding figures were Menashe ben Yisrael (1604–57), the kabbalist Yaakov Sasportas (1610–98), Antonio Enriquez Gomez (1600–after 1660), David Franco Mendes (1713–92), Uriel da Costa (1585–1640), and Barukh Spinoza (1632–77). Spinoza was excommunicated by the rabbis of A. in 1656 for his heretical views. The first Hebrew printing press in A. was founded in 1627, making the city a center of Hebrew printing. Additional Hebrew presses were opened in the 17th–19th cents. A Talmud Torah Society founded in 1616 opened a J. school and a Mikra Kodesh Society founded in 1740 promoted religious study. The Ashkenazi congregation published newspapers and books, including a translation of the Bible into Yiddish. R. Moshe ben Shimon Frankfort (1672–1762) published a commentary on the *Shulhan Arukh*. In 1811 a few dozen schools and *hadarim* were being maintained by the Sephardi and Ashkenazi congregations, with a total attendance of 684. From the 17th cent. on, Jews played an important role in the export trade, especially to Germany, Eastern Europe, the Iberian Peninsula, England, Italy, and India. In the 17th and 18th cents., the Jews were also prominent in banking and the stock exchange as well as in the precious stone trade and diamond polishing, a profession which many Jews were entering well into the 20th cent. In 1796, the J. pop. was 23,549 (11.7% of the

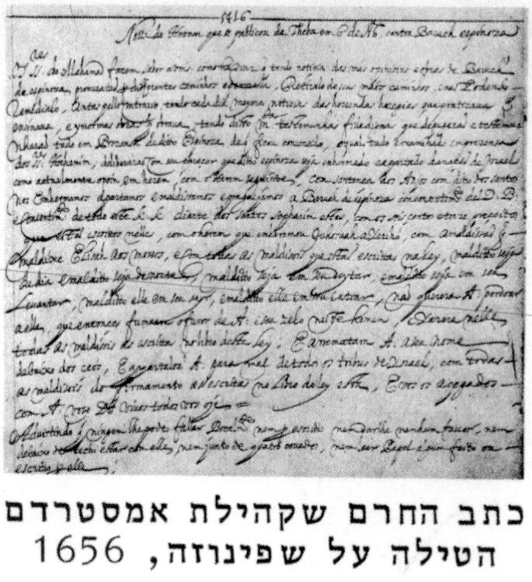
כתב החרם שקהילת אמסטרדם
הטילה על שפינוזה, 1656

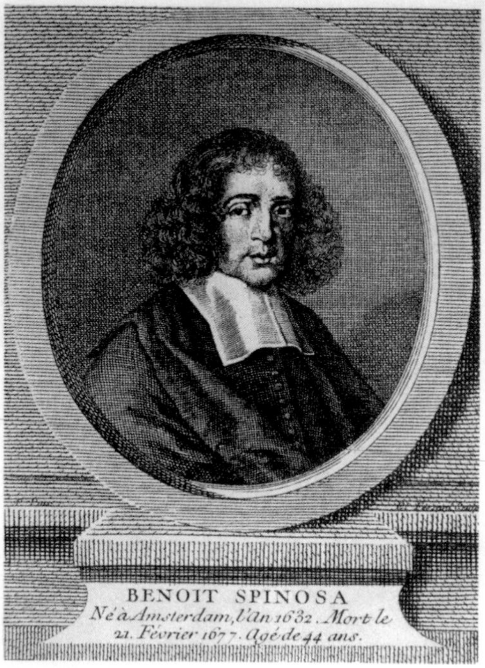
BENOIT SPINOSA
Né à Amsterdam, l'an 1632. Mort le
21. Février 1677. Agé de 44 ans.

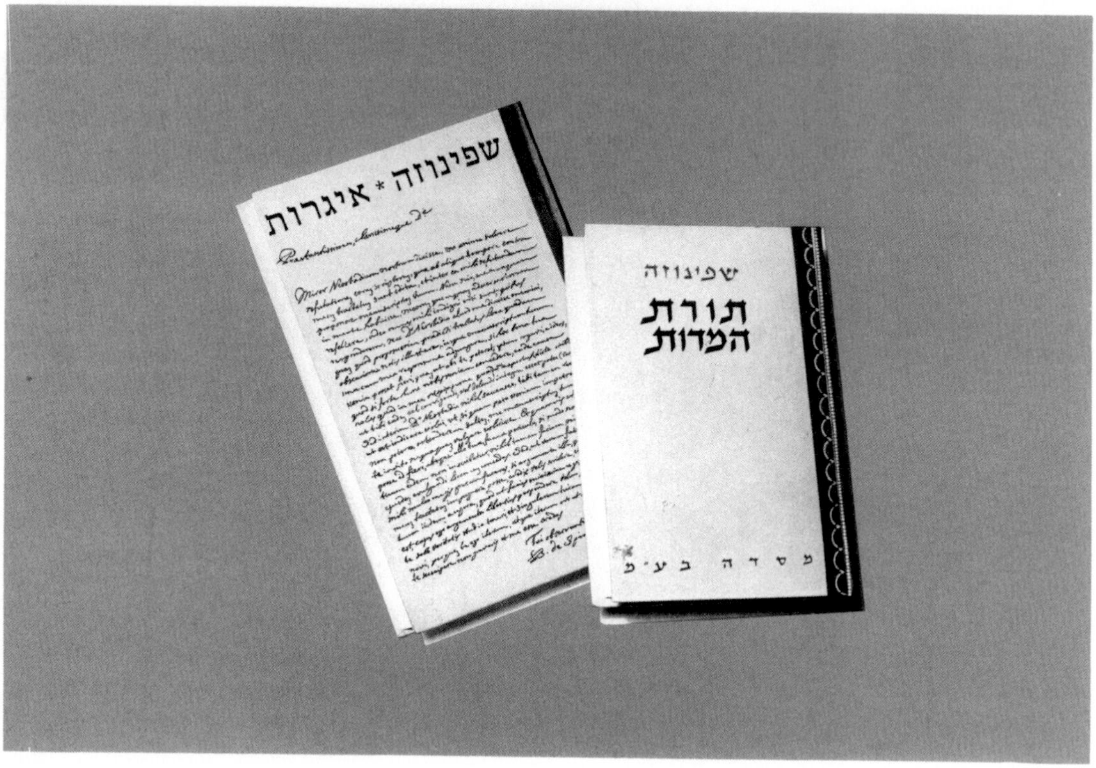
שפינוזה * איגרות
שפינוזה
תורת
המדות
מסדה בע״מ

*Document excommunicating Benedikt (Barukh) Spinoza from the Amsterdam community (*top left*); an engraving of the Dutch-Jewish philosopher (*top right*); and a page from his writings (*bottom*) (Ministry of Education and Culture/photo courtesy of Yad Vashem, The Holocaust Martyrs' and Heroes' Remembrance Authority, Jerusalem)*

total). At the end of the 18th cent., the Felix Libertate society struggled to achieve equal political and civil rights for the Jews of Holland. It also attempted to institute changes in community institutions. The organization founded the Adass Jeshuran synagogue, introducing moderate reforms in the prayer service which aroused the ire of community leaders. The organization was soon dismantled. In the late 19th cent., J. writers, artists, and professionals became part of the city's cultural and intellectual life. Outstanding among the writers were Herman Heyermans (1864–1924), Israel Querido (1872–1932), J. I. Haan (1881–1921), and Carry van Bruggen de Haan (1881–1932). The painter Jozef Israels (1824–1911) was one of the leaders of the Amsterdam School of painting. Nathan Judels (1815–1903) was a well-known stage actor. The statesman and jurist Tobias Michael Carel Asser (1838–1913)

was awarded the Nobel Peace Prize in 1911. Between the late 19th cent. and the outbreak of WWI, the Zionist movement gained considerable strength, clashing with both assimilationist and Orthodox circles. At the turn of the 19th cent., J. refugees from Eastern Europe flooded the city, receiving support from the community and its institutions. The J. pop. subsequently rose to 68,758 in 1920, dropping to 65,523 in 1930. The economic position of the J. middle class worsened between the World Wars owing to the crisis in the diamond and textile markets. To deal with the situation, the community expanded its welfare operations. Most J. children attended public schools but they were also enrolled in a number of J. educational institutions in order to ensure that they received a J. education, such as a *talmud torah* and a Dat ve-Yare Sunday school. However, the influence of these two schools

Celebrating the opening of Amsterdam's Great Sephardi Synagogue, Holland, 1675 (Ministry of Education and Culture/photo courtesy of Yad Vashem, The Holocaust Martyrs' and Heroes' Remembrance Authority, Jerusalem)

was marginal and their attendance in perpetual decline. In 1932, the number of J. schoolchildren in the city was about 2,000, dropping to 1,514 in 1938. In order to attract children from well-to-do families to J. educational frameworks, a J. secondary school was opened in 1927 and an academic high school in 1928. The Zionists, particularly the youth movements at both ends of the political spectrum, continued to grow in strength. Their membership increased from 350 in 1929 to 800 in 1939.

The rise of Hitler to power in 1933 sparked an influx of German-J. refugees. To assist them a special committee (Comite voor Bijzondere Joodse Belangen) was set up to raise funds and to open schools and relief agencies for the refugees. After the German occupation in 1940, an edict was published in Holland for the registration of J. businesses. In 1941, with refugees still arriving, the J. pop. of A. rose to 79,497 "full Jews" and 5,359 "half Jews." In late Nov. 1940 and early 1941, Dutch Nazis staged demonstrations and riots in the J. quarter and damaged J. property. The Jews organized defensive action and on 11 Feb. 1941, in the midst of clashes between Nazis and Jews, a Dutch Nazi was killed. In 1941, J. property began to be expropriated through the "Aryanization" of business enterprises and the freezing of bank accounts. In Feb. 1941, a J. Council (Joodse Raad) was established headed by Abraham Asscher and David Cohen. It rendered as much assistance as possible to the community's needy. On 22 Feb., following an incident involving Jews and German police, 389 young Jews were arrested and dispatched to the Buchenwald concentration camp. Those who survived there were transferred to the Mauthausen concentration camp after a

Anthony St., once the main street of the Jewish quarter of Amsterdam, Holland. In the 17th cent., most of the houses were owned by the Portuguese Jew De Pinto

few months and soon met their deaths. In protest against the arrests and deportations, a strike joined by broad sectors of the non-J. pop. was staged on 25–26 Feb., paralyzing public services and the big factories. Mobilization of Jews for forced labor camps commenced in late 1941, at first voluntarily but when that failed, under compulsion. Most were sent to the Westerbork camp. The concentration of Jews from the rest of Holland for deportation to the death camps in the east began in Jan. 1943. Some were brought to A. and housed in J. quarters that in effect became ghettoes. On 29 April 1942, the Jews were made to wear special badges. The first transports left for Auschwitz via Westerbork on 15 July 1942. The Germans made special efforts in Oct. to meet their deportation quotas. In May 1943, the deportations to the Auschwitz and Sobibor death camps were again stepped up. Major *Aktions* were also organized in June and Sept. 1943. After Nov., transports left Westbork for Auschwitz at the rate of one a month, each carrying 1,000 Jews. The number dropped somewhat in March 1944. The transports included Jews from both A. and other parts of Holland. The Dutch, acting through the municipal authorities, railway workers, and local police, also took part in the roundups and deportations. Some Jews of Portuguese origin tried to argue that they were not Jews by race but only by religious affinity and in this way tried to evade deportation. But in Feb. 1944, they were also rounded up and deported to Auschwitz via Westerbork. The expropriation of J. private and public property continued commensurately. The famous Bibliotheca Rosenthaliana library was transferred to Germany (but restored after the war). Starting in mid-1942, Jews tried to avoid deportation by hiding. Some Dutch hid Jews out of humanitarian impulses, others against payment. In 1943, underground groups began helping Jews find places of refuge and in early 1944 a nationwide underground fund was used to assist Jews in hiding. Some groups concentrated their efforts on hiding J. children and managed to save hundreds. There were also attempts at flight to Switzerland via Belgium and France. Another escape route, via France and Spain, was used by the underground run by the Hehalutz movement. Between 100 and 150 reached Spain in this way, including about 70 pioneers, most emigrating to Palestine. Jews also joined general underground organizations, initiated underground newspapers, and took part in armed clashes against the Germans and Dutch Nazis. After the war, survivors found it necessary to engage in a public campaign against the authorities, banks, and insurance companies to regain their property. It was frequently difficult to get their children back from the families who had sheltered them. The Jews of A. were active in the prosecution of German war criminals and Dutch collaborators. The J. pop. of A. was 6,671 in 1960 and 15,687 in 1966. The congregations active before the war — Ashkenazi, Sephardi, and Liberal — renewed their activities and some synagogues were restored and placed at the disposal of the worshipers. The community maintained health and welfare services and cultural centers. In 1969, seven J. schools were in operation, attended by 450 children. The Holocaust is commemorated in the Anne Frank House.

AMSTETTEN Lower Austria, Austria. Although a J. cemetery was opened in 1859, Jews were allowed to settle in A. only in 1865. A community was established in 1881. A few years later a small synagogue was inaugurated and in 1894 a new cemetery was consecrated. Jews were engaged in trade and owned small factories. The J. pop. stood at 45 in 1900, rising to 200 in 1934. During the 1920s antisemitic agitation was intense in A., although not violent. After the *Anschluss* (13 March 1938), Jews with Czechoslovakian citizenship were expelled over the border. On *Kristallnacht* (9–10 Nov. 1938), the interior of the synagogue was destroyed, windows of J. houses were smashed, and some men were arrested. Most of the Jews succeeded in emigrating. In May 1940, the remaining 53 Jews were sent to Vienna and from there to the east.

ANANEV Moldavia, today Ukraine. An organized J. community existed by the early 19th cent. and numbered 3,527 (total 16,684) in 1897. Jews were victimized by pogroms in 1881, 1905, and 1919, the latter claiming 14 lives. In 1921, under Soviet rule, the J. pop. was 3,516, with a J. school in operation, and 1,779 (total 5,918) on the eve of WWII. German and Rumanian forces captured A. on 7 Aug. 1941. The Germans immediately executed 600 Jews. Throughout the month of Aug., Jews from A. and its environs were executed at the rate of 150–250 a day, including Jews expelled from Rumania and en route to Transnistria. In Oct. 1941, about 300 surviving Jews were expelled to the Dubossary ghetto and in Nov. about 150 were sent to the Gvozdevka camp. Almost all were murdered.

ANARCS Szabolcs dist., Hungary. Jews, first mentioned in 1747, numbered 105 in 1880 with a synagogue and cemetery and 91 in 1930. On 29–31 May 1944, they were deported to Auschwitz via Kisvarda.

ANCONA Marche, Italy. An organized J. community in this Adriatic seaport is known from the 14th cent. In 1427, the local Jews were forced to wear the J. badge and reside on a single street. In 1492, the community absorbed refugees from Sicily, and also from the Kingdom of Naples after 1510. It also attracted immigrants from the Levant. In 1494, the Jews of A. were authorized to open a loan bank or *Monte di Pieta*, which functioned until 1547. The order to wear a yellow hat, issued in 1524, was abolished in 1528. The visit of the pseudo-messiah Shelomo Molcho in 1529 stimulated messianic expectations. When A. came under papal authority in 1532, Popes Paul III and Paul IV issued anti-J. measures, among them the Bull of 12 July 1555, which obliged Jews to wear a badge and to live in a ghetto. There were also prohibitions against owning real estate property and against trading in second-hand clothing. In 1541, due to A.'s status as a free port and the desire to advance mercantile interests, Paul III encouraged Jews expelled from Naples to settle in A. In 1547, he extended an invitation to the Marranos to settle. Failure to protect these Marranos against the Inquisition resulted in 23 men and a woman being burnt at the stake in 1556. Elegies composed at the time are still recited locally on the 9th of Av. A Portuguese Marrano leader Dona Gracia Mendes declared a boycott against A., but it caused dissension within the J. world. When all the Jews in the Papal States were expelled, Popes Pius V in 1569 and Clement VIII in 1593 exempted those in Rome and A. because of their economic utility in the Levant trade. A local Purim festival observed on 21 Tevet commemorates the deliverance of the A. community from an earthquake on 29 Dec. 1690. The present synagogue is a 17th cent. building. Napoleon Bonaparte entered A. in Feb. 1797, abolishing the old regime. The ghetto gates were removed and Jews were invited to sit on the city council. But in 1814, A. returned to the papacy and the former discriminatory legislation was restored. Jews only obtained full civil rights in 1861, when A. and the other communities of the Marche were included in the Kingdom of Italy. In 1873, the community numbered 1,740 Jews. On 9 Sept. 1901, the first convention of the Italian Zionist Feder-

ation was held in A. and a local group was established. In 1925, the J. pop. was reduced to 850. According to the 1930 law reforming the J. communities in Italy, A. became one of 26 communities and included under its jurisdiction the other Marche communities: Pesaro (140 Jews in 1873, 100 in 1923, and 15 in 1936); Urbino (181 in 1869, 80 in 1925, and 38 in 1931); Senigallia (300 Jews in 1886, 109 in 1901, 60 in 1936); and Ascoli Piceno.

According to the daily newspaper *Corriere Adriatico* of 27 Nov. 1938, there were 1,078 Jews in the A. district. The J. pop. included 75 businessmen, 18 commercial agents, nine industrialists, 15 teachers, 12 doctors. The newspaper launched a racist campaign against the Jews in its columns. In mid-1939, there were 914 Jews in A. and 117 in the district. On 15 May 1940, windows of J. shops were smeared with anti-J. slogans. In 1940, the rabbi of Livorno, Elio Toaff, was invited to A. to serve as its spiritual leader. A. was the site of the Center for the Study of the J. Problem in Italy, inaugurated on 28 Oct. 1941. A roundup of Jews scheduled for 9 Oct. 1943 failed when a Catholic priest, Don Bernardin, urged R. Toaff to encourage all Jews to go into hiding. On 15 Jan. and 12 March 1944, Jews from A. were deported to the Fossoli concentration camp. Altogether ten Jews from the city were deported; one returned. In 1948, the community numbered 400 members. In 1971, there were 400 Jews living in the district of A., including also those in Senigallia and Urbino.

ANDERNACH Rhineland, Germany. Benjamin of Tudela numbered A. among the 13 cities on the Rhine with important J. communities in the 12th cent. J. homes were destroyed in anti-J. riots in 1287 and Jews suffered in the Armleder disturbances of 1337 and in the Black Death persecutions of 1348–49. The community was renewed in the 14th cent., but by 1448 no Jews were present. The modern community dates from the development of the local malt industry in the mid-19th cent. From 1890, a religious school was operating here. The J. pop. rose from 53 in 1871 to 141 (total 10,771) in 1925. The synagogue, consecrated in 1933, was the only one to be built in the Rhineland after WWI. On *Kristallnacht* (9–10 Nov. 1938), it was set on fire, J. homes were destroyed, and most of the young men were taken to the Dachau concentration camp. In 1939, 45 Jews were left; at least 11 perished in the Holocaust.

ANDREAPOL   Kalinin dist., Russia. Jews probably settled in the late 19th cent. Their pop. was 327 in 1926 and 133 in 1939. During the German occupation of Sept. 1941–Jan. 1942, the few who had not fled or been evacuated were murdered.

ANDREEVO-IVANOVKA   (Chernovo, Kulikovo Pole) Odessa dist., Ukraine. The J. pop. was 546 (total 1,458) in 1897 and 330 in 1939. The Germans and Rumanians captured the town on 5 Aug. 1941, shortly afterwards murdering 60 Jews from the area (mostly from A.). On 1 Sept., A. was transferred to Transnistria. In March 1942, 165 Jews from Odessa were murdered in the town. In all, 236 Jews from the area were murdered during the occupation, most from A.

ANDRIEJAVAS   Kretinga dist., Lithuania. The J. pop. was 66 in 1923. The Jews were killed in the Holocaust.

ANDRUSHEVKA   Zhitomir dist., Ukraine. Jews are first mentioned in the mid-18th cent. as numbering 12. By 1897, their number stood at 430 (total 2,682) and in 1927 at 300. In the Soviet period, 80% of the Jews were artisans or laborers. A J. elementary school (three grades) was operating. In 1939 the J. pop. was 658. The Germans arrived on 16 July 1941. During the occupation, they murdered 1,747 people, including Jews from A. and its environs.

ANDRYCHOW   (Yid. Yandrichov) Cracow dist., Poland. Jews settled in the first half of the 19th cent., dealing mainly in cloth, and were behind the establishment of the first mechanized knitting plants in the second half of the cent. The community grew to 635 (total 3,866) in 1880, building a splendid 600-seat synagogue in 1884. However, there was a subsequent drop in the J. pop. as tradesmen outside the textile industry had to struggle to earn a living. Despite economic hardship the community maintained a rich cultural

Opening of Jewish community center, Andrychow, Poland, 1924

life and Zionist activity was widespread. The J. pop. in 1939 was 370. Many fled east with the coming of the Germans on 3 Sept. 1939. Those remaining faced a regime of persecution and forced labor. The synagogue was burned to the ground on 25 Nov. and in Sept. 1941 a ghetto was set up, where a semblance of traditional J. life was maintained in the face of deteriorating conditions. Expulsion came on 2 July 1942: 100 Jews were loaded on a train to the Belzec death camp, 40 were sent to Auschwitz, over a hundred to labor camps, and 60 to the Wadowice ghetto, subsequently to be returned to a labor camp in A. The women were ultimately deported to Auschwitz and the men transferred in the summer of 1943 to other labor camps, where they died.

ANDRZEJEWO Bialystok dist., Poland. Founded in the second half of the 19th cent., the community numbered 277 out of a total pop. of 800 in 1921. In WWII, the Germans deported its Jews to larger centers but some escaped to Soviet Russia.

ANDRZEJOW Lodz dist., Poland. The J. community was founded in 1805 at this vacation resort, eventually a suburb of Lodz. In 1921, 99 Jews lived there.

ANGENROD Hesse, Germany. Owing to their useful role in the cattle trade, Jews were welcomed and by 1797 had established a community—dubbed "New Jerusalem"—which numbered 247 (42% of the total) in 1861. Reduced to 63 by the time Hitler came to power in 1933, it had virtually disintegrated by 1939. The last eight Jews were deported in 1942.

ANGERBURG (Pol. Wegorzewo) East Prussia, Germany, today Poland. The J. pop. grew from 27 in 1843 to 72 in 1871. By 1880, the J. pop. numbered 54. During WWI, the rented prayer room was closed and the religious instruction teacher dismissed for lack of funds. When the Nazis came to power, the J. pop. numbered 42. By May 1939 there were only 15 Jews in A. No further information on the fate of the community under Nazi rule is available.

ANGERMUENDE Brandenburg, Germany. The earliest evidence of Jews in A. dates from 1681. In 1709, the four J. families in A. acquired a burial ground. In 1815, a synagogue was set up to serve the 20 J. families in the town. In 1880, the J. pop. was 135.

When the Nazis came to power in 1933, there were 60 Jews. Economic harassment and hostility forced most Jews to sell their businesses and leave the town. On *Kristallnacht* (9–10 Nov. 1938), the synagogue was burned down and the cemetery desecrated. Four Jews were arrested. On 13 April 1942, the last Jews, a couple and a family, were deported to the east and were probably murdered in Auschwitz.

ANGERS Maine-et-Loire dist., France. The renowned talmudist R. Yosef ben Shemuel Tov Elem-Bonfils, lived in A. at the end of the 11th cent. The local Jews lived on the Rue de la Juiverie until the general expulsion from France in the 14th cent. In the 19th cent. Jews settled again in A., numbering 21 in 1850. In 1940, there were 400 Jews in A. Arrests started in July 1942 and continued in Oct. 1942. The Jews were deported to Auschwitz via Drancy. Of the 824 persons deported, only 14 returned. With the influx of Jews from North Africa, the community numbered 180 in 1964.

ANKLAM Pomerania, Germany. J. moneylenders in A. were burned to death in the Black Death persecutions of 1348–49. Jews only settled permanently in A. after the regulations regarding Jews in Prussia were revised in 1812. In 1816, the J. pop. of A. came to 33 and in 1861 to 300. The community set up a synagogue (1841), an elementary school (1855–61), and a cemetery (1817). When the Nazis assumed power in 1933, there were only 43 Jews in A. In 1936, a Jew was arrested on suspicion of racial defilement (*Rassenschande*). On *Kristallnacht* (9–10 Nov. 1938), the synagogue was set on fire. By 1939, 14 Jews and ten individuals of partial J. origin (*Mischlinge*) were still living in A. Eight Jews were deported to the Lublin dist. of Poland on 12–13 Feb. 1940 together with the Jews of Stettin and probably perished then. By 1941, there were no Jews left in A.

ANNABERG Saxony, Germany. Jews did not settle in A. until 1867. In 1890, the community numbered 78 individuals. The community gave complete equality to J. immigrants from Eastern Europe. In 1897, a synagogue was established and a religious education teacher engaged. A cemetery was set up in 1905. At this time, the J. pop. was 137, dropping to 55 in 1925. Jews served on the town council from the turn of the century and played an important role in the town's eco-

nomic development. In 1930, Jews owned one of the biggest department stores in the area as well as 15 textile factories. When the Nazis came to power in 1933, the community numbered 58 members; 39 were residents of the town itself. In the boycott of J. businesses on 1 April 1933, SA and SS troops laid siege to J. stores. Customers who did not observe the boycott had a stamp placed on their faces reading "We are traitors who buy from Jews." On *Kristallnacht* (9–10 Nov. 1938), the synagogue was blown up and the cemetery desecrated. By 1939, there were only eight Jews, two married to non-J. partners, and six of partial J. origin (*Mischlinge*) in A. One was taken to a concentration camp, but survived. No further information about the fate of the others is available.

ANNOPOL Kamenets-Podolski dist., Ukraine. Jews numbered 395 in 1765 and 1,812 (82.5% of the total) in 1897. Dov Baer of Mezhirech (1704–72), one of the greatest hasidic figures, is buried in the town. The J. pop. dropped to 1,259 in 1926 and presumably declined even further by 1939. A. J. rural council was active between the World Wars. The Germans arrived on 9 July 1941. The Jews were transported to Slavuta and executed on 26 June 1942 together with the local Jews and Jews from other towns.

ANNOPOL-RACHOW Lublin dist., Poland. Jews arrived in the early 17th cent. as innkeepers, distillers, and grain and cattle merchants as well as artisans and petty traders. In the 19th cent., A. was a center of Torah learning. Three generations of the Rubinstein family served as rabbis: R. Nahman (1828–78), R. Elimelekh (1878–1923), and R. Nahman Barukh (until 1935). Economic conditions worsened at the turn of the 19th cent. and the community suffered severe food shortages in WWI. Zionist activity commenced at this time and the J. pop. rose from 575 in 1897 to 1,251 (total 1,714) in 1921. After the war, Agudat Israel, representing Gur Hasidism, contended with the Zionists for influence. After the German occupation of 15 Sept. 1939, a *Judenrat* and ghetto were set up and a regime of forced labor was introduced. An influx of refugees, believing that conditions were reasonable in A., brought the J. pop. up to 1,943 in May 1942. On 15 Oct. 1942, after 400 were selected for the Guszczardow and Janiszow labor camps, the remaining Jews were sent to the Krasnik ghetto and from there to the Belzec death camp in Nov. A small group organizing in the forest

as partisans liberated hundreds of Jews from the Janiszow camp in early 1943 after a bold attack.

ANRATH Rhineland, Germany. The J. pop. was 116 in 1852 and 44 in 1925. The community maintained a synagogue, a school, and a cemetery. It was affiliated to the Krefeld community. The Nazis deported 13 J. residents, who perished.

ANROECHTE Westphalia, Germany. Jews are first mentioned in 1614. Their pop. never exceeded a few dozen (3–4% of the total). A synagogue was in use in the 18th cent. and a school was opened in 1855 with 24 children in attendance. Jews were prominent in the cattle trade and participated in public and social life despite certain manifestations of antisemitism in the village. In the Nazi era, J. businesses were gradually eliminated and in 1938, the synagogue was vandalized along with J. homes and stores. Of the 72 Jews present in 1933, 26 emigrated, 34 were deported to the Zamosc ghetto on 24 April 1942, and five to the Theresienstadt ghetto on 27 July. In all, 41 Jews perished in the Holocaust.

ANSBACH (in J. sources, Onolshbach) Middle Franconia, Germany. Jews first settled in the early 14th cent. Most were murdered in the Black Death persecutions of 1348–49. The community reestablished itself in the second half of the 14th cent. under the protection of the margrave Friedrich V. A J. quarter and synagogue are known from the 1470s. Anti-J. agitation intensified in the early 16th cent., leading to the expulsion of the Jews in 1560. In 1609 they were again permitted to settle and quickly came to dominate trade, especially in cattle and horses. The community played a leading role in the Landjudenschaft organization of the 48 J. communities (as of 1714) in the Ansbach principality. In the 18th cent. the Model and Fraenkel families were prominent as Court Jews. However, the prosecution of one of the Fraenkels on charges of witchcraft led to the impoundment of J. religious books throughout the principality. Restrictions and disabilities lasting until the Emancipation were introduced in the 18th cent., though the community remained one of the wealthiest in the region, with 30 merchants visiting the Leipzig fair each year. In 1837 the J. pop. was 450 (total 14,100). A. J. public school was opened in 1828 and a small yeshiva in the 1850s. From 1896 to 1916, R. Pinchas Kohn,

one of the leaders of Agudat Israel, served as rabbi. Antisemitism was widespread in the post-WWI period, with Nazi propaganda stirring up anti-J. feelings. The J. cemetery was desecrated in 1927 and 1932. In 1933 there were 197 Jews in A. Communal property included a synagogue built in the baroque style in 1744-46 by the well-known Italian architect Leopold Retty. The Zionist Organization and Central Union (C.V.) were active. In 1933 J. traders were banned from the livestock market and Jews were also banned from various public places. The community reacted by maintaining welfare services and cultural activities (through the Juedischer Kulturbund). All the Jews of A. were arrested by local SA troops on *Kristallnacht* (9-10 Nov. 1938) but largely through the efforts of the mayor no physical harm came to them and the damage to J. property was minimal. He saved the synagogue by symbolically lighting a fire and quickly extinguishing it. The synagogue was soon after sold to the municipality. Until that time, 87 Jews had left the city. In Dec., another 84 were expelled and 17

more left in 1939-40, bringing the community to an end. Of the total, 44 left Germany, 19 of them to the U.S. After the war, 191 Jews gathered in the city but most soon emigrated.

ANTALIEPTE (Yid. Antalapt) Zarasai dist., Lithuania. The J. pop. in 1897 was 474 (85.5% of the total). After WWI many Jews emigrated to South Africa, the U.S., Uruguay, and Palestine. When the Germans entered A. on 26 June 1941, they together with the Lithuanians immediately began to persecute the Jews. Able-bodied Jews were sent to forced labor. On 26 Aug. 1941, all the Jews were taken to the Paziemiai forest and murdered.

ANTANAVAS Marijampole dist., Lithuania. The J. pop. in 1923 was 192. All Jews were killed after the German conquest of 1941.

ANTONINY Kamenets-Podolski dist., Ukraine. The J. pop. in 1939 was 110 (3.5% of the total). The Ger-

The Levin family store, Antaliepte, Lithuania

mans occupied A. on 7 July 1941 and in July 1942 executed the Jews at the village of Manivtsy.

ANTONOVKA Mogilev dist., Belorussia. A. was founded in 1837 as a J. farm settlement. In 1924–25, under the Soviets, 39 J. families were engaged in agriculture. In 1930 the settlement became a kolkhoz with only ten of the J. families continuing to farm. On 14 Nov. 1941, during a major German *Aktion* in the villages of the Krichev dist., 18 Jews from A. were murdered.

ANTONOWKA Volhynia dist., Poland, today Ukraine. A. was founded as a J. farm settlement in 1833 on 900 acres of land and numbered 620 Jews in 1897 and 482 (total 535) in 1921. After A. was captured by the Germans in July 1941, all Jews were brought to the Tuczyn ghetto in fall 1942 to meet their end.

ANTOPOL Polesie dist., Poland, today Belarus. J. settlement dates from 1604 and grew considerably in the 19th cent. with highway, canal, and railway links bringing prosperity and the J. pop. reaching 3,137 in 1897 (total 3,867). Jews operated flour mills, hide-processing plants, and oil presses; others farmed. There were seven synagogues in A. The Zionists became active in the 1880s and the Bund in the early 20th cent. In WWI, many homes and synagogues were destroyed in the fighting and the Jews suffered under a harsh German occupation. The J. pop. dropped to 1,792 (total 2,206) in 1921. Between the wars the community received aid from the Joint Distribution Committee and former townsmen in the U.S. The Germans took the town on 25 June 1941 and set up an open ghetto in Oct. when 150 young Jews were arrested and murdered despite a ransom payment by the community. The ghetto with its 2,500 Jews including refugees was liquidated in the second half of 1942. Most were brought to Brona Gora and murdered in July, the skilled workers in Aug., and a final 300 on 16 Oct.

The poet Hayyim Nahman Bialik (front row, sixth from left) visiting the Tahkemoni school in Antwerp, Belgium (Brachfeld Sylvain/photo courtesy of Yad Vashem, The Holocaust Martyrs' and Heroes' Remembrance Authority, Jerusalem)

ANTWERP (Flem. Antwerpen; Fr. Anvers) Belgium. The arrival of J. craftsmen, Marranos from Portugal, contributed to the expansion of the diamond industry which was established in A. in the 15th cent. In the 16th, 17th, and 18th cents. there was a significant number of Jews living in A., which was already at that time a major international commercial center. The Jews were also engaged in the tobacco trade. A community with 36–38 families (about 100 persons) was formally established during the Dutch occupation (1815–30). After Belgian independence was achieved in 1830, Jews obtained religious freedom and inaugurated a synagogue in 1832. By 1846, the community numbered 345 Jews. An influx of Jews from eastern Germany increased the J. pop. to between 800–1000 in the 1870s. This was followed by the arrival of East European Jews. The first Great Synagogue was inaugurated in 1893, and five years later, the Portuguese congregation headed by R. Hayyim Mizrahi was established. Spiritual leaders were Rabbis N. Z. Ullman and Marcus Rottenberg, as well as Dr. Joseph Wiener, chief rabbi of A. and then of Belgium. The community, headed in 1901 by Baron von Stein, a tobacco merchant and diplomat, increased rapidly between the World Wars, from 8,000 in 1900 to 55,000 in 1939 (20% of the total). The majority of Jews in the community were of East European origin. In addition to the two Ashkenazi congregations, there was also a Sephardi synagogue. The city developed into a major embarkation point for the mass migration of East European Jews to the U.S. Communal societies, such as Ezra, extended charitable relief. As A. developed into a world diamond center, Jews began entering the trade as cutters, polishers, or dealers. In 1919, J. artisans organized. Between the World Wars, there were 34 synagogues and prayer houses in the city and two comprehensive elementary schools were established in 1903 and in 1920. The community also maintained four Hebrew schools, two yeshivas, and 22 social organizations. The Zionists became active and in 1914 the Zionist Federation was established. Most Zionist parties and youth movements were represented. The

Jewish tailors, Antwerp, Belgium, 1929 (Brachfeld Sylvain/photo courtesy of Yad Vashem, The Holocaust Martyrs' and Heroes' Remembrance Authority, Jerusalem)

Shomre Hadath congregation became a center for Zionist thought under the prominent religious thinker R. Moshe Avigdor Amiel (1883–1946). In 1920 he served as chief rabbi of A. A J. press in Flemish, Yiddish, Hebrew, and German flourished.

When the Germans invaded Belgium, many Jews from A. tried to flee, mainly to the south of France. About 30,000, representing about 40% of the country's total number of Jews, returned after the Belgian surrender (28 May, 1940). At first, no special measures were taken against the Jews and the diamond industry was reactivated and even flourished for awhile. With the first anti-J. decrees, on 28 Oct. 1940, more than 13,000 A. Jews were required to register and J. businesses were marked with trilingual signs. Further decrees forbade Jews from entering public parks or living in cities other than Brussels, Antwerp, Liege, and Charleroi. On 10 April 1941, the eve of Passover, right-wing groups incited riots in the J. quarter. On 14 April 1941, members of a pro-Nazi organization ("Volksverwering" – the People's Defense) looted J. shops as well as the two main synagogues and the residence of R. Rottenberg. The Germans ordered the establishment of a *Judenrat*. According to the German census of Oct. 1941, there were 17,242 Jews in A. From May, all Jews were forced to wear the yellow star. Large-scale deportations started in 1942. Four transports were sent to northern France for forced labor (mostly for the Todt organization), but later the deportees were sent to Auschwitz. The last deportation took place on the night of 3-4 Sept. 1943 and included Jews of Belgian origin and members of the *Judenrat*. During the occupation, in late 1941, a branch of the Association des Juifs en Belgique (AJB) was set up in A. Also, many local Jews were connected with the Comite de Defense des Juifs and took part in the effort to provide hiding places, food, and other essentials. Others joined various resistance movements, such as the Mouvement National Belge. Upon liberation, on 4 Sept. 1944, the Hulp aan Joodse Slachtoffersvan de Oorlog – Help for J. War Victims was organized to aid returning and displaced persons. Soldiers of the J. Brigade also helped in the rehabilitation efforts. In 1969, there were 10,500 Jews in the community.

ANYKSCIAI   Utena dist., Lithuania. A.'s J. community began in the 17th cent. It was hit hard by repeated fires in the late 19th and early 20th cents. The J. pop. in 1897 was 2,754 (70% of the total). On 14

July 1915 a Russian regiment staged a pogrom against A.'s Jews. The J. pop. in 1940 was about 2,000. Zionist parties were very active. On 26 June 1941, the Germans took the city and all Jews were ordered to the synagogue, where they were tortured. They were kept in a forest outside of town for weeks without shelter. Between 28 July and 29 Aug. most were murdered at nearby Liudiskiai, by Lithuanian nationalists.

APA   N. Transylvania dist., Rumania. Jews settled in the mid-18th cent. The J. pop. in 1920 was 69 (3% of the total). In May 1944 the community was transferred to the Satu Mare ghetto and in June deported to Auschwitz.

APAGY   Szabolcs dist., Hungary. Jews are first mentioned in 1747. Their pop. was 160 in 1880 and 109 in 1930. On 14 April 1944, they were brought to Szabolcs and from there deported between 17 May and 6 June to Auschwitz.

APATIN   Vojvodina dist., Yugoslavia. Jews lived in A. from the late 19th cent. until the 1940s. There were 251 in 1921 and 61 in 1940 (total 17,000). Most perished in the Holocaust.

APC   Heves dist., Hungary. Jews apparently settled in the early 19th cent. and numbered 116 in 1930. They maintained a synagogue and school. Most of the Jews, about 30 families, were deported to Auschwitz via Hatvan from 12 June 1944.

APE   Vidzeme (Livonia) dist., Latvia. The J. pop. early in the cent. was 200 but by 1935 dropped to 82 (total 922). Most stores were J.-owned. The Jews were murdered by the Germans in summer 1941.

APELDOORN   Gelderland dist., Holland. Jews first settled in A. in the late 18th cent. In the 19th cent. the community grew slowly and achieved independence in 1890. The J. pop. in 1888 was 53. In the 20th cent. the J. pop. growth accelerated, primarily due to the establishment of central J. medical institutions there, a mental hospital, and an institution for retarded children. Welfare organizations were also founded as well as a branch of the Zionist Organization and a Zionist youth movement. In 1941 there were 1,549 Jews (total 74,447). In Oct. 1941, 13 men were deported to the Mauthausen concentration camp. Between

Studying the Talmud in Anyksciai, Lithuania

Aug. 1942 and March 1943 the rest of the Jews were deported, most via the Westerbork transit camp. The patients of the medical institutions were taken directly to Auschwitz-Birkenau. Dozens survived in hiding and a few survived the camps. The community was reestablished after the war.

APLERBECK   Westphalia, Germany. Six Jews were present in 1818. The community reached a peak pop. of 125 (total 9,772) in 1905, becoming independent in 1911 with three attached communities: Soelde, Schueren, and Berghofen. Most Jews engaged in trade and crafts and were active in the town's public and social life. In the Nazi era, they were gradually isolated. Of the 100 Jews present in 1933, over 50 left before *Kristallnacht* (9–10 Nov. 1938), including 15 for Holland. On *Kristallnacht* most J. homes and stores were wrecked and the cemetery was desecrated. The remaining Jews were then deported to the camps, where they perished along with most of the Jews who had previously left the town.

APOLDA   Thuringia, Germany. Jews settled in A. in the 19th cent., engaging in the knitting and embroidery trades and opening small businesses. The J. pop. grew from 12 in 1880 to 39 in 1885 and 60 in 1900. During the first years of Nazi rule, four Jews from A. were incarcerated in concentration camps. On *Kristallnacht* (9–10 Nov. 1938), 11 J. men were arrested and deported to the Buchenwald concentration camp. J. shops and homes were vandalized. Most Jews from A. managed to make it to safe havens in Palestine and the Americas before the outbreak of war. Those who remained were subjected to deportations to the east on 10 May 1942 and on 20 Sept. 1942. At least seven perished in the Holocaust.

APOLLONIA   (Marsa Susa) Cyrenaica dist., Libya. Egyptian Jews settled in A. in the Greek and Roman period (4 B.C.E.–1 C.E.). The Jews maintained close ties with J. centers in Egypt and Eretz Israel, suffering severely in the rebellion of 115–17 C.E. Although there were Jews in A. during the Byzantine and Muslim

eras, little is known about how they lived. In 1906, there were 45 Jews in A. The community never prospered. It was geographically isolated and the Arab Revolt of 1915–22 fostered a sense of insecurity. In 1931, under Italian rule, the community began to develop. The J. pop. in 1936 was 110 (0.7% of the total). A single community was forged with that of Cyrene, sharing a leader, a rabbi, who was also *shohet*, teacher, and treasurer. Roman caves served as homes for some; one functioned as a *genizah*. Relations with the Arab neighbors were tense, though moderated by the influence of the Sanusi brotherhood. When the Italians built a modern port, A.'s Jews came under Italian cultural influence. Though there was no Zionist activity, from the 1930s Jews contributed to the JNF. The Fascist regulations of 1938 affected the Jews but disruptions were minimal. Following massive Allied bombing in early 1941, many Jews fled the city and sought refuge in caves or – for pay – among the Bedouin. In 1942, A.'s Jews were sent to the concentration camp at Giado. Survivors returned to find their homes looted and destroyed. Isolation, tension, and hostility against the Jews led in the late 1940s to the Jews of A. leaving for Derna and Benghazi. In 1949–51 most of the community emigrated to Israel.

APOSTAG Pest–Pilis–Solt–Kiskun dist. Hungary. Jews arrived in the first half of the 17th cent., fleeing the Christian reconquest from the Turks. A new community was formed in the 18th cent. by Jews from Austria, Czechoslovakia, and Moravia, growing to 783 in 1840 but afterwards declining through emigration to the cities. A magnificent synagogue built in 1822 was declared an historic site after WWII. In 1940, J. men were drafted into labor battalions and sent to the Ukraine, where eight perished. On 25–27 June 1944, the town's 100 Jews were deported to Auschwitz via Kalocsa and Kecskemet.

APOSTOLOVO Dnepropetrovsk dist., Ukraine. The J. pop. in 1939 was 81 (total 9,997). The Germans captured A. on 17 Aug. 1941 and probably in fall 1941 murdered 129 Jews there.

APPINGEDAM Groningen dist., Holland. J. settlement dates back to 1563, when a Jew received permission to settle there. Jews lived there continuously until the Holocaust. In the 18th cent. the community developed and grew. The J. pop. in 1809 was 130. During the 19th cent. a few welfare organizations were founded. In 1801 a synagogue was built and a J. school established. There were 93 Jews in 1941 (total 6,847). They were deported in the Holocaust; only one survived and returned after the war, while five others managed to hide.

ARAD S. Transylvania dist., Rumania. Jews first settled in the mid-18th cent. A synagogue was built in 1759. In 1868 the community joined the Neolog association. R. Aharon Horin (1766–1844) was one of the founders of Reform Judaism in Hungary. He established the first J. school in 1832, planned a rabbinical seminary, advocated that Jews take up a craft or agriculture rather than engage in peddling, and permitted worshipers to pray without a head covering and to write and travel on the Sabbath. His successor, R. Yaakov Steinhardt, introduced sermons in Hungarian. An Orthodox community was established in 1903 which opened a school and a yeshiva. The Vizhnitz Rabbi had a hasidic court in A. Jews were responsible for A. becoming one of the leading centers of commerce and industry in the Austro-Hungarian monarchy. In 1841, 500 Jews volunteered for military service and fought in the Hungarian war of independence (1848–49). Jews became involved in local politics and Dr. Franz Sarkany was elected mayor in 1867. Jews founded the *Arader Zeitung*, the first evening newspaper in Hungary, and were active in journalism, literature, and the plastic arts with the sculptor Yaakov Guttmann and artist Isidor Kaufmann achieving prominence. Zionist activity began in 1920 and some 30–40 young people underwent pioneer training. The community operated a *matza* factory and maintained an orphanage and old age home. The J. pop. came to 7,000 in 1928 (10% of the total). Antisemitic manifestations were rife in the 1930s and the Iron Guard persecuted the Jews in 1940–41. In Aug. 1941, all J. males aged 18–55 were drafted into labor battalions. The J. pop. of the surrounding villages and small towns were brought to A. 120 Jews were transferred to the Vapniarca camp in Transnistria. Most of the remaining J. pop. succeeded in escaping to Timisoara in Aug.–Sept. 1944, but returned after A. was liberated. The J. community was active in providing assistance to Holocaust survivors and the Zionist Organization in A. helped prepare the majority to immigrate to Palestine.

ARBAYTHEYM Zaporozhe dist., Ukraine. A. was

Synagogue in Arad, Rumania

founded as a J. colony, probably in the early 1920s, and was attached to the Novo-Zlatopol J. Autonomous Region when it was established in 1929. The Soviet secret police (NKVD) uncovered a clandestine Zionist cell in 1940 and arrested its members. The Germans captured A. in Oct. 1941 and at the end of the year murdered about 50 Jews near the Spetsdorf kolkhoz.

ARBUZINKA   Odessa dist., Ukraine. The J. pop. in 1939 was 99 (total 6,772). The Germans captured A. on 5 Aug. 1941 and probably murdered the Jews who had neither fled nor been evacuated in the fall.

ARCHANGELSKAYA   Krasnodar territory, Russia. In late Nov. 1942, a few Jews were arrested and mur-

dered in the village. After it was liberated, 70 bodies were found in several pits, apparently all Jews.

ARCHSHOFEN   Wuerttemberg, Germany. Jews could settle from the early 18th cent. but the community was limited to 15 families. They were permitted to engage only in the cattle trade, which remained their main source of livelihood even when restrictions were removed in 1810 after annexation to Wuerttemberg. The community reached a peak pop. of 180 in 1870 and declined steadily thereafter. Until the Nazi era, relations with the local pop. were satisfactory and Jews participated in public life. By 1938 all J. businesses were closed and Jews socially ostracized as persecution intensified. Of the 23 Jews in A. in

1933, 12 emigrated by 1939. Some of those remaining died in A.; the others perished after deportation to the east.

ARCIZ Bessarabia, Rumania, today Republic of Moldova. Jews first settled in the mid-19th cent. In 1900, 44 families were on the verge of starvation caused by drought and were helped by other communities. The J. pop. in 1930 was 842 (29% of the total). A J. elementary and high school were founded in the 1920s. The situation of the Jews declined from 1935 due to the boycott by German inhabitants. After the Soviet annexation in May 1940, J. businesses and institutions were closed. The invading Rumanian and German armies murdered Jews and deported the remainder to their death in Transnistria.

ARDED (Hung. Erdod) N. Transylvania dist., Rumania. Jews settled in the mid-18th cent. and engaged in agriculture. The J. pop. in 1930 was 124 (3% of the total). In May 1944 the community was transferred to the Satu Mare ghetto and in June deported to Auschwitz. In 1947, 80 Jews were living there but soon left.

ARGENSCHWANG Rhineland, Germany. Jews probably settled in the mid-18th cent., numbering 66 (total 454) in 1858 and 29 in 1932. Jews worked as cattle dealers, butchers, and horse traders. The community maintained a J. school in the second half of the 19th cent. and at the outset of the Nazi era had a synagogue, cemetery, and *mikve*. On *Kristallnacht* (9–10 Nov. 1938), the synagogue, J. homes, and stores were extensively damaged. Although some Jews left for other German cities, they too were deported like the Jews who stayed behind.

ARHEILGEN Hesse, Germany. Established around 1800, the community numbered 111 in 1828 but dwindled to 24 (0.4% of the total) in 1910. The Nazis, who failed to gain wide support in A. before 1933, organized murderous outrages on *Kristallnacht* (9–10 Nov. 1938). The synagogue (previously acquired by non-Jews) remained intact, but Torah scrolls removed to Darmstadt were burned there. Some of the remaining Jews emigrated; others perished in the Holocaust.

ARINIS (Hung. Egerhat) N. Transylvania dist., Rumania. Jews settled in the late 18th or early 19th

cent. J. pop. (1920): 92 (13% of the total). In May 1944 the J. community was transferred to the Simleul Silvaniei ghetto and then deported to Auschwitz.

ARIOGALA (Yid. Eragala or Ragala) Kedainai dist., Lithuania. A.'s J. community began in the 18th cent. By 1897 the J. pop. was 1,541 (65 %) of the total. The tribulations of WWI, fire, and emigration to the Russian interior, the U.S., South Africa, and Palestine left the 1923 J. pop. at 456 (38%). Lithuanian incitement against Jews began in the 1930s, including a death resulting from a blood libel attack. After the German invasion of June 1941, Lithuanian nationalists started killing off Jews, among them three J. communal leaders. On 9 Aug. all 662 Jews were taken to prepared pits outside the town and together with Jews from neighboring towns were shot by Lithuanians.

ARLON (Flem. Aarlen) Belgium. Established after the independence of Belgium in 1831, the J. community numbered 102 in 1834 and 147 in 1864. The Jews had originally come from Lorraine and Germany. Most were merchants and relatively prosperous. The new synagogue inaugurated in 1865 is the oldest synagogue in Belgium. In 1889, the community numbered 188 members. The Fribourg family established a major international wheat trading company. The journalist Camille Cerf was born in A. After the German invasion of Belgium on 10 May 1940, half of the J. pop. left for France. On 23 Oct. ritual slaughter was forbidden and the Nuremberg Laws defining who was a Jew were introduced. In Nov., the municipality listed all the Jews of A. On 29 July 1941, the identity cards of the Jews were stamped with the word "Jew." According to the German census of 1 Oct. 1941, there were 59 Jews in A. On 27 May 1942, Jews were ordered to wear the yellow badge. Deportation to Auschwitz began on 12 Aug. Some who had escaped to the south of France were deported too.

ARMAVIR Krasnodar territory, Russia. The first Jews, settling in the late 19th cent., were demobilized soldiers and their families, members of the intelligentsia, well-to-do merchants, and artisans whose skills were in demand. There was a trend toward emigration at the turn of the 19th cent. In 1917, the J. pop. comprised 70 families, half of whom were converts. In the entire autonomous region of A., there were just 222

Jews (0.04% of the total). The Germans occupied A. on 7 Aug. 1942, murdering, outside the city, all the Jews of A. and its environs, including refugees from the western parts of the Soviet Union. In all, 550 were murdered. From among the Odessa orphans evacuated to A. – 70% of whom were Jews, as were six teachers – four J. children were gassed in late Aug. 1942.

ARMYIANSK Crimea, Russia, today Ukraine. Jews probably settled in the late 19th cent. A Zionist group was already active in the early 20th cent. and the community had its own rabbi before WWI. In 1926, the J. pop. was 156, dropping to 107 (total 3,963) in 1939. The Germans occupied A. in late Oct. 1941, murdering 11 Jews in 1942. The rest of those who remained behind were apparently murdered at the village of Voyenka in Feb. or March 1942.

ARNHEM Gelderland dist., Holland. J. settlement began in the 13th cent. The Jews suffered in the Black Death persecutions of 1348–49. A community was officially recognized in 1765. A synagogue was built in 1799 and a larger one in 1853. In the 19th cent., J. community life developed and welfare organizations were founded. A school was opened in 1817 and in 1881 the seat of the Gelderland chief rabbinate was established in A. The J. pop. in 1892 was 1,248. Between the World Wars, Zionist activity took root. German refugees arrived during the 1930s and when the Germans arrived (May 1940) there were over 2,000 Jews (total 90,000). In Sept. 1940 some 300 Jews were transferred there from the coastal regions. In Sept.–Oct. 1941, a number of Jews were arrested and taken to the Mauthausen concentration camp, where they perished. Some Jews fled to western Holland and others found hiding places. In Jan. 1942, 163 J. families were ordered to transfer to Amsterdam, while others were taken to forced labor. In Oct.–Dec. 1942 the remaining Jews were deported to the Westerbork transit camp. More than 1,600 were sent to camps in Eastern Europe. Some 400 survived the Holocaust. A few returned to A. after the war and a community was reestablished.

ARNSBERG Westphalia, Germany. Jews may have been present as early as the mid-14th cent. but only from 1810, under Hessian rule, did the community begin to grow, reaching a pop. of 140 (total 20,360) in 1821. An organized community existed from 1824

and a synagogue, cemetery, and J. school were opened. A new synagogue was completed in 1853. Most Jews engaged in trade and crafts. The J. pop. subsequently declined to 90 in 1926 and 40 in 1933. By 1938, all J. businesses had been "Aryanized" and Jews expelled from social organizations. On *Kristallnacht* (9–10 Nov. 1938), SA troops and local mobs destroyed J. homes and stores; the contents of the synagogue were burned; the J. cemetery was desecrated; and most J. men were sent to the Sachsenhausen concentration camp, where they were held for a number of weeks. Seventeen Jews left for other cities in Germany. Of those who emigrated, seven reached Holland, six South America, and five Palestine. Thirteen perished in the Holocaust.

ARNSTADT Thuringia, Germany. The community, which had a synagogue (mentioned in 1347), suffered persecutions in the mid-13th century and was almost entirely destroyed in the Black Death disturbances of 1348–49. A J. settlement developed only in the mid–19th century, with Jews founding department stores and banks or engaging in the local cattle trade. In 1883, 65 Jews (15 families) lived in A. A synagogue was dedicated in 1913 and a new J. cemetery in 1921. The J. pop was 125 in 1925 (total 20 000). During the Nazi boycott of 1 April 1933, the SA picketed J. shops and from summer 1935, Jews were limited to buying only in three specified shops. On *Kristallnacht* (9–10 Nov. 1938), the synagogue in A. was burned down and J. men deported to the Buchenwald concentration camp, where one died. Only 39 Jews were left in A. by 1939. The remaining Jews were deported to the death camps in spring and autumn 1942 and again in June 1944.

ARNSTEIN Lower Franconia, Germany. Jews were present at the time of the Rindfleisch massacres in 1298 and operated a synagogue and school in the first half of the 19th cent. The J. pop. declined steadily from 81 in 1814 to 29 in 1933 (total 1,652). Twenty-five left in 1937–38, most to other German cities. The last two left for Frankfurt after the *Kristallnacht* disturbances (9–10 Nov. 1938).

ARNSWALDE (Pol. Choszczno) Brandenburg, Germany, today Poland. A J. community is mentioned in A. from 1321. In the 16th cent. and most of the 17th cent., there is little evidence of Jews. The community

Izbica in the Lublin dist. of Poland and the Theresienstadt ghetto.

ASCHENHAUSEN Thuringia, Germany. Jews first settled in A. in 1695 and the J. pop. was seven families in 1707. The community established a synagogue and a cemetery. In the 19th cent., Jews made up half of the total pop., reaching an absolute majority in 1848 with 50 families. Until 1919, the chairman of the local council was generally a Jew. After 1900, the community rapidly declined, dwindling to 12 members on the eve of the Nazi takeover in 1933. Together with the affiliated communities of Kaltennordheim (35 Jews), Kaltensundheim (5) and Opferhausen (2), the combined J. pop. in the area was 52 Jews. Those who still remained after 1939 were deported and in 1943 the four last Jews were sent to the Theresienstadt ghetto.

ASCHERSLEBEN Saxony, Germany. Jews are first mentioned in 1325. They lived outside the town in the Jews' village (*Jodendorp*) until their expulsion in 1494 on the orders of the Bishop of Halberstadt. It was not until after 1767 that a community once again emerged, numbering 145 in 1864. A cemetery was established at the beginning of the 19th cent. and a synagogue in 1852. When the Nazis came to power in 1933, the community included 77 individuals. On *Kristallnacht* (9–10 Nov. 1938), the synagogue and the mortuary were destroyed and businesses and homes were looted and vandalized. In 1939, there were 23 Jews in A. Most were finally deported to the Theresienstadt ghetto. Altogether at least 34 Jews perished in the camps, including those who sought shelter in other towns or neighboring countries. In 1941–43, there was a forced labor camp in A. for J. women. Its remaining inmates were deported to Auschwitz at the end of 1943.

ASKANYIA NOVA Zaporozhe dist., Ukraine. J. scientists and academicians were drawn to the town in the Soviet period when it became a scientific center. In 1939, 22 remained. The Germans captured A. on 14 Sept. 1941 and on 5 March 1942, at the nearby mines, murdered 200 Jews from A. and the surrounding area.

ASSEN Drenthe dist., Holland. A few Jews settled in the 18th cent. Their numbers increased from 26 in 1809 to 498 in 1883. The community continued to develop between the World Wars. There were about 420 Jews in 1941 (total 20,566). On 2 Oct. 1942, the Jews were arrested and sent to the Westerbork transit camp, and from there to Poland. In March 1943 a few Jews in an institution for the mentally ill were arrested. Only 11 Jews survived in hiding. A community was reestablished after the war.

ASSENHEIM Hesse, Germany. Jews lived there around 1277–1349 and from the late 15th cent. onward. Prominent in the cattle trade, they numbered 87 (9% of the total) in 1861. The last few were deported to Poland on 30 Sept. 1942.

ASSLAR Hesse Germany. Jews lived there from the 18th cent. and (together with those in Hermannstein) numbered 55 in 1835. By 1910 the community had dwindled to 31 and most of the remaining Jews left before WWII.

ASTI Piedmont, Italy. The J. presence in A. originated at the beginning of the 14th cent., when Jews expelled from France took refuge there. They were followed by Jews from Germany, and after 1492, from Spain. The concessions they received from the authorities were related to their economic functions, primarily moneylending. The local Jews adopted the J. liturgy practiced in France. Shared by the Jews of Fossano and Moncalvo, it is called the APAM rite, more correctly AFAM, after the Hebrew initials of A., Fossano, and Moncalvo, where it was employed. In 1553, the community suffered as a result of a blood libel. As in all Piedmontese cities, the local Jews were restricted to a ghetto in 1723. In 1761, the community numbered 136 Jews. In 1873, it numbered 470, but subsequently the community dwindled. With the French Revolution and the annexation to France, the Jews were entitled to reside outside the ghetto, but only the rich could afford to do so. In 1803, there were riots against the local Jews. In 1848, the Jews received full equality, and some entered politics. In 1889, the synagogue was rebuilt by Count Leonetto Ottolenghi, a distinguished philanthropist. By 1901, only 312 Jews resided in A. In the mid 1920s, the community numbered 80 Jews. According to the 1930 edict reforming the J. communities in Italy, A. was included in the district of Alessandria. In 1936, the community numbered 85 Jews. During WWII, 51 members of the

community were killed. In Feb. 1944, the community was dissolved by the district governor. In 1946, the synagogue reopened, but the community was not revived. In 1948, 59 Jews lived in A. By 1970, only 20 remained.

ASUNE Latgale dist., Latvia. The J. pop. in 1930 was 24; murdered by the Germans in summer 1941.

ASZOD Pest–Pilis–Solt–Kiskun dist., Hungary. Jews, mainly from Moravia, settled in the early 18th cent. About 200 Jews left for Adony in the mid-19th cent. after the J. pop. reached a peak of 530 in 1840. The community formed a Neologist congregation after 1868, with about 20 smaller communities affiliated to it. R. Yehuda Aszod (1794–1866) was one of the country's most prominent Torah scholars and R. Shimon Hevesi (1868–1943) became chief rabbi of Budapest. In 1941, 278 Jews remained in A. which was a dispatch point for forced labor to the Ukraine. On 10 July 1944, they were deported to Auschwitz via Rakoscsaba.

ATHENS (Athenes, Atina, Athinai, Athine) capital of Greece. The roots of this community stretch back to antiquity. Jews settled in A. by the second cent. B.C.E. and inscriptions testifying to the presence of a community date from the first centuries C.E.. This was the largest Romaniot community (i.e., dating from the Byzantine period) on the Greek mainland. The Talmud often mentions J. sages of A. and reflects on the differences between the J. spirit and Athenian culture and philosophy. No records of Jews in A. are found from the fourth to 14th cents. Only in the 15th cent. were a number of refugees from the Spanish Inquisition found there. In the 17th cent., Shabbetai Zvi visited and mingled with the local Jews, while a French traveler in 1650 mentions 15–20 J. families. A small number were present during the Greek revolt of 1821–29. An organized community of Romaniot, Sephardi, and Ashkenazi Jews was founded in the mid-19th cent. Max Rothschild, a scion of the Frankfurt Rothschilds, settled here in 1833. His son Karol became the first president of the J. community. The community then grew in size and influence, absorbing numerous Sephardi immigrants from Izmir, Istanbul, Chios, and other Aegean islands. The J. pop. in 1887 was 250. Community prayers were organized and in 1889 the community formed a philanthropic association that as-

sisted the poor and sick. The community also assisted victims of the 1891 blood libel in Corfu and of the 1893–94 earthquakes in Zakinthos. Antisemitic incidents also took place in A. during this period. In the first quarter of the 20th cent., the community stabilized. A synagogue (the "Old Synagogue"), at 8 Melidoni Street, was built in 1904–06. Among the donors to the synagogue funds was one of the pillars of the community, Avraham Constantini. A successful businessman, he followed Rothschild as president of the community, was active in the Alliance Israelite, and was a pioneer of the Greek Zionist movement. The success of such Jews sometimes aroused anti-J. feeling, which found expression mainly in the Greek press. Following the Balkan wars (1912–13), the Jews' financial situation improved while more Jews from various locations settled there. They mostly dealt in trade, import, and export. As entrepreneurs, the Jews established two banks, an electronics plant, and a cigarette factory. Zionist organizations were established after 1913, alongside a number of welfare associations. The J. pop. in 1913 was about 500. Many Salonika Jews relocated in A. after the great fire in Salonika (1917). In 1923, a J. school was opened and in 1924 a branch of B'nai B'rith was inaugurated, the latter sponsoring a school and a youth organization. According to the 1928 census, A. was the fifth largest J. community in Greece (1,578 Jews), after Salonika, Kavala, Janina, and Corfu. In the early 1930s, Greece experienced an economic crisis and the Jews became victims of nationalist, anti-foreign propaganda that ostracized J. tradesmen. While rumors spread of persecution in Germany and antisemitism escalated in A., the community approached the government for financial assistance and the police for protection. In the mid-1930s, however, the economy improved somewhat and the Jews enjoyed renewed tolerance.

On the eve of the Holocaust, although there were some 3,000–3,500 Jews in A., there were no J. welfare organizations or schools. In May 1941, Germany invaded Greece, A. came under Italian occupation, and a Greek puppet regime was installed by the Germans. Within the next two years, the J. pop. grew to 8,000–10,000, as thousands from the German and Bulgarian occupation zones fled to Athens. Among those were 3,000 Jews who fled Salonika when Eichmann's deputies R. Gunther and D. Wisliceny arrived there in Jan. 1943 to oversee the implementation of the "final solution." Under Italian rule, the Jews lived relatively free

of persecution, although the Germans conducted searches in all institutions and many homes for documentation that indicated anti-German activity. In summer 1941, Greek youths, encouraged by the Gestapo, tormented Jews, disseminated anti-J. propaganda, and raided the Old Synagogue. The community was officially dismantled, but secret committees assisted the Greek underground movement. As information reached A. about the Salonika deportations, the underground movement – with the assistance of Greek Archbishop Damaskinos, the A. police, and members of the municipality – formulated its intentions and plans to save the Jews of A. Following the example of Archbishop Damaskinos, who published a letter denouncing the maltreatment of the Greek Jews, many heads of national, religious, professional, and cultural organizations also became involved in the struggle to save the Jews of A. After the Italian surrender in Sept. 1943, the Germans entered. D. Wisliceny arrived and proceeded to implement the "final solution." When R. Eliyahu Barzilai, was ordered to draw up lists of all the Jews and their property, he destroyed all community records. The rabbi and his family were then "kidnapped" by the underground movement and taken into hiding. This encouraged many Jews to go into hiding in Christian homes and institutions. In Oct., the Germans commanded all Jews to return to their homes and register in the synagogue. Within a month only some 2,000 had registered, mostly those with no means to relocate. At the same time the underground movement and the Greek embassy in Istanbul made appeals to the Greek pop. to assist the Jews in escaping from the transit camp in A. and en route to Poland. False documents were issued for many Jews and places of hiding were proffered. Some 3,000 Jews of A. acquired false identity cards and about 600 were able to flee to Palestine by boat. On 20 Oct. the Germans began confiscating J. possessions. On 23 March 1944, a few hundred Jews were captured in the synagogue. They were taken to the Haydari transit camp and were joined by their families and other Jews. Some 3,000 were in the camp until 2 April, when Swiss and Turkish subjects were transferred to their countries of origin and the rest were transported to Auschwitz. Most were killed in the gas chambers; 648 were "selected" by Josef Mengele for medical "research." Only 40 inmates survived. En route to Auschwitz, 174 subjects of Spain and Portugal were rerouted to Bergen-Belsen and survived. Another few dozen Jews were taken to Auschwitz in May. In the meantime, the general pop. of A. increased its opposition to the Nazi terror and staged mass demonstrations and a general strike. The J. partisans and the Red Cross managed to distribute supplies to those in hiding in and about A., and continued to do so until liberation. Thus, thanks to the concerted efforts of Greek leaders to save the endangered Jews, as well as the help extended by the extensive underground movement, only 1,300 Jews were deported from A. to the death camps. After the war some 5,000 Jews returned to A., most from their hiding places in the area and a few from the death camps. About 1,500 subsequently immigrated to Palestine. The community was rehabilitated and by 1991 was the largest J. community in Greece, with 3,000 Jews.

AUB (in J. sources, Ava, Oyb) Lower Franconia, Germany. Jews are mentioned as victims of the Rindfleisch massacres of 1298. The modern community is known from the early 17th cent., and suffered greatly

Embroidered Ark curtain, Aub (Bavaria), Germany

in the Thirty Years War. During the 17th cent. many J. refugees from the Wuerzburg bishopric and other localities settled there. A synagogue was erected in 1754. In 1890, the J. pop. was 115 (total 1,062) and in 1933, 73. On *Kristallnacht* (9–10 Nov. 1938), SA and SS troops destroyed J. homes and beat J. men. Fourteen Jews left in the next two months and the last 23 by around mid-1939. In all, 21 emigrated, 16 of them to the U.S., and 55 left for other German cities, including 25 for Wuerzburg.

AUCE   (Yid. Oitz) Zemgale (Courland) dist., Latvia. Jews arrived with the founding of the town in the 18th cent. The community was under the jurisdiction of Tukums until 1905. During WWI, J. homes and property were destroyed. In 1935 the J. pop. was 147 (total 3,320). Under Soviet rule from 1940 J. businesses were nationalized and public life was curtailed. The Germans captured the town in July 1941 and murdered all the Jews in late summer or early fall.

AUERBACH   Hesse, Germany. Established around 1770, the community numbered 120 (8% of the total) in 1861 and had close ties with the Jews of neighboring Bensheim. By 1933 it had dwindled to 49 and in 1938 the synagogue was purchased by a non-Jew. On *Kristallnacht* (9–10 Nov. 1938) stormtroopers destroyed J. homes and property. The remaining Jews emigrated or moved elsewhere, but eight survivors were deported in 1942. The synagogue was restored in 1987.

AUFHAUSEN   Wuerttemberg, Germany. Jews first settled in the 16th cent. and maintained a continuous presence from the late 17th, engaging in the cattle and grain trade and reaching a peak pop. of 378 in 1854. Thereafter their number declined rapidly, with only five remaining in 1933; only one emigrated and survived.

AUFSESS   (also Oberaufsess) Upper Franconia, Germany. Jews were present in the first half of the 14th cent., fleeing in the Thirty Years War and renewing the settlement in the latter 17th cent. under the protection of Carl Heinrich, the ruler of A., who built the community a synagogue after the disturbances of 1699. A J. public school was opened in 1879 and a new synagogue around 1900, when the J. pop. was 56 (total 770). In 1933, 11 Jews remained; three emigrated and seven left for other German cities.

Synagogue in Aufsess (Bavaria), Germany

AUGSBURG   Swabia, Germany. The J. community probably dated from the second half of the 12th cent. During the medieval period the Jews lived in a quarter called *Judenberg* with a synagogue, bathhouse, and wedding hall known from the 13th cent. A rabbi (*Judenmeister*) headed a community council (*Judenrat*) consisting of 12 elected elders. In 1276 a municipal statute that served as a model for other communities in South Germany and Switzerland fixed the social and economic rights of the Jews. A. had a famous yeshiva, where a special method of deep talmudic study known as the A. *hillukim* was developed. Among its illustrious rabbis was Meir ben Barukh (Maharam) of Rothenburg (active there in the mid-13th cent.). Untypically, local townsmen protected the Jews during the Rindfleisch (1298) and Armleder (1336) disturbances. The community grew and flourished in the first half of the 14th cent. However, in

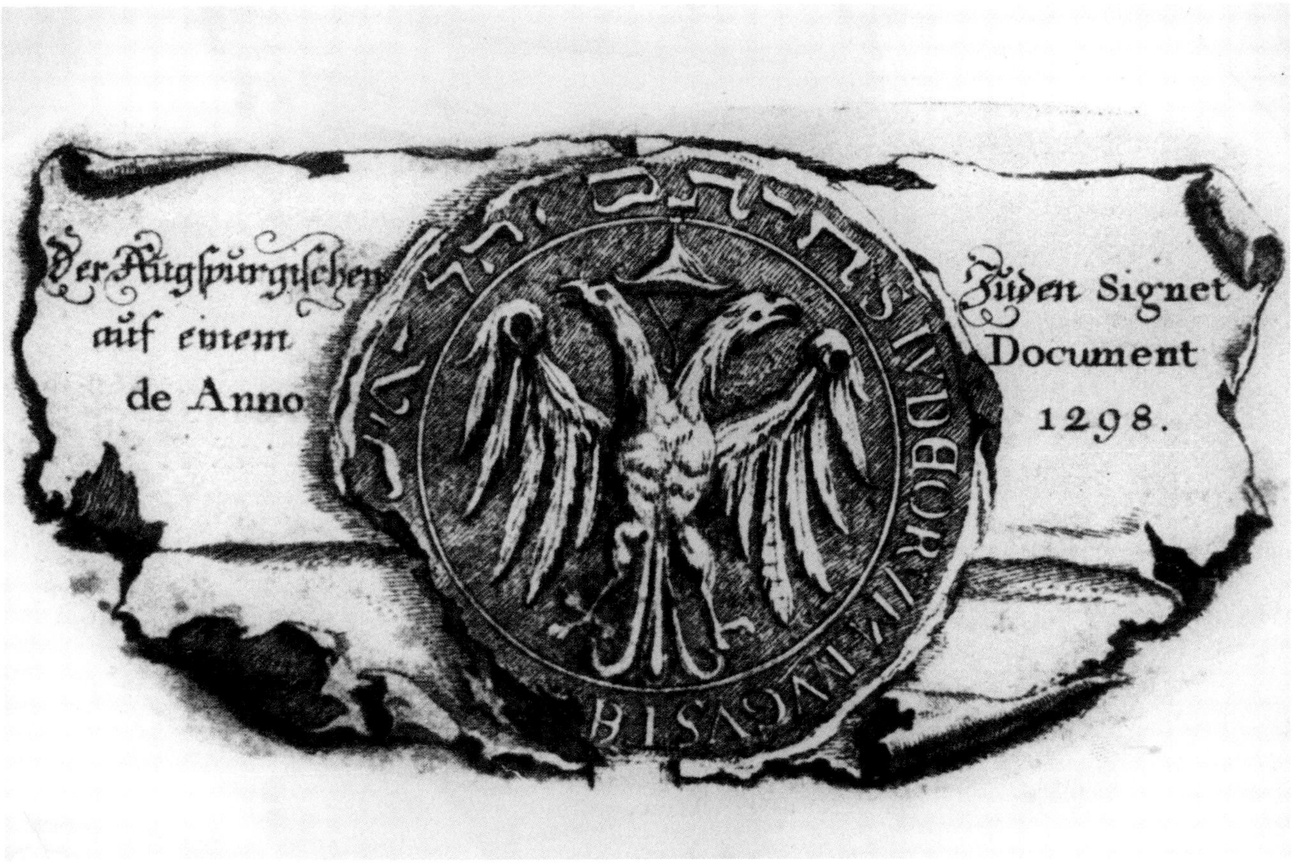
de Anno
Signet
Document
1298.

Seal of Augsburg Jewish community, Germany, 1298

the Black Death persecutions of 1348–49, most were massacred by the local pop., many being burned alive together with their promissory notes. The few survivors reestablished the community almost immediately but in 1438 the municipality published an expulsion order forcing all 300 Jews to leave the city. During this period the yeshiva flourished under R. Yaakov ben Yehuda Weil (1390–1457), one of Germany's outstanding rabbis at the time. In the 16th cent., a Hebrew press run by Hayyim Schwarz of Prague produced such works as Rashi's Pentateuch commentary (1533) and an illustrated Passover *Haggadah* (1534). For the next few hundred years Jews were allowed to visit the city for purposes of trade, though during the wars of the 18th cent. such Court Jews as Samuel Oppenheimer and Josef Guggenheimer were active there. In the second half of the 18th cent. the Kaulla banking family did extensive business in A. and in 1808 Arnold Seligmann founded the largest bank in the city. Permanent settlement was officially renewed in 1803 and after the Bavarian annexation in 1806 the remaining residence restrictions were gradually removed. In 1861, A. became the seat of the district rabbinate. Though Liberals formed a majority and an organ was introduced into the synagogue in 1865, prayer services remained by and large traditional, preserving the unity of the community. The J. pop. grew to 449 (total 50,057). By 1880 the J. pop. was 1,031 with Jews a major factor in the city's commercial life, controlling wholesale and retail trade, operating 20 banks, and pioneering industry (especially cloth, shoes, and chemical products), where at least 10,000 workers were employed in J.-owned factories. Many of the city's outstanding doctors and lawyers were also Jews and among the prominent J. cultural figures were the director of the municipal theater and the conductor of the local orchestra. A new synagogue, one of the most magnificent in Germany, was dedicated in 1917. The J. pop. in 1933 was 1,030. Under the Nazi regime Jews maintained an active communal life, offering a broad range of cultural and social services. A J. public school and old age home were main-

Young Jewish pioneers from Luzhki harvesting hay at an agricultural training farm in Augustow, Poland

tained, various institutions offered vocational and foreign language study preparatory to emigration, and the Central Union (C.V.), Zionist Organization, and Juedischer Kulturbund with its concerts and theater performances were all active. A total of 445 Jews managed to emigrate, half to the U.S. and a third in 1938–39 after the synagogue was destroyed and J. stores looted on *Kristallnacht* (9–10 Nov. 1938). Another 113 left for other German cities. The remaining 170 Jews were herded into a ghetto in late 1941; 19 were deported to the Riga ghetto via Munich on 20 Nov. 1941, another 129 to Piaski (Poland) via Munich on 3 April 1942, and most of the others to the Theresienstadt ghetto up to 1945. A postwar community, composed of former residents and East European concentration camp survivors, numbered 229 in 1970.

AUGUSTOW   Bialystok dist., Poland. The first Jews settled in 1564. In 1578 they were granted a charter from King Stephen Bathory permitting them to engage in trade and crafts, including the sale of alcoholic beverages. In the 17th cent. Jews were particularly active in the freshwater fish trade. The community grew from 462 in 1800 to 3,669 (total 7,998) in 1857. In the second half of the 19th cent. Jews operated three flour mills, two sawmills, a brickyard, a hide-processing plant, and a porcelain tile factory. They also supplied services to the Russian soldiers stationed in the area from 1868. A series of fires in the late 19th cent. curtailed economic prosperity. Some entered the small-scale textile industry developing in the city. In the 1890s small groups of Hasidim appeared. The first Zionist group was organized in 1885 and the Bund began operating in 1905, participating in strikes and demonstrations. Many Jews fled in WWI, never to return. The J. pop. dropped to 2,397 in 1931. Under Polish rule between the World Wars, the community experienced economic hardship. A Cooperative Bank founded in 1922 with the help of the Joint Distribution Committee offered financial aid. Political life, however, expanded, with the Zionists and their youth movements active along with the Bund and Agudat Is-

rael. A modernized *heder* set up in 1917 developed into a J. public school enrolling 230 children in 1939. With the city occupied by the Soviets from Sept. 1939 most Jews found employment in the new cooperatives under a regime of nationalization. All J. community institutions were shut down. The Germans captured the city on 22 June 1941. Dozens of Jews were executed within two weeks and on 15 Aug., 800–900 J. men were murdered. The remaining 2,000 Jews were confined to a ghetto. On 2 Nov. 1942 they were brought to the Bogusze transit camp near Grajewo and from there deported to the Treblinka death camp and Auschwitz in Dec. and Jan.

AUKSTADVARIS (Yid. Visoki–Dvor) Troki dist., Lithuania. Jews began settling by the 17th cent. The J. pop. in 1888 was 194 (28% of the total). In the late 19th cent. Vilna, 40 miles away, was the source of A.'s J. cultural, educational, and economic life, including the ideas of the Enlightenment and Zionism. During WWI, most Jews fled because of the war conditions and returned after the German conquest of Lithuania. Between the wars two Jews were elected to the local council. The J. pop. in 1941 was 230. After Germany's invasion of the USSR in June 1941, Lithuanians executed five Jews. Jews were taken to forced labor. On 22 Sept. 1941 (Rosh Hashanah) all the Jews were taken to Troki and on 30 Sept. (the eve of Yom Kippur), they were killed by Lithuanians.

AUKSTOJI-PANEMUNE (Yid. Panemon) Kaunas dist., Lithuania. The J. pop. in 1897 stood at 775 (49% of the total), dropping to a few hundred in 1935. The Jews earned their living as artisans, as tradesmen, and from small industry. Prior to WWII, A.-P. was annexed by Kaunas, but the J. community remained independent. For the fate of A.-P.'s Jews in the Holocaust, see KAUNAS.

AUMUND-VEGESACK Hanover, Germany. Evidence of the first "protected Jew" (*Schutzjude*) dates from 1758. By 1844, the J. pop. in A. numbered 81. In 1909, the community had 140 members. Its management moved to Vegesack in 1903. The synagogue was established in A. (probably in the 1850s). It was damaged in an arson attack in 1888. The religious instruction teacher held classes in A. as well as in Vegesack and in the affiliated community of Blumenthal. When the Nazis took power in 1933, the community numbered about 80 members. On *Kristallnacht* (9–10 Nov. 1938), the synagogue was burned down and SA troops murdered three Jews. From autumn 1941, those who did not manage to emigrate were deported to the east where nearly all perished.

AURELOW Lodz dist., Poland. A small community existed here between the World Wars. During WWII Jews were assembled from the region and transported to extermination camps.

AURICH Hanover, Germany. Jews settled in A. in 1635, their number growing from nine families in 1645 to 219 Jews in 1824 and 406 in 1885. The community established a synagogue (1810), a school, and a cemetery (1764). A rabbi was employed until 1826. The community's religious orientation was Orthodox. In 1848 and again in 1913, a Jew was elected a member of the city council. When the Nazis came to power in 1933, there were 398 Jews in A. Boycott measures were directed especially against the 50 (of a total 58) J. cattle traders and butchers who were falsely accused of fraud and cruelty to animals. On *Kristallnacht* (9–10 Nov. 1938), the synagogue was burned down, J. men were rounded up and maltreated, and 40–50 men were detained for several weeks in the Sachsenhausen concentration camp. In early 1940, there were about 155 Jews in A. They fled to the bigger towns upon hearing about plans for their evacuation. In March 1940, there were 20 Jews and they also left A. before long. About 150 local Jews managed to emigrate, about 160 perished. Many who had fled to Holland were rounded up again when the Nazis occupied the country.

AUSCHWITZ see OSWIENCIM.

AUTENHAUSEN Upper Franconia, Germany. The community was founded around the turn of the 17th cent., opening a synagogue and public school in 1828. The J. pop in 1890 was 64 (total 332). The last two J. families left for Coburg in 1923 after being beaten by Nazi youth.

AVIGNON Vaucluse dist., France. The first archeological evidence of a J. presence in A. dates from the fourth cent. with documentary evidence from 1178. The statutes of the municipality of A., dating from 1243, put in force the rules dictated by the Fourth Lateran Council of 1215, requiring the Jews to wear the

Rouelle badge. The Jews of A., together with those of Carpentras, Cavaillon and L'Isle-sur-Sorgue, formed the Four Holy Communities of Comtat-Venaissin, part of the papal territory in France. They shared a unique liturgy, called *Comtadin*, which greatly resembled Portuguese rites. A local Purim festival was observed on the 8th of Shevat to celebrate the providential escape of the community from tragedy in 1757. Following A.'s incorporation into France in 1791, the Jews were granted full civil rights. With the Napoleonic decree of 1808, the community was included in the regional consistory of Marseilles. When the local synagogue burned down a new one was inaugurated in 1849. In the second half of the 19th cent., two J. religious periodicals, *La Loi Divine* and *La Famille de Jacob*, were published in A. By 1892, the community consisted of a total of 54 families. During WWII, many refugees, especially from the Alsace region, settled in A. The census of June 1941 listed 300 Jews. On 17 April 1943, several J. families were arrested and deported, including Chief Rabbi Joseph

Sachs. Altogether 75 Jews from A. perished in the Holocaust. After the war, with the North African influx to France, the J. pop. in A. increased to 500 in 1960 and 2,000 in 1968.

AZOV   Rostov dist., Russia. Jews inhabited A. during the old period when it was called Tanais. The modern community dates from the mid-19th cent. A synagogue was built at this time. In the early 20th cent., the J. pop. was 340 (total 26,000). A private J. school for boys was opened in 1907. In 1939, the J. pop. was just 19, with 88 Jews in the surrounding area. The few who had neither fled nor been evacuated were murdered after the arrival of the Germans on 27 July 1942.

AZUOLU BUDA   (Yid. Dambava Buda) Marijampole dist., Lithuania. In 1899 a Zionist organization was founded here. Prior to WWI there were about 15 J. families. In July 1941 A.'s Jews were transported to Prienai or Marijampole and shared the fate of the Jews there.

B

BABENHAUSEN Hesse, Germany. In medieval times, Jews lived there until the Black Death persecutions of 1348–49. The modern community developed in the 19th cent., when Jews began to prosper in the livestock trade. From 100 in 1871, their number declined to 50 (1.8% of the total) in 1933. The Nazi economic boycott led to the community's virtual disappearance before 1939. On *Kristallnacht* (9–10 Nov. 1938) SA troops refrained from burning the synagogue down, as it had been sold to a non-Jew, but vandalized its interior. Some townspeople helped them loot J. homes. Most Jews emigrated, but some were deported in 1942.

BABENKA Kiev dist., Ukraine. Jews numbered 42 in 1790 and under the Soviets in 1939, 103 (total 4,043). The Germans captured B. on 5 Aug. 1941, murdering the Jews in Sept.

BABIAK Lodz dist., Poland. In 1857, 240 Jews, some of them farmers, were living here. In 1940, the 240 Jews were transported to Bugaj, and then to Chelmno.

BABINOVICHI Vitebsk dist., Belorussia. The J. pop. was 552 (total 1,157) in 1897 and 332 in 1926 under the Soviets. The Germans occupied the town in July 1941. In late April 1942, the 100 remaining Jews who had not fled or been evacuated were brought to Liozno and executed there together with other Jews from the area.

BABOCSA Somogy dist., Hungary. Jews settled in the first half of the 18th cent. and numbered 127 in 1880 and 53 in 1930. A synagogue was built in 1924. On 6 July 1944, they were deported to Auschwitz via Barcs.

BABTAI (Yid. Babet) Kaunas dist., Lithuania. In the 19th cent., J. merchants developed lumber and agricultural exports to Prussia. The J. pop. in 1913 was 900 (75% of the total) and dropped to 153 in 1923. On 28 Aug. 1941 Lithuanian nationalists carried out a pogrom killing 83 Jews, who were buried in pits just outside the town.

BABTSHINCY Vinnitsa dist., Ukraine. The J. pop. was 105 in 1847 and 192 (total 7,344) in 1939. The Germans occupied B. on 20 July 1941 and murdered about 130 Jews on 22 July and 94 more a month later.

BAC Vojvodina dist., Yugoslavia. Jews lived there from the 19th cent. until the Holocaust. They numbered 164 in 1921 and 42 in 1931 (total 4,052).

BACAU Moldavia dist., Rumania. A J. community existed in the late 18th cent. In 1824, 1838, and 1886, blood libels against the Jews sparked pogroms and in 1884 J. merchants were persecuted and local rioters plundered J. property. Up to the mid-19th cent., Jews monopolized many trades. Shoemakers and tailors established unions and had their own synagogues. Jews dominated the transport of goods in their wagons. With the coming of the railroad in 1868, these carters turned to agriculture. At the beginning of the 19th cent., Jews were the first to practice medicine and the last J. doctor holding an official position in the health services was dismissed in 1886. In 1896, the community census recorded that of the 7,924 Jews, 1,529 were artisans. In 1890, the first "modern" J. school was opened and by 1896 it had 370 pupils. The community had 30 prayer houses (in 1939), a hospital, a maternity clinic, an old age home, an orphanage, and a nursery school. Members of the thriving Zionist movement in B. were among the founders of Rosh Pinna and Zikh-

Staff of Jewish community hospital, Bacau, Rumania, 1942

ron Yaakov. The J. pop. in 1915 was 11,500 (60% of the total). Between the World Wars, B. became an important trading center and the majority of the 1,200 businesses and shops were owned by Jews, whose factories made B. a leading manufacturing center. Toward the end of WWI, 34 J. soldiers were unjustly sentenced to death. Antisemitism was rife during the 1930s and from 1940 Jews were persecuted by the local Iron Guard Legionnaires. Over 5,000 J. refugees expelled from neighboring towns and villages swelled the community. J. schools were opened to accommodate the J. pupils expelled from government schools and 300 Jews were sent to Ucea de Jos to work on laying the railroad. In 1943 another group was sent to forced labor in Bessarabia. From 7 May 1944, all Jews aged 18–50 (of the 12,000 J. pop.) were compelled to report daily for menial work. When the Soviet army captured the city, the Jews were ordered to provide services for the town. After the armistice in Aug. 1944, the B. Jews provided accommodation and livelihoods to those who returned from Transnistria and the 800 who returned from the Soviet Union. In 1969, 18,000 Jews were living there but they later left, mostly for Israel.

BACESTI Moldavia dist., Rumania. Jews settled here in the mid-19th cent. The J. pop. in 1899 was 526 (28% of the total). Under the Goga-Cuza regime (1937) peasants were incited to attack the Jews. On 22 June 1941, males up to age 50 were sent to the Targu-Jiu concentration camp. The next day the remaining Jews were expelled to Roman, where they were joined on 1 Sept. by the menfolk, who were put to forced labor.

BACHARACH Rhineland, Germany. Three local J. families found shelter in the nearby Stahleck fortress in 1146 during disturbances accompanying the Second Crusade. The heads of the families were later murdered. In 1283, 26 Jews were slaughtered in the aftermath of the Mainz blood libel and Jews were again attacked in the Armleder (1337) and Black Death (1348–

49) persecutions. J. life continued into the modern era. The community numbered 72 (total 1,601) in 1858 and 38 in 1933. Five Jews perished in the Holocaust.

BACKA PALANKA Vojvodina dist., Yugoslavia. A J. settlement existed in the Roman period and was renewed from 1771. A J. school existed in 1835–1900. There were 265 Jews (total 5,524) in 1931 and 254 in 1940. Most perished during the Holocaust.

BACKA TOPOLA Vojvodina dist., Yugoslavia. Jews settled during the 19th cent. The Zionist movement was active in the 1920s and 1930s. In 1941 there were 130 J. families (total pop. 15,000). With the Hungarian occupation, Jews were killed or sent to labor camps, where many died. Others were sent to Auschwitz and other camps from 1944.

BACKI PETROVAC Vojvodina dist., Yugoslavia. Jews settled there at the end of the 18th cent. The J. pop. in 1940 was 100. Most were killed by the Germans and Hungarians during the Holocaust.

BACKO PETROVO SELO Vojvodina dist., Yugoslavia. A J. community was established in the 18th cent. Antisemitism culminated in 1903 with a blood libel. All the Jews (300 in 1940; total pop. 11,000) perished during the Holocaust.

BACOVO (Hung. Bacso or Bacsava; Yid. Batschive) Carpatho-Russia, Czechoslovakia, today Ukraine. Jews probably settled in the early 19th cent., numbering 118 in 1880, 165 (total 570) in 1921 under Czechoslovakian rule, and 202 in 1941 under the Hungarians. The latter drafted a number of Jews into labor battalions in 1941 and in late July expelled a few J. families without Hungarian citizenship to the occupied Ukraine, where they were murdered. The rest were deported to Auschwitz in the second half of May 1944.

BACSALMAS Bacs–Bodrug dist., Hungary. Jews settled in the mid-18th cent. and numbered 189 (2% of the total) in 1880. In 1846, they opened a J. school and in 1888 a synagogue. They suffered from two blood libels, in 1763 and 1897. After WWI, they suffered from attacks and in 1941 their farms were confiscated and "Aryans" placed in charge of their businesses. The J. pop. was 186 in 1941. The Germans converted the local flour mill into a ghetto in April

1944 and on 25–28 June sent the Jews to Austria and Auschwitz. After 1946, those who had returned left because of the hostility of their neighbors.

BACZKI Lublin dist., Poland. Jews first settled in the 1860s, most finding employment in factories owned by the Perlis family, which also helped Jews settle in B. by providing them with land allotments and supplies. By the end of the 19th cent., the community maintained a synagogue and a 2,000-vol. library. The pop. remained around 150 until WWI. Between the World Wars, the Zionists and the Bund were active. Refugees arriving after the German occupation of Sept. 1939 brought the J. pop. of B. and environs up to 1,665 by Jan. 1942. All were deported to the Treblinka death camp on 23–25 Sept. 1942. Those who escaped to the forest were hunted down or turned in by Polish farmers.

The Perlis workshop, Baczki, Poland

BAD BUCHAU Wuerttemberg, Germany. Jews were present in the 16th cent. and perhaps earlier. Throughout the 18th cent., the community was subjected to residence and trade restrictions as well as high taxes leading 12 families to move to the neighboring village of Kappel, where a synagogue was built. The J. pop. grew to 155 in 1843 before dwindling to

Synagogue in Bad Buchau, Germany, built in 1837-39

zero in 1900. Chaila (Caroline) Kaulla (1739–1809), one of the few women court agents in Germany and founder of a great J. banking dynasty, was born in B. A J. school was opened in 1826 and in 1839 a new synagogue was inaugurated. Its belfry, to summon Jews to prayer, was the only one in Germany. The community grew to 724 by 1854, thereafter shrinking as emigration and the attractions of city life claimed the young. In the second half of the 19th cent., J. economic life expanded into the textile, food, and leather trades as well as into cattle and land dealings. At the outset of the Nazi era, there were 165 Jews and 38 J. business establishments in the town. A Zionist society was also active. Emigration was stepped up after *Kristallnacht* (9–10 Nov. 1938), when the synagogue was burned, Jews beaten, and J. property pillaged. In all, 80 Jews left Germany; the rest lost their lives in the Holocaust. The ancient J. cemetery with its 1,000 burial plots has been preserved by the local city council.

BAD DRIBURG Westphalia, Germany. Jews are first mentioned in 1652. A synagogue was opened in the early 19th cent. and a J. school in the early 20th. The J. pop. consistently numbered around 50 (2% of the total). On *Kristallnacht* (9–10 Nov. 1938), the synagogue was burned and J. homes and stores were damaged. The men were sent to the Buchenwald concentration camp. Twenty-one Jews perished in the Holocaust.

BAD DUERKHEIM Palatinate, Germany. Jews are mentioned in 1309, making the community one of the oldest in the Palatinate. It was destroyed in the Black Death persecutions of 1348–49. Jews were again living there in the second half of the 17th cent., employed as butchers and merchants. In 1700, they were forced to move to an out-of-the-way alley and prohibited from trading in food products other than meat. In the mid-18th cent., the community numbered 15 families. A synagogue was erected in 1748 and in the 19th cent. the community began to grow significantly, reaching

a pop. of 305 (total 6,089) in 1880. Jews were active in trade, especially in textiles, and as artisans. In the 20th cent. Jews became winegrowers and wine merchants. Jews served on the municipal council and were active in public affairs. In 1865, the Hungarian-born Dr. Adolf Salvendi became community rabbi, serving for 44 years. As the only Orthodox rabbi in the Palatinate he came into frequent conflict with Liberal circles throughout the province. A new synagogue was consecrated in 1892. The J. elementary school founded in the 1840s closed in 1870. A private business school set up by a Jew at around the same time developed into one of the most important educational institutes in the town, becoming a municipal high school with its J. principals occupying leading public positions. The Liberal proclivities of the congregation found expression in the introduction of an organ and choir into the synagogue. In 1920, a woman served as beadle (*shamash*). Ludwig Strauss, who as director of the high school dormitory was chosen to head the community in 1907, served continuously on the municipal council from 1918 until the Nazi era. The J. pop. fell to 185 in 1925

Interior of Bad Duerkheim synagogue, Germany

and 152 in 1933. With the advent of the Nazis, Jews were removed from public positions. In 1935, they were banned from municipal baths and resort areas. By 1937, about half the Jews had left the town, at least 20 reaching the U.S. On *Kristallnacht* (9–10 Nov. 1938), SA troops wrecked the synagogue and about 25 J. homes and stores. Four men were sent to the Dachau concentration camp. By the end of 1939, the last five J. business establishments were transferred

to German ownership. The remaining 28 Jews were confined to four buildings. On 22 Oct. 1940, 19 Jews were deported to the Gurs concentration camp in southern France. At least 25 Jews perished in the Holocaust. Among B.'s satellite communities were Kallstadt (63 Jews in 1848 with a synagogue and J. school), Ungstein (42 Jews in 1875), Freinsheim (65 in 1835), Friedelsheim (61 in 1848), and Weisenheim am Berg (42 in 1848).

BAD EMS Hesse–Nassau, Germany. The community, established by eight families around 1738, provided Jews visiting the spa with kosher facilities and opened one of the first hotels. Following the resort's development in the 19th cent., a synagogue (1837) and other J. hotels were built, with physicians helping to expand the community. The J. pop. rose to 181 (3% of the total) in 1885. A society endowed by the Rothschilds and other benefactors (1887) offered free medical treatment to needy Jews; an Orthodox home for orphaned girls was opened (1897); and communal life flourished during the Weimar Republic. Once Nazi persecution developed, the community's last rabbi, Dr. Friedrich Laufheimer (1932–39), endeavored to sustain J. morale. The synagogue's interior was destroyed on *Kristallnacht* (9–10 Nov. 1938) and the aged were among those attacked in the pogrom. The last remaining Jews were deported in 1941.

BADEN Lower Austria, Austria. Jews first settled here in 1806. In 1874, a J. burial society (*hevra kaddisha*) was founded, which gained international recognition, since B. was well known in Europe for its spa facilities and Jews who died here had to be transported to their home residence. Jews were engaged in trade and represented in the professional class as doctors. In 1873, a splendid synagogue was consecrated. In 1878, the community was acknowledged as a religious corporation (*Kultusgemeinde*). Wilhelm Reich served as the community's first rabbi and succeeded in bringing about a compromise between Orthodox and Liberal elements. He was active in founding the Agudat Israel orphanage. In 1928, the J. pop. numbered 1,500 (total 22,388), declining to 1,108 in 1934 and 1,000 in May 1938. Most community members were of Hungarian origin. On *Kristallnacht* (9–10 Nov. 1938), the synagogue and the administration offices were blown up and the Jews were arrested. Many succeeded in emigrating or in escaping over the Czechoslovakian bor-

der. By May 1940 the remaining 43 Jews were sent to Vienna and then deported to the east. The community was reconstituted in 1946.

BADEN-BADEN Baden, Germany. Jews were already visiting the local mineral springs in the 17th cent. but permanent residence was only permitted in 1862 after the emancipation of Baden Jews. The community grew rapidly to 156 in 1895 and 435 in 1925 (total 25,692). A splendid synagogue in the Romanesque style was completed in 1898 and a cemetery was consecrated in 1921. The national convention of Agudat Israel was held in B. in 1921 and most of the J. organizations in Germany had offices there. Antisemitism intensified after WWI, often driving away J. vacationers and reducing the J. pop. to 260 in 1933. In 1937 health facilities and public parks were closed to the Jews. The Zionist Organization engaged in widespread activity throughout this period. Sixty-five Jews left B. between 1933–38, including 27 to Western Eu-

rope. On *Kristallnacht* (9–10 Nov. 1938), around 80 J. men were brought to the synagogue and one was forced to read from *Mein Kampf.* Most were then sent to the Dachau concentration camp after being beaten. The synagogue was burned and J. stores and homes were pillaged. In all, 154 Jews left the city by 1942. Of these, 46 were later trapped and deported, as were the 114 sent to the Gurs concentration camp in southern France directly from the city on 22 Oct. 1940. The community was reestablished after the war and numbered 53 in 1976.

BAD GODESBERG Rhineland, Germany. J. settlement commenced in the 17th cent. In 1861, the J. pop. was 73. Jews engaged in trade and worked as butchers. In the last quarter of the 19th cent., most belonged to the lower or middle class. The community was attached to the Bonn Consistory in Napoleonic times and became independent in 1875. A synagogue was consecrated in 1850. After WWI, the number of J.

President of Baden-Baden Jewish community being led by congregants to the synagogue, Germany

artisans grew somewhat and for the first time Jews were employed as white collar workers. The community remained Orthodox. Of the 121 Jews in B. and its satellite communities present in 1933, including Mehlem, 48 emigrated by 1938, most in the first years of Nazi rule. On *Kristallnacht* (9–10 Nov. 1938), the synagogue was burned and J. homes and stores were destroyed. Another 36 emigrated by the end of 1939. The rest were moved to a single house. On 20 Jan. 1942, nine were transferred to Cologne and on 23 Jan., 23 were sent to the expropriated Benedictine monastery in Bonn-Endenich. Most were deported to the Theresienstadt and Lodz ghettoes in June–July 1942. In 1944, Jews in mixed marriages were deported as well.

BAD HERSFELD Hesse–Nassau, Germany. After the Black Death massacres (1348–49), Jews lived there until the 17th cent. The modern community, numbering 76 (1% of the total) in 1871, maintained an elementary school (1878–1938), opened a new synagogue (1900), and was affiliated with the rabbinate of Fulda. Branches of Agudat Israel, the German Zionist Organization, and the J. War Veterans Association

were established and by 1925 the community had grown to 325 (3%). As a result of the Nazi boycott, however, it dwindled to 90 by *Kristallnacht* (9–10 Nov. 1938), when the synagogue was burned down and townspeople looted or destroyed J. property. Of the 273 J. residents in 1933, 116 emigrated (54 to the U.S. and 17 to Palestine); 140 moved to Frankfurt and other German cities before WWII; and at least 23 are known to have perished in the Holocaust.

BAD HOMBURG Hesse–Nassau, Germany. Jews lived there in the 14th cent. but a permanent community was only established 350 years later, when the landgrave invited Jews and Huguenots to settle in Homburg vor der Hoehe (1684). A synagogue was opened (1731) and a Hebrew printing house published 45 works (1710–48). Jews contributed to the town's development as a health resort. By 1865 their number had grown to 604 (9% of the total). They built an imposing new synagogue (1866) with a community center (1877), also opening three sanatoriums and two famous kosher hotels that had an international clientele. The establishment of Agudat Israel was first mooted at a

The butcher Moritz Kahn, Bad Homburg, Germany

conference held in the town (1909); Aharon Roke'ah of Belz, Hayyim Soloveichik, and Yitzhak Volozhiner paid regular visits; while the sculptor Mark Antokolski and World Zionist Organization president David Wolffsohn both died there. After WWI, Shoshana and Yehoshua Persitz transferred the Omanut publishing house from Moscow to B. and their home served as a meeting place for Russian-J. writers and intellectuals (1920–25). The community, persecuted by the Nazis, dwindled from 300 (2%) in 1933 to 70 on *Kristallnacht* (9–10 Nov. 1938), when SA troops burned the synagogue to the ground in a general pogrom. The last Jews were deported in 1942–43; at least 45 perished in the Holocaust.

BAD HONNEF Rhineland, Germany. Three Jews under letters of protection were present in 1622. The J. pop. never reached more than 30–60 (less than 1% of the total). The Central Union (C.V) opened a branch in 1919. In the Weimar period, Jews were involved in public life, but antisemitism also intensified. In the Nazi era, J. businesses were closed down. The synagogue was burned on *Kristallnacht* (9–10 Nov. 1938). Of the 34 Jews present in 1933, 22 emigrated, including ten to the U.S. In 1941–42, at least eight were deported to the east where they perished.

BAD KISSINGEN (in J. sources, Kischa) Lower Franconia, Germany. Jews were victims of the Rindfleisch massacres of 1298. In 1705 a synagogue was dedicated and in 1801 a cemetery. B. served as the seat of the regional rabbinate from 1839, embracing 2,500 Jews in numerous communities. Among the chief rabbis were Lazarus Adler (1839–52), Gabriel Lippmann (1853–64), and Moshe Aryeh Leib Bamberger (1865–1902). A new synagogue was built in 1902 as the J. pop. grew from 210 in 1837 to a peak of 504 in 1925 (total 9,517). B. was famous for its mineral baths, attracting thousands of visitors each year, including many Jews, and providing employment for 90% of the J. community. Jews owned hotels and restaurants and worked as doctors at the health facilities. A J. children's clinic founded in 1905 on the initiative of the chief rabbi, Yitzhak Seckel Bamberger (serving 38 communities in 1902–32), accommodated as many as 400 children. In 1933, 344 Jews remained in B. The

Prayers in the Bad Honnef synagogue, Germany, 1938

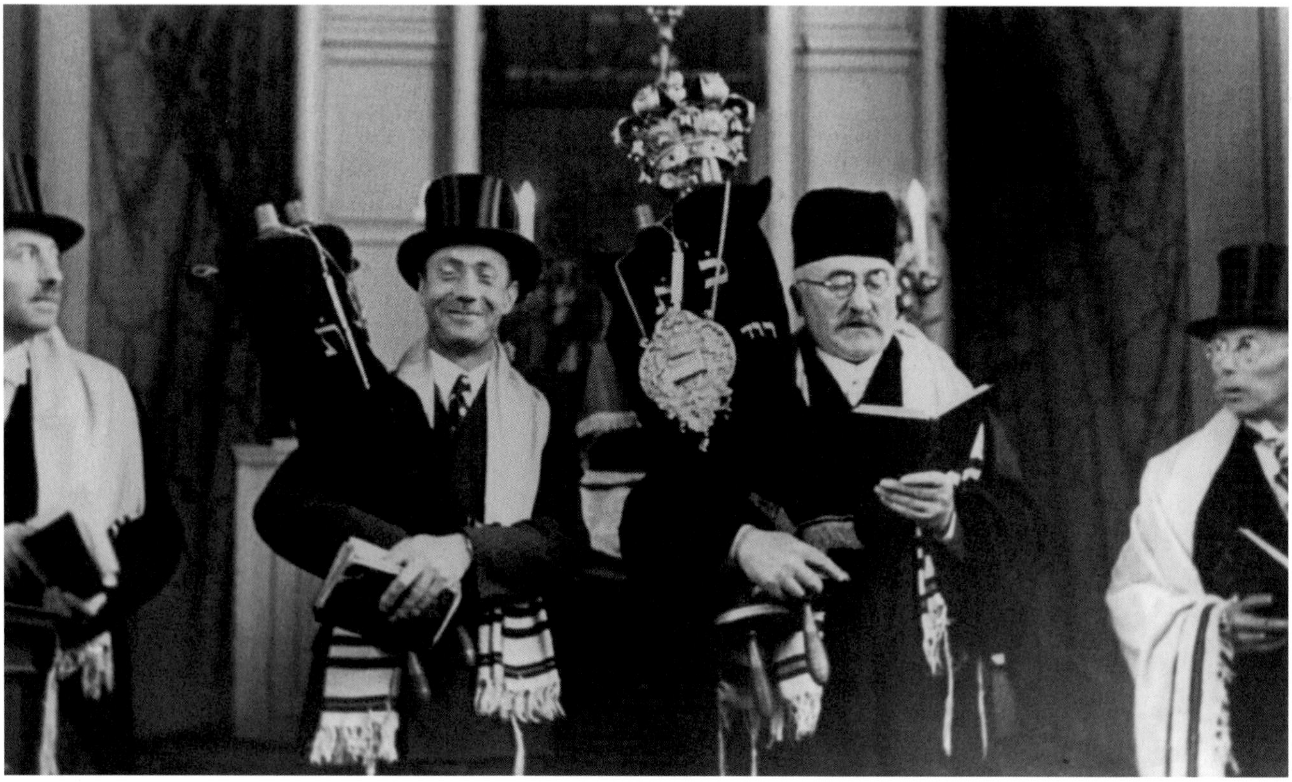

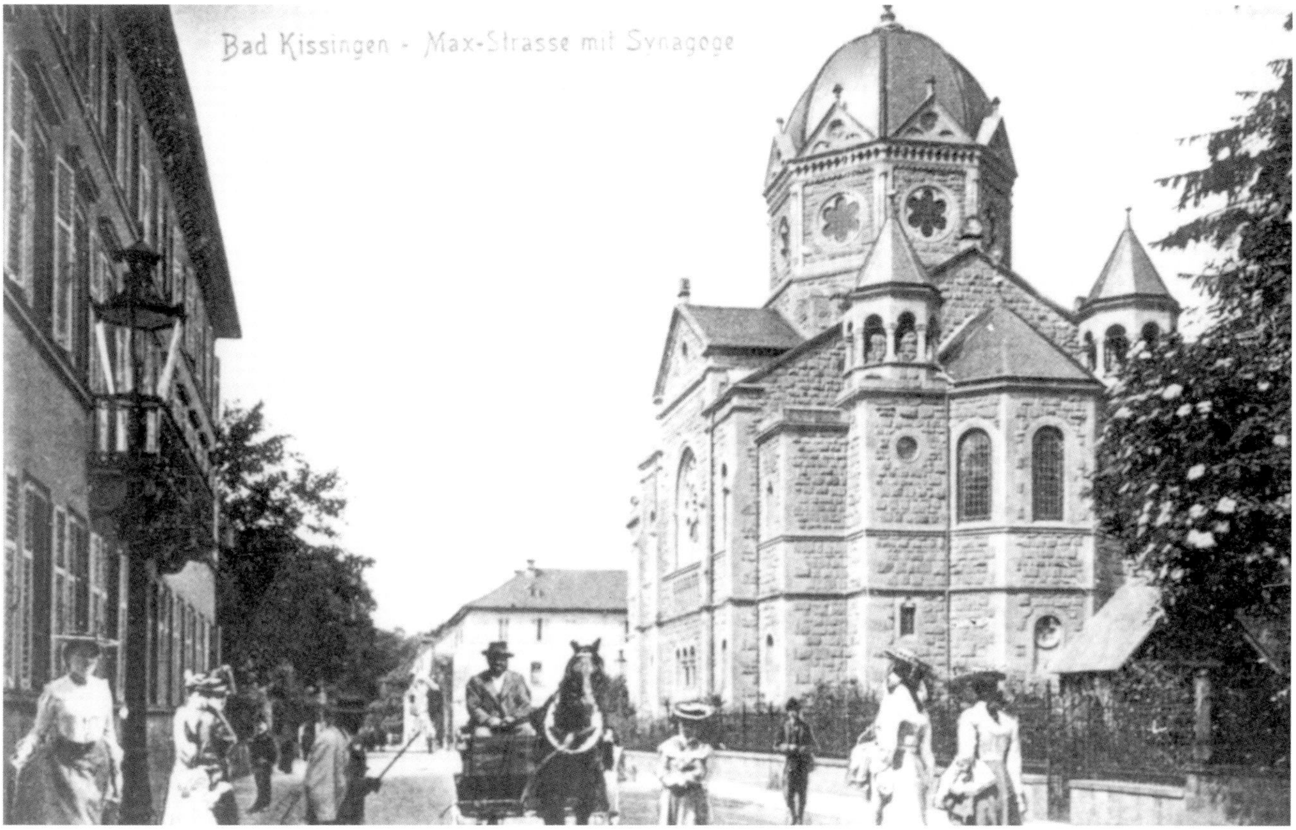
Bad Kissingen - Max-Strasse mit Synagoge

Synagogue in Bad Kissingen, Germany

economic boycott under the Nazi regime struck hard at their tourist-based livelihoods as severe persecution ensued. Nonetheless, 15 J. boarding houses were still open in 1935 with 600 guests. On *Kristallnacht* (9–10 Nov. 1938), J. homes and stores were destroyed along with a J. hotel and J. health facilities. All J. men under 70 were sent to the Dachau concentration camp. Emigration, which had commenced in 1933 with an exodus of younger Jews, reached a total of 121 through 1939, including 64 to the U.S. Another 143 left for other German cities, including 31 to Frankfurt and 29 to Berlin. Of the 43 Jews remaining in 1942, 23 were deported to Izbica in the Lublin dist. of Poland via Wuerzburg on 24 April and others were later sent to the Theresienstadt ghetto.

BAD KOENIG Hesse, Germany. Established in the late 18th cent., the community promoted the town's development as a health resort, which attracted a largely J. clientele. Known for their religious observance, the Jews numbered 100 (5.1% of the total) in 1880 and 71 (2.9%) in 1933. After *Kristallnacht* (9–10 Nov. 1938), when Nazis desecrated the synagogue, beat Jews, and looted J. property, the community dispersed. Not one Jew remained, some youngsters joining pioneer training programs in the hope of emigrating to Palestine.

BAD KREUZNACH Rhineland, Germany. A number of J. moneylenders were present in the 13th cent. In 1336, Count Sponheim was authorized to settle 60 Jews on his estate and in 1338 the community had its own rabbi. The community ended in the Black Death persecutions of 1348–49, when the Jews were murdered or expelled. Jews were again present in the last quarter of the 14th cent. but in 1404 all were arrested and their property confiscated. Jews were arrested again c. 1434, when the community included around ten families. In 1525, the Jews were allowed to engage in trade in addition to moneylending. A new cemetery was opened in 1661 and a synagogue that remained in use for 200 years was constructed in 1737. In 1746, the J. pop. reached 30 families. In 1808, under French rule, the number of Jews increased

to 286 with the community becoming one of the most important in the region. In the same year it was attached to the Bonn Consistory. A private J. school was opened in 1820 but it soon closed and other attempts to establish J. schools failed. A community center was built in 1844–45. Most Jews engaged in trade. The J. pop. subsequently grew to 506 in 1848 and 601 (total 15,321) in 1880. In the Weimar period, the economic position of the Jews remained satisfactory. Although there were doctors, lawyers, artisans, and brokers, most remained tradesmen, selling textiles, shoes, furniture, hardware, musical instruments, household silver, and antiques. There were also butchers and wine and grain merchants. Jews were members of local choirs and sports clubs, the Barukh brothers winning national and European championships in weightlifting and wrestling. A J. school for religious education enrolled 75 children in 1932. The communities of Muenster am Stein and Planig were attached to the congregation. In 1933, the J. pop. was 713 but already in the first months of Nazi rule about 200 Jews left the city. A children's sanatorium founded in 1920 became one of the two largest in Germany for J. children with 118 beds in 1933. Social and cultural life continued to flourish in the Nazi era. A Zionist youth group was founded in 1933 and numerous courses were offered in the community. A J. public school was opened in 1937 with 34 children. However, unrelenting anti-J. agitation accompanied daily life. On *Kristallnacht* (9–10 Nov. 1938), the children's sanatorium was shut down for good and SA troops and Hitler Youth wrecked the synagogue and caused serious damage to at least 22 J. homes and stores. J. men were sent to the Buchenwald and Dachau concentration camps. J. emigration continued throughout the period. In mid-1939, barely 200 Jews remained. Those who stayed were deported to the east: 58 on 1 May 1942; 16 on 14 June; 50 on 28 July; and two in Jan. 1945.

BAD MERGENTHEIM Wuerttemberg, Germany. A few J. families were present in 1292; 16 Jews were murdered in the Rindfleisch massacres of 1298 and others in the Armleder massacres of 1336–39 and the Black Death persecutions of 1348–49. In 1495 the Teutonic Order assumed responsibility for the small J. community, which only began to develop during the Thirty Years War (1618–48) when a new charter permitted Jews to trade in farm produce while imposing

residence restrictions and continuing the ban on moneylending. In the first half of the 19th cent., when the town was attached to the Wuerttemberg principality, many Jews were numbered among the poor and tensions with the local pop. led to violent anti-J. outbursts in 1819 and 1848. Economic conditions improved with the discovery of mineral springs at midcent. Jews prospered in the wholesale and retail trade, dealing in food and clothing, horses and cattle. The community hosted regional conferences of Agudat Israel and other Orthodox bodies. In 1900 it reached a peak pop. of 276 (around 6% of the total) and in 1933 numbered 196. On *Kristallnacht* (9–10 Nov. 1938) the synagogue was desecrated, Jews were severely beaten, and J. stores looted. Emigration consequently accelerated and, in all, 123 Jews managed to leave Germany until 1941, 69 of them reaching the U.S. and 36 Palestine. None of the others survived the Holocaust, many ending their days in the Theresienstadt ghetto.

BAD MINGOLSHEIM Baden, Germany. Jews first settled in the 18th cent. Their pop. reached 77 in 1875 (total 1,972). In the early 20th cent. they opened eight cigarette factories and continued to be active as cattle traders, brokers, and shopkeepers. The exodus of the young reduced the J. pop. to 11 in 1933. All but four Jews left by 1938. The latter were deported to the Gurs concentration camp on 22 Oct 1940.

BAD NAUHEIM Hesse, Germany. The first Jews living in the medieval village of Nauheim were expelled in the Black Death persecutions of 1348–49 and again in 1539. Unfair taxation known as *Schutzgeld* or "protection money" retarded the community's growth until 1830. The discovery of medicinal waters, however, transformed N. into an expanding health resort (renamed "Bad" Nauheim) and led to the opening of guest houses for Jews visiting the spa. The community, numbering 67 (2.5% of the total) in 1880, grew to 119 in 1900 after many J. physicians, lawyers, and businessmen took up residence there. They opened 11 kosher hotels and seven other establishments that served visitors seeking a cure for their ailments. Between 1880–1935, the number of J. physicians rose to 50. Their successful treatment of heart disease enhanced the renown of B. and attracted patients from all over the world. From 1875 the community enabled poor Jews to be treated free of charge and a large children's clinic was opened in 1893. Religiously Orthodox,

prises and children's homes to close. The synagogue was vandalized on *Kristallnacht* (9–10 Nov. 1938). By 1939 the community had vanished. Three Jews committed suicide, 14 emigrated, and about 15 (including three who moved to Holland) perished in the Holocaust. Only one (hidden by a friendly policeman) survived. The former synagogue, which housed refugees after WWII, was demolished in 1962.

BAD SODEN   Hesse–Nassau, Germany. Jews in medieval Soden fell victim to the Black Death persecutions of 1348–49 and an independent community was not established until 1849. Transformed into a flourishing spa (and renamed "Bad" S.), the town attracted wealthy J. visitors from Frankfurt—and the baptized composer Felix Mendelssohn. In 1885 Baron Rothschild endowed a sanatorium treating needy Jews (213 in 1912). By 1925 the community numbered 49 (2% of the total.). On *Kristallnacht* (9–10 Nov. 1938), Nazis destroyed the synagogue's interior and a mob burned the sanatorium. Some Jews emigrated (1933–37), others probably died in the Holocaust.

BAD WILDUNGEN   Hesse–Nassau, Germany. A community was not established there until 1866, numbering 77 (over 3% of the total) in 1880. Contributions from Jews visiting the local spa helped to build a synagogue center (1814). During the Weimar Republic, there were four J. hotels (two kosher) and the community—affiliated with the rabbinate of Kassel—numbered 152 (1925). As a result of the Nazi boycott from 1933 the J. pop. declined. On *Kristallnacht* (9–10

Stained glass windows of Bad Wildungen synagogue, Germany

Nov. 1938), SA troops looted and destroyed the synagogue in a murderous pogrom. Of the 150 Jews living there in 1933, 76 left (52 emigrating) and the remainder (67) were expelled by the end of 1939. At least 50 perished in the Holocaust.

BAEVO   Vitebsk dist., Belorussia. The J. pop. was 505 (total 906) in 1897 and 243 in 1923 under the Soviets. In 1930, 15 J. families were employed at a nearby kolkhoz and also engaged in crafts. The Germans occupied B. in July 1941. In early Oct., the town's 200 Jews were executed at the nearby village of Pakhomovo.

BAGAMER   Bihar dist., Hungary. Jews settled in the second half of the 18th cent. and numbered 91 in 1938. They were deported to Auschwitz via the Nagyvarad ghetto from 20 May to 3 June 1944.

BAGASLAVISKIS   Ukmerge dist., Lithuania. B. had 50 J. families prior to WWI. Being a small, poor community, it had no doctor or school and only a visiting rabbi. In summer 1941, Lithuanian nationalists persecuted Jews with much cruelty. B.'s Jews were transferred to Ukmerge, where they were murdered on 5 Sept. 1941.

BAGNOLET   Seine-Saint-Denis dist., France. Jews settled in B. at the end of the 19th cent. The immigrant community was composed mainly of Jews from Poland and Russia. Prior to WWI, the J. community in B. numbered 609 persons. Arrests began in spring 1942 and continued in 1943. Two hundred and two Jews (including 128 foreign nationals) were deported to Auschwitz via the Drancy concentration camp.

BAIA MARE   (Hung. Nagybanya) N. Transylvania dist., Rumania. A J. community existed from 1860 and Jews were invoved in the development of the mining industry. During WWI, 288 Jews were drafted into the army and 20 J. soldiers were killed in battle. The J. pop. in 1920 was 1,792 (14% of the total). In the 1920s an additional 1,500 Jews were attracted to settle by the increased industrialization to which the Jews contributed greatly. The community's last rabbi, Dr. Moshe Aharon Hacohen Krauss (1919–44), opened a yeshiva with 50 students in the 1930s. From 1924 Zionist youth movements were established. From late 1940, Fascist and Nazi organizations incited the

pop. against the Jews, who suffered economically. In 1943 many were sent to forced labor to Hungary and the Ukraine. At the beginning of May 1944, 14,000 Jews from B. and the surrounding area were ghettoized and on 27 May deported to Auschwitz. After the war, 950 survivors returned but the numbers gradually diminshed.

BAIA SPRIE (Hung. Felsobanya) N. Transylvania dist., Rumania. Jews settled in this mining town in the late 1850s. The J. pop. in 1920 was 193 (5% of the total). In May 1944 community members were transferred to the Baia Mare ghetto and on 27 May deported to Auschwitz.

BAIERSDORF (Yid. Fayersdorf, etc.) Middle Franconia, Germany. Jews may have been present as early as the 14th cent. and constituted one of the most important communities in the Bayreuth margravate in the 16th cent. The Court Jew Salomon Samson was prominent in the principality at the turn of the 17th cent. In 1702, B. was fixed as the seat of the margravate's chief rabbi, a position occupied since 1728 by one of the sons of Glueckel of Hameln, the famous female diarist. In 1717 residence was restricted to one son per family and various trade restrictions were added in 1771. In 1837, the J. pop. was 440 (total 1,550), thereafter declining rapidly and numbering only 19 in 1933. All but one of the Jews left by 1938, ten emigrating.

BAIERTAL Baden, Germany. The first Jews arrived after the Thirty Years War and the J. pop. grew to a peak of 160 in 1863 (15% of the total). A synagogue was in existence by 1740 and a new one was built in 1833 while a J. elementary school was opened in 1839. The J. pop. dropped steadily to 25 in 1933. On *Kristallnacht* (9–10 Nov. 1938) the synagogue and J. homes were vandalized and J. stores looted. Nine Jews left B. in 1936–40. The last 13 were deported to the Gurs concentration camp on 22 Oct. 1940.

BAINETI Bukovina, Rumania, today Ukraine. The Jews were attached to the Siret community and had no independent institutions. The J. pop. in 1930 was 23. In 1941 the J. pop. was force-marched to Suceava and transferred to the Calafat and Craiova internment camps. Approximately 80% died on the way to Transnistria.

BAISINGEN Wuerttemberg, Germany. Jews were present in the 14th cent. but the permanent settlement dates from 1640, with Jews subjected to various restrictions and a heavy tax burden. In the 18th cent. most were peddlers. Their economic situation improved somewhat in the 19th cent. when efforts were made to find them more productive occupations. The J. pop. reached a peak of 235 in 1843 and declined steadily thereafter. Another 109 Jews in the neighboring village of Unterschwandorf were also part of the community but by 1869 only one was left there. In 1848 local gangs attacked J. homes, causing much damage. By 1933 the J. pop. stood at 86, with most engaged in the cattle trade. On *Kristallnacht* (9–10 Nov. 1938), SA units vandalized the synagogue, cemetery, and J. homes. Subsequently, in the face of increasing economic and social isolation, emigration was stepped up and 60 Jews managed to leave the country. All but a few of the others met their end after expulsion to the east in 1942. The J. cemetery was desecrated in 1949 and 1971.

BAISOGALA (Yid. Baisegale) Kedainiai dist., Lithuania. The J. community began at the end of the 18th cent. The J. pop. in 1897 was 634 (53% of the total). The 100 Jews who lived in B. at the beginning of WWI were exiled by the Russian authorities. After the war, some returned to find the synagogue destroyed and their homes occupied by non-Jews. The few Jews remaining by the beginning of WWII were sent to Krakes and murdered on 2 Sept. 1941.

BAJA Bacs-Bodrog dist., Hungary. Jews settled in the first half of the 18th cent., gradually gaining a prominent role in the economic life of B. Besides dealing mainly in alcoholic beverages, tobacco, hides, wool, and grain, Jews owned the largest store in the region and dominated exports from all its pig farms. The J. pop. reached a peak of 2,542 (13% of the total) in 1880. After a devastating fire in 1840, a new J. school was built in 1841 and a new synagogue in 1845. A J. hospital was opened in 1882 and an old age home in 1901. Despite local hostility, two Jews served as mayors of the city and in 1902 a local Jew was elected to Parliament. In 1941, 1,378 Jews remained. About 120 Jews were sent to the Bacstopolya labor camp on 14 April 1944 and the rest confined to a ghetto in May. Most were deported at the end of June to Auschwitz and Austria via Bacsalmas and Kassa. When the Germans left on 13 Oct. they tried to take the remaining

Jews with them, but the mayor intervened. Eighty Jews taken by the Germans to Austria managed to escape. Some 400 survivors reestablished the community and in 1953, 180 Jews remained.

BAJMOK Vojvodina dist., Yugoslavia. Jews lived in B. from the late 19th cent. There were 142 Jews in 1940 (total 6,000). They perished in the Holocaust.

BAKALARZEWO Bialystok dist., Poland. In the late 19th cent. B. became a resort and this provided many of its Jews with new livelihoods. Large numbers fled during WWI, leaving 141 out of a total pop. of 705 in 1921. Expelled by the Germans in Oct. 1939, almost all perished in the Holocaust.

BAKHCHISARAY Crimea, Russia, today Ukraine. Krimchaks lived in Chufat-Kale (part of new B.) in the early 13th cent. A Karaite printing press was founded in 1734 and in 1793–94 the J. pop. was 1,162. The figure dropped to 210 (total 12,959) in 1897 and remained at a stable level throughout the Soviet period (228 in 1939). The Germans arrived on 2 Nov. 1941. On 13 Dec., *Sonderkommando 11a* troops murdered about 90 Jews. In the first half of July 1943, the Nazis murdered over 1,000, some from B. but most from the surrounding area.

BAKHMACH Chernigov dist., Ukraine. B. developed as a railroad junction in the 1860s and 1870s and had a J. pop. of 491 in 1897. Pogroms were staged in 1905 and in Sept. 1919. In 1939, the Jews numbered 295 (total 10,226). The Germans arrived on 10 Sept. 1941 after most of the Jews had fled. Six remaining families were murdered.

BAKSZTY Nowogrodek dist., Poland, today Belarus. The J. pop. was 172 in 1897 (total 1,461), declining to 55 in the 1920s. The Germans transferred most to the Iwie ghetto where they were murdered on 12 May 1942.

BAKTALORANTHAZA Szabolcs dist., Hungary. Jews were present by the early 18th cent. and numbered 211 in 1930. In spring 1944, they were expelled to the Kisvarda ghetto and then deported to Auschwitz on 25–27 June.

BALABANOVKA Vinnitsa dist., Ukraine. About ten Jews were present in the latter half of the 18th cent. In 1897, they numbered 493 (total 3,089) and 124 in 1926. The Nazis murdered 38 by Dec. 1942.

BALACEANA Bukovina, Rumania. Jews settled in the late 19th cent. The J. pop. in 1930 was 134. Zionist activity took place in the interwar period. In Jan. 1941, the J. pop. left for Suceava and then was deported to Transnistria. Few survived.

BALAKLAVA Crimea, Russia, today Ukraine. A council of Russian Zionists convened here on 18–22 Sept. 1919 with the participation of Meir Dizengoff, future mayor of Tel Aviv. In 1939, the J. pop. was 104 (total 5,148). The Germans occupied B. on 30 Nov. 1941, murdering in Dec. those Jews who had neither fled nor been evacuated. In all, they murdered 171 people in the area; most were Jews.

BALASSAGYARMAT Nograd dist., Hungary. Jews were present in the late 17th cent. The J. pop. was 2,033 (32% of the total) in 1869 and 2,013 in 1930. At the turn of the cent., Jews opened factories and banks in an atmosphere of general prosperity. A J. school had 286 students in 1885 but was opposed by the Orthodox because the language of instruction was Hungarian. They established a *talmud torah* and a yeshiva which enjoyed a distinguished reputation. R. Meir Eisenstadt (Maharam Esh; d. 1892) was an outstanding Torah scholar and R. Aharon David Deutsch, who served in 1851–78, was a leader of the Orthodox movement in Hungary. In 1942, young Jews were drafted into labor battalions and sent to the Ukraine where many perished. At the end of May 1944, 2,100 Jews were sent to Nyires ghetto and deported from 12–14 June to Auschwitz. The postwar community of 182 survivors gradually vanished through emigration.

BALATONBOGLAR Somogy dist., Hungary. Jews settled in the mid-18th cent. and became active in the burgeoning lakeside resort trade, numbering 240 in 1880. In 1890, a synagogue and J. school were inaugurated. In 1930, the Jews numbered 213. They were deported to Auschwitz via Kaposvar on 6 July 1944.

BALATONFURED Zala dist., Hungary. Jews are first mentioned in 1746. A synagogue was erected in 1840. The first licensed J. doctor in Hungary, Yosef Osztreicher (1786–1830), came from B. and estab-

lished a convalescent home here that attracted convalescents from all over the country. The Jews numbered 117 in 1880 and 143 in 1930. The young were seized for forced labor in 1942, most perishing. On 16 May 1944, 130 were taken to the Tapolca ghetto, from where they were sent to Auschwitz via Zalaegerszeg on 6 July.

BALATONSZEMES Somogy dist., Hungary. Jews arrived in the 18th cent. The Neologist community numbered 54 in 1930. On 1–2 July 1944, they were deported to Auschwitz via Kaposvar.

BALBIERISKIS (Yid. Balbirishok) Marijampole dist., Lithuania. The J. community began in the mid-17th cent. The J. pop. in 1897 was 925 (45% of the total). By 1923 the J. pop. had fallen to 507, economic conditions caused further emigration, and by 1940 the J. pop. was about 350. Most supported Zionist parties. After the German invasion in June 1941, local Lithuanians rounded up J. males, beat them, and sent them to forced labor. They were all forced to walk to Prienai, where they were murdered on 27 Aug. The women and children were taken to Marijampole and murdered on 1 Sept. 1941.

BALBRONN Bas-Rhin dist., France. The J. community numbered 170 members in 1784 and 184 in 1805. The local synagogue was inaugurated in 1895. By 1936, the community consisted of 62 members. During WWII, all were expelled from their homes with the rest of the Jews from Alsace-Lorraine, to the south of France. Twelve were deported.

BALIGROD Lwow dist., Poland. The first Jews arrived from Lesko and Sanok in the late 18th cent. The community led a typical village life under hasidic dominance. Tradesmen set up their stalls and carts on market and fair days, some ran inns, and a few wealthy merchants dealt in wine and lumber. In 1900 the J.

Class of 1922, first graduates of the Hebrew elementary school in Balbieriskis, Lithuania

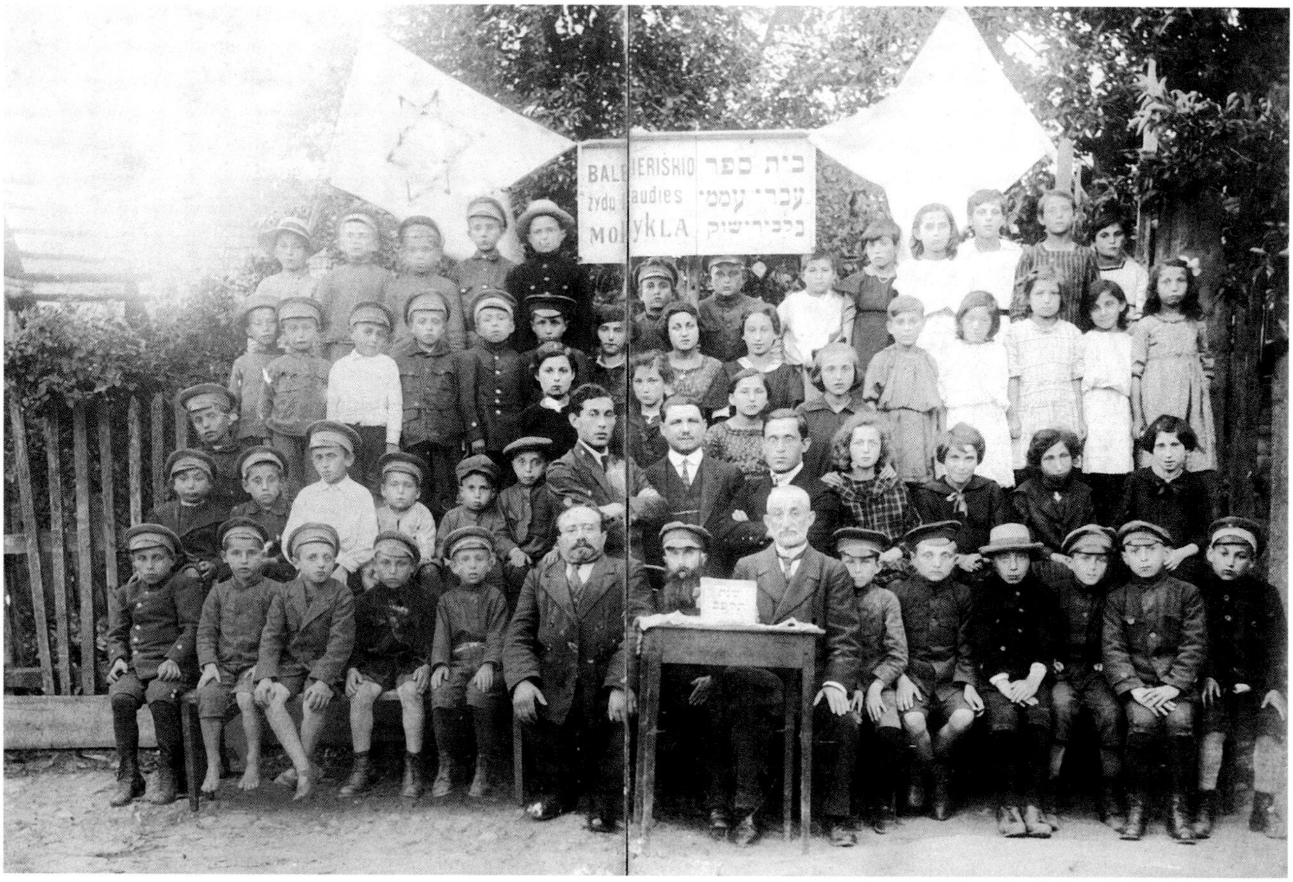
BAL IERIŠKIO
žydu audies
MO YKLA
בית ספר
עברי עממי
בלבירישוק

pop. stood at 988 (61%), but dropped to 515 in 1921 after increasing emigration and the severe hardship of WWI. Between the World Wars the Zionists exercised a dominant influence. The community was expelled by the Germans to the Zaslawie concentration camp in the summer of 1942 and later sent to the Belzec death camp.

BALKANY Szabolcs dist., Hungary. Jews arrived in the early 18th cent, building a synagogue in 1840 and also operating a J. school and yeshiva. Most were merchants and artisans. The J. pop. stood at 590 in 1840 and 417 in 1941. On 14 April 1944, the Jews were concentrated in Nyiregyhaza and later dispersed by the Germans among abandoned farms before deportation to Auschwitz on 17 May 1944. The community was reestablished but local residents drove the Jews out in 1956.

BALLIN Kamenets-Podolski dist., Ukraine. Jews settled in the 18th cent., dwindling in number after Haidamak attacks. In 1897, the J. pop. was 357 (22% of the total). A J. kolkhoz was active between the World Wars. The Germans captured B. on 10 July 1941, executing 150 Jews outside the town in the fall. In Sept. 1942, 250 Jews were executed and the artisans were sent to Kamenets-Podolski and later killed.

BALMAZUJVAROS Hajdu dist., Hungary. Jews were present by 1784. A synagogue was built in 1850, a J. school opened in 1878, and a yeshiva in 1896. The J. pop. reached a peak of 508 (4.3% of the total) in 1900. After WWI, the Jews suffered from antisemitic incidents and the Mizrachi movement attracted many members until Zionism was declared anti-religious by the community heads at the urging of the town rabbi. In WWII, the men were subjected to forced labor. After the Germans arrived in May 1944, they dispatched the remaining 388 Jews of B. to Austria and Auschwitz (between 25–28 June). The postwar community of 86 survivors dispersed by 1956.

BALNINKAI (Yid. Balnik) Ukmerge dist., Lithuania. The J. community was established at the end of the 18th cent. The J. pop. in 1897 was 255 (44% of the total) and dropped to 142 in 1933. Lithuanian nationalists took control of B. after the German invasion

and murdered all of B.'s Jews in the Pivonija forest on 5 Sept. 1941.

BALTA Moldavia, today Ukraine. J. settlement commenced in the early 16th cent., when the city was located on the border between Poland and the Ottoman Empire. In 1768, the Jews were victimized in Haidamak pogroms. In 1791, the city was annexed to the Russian Empire. New and violent pogroms in 1882 undermined J. economic life and further pogroms were staged in 1905 and in 1919 during the civil war, with Jews fleeing to Odessa as B. changed hands between the Bolsheviks and the Petlyura gangs. In the Soviet period, the J. pop. dropped from 13,235 (total 23,363) in 1897 to 9,116 in 1926 and 4,711 in 1939. A J. kolkhoz operated in the 1930s. German and Rumanian forces captured B. on 5 Aug. 1941. On 8 Aug., the Germans murdered 200 Jews on the outskirts of the city, mostly refugees from Bessarabia. A ghetto under a *Judenrat* was established for nearly 4,000 Jews, including 1,500 from B. In winter 1941, over 1,000 Jews were expelled to Voytovka and Nikolayev, most dying of starvation or being murdered. Two orphanages were maintained in the ghetto. Assistance was received from Bucharest and in 1944 most of the children were brought to Rumania. A total of 1,795 Jews survived the war in the ghetto.

BALTI (Beltsy) Bessarabia, Rumania, today Republic of Moldova. Jews were among the founders of B. in the late 18th cent. The J. pop. in 1897 was 10,348 (56% of the total). In 1918 a J. elementary school and high schools for boys and girls were opened with an attendance of 1,200 pupils. Zionist activity began in the early 20th cent. and branches of most Zionist organizations and youth movements were active. Over 100 youth were trained at two Hehalutz training farms here. The only Hebrew periodical in Bessarabia, *Shurot*, was published during 1935–38, dealing with literature and education. J. party representatives gained 14 seats on the municipal council in 1929 and ten in 1933. A Jew was appointed deputy mayor on both occasions. In 1930, under the Goga-Cuza regime, antisemitic ruffians physically abused Jews, J. schools were closed, and J. officials dismissed from government service. The J. pop. in 1930 was 14,229 (60% of the total). When the Russians took B. on 28 July 1940, J. community institutions were

closed. Zionist and communal leaders were expelled to Siberia. In June 1941 Jews were killed during the German air raids and houses were wrecked. As Jews fled to nearby village, their goods were stolen by peasants and German and Rumanian soldiers and they were beaten and the women raped. B. Jews were forced to return and were incarcerated in two camps. In July 1941, 814 Jews were sent to forced labor, the majority of whom were deported to Transnistria. On 30 Aug., the remaining 3,000 Jews were transferred to Marculesti and the survivors deported to Transnistria. A sizable J. community was reestablished after the war and numbered 3,000 in 1996.

BALTINAVA Latgale dist., Latvia. Jews began to settle in the late 19th cent. Half their homes were destroyed in WWI. Between the World Wars most Jews engaged in trade and operated small auxiliary farms. The Zionists were active. In 1935, the J. pop. stood at 164 (total 478). The Germans took the town in early July 1941. Over 40 Jews were executed that same month and the able-bodied put to forced labor on peasant farms. All were murdered in the Baltnice forest on 11 Aug. 1941.

Hevra Kaddisha Book of Regulations, Bamberg, Germany, 1778

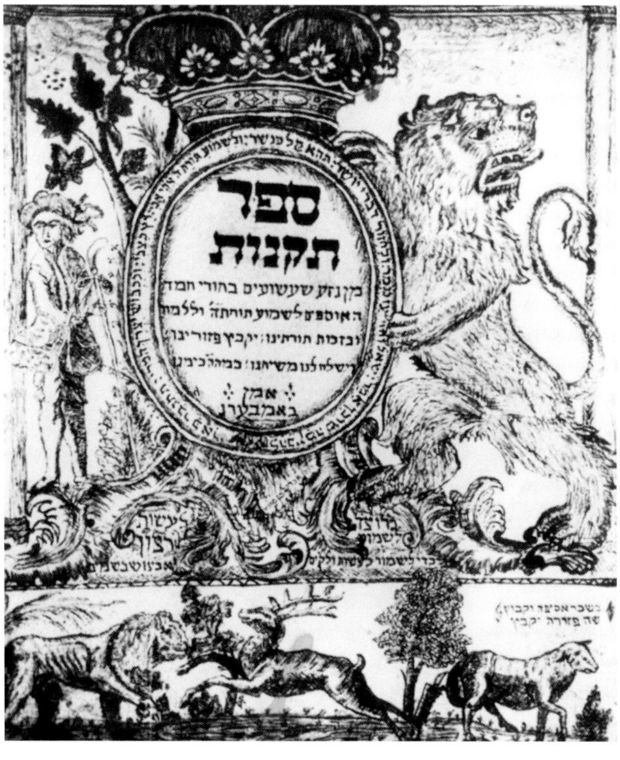
ספר
תקנות

BALVI Latgale dist., Latvia. Jews from the nearby village of Werfelovo settled in the newly founded town in the early 20th cent. and numbered 487 (half the pop.) in 1925. Between the World Wars most Jews owned stores or engaged in wholesale trade (flax and lumber). The center of community life was its single wooden synagogue and the prevailing atmosphere was pro-Zionist, with the pioneer movements active. The J. pop. in 1935 was 379. Under Soviet rule (1940–41), J. commercial and public life was curtailed. The Germans entered the town in July 1941 and immediately set up a ghetto and subjected the Jews to forced labor and random killing. On 9 Aug. all were executed outside the town together with a few hundred J. refugees from Riga and Lithuania. A total of 362 of B.'s Jews perished in WWII.

BAMBERG (in J. sources, Babenberk, Bonfir) Upper Franconia, Germany. Jews were present in the 11th cent. under the protection of the bishop. In 1096, during the First Crusade, they were forcibly converted, though afterwards allowed to return to their faith. The Jews lived in a special quarter (*Vicus Judaeorum*) with a synagogue, wedding hall, and other facilities and engaged mainly in moneylending. The first known rabbi was Shemuel b. Barukh (about 1220), one of Germany's most important tosafists and founder of a well-known yeshiva. The Jews were persecuted throughout the 13th and 14th cent. with 135 murdered in the Rindfleisch massacres of 1298 and the J. quarter destroyed in the Black Death persecutions of 1348–49. Survivors renewed the community but were again subjected to persecution in the 15th cent. and finally expelled in 1478, finding shelter in neighboring villages. R. Moshe Mintz, one of the most influential talmudists of his time, was the community's last rabbi for 200 years. In 1499, refugees from the Nuremberg expulsion began to arrive in B., joined by others in the 16th cent. In 1561 a synagogue was dedicated. By the end of the 17th cent. the community had expanded to 24 families, engaging now in some trade in addition to moneylending, despite severe restrictions. In 1699, anti-J. riots spread from B. to 24 other settlements in the area over false charges of J. grain sales abroad producing famine. In B. violence was averted when a Jew poured down sacks of plums on the mob from a rooftop to show that the Jews were not hoarding grain (it turned out that the bishop was the culprit); the anniversary of

this deliverance was commemorated thereafter in a local J. "plum fast." In the second half of the 18th cent., frequent wars brought to the fore a number of Court Jews as army contractors and bankers, the most prominent of whom was Shemuel Seligmann Hesslein. In 1803, B. was annexed to Bavaria and the Jews came under the protection of Duke Maximilian Joseph. In 1806 the state rabbinate was dissolved and in 1813 the "Jew decree" restricted J. settlement after the J. pop. stood at 287 (total 18,143). A J. public school was opened in 1805 (closing in 1821) and a *talmud torah* in 1823. In 1825 R. Shimon Rosenfeld became rabbi of the community, the first in Bavaria to deliver his sermons in German. A new cemetery was consecrated in 1851. In the second half of the 19th cent. the community reached its peak growth, numbering 1,269 in 1880. A new synagogue was dedicated in 1910. In the 1920s the Jews suffered from antisemitic agitation and violence, promoted by the budding Nazi party. Nonetheless the community was one of the most economically important in Germany. The Wassermann bank was among the leading financial institutions in the country. Oskar Wassermann (1869–1934) was a patron of J. learning and president of Germany's Keren Hayesod while August von Wassermann (1866–1925) was an outstanding bacteriologist, devising the well-known test for syphilis. Jews were also pioneers in local industry, traded in cattle and horses, and operated a local branch of the Tietz department store. Many national organizations, like the Zionist Organization and the Central Union (C.V.), were represented in B. and the community itself operated extensive welfare services. In 1933 the J. pop. stood at 812 (total 54,161).

With the Nazi rise to power in 1933 a period of severe persecution commenced. Three Jews were murdered at the Dachau concentration camp in 1933. In 1934, J. municipal workers and newspaper employees were fired, lawyers were banned from appearing in court, and doctors from treating non-J. patients. The economic boycott was enforced against J. stores and factories, which underwent a process of "Aryanization." In 1936, J. students were expelled from the public schools and in 1938 Jews were banned from various public places. Throughout the period the community intensified its cultural and social services. The J. Cultural Association (Juedischer Kulturbund) put on concerts and other performances and Zionist youth were prepared for *aliya*. Between 1933–41,

443 Jews emigrated from Germany, including 164 to the U.S., 77 to England, and 61 to Palestine. Another 66 left for other German cities, including 21 for Berlin. On *Kristallnacht* (9–10 Nov. 1938) the Great Synagogue was burned to the ground, and with it nearly 40 Torah scrolls. The old synagogue and community center were vandalized along with numerous J. homes. The chairman of the community council, Willy Lessing, was mercilessly beaten and died two months later. In 1939 the Jews were evicted from their homes and placed under a curfew. In 1941 they were subjected to arduous forced labor, the old as well as the very young. In Nov. 300 Jews remained in B. Of these, 106 were deported to the Riga ghetto via Nuremberg on 29 Nov., 105 were deported to Izbica (in the Lublin dist. of Poland) via Nuremberg on 25 April 1942, and many of the others were sent to the Theresienstadt ghetto and Auschwitz through Feb. 1943. After the War, B. became one of the three largest Displaced Persons centers in Bavaria, housing over 14,000 Jews in 37 camps in 1947.

BANHIDA   Komarom dist., Hungary. Jews settled in the late 18th cent. and numbered 22 in 1869 and 69 in 1941. They were deported to Auschwitz on 16 June 1944.

BANILA PE CEREMUS   (Ger., Rus. Banila) Bukovina, Rumania. Jews first settled in the late 19th cent. The J. pop. in 1930 was 517. In June 1941, Rumanians and Germans murdered 263 Jews. The remainder were deported to Transnistria.

BANILA PE SIRET   Bukovina, Rumania, today Ukraine. Jews first settled in the early 19th cent. The J. pop. in 1930 was 687. In July 1941, 15 Jews were murdered by the local pop. and the remainder were deported to Transnistria. About 50-60 returned after the war.

BANJA LUKA   Bosnia-Hercegovina, Yugoslavia, today Republic of Bosnia. Sephardi Jews first settled in the early 18th cent. and Ashkenazim from 1878. Many professionals contributed to the town's economy. In 1921 there were 484 Jews (total 18,000) and 383 in 1940. There was considerable Zionist activity between the World Wars. Most were killed by armed members of the Ustase fascist organization in summer 1941.

BANOVCE (Hung. Banoc) Slovakia, Czechoslovakia, today Republic of Slovakia. Jews probably settled in the 17th cent. Under the protection of Count Illeshazy the community became the second largest in the dist. after Trencin with a pop. of 259 in 1787 and 395 in 1818. A synagogue was erected in the 1770s and one of the first J. schools in the dist., combining religious and secular studies, was operating by 1784. Most Jews at the time were peddlers and shopkeepers. In 1848, Jews successfully warded off attacks in peasant riots. A new synagogue was built in 1862 as the J. pop. reached a level of about 500 (nearly 20% of the total), where it remained until WWII. R. Moshe Reich served the community from 1910 until 1942 and was one of the leaders of Agudat Israel in Czechoslovakia. Jews served on the local council before and after WWI and the Zionists were active from the late 19th cent. Hashomer Hatzair founded a branch in 1923 and Bnei Akiva operated a pioneer training farm in the 1930s. Jews owned most of the businesses in the town, dealing especially in textiles and farm produce, while about 30 were artisans. In 1938, under Slovakian

rule, 46 Jews holding Hungarian citizenship were expelled from B. From 1940 Jews were seized for forced labor and in 1941 they were pushed out of their businesses. About 50 young J. men were deported to the Majdanek concentration camp on 27 March 1942 and 46 young women were dispatched to Auschwitz on 1 April. Families were sent to the death camps in April–June. In all, 387 Jews were deported in 1942. Of the 110 who remained, the Germans murdered 40 on 3 Sept. 1944 after retaking the town from the partisans who held it for a week. Dozens more were executed beside a mass grave in the fall.

BANSKA BYSTRICA (Hung. Besztercebanya) Slovakia, Czechoslovakia, today Republic of Slovakia. Jews arrived c. 1855, establishing an independent community in 1862. At the synagogue erected in 1867, prayers were accompanied by a female choir and the congregation became Neologist after the split of 1869. A private J. school was started in 1866. The Zionist society founded in 1897 was one of the first in Hungary. The J. pop. rose from 247 in 1869 to

Opening ceremony of Second Maccabiah Games, Banska Bystrica, Czechoslovakia, 1936

561 in 1880 and 1,025 (total 9,264) in 1900. In the 1920s, dozens of J. families arriving from Radvan and environs formed an Orthodox congregation. The joint school was attended by 100 children. The Zionists were active from 1922 and in the 1930s, Hashomer Hatzair ran a training program geared toward *aliya* to Palestine. Relations with the local pop. were generally satisfactory and Jews were active in public affairs. They owned 115 stores and 32 workshops as well as a number of factories, including one of the biggest furniture factories in Czechoslovakia. In 1940, the J. pop. was 1,327. In 1941, a government decree closed down 181 J. businesses and in early 1942, 136 J. men were seized for forced labor. Deportations began on 24 March 1942, when 78 young Jews were sent to the Majdanek concentration camp via Zilina. On 3 April, 83 girls were deported to Auschwitz. Subsequently hundreds of families from B. and its environs were transported to concentration camps and ghettoes in the Lublin area. About 400 Jews deemed economically useful remained behind. Thousands of J. refugees began to arrive after the Slovakian national uprising in Aug. 1944. The Germans rounded up about 1,000 Jews and murdered most near the village of Kremnicka, including J. paratroopers from Palestine like the locally born Haviva Reik. Dozens of local residents helped the Jews and Yad Vashem subsequently honored them as Righteous among the Nations. A new community was established after the war, numbering 296 in 1946 and about 50 in 1990.

BANSKA STIAVNICA (Hung. Selmecbanya) Slovakia, Czechoslovakia, today Republic of Slovakia. Jews are mentioned in 1367, probably employed as mintmasters. The modern community began about 1867, numbering 30 families in 1879 and reaching a peak of 527 Jews (total 16,376) in 1900. A J. elementary school was opened in 1887 and a fine synagogue in the neoclassical style was built in 1892. Jews pioneered local industry (wood, textiles, shoes) and many belonged to the merchant and professional class. In late 1918, demobilized J. soldiers fought off local rioters. Most of the young belonged to Zionist groups like Hashomer Hatzair and Maccabi Hatzair. In 1940, the J. pop. was 404. The creation of the Slovakian state in March 1939 was accompanied by the persecution of the Jews. J. children were expelled from public schools and J. businessmen were forced to liquidate their businesses. Thirty-seven young men

and 23 young women were deported to the Majdanek concentration camp and Auschwitz, respectively, in March and April 1942 and dozens of J. families were divided between the Majdanek concentration camp and the Sobibor death camp in June. A hundred Jews were left behind, joined by refugees during the Slovakian national uprising in fall 1944. Some joined the rebels while most survived hiding out in the forests and nearby villages.

BAR Vinnitsa dist., Ukraine. Jews settled in the 16th cent. In 1648 Chmielnicki's troops killed 2,000 Jews who, together with the Poles, were defending the local fortress. The J. pop. was 547 in 1787 and 5,773 in 1897. The community maintained a synagogue and 17 prayer houses. Most Jews were Hasidim. In 1918, the Petlyura gangs murdered 20 Jews and pillaged J. property. In the Soviet period, many Jews worked in factories (sugar, clothing, tractors, and a powerhouse). A J. kolkhoz was started in 1929 and a Yiddish school was also opened. In 1939, the J. pop. was 3,869. The Germans occupied B. on 16 July 1941. A ghetto was set up in late July and on 19 Aug., 2,000 Jews were murdered. The children were thrown into pits while still alive.

BAR-LE-DUC Meuse dist., France. The J. presence dates from the 12th cent. but was interrupted by expulsions, the last occurring in 1477. In 1789, the community was renewed. It was affiliated from 1808 to the consistory of Nancy and administered by the rabbinate of Verdun. The local synagogue was inaugurated in 1872. In 1892, the J. pop. numbered 170. During WWII, there was a regional camp in B. with 263 internees. Eighteen Jews living in B. were deported or shot. In 1968, there were 40 Jews in B.

BARA Moldavia dist., Rumania. A flourishing J. community existed here before 1618, declined, and was revived in the mid-19th cent. The J. pop. in 1899 was 308. After the outbreak of WWII, the Jews were expelled to Roman.

BARABAS Bereg dist., Hungary. Jews are mentioned in 1851 and numbered 88 in 1930. A synagogue was established in 1910. All were deported to Auschwitz at the beginning of July 1944.

BARAN Vitebsk dist., Belorussia. In 1929, 17 J.

families worked on a kolkhoz and in 1939 the J. pop. was 81 (total 1,589). The Germans arrived on 16 July 1941. In Sept. all the Jews were brought to two houses and held there for months. On 8 April 1942 about 45 were murdered.

BARAND Bihar dist., Hungary. Jews settled in the late 19th cent. and in 1930 numbered 54, mostly merchants and artisans. They were deported to Auschwitz via Nagyvarad at the end of May 1944.

BARANOVKA Zhitomir dist., Ukraine. Jews were present in the 17th cent. and in the course of the 19th cent. reached a pop. of 1,990 to form a majority in the town. Russian-language J. elementary schools for boys and girls were opened in the early 20th cent. In the civil war (1918–21) Jews escaped a pogrom at the hands of the Petlyura gangs by paying a tribute. In the late 1920s, under the Soviets, there were 208 J. laborers, 162 artisans, 81 tradesmen, and 126 "classless" Jews. In 1939, the J. pop. was 1,447 (total 6,312). The Germans captured the town on 10

July 1941, confining the Jews in a ghetto consisting of a few small houses. On 19 July, they murdered 74 J. males in the town center and a few weeks later executed a few hundred more outside the town. Another 180 were murdered on 19 Aug. Jews were murdered individually or in small groups until Jan. 1942. On 6 Jan. 1942, Jews from the villages in the area were brought to B. and 595 were murdered on the Novograd–Vohlinsk road.

BARANOW (I) Lwow dist., Poland. Jews are mentioned from the 14th cent. but the community apparently ceased to exist with the upheavals of the mid-17th cent. After renewal in the 18th cent., the J. pop. grew to 1,491 (total 2,371) in 1890, at which time all trade was in J. hands as well as all crafts with the exception of shoemaking. The coming of the railroad in the 1890s cut into the J. grain trade and two great fires, in 1890 and 1896, left many Jews homeless and without a source of income, leading to increased emigration. Fleeing in WWI in the face of the advancing Russians, the Jews returned in 1915 to find their homes

Mizrachi delegates from Baranow, Poland, 1920

munity grew from 181 in 1835 to 1,011 (total 5,307) in 1869 after restrictions were lifted. Jews owned 220 stores and business establishments and another 89 were artisans. Jews also contributed to the development of the town as a health resort. B. was a center of Hasidism and the community maintained a *heder, talmud torah*, and yeshiva. The Zionist movement became active in the late 19th cent. Though many left during WWI, the J. pop. reached 2,119 in 1919 with 40 surrounding settlements under the auspices of the local rabbinate. Children attended public schools. In 1935, ten of 22 municipal council members were Jews. A branch of Mizrachi was founded in 1921 with the General Zionists, Po'alei Zion, and WIZO also active along with such youth movements as Hashomer Hatzair, Bnai Akiva, and Betar. Among the Orthodox, Agudat Israel was influential, running its Beth Jacob movement for girls. In 1940, the J. pop. was 2,441. In the Slovakian state created in March 1939, Jews were pushed out of their businesses and in Sept. 1940, 200 were sent to labor camps. Many J. refugees also arrived in the town from the nearby Polish ghettoes. About 400 Jews were deported to Auschwitz via Zilina on 18 April 1942. Jews from the surrounding settlements were then concentrated in the town and deported together with local Jews to the Lublin area: 261 to the Pulawy ghetto on 15 May; 140 to Opole on 16 May; 1,100 to Nalenczow on 17 May; and hundreds more to Rejowiec on 24 May. In all, 3,280 Jews were deported from the county in 1942 and 2,100 from B. Of the few hundred Jews spared as essential workers, dozens were hunted down and deported or executed in Slovakia in Sept. 1944. After the war, a community of 300 was reestablished (200 in 1949).

BARKASOVO (Hung. Barkaszo) Carpatho-Russia, Czechoslovakia, today Ukraine. Jews probably arrived in the mid-19th cent. and numbered 124 (total 978) in 1880. Their pop. rose to 151 in 1921, with some engaging in agriculture, and then dropped to 136 in 1941 after the Hungarian occupation of Nov. 1938. All were deported to Auschwitz in mid-May 1944.

BARLAD Moldavia dist., Rumania. In 1762 a Street of J. Merchants existed in B. In 1862, R. Yitzhak Taubs was officially recognized by Prince Cuza as community rabbi, and was the first to give sermons in Rumanian. He wrote several works on the B. J. community which were translated into a number of languages.

From 1899 (when the J. pop. was 5,883, 24% of the total) to 1902, 600 Jews emigrated. In 1907 an organization set up by teachers, priests, and politicians incited students to antisemitic activities. Zionist activity began in the 1890s. In 1918, Rumanian citizenship was granted to 235 Jews, and in 1919 to a further 736. In Nov. 1940, the Iron Guard arrested all J. men, who were sent to forced labor. On the outbreak of the Soviet-Rumanian war, Jews from the surrounding district were brought to B. J. pupils were expelled from the government high school and the community set up its own facility. The needy increased from 200 in 1940 to 600 in 1943. The community took care of 167 orphans returned from Transnistria. After the war the 3,100-member (1947) J. community continued to function.

BARR Bas-Rhin dist., France. The J. community was established in the second half of the 19th cent. A synagogue was inaugurated in 1878. In 1936, the community consisted of 108 members. During WWII, the Jews were expelled from their homes and deported to the south of France. In 1950, the synagogue was renovated. The community numbered 46 members in 1965.

BARSANA (Hung. Barcanfalva; Yid. Birsanov) N. Transylvania dist., Rumania. Jews settled in the early 18th cent. The J. pop. in 1920 was 485 (14% of the total). In late April 1944 the Jews were transferred to the Viseul de Sus ghetto and then deported to Auschwitz. Sixty survivors returned after the war but soon left.

BARSINGHAUSEN Hanover, Germany. Established in 1843, the district community numbered 47 (2% of the total) in 1871. Affiliated with the Hanover rabbinate in 1901, it grew to 67 in 1913. It maintained a synagogue and an elementary school, with branches of the Central Union (C.V.) and J. War Veterans Association becoming active after WWI. From 1933, Jews displayed greater interest in Zionism. The synagogue's interior was destroyed on *Kristallnacht* (9–10 Nov. 1938). Seven Jews were arrested and deported to the Buchenwald concentration camp. At least 17 Jews died in the Holocaust.

BARSTYCIAI (Yid. Barshtitz) Mazeikiai dist., Lithuania. In 1923 the J. pop. was 87. All B.'s Jews were killed in the Holocaust.

BARTENSTEIN (Polish Bartoszyce) East Prussia, Germany, today Poland. The first evidence of a J. presence in B. dates from 1737. The J. pop. numbered 86 in 1880, declining to 60–65 in the Weimar years. The community established a cemetery (about 1820) and a synagogue (about 1857). By 1935, J. businesses were in decline due to boycott measures. Many Jews left and by May 1939 only 12 remained. Since there were only two Jews in B. by Oct. 1942, it may be assumed that those who failed to emigrate or were not protected by marriage to a non-J. partner were deported.

BARTININKAI (Yid. Bartinink) Vilkaviskis dist., Lithuania. The J. pop. in 1923 was 93 (24% of the total). All Jews were killed in the Holocaust.

BARYSZ Tarnopol dist., Poland, today Ukraine. The J. community of a few hundred constituted 5–10% of the total J. pop. from the late 19th cent. on. The Jews were expelled to Buczacz by the Germans in Oct. 1942 and shared the fate of the local Jews.

BARYSZEVKA Kiev dist., Ukraine. Jews numbered 462 in 1897 and 134 (total 2,401) under the Soviets in 1939. The Germans captured B. on 17 Aug. 1941 and murdered the Jews shortly afterwards.

BASHTANKA Nikolaiev dist., Ukraine. A number of J. colonies and, from the 1930s, J. kolkhozes were established around B. In 1939, the J. pop. of B. was 61 (total 6,749) and of the surrounding region 1,730. Almost all were farmers. The Germans arrived in mid-Aug. 1941 and murdered the Jews, probably in Sept.

BASSUM Hanover, Germany. The community opened a synagogue in 1830 and numbered 32 (5% of the total) in 1861. By the time the Nazis came to power, the synagogue was no longer in use. On *Kristallnacht* (9–10 Nov. 1938), Jews were abused and three were arrested and deported to the Buchenwald concentration camp. All 26 Jews registered in B. in 1933 left by 1940, with 12 emigrating. Two joined the ill-fated voyage of the *St. Louis* in 1939. They were deported after their return and perished in the Holocaust.

BASTHEIM Lower Franconia, Germany. Jews numbered 50 in 1837 and steadily declined thereafter to 17 in 1933 (total pop. 537). Twelve left in 1937–39, four to the U.S. and four to France. The interior of the synagogue was destroyed in the rioting that accompanied the Sudetenland crisis of Sept. 1938. The last two Jews were deported in 1942.

BASTIA Corsica (France). Pascal Paoli, an 18th cent. Corsican patriot, invited 500 J. families to settle on the island to encourage and develop local commerce. Their integration was so thorough that no trace of J. origin is left today, except local family traditions. From WWI, Jews from Syria and Palestine established a small J. community and synagogue in B. In the 1970s, the total J. pop. of Corsica consisted of 300 Jews, including those living in Ajaccio, Corste, Ile Rousse, and Porto-Vecchio.

BATAKIAI (Yid. Batok) Taurage dist., Lithuania. Before WWI B.'s J. pop. was approximately 50 families, most of whom were expelled during the war. In 1940 there were approximately ten families. After the Germans entered B. on 22–23 June 1941, J. women and children from B. and surrounding villages were shot at a mass grave; the men had already been murdered.

BATARCI (Hung. Batarcs) N. Transylvania dist., Rumania. The community was founded mainly by the Leibi, Landau, and Soldan families from Galicia in the late 18th cent. The J. pop. in 1920 was 150 (10% of the total). In May 1944 the Jews were transferred to Halmeu and then to the Nagyszollos ghetto. In June 1944 they were deported to Auschwitz.

BATASZEK Tolna dist., Hungary. Jews are first mentioned in 1640. Until 1880, when their pop. reached 200, they were mainly employed in the wine industry. With its collapse, many left B. In 1930, the pop. was 122. After the arrival of the Germans on 19 March 1944, local Nazis and SS troops attacked and robbed the 100 remaining Jews, who were subsequently sent to the Bonyhad and Pecs ghettoes before deportation to Auschwitz on 3–4 July. Some women were sent to Stutthof and its sub-camps where many perished.

BATAYSK Rostov dist., Russia. Jews probably settled in the early 20th cent. In 1939, the J. pop. was 186 (total 49,614). After their arrival on 27 July

1942, the Germans murdered the few Jews who had neither fled nor been evacuated.

BATELOV Moravia, Czechoslovakia. Jews apparently settled in the 15th cent., reaching a pop. of 190 in 1846. In 1930, 31 remained (1.7% of the total). In May 1942, the Jews were deported to the Theresienstadt ghetto via Trebic. Subsequently half were sent to the Lublin dist. of Poland in the same month; others were dispatched to Treblinka in Oct.; and the rest to Auschwitz in 1943–44. Few survived.

BATIATYCZE Tarnopol dist., Poland, today Ukraine. The J. pop. in 1921 was 195. Its Jews were possibly expelled to Kamionka Strumilowa for liquidation in summer–early fall 1942.

BATOROVE KESY (Hung. Batorkeszi) Slovakia, Czechoslovakia, today Republic of Slovakia. Jews probably arrived in the 17th cent. An organized community was apparently formed in the 1760s, reaching a peak pop. of 324 in 1840 and extending its rabbinical jurisdiction to 20 nearby settlements. An impressive synagogue was built in the latter half of the 19th cent., with the Orthodox community maintaining a *heder*, *talmud torah*, *beit midrash*, and in different periods, a yeshiva in addition to a regular school. R. Yisrael (Izidor) Goldberger, who served as rabbi in a number of major Hungarian communities, was born in B. in 1876. A Zionist society operated from the 1920s. In 1941 the J. pop. was 100 (total 3,636). After the town was annexed to Hungary in Nov. 1938, the Jews were persecuted and in June 1944, after the arrival of the Germans, they were deported to Auschwitz.

BATOVO (Hung. Batyu) Carpatho-Russia, Czechoslovakia, today Ukraine. Jews probably arrived in the first half of the 19th cent. In 1880 their pop. was 59 (total 845). In 1921, under the Czechoslovakian Republic, it was 197 and in 1939, under the Hungarians, 130. The Hungarians occupied B. in Nov. 1938 and in 1941 drafted a number of Jews into labor battalions, assigning most to the eastern front, where some perished. The rest were deported to Auschwitz in mid-May 1944.

BATTENFELD Hesse–Nassau, Germany. Established around 1750, the J. community numbered 29 (about 6% of the total) in 1871–95, not including members in Battenberg (78 in 1861) and Rennerthausen. Affiliated with the district rabbinate of Marburg, it maintained a synagogue (dating from 1777) and an elementary school (1825–1925). The synagogue was burned down on *Kristallnacht* (9–10 Nov. 1938), but Jews still remained in B. and Battenberg at the outbreak of WWII; 12 perished in the Holocaust.

BATTONYA Csanad dist., Hungary. Jews are believed to have settled in the late 18th cent., reaching a peak pop. of 256 in 1900 (2% of the total), which dropped to 152 in 1930 as many moved to the larger cities. Jews owned a brickyard, two carpet factories, and a flour mill. A synagogue was built in 1896. Mizrachi was active in the 1930s. On 26 June 1944, 100 Jews were sent to Strasshof in Austria; 80 survived the war. Another 22 were deported to Auschwitz.

BATURINO Smolensk dist., Russia. Near Ilino the Germans murdered 80 Jews from B. and the neighboring villages in fall 1941.

BAUMBACH Hesse–Nassau, Germany. The community, which had a synagogue (1830) and an elementary school (1860–1934), numbered 79 (14% of the total) in 1895. The synagogue was burned down on *Kristallnacht* (9–10 Nov. 1938). Thirteen of the 39 Jews (1933) emigrated; at least 11 others perished in the Holocaust.

BAUMHOLDER Rhineland, Germany. Jews settled in the late 17th cent. and reached a peak pop. of 42 (total 1,707) in 1871. They engaged in peddling and cattle trading. At the turn of the 19th cent., community life all but ceased. In the Nazi era, Jews began to leave the town. Eleven perished in the Holocaust.

BAUSENDORF Rhineland, Germany. Fourteen Jews lived in B. at the start of the 19th cent.; 27 in 1843; and 46 (total 585) in 1895. In 1932, the J. pop. was 33. The community maintained a synagogue and a cemetery (opened in the late 19th cent.). By June 1939, there were no Jews in the village. Eleven emigrated to the Americas, a few died, and the rest moved to other places in Germany. The cemetery was desecrated in the Nazi period and again in 1950.

BAUSKA Zemgale (Courland) dist., Latvia. Lithuanian Jews first settled in the Sloboda suburb of B.

across the Lielupe River in the late 18th cent. and were only permitted to settle in the town proper under Russian rule, establishing an organized community by around 1820. The J. settlement grew rapidly in the 19th cent., set back only by the resettlement of 692 Jews in the Kherson province of S. Russia in 1820 and a cholera epidemic in 1848. It reached a peak pop. of 3,631 (total 6,113) in 1881. J. merchants were prominent in the important flax trade with Germany but many Jews were also poor. Among the town's many illustrious rabbis were Mordekhai Eliasberg, an early Hovevei Zion leader, and Avraham Yitzhak Kook, one of the central figures of religious Zionism and a future chief rabbi of Palestine. The Hasidim gained a foothold in B. in 1856, setting up their own prayer house, as did Jews from Lithuania settling illegally late in the cent. and maintaining a more or less independent community life. Throughout the period Zionist activity was marked by the support of Orthodox circles, including Habad Hasidim. In 1915 the Jews were expelled from B. by the Russians, returning in 1918 and then suffering at the hands of Latvian soldiers as the regimes changed. Only 604 Jews remained in 1920 (total pop. 2,902) but by 1925 there were 919. Between the World Wars the Jews still claimed a large share of the town's trade, owning half of its larger stores and backed by an active cooperative bank. Soviet rule (1940–41) saw the nationalization of all J. businesses and the phasing out of J. public life. The Germans captured the town on 26 June 1941. On 3 Aug., 50 Jews were executed by Latvian auxiliary police after being made to dig their own graves. B. also became the only place in Latvia where J. men are known to have been sterilized. On 30 Sept. 1941 the community was liquidated when about 800 Jews were murdered at the site of the previous execution.

BAUTZEN   Saxony, Germany. There is evidence of Jews in B. at the end of the 13th, 14th, and 15th cents. A permanent settlement began in the 19th cent. and in 1890 there were 49 Jews in B. The community established a prayer room and a cemetery. When the Nazis came to power in 1933, the community numbered 104 individuals; 73 were living in the town itself. In the wake of the boycott of 1 April 1933, J. businesses declined. By 1938, the community numbered 45. On *Kristallnacht* (9–10 Nov. 1938), prayer room furnishings were burned and businesses and homes

wrecked. The Jews were dragged from their houses and marched through the streets, cursed and abused by the pop. The male Jews were taken to the Buchenwald concentration camp. By 1939, 13 Jews had managed to emigrate. With the exception of two or three individuals married to non-Jews, the remaining Jews were deported to the east. Only one survived.

BAYONNE   Basses-Pyrenees dist., France. In the beginning of the 16th cent. Marranos from Spain and Portugal began to settle in the suburb of Saint-Esprit. By 1550, the central authorities granted these "New Christians" rights of residence. In the middle of the 17th cent. a community, called the Dispersed of Judah (*Nefutzot Yehuda*) was organized. A cemetery was established in 1660 in the Saint Etienne section of Saint-Esprit. From 1723, Judaism was observed openly. Comprising only 700 members at the beginning of the 18th cent., the community developed rapidly, numbering 3,500 in 1753. B. with its rabbinical court claimed jurisdiction over the small communities in the vicinity, including Biarritz, Saint-Jean de-Luz, Bidache, and Peyrehorade. The local Jews monopolized the import of salt and glue and helped to introduce the chocolate industry into France. They were among the first to establish trade connections with the French West Indies. In 1790, the Jews of B. were recognized as French citizens. At the height of its prosperity in the 19th cent., the community maintained seven synagogues. In 1844, the J. pop. numbered 1,293. By 1897 the community numbered only 865. Rene Cassin (1887–1976), Nobel Prize winner and president of the Alliance Israelite Universelle, was born in B. By 1926 the community numbered only 45 families. After the Franco-German armistice in June 1940, many refugees from Belgium and Luxembourg arrived in B. Since many were unable to get to Spain, the official police census of 15 March 1942 numbered 308 J. families as living in B. In April 1943, almost all Jews in B. and the surrounding district (about 300 Jews altogether) were forcibly evacuated, deported, and then murdered by the Germans. Many holy religious objects were hidden at that time in the Basque Museum and subsequently returned to the community after liberation. After the war, with the influx of North African Jews to France, the community of B. reestablished itself, numbering 700 in 1969. Its synagogue was restored and services are conducted according to Sephardi rites.

BAYREUTH Upper Franconia, Germany. Jews appeared in 1248 after receiving permanent residence rights from the Hohenzollern burgrave Friedrich III. The community was virtually destroyed in the Black Death persecutions of 1348–49 and renewed after receiving a letter of protection from Friedrich V. B. was also made the seat of the chief rabbi (*Hochmeister*) of the principality. Jews engaged mainly in moneylending and moneychanging and over the next two centuries were forced to remit debts and leave the city a number of times in the face of local pressure. They were finally expelled in 1564. The community was renewed in the mid-18th cent. by Court Jews facing similar threats of expulsion and various measures to limit the J. pop., which nonetheless grew to 79 families by 1771. A magnificent synagogue was consecrated in 1760 and a cemetery in 1787. Conditions improved after the annexation of the principality to Bavaria in 1810. In 1824 a J. public school was opened. The pop. increased to a peak of 530 (total 13,530) in 1837, declining to 261 in 1933. During the Nazi era the Jews suffered from the economic boycott and in 1936, all J. girls were expelled from the municipal high school. Thirty-nine Jews are known to have emigrated in this period, 25 to the U.S. In Nov. 1938, 120 Jews remained. On *Kristallnacht* (9–10 Nov. 1938) the synagogue was vandalized and J. stores and homes were looted. In late 1939, 80 Jews were evicted

Sinai, *weekly newspaper published in Bayreuth for religious Jews, Germany, 1846*

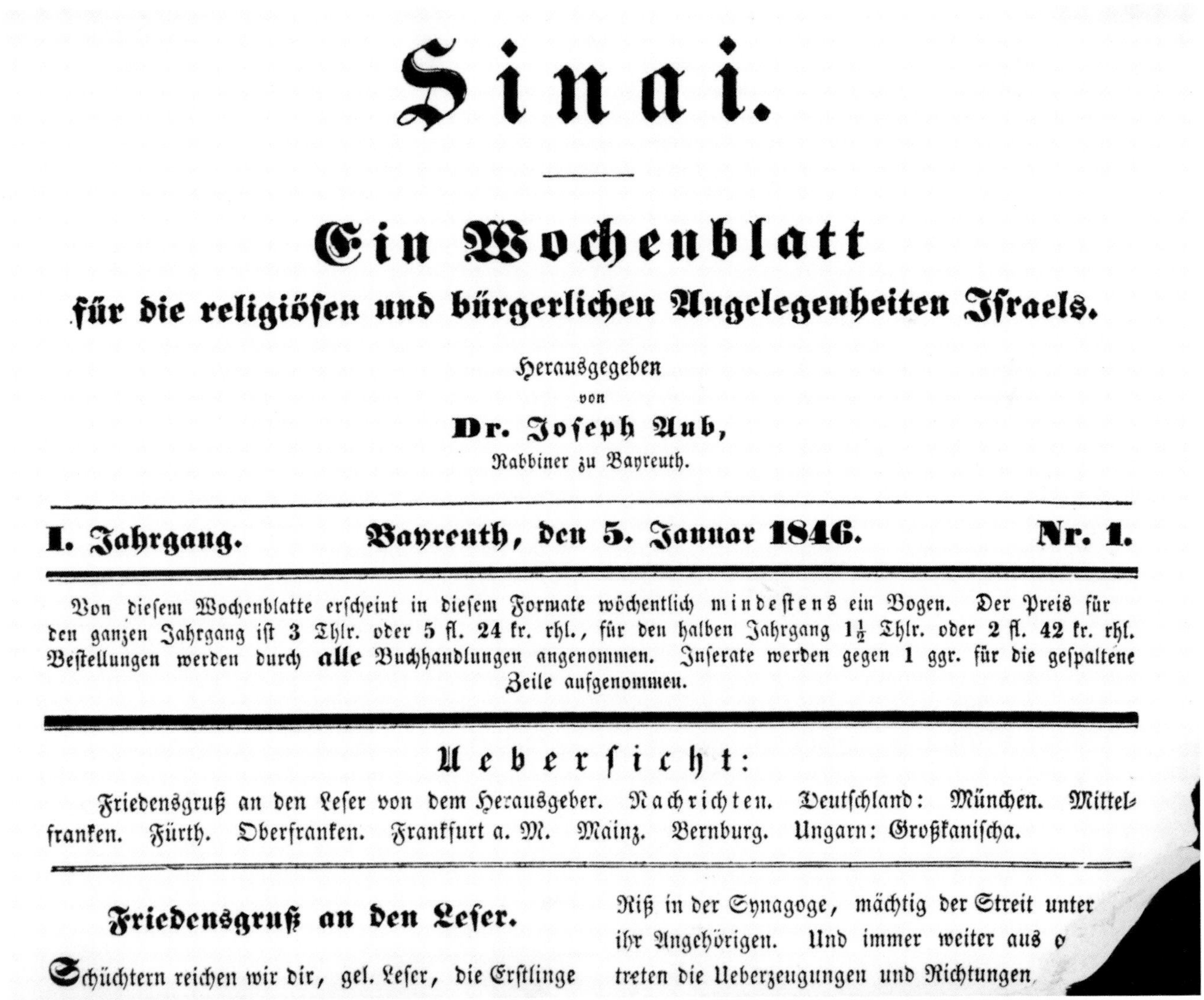

Sinai.

Ein Wochenblatt

für die religiösen und bürgerlichen Angelegenheiten Israels.

Herausgegeben
von
Dr. Joseph Aub,
Rabbiner zu Bayreuth.

I. Jahrgang. Bayreuth, den 5. Januar 1846. Nr. 1.

Von diesem Wochenblatte erscheint in diesem Formate wöchentlich mindestens ein Bogen. Der Preis für den ganzen Jahrgang ist 3 Thlr. oder 5 fl. 24 kr. rhl., für den halben Jahrgang 1½ Thlr. oder 2 fl. 42 kr. rhl. Bestellungen werden durch alle Buchhandlungen angenommen. Inserate werden gegen 1 ggr. für die gespaltene Zeile aufgenommen.

Uebersicht:

Friedensgruß an den Leser von dem Herausgeber. Nachrichten. Deutschland: München. Mittelfranken. Fürth. Oberfranken. Frankfurt a. M. Mainz. Bernburg. Ungarn: Großkanischa.

Friedensgruß an den Leser.

Schüchtern reichen wir dir, gel. Leser, die Erstlinge

Riß in der Synagoge, mächtig der Streit unter ihr Angehörigen. Und immer weiter aus- treten die Ueberzeugungen und Richtungen,

from their apartments and crowded into a ghetto. On 27 Nov. 1941, 60 were deported to the Riga ghetto via Bamberg; another 11 were sent to the Theresienstadt ghetto on 9 Sept. 1942 after being expelled to Bamberg on 12 Jan. After the war, 350 refugees organized a new community in B. Over the years most left for Israel or the U.S.

BAZALIYA Kamenets-Podolski dist., Ukraine. Jews settled in the late 17th cent. and in 1765 they numbered 240 (including the surrounding area). One of the first J. printing presses in Volhynia was founded in B. The hasidic *tzaddik* R. Yosef David was active there in the early 20th cent. The J. pop. was 820 (24.4% of the total) in 1897 and 410 in 1939. The Germans occupied B. on 6 July 1941. Most Jews in the area were executed in July 1942 at the village of Manivtsy in Krasilov prov.

BAZAR Zhitomir dist., Ukraine. The J. community probably developed from the late 18th cent., reaching a pop. of 833 (total 1,976) in 1897. A Zionist society and Hebrew school were founded in 1917. During the civil war (1918–21), J. self-defense groups formed to protect Jews against pillaging and the demand for tributes. During the Soviet period, a J. kolkhoz with 60 families was set up. A regular *minyan* was maintained until R. Shmaryahu Shinderman was forced to emigrate to Palestine. On the eve of WWII, the J. pop. was about 1,000. The Germans took B. on 22 Aug. 1941 and in Sept. arrested 176 Jews, murdering them on the way to Korosten. Another 21 Jews were murdered on 21 Nov. Later on, Jews were murdered in small groups. The Germans murdered nearly 300 people.

BAZILIONAI (Padubysys) Siauliai dist., Lithuania. The J. community developed in the 19th cent. Prior to WWI, 40 J. families lived here, a third of whom emigrated. After the Germans conquered Lithuania, Lithuanian nationalists forced all Jews into a ghetto. At the end of Aug. 1941 they were transferred to Zagare and killed on Yom Kippur, 2 Oct. 1941.

BEBRA Hesse–Nassau, Germany. Numbering 111 (8% of the total.) in 1861, the J. community had members in neighboring Iba (27) and Weiterode (19). After WWI, it was affiliated with the rabbinate of Kassel. The synagogue, reconstructed in 1924, was attacked by a mob on *Kristallnacht* (9–10 Nov. 1938), its interior

being destroyed. A J. woman was raped in the pogrom. Of the 166 Jews registered after 1933, 29 emigrated and 109 moved elsewhere (some emigrating) by the end of 1939. At least 22 are known to have perished in the Holocaust.

BECEJ (Stari) Vojvodina dist., Yugoslavia. Early in the 19th cent. Jews settled in B. from Hungary and Moravia. A community was established in the 1860s. Zionism was introduced in the early 1900s. The J. pop. in 1931 was 741 (total 20,519). In Jan. 1942, all the Jews were killed by Hungarian forces.

BECHHOFEN Middle Franconia, Germany. A J. settlement of 20 families existed in the late 16th cent. The synagogue was destroyed in the Thirty Years War. A new wooden one, built in 1684, was called the Barn (*Scheunensynagoge*) because of its shape. In 1732 the interior was decorated by the master painter Eliezer Sussmann, making it famous throughout Germany. Most Jews left the town in the early 1760s because of severe persecution. They returned to improved conditions at the beginning of the 19th cent. The Jews numbered 170 (total 810) in 1837. In the Nazi era, J. homes and stores were "Aryanized." All the Jews left in 1934–38, ten to the U.S. and 26 to other German cities. Though the synagogue was placed under the control of the Bavarian Office of Antiquities, it was burned to the ground on *Kristallnacht* (9–10 Nov. 1938) by local rioters.

BECHYNE Bohemia, Czechoslovakia. Jews were present by the late 16th cent. Many left in the early 18th cent. in the face of severe housing restrictions. The J. pop. was 145 in 1902 and 32 in 1930 (1.5% of the total). The few Jews who remained after the German occupation were deported to the Theresienstadt ghetto in Nov. 1942 and from there to Auschwitz in Jan., Sept., and Oct. 1943. None survived.

BECKOV Slovakia, Czechoslovakia, today Republic of Slovakia. J. refugees from Moravia settled in the late 17th cent. Their pop. rose to a peak of 348 (total 1,670) in 1828 and then commenced to decline steadily. In May 1848, rioting peasants looted J. homes and stores and damaged much property. The J. pop. was 152 in 1900 and 53 in 1940 with many leaving after the establishment of the Slovakian state in March 1939. When most J. businesses were liqui-

Synagogue in Bechhofen, Germany

dated or "Aryanized" in 1941 under government pressure, the Jews who were left without work were sent to labor camps. Deportations began in April 1942 with most Jews concentrated first at Nove Mesto and then transported to the Opole ghetto in the Lublin dist. of Poland where most perished.

BECKUM Westphalia, Germany. Individual Jews were living in B. in the first half of the 14th cent. and towards the end of the 17th cent., but community life did not begin to develop until the mid-18th cent., when a community center was set up in 1740, comprising prayer and teaching rooms. The community grew to 72 individuals by 1835, and in 1925 peaked at 111 members. It was able to expand its religious school into an elementary school in 1835 and to dedicate a new and bigger synagogue in 1867. In June 1933, about four months after the Nazis took over, there were 86 Jews living in B. On *Kristallnacht* (9–10 Nov. 1938), the synagogue and school were utterly wrecked,

along with J. stores and homes. A number of Jews were hounded through the streets and physically assaulted, one being beaten to death. Nearly all Jews subsequently left the town. The only two Jews who were still living in B. by May 1939 were deported to the Theresienstadt ghetto on 28 July 1942.

BECLEAN (Hung. Bethlen) N. Transylvania dist., Rumania. Jews first settled in the early 18th cent. A yeshiva was opened in 1866 and continued to function until 1944. A Hebrew press, established in 1908, printed rabbinical tracts by local and other scholars. The J. pop. in 1920 was 666 (21% of the total). Between the World Wars the community had an influx of 300 Jews from the surrounding villages. Jews opened a number of factories employing hundreds of J. and non-J. workers. Zionist activity began in 1920 with the organization of Hebrew classes, and Zionist youth movements began to function in summer 1922. In summer 1941 a number of families were expelled

to Kamenets-Podolski, where they were murdered. In June 1942, 44 men aged 21–40 were sent to labor battalions in the Ukraine, where they died. On 5 May 1944, 822 Jews were transferred to the Dej ghetto; 44 survived. Survivors returned after WWII but by the early 1950s all left.

BEDBURG Rhineland, Germany. Jews were present in the 17th cent. and a synagogue was in use in 1801. In 1834, anti-J. riots and the vandalizing of the synagogue followed the murder of a Christian child (by a German soldier, as it turned out). Jews mainly traded in farm produce. Adolf Silverberg, a leading industrialist in the town, opened a textile factory and helped develop the local coal-mining industry. The J. pop. reached a peak of 73 (total 2,468) in 1911 and numbered 65 in 1933. On *Kristallnacht* (9–10 Nov. 1938), the synagogue was wrecked and five Jews were sent to the Dachau concentration camp. Most emigrated. The last 13 were deported in Nov. 1942. In all, 20 perished in the Holocaust.

BEDEVLA (Hung. Bedohaza) Carpatho-Russia, Czechoslovakia, today Ukraine. J. settlement probably dates from the mid-18th cent. In 1768, the J. pop. was 39, rising to 115 in 1830 and 304 in 1880. B. became an important center of Vizhnitz Hasidism. Most Jews earned their livelihoods from trade, crafts, and farming. Jews also owned a flour mill. The Hungarians occupied B. in March 1939 and in 1940 drafted a few dozen Jews into labor battalions, sending some to the eastern front and some to labor camps. In late July or early Aug. 1941 a number of J. families without Hungarian citizenship were expelled to Kamenets-Podolski, where they were murdered. The rest were deported to Auschwitz in late May 1944.

BEEK Limburg dist., Holland. Jews settled there in the 17th cent. The J. pop. in 1941 was 34 (total 6,704). About half the Jews were deported in the Holocaust, while 12 survived in hiding.

BEELITZ Brandenburg, Germany. Although there is some indication that Jews may have been present in the 13th cent. J. settlement in B. started only in the 18th cent. when a Jew received civil rights (1710) and a J. cemetery was established. In 1910, the J. pop. was 92. The community maintained a synagogue, but services and religious instruction were not held on a regular basis. In 1908, with the aid of B'nai B'rith, a J. educational institution for mentally handicapped children, the only one in Germany, was established. It was called the Wilhelm-Auguste-Victoria Stiftung or, popularly, the J. Orphanage. When the Nazis came to power in 1933, there were 79 Jews in B. (probably excluding the children of the orphanage). In 1936, there were five community members entitled to vote. On *Kristallnacht* (9–10 Nov. 1938), windows of J. shops were smashed and the cemetery was desecrated. The orphanage's 71 children and teachers were transferred to Berlin in April 1942, and probably deported from there to the Warsaw ghetto. No further information about the fate of the Jews of B. is available. A mass grave in B. of 24 J. girls, probably forced laborers from Eastern Europe, testifies to an execution in 1945.

BEERFELDEN Hesse, Germany. Numbering 187 (6.7% of the total) in 1861, this Orthodox community acknowledged R. Seckel Wormser, the "Ba'al Shem of Michelstadt" (d. 1847), as its first religious authority. The synagogue's completion took many years (1797–1850) owing to local Protestant hostility. From 1924 Nazism gained support and Jews received scant justice from the courts. On *Kristallnacht* (9–10 Nov. 1938) the synagogue was burned down and Jews were sent to the Dachau concentration camp. Of the 105 living there in 1933, only 23 remained at the end of 1938. Most were deported in 1942.

BEGOML Minsk dist., Belorussia. Jews probably settled in the first half of the 19th cent. In the Soviet

Children's orchestra, Beelitz, Germany

period, many Jews (50 in 1930) worked in a kolkhoz founded in 1925. A J. school (of apparently four grades) was still operating in 1931. In 1939, the J. pop. was 206 (total 2,038). The Germans captured the town on 2 July 1941, murdering the Jews who failed to escape with the retreating Red Army. In all, 800 Jews were murdered in the area.

BEILEN   Drenthe dist., Holland. A J. community was organized in 1850 and 71 Jews were living there in 1860. In 1939 the Westerbork refugee camp was established in B. In the 1940s, it was used as the main transit camp for the deportation of Dutch Jews to Eastern Europe. The J. pop. in 1941 was 65 (total 9,554). In the Holocaust, 34 Jews were deported and perished in Poland.

BEISEFOERTH   Hesse–Nassau, Germany. Jews living there from the 17th cent. originally formed part of a regional community but established one of their own, numbering 78 (10% of the total) in 1861, and 20 in 1925. Rebuilt on its 75th anniversary (1928), the synagogue closed ten years later and by Oct. 1939 most of the remaining Jews had left. At least two died in Auschwitz.

BEIUS   (Hung. Belenyes) S. Transylvania dist., Rumania. Jews first settled in the early 19th cent., building a synagogue in 1858 and opening a J. elementary school in 1886, one of the first in Transylvania. B.'s geographical situation attracted J. settlers after WWI. The position of the Jews declined in the 1930s. The J. pop. was 483 in 1930 (11% of the total). On 31 Dec. 1940, Iron Guard Legionnaires attacked the synagogue and communal property. Young Jews were sent to forced labor and others to Transnistria. The non-J. pop. prevented B.'s mayor from turning the synagogue into a club. The J. pop. was transferred to Ginta. All the remaining Jews fled to Deva in Sept. 1944. Those who returned in Oct. to B. following liberation soon left because of the extreme nationalist atmosphere.

BEJA   Beja dist., Tunisia. In the 17th cent., when B. became an urban center occupied by a Turkish garrison, Jews from the western Maghreb — descendants of the Spanish exiles in Algeria and Morocco — began arriving, finding both economic opportunity and physical security. Their Spanish-influenced language left its mark on the Judeo-Arabic spoken in B. According to tradition, the well-known *paytan* or poet Fraji Chaouat of Fez was among them. The circumstances of his burial became a subject of popular legend and his grave in nearby Testour a place of pilgrimage. Under the French Protectorate (from 1881), emigration of Jews from Algeria to Tunisia was renewed as many sought a more traditional J. environment. Leghornian Jews attracted by the city's economic prosperity also arrived. The Jews originally lived in the old Arab quarter, where a synagogue was built. Most Jews subsequently moved to the modern new quarter, living alongside the French and Italians. A Great Synagogue was also built there. Middle-class Jews, as merchants and brokers, traded in farm produce, known throughout Tunisia for its high quality. A J. school was founded in the late 19th cent. A number of local children studied at the Alliance school in Tunis or at the Djdeida agricultural school founded in 1895. In the 1920s and 1930s, J. children attended the French public school in the city. In the afternoons they attended the *talmud torah*. In 1901 the community council was given official status, becoming known as the J. Relief Fund (Caisse de Secours et de Bienfaisance). In 1907, a youth organization named La Jeunesse Israelite de B. was founded, engaging in cultural activity in a Zionist spirit. Benei Zion, a distinctly Zionist organization, was founded in 1913 as an auxiliary of the Agudat Zion in Tunis. It was supported by most of the community and headed by one of the local rabbis. With 71 members, it was the fourth largest Zionist group in Tunisia (after those in Tunis, Sousse, and Nabeul). However, in the late 1920s, Zionist activity in B. ground to a halt, mainly for organizational reasons. Violent anti-J. rioting broke out on 28 Aug. 1917. Arab soldiers on leave and local Bedouins attacked J. stores and injured a number of Jews. A J. soccer team, Stade Bejaoua, later joined by Arab, French, and Italian players, became the leading team in the Tunisian league. The 1929 economic crisis left its mark on local Jews and many left for Tunis, but the J. pop. remained stable, owing to an influx of Jews from the southern towns of Gabes and Djerba. Thus the J. pop. remained around 1,000 between the World Wars (total 13,292 in 1936). In WWII, B. was spared the six-month German occupation of Tunisia. However, dozens of Jews were killed in the German air attack of 20 Nov. 1942 and nearly all the Jews fled the city, staying at distant farms.

Some were able to obtain entry permits to Free Algeria as war refugees, staying in Algiers, Mila, Gelma, and Setif until the end of the war. Those who returned to the city began rebuilding their businesses, serving as food suppliers to the French army and the Arab pop. Almost all returned with the liberation of Tunisia in spring 1943. In the same year, a Tze'irei Tziyyon group was founded, seeking to propagate the idea of *aliya*. Already in 1946, a few left for Israel, settling in Kibbutz Regavim. The community council continued to function and by the mid-1950s B. was a flourishing J. community. The mass exodus of B.'s Jews commenced in 1956 when Tunisia became independent. Some left for Israel but the majority went to France, continuing to maintain close ties with those who remained behind.

BEKECS   Zemplen dist., Hungary. Jews settled in the 18th cent., numbering 109 in 1880 and 101 in 1930. They were deported to Auschwitz via Satoraljaujhely on 16 and 22–25 July 1944.

BEKES   Bekes dist., Hungary. Jews from Adony settled c. 1840. The J. pop. was 537 (2.5%) in 1869, thereafter declining steadily to 228 in 1941. A school was established in 1861 and a synagogue in 1908. On 26 June 1944, most were deported to Auschwitz via Bekescsaba.

BEKESCSABA   Bekes dist., Hungary. Jews probably settled in the late 18th cent. With fertile land and as an important rail junction, B. attracted Jews from all over Hungary, their numbers growing to 1,511 (4.4% of the total) in 1890. The enterprises they established included a flour mill, textile factory, cold storage plant, printing press, department store, and a factory for producing farming implements. The community had three synagogues and started a school in 1865. Zionist activity was extensive, starting in 1927, with Mizrachi, the Revisionists, and Habonim operating branches. Hungary's racial laws of 1938 undermined the economy of the Jews, who were subjected to forced labor from 1940. The J. pop. in 1941 was 2,433. The Germans arrived in March 1944, instituting a regime of persecution and property expropriations. A *Judenrat* was established and on 25–26 June the Jews were deported to Auschwitz. The postwar community of 300 survivors numbered 151 in 1968.

BEKESMEGYER   Pest–Pilis–Solt–Kiskun   dist., Hungary. The J. pop. was 136 in 1930. In March 1944, the Jews were confined to a ghetto together with others from the area. Some left for Budapest and others were sent to forced labor. The remaining Jews were deported to Auschwitz on 30 June 1944.

BEKESSZENTANDRAS   Bekes dist., Hungary. The well-established J. community of 215 in 1880 dwindled to 50 in 1930. The Jews were probably deported to Auschwitz via Bekes on 26 June 1944.

BELA CRKVA   Vojvodina dist., Yugoslavia. Jews settled there at the end of the 19th cent. All 30 Jews living there in 1940 perished in the Holocaust under the Germans.

BELAYA GLINA   Krasnodar territory, Russia. The Germans murdered a number of Jews after arriving on 1 Aug. 1942 (about 15 names are known).

BELAYA TSERKOW   Kiev dist., Ukraine. Jews settled in the early 17th cent. Six hundred J. families were massacred in the Chmielnicki disturbances of 1648–49. The J. pop. was 1,457 in 1765 and 18,720 in 1897. In 1904, Jews owned 250 workshops and 25 factories engaging in light industry and employing 300 Jews. The Zionists and Bund were active. In 1929, under the Soviets, 240 J. artisans were organized in cooperatives; 3,628 Jews classified as lacking rights were unemployed. Of these, 2,655 were hired by the local sugar refinery and 847 taken in by kolkhozes. A Yiddish-language school and a vocational school were opened. In 1939, the J. pop. was 9,284. The Germans captured B. on 16 July 1941. J. belongings were confiscated in Oct. 1941 and the Jews were subsequently transferred to prisoner-of-war camp No. 334, where 6,000 were executed.

BELED   Sopron dist., Hungary. Jews arrived in the late 18th cent., establishing a synagogue in 1790. Jews controlled trade in B., but were only allowed to buy land or engage in agriculture in the second half of the 19th cent. The J. pop. was 239 in 1831 and 360 in 1944, with the community crushed by Hungary's racial laws of 1938. In 1944, the Jews were confined in a ghetto together with 72 from nearby settlements. Some were transferred to Szombathely on 30 June and the rest deported to Auschwitz on 4 July.

Forty-four Jews returned after the war; 29 were still present in 1957.

BELEV Tula dist., Russia. Jews probably settled in the late 19th cent. Their pop. was 238 in 1926. The few who had not fled or been evacuated were murdered during the short German occupation of the town (23 Oct. to 31 Dec. 1941).

BELFORT Belfort dist., France. The J. community was established in 1808, and 50 families inaugurated its synagogue in 1857. The government only officially recognized the community in 1906. On the eve of WWI, it numbered 200 families. There was a J. mayor in 1919–20. During the 1920s, there was a rich religious and social life in the dist., centered around B. On the eve of WWII, the J. pop. numbered 383. During WWII, the Germans deported and murdered 245 members of the community. In 1964, there were 1,300 Jews living in B.

BELGARD (Pol. Bialogard) Pomerania, Germany, today Poland. A small J. settlement existed at the end of the 17th cent. In 1764, it comprised only four families. In 1880, the community numbered 281 members and 135 in 1909. The community maintained a synagogue (1829) and a cemetery. In 1920, J. citizens were arrested and J. businesses looted in connection with the abortive Kapp putsch against the Weimar Republic. When the Nazis assumed power in 1933, there were 112 Jews living in B., dropping to 62 by May 1934. After *Kristallnacht* (9–10 Nov. 1938), the SA began using the synagogue for its own purposes. By May 1939, only ten Jews and five persons of partial J. origin (*Mischlinge*) remained in the town. No information about their fate is available, but it may be assumed that those who did not emigrate were deported to the east. By Oct. 1942 there was only one Jew left in B., probably protected by marriage to a non-Jew.

BELGOROD Kursk dist., Russia. Jews probably settled in the late 19th cent. A synagogue was in use in the early 20th cent. In 1926, the J. pop. was 631 (total 31,036). The Germans arrived on 2 Oct. 1941 and murdered, at the village of Mikchayilovka, the few Jews who had neither fled nor been evacuated.

BELGRADE (Beograd) capital of Yugoslavia. Jews seem to have lived in B. in Second Temple times and took part in developing the town into a thriving center of trade that absorbed Jews expelled from Germany and Hungary. They first lived along the Sava River but began building a J. quarter on the Danube River in the 16th cent. During that period (under the Ottoman Empire) the community became more established, founded welfare organizations, and enjoyed the general economic well-being of the time. In the 17th cent. B. was home to many well-known J. scholars and the community reached a cultural, spiritual, and economic peak. In Sept. 1688, B. was captured by the Austrians, the battles bringing destruction to the J. quarter and resettlement of the Jews in a concentration camp, where only one-quarter of the 800 Jews survived the harsh conditions until they were ransomed by other European communities. In 1690 the Turks reoccupied B. and some Jews returned to restore the community. By the early 18th cent. the Jews held some notable positions in the politics and economy of B. In 1717, B. came under Austrian rule and many Jews were deprived of their rights as citizens and their conditions deteriorated. Improvement came with Turkish rule from 1791. In 1794 many Jews lost their lives in a plague. In 1804–07 the Jews suffered during the Serbian rebellion against Ottoman rule; many were killed and hundreds expelled. The Turks eventually regained B. in 1813 and some Jews returned. After 1815, B. came into Serbian hands again, but this time the Jews enjoyed full civil rights and many privileges. In the 1830s the Serbian prince was deposed and the Jews again suffered anti-J. laws. Their economic stability plummeted and they became victims of a blood libel in 1840. Many Jews were expelled and the others were not allowed out of the J. quarter. In 1862 a war broke out between the Serbs and Austrians. J. homes in B. were destroyed, and their equal rights revoked. The problem was brought up at the Berlin peace talks of 1878 but the Serbians renewed J. rights only in 1888. By 1895 the Jews numbered 3,097 (5.23% of the total pop.). After 1888 most Jews worked in trade, but in 1893 the government ruled that the Jews were not to sell tobacco and liquor. Sephardi and Ashkenazi Jews lived side by side until a conflict arose between the Ashkenazim and Sephardim in 1860. The community as a whole tried to maintain its activities even throughout the trying period of the 1840s–80s. From 1837 Hebrew books were printed in B. From the end of the 19th cent. the Se-

Moshe Mendel (standing second from right), soldier in the Carrier Pigeon Corps of the Yugoslavian army (Beth Hatefutsoth Photo Archive, Tel Aviv/courtesy of Gavra Mandil, Tel Aviv)

phardi community's activities and organizations (which included education, welfare, and a branch of the Alliance Israelite) were coordinated by a committee. In 1897, David Alkalai was elected to represent the Jews of Serbia at the First Zionist Congress in Basel. Upon returning to B. he established a movement called "Zion," which sent representatives to the following Congresses and also worked to unite the Ashkenazi and Sephardi communities. Zionism became widespread, but all Zionist activity was halted with the outbreak of WWI and only renewed when the Balfour Declaration was recognized by the Serbian authorities in 1917. The J. pop. in 1910 was 4,192 (total 89,876). Many Jews fought in the Balkan wars from 1912 and in WWI while others were very active in the war effort on the home front. Later to become chief rabbi of Serbia (1923; Yugoslavia from 1929), Yitzhak Alcalay promoted J.-Serbian patriotism. After WWI the Jews enjoyed equal rights. J. involvement in art, literature, music, and other fields of culture increased in the 1920s and J. journalism and publishing became most pronounced in the 1930s. The J. pop. numbered 7,906 in 1931 (3.31% of the total pop.).

With Hitler's rise to power in Germany, antisemitic articles began to be published. Many J. youths then joined the underground Communist party. Some were arrested, and of those only a few survived. From 1940, J. children were not permitted to study in the Yugoslav schools and limitations on J. business and education followed. In 1941 the J. pop. peaked at 12,000. In March 1941 the Germans bombed B., and in April the army entered the city. The J. neighborhoods were destroyed. Some Jews fled, but most remained and were forced to wear the yellow badge. Men and wom-

"Smoking and drinking" party, Belgrade, Yugoslavia, 1890 (Beth Hatefutsoth Photo Archive, Tel Aviv/courtesy of Dr. Rafael Fiazza, Israel)

en were sent to forced labor. Some youths escaped in June 1941 and later joined the partisans. In July and Aug. most of the J. men were taken to concentration camps, where the majority died. The women and children who were left in B. were taken in Dec. to the Sajmishche camp on the outskirts of B. and were killed in gas vans and their bodies buried in trenches in the village of Jaintsi, southeast of B. Many Jews who had fled B. were eventually caught by the Germans and some underground fighters (such as Dora Alkalai) were caught and tortured by the Gestapo. The Sephardi synagogue, built in 1908, was bombed by the Germans in 1941. The Ashkenazi synagogue, rebuilt in the grand style in 1926, was used as a brothel for the German soldiers during WWII. J. survivors of the WWII camps, partisans, and prisoners of war returned to B. and revived the community. Despite their small numbers, the Jews played an important role, especially in the intellectual life of the city. Most of the survivors—some 7,000—moved to Israel after 1948.

BELILOVKA Zhitomir dist., Ukraine. Jews were

present in the early 18th cent. Three were killed in Cossack attacks in 1735. The J. pop. was 124 in 1765 and 2,223 (total 4,851) in 1897. The Jews were attacked by the Petlyura gangs in 1918 and by Anton Denikin's White Army troops in 1919–20. Consequently, and also through internal migration, the J. pop. dropped to 1,897 in 1926 and to even less by 1941. The Germans captured the town on 15 July 1941, murdering the Jews there shortly afterwards.

BELIU (Hung. Bel) S. Transylvania dist., Rumania. Jews first settled in the early 19th cent. and in 1869 joined the Neologist association. The J. pop. stood at 64 in 1930 (3% of the total). In the 1930s, with the increase of antisemitism, about a third of the community left for the larger cities. At the outbreak of the Soviet-Rumanian war in June 1941, the J. pop. was transferred to Ginta. Seventy Jews returned after the war.

BELKHATOW Lodz dist., Poland. In 1808, 17 Jews lived here and by 1857 the 1,100 Jews (73% of the total) engaged mainly in the textile industry. At

The bus from Szczercow to Belkhatow, Poland, 1920

the end of the 19th cent. over 900 of the 2,987 Jews were weavers; others engaged mainly in transport. In 1893, the Gur Hasidim nominated Shemuel Shelomo Braun as town rabbi, and he founded a yeshiva. The first members of the Haskala movement here were among the students at this institution. The Bund was active in the J. labor unions established from the beginning of the 20th cent. In the 1920s and 1930s the political parties, youth movements, and hasidic groups became the centers of cultural activity. The Mizrachi movement, founded in 1917, gained the majority of votes in elections to the Zionist Congresses. Together with Agudat Israel they dominated the leadership of the community. By 1938 the Agudat Israel youth movement had the largest following. In 1925 the J. community sent 13 representatives to the 24-member municipal council, but in 1927 this number was reduced to seven. Under the German occupation the community numbered 6,000, including refugees who came from border towns. The Jews were confined to the existing J. quarter, which was turned into an open ghetto, enabling them to work clandestinely in the tex-

tile trade and sell the goods to Poles. Many worked in textile factories taken over by the Germans, manufacturing uniforms for the German army. Over 1,000 were employed in carpentery, dressmaking, and shoemaking workshops. Schools and cultural institutions functioned secretly until mid-1941 when 700 men aged 18–45 were sent to labor camps from which few returned. The Germans intervened frequently in the composition of the *Judenrat*. Some members were arrested and even executed. On 18 March 1942 (Purim) ten Jews were hanged publicly for smuggling and about 400 Jews were transported to labor camps and other cities. The final annihilation of the community began in Aug. 1942 when most Jews were deported to the Chelmno death camp.

BELLERSHEIM Hesse, Germany. The Jews of Wohnbach, Obbornhofen, and B. formed one community, numbering several dozen in the 19th cent. On *Kristallnacht* (9–10 Nov. 1938) the synagogue was desecrated. The last few Jews were probably deported in 1941–42.

BELOGORODKA   Kamenets-Podolski dist., Ukraine. Jews in small numbers are known from the early 17th cent. The J. pop. was 100 in 1765 and 1,846 (34% of the total) in 1897. Eighteen Jews were murdered and many injured in a pogrom during Easter 1918. In 1926, the J. pop. was 1,194. The Germans entered B. on 4 July 1941. The Jews were murdered during the occupation.

BELOPOLYE   Vinnitsa dist., Ukraine. Jews settled in 1721 and numbered 1,141 (total 2,619) in 1897 and 1,255 in 1926 under the Soviets. A J. council was active in the town for awhile. Most children attended a Yiddish school. The Germans arrived in early July 1941, murdering the Jews at the local cemetery in May 1942.

BELORECHENSKAYA   Krasnodar territory, Russia. The Germans murdered a few dozen Jews in the village in mid-Sept. 1942.

BELOVAREC   (Hung. Kiskirva) Carpatho-Russia, Czechoslovakia, today Ukraine. Jews probably settled at the turn of the 18th cent. and numbered 101 (total 528) in 1880 and 142 in 1921. The Hungarians arrived in March 1939 and in summer 1941 expelled many of the Jews to Kamenets-Podolski, where they were murdered. The rest were deported to Auschwitz in the second half of May 1944.

BELUSA   Slovakia, Czechoslovakia, today Republic of Slovakia. Jews settled in the first half of the 18th cent., forming a Neologist congregation after the 1869 split. They reached a peak pop. of 108 (total 2,270) in 1880. After WWI most of the young joined Hashomer Hatzair. In 1930 the J. pop. was 56. Most Jews were deported via Zilina to Auschwitz and the death camps of the Lublin dist. of Poland in spring 1942.

BELYI   Smolensk dist., Russia. Jews probably settled in the mid-19th cent. and numbered 287 (total 6,952) in 1897. In the Soviet period, the J. pop. fell to 218 in 1926 and 92 in 1939. The Germans first murdered 75 Jews on 4 Oct. 1941 and then another 200 from the area in the course of the same fall.

BELYNICHI   Mogilev dist., Belorussia. The J. pop. was 1,087 in 1847 and 1,063 in 1897. In 1924, under the Soviets, Jews were employed in three artisan cooperatives. In 1925, 47 J. families earned their livelihoods from agriculture, founding an agricultural cooperative in the town. The Jews remained observant and in the late 1920s those in the cooperatives did not work on the J. Sabbath. In summer 1926, unregistered *hadarim* stepped up their activity. A four-year J. school was also in operation. The Germans occupied the town on 6 Aug. 1941, murdering 150 J. men in early Sept. The remaining 600 Jews were concentrated in a ghetto. On 12 Dec. they were executed outside the town.

BELZ   Lwow dist., Poland, today Ukraine. There is a complaint against J. tailors in 1413, but the Jews may have been present much earlier. J. residence rights were assured by the king. About 200 died of hunger and plague during the Chmielnicki disturbances in 1648–49 and 60 children were murdered by the Swedes during their invasion in 1660. To attract the fleeing Jews back to the town, they were accorded trade privileges and the community flourished, its importance fixing it as the seat of many outstanding rabbis, like Yehoshua Falk and Yoel Sirkes. A decline set in with Austrian rule when B. lost its status of provincial capital, but a new era was inaugurated when R. Shalom Roke'ah founded a hasidic dynasty there in 1817. Thousands of followers flocked to him and B. became the center of Galician Hasidism. By the end of the 19th cent. the pop. had grown to 2,872 out of a total 5,075. Most, including the hasidic court, fled before the Russian armies in 1914 and many did not return after WWI. With the return of the court in 1925, a process of economic rehabilitation commenced but new hardships set in during the 1930s owing to competition with the Poles and Ukrainians. The German occupation on 10 Oct. 1939 initiated an exodus of local Jews and only

The Great Synagogue in Belz, Poland

30 remained. An influx of refugees brought the pop. up to 1,540 by May 1942. A thousand were deported to Hrubieszow on 2 June and from there to the Sobibor death camp. Another 504 were brought to Hrubieszow in Sept. after the harvest when they were no longer needed on the farms in the area. They suffered the fate of other Jews in the region.

BELZEC Lwow dist., today Poland. Jews lived there from the second half of the 19th cent., numbering between 100 and 150. With the German occupation in WWII the town became the center of a network of forced labor camps. The notorious death camp operated from mid-March 1942 to the spring of 1943 and claimed over 600,000 J. lives, the Jews being brought in from the regions of Lublin and Galicia as well as the eastern Cracow and Radom districts, Germany, Austria, Czechoslovakia, and Rumania.

BELZHYCE Lublin dist., Poland. A J. settlement existing in the 1560s was sufficiently important to host meetings of the Council of the Four Lands in 1625 and 1643. The community suffered grievously in the Chmielnicki massacres of 1648–49 and only regained its former economic prominence in the early 18th cent. In the early 19th cent., R. Yitzhak Moshe Azriel Licht (d. 1831) headed an important hasidic congregation. The J. pop. numbered 832 in 1857 and 1,882 (total 3,694) in 1921. Most were artisans and peddlers. Organized Zionist activity commenced in 1920 and a Tarbut Hebrew school was founded in 1929. On the eve of the German occupation of Sept. 1939, Jews numbered 2,100, increasing to 4,000 in mid-1941 with the influx of refugees from Stettin, Cracow, Lublin, and other places. A *Judenrat* was established in early 1941 and later a ghetto, where a typhoid epidemic broke out in the summer. Some were expelled to Poniatowa in the fall and in late 1941 a group was sent to Majdanek to help erect the concentration camp. Around May 1942, most of the others were deported to the Sobibor death camp. Those in B.'s labor camp (established in summer 1942), reaching a peak of 1,200 in late 1942, were murdered or transferred to Bendzin in May 1943.

The Belz Rebbe attending a funeral, 1851

BENATKY NAD JIZEROU   Bohemia, Czechoslovakia. J. settlement commenced at the turn of the 18th cent. The J. pop. was 49 in 1930 (1.3% of the total). Those who remained after the German occupation were deported to the Theresienstadt ghetto in mid-Jan. 1943 and from there to Auschwitz in the same month. Few survived.

BENDKOW   Lodz dist., Poland. In 1857, 248 Jews lived here. With the German conquest the remaining 228 Jews left.

BENDORF AM RHEIN   Rhineland, Germany. A J. moneylender dealing with the mother superior of the local monastery is mentioned in 1339. Jews are again mentioned only in 1592. A synagogue is known to have existed in 1711. It burned down in 1825 and a new one was consecrated in the same year. After the French period, Jews continued to trade, as they had down through the years, in livestock, and to work as butchers. Their pop. grew from 86 in 1816 to 156 in 1858. In 1869, a J. psychiatric hospital was founded in B. by Meir Jacobi. In 1873, it was transferred to new and spacious premises on the road to nearby Sayn. In 1892 it housed 120 patients. Relations with the local pop. were generally good. In 1933, the J. pop. was 209. In 1939, 261 were recorded but this probably included about 200 at the Sayn hospital. On *Kristallnacht* (9–10 Nov. 1938), the synagogue was wrecked as were J. homes. Since by early 1939 the Sayn hospital remained the only one in Germany where J. psychiatric patients could be admitted, all the J. psychiatric patients in Germany, over 500, were ordered to be brought there in 1940. In March 1942 all, including the staff, were deported to Izbica in the Lublin dist. of Poland. Over a period of a few months, more than 1,000 Jews were deported via the hospital, including 32 from B.

BENDZIN   Kielce dist., Poland. The first Jews settled in the surrounding villages in 1226 and in the late 13th cent. were present in the town itself, thenceforth consolidating their position as they obtained down through the years a number of royal privileges.

Zionist youth brass band, Bendzin, Poland, April 1935 (Abasma Archives, Tel Yitzhak/photo courtesy of Yad Vashem, The Holocaust Martyrs' and Heroes' Remembrance Authority, Jerusalem)

A cemetery consecrated in 1592 and also serving smaller communities was in use until 1831. By the 17th cent., most of the wholesale trade was in J. hands and commercial ties were maintained with Silesia and Germany. In the 18th cent., Jews leased beer breweries and flour mills and traded locally in farm produce. The development of the mining industry in the early 19th cent. created new jobs for the Jews in the coal mines as well as opportunities for joint leasing ventures with Polish partners. Jews sided with the Poles against the czar in the rebellion of 1830–31. Over 100 died in a cholera epidemic around that time. The J. pop. grew from 2,418 in 1857 to 10,839 in 1897 and 24,862 (total 49,623) in 1910. In the late 19th cent., the first modern J. schools were opened in the city, teaching European and Slavic languages, history and geography, mathematics, etc. Zionist activity commenced in the Hovevei Zion period. Mizrachi opened an office in 1898. In 1905, the Bund and Po'alei Zion began operating. After WWI, Jews were prominent in B.'s industrialization, initiating the establishment of factories to manufacture metal products, chemicals, and electric bulbs. In addition, Jews operated 672 mostly small workshops and factories, two-thirds in the garment industry. Zionist activity was extensive. The Left Po'alei Zion Party founded five trade unions for 320 J. workers in 1921 and another three in 1926 for tailors, porters, and domestics. It also opened a kindergarten and day care center. Among the pioneer youth movements, Hehalutz and Gordonia were active, the latter with one of the biggest branches in Poland in the 1930s. In 1917, a Mizrachi-sponsored Yavne secondary school was opened, reaching an enrollment of 270 in 1927. Mizrachi also opened a modernized *heder* in 1920. Another 420 children attended a *talmud torah* set up by Agudat Israel, which throughout the period contended with the Zionists for community leadership. B. was a Zionist stronghold and many leading figures from the World Zionist Movement visited the city during the 1930s, including D. Ben-Gurion, Y. Ben-Zvi, V. Jabotinsky, and H. N. Bialik. In 1931, the J. pop. of 21,625 was struggling to subsist in the general economic crisis. It later faced growing antisemitism and anti-J. boycotts.

On the outbreak of WWII, about 4,500 Jews fled east. The Germans entered B. on 5 Sept. 1939. The next day the SS arrived, murdering two J. bakers for supposedly overcharging. Three days later, local *Volksdeutsche* set the synagogue on fire. The conflagration spread to J. homes and 60 Jews were burned alive. A few days later, 17 J. men were executed, charged with shooting at German troops. In early 1940, the Germans began to force Jews out of their businesses and evict them from choice apartments. Refugees arriving in 1940–41, including 3,000 from the town of Oswiencim (Auschwitz), along with returning residents, brought the J. pop. up to 25,171 in 1941. The youth movements resumed their activities in early 1940 and in May 1940, 60 youngsters were permitted to set up a 100-acre farm on the outskirts of the city which became a focus of movement activity. In all, about 1,400 were active in the youth movements, which turned to the idea of creating an underground after a visit by Mordekhai Anielewicz from Warsaw in May 1942. At the same time, large numbers of young Jews were being sent to labor camps – by April 1942, 6,500 from B. and neighboring Sosnowiec along with other settlements in the area. Many others were employed in local "shops" manufacturing clothing and boots for the German army. The "shops" earned their directors substantial profits while Jews regarded working in them as better than at a labor camp. Deportations commenced in May and June 1942 when 2,400 "nonproductive" Jews were transported to Auschwitz in two *Aktions*. On 15 Aug., another 8,000–10,000 were sent there. Deportations continued in groups of 10–50 over the next year. In spring 1943, the Jews were confined to a ghetto in the Kamionka suburb and on 22 June, 4,000 Jews were rounded up for deportation to Auschwitz. The final liquidation of the ghetto commenced on 1 Aug. when a special German force of 800 arrived in the area. By 7 Aug., 30,000 Jews from B. and Sosnowiec had been deported to Auschwitz. The J. underground had by this time created six bunkers and collected about 20 handguns and a few dozen grenades. The underground was opposed by the head of the *Judenrat*, who felt that its existence endangered the community. As the Germans closed in, one bunker held them off for half an hour. Fifteen managed to hide from the Germans with several making their way to Palestine in 1944.

BENEDIKOVCE (Hung. Benedeki) Carpatho-Russia, Czechoslovakia, today Ukraine. Jews probably settled in the mid-18th cent. In 1880, they numbered 177 (total 526), their pop. remaining stable throughout the existence of the Czechoslovakian Republic (163 in 1921 and 188 in 1941 under the Hungarians). Jews owned a factory manufacturing alcohol. The Hungar-

ians arrived in March 1939 and in 1941 drafted a number of Jews into forced labor battalions. The remaining 150 Jews were deported to Auschwitz in mid-May 1944.

BENESOV Bohemia, Czechoslovakia. Jews are mentioned in 1385. The modern community was established in 1845 along with a synagogue. A J. elementary school was in operation in 1867–97. The J. pop. reached a peak of 447 (6.5% of the total) in 1900. In 1940, 362 remained, with the rate of intermarriage reaching 45%. Ten local Jews were sent to the Buchenwald concentration camp in fall 1939, only one surviving. After the assassination of the Bohemia and Moravia *Reichsprotektor* Reinhard Heydrich in May 1942, the Jews were evicted from their homes and the able-bodied subjected to forced labor until most were deported to the Maly Trostinets death camp near Minsk and gassed to death on 12 Sept. 1942. A detention center for intermarried Jews residing in the Bohemia-Moravia Protectorate was set up in summer 1944 and held 1,500 inmates by the end of the war.

BENFELD Bas-Rhin dist., France. The J. presence dates from the mid-14th cent. The community disappeared due to expulsions; it was renewed in 1830. The J. pop. of B. was 236 in 1836. The synagogue was inaugurated in 1846. The community numbered 171 members in 1936. During the occupation, all were expelled to the south of France, with the rest of Alsace-Lorraine Jews. Altogether, the Germans deported 31 B. Jews. The synagogue and cemetery were severely damaged. In 1968, the community numbered 75 persons.

BEN GARDANE Orgama dist., Tunisia. Jews apparently settled in the early 19th cent., arriving primarily from Djerba and profiting from the border trade, mostly illegal, with Libya. Most Jews lived under straitened economic circumstances. J. women were known for their fine embroidery work. Between the World Wars, the urban settlement was mainly J., with a Bedouin pop. living on the outskirts of the town. In 1936, the J. pop. was 489 (total 1,395 including the Bedouin). In this period, Shaul Hadad, Jerusalem-born of parents from Djerba, became rabbi and head of the community. The large, well-appointed synagogue could seat several hundred worshipers. The children studied at the synagogue's *talmud torah* rather than at the French school. They continued their studies, if they wished, at the *yeshivot* in Djerba. Relations with the Arabs were confined to business. A French garrison provided security. WWII brought shortages in basic necessities and a drop in J. income as the border with Libya was closed. The Vichy regime had little impact on the J. community. The Germans, who arrived in Nov. 1942, also caused little hardship beyond their demand for supplies. Most Jews fled to Djerba and Zarzis when Allied bombardments began soon afterwards. When they returned, they found their homes in ruins and their property pillaged. The community only partially recovered, mainly through the assistance of the Joint Distribution Committee and OZE. The Zionists became active in the postwar period and a branch of Ataret Zion was established in 1945. In 1950 the J. Agency provided a Hebrew teacher. In 1946, the J. pop. was 675. Arab nationalism created tensions in Arab-J. relations. Owing to the isolation of the settlement and its J. character, combined with the revival of commerce, Jews only began to leave in 1956. About 80 still remained in 1976.

BENGHAZI Cyrenaica dist., Libya. The J. settlement apparently dates from the fourth cent. B.C.E. under the Ptolemies and is thus among the oldest in North Africa. Subsequently J. exiles, including a number of Sicarii, found refuge there after the destruction of the Second Temple and were influential in fomenting the rebellion against Trajan and Roman rule in 115–17 C.E. As a consequence, the community was left in ruins and remained insignificant throughout the period of Moslem rule in the 7th to 16th cent. The renewal of the community and its institutions probably commenced in the early 16th cent. with the arrival of J. exiles from Spain and Portugal, though in the early 17th cent. only four J. families were present. The growth of commerce served to attract additional Jews, who were active in the caravan trade from Central Africa and the maritime trade with Egypt, Crete, and Europe. Like all non-Moslem minorities in the Ottoman Empire, the Jews were subjected to various discriminatory measures, such as the ban on riding animals and bearing arms and the obligation to wear a black hat. At the same time, the Jews, particularly the wealthy among them, were granted broad communal autonomy and enjoyed numerous dispensations. Under Qaramanli rule from 1711, B. became a major commercial crossroads in Cyrenaica, thanks largely to J. activity. Jews re-

Jewish cemetery in Benghazi, Libya (Rafaelo Fallach, Rome/photo courtesy of Yad Vashem, The Holocaust Martyrs' and Heroes' Remembrance Authority, Jerusalem)

mained loyal to the regime throughout the period. In 1793, when the despotic Algerian pirate Ali Burgul seized power in Cyrenaica and Tripolitania, B. became the base from which the Qaramanlis reconquered Tripoli. The Jews celebrated the event with a "Purim of Ali Burgul" in addition to the traditional festival. The transfer of Libya to direct Ottoman rule in 1835 produced many changes in the situation of the Jews as the influence of the European powers was increasingly felt, bringing exposure to western culture and significant reform. In the 19th cent., B. became a large, overcrowded city whose economic prosperity attracted many Jews. In 1850, the J. pop. included about 400 families, forming two congregations according to local or Tripolitan origin, with R. Yitzhak Khalfon serving as *hakham* for both. Jews frequently represented the business and diplomatic interests of the European countries in B. and thus contributed to the westernization of the city. In the late 19th cent., the

chief rabbi and president of the community, R. Rahamim Farjon, represented the Florio Rubattino shipping company of Italy. Most employees at the Banco di Roma branch founded in B. in 1910 were also Jews. Jews dominated trade and the crafts, owning most of the shops in the market, though they soon met with Moslem and Christian competition, frequently accompanied by persecution. The Jews, however, prospered and by 1880, a wealthy J. merchant class could be found in B., comprising about 50 families. The community maintained a number of synagogues, a rabbinical court, and a *talmud torah*. The ancient synagogue of B. was torn down in 1862 and replaced by a new one. A second synagogue, seating 500, was started in the late 19th cent. and completed in 1914. The third synagogue was consecrated in 1906 and included a *talmud torah*, one of several in B. Following Ottoman reforms, Jews were permitted representation in the municipal council, but few were employed in the civil

service. Ottoman interests continued to include protection of the Jews, who controlled the city's commerce, assured the flow of goods from Central Africa to Istanbul, and served as bankers. In daily life, despite the formal abrogation of the Dhimmi (Protection) laws, Jews continued to address Moslems as "Sir" (*sidi*) and step aside for them in the street. Anti-J. incidents also occurred from time to time, particularly with the weakening of the central government in the late 19th cent. A blood libel instigated by European Christians in the city in 1862 led to the arrest of a number of Jews and in 1868 the synagogue and J. cemetery were vandalized when Jews protested the conversion of a J. girl to the Islamic faith. In 1906, a fire in the J. market was exploited to loot J. stores. By 1902, the J. pop. was around 2,000 (total 15,000). The westernized Jews within the community helped the Italians penetrate into Cyrenaica prior to the Italian naval attack on 19–20 Oct. 1911 and the subsequent surrender of the city. Traditional Jews, however, were seen as remaining loyal to the Ottoman regime and the loyalty of J. foreign subjects was also doubted. In the Arab Revolt (1915–22), the J. community remained neutral but Italian doubts and suspicions grew when first the Senusi leader Muhammad Idris and later the militant Umar al-Mukhtar raised the banner of revolt. In 1923–24, new Italian regulations defined the Jews as "natives" and many J. civil servants were dismissed from their jobs. At the same time, Italian sympathies for westernized Jews remained and as Italian culture and assimilationist tendencies took hold, a greater proportion of local Jews than in Tripoli applied for Italian citizenship. Mussolini's desire to appear as the defender of Islam in his struggle against France and England expressed itself in discrimination against the Jews in the 1930s. However, the stability and economic prosperity the Jews enjoyed under the Italian regime led most of them to support it. Many joined the Fascist Party and J. students in the Italian schools were quick to join the Fascist youth movements. When Ethiopia was conquered in 1935, the Jews of B. extended aid to the Falashas. They also collected silver and gold for Italy as a demonstration of their patriotism. About half the Jews of B. were engaged in trade and in general the community was more prosperous than Tripoli's, with fewer children and adults past retirement age forced to work. The growth rate of the J. pop. was slow and steady, rising from 2,767 in 1931 to a peak of 3,654 (total 66,800) in 1937. The chief rabbi

of B. was also the chief rabbi of Cyrenaica. The appointment of an Italian chief rabbi remained a sore point in the community, as in Tripoli. In Sept. 1919, Prof. Gustavo Calo arrived from Mantua to assume the office. He returned a year later to Italy because the community could not afford his salary and due to difficulties in dealing with the Arab pop. Efrayyim Khalfon, whose family was prominent in shipping and banking, headed the community until 1918. He was succeeded by Eliyahu Farjon, also active in shipping and a founder of the local Dante Alighieri Society for Italian Culture. In 1933 the community council was dissolved by the Italians in an attempt to appease the Arabs and Farjon became a government-appointed commissioner, resigning in 1935. Most children (306 in 1934) studied in Italian public schools in the mornings and attended the *talmud torah* in the afternoon. In 1934, the Italians opened a J. elementary school, which also reached an enrollment of 300 in the course of time. In 1935 the *talmud torah* was modernized, Hebrew instruction was introduced, and a cafeteria and eye clinic were added. A J. Hebrew-language kindergarten was also started. Zionism in B. was rooted in the consideration of Cyrenaica for autonomous settlement by the Zionist Territorialists in 1906. A Herzl society was founded in 1919 and a Chaim Weizmann group in 1924 but Zionist activity declined in the 1930s, reducing itself to cultural and social interests. The decline was due to the rise of Fascism in Italy and the desire of the community itself to maintain a low profile against a background of Arab riots in Palestine. Also active in the 1930s was the ADEI Zionist women's organization, the Italian counterpart to WIZO. Relations with the Arab pop. remained ambivalent, as Jews were both suspected of collaboration with the Italians and seen as fraternal "natives" ranged against the colonial power. Strong commercial ties prevailed between J. merchants and Bedouin tribesmen, even after the publication of Italy's racial laws in 1938.

The Italian racial laws published on 6 Oct. 1938 excluded J. children from Italian secondary schools and J. clerks from government employment. In 1938–40, about 100 Jews left B., most for Tunisia, but the enforcement of the laws until 1940 was less strict in B. and in Libya as a whole owing to the opposition of the Italian governor, Italo Balbo. Balbo's death and Italy's entry into the war alongside Germany on 10 June 1940 marked a deterioration in conditions for the Jews. Between 1940 and 1943, B. changed hands five times

as the British and Italians contended for its possession. In the first period of British rule (9 Dec. 1940–April 1941), the racial laws were lifted and other forms of discrimination eliminated. J. soldiers serving with the British forces mingled with local Jews, trying to revive Zionist activity and also providing material assistance. About 200 Jews left with the British on their withdrawal from B. Immediately J. property was looted, mostly by the local Italian pop., and two Jews were killed. The return of the Italians saw the appearance of the first German soldiers in B., members of Rommel's Afrika Korps. The British returned on 18 Nov. 1941 and held the city until 28 Jan. 1942. When the Italians returned they stepped up anti-J. measures. New edicts were published circumscribing J. commercial activity and banning publication of all but strictly religious writings. On 7 Feb. 1942, Mussolini personally ordered the J. pop. of Libya to be "thinned out." Deportations were carried out in Aug.–Oct. 1942., with the Jews of B. the last to go. Jews of British nationality (300 in all of Libya) were sent to detention facilities in Italy. After the German occupation of Italy on 8 Sept. 1943, they were put to forced labor, working on fortifications in Italy. In early 1944, 100 were sent to Insbruck in Austria and 200 to Bergen-Belsen. Jews of French nationality (1,600 in Libya) were deported to detention camps in Tunisia and Algeria. About 50 J. families from B. were held in the Sfax camp in Tunisia. Unlike the Jews of Tripoli after the liberation of Tunisia by the Allies in May 1943, they remained there for another year for lack of transportation facilities to take them home. Jews of Libyan nationality were sent to concentration camps in Tripolitania, most to Jado and the others to Gharian and Yefren. The Jado camp held 2,600 Jews under the harshest of conditions. Over 500 died of starvation, exhaustion, and typhus. The camp was located 145 mile south of Tripoli and commanded by Ettore Bastico, an Italian general with marked antisemitic prejudices. The Jews were housed in barrack-like structures holding 300–350 prisoners and partitioned by families with sheets for privacy. The men worked 12 hours a day shifting earth and rocks. On the approach of the British in Jan. 1943, the Italians and Arab guards fled. About 200 Jews also ran away. Under the British, the survivors gradually made their way back to B., where about 260 Jews had remained throughout the period. Few were able to recover economically and they required assistance from the community. J. soldiers from Company 462 of the Palestine Regiment also assisted in the reha-

bilitation of the community, even helping smuggle young Jews into Palestine. They set up a Hebrew school which attracted J. children from all of Cyrenaica and also conducted Hebrew classes for adults. By early 1944, it was attended by over 400 children up to the age of 14. In Feb. 1944, the J. soldiers also founded a local Hehalutz organization. Moshe Sharett (Shertok) visited the community in May 1944 on behalf of the J. leadership in Palestine. After the war preparations began for *aliya*. During this period, Arab nationalists were attacking Jews in B. By Sept. 1949 about 2,000 Jews from B. and the rest of Cyrenaica had liquidated their businesses and left for Tripoli in anticipation of departure to Israel. Despite the extensive preparations, B.'s Jews only left for Israel in 1951.

BENI KHALED   Grombalia dist., Tunisia. Jews arrived in the early 20th cent. and numbered 52 in 1926, mostly trading in the local market. In the riots of 1917, J. stores were destroyed and by 1936 only nine Jews remained, all leaving during WWII.

BENSHEIM   Hesse, Germany. The medieval community – including Jews expelled from France in 1306 – suffered martyrdom during the Black Death persecutions of 1348–49 and banishment in 1461. The community was reestablished in 1634, but socio-economic factors limited its growth until the 19th cent. Following the award of civil rights (1850), Jews engaged in a variety of occupations and their number grew to 167 (2.8% of the total) in 1880. Many Christian residents attended the opening of a new and larger Orthodox synagogue in 1892. On *Kristallnacht* (9–10 Nov. 1938), however, it was burned down and J. residents throughout the area were attacked. Of the 168 Jews living there in 1933, nearly all had left (many emigrating to the U.S.) by 1939 and in Feb. 1942 the last 17 were deported. After WWII, Displaced Persons camps in the neighborhood housed up to 4,000 Holocaust survivors, most of whom left for Israel.

BENTHEIM   Hanover, Germany. After the Black Death persecutions of 1348–49, Jews did not live there until the 17th cent. They established a district community under the Emden rabbinate's jurisdiction in 1844, opened a synagogue in 1853, and maintained an elementary school from 1864 to 1922. The community numbered 85 (about 4% of the total) in 1880 and 120 in 1926. Two associated communities, Gilde-

haus and Schuettorf, were absorbed in 1928. After the synagogue's destruction on *Kristallnacht* (9–10 Nov. 1938), nine Jews emigrated from B., 12 from Gildehaus, and seven (including five who went to Palestine) from Schuettorf. At least 50 others who remained in Germany were deported, 16 (originally from B.) to Auschwitz and to the Sobibor death camp where they are believed to have perished.

BERBESTI   (Hung. Bardfalva) N. Transylvania dist., Rumania. A J. community was founded in 1850. The J. pop. in 1920 was 550 (24% of the total). The Jews were ghettoized in April 1944 and together with those from surrounding villages numbered 3,000. In May they were transferred to the Sighet ghetto. All were deported to Auschwitz and 80% perished there.

BERCEL   Nograd dist., Hungary. Jews settled in the early 19th cent., erecting a synagogue in 1875 and founding a yeshiva c. 1908. The J. pop. was 128 in 1880 and 179 in 1930. The Jews were deported to Auschwitz on 12–14 June via Balassagyarmat and Geres.

BERDICHEV   Zhitomir dist., Ukraine. Jews are first mentioned in 1593 and numbered 1,220 in 1765. The J. pop. grew significantly in the 19th cent., reaching 41,617 (total 53,351) in 1897 and 55,876 on the eve of WWI. Among the prominent rabbis serving the community were Levi Yitzhak, whose presence made B. a center of Ukrainian Hasidism. In the early 19th cent., B. became a center of the Ukrainian Haskala, with modern schools, a public library, and numerous J. printing presses putting out both halakhic and Haskala literature. A number of world-famous musicians were born in the city, including Anton and Nikolai Rubinstein and Vladimir Horovitz. The Zionists and Bund became active at the turn of the 19th cent. The latter dominated the leadership of the J. community from the eve of the Feb. 1917 Revolution until 1919, with a Bund member serving as mayor and head of the community council. In early Jan. 1919, the Petlyura gangs staged a pogrom and killed 23 Jews and injured many others. The Soviet period saw the establishment of the first J. law court in the Ukraine (1924); the first J. police commissariat (1926); and local government offices using Yiddish as an official language alongside Ukrainian and Russian. Yiddish-language elementary and vocational schools

were also founded. In the late 1920s, some Jews earned their livelihoods from agriculture in nearby kolkhozes. Among the well-known writers born in B. were Pinkhes Kahanovich (Der Nister; 1884–1950), Vasili Grossman, (1905–64), and Yosef Yehuda Lerner (1849–1907). The J. pop. in 1939 was 23,266. B. was captured by the Germans on 7 July 1941. About 1,000 Jews managed to flee the city. On 10 July, 300 Jews were executed for supposedly killing a German officer. Another 148 were executed at the end of the month for alleged Communist activity and for "stealing" Christian property. The first *Aktion*, in which 850 Jews were murdered, took place around the end of July. Subsequently a ghetto was established crowding together thousands of Jews. In the second *Aktion*, in late Aug., 2,000 Jews were executed near the village of Bistrik. A third *Aktion*, took place near the village of Khazhin on 5 Sept. 1941 and claimed another 4,300 J. lives. In a major *Aktion* in the last quarter of 1941, 15,000 Jews were massacred near the village of Radienskoye. The few remaining

Synagogue in Berdichev, Ukraine (The Russian Ethnographic Museum, Petersburg/photo courtesy of Yad Vashem, The Holocaust Martyrs' and Heroes' Remembrance Authority, Jerusalem)

Jews were murdered by mid-1942. In all, about 30,000 Jews were murdered, most from B. itself and some from the surrounding settlements. About 6,300 Jews were living in B. in the late 1950s; most left for Israel in the 1990s.

BERDINOVO Odessa dist., Ukraine. A J. council (soviet) was active in the town, which the Germans captured on 7 Aug. 1941. On 14 Nov., they murdered 41 local Jews and 30 from the neighboring settlements.

BEREGSURANY Bereg dist., Hungary. The J. pop. in 1930 was 65. The Jews were deported to Auschwitz via Beregszasz on 20 May 1944.

BEREHOVO (Hung. Beragszasz) Carpatho-Russia, Czechoslovakia, today Ukraine. J. settlement began in the mid-18th cent. Four J. families were present in 1768. The J. pop. then grew to 200 in 1830 and 1,795 (total 6,930) in 1880. An organized community with its own rabbi was formed by the mid-19th cent. In 1861, R. Avraham Yehuda ha-Kohen Schwarz, author

Two Jews walking in Berehovo, Czechoslovakia, 1936

of *Kol Aryeh*, began to officiate there, also founding a yeshiva for 50 students. The yeshiva entered its most flourishing period under R. Shelomo Schreiber (Sofer), who served as rabbi from 1884 to 1930. In the late 1930s, R. Asher Staynmetz opened a yeshiva of his own with 150 students. The J. pop. grew to 4,592 in 1921 and 5,865 (total 19,379) in 1941. During the 1920s and 1930s, the community also maintained a number of prayer houses, welfare and charity institutions, a *talmud torah*, a few *hadarim*, and a J. elementary school. In addition to trade and crafts, Jews were represented in the professions (22 doctors, 17 lawyers) and they also owned two banks, 16 factories, and three flour mills. A few dozen J. families worked on three J. farms. Most of the Zionist parties and organizations were active, especially among the young, including Betar, Hashomer Hatzair, Bnei Akiva, and others. A few dozen Jews emigrated to Palestine before WWII. Hungary annexed the city in fall 1938. In 1941, about 500 Jews were drafted into labor battalions, most being sent to the eastern front, where they perished. About 250, lacking Hungarian citizenship, were deported to German-occupied territory in the Ukraine and murdered there. After the German occupation of Hungary in winter 1944, a temporary ghetto and *Judenrat* were set up in the city. In mid-May, nearly 11,000 Jews were deported to Auschwitz from the ghetto in four transports: 3,600 from B. and 7,400 from the surrounding area.

BEREHY (Hung. Nagybereg; Yid. Bereg) Carpatho-Russia, Czechoslovakia. Jews probably settled at the turn of the 18th cent, numbering 72 in 1880, 142 (total 2,001) in 1921, and 176 in 1941. The Hungarians occupied B. in March 1939 and in 1941 drafted a number of Jews into labor battalions, sending them to forced labor camps. In July 1944, a few J. families without Hungarian citizenship were expelled to Kamenets-Podolski, where they were murdered. The rest were deported to Auschwitz on 18 May 1944.

BEREKBOSZORMENY Bihar dist., Hungary. Jews settled in the early 19th cent., erecting a synagogue in 1880 and numbering 80 in 1930. On 20 May 1944, they were deported to Auschwitz via Beregszasz.

BERESTECZKO Volhynia dist., Poland, today Ukraine. The community dates from the mid-16th cent.

Only 12 of the town's 1,000 Jews survived the Chmielnicki massacres of 1648–1649. The community grew when B. became a transit point for Russian-Austrian trade after the late-18th cent. partition of Poland, reaching 2,251 (total 4,953) in 1897. The rivalry between Olyka and Turzysk Hasidism reflected the social division of the community between rich and poor. The Zionists were active from the early 20th cent. with the youth movements becoming prominent between the World Wars and 200 scouts in Hashomer Hatzair. A Hebrew school and library existed from 1918. In the generally depressed economy, most crafts and trades were in J. hands. Twenty J. firms exported grain, flax, honey, mushrooms, and dairy products to central and western Poland. The. pop. in 1931 was 2,210. The Germans captured B. on 23 June 1941. Around 300 J. men were murdered near the local castle on 8 Aug. A *Judenrat* was appointed and a ghetto was set up in Oct. and the residents put to forced labor. The community was liquidated on 7–9 Sept. 1942.

BERESTI Moldavia dist., Rumania. Jews first settled in 1838 and numbered 560 in 1899 (15% of the total). In 1907 Jews were expelled to Bacau. Persecution led Jews to leave from Sept. 1940 and by early 1941 none remained.

BERETTYOUJFALU Bihar dist., Hungary. Jews settled in the 19th cent., dominating the town's trade and operating a number of factories. A synagogue was built c. 1840 and a J. school was in operation by 1876. The Jews numbered 811 (12% of the total) in 1890 and 982 in 1941. Zionism never took root in B., but in 1938 the community helped ten youngsters go to Palestine. After the German occupation of spring 1944, the Jews were sent to the Nagyvarad ghetto and from there deported to Auschwitz on 29 June. Most of the few dozen Jews of the postwar community emigrated to Israel.

BEREZA KARTUSKA Polesie dist., Poland, today Belaurus. An organized J. community is known from 1662, growing to 2,623 in 1897 (total pop. 6,226) with six synagogues and J. tradesman benefiting from the railway link and the presence of permanent army barracks. Most of the young were attracted to revolutionary circles in the early 20th cent., to the detriment of the budding Zionist movement. Yaakov Klatzkin, an outstanding J. thinker, was born there in 1882. In

WWI much of the town was destroyed. Under the German occupation Jews became prominent in the newly established lumber industry and a Jew served as mayor until the late 1920s. Between the World Wars as well, when the J. pop. dropped to 2,163 (total 3,526), a Jew served as mayor. Zionist activity was extensive and the Bund contended with nationalist circles for domination of the artisan organizations. Hebrew and Yiddish schools existed. The Germans entered the town on 23 June 1941. A *Judenrat* was set up under a regime of forced labor and extortion. In July 1942, 2,500 Jews including refugees were crowded into adjoining ghettoes for the "productive" and the nonworking pop. The latter were brought to Brona Gora on 15 July and murdered. On 15 Oct., as a second *Aktion* commenced, the remaining Jews set the ghetto on fire. Some *Judenrat* members committed suicide; 100 Jews escaping through a tunnel suffocated in the smoke; and 1,800 were brought outside the town the next day and executed. Some J. youth joined partisan groups.

BEREZDOV Kamenets-Podolski dist., Ukraine. Jews numbered 205 in 1765 and 1,319 (49% of the total) in 1897. Sixty of the 100 workers in a J.-owned leather goods factory were Jews. In 1919, during the Russian civil war (1918–21), Jews were attacked in a pogrom. A. J. rural council was active in the 1920s and 1930s. In 1939, the J. pop. was 778. The Germans captured B. on 9 July 1941, executing 1,200 Jews by the end of the year. On 4 March 1942, they expelled 175 Jews to Krasnostav, later bringing them to Slavuta for execution.

BEREZINO Mogilev dist., Belorussia. The J. pop. was 208 in 1766 and 3,377 (total 4,871) in 1897. Peasants from the neighboring villages attacked Jews in 1906 and a pogrom was staged during the Russian civil war (1918–21). In 1930, under the Soviets, 20 J. families worked in a multinational kolkhoz. Many Jews worked in a cooperative. In 1939 their pop. was 1,536. The Germans captured the town on 3 July 1941, concentrating Jews from the surrounding area there in late July. In Aug., 150 Jews were shot and in a major three-day *Aktion* starting on 25 Dec., 1,000 were executed. Most of the children were thrown alive into the mass graves.

BEREZNA Chernigov dist., Ukraine. Jews settled in the early 19th cent. and numbered 1,357 (total 9,922)

THE CHURCH STREET.—TOP LEFT: THE JEWISH HOSPITAL.

קארטוזבערעזע: די צערקאוונע
גאס. אויבן: דער בית החולים.

Church St., Bereza Kartuska, Poland; top left: *the Jewish Hospital*

in 1897. J. property was pillaged and destroyed in a 1905 pogrom. The J. pop. fell to 211 in 1939 after much internal migration. Most Jews fled before the Germans occupied the town on 5 Sept. 1941. Ten were murdered on 5 Dec. and at the end of the month, J. children at the regional children's home were also put to death.

BEREZNE Volhynia dist., Poland, today Ukraine. Jews settled in the mid-16th cent. Fifty J. families lost their lives in the Chmielnicki massacres of 1648–49 and the community did not grow significantly until the 19th cent., the J. pop. reaching a peak of 2,765 (total 4,059) in 1897. Thereafter it declined somewhat in the face of economic stagnation. Spiritual life was dominated from the early 19th cent by the hasidic court founded by Yehiel Mikhal Pechenik of the Stolin-Karlin dynasty. Between the World Wars,

the Zionist parties were active as well as a small Bund group. A Hebrew school and a library existed. The Germans entered the town on 6 July 1941 and established a *Judenrat*. On 6 Oct. 1941, 1,500 Jews were packed into a ghetto after 300 were sent to the Kostopol labor camp; another few hundred were housed in a second ghetto for skilled workers and their families. On 25 Aug. 1942, 3,000, including refugees, were murdered near the J. cemetery. About 150 survived the war, some as partisans.

BEREZNEGOVATOE Nikolaiev dist., Ukraine. J. settlement probably commenced in the mid-19th cent. A pogrom was staged on 30–31 March 1882. The J. pop. in 1939 was 271 (total 6,386). The Germans captured B. on 18 Aug. 1941 and on 15 Sept. murdered the Jews in groups outside the town. Over 2,000 people from the region were murdered during

the war; many were Jews. Over 100 Jews were murdered in Oryanda.

BEREZNICA Volhynia dist., Poland, today Ukraine. After 100 Jews lost their lives in the Chmielnicki massacres of 1648–49, the community only began to grow in the 19th cent., reaching a peak pop. of 2,160 (total 2,964) in 1897 but declining to 1,372 in 1921 as neighboring Sarny with its railway junction attracted many. In 1896, R. Yoel Shurin founded a yeshiva which was transferred in 1903 to Zviahel. The community identified mainly with Stolin and Turzysk Hasidism. The Ukrainians staged a pogrom after the German occupation of July 1941. On 26 Aug. 1942, 1,000 were marched to Sarny; 500 were murdered along the way.

BEREZOVKA Odessa dist., Ukraine. A pogrom took place on 26–27 April 1881. In 1897, the J. pop. was 3,458 (total 6,154). A government school for J. children was operating in the early 20th cent. In the 1920s, under the Soviets, a J. elementary school was founded (still open in 1939) as well as a Yiddish-language night school, a J. club, and a library. Many Jews were employed in artisan cooperatives or in J. kolkhozes (one of them operating until 1939). In 1939, the J. pop. was 1,424. The Germans captured B. on 10 Aug. 1941 and murdered 41 Jews on 14 Aug. Another 100 were murdered on 25 or 26 Aug. and the rest over the following days. In all, 211 Jews were murdered by early Sept. The Rumanians expelled thousands of Jews from Bessarabia and Odessa to the B. region; nearly 7,000 perished.

BEREZOVO (Hung. Berezna; Yid. Berezyv) Carpatho-Russia, Czechoslovakia, today Ukraine. J. settlement probably commenced in the late 18th cent. Over 20 J. families lived in the town in 1830. The J. pop. then grew to 236 (total 1,104) in 1880, 369 in 1921 under Czechoslovakian rule, and 376 in 1941 under the Hungarians. During the Czechoslovakian period, all the town's business establishments were in J. hands. J. youth belonged to Zionist and Orthodox organizations. The Hungarians arrived in March 1939 and in 1941 drafted dozens of Jews into forced labor battalions. In late July 1941, a number of J. families without Hungarian citizenship were expelled to Kamenets-Podolski, where they were murdered. The rest were deported to Auschwitz on 19 May 1944.

BEREZOW Volhynia dist., Poland, today Ukraine. Jews numbered around 100 in the 1930s, increasing to 303 owing to an influx of refugees. The Germans murdered all but 50.

BERGEN Hesse–Nassau, Germany. Established in the early 18th cent., the community numbered 129 (10% of the total) in 1835. It maintained an elementary school, built a new synagogue (1854), and grew to 223 in 1895. Affiliated with the rabbinate of Hanau, it also had members in nearby Fechenheim and a pop. numbering 148 in 1925. The Nazi boycott forced Jews to leave and only nine remained on *Kristallnacht* (9–10 Nov. 1938) when the synagogue's interior was destroyed. Among the 55 Holocaust victims were 28 Jews deported in 1942.

BERGEN OP ZOOM Noord-Brabant dist., Holland. The J. presence dates back to the 18th cent. The J. pop. in 1941 was 73. In Nov. 1942 the Jews were deported to their death in Poland; 21 survived in hiding.

BERGZABERN Palatinate, Germany. A few Jews lived in B. in the mid-14th cent. None remained after the Black Death persecutions of 1348–49. The community was reestablished in the 17th cent, numbering six families in 1681 and 1768. Nineteen families (106 Jews) were present in 1848, including 13 merchants, three artisans, and three merchant-farmers. The J. pop. rose to 123 in 1880 but then declined to 81 in 1900 and 43 in 1932. A synagogue was consecrated in 1850. The J. elementary school, opened in 1837, was recognized as a municipal institute in 1870 but closed in 1915 for lack of students. On *Kristallnacht* (9–10 Nov. 1938), rioters razed the synagogue. Seventeen Jews remained in May 1939, most leaving by the end of 1940. Nineteen emigrated in the Nazi era and the rest moved to other localities in Germany. In addition to two Jews who were deported to the Gurs concentration camp on 22 Oct. 1940, at least 12 more perished in the Holocaust.

BERHOMET PE SIRET Bukovina, Rumania, today Ukraine. Jews first settled in 1804 and were instrumental in making B. the largest village in Bukovina. The J. pop. in 1930 was 979 (10% of the total). The majority of the J. pop. were members of Mizrachi. In May 1941, the J. pop. was force-marched to Storojineti

and then to Vascauti. In Aug. the Jews were deported to Transnistria. Few survived; five were murdered by Ukrainian nationalists.

BERISLAV Nikolaiev dist., Ukraine. J. settlement began in the early 19th cent. In 1882 Jews were attacked and J. property was destroyed in a pogrom. The J. pop. was 2,642 (total 12,149) in 1897 and 230 in 1939 under the Soviets. During the 1930s, a few J. kolkhozes were active in the region, including the Frayer Arbeter kolkhoz with 69 families and a two-grade J. school and the Kaganovich kolkhoz, which also maintained a J. school. A number of Jews from B. earned their living there. The Germans captured B. on 23 Aug. 1941 and on 22 Sept. murdered about 400 Jews from B. and its environs. On 25 Sept., 16 Jews from the Kaganovich kolkhoz were murdered. In early Oct., another 35 Jews from B. were murdered.

BERKACH Thuringia, Germany. Jews first settled there in the 18th cent. and by 1833 the community grew to 152 (33% of the total). The community had a synagogue (1854), its own cemetery (1846), and a school. The J. pop. was 98 in 1895 and 38 in 1895. The 20 to 30 Jews who still lived in B. at the time of the Nazi takeover in 1933 were persecuted and harassed. In spring 1938, the J. community was forced to hand over the synagogue for demolition to the local authorities. The demolition was never carried out and the synagogue, now owned by the municipality, was spared on *Kristallnacht* (9–10 Nov. 1938). On the night of the pogrom, nine Jews were arrested and deported to the Buchenwald concentration camp, where one died. Ten community members made it to safe havens (U.S., Australia, Palestine) before the outbreak of war. At least 14 Jews from B. perished in concentration camps to which they were deported in 1942. After 1989, the old synagogue was restored.

BERLEBURG Westphalia, Germany. Jews are first mentioned in 1640. Four were living under letters of protection in the late 17th cent. and 18 families were present in 1770. In 1812, under the Prussians, Jews living under letters of protection were accorded civil rights; the rest received such rights in 1847. A synagogue was erected in 1800 with a J. school operating within its walls. After it burned down in 1825, construction began on a new synagogue in 1835. The J. pop. reached a peak of 119 in 1843, thereafter declin-

ing steadily to 39 in mid-1933. Under the Nazis, local residents continued to patronize J. stores and merchants despite the boycott. The last J. student at the local secondary school was expelled in Nov. 1938. On *Kristallnacht* (9–10 Nov. 1938), the synagogue was wrecked and J. men were sent to the Oranienburg concentration camp. In the 1934–42 period, 13 Jews moved to other localities in Germany. At least ten emigrated, six to the U.S. Three Jews were deported to the east on 28 April 1942 and the last 15 to the Theresienstadt ghetto on 27 July 1942. Fifteen Jews are known to have perished in the Holocaust.

BERLICHINGEN Wuerttemberg, Germany. The J. community, founded in 1632 by descendants of Jews expelled from Spain, contributed to making the town a center of commercial life. Jews dealt in sheep, cattle, and fish, engaged in moneylending, and ran inns. The pop. reached a peak of 249 in 1854 (total 1,524), with another 50 from Biringen attached to the community

Synagogue in Berlichingen, Germany

and 218 in neighboring Ernsbach (ultimately attached as well when the pop. dwindled to two in 1925). Due to emigration, the J. pop. of B. declined steadily, but after WWI public life intensified. A pioneer training farm, one of the first in Germany, was set up on a nearby estate. In 1933, 68 Jews remained in B. Anti-J. propaganda intensified and J. commercial life increasingly suffered. The synagogue was vandalized on *Kristallnacht* (9–10 Nov. 1938) and later dismantled. Out of 70 Jews remaining in 1939, 43 Jews saved themselves by emigrating, mainly to Palestine, the U.S., and Switzerland; nearly all the others died in the Holocaust.

BERLIN capital of Germany. Jews were probably present in B. soon after it was founded in the late 12th cent. A tombstone found in the J. cemetery of nearby Spandau – which also served the B. community – dates back to 1244, the same year in which the name "Berlin" first appears in a written document. Fifty years later, Jews were mentioned in a document issued by the city council. Although the Jews in B. were not confined to a ghetto, they lived in a narrow section of the town (*Grosser Juedenhof* and *Juedenstrasse*) and until the second half of the 16th cent. buried their dead in Spandau. The medieval J. settlements in Berlin-Coelln and in Spandau were exposed to recurring persecutions and expulsions. The cemetery in Spandau was destroyed in 1350 in the Black Death persecutions, and in 1510, 50 Jews of Berlin, falsely accused of church theft, were tortured to death. All remaining Jews had to take an oath to leave the Brandenburg Mark "forthwith and forever." Nonetheless, individual Jews – notably the mintmaster, Lippold – arrived a few decades later at the summons of the ruling elector. However, when the latter suddenly passed away in 1571, his death was imputed to his hated J. mintmaster, who was executed after a show trial. A fresh start for the J. community only came nearly a hundred years later, when on 21 May 1671, the Great Elector of Brandenburg, Friedrich Wilhelm, issued "an edict concerning the admission of 50 families of protected Jews provided that they do not keep synagogues." The settlement edict was promulgated with an eye to attracting the recently expelled Viennese Jews, but only rich Jews were invited and residence permits were limited to 20 years. The Jews had to pay extra taxes and were forbidden to have public synagogues. Nonetheless, at least 12 J. families were living in Berlin by 1674, their number expanding to

40 by 1688 and to no fewer than 117 in 1700 (2% of the total.) A plot of land for a cemetery was already acquired in 1672 and in 1714 the first public synagogue was festively dedicated in the Heidereuthergasse in the presence of Queen Sophie Dorothea and her court. The Great Elector's successors, King Frederick I and Frederick William I, continued his policy of favoring (and financially squeezing) affluent Jews. In 1724, and again in 1734, poorer Jews, mainly of East European origin, were expelled from B. This notwithstanding, and despite increasingly draconian regulations, the J. pop. of B. continued to expand over the next decades, numbering 2,188 persons in 1750. In the same year, King Frederick II of Prussia (Frederick the Great) published "revised general privileges and regulation for the Jews" which decisively changed their social position for the worse. The new regulation differentiated between two kinds of protected Jews. Ordinary protected Jews (*Schutzjuden*) were entitled to bequeath their "letter of protection" to one of their descendants while the right of "extraordinary" Jews expired with their death, unless they were willing and able to pay the exorbitant sum of 10,000 thalers. Poor Jews were not allowed to marry at all and the J. community was made collectively responsible for debts, thefts, or illegal sojourn of alien Jews. As a result of the restrictive admission policy practiced by the rulers of Brandenburg-Prussia, the B. J. community was from the outset relatively well-to-do. In the course of the 18th cent., some Jews carved a fortune for themselves as tax collectors, court and army suppliers, bankers, wholesalers, or manufacturing entrepreneurs. During the Seven Years War (1756–63), King Frederick II farmed out the minting prerogative to the head of the J. community, Ephraim, who in 1761 acquired a palace which he extended and sumptuously decorated. In 1782, the Ephraim family employed more than 800 persons in its silver and gold factories.

The first decades following the end of the Seven Years War (1763) were a period of economic transformation and spiritual and religious fermentation for the J. community of Berlin, which under the leadership of Moses Mendelssohn (1729–86) and his disciples became a focal point of the Haskala movement. Beginning in the 1770s, Mendelssohn gathered around him a growing circle of young J. scholars, *maskilim*, who like himself were well versed both in the secular world of general learning and in the specifically J. tradition of the Talmud and the Torah. Mendelssohn's disciples

Renowned philosopher Martin Buber lecturing, Berlin, 1934 (Deutsche Bibliothek/photo courtesy of Yad Vashem, The Holocaust Martyrs' and Heroes' Remembrance Authority, Jerusalem)

took over the direction of the Hebrew periodical *Ha-Me'assef,* which, initiated in Koenigsberg, soon became the chief organ of the Hebrew Enlightenment in both Western and Eastern Europe. An integral part of the social milieu of the Berlin Haskala was a new J. economic elite, notably the Itzig and Ephraim families, who engaged the *maskilim* as private tutors, supported them financially, and often intermarried with them. The J. Free School (Juedische Freischule), founded in Berlin in 1778, by Itzig's son and his son-in-law, David Friedlaender, was the first modern J. school that also gave instruction in secular subjects. Towards the end of the 18th cent., a small group of upper class J. women — notably Rahel Varnhagen-Levin and Henriette Herz — operated salons where J. and Christian intellectuals of both sexes could converse on equal terms. Christian Wilhelm Dohm, one of Mendelssohn's gentile friends, formulated in 1781 for the first time a political theory of the emancipation of the Jews. Dohm's ideas were first implemented in the context of the political reforms carried out in Prussia in the wake of its

1806 defeat by Napoleon. In accordance with the Prussian urban ordinance of 1808, associated with the reform of Baron Karl vom Stein, the Jews became citizens entitled to the equal rights in their respective cities. Jews who owned either a business or a home were entitled to vote and to hold honorary offices in town councils. The first Jews to be elected to the Berlin City Council and Parliament (Stadtverordnetenversammlung) were respectively the *maskil* David Friedlaender and the banker Salomon Veit (1751–1827). Both were widely popular among the non-J. pop. The decisive step was taken in 1812, when at the end of a protracted debate initiated by the liberal state chancellor, August von Hardenberg, the Prussian Edict was enacted. This granted all Jews legally living in Prussia at that time the status of "native residents and Prussian citizens." However, in the wake of the Congress of Vienna (1815), the Edict was restricted to Prussia within its 1812 borders; newly won or returned territories were excluded from its scope. Soon after the announcement of the 1812 Edict, David Friedlaender published a

brochure proposing a fundamental reform of the J. religious service. Friedlaender's initiative was seconded
by Israel Jacobson, who in 1810 had instituted in See-
sen\Westphalia the first reformed service in Germany.
Moving to Berlin at the end of 1814, Jacobson instituted a regular modernized service, whose features included an organ and sermons in German delivered by
lay preachers—for the most part young university students. Attracting in their heyday close to a thousand
Berlin Jews, the Jacobson services were moved after
awhile from his private home to a decorous temple
in the spacious house of the wealthy sugar refiner, Jacob Herz Beer (1769–1825). They were, however,
abruptly terminated towards the end of 1823, when
the Prussian government, wary of change and responding to the protests of the traditionalists in the community, ordered their suspension. In 1819, Leopold Zunz
(1794–1886), Eduard Gans (1798–1839), and Moses
Moser (1796–1838) founded in Berlin the Association
for Culture and the Scientific Study of the Jews (Verein fuer Cultur [sic] und Wissenschaft der Juden). The
Verein sought to instill in the Jews a new sense of their
collective identity, to be attained by the study of their
common past. This purpose was served by the publication of the *Zeitschrift fuer die Wissenschaft des Judentums*, the first scientific J. periodical, edited by Zunz.
Both the scholarly project and the spiritual impulses
generated by it outlasted the demise of the first organization, which was dissolved in 1824. In the first decades of the 19th cent., the J. community was afflicted
by a wave of conversions to Christianity. No less than
7% of all the 3,493 Berlin Jews listed in the 1812
Emancipation Edict later converted. Especially affected were the upper strata and the young. In all, it
may be estimated that more than 1,200 Berlin Jews
converted between 1812 and 1847, among them the
descendants of Moses Mendelssohn. The demographic
deficits were offset by the influx of new settlers from
the three eastern provinces: Silesia, West Prussia, and
Posen. The size of the J. pop., which more or less stagnated between 1770 and 1822, began to grow rapidly.
In 1831 there were still 5,000 Jews in Berlin and by
1849 their number had doubled. The newcomers, for
the most part from traditional J. homes, were far less
susceptible to the temptation to convert. In any case,
the wave already appeared to have spent itself; while
326 Jews converted between 1830 and 1836, only sev-
en did so in 1847. After Frederick William IV as-
cended the throne in 1840, the religious controversy

*Peter Fingesten sculpting "Eternity," Berlin, Germany (Deutsche
Bibliothek/photo courtesy of Yad Vashem, The Holocaust Martyrs' and
Heroes' Remembrance Authority, Jerusalem)*

between reform and tradition flared up again. In
1845, the more radical reformers set up their own congregation, which had a nominal membership of only
300 but enjoyed wide support. The Reform congregation was unique in Germany because it held its main
services on Sundays, practically removed Hebrew
from the prayer book, dispensed with the head cover
(*kippa*) for men, and accommodated men and women
during prayer without partition. Rabbi Samuel Hold-
heim (1806–60) led the Reform congregation from
1847. In the 1860s the Liberals succeeded in advancing two of their nominees to the position of rabbi: Joseph Aub and the well-known reformer Abraham Geiger. Introduction of an organ, choir, and German prayers into the service signalized the Liberal dominance
of the New Synagogue in the Oranienburger Strasse.
The consecration of the magnificent Liberal syna-

The Maccabi Berlin and Maccabi Petah Tikva netball teams, Berlin, Germany (Juedisches Museum im Stadtmuseum, Berlin/photo courtesy of Yad Vashem, The Holocaust Martyrs' and Heroes' Remembrance Authority, Jerusalem)

gogue in the presence of Prime Minister Otto von Bismarck in 1866, was a symbol of the new confidence of the J. minority in B. Three years later, the extreme Orthodox, led by Azriel Hildesheimer (1820–99), separated from the B. community, founding their own Orthodox Adass Jisroel congregation, with some 300 members. Already by the late 1840s, the Jews appeared to be well integrated into the life of B. Jews were especially prominent as bankers, traders, and textile entrepreneurs. Half of all the bigger firms and industrial concerns in B. in 1848–49 were in J. hands. Several Jews served as city councilors and a number of Jews from B., some baptized, rose to fame around the mid-19th cent. Mendelssohn's grandson, the com-

poser Felix Mendelssohn, and the poet Heinrich Heine were both converted Jews. On the other hand, without departing from Judaism, the composer Giacomo Meyerbeer (son of the banker Jacob Herz Beer) served between 1842 and 1847 as the general musical director of the Royal Opera in Berlin. Most Jews in Berlin enthusiastically embraced the March 1848 revolution. Zunz took an active part in the preparations for the Prussian and the Frankfurt National Assemblies and in early 1849 was one of the founders of the Democratic People's Party (Demokratische Volkspartei). Koenigsberg-born Johann Jacoby entered the Frankfurt Assembly after winning a seat in the Prussian Assembly in Berlin, becoming one of the prominent

The Jewish Cultural Association Orchestra, Berlin, Germany

spokesmen for the democratic movement. However, the J. hope that the revolution would bring in its wake complete and unqualified equal rights was only partly fulfilled. Although the Prussian state was forced to incorporate in its constitution the Frankfurt bill of rights of Dec. 1848, which promised equal status to all religious minorities, this was largely revoked through the revised constitution of Jan. 1850. During the reactionary backlash of the 1850s, Jews were once again excluded from any civil, judicial, military, or academic office which required its holder to take a Christian oath. Formal legal discrimination was only removed when the "Law of the Equality of Religions as regards Common and State Civil Rights" was passed in July 1869 in the course of establishing the North German Confederation.

With the establishment of the German Reich in 1871, B. became the capital city of Germany and a leading European metropolis. Freed of the former legal constraints, especially those pertaining to their freedom of movement and settlement, Jews began to stream into the capital city. In 1852, there were still fewer than 10,000 Jews in B. By 1871 there were already 36,326 — a more than threefold increase in less than 20 years. In the following decades, the J. pop. of Greater B. more than quadrupled, rising from 64,355 in 1885 to 144,043 in 1910 and peaking at 172,672 in 1925. The increase in the J. pop. kept pace with that of the general pop. of B., the relative proportion shifting from 3.9% in 1871 to 3.86% in 1910 and 4.29% in 1925. In the latter year, B. had the fourth largest J. pop. in Europe and the seventh in the world. In the course of the last third of the 19th cent., a concentration of poorer J. immigrants from Eastern Europe, driven from their na-

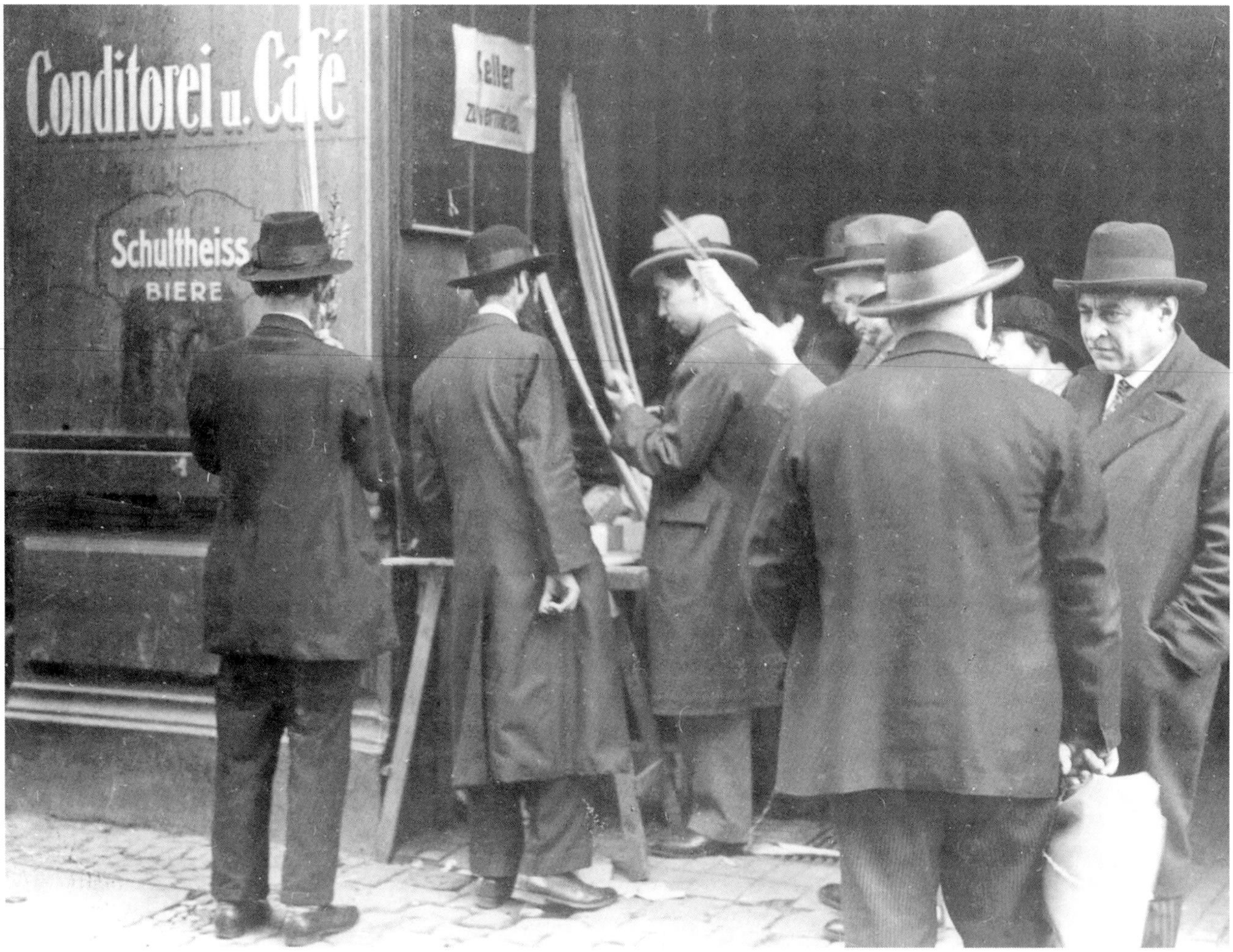
Conditorei u.
Schultheiss
BIERE

Examining lulavim (palm shoots) *before Sukkot at a Grenadier St. stand, Berlin, Germany, 1933 (Bundesarchiv/photo courtesy of Yad Vashem, The Holocaust Martyrs' and Heroes' Remembrance Authority, Jerusalem)*

tive lands by economic hardship and pogroms, began to develop in the Scheunenviertel neighborhood. The Scheunenviertel seemed to replicate an East European *shtetl*, complete with its own J. hotels, groceries, butcher shops, street stands, peddlers, and idlers. The Jews from Eastern Europe (*Ostjuden*) constituted a social and cultural enclave within the established and acculturated J. minority, which tended to view them as unwelcome intruders, preventing a complete and seamless integration of Jews into the German environment. The percentage of foreign-born Jews – coming for the most part from Poland, Russia, and Galicia – within the J. pop. of the city rose from 19% in 1910 to more than 25% in 1925. At the other pole of the social scale, the J. upper class had its homes in the villa colony of the fashionable Grunewald neighborhood. During the peak period of the Weimar Republic, the soaring rate of mixed marriages, more frequent in Berlin than in the less urbanized parts of Germany, was a troublesome phenomenon. The percentage of mixed marriages rose from 27% in 1900 to 34% in 1921, reaching more than 45% in 1929, i.e., for every two J. marriages there was one mixed marriage. J. prominence in the life of Berlin was also a function of the uneven J. occupational distribution, Jews being especially conspicuous in those branches of the economy that had to do with commerce and trade. More than a half of the J. breadwinners were in commerce as shopkeepers, merchants, sellers, apprentices, bookkeepers, brokers, etc. Jews dominated the readymade clothing industry in Berlin both as company owners and as workers. Most workers in this trade were new immigrants from the east and

women. With their greater economic flexibility and their traditional specialization in finance and brokerage, the Jews seemed better attuned to the spirit of the new capitalistic age than the German pop. Especially notable was the pioneering role of Jews in the introduction of the modern institution of department stores, with its revolutionary new concept of consumption. Among the most outstanding J. figures in the economic life of B. in the second half of the 19th cent. were the bankers Gerson von Bleichroeder (who served as financial adviser to the Prussian government and to Bismarck) and Carl Fuerstenberg; the publishers Mosse, Ullstein, and Fischer; the department store owners Nathan Israel, Arthur Wertheim, Hermann Tietz (Hertie), Adolf Jandorf (founder of the Ka De We); the industrialist Emil Rathenau (founder of the AEG). Jews comprised half of the 60 wealthiest taxpayers in B. during the Wilhelminian period. With their traditional emphasis on education and learning, Jews were not slow to take full advantage of the new opportunities opened to them in the age of emancipation and acculturation. By 1893, almost a fourth of all grammar school pupils in B. were Jews. J. girls constituted a third of all those enrolled in the women's colleges. More than 66% percent of all J. children in B. received secondary school education compared to 8% of all children in Prussia in 1906-07. In 1886-87, 37% of all students at the University of Berlin medical school were Jews. In 1905–06, 41% of all J. students in Prussia studied law and in 1907 there were already 526 J. lawyers in B. alone, more than half of all the attorneys there. In 1911, the Kaiser Wilhelm Society for the Advancement of the Sciences counted amongst its members several J. scientists, including three who subsequently became Nobel Prize winners: Albert Einstein, Richard Willstaetter, and (the baptized) Fritz Haber. From the 1848 Revolution, Jews played an increasingly active role in the political life of the capital, both at the local and at the Reich level. The liberal politician Wolfgang Strassmann served from 1876 as chairman of the city parliament; Eduard Lasker became leader of the National-Liberal party in the Prussian Landtag (state parliament); the Breslau-born Ferdinand Lassalle worked out his socialist theories in B.; and Paul Singer was for many years a leader of the Social Democratic faction in the Berlin city parliament. On the extreme reactionary right of the political spectrum, the baptized politician Friedrich Julius Stahl became a leading exponent of the ultra-conservative "Christian State." In

their voting behavior, however, the majority of the Jews of B. steered clear of radical politics. Some 70% of the J. vote of B. in the 1860s and 1870s went to the middle-class party of the National-Liberals. After its foundation, the Jews shifted their loyalty to the leftist liberal German Democratic Party (DDP), dubbed by antisemites as the "Jew party." J. participation in German politics in Imperial Germany was overshadowed by a resurgence of antisemitism which colored the political scene during the last two decades of the 19th cent. To B. belongs the dubious distinction of being the birthplace of modern antisemitism. The very word "antisemitism" was coined there in 1879 by the journalist Wilhelm Marr, author of the pamphlet "The Victory of Judaism over Germanic Culture" and founder of the "Antisemitic League." The psychological impact of the stock exchange crash in 1873 provided fertile ground for a concerted publicity campaign, conducted by the Catholics and the Protestant Conservatives, against Bismarck and his supposed Lib-

World-famous physicist Albert Einstein, Berlin, Germany (Landesbildstelle, Berlin/photo courtesy of Beth Hatefutsoth, Tel Aviv)

Irmingard Willner's dance school, Berlin, Germany, 1936 (Juedisches Museum im Stadtmuseum, Berlin/photo courtesy of Yad Vashem, The Holocaust Martyrs' and Heroes' Remembrance Authority, Jerusalem)

eral and J. allies. Adolf Stoecker, the court preacher, took advantage of the public mood to organize the first antisemitic political party anywhere. The University of Berlin professor Heinrich Treitschke, author of the slogan "The Jews are our misfortune," helped make the movement socially acceptable. A declaration signed in spring 1881 by 75 Christian notables, among them the classical historian Theodor Mommsen, warned against the revival of ancient prejudices. It was the sensational success of the antisemitic parties in the Reichstag elections that prompted the Berlin J. lawyers Maximilian Horowitz and Eugen Fuchs to found in 1893

the Central Union of German Citizens of the J. Faith (C. V.). Founded to defend the J. minority against antisemitism, the Central Union became in time a mass organization, claiming to represent the great majority of the German Jews. In 1897, four years after the Central Union, the German Zionist Organization (Zionistische Vereinigung fuer Deutschland, ZVfD) was set up, representing a completely different type of response to antisemitism. While the Central Union was predicated on the Liberal assumption that Judaism was merely a religion and that German Jews differed from their non-J. compatriots only by their faith, the point of departure

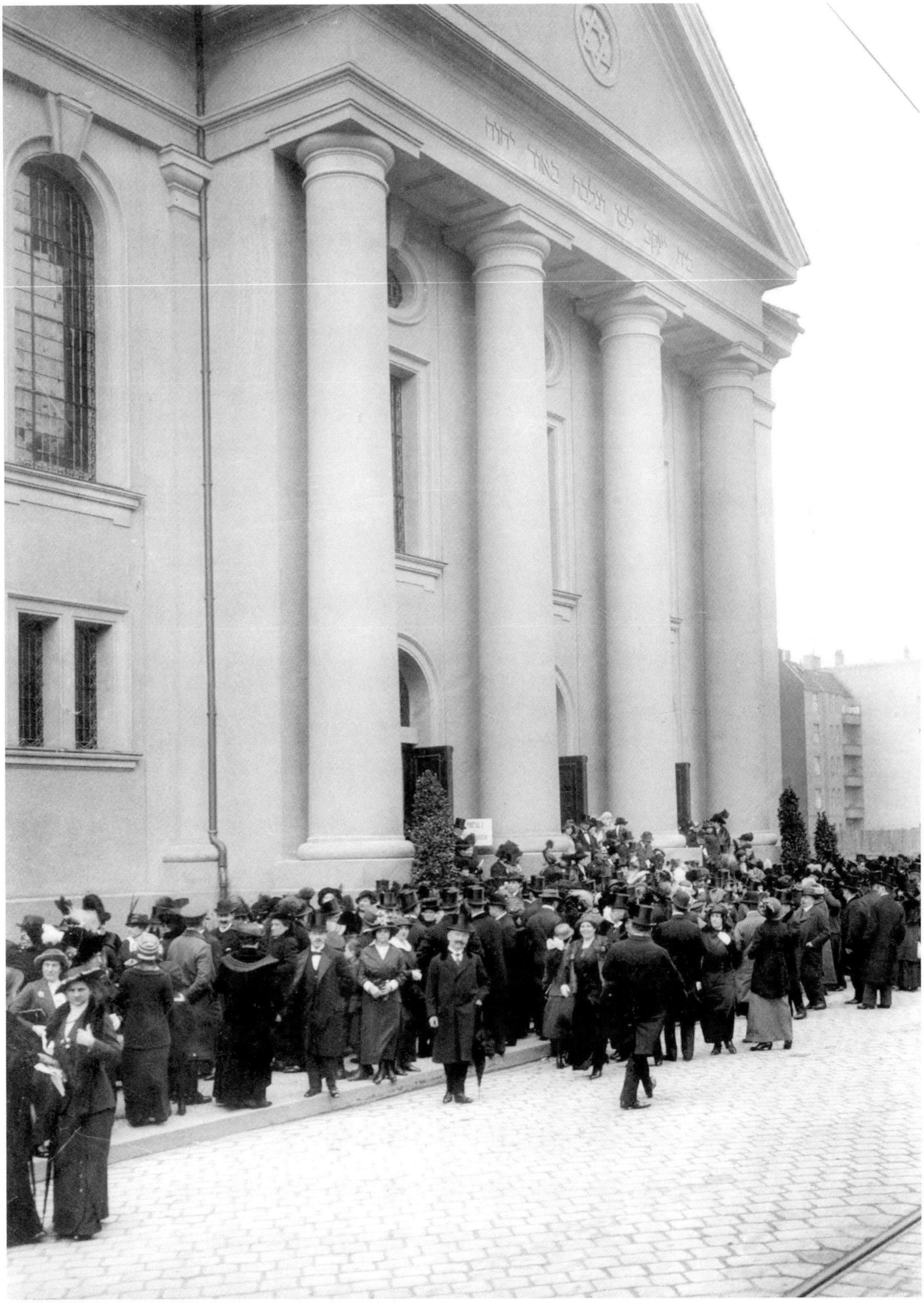

The Moabit Synagogue, Berlin, Germany, 1912

of the Zionists was the belief in the ethnic-national uniqueness of the Jews and the futility of fighting anti-semitism in the Diaspora. At the same time, the Zion-ists, in keeping with their ideology, emphasized their solidarity with East European Jews. It was a young Zionist medical student, Siegfried Lehmann, who in May 1916 founded the J. People's Home in East Berlin to take care of the new immigrants. The Zionists, how-ever, failed to convince the majority of the Berlin Jews, who subscribed overwhelmingly to the Liberal point of view. The first notable Zionist breakthrough in Berlin was achieved in 1928, when G. Kareski, representing the Zionist-related J. People's Party, was elected chair-man of the J. community. Kareski held the office for two years until the Liberals returned to power in late 1930. In its bid to "conquer" the community, the J. People's Party was operating against the official, Pales-tine-centered line of the German Zionist Organization headed by Kurt Blumenfeld. At the outbreak of WWI in 1914, German Jews of every ideological conviction and shade were gripped by the super-patriotic wave that swept across Germany in the initial stages of the war. Even figures like the Zionist philosopher Martin Buber and the Liberal Rabbi Leo Baeck joined the pa-triotic chorus. Close to 20,000 Berlin Jews fought for their German fatherland in the war; many paid with their lives. The initial enthusiasm soon gave way to disillusionment at the spectacle of the revival of anti-semitism during the war, manifested most dramatically in the J. census of 1916, which purported to determine the truth of the allegations that the Jews were shirking military service and particularly combat duty. The anti-semitic libel was fanned by the humiliating German de-feat and the legend of the J. "stab in the back." During the Weimar Republic, several Berlin Jews came to oc-cupy high state offices. Hugo Preuss, a constitutional lawyer, drafted the Weimar constitution. Preuss, Walther Rathenau, son of the founder of the AEG, and Rudolf Hilderling were Reich ministers. Paul Hirsch became minister-president of Prussia. At the municipal level, Bernhard Weiss served as deputy di-rector of the Berlin police. The J. contribution to the cultural life of the capital — what came to be known as "Weimar culture" — was crucial, be it as producers, consumers, or patrons of the arts. Among the J. musical composers and directors who were active in Berlin were Otto Klemperer, Bruno Walter, Arnold Schoen-berg, and Kurt Weil. Max Reinhard was a leading the-ater director. Ernst Lubitsch and Carl Mayer were well-

known film directors. Alfred Doeblin was an innova-tive novelist. The painter Max Liebermann was elected in 1919 president of the Prussian Academy of Arts. The Hebrew novelist and later Nobel Prize winner, S. Y. Agnon, lived in Berlin from 1912 to 1924. The J. community and its institutions continued to play a vital role in the life of the Jews in Imperial and Weimar Ger-many. Some 1,500 permanent employees worked in the Berlin J. community during the 1920s. The community maintained synagogues, schools, libraries, and ceme-teries as well as social welfare institutions like hospi-tals, old age homes, and kindergartens. One-seventh of all J. children attended J. schools. For the majority who attended public schools, the community provided 48 religious instruction schools. Berlin in the 1920s boasted more synagogues than any other European city, including 12 large community synagogues, with an average capacity of 2,000 seats; 70 private syna-gogues; and numerous smaller prayer rooms set up mainly by East European Jews. Most synagogues be-longed to the Liberal majority stream. In 1872 Abra-ham Geiger and Moritz Lazarus opened in Berlin the Hochschule fuer die Wissenschaft des Judentums, which was destined to become one of the most signifi-cant teaching seminaries in the modern J. world. Although formally professing to be non-partisan, the Hochschule was clearly biased in the Liberal, progres-sive direction. Some leading J. thinkers of the age ei-ther taught or studied there, including Martin Buber, Leo Baeck, and Salomon Schechter, one of the found-ers of the Conservative movement in the U.S. A year later, in 1873, the leader of the Orthodox Adass Jisroel congregation, Azriel Hildesheimer, founded his own rabbinical seminary. Berlin was the seat of a host of J. organizations. Aside from the two main ideological adversaries, the Central Union and the German Zionist Organization, there was the National Association of J. War Veterans (Reichsbund Juedischer Frontsoldaten, RjF). Founded in 1919 by retired army captain Leo Loewenstein (1879–1956), the association set itself the task of refuting the antisemitic slander and redeem-ing the honor of the German J. soldiers who fought and died in WWI. The League of J. Women (*Juedischer Frauenbund, JFB*) was founded in 1904 by Bertha Pappenheim, an early J. feminist. Apart from these ma-jor organizations, there were also numerous sports, youth, religious, welfare, and cultural associations. Under the ever-lengthening shadow of racial antisemit-ism, the extreme right-wing parties conducted mali-

cious hate propaganda against the "J. republic" and the J. "traitors." In 1922, Foreign Minister Rathenau was gunned down on the streets of Berlin. The new J. immigrants from the east formed an ideal target for those fanning the flames of racial hatred. In 1923, unemployed workers attacked J. residents of the Scheunenviertel neighborhood. In Sept. 1931, Nazi hooligans stormed a J. coffee house and assaulted passers-by in the luxurious Kurfuerstendamm lane in the west of the city.

Until Hitler's accession to power, Berlin could not be reckoned as a Nazi bastion. In the last free Reichstag elections of Nov. 1932, the Nazis won only 26% of the vote there – below the national average of 33%. After 1933, Berlin became the capital of the Third Reich and the nerve center of Nazi persecution policy. Not only the Reich ministries, but also the Nazi party and the Nazi instruments of terror – the Gestapo, the SS and, after 1939, the Reich Security Head Office – had their head offices in Berlin. The future propaganda minister Joseph Goebbels, who had been appointed by Hitler as Gauleiter (Nazi administrative head) of Berlin in 1926, regarded it as his special mission to rid the capital city of the Nazi Reich of its J. pop. The first J. victims were party activists, intellectuals, and artists of J. descent who had identified themselves in the past as the political opponents of the Nazis. Many were apprehended, maltreated, and thrown into makeshift concentration camps without trial. At the same time, the police and the SA carried out demonstrative raids in the Scheunenviertel neighborhood, for instance on 9 March – body-searching and arresting passers-by, especially Orthodox Jews. Anticipating the general boycott of 1 April and the Civil Service Law of 7 April, the municipality already took steps in March 1933 to remove J. judges and lawyers from the courts and to cancel the contracts of J. medical doctors working in city hospitals. On the day of the boycott, SA and SS troops stood guard before J. shops as well as the work places of J. lawyers, estate agents, and medical doctors. In the next months numerous J. civil servants were fired. In June 1933, there were 16,643 Jews listed as unemployed. The economic effect of the discriminatory legislation of spring 1933 was in fact uneven. While thousands of J. lawyers, physicians, and public employees lost their livelihood, most private businesses were still able to operate during the first years. By Aug. 1935, the J. pop. of B. had declined from the 160,564 registered in the Nazi census of June 1933

to just over 153,000 and by the beginning of 1938 to 140,000. An estimated 28,000 Jews had left Berlin during the first three years and a further 20,000 during the years 1936–37. However, their number was partly offset by an influx of Jews from all over Germany. A directory of addresses prepared in June 1936 lists some 19 leading J. organizations which had their main offices in Berlin. The Reichsvertretung, the main umbrella organization, was set up in Sept. 1933 by all the major constitutive forces of German Jewry to coordinate J. activity and represent the German Jews before the regime. Leo Baeck, the Berlin Liberal rabbi, was chosen by unanimous consent as president. The Berlin J. community, chaired since May 1933 by Julius Stahl (Liberals), tried to cope with the disastrous effects of Nazi discrimination policy to the best of its limited ability. In 1933, the community was assisting more than 19,000 needy persons, apart from an additional 21,000 aid recipients in the framework of J. Winter Relief. The Central Bureau for J. Economic Relief of the J. community and the credit associations extended short-term loans to hard-hit self-employed Jews. J. institutions were encouraged to give preference to J. artisans and suppliers. The Kulturbund staged concerts, theater productions, and lectures, providing jobs to many unemployed J. artists. The J. educational system was greatly expanded to accommodate the growing number of J. pupils ejected from German public schools. By the end of 1937, there were still 2,122 J. children attending public schools in Berlin compared to 6,846 at 24 J. schools. The Juedisches Lehrhaus offered courses in J. history and philosophy to adults intent on rediscovering their J. identity. The Zionist paper, the *Juedische Rundschau*, and its ideological rival, the *CV-Zeitung*, counted among their readers thousands of Berlin Jews. The Berlin Palestine Office, affiliated to the Zionist Organization, was flooded by thousands of applications for precious immigration certificates to Palestine. The Zionist Hehalutz provided much sought-after training courses for youths preparing for future emigration to Palestine. The Hilfsverein offered counseling and aid to those seeking to emigrate to countries other than Palestine. In autumn 1937, Goebbels and Count Helldorf, the Berlin police chief, intervened to speed up the process of segregation and isolation of the J. pop. Emulating the Gestapo, the municipality, for its part, began to prepare its own list of Jews. In Nov. 1937, it published a list of all J. medical doctors in the capital city, together with their addresses. The

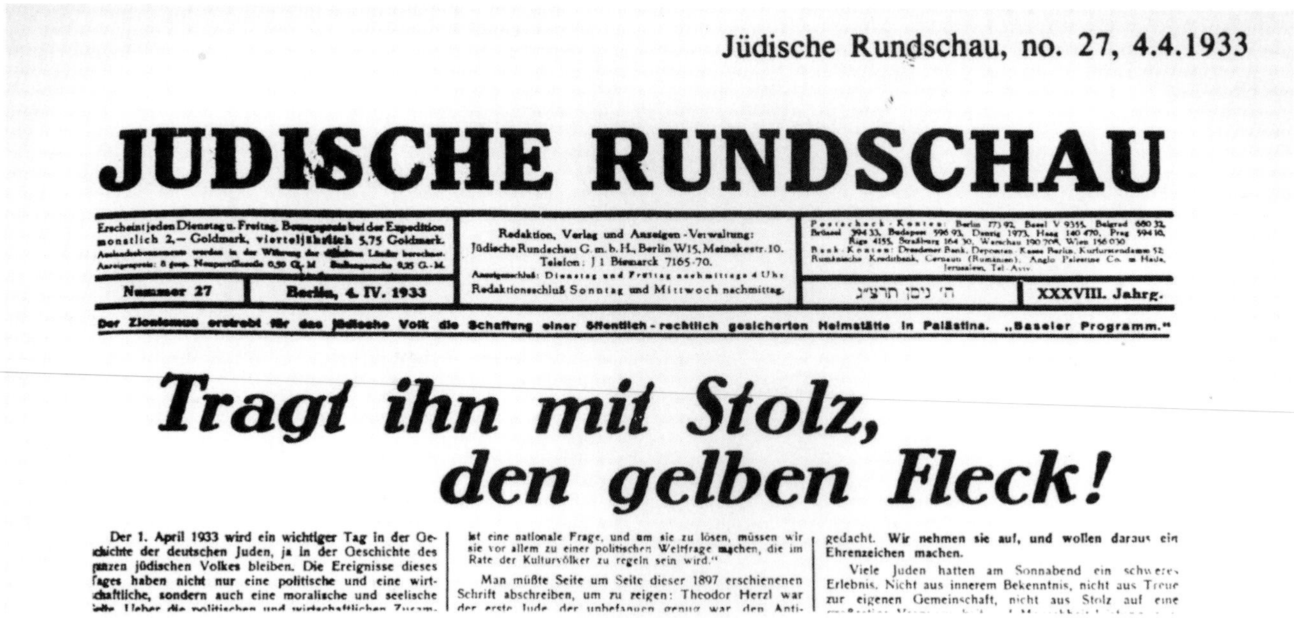

Jüdische Rundschau, no. 27, 4.4.1933

JÜDISCHE RUNDSCHAU

Erscheint jeden Dienstag u. Freitag. Bezugspreis bei der Expedition monatlich 2,– Goldmark, vierteljährlich 5,75 Goldmark.

Redaktion, Verlag und Anzeigen-Verwaltung: Jüdische Rundschau G. m. b. H., Berlin W15, Meinekestr. 10. Telefon: J 1 Bismarck 7165-70.

Redaktionsschluß Sonntag und Mittwoch nachmittag.

Nummer 27 | Berlin, 4. IV. 1933 | ה׳ ניסן תרצ״ג | XXXVIII. Jahrg.

Der Zionismus erstrebt für das jüdische Volk die Schaffung einer öffentlich-rechtlich gesicherten Heimstätte in Palästina. „Baseler Programm."

Tragt ihn mit Stolz, den gelben Fleck!

Der 1. April 1933 wird ein wichtiger Tag in der Geschichte der deutschen Juden, ja in der Geschichte des ganzen jüdischen Volkes bleiben. Die Ereignisse dieses Tages haben nicht nur eine politische und eine wirtschaftliche, sondern auch eine moralische und seelische Seite. Ueber die politischen und wirtschaftlichen Zusam-

ist eine nationale Frage, und um sie zu lösen, müssen wir sie vor allem zu einer politischen Weltfrage machen, die im Rate der Kulturvölker zu regeln sein wird."

Man müßte Seite um Seite dieser 1897 erschienenen Schrift abschreiben, um zu zeigen: Theodor Herzl war der erste Jude, der unbefangen genug war, den Anti-

gedacht. Wir nehmen sie auf, und wollen daraus ein Ehrenzeichen machen.

Viele Juden hatten am Sonnabend ein schweres Erlebnis. Nicht aus innerem Bekenntnis, nicht aus Treue zur eigenen Gemeinschaft, nicht aus Stolz auf eine

Front page of the German Zionist newspaper Juedische Rundschau *with an article by Robert Weltsch, "Wear the Yellow Badge Proudly!" Berlin, 4 April 1933*

list was to be hung in all municipal offices and other public institutions. In Feb. and March 1938 similar lists were prepared for J. dental surgeons and dentists. Goebbels urged the Berlin police to work out more radical methods for pushing forward the process of displacing the Jews. In summer 1938, Albert Speer also began to contribute his share. As the "General Inspector of Building for the Replanning of Berlin," he demanded that the Ministry of Justice lift the legal protection of J. tenants. Goebbels, more than any other Nazi, was responsible for instigating the *Kristallnacht* pogrom of 9–10 Nov. 1938. Berlin, where more than a third of the German Jews lived at the time, was especially hard hit. J. shops were looted and destroyed and a carpet of glass splinters covered the streets where most J. shops were located: Kurfuerstendamm, Tauenziehenstrasse, and the Wilmersdorfer Strasse. More than 40 synagogues were burned and destroyed. The Liberal synagogue in the Fasanenstrasse was invaded on the evening of 9 Nov. by a unit of SA troops who, after systematically wrecking its interior, set fire to the whole building. Other famous synagogues suffered a similar fate. The oldest synagogue in the Heidereuthergasse and a number of synagogues in the Pestalozzi- and Rykestrasse were desecrated and plundered but not destroyed because of their proximity to other buildings. Dozens of Jews were murdered on the night of the pogrom and some 12,000 men were arrested. Many were deported to the Sachsenhausen concentration camp, where they were incarcerated during the harsh winter months. The remaining J. associations, including the Zionist Organization and the Central Union, were closed down. J. newspapers had already been banned on the eve of the pogrom. In May 1939, there were still 78,713 "Jews by religion" registered in B. About 80,000 Jews had left Berlin between 1933 and the outbreak of war in Sept. 1939. Those who remained were mostly older and poorer Jews. All J. property had been forcibly "Aryanized" (that is, confiscated) and Jews were prohibited from practicing their professions. From April 1940, practically all men between 18 and 55 and women between 18 and 50 were required to register with the labor office for work assignments. In 1940, there were more than 20,000 Jews deployed as forced laborers in Berlin and by July 1941, there were 26,000–28,000 persons – 45% of them women – working in more than 230 German firms and concerns. In April 1939, all protection for J. tenants was rescinded by law and, in accordance with the previous arrangement between Speer and the Berlin police chief, the remaining J. pop. was increasingly concentrated in so-called J. houses (*Judenhaeuser*). A ban issued by the police on 3 Dec. 1938 had already denied access of all Jews to public theaters, cinemas,

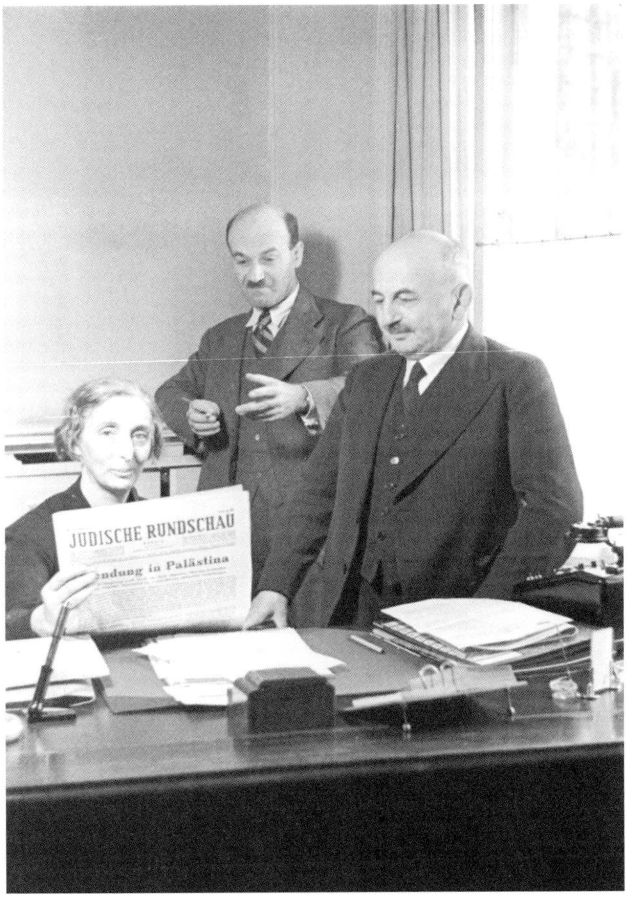
JUDISCHE RUNDSCHAU

Robert Weltsch (center), *editor of the* Juedische Rundschau, *the German Zionist newspaper, and Kurt Blumenfeld* (right), *former chairman of the German Zionist Organization, Berlin, Germany, 1937 (Juedisches Museum im Stadtmuseum, Berlin/photo courtesy of Yad Vashem, The Holocaust Martyrs' and Heroes' Remembrance Authority, Jerusalem)*

concerts, museums, fairgrounds, exhibition halls, parks, swimming pools, sports facilities, ice rinks, etc. After the start of the war, the remaining Jews were subjected to an endless series of humiliating prohibitions: their telephone connections were cut, their radios confiscated, and their use of public transport restricted. They were limited to specific hours and specific shops when purchasing food. Perhaps the most bitter blow of all was the order of 8 Sept. 1941 directing all Jews over the age of six to wear a yellow Star of David, sewn to the upper left front of their clothing. As of July 1939, the Berlin J. community was integrated into the Reich Union of the Jews of Germany (Reichsvereinigung der Juden in Deutschland), the Nazi-imposed organization which succeeded the voluntary Reichsvertretung. Heinrich Stahl, who had headed the B. community since May 1933 and in early 1940 had fallen out with the Gestapo over his intention to emigrate, was replaced by Moritz Henschel. At that time, the B. community leadership became increasingly the captive of the Gestapo and an unwitting link in the machinery of destruction. Employment with the community organization became a coveted privilege, the only way to dodge the forced labor requirement and – after 1941 – a chance to delay deportation. On Yom Kippur 1941, several leading officials of the J. community – including Chairman Henschel, his deputy (Philipp Kozower), and Dr. Martha Mosse, the director of the community's housing office – were summoned by the acting director of the J. section of the Gestapo, who informed them of the impending deportations. The J. officials were ordered to fill out 3,000 questionnaires and to make the Levetzowstrasse synagogue ready for the reception of 1,000 persons. Throughout the deportations of Jews from Berlin – some 180 in all – the Gestapo was to rely on the J. community's list for the names and addresses of Jews. The first transport left on 18 Oct. 1941 with 1,013 persons in the direction of the Lodz ghetto. By the end of Jan. 1942, there were still 58,637 Jews living in Berlin, of which 21,000 were working as forced laborers. About 2,000 were employed in J. institutions. In May 1942, the "Baum group," a J.-Communist resistance organization, carried out an arson attack on the Nazi propaganda exhibition "Soviet Paradise." The head of the group, Herbert Baum, and other ringleaders were caught and later executed. In response, the Gestapo arrested 500 J. hostages in Berlin. Half were shot and half were deported to Auschwitz. The leaders of the J. communities in Berlin and Vienna, as well as the Reichsvereinigung, were summoned by the Gestapo, informed of the decision to shoot the hostages, and threatened with further reprisals. The transports of the elderly and "privileged" to the Theresienstadt ghetto began in June 1942. Among the first deportees was Heinrich Stahl, the chairman of the Berlin community for many years. By Sept. 1942 there were only 46,658 Jews in B. In Oct. 1942, the Gestapo carried out for the first time a selection of community employees which led to the arrest of 345 persons and deportation to the Riga ghetto. Twenty were able to escape. In response, the Gestapo arrested in Nov. 20 leading personalities of the J. community and the Reichsvereinigung. Eight were shot and the members of their families deported later. The dwindling J. pop. was making it increasingly difficult to meet the re-

quired deportation quotas. At this stage, Alois Brunner and his Viennese team of deportation experts, including four J. orderlies, were brought to B. Brunner introduced new terrorist methods by which Jews destined for deportation were rounded up in their homes and on the streets without prior notice. J. employees of the community were forced to accompany Gestapo search parties. The J. old age home in the Grosse Hamburger Strasse was transformed into a transit camp, capable of holding up to 1,500 Jews. In Dec. 1942, the last big deportation phase began and by Feb. 1943 there were only 27,000 Jews living in Berlin, more than half of the remaining J. pop. in Germany. In the last big roundup of Jews in Berlin beginning on 27 Feb. 1943 — nicknamed *"Fabrik-Aktion"* — Jews were arrested at their workplaces in the factories. Of the more than 11,000 Jews arrested in the last, final roundup, 8,568 "unprotected" Jews were deported in March 1943. Jews in mixed marriages were separated from the rest and held in a building belonging to the J. community in Rosenstrasse. After vigorous protests and demonstrations by their non-J. spouses, they and the so-called racial half-Jews raised as Jews (*Geltungsjuden*) were released in the course of March 1943. After the March transports, there were still 18,515 Jews living in Berlin. In the ensuing transports, the Gestapo deported the remaining community officials — including the last community chairman Moritz Henschel. The Berlin J. community had already been dissolved on 28 Jan. 1943 and all its assets confiscated. The last J. "colony" in the capital — some 800 persons — was located in the J. hospital in the Iranische Strasse. The main activity of the hospital was to provide medical help to the few thousand Jews who still remained in Berlin — for the most part Jews in "privileged" mixed marriages. After the war, there were about 7,500 Jews in Berlin: 4,200 escaped deportation by dint of their "privileged" mixed marriage status; 1,400 were so-called *"U-Boote"* Jews who evaded deportation by going underground; 1,900 returned to Berlin from the concentration camps (especially from the Theresienstadt ghetto). All in all, about 35,500 Berlin Jews were deported to the death camps in the east in more than 60 transports and about 15,000 were deported to the Theresienstadt ghetto in more than 120 trains. The last transport to Theresienstadt left Berlin on 27 March 1945. It is estimated that more than 55,000 Jews from Berlin perished under the Nazis. The latter figure also includes those who died in concentration camps and

pogroms before the war and hundreds who committed suicide under persecution and the threat of deportation. A provisional J. community had already been set up a few days after liberation on the initiative of a few Jews and in Feb. 1946 it was recognized as a corporate association under public law. The three synagogues that survived the Nazis were renovated and rededicated. Elections to the J. community executive were held for the first time in Jan. 1948 and Heinz Galinski (1912–92), born in the north German town of Marienburg, was chosen in 1949 as chairman of the community, a post he was to retain for the next 44 years until his death in 1992. With the division of Berlin between the powers, the J. community was split in Jan. 1953 between East and West Berlin. Only a small community of a few hundred continued to exist in East Berlin, its numbers declining from 1,500 in 1949 to 450 in the 1970s and a token 200 in the 1980s. In contrast to West Berlin, the Jews living in East Berlin were for the most part assimilated German Jews who did not feel themselves Jews either in the religious or in the ethnic-national sense. Under the German Democratic Republic, the community in East Berlin was poor, cut off from the J. centers in the west and Israel, and its managing board reduced to subservient obedience. A change in the official line made itself felt only in the late 1980s, when the government allocated money for the reconstruction of the Neue Synagoge and began to support J. cultural events, especially those commemorating the 50th anniversary of *Kristallnacht*. A short time before its fall, the Communist regime sanctioned the reestablishment of the Orthodox Adass Jisroel in East Berlin, which by 1998 had 300 members. By contrast, the West Berlin community, under the dynamic leadership of Galinski, enjoyed the good will of the Federal Republic, which supported its existence and financed its activities. A new community center was dedicated in 1959 and a J. adult education center was opened in 1961. In 1971, the Berlin Senate undertook to support the J. community in the execution of its tasks. This agreement was replaced in 1993 by a formal state treaty. With the German reunification of 1990, the East and West Berlin J. communities also united. About half of the 6,000-strong Berlin J. community in 1980 consisted of J. emigrants from Russia. The influx of J. emigrants after the fall of Communism increased and from 1997, the community bulletin has been published in German and Russian. In June 1997, Andreas Nachama was elected chairman. Numbering

over 12,000 members (1998), the Berlin community is among the fastest growing J. communities in the world.

BERLINCHEN (Pol. Barlinek) Brandenburg, Germany, today Poland. The community of B. numbered 130 Jews in 1880. It had a synagogue and a cemetery and from 1860 employed a religious education teacher. When the Nazis came to power in 1933, there were 26 Jews in B. No further information about their fate is available.

BERNBURG Anhalt, Germany. A J. resident is mentioned in 1301, and in the second half of the 15th cent. there is evidence of a J. settlement. A modern community developed from the end of the 17th cent. With more than 200 individuals at the beginning of the 19th cent., the J. pop. of B. peaked in 1887 at 400. The community established two synagogues in 1731 and 1835. It maintained two cemeteries (the second one from 1826) and employed rabbis from 1831 to 1916. From the 1830s, the community defined itself as Liberal. By 1933, the J. pop. had shrunk to 172 individuals. On *Kristallnacht* (9-10 Nov. 1938), the synagogue was looted and burned down, J. businesses and homes were wrecked, and J. men were taken off to the Buchenwald concentration camp. By May 1939, 75 Jews remained in the urban district of B. Of those who did not manage to emigrate, most were deported, including 16 in 1942 to the Theresienstadt ghetto. Only Jews married to non-Jews remained in B. B. also served as the location of one of the Third Reich's "euthanasia" centers, and about 20,000 people, including Jews, were gassed there.

BERNKASTEL-KUES Rhineland, Germany. Jews are first mentioned in the late 13th cent. Fourteen were murdered in 1289 following the Oberwesel blood libel and most left in the persecutions later in the cent. Jews are again mentioned in 1344 but were subjected to a number of subsequent expulsions (1418, 1589). Only from the early 17th cent. did the Jews permanently inhabit the town, though under an official quota of just three families until the late 18th cent. Residence restrictions were lifted under French rule and the J. pop. grew to over 60 in 1808 and a peak of 110 (about 4% of the total) in 1866. Most engaged in petty trade, cattle dealing, or moneylending. A synagogue was consecrated in 1852 and rebuilt in

1882 after a fire. A J. elementary school for 30-40 children was started in 1850 but closed in 1866, reopening as a private school for religious instruction in 1885. In 1926, the community was united with neighboring Kues. Together they had a pop. of 59 in 1933. Most Jews operated commercial establishments. By Nov. 1938, just 15 Jews and three J. businesses remained. On *Kristallnacht* (9-10 Nov. 1938), the synagogue was wrecked. In all, 32 Jews emigrated from Germany, including 20 to the U.S., while in 1937-40, 15 moved to other places in Germany. The last four Jews in B. were deported to Lodz via Trier on 16 Oct. 1940.

BERNSTADT (Pol. Bierutow) Lower Silesia, Germany today Poland. Jews were present in the first half of the 14th cent. but are not heard from again for a long period of time. In 1780, their pop. was already 101 and in 1871 it was 245. The community maintained a synagogue, cemetery, welfare agencies, and other communal institutions and a number of Jews served on the municipal council. B. was the birthplace of the J. painter Ludwig Meidner (1884-1966). At the time of the Nazi rise to power, 52 Jews remained. With many emigrating to European countries, the number dropped to 46 in 1935 and 22 in 1937. On *Kristallnacht* (9-10 Nov. 1938), the synagogue was set on fire and a number of J. stores were destroyed. By 19 Nov. 1942, just one intermarried Jew remained. No further information about the community in WWII is available. Presumably those who did not emigrate to safety perished after deportation.

BERNSTEIN (Pol. Pelczyce) Brandenburg, Germany, today Poland. The J. community numbered 37 members in 1801 and peaked at 70 individuals in 1871. It maintained a synagogue and a cemetery. In 1932, the J. pop. was 20. No information concerning their fate under Nazi rule is available.

BEROUN Bohemia, Czechoslovakia. The community was late to form. In the early 20th cent., it had 30 small settlements affiliated to it. A J. elementary school was opened in 1877. The J. pop. was 133 (total 11,448) in 1921 and 113 in 1930. Some Jews emigrated at the outset of WWII, mainly to England and Palestine. The synagogue was closed in Oct. 1941 and religious articles and community documents were transferred to the Central J. Museum in Prague. The remaining Jews were deported to the Theresienstadt ghetto and

from there to the death camps in Feb.–Sept. 1942. Few survived.

BERSHAD   Vinnitsa dist., Ukraine. J. settlement probably began in the 16th cent. In the 17th and 18th cent., Chmielnicki's Cossacks and the Haidamaks attacked the Jews. In the 17th cent., many Jews came under the influence of Shabbateanism and in the 18th cent. Hasidism under R. Rafael, a student of R. Pinhas of Korets, was prominent in B. The J. pop. was 438 in 1765 and 6,603 in 1896. B. was famous for the prayer shawls manufactured there and sold throughout the Pale of Settlement. The Zionists and the Bund became active at the turn of the 19th cent. In 1905, J. homes and stores were looted and burned in anti-J. riots. During the civil war (1918–21), Petlyura gangs, Denikin's White Army troops, and other rampaging bands murdered 150 Jews. In the Soviet period, J. artisans were organized in nine cooperatives according to trade. Twenty-one J. families founded a kolkhoz. In the 1920s, a J. section was opened in the law courts and in 1923–31 a Yiddish school, including vocational training, was operating. In 1939, the J. pop. dropped to 4,271 after many of the young left. Many fled to the east on the approach of the Germans but 800 remained behind when they occupied the city. In Aug. 1941, B. was attached to Rumanian-administered Transnistria and in early Sept. a ghetto was established where Jews expelled from Bukovina and Bessarabia were brought a month later. Mortality in the ghetto reached a rate of 50–70% for adults and 80% for children. Additional Jews from Bukovina were brought in during the winter. In Aug. 1943, 1,203 Jews were mobilized for forced labor in the Nikolaev region; none returned. Four hundred, most from B. were murdered in a ghetto *Aktion* in late 1943. Jews from B. organized and led an underground of 50 Jews. Among its leaders was Yaakov Tales, a locally born senior officer in the Red Army. In late 1943, members of the underground joined a partisan unit operating in the area. The Nazis caught and murdered many prior to the liberation.

BERWANGEN   Baden, Germany. The J. settlement dates from the late 18th cent. and rose steadily in the 19th cent. to 146 in 1887 (15% of the total). A synagogue and cemetery were inaugurated in 1845. In 1933, 33 Jews remained. In 1933–38, 13 left for the U.S. Another 12 left in 1939–40 after the synagogue and J. homes were vandalized on *Kristallnacht* (9–10

Nov. 1938). The last eight Jews were deported to the Gurs concentration camp on 22 Oct. 1940.

BERZPILS   Latgale dist., Latvia. The J. pop. in 1935 was 30 (total 173). The Jews were murdered by the Germans at the outset of the German occupation in 1941.

BES   Slovakia, Czechoslovakia, today Republic of Slovakia. Jews settled in the mid-18th cent., maintaining a pop. of about 80 (3% of the total) in the 1900–40 period and having the use of a synagogue and cemetery. All were deported to Auschwitz on 16 June 1944.

BESANCON   Doubs dist., France. Jews are first mentioned in 1245. The community ceased to exist in the 15th cent. Jews managed to acquire temporary residence permits from time to time, but it was not until the French Revolution that Jews resettled in B. In 1809, the J. community numbered 28 families (55 individuals), mostly from Alsace. They were mainly itinerant merchants, watchmakers, and butchers. The community grew and by 1839, the J. pop. was 670. A charitable society was founded in 1865 and a synagogue in the Moorish style was inaugurated in 1869. Until 1858, the community belonged to the consistory of Nancy, then to that of Lyon. In 1872 an independent consistory was set up in B. After the Franco-Prussian War of 1870, Jews from Alsace settled in B. At the beginning of the 20th cent., there were 170 J. families in B. Between the World Wars, the community continued to absorb immigrants, mostly from Poland. In WWII, the Germans established a regional camp in B., mostly for British internees. One hundred Jews who did not manage to leave B. in May 1940 were deported by the Germans. After liberation, the community gradually revived with the influx of North African Jews, and numbered 120 families in 1960. In 1964, there were 600 Jews living in B.

BESHENKOVICHI   Vitebsk dist., Belorussia. Jews settled in the first half of the 18th cent. and reached a pop. of 3,182 (total 4,423) in 1897, dropping to 1,487 in 1926 in the wake of internal migration under the Soviets. A J. council, established in 1927, was in existence until the mid-1930s. A J. elementary school was also in operation. About half the Jews were engaged in crafts. A J. kolkhoz was started in the late 1920s and supported 37 J. families in 1930. In 1939,

he was sentenced, the Nazis in the city again rioted. The Nazi racial laws first published in 1933 were not applied in B. until July 1937 since the Jews came under the protection of the League of Nations' minority rights convention. By 1933, the Rabbinical Association of Upper Silesia had transferred its seat to B. In the same year, the J. pop. was about 3,500. The number dropped to 2,930 by 1936. As in other places in Germany, Jews of Polish nationality were expelled from the city in Oct. 1938. A few day after *Kristallnacht* (9–10 Nov. 1938), the synagogue was set on fire and about 70 J. stores were destroyed. In addition, 370 J. men were arrested and about 145 sent to the Buchenwald concentration camp. Subsequently many Jews emigrated, leaving a J. pop. of 1,326 in 1939. On 2 Feb. 1942, most of the remaining Jews – about 1,000 – were expelled to General Gouvernement territory. The 300 Jews left behind were almost all deported in the course of 1942. They apparently perished. In late 1942, 51 Jews in mixed marriages remained in the city. A small community was reestablished after the war with an office and prayer room at its disposal.

BEVERUNGEN Westphalia, Germany. The Bishop of Paderborn granted two J. families residence rights in 1586. The community grew in the mid-17th cent. with Jews mainly trading in flax, thread, and fruit and engaging in moneylending as a sideline. In the mid-18th cent., Jews could purchase stalls for their trade but not until 1788 were they allowed to own land. The creation of the Kingdom of Westphalia under Napoleon in 1807 brought equal rights to the Jews. J. emancipation was abrogated when Westphalia was returned to Prussia, but the position of the Jews continued to improve. Jews were elected to the municipal council and participated in local social and cultural activities. A new synagogue was consecrated in 1821. Another one was completed in 1852 and served a number of other communities as well. In 1824, 17 of 39 J. breadwinners practiced various trades and in 1851 five well-to-do Jews were among the founders of a spinning mill. In the late 19th cent., Jews opened three wood-processing plants. In 1900, Jews owned 13 of the town's stores selling grain, hides, feed, etc. The J. pop. reached a peak of 207 in 1834 and then dropped to 131 (total 1,983) in 1895 as a result of emigration, the exodus of the young to the big cities, and a declining birthrate. In 1904, the community school was recognized as a public school; in 1911, 30 children were attending the school as the J. pop. dwindled. The economic crisis following WWI seriously affected the Jews but on the eve of the Nazi rise to power in 1933 they continued to play a leading economic role in the town. The two wood-processing plants still in operation employed 250 workers and eight stores and two butcher shops were in J. hands. In 1933, 64 Jews remained, subjected to economic boycotts, persecution, and violence. In 1933–38, 24 Jews emigrated, six to the U.S. and five to Palestine. On *Kristallnacht* (9–10 Nov. 1938), the synagogue was vandalized and two J. homes and two J. stores were seriously damaged. The last J. business was "Aryanized" in April 1939. The remaining J. men were mobilized for forced labor. Another nine Jews emigrated by 1941. Of the 29 remaining Jews, seven were deported to the Riga ghetto in Dec. 1941; 11 to Poland in March 1942; five to Auschwitz in May 1942; four to the Theresienstadt ghetto in July 1942; and the last two J. men, married to German women, to Theresienstadt in Feb. 1945. Another 15 Jews were deported from their places of refuge in occupied Europe and other German cities. In all, 41 Jews died in the concentration and death camps.

BEVERWIJK Noord-Holland dist., Holland. A J. community existed in 1800. Its numbers reached about 60 in 1840. The J. pop. in 1937 was 91. There was an agricultural training farm run by Mizrachi in 1935–38. In March 1942 the Jews were transferred to Amsterdam. They were deported to the camps along with Amsterdam Jewry, 37 survived in hiding while at least 26 deportees returned. The fate of some 140 others is not known.

BEZDAN Vojvodina dist., Yugoslavia. Jews settled in B. in 1740. In 1931 they numbered 116 (total 6,449). Almost all the Jews perished in the Holocaust.

BEZHANITSY Kalinin dist., Russia. After the arrival of the Germans in the second half of July 1941, 120 Jews were executed outside the town.

BEZIDUL NOU (Hung. Bozodujfalu) N. Transylvania dist., Rumania. In 1868–69 a group of about 100 Seventh Day Adventists living in B. converted to Judaism and founded a community which worked the land. A number of Jews joined them in the early 20th cent. In 1940, when B. came under Hungarian control, the

community was persecuted and most converted to Unitarianism. In spring 1944, the community was transferred to the Marosvasarhely ghetto. Some received permits to remain there while others were deported to Auschwitz with the other Jews. After the war about 50 of the converts moved to Israel.

BEZIERS   Herault dist., France. The J. community of B. was an important center of learning, known to medieval Jews as "Little Jerusalem." The synagogue in B. was built in the middle of the 12th cent., probably in 1144. An inscription relates that R. Shelomo Halafta, whom Benjamin of Tudela met in 1165, purchased the ground. The Jews were expelled from B. in 1306 and in 1394. Before WWII no more than four or five J. families lived in B. During the war, 300 J. refugees found refuge here; many were from Belgium. They had two prayer rooms at their disposal. After the war, a new community was formed. It numbered 280 in 1964. After 1968, it consisted of around 400 individuals, mostly from North Africa.

BIALACHOW   Lodz dist., Poland. Jews first settled here in 1860 and were affiliated with the community at Zarnow. The majority were Gur and Aleksander Hasidim. The 100-member J. community in 1939 grew to 350 with the influx of refugees by 1941. In Oct. 1942 the Jews were sent to Opoczno en route to the Treblinka death camp.

BIALA PODLASKA   Lublin dist., Poland. An organized community with a synagogue and cemetery existed in the first half of the 17th cent., under the jurisdiction of Brest-Litovsk. The community prospered and grew rapidly in the 18th cent. The well-to-do traded in grain and lumber, leased concessions, and supplied the royal court. In the 19th cent., B. was the seat of a number of hasidic courts. The J. pop. grew from 2,394 in 1860 to 6,549 (total 13,090) in 1897. Jews opened numerous factories (for wooden pegs, shoes, and soap), hide-processing plants, sawmills, brickyards, flour mills, and a beer brewery. Many also lived in penury and were supported by the community. The existence of a J. proletariat paved the way for the J. labor movements, with the Bund and Po'alei Zion becoming active in the early 20th cent. A Hebrew school and an orphanage operated until 1918. In WWI, the Jews suffered from hunger and disease under a German regime of heavy taxes, expropri-

ations, and forced labor. However, community life flourished and Zionist activity intensified. In the aftermath of the war, the Polish soldiers and the peasant pop. victimized the Jews. Despite assistance from the Joint Distribution Committee, many young people emigrated to the U.S., Argentina, and other countries. Mutual aid societies, credit organizations, and charitable institutions also operated extensively in the community. A *talmud torah* school had an enrollment of 250 mostly needy children and the TOZ organized summer camps for around 200. Jews were extensively represented in the city administration, but their influence diminished during the 1930s. The anti-J. economic boycott of the 1930s further undermined the position of the Jews, whose pop. reached 6,923 in 1931. The Germans took final possession of the city on 10 Oct. 1939 in the wake of the Molotov-Ribbentrop agreement. About 600 Jews fled to Soviet-controlled Eastern Poland. In Nov., a *Judenrat* was set up, charged with supplying forced labor and collecting "contributions." In late 1939, 2,000 Jews from Suwalki and Serock arrived, confined with local Jews to a ghetto where a typhoid epidemic soon broke out. J. prisoners of war were also sent to the ghetto. On 11 June 1942, 3,000 Jews deemed unfit for labor were deported to the Sobibor death camp. These were replaced in Sept. by 3,000 from Janow and Konstantin. Most of the Jews were transferred to the Miendzyrzec ghetto in late Sept.–early Oct. 1942 and subsequently deported to the Treblinka death camp.

BIALA RAWSKA   Lodz dist., Poland. Jews lived in B. from the late 18th cent. By the 1920s, 1,429 Jews lived there (61% of the total) and Jews owned the majority of its 66 stores. In Oct. 1941 the 4,000 J. inhabitants and refugees were ghettoized and on 27 Oct. 1942 sent to Treblinka.

BIALOBRZEGI   Kielce dist., Poland. Jews settled in the early 19th cent., numbering 436 in 1857 and 1,418 (total 2,419) in 1921. In 1910 a great fire destroyed 100 J. homes and the synagogue. The community recovered with assistance from the Jews of Radom. R. Shraga Yair Rabinovitz (1815–1912) maintained a large hasidic court in B., transferring it to Radom after the fire. The Orthodox controlled community institutions but Zionist groups were active and a modern J. school was founded in 1932. After the German occupation of Sept. 1939, a *Judenrat* and

Jewish officials on construction site, Bialystok, Poland

Jews were also employed in the food, construction, wood, and metal industries, most of them in small factories and workshops under very bad working conditions. The Bund remained the most influential political body, followed by such Zionist parties as the General Zionists, Mizrachi, and the Revisionists. The Zionist youth movements were also active. A few youths belonged to the underground Communist youth movement. Between the World Wars the J. educational system developed extensively. The Hebrew Tarbut system, affiliated with the Zionists, maintained several elementary schools, kindergartens, and a high school. Others were the Grosser elementary schools and the Yiddish Mendele Mokher Sefarim School for handicapped and neglected children of the J. League for Culture (transferred after 1921 to the CYSHO network), the Hebrew elementary school operated by Mizrachi, and an Orthodox Beth Jacob elementary school for girls. There were also a private Hebrew school opened in 1919; two schools (for boys and for girls) opened in 1925 by the Society for Education; two private schools teaching in Polish which also took in non-J. children; and a Takhkemoni high school. There were also several

vocational schools, including the Hantwerker Schule established in 1906 and reopened during the 1920s and an ORT school for girls established in 1923. J. cultural life flourished in every field. Among the Yiddish daily newspapers were *Dos Naye Leben, Unser Leben,* the Bund's *Bialistoker Werker,* the Zionist *Unser Weg,* the *Bialistoker Tagblatt,* and others.

On the eve of WWII (1939) the J. pop. was 43,000. On 22 Sept. 1939, B. was occupied by the Soviets. The business sector was closed down and J. public and political life ended. Most Jews were incorporated into the new economic regime and some "capitalists" were arrested or deported to Siberia. The Yiddish *Bialistoker Shtern* remained the only official J. newspaper for the whole region. Thousands of J. refugees from German-occupied Poland escaped to B., swelling the J. pop. The Germans captured the city on 27 June 1941, holding it until 27 July 1944. At this time, some 50,000 Jews lived in B. On 28 June ("Red Friday") the Germans burned down the J. quarter, including the synagogue with 1,000–2,000 Jews inside. Similar events followed in rapid succession: on 3 July, 300 J. intellectuals were executed at Pietrasze, outside the city, and on 12 July, another 3,000 (according to a different source, 4,500) were murdered in the same place. For administrative purposes, B. was incorporated into the Reich (late July 1941) as an autonomous district (*Bezirk*) of East Prussia, under Governor (*Gauleiter* and *Oberpraesident*) Erich Koch. Under this setup, various Nazi authorities in Berlin, in B., and in Koenigsberg frequently issued contradictory orders concerning the ghetto and the Jews. On 26 July 1941, a *Judenrat* of 12, all former public figures, was established. Formally its chairman was Dr. Gedalya Rosenmann but its effective head was his deputy, Efrayyim Barash. After a month a new *Judenrat* was appointed, now headed formally by Barash. On 1 Aug., the Jews were sealed into a ghetto with three gates guarded by gendarmes. The German civil administration supplied the ghetto pop. with its meager rations, irregular except for bread, through the *Judenrat*. The *Judenrat* encouraged inhabitants to grow vegetables and fruit on plots of land. The Germans confiscated property, exacted "contributions," and levied head and apartment taxes in addition to the taxes collected by the *Judenrat* to cover its own expenses. The first year of ghetto life was relatively quiet. The *Judenrat* headed by Barash maintained departments for industry and crafts, labor,

finances, supply, health, welfare, housing, culture, and even vegetable gardening and such facilities as soup kitchens, two hospitals, an outpatient clinic, three pharmacies, first aid, two schools, a law court, etc. In fall 1941 Barash was made responsible for selecting 5,000 Jews to be expelled to the Pruzhany ghetto (where they perished in Jan. 1943). Jews aged 15-65 were recruited for forced labor, working in German-operated factories and enterprises. Two thousand were employed by the *Judenrat* in a number of workshops and small enterprises. B. was an important center of anti-Nazi underground activity. J. youth movements, banned under the Soviets, resumed activities, starting underground cells and becoming active by early 1942. The organizers and leaders were Mordekhai Tenenbaum (Tamaroff), Haika Grosman, Edek Boraks, and others. By Aug. 1942, a united underground was formed. Discussions were held about strategy — whether to promote an uprising in the ghetto or escape to the forests to join the partisans. On Tenenbaum's initiative, an underground archive was also set up, headed by Tzevi Mersik. On 5–12 Feb. 1943, the first *Aktion* was conducted in the ghetto. Two thousand Jews were shot and 10,000 were deported to the Treblinka death camp. On 13 March 1943 the last 1,148 Jews in the Grodno ghetto at the time of its final liquidation were brought to B. The period following the first *Aktion* was marked by intensive preparations for armed resistance in case deportations were renewed. Tenenbaum approached the Armia Krajowa (part of the Polish underground) in an effort to acquire arms but there was no response. However, the J. underground received aid from a German anti-Fascist group, which supplied it with arms, maps, medical supplies, and intelligence information. Thanks to this a number of J. lives were saved. On the eve of the Aug. 1943 *Aktion* the underground included 200 fighters and possessed 130 guns, a few homemade grenades, and explosives. On the night of 15–16 Aug. the ghetto was surrounded by German soldiers and SS troops, assisted by Ukrainian auxiliaries. On 16 Aug. the *Judenrat* announced to the ghetto pop., numbering about, 30,000, that it had to report for immediate evacuation. In the wake of this announcement the underground called for an uprising and mobilized its cells. The fighting lasted five days, during which the commander, Tenenbaum, fell. Some fled to the forests, joining partisan units, mainly the Kadima group. Deportations commenced on 18 Aug. and went

on for three days. Jews fit for work were sent to the Poniatowa and Blizhyn labor camps in the Lublin dist. of Poland. The remaining 12,000 were dispatched to the Treblinka death camp (in ten transports) and to Auschwitz (two transports). A train with 1,200 children was sent to the Theresienstadt ghetto. A month later they too ended up in Auschwitz. After the big *Aktion* some 1,000 Jews were transferred to a "small ghetto" and employed cleaning up. On 8 Sept. 1943 the "small ghetto" too was liquidated and its occupants (among them, Barash, Rosenmann, and the chief of the J. police, Markus) were deported to the Majdanek concentration camp, Poniatow, Belzec, and Treblinka. On 3 Nov. 1943, when the *Erntefest Aktion* was launched, about 42,000 Jews were murdered in these camps, including 11,000–15,000 from B. Soon after the war, 1,085 Jews assembled in B., 900 of them former residents and the rest from neighboring villages.

BIARRITZ Basses-Pyrenees dist., France. The J. community dates to the beginning of the 17th cent. In 1619, after disorders in Saint-Jean de-Luz, Marranos left the town and settled in B. More than 2,000 Jews resided in B. The synagogue was built in 1904. The Torah scrolls, the ark, and silver candelabrum came from the former synagogue in Peyrehorade that was destroyed. During WWII, B. was located in the occupied German zone. According to the 1942 census of Jews, 168 families in B. at this time were deported. In 1968, the community had 150 members, mostly Jews from North Africa.

BIBERGAU (in J. sources, Biberich) Lower Franconia, Germany. Jews are known from the late 17th cent. and numbered 131 (total 499) in 1816. The few remaining in 1907 were attached to the Dettelbach community and the last two were deported to Theresienstadt in Sept. 1942.

BIBLIS Hesse, Germany. This Orthodox community, numbering almost 200 (8% of the total.) in 1871, was noted for its J. educational work and industrial enterprise. Mauricio Hochschild, whose family ran a metal-trading company, later became one of Bolivia's wealthiest mining magnates. By 18 Nov. 1938, a week after *Kristallnacht* (9–10 Nov. 1938), the last Jews had fled—mostly emigrating to the U.S. and Palestine.

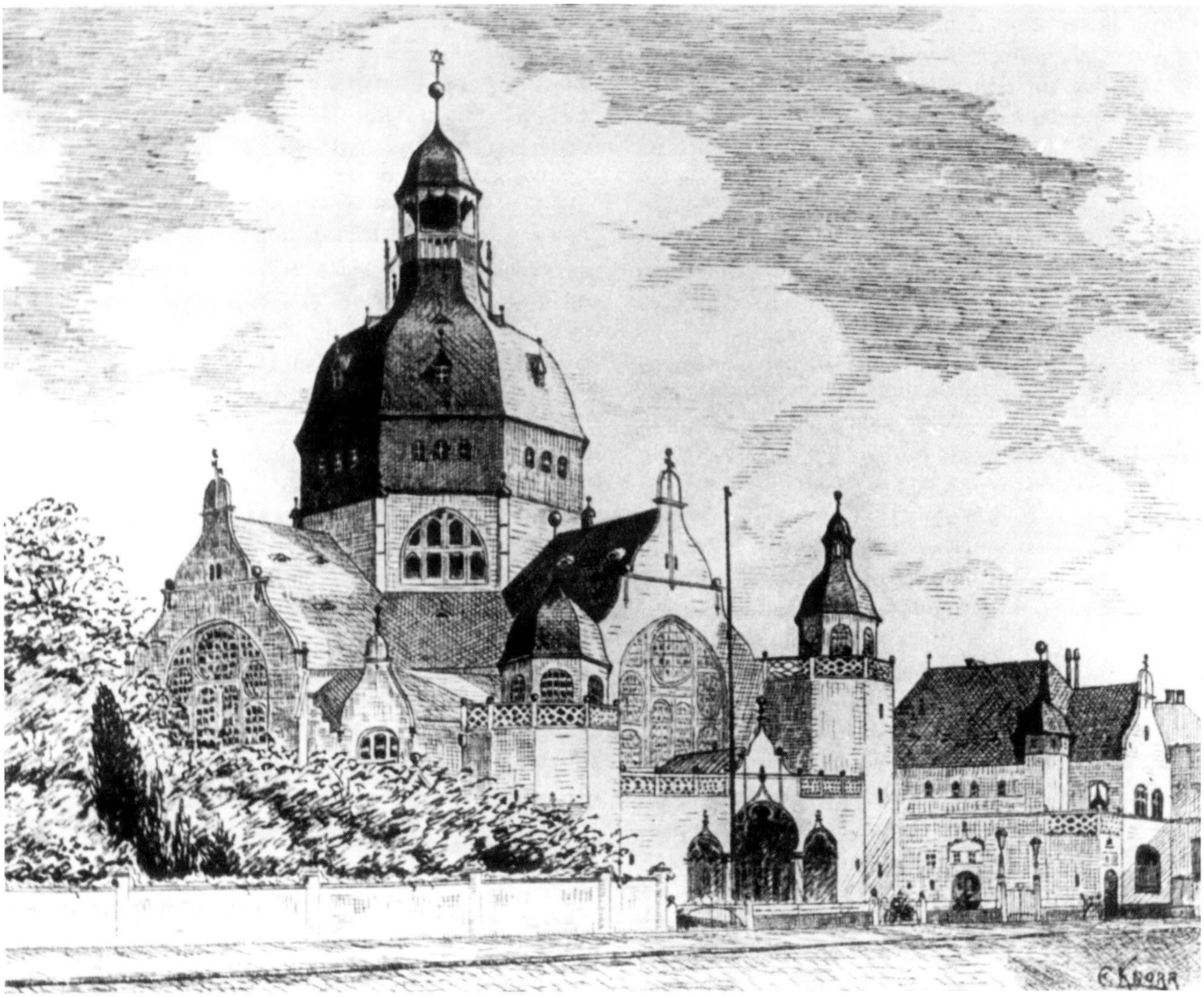
E. Knorr

Synagogue in Bielefeld, Germany, 1929

tendance of 41 in 1862. Over 40% of J. children also attended secondary schools (67% in 1896). In 1925, in the Weimar period, the J. pop. reached a peak of 883. Jews continued to play a dominant role in the textile industry and were also prominent in the legal profession, comprising 21% of the city's lawyers. Over half the Jews engaged in trade, 18% were white-collar workers, 11% artisans, and 9% blue-collar workers. There were also 12 J. doctors in the city. The community was a regional J. center for charity work, for organizational affairs, and for the J youth movements of northwest Germany. The Orthodox East European community had little contact with the Liberal majority. Out of its small *minyan* came the first stirrings of Zionism, with a local group numbering 38 members in 1921 and Hehalutz active from 1925. The J. Scouts, organized in 1930, also had Zionist leanings. ORT was also active. During this period anitisemitism intensified with occasional outbursts of violence. Nazi party offices were opened in 1925 and in 1930 the Nazis received 17.4% of the vote in the Reichstag elections. In 1933, they became the city's largest party with 37.7% of the vote.

In mid-1933, the J. pop. was 797 (total 121,031). With the Nazi rise to power, measures were immediately instituted to remove the Jews from economic and public life. Boycotts were directed against J. doctors and lawyers as well as J. businesses. J. incomes dropped sharply and in 1935 numerous J. businesses were sold. Jews were banned from places of entertain-

ment and physical attacks became more frequent. Nonetheless, the rate of emigration in the first years of Nazi rule was well below the national average (26 Jews in 1933, 32 from Jan. 1934 to Sept. 1935). Most of these Jews left for neighboring countries. The community organized help for emigrants as well as vocational retraining through the Regional Bureau for J. Economic Relief (Provinzialstelle fuer Juedische Wirtschaftshilfe). Zionist activity among the young was also expanded. Hebrew and other courses were organized and a WIZO branch was started up. In Aug. 1938, 79 of the 151 J. business establishments operating in 1933 were still open; in early Nov. only 58 remained. After the publication of the Nuremberg Laws (1935), emigration began to increase. From Sept. 1935 up to *Kristallnacht* (9–10 Nov. 1938), 184 Jews left the city. Others, however, arrived (105 in 1936). On 28–29 Oct. 1938, at least 11–13 Jews of East European origin were expelled, leaving a total J. pop. of about 500. On *Kristallnacht*, the synagogue was burned and at least 18 J. stores were vandalized. About 40–50 J. men were arrested, most of them shopkeepers. About 30 were sent to the Buchenwald concentration camp, where they were kept for some months. J. children still attending German schools were expelled. By Jan 1939 only four J. businesses were still open. By May–June these too were "Aryanized." Jews were now increasingly mobilized for forced labor. From *Kristallnacht* until the outbreak of war on 1 Sept. 1939, another 196 Jews emigrated. The remaining Jews were moved to at least 19 "J. houses," with another 48 managing to emigrate until the ban on emigration on 23 Oct. 1941. The community started a J. school for 17 J. students in Sept. 1939. A J. old age home housed another 20–30 Jews. A camp, holding an average of 75 nonresident Jews engaged in forced labor, was also set up. From the second half of 1941, Jews were only allowed to shop one hour a day and from around Sept. they were banned from the weekly market. In fall 1941, 400 Jews were left in the city in addition to another 100 in mixed marriages. Of the 495 Jews who had emigrated, 122 reached the U.S.; 91 England; 79 Holland; 57 Palestine; and 52 South Africa. Deportations began in late 1941, including 431 Jews in seven transports: 88 to the Riga ghetto on 13 Dec.; 45 to the Warsaw ghetto or to the Lublin dist. (Poland) on 31 March 1942; 32 to an unknown destination (perhaps Minsk or Trostyanets) on 8–11 July; 145 to the Theresienstadt ghetto on 31 July (mostly elderly Jews); 84 to Auschwitz on 2

March 1943 (including about 63 from the forced labor camp); 29 to Theresienstadt on 12 May; and eight to Theresienstadt on 28 June. Subsequently another 20 were deported in small groups and on 19 Sept. 1944, 30–40 Jews in mixed marriages were deported to Zeitz and Elben. At least 509 Jews perished in the Holocaust. In the satellite community of Brackwede, 13 of the 20 Jews there emigrated. A community of 50–60 survivors was established after the war, with a synagogue and community center dedicated in 1963. In the 1980s, about 30 Jews remained.

BIELICA Nowogrodek dist., Poland, today Belarus. Jews apparently arrived in the 16th cent., engaging in the lumber trade and opening hostels near the town. Their pop. reached a peak of 679 (total 1,686) in 1897 but fell to 483 in 1921. Between the World Wars Jews were shopkeepers and petty traders. Most children studied at a Mizrachi Horev school. Shortly after their arrival on 28 June 1941 the Germans murdered 11 Jews and organized the burning of J. homes, the synagogue, and the J. school building. Another 36 Jews were murdered soon after and on 10 Nov. 1941, 600 Jews were expelled to Lida, Zdzieciol, and Szczuczyn, sharing the fate of local Jews.

BIELLA Piedmont, Italy. The first documented evidence about Jews in B. dates back to the 16th cent. They were engaged in moneylending and commerce. The ghetto was officially introduced in 1723. By 1761, there were six families (26 individuals) listed. Local Jews also engaged in the cloth industry and in 1798, two local firms attained national importance. By 1848, the industry and the J. community were flourishing. In 1873, the community included 80 Jews, peaking at 100 in 1886. Socially, the Jews were well integrated. The local synagogue was renovated in 1893. According to the 1930 law reforming the J. communities, B. was included in the district of Vercelli. In 1936, the community numbered 75 Jews. During the Holocaust, one local Jew was deported to Auschwitz.

BIELOPOLIE Sumy dist., Ukraine. The J. pop. was 105 (1% of the total) in 1897 and 125 in 1939. The Germans arrived on 7 Oct. 1941, registering 30 Jews. In early 1942, the Jews were sent to labor in the peat bogs. Afterwards they were sent to Konotop for execution.

BIELSK Warsaw dist., Poland. The J. community began to develop initially under the auspices of Plock in the 19th cent. Most of the J. craftsmen were tailors and some farmed. Many fled during WWI. The J. pop. reached 249 in 1921 (total 1,573) and dropped to around 200 at the beginning of WWII. After being put to work at forced labor, most of the Jews were expelled in March 1941 to Nova Slupie.

BIELSKO-BIALA (Yid. Biala-Bielitz) Silesia and Cracow dists., Poland. The two cities, on opposite banks of the Biala River, had a closely intertwined history. Jews settled in Bielsko in the second half of the 17th cent. but the community only began to grow significantly in the second half of the 19th when residence and trade restrictions were lifted. J. livelihoods were mainly connected with the textile industry though the larger factories were in the hands of the German pop. The Jews were also well represented in the professional class, supplying half the city's doctors and almost all its lawyers. The cultural orientation of the community, in keeping with its Austro-German origins, was pro-German and modern. Only a minority of East European Jews clung to a traditional way of life, which gradually

weakened as they too went over to worship in the magnificent "Temple" erected in 1881. With the community controlled by assimilationists, the Zionists were slow to start organizing in the 1890s. Most children studied in public schools and were very active in sports. The Maccabi club founded in 1906 became one of the largest in Poland with 400 members between the World Wars. Many of the young fought in WWI. Biala's J. history commenced in 1600 but with the granting to the city of a royal *de non tolerandis Judaeis privilege* in 1669, J. settlement was banned until 1850 and Jews only lived in neighboring Lipnik, which subsequently became a suburb of Biala with its 120 J. families. Unlike Bielsko, Biala was dominated by its E. European pop., mostly engaged in trade and the crafts, with the more successful moving to the sister city and assimilating. The prosperity of Bielsko continued to attract Jews from all over Poland. The J. pop. rose from 1,977 in 1890 to 3,928 (total 19,785) in 1921 and around 6,000 on the eve of WWII. In Biala, the J. pop. rose from 1,343 in 1921 to 2,903 in 1931 (total 22,702). Under Polish rule between the World Wars the Jews suffered from discrimination at the hands of the authorities and from the general economic crisis

Jewish soldiers from the Third Riflemen's Regiment of Podhale in front of the Bielsko-Biala synagogue, Poland, 1938

as well as from rising antisemitism, but the big J. factories were able to maintain their position and J. public institutions, welfare services, and professional organizations were highly active. From 1931, the Zionists controlled the Bielsko J. community council and the J. school enrolled over 500 children. The approach of the Germans on the outbreak of WWII led to mass flight, leaving only 400–500 Jews behind when the Germans arrived on 3 Sept. 1939. With many cut off and returning, the number rose to 2,000 in the two cities. On 4 Sept., the Germans blew up all the temples and synagogues as well as J. public buildings. At the end of the month the homes and stores of Jews who had fled were impounded. A regime of forced labor ensued, with groups of Jews being deported to the Nisko reservation (near Lublin). A *Judenrat* was set up at the end of 1939 and a ghetto late in the summer of 1940. Through 1941 men and women were increasingly sent to labor camps and in 1942 hunger and disease intensified. On 20 June 1942 the remaining 400 Jews, mostly women, children, the sick, and the old, were sent to Auschwitz, where they perished. After the war around 5,000 J. refugees passed through the two cities on their way west and to Palestine and a J. welfare committee was set up to provide for them.

BIELSK PODLASKI   Bialystok dist., Poland. The first Jews settled in the late 15th cent., leasing the local customs house. A synagogue was built in 1542 but no Jews were present in the 17th–18th cents. The modern community was founded in the early 19th cent. and numbered 94 in 1816, growing with the coming of the railroad to 4,079 (total 6,464) in 1897 and developing the wholesale trade in grain, fruit, and lumber. In the late 19th cent., Jews opened flour mills and a small tobacco-processing and ciga-

The old beit midrash *of Bielsk Podlaski, Poland, 1962*

rette factory. Almost all the town's bakers were Jews as were 70% of its artisans. Most Jews had auxiliary farms. Under the German occupation in WWI, economic life came to a virtual standstill and Jews were subjected to forced labor, but community life continued with the Bund and Zionists active. The anarchy at the close of the war further undermined J. livelihoods, which continued to deteriorate under the discriminatory measures of the Polish government. A Yiddish school for 250 children was founded in 1920 and numerous Zionist youth movements had branches in the city and many young people underwent pioneer training. During their two-year occupation the Soviets organized cooperatives for artisans and a large state-run store instead of the J. shops which were closed down. The Germans entered the city on 25 June 1941. In late July they murdered 30 J. intellectuals and in early Aug. packed 5,000 Jews into a ghetto, exacting large contributions of goods and money. A few hundred refugees arrived in Nov. 1942 and in early 1943 a group of skilled workers was sent to the Bialystok ghetto. In Feb. Gestapo troops together with Ukrainian and Polish police executed the sick and old outside the city. The rest of the Jews were deported to the Treblinka death camp.

BIERSTADT Hesse–Nassau, Germany. Established in 1827, the community had members in three neighboring villages; it numbered 72 (2% of the total.) in 1925 and 48 in 1932. Jews who remained after *Kristallnacht* (9–10 Nov. 1938), when the synagogue was vandalized, probably died in the Holocaust.

BIEZUN Warsaw dist., Poland. By the beginning of the 19th cent. the Jews constituted an independent community. In WWI they suffered greatly from both Cossack and German invaders. After the war, when the J. pop. reached 779 (total 2,344), there was increased Zionist activity. B. was occupied by the Germans on 4 Sept. 1939. Expelled in Nov. 1939, most Jews found shelter in other towns but ultimately perished in the extermination camps. Few survived—some thanks to help from Poles, others by fighting in the partisan units.

BIGGE Westphalia, Germany. Eight J. families were present in 1846 and a peak of 80 Jews (total 1,116) in 1910. A J. elementary school operated in the early 20th cent. and a synagogue and cemetery were in use

through the Nazi period. Of the 49 Jews in B. in 1933, at least 18 emigrated across the sea (11 to the U.S.) and survived the war. At least 24 perished in the camps.

BIHAC Bosnia-Hercegovina, Yugoslavia, today Republic of Bosnia. Jews probably settled during Ottoman rule. In 1928 they were represented on the town council. Most of the Jews (156 in 1940; total pop. 6,000) were killed in Jasenovac; only 25 survived.

BIHARKERESZTES Bihar dist., Hungary. Jews were apparently present in the mid-19th cent. In 1930 the J. pop. was 164. In 1942, most men were taken to forced labor and at the end of May 1944, the remaining Jews were deported to Auschwitz via Nagyvarad. Survivors reestablished the community, but gradually left.

BIHARNAGYBAJOM (also Nagybajom) Bihar dist., Hungary. Jews settled in the early 19th cent., numbering 208 in 1880 and 144 in 1930. On 3 June they were deported to Auschwitz via the Nagyiarad ghetto.

BIJELJINA Bosnia-Hercegovina, Yugoslavia, today Republic of Bosnia. The J. community was established in the 19th cent. or earlier. Zionism found expression from the beginning of the 20th cent. The J. pop. in 1931 was 328 (total 12,389). During WWII the Jews were persecuted by the Ustase fascist organization assisted by local Germans and the German army. All the Jews perished in the camps; 18 fell as partisans.

BIKOVKA Zhitomir dist., Ukraine. Jews numbered 92 in 1897 and 151 (total 1,872) in 1939. The Germans captured B. on 9 July 1941, murdering the few Jews who had neither escaped nor been evacuated.

BILA CIRKEV (Hung. Fejeregyhaza; Yid. Vais Feld) Carpatho-Russia, Czechoslovakia, today Ukraine. Jews probably settled in the mid-18th cent., numbering ten in 1768 and 42 (total 284) in 1880. The J. pop. rose to 230 in 1921 under Czechoslovakian rule and then dropped to 176 (total 1,714) in 1941. The Hungarians occupied the town in March 1939 and in 1941 drafted a number of Jews into labor battalions. In Aug. 1941, a few families without Hungarian citizenship were expelled to Kamenets-Podolski and mur-

dered there. The rest were deported to Auschwitz in the second half of May 1944.

BILCZE ZLOTE Tarnopol dist., Poland, today Ukraine. Between 20 and 30 J. families lived here mostly as farmers over the years. With the Russian retreat in 1941, their Ukrainian neighbors terrorized them and the Germans expelled them in 1942 to nearby Borszczow to await their fate.

BILGORAI Lublin dist., Poland. The J. settlement was one of the oldest in the Lublin area, dating from the late 16th cent. It was destroyed in the Chmielnicki massacres of 1648-49 and renewed in the 18th cent. Early in the 18th cent., the Kronenberg family established a renowned printing and publishing house. A synagogue was built later in the cent. In the 19th cent., Jews were prominent in the manufacturing and marketing of screens and sieves. Their pop. grew from 1,019 in 1827 to 3,486 (total 5,311) in 1897. B. was the birthplace of Nobel Prize author Isaac Bashevis Singer and his brother Israel. At the beginning and end of WWI, the Jews suffered from the depredations of Russian and Polish soldiers and under the Austrian occupation of 1915-18 endured starvation and epidemics. J. economic activity was renewed in the aftermath, bolstered by mutual aid societies and three J. banks. Many were active in the horsehair-weaving industry, some dealt in lumber, and a J. group operated a bus in B. Most of the J. political parties and Zionist movements were active as the J. pop. grew to 4,596 in 1931. The Germans entered B. on 17 Sept. 1939, placing the Jews under a regime of forced labor and sending groups to labor camps. Approximately 1,500 fled with the retreating Red Army. A *Judenrat* was established in late 1939 and J. property confiscated. A ghetto, crowding together 3,500 Jews, was set up in the second half of 1940. On 9 Aug. 1942, over 1,000 were deported to the Belzec death camp. Of the 1,500 remaining Jews, all but 70 skilled workers and their families were deported to Belzec on 2 Nov., with 50 murdered along the way and 200 left dead in the ghetto. The workers' families were murdered in Jan. 1943.

BILINA Bohemia (Sudetenland), Czechoslovakia. Jews are first mentioned in 1417. The modern community reached a pop. of 70-80 (nearly 1% of the total). A synagogue was opened in 1895. Jews maintained good relations with their neighbors and served on the municipal council. The Zionists were also active. After the annexation of the Sudetenland to the Third Reich in fall 1938, the Jews fled to other settlements in Bohemia and Moravia, most subsequently emigrating, mainly to England and Palestine. The Nazis destroyed the J. cemetery and in late 1942 the few who remained were deported to the Theresienstadt ghetto and to the death camps.

BILKY (Hung. Bilke) Carpatho-Russia, Czechoslovakia, today Ukraine. J. settlement dates from the first half of the 18th cent. Six J. families were present in 1736. The J. pop. then rose from 40 in 1830 to 620 (total 3,347) in 1880. With the community continuing to grow in the early 20th cent., it was accorded the right to appoint its own rabbi. The first was A. Lieberman. The community also maintained an elementary school, a *talmud torah*, and a number of *hadarim* as well as a yeshiva for 70 students. The J. pop. increased to 1,081 in 1921 and 1,103 in 1941. Betar, Hashomer Hatzair, and other Zionist youth groups were active in the 1920s and 1930s. Jews owned over 30 business establishments, including two flour mills, a brickyard, a tannery, and a factory for producing building materials. A few dozen J. workers were employed in these industrial enterprises. The Hungarians occupied the town in March 1939, drafting a few dozen young Jews into forced labor battalions. In late July or early Aug., a number of Jews without Hungarian citizenship were expelled to Kamenets-Podolski, most perishing there. The hundreds who remained were deported to Auschwitz in late May 1944.

The central milk cooperative, Bilky, Czechoslovakia, 1930. (YIVO Archive, New York/photo courtesy of Beth Hatefutsoth, Tel Aviv)

murdered in B.'s J. cemetery. A small number of young Jews succeeded in fleeing to the USSR and serving in the Red Army.

BISCHHEIM AU SAUM   (Bischeim-Schiltigheim) Bas-Rhin dist., France. A. J. community is first mentioned around 1600. Up to the French Revolution, B. was considered one of the most important communities in Alsace. In 1766, 32 J. families resided in B., increasing to 79 families (473 persons) in 1784. In 1792, 148 Jews (men only) were listed, and five years later they founded a cemetery. From the middle of the 18th cent. the community owned a hospice and several charitable societies were active. A musical society was founded in 1868. B. was the home of H. Cerf Berr, head of the Jews of Alsace, and his brother-in-law, Yosef David Sinzheim, who presided at the Paris Sanhedrin of 1806 and became the first chief rabbi of France in 1808. Cerf Berr constructed a ritual bath for his brother-in-law in 1780 and established a foundation on behalf of the community for charitable and educational causes. The synagogue built in 1781 was replaced by a new one inaugurated in 1838 when the community numbered 158 families (798 persons). In 1830 a J. school was opened. In 1936, the community numbered 148 members. During WWII, between July–Oct. 1940, the Jews of B., together with the rest of the Jews of Alsace-Lorraine, were expelled from their homes to the south of France. The synagogue was looted and subsequently destroyed in 1944 by bombardment. The cemetery was largely left intact. Twenty-eight Jews from B. with its suburbs of Schiltigheim and Hoenhem perished during the Holocaust. In 1959, a new synagogue was built. In 1968, the community consisted of 360 members.

BISCHOFSBURG   (Pol. Biskupiec) East Prussia, Germany, today Poland. J. settlement started probably only in the 19th cent. In 1871, the J. pop. numbered 134, declining to 79 in 1905. The community maintained a synagogue and a cemetery. On the eve of the Nazi assumption of power in 1933, the number of Jews declined to about 30. J. businesses suffered due to Nazi boycott measures. No further information about the fate of the community under Nazi rule is available.

BISCHOFSHEIM   Hesse, Germany. Thanks to this village's transformation into an industrial center, the community also grew, numbering 82 (about 5% of the total) in 1871 and enjoying good relations with working-class neighbors. The last 30 Jews mostly fled after *Kristallnacht* (9–10 Nov. 1938), when a non-J. family purchased the synagogue, thus preventing its destruction by the Nazis.

BISCHOFSWERDER   (Pol. Biskupie) East Prussia, Germany, today Poland. Jews settled in B. in the mid-18th cent. They numbered 18 families in 1812 and 190 individuals in 1880. By 1925, the J. pop. came to 35. The community maintained a synagogue (from about 1863) and a cemetery. On the eve of the Nazi assumption of power in 1933, the pop. of the J. community was 22. By mid-1938, only five Jews remained in B. There are indications they intended to sell the synagogue. No information about the community under Nazi rule is available.

BISCHWILLER   (Ger. Bischweiler) Bas-Rhin dist., France. The Jews of B. were massacred during the Black Death persecutions of 1348–49. Jews only returned to settle in 1845, inaugurating a synagogue in 1859. The community numbered 193 members in 1936. During the occupation in WWII, the Jews were expelled to the south of France, together with the rest of Alsace-Lorraine Jews. The synagogue was completely destroyed. There were 19 Jews deported from B. In 1965, there were 50 Jews living in B.

BISKUPICE   Lublin dist., Poland. A small J. community was present in the mid-18th cent., growing to 543 (total 1,476) in 1897 but dropping to 129 in 1921 after many left in WWI. Under the German occupation from Sept. 1939, refugees swelled the J. pop. to 650 in 1941, reduced to 450 in early 1942 as many died from lack of food and the intolerable conditions. They were deported in March 1942, apparently to the Majdanek concentration camp.

BISTRA   (Hung. Bisztra) N. Transylvania dist., Rumania. A J. community was established in the mid-19th cent. The J. pop. in 1930 was 303 (32% of the total). In April 1944 Jews were handed over to the police by peasants and deported to Auschwitz.

BISTRITA   (Hung. Besztece) N. Transylvania dist., Rumania. A J. community was organized in the 1860s, and in 1893 a synagogue was consecrated,

one of the largest and most magnificent in Transylvania. In WWI, 138 B. Jews were conscripted and 12 were killed in action. The J. pop. in 1920 was 2,018 (16% of the total). A J. school was founded in 1924 and continued to function until 1942. The first Zionist youth association in Rumania, *Ivriah*, was established in 1901, and after WWI other Zionist youth movements were organized. In summer 1941, Jews were expelled to Kamenets-Podolski, where they were murdered by Hungarian soldiers. Jews aged 21-45 were drafted into labor battalions in the Ukraine in 1942–44. After the Germans captured B. in March 1944 the J. community was oppressed and leaders were sent to concentration camps in western Hungary. On 3 May 1944 the 7,000 Jews of B. and the district were ghettoized in an open field north of the city. They were deported to Auschwitz on 1 and 4 June 1944.

BITBURG Rhineland, Germany. Five Jews were present in 1808 and a peak of 73 (total 3,167) in 1905. On *Kristallnacht* (9–10 Nov. 1938), the synagogue was destroyed. Of the 40 Jews living in B. in the Nazi period (of whom 12 arrived after May 1933), 17 emigrated (15 to the U.S.). Another 15 moved to other localities in Germany and some of these presumably emigrated as well. Eight Jews were deported in 1942 to the east where they perished.

BITOLA Monastir (Macedonia), Yugoslavia. Jews settled in B. in the 15th cent. or earlier. In the late 15th cent. J. refugees arrived from Spain and Portugal and established their own community, which remained separate from the earlier Romaniot community. The Spanish and Portuguese were long in conflict between themselves. The Ottoman Sultan decreed a dress code and taxes for the Jews and other non-Muslims in 1622. B. was home to many well-known sages. In 1894 the Jews numbered 6,500 – 11% of the total pop. – and were involved in the town's international trade. Early in the 20th cent., thousands of Jews left for other towns and the U. S., and in the 1930s to Palestine. The J. quarter was not closed within walls and it housed the two main synagogues (one for the Spanish community and the other for the Portuguese). Many studied the Kabbalah, and ties with Eretz Israel were strong. The Alliance Israelite organization was

The Bitola band, Yugoslavia (Beth Hatefutsoth Photo Archive, Tel Aviv/courtesy of Jenny Lebel, Tel Aviv)

active, opening schools in 1893 (boys) and 1903 (girls), which were closed in 1914. By 1939 very few J. children were permitted to study in the government's schools. With the Balkan wars of 1912–13, Jews were drafted into the army and B. came under Serbian rule. In 1913 the Jews numbered 6,000 (10% of the total). In WWI Bulgarian armies entered B. and most inhabitants left for other towns. Those who returned found B. in a state of destruction. Jews had no source of livelihood and a few migrated. The J. pop. in 1921 was 2,640 (out of 28,420). Various Zionist youth movements operated between the two World Wars and J. welfare organizations were very active, caring for the widespread local needs as well as welfare in Palestine, to where a few groups emigrated in the late 1920s. Destitution became most extreme during 1928–31 when living conditions were severe. The region was annexed to Bulgaria in April 1941, and the J. inhabitants of B. were deprived of all civil rights and citizenship. The J. pop. in 1940 was 3,269 (10%). In May the J. youth were taken to forced labor facilities, moving ammunition from military storage to train stations. They managed to throw some aside to be collected in the dark and used in an uprising against the Nazis. In the J. quarter of B. the Jews engaged in underground activities – distributing propaganda, maintaining the ammunition and first-aid supplies, and sheltering partisans. Most of the community's leaders, including Leon Kimchi, were eventually arrested, in Dec.1942, for their underground activities. On 11 March 1943 they were taken to a factory storage room and executed. The Jews of B. were taken to the Treblinka death camp on 22, 25, and 29 March 1943. None survived.

BITTERFELD Saxony, Germany. There was a J. community in B. in the 13th cent, but it was wiped out in the Black Death persecutions 1348–49. A J. settlement was established around 1880. It numbered 74 individuals in 1925. The Jews were members of the Delitzsch community and used its cemetery. At the end of the 1920s, they organized their community, but never established a cemetery or a prayer room. At the beginning of 1933, the community numbered about 60. Immediately after *Kristallnacht* (9–10 Nov. 1938), 15 J. businesses closed down or were handed over to non-Jews. Mass emigration began, which left only 14 Jews in 1939. The eight Jews remaining in B. in 1941 were deported to the east.

BIUK-ONLAR (from 1944, Oktyabrskoye) Crimea, Russia, today Ukraine. The first Jews to arrive and settle illegally in the early 20th cent. were well-to-do merchants exporting grain via the port of Teodosya. In the Soviet period, the region became a center of J. agricultural settlement. Two J. rural councils existed in the county in the 1920s and 1930s and in 1932 over 600 J. families were employed at 11 J. kolkhozes. In 1938, 98 Jews were living in the town. The Germans occupied the area in late Oct. 1941. In April 1942, they murdered nine Jews. At the Lenindorf kolkhoz, where 92 J. families lived in 1932, the Germans murdered 16 Jews in the second half of Nov. 1941 and another 18 in Jan. 1942. During the entire occupation, 45 Jews were murdered.

BIVOLARI Moldavia dist., Rumania. Jews settled in the early 19th cent. The J. pop. in 1885 was 1,000 (83% of the total). The poet Yona David was born there. In May–June 1941 Jews were arrested and sent to forced labor. At the end of June, all the Jews were expelled to Iasi. Few returned after the war.

BIXAD (Hung. Bikszad) N. Transylvania dist., Rumania. Jews from Galicia settled in the late 18th cent. The J. pop. in 1930 was 119 (6% of the total). In May 1944 the community was transferred to the Satu Mare ghetto and in June deported to Auschwitz.

BIZERTE (also Benzert) Bizerte dist., Tunisia. There is evidence of a J. community in the Phoenician, Roman, and Byzantine periods. At this time Jews engaged in fishing, commerce, and some farming. According to Arab sources, Jews served as governors of the city until the Arab conquest in 698 and one commanded the Byzantine forces defending the city during the invasion. In the Arab period, the status of the Jews diminished but they still played an important role in the city. B. is not numbered among the J. communities which suffered in the Almohad disturbances of 1159. Many seem to have already left for bigger cities like Kairouan and Mahdia under the Fatimids and Zeirids in the 10th–11th cent. The community was renewed in the early 17th cent. when Leghornian Jews – descendants of the Spanish exiles – arrived from Italy. In the early 19th cent., the community numbered about 500 Jews (total 6,000), organized around a synagogue and served by four rabbis. R. Yisrael Iman is attributed with founding the community's

institutions. He arrived from Tiberias after the earthquake there in 1837 and served in B. until his death in 1897. Another prominent rabbi, officiating in the late 19th cent., was Meir Shelomo Pariente, of Leghornian extraction, author of *Imrei Shefer* (1924). Most Jews earned their livelihoods as peddlers and artisans, with a few wealthy Leghornians active in international trade. In the late 19th cent., under the French Protectorate, a process of modernization set in and many Jews moved to the new European quarter built outside the city walls. J. residents of B. commuted to work in Tunis and the community came under the religious jurisdiction of the capital. With B. becoming France's most important military port in Tunisia and with the development of a local military industry, new job opportunities were created for J. craftsmen and suppliers. The J. pop. reached 1,125 in 1909 and 1,522 in 1921 (total 12,341 non-European residents). Between the World Wars, acquiring French citizenship now became possible for the Jews and many entered the professional class, particularly as lawyers; others became officials in the French civil service, especially as customs clerks. Jews owned and staffed the local branch of the Bank of Tunisia. In 1936, 52 of the community's 431 breadwinners were professional people, a very high percentage for a provincial town, while 284 were artisans and 61 merchants. After WWI, in the wake of the Arab riots of 1917 and the world economic crisis of the late 1920s, the J. pop. dropped somewhat as many moved to Tunis. From 1904 the community council was styled the J. Relief Fund (Caisse de Secours et de Bienfaisance) and mainly charged with welfare work. In 1908 it began building a J. hospital. One of the central figures in the council was the journalist Yisrael Archi, who worked untiringly to obtain French citizenship for all the Jews of Tunisia. In the 1920s and 1930s, he served as president of the Societe de l'Hopital and in the 1950s as chairman of the community council. Most J. children (boys and girls) attended the French public school founded in 1883. Two *talmudei torah* operated in the afternoons. A Zionist group was active in 1919 and in 1924 the Union Universelle Jeunesse Juive (UUJJ) organized a scout den. Attempts to maintain active Betar and Hashomer Hatzair groups in the 1930s failed. The link with Palestine was for the most part maintained through the synagogue, which was the focus of the community's social life and was visited by fundraisers from the Holy Land. It

also organized modern Hebrew courses for adults. Arab-J. relations were marked by continuing tension under French rule, with a violent outburst in the 1917 riots that spread through Tunisia. In 1936 the J. pop. was 1,342. In WWII, Jews suffered from food shortages and from Sept. 1941, from the anti-J. laws of the Vichy regime. Following the German occupation of the city on 10 Nov. 1942, heavy bombing attacks by Allied planes caused many Jews to flee and destroyed many buildings, including the synagogue. During their six-month occupation of B., the Germans ran the largest and hardest forced labor camp in Tunisia there, holding 400–500 Jews, mainly from Tunis. German guards murdered three internees and in the Allied bombardments of Feb 1943, 11 were killed and 19 wounded. With the return of the Allies in May 1944, J. life slowly returned to normal, bolstered by Joint Distribution Committee and OZE aid. Betar became the most influential Zionist group and the use of the local port as a place of anchorage for *ma'pilim* ships further awakened interest in the Zionist idea. After the Betar leaders left for Israel, Hashomer Hatzair became the torchbearer of the Zionist movement. Only a quarter of the city's Jews emigrated in the 1946–56 period, half to France and half to Israel. B. with its large naval base was the only city in Tunisia to remain in French hands after Tunisian independence in 1956. In the 1961 fighting between the two, over 1,000 people were killed in the city. French nationals among the 1,200 Jews there were evacuated as French citizens. Another 300 were smuggled out of the country by the Israeli Mossad.

BJELOVAR Croatia, Yugoslavia, today Republic of Croatia. The J. community was established in 1877. Under Austrian rule the Jews were close to the Croatian national government. Zionism was widespread from the 1920s. The Jews eventually worked in the free professions and crafts, as well as in local industry. They numbered 501 in 1921 (total 7,859) and 429 in 1940. Little antisemitism was suffered until the Holocaust, when the Jews were hunted down and perished in camps.

BLAGOEVO (until 1923, Bolshoyi Buyalik) Odessa dist., Ukraine. The J. pop. in 1939 was 105 (total 5,191). Shortly after their arrival in early Aug. 1941, the Germans presumably murdered the few Jews who had neither fled nor been evacuated.

BLAJ (Hung. Balazsfalva; Ger. Blasendorf) S. Transylvania dist., Rumania. A J. community was founded in 1871. Shimon Mendel, grandson of the chief rabbi of Transylvania, donated land for the community's institutions. R. Yosef Gruenbaum (1895–1920) was one of the first Zionists in Transylvania and Dr. Janos Ronai was the only J. from Transylvania at the First Zionist Congress in 1897. Relations with the general community, especially the clergy, were cordial up to the 1930s but when the economy declined, many Jews left. In 1941, the J. pop. increased from 193 to 1,185 (and in 1942 to 1,348) due to the influx of refugees from the surrounding villages. In 1942, J. communal property was confiscated, J. males were drafted into labor battalions, and others were deported to Transnistria and died there. After the liberation, some refugees remained but he majority left for larger towns, and during 1945–47 emigrated to Palestine.

BLAMONT Meurth-et-Moselle dist., France. The synagogue in this village was inaugurated in 1844. According to the 1939 census, 32 Jews were listed as living in B. and 44 in 1942. Arrests began on 14 July 1942. On 13 Oct. 1943, 33 Jews were arrested and five Jews on 13 July 1944.

BLASZKI Lodz dist., Poland. By 1764, 56 Jews earned their living here from trading in grain, seeds, and export of eggs. The J. pop. in 1921 was 2,186 (56% of the total). Antisemitic manifestations were frequent in the 1930s. In Dec. 1939 the Jews were expelled to various towns in the General Gouvernement. The single J. survivor was murdered by local Poles.

BLAZOWA Lwow dist., Poland. The J. settlement dates from the 18th cent. and was known for the hasidic court established by Tzevi Elimelekh Shapira, the founder of the local dynasty. The J. pop. reached a peak of 942 in 1890 (20% of the total). After WWI antisemitism was rife. In 1918, 200 J. homes were pillaged by local peasants and in 1919 they initiated a boycott on the sale of food to Jews. During the German occupation the *Judenrat* operated a communal kitchen for awhile that fed 300 needy Jews. The Germans tortured and murdered 22 Jews on their arrival in the city. The community was liquidated in June 1942 when the J. pop. was expelled to Rzeszow. Most were deported to the Belzec death camp a month later.

Young Jews from Blazowa, Poland

BLEICHERODE Saxony, Germany. Jews were living in B. in 1290. The community was spared the Black Death persecutions of 1348–49, but in 1593 all the Jews were expelled from the city. A new J. settlement started around 1700, numbering 177 individuals in 1746. The community maintained a cemetery (1728) and a synagogue (1872). The Jews played an important role in the weaving industry and several Jews were elected members of the city council. When the Nazis came to power in 1933, the community numbered about 100, but soon many, the affluent Jews in particular, moved away, following the extensive "Aryanization" of the larger J. businesses. Hans Beyth (1901–47), a native of B., was among the main organizers of Youth Aliya from Germany. In 1937, 77 Jews (29 families) were still living in the town. On *Kristallnacht* (9–10 Nov. 1938), the synagogue was destroyed, the cemetery was desecrated, and J. stores were vandalized. By 1939, 18 families and nine individuals had emigrated. The remaining 11 J. families were deported to the east, one person

committing suicide beforehand. One Jew survived because of his non-J. wife.

BLENDUV Warsaw dist., Poland. Jews appeared with the founding of the town as an industrial settlement in the 1820s. With the decline of the weaving industry they turned to small businesses and crafts and from the 1920s, when the J. pop. reached 815 (out total of 1,879), many became hatmakers. Despite economic hardship and antisemitism, community life persevered under the spiritual leadership of R. Yaakov Yitzhak Shapira and his descendants. Zionism flourished between the World Wars. The German occupation of 8 Sept. 1939 instituted a regime of persecution and forced labor with the large German pop. of the town unstinting in their cooperation with the Nazis. A ghetto was set up at the end of 1940 and at the beginning of 1941, 1,030 Jews, including refugees, were deported to the Warsaw ghetto. None survived.

BLEZEWO Volhynia dist., Poland, today Ukraine. Jews numbered 101 in 1921 (total 878). They were murdered by the Germans on 11 Sept. 1942 after being transferred to the Berezow ghetto.

BLOIS Loir-et-Cher dist., France. The earliest reference to Jews in B. is in 992. A blood libel in 1171 was the first ritual murder accusation in France. It resulted in Count Theobald ordering the whole community of 31 Jews to be burnt at the stake on 26 May. Yaakov ben Meir Tam established the day of the martyrdom as a fast day for the Jews in France, England, and the Rhineland. Jews resettled in B., and in 1345 a quarter known as *La Juiverie* was reported. There is no further information about the Jews until WWII. According to the census of 1942, 16 Jews were reported as residing in B. Large numbers of Jews from Alsace were evacuated to B., which was a site of a local camp for foreigners. In 1964, there were 250 Jews living in B., most from North Africa.

BLOMBERG Lippe, Germany. Jews had a cemetery there as early as 1500. They built a synagogue in 1808. The community numbered 50 (2% of the total) in 1892, with members in Cappel and Schwalenberg. The community dwindled to six by 1933 and only one Jew remained in 1938.

BLONIE Warsaw dist., Poland. With the removal of

residence restrictions in 1862 a community emerged numbering 1,027 at the end of the 19th cent. With the arrival of the Germans in early Sept. 1939, Jews were put to forced labor and at the end of 1939, 600 deportees from other communities were sent there. A ghetto with a *Judenrat* was set up in the fall of 1940 but razed by the Germans in Feb. 1941, the Jews being sent to the Warsaw ghetto and from there to the Treblinka death camp.

BOBENHAUSEN Hesse, Germany. Established in the second half of the 18th cent., the community numbered 61 (10% of the total) in 1880 but dwindled to a handful in 1942, when the Jews were transported to death camps.

BOBER Kiev dist., Ukraine. B. was a J. agricultural colony in the 19th cent. with a pop. of eight J. families in 1878. In 1897 Jews numbered 208 (total 633 residents) and engaged mostly in fishing. In 1926, under the Soviets, the J. pop. was 99. The Nazis murdered all those who had neither fled nor been evacuated.

BOBINICHI Vitebsk dist., Belorussia. Jews numbered 170 (total 219) in 1920. The Germans occupied the town in early July 1941. In Jan. 1942, 108 Jews were murdered at the Christian cemetery.

BOBOWA (Yid. Bobov) Cracow dist., Poland. A community of 44 families lived there in 1765. In 1893 the hasidic Bobow dynasty established its court in B., creating additional sources of income. A yeshiva accommodating 300 students was also established and Bobowa Hasidism won renown for its melodies. The J. pop. reached 749 (half the total) in 1900. At the end of WWI, local peasants and Polish soldiers pillaged J. homes and subsequently the Polish anti-J. boycott contributed to a deterioration in economic conditions. The Germans occupied B. on 7 Sept. 1939. The ghetto set up in Oct. 1941 was liquidated in Aug. 1942. Refugees had swelled the J. pop. there from 658 in 1939 to 1,500. About 400 women, children, and elderly people were murdered in the forest; the rest were deported to the Belzec death camp after expulsion to the Gorlice ghetto; and 210 young men were sent to the Biezhanow labor camp.

BOBR Minsk dist., Belorussia. Jews probably settled in the first half of the 18th cent., numbering 168 in

Bobowa Hasidim with R. Halberstam, Poland

1766 and 1,479 (total 2,483) in 1897. In 1926, under the Soviets, their number fell to 1,018. Some Jews worked in agriculture. A J. kolkhoz founded in 1924 employed 22 families (nine in 1930). A J. school for 90 children was also opened in 1924. The Germans arrived on 6 July 1941 and on 10 Oct. murdered 961 Jews from B. and its environs beside a ditch just outside the town. Those remaining were expelled to Borisov, where they perished.

BOBRINETS Kirovograd dist., Ukraine. Jews probably settled in the early 19th cent. and numbered 3,481 (total 14,281) in 1897. Two *talmudei torah* existed by the 1880s. In the Soviet period, the J. pop. dropped to 2,265 in 1926 and 654 in 1939. The Germans captured the city on 6 Aug. 1941, murdering five Jews on 10 Aug. A ghetto was soon established and in Dec. 1941, 388 Jews were murdered, including about 120 children. The remaining Jews in B. and its environs were murdered in the following months. In all, 530 people were killed in the Nazi period, most of them Jews.

BOBRKA (Yid. Boibrik) Lwow dist., Poland, today Ukraine. The community, probably founded in the late 17th cent., was based mainly on trade and crafts and included a number of wealthy merchants at the turn of the 19th cent. The J. pop. in 1900 was 2,500 (almost half the total). The Vitalis family (Belz Hasidim) dominated spiritual life throughout the 19th cent. and the Zionists became active in the 1890s. With the outbreak of WWI, the Jews who did not manage to flee to the interior of the country suffered greatly from Russian soldiers, who burned homes and synagogues. Subsequently, under the Polish regime the number of Jews declined to 1,480 in 1921. Up to 1933 the Jews constituted a third of the city council. At the beginning of WWII refugees swelled the J. pop. to 2,700. After two years of Soviet rule, B. was occupied by the Germans on 30 June 1941. In a pogrom organized by the Ukrainians, some 60 Jews were killed or injured. In July a *Judenrat* was set up and forced labor was imposed. In Aug. 1942, 1,200–1,500 Jews were deported to the Belzec death camp and around 200 among the disabled and those attempting to escape murdered on the spot.

The remaining 1,500 or so Jews were herded into a ghetto. The second *Aktion* took place on 8 Dec. and another few hundred Jews were deported to Belzec. Starvation and typhus caused many deaths and bodies were scattered on the sidewalks. In the third and final *Aktion* of 13 April 1943, the Jews were taken to the cemetery of a neighboring village and shot at the edge of a ditch. The last 159 young Jews were sent to the Janowska camp in Lwow, where only four survived.

BOBROVITSA Chernigov dist., Ukraine. Jews settled in the latter half of the 19th cent. and numbered 671 (total 5,120) in 1897. Anton Denikin's White Army staged a continuing pogrom from Dec. 1919 to Feb. 1920. In 1939, 122 Jews remained. After their arrival on 15 Sept. 1941, the Germans murdered those who had not fled or been evacuated.

BOBROVYI KUT Nikolaiev dist., Ukraine. B. was founded in 1807 by Jews from Mogilev. The J. pop. was 408 in 1810 and 1,248 (total 1,469) in 1897. Aside from farming, the few dozen families here engaged in crafts (as cobblers, etc.). A kolkhoz was established within the settlement in the 1920s. In 1936, 600 Jews (136 families) remained, with a J. school still in operation. The Germans captured B. on 27 Aug. 1941, murdering 850 Jews from the settlement and its environs on 16 Sept. Another 300 Jews from various kolkhozes in the region were also murdered.

BOBROWNIKI Lublin dist., Poland. In the absence of residence restrictions, Jews were probably present in the Middle Ages but apparently only formed an organ-

Synagogue in Bobrovyi Kut, Ukraine

ized community in the 18th cent. Their pop. dropped from 519 in 1857 to 282 (total 1,273) in 1897 after attempts at industrialization failed. On the arrival of the Germans in Sept. 1939, 200 remained. On 6 May 1942, in an *Aktion*, the old and sick were shot. The rest were brought to Demblin-Irena and from there deported to the Sobibor death camp after a selection for the local labor camps.

BOBRUISK Mogilev dist., Belorussia. The J. pop. grew from 359 in 1776 to 8,866 in 1861 and 20,759 (total 34,336) in 1897. In the late 19th cent. J. breadwinners included 87 wholesale merchants, 1,706 petty traders, 70 farmers, 2,438 artisans, 1,034 day laborers and professional workers, and 374 white-collar workers. The community's three *yeshivot*, the first founded in 1823, had a total of 300 students in 1912. The community also maintained various social welfare agencies. The *maskilim* in the city founded a Te'uda be-Yisrael society. A Hovevei Zion group was formed in 1885 and in the early 20th cent. the Zionist movement and the Bund became active. The J. pop. in 1914 was 25,876. B. was the birthplace of Berl Katznelson (1877–1944), leader of the Zionist labor movement; Kadish Luz (1895–1972), leader of the kibbutz movement and future speaker of Israel's Knesset; R. Yitzhak Nissenbaum (1864–1942), an important figure in religious Zionism; Yitzhak Tabenkin (1887–1971), one of the founders of the Kibbutz ha-Me'uhad movement; and the writers Pauline Wengeroff (1833–1916) and David Shimoni (1886–1956). In Aug.–Sept. 1919, during the civil war, Polish soldiers mobilized Jews for forced labor and murdered a J. family of nine. In spring 1921, peasant gangs rioted against the Jews. In 1926, under the Soviets, the J. pop. was 21,558, rising to 26,703 (total 84,078) in 1939. In 1926, 23 J. families worked at J. farm settlements near the city. Artisan cooperatives started in 1927 had 638 members. Their workshops were converted into a state factory in 1930, employing 650 workers in 1938, mostly Jews. A factory for producing wood products had 2,000 workers, many of whom were presumably Jews. In 1928, there were 40 *battei midrash* and synagogues in the city. In the same year, the municipal council closed 14 of them. R. Shemuel Alexandrov started an *Ohavei Torah* circle in the community for Talmud study which was opposed by J. Communists. In the late 1920s, the Zionist activities of Hehalutz, Kidma, Hashomer Hatzair, Maccabi, and other organ-

Facility for needy Jews, Bobruisk, Belorussia

izations were outlawed. Twelve J. schools were opened in the city, some going up to the seventh grade, others only up to the fourth. In 1926–27 their total enrollment was 2,400 and in 1936, 3,000 (out of the total 12,000 students in the city). All J. schools were closed in 1939. The Germans captured B. on 28 June 1941. About 7,000 Jews managed to flee to the east beforehand. In the beginning of July, the Germans executed 3,500 Jews. On 5 Aug., they rounded up 800 J. men, supposedly for a labor camp, but they were never heard from again. A few days later a ghetto was established in an open field near the airport. Jews from Glussk, Slutsk, and Starye Dorogi were brought there. In Sept., the Nazis executed 380 Jews and on 7 Nov. they carried out their major *Aktion* in which 20,000 Jews were murdered. The head of the J. police, Weiss, was shot on the spot when he refused to hand over J. children. A subsequent *Aktion* claimed 5,281 after the Jews rebelled against wearing the yellow badge and working at forced labor. Before the *Aktion*, small groups of Jews escaped to the forests, some joining the partisans.

BOCHEYKOVO Vitebsk dist., Belorussia. The J. pop. was 323 (total 722) in 1897 and 183 in 1923 under the Soviets. In 1925, seven J. families earned their livelihoods in agriculture. The Germans occupied the town in July 1941 and murdered in Feb. 1942 those Jews who had neither been evacuated nor succeeded in fleeing.

BOCHNIA Cracow dist., Poland. Jews settled in the 13th cent. following the discovery of salt mines and were active in the trade. The organized community was accorded a number of privileges in 1555, but in 1605, following a Host desecration libel, the Jews were expelled from the town. Permanent settlement was only renewed under the Austrians in 1867 with the achievement of equal rights throughout Galicia. The Halberstam hasidic dynasty was a leading force in the new community. In the 1880s the J. pop. stabilized at around 2,000 (about a fifth of the total) and signs of political and social modernization began to be seen as Zionist groups organized. In 1918, anti-J. rioting in the surrounding villages sent a stream of refugees to B. but the town itself was untouched. While the pop. rose by a few hundred after WWI, economic conditions deteriorated and in the 1930s antisemitism intensified. Many fled east with the approach of war. The Germans entered B. on 3 Sept. 1939 and instituted a reign of terror and forced labor, with a ghetto set up on 16 March 1942. The first *Aktion* commenced on 24 Aug. All Jews were ordered to report to the army barracks in the town and from there were dispatched to the Belzec death camp. Those trying to hide were murdered on the spot. Another 1,500 Jews from the surrounding area were then packed into a smaller ghetto area along with local survivors. All those without employment, including women and children, were deported to Belzec on 2 Nov. 1942. Patients at the ghetto hospital were murdered. The remnant of the community was deported to the Plaszow and Szewenia camps in Aug. and Sept. 1943. Justyna and Shimon Draenger of the J. Fighting Organization in Cracow hid in B. after they fled from prison, and were killed there in Nov. 1943.

BOCHOLT Westphalia, Germany. Continuous J. settlement started in the 17th century. The community grew from three families in 1683 to 120 individuals in 1871 and peaked in 1905 at 296 individuals. In 1932, 227 remained. A J. cemetery was opened about 1700

and a synagogue was consecrated in 1798. Jews were well integrated in the life of the city. One served as a judge in magistrates court and in 1919 a J. woman was elected to the municipal council. On 1 April 1933, several J. stores were vandalized, part of the Nazi boycott operations. In June 1933, the J. pop. was 204, about 90 leaving until Nov. 1938. On *Kristallnacht* (9–10 Nov. 1938), the contents of the synagogue were burned in the street and J. homes and stores were vandalized and pillaged. Several Jews were beaten. During the next two months, about 50 Jews left the city, about half fleeing to Holland. On 1 Oct. 1941, 36 Jews remained; 35 were deported to the ghettoes and concentration camps. There was one Jew living in the city in Sept. 1944. In all, about 80 Jews from B. perished in the Holocaust.

BOCHUM Westphalia, Germany. A permanent J. settlement dates from the late 16th cent. though Jews also seem to have been present in the 14th–15th cents. The five families there in 1590 had a synagogue. In the 18th cent., Jews were allowed to purchase houses and building lots, unlike other places in Germany. In 1765, Jews prayed in a makeshift synagogue. Their cemetery probably dated from the 17th cent. Jews earned their livelihoods as merchants, butchers, and sometimes as moneylenders. Economic conditions deteriorated in the second half of the 18th cent. and did not improve until the early 19th cent. In 1789, about a quarter of the Jews worked as servants. Most residence restrictions were lifted in the early 19th cent., leading to the growth of the community from 74 in 1812 to 370 in 1871 and 1,002 (total 66,000) in 1900. Most new J. residents came from Westphalia, the Rhineland, the Palatinate, and North Hesse; others came from Holland. Towards the end of the 19th cent., a number of Jews arrived from Eastern Europe. During the 19th cent., emancipation led to a small number entering the professional class. J. women worked in family businesses while those belonging to the lower classes were employed as maids, "graduating" in the second half of the 19th cent. to the positions of housekeepers and cooks. The consecration of a synagogue in 1863 was a citywide social event. Notwithstanding, antisemitism also made itself felt in daily life. The synagogue was designed to serve a Reform community and included an organ. In 1828, a J. elementary school was founded, reaching an enrollment of 41 in 1863 and then rising to 80 in 1882 and 125 in 1886 as the pop. rose. J. children continued their studies in municipal secondary schools. In the late 19th cent., over half the Jews still engaged in commerce. About a quarter practiced trades. Few were active in the city's burgeoning heavy industry and mining, though some were innovators, one being the first to run an advertising agency in the city and another opening the biggest and most modern movie theater there in 1910. Still others were doctors, jurists, and bankers. Women's occupations also expanded. In the 1870s, some opened their own stores or worked as milliners. From the early 20th cent., women worked as insurance agents, bookkeepers, and secretaries. Antisemitism increased still further in the 1880s though it met with local opposition and declined somewhat in the 1890s. A third cemetery was opened in 1884. Cultural activity also expanded in the late 19th cent. A J. literary society, the first of its kind in Germany, was founded in 1886. Theater and dance groups were later added and membership reached 100 in 1888. A summer camp society was founded in 1905 to help needy children and the Central Union (C.V.) opened a branch in the city. The Zionists also became active. The Jews reached a peak pop. of 1,244 in 1930, making the community the third largest in Westphalia after Dortmund and Gelsenkirchen. Many more Jews now arrived from Eastern Europe, most of them Orthodox. Their children increased attendance at the J. school, which had fallen to 54 by 1924 as assimilation continued to prevail. By 1933, 125 children were enrolled there; another 100 studied at a Hebrew school. There were 20 children in the local *heder*, while 175 attended religious classes after school. A J. kindergarten was also in operation. In 1925, a Jew, Otto Ruer, was elected mayor, an unusual event for a large German city at this time. The Alsberg family of Cologne established a large department store and many Jews were now entering the professional class. In 1922, the Zionist movement had just 30 members. In 1932, the Nazis constituted the city's largest political party and in the 1933 Reichstag elections they won 36.3% of the votes.

In mid-1933 the J. pop. was 1,069 (total 314,547). SA troops physically attacked Jews and enforced economic boycotts. In one case, a Jew was beaten to death and schoolchildren were abused. On 29 March 1933, the mayor of B. prohibited all business contacts between the municipality and J. establishments, including shopping by municipal workers in J. stores. On 4 April, J. lawyers were ordered to transfer their cases to German colleagues and on 12 April J. doctors were thrown

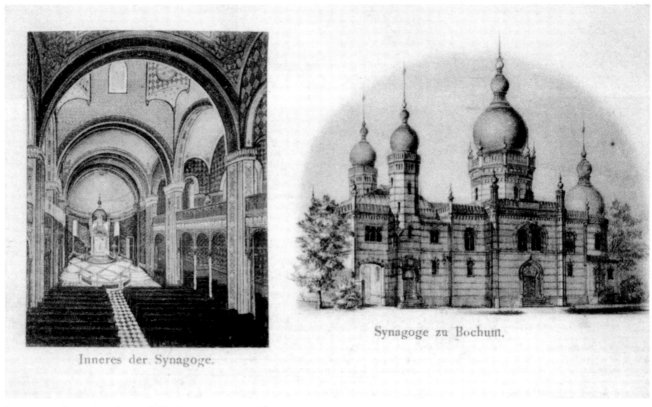

Inneres der Synagoge.

Synagoge zu Bochum.

Interior and exterior views of Bochum synagogue, Germany

out of the Ruhr medical association. During the year, the local boycott list was expanded to include 150 J. businesses and 50 J. doctors, lawyers, brokers, and agents. From June to Oct. 1933, the J. pop. dropped by 148 and in April 1934 by another 82. The community marshaled its resources and tried to present a united front, with two Zionists added to the community council. Zionist activity intensified and Habonim attracted the young. J. artists thrown off the German stage initiated the J. Cultural Association (Juedischer Kulturbund), which staged, in B. and other large German cities, theater productions from the J. repertoire. A Maccabi sports club was founded around the end of 1934. By 1937 only one J. doctor and three J. lawyers were still practicing and only half of the 111 J. retail establishments which had operated in 1933 were still open. In 1936, the J. pop. was about 700 and in 1937 it dropped further to about 600, but Jews fleeing from villages and small towns brought it back up to 644 in Oct. 1938. Many children were now studying Hebrew or English privately as they prepared to emigrate. In late Oct. 1938, a number of Polish Jews were among the hundreds in Westphalia expelled to Poland.

On *Kristallnacht* (9–10 Nov. 1938), the synagogue was set on fire, two cemeteries were desecrated, and J. homes and stores were wrecked by SA troops. Over 100 Jews were arrested; most were sent to the Sachsenhausen concentration camp. In 1939, about half the remaining Jews left, many preferring to emigrate to Holland. Eleven groups of children were able to reach Holland and England. Most of the community's leaders also left at this time. In May 1939, 326 Jews remained. Another 1,000 were defined as Jews by Germany's racial laws, a third of them third-generation descendants of mixed marriages. The remaining Jews were held in five or six "J. houses." By Feb. 1941, the J. pop. dropped by another 80. Mass deportations commenced in Jan. 1942 and lasted until Sept. 1944. The Jews of B. were included in five transports leaving for the east from Dortmund: on 25–27 Jan. 1942 a total of 1,350 Jews to the Riga ghetto; on 27 April 2,100 to Zamosc; on 29 July 1,000 to the Theresienstadt ghettto; on 1 March 1943 1,000 to Auschwitz; and on 5 May an unknown number to Theresienstadt. Subsequently only Jews in mixed marriages remained. These were sent to labor camps, some reaching Theresienstadt in Feb.

1945. At least 200 Jews perished in the Holocaust. From 1943 a branch of the Buchenwald concentration camp operated as a forced labor camp in the city. Another camp was set up in July 1944 on the grounds of the Bochumer Verein military industries plant with 434 Hungarian Jews sent there from Auschwitz. Others who later arrived here brought the total up to 1,706 in Nov. At least 125 died. In Aug. 1944, another camp serving the steel industry held 400-650 prisoners, mostly Jews. In March 1945, about 2,000 workers were sent from the camps to Buchenwald. Most were presumably murdered. After the war a community of 42 survivors was reestablished. It united with the Herne and Recklinghausen communities in 1953, reaching a combined pop. of about 100 in 1960.

BOCICOIUL MARE (Hung. Nagybocsko) N. Transylvania dist., Rumania. Jews first settled in the early 18th cent. The majority engaged in agriculture. The J. pop. in 1920 was 338 (34% of the total). Antisemitic manifestations began with the arrival of the Hungarians in Sept. 1940. Jews were stripped of their landholdings, merchants and tradesmen were forbidden to sell their wares. In April 1944, the community was transferred to the Sighet ghetto and later deported to Auschwitz.

BOCKI Bialystok dist., Poland, today Belarus. Founded in the 16th cent., the J. settlement was one of the oldest in Poland. Many Jews ran inns and the more substantial merchants dealt in grain, cattle, and hides and helped develop Poland's economy, exporting tobacco and importing consumer goods as well as raw materials for Polish artisans. In the 19th cent. J. commerce was hampered by new restrictions. The J. pop. reached a peak of 2,576 in 1847, declining thereafter, through emigration and two epidemics to 1,409 in 1897 and 725 in 1921. Economic conditions deteriorated further between the World Wars. Zionist activity intensified. After the German occupation of June 1941, the Jews were concentrated in two ghettoes under a regime of forced labor. On 2 Nov. 1942, most of the town's 600 Jews were deported to the Treblinka death camp via Bielsk Podlaski. A group of skilled laborers was later killed off in labor camps and at Auschwitz.

BODENFELDE Hanover, Germany. J. residents founded an elementary school in 1819 and opened a synagogue in 1825. Together with the Jews of Uslar (1843) and Lippoldsberg (1867), they formed a regional community. They engaged in various trades and numbered 65 in 1861, dwindling to 30 in 1913. Having disposed of its synagogue, the community was forced to disband on 17 June 1937. Twelve Jews emigrated (four to Palestine); seven perished in Nazi camps.

BODENHEIM Hesse, Germany. The Jews, who traded in livestock and wine, numbered 118 in 1853 but soon dwindled. On *Kristallnacht* (9-10 Nov. 1938), J. property was vandalized and by the spring of 1939 all the Jews had left, many emigrating.

BODERSWEIER Baden, Germany. Jews first settled in the early 17th cent. A new synagogue was built in 1811 and the J. pop. grew to 116 in 1875 (total 1,124). Thereafter it declined steadily to 34 in 1933. On *Kristallnacht* (9-10 Nov. 1938) the synagogue was vandalized and eight Jews were detained at Dachau for a few weeks after being severely beaten. Fifteen Jews left B. until 1940. Twenty-two were deported to the Gurs concentration camp and other camps; six survived.

BODROGKERESZTUR Zemplen dist., Hungary. Jews arriving from Poland are first mentioned in 1726, protected by estate owners whose produce they marketed. Most dealt in alcoholic beverages, making a name for themselves as winegrowers. The first synagogue was erected in 1767 and a J. school was opened in 1784 by order of Emperor Joseph II. The hasidic court established by R. Yeshayahu Steiner (1851-1925) dominated community life and boosted the J. economy through the development of services for the influx of his followers. The J. pop. was 336 in 1880 and 535 in 1930 after hundreds of WWI refugees from Galicia settled in the town, arousing antisemitism and increasing Zionist influence. In 1941, 455 Jews remained. With the German occupation of spring 1944, they were transferred to the Satoraljaujhely ghetto and then deported to Auschwitz on 16 May. Of the fewer than 100 who survived the war, most emigrated to Israel.

BODZANOW Warsaw dist., Poland. A community existed from the late 19th cent. In 1919, Jews were plundered and maltreated by Polish soldiers and later suffered economic hardship. The J. pop. in 1921 was

807 (total 2,093) In March 1941 they were expelled to the General Gouvernement and perished.

BODZENTYN Kielce dist., Poland. Jews first settled in the early 19th cent. They numbered 934 (total 3,039) in 1921 and 700 on the eve of the German occupation in Sept. 1939. Their numbers increased to 1,400 with the arrival of refugees in 1940. All were deported to the Treblinka death camp on 20–21 Sept. 1942.

BOECHINGEN Palatinate, Germany. A synagogue was in use in the 18th cent. and a J. elementary school was in operation in 1834, attended by 41 children. In 1846, the J. pop. included 41 families (178 Jews); 30 of the breadwinners were merchants and 11 artisans. The J. pop. was 160 (total 940) in 1871 and then dropped steadily to 115 in 1900 and 42 in 1933. All left before the outbreak of war in 1939, most in the wake of *Kristallnacht* (9–10 Nov. 1938), when the synagogue was set on fire. At least ten Jews left Germany.

BOEDIGHEIM Baden, Germany. The J. settlement began in 1345 and continued to grow thanks to the favorable attitude of the nobility to J. refugees from Wuerzburg. In the early 18th cent., the Jews lived in a separate quarter and enjoyed extensive trade rights. A synagogue was erected in 1818 and the local cemetery served more than 30 communities for hundreds of years. The 1848 revolution was accompanied by anti-J. violence. Jews maintained a stable pop. of around 90 through the 19th cent (10% of the total) but dropped to 14 in 1933. Eight left by 1939 and six were deported to the Gurs concentration camp in 1940.

BOENSTADT Hesse, Germany. Numbering 51 (7.6% of the total) in 1861, the community declined and after WWI its synagogue was closed. Seven Jews living there in 1939 were eventually deported.

BOESINGFELD Lippe, Germany. In 1890, the J. pop. was 35. The community maintained a synagogue (established in 1903) and a cemetery. In June 1933, about four months after the Nazi assumption of power, 23 Jews remained. On *Kristallnacht* (9–10 Nov. 1938), the interior of the synagogue was destroyed, the J. cemetery was desecrated, and a J. store was vandalized. Nineteen Jews remained in

May 1939. Those who failed to emigrate were deported to the east.

BOGACHEVKA Odessa dist., Ukraine. B. was founded as a J. farm settlement in 1850 and had a pop. of 84 families (418 people, including 146 children). In 1897, the pop. was 506 (all Jews) and in 1926, 2,578 (including 326 Jews). A three-grade J. school was still active in 1931–32. The Germans and Rumanians arrived on 5 Aug. 1941 and on 11 Aug. murdered 131 Jews near the village of Berezki.

BOGDANOVKA Stavropol territory, Russia. The founders of the J. village were Mountain Jews (Tats). Expelled from Persia in the early 19th cent., they settled in the village of Dzeganas, where they formed a community with a rabbi. In 1897, their pop. was 322 (total 682). Anti-Soviet White Russian gangs murdered many of their descendants (127 families numbering about 650 people in 1918). In June 1918, the survivors, dispersing in the North Caucasus area, demanded that the Soviet authorities allow them to return. In the late 1920s, they resettled at a site in the Mozdok area which they named B. In 1930 they numbered 111 families. A number of Jews joined the new Druzhba kolkhoz there in the same year. Some Jews continued to work in crafts. The J. pop. reached an apparently stable level of 125 families (about 550 Jews) in 1934. Until 1933–34, along with a J. rural council (soviet), a J. school teaching in the Tat dialect of the Mountain Jews was active. The Germans occupied B. in late Aug. or early Sept. 1942, murdering 472 Jews either on 20 or 25 Sept. A few were saved by their non-J. neighbors. A monument to the Nazi victims was put up after the war

BOGODUKHOV Kharkov dist., Ukraine. Jews numbered 89 (total 11,702) in 1897 and 136 in 1939. The Germans captured the city on 12 Oct. 1941 and in Nov. 1942 murdered, near the local hide-processing plant, the Jews who had neither fled nor been evacuated.

BOGORJA Kielce dist., Poland. A J. community of 125 was present in 1789. At the turn of the 18th cent., it built a wooden synagogue renowned for its mirrored ceiling and decorative walls. The J. pop. rose to 450 (total 1,189) in 1921. Many fled eastward at the approach of the Germans in Sept. 1939 but refugees

brought the J. pop. up to 600 in April 1942, all confined to a ghetto. In Oct. 1942, the Jews were deported to one of the death camps.

BOGORODITSK Tula dist., Russia. Jews probably settled in the early 20th cent. In 1926 their pop. was 54. The few who neither had fled nor been evacuated were murdered during the short German occupation of the town (15 Nov. to 15 Dec. 1941).

BOGUSHEVSK Vitebsk dist., Belorussia. The J. pop. was 144 in 1811 and 569 (total 3,280) in 1939. In the Soviet period, a J. elementary school (four grades) was active in the town. Prior to the arrival of the Germans in July 1941, some Jews fled. On 5 Sept., about 60 were murdered.

BOGUSLAV Kiev dist., Ukraine. J. settlement commenced in the early 17th cent., with the J. pop. reaching 574 in 1765 and 7,445 in 1897. R. Hirsch Menahem and R. Moshe Eikel were among the well-known rabbis who officiated and were buried in the city. Both the Zionists and the Bund were active. In April 1917, rioting Ukrainians murdered 20 Jews and injured 50. On 12 May 1919 General Denikin's White Army troops killed 40, raped women, and pillaged property. About 1,000 young Jews subsequently organized self-defense units. In the Soviet period, J. artisans constituted a majority in the trade unions, where deliberations were in Yiddish. In the 1930s, many Jews were employed in local factories as production workers and clerks. In 1939, the J. pop. was 2,230. The Germans captured B. on 26 July 1941, murdering most Jews by the end of the year. Skilled workers were executed in July 1943.

BOHDAN (Hung. Tiszabogdany) Carpatho-Russia, Czechoslovakia, today Ukraine. Jews settled in the mid-19th cent. In 1880, the J. pop. was 123 (total 2,060), rising to 275 in 1921 in the Czechoslovakian Republic and 329 in 1941 under the Hungarians. A number of Jews were farmers (mainly raising cattle). Jews were very active in local life with a few elected to the municipal council and one chosen as deputy chairman. Bnei Akiva, Hehalutz, Ha-Oved, and other groups were active among J. youth. After the Hungarian occupation of March 1939, a few dozen Jews were drafted into labor battalions, some being sent to the eastern front and perishing there. Others were sent to the forced labor camp set up near the town. A rescue committee operating in B. helped J. refugees from Poland reach Budapest. The remaining Jews were deported to Auschwitz in the second half of May 1944.

BOHORODCZANY (Yid. Bradshin) Stanislawow dist., Poland, today Ukraine. Jews appear with the founding of the town at the end of the 17th cent. The community grew to a peak of 2,505 (total 4,781) in 1890, after which a decline set in. In the 19th and early 20th cent. Jews were active in the cloth and lumber industries. From the late 19th cent., Zionism made significant inroads. A Cossack pogrom in 1915 was marked by murder, rape, and looting. The community was liquidated in Sept. 1942.

BOHUMIN Silesia, Czechoslovakia. A J. soap manufacturer and a J. distiller are mentioned in 1655. A synagogue was opened in 1900 and a community center in 1924. The community also maintained an elementary school. The J. pop. reached 801 (total 9,607) in 1921 and numbered 722 in 1930. The Maccabiah Games were held in the city in 1933 and Zionist activity was widespread. Under the Germans, the Jews were subjected to forced labor and subsequently many were sent in 1940 to the Nisko camp in Poland. The synagogue was destroyed in Sept. 1939.

BOIAN Bukovina, Rumania, today Ukraine. Jews were granted permission to settle in 1860. R. Yitzhak Friedmann of Sadagora set up his hasidic court in 1886. In 1914, Russian troops burned the J. quarter and the majority of the 2,573 Jews left. The J. pop. in 1930 was 118. The remaining Jews were deported to Transnistria in 1941.

BOJARKA Kiev dist., Ukraine. Jews numbered 13 in 1765 and 721 in 1897. B. attracted J. summer vacationers, among them the historian Simon Dubnow (1860–1940). Shalom Aleichem (1859–1916) lived and wrote in the town for many years. In July and Sept. 1919, Jews were attacked in riots. In 1939, under the Soviets, the J. pop. was 294. The Germans arrived in the area on 1 Aug. 1941. On 14 June 1942 they executed 1,500 Jews from Zwenigorodka prov., including the Jews of B.

BOJNA Slovakia, Czechoslovakia, today Republic of Slovakia. An independent community (in the vicin-

ity of Topolcany) existed in the village from the early 19th cent., reaching a pop. of 125 in 1880 and maintaining a synagogue, cemetery, and elementary school. In 1920, about 70 Jews remained. Most were deported to the death camps of the Lublin dist. of Poland in spring 1942.

BOKONY   Szabolcs dist., Hungary. Jews settled in the late 18th cent., numbering 197 in 1880. After widespread pillaging following WWI, many left and the pop. stood at 137 in 1930. The 75–80 Jews there in spring 1944 were transferred to Nyiregyhaza and then deported on 17 May 1944 to Auschwitz.

BOKOVO-ANTRATSIT   Voroshilovgrad dist., Ukraine. The J. pop. in 1939 was 118 (total 13,297). The Germans captured the town on 18 July 1941. On 11 Aug. 1942, the German police apprehended and brutally tortured the J. partisan Valentina Ozhogina before executing her on 17 Aug.

BOLDVA   Borsod dist., Hungary. Jews were present in 1747 and numbered 65 in 1930. They were deported to Auschwitz via Edeleny and Miskolc on 10 June 1944.

BOLECHOW   Stanislawow dist., Poland, today Ukraine. Jews appeared with the founding of the town in 1612 and enjoyed equal rights under its proprietors. The town was burned by the Tartars in 1669 and captured by the Swedes at the beginning of the 18th cent. with the Jews organizing themselves into armed self-defense units. The Hebrew writer and memoirist Dov Ber Birkenthal (Ber of Bolechow, 1723–1895) was a leader of the community in the mid-18th cent. Jews were active in the salt trade and wealthy merchants imported wines and spices from Hungary and the Ottoman Empire. In the early 19th cent., after the Austrian annexation, tanning became a significant source of income and later, with the decline of the salt industry, the lumber industry as well. Many Jews emigrated to the U.S. in 1880–1910, the J. pop. having reached a peak of 3,323 (nearly 80% of the total) in 1890. Both Haskala and Hasidism were prominent in the town throughout the 19th cent. and the Zionists began their activities in the 1890s. Despite the opposition of the Orthodox majority, a secular school, where Hebrew, Polish, and German were taught, was set up in 1856. A Jew was elected mayor for the first and only time

in 1874. The J. pop. dropped by 25% in WWI when many fled out of fear of the Russians and never returned. With the end of the war the Jews were employed as factory workers and tradesmen. A J. bank was set up with the help of the Joint Distribution Committee as well as welfare services. By 1924 the Zionists constituted the majority in the community council and maintained control of community affairs. The J. pop. in 1931 was 2,986. Under the Soviet regime at the outset of WWII, J. institutions were dissolved and economic hardship ensued. Ukrainian rioting directed against the Jews greeted the occupation of the town by the Slovakian and Hungarian armies on 3 July 1941. With the arrival of the German authorities the following month, a *Judenrat* was set up and restrictions introduced along with a regime of extortion and forced labor. The first *Aktion* took place on 28–29 Oct. when 1,850 Jews were murdered in the Tanjawa forest. Starvation and typhus further decimated the pop., at the rate of 40 dead a day, in the harsh winter of 1941–42. On 3 Aug. 1942 some 2,000 Jews were sent to the Belzec death camp. The others were confined to a ghetto and deported to forced labor camps in other towns. Between March and 29 Aug. 1943, the Jews in the camps were murdered. Of the 300 who fled to the forests, only 45 survived.

BOLESLAWIEC   Lodz dist., Poland. Jews first settled in the mid-17th cent. and numbered 504 in 1939, dropping to 474 in the following year. By the end of Aug. 1941, none remained. In Oct. 1945 the eight survivors were murdered by a Polish right-wing underground unit.

BOLESOV   Slovakia, Czechoslovakia, today Republic of Slovakia. J. refugees from Moravia may have settled in the late 17th cent. A few J. families were present in the first half of the 18th cent., the J. pop. reaching a peak of 112 (total 554) in 1828. In the mid-19th cent., the local rabbinate was responsible for Jews in 24 settlements. In the 1869 congregational split, the community defined itself as Status Quo. It maintained a synagogue, cemetery, community center, school, *mikve*, and poultry slaughterhouse. Jews engaged in trade and agriculture. In 1940, there were 39 Jews in B. Most were deported to the death camps in spring 1942.

BOLGRAD   Bessarabia, Rumania, today Republic of

Moldova. It is not known precisely when the Jews began to settle in B. In 1869, the Turks, who controlled B. from 1856 to 1878, tried to expel them from the town. A synagogue and a prayer house for craftsmen were constructed in about the mid-19th cent. Under Russian rule in 1897, the J. pop. numbered 1,196 (total 12,300). R. Matis Morgenstern, who served from 1894, was succeeded in 1908 by R. Yitzhak Meiler. A Bikkur Holim society was set up in 1903, and a year later a library. By 1910, the J. pop. had increased to 1,419. During the civil war (1918–21), the Jews formed self-defense units, equipped with arms provided by the J. community. B. was ruled by Rumania from 1918 to 1940 and in 1940 was annexed by the Soviet Union. The Germans occupied B. on 22 July 1941. For the next month J. men were brutalized. Many of them died. On 2 Sept. the Germans executed 121 J. men outside the town. About 1,000 J. women and children were subsequently assembled in the synagogue and transferred to a ghetto, which also held Jews from other localities in Moldavia. From the beginning of the German occupation until Oct. 1941, the Nazis murdered about 400 Jews from B. A few hundred were deported in Oct. 1941 to Transnistria. Many were shot on the way; others died of cold and hunger.

BOLIMOW Lodz dist. Poland. In the mid-18th cent. a number of J. innkeepers settled here. The community numbered 339 in 1897. Many of the J. artisans were carpenters. In WWI, after heavy fighting and the use of poison gas, B. was in ruins and the Jews fled to Warsaw and Lowicz. The J. pop. in 1939 was 235. In 1940 a ghetto was established with a *Judenrat*. The Jews were transported to the Warsaw ghetto in March 1941.

BOLLENDORF Rhineland, Germany. Jews first settled in the mid-19th cent. and reached a peak pop. of 110 (9% of the total) in 1914. Most were merchants, some trading in cattle and horses; some acted as moneylenders. Jews were active in public and social life but there were also occasional violent outbursts of antisemitism. Most were Orthodox in religious outlook. In 1932, 65 Jews remained. On *Kristallnacht* (9–10 Nov. 1938), their homes and stores were wrecked and the synagogue was burned. At least 20 Jews emigrated in the Nazi period. Those remaining were mobilized for forced labor. The last 11 were deported to camps in the east in April 1942. At least 23 Jews perished in the Holocaust.

BOLOGNA Italy. The first J. settlements date back to the third and fourth cents. The Jews are mentioned in 1171, when they were temporarily expelled. In 1366 they were confined within a separate quarter, and in 1417 they were compelled to wear the J. badge and limit their activities to moneylending. In the 15th and the 16th cents, B. developed into one of the most important Italian J. communities. Among its renowned rabbis were Obadiah Sforno, Yaakov Mantino, Azariah dei Rossi, and Shemuel Archivolti. There were 16 synagogues in B. in the middle of the 16th century. Local Jews were involved in silk spinning and in printing. The first printing press was set up in 1477–82 and the second in 1537–40. B. reverted to direct papal rule in 1513, and in 1556 Pope Paul IV ordered the Jews confined to a ghetto. In 1568, Pope Pius V established a House of Catechumens in B. (a Catholic institution designed to assist and win converts) and then he banished the Jews. They returned in 1586, only to be expelled in 1593 by Clement VIII. Two hundred years later, after the French Revolution, Jews returned to B., but once again suffered from renewed papal rule, leading to expulsion in 1836. In 1829, the community established a synagogue. In June 1858, a six-year-old J. child, Edgaro Mortara, was kidnapped from his parents' home by papal gendarmes and immediately carried to Rome, where he was confined within a House of Catechumens. This affair aroused a universal outcry, but the parents were unable to get their child back despite all their efforts. When in 1859, B. was annexed to Piedmont, equal rights were granted to the Jews. According to the 1861 census, there were 229 Jews living in B. They earned their livelihood from commerce, industry, printing, and as professionals. Amilcare Zamorani founded the local newspaper *Il Resto del Carlino*. The first congress of Italian Jewry was held in B. in 1863. A local Zionist organization was established in B. in 1902, and in 1918 the Italian Zionist Federation was founded in B. Officially the J. community was recognized in 1928. With the 1930 reform of the J. community B. was included among the 26 communities recognized by Italian law. According to the 1936 census the B. community comprised 1,400 members. During WWII, a branch of the Center for the Study of the J. Problem in Italy, established in Ancona by Guido Podaliri, operated in B. In autumn and winter 1943, 84 local Jews were deported to extermination camps. Among the victims was R. Alberto Orvieto, who served the community, for 44 years. Additional Jews,

arrested in B. but not members of the community, were deported from the city. Altogether 108 died in the camps. Only four returned. During the war, the synagogue was destroyed in a Nov. 1943 bombardment. Local Jews were active in the resistance. After the war, the community, numbering 390 members, was re-organized. The synagogue was rebuilt in 1954. By 1970, there were only 270 Jews in B.

BOLSHAIA VRADIEVKA Odessa dist., Ukraine. The J. pop. in 1939 was 481 (total 7,022). The town was captured by the Germans in Aug. 1941 and by early Sept. 6,500 Jews from the region were murdered near the village of Berezki. The Rumanians expelled thousands of Jews from Bessarabia, Bukovina, and Odessa to the region. Many died of disease or starvation or were shot. Only 27 Jews remained in B. in late 1943.

BOLSHAYIA ALEKSANDROVKA Nikolaiev dist., Ukraine. Jews settled in the mid-19th cent and numbered 111 (total 6,266) in 1939. The Germans occupied B. on 28 Aug. 1941 and probably murdered 124 local residents in Sept., most of them Jews.

BOLSHIYE NEZGORTSI Zhitomir dist., Ukraine. The J. pop. was 339 in 1897 and 114 (total 1,472) in 1926 under the Soviets. The Germans captured B. in Aug. 1941. Most of the Jews perished in the Holocaust.

BOLSHOY TOKMAK (also Vel. Tokmak) Zaporozhe dist., Ukraine. Jews numbered 2,421 (total 19,326) in 1897 and 1,356 in 1939 under the Soviets. The Germans arrived on 7 Oct. 1941, murdering 837 people (most of them Jews) on the outskirts of the city and 164, including 23 children, in B. itself.

BOLSZOWCE (Yid. Bolshevits) Stanislawow dist., Poland. Jews are recorded from 1635 with an independent community in the late 18th cent. The sufferings of WWI led to a radical decline in the J. pop., from 2,256 (60% of the total) in 1900 to 825 (40%) in 1921. Most were deported to the Belzec death camp in Sept. and Oct. 1942.

BONFELD Wuerttemberg, Germany. The permanent J. settlement dates from the second half of the 18th cent., reaching a peak pop. of 129 in 1854. Jews played a leading role in B.'s economy, owning stores and engaging in the cattle trade. In the Nazi era J. businesses closed down and the synagogue was destroyed in the *Kristallnacht* disturbances (9–10 Nov. 1938). Half the town's 40 Jews emigrated until 1941; the rest were deported to the east and perished.

BONN Rhineland, Germany. Jews were present by the 11th cent. at the latest. In the mid-12th cent. the flourishing community became a leading center of talmudic studies. Among its outstanding scholars were the tosafists R. Shemuel ben Natronai and his brother-in-law R. Yoel ben Yitzhak ha-Levi as well as the *paytan* R. Efrayyim ben Yaakov. The community was subjected to several persecutions. In 1288, 104 Jews, including 38 children, were killed in the wake of the Oberwesel blood libel. In the Black Death persecutions of 1348–49, those Jews who were not murdered were expelled. The renewed community was expelled about the middle of the 15th century. Jews are known to have been present again in the last decades of the 16th cent. The community grew from five families in 1650 to 296 individuals in 1784, reaching 536 in 1871 and a peak of 1228 in 1910. In 1715, Archbishop Josef Clemens of Cologne (1688–1723), bowing to local pressure had the Jews move to a single street, where they were allowed to build a synagogue and 16 houses but were locked behind a gate at night. This suppression notwithstanding, several Jews succeeded in attaining important positions as bankers, contractors, and doctors at the court of Josef Clemens and his successors. The best known among them were Salomon Herz Oppenheim and his grandson Salomon Oppenheim, who at the end of the 18th cent. founded a famous banking house in Cologne. In 1797, under French rule, the gates of the J. quarter were torn down, symbolizing the achievement of equal rights. Two Jews were delegates to the Assembly of J. Notables convened by Napoleon in Paris in 1806 to discuss the status of the Jews in the French Empire. Under Prussian rule (from 1815) three Jews became members of the municipal council well before the 1848 revolution. Jews participated in the revolutionary events themselves, playing a prominent role as writers and editors of democratic newspapers. Socially, the Reading and Recreation Society became the elite club of local Jews. From the mid-19th century, J. lecturers held positions at the local university. Among the J. students was Zionist thinker Moses Hess (1812–75), a native of Bonn. From the 1840s, religious reformers consti-

Children at the Bonn Jewish school, Germany, 1938 (Talma Shiloni/photo courtesy of Yad Vashem, The Holocaust Martyrs' and Heroes' Remembrance Authority, Jerusalem)

tuted a significant group in the community. They became stronger with the arrival in 1862 of the Liberal leader Dr. Ludwig Philippson. However, only in 1875, when the predominantly Orthodox Jews of neighboring localities set up their own communities, did the Bonn community as a whole become reformed. In 1879 a new imposing synagogue, equipped with an organ, was dedicated. The community had an impressive range of social and welfare associations. Branches of the Central Union (C.V.) and the Zionist Organization were opened before WWI.

After the Nazi rise to power, the J. pop. dropped from about 1,000 in June 1933 to 674 in summer 1937. J. lecturers were dismissed from the university and J.-owned businesses were subjected to "Aryanization." J. organizations continued to serve the community throughout the period. Hebrew courses proliferated under Zionist auspices and the J. school reached a peak enrollment of 85 in 1935. In 1936,

the Zionists reached a membership of 196, making it the largest organization in the community and Hehalutz ran a pioneer training camp for 36. On *Kristallnacht* (9–10 Nov. 1938), the synagogue was set on fire and SA and SS units vandalized J. stores and apartments. J. men were arrested and sent mainly to the Dachau concentration camp. In May 1939, 464 Jews remained in the city. Beginning in the same year, Jews were concentrated in "J. houses," which reached a total of 32 in 1941. On 10 Feb. 1941, Jews in two local sanatoriums were removed to the Andernach sanatorium and subsequently killed. In summer 1941, the remaining Jews were moved to the Benedictine monastery in Endenich, which had been sequestered by the Gestapo. Jews from the entire region were also moved there somewhat later. In June and July 1942, the Jews were deported in four transports: 47 (35 from B.) to the Theresienstadt ghetto on 14 June; 93 (43) to the Lodz ghetto on 14 or 15 June; 164 (69) to the Theresienstadt ghetto or

Ark of the Law in the rebuilt Bonn synagogue, Germany

Lodz on 19 or 21 July; and 89 (70) to the Theresien-stadt ghetto on 27 July. Jews in mixed marriages were sent to forced labor camps in Sept. 1944. A community of about 60 was established after the war. A new synagogue was consecrated in 1958. In 1977, the congregation numbered about 200.

BONNLAND Lower Franconia, Germany. Jews numbered 73 in 1816 and eight in 1933 (total 273); three are known to have emigrated to the U.S. in 1937–38.

BONN-POPPELSDORF Rhineland, Germany. Jews are mentioned in 1624 and in 1685–86, six Jews had letters of protection. In 1808 the J. pop. numbered 42. The community was attached to the Bonn consistory in 1809 and to the Bonn regional congregation in 1855 under Prussian law. In 1852 it consecrated its own synagogue; in 1861 a cemetery was established in neighboring Endenich; and in 1875 the community

became independent, though remaining under the aegis of the Bonn rabbinate. The J. pop. of B. reached 62 in 1890. Together with the Jews of adjacent localities, who also belonged to the community, the community numbered 230. A new and larger synagogue was completed in 1902. Relations with the non-J. pop. seem to have been satisfactory in the late 19th cent. despite the rising tide of political antisemitism. The community numbered 162 in 1931. After the rise of the Nazis to power, the J. pop. declined and the community was disbanded before the end of 1936. On *Kristallnacht* (9–10 Nov. 1938), the synagogue was set on fire. Jews remaining in B. were presumably deported to the east in 1941, where they perished.

BONYHAD Tolna dist., Hungary. Jews from Austria, Germany, and Moravia arrived, under the protection of estate owners, after the expulsion of the Turks in the early 18th cent. They became known as manufacturers of smoking pipes and some also joined the

professional class. In 1826, they numbered 1,662 (35.2% of the total) and from the mid-1850s to WWII maintained a pop. of 1,000–1,200. The first synagogue was built in 1764 and a J. elementary school was opened in 1784. In 1869, the community split into Orthodox and Neologist congregations. The Zionists were not active in B., but some youngsters came to Palestine in the 1920s and 1930s. The situation of the community deteriorated radically with the publication of Hungary's race laws in 1938. In 1940–43, nearly all J. males were seized for forced labor and sent to Transylvania, Poland, the Ukraine, and the Russian front. The remaining 1,180 Jews were confined in a ghetto in May 1944 and deported to Auschwitz via Pecs and Lakics on 6 July. About 1,200 J. forced laborers in B. were murdered at the local parade grounds by SS forces on 17 Oct. The 352 Jews who returned after the war gradually emigrated.

BOPPARD Rhineland, Germany. A J. community existed in the 12th cent., augmented at the turn of the 12th cent. by Jews expelled from France by Philip II. Jews lived in a Street of the Jews and had the use of a synagogue. They were subject to repeated persecutions during the Middle Ages and the community was finally destroyed in the Black Death persecutions of 1348–49. Jews are again mentioned in 1462 and were present in limited numbers until a permanent settlement was established in the mid-18th century (a cemetery had been opened at the beginning of the 17th century). The J. pop. rose from 51 in 1808 to a peak of 127 in 1905 (total 6,583). A synagogue was consecrated in 1867. In June 1933, about four months after the Nazis came to power, the J. pop. was 92. On *Kristallnacht* (9–10 Nov. 1938), J. homes and stores were wrecked, Jews were beaten, and the Torah scrolls and other objects were taken out of the synagogue and burned. J. men were sent to a concentration camp. In 1933–41, most of the Jews left, emigrating to the U.S., South America, and South Africa. The 32 Jews present in 1942 were deported to the east.

BORCULO (Borkelo) Gelderland dist., Holland. Jews first settled in the 17th cent. A community existed in the 18th cent. and grew significantly in the mid-19th cent., when its activities were also developed. The J. pop. in 1941 was 123. In 1942 some 70 Jews were deported and perished. About 50 survived in hiding.

BORDEAUX Gironde dist., France. The first reference to Jews in B. dates to the second half of the sixth cent. Since B. was under English sovereignty between 1154–1453, the Jews were spared the edicts of expulsion issued by the kings of France, but they were nomimally expelled in 1284, 1305, and 1310–11. At the end of the 15th cent. Marranos from Spain and Portugal settling in B. were granted privileges. They only began to profess Judaism openly in 1710. They established a communal institution for charitable activity, first called Sedaca, later "Nation." A *talmud torah* was established before 1710. The community grew with the arrival of Jews from Avignon in the 17th cent.. The two communities did not mingle with the Portuguese. In 1759, the Jews from Avignon also constituted a "Nation," a term used to describe what was in essence a community structure. In 1769, Louis XV approved the status of Nation for the Portuguese Jews. The Portugese engaged in finance and maritime trade with the West Indies. They also owned their own boats and acted as suppliers of equipment. The Jews of Avignon origin traded in textiles and clothing, new and secondhand. In 1806 there were 2,131 Jews in B. of whom 1,651 were of Spanish or Portuguese origin; 144 were Avignonese; and 336 of German, Polish, or Dutch origin. In 1806, two delegates represented the community at the Assembly of J. Notables—Abraham Furtado, who became president of the Assembly, and Isaac Roderigues. B. became the seat of a consistory with jurisdiction over ten districts. A synagogue built in 1810 and destroyed by fire in 1873 was replaced by a synagogue that was noted for its size and for the beauty of its interior. This synagogue was inaugurated in 1882, at a time when B. was considered the center of Sephardi Judaism in France. In 1900, the J. pop. in B. numbered 1,940. Between the World Wars, the Jews were fully integrated in the economic, administrative, and intellectual life of the city. They maintained several mutual-aid organizations and the Zionists were active. During WWII, B. became a center to which refugees from northern France fled during May–June 1940. The head office of the international rescue organization, HIAS-ICA, was transferred to B. After the Franco-German armistice (21 June 1940), the Institut d'Etude des Questions Juives in Paris opened a wing in B. According to the census of June 1941 there were 5,722 Jews in B. During the occupation, gangs of French fascists wrecked the synagogue and in 1944, it was turned into a prison

for deportees. On 13 Jan. 1944, 350 Jews were arrested. Between July 1942 and Feb. 1944, the Germans deported 1,279 Jews via Drancy to Auschwitz. After the war, the community was revived with the arrival of new immigrants, including a new Ashkenazi congregation. The synagogue was reconstructed in 1956. In 1960 there were 3,000 Jews in B., and 5,500 in 1969 with the arrival of Jews from North Africa.

BOREMEL (Michalowka) Volhynia dist., Poland, today Ukraine. Jews settled shortly before 1782 and numbered 1,047 in 1897 and 857 (95% of the total) in 1921. Olyka and Turzysk Hasidim had their own synagogues and the Zionists were active from the early 20th cent. The Germans took the town on 25 June 1941 and engaged in sporadic killing. A ghetto was set up in summer 1942. On 8 Oct. 1942, the Jews were led out of the town and executed.

BORGHORST Westphalia, Germany. Jews settled in 1720, building a synagogue in 1854 and opening a cemetery in 1900. Their pop. from the mid-19th cent. to 1933 was 40–50 (usually less than 1% of the total). The synagogue was burned on *Kristallnacht* (9–10 Nov. 1938). Out of the 40 Jews living in B. in 1933, some of the young emigrated to the U.S. Twenty were deported in 1941–42, 16 of them to the Riga ghetto.

BORISOV Minsk dist., Belorussia. J. settlement began in the 16th cent. The community was one of the most important in Lithuania at the time, with a pop. of 266 in 1766. In 1811, the J. pop. was 865, rising to 7,722 (total 15,063) in 1897. Israel's fifth chief of staff, Lt.-Gen. Hayyim Laskov, was born in B. in 1919. The Hebrew writer Shemuel Alexandrov was born here in 1865. In the early 20th cent., two private schools and a *talmud torah* attended by 140 children were active. Jews played an important part in the industrialization of the city. Jews owned all its match factories. In many of them, all or most of the workers were Jews. Most houses were built of wood and thus were frequently destroyed in fires. On 25 May 1910, 300 went up in flames, most belonging to Jews. In summer 1915, during WWI, the city suffered because of its proximity to the front. By late 1916, 900 refugees had gathered there. During the short-lived period of Polish rule, in summer 1920, Polish soldiers staged a pogrom, killing and injuring 300 Jews. In the Soviet period, dozens of J. families worked in agriculture

(54 at a kolkhoz in 1931). In 1929, many were employed in artisan cooperatives and factories, including 124 at a glass factory. Two J. schools (seven and ten grades, respectively) were still open in the 1930s. During the 1920s, Yiddish was officially used in local law courts. In 1939, the J. pop. was 10,011 (total 49,108). The Germans captured the city on 2 July 1941. In Aug., they murdered 739 Jews, labeling 439 of them "saboteurs and robbers." Subsequently 176 were murdered for protesting against the creation of a ghetto. The ghetto, enclosed by barbed wire, was established in the eastern part of the city in Aug. and housed 7,000 Jews. Jews were required to wear the yellow badge. On 20–21 Oct. 1941 (7–9 Oct. according to other sources), 7,000–8,000 Jews were executed at the local airfield. The Germans opened the graves in Oct. 1943 and burned the bodies. Local collaborators took part in the executions.

BORKEN (I) Hesse–Nassau, Germany. Established in the 18th cent., the community maintained a J. elementary school (1823–1934), numbered 204 (16% of the total) in 1895, and was affiliated with Kassel's rabbinate. Of the 141 Jews living there in 1933, 71 emigrated; the last three were deported to the Theresienstadt ghetto in 1942.

BORKEN (II) Westphalia, Germany. Jews were occasionally present from the early 14th century but permanent settlement began in the 1660s. Eight families were present in the latter half of the 18th cent. and by 1871 the J. pop. had grown to 90. A synagogue was erected in 1818 and a J. elementary school was opened in 1830. The community established three cemeteries, the oldest already in the 16th century. B. was among the communities that founded the Westphalian branch of the Orthodox Association for the Proctection of the Religious Interests of Judaism. The Haas brothers operated a wood veneer factory with branches in Hamburg and Paris. Jews were active in local life, joining the Red Cross and various sports clubs. On the eve of the Nazi rise to power in 1933, the J. pop. numbered 102. On *Kristallnacht* (9–10 Nov. 1938), the interior of the synagogue was wrecked, the J. cemeteries were desecrated, and J. homes and stores were vandalized. In 1939, the J. school was closed and 40–50 Jews were still living in the town. Starting in Dec. 1941, those who remained were deported to the east.

BORKOVICHI Vitebsk dist., Belorussia. The J. pop. was 92 (total 180) in 1920. A J. elementary school served the area and until the mid-1920s, Jews operated private farms. The Germans arrived in July 1941 and murdered the few remaining Jews who had not fled or been evacuated.

BORNE Overijssel dist., Holland. J. settlement began in the late 17th cent. The J. pop. in 1860 was 68. Much of the community's development was due to the influential Spanjaard family. The J. pop. in 1941 was 116 (total 10,722). The Germans deported 80 Jews; only seven returned. The rest survived in hiding.

BORNHEIM Rhineland, Germany. Individual Jews were present in the 17th cent. In 1843, the J. pop. was 73, served by the community's 17th cent. synagogue. A new synagogue was consecrated in 1866. Jews were active in local life, particularly from the mid-19th cent., joining the marksmen's club, volunteer fire department, and men's choir. The J. pop. grew to 107 (total 2,464) in 1871 and 140 in 1913. In June 1933, four months after the Nazi rise to power, the J. pop. numbered 116. On *Kristallnacht* (9–10 Nov. 1938), SS forces set the synagogue on fire and vandalized J. homes and stores. In 1939, 97 Jews were still living in B. Eighteen were sent to the Benedictine monastery in Endenich in summer 1941 and from there deported to the concentration and death camps. In all, 72 were deported to the east, where most perished. Also deported to the east were Jews from neighboring settlements: at least eight from Roisdorf; 15 from Alfter; 15 from Waldorf; six from Walberberg; and eight from Hersel.

BORODIANKA Kiev dist., Ukraine. Jews settled in the 18th cent., numbering 353 in 1765 and 621 in 1897. Most were Hasidim. In fall 1917, Jews were attacked by gangs and on 23 Feb. 1923, by Petlyura's bands. Two were murdered. In 1939, under the Soviets, the J. pop. was 284 (total 4,234). The Germans arrived on 23 Aug. 1941, murdering the Jews of B. and its environs in the fall. Many Jews belonged to an underground organization active in the area.

BOROVAJA (Antopol; among Jews, Borovka) Latgale dist., Latvia. This 20th cent. J. community was one of the youngest in Latvia and numbered 176 (total 715) in 1935, living in an atmosphere of general prosperity and communal harmony. Habad Hasidim and *Mitnaggedim* prayed in the same synagogue and most identified with Zionism. All but a few were murdered by the Latvians in fall 1941.

BOROVKA Vinnitsa dist., Ukraine. Jews numbered 48 in 1784 and 126 in 1847. A J. kolkhoz founded in 1929 had a pop. of 419 in 1931. A J. elementary school was opened in the mid-1920s and a J. rural council was established in 1931. In 1939, the J. pop. was 296 (total 6,507). The Germans occupied B. on 20 July 1941 and murdered 252 Jews on 8–9 Aug. Sixteen who eluded the *Aktion* were caught and most were murdered.

BOROVSK Moscow dist., Russia. Jews numbered 43 in 1926. The few who remained and had neither fled nor been evacuated were murdered after the arrival of the Germans on 15 Oct. 1941.

BOROWA Cracow dist., Poland. The Jews numbered 186 (total 1,256) in 1921. Restriction of movement and confiscation of property under the Germans in WWII left them without a means of livelihood. The community was expelled to Radomysl and were caught up in the *Aktion* of 19 July 1942. Survivors were sent on to Dembica to share the fate of the local Jews.

BOROWAYA Kiev dist., Ukraine. The J. pop. in 1939 was 176. After their arrival on 30 July 1941, the Germans murdered the Jews.

BORSA N. Transylvania dist., Rumania. Jews from Galicia settled in the mid-18th cent., buying and leasing land. The pop. in 1891 was 1,432 (23% of the total). In the late 19th cent. R. Pinhas Hager set up his hasidic court in B. and it became the strongest element in the community. Zionist activity began prior to WWI, and between the World Wars Mizrachi and Bnei Akiva were the strongest movements. After the war returning Rumanian soldiers plundered J. property. The J. pop. in 1930 was 2,486. On 4 July 1930, peasants from the surrounding villages, incited by antisemites, set fire to the J. quarter and 2,000 Jews were left homeless. A committee to aid the victims was set up with contributions from Rumanian Jewry and overseas organizations. In summer 1941, 40 families were expelled to Poland, where they were killed, and in 1942–43 Jews were sent to labor battalions in the Uk-

Soup kitchen run by the Joint Distribution Committee, Borsa, Rumania, c. 1930 (Beth Hatefutsoth Photo Archive, Tel Aviv/photo courtesy of Yad Vashem, The Holocaust Martyrs' and Heroes' Remembrance Authority, Jerusalem)

raine. In April 1944 the community was transferred to the Viseul de Sus ghetto and then deported to Auschwitz. About 300 survivors returned after the war; almost all left for Israel.

BORSEC (Hung. Borszek) N. Transylvania dist., Rumania. Jews settled in this health spa in the late 19th cent. and supplied services to the vacationers. The J. pop in 1920 was 92 (6% of the total). The majority left in 1942 for other towns in Rumania. In May 1944, those remaining were transferred to the Reghin ghetto, and in June deported to Auschwitz.

BORSHCHAGOVKA Vinnitsa dist., Ukraine. Four J. families were present in 1763. The J. pop. was 1,853 (total 3,196) in 1897, dropping to 230 in 1926 after most Jews left in the wake of a pogrom staged on 3 July 1919. Twelve families (50 Jews) remained on the eve of WWII. The Germans took the town on 22 July 1941 and murdered 36 Jews. Others who fled to Pogrebishche shared the fate of the Jews there.

BORSZCZOW Tarnopol dist., Poland. Though there is evidence of J. settlement in the 17th cent., significant development can only be traced to the 18th cent., with the pop. reaching a peak of 1,808 in 1890 (out of a total 4,331). Emigration, mostly to the U.S., up to WWI reduced it by a third. The arrival of war refugees again boosted the pop., but between the World Wars economic conditions deteriorated further under anti-J. Polish policy. The Zionists were widely active and the community enjoyed a rich cultural life with lectures and theater as well as a 2,000-volume library and a Hebrew school. Much activity ceased with the Soviet annexation from 17 Sept. 1939, but religious life continued. B. was occupied on 7 July by Hungarian troops and the Germans took over the town in Sept. 1941. A ghetto was set up on 1 April 1942 and in the first major *Aktion* on 26 Sept., 800 Jews were deported to the Belzec death camp and another 100 murdered on the spot. A harsh winter brought starvation and disease. On 13 March 1943, 400 more Jews were sent to the Belzec death camp and in April and June 3,300 were murdered in the J. cemetery and the town was declared *Judenrein*, though another few hundred were later flushed out of hiding and executed. An underground group calling itself the Borshchever Band carried out a number of successful raids outside the ghetto and even fought a pitched battle with the Germans, afterwards dispersing with heavy losses, the survivors joining partisan groups.

BORYNIA Lwow dist., Poland, today Ukraine. In 1880 there were 86 Jews in a pop. of 1,323. With the arrival of the Gestapo a few months after the Germans took the town on 1 July 1941, the Jews were systematically murdered through the end of 1942. Only a few survived.

BORYSLAW Lwow dist., Poland, today Ukraine. The small J. community of the early 19th cent. grew to 7,752 in 1890 (75% of the total), owing largely to the development of the oil industry which Jews helped to pioneer. By 1880 the industry employed 3,000 Jews from B. and its environs. Modern methods and bank takeovers wiped out many of the smaller producers

Schoolchildren dressed for a Purim party, Borszczow, Poland, 1928

and brought about an economic crisis, with only 750 remaining as salaried workers by 1914. As a result, emigration to the U.S. increased. Nonetheless Jews continued to be active in the industry, also pioneering the exploitation of natural gas. The economic crisis intensified between the World Wars, with Polish competition threatening the J. monopoly on the wholesale and retail trade. Wide-ranging welfare services were instituted, including soup kitchens and loan societies. By the time the community gained independent status in 1928 from the Polish authorities the Zionist parties had become the dominant factor in public life. Although Zionist youth movements were active, most youngsters attended non-J. public schools where the growing antisemitism that reached a peak in the 1930s was clearly felt. When units of the German army began to arrive in Sept. 1939, the J. pop. of the town and its suburbs stood at around 13,000. Both the Germans and the local Ukrainians proceeded to terrorize the Jews, only the arrival of the Red Army on 12 Sept. bringing relief. However, the Soviets quickly nationalized the oilfields and dissolved all J. institutions,

allowing only religious life to continue. The Germans retook B. on 1 July 1941. The next day 300 Jews were brutally murdered in the streets in a pogrom staged by the Ukrainians with German help. A few days later a *Judenrat* was set up and a regime of forced labor begun. The first mass murders took place on 29–30 Nov. when 1,500 Jews, selected according to a list drawn up by local Ukrainians, were shot in a nearby forest. Hunger and disease further decimated the community during the winter. In a massive *Aktion* during Aug. 1942, 5,000 Jews were deported to the Belzec death camp. Those remaining were crowded into two ghettoes. In Oct., another 1,500 were deported to Belzec and in Nov. a new selection was made with the able-bodied taken for forced labor. Around 2,000 of the others were deported or murdered. On 16–17 Feb. 1943, 600 Jews were executed near the municipal slaughterhouse and dumped into mass graves, leaving only essential workers in the ghetto along with some 1,200 Jews in the labor camp. The ghetto residents were systematically murdered and the Jews in the labor camp deported to the concentration camps be-

a congress in B. During the 1907 peasant revolt, 1,500 farmers attacked Jews, destroyed their property, plundered their shops and houses, killing two and wounding many more. In 1832, Jews constituted 40% of the artisans and in 1900, 90%. A J. hospital was established in 1817. A school for boys opened in 1865 with 438 pupils and for girls in 1896. In 1889, there were 32 *hadarim* with 2,000 pupils; a *talmud torah* had 500 pupils in 1910. B. had two synagogues and 60 prayer houses. A controversy over the appointment of a rabbi to the community in the new city flared up in 1889 with the arrival of R. M. Maierson. It continued during the term of R. Leibush Mendel Landau, a *maskil* who in 1898 founded a Zionist group. The conflict ended in 1921 with the appointment of a chief rabbi for both communities. The J. pop. in 1899 came to 16,817 (51% of the total), including 600 expelled from surrounding villages. The Zionist movement was especially active in B. and in 1882 a Hebrew periodical *Ha'or* appeared. In 1921, four of the 15 municipal councilors were Jews and in 1930 a Jew was appointed deputy mayor. The J. pop. in 1930 stood at 11,840 (37% of the total). During 1918–40, 7,036 pupils attended the boys' school and 6,038 the girls' school. In 1931, a vocational school for girls was founded. Zionist youth movements were active between the World Wars and a training farm existed on the outskirts of the city. From 1940, the Iron Guard Legionnaires persecuted Jews and 8,000 B. Jews were drafted into labor battalions working on roads, dams, bridges, and for the Rumanian army throughout Rumania during 1940-43. Groups of Jews were arrested and held as hostages (3 July 1941) and were expelled to Transnistria (148 during Sept.–Oct. 1942). Following the outbreak of the Soviet-Rumanian war (June 1941), 11,000 Jews from Rumanian communities and from Poland found refuge in B. Two high schools which the community opened together with the vocational school, the elementary schools, and the *talmud torah* provided education for 1,390 children in the J. pop., which numbered 15,502 in 1942. In spring 1944, 186 J. orphans brought from Transnistria were cared for by the community. On 7 March 1944, Jews were forced to build trenches against the approaching Soviet forces. When the Rumanian forces left B., Jews took over the municipal administration. After the war a community of 19,550 existed; over the years the majority immigrated to Israel.

BOTTROP Westphalia, Germany. Two Jews were present in 1842 and the J. pop. grew to 68 in 1905, reaching its peak in 1925 with 237. From 1848, the J. inhabitants were attached to the Dorsten congregation. In 1901, a cemetery was established. In 1910, with the number of Jews exceeding that of Dorsten, B. achieved the status of a daughter community. The community established a prayer room in the early 1920s and became independent in 1932. Jews from Eastern Europe arrived during and after WWI, many of them working at first in the factories and in the mines. In June 1933, four months after the Nazi rise to power, there were 194 Jews in the city, including 96 of East European origin. By 1938, about half the Jews had left the city. On 28 Oct. 1938, 55 Jews of Polish origin were expelled to the Bentschen-Zbaszyn camp on the Polish border and a year later transferred to occupied Poland. On *Kristallnacht* (9-10 Nov. 1938), J. homes and stores were destroyed and 35 Jews were arrested, including 17 children. By May 1939 only 28 Jews remained. The last nine remaining Jews were deported in Jan.–Feb. 1942.

BOULAY Moselle dist., France. Jews lived in B. from the end of the 14th cent. The only synagogue permitted in Lorraine was located here from 1699. In 1671, a false ritual murder accusation led to the death of a young rabbi, Raphael Levy, who was burned at the stake. In 1721, Duke Leopold confirmed the right of 19 J. families to reside in B. The synagogue designated the main one in the duchy of Lorraine was inaugurated in 1854. The J. pop. of B. numbered 137 in 1808; 265 in 1831; and 120 in 1931. In the B. district there were 663 Jews in 1885; 615 in 1895; 578 in 1910; and 432 in 1931. During WWII, the Germans expelled all the local Jews to the south of France. Eleven Jews from B. were deported. The synagogue, completely destroyed during the war, was rebuilt in 1955. In 1968, there were only 35 Jews in B.

BOULOGNE-SUR-MER Pas-de-Calais dist., France. Jews settled in B. from the first half of the 19th cent., inaugurating a synagogue in 1873. In autumn 1940, persecutions of Jews in northern France began. The actual takeover of J. businesses in B. started early in 1941. In Dec. 1940, the Jews of B. were expelled and confined in a camp for civilian prisoners near Troyes The local synagogue was destroyed. The Todt

organization maintained a group in B. In 1965, there were 100 Jews living in B.

BOULOGNE-SUR-SEINE (Boulogne-Billancourt) Hauts-de-Seine dist., France. The synagogue was inaugurated in 1911. A J. high school was founded in 1935 and the community maintained a charitable association for assisting poor children. During WWII, the 1941 census listed 921 Jews in B. In July 1942, 96 Jews were arrested.

BOURG-EN-BRESSE Ain dist., France. Jews are first mentioned in B. In 1277. In 1438, 11 J. families signed an agreement to share the expenses of fortifying the village. In the beginning of the 16th cent., Jews were no longer living in B. At the beginning of WWII, there were between 10–15 J. families. Seven Jews were arrested on 10 July 1944, and executed in Marlieux on 14 July. The bodies of another ten who were executed were found on 20 July in the Seillon forest. The community never reestablished itself.

BOURGES Cher dist., France. The first reference to local Jews dates from the sixth cent. Saint Germain is mentioned as having converted several Jews in B. in 568 and a local bishop (624–647) also converted many Jews, expelling those who resisted him. There are records of a J. quarter in B. in 1020. The Jews were expelled in 1182 but returned in 1198. The B. community ceased to exist in 1394, when the final expulsion of Jews from France took place. After 1940, hundred of J. refugees settled in B. In 1947, a new community was established, which consisted of 90 Jews in 1964.

BOURTANGE (Boertange) Groningen dist., Holland. J. settlement began in the 18th cent. and 81 Jews lived there in 1892. The J. pop. in 1938 was 55. The Jews were deported to Poland in WWII; only two survived in hiding.

BOXMEER Noord-Brabnamt dist., Holland. A community was established in the 19th cent. The J. pop. in 1941 was 23 (total 4,075). All the Jews were deported in WWII; none returned.

BOZIENI-BALS Moldavia dist., Rumania. J. families first settled in 1838. The J. pop. in 1899 was 349 (22% of the total). In summer 1941 the Jews were expelled to Roman.

BRAD S. Transylvania dist., Rumania. Jews settled here in the mid-19th cent. and were attached to the Deva community. They made their living mainly as engineers and clerks in the mining industry. The J. pop. in 1930 stood at 102 (2% of the total). On 29 Nov. 1940, Iron Guard Legionnaires plundered J. property. The men were drafted into labor battalions and were released in Sept. 1944. In 1950, only three J. families remained.

BRAGIN Polesie dist., Belorussia. Jews are first mentioned in the mid-17th cent. Jews were victimized in the Chmielnicki massacres of 1648–49 and in Haidamak attacks in 1750. Their pop. was 260 in 1765 and 2,254 (total 4,311) in 1897. In the Soviet period, a J. elementary school was in operation until the late 1930s. A Hehalutz group was active in the mid-1920s and three kolkhozes supporting 50 J. families were founded in the early 1920s. In 1939, the total J. pop. was 958. The Germans occupied the town on 28 Aug. 1941. A small number of Jews fled. On 13 Sept., about 300 Jews were murdered outside the town. The rest were murdered shortly afterwards near the local police station.

BRAILA Walachia dist., Rumania. Jews first settled in the 15th cent. and from 1829, when B. was decreed a free port, Jews worked as stevedores. After 1863, the influx of Rumanian merchants from N. Transylvania caused an outbreak of antisemitism. The livelihoods of 300 J. families were adversely affected by the 1855 law against peddling. The J. pop. in 1899 was 9,830 (18% of the total). Jews played a prominent part in the trading of grain. A community council was selected by democratic elections in 1905. The first synagogue (Sephardi) was built in 1830 and prior to WWI, eight prayer houses were functioning. In 1888, a home for the aged was established with 30 beds. In 1895, an evening school for J. adults was opened. B. Jews played a leading role in Zionist activities in Rumania. A B'nai B'rith lodge was founded in 1873 which supported the Settlement in Eretz Israel movement. On 26–27 Dec. 1895, the second national convention of Hovevei Zion was held in B. with representatives from 13 cities. The founding conference of J. Teachers in Rumania took place on 26–27 Dec. 1908, and a resolution was

passed proposing the teaching of Hebrew as a living language. In 1881, a branch of the Settlement in Eretz Israel movement was active in supporting the establishment of Zikhron Yaakov and Rosh Pinna. At the outbreak of WWI, B. was occupied by the German army and Jews were taken to build trenches. In 1918–19, 2,280 Jews were granted citizenship and until the Goga–Cuza regime (1937) J. representatives served on the municipal council. The Zionist movement was reestablished with 700 members, and in 1920 the Zionists gained the majority in the community elections. The J. pop. in 1930 was 7,246. In 1940, Rumanian Iron Guard Legionnaires persecuted the J. pop. In Sept., J. merchants were prevented from entering the port to receive their grain supplies. In Nov. Jews were

attacked, their property confiscated, and heavy taxes imposed. Those aged 16–60 were drafted into labor battalions from 4 Aug. 1941 up to Aug. 1944. After the war, the community continued to function. There was a larger J. pop. than in the prewar period due to the influx of survivors from Bessarabia and northern Bukovina. The majority later emigrated to Israel.

BRAILOW   Vinnitsa dist., Ukraine. Jews numbered 638 in 1765 and 3,721 in 1897. On 10 July 1919, the Petlyura gangs attacked Jews and looted J. property. The J. pop. fell to 2,393 in 1926. A J. council was active in the Soviet period. The Germans captured B. on 17 July 1941, with a few Jews managing to flee. Fifteen Jews were murdered immediately. Afterwards

Avraham Rechtman of the Jewish Ethnographic Society taking notes from informant, Brailow, Ukraine (YIVO Archive, New York/photo courtesy of Yad Vashem, The Holocaust Martyrs' and Heroes' Remembrance Authority, Jerusalem)

the Jews were made to pay a large tribute and wear the yellow patch. In Feb. 1942, 2,000 of the city's 3,000 Jews were executed. Skilled workers and their families were then concentrated in a ghetto along with 200 Jews who had escaped the *Aktion* and others who had been expelled from Dorohoi in Rumania. In a second *Aktion*, in mid-April 1942, about 250 Jews were killed and 300 escaped to the Zhmerinka ghetto in Transnistria. The rest of the Jews were executed in a third and final *Aktion* in May 1942.

BRAKEL Westphalia, Germany. Jews are first mentioned in 1560. A community of seven families was present in 1651 and a synagogue was in use in 1691. The J. pop. comprised 11 families in 1704 and 65 individuals in 1806, rising to a peak of 174 in 1843 and declining to 101 in 1905. The synagogue moved to a new building in 1844; a new cemetery was opened in 1854. Economic circumstances improved in the late 19th cent. as the Jews came to constitute a community of well-to-do merchants. Jews were also active in public life, with two serving on the municipal council in 1874. Among the town's leading commercial establishments were the Weiler, Flechtheim and Heinberg grain stores, whose business extended beyond the borders of Germany, and the Delberg leather goods company, which sold extensively in western and northern Germany. In June 1933, some four months after the Nazi assumption of power, the J. pop. numbered 99. Under Nazi rule, the Jews were subjected to the usual persecution and harassment. In 1938, the community's *shohet* died of wounds inflicted by SA thugs. On *Kristallnacht* (9–10 Nov. 1938), the windows of the synagogue were smashed and ten J. stores were vandalized. J. men were sent to the Buchenwald concentration camp. By May 1939 only 36 Jews remained – seven had died and 46 left. The last Jews in the town were deported from late 1941, to the Riga ghetto on 10 Dec.; to the Warsaw ghetto on 28 March 1942; and to the Theresienstadt ghetto on 28 July 1942.

BRANDENBURG AN DER HAVEL Brandenburg, Germany. The first Jew in B. is mentioned in 1313, and an organized community with a synagogue existed as early as 1322. Following the Berlin trial for desecration of the Host in 1510, five Jews from B. were executed. The remaining B. Jews together with the Jews from Brandenburg province were expelled. After the second general expulsion of Jews from Bran-

denburg in 1573, no Jews lived in B. until 1671. The new, growing community established two synagogues (1781–82 and 1883) and two cemeteries (before 1720 and 1747) and from 1859 employed a rabbi. Toward the end of the 19th cent., Jews were serving on the city council. By 1925 the J. pop. was 483. When the Nazis came to power in 1933, there were 350 Jews in B. On *Kristallnacht* (9–10 Nov. 1938), the synagogue was set on fire; the cemetery desecrated and its mortuary pulled down; and J. stores were wrecked and looted. Jews were arrested, tormented, and beaten. One woman committed suicide. At the beginning of the 1940s, 90 Jews who did not manage to emigrate were deported to the east; 28 were sent on 13 April 1942 to the Warsaw ghetto. At the end of WWII, only ten Jews, probably protected by marriage to non-Jews, still lived in B.

BRANDOBERNDORF Hesse–Nassau, Germany. The J. community numbered 25 (3% of the total) in 1925. A synagogue in nearby Kroeffelbach, destroyed on *Kristallnacht* (9–10 Nov. 1938), served the Jews of B., Kroeffelbach (five families), and Kraftsolms (four families). All left by Sept. 1940.

BRANDYS NAD LABEM Bohemia, Czechoslovakia. The J. settlement was founded in the Hradek quarter in the early 16th cent. After the expulsion from Moravia in 1559, the Jews of B. emigrated to Poznan in Poland, returning to B. in 1568. A small J. quarter was maintained in the 17th–19th cents. In 1921, B. reached a peak pop. of 272 (total 5,031). In 1930, 60 Jews remained. Some fled prior to deportation in 1942. The synagogue was converted into a warehouse in Oct. 1941 and religious articles were transferred to the J. Museum in Prague. The remaining Jews were sent to the Theresienstadt ghetto in Jan.–Sept. 1942 and from there to the east. Few survived.

BRANSK Bialystok dist., Poland. A small number of Jews were present in the 17th–18th cents., leasing flour mills and inns. In the 1860s, Jews from the surrounding villages settled in B., many of them Hasidim (Kotsk, Gur, Radzymin, Aleksandrow). By 1897, the J. pop. was 2,374 (total 4,087). Economic hardship led to organized emigration to the U.S., Latin America, and South Africa. R. Shimon Yehuda Hacohen Shkop served as rabbi in 1906–20 and transferred his famous yeshiva there. Haskala influence increased in the late

19th cent. and Hovevei Zion and socialist groups became active. Under the German occupation in WWI the Jews were subjected to forced labor, heavy taxes, and property expropriations. The arrival of General Haller's Polish troops at the end of the war unleashed a reign of persecution, pillage, and rape. Between the World Wars the Zionist youth groups were active and a Tarbut Hebrew school was founded. J. trade was undermined by the Polish cooperatives and the economic boycott. The Germans captured the city from the Soviets on 25 June 1941, subjecting the town's 2,700 Jews to a regime of forced labor and extortion. A ghetto was established in July. On 2 Nov. 1942 the Jews were expelled to Bialystok and from there deported to the Treblinka death camp About 100 hiding out in bunkers were subsequently rounded up and murdered. Some managed to join the partisans.

BRANSZCZYK Bialystok dist., Poland. The J. pop. in 1921 was 140 (total 731). The Jews were expelled by the Germans in fall 1939 to Wyszkow and other places, sharing the fate of the local Jews.

BRASLAW Vilna dist., Poland. A few J. families were present in the mid-16th cent. The community grew in the 19th cent., with J. merchants dealing mainly in flax and grain and others operating inns. The J. pop. reached 1,234 (total 1,501) in 1897. By 1884 three synagogues were operating in B. but were closed that year because of a dispute between Hasidim and *Mitnaggedim*. Later in the year they burned down. After the Russo-Japanese War of 1905, a pogrom broke out when Jews were blamed for the Russian defeat. Many merchants emigrated to Danzig; their places were soon taken by Jews from the surrounding towns as J. commerce thrived in the pre-WWI years. The J. pop. in 1925 was 1,900. Most children studied at a CYSHO Yiddish school and among the Zionist organizations Hehalutz sent a number of pioneers to Palestine. The Germans captured the city on 27 June 1941 after two years of Soviet rule. A ghetto was established on 15 April 1942, crowded with refugees. On 3 June, 2,500 Jews were executed near the local railway station. The remaining 1,000 were killed on 12 March 1943 after an effort at resistance failed.

BRASOV (Hung. Brasso; Ger. Kronstadt) S. Transylvania dist., Rumania. A J. community was established in 1828 and joined the Neologist association in 1868. An Orthodox community was founded in 1877. The Neologist community built a synagogue in 1899–1905 with 800 seats. Between the World Wars, both communities had separate institutions, except for the J. school, opened in 1940 and jointly managed. Zionist organizations were founded in 1920. The J. pop. was 2,594 in 1930 (4% of the total). In fall 1940, the Iron Guard nationalized all J. institutions and most J. shops were seized. In 1941, Jews from throughout S. Transylvania who were drafted for forced labor were brought to B. Another 200 refugees came from Ploiesti. In Aug. 1942, 850 Jews aged 18–50 were drafted into labor battalions and put to work in B.; some were sent to Predeal and Bran. In spring 1943, 250 youths were sent to the Suraia camp to build fortifications. By Aug. 1944, only 250–300 remained in the labor battalions after most of the Jews had succeeded in obtaining their freedom. In 1945–46, the J. pop. increased to 3,500.

BRATISLAVA (Ger. Pressburg; Hung. Pozsony) Slovakia, Czechoslovakia, today Republic of Slovakia. A community apparently existed in the 12th cent. Under royal protection until 1345, it enjoyed equality and economic stability, probably reaching a pop. of a few hundred Jews inhabiting their own quarter and maintaining a synagogue and other communal institutions. In 1360, the Jews were expelled following a period of severe persecution, returning in 1368 and again building a viable community despite ongoing harassment. In the first half of the 15th cent., the Street of the Jews numbered 39 J.-owned houses. The Jews themselves were forced to wear special dress. They were again expelled in Oct. 1526 after the Turks defeated the Hungarians at Mohacs. Most settled on Austrian territory just across the Danube River and some at a place called Schlossberg ("Castle Hill") outside the city limits. The new community, under the protection of the House of Palffy from 1599, again grew and prospered, augmented by J. refugees from Vienna in 1670, including R. Yom Tov Lipmann, who officiated as rabbi from c. 1690. In the early 18th cent., the J. pop. of Schlossberg was officially 40–50 families with another few in the Zuckermandel quarter; including refugees and temporary residents, the J. pop. probably reached about 200 families. The well-known Court Jew Shimon Mikhael headed the community, which enjoyed broad autonomy. During the first half of the 18th cent., B. became an important religious cen-

Emperor Francis Joseph visiting the Bratislava Jewish community, Czechoslovakia

ter, maintaining a large yeshiva. However, from the mid-18th cent. a debilitating "tolerance tax," the highest in Hungary (and remaining in force until 1848), sowed economic distress. The situation improved at the turn of 18th cent. as the J. pop. increased to over 2,000 and an increasing number of Jews moved to within the city walls. Under the stewardship of R. Moshe Sofer (Schreiber), known as Hatam Sofer, from 1806 to 1839, B. again became a great religious center, the most important in Central Europe, with R. Sofer shaping the spiritual life of Slovakian Jewry. His descendants served as the community's rabbis until WWII. By the mid-19th cent., the J. pop. was about 4,000. Anti-J. riots broke out twice in 1848 and in the second half of the 19th cent., causing great damage to J. property. A Great Synagogue was consecrated in 1864. In 1872, 60 families formed a separate Neologist congregation, a step accompanied by growing religious friction within the community which continued into the Holocaust period. The Neol-

ogists took over the J. elementary school founded in 1820 under Haskala influence and built their own synagogue in 1895. In the 1870s, the Orthodox congregation also opened an elementary school, adding junior high school classes in 1885-86. The yeshiva, which had flourished under R. Sofer, reached an enrollment of over 500 in the late 19th cent. In the early 20th cent., Jews became more active in the city's public and economic life. Twenty-four served on the municipal council in 1900 as the J. pop. grew to 7,111 (total 65,867). Jews owned about 720 business establishments, dealing in textiles, clothing, groceries, farm produce, etc. A fire in 1913 destroyed many homes in the J. quarter, causing many families to move to the town center. Most Jews identified with German culture while the educated class inclined more to Hungarian culture. The first Zionist society was founded in 1897 with Mizrachi becoming active in 1902 and Po'alei Zion and Tze'irei Tziyyon by 1912, when Agudat Israel also opened a branch. After WWI, WIZO and such

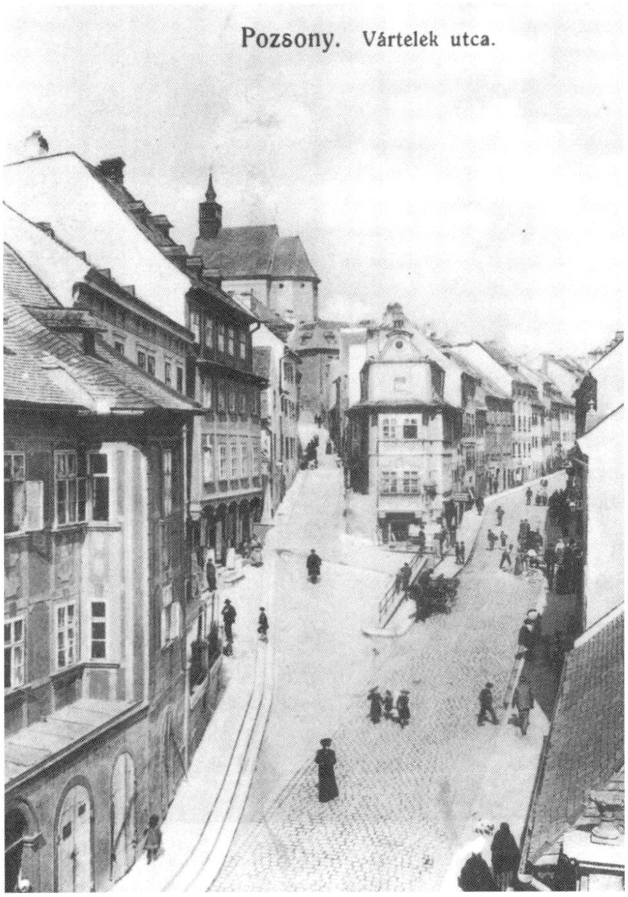
Pozsony. Vártelek utca.

The Jewish quarter of Bratislava, Czechoslovakia, 1920 (Jewish Museum, Prague/photo courtesy of Beth Hatefutsoth, Tel Aviv)

youth movements as Hashomer Hatzair, Bnei Akiva, and Betar became active along with the Maccabi sports club. The Zionists also published the *Juedische Rundschau* (later called the *Juedische Volkszeitung*). New riots shook the community in the aftermath of WWI, with the situation stabilizing somewhat under Czechoslovakian rule. With the total J. pop. rising from 10,973 in 1921 to 18,102 in 1940, the dominant Orthodox congregation also maintained 15 prayer houses, 11 *battei midrash*, two cemeteries, a big community center and library, a hospital, an old age home, and an orphanage. Jews continued to dominate trade, also operating five banks and seven pharmacies and insurance and shipping agencies as well as providing the city with about 50 doctors, 65 lawyers, 30 engineers, and other professional and academic personnel.

Persecution of the Jews intensified after the establishment of Slovakian autonomy in Oct. 1938. Synagogues and community facilities were vandalized and Jews were attacked in the streets. In Nov., dozens of J. families without Slovakian citizenship were expelled from the city. Jews were also removed from public positions, their livelihoods were undermined, and they were forced out of their homes. During 1941, about 950 J. businesses were closed down, a third of the largest ones were "Aryanized," and hundreds of Jews were seized for forced labor. In Oct. 1941, 6,743 Jews were expelled to 16 provincial towns (most to Trnava, Nitra, and Nove Mesto). In early 1942, 8,380 Jews remained. In late March, hundreds of young Jews were deported to the Majdanek concentration camp and 380 young women from B. and the surrounding settlements were sent to the Patronka camp en route to Auschwitz. Deportations of J. families to Auschwitz commenced in the second half of April. About 2,000 Jews from B. and environs were transported to the Lublin dist. (Poland) on 2 and 8 June, able-bodied men to the Majdanek concentration camp, the rest to the Sobibor death camp. About 250 more were sent to the Lublin dist. in mid-June and 650 to Auschwitz in July, all via Zilina. A final group of about 320 left for Zilina on 25 Sept. The remaining Jews, numbering 5,231 in early 1944, continued to suffer persecution and abuse. The 2,000 or so who did not manage to flee before the arrival of the Germans in Sept. 1944 were sent to the Sered concentration camp on 29 Sept. and from there to Auschwitz. Towards the end of the war, the Nazis set up a labor camp for about 500 Hungarian Jews across the river, murdering all of them before evacuating the area. After the war, a community numbering 7,000 Jews in 1947 was established, all but a few hundred of them newcomers. With assistance from the Joint Distribution Committee, community services were revived and J. life again flourished, with intense Zionist activity. About 4,000 Jews left the city in 1948–49, most for Israel. In the mid-1990s, the J. pop. was about 800 and community life again began to revive after a period of relative decline.

BRATOLIUBOVKA Kirovograd dist., Ukraine. The J. pop. was 1,193 (total 2,330) in 1897, with one of the community's two synagogues built in the early 19th cent. A *talmud torah* enrolled 20 children at the turn of the cent. The J. pop. dropped rapidly after the Oct. 1917 Revolution and the civil war (1918–21), numbering 45 in 1926. Following the German occupation in Aug. 1941, the few remaining Jews in B. were apparently murdered immediately.

BRATSKOYE Odessa dist., Ukraine. Jews numbered 241 (total 1,403) in 1897 and 203 in 1939. The Germans captured B. on 7 Aug. 1941 and in Oct., they murdered 26 local families and 24 from Bukovina and the Western Ukraine on the road leading to the village of Viktorovka.

BRATSLAW Vinnitsa dist., Ukraine. Jews settled in the 15th cent. In 1479, 400 were killed in a Tartar attack and the town was abandoned by the Jews until the early 17th cent. In 1648, the Jews were murdered in the Chmielnicki massacres of 1648-49, including those who fled to Nemirov and Tulchin. In 1765, the J. pop. was 101, growing to 3,920 in 1897. In 1910, Jews owned most of the town's 16 small factories (candles, hide processing, soft drinks, etc.) Most of the Jews were followers of Nahman of Bratslav, who arrived in B. in 1802 and served as rabbi until 1808. During the civil war (1918–21), the Petlyura gangs murdered 239 Jews. In the Soviet period, a Yiddish elementary school operated until 1931. Half the members of the local council were Jews, whose pop. stood at 1,010 in 1939. On 22 July 1941, the German and Rumanian armies captured B., which was then attached to Rumanian-administered Transnistria. In Nov., some local Jews were taken to the Pechera concentration camp. Another 747 skilled workers and their families were held at two local labor camps. In Aug. 1942, 1,200 Jews expelled from Bukovina and Bessarabia were brought to the two camps. All worked in a quarry or paving the road to Stalino. In Sept. 1942, 400 Jews were executed, including 85 children. Another 15 were shot on 18 Jan. 1943. Only 227 Jews survived in the two camps.

BRAUNFELS Hesse–Nassau, Germany. An independent J. community was first established in 1697 and two rival synagogues were maintained there during the 18th cent. Augmented by Jews from neighboring villages, the community opened a new synagogue (1852) and numbered 105 (6% of the total) in 1880, but soon declined. It disbanded in 1938, when only 13 Jews remained; the last four perished in the Holocaust.

BRAUNSBACH Wuerttemberg, Germany. Jews are first mentioned in 1673. By 1843 they numbered 293 (total 1,091) and were prominent in the town's commerce, dealing in land and cattle, but as Jews emigrated the town's fortunes also declined. Good relations prevailed with the local pop. in an atmosphere distinctly liberal in outlook. In 1933, 39 Jews were left, with another eight from neighboring Duensbach attached to the community. The pop. in 1854 was 100. On *Kristallnacht* (9–10 Nov. 1938), the synagogues in both B. and Duensbach were vandalized by SD gangs. Under increasing economic and social pressure, 17 Jews emigrated; the others were deported, nearly all to their deaths (to the Riga and Theresienstadt ghettoes and to Auschwitz).

BRAUNSBERG (Pol. Braniewo) East Prussia, Germany, today Poland. The first evidence of Jews dates from 1744. By 1884, the community had grown to 169 members, dropping to 99 in 1905 and to about 50 by 1925. The community maintained a synagogue (1855) and a cemetery. On *Kristallnacht* (9–10 Nov. 1938), the synagogue was set on fire. By May 1939 there were only ten Jews in B. No further information about their fate under Nazi rule is available.

BRAUNSCHWEIG Brunswick, Germany. First evidence of a J. presence dates from 1282 and in 1320 there was a community which had a synagogue and comprised at least 24 families. In the Black Death persecutions of 1348-49, more than half of the Jews were murdered, but the community continued to exist until its expulsion in 1510. There were attempts at resettlement and individual Jews were allowed to live in B. but it was not until the 18th cent. that a J. community started to develop again. During the fairs, there would be 300–600 Jews in the town. About 1770, a Court Jew maintained a rabbinical house of learning and from 1779 onward, the synagogue was located in his house. In 1786, the J. pop came to 206 and in 1812 to 379. At this time, although there were several J. bankers and rich businessmen, half the Jews were considered indigent. The first J. town councilor took office in 1845. The community, which in 1825 became the center of a district rabbinate, dedicated a new synagogue building in 1875. In the wake of immigration from Eastern Europe, the J. pop. grew to 710 in 1890 and 1,100 in 1927. The newcomers were not given an equal share in the community's leadership. In 1933, 980 Jews were living in B. At the start of the anti-J. boycott, 1 April 1933, 11 members of the youth group of the J. War Veterans Association (RjF) were arrested and maltreated with one subsequently

The Jacobson School, Braunschweig, Germany,1930 (Beth Hatefutsoth Photo Archive, Tel Aviv)

dying. The various boycott measures continued and by fall 1938, most J. businesses had been "Aryanized" and B.'s 19 J. doctors were no longer practicing. Sixty-nine Jews of non-German citizenship were deported to Poland in Oct. 1938. On *Kristallnacht* (9–10 Nov. 1938), the synagogue was burned down, J. stores were wrecked, and 71 men were arrested and taken to the Buchenwald concentration camp. At this time, 620 Jews remained in B. About 200 managed to escape by 1941. The remaining Jews were billeted in eight "J. houses" and deported in 14 transports from 1941. 377 Jews from B. died in the Holocaust.

BRCKO   Bosnia-Hercegovina, Yugoslavia, today Republic of Bosnia. Jews lived in B. before the 19th cent. They numbered 126 in 1931 (total 7,780). Armed members of the Fascist Ustase organization cruelly persecuted and killed 130 in the Holocaust.

BREAZA   Bukovina, Rumania. Jews first settled in the late 19th cent. The J. pop. in 1930 was 140. The

Iron Guard confiscated J. shops and factories and incited the local pop. against the Jews. In 1940, the J. pop. was transferred to the Campulung ghetto, and in Oct. 1941 deported to Transnistria. Only 20 survived the war.

BREB   N. Transylvania dist., Rumania. A J. community existed in this resort village in the mid-19th cent. The J. pop. in 1920 was 224 (14% of the total). In 1944 the community was transferred to the Berbesti ghetto and then deported to Auschwitz.

BRECLAV   Moravia (Sudetenland), Czechoslovakia. Jews are first mentioned in 1411 and in the mid-16th cent. were part of a large community with a synagogue and rabbi. They were attacked in riots in 1574, 1605, and 1622. The community was totally destroyed in 1643 during the Swedish occupation. The J. quarter was reestablished in 1671 under the auspices of Beatrix of Liechtenstein and a synagogue was built in the following years as J. refugees from Vienna arrived. In

1702, all the houses in the city went up in flames and in 1812 all J. homes again burned down. The renowned historian Heinrich Graetz (1817–91) taught in the local J. school in 1850–52. A new synagogue seating 417 was completed in 1868 as the J. pop. rose steadily from 325 in 1797 to 532 in 1869 and 783 (total 8,839) in 1910. Most Jews belonged to the middle class and were pioneers in the city's industrial development. The Zionists were active before WWI. In 1930, the J. pop. was 589. Following the Munich Agreement of Sept. 1938 and the annexation of the Sudetenland to the Third Reich, those Jews who had not fled were expelled to the Czechoslovakian border on 15 Oct. Denied entry, 65 J. refugees remained for weeks without shelter in an open field, until the British ambassador in Prague intervened and 51 were brought to a refugee camp in Ivanice on 7 Nov. In April 1942, the Jews of B. were deported to the Theresienstadt ghetto and from there sent to the death camps. About 50 of the 100 surviving Jews emigrated to Israel after the war.

BREDA Noord-Brabant dist., Holland. Organized J. settlement began in the early 19th cent. and by 1893 there were 175 Jews. In 1941 over 200 Jews lived there. In Dec. 1942, 176 were deported via the Westerbork transit camp. Only three of these survived, as did 26 who had gone into hiding. A community was reestablished after the war.

BREISACH (in J. sources, Bizach, Brizche) Baden, Germany. The J. settlement probably began in the early 14th cent. All the Jews were burned alive in the Black Death persecutions of 1348–49. A letter of protection was granted by Duke Albert in 1446 and remained in effect for hundreds of years. The revived J. community, the only one in the region, maintained continuous settlement until WWII. The J. quarter was heavily damaged in the French invasion of 1793. In 1827–86, B. was the seat of the district rabbinate. A new synagogue and a second cemetery were opened in the 1830s, when the J. pop. reached a peak of 572 (total 3,050), and a J. elementary school operated in 1835–76. The majority of Jews were cattle traders. After WWI the J. pop. dropped sharply, standing at 231 in 1933. By 1940, 157 Jews had left the town, most emigrating (many to nearby France). On *Kristallnacht* (9–10 Nov. 1938), the synagogue was burned down and 30 Jews were taken to the Dachau concentration camp. The last 34 Jews were deported to the Gurs concentration camp on 22 Oct.

1940. Another 29 were deported from their places of refuge after leaving B. All perished, 31 of them in Auschwitz.

BREITENBACH AM HERZBERG Hesse-Nassau, Germany. Jews lived in B. from the mid-18th cent., numbering 80 (10% of the total) in 1905 and 75 in 1933. Not one remained after 1939.

BREMEN Free Hanseatic city, Germany. There is evidence of individual Jews in B. from the 14th cent. The first community within the city came about following the annexation by B. in 1803 of the neighboring town of Hastedt, which had a J. community from the 18th cent. Jews were only allowed to live within city limits under French rule (1811–13). In 1825, 50 Jews were living in Hastedt and only 13 within the city limits. After 1848, practically all of the Hastedt Jews moved to B., where the religious services were now performed. The J. pop. was 100 in 1860, but then swelled to 798 in 1900 and 1,329 in 1922 due to an influx of J. immigrants from Eastern Europe,. In 1876, the community dedicated a synagogue and in 1898 engaged Leopold Rosenak as its first rabbi; the newcomers from Eastern Europe, mostly Orthodox, maintained two prayer rooms. Since the city was a port for overseas emigration thousands of Jews spent some time in B. For these temporary residents, the community established a small synagogue. Relief organizations distributed 14,600 kosher meals in 1908. For its own needs, it set up an old age home (1922) and a community center (1927). Both the liberal Central Union (C.V.) and Zionist organizations found supporters among community members. In the 1920s, brutal antisemitic attacks foreshadowed coming events. At the time of the Nazi takeover in 1933, there were 1,314 Jews living in B. Riots took place even before the boycott of J. businesses on 1 April 1933. The boycott measures continued and by 1935 various businesses had to be closed down. The community was unable to maintain several of its institutions for financial reasons, but it did manage to step up its internal cultural life and to counter growing social isolation. On *Kristallnacht* (9–10 Nov. 1938), the synagogue, which had already previously been the target of acts of violence, was set on fire and the cemetery was desecrated. J. men were arrested and until mid-Dec. 1938 were imprisoned in the Bremen-Oslebshausen jail. By 1941, at least 431 Jews from B. had managed to emigrate abroad. Deportations

families were classified as "generally privileged" (*Generalprivilegierte*); 160 (relatives of the first class) as *Stammnumeranten*; and the rest *Extra-Ordinaere*. Although this latter group comprised the majority, its members were not recognized as members of the community. This guaranteed control of the community by its wealthy families. Among these families, Haskala, perceived as the right approach to gaining full entry into Christian society, had already made inroads in the late 18th cent. With the backing of Count Hoym, the minister for Silesia, these same wealthy families were allowed to set up in 1791 a J. state school (the Koenigliche Wilhelmsschule), emphasizing humanistic studies as an alternative to the 20 *hadarim* of the traditional system. In 1801, a J. state school for girls was added. Two of the teachers in the boys' school edited *Ha-Me'assef* in 1794–97, where the ideas of Haskala were disseminated. One of the figures connected with Haskala was Ephraim Kuh (1731–90), the first J. poet to write in German. Nonetheless, few of the Jews of B. were involved in these developments. The majority opposed Haskala vehemently and one of the community's rabbis published a ban on Mendelssohn and his writings in 1787. Consequently, Haskala proponents started their own synagogue in 1796, the Synagoge zum Tempel, where reforms and sermons in German were first instituted. A new burial society was also founded, as the existing one refused to conduct funerals postponed for a few days after the death.

In 1812, when Prussian law emancipating the Jews went into force in Silesia, the Jews of B. achieved the status of citizens and there was, therefore, no longer any justification for the division of Jews into classes within the J. community. J. life could now flourish. Jews began arriving from Silesia, Galicia, and Russian Poland. This influx made B., with a pop. of 7,384 in 1850, one of the three largest J. communities in Germany. This was just the beginning of its growth. Thirty years later, in 1880, the J. pop. had grown by 150% to stand at 17,500. In 1905, the J. pop. was 20,356 and in 1925, 23,240. This growth was accompanied by impressive economic gains. Jews played an important role in the grain, wool, leather, and textile trade, in the chemical and mining industries, and in the development of the railroad and banking. In 1906, 56.9% of J. breadwinners belonged to the bourgeoisie and only 15.6% to the lower class. This was the opposite of the picture for the Christian pop., where 65.5% of the Protestants and 73.2% of the Catholics belonged

to the lower class. Through their strong economic position, the Jews of B. acquired a measure of political influence both at the local and the national level. The first Jew was elected to the municipal council in the early 1840s. Jews also took part in the 1848 revolution and two were elected to the national assembly in Frankfurt. The Prussian three-class franchise system made it possible for Jews to win representation on the municipal council far beyond their share in the pop. (about 4%). About 40% of the Liberal faction was comprised of Jews. In the 1887–1923 period, three J. jurists served consecutively as chairmen of the council and in the late 1870s, two Jews were elected to the Reichstag. The institution of the equal vote in 1919 put an end to both Liberal dominance in the council and the overrepresentation of Jews. Nonetheless, Jews still found a place in the new liberal party, the German Democrats (DDP). Paula Ollendorff (1860–1938), who was very active in the community's charity institutions, represented the party in the municipal council from 1918. Eugen Schiffer (1860–1954) was one of the party's founders and served as minister of finance, minister of justice, and deputy chancellor. Others joined the Left, now the leading political force in the city. The forerunner was Ferdinand Lassalle (1825–64), the most famous of the J. politicians born in B., who founded the Allgemeiner Deutscher Arbeiterverein (1863), the predecessor of the Social Democratic Party. Ernst Eckstein was among the founders of the Socialist Workers Party (1931). Another area where Jews left their mark was intellectual life. The foundations were laid at the pre-academic level. From the mid-19th cent., the community began to relinquish its own general institutions of learning. The Wilhelmsschule, which the community had opened at the end of the 18th cent. to provide a modernized education, was closed in 1848 and the overwhelming majority of J. children attended public schools. Only in the Weimar period did the community again open a school of its own, an Orthodox elementary school (1920) that was expanded into a secondary school but attracted only a small number of children. Among the preferred schools among Jews was the prestigious Johannesgymnasium. Founded in 1872 as an interdenominational school, it soon included six Jews on its teaching staff. For the first time in Germany (until canceled by the Ministry of Education in 1876) classes in J. religion were mandatory and the subject was part of matriculation exams. Not only were Jews admitted to the same

educational institutions as Christians, they also exploited the opportunity more fully. While the overwhelming majority of Breslau's Christian children in the Second Reich received only primary school education, 80% of the J. students continued with their secondary education. At the turn of the 19th cent., the University of B. had the second highest percentage of J. students after Berlin (222 or 20% in 1886–87; 210 or 13.5% in 1902–03). Against this background, it was not surprising to find Jews occupying key positions in the humanities, the sciences, and the arts in B. There were many Jews among the lecturers at the local university, especially in the natural sciences, and a few served as rectors. Two B. Jews won Nobel Prizes: the chemist Fritz Haber (1868–1934) in 1918 and the physicist Max Born (1882–1970) in 1954. The architects Paul and Richard Ehrlich and the painter Eugen Spiro (1874–1972) were important contributors to the development of the *Jugendstil* style in B. Many Jews, among them Paul Muehsam (1876–1960), belonged to the "B. School" (*Breslauer Dichterschule*). The well-known theater critic Alfred Kerr (1867–1948) was also born in B. Jews owned a number of publishing houses and three newspapers. Also worthy of note is Edith Stein (1891–1942), who was born into an Orthodox J. family, studied philosophy under Edmund Hussserl, and having converted to Catholicism, entered a Carmelite convent. The Nazis murdered her in Auschwitz. One of the most striking expressions of the degree of J. assimilation into Christian society was the high rate of intermarriage. During WWI, it reached a peak of 52.8% and in the mid-1920s was still at a level of 39.2%. During the war, the Jews also paid a heavy price as citizens with equal rights: 450 fell in battle. The religious strife that commenced in the late 18th cent. continued into the first half of the 19th cent. Solomon Titkin (1791–1843), the chief rabbi from 1820, stood for undeviating Orthodoxy. Likewise, the first Great Synagogue erected in 1829 (the Storch-Synagoge) belonged to the Orthodox camp. Tensions reached their peak when Dr. Abraham Geiger (1874–1910), an uncompromising exponent of religious reform, was elected rabbi by the demand of the 120 Liberal voters (total 900) in the community and charged with delivering sermons in German. Conflicts over the division of responsibilities led to the dismissal of R. Tiktin in 1842 by the community's executive board and his replacement by Dr. Geiger. The Orthodox continued to recognize R. Tiktin as their rabbi and chose

his son Gedalya (1810–86) to replace him when he died. In 1854, a compromise was reached between the parties to the dispute. The community issued a statute recognizing the Liberal and Orthodox factions as representing two trends with equal rights under two religious commissions responsible for their own rabbis, synagogues, and schools. The "united community" thus created served as a model for many other communities in Germany. When Dr. Geiger left B. in 1863, Manuel Joel (1826–90), considered more moderate, was chosen as the new Liberal rabbi. Under his ministry, a new Liberal synagogue was consecrated in 1872, a magnificent structure equipped with an organ and the second largest synagogue in Germany. The unity of the community was illustrated by the fact that R. Gedalya Titkin attended the inaugural ceremony. The stability of the religious compromise between Orthodox and Liberals was fortified by the Juedisch-Theologisches Seminar founded in 1854, at the same time that the united community was formed. Zacharias Frankel (1801–75), then rabbi of Dresden, was appointed its director. He sought to distance himself from Abraham Geiger's uncompromising Reform tendencies and was an advocate of blending the traditional way of life with modern needs with the aid of unfettered scientific research. It was in this spirit that the Seminary became the first modern J. theological seminary for rabbinical training and a model for others in Europe and the United States. Frankel refused to align the Seminary with any theological stream and its faculty over a period of 85 years embraced a broad range of teachers, from the Hungarian Neologist Michael Guttmann (1921–33) to Isaak Heinemann (1918–38), representing Frankfurt Community Orthodoxy, and Yisrael Rabin (1921–34), a Lithuanian yeshiva graduate and Mizrachi activist, the first Zionist among the teachers. Frankel's own theological approach was basically shared by the most famous of the Seminary's teachers, the great historian Heinrich Graetz (1817–91), who taught there from the beginning and wrote 10 of the 11 volumes of his *History of the Jews* in B. Students too came from different streams and different countries. Aside from Germany, most came from Poland and Hungary. The Seminary reached the peak of its growth in 1930 when it had 79 students. In association with the Seminary, secondary schooling including J. studies was offered (until 1887) and a teachers seminary was opened (1856–67), revived somewhat in 1926 with a program for external students. The

Seminary's library contained valuable manuscripts and books. The journal *Monatsschrift fuer Geschichte und Wissenschaft des Judentums*, which Frankel had founded in Dresden in 1851, was also identified with the Seminary and it became the leading forum for J. studies. The *Germania Judaica* project was also connected with the Seminary. It was started in 1903 by Marcus Brann (1849–1920), Graetz's successor at the Seminary. The connection between the Seminary and the local community could be seen in the fact that since 1891 the latter's Liberal rabbis were graduates of the Seminary (Jacob Guttmann, 1891–1919; Hermann Vogelstein, 1920–38; Reinhold Lewin, 1938–43). In addition, in the Weimar period, the Seminary ran courses for youth movement members interested in leadership positions while teachers and advanced students began to teach in the J. adult education center (Freie juedische Volkshochschule) founded in 1919. From the latter part of the 19th cent., a new element entered J. life in B.: immigrants from Eastern Europe. Their percentage in the J. pop. of B. was indeed lower than in the other large J. communities in Germany – 7.2% in 1910 and 9% in 1925 – but these figures only reveal part of the picture. B. was an important stopover point for thousands of East European Jews on their way west, and thousands of them stayed in the city for a short period. Although in the final reckoning, the 11,055 immigrants who arrived in the 1882–1914 period must be set against the 10,000 who left, their presence in the J. pop. was conspicuous. The crystallization of B. as a Zionist center from the early 20th cent. was probably linked to the arrival of these East European immigrants, with their pronounced J. ethnic identity. In 1901, the first Zionist newspaper in Germany, *Der Zionist*, was founded in the city and in 1912 Yosef Marcus started the Zionist Blau-Weiss youth movement. During the Weimar period, a broad spectrum of Zionist groups was active, from the German Zionist Organization and Mizrachi to youth groups and student organizations. The growing influence of the Zionists was also reflected in the Seminary's curriculum – greater prominence was given to Hebrew language study and a Hebrew school was set up in the 1920s. Alongside the Zionist organizations many organizations with a Liberal character also existed in the community: the Lehr- and Leseverein, dating back to 1842, the Central Union (C.V.), the RjF (the J. War Veterans Association), the Verband nationaldeutscher Juden, and B'nai B'rith. Orthodox organizations were also to be found. The strength of the different factions could be seen on the community council in 1925: the Liberals held 13 seats; the Orthodox four; and the Zionists four. Other newspapers published in B. were the *Juedisches Volksblatt* (from 1895), whose name was later changed to *Juedische Zeitung fuer Ostdeutschland* and which also had a Zionist orientation, and the community bulletin (from 1924). A J. museum was founded in 1928. J. charity services were also highly developed in the community. Despite the community's prosperous image, there were many poor, especially after WWI when immigration from Eastern Europe was stepped up. The first charity organizations began to operate as early as the 18th cent. along with a sanatorium in 1726 which became a hospital in 1784. An orphanage was founded in 1805. Thanks to Jonas Fraenckel (1773–1846), chairman of the community in 1841–46 and whose bequest made possible the founding of the Juedisch-Theologisches Seminar, a fund was set up for the construction of inexpensive housing, an apartment building for needy J. families, a loan institute to fight poverty, and an institute for the furtherance of the arts and crafts among the Jews. Later a kindergarten and day care center were started along with a hospital for the chronically ill, the Beate-Guttmann-Heim (a home for elderly women without families, 1928), an old age home, a dormitory for J. nurses, and a homemaking school. The national-racist antisemitism that proliferated in Germany in the last third of the 19th cent. did not bypass B., although the liberal town council opposed the demands of the antisemites. Their efforts to keep J. teachers out of public schools and J. doctors out of executive positions in a local hospital failed. Only in their campaign to restrict East European immigration were they partially successful, as policy was not set by the liberal municipal authorities alone but also by the Prussian government. While the municipality approved all 48 applications for citizenship made by Jews between 1908 and 1914, the Prussian government only allowed eight. The antisemites also succeeded in gaining a foothold in the local university and, in particular, among the student organizations. The creation of the first J. students union in 1886 was a response to increasing attacks. After WWI, when B. became a border town where the dispute between Germany and Poland over Upper Silesia was keenly felt, nationalism and antisemitism intensified. J. membership in local societies was affected. Whereas in the past only those with an antisemitic or clear-cut Christian character banned Jews,

now, in 1924, the doors to the Alpenverein were closed to them. In 1925, antisemitic doctors founded a new medical association that did not accept J. members and called for a boycott of J. doctors. In many secondary schools, swastikas were drawn on the walls and students distributed antisemitic flyers. The antisemitic atmosphere in the city even produced a blood libel following the brutal murder of two children in 1926. The antisemitism soon developed into violence against the Jews and their institutions. In 1926, the old J. cemetery was desecrated. Lassalle's grave, in the second cemetery, was desecrated in 1932. In a number of instances, Jews were harassed and beaten in the street by antisemites. When the Volunteer Corps (*Freikorps*) and the Navy took control of Breslau during the Kapp Putsch in March 1920, they murdered six of their adversaries, including, with particular brutality, Bernhard Schottlaender, a leading J. member of the Independent Social Democrats (USPD) and editor of the socialist newspaper *Schlesische Arbeiterzeitung*. Some five months later, in Aug., an antisemitc mob looted a J. department store and smashed the windows of a hotel where East European Jews generally stayed. Only police intervention prevented the total destruction of the building. The outburst repeated itself on a larger scale in July 1923. A demonstration against unemployment and inflation deteriorated into an anti-J. riot with over 100 stores looted, almost all owned by Jews. With the increase of Nazi strength in the city in the early 1930s, verbal and physical assaults against Jews also multiplied. A local pro-Nazi newspaper called for a boycott of J. stores in spring 1932. In Nov., when a J. jurist was appointed to a professorship at the university, Nazi students disrupted his lectures, hurling tear gas bombs and injuring J. students. Finally, under Nazi rule, the professor was dismissed.

After Jan. 1933, the J. pop. in B. was subjected to intensifying antisemitic assaults and boycott measures even before Boycott Day on 1 April 1933, the new regime's first official and nationwide antisemitic measure. In Feb., Nazi hooligans stabbed a J. student to death. In March, the J. artistic director of the united theaters of B. was pressured to resign and subsequently arrested and tortured. In the same month, SA troops posted themselves in front of J. business establishments. J. judges and lawyers were forcibly removed from courtrooms and forbidden to work in their profession until further notice (which temporarily paralyzed the city's legal system). In April, as in all of Germany,

a wave of dismissals commenced among J. professors, jurists, doctors, and teachers in the public service. But beyond all this, the B. Jews were subjected to what the *J. Chronicle* (5.5.1933) termed "a veritable reign of terror." J. passports were specially stamped to prevent Jews from leaving Germany. At any time Jews were liable to be attacked in the streets. Many were falsely accused by informers and tortured. A local J. leader of the Social-Democrat Reichsbanner was sent to a concentration camp, where he died. A J. industrialist was murdered in B. itself by the Nazis. In Aug., the J. community bulletin was temporarily closed down after an editorial supposedly spread lies about the situation of the Jews in Germany. The chairman of the community, who also served as editor of the paper, and the author of the article were both imprisoned. Serious incidents also occurred in the following years. In Sept. 1935, Nazis attacked J. youngsters watching a soccer game in defiance of "Jews Not Welcome Here" signs. One died of his injuries. The economic boycott was stepped up, forcing many Jews to liquidate or sell their businesses. J. unemployment increased and in 1936 about 4,000 Jews, representing 20–25% of the J. pop., were on welfare. Welfare payments were one of the measures taken by the J. community to contend with the deteriorating situation. In April–May 1933, it had already started a consulting service and foreign language courses preparatory to emigration. Vocational training facilities were expanded. Nonetheless, in the first years of Nazi rule, emigration did not reach large numbers. In June 1933, the community numbered 19,722; on 30 Sept. 1935 it was 18,652; and still 17,223 on 31 March 1937. More and more parents desired to transfer their children to the community's educational institutions. The Orthodox school was already full by May 1933 and in 1934 a Liberal elementary school was opened. In early 1937, about 1,300 children were enrolled in J. schools and nearly 60 teachers were teaching in them. The Hebrew school at the Seminary was expanded and in 1935, it was involved in setting up courses to prepare students for enrollment in teachers' seminaries in Palestine. Over 400 students signed up in the same year. The Seminary itself added non-J. subjects to its curriculum in light of the fact that J. attendance at the universities was now restricted. At the same time, it tightened its admission requirements on the assumption that there would be little future in Germany for rabbinical students. Students in the upper classes also left, especially foreign nationals, as did some of the

lecturers. In early 1937, 50 students remained, a drop of 30 from the 1930 peak. In response to the increasing isolation of Jews from the city's social and cultural life, a flourishing branch of the J. Cultural Association (Juedischer Kulturbund) was opened in 1934, reaching a membership of 4,000 in 1937. A sports hall and swimming pool were inaugurated. The young increasingly joined Zionist groups and Zionist influence increased in the adult community as well. In fall–winter 1935, the Zionists received the same number of seats as the Liberals on the community council. A great loss to the community was the closing of the newspaper *Juedische Zeitung fuer Ostdeutschland* in 1937. The first sign of further exacerbation of the situation of the Jews was the expulsion of the Polish Jews in late Oct. 1938, which included most of the 3,000 Jews of B. who were Polish subjects. A few days later, on 9–10 Nov., the infrastructure of the entire community was destroyed in the *Kristallnacht* riots. The Liberal synagogue was put to the torch along with its Torah scrolls. The Polish Altglogauer Schule was destroyed and the Orthodox Storch synagogue was damaged (though not burned for fear of the fire spreading to adjoining buildings). The Seminary was also vandalized. What remained of its library was impounded, as were the community and school libraries. J. business establishments were destroyed and looted. Many J. men, including Seminary students as well as doctors and patients at the J. hospital, were arrested. Most were sent to the Buchenwald concentration camp. Not a few died during the detention process. After the disturbances, the community still tried to salvage something of its life. The damages to the Storch synagogue were repaired and prayer services renewed there for both the Orthodox and Liberal congregations. Prayer services were also held in synagogues in community institutions (the Orthodox school, the hospital, the Beate-Guttmann-Heim). While the Liberal school closed down, the Orthodox school continued to operate, with additional classes opened in the community center. The Cultural Association renewed its activities in late Nov. The Seminary still held lectures on a modest scale, but faculty meetings were outlawed. Lecturers examined senior students clandestinely in order to give them their matriculation certificates. After the last exam on 21 Feb. 1939 the seminary closed its doors. One more volume of the *Monatsschrift* was published in 1939 with Leo Baeck as editor, but its distribution in Germany was by then impossible. According to the census of 17 May 1939, there were 10,309 Jews in the B. urban district, about half the number in 1933. Another 559 were classified as Jews according to the Nuremberg Laws and 2,507 were of mixed J. origin (*Mischlinge*), 350 of them being Jews by religion. Most of the remaining Jews lived in straitened economic circumstances. About 8,200 were in need of assistance. To make matters worse, they were seized for forced labor and subjected to additional restrictions, such as bans on assembling in groups larger than two people; leaving their homes after 8 p.m.; shopping other than in special stores open two and a half hours a day. In Sept. 1939, the High Holiday prayer services were banned except for two Yom Kippur services for schoolchildren in their school and for 150 teachers and community workers in the community center. In spring 1940, 300 Jews were arrested because the names "Israel" and "Sarah" designated by the authorities for use by J. men and women did not appear on their food cards. J. buildings housing community institutions were systematically expropriated: the J. hospital in Aug. 1939; the hospital for the chronically ill in Dec. 1939; the orphanage in Sept. 1940; the school in late 1940; and the Beate-Guttmann-Heim in June 1941. The fixed assets of individual Jews were also expropriated. The Cultural Association branch was closed in Sept. 1941. Despite the confiscation of their buildings, some institutions continued to operate. The J. school was transferred in part to the community center and partly to a building used by one of the community's societies. In Oct. 1941, 512 students and 21 teachers were still there, in 17 classes. The care of the sick was carried on in the community center and in a private hospital. Orthodox and Liberal prayer services were ultimately unified in a single *minyan*. Emigration continued after May 1939 and even in the first two years after the outbreak of WWII over 600 Jews managed to leave the country. Deportations on a small scale were carried out at the same time: in early Oct. 1939, about 50 Polish Jews, who had not been expelled in Oct. 1938 or had been permitted to return, were deported; in Nov., after the failed attempt on Hitler's life on the 9th, 120–150 J. men were deported to the Buchenwald concentration camp. On 1 June 1941, the eve of mass deportations, the number of Jews in B. totaled 8,129. In the last stage before deportation to the east, most were forced to move to "J. houses" in B. itself, starting in Sept. 1941. About 1,500 were transferred to three transit camps outside the city: 700 to Tormersdorf (Predocice) from June–July 1941; about 500 to Riebnig

Jewish kindergarten, Brest-Litovsk (Brzesc n. Bugiem), Poland, 1921 (The Joint National Distribution Committee/photo courtesy of Yad Vashem, The Holocaust Martyrs' and Heroes' Remembrance Authority, Jerusalem)

(Rybna) from Oct.; and the rest to the Gruessau (Krzeszow) monastery, also in Oct. Deportation to the death camps subsequently commenced together with the rest of the Jews of Lower Silesia. The first transport was to Kovno on 25 Nov. 1941. The following transports were destined for the Lublin dist. in Poland, Auschwitz, and the Theresienstadt ghetto. In early June 1943, the last patients at the old age home and J. hospital were deported to the Theresienstadt ghetto and on 16 June the last Jews not protected by mixed marriage were deported, including the last chairman of the community. Among the deportees were the last two rabbis of the community, the Liberal rabbi Reinhold Lewin and the Orthodox rabbi Bernhard Hamburger. Still remaining were 600–700 Jews. Many of these were deported during 1944 and through early 1945, leaving just 150 when the Nazi regime collapsed. After the war, about 10,000 J. refugees from Eastern Europe arrived in B., which was now a Polish city. They founded

a community, using the Storch synagogue for prayer services and opening a school. In 1962, the community still numbered 8,000 Jews, but by the end of the decade their number had dwindled to a small remnant, most having left for Israel. The school was closed in 1967 and the last public prayer service in the Storch synagogue was held in 1969. In 1990, the J. pop. was about 70. Of the three J. cemeteries of the modern community, the oldest was plowed under by the Nazis in 1944; the one where Lassalle is buried was turned into a museum in 1988; and the third is still open.

BREST-LITOVSK (in 1921–45, Brzesc nad Bugiem; Yid. Brisk [Brisk de-Lita]) Polesie dist., Poland, today Belarus. Jews probably began to settle in the mid-14th cent., receiving a liberal charter from the Lithuanian Prince Vitold in 1388 that served later as a model for the entire duchy. Most economic activity in Lithuania was controlled by the Jews of B. as mer-

chants, moneylenders, tax farmers, and proprietors of estates and villages. In 1523, Michael Jozefowicz of the powerful commercial family became the only Jew elevated to the nobility (by King Sigismund I) without converting. After a fire in 1568, a synagogue considered one of the most beautiful in Poland–Lithuania was built. Another synagogue, along with a renowned yeshiva attracting students from Italy, Germany, and the Crimea, was financed by Shaul Wahl, who arrived from Padua and became one of Lithuania's most prominent merchants. B. was among the three communities that founded the Council of Lithuania in 1623 and maintained its position as the leading community of Lithuania with 30 communities attached to it. Nineteen of the Council's 42 meetings convened there until the first half of the 18th cent., when it was superseded by Vilna. Throughout its history the community was plagued by devastating fires along with occasional outbursts of violence, especially by students at the Jesuit college. In the Chmielnicki massacres of 1648–49, about 2,000 Jews were murdered. Others were murdered by the Russian army in 1660. Despite economic decline after the mid-17th cent. wars, the commmunity continued to grow, numbering 3,175 in 1766. It was served by many well-known rabbis, such as Efrayyim Zalman Schorr, son-in-law of Shaul Wahl (1541–1617), Yoel Sirkes (1561–1640), and his grandson Aryeh Yehuda Leib (1614–1676), Moshe ben Yehuda Liva, Aharon Shemuel Koidanover, and Mordekhai Ziskind Rutenberg. New fires in 1802 and 1828 destroyed most of the J. quarter, including five synagogues. When a fortress was built in the neighborhood the Jews were forced to pull down the Shaul Wahl synagogue and move to a new quarter, where another magnificent synagogue was built. In the 19th cent., the city developed as an important transportation junction, with the Dnieper–Bug river system connecting the Black and Baltic Seas and the Kiev–Warsaw and Moscow–Warsaw railroads running through it. Jews now expanded their trade into lumber, grain, fruit, and cattle as the J. pop. grew from 8,136 in 1847 to 30,608 (total 46,568) in 1897. About 40% of the J. pop. engaged in crafts in small workshops. Great fires in 1895 and 1901 again destroyed most J. homes. A number of J. banks served the community from the latter half of the 19th cent. An old age home was opened in 1876 and the J. hospital developed into a highly esteemed facility in the late 19th cent. A *talmud torah* founded in 1856 enrolled 500 children and four J. pub-

lic schools served about 1,700. In the early 20th cent. there were two big synagogues and about 30 prayer houses in the city. Leading rabbis were Tzevi Hirsch Orenstein (1865–74), Yehoshua Leib Diskin (1874–77), and Yosef Dov Baer Solveitchik (1878–92) and his son Hayyim (1892–1918), who was prominent in his opposition to Haskala and Zionism. Also well known were Avraham Goldberg and Noah Finkelstein, editors of the Zionist Yiddish daily *Haynt*. The Zionists became active in 1884 and a large branch of the Bund operated in the early 20th cent. Despite the J. majority, only three of the city's 32 council members were Jews at the turn of the cent. In 1905 a pogrom was staged, warded off by J. self-defense forces. In Aug. 1915 the city was evacuated under Russian orders and the Jews returned to find many of their homes burned by soldiers. In 1921, the J. pop. was 15,630, rising to 21,769 in 1929. Most Jews were engaged in petty trade and crafts. Between the World Wars, a Hebrew school system began to operate, with an enrollment of 500 in 1929. Among the Zionists, Betar had 800 members in the late 1930s. Under Soviet rule in 1939–41, J. community life was curtailed. The Germans arrived in June 1941, immediately murdering dozens of Jews. On 28–29 June about 5,000 J. men were taken out of their homes and executed at a brickyard in the city's Kotelna suburb. A *Judenrat* was appointed in Aug. In Nov.–Dec. 1941, the Jews were concentrated in two ghettoes. In early 1942 Jews began organizing a revolt, accumulating weapons that included machineguns, but they were unable to act when the ghetto was surrounded on the night of 15 Oct. 1942 and the Jews removed in a lightning *Aktion* to Brona Gora, where they were all murdered.

BRETTEN Baden, Germany. Jews were present in the early 14th cent. Some lost their lives in the Armleder massacres of 1336–39 and all were slaughtered in the Black Death persecutions of 1348–49. A viable J. settlement was only reestablished after the Thirty Years War. In 1710 the Jews were granted a letter of protection. A synagogue was erected in 1822 and in 1827 B. became the seat of the district rabbinate with jurisdiction over 20 communities. A J. elementary school operated in 1835–62. In anti-J. riots during the 1848 revolution, J. homes were destroyed. The J. pop. reached a peak 263 in 1900 (total 4,781). In the early 20th cent., most Jews were cattle traders and shopkeepers, with the J. pop. falling to 114 by 1933 but aug-

mented by new arrivals in the Nazi era. Community life expanded and the Zionist youth movements became active. On *Kristallnacht* (9–10 Nov. 1938), the synagogue was burned down, J. stores destroyed, and J. men sent to the Dachau concentration camp. In all, 76 Jews emigrated in 1936–40, as did many of the 36 who moved to other German cities in the period. The last 18 were deported to the Gurs concentration camp on 22 Oct. 1940.

BRETZENHEIM Hesse, Germany. Jews lived there from the 16th cent. Numbering 84 (4.6% of the total) in 1861, the community dwindled to 26 in 1933. Most Jews emigrated after *Kristallnacht* (9–10 Nov. 1938), the last few being deported in 1942.

BREUNA Hesse–Nassau, Germany. Jews lived there from the mid-18th cent., had a regional synagogue (1876), and numbered 43 (4% of the total) in 1861. Only 17 Jews remained by Sept. 1937; the last six were deported in 1942.

BREYELL Rhineland, Germany. Jews are mentioned in the early 19th cent. They numbered 44 in 1905 and 32 in 1925. Under the Nazis, 11 were deported to Riga on 11 Dec. 1941 and 12 to the Theresienstadt ghetto on 25 July 1942, all perishing.

BREZNICE Bohemia, Czechoslovakia. The J. quarter was founded in 1570. The synagogue erected in 1725 burned in 1821 and was rebuilt in 1874. In the mid-19th cent., the J. pop. was 190, dropping to 118 in 1900 and 30 in 1930. Those remaining after the Nazi occupation were probably deported to the Theresienstadt ghetto via Pilsen in Jan. 1942 and from there to the death camps in the east.

BREZNO (Hung. Breznobanya) Slovakia, Czechoslovakia, today Republic of Slovakia. Jews probably settled in the 1850s. In 1869, they formed a Status Quo and later a Neologist congregation. A new synagogue was consecrated in 1902, when the J. pop. was about 170 (4% of the total). Most engaged in trade, including a few wealthy lumber merchants. The Zionists were active from the 1920s with Hashomer Hatzair organizing pioneer training for *aliya* in the 1930s. In 1940, the J. pop. was 200. A J. school (nine grades) was opened in the same year after J. children were expelled from the public schools. In 1941,

Jews were forced out of their businesses and some were mobilized for forced labor. In spring 1942, young J. men and women were deported to the Majdanek concentration camp and to Auschwitz, respectively. In June, J. families were deported to death camps in the Lublin dist. (Poland). Altogether, 130 Jews were deported in 1942. Six J. families remained, joined by 400 refugees during the Slovakian national uprising in fall 1944. The Germans murdered about 150 while others hid out in the forests and villages.

BREZOVA Slovakia, Czechoslovakia, today Republic of Slovakia. J. refugees from Moravia may have arrived in the late 17th cent. The first synagogue was built towards the end of the 18th cent. and the community grew to a peak of 334 (total 3,644) in 1869. J. homes and stores were looted in peasant riots in 1848. The community maintained a *talmud torah* and, until 1918, a J. elementary school. The Schick family produced rabbis and scholars known throughout the J. world. R. Moshe Schick (1808–80) was the spiritual leader of Orthodox Jewry in the Austro-Hungarian Empire and in the forefront of the struggle against Neologism. Jews were active as tanners and livestock dealers. In 1940, they numbered 92. In 1941, most were forced out of business and in March and April 1942 young men and women were deported to the Majdanek concentration camp and Auschwitz, respectively. Another 92 Jews were sent to the death camps in the east soon after.

BREZOVICA Slovakia, Czechoslovakia, today Republic of Slovakia. Jews from Galicia probably settled in the mid-18th cent. A wooden synagogue was erected in 1828 when the community numbered 148. There were 13 settlements affiliated to the congregation. A new synagogue was consecrated in 1870 and the community reached a peak pop. of 272 (total 1,652) in 1880, after which it declined steadily as the young left for the big cities. After WWI, the community maintained a regional J. school, yeshiva, and *talmud torah*. In 1940, 85 Jews remained. Under Slovakian rule, most J. businesses were closed down in 1941. The young were sent to the Poprad and Zilina camps in late March 1942 and the rest of the Jews were deported via Sabinov to the Rejowiec ghetto in the Lublin dist. (Poland) on 23 May.

BRIANKA Voroshilovgrad dist., Ukraine. The J.

pop. in 1939 was 545 (total 37,021). After their arrival on 12 July 1942, the Germans murdered the remaining Jews.

BRIANSK Oriol dist., Russia. Jews lived in B. in the 15th cent. but their residence was banned in the following centuries and only renewed in the late 19th cent. A burial society (*hevra kaddisha*) was founded in 1877 and a *talmud torah* was active. In 1897, the J. pop. was 1,321 (total 25,000). A pogrom was staged against the Jews in Oct. 1905. During the Soviet period, the J. pop. grew to 2,500 in 1926 and 5,102 (total 87,490) in 1939. The Germans captured the city on 6 Oct. 1941. The Jews were murdered in Aug. 1942, on the way to Karachev. After the war, 7,500 bodies of Jews and gypsies from B. and its environs were discovered in 14 mass graves.

BRICENA Bessarabia, Rumania, today Republic of Moldova. Jews first settled in 1760. A J. social body, the Society for Assisting the Poor, was organized only in the 19th cent. and served as a substitute for a community. J. artisans set up an organization to attend to their needs, and it eventually provided economic and medical aid to the entire community. It also established the first J. secular school in 1909. Zionist activity began in 1897 with the establishment of a synagogue and an adjoining club. A branch of Hovevei Zion opened in the early 20th cent. and a new *talmud torah* with a nationalist curriculum was set up by Zionists in 1924. Jews suffered from antisemitic outbursts and during the Feb. 1917 Revolution and in 1918 when the Rumanians entered B. they were the victims of pogroms, despite attempts at self-defense by the youth. Between the World Wars Jews engaged in trading in cattle and hides for fur. The official community was established in 1934; its chairman through 1940 was Dr. A. Trachtenbroit who also headed the Zionist movement in B. The J. pop. in 1930 was 5,354 (95% of the total) and on the eve of the Holocaust it was estimated at 10,000. When the Red Army took B. in June 1940, 80 Jews, mainly community leaders, were sent to forced labor in Siberia. On 22 July 1941 the Rumanian army entered and on 28 July 1941, the J. pop. was marched to Secureni. On 4 Aug. those who were not shot or did not die of starvation or weakness reached Mogilev and then were returned to Secureni and finally taken to Transnistria, where most died under the harsh conditions. During 1944–46, 2,500 Jews from B. and

the surroundings returned and reestablished a community.

BRICEVA Bessarabia, Rumania, today Republic of Moldova. Jews from Yekaterinoslav (Dnepropetrovsk) were the first to settle in this J. colony in 1836 (or 1838) and engage in agriculture. At the end of the 19th cent. there were 83 families with seven (later nine) synagogues and a J. school operating on the lines of Haskala institutions in Russia. The Jews of B. did not suffer economically during WWI and their situation improved after the war. Deserters from the Russian and Rumanian armies found refuge from 1916 in this J.-dominated town. During 1919–20 it served as a way station for J. refugees from the Ukraine. After annexation by Rumania following WWI, a J. elementary school and Hebrew intermediate school were opened. B. became a center of Yiddish culture. The J. pop. in 1930 was 2,431 (89% of the total). During the 1930s, there were outbursts of antisemitism and the J. community organized self-defense. When the weekly market was closed down in 1936 the economic situation of the Jews declined and worsened in June 1940 when Bessarabia was annexed to the USSR. When the Rumanian army returned in June 1941, soldiers killed Jews, plundered their property, and raped J. women. The Jews were rounded up and marched through neighboring villages to a camp in the Rublenita forest, transferred to Vertujeni, and then to the Cosauti forest where they were shot. Others were taken to Rezina and then deported to Transnistria where they were shot or died of starvation and disease. After the war the few survivors found this former J. town populated by non-Jews and soon left.

BRIEG (Pol. Brzeg) Lower Silesia, Germany. Jews settled in the 14th cent. and established a synagogue and cemetery. The community was spared the Black Death persecutions of 1349–50 and continued to exist until it was finally expelled in 1453. Jews are again mentioned in the 16th and 17th cents., with a Jew allowed to open a Hebrew-Yiddish printing press in 1689. There was an organized community in the last third of the 18th cent. It maintained a synagogue (consecrated in 1799) and a cemetery (1781), but large-scale J. settlement only occurred in the mid-19th cent. In 1846, the J. pop. was 373, rising to a peak of 448 in 1885. The community was Orthodox in character though there was also an organization of Liberal

Jews. In 1933, the J. pop. was 255, dropping to 160 in 1938. On *Kristallnacht* (9–10 Nov. 1938), the synagogue and nine J. stores and taverns were destroyed while four Jews were arrested. A number of J. families subsequently emigrated to Europe, leaving 123 Jews in the city. Deportations to the Theresienstadt ghetto and General Gouvernement territory commenced in March 1942. In Oct. 1942, nine intermarried Jews remained.

BRIELLE Zuid-Holland dist., Holland. Jews first settled in 1756 and numbered 126 in 1883. As the town lost its commercial importance, the community dwindled. The J. pop. in 1941 was 29 (total 3,389). In the Holocaust all were deported and perished in Poland (1943).

BRILON Westphalia, Germany. The first indisputable evidence of a J. presence in the town dates from 1578. The J. pop. grew from six families in 1672 to 12 in 1803, peaking at 131 in 1864. In 1832, Yosef Avraham Friedland was appointed state rabbi of Westphalia and Wittgenstein with B. as his seat. His Reform tendencies divided the community. Meir Friedland, the state rabbi's grandson, opened the only J. printing

house in Westphalia in 1842. He also began publishing the town's only local newspaper in the same year. The J. pop. dropped to 75 in 1900. A new synagogue was consecrated in 1931. In June 1933, about four months after the Nazi assumption of power, the J. pop. numbered 72. One family of three was expelled to Poland on 27 Oct. 1938. On *Kristallnacht* (9–10 Nov. 1938), the synagogue was set on fire and J. homes and stores were destroyed. Eleven Jews were sent to the Sachsenhausen concentration camp. After April 1939, the remaining Jews were confined to two special houses. Of the total 56 who left, 21 emigrated to the U.S. and 21 moved to other German cities. Those who remained were deported to the east during the years 1942–43.

BRNO Moravia, Czechoslovakia. A J. community existed in the first half of the 13th cent. In 1254, King Premysl Otakar of Bohemia granted the Jews a wide-ranging charter. A new charter, which Charles IV issued in 1345, encouraged further J. settlement, particularly of J. refugees from Germany, and helped increase the J. pop. to 600–800 in the late 14th cent. In 1454, the Jews were expelled at the instigation of

Jewish dancing students with their instructor, Brno, Czechoslovakia, 1926 (Beth Hatefutsoth Photo Archive, Tel Aviv/courtesy of Hannah Landes, Tel Aviv)

stroyed 800 homes mostly of Jews. It also operated a hospital, old age home, and orphanage. B. was a leading center of Haskala and unlike such cities as Cracow and Lwow displayed a pro-German orientation. The Haskala leader Nahman Krochmal (1785–1840) was born there and Yehoshua Heschel Schorr (1815–95) published the Hebrew periodical *Hehalutz* there from 1852 to 1889. Haskala adherents were among the forerunners of Hebrew and Yiddish literature in Galicia and founders of the first Yiddish theater circle. The modern J. public school founded in 1854 enrolled 1,132 boys and girls in 1905. At the same time the traditional *heder* system accommodated 574 children. The Zionist movement became active in 1890 and by the outbreak of WWI dominated the community council. The Russian occupation of Aug. 1914 ushered in a reign of Cossack terror marked by rape and pillage. Most wealthy Jews fled and many J. homes were burned. The proximity of the front continued to disrupt daily life even after the Austrians returned in July 1915. Under the shortlived West Ukrainian Republic created in 1918 the Jews suffered severe persecution. Stability returned with the advent of Polish rule but the Jews continued to live in straitened economic circumstances. J. trade was undercut by the Polish and Ukrainian cooperatives as well as economic crises and boycotts. In 1921 the J. pop. stood at 7,202 (total 10,860), receiving extensive aid from the Joint Distribution Committee. Most of the Zionist parties and youth movements were now active. The Soviets annexed the city in Sept. 1939, nationalizing stores and factories and putting an end to J. communal and political life. Many Jews were drafted into the Red Army. The Germans captured B. on 1 July 1941 and immediately instituted a regime of severe persecuton, including curfews, public bans, and forced labor for men aged 14–65 and women aged 18–45. On 15–17 July, 250 of the community's leading figures were executed near the J. cemetery. A *Judenrat* was set up in the same month. Thereafter Jews were regularly robbed and beaten by Ukrainians as well as Germans; homes and property were impounded. To supplement their meager rations and avoid being sent to the labor camps, the Jews sought local employment and set up a factory with 400 J. workers to supply German needs. Over 1,500 Jews were nonetheless sent to the labor camps, most perishing under their severe living conditions. On 19 Sept. 1942, the first large-scale *Aktion* was carried out. All those hiding or trying to escape were shot on sight along with the sick; all the Jews in the old age home and orphanage were murdered. In all there were 250–300 victims. Another 2,000–2,500 were loaded on railway cars and transported to the Belzec death camp. The process was repeated on 2 Nov. 1942, claiming a further 2,000–3,000 victims. Jews now came into the city from other settlements and all, numbering 5,000-7,000, were sealed into a ghetto in Dec. or confined to a local labor camp. Hunger and disease decimated the pop., littering the streets with the dead. A new series of *Aktion*s commenced in April 1943. Many prepared hiding places, in cellars, attics, and underground shelters, while others found refuge in the forest. Some were helped by Christians, others were hunted down by the German and Ukrainian police as well as by local peasants. Attempts to organize resistance were made in the ghetto and in the forests there were instances of armed resistance. The ghetto and labor camp were liquidated in a final *Aktion* on 21 May 1943. To force all the Jews into the street, houses were set on fire. The disabled were murdered on the spot, children's heads were smashed in, and the living were thrown into the flames. About 3,500 were packed into railway cars and deported to the Majdanek concentration camp. Around 250 Jews survived the war.

BROK Bialystok dist., Poland. Jews from Plock first settled in the 17th cent. With the town's development as a resort at the end of the 19th cent. they enjoyed new economic horizons, including the baking of *matzot*, which were marketed in the large towns. Most of the town's 1,000 Jews, a third of the overall pop., was forced to flee into Soviet-annexed territories with the coming of the Nazis on 8 Sept. 1939. Around 300 survived the war.

BROSZNIOW Stanislawow dist., Poland, today Ukraine. The town developed in the 20th cent. around its lumber industry, with 226 Jews (total pop. 1,631) in 1921. Zionist activity was extensive between the World Wars. The community was probably expelled to Dolina in 1942 and liquidated with all the other Jews there on 3 Aug. 1942.

BROTDORF (from 1938, part of Merzig) Saar, Germany. The first Jew settled in B. at the beginning of the 18th cent. The J. pop. was 75 individuals in 1895. Although affiliated with the Merzig community, the B. community consecrated its own synagogue in

1854. When the Saar was annexed to the German Reich in 1935, there were 31 Jews in B. On *Kristallnacht* (9–10 Nov. 1938), the synagogue, was burned down and J. homes were wrecked. By 1940, there were only six Jews in B. They were deported on 22 Oct. 1940 to the Gurs concentration camp. At least seven Jews from B. perished under Nazi rule.

BROVARY Kiev dist., Ukraine. J. residence was banned for a long time because of the town's proximity to Kiev. In 1897, the J. pop. was 888 (total 3,817). Pogroms were staged against the Jews in March 1918 and Feb. 1919. In 1939, under the Soviets, the J. pop. was 485. The Germans arrived on 19 Sept. 1941 and murdered the Jews at the end of the month.

BRUCHSAL (in J. sources, Broshele, Broisl) Baden, Germany. A J. settlement existed by the latter 13th cent. with an organized community concentrated in a J. quarter in the first half of the 14th cent. The community was destroyed in the Black Death persecutions of 1348–49. The new community suffered religious persecution in the 15th cent. and lost all its property in the Thirty Years War (1618–48). Throughout the 18th cent. the Jews were subjected to political and economic pressure by the ruling bishops. The first synagogue was consecrated in 1802 and in 1827 B. became the seat of the district rabbinate with jurisdiction over a dozen communities. Jews came to play a leading role in the city's economy, trading in beer hops and other farm produce and operating a major knitwool factory. The J. pop. grew steadily, rising from 178 in 1825 to 743 (total 12,614) in 1895. Antisemitism made itself felt in the 1880s and 1890s, with occasional violent outbursts, and again after WWI. From the early 20th cent., the J. pop. began to decline through emigration and by 1933 numbered 501. The community remained prominent economically, with Jews owning 21 factories (12 of them making cigarettes) and being well represented in the professional class. Under Nazi rule, discriminatory laws were applied and the economic boycott was enforced. In 1936–37, 110 Jews left the city, 76 of them emigrating from Germany. In 1938 Jews of Polish and Czech origin were expelled to the Polish border and on *Kristallnacht* (9–10 Nov. 1938), the synagogue was burned to the ground, J. homes and stores were wrecked, and J. men were sent to the Dachau concentration camp. The last 79 Jews in the city were sent to the Gurs concentration camp in Oct. 1940, joined by another 37 who had previously left and were subsequently caught up in the deportations; 86 perished in the camps.

BRUECKENAU Lower Franconia, Germany. Jews are mentioned in the late 16th cent. The modern community was founded in the mid-19th cent. by Jews from Zuentersbach in Prussia. The synagogue and *talmud torah* were destroyed in a fire in 1876 that left most of the Jews homeless. A new synagogue was built in 1913 and a J. public school was opened in 1924. B. was a J. health resort with three kosher hotels and summer camps for children. The J. pop. grew from 55 in 1880 to 114 in 1910 (total 1,627). With the Nazi economic boycott in 1933 the wealthier Jews began to leave. On *Kristallnacht* (9–10 Nov. 1938), the synagogue was burned and nearly all J. men were sent to the Dachau concentration camp. In all, 29 Jews emigrated in 1933–40 (13 to the U.S.) and 95 left for other German cities, including 58 to Frankfurt. The last seven Jews were deported to Izbica in the Lublin dist. (Poland) and the Theresienstadt ghetto in 1942.

BRUEHL Rhineland, Germany. Jews are first mentioned in 1177 and there is evidence of the existence of a J. community with a prayer room and a cemetery during the 14th and 15th cents. The Jews were apparently expelled in 1480. Jews were present again in the 17th cent., the J. pop. of four individuals in 1607 rising to 36 in 1747, reaching 72 in 1843, and peaking at 168 in 1911. A synagogue was consecrated in 1882. In 1933, the J. pop. was about 100. Under Nazi persecution, about half the Jews left before Nov. 1938, but their number was partly offset by 44 newcomers, mostly relatives of the local Jews. On *Kristallnacht* (9–10 Nov. 1938), 20–30 SA troops, accompanied by Hitler Youth and some local residents, destroyed ten J. stores and set the synagogue on fire. J. homes were also wrecked and looted and Jews beaten. Almost all J. men were arrested and some sent to the Dachau concentration camp. By May 1939, only 39 Jews were left. In June–July 1942 the remaining 22 Jews were deported; only one survived. In all, at least 59 Jews perished in the Holocaust.

BRUMATH Bas-Rhin dist., France. The J. pop. numbered 400 in 1865. In 1884, the synagogue was inaugurated and then renovated in 1922. In 1936, the community numbered 185 members. During WWII,

brought into B. In June 1942, about 180 Jews were murdered in the streets and another 560 deported to the Belzec death camp. In July a ghetto was set up and sealed off with refugees swelling the pop. to over 5,000. Starvation and a typhoid epidemic struck down many. On 12 Sept, over 4,000 were sent to the Belzec death camp and a few hundred left dead in the ghetto. Survivors were hunted down and murdered or subsequently deported.

BRZESKO NOWE   (Yid. Bzhisk) Kielce dist., Poland. Jews were allowed to settle in B. in the late 19th cent. and numbered 457 (total 1,845) in 1921. Difficult economic conditions between the World Wars reduced the J. pop. to about 300 when the Germans captured B. in Sept. 1939. Since there was no permanent German presence in B., the tolerable conditions attracted other Jews. On 8 Nov 1942, all were deported to the Belzec death camp. The many who hid in anticipation of the *Aktion* were rounded up and held in other settlements until liquidated with a

group of 600 Jews on 18 Nov. in the forests near Zagorze.

BRZEZANY   (Yid. Brizan) Tarnopol dist., Poland, today Ukraine. Jews may have been among the first settlers in the town when it was founded in 1530 and soon were monopolizing trade. The community became independent in 1638 and in 1718 built a luxurious new synagogue that was to stand until the end of the community. Austrian rule from 1772 brought heavy taxation but the community continued to grow, reaching 4,712 out total of 10,899 in 1880, with many Jews now engaged in crafts and some in the professions. Outstanding among the community's rabbis was Shalom Mordekhai Shvadron (1880–1911), known as the Maharsham and author of many books. Zionist activity began in 1893. By 1908, 186 J. youngsters were receiving a secular education in the local high school and in 1907 a Hebrew school was founded. Two great fires swept the town during WWI and the upheavals following the war brought further hardship

The "Jewish Art" drama circle in Brzezany, Poland, 1938

until Polish rule was established and normal life resumed. Between the World Wars the Zionists dominated public life and the community enjoyed rich and varied cultural and social services: drama and music circles, youth and sports clubs, an orphanage and old age home. The Russian occupation of 1939–41 put an end to J. community organizations, including the refugee committee extending aid to the thousands of Jews arriving from the western part of Poland and which now had to operate in secret. The city was bombarded at the end of June 1941, damaging the J. quarter in the center of the town. The Germans arrived on 7 July and the Jews were forced to collect the corpses in the streets as Ukrainian police beat them. Later the same police murdered 12 men and women and Ukrainian peasants also came in and pillaged J. property. The Germans quickly instituted anti-J. measures and through the *Judenrat* carried out their policy of extortion and forced labor. The first instance of mass murder occurred on 1 Oct. 1941 (Yom Kippur) when a selection was made from the thousands of Jews gathered in the city square. About 500–700 were brought to the nearby quarries, ordered to undress, and gunned down. On 18 Dec. around 1,200 appearing on a list of the poor compiled by the *Judenrat* for the purpose of expulsion were murdered by the Germans in the forest. The young continued to be sent to the labor camps and during the winter the Gestapo went through the J. hospital a number of times to murder typhoid patients. Further *Aktion*s followed and on 21 Sept. 1942, again on Yom Kippur, between 1,000 and 1,500 were deported to the Belzec death camp while another few hundred were murdered in the streets and in their homes. The remaining Jews were herded into a ghetto and further decimated in the next *Aktion* on 4–5 Dec. 1942 (Hanukkah) when another few hundred were sent to the Belzec death camp. The final liquidation of the ghetto and labor camp (housing around 400 Jews) took place on 12 June 1943, claiming over 1,700 victims. Few of the town's J. residents survived the war.

BRZOSTEK Cracow dist., Poland. Jews first settled in the late 18th cent. under Austrian rule, but the isolation of the town and the hostility of the local pop. slowed the development of the community, which reached a peak pop. of 514 in 1910 (35% of the total). Cossack pillaging and arson left the Jews destitute after WWI. The traditional hasidic character of the community delayed the spread of Zionism until the 1920s. Many fled with the approach of the Germans in 1939. Under the German occupation, there existed a communal kitchen. Young Jews were sent to labor camps. Almost all were executed in the nearby forest on 12 July 1942.

BRZOSTOWICA WIELKA Bialystok dist., Poland, today Belarus. About 1,100 Jews were present during the second half of the 19th cent. By 1921 their pop. fell to 720 (total 1,371) as their economic position deteriorated under discriminatory government policy. Between the World Wars the Zionists were active and most children attended a Tarbut Hebrew school. With the arrival of the Germans in late June 1941 after two years of Soviet rule, the aged were expelled to Krynki. In summer 1942 they were joined by the rest of the J. pop. In Nov. 1942 all 500 were deported to the Treblinka death camp.

BRZOZDOWCE (Yid. Brizdovits) Lwow dist., Poland, today Ukraine. The community apparently dates from the late 17th cent. and numbered around 500 (a fifth of the total) at the end of the 19th cent. The Germans transferred the Jews to the Bobrka ghetto in the second half of 1942 and they shared the fate of the local Jews.

BRZOZOW Lwow dist., Poland. Permanent settlement began in the 18th cent. with Austrian rule. The J. pop. grew continuously, reaching 1,255 in 1910 (total 4,438) but dropping to 1,046 in 1931. A. J. self-defense group expelled rampaging peasants from the town in 1918 after they pillaged 104 J. homes. Economic conditions deteriorated between the World Wars while Zionist influence increased. In the first days of German occupation, 300 Jews were shot outside the town. A ghetto was established in the second half of 1941. Most of the remaining Jews, around 800, were executed in the nearby forest on 10 Aug. 1942.

BUBLITZ (Pol. Bobolice) Pomerania, Germany, today Poland. The first J. family is mentioned in 1728. The community reached a peak pop. of 189 in 1861 and maintained a cemetery and a synagogue. The latter as well as J. houses suffered in the antisemitic riots which broke out in Pomerania in 1881. By 1924, the J. pop. was 90. When the Nazis came to power in 1933, there were 52 Jews in B. They began

Zionists meeting in Brzozow, Poland, 1930

to leave the town in 1937. On *Kristallnacht* (9–10 Nov. 1938), the synagogue was destroyed. No further information is available about the fate of the community's members under Nazi rule.

BUCECEA Moldavia dist., Rumania. Jews settled here in the early 19th cent. and from 1831 to 1930 constituted the majority of the pop. The J. pop. in 1899 was 1,281 (72% of the total). On 18 March 1907, 1,000 rioting peasants plundered J. property during their revolt. In 1937, there was a J. school and kindergarten. In June 1941 all the Jews were expelled to Botosani and the males sent to forced labor. A small community was founded after the war.

BUCHAREST (Rum. Bucuresti) capital of Rumania. J. Sephardi traders from Bulgaria settled in the mid-16th cent. On 13 Nov. 1593, Jews holding promissory notes of Prince Mihai Viteazul were murdered and the Christian pop. slaughtered the remaining community. Jews from Poland and the Ukraine settled in the mid-17th cent. Synagogues were built (the first in the early 17th cent.) and destroyed. During the Russo-Turkish war (1773), Jews were imprisoned and attempts were made to convert them to Christianity, but they were released by the Russian army. In an

1801 blood libel and ensuing riots 128 Jews were killed and many were injured. In the early 19th cent., Jews were persecuted by revolutionary groups and by the conquering Turks. Jews from Moldavia settled in the 1820s. Hillel Manoach served as "Banker of the Emirate" and was awarded the title "Court Banker" by the sultan. Other J. bankers played a cardinal role in the development of the economy. On 18 July 1866, Jews were attacked by antisemites, following attempts by the French J. statesman Adolphe Cremieux to obtain equal rights for Jews in Rumania. One of the outstanding rabbinical scholars of the period, R. Meir Leibush, son of Yehiel Mikhal (known as the Malbin), served the main community from 1858 to 1864. Among his works are commentaries on the Bible and the *Shulhan Arukh*. In 1830, the Sephardi Jews broke away from the predominantly Ashkenazi community and set up a home for the aged (1895), a school for boys (1868), for girls (1878), and a nursery school (1911). A. I. Papo, one of the leading rabbis of the Sephardi communities in the Balkans, served the B. Sephardi community during 1819–28. In 1863, 300 J. families of Austrian and Prussian origin established a separate community. Renewed attempts to unify the community failed, despite the involvement of the authorities. From 1840, the J. educa-

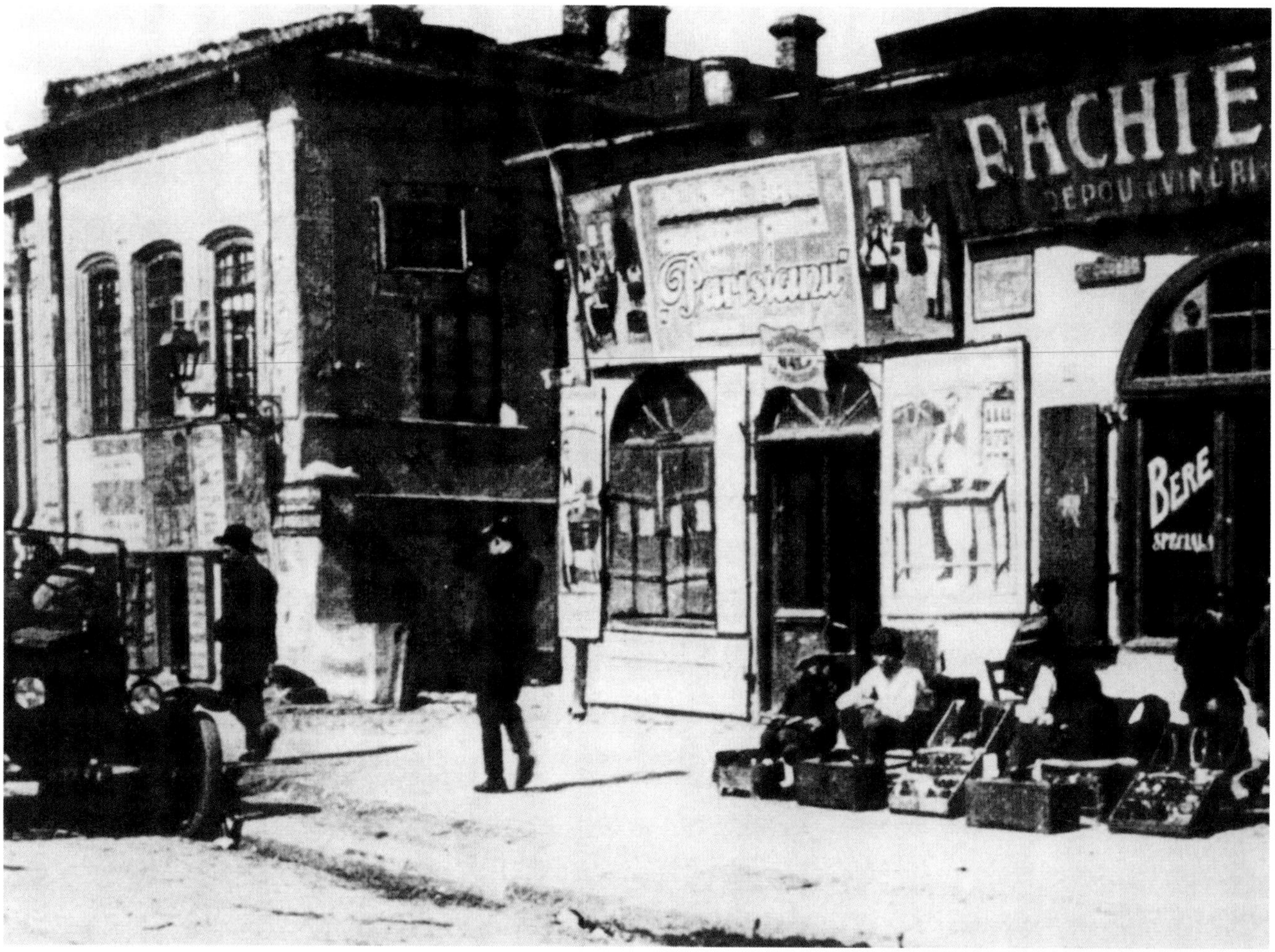
RACHIE
BERE

The Jewish quarter of Bucharest, Rumania, turn of the 19th cent. (Dr. Th. Lavi, Jerusalem/photo courtesy of Yad Vashem, The Holocaust Martyrs' and Heroes' Remembrance Authority, Jerusalem)

tional system included 12 *hadarim*, a *talmud torah*, and elementary schools for boys and girls. A modern school (opened in 1852) graduated 1,884 pupils up to 1916. The Cultura organization opened its own high school in 1895 and other J. schools were established in new neighborhoods. In 1897, the Ciocanul vocational school was opened with aid from the Jewish Colonization Association (ICA). In 1898 the community opened a high school with 167 pupils and a nursery school. The J. pop. in 1899 was 40,533 (15% of the total). The local branch of B'nai B'rith was active in the struggle to obtain J. emancipation and raised funds for J. educational institutions. An association of J. academicians, Unirea, was founded in 1909 with 80 members and existed until 1948. Fifteen J. welfare institutions functioned in B. providing aid to the needy. A home for the aged, Elisabeteu, was founded in 1875 and the Ospitalitatea home opened in 1905. Up to 1917, 4,000 J. aged were provided for. Newspapers and periodicals in many languages were published in B. *Israelitul Roman*, the first J. periodical in Rumanian and French, appeared in April 1857, advocating J. civil rights. A widely read Yiddish newspaper was published from 1874 to 1896 and served as the official organ of the Eretz Israel Settlement movement. *Egalitatea*, a weekly supporting the struggle for equal rights, appeared from 1890 for over a quarter century. A pre-Zionist youth group was established in 1882, inspired by the visit of Sir Laurence Oliphant. A branch of Hovevei Zion opened in 1894 and Zionist activities flourished at the turn of the century. The community reorganized after WWI and held elections with representatives of all communal bodies. The following institutions were registered

Bourgeois Jewish family, Bucharest, Rumania, early 20th cent.

with the Ministry of the Interior: 36 synagogues, 12 elementary schools, a commercial school, two high schools, two vocational schools, two old age homes, two orphanages, and a cemetery. The community consisted of 11,500 families. The power struggle between the various factions within the community continued until 1931 when it was granted official recognition. In May 1921, the community appointed the Sephardi rabbi Dr. I. Niemirower as chief rabbi and he set up a rabbinical commission of 12 rabbis. In 1927, he was appointed to the Senate as representative of the J. religion. Between the World Wars, the Sephardi community numbered 8,000 and was active in disseminating its cultural tradition. Jews fleeing the Russian Revolution (1917) and many who migrated from smaller towns settled in B. during the 1920s, strengthening the community's educational institutions. After

the Jews were granted emancipation in 1921, the number of pupils attending J. schools dropped owing to assimilation, but increased once again after antisemitic manifestations in 1933 led to the ouster of J. children from government schools. Between the World Wars, Jews were active in developing the economy, building factories, and expanding their banks. Jews were active in the field of publishing, including the translation of world literature. Most J. organizations and political parties had their headquarters in B. The official publication of Rumanian Jewry, *Curierul Israelit*, appeared weekly. Jews owned Rumanian newspapers and many of their journalists were Jews. A popular university was established by the Union of Rumanian Jewry and provided adult education for the community. A J. studies library with 7,000 volumes was opened in 1933 and published its own periodical in 1933–36.

The headquarters of the Rumanian Zionist Organization moved to B. in 1919. Zionist political parties were active and youth movements flourished. Their members set up self-defense units against attacks by antisemites. Maccabi opened a sports facility in the J. quarter and its members competed throughout Rumania. Hebrew-language classes were held for youth and adults. A Zionist daily, *Mantuirea*, appeared until 1922. This was replaced by the weekly *Renasterea Noastra* until it was closed by the Antonescu government in 1942. In 1922–23, antisemitic student organizations introduced the *numerus clausus* in the university, which radically reduced the number of J. students in the medical and law faculties. The 1931 economic crisis hit J. bankers, merchants, and traders hard and many went bankrupt. The situation further deteriorated with the rise of the Nazi Party in Germany and during the Goga-Cuza regime (1938). Jews were ousted from trade unions in 1938 and J. government officials were dismissed.

The J. pop. increased from 76,480 in 1930 (12% of the total) to 102,018 in 1941 (10% of the total), making B. the largest J. community in Rumania. The headquarters of most J. organizations situated in B. were instrumental in reducing the hardships and suffering of the J. pop. After 1942, refugees streamed into B. not only from areas of Rumania, but also from Hungary and Poland. This required reorganization by the community authorities and their immediate task was to provide welfare services for the increasing numbers of impoverished members of the community as well as the refugees. Immediately after Antonescu began his rule (6 Sept. 1940), the Iron Guard Legionnaires, whose headquarters were in B., immediately set about persecuting the Jews and plundering their property. On 6–13 Sept., 1,302 of the 1,479 J. lawyers in B. were ousted from their professional association. Associations of engineers, journalists, writers and artists also expelled their J. members. The opera and theaters fired J. workers and Jews were not permitted to transact business at the stock exchange. J. teachers were expelled from government schools and the universities. J. commerce was badly hit; J. shops were boycotted and Jews forced to sell their property to the Green Shirts at undervalued prices. The latter rounded up Jews, brutally tortured them, closed the synagogues, and expropriated the J. school buildings to billet Rumanian and German soldiers. On 21 Jan. 1941, the Iron Guard

used their revolt against Antonescu as a pretext to imprison several hundred Jews, including community leaders, in army camps and jails where they were tortured mercilessly and then murdered. J. houses were destroyed and their content plundered. The Guard burned down synagogues and J. public buildings. In Sept. 1942, about 600 Jews who had applied to the Soviet legation in 1940 to migrate to Bessarabia were deported to Transnistria. In 1942, 28,177 Jews aged 16-60 were drafted into labor battalions and by spring 1944 they numbered 50,000. Some worked within B. while others were sent to neighboring districts or distant locales. Those in penal units were sent to army camps as well as to Transnistria, where they lived in concentration camp conditions. A special committee was appointed to provide warm clothing, food, and money to the these laborers. The Rumanian Red Cross assisted in opening clinics manned by J. doctors in several neighborhoods. The community also ran three hospitals and three clinics. Schools were expanded to provide for children expelled from government institutions. Throughout the entire war period, the schools functioned daily and school books in Hebrew were published. The Zionist movement made its impact on the curriculum of the J. schools and set up its own Tarbut school with Hebrew as the language of instruction. The Zionist youth movements played an important part in the educational system during this period and many of its graduates immigrated to Palestine. Three institutions were set up to provide graduate education for students ousted from the universities. The synagogues provided spiritual inspiration for the J. pop. The Sephardi community also expanded its activities during the Holocaust, in particular providing aid to its impoverished members whose property was confiscated. It also doubled the numbers in its schools. The Mother and Child Center run by Mella Jancu provided meals and clothes to over 500 children. It also opened schools in outlying districts, providing aid to the needy. Expelled from the Rumanian theater, J. actors opened a theater and produced plays on J. themes. A children's theater presented plays on themes connected with their daily life. Between Sept. 1940 and Jan. 1941, the Zionist movement was forced underground, but in early 1941 it was permitted to hold cultural events. Training farms functioned on the outskirts of the city. B. was the center of immigration to Palestine and pioneers were billeted there until they were able to move on. In fall 1943, parachutists from

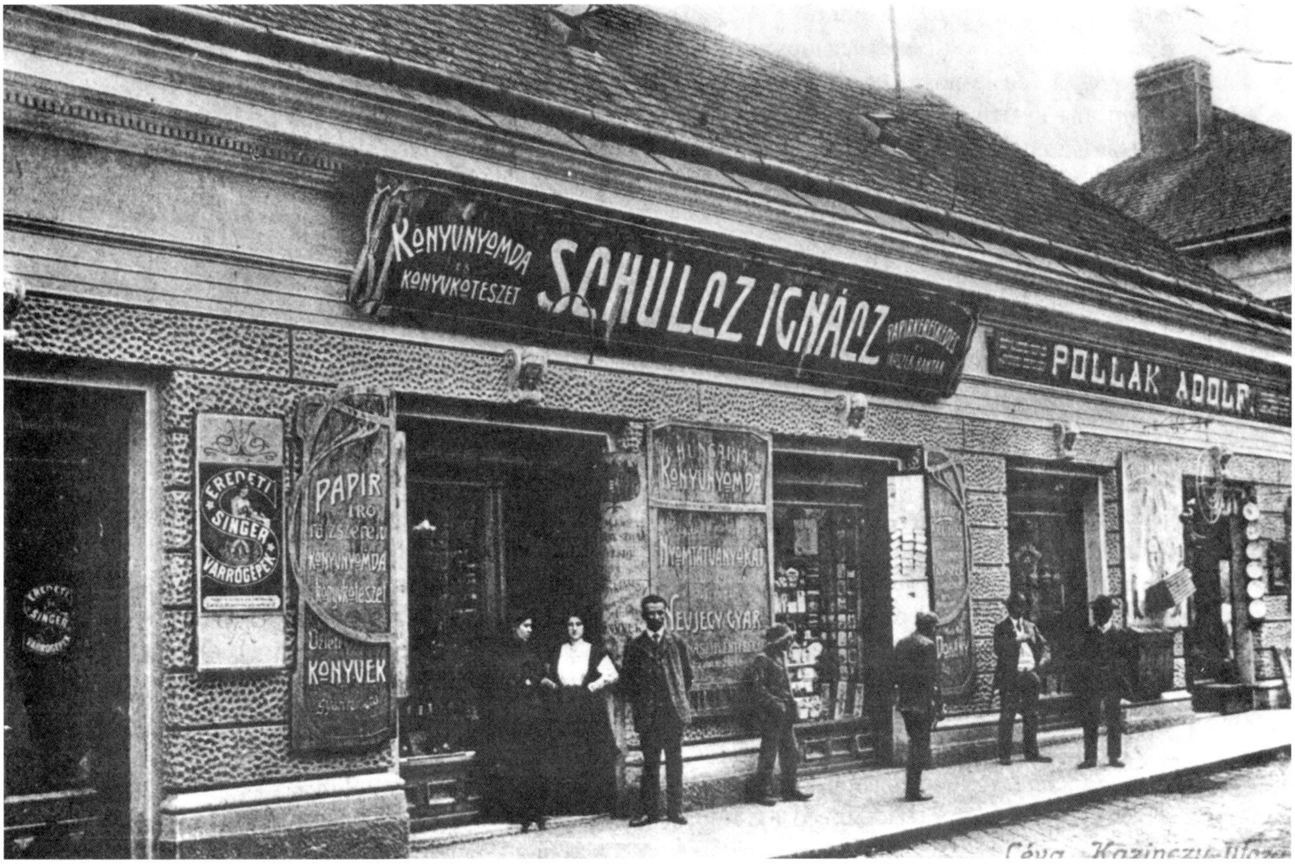
SCHULCZ IGNÁCZ
POLLAK ADOLF
PAPIR
SINGER

Jewish stores in Budapest, Hungary

fication of the city in 1872. The latter community developed with the growth of the city and became one of the largest and best organized J. communities in the world. The first Jews opened kosher restaurants, some 17 in all. In the late 18th cent., Emperor Joseph allowed Jews to settle officially, but this was canceled after his death (1790). Conflicts between city and national authorities led to a distinction between "tolerated Jews," officially given residence rights in 1780 and numbering 310 in 1799, and 765 Jews without rights. Subsequently Jews contributed to the industrial and cultural development of the city and by 1857 numbered 27,101. Anti-J. agitation continued throughout the 19th cent. and the Jews continually sought to prove their loyalty, with the young volunteering to fight in Hungary's wars and their elders donating generously to various social and cultural causes. In 1867, the community received royal recognition from Emperor Francis Joseph. Several J. families led the way in the city's economic growth: the Wahrmanns operated some of the largest flour mills in the country; the Ullmanns owned a number of important banks; the Hatvani-Deutsch family were leaders in the food industry; and the Wodianers were active in shipping, printing, and the farm produce trade. By 1900, most of the city's 168,975 Jews were employed in commerce and industry and there was a large professional class. An organized community, affiliated with the Obuda congregation, existed from 1790 with the founding of a burial society (*hevra kaddisha*). The community maintained a ramified network of welfare services, including an old age home, and founded the first orphanage for girls in Hungary (1867). An institute for the deaf and dumb was founded in 1876 and cared for 736 youngsters in 1927 while an institute for the blind started operating in 1908. The first J. hospital was opened in 1802 and eventually, by 1925, there were six J. hospitals, providing the community with a full range of medical services. In 1868, when the Jews of Hungary split into three denominations, the majority became Neologists. The Orthodox founded their own congregation in 1870, led by R. M. Trebitsch.

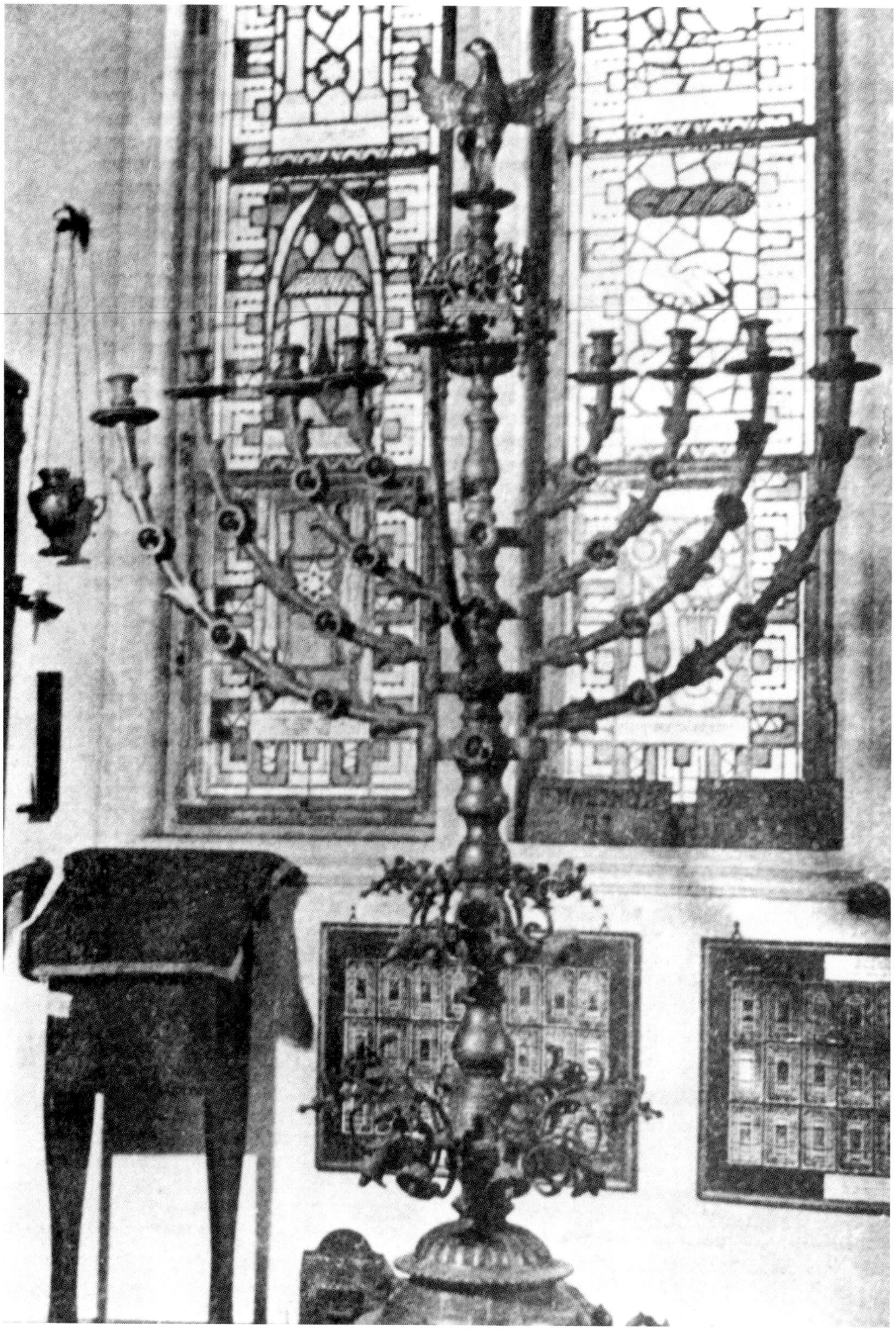

The Jewish Museum in Budapest, Hungary, 1930 (Ministry of Education and Culture/photo courtesy of Yad Vashem, The Holocaust Martyrs' and Heroes' Remembrance Authority, Jerusalem)

The congregation was later led by R. Adolph Frankl, head of the National Federation of Orthodox Communities in Hungary from 1905, and numbered about 10,000 members between the World Wars. The first synagogue was built in 1784. The monumental Great Synagogue on Dohany Street, with its 3,000 seats and one of the most magnificent in Europe, was completed in 1859. Among its rabbis, Shemuel Cohen was the first in B. to deliver sermons in Hungarian. Orthodox life was furthered in 1890–1929 by the influential R. Yaakov Koppel Reich, who was named a royal consultant and appointed to represent the Orthodox in the upper house of parliament. The first J. school was opened in 1814 and by 1850 enrolled 413 children. The community also provided religious instruction for children attending non-J. schools, about 8,000 in 1869 and 20,000 in 1925. Between the World Wars, the community maintained 15 J. schools serving 3,600 children and employed 160 teachers in its institutions for orphans, the deaf and dumb, and the blind. A J. secondary school, opened in 1919 with separate facilities for boys and girls, gave five hours of Hebrew instruction a week. In 1931, the girls' section was transferred to a separate building and numbered nearly 700 students. The Orthodox congregation, with about 50 teachers, had its own school system. Among cultural institutions, the Hungarian-J. Literary Society (Izraelita Magyar Irodalmi Tarsulat), founded in 1894, initiated the first complete Hungarian translation of the Old Testament made by Jews and published original research and collections of source materials in Hungarian-J. history as well as a J. yearbook. Its leading spirit until the end of WWI was Samu Szemere. Though banned by Orthodox rabbis, another important institution was the rabbinical seminary founded in 1877. Emperor Francis Joseph provided the funds, derived from taxes imposed by the Austrians on the Jews of Hungary for their part in the revolt of 1848. Among its teachers were David Kaufman, Yehuda Aryeh Blau, and Shemuel David Levinger. A J. teachers' college founded in 1857 graduated 1,589 teachers by 1930. The community's library contained 10,000 volumes in 1930 and when its collection was incorporated into the rabbinical seminary's library after WWII the number grew to 60,000. Among the city's leading J. periodicals was the weekly *Magyar Izraelita*, founded in the 1860s and the first in the Hungarian language. After WWI, the periodical became very anti-Zionist and pro-assimilationist. The *Egyenloseg* ("Equality")

appeared from 1882 to 1938. In 1907–38 the Zionist journal *Zsido Szemle* appeared and in 1925–38, *Zsido Ujsag*, a weekly for the Orthodox community. In 1911–40, a Hebrew quarterly for Judaic studies appeared with intervals, *Ha-Tzofeh me-Eretz Hagar*. By 1910, nearly half the city's journalists were Jews. Among J. professionals, doctors were the most prominent, medicine being the only field where university training was open to the Jews before the Emancipation. Zionist activity commenced in the 1890s and received a big boost when Theodor Herzl (born in B.) revisited the city in 1899. The first organized group of Jews, members of Maccabi, emigrated to Palestine soon after WWI. The Zionist Association, founded in 1902, eventually had 300 branches throughout Hungary. By 1937, there were seven training camps for Zionist youths. During WWI the combined communities cared for about 20,000 J. refugees. After the war, the Jews suffered from the White Terror and many were kidnapped and murdered at its headquarters in the Britannia Hotel. Antisemitic riots and discriminatory government measures marked the period between the World Wars: Jews were fired from government positions; a law was enacted forbidding them to trade in wine and tobacco; in 1920, the *numerus clausus* was enacted; 15,000 of B.'s Jews were expelled from Hungary as aliens (1922); nine were killed and 23 injured in a bomb attack (1923); and Jews were attacked in the city's universities (1927). Despite the discrimination, many important J. institutions and activities, both social and cultural, were initiated at this time and there was greater self-identification with the community among Jews, with many who had assimilated returning to Judaism. From 1910 through the 1940s, the J. pop. was about 200,000 (20–23% of the total).

Hungary's racial laws severely undermined J. life starting in 1938 and the situation deteriorated still further with the institution of forced labor for Jews in 1940. In reaction to the racial laws, about 14,000 Jews converted in 1938–43. The Germans invaded Hungary on 19 March 1944, immediately dismantling all J. organizations and replacing them with a single J. Council (*Zsido Tanacs*). Jews were arbitrarily arrested at train stations and sent to the Kistarcsa political prisoner camp while J. leaders were rounded up according to special lists. In April, Jews were evicted from 1,500 apartments on orders given personally by Adolf Eichmann at the city's Gestapo headquarters. Another 800

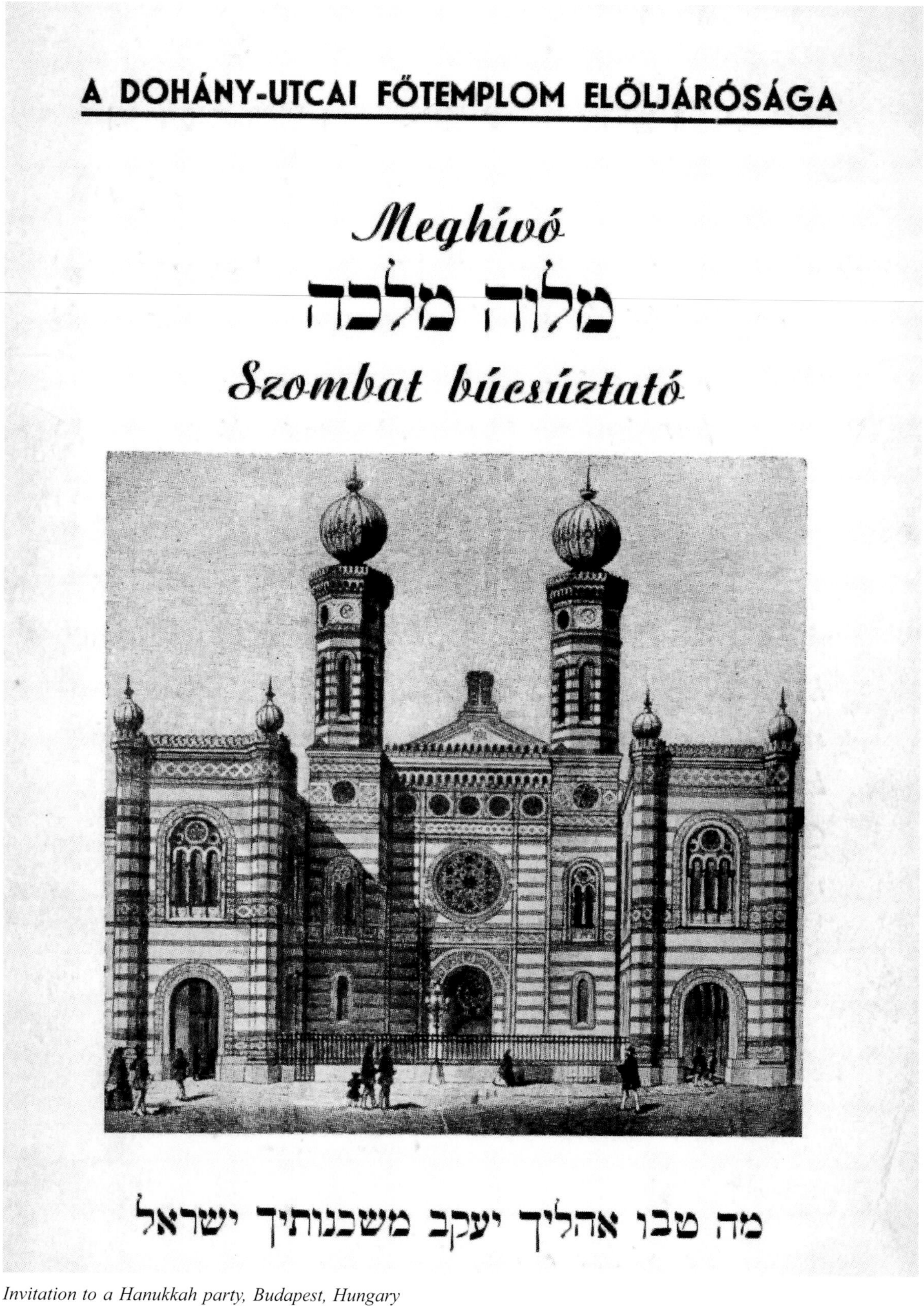

A DOHÁNY-UTCAI FŐTEMPLOM ELŐLJÁRÓSÁGA

Meghívó

מלוה מלכה

Szombat búcsúztató

מה טבו אהליך יעקב משכנותיך ישראל

Invitation to a Hanukkah party, Budapest, Hungary

buildings with a majority of J. tenants were impounded in June and a ghetto was organized. As Jews were being rounded up and deported, the J. Council was perceived by many B. Jews as too willing a tool of the Gestapo. The Zionists, on the other hand, played an active role in revealing the truth about the deportations and in providing forged papers that helped many escape. International and local pressure temporarily put a stop to deportations, but not before 17,500 of B's Jews were sent to concentration camps. About 2,600 Jews together with their families were granted safe-conduct passes by the neutral powers. On 19 July, after being foiled in his deportation efforts, Eichmann had the 1,220 J. inmates of Kistarcsa sent to Auschwitz on his own initiative. Among the most active of the foreigners trying to save Jews was Raoul Wallenberg, working out of the Swedish Embassy and in cooperation with the Zionist groups. Wallenberg authorized the forging of about 8,000 Swedish passports on the understanding that they were to be used only for the duration of the war. Others who gave their protection were the Swiss and Spanish embassies. Hungarian Church leaders did not help very much but 2,718 Jews were hidden in monasteries. With a new government formed under the virulent antisemite Ferenc Szalasi of the Arrow Cross Party, Eichmann returned to B. on 17 Oct. 1944 to implement the Final Solution there. On 20 Oct., all J. males between the ages of 16 and 60 were ordered out of their homes and some 50,000 were led in a cruel death march to the Austrian border, followed a few days later by women with their infants. Wallenberg was instrumental in bringing five truckloads of food and distributing medicines among the marchers. Thanks to the approach of the Russian army, about 60,000 marchers were saved from Auschwitz. Jews continued to be murdered by the Nazis within B. By Jan. 1945, about 70,000 were left in the ghetto. The Russians reached the city on 17 Jan., liberating the ghetto the next morning. The postwar community numbered 96,500 Jews in 1946.

BUDESTI (Hung. Budfalva) N. Transylvania dist., Rumania. Jews settled in the early 18th cent. and many became wealthy from gold mining and the lumber industry. The J. pop. in 1920 was 452 (18% of the total). Members of the rival Spinka and the Sighet hasidic sects were dominant in the community. Zionist activity was particularly strong in B. during the 1930s. In April 1944 the J community was transferred to the Ber-

besti ghetto and then deported to Auschwitz. About 100 survivors returned after the war but soon left.

BUDKOVCE (Hung. Butka) Slovakia, Czechoslovakia, today Republic of Slovakia. Jews were present in the first half of the 18th cent. and numbered 125 (total 1,127) in 1880. In 1940, 112 remained. Most were deported to the Lukow ghetto in the Lublin dist. of Poland on 6 May 1942.

BUDSLAW Vilna dist., Poland, today Belarus. A few J. families lived there in the latter 18th cent. and 175 in 1847. About 150 Jews were present between the World Wars, benefiting in trade from the presence of a large army camp, which offset the competition of the Polish cooperatives. The Germans captured B. in June 1941. On 13 Sept. they executed 50 Jews outside the town. Most of the others were murdered in a nearby forest in Sept. 1942.

BUDSZENTMIHALY Szabolcs dist., Hungary. Jews were present by the late 18th cent., engaging in the grain trade and maintaining a J. school, *talmud torah*, and yeshiva. They numbered 495 in 1880 and 684 in 1941 (5.7% of the total). The young men were sent to forced labor in 1942 and the remaining Jews were deported on 17 May 1944 to Auschwitz via Nyiregyhaza. Survivors tried to reestablish the community but soon left.

BUDZANOW (Yid. Bizinev) Tarnopol dist., Poland, today Ukraine. The first Jews are mentioned in 1628 and an organized community existed by the early 18th cent., with the pop. growing to around 1,700 (nearly a third of the total) by the end of the 19th. J. livelihoods centered around the town's weekly trade fair. The community was exceedingly poor and on the whole lived a simple traditional life. Most of the Jews abandoned the town as a result of the sufferings of WWI and its aftermath. The community was only fully rehabilitated toward the outbreak of WWII, with Zionist activity expanding greatly in the interim. The J. pop. in 1931 was 1,213. The Soviet regime of Sept. 1939 brought with it nationalization of J. assets and further hardship. The Germans entered the town on 2 July 1941, established a *Judenrat*, and sent Jews to various labor camps. In the fall of 1942 the Jews were expelled to the Trembowla ghetto and liquidated in the various *Aktion*s. Those hiding in B. were

rounded up and murdered by the Ukrainian police. A few dozen survived the war.

BUDZISKA Lublin dist., Poland. The J. pop. was 119 in 1921 (total 425). Most were employed in the Perlis factories in Baczki and Ostrowsk. In Sept. 1942, the Germans deported the Jews to the Sobibor death camp via Baczki.

BUECKEBURG Schaumburg–Lippe, Germany. The town's growth as an administrative and commercial center fostered the establishment of a small J. community in 1660. The Jews were expelled between 1717 and 1728, but afterwards the community revived. The Court Jew Isaak Heine (1700) headed a long line of bankers and merchants, his most famous descendant being the poet Heinrich Heine (1797–1856). Numbering 90 (over 4% of the total) in 1771 and 79 in 1853, the community adopted in its new synagogue, established in 1866, some features of Liberal Judaism – "modernized" education and reformed services with a choir. The J. pop. of 110 (2%) in 1913 declined to 60 (1925) and an amalgamation with the Obernkirchen and Rinteln communities took place in 1932. Before 1938, only five Jews had left B., driven by Nazi boycott and "Aryanization" measures. Many more left in the wake of *Kristallnacht* (9–10 Nov. 1938) and the tightening of the Nazi noose in 1939 and 1940. About 20 made it to safe havens; only one of the 25 deported (1941–42) to the east and the Theresienstadt ghetto survived.

BUEDESHEIM Hesse Germany. The community, numbering 76 (3.5% of the total) in 1861, mainly engaged in the livestock trade. On *Kristallnacht* (9–10 Nov. 1938), the synagogue was devastated and J. property looted. Of the 57 Jews living there in 1933, 40 had emigrated or moved elsewhere by 1939 and the rest were deported in 1942.

BUEDINGEN Hesse, Germany. Established around 1680, the community numbered 161 (4.7% of the total) in 1905. During the Weimar Republic, local Jews (mostly livestock dealers and storekeepers) were active in social and political life. The J. pop. numbered 146 (3.9%) in 1933 but the community disbanded in 1938, after many Jews had emigrated or fled to other towns. Five families remained on *Kristallnacht* (9–10 Nov. 1938), when a mob attacked J.

homes and stores. After the men were released from the Buchenwald concentration camp, all but one of the Jews left.

BUEHL Baden, Germany. Jews are first mentioned in 1579 but the few J. families there were forced to leave in the early 17th cent. and the J. settlement was only renewed during the Thirty Years War (1618–48). A synagogue was dedicated in 1832 and a cemetery in 1833. In 1830–76 a J. elementary school was in operation as the J. pop. grew to a peak of 301 in 1865 (total 2,888). In 1827, B. became the seat of the district rabbinate. Among its leading rabbis was Leopold Schott (1807–69), one of the first rabbis in Baden with a university education, who introduced a Reform style of worship. There were anti-J. riots in the 1848 revolution. Jews were regularly elected to the municipal council. From the last third of the 19th cent., the J. pop. began to decline through emigration and the shift to the big cities, dropping to 72 in 1933. When the Nazis came to power, the Jews were immediately subjected to persecution. Torah scrolls were vandalized in 1935 and Jews were gradually forced to liquidate their businesses. On *Kristallnacht* (9–10 Nov. 1938), the synagogue was burned and J. stores damaged. Up to 1940, 21 Jews emigrated and 13 left for other German cities. The community ended when 28 were deported to the Gurs concentration camp on 22 Oct. 1940.

BUENDE Westphalia, Germany. Jews numbered six families in 1808 and reached a pop. of 137 (total 2,052) in 1871. A J. school was in operation until 1890. Jews were active in public and social life, serving on the municipal council and joining sports and glee clubs. In June 1933, about four months after the Nazi rise to power, 56 Jews were counted. On *Kristallnacht* (9–10 Nov. 1938), the synagogue was destroyed; the J. cemetery desecrated; J. homes and stores vandalized; and most J. men sent to the Buchenwald concentration camp. By May 1939, only 11 Jews remained; most fell victim to deportation during the war.

BUER Westphalia, Germany. Jews arrived in B. only in the last third of the 19th cent., with the industrialization of the Ruhr region. Jews provided the workers with cheap food, clothing, and household items and some even opened department stores. They were affiliated to the Dorsten community, numbering 79 in 1905

and a peak of 171 (total 99,058) in 1925. A splendid synagogue with 300 seats was consecrated in 1922 but the community only become independent in 1932. In 1932, the J. pop. was 150. Emigration commenced even before the Nazis gained power in 1933. In mid-1933, a Zionist group was formed and Hebrew lessons were offered. On *Kristallnacht* (9–10 Nov. 1938), the synagogue was set on fire and all J. men were arrested. The last Jews were deported to the east in 1942–43. At least 62, including 21 children, died in the camps.

BUEREN Westphalia, Germany. Jews lived in B. in the 13th cent. but were massacred by the local pop. at the end of the cent. following a Host desecration libel. Jews were apparently again present in the 16th cent. and reached a peak pop. of 123 (total 2,196) in 1880. A J. cemetery was in use in 1837 and a J. school in 1851. A synagogue was consecrated in 1862. Jews owned stores selling spices, grain, and shoes. In June 1933, 39 Jews lived in B., their number being augmented by newcomers. Under Nazi rule, many left, mostly to other places in Germany. On *Kristallnacht* (9–10 Nov. 1938), the synagogue was vandalized and in May 1939 only nine were left. In 1941, six Jews were sent to camps in the east where they perished.

BUERGEL Hesse, Germany. Numbering 233 (26.7% of the total) in 1828, the community grew to 304 (21%) in 1861. Isaac Eberst, father of the composer Jacques Offenbach, once served there as cantor (*hazzan*). Around 1860 the synagogue adopted a Reform style of worship (with organ and choir). On *Kristallnacht* (9–10 Nov. 1938), Nazis destroyed the synagogue's interior and by 1939 most of the remaining 60 Jews had left. In 1952, a bronze menorah donated to the synagogue in 1767 was given to U.S. President Harry S. Truman by Israel's Prime Minister David Ben-Gurion.

BUERSTADT Hesse, Germany. Numbering 45 (1% of the total) in 1861, the community declined to 23 in 1933 and by 1939 most of the Jews had left.

BUETOW (Pol. Bytow) Pomerania, Germany, today Poland. Jews began to settle in B. after 1720. In 1812, there were already 34 J. families, and by 1889 the J. pop. reached its peak of about 550

(about 10% of the total). The community established a synagogue (1856) and a cemetery. At the end of the 19th cent., antisemitism grew and the windows of the synagogue and of J. apartments were repeatedly smashed. By 1909, the J. pop. had shrunk to 250. When the Nazis came to power in 1933, there were 114 Jews in B. and 70 in March, 1934. The boycott measures severely hurt J. businessmen, and by Sept. 1935 they had either sold their businesses or were facing economic ruin. On *Kristallnacht* (9–10 Nov. 1938), the synagogue was burned down. By May 1939, only 37 Jews and five individuals of partial J. origin (*Mischlinge*) remained in the town. No further information about their fate is available, but it may be assumed that those who did not manage to emigrate abroad were deported to the east. By Oct. 1942, only one Jew was still living in B., probably protected by marriage to a non-Jew.

BUETTELBORN Hesse, Germany. The community, numbering 42 (3.5% of the total) in 1861, had practically disappeared by *Kristallnacht*, when the synagogue was vandalized.

BUETTHARD Lower Franconia, Germany. Jews numbered 63 (total 771) in 1867 and ten in 1933 with a synagogue and community center at their disposal. Five left in 1937. On *Kristallnacht* (9–10 Nov. 1938) J. homes were vandalized with the help of local residents. Of the last five Jews (all over 65) three emigrated in 1939 and two were deported to the Theresienstadt ghetto in 1942.

BUGOJNO Bosnia-Hercegovina, Yugoslavia, today Republic of Bosnia. Jews settled there at the end of the 19th cent. In 1931 there were 46 Jews (total 15,960). In WWII the Ustase fascist orgnaizaion massacred the Jews.

BUGYI Pest–Pilis–Solt–Kiskun dist., Hungary. Jews were present by the 17th cent., numbering 104 in 1880 and 60 in 1930. They were deported to Auschwitz via Lajosmizse and Monoy at the end of June 1944.

BUHUSI Moldavia dist., Rumania. J. settlement began in 1823. A stone synagogue was built in 1824. R. Yitzhak Friedmann of the Ruzhin dynasty started a hasidic court in B. in 1866. Zionist activity began

in 1893. The J. pop. in 1899 was 1,732 (48% of the total). In 1908, R. Ben-Zion Roler established a yeshiva which existed until 1940. During the 1907 peasant revolt, J. property was vandalized. Antisemitic outbreaks were common between the World Wars. In 1940, the Iron Guard forced Jews to pay large sums to their coffers and sent J. males to forced labor. Jews from surrounding villages were brought to B. In 1944, 70 orphans returning from Transnistria were cared for by the community. The J. pop. in 1947 was 2,000.

BUJ Szabolcs dist., Hungary. Jews are mentioned in 1770, numbering 247 in 1880 and 104 in 1930. Most of the men seized for forced labor in 1941 perished. On 17 May 1944, the remaining Jews were deported to Auschwitz via Simapuszta.

BUJOR Moldavia dist., Rumania. Jews settled in 1825. The J. pop. in 1930 was 181 (19% of the total). In June 1941 all the Jews were expelled to Galati.

BUK Poznan dist., Poland. A J. settlement existed at the beginning of Prussian rule in 1793. A year-old synagogue was destroyed in 1848 by rioting Poles, when 60 J. families lost their property. A new synagogue and a J. elementary school were opened in the 1860s. The J. pop. was 241 in 1840 and 156 (total 3,737) in 1913, dropping to 33 in 1939 as most left independent Poland. All were expelled by the Germans via Melinow to General Gouvernement territory around late 1939 as were 1,300 Jews in a local transit camp.

BUKACZOWCE (Yid. Bokshevits) Stanislawow dist., Poland, today Ukraine. A permanent J. community developed during the 18th cent., growing to a peak pop. of 1,216 (50% of the total) in 1900. The sufferings of WWI and its aftermath led to a drop in the J. pop. by nearly half. The Zionists were active from the beginning of the century, organizing a Hebrew school and cultural activity. After Soviet rule (1939–41), the Germans entered the town on 3 July 1941, immediately instituting repressive measures. Refugees filled the town the following spring and typhoid broke out. The community was liquidated in three separate *Aktion*s (21 Sept. 1942 [Yom Kippur], 26 Oct. 1942, 19 Jan. 1943) sending nearly all the Jews to the Belzec death camp.

BUKCHA Polesie dist., Belorussia. The J. pop. was 123 (total 635) in 1897. In the early 1920s, Jews earned their livelihoods as farmers and artisans. The Germans captured B. in July 1941 and murdered the Jews still there.

BUKI Kiev dist., Ukraine. Jews numbered 1,182 in 1847 and 2,298 (total 3,923) in 1897. A *talmud torah* and a private school for girls were founded in 1909. On 12-14 May 1919, Ukrainian gangs attacked Jews. In 1939, under the Soviets, the J. pop. was 546. The Germans arrived on 14 July 1941. A small number of Jews managed to flee to the east; the rest were murdered.

BUKOWSKO (Yid. Bikavsk) Lwow dist., Poland. Jews settled in the 18th cent., much of their livelihood revolving around the town's annual trade fair and later bolstered by the establishment of a dominant hasidic court connected with the Dynow dynasty. The J. pop. stood at 748 (total 991) in 1900, but dropped to 494 in 1921 after emigration and the tribulations of WWI took their toll, with many on the verge of starvation. The advance of the Germans in 1939 brought a stream of refugees and subsequently a regime of forced labor and extortion. Those Jews not sent to labor camps were deported to the Belzec death camp in the summer of 1942, probably via Zaslawie.

BUNDE Hanover, Germany. Jews of Portuguese Marrano origin first lived there (1671-1720), but a community was only established in the 19th cent. It maintained a synagogue and a religious school, numbering 78 (4% of the total) in 1922. The Jews disbanded the community and disposed of the synagogue in July 1938. Most left, 34 emigrating to Holland. At least 33 Jews from B. perished in the Holocaust.

BUNZLAU (Pol. Boleslawiec) Lower Silesia, Germany, today Poland. Jews were present by 1370 at the latest, occupying a Street of the Jews numbering 31 houses and 360 residents. The Jews were expelled a number of times and after 1454 did not reappear for hundreds of years. A few Court Jews were present in the 18th cent., but only in 1812 was a community reestablished. The J. pop. rose from 21 in 1822 to 99 in 1849 and 194 in 1880. The community maintained a cemetery (opened in 1817) and a synagogue (1878). The J. pop. began to drop in the early 20th

cent. and in 1925 stood at 103. On *Kristallnacht* (9–10 Nov. 1938), the synagogue was burned and many J. stores were destroyed. In 1939, 64 Jews remained and in Nov. 1942 just one intermarried Jew. There is no additional information as to the fate of the community under the Nazis. Presumably those Jews who did not leave in time were deported and perished.

BURDUJENI Moldavia dist., Rumania. In the late 18th cent., J. inhabitants of Serpineti (Bukovina) crossed the border and settled in B. The J. pop. in 1899 was 2,059 (78% of the total). During the 1907 peasant revolt, 287 J. houses and six synagogues were destroyed and 446 families left destitute. In Feb. 1941, 110 Jews were expelled across the Russian border; not all succeeded in crossing and 58 were deported to Targu-Jiu in May 1941. On 9 Oct. 1941 the J. pop. was expelled to Transnistria. Survivors returned after the war.

BURG Saxony, Germany. References indicate a Street of the Jews in 1365, but the settlement was probably several decades older. In 1493, the Jews of B. were expelled together with all Jews of the Magdeburg archbishopric. There was a new community in the second half of the 18th cent. It established a prayer room and cemetery. In 1850, the community numbered 122 members and two years later consecrated a synagogue. In the 1890s, there were only three J. families in B. and from 1893 on, the synagogue was no longer used. It was finally sold and the remaining Jews of B. used the synagogue in Genthin. By 1925, the community numbered 82. When the Nazis came to power in 1933, there were 74 Jews living in B. They prepared for emigration by organizing a Hebrew-language course. Since the synagogue was no longer J.-owned, it survived *Kristallnacht* (9–10 Nov. 1938). In 1939, 22 Jews still lived in the city. It may be assumed that those who did not manage to emigrate were deported to the east, with the exception of two persons who, probably protected by marriage to non-Jews, were still living in B. in Oct. 1942.

BURGBROHL Rhineland, Germany. The J. pop. was 87 in 1843 and 16 in 1933. Four Jews perished in the Holocaust.

BURGDORF Hanover, Germany. Numbering 29 in 1738, the J. community rebuilt its synagogue in 1810 and grew to 114 (nearly 4% of the total) in 1871. It absorbed the three outlying communities of Burgwedel, Isernhagen, and Lehrte, and maintained a J. elementary school (1889–1932). Nazi boycott measures forced most Jews to leave well before the end of 1938. On *Kristallnacht* (9–10 Nov. 1938), the interior of the synagogue was vandalized. The building was sold to the municipality in Feb. 1939. Nine emigrated from B. (seven to England) and nine from Lehrte (six to the U.S.) by Aug. 1939. At least 25 perished in the Holocaust.

BURGGRAEFENRODE Hesse, Germany. Numbering 62 (11.3% of the total) in 1861, the community disintegrated after WWI. The few Jews remaining in 1939 perished in the Holocaust.

BURGHASLACH Middle Franconia, Germany. Jews are mentioned in the mid-16th cent. Thirty families were present in 1733, when a synagogue was dedicated. In 1809 the J. pop. was 209 (total 870). Jews traded in glass, textiles, beer hops, and cattle. A J. public school was opened in 1869. In 1933 the Jews numbered 60. The synagogue was burned down on *Kristallnacht* (9–10 Nov. 1938). Later in the morning, all the Jews were arrested and their homes wrecked. By Dec. all but ten left the city, 14 emigrating to the U.S. and six to Palestine. The last ten left in 1939–40.

BURGHAUN Hesse–Nassau, Germany. Established in the 17th cent., the J. community ran an elementary school (1867–1933), numbered 176 (15% of the total) in 1885, and dedicated a new synagogue in 1910. By 1933 the community had dwindled to 112. Torah scrolls were removed from the synagogue before a mob burned it to the ground on *Kristallnacht* (9–10 Nov. 1938). Most of the remaining Jews were deported (1941); at least 26 perished in the Holocaust.

BURGKUNSTADT Upper Franconia, Germany. Jews are mentioned as victims of the Rindfleisch massacres of 1298. In 1620 the community consecrated a cemetery serving numerous settlements in the area for hundreds of years. In the Bamberg riots of 1699, the Jews fled the town as 14 of their homes were destroyed. Leopold Stein, one of the spokesmen of the Reform movement in Germany, served as rabbi in 1835–43. In 1837 the J. pop. reached a peak of 420 (total 1,305). In 1933, 53 Jews remained; 40 left in 1935–39, with 16

going abroad and 24 to other German cities. In 1937, the J.-owned shoe factory, employing 400, was impounded and on *Kristallnacht* (9–10 Nov. 1938), the synagogue was vandalized. Of the remaining Jews, ten were deported to Izbica in the Lublin dist. (Poland), in April 1942. The four Jews in the attached community of Hochstadt am Main met similar fates.

BURGPREPPACH Lower Franconia, Germany. Jews were probably present during the Thirty Years War (1618–48). From 1681 B. was the seat of the chief rabbinate (or rabbinical court) of the Grabfeld region. Among its outstanding rabbis was Yosef Breslau (1691–1752), author of *Shoresh Yosef* and *Hok Yosef*. In 1875 a *talmud torah* encompassing secular studies was founded according to the system of Shimshon Rafael Hirsch of Frankfurt. The J. pop. grew to 198 in 1890 (total 602), but from the early 20th cent. economic conditions deteriorated and the pop. declined steadily to 78 in 1933. The community operated two synagogues, a cemetery, and an elementary school (the old *talmud torah*). In 1934 a blood libel originating in Manau led to the arrest of six local Jews. Sixteen Jews left B. up to Feb. 1938. On *Kristallnacht* (9–10 Nov. 1938), the old synagogue (built in 1764) was burned down and J. homes were vandalized. Most of the remaining Jews left in 1939, 14 emigrating and 24 moving to other German cities. The last Jew fled to Berlin in Feb. 1942.

BURGSINN Lower Franconia, Germany. Jews numbered 87 in 1867 and 49 in 1933 (total 2,000). Jews were attacked in March 1938 after the Austrian *Anschluss*. On *Kristallnacht* (9–10 Nov. 1938), the synagogue and J. homes were vandalized. Of the 41 Jews who left B. in the Nazi period, 23 moved to other German cities and 18 emigrated, 13 of them to the U.S. The last Jews were deported in 1942.

BURGSTEINFURT Westphalia, Germany. Jews are first mentioned in 1337 and in 1347 the J. pop. numbered 109. Three years later the community was destroyed in the Black Death persecutions. The modern J. community grew from one family in 1662 to four families in 1735, reaching 126 individuals in 1811 and a peak of 227 in 1895. The community consecrated a synagogue in 1764 and had two cemeteries (16th cent.; 1884). A local *matza* factory, owned by Ernst Marcus, was said to be the largest in Europe. Emigra-

tion to the big cities from the late 19th cent. reduced the J. pop. to 117 (total 6,565) in 1933. Under the Nazis, 67 Jews emigrated up to 1940, including 22 to Holland and 18 to Chile; 17 left for the larger German cities. On *Kristallnacht* (9–10 Nov. 1938), the synagogue was set on fire and J. homes and stores were damaged. In May 1939, 39 Jews remained in B. In 1941–42, the last Jews were deported to concentration camps in the east where they perished.

BURIN Sumy dist., Ukraine. The J. pop. in 1939 was 113 (2% of the total). After their arrival on 19 Sept. 1941, the Germans murdered the Jews who had neither fled nor been evacuated.

BURKANOW Tarnopol dist., Poland, today Ukraine. The J. pop. in 1921 was 110. The Jews were murdered locally or expelled to Podhajce for liquidation in fall 1942.

BURSZTYN Stanislawow dist., Poland, today Ukraine. Jews probably arrived in the early 17th cent. and enjoyed relatively secure conditions under the Polish kingdom. A committee for the redemption of prisoners was particularly active in the face of Tartar incursions. The first synagogue was built in the mid-18th cent. With the Austrian conquest in 1772, conditions worsened under heavy taxes and other disabilities, but improved with the institution of J. equality and the development of the town in the second half of the 19th cent. when the J. pop. rose to around 2,000 (50% of the total). Hasidism and Haskala were well represented and at the end of the cent. the Zionist movement made its appearance. The sufferings of WWI and three separate fires that destroyed large parts of B., including its synagogues, reduced the J. pop. to as little as 1,000 at the end of the war with another 400 or so arriving from the surrounding villages. These hardships were compounded by the economic crisis of the 1930s. Despite its policy of nationalization, the Soviet regime of 1939–41 brought a measure of relief. The Germans took the city on 2 July 1941. Ukrainian anti-J. riots followed and a *Judenrat* was set up. In Sept. 1941 the Jews were concentrated in an open ghetto. Expulsions began in Sept. 1942 to Bukaczowce and Rohatyn, where the Jews met their deaths. A partisan group, mostly composed of J. escapees, operated in the Bukaczowce woods.

BUSENBERG Palatinate, Germany. A J. community existed in the early 19th cent., maintaining a synagogue and a cemetery (the latter opened in 1833). In 1848, the J. pop. comprised 31 families (170 Jews), including seven farmers, six artisans, and 18 merchants. In 1867, there were 24 families (129 Jews, or 16.6% of the total), barely eking out a living as junk dealers and small-scale livestock traders. The J. pop. was 74 in 1875, 50 in 1900, and 28 in 1932. All left before *Kristallnacht* (9–10 Nov. 1938), four emigrating and the rest moving to other localities in Germany.

BUSK Tarnopol dist., Poland, today Ukraine. Jews are already mentioned in 1454 and lived in relative security until the Chmielnicki massacres of 1648–49, which claimed around 100 J. lives. In the 18th cent., Jakob Frank (1726–91) visited the town and about 103 of his followers there converted to Christianity, among them the local rabbi. In the 19th cent. Belz and Olesko Hasidism predominated. At the beginning of the 20th cent., when the J. pop. was 2,340 (total 6,671), many emigrated to the U.S. and a further flight of Jews took place during WWI, with the pop. declining to 1,600 by 1931. Between the World Wars the Zionists became the dominant political force in the community, but political and community life was disrupted by the Soviet occupation in Sept. 1939. The Germans entered the town on 1 July 1941, set up a *Judenrat*, and instituted forced labor. Disease, hunger, and unremitting persecution followed. The first *Aktion* took place on 21 Sept 1942 (Yom Kippur), when around 700 Jews were taken to a village near Zloczow and murdered. The ghetto was set up thereafter, receiving the remnants of the Jews from nearby towns. A labor camp was established later. Final liquidation commenced in May 1943 with deportations to the Janowska camp in Lwow and the murder of women and children in the forest and in the ghetto itself. Those who escaped to the forests were found and murdered by the Germans and Ukrainians.

BUSKO Kielce dist., Poland. Jews settled in the late 19th cent., numbering 895 in 1897 and 1,464 (total 3,949) in 1921. Some became involved in the tourist trade with B.'s development as a health resort. A synagogue was established in 1930. In 1933, following quarrels with Polish tradesmen and the murder of a J. merchant, the municipal authorities severely restricted the commercial rights of Jews. The Zionists were ac-

tive between the World Wars and maintained a 3,500-volume library. After the German occupation of Sept. 1939, a central *Judenrat* responsible for smaller J. communities in the area was established. In April 1941, an open ghetto was set up. Despite German restrictions, refugees continued to arrive and the J. pop. reached 1,728 in Nov. 1941. In Oct. 1942, after a selection for the labor camps, those remaining were deported to the Treblinka death camp

BUSSUM-NAARDEN Noord-Holland dist., Holland. Jews settled in Naarden during the 17th cent. and in Bussum in the early 20th cent. In 1911 the J. pop. was 75 in Bussum and 34 in Naarden. The two communities were united in 1933. The J. pop. in 1938 was 377. German refugees arrived in the 1930s and Jews were transferred there from the coastal regions in 1940. In June 1942 all were moved to Amsterdam and later deported to Poland; 220 perished in the Holocaust. A community was reestablished after the war.

BUSTINO (Hung. Bustyahaza) Carpatho-Russia, Czechoslovakia, today Ukraine. J. settlement apparently dates from the first half of the 18th cent. A single family (six Jews) was present in 1746. After the Jews abandoned the town, J. settlement was only renewed in the late 19th cent. In 1880, the J. pop. was 142. Its number rose considerably during the time of the Czechoslovakian Republic, reaching 1,042 in 1930 before dropping to 994 (total 3,965) in 1941. A number of Jews farmed and a few were administrative officials. The Zionists and Agudat Israel were mainly active among the young. The Hungarians occupied the town in March 1939. In 1940–41, they drafted dozens of Jews into forced labor battalions. In Aug. 1941, a few families without Hungarian citizenship were expelled to German-occupied Ukrainian territory, where they were murdered. The rest were deported to Auschwitz in late May 1944. After the war a number of survivors returned but soon left, mostly for Czechoslovakia.

BUSTINSKY HANDAL (Hung. Handalbustyahaza; Yid. Handel Byshtyne) Slovakia, Czechoslovakia, today Republic of Slovakia. Jews arrived in the mid-19th cent., numbering 30 in 1880 and 256 (total 860) in 1921. Jews owned a sawmill and flour mill and there were a few wealthy lumber merchants. The Hun-

garians occupied the town in March 1939 and in 1941 drafted a number of Jews into labor battalions. In July 1941, a few J. families without Hungarian citizenship were expelled to Kamenets-Podolski, where they were murdered. The rest were deported to Auschwitz in late May 1944.

BUTENI (Hung. Korosbokeny) S. Transylvania dist., Rumania. Jews first settled in the late 19th cent. They were attached to the Sebis Neologist congregation. After WWI many Jews moved to nearby towns. The J. pop. was 59 in 1930 (2% of the total). On 24 June 1941, the J. pop. was transferred to Arad and never returned to B.

BUTLA Lwow dist., Poland, today Ukraine. The J. pop. in 1921 was 182. The Jews were deported via Turka or directly to the Belzec death camp in the second half of 1942.

BUTRIMONYS (Yid. Butrimanz) Alytus dist., Lithuania. B., one of Lithuania's first J. communities, had a J. pop. of 1,919 (80% of the total) in 1897. Zionism was strong already in the Hovevei Zion period. With Lithuania's independence in 1918, a community council was established which administered most areas of J. life. In 1920 a Hebrew-language school was started. In addition to Zionist parties, Agudat Yisrael and the Communists were active. Most of the latter were Jews. A German army unit entered B. in late June 1941. It was joined by Lithuanian nationalists and Red Army deserters who beat, raped, and robbed Jews and seized them for forced labor. On 12 Aug. 1941, 83 J. men and 17 young women were taken to Alytus and executed. On 21 Aug. the same fate befell another 115 young men. Groups of Jews from other towns were brought to B. and forced into a ghetto with B.'s Jews. On 9 Sept. they all were all forced to enter prepared mass graves and shot.

BUTTENHAUSEN Wuerttemberg, Germany. J. settlement began in 1787 when 25 families received residence rights from the local ruler. By the mid-19th cent. the Jews formed the majority of the total and constituted its wealthy class, reaching a peak pop. of 442 in 1870. B. became one of the region's centers of commerce and culture, with the Jews remaining prominent even as their numbers began to dwindle, primarily due to emi-

Winter in Butrimonys, Lithuania

gration to the U.S. and the larger German cities and a sharply declining birthrate (from 10.3 per family in 1850 to 2.1 in 1925). In 1912, most Jews were engaged in the cattle trade; the wealthiest owned a cigarette factory. Throughout the period relations with the local pop. were excellent and little cooperation was extended to the Nazi authorities, with local residents removing the contents of the synagogue for safekeeping when SA troops set it on fire on *Kristallnacht* (9–10 Nov. 1938). Few of the town's 89 Jews had left at that point; 39 emigrated by 1941; 109, including refugees from Stuttgart and Heilbronn-Sondheim, were expelled to the Riga ghetto on 16 Dec. 1941 and to the Theresienstadt ghetto on 22 Aug. 1942. After the war, local townsman erected monuments to commemorate the fallen and mark the site of the razed synagogue.

BUTTENHEIM Upper Franconia, Germany. Jews were possibly present from the late 16th cent. In 1740 they erected a beautiful synagogue in the rococo style. The J. pop. reached 176 in 1810 (total 822) but many emigrated to the U.S. in the 1827–39 period and the pop. continued to decline steadily, leaving 18 in 1933. All emigrated in 1934–39, including 11 to England and six to the U.S.

BUTTENWIESEN (in J. sources, Patavieza, Potivich) Swabia, Germany. An organized community existed in the first half of the 17th cent. A cemetery was consecrated in 1633 and additional Jews, expelled from the principality of Pfalz-Neuburg, arrived in the 1740s. A J. public school enrolled 116 children in 1846 and in 1857 a new synagogue was opened. The J. pop. stood at 344 in 1867 (total 806), afterwards declining steadily to 73 in 1933. On *Kristallnacht* (9–10 Nov. 1938), the synagogue and cemetery were damaged along with J. homes and stores. Twenty-seven Jews left B. in 1934–41, 13 of them emigrating. The last 37 were deported to Piaski (Poland) via Munich on 3 April 1942.

BUTZBACH Hesse, Germany. Established in the 14th cent and expelled in 1667, the community was not revived until 1848. Its members upheld the Orthodox tradition of Frankfurt am Main and numbered 122 (4.9% of the total) in 1890. By 1933 the J. pop. had risen to 148 (2.6%), but the Nazi economic boycott made it impossible for Jews to remain. Ninety-seven left before Dec. 1938, most emigrating to the U.S.

and British Commonwealth countries. On *Kristallnacht* (9–10 Nov. 1938), the synagogue was desecrated and then burned down, Jews were attacked, and their property was looted or destroyed. Some Germans, however, defied the Nazis and protected local Jews, hiding their valuables and rescuing a Torah scroll.

BUTZWEILER Rhineland, Germany. The first Jew is mentioned in 1753. A cemetery was opened in 1846 and the community reached a peak pop. of 93 in 1860, with a Jew sitting on the village council. A synagogue was consecrated in 1892. In June 1933, the J. pop. was 49. On *Kristallnacht* (9–10 Nov. 1938), SA forces and local residents wrecked the synagogue and J. houses and descrecrated the cemetery. On the following night, the J. residents were driven toward Luxembourg, but as they were not allowed to cross the border, they returned. In May 1939, 16 Jews remained, many of them moving to Trier. The last five Jews were deported in Feb. 1943. About 19 Jews from B. were deported from Trier.

BUZAU Walachia dist., Rumania. Jews lived in B. from the early 17th cent. and an organized community existed from 1838. The J. pop. in 1890 was 2,112 (12% of the total). A blood libel trial, moved from Chilia (Transylvania) in 1871, set off pogroms. A B'nai B'rith lodge functioned from 1874. In 1897, the eighth congress of the Association of Indigenous Jews (Uniunea Evreilor Pamanteni) was held in B. with representatives from 16 towns. By 1899, four Zionist organizations were active. During the 1907 peasant revolt J. property was attacked. The Zionist parties won a majority in the 1920 community council elections. An all-J. party received almost all the J. votes in the 1931–32 parliamentary elections. During 1933–40, a bi-monthly devoted to Zionist and communal matters, *Viata Evreeasca*, appeared. The theological seminary run by the antisemitic bishop Ghenadie Niculescu became a center of antisemitic provocation. Under Iron Guard rule, the J. cemetery was destroyed and headstones used for building a church. In 1940, Jews aged 18–60 were arrested and held until the end of 1941. In April 1944, the community took care of 900 J. orphans returning from Transnistria. The J. community continued to function after the war.

BUZHENIN Lodz. dist., Poland. Jews first settled here in 1793; by 1884 the community had grown to

329. In 1941 the 180 Jews were deported to the ghetto in nearby Zdunska Wola.

BUZIAS   (Hung., Buziasfurdo) S. Transylvania dist., Rumania. A J. community existed in 1848. In 1869, the community joined the Neologist association. Most made their livings from services centered around B.'s health spas. The J. pop. was 73 in 1930 (2% of the total). Under the rule of the Iron Guard in 1941, J. property was confiscated. In 1942 all the Jews were exiled to Blaj and never returned to B.

BUZINOVO   Odessa dist., Ukraine. The J. pop. was 235 (total 760) in 1897 and 63 in 1926. After occupying the town on 10 Aug. 1941, the Nazis murdered the few Jews who had neither fled nor been evacuated.

BYCHAWA   Lublin dist., Poland. Jews were present in the mid-17th cent., their pop. growing to 1,447 (total 1,837) in 1884. R. Nehemia Yehiel Rabinowitz, son of R. Yaakov Yitzhak of Przysucha ("the holy Jew"), founded a hasidic dynasty in B. in the mid-19th cent. that lasted until the Holocaust. The Zionists became active in 1904, intensifying their activity after the publication of the Balfour Declaration in 1917. In 1921, the J. pop. stood at 1,876 with 44% of the Jews working as salaried employees and the rest in family workshops or businesses. A Tarbut Hebrew school was started in 1921 despite vehement Orthodox opposition. Economic conditions worsened in the late 1930s following the economic boycott. On the eve of the war, local Poles linked up with gangsters to pillage J. property. Under the German occupation from Sept. 1939, the J. pop. grew from 2,000 to 2,850 with the arrival of refugees. The community was subject to forced labor and extortionate "contributions." On 11 Oct. 1942, most of the Jews were expelled to Belzhyce and from there presumably deported to the Belzec death camp. The local labor camp with 500 Jews was liquidated on 8 May, some being sent to the Budzyn labor camp, others to the Majdanek concentration camp.

BYDGOSZCZ   Poznan dist., Poland. Jews were invited to settle by King Casimir the Great in 1346 and engaged in the grain trade with Danzig (Gdansk). In 1555 they were expelled by King Sigismund III under local pressure and settled in nearby Fordon. During the 17th cent. Jews found their way back to the city and in the late 18th cent. were active in the cloth trade. In 1802 they were allowed to work as jewelers, watchmakers, embroiderers, and in a number of other crafts. In 1847 all remaining disabilities were lifted and B. began to attract Jews from the entire region, their pop. rising to 1,364 in 1859 and 1,889 (total 34,044) in 1880. Jews played a central role in banking and the development of the transportation system as well as in trade and industry. When B. came under Prussian rule in 1772, a J. delegate was sent to the Prussian Landtag. In 1831 a new synagogue was erected. Another one was built in 1885 incorporating reforms in the prayer service. In 1867 a number of smaller communities were attached to B. A J. elementary school operated under government supervision from the first half of the cent. Jews also attended German universities in increasing numbers, creating a J. professional class in the city. The inclusion of B. in independent Poland after WWI accelerated the process of emigration that had commenced in the late 19th cent., but the process was reversed in the 1930s, when Jews from former Congress Poland arrived. Another 240 Jews from among the Polish nationals expelled from Germany in 1938 were also taken in by the community. In 1939 there were about 3,000 Jews in B., with the Zionists and their youth movements active and 270 children receiving supplementary religious education. The Germans captured the city on 5 Sept. 1939. Immediately they murdered 3,000 Jews and Poles in nearby Fordon. Shortly afterwards the remaining Jews were expelled to General Gouvernement territory and B. became one of the first cities in Poland to be "free of Jews" (*judenrein*).

BYKHOV   Mogilev dist., Belorussia. An organized J. community was already in existence in the early 17th cent., suffering in the Chmielnicki massacres of 1648–49. In 1662 the community helped the Polish General Grokhowski against the Russians. In appreciation King Michael Wisniowiecki in 1669 granted the Jews tax exemptions for 20 years. The J. pop. reached 887 in 1766 and 3,037 in 1897. In 1925, under the Soviets, 11 J. families joined a J. kolkhoz founded next to the town. Another 33 families joined a second kolkhoz founded in 1929. A J. school operated in the town. In 1939, the J. pop. was 2,295 (total 11,026). The Germans occupied B. on 4 July 1941 and in Sept. murdered 250 Jews outside the town. In Nov., 4,000 Jews from B. and the surrounding area were brought to the town's old castle, held there for a few days with-

out food or water, and then executed on the banks of the Dnieper River. In 1943, the children of mixed marriages were also murdered.

BYSHEV Kiev dist., Ukraine. The J. pop. was 142 in 1765 and 597 (total 3,523) in 1897. In 1926, under the Soviets, only 32 Jews remained. Those who had neither fled nor been evacuated perished under the occupation when the Germans arrived on 9 July 1941.

BYSTRA Slovakia, Czechoslovakia, today Republic of Slovakia. Jews numbered 110 in 1828, maintaining a synagogue and cemetery. In 1940, 70 remained. Most were deported to the death camps in 1942.

BYSTRZYCA Vilna dist., Poland, today Belarus. A few J. farmers settled in the late 19th cent. The J. pop. rose to 154 in 1919 as Jews opened stores and workshops between the World Wars. A ghetto was established by the Germans after their arrival in June 1941. Subsequently some Jews were sent to labor camps while the rest were expelled to the Kiemieliszki ghetto and executed in a nearby forest on 24 Oct. 1942.

BYTEN Nowogrodek dist., Poland, today Belarus. Jews were probably present from the turn of the 16th cent. In the 18th cent. they leased distilleries, flour mills, and inns from the town's proprietor. The J. pop. grew to 573 in 1847 and 1,614 (total 2,682) in 1897. Many Jews were employed in J.-owned kerchief and hide-processing factories and in the lumber trade, but with the closing of the factories in the early 20th cent. many were left without a livelihood and a process of emigration set in. The Bund and Po'alei Zion became active and organized a self-defense group during the disturbances following the 1905 revolution. In WWI, retreating Cossacks burned down most of the town. Under the hardships of the German occupation of 1915-18, about 300 Jews died, leaving 739 in 1921, with many emigrating to Latin America. The government curtailment of the J. lumber trade in 1929, coupled with the general economic crisis, impoverished many Jews. After two years of Soviet rule (1939-41) the Germans arrived on 28 June 1941, appointing a *Judenrat* and seizing Jews for forced labor. J. refugees began arriving from the surrounding villages in Aug. and in June 1942, 1,200 Jews were

packed into a ghetto, 18-20 to a room. In July, 840 were murdered outside the town. Another 200 fled to the forests and were able to subsist for awhile in family camps and with partisan groups. The 140 remaining in the ghetto were executed on 29 Aug. and 19 Sept. 1942.

BZENEC Moravia, Czechoslovakia. Jews were apparently present in the 14th cent. The city was destroyed in the wars of the mid-16th cent. but Jews returned by 1604, trading in salt and alcoholic beverages. In 1605, the city was again destroyed, by the Transylvanian prince Stephen Bocskay. In 1798, J. residence was restricted to 130 families. In 1857 the J. pop. reached a peak of 965, then declined steadily to 138 (total 4,562) in 1930. A new synagogue was consecrated in 1863. Between the World Wars, Jews operated a *matza* (unleavened bread) factory and a sugar refinery. The Zionists were active at this time. *Reichsprotektor* Reinhard Heydrich ordered the synagogue closed down in Oct. 1941. The Jews were deported to the Theresienstadt ghetto in one of the transports that left from neighboring Kyjov in Jan. 1943. Most were sent on to Auschwitz in the same year. Religious articles and community documents were transferred to the Central J. Museum of Prague before the deportations.

BZHEZINY Lodz dist., Poland. Jews lived here in the early 17th cent. At the end of the 19th cent., a group of Jews from Moscow who specialized in readymade wear settled there and exported to Russia, China, and Persia. Prior to WWI, B. became a leading center of J. tailors. Modern schools were opened. At the end of the 19th cent., the community numbered 3,917. Jews were active in the 1905 revolution and most of the J. apprentice tailors took part in the general strike. Between the World Wars, when markets in the east were no longer available, 300 of the 2,000 workshops remained, operating four months a year. Jews were helped by loans from J. loan funds, and the Lodz Chamber of Commerce and Industry arranged for orders of readymade clothing from customers in western Europe. Representatives of the J. tailors were elected to the community council led by Agudat Israel. In 1931 the council chairman was a representative of the Aleksander Hasidim. In 1929, the 12 J. city councilors constituted 50% of the municipal council. The J. community numbered 6,850 when the Germans captured the city on 9 Sept. 1939. B. became a center

for supplying the German military with clothing, even when the Jews were in the ghetto set up in April–May 1940, and which had 6,000 inhabitants with a *Judenrat* by 1942. Many Poles brought supplies to the Jews in the ghetto. On 14–15 May 1942, 1,700 Jews were sent to Chelmno and on 18 May another 4,000 were transported to the Lodz ghetto. Only 300 remained and the Germans shot them in Aug. 1942. Some 200–300 B. Jews survived the Holocaust but none resettled there.

BZHEZNICA Lodz dist., Poland. Jews settled here at the end of the 18th cent. and the community served as a center for Jews in surrounding villages. Between the World Wars, the Jews suffered from the boycott of their shops as well as other manifestations of antisemitism. On 3 Sept. 1939 the marketplace and part of the district inhabited by the 150 J. families was gutted by fire. By Passover 1942 nearly all the Jews had been expelled to the ghetto in Pajeczno, and from there to the Lodz ghetto and Chelmno death camp.

C

CABAJ CAPOR Slovakia, Czechoslovakia, today Republic of Slovakia. A community of about 400 Jews was present in 1830. In the early 20th cent., the J. pop. began to dwindle, with 36 Jews remaining in 1940. Most perished in the Holocaust.

CABESTI Bukovina, Rumania, today Ukraine. The J. pop. in 1930 was 120. On 5 July 1941, almost all the Jews were murdered by the local pop. The few survivors were deported to Transnistria.

CACHTICE (Hung. Csejte) Slovakia, Czechoslovakia, today Republic of Slovakia. Jews are mentioned in 1614. In 1689, 11 J. families settled under the protection of Count Pongrac. The community become one of the largest in the Trencin dist., reaching a pop. of 309 in 1787. A synagogue was erected in 1820. Following the exodus to the cities, the J. pop. dropped from 290 in 1869 to 65 in 1910 and 12 in 1940. On 25 April 1942, the Jews were deported to the Opole ghetto in the Lublin dist. of Poland.

CADCA (Hung. Csaca) Slovakia, Czechoslovakia, today Republic of Slovakia. Jews are known from the first half of the 18th cent. A wooden synagogue was built c. 1800. Most Jews lived in straitened economic circumstances and earned their living as itinerant peddlers. Their pop. rose to 132 in 1828 and a peak of 400 (total 5,207) in 1910, maintaining nearly that level until WWII. A J. school was started in the late 19th cent. and a new synagogue was consecrated in 1864. Jews became more active in the economy, running two large sawmills and also operating as lumber merchants. They served on the local council both before and after WWI. In postwar riots, J. stores were looted and Jews attacked. Jews owned 70 business establishments, 15 workshops, and six factories. All doc-

tors in the town were Jews. In 1928, the congregation joined the Liberal Jeshurun organization. The Zionists were active. In the Slovakian state (1938), Jews were forced out of their businesses. In March and April 1942, young J. men were deported to the Majdanek concentration camp and the women to Auschwitz. In June, about 200 Jews were deported to the death camps in the Lublin dist. of Poland.

CAIUTI Moldavia dist., Rumania. Jews first settled in the early 19th cent. A synagogue was built in 1868 on land donated by a Christian noblewoman. A branch of Hovevei Zion was opened in 1898. In 1899, the J. pop. peaked at 219, but then dropped in 1930 to 111 (28% of the total). Antisemitic acts were incited by the Goga-Coza regime in 1937. On 21 Jan. 1941 the Jews were given 24 hours to leave. Four or five Jews left for Tecuci and the rest for Bacau. Prior to their exodus, the local pop. began robbing J. homes, forcing the Jews to leave everything behind.

CAJLA Slovakia, Czechoslovakia, today Republic of Slovakia. Jews numbered about 200 in 1780 and 147 in 1840, maintaining a synagogue and cemetery. Only 38 remained in 1919.

CAKOVEC (Hung. Csaktornya) Croatia, Yugoslavia, today Republic of Croatia. A community was established in 1740 and by 1910 there were 300 Jews (total 5,887). Most of the commerce and industry was in J. hands. Zionism dominated from 1915 to 1941. In 1940 the Jews numbered 500 (total 7,000). In 1941, C. was annexed to Hungary and in 1943 all Jews aged 18–48 were drafted into labor battalions and sent to the Ukrainian front. Only a few returned. On 19 March 1944 the Germans took over and established a *Judenrat*. All the Jews were sent to the Najka-

nizha ghetto and from there to Auschwitz. In all, 430 Jews from C. were killed in the Holocaust.

CALAFAT Oltania dist., Rumania. Jews settled in the mid-19th cent. Due to the fierce antisemitism of the mixed Rumanian, Greek, and Bulgarian pop., their numbers declined from 293 in 1910 to 57 in 1930. From Sept. 1940 to Jan. 1941, half the J. pop. moved to Craiova; the remainder joined them in June 1941. After the war, the Jews never returned to C.

CALARASI Walachia dis., Rumania. Jews, primarily Sephardim from the Balkans, first settled in 1843. In 1898, the Hovevei Zion branch included all 73 heads of families. The J. pop. in 1930 was 327. On 23 Nov. 1940, all the 50 J. men in C. were arrested and tortured by members of the Iron Guard. On 6 July 1941, the train carrying 1,021 Jews from Iasi stopped at C. The 25 on the transport who had died were buried; the others were locked up in a barracks. In Aug. 1941, the remaining 980 Jews were returned to Iasi. From 1942 to 1944, C. Jews worked in forced labor battalions. After the war, about half the J. pop. immigrated to Israel.

CALARASI-TARG Bessarabia, Rumania, today Republic of Moldova. A J. community existed in the early 19th cent. and traded in agricultural products, especially plums, for which C. was famous. Jews were the main exporters of wines, fruit, and grain to Russia. With the arrival of the railway, they bought land, built houses, and set up factories. At the end of the 19th cent., J. schools were established with Hebrew as the language of instruction. The J. pop. in 1897 was 4,593 (89% of the total). On 23 Oct. 1905, local gangs and peasants attacked the J. pop., killing 60 and injuring 220. They burned 500 J. homes and destroyed most of the J. stores and workshops. About 600 Jews emigrated to the U.S., Canada, and Argentina. After WWI, antisemitic manifestations continued. Most of the Zionist youth movements were active. The J. pop. in 1930 was 3,631 (76% of the total). In 1940, after annexation to the USSR, the Soviets exiled Zionists, community leaders and wealthy Jews to Russia; most survived. The majority of the J. pop. fled with the retreating Soviet forces in 1941 and were saved. Others fled to Chisinau and shared the fate of the community. The remaining Jews were taken to the Vetomineasa woods and murdered.

CALATELE (Hung., Kiskalota) S. Transylvania dist., Rumania. A J. community was organized at the end of the 19th cent. Zionist activities developed between the World Wars. The J. pop. in 1930 was 61 (5% of the total). Exact details about the community are unavailable but it is assumed that after the outbreak of WWII, the J. pop., together with the rest of the Jews in the district, was transferred to Sarmas, Turda, and Ludus.

CALBE Saxony, Germany. A medieval J. community, which is first mentioned in 1365, came to an end in 1493, when all Jews of the Magdeburg archbishopric were expelled. From the 17th cent. on, Jews were living again in C., but their numbers remained small. It was not until 1840 that a prayer room was set up. A cemetery was established in 1863. In 1867, the community numbered 72. In 1933, only 26 Jews were still living in C. By 1936, four families and two individuals had emigrated, primarily abroad. On *Kristallnacht* (9–10 Nov. 1938), stores were wrecked and two couples were arrested, the men apparently taken to a concentration camp. Of the 12 Jews still living in C. in 1939, five were deported to the east.

CALINESTI (I) (Hung. Felsokalinfalva) N. Transylvania dist., Rumania. Jews settled in the late 18th cent. The J. pop. in 1930 was 148 (7% of the total). At the end of April 1944, the Jews were transferred to the Berbesti ghetto and in June deported to Auschwitz.

CALINESTI (II) (Hung. Kanyahaza) N. Transylvania dist., Rumania. Jews settled in the late 18th cent. The J. pop. in 1930 was 187 (9% of the total). In May 1944, the J. pop. was transferred to the Satu Mare ghetto and in June deported to Auschwitz.

CAMARZANA (Hung. Komorzan) N. Transylvania dist., Rumania. Jews settled in the late 18th cent. The J. pop. in 1930 was 134 (6% of the total). In May 1944, the community was transferred to the Satu Mare ghetto and in June deported to Auschwitz.

CAMBERG (now Bad Camberg) Hesse–Nassau, Germany. The J. community, established in the 18th cent., opened a new synagogue (1837) and numbered 115 (5% of the total) in 1880. Jews participated in the town's social life and were elected to the town council. By 1925 the community (excluding members

in Eisenbach and Steinfischbach) had declined to 72. On *Kristallnacht* (9–10 Nov. 1938), a mob vandalized and then demolished the synagogue. Of the 63 Jews living there in 1933, 34 emigrated and four committed suicide; at least 17 perished in the Holocaust.

CAMMIN (Pol. Kamien Pomorski) Pomerania, Germany, today Poland. Jews were trading in C. as early as 1663. At the beginning of the 18th cent. two J. families were given permission to live in the town. The community peaked at 113 members in 1880 and maintained a synagogue and a cemetery. When the Nazis came to power in 1933, there were 33 Jews in C. On *Kristallnacht* (9–10 Nov. 1938), the synagogue was set on fire, J. businesses were wrecked, and eight J. men were arrested. No further information about the fate of the Jews of C. is available.

CAMPIA TURZII (Hung. Aranyosgyeres) S. Transylvania dist., Rumania. A J. community existed in the late 19th cent. The J. pop. in 1930 was 208 (5% of the total). During the 1930s, many moved to Hungary. The J. pop. was expelled in summer 1941 to Turda, Sarmas, and Ludus. About 60 returned after the war.

CAMPINA Walachia dist., Rumania. J. oil experts settled near the refinery at the end of the 19th cent. A synagogue was built in 1902 and in 1910, 37 pupils attended the J. school. The J. pop. in 1930 was 319 (2% of the total). On 15 July 1941, after the Soviets bombed the refinery, the J. males were taken to the Teisi concentration camp. The women and children were expelled to Ploiesti. The majority returned after the war.

CAMPULUNG LA TISA (Hung. Hosszumezo) N. Transylvania dist., Rumania. A J. community existed from the 1870s. The J. pop. in 1930 was 317 (11% of the total). The Jews were transferred to the Aknaszlatina ghetto in April 1944 and on 25 May deported to Auschwitz.

CAMPULUNG-MOLDOVENESC Bukovina, Rumania. Jews settled in the mid-18th cent. Under Austrian rule, they dominated the lumber industry and owned several vacation hostels in the area. Branches of the Zionist youth movements were founded after WWI. The J. pop. in 1930 was 1,488 (15% of the total). Antisemitism was rife during the 1930s. In

1940, the Iron Guard plundered J. property. In Oct. 1941, the J. pop. was transferred to Atachi; the elderly and sick were murdered on the way. The Jews were subsequently moved to Zhmerinka, Shargorod, and Murafa. Many died in the 1942–43 typhus epidemic. When Transnistria was captured by the Soviets in 1944, the men were conscripted into the army and the women sent to work. In 1947, 1,350 Jews, mainly from north Bukovina, lived in C. The majority immigrated to Israel.

CANA (Hung. Hernadcsany) Slovakia, Czechoslovakia, today Republic of Slovakia. Jews probably settled in the 1740s, reaching a pop. of 60 in 1828 and 151 (total 1,425) in 1910. The community maintained a synagogue and cemetery. In 1941, 107 Jews remained. The Jews of C. earned their livelihood from trade and agriculture and as artisans. In 1940, they were seized for forced labor in the Hungarian army. In April 1944 they were moved to Kosice and from there deported to Auschwitz on 17 May.

CANTAVIR Vojvodina dist., Yugoslavia. The community dates from the mid-19th cent. The J. pop. in 1931 was 78 (total 11,287). The community was completely destroyed in the Holocaust.

CAPRESTI Bessarabia, Rumania, today Republic of Moldova. Jews founded C. in 1853 and engaged in agriculture. Between the World Wars Communists and members of Alexandru Cuza's fascist organization incited the local pop. against the "J. parasites." The J. pop. in 1930 was 1,815 (90% of the total). In 1934, the community split into two. The communal institutions were reorganized. Zionist organizations were active. The majority of the J. pop was annihilated during WWII, but no specific details are available.

CARACAL Oltania dist., Rumania. The J. pop. in C. stood at 230 in 1894 and a J. community was established in 1898. A Hovevei Zion branch was founded in the same year. A synagogue and elementary school were built in 1901. The J. pop. in 1930 was 118 (1% of the total). The Jews were persecuted by the Iron Guard in 1940, and in 1941 most Jews left. After the war, the majority returned.

CARANSEBES (Hung. Karansebes) S. Transylvania dist., Rumania. Jews first settled in the mid-18th

cent., but a community was only established in 1874. During the following decades it developed. The economic situation in the community was good and there were several wealthy members involved in the mining industry. The J. pop. in 1930 was 329 (4% of the total). Zionist youth movements were very active between the World Wars. At the outbreak of WWII, the Jews were forced to forfeit their property. After the war, communal activities were renewed.

CARASEU (Hung. Szamoskrasso) N. Transylvania dist., Rumania. Jews settled in the late 18th cent. The J. pop. in 1930 was 91 (6% of the total). In May 1944, the community was transferred to the Satu Mare ghetto and then deported to Auschwitz.

CAREI (Hung. Nagykaroly) N. Transylvania dist., Rumania. Twelve J. families from Pressburg, Moldavia, and Galicia were brought here in 1720 by the local count, who built houses for them and granted permission to trade. In the late 18th and early 19th cents. restrictions on additional J. settlement and trade were imposed. The J. pop. in 1869 was 2,106 (17% of the total). In 1871 a very elegant synagogue seating over 1,000 was consecrated. A J. school was established in 1785 and had 206 pupils in 1894. Jews fought in the Hungarian war of independence (1848-49) and served in the Hungarian national guard. The first Hasidim to enter Transylvania were R. Levi Yitzhak of Berdichev and R. Aharon of Zhitomir, who were forced to leave after three years. From the 1850s, Jews were permitted to trade freely and some entered the free professions. At the end of the 19th cent., most financial institutions in C. belonged to Jews. In 1881, 60 Jews left the community and joined the Orthodox movement and set up a community with its own facilities and rabbi, Moshe Shwartz, who opened a yeshiva that became one of the largest in Transylvania. In 1901, the Great Synagogue of the Orthodox community was dedicated. The declining economic situation after the war forced hundreds of Jews to leave. Under the influence of the noted hasidic rabbi, Yoel Teitelbaum, who came to C. in 1926 the Orthodox community followed hasidic customs and wore hasidic dress, and 250 pupils attended his yeshiva. After R. Teitelbaum left in 1934, a split occurred in the hasidic community with reverberations throughout the country. The conductor, Miklos Brodi, some of whose works were based on biblical themes, was

born in C. Zionist activity developed in the 1930s. The annexation of Transylvania to Hungary in Sept. 1940 brought a deterioration in the situation of the Jews, caused by the predominant Hungarian and German pop. who joined Nazi-supported organizations. Trading permits were revoked and Jews were forced to forfeit their factories and shops to Hungarians and Germans. The J. pop. in 1941 was 2,255 (14% of the total). On 1 July 1942, 150 Jews aged 21-42 were drafted into labor battalions in the Ukraine, where 80% died. The community was persecuted by local Nazis and Hungarian soldiers. After the German conquest on 19 March 1944, further restrictions were imposed on Jews. On 13 May, the community was transferred to Satu Mare and on 20 May deported to Auschwitz. After the war, 400 survivors returned and by 1947 the community increased to 600, but during the 1950s Jews began to leave. Only a small number remained.

CARLIBABA (Ger. Kirlibaba), Bukovina, Rumania. The J. pop. in 1930 was 154. There was Zionist activity between the World Wars. In 1942, the young men were drafted into labor battalions in the Ukraine. In spring 1944, the J. pop. was deported to Auschwitz.

CARLSRUHE (Pol. Pokoj) Upper Silesia, Germany, today Poland. An organized community of 96 was in existence in 1842, reaching a peak pop. of 128 in 1861. The community maintained a synagogue and cemetery along with J. educational facilities. On the eve of the Nazi rise to power in 1933, 42 Jews remained. The Nazi racial laws were not applied until 16 July 1937 since the Jews were under the protection of the League of Nations' minority rights convention. On *Kristallnacht* (9-10 Nov. 1938), the synagogue was set on fire and a number of J. homes and stores were destroyed. Most of the Jews emigrated.

CARPATHOS (Karpathos) Dodecanese Islands, Greece. In 1901, 15 J. Romaniot tradesmen lived in C.

CARPENTRAS Vaucluse dist., France. The J. presence in C. dates to the 12th century. The Jews of C. together with those of Avignon, Cavaillon and L'Isle-sur-Sorgue, formed the Four Holy Communities of Comtat-Venaissin, part of the papal territory in France. They shared a unique liturgy called *Comtadin*, which was based on old Provencal rites and similar to Portu-

guese practices. The Jews were expelled at the beginning of the 13th cent. but returned and were expelled again in 1269. In 1276, 64 heads of J. families signed an agreement with the papal administration, regarding payment for the privilege of residence. The Jews of C. welcomed exiles from France after the expulsions of 1306 and 1322, but then they, too, were forced to leave the locality. The community was renewed in 1343 and its new synagogue was built in 1367. At this time, the community numbered 98 families, most engaged in brokerage, moneylending, and commerce in agricultural products. After a riot in 1459 in which 60 Jews were killed, restrictions, primarily economic, were imposed on the Jews. In 1473 there were 69 J. families (298 persons), who four years later were transferred to a special street, the Carriere in the center of the town. A century later, the community had dwindled, numbering only six families in 1571. Due to the influx of Jews from neighboring localities in Comtat-Venaissin, there were 83 families in C. in 1669. A synagogue was built between 1741–43. The community had reached its maximum size in the second half of the 18th cent., numbering 1,200 persons in 1760 and 2,000 in 1789. Afterwards it dwindled, numbering 360 members in 1811. In the 1920s, religious services were held only on Yom Kippur. The synagogue, declared an historical building in 1924, was partly restored in 1930. During WWII, there were no more than 12 families in C., which was located in Vichy France. After the war, the synagogue was repaired (in 1953) and in 1959 it was declared a national historic site. With the influx to France of Jews from North Africa, the community numbered 140 members in 1964.

CARTHAGE   Tunis dist., Tunisia. The ancient J. community is known only from the first cent. C.E. in the Roman period, its size attested by the writings of Josephus and the Church Fathers and by a large cemetery discovered by archeologists. The *amoraim* R. Abba and R. Hinna were active there after the destruction of the Second Temple, when the community grew considerably. The conversion of Berbers to Judaism in this period may have contributed to its size. The city declined under the Moslems, with the center of J. life shifting to Kairouan. Jews were not heard from again in C. until after WWII, when over 1,000 refugees from Tunis arrived to escape the Allied bombings. These returned home after the war. A 1946 census recorded the presence of 1,064 Jews (21.8% of the total).

CASALE MONFERRATO   Piedmont, Italy. The Jews are mentioned as settling in C. in the 1430s when the town was ruled by the Paleologi. During the rule of the Gonzaga dukes, between 1536–1708, the number of Jews increased and they established an organized community. In 1551, seven families bought land for a cemetery. In 1570, Duke Gugliemo of Mantova and Monferrato granted them privileges. By 1590, communal life was organized and 27 families bought land for another cemetery. A synagogue dedicated in 1595 was enlarged in 1662 and completely restored in 1866. The local Jews were mainly engaged in moneylending as well as commerce. In 1611, they were accused of a blood libel which led to anti-J. measures. The Jews were forced to reside in a separate quarter, to wear the J. badge, and to pay heavy taxes. By 1709, when C. was passed to the dukes of Savoy, the condition of the Jews deteriorated. In 1724 a ghetto was established in C. and from that time on the Jews were no longer entitled to own real estate. According to the 1761 census, there were 136 J. families (673 persons) in C. The French Revolution signaled the beginning of freedom for the local Jews, who received civil rights. However these were abrogated in 1814 and they were once again restricted to living in the ghetto. A general council was established in Piedmont to improve the political and civil status of the local Jews. The community, numbering 850, was fully emancipated in 1848. When in March 1849, during the war of Piedmont against Austria, Austrian troops marched into C., Jews actively participated in defending the city. The success in defeating the enemy is commemorated in local tradition by a special Purim festival held on the second month of Nissan every year. *Vessillo Israelitico*, founded by R. Flaminio Servi in 1874 and published in C., was a popular periodical among Italian Jews until 1922. In 1888 the C. community consisted of 750 members, dropping to 109 in 1938. During WWII, there were only 79 Jews in C. (1940). Fourteen converted to Christianity. The number of Jews diminished in 1942–43. After Sept. 1943 and Italy's capitulation, the majority found refuge in neighboring cities or in Switzerland. Those who remained were sent to forced labor camps. Several old and poor Jews were arrested in Feb. and April 1944. Altogether 19 were deported from C., but there is evidence that an additional 40 Jews from C. were deported from other cities to extermination camps. There was only one survivor. After the war,

the community consisted of 44 persons, dropping to 20 in the 1960s.

CASLAV Bohemia, Czechoslovakia, today Czech Republic. Jews settled after the 1848 revolution and numbered 300 by 1870. A synagogue was opened in 1900 and the community also maintained a J. school. In 1930, 119 Jews remained (total 10,635). The film director Milos Forman was born (1932) in C. In 1942, the Jews were deported to the Theresienstadt ghetto together with the Jews of Prague and from there to the death camps of Poland.

CASTA Slovakia, Czechoslovakia, today Republic of Slovakia. Jews arrived in the 17th cent., if not before, forming an independent community in the early 18th cent. and erecting synagogues in 1759 and 1884. Their pop. reached a peak of 270 (total 1,538) in 1828 and then declined steadily to 171 in 1880 and 28 in 1940. In the Slovakian state, J. businesses were closed down or "Aryanized" and in 1942 the remaining Jews were deported to the death camps in the east.

CASTROP-RAUXEL Westphalia, Germany. Jews were present in small numbers from the late 16th cent. with a community beginning to form in the late 19th cent. A synagogue was consecrated in 1845, also housing a J. school. The J. pop. rose to 81 in 1849 and 130 in 1900. The economic position of the Jews improved following the industrial development of the Ruhr region in the early 20th cent. All but one of the city's major business establishments was in J. hands. In 1932, the J. pop. was 160 (about 3% of the total). By 1939, about three-quarters had left the city, many to the U.S. and Palestine. The synagogue was destroyed on *Kristallnacht* (9–10 Nov. 1938), and the last nine Jews were deported to death camps in the east in 1942.

CAUSANII-NOUI Bessarabia, Rumania, today Republic of Moldova. A J. community existed here in 1760 and up to WWI suffered from poverty. It dwindled from 800 to 500 families, but after the war the economic situation improved. Six synagogues served the Zionists and the various artisans' unions. Zionist activity among the youth began in the late 1920s. The J. pop. in 1930 was 1,870 (35% of the total). In 1940, Zionists and those considered wealthy by the Soviet rulers were exiled to Siberia; most died there. Others escaped to

Odessa with the retreating Red Army in 1941 and shared the fate of the Jews there. The remaining Jews were murdered in C. by Ukrainians.

CECE Fejer dist., Hungary. Jews were present in the 17th cent. and a synagogue was built by the end of the 18th cent. The J. pop. was 398 in 1840, afterwards dropping as Jews left for the big cities. After WWI, C. became a center of the antisemitic Arrow Cross Party. In 1941, the men were drafted for forced labor in the Ukraine, where many died. The 50 remaining Jews were brought to the Sarbogard ghetto at the end of May and then to the Kaspovar ghetto towards the end of June, before final deportation to Auschwitz at the beginning of July 1944.

CECHOWKA Warsaw dist., Poland. The J. pop. in 1921 was 143 (total 792). All 600 Jews including refugees were expelled by the Germans to the Warsaw ghetto on 27 March 1942, sharing the fate of the Jews there.

CEGLED Pest–Pilis–Solt–Kiskun dist., Hungary. Jews settled in the first half of the 19th cent., forming a Neologist congregation in 1869 and reaching a peak. pop. of 1,121 (3% of the total) in 1910. A J. school established by the end of the 19th cent. was in operation until the Holocaust and a magnificent synagogue was built in 1905. Jews suffered in the White Terror after WWI and their economic life was undermined by Hungary's racial laws of 1938. In 1941, male members of the community, young and old, were sent to forced labor in the Ukraine, where most died. In 1941, 659 Jews remained. They were deported to Auschwitz after being expelled to Kecskemet at the end of June 1944. In 1946, 150 survivors reestablished the community.

CEHUL SILVANIEI (Hung. Szilagycseh) N. Transylvania dist., Rumania. An organized J. community existed in the early 19th cent. In 1901 a synagogue was consecrated and the *mikve* erected nearby also functioned as the public bathhouse. R. Moshe Klein served the community from 1870 and established a yeshiva for students from the Salaj dist. In WWI, 60 Jews were conscripted into the Hungarian army; five fell in battle. During the chaos following WWI, a gang organized by Sandor Szekely plundered J. property and a J. self-defense group fought back. Zionist

Sept. 1939 and instituted a regime of unremitting persecution. On 28 Aug. 1942, 34 Jews were murdered in C. prior to transfer to Slomniki, from where they were deported to the Belzec death camp. A small group left behind in C. to arrange J. property and possessions was brought to the nearby forest and killed at the end of 1942.

CHASHNIKI   Vitebsk dist., Belorussia. Jews settled in the 17th cent. Their pop. was 215 in 1766 and 3,480 (total 4,590) in 1897. In 1910 state-run and private J. schools were in operation. In 1924, under the Soviets, a J. council (soviet) was established and a J. elementary school was open until the late 1930s. Thirty-nine percent of the Jews were artisans and 18 J. families worked on a number of kolkhozes founded nearby in the late 1920s. In 1939 the J. pop. was 1,109. The Germans occupied the town on 4 July 1941. J. homes were marked and Jews forced to wear the Star of David. Tributes in gold and silver were exacted from the community. On 14 Feb. 1942, 1,000 Jews were herded into a church and the next day murdered beside freshly dug pits.

CHASOV YAR   Stalino dist., Ukraine. The J. pop. in 1939 was 254 (total 24,312). The Germans captured C. on 31 March 1941 and those Jews who had neither fled nor been evacuated perished during the occupation.

CHATEAU-SALINS   (during the German occupation, Salzburgen) Moselle dist., France. The synagogue was inaugurated in 1844. In 1885 there were 816 Jews in C., but then their number dwindled, to 495 in 1910 and 289 in 1931. During WWII, the Germans expelled the local Jews to the south of France. The synagogue was partly destroyed. In the 1960s only 12 Jews remained in C.

CHAUSY   Mogilev dist., Belorussia. Jews were already present at the time of the Russo-Polish war of 1654. The Russians took many Jews as prisoners and they died far from home, with the municipality confiscating their property. In 1623, King Michael Wisnio-wiecki of Poland ordered their property restored and accorded the Jews a charter of rights confirmed by subsequent kings. The J. pop. rose from 283 in 1765 to 1,325 in 1785. Of the town's 134 merchants, 118 were Jews. In 1897, the J. pop. was 2,515 (total 4,960), dropping to 1,757 in 1926 under the Soviets.

Two J. kolkhozes were set up near the town, one in 1927 with 20 families and the other in 1928 with 12 families. Many Jews worked in artisan cooperatives, mainly as tailors and shoemakers. A J. elementary school was active in 1931. In 1939, the J. pop. was 1,272, with J. refugees arriving from occupied Poland. The Germans captured C. on 15 July 1941. In Aug., they concentrated the Jews in a ghetto and in the fall took them outside the city and murdered them on the way to the village of Dranukha. Children of mixed marriages were murdered later.

CHEB   Bohemia (Sudetenland), Czechoslovakia, today Czech Republic. The community, one of the oldest in Bohemia, most likely in existence from the 13th cent., enjoyed various privileges. It reached a pop. of 1,000–3,000 in the first half of the 14th cent. In 1350, almost all the Jews were massacred within a few hours by their Christian neighbors, incited by the local priest. The street in which they lived came to be known as "Murder Lane" (*Mordgaesschen*). A new ghetto was established in 1352, but after subsequent expulsions in 1430 and 1502, a new community was only founded in 1853. A splendid new synagogue was consecrated in 1893 as the pop. reached a peak of 500–550 (about 2% of the total), maintained until the 1930s. C. was the birthplace of the pianist Rudolf Serkin (1903–91). The Jews left after the Germans destroyed their stores on 12 Sept. 1938. The city's two synagogues were burned on 23 Sept.

CHECHELNIK   Vinnitsa dist., Ukraine. In 1765 the J. pop. was 485. Jews suffered grievously from Cossack and Haidamak attacks on the town. In 1897, their pop. was 3,388 (total 8,000). In the 1920s, a J. council (soviet) and J. elementary school were established along with a J. kolkhoz. In 1939 the J. pop. was 1,327. The Germans captured the town on 24 July 1941. After its annexation to Transnistria, the Rumanians set up a ghetto there and appointed a *Judenrat*. The ghetto held 600–800 local Jews and probably over 1,000 from Bessarabia and Bukovina. Of the refugees, 475 were still there on 1 Sept. 1943. Many died of disease and from the regime of hard labor under the occupation.

CHECHERSK   Gomel dist., Belorussia. The J. pop. was 301 in 1766 and 1,700 (total 2,316) in 1897. A synagogue and two prayer houses served the commun-

ity and in 1903 a modernized *heder* was opened. In 1905, a J. self-defense group was formed. In the first half of the 1920s, under the Soviets, teachers at the *hadarim* still operating were prosecuted. In 1930, 37 J. families were employed in two kolkhozes. A J. elementary school was active. In 1939 the J. pop. was 977. The Germans captured the town on 14 Aug. 1941 after most of the Jews fled. A ghetto for the 200 remaining Jews was established immediately. In late Nov., 80 were executed beside an antitank ditch. The rest of the Jews were murdered there together with gypsies in late Dec. in an *Aktion* that took 350 lives.

CHELM Lublin dist., Poland. Jews may have been present in the 12th cent. and constituted one of the largest and most important communities in Poland by the 16th cent., standing at the head of an autonomous district. Its first rabbi, Yehuda Aharon, received the title *doctor legus mosaicae* and also presided over the Lublin and Belz districts. His son R. Eliyahu Ba'al Shem of C. (d. 1590) was among the outstanding

Zionist workers demonstrating in Chelm, Poland, 1932 (YIVO Archive, New York/photo courtesy of Yad Vashem, The Holocaust Martyrs' and Heroes' Remembrance Authority, Jerusalem)

kabbalists of the age. R. Shemuel Eliezer ben Yehuda Edels (1555–1631), one of the greatest of the J. sages, officiated in 1605–15. Reference to the slaughter of the 400-member community in 1648 during the Chmielnicki massacres is made in the *El Ma'ale Rahamin* prayer which was composed at this time. Recovery was apparently rapid and in the 17th cent. the community was active in the Council of the Four Lands. It was also one of the first to come under the influence of Hasidism. R. Yosef Kazis, R. Natan Nota (d. 1812), and R. Avraham Yehoshua Heschel Leiner founded dynasties that endured until WWII. Economic conditions improved in the 18th cent. as Jews engaged in the hide and horse trade. However, their position was weakened when the Polish Sejm instituted discriminatory measures in 1789 as well as after the Third Partition of Poland in 1795, when traditional trade routes were closed off and Russian rule undermined economic stability. The J. pop. grew from 1,902 in 1827 to 7,226 in 1897 and 12,064 (total 23,221) in 1921. Over time, the Jews of C. inexplicably earned a reputation for simplemindedness, giving rise to numerous entertaining stories and making "Chelm" and "Chelmer" bywords in the J. world. Despite the rise of modern political movements in C. after WWI, Hasidism preserved its strength, though a number of Hebrew schools now competed with the *heder* system that had prevailed for hundreds of years. Zionist activity intensified after the publication of the Balfour Declaration in 1917, with Hashomer Hatzair becoming the first youth movement to open its doors. The Bund operated from 1905 but declined after 1924 when many of its leaders emigrated to the Americas. Three Yiddish newspapers were published in C. The community supported numerous welfare services, with WIZO helping orphans and needy children and TOZ providing health care. On the eve of WWII there were about 15,000 Jews in C. The Germans occupied the city on 9 Oct. 1939, immediately instituting a regime of severe persecution. On 1 Dec., they led 2,000 Jews in a death march to the Bug River. Only 150 survived. A *Judenrat* was then appointed and in Oct. 1940 the Jews were confined to a ghetto, which was sealed off in late 1941. Hunger and disease claimed many lives. Deportations to the Sobibor death camp commenced on 22 May 1942, when 3,000 Jews were packed into cattle cars and transported there for extermination, followed by 2,000 Jews from Slovakia who arrived in the ghetto on the same day. In June, another 600 were sent to So-

bibor as able-bodied workers. On 27–28 Oct., 3,000 were led in a forced march to Wlodawa for deportation. Few survived. The last Jews were sent to Sobibor on 6 Nov. 1942. After the war, a few hundred Jews, mostly from places of refuge in the Soviet Union, returned to C., but all soon left in the face of the violent antisemitism that persisted in the city and in Poland as a whole.

CHELMNO   (Ger. Kulm) Pomerania dist., Poland. J. settlement began after the annexation to Prussia in 1772. By 1815, 11 J. families were living there under "protected" status, earning a livelihood in the grain trade. Despite the city's antisemitic atmosphere and stiff competition from German merchants, the J. pop. grew rapidly to 1,075 in 1855 and economic conditions improved. In the religious sphere, the Liberals were highly influential. Subsequently emigration was stepped up and the J. pop. fell to 463 in 1895 (total 10,523) and 74 in 1921. Those remaining were presumably expelled from the city immediately after its capture by the Germans in Sept. 1939.

CHELMNO CAMP   (Ger. Kulmhof) extermination camp, south of the city of C., in a village of the same name. This was the first Nazi death camp and began to operate in Dec. 1941. Victims were sealed into trucks 50–70 at a time and asphyxiated by exhaust fumes while the vehicle was en route to the mass graves dug at the burial site. The killing continued until March 1943 and, after a pause, from April to Aug. 1944. From then until Jan. 1945 the Nazis tried to destroy the evidence of their crimes. Among their victims were the Jews of the Lodz ghetto and other settlements in the Warthegau dist. Also killed in C. were hundreds of Poles, Russian prisoners of war, and children from the Czech village of Lidice. In all, about 250,000 died there.

CHELMZHA   (Ger. Culmsee) Pomerania dist., Poland. Jews first settled after the annexation to Prussia in 1772. With the achievement of equal rights in the first half of the 19th cent., they branched out into a variety of occupations, including farming, innkeeping, building, and banking. The J. pop. reached a peak of 664 in 1885, with a well-to-do minority displaying assimilationist and Liberal religious tendencies. Emigration reduced the J. pop. to 72 in 1921. The Zionists were active between the World Wars. The last remain-

ing Jews were expelled by the Germans to General Gouvernement territory in Nov. 1939.

CHEMEROVTSY   (Yid. Chemirovits) Kamenets-Podolski dist., Ukraine. Jews are first mentioned in 1578. In 1897, they numbered 1,231 (41% of the total). In the Soviet period, a J. council and kolkhoz were functioning. In 1939, the J. pop. was 1,139. The Germans occupied the town on 9 July 1941. In the second half of July 1941, local Ukrainians murdered 161 Jews in a pogrom instigated by a Russian Orthodox priest. The remaining Jews were transferred to the Kamenets-Podolski ghetto in summer 1942 and murdered in the fall. Eighteen Jews, including children, were shot in the market square on 4 Oct. 1942.

CHEMNITZ   (from 1953 until 1990 Karl-Marx-Stadt) Saxony, Germany. The first documentary evidence of Jews living in C. dates from 1357. After a residence ban on Jews was issued in 1539, no Jews settled in C. until the middle of the 19th cent. Despite virulent antisemitism, a community of 101 developed in 1871. From 1875, welfare organizations were founded and religious services were held in private apartments. In 1876 a religious school was set up; a cemetery was established in 1879; and a rabbi was engaged in 1881. By 1890, the community numbered 955 people, and in 1899 a synagogue was consecrated where services were held in accordance with Liberal practices, including a synagogue choir. In 1903, a branch of the Central Union (C.V.) was founded, followed in 1906 by a local Zionist group. Around this time, Jews from Eastern Europe arrived in C. and during WWI some 1,200 East European Jews, who were expelled from Leipzig and Dresden, were interned near C. The C. community council cared for these internees, many of whom became residents of the city. In 1925, the J. pop. was 3,500, of whom only 1,400 were German nationals. However, the immigrant East European Jews gained the right to vote in communal elections only after a bitter fight—waged primarily by the Zionists. Even then they were not allowed to run for office. In the 1920s, in addition to the synagogue, there were two Orthodox prayer rooms and in 1922, Orthodox Jews set up a *talmud torah* school, which had an enrollment of 200 children; 155 children attended the Liberal religious school. The community maintained welfare and sports associations, youth groups, and various Liberal and Zionist organizations. A cultural and administrative

center opened in 1932. Most community members were self-employed (including, in 1930, 25 J. physicians and 12 lawyers) or employed as white-collar personnel. There were very few blue-collar workers. J. firms controlled 35% of the city's textile industry. In the Weimar period, two Jews served on the city council and one community member was the editor of a Communist newspaper. In 1927, Nazis attacked a Jew, who died from his injuries.

When the Nazis came to power in 1933, the J. pop. was 2,796 (0.68% of the total). In the boycott of J. businesses that began on 1 April 1933, apartments were also searched and arrests made. A J. attorney was murdered and a J. manufacturer shot himself in order to escape "protective" custody. Even after the official end of the boycott, the measures continued. The city's J. theater director fled when he heard that the Nazis were searching for him. In 1935, there were still 2,387 Jews in C. and, according to Nazi statistics, there were still 118 J. stores and workshops. Eighteen physicians, seven dentists, and five lawyers were still practicing. From 1935, the clientele of J. businesses was increasingly harassed, and "Aryanization" measures were stepped up considerably.

The community, which had published a community newspaper since 1933, expanded its internal cultural life with a whole range of sports, cultural, and educational activities. A ski lodge, which the community had in the Erz Mountains, served as a hiding place for members of the German Social Democratic Party (SPD) escaping to Prague. In spring 1938, the community finally received permission to set up a J. school, which in Oct. 1938 was attended by 150 students. At this time a ban was imposed on the publication of the community newspaper, and 318 Jews of non-German citizenship were deported to Poland. On *Kristallnacht* (9–10 Nov. 1938), the synagogue was set on fire and 171 Jews were arrested and brutally treated before they were taken to the Buchenwald concentration camp. One man was shot, another died in Buchenwald. Two died after their release from the aftereffects of their imprisonment. Rabbi Dr. Fuchs (in office since 1907) escaped arrest because a non-J. physician protected him. The community was presented with the bill for the clearing-up operations after the rioting and in April 1939, it was compelled to sell the synagogue site. A prayer room was established elsewhere on a makeshift basis. In 1939, there were 2,096 Jews in C.; only a small percentage had emi-

grated. From this time on, Jews were billeted in "J. houses" and conscripted for forced labor. In 1942, the Nazis closed down the J. school. There were six deportations to the east, from Jan. 1942 to June 1943. There were two further operations aimed at those of partial J. descent (*Mischlinge*) in Jan. 1944 and Feb. 1945. A total of 2,000 C. Jews were deported. Almost all perished. A small community with 57 members was reestablished in 1945. By 1960 its membership had dwindled to 20.

CHENCINI   Kielce dist., Poland. Jews settled in the mid-16th cent. and in 1602 received a royal privilege lifting all residence restrictions and permitting them to produce and sell alcoholic beverages. In the wake of the mid-17th cent. Swedish war, just 34 J. families remained in the town but their privileges were renewed and the J. pop. grew to 912 in 1765, when Jews owned 14 bakeries, 11 distilleries, and five slaughterhouses. In 1897, the J. pop. reached 4,361 (total 6,177) but it dropped to 2,835 in 1921 after many left for nearby Kielce with its burgeoning industry. Jews in C. were mainly employed as artisans, owning 55 of the city's 66 workshops. In the 1930s their economic position deteriorated further in the face of Polish competition and anti-J. agitation, with just 10% of the labor force finding employment locally. The Germans captured the city on 5 Sept. 1939, murdering Jews at random, including the rabbi, while Poles forcibly took over J. businesses and a regime of forced labor and extortion was instituted. On 11 Dec., the Germans appointed a *Judenrat* and on 10 July 1941 they set up a ghetto, crowding together 4,000 Jews. On 13 Sept. 1942, nearly all were deported to the Treblinka death camp. There were only 30 survivors after the war. Several returned to C. but soon left.

CHEPA   (Hung. Csepe) Carpatho-Russia, Czechoslovakia, today Ukraine. J. settlement began in the latter half of the 18th cent. with a total of four J. families present in 1768. In 1880, the J. pop. was 80. A few families farmed and Jews owned two flour mills. The J. pop. rose to 179 (total 975) in 1921 and then dropped to 158 in 1941. C. was the birthplace of R. Yisrael Yehuda Berkovits, one of the leaders of Mizrachi in Czechoslovakia. The Hungarians occupied C. in Nov. 1938 and in 1941 drafted dozens of Jews into forced labor battalions. In late July 1941 a number of Jews without Hungarian citizenship were expelled to the German-oc-

cupied Ukraine and murdered. In the second half of May 1944, the rest were deported to Auschwitz.

CHEREYA Vitebsk dist., Belorussia. Jews settled in the late 17th cent. Their pop. was 399 in 1766 and 1,829 (total 3,039) in 1897, dropping to 1,098 in 1926 under the Soviets. A J. elementary school was active. The Germans captured C. on 4 July 1941. Only a few Jews escaped. The Germans instituted a regime of forced labor and on 5 March 1942 executed the Jews. Some skilled workers, who had been allowed to live, were murdered later on.

CHERIKOV Mogilev dist., Belorussia. Jews settled in the early 17th cent., receiving a charter of rights from King Wladyslaw IV in 1648. In the Chmielnicki massacres of 1648–49 Cossack troops attacked the Jews but the settlement was renewed and a community again organized. King Augustus II confirmed the old charter in 1720. In 1766, the J. pop. was 186, increasing to 2,698 in 1897. A J. school was opened in 1882. In the late 19th cent., the Zionists became active, founding a library with a reading room and lectures. Five Jews were elected to the municipal council in 1917. In 1924, under the Soviets, J. breadwinners included 17 blue-collar workers, 80 artisans, and 352 farmers. In 1925, a J. kolkhoz was started nearby, employing ten J. families in 1930. Two other kolkhozes employed another 39 J. families in 1930. In 1939, the J. pop. of C. was 949 (total 6,411). The Germans captured C. on 17 July 1941 and on 28 Oct. executed about 500 Jews at the flour mill on the outskirts of the town. Jews in mixed marriages along with their children and other Jews caught in hiding were murdered in Nov. 1941 and winter 1942.

CHERKASY Kiev dist., Ukraine. J. settlement commenced in the 16th cent. In 1765, the J. pop. was 171

Jewish children in classroom, Cherkasy, Ukraine, 1917 (The Central Archive for the History of the Jewish People, Jerusalem/photo courtesy of Yad Vashem, The Holocaust Martyrs' and Heroes' Remembrance Authority, Jerusalem)

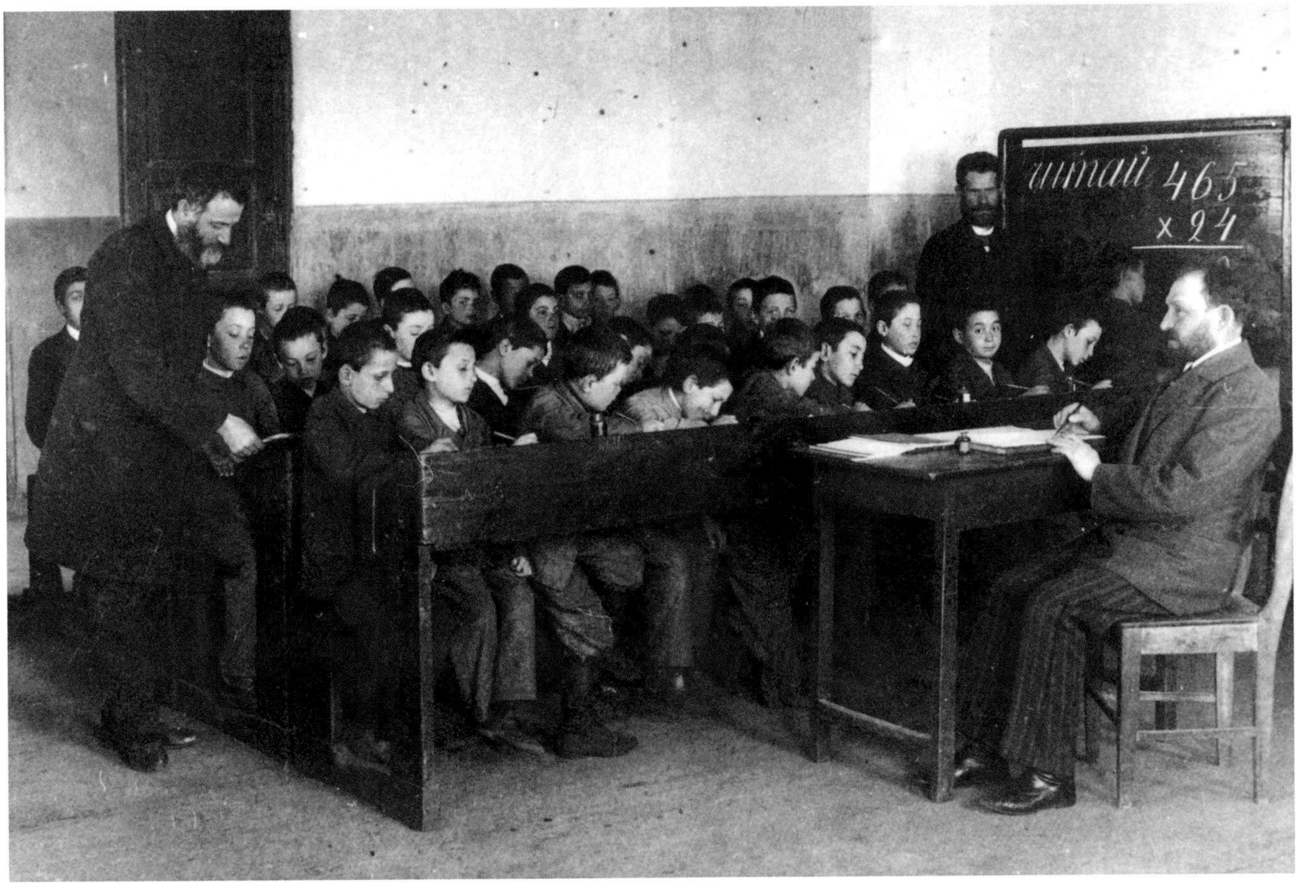
465
x 94

but Haidamak attacks put an end to the community. The J. pop. again grew in the 19th cent., reaching 10,950 in 1897. Jews contributed significantly to the development of the local food industry. In 1910, a group of J. tailors founded a cooperative. Most Jews were Hasidim. Among the community's better-known rabbis were Nahum Zalman Schneersohn and R. Twersky. A Zionist society was founded in the early 20th cent. and Hehalutz opened a branch in 1920. A third of the representatives on the municipal council were Jews. Anton Denikin's White Army soldiers murdered 700 Jews on 16–20 May 1919. In Aug., the Petlyura gangs attacked the Jews, causing heavy damage to J. homes and other property. In 1924, under the Soviets, 67 J. families (337 people) founded a kolkhoz. In 1925, a J. law court and a J. section in the police were set up. Two Yiddish-language schools, one vocational and the other including high school classes, were operating in the city. In 1939, the J. pop. was 7,637. The Germans captured C. on 22 Aug. 1941. On 10 Nov., a ghetto was established and in late Nov. about 900 Jews were murdered in a first *Aktion*. Almost all the rest were murdered in a second *Aktion* in 1942. A Ukrainian woman hid and saved 25 J. orphans.

CHERNA (Hung. Csarnato) Carpatho-Russia, Czechoslovakia, today Ukraine. Jews probably settled in the mid-19th cent., numbering 39 (total 410) in 1880 and 128 in 1921 and 1941. Following the German occupation in March 1944, they shared the fate of the rest of the Jews in the region.

CHERNEVKA Mogilev dist., Belorussia. In the mid-1920s, under the Soviets, 32 J. families were employed in agriculture and in 1930, 43 J. families worked at a kolkhoz. The Germans arrived in July 1941. In Aug. they murdered 200 local residents (probably most of them J. men) and in Sept. another 600 Jews (women and children) from C. and its environs.

CHERNEVTSY Vinnitsa dist., Ukraine. Jews numbered 53 in 1784 and 2,274 (total 8,994) in 1897. In the Soviet period, about 200 children attended a J. school in the mid-1920s. In the late 1930s, many of the town's 400 factory workers were Jews and some worked at a J. kolkhoz. In 1939, the J. pop. was 1,455. The Germans occupied C. on 21 July 1941. In July–Aug., they murdered 479 Jews from the region, including many from C. After the town was annexed to Transnistria in early

Sept., the Rumanians established a ghetto there under a regime of forced labor and extortionate fines. They also transferred to C. 170 Jews from Bessarabia and 279 from Bukovina.

CHERNIAKHOV Zhitomir dist., Ukraine. Jews are first mentioned in 1629. The community was destroyed in the Chmielnicki massacres of 1648–49 and only in 1721 are Jews mentioned again. In 1897 their pop. was 1,774 (total 3,878). During the Russian civil war (1918–20), the Jews were victimized in a number of pogroms, the most serious occurring on 20 and 24 June 1919. Consequently the J. pop. dropped to 437 in 1926. In 1929, most breadwinners (211) were artisans, with 104 still in trade. The Germans captured C. on 13 July 1941 and in the first few months of the occupation murdered all 568 Jews in the town.

CHERNIGOV Chernigov dist., Ukraine. Jews were present in the 13th cent. A R. Yitzhak (Itze) is known from the period. Jews were again present in the 17th cent. but were periodically expelled, a result of local complaints to the Polish king. All the Jews were killed in the Chmielnicki massacres of 1648–49. The J. community was only reestablished in the late 18th cent. In 1897, the J. pop was 8,779 (32% of the total). The community maintained charitable institutions and in addition to *hadarim*, a *talmud torah* enrolling 110 students, elementary schools for boys and girls, and a girls' vocational school. In a pogrom staged in Oct. 1905, a number of Jews were killed, many were injured, and J. homes and stores were looted. The poet, physician and scholar Dr. Yehuda Leib Binyamin Katzenelson (Buki ben Yogli, 1846–1917) was born and raised in C. The poetess Zelda Schneersohn-Mishkovski was also born there in 1914. The J. pop. rose between the World Wars, reaching 12,204 in 1939. Many Jews were presumably employed in the Soviet bureaucracy, government stores, and artisan cooperatives. Many others worked in a large textile plant originally set up as a cooperative with the assistance of ORT. A sewing school for girls was attended by over 100 in the 1920s and another 60 boys were enrolled in technical courses. These, too, were supported by ORT. The Germans captured the city on 9 Sept. 1941. By late Oct., 400 Jews had been murdered. In early Nov. 3,000 were brought to the grounds of the city jail and murdered. In 1959 the J. pop. of C. was 6,600.

Jewish self-defense force, Chernobyl, Ukraine (Elias Tcherikower/photo courtesy of Yad Vashem, The Holocaust Martyrs' and Heroes' Remembrance Authority, Jerusalem)

CHERNOBYL Kiev dist., Ukraine. An organized J. community under the jurisdiction of the Lithuanian Council existed in the late 17th cent. In 1710 the community was attached to the Council of the Four Lands. The J. pop. of C. was 696 in 1765 and 5,526 (total 9,351) in 1897. The *tzaddik* Menahem Nahum of C. lived here and inspired the foundation of several famous hasidic dynasties. Summer vacationers were an important source of income for local Jews. In 1916, a rabbi and the local Zionists initiated the establishment of a Hebrew school. Immediately after the Oct. 1917 Revolution, its enrollment rose to about 300 children. On 1 April 1919, General Denikin's White Army troops staged a pogrom in which they murdered 150 Jews, raped women, and pillaged property. In the early 1920s, the Soviets closed the Hebrew school and opened a Yiddish elementary school instead. A number of J. families founded a kolkhoz nearby. Yiddish flourished as an official language until 1937, when all J. institutions were closed down. In 1939, the J. pop. was 1,783. The Germans arrived on 25 Aug. 1941 and on 7 Nov. executed a large group of Jews.

CHERNUKHI Poltava dist., Ukraine. Jews numbered 275 (total 2,631) in 1897, dropping to 89 by 1939 in the town and to 50 in the rest of the province. The Germans arrived on 17 Sept. 1941, murdering 132 Jews in the same month.

CHERNY ARDOV (Hung. Fekete Ardo) Carpatho-Russia, Czechoslovakia, today Ukraine. Jews settled in the first half of the 18th cent. and maintained a pop. of two or three families until the 19th cent. In 1880 they numbered 284 (total 1,283) and between the World Wars slightly more than 300. Among them were 20 tradesmen, 12 artisans, and three flour mill operators. The Hungarians occupied the town in Nov. 1938 and in 1941 drafted a few dozen Jews into labor battalions for forced labor on the eastern front. In Aug. 1941, a number of J. families without Hungarian citizenship were expelled to Kamenets-Podolski and murdered. The rest were deported to Auschwitz in the second half of May 1944.

CHERNYI OSTROV Kamenets-Podolski dist., Ukraine. Jews settled in the early 18th cent. and numbered 226 in 1765 and 2,216 (79% of the total) in 1897. In the Soviet period, the J. pop. declined, reaching 1,200 in 1939. The Germans entered the town on 7 July 1941. In the course of the year, 109 Jews were murdered. Most were transferred to the Proskurov ghetto in 1942 and died in the following months.

CHERVEN (until 1925, Igumen) Minsk dist., Belorussia. J. settlement probably commenced in the late 18th cent. In 1794–95 the J. pop. was 91 and in 1897, 2,817 (total 4,573). In the early 1880s, most of the town's 136 registered artisans were Jews. A J. elementary school was started in 1920, reaching an enrollment of 250–260 in 1926–35. A J. club with a

drama circle was also active. A few dozen J. families worked in kolkhozes. In 1939, the J. pop. was 1,491. The Germans captured the town on 2 July 1941 and established a ghetto. On 1 Feb. 1942, they murdered 1,500–1,750 Jews from C. and its environs, probably at the J. cemetery.

CHERVONNOYE Zhitomir dist., Ukraine. Jews were probably present by the 18th cent. and numbered 711 (total 2,638) in 1897. In the late 1920s, the community had a J. school, rabbi, community head, and a *beit midrash* converted into a clubroom in 1929 under pressure from the *Yevsektsiya* (J. section of the Communist Party). About 100 breadwinners were factory hands, mainly at a sugar refinery. In the wake of the Russian civil war (1918–20) and internal migration, the J. pop. dropped to 411 in 1939. The Germans captured C. on 7 July 1941 and murdered all but a few J. families.

CHERVONOARMEYSKOYE (until 1935, Sofyevka; in 1935–39, Krasnoarmeyskoye) Zaporozhe dist., Ukraine. Jews settled in the late 19th cent. and numbered 390 (total 9,327) in 1897 and 157 in 1939. The remaining few who had neither fled nor been evacuated, were murdered after the German occupation of Oct. 1941.

CHIGIRIN Kirovograd dist., Ukraine. J. settlement apparently commenced in the first half of the 17th cent. Shortly after the return of C. to Polish rule in 1758, Jews numbered 66. In 1897, the J. pop. was 2,922 (total 9,872). Throughout the 19th cent., most trade was in J. hands. In a pogrom staged on 24 Oct. 1905, local residents and peasants from the area pillaged J. property. Another pogrom occurred on 25 May 1919, resulting in a sharp drop of the J. pop. to 402 in 1926. Only 74 Jews remained in 1939; they were murdered by the Germans after their arrival in early Aug. 1941.

CHIOS (Chio, Khio, Sakiz, Hios, Syo, Sio, Scio) North Aegean Islands, Greece. Jews are mentioned as residing in C. as early as the second cent. B.C.E.. Benjamin of Tudela, the 12th cent. traveler, recorded the presence of some 400 Jews in C. The community was augmented by a large Spanish immigration in the mid-15th cent. as well as by refugees following the Spanish and Portuguese expulsions. The Sephardi community soon predominated over the Romaniot body. From 1566 C. was under Turkish rule and organ-

ized J. life began to develop. A J. school was opened in 1613 and in 1639 the J. pop. stood at 300. In the 19th cent., most Jews dealt successfully in trade. During the Greek revolt of 1821, the J. support of the Turks and the benefits gained led to Greek resentment. Along with the rest of the pop., the Jews suffered losses and financial difficulties following an epidemic in 1865 and a fire in 1875. In 1885, the J. pop. had dropped to 180 from 350 in 1881 following a severe earthquake that year which destroyed the J. ghetto, killed dozens, and left hundreds homeless. About 200 J. refugees found shelter in Izmir. The remaining Jews moved into Greek Orthodox, Catholic, and Protestant neighborhoods. Assistance was received from the Alliance Israelite, Baron Rothschild, the Anglo-J. Association, and other sources. The Jews built a new synagogue and began to rehabilitate the community with the donations received. In 1894, an Alliance Israelite school was opened. Towards the end of the 19th cent., a central figure in the community, Yehuda Issachar, became mayor of C. Tension between the religions culminated in anti-J. blood libels and riots in 1892 and 1900. In the last decade of the 19th cent. the community absorbed refugees from Crete and Russia. The J. pop. in 1897 was 200. After the Balkan wars (1912–13) C. was annexed to Greece. J. emigration increased and by 1928–38 only 4–10 Jews remained. In 1941, the Germans deported the last remaining family to Saloniki. Claiming to be Italian subjects, they survived the war in Athens.

CHISINAU (Kishinev) Bessarabia, Rumania, today Republic of Moldova. A J. community of 144 families existed here in 1773. They controlled the trade in pro-

Desecrated religious books being buried, Chisinau (Kishinev), Rumania, 1903 (Central Zionist Archives, Jerusalem/photo courtesy of Beth Hatefutsoth, Tel Aviv)

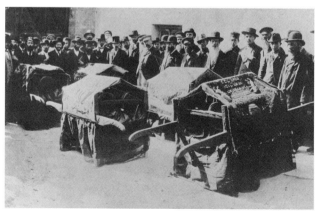

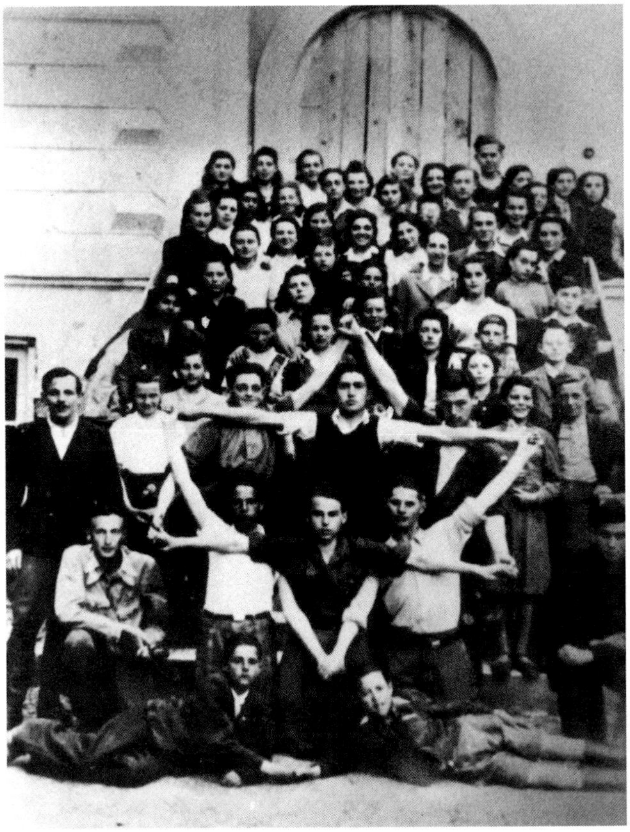

Hehalutz group, Chisinau (Kishinev), Rumania, 1920s (Labour Movement Archive, Tel Aviv//photo courtesy of Yad Vashem, The Holocaust Martyrs' and Heroes' Remembrance Authority, Jerusalem)

duce, both internal and export. Under Russian rule from 1812, Jews were granted equal rights except for that of holding government positions. In 1839, they were forbidden to settle along the border, although those living there were allowed to continue to do so. In the 1817 census a large number of Jews stated their occupation as "street begging." These mendicants were organized in a guild of their own from 1823 and their numbers increased rapidly, especially toward the end of the century with the influx of Jews from surrounding villages impoverished by the drought and the drop in grain prices. From 1851 Jews were drafted into the army. During the mid-19th cent., the authorities encouraged Jews from Rumania, Austria, and Russia to settle in C. and engage in trade with these countries. These Jews were exempt from military service and many Jews hastened to renounce their Russian citizenship and become Turkish, Austrian, or Rumanian nationals in order to gain this privilege. In the 1880s foreign citizens lost their trading permits and their children were forbidden to attend state schools. Jews began to revert to their former nationality and in 1914–18 those who had not succeeded in doing so were expelled to Siberia. The majority of the wage earners were artisans, although some were employed in agriculture, in viticulture, and in the growing and processing of tobacco. During the 1830s, proponents of Haskala (Enlightenment) movement settled in C. By mid-century conflicts with the Hasidim became rife, especially concerning the decision of the hasidic leader, R. Yisrael of Ruzhin, to settle there. The number of J. doctors and teachers and Jews in the free professions increased rapidly. One of the first J. secular schools in Russia was opened by the *maskilim* in C. in 1839. It was replaced in 1850 by two government schools. A yeshiva was opened in 1860 which by 1876 had 280 students. In 1893 a vocational school for girls was opened and by 1902 it had 207 pupils. The J. pop. in 1897 was 50,237 (46% of the total). Jews were

Poster for Jewish National Party in parliamentary elections, Chisinau (Kishinev), Rumania, 1931 (Jewish National and University Library, Jerusalem/photo courtesy of Beth Hatefutsoth, Tel Aviv)

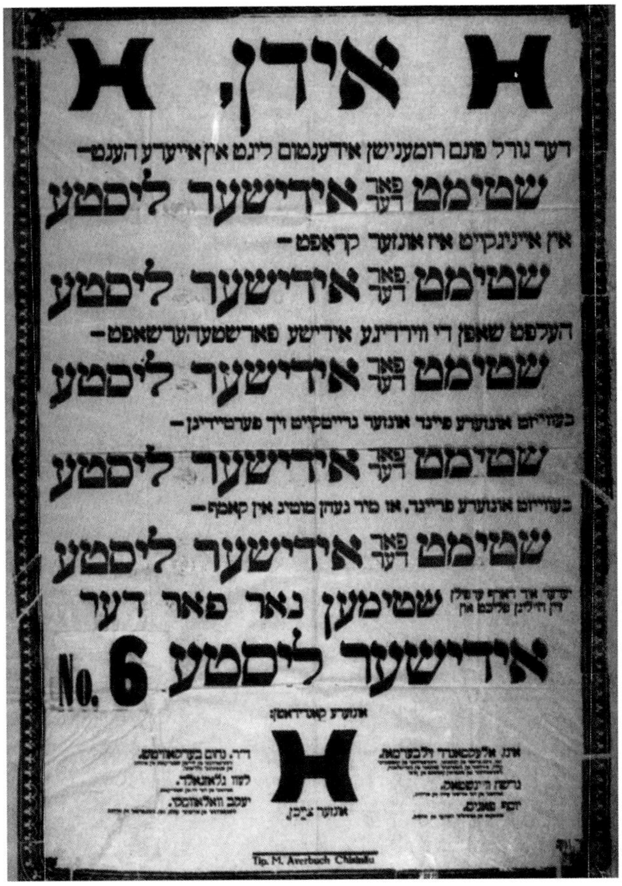
אידן,
שטימט פאר דער אידישער ליסטע
No. 6
אידישער ליסטע

Jewish street, Chisinau (Kishinev), Rumania

constantly subjected to antisemitic attacks. On 6–7 April 1903 Russian and Ukrainian inhabitants incited local Rumanians to set upon the Jews. Events began with a blood libel charging the Jews with the murder of a Christian boy in nearby Dubosari as well as causing the suicide of a Christian girl in the J. hospital. In the ensuing pogrom, incited by the local antisemitic newspaper *Bessarabetz*, 44 Jews were killed, 92 seriously injured, and over 500 hurt. Over 700 houses, shops, and warehouses were plundered and ruined. More than 2,000 J. families were left homeless. The attackers were joined by students from the local theological seminary as well as high school pupils. Neither the 5,000 soldiers garrisoned in C. nor the authorities took steps to stop the assaults; it was later proved that the latter had supported them. This was the most notorious of all pogroms and aroused protest among Jews and non-

Jews in many parts of the world. The Hebrew poet Hayyim Nahman Bialik, who was sent by the J. Historical Commission in Odessa to report on the atrocity, was moved to write two of his best-known works, *Al he-Shehita* and *Be-Ir ha-Harega*, which stimulated the J. self-defense movement in Eastern Europe. The Russian authorities went through the motions of bringing the inciters to justice, but the sentences imposed were extremely light. This pogrom was a warning to the Jews that the Russians would no longer be content with imposing restrictions through economic decrees but were now determined to harm the Jews physically. On 19–20 Oct. 1905, in yet another pogrom, 19 Jews were killed, 56 injured, and many shops ransacked. Over 7,000 Jews emigrated to the U.S. or to towns in Russia. A branch of Hovevei Zion was opened in 1886 led by Meir Dizengoff (future mayor of Tel Aviv). After the

First Zionist Congress in 1897, C. became one of the important centers of Russian Zionism. A Zionist socialist party was formed and many of its leaders immigrated to Eretz Israel with the Second Aliya. Distinguished Zionists emanating from C. included Dr. Yaakov Bernstein-Cohen, Hayyim Greenberg (1889–1933), and Yosef Baratz (1890–1968). Between the World Wars the Zionist movement expanded and branches of most of the youth and adult movements were opened. The Bund became active at the beginning of the 20th cent. and was one of the important political parties in the community. Following the annexation of Bessarabia to Rumania in 1918, the J. pop. was granted equal rights enabling their representatives to be elected to the municipal council and to establish their own political party with the community's rabbi as its representative in the Rumanian senate. Owing to the suspicion that the Jews were Communist sympathizers, senior positions in the government, the judiciary, and the police were closed to them. In the 1930s there was an upsurge of antisemitism led by the Cuza Party. Between the World Wars the Jews' economic situation declined because of the loss of their foreign markets, especially Russia. J.-owned businesses and factories closed down and hundreds of young Jews were forced to seek employment in other Rumanian cities or overseas. Even so, the majority (82% in 1924) of stores and workshops remained in J. hands. The J. pop. figures for 1930 (41,405, 36% of the total) reveal a decline in the community with the number of deaths exceeding births by 25%. In 1938 the difference was 40%. Government schools were opened to Jews and in some of the high schools they constituted over 50% of the pupils. The Tarbut organization opened schools where the language of instruction was Hebrew. In 1923 a J. high school was opened. During 1920–40 the J. press flourished and daily Yiddish newspapers appeared, such as *Unzer Tsayt* (1922–38), as well as a variety of periodicals. From 1938, all publications in Hebrew and Yiddish were banned.

It is estimated that in June 1941 the J. pop. including refugees (especially from the Ukraine) reached 60,000.

Drawing water in the Chisinau (Kishinev) ghetto, Rumania, Aug. 1941 (Bundesarchiv/photo courtesy of Yad Vashem, The Holocaust Martyrs' and Heroes' Remembrance Authority, Jerusalem)

Large numbers of Jews were killed in the German air raid on 21 June 1941. Thousands of Jews fled eastward, but up to 10,000 were murdered by the approaching German and Rumanian armies. The German *Einsatzkommando* under the command of SS *Sturmbannfuehrer* Paul Johannes Zapp entered C. on 16–17 July and set about the systematic annihilation of the Jews. During the ensuing two weeks over 10,000 Jews were murdered in their homes and on the streets. On 24 July the remaining 11,000 were forcibly marched to the old market area and ghettoized in the ruins there. The conditions were overcrowded and there were neither sanitary facitilites nor running water. The Rumanian soldiers stole all their valuables as the Jews entered the ghetto. A group of 500 Jews was taken into the nearby woods and shot. At the end of July another group of 450 intellectuals was taken to nearby antitank ditches and shot by German and Rumanian troops. Further groups of Jews were taken to various sites, forced to dig their own graves, and then shot. Others were sent to work in forced labor units but few returned. On 4 Oct., 1,600 were taken out of the ghetto in wagons and were murdered as they crossed the Dniester River. During Oct. groups of Jews were deported to Transnistria. Rumanian peasants robbed the Jews on the way and those who lagged behind were shot. The last transports of 1,004 and 257 left the ghetto on 25 and 31 Oct. 1941. The ghetto was not destroyed immediately; 200 Jews from other areas in Bessarabia were brought there and on 21 May 1942 all were deported to Transnistria. A community was reestablished after the war numbering about 5,500 in 1947, 43,000 in 1959, and 25,000 in 1996.

CHISINEU-CRIS (Hung. Kisjeno) S. Transylvania dist., Rumania. A J. community existed here in 1889 and joined the Neologist association. The J. pop. in 1930 was 233 (4% of the total). At the outbreak of the Soviet-Rumanian war (June 1941), the J. pop. of 169 was transferred to Arad.

CHISTIAKOVO Stalino dist., Ukraine. The J. pop. in 1939 was 341 (total 49,451). The Germans captured C. on 30 Oct. 1941 and during the occupation, those Jews who had neither fled nor been evacuated perished.

CHIUESTI (Hung. Pecsetszeg) N. Transylvania dist., Rumania. Jews first settled in the mid-18th

cent. and, among other occupations, manufactured kosher wine. The J. pop. in 1930 was 91 (8% of the total). In May 1944 the J. pop. was transferred to the Dej ghetto and then deported to Auschwitz.

CHKALOVA Zaporozhe dist., Ukraine. C. was founded as a J. colony, probably in the 1920s. After the German occupation of Oct. 1941, 157 Jews were murdered, including 57 expelled to C. from other places.

CHLEWCZANY Stanislawow dist., Poland, today Ukraine. The J. pop. in 1921 was 125. The Jews were deported to the Belzec death camp in summer-fall 1942, directly or via Rawa Ruska.

CHMELNIK (Hung. Komlos; Yid. Kalmoyish) Carpatho-Russia, Czechoslovakia, today Ukraine. Jews probably settled in the mid-18th cent. Three J. families were present in 1768. In 1880, the J. pop. was 121 (total 612), maintaining that level until WWII. A few Jews were farmers. The Hungarians occupied C. in March 1939. In mid-May 1944, the Jews were deported to Auschwitz.

CHMIELNIK Kielce dist., Poland. Jews were present in the 13th cent. The community was virtually wiped out during the Swedish war of 1656 when Stefan Czarniecki's irregular Polish troops massacred about 150 Jews. The community was reestablished in the second half of the 17th cent. Jews dominated the grain, cattle, and lumber trade, achieving a measure of prosperity in the 18th cent. and constructing one of the finest synagogues in Poland. In the mid-19th cent., Jews opened textile factories and towards the end of the cent. began to enter professional life. Their pop. grew from 1,195 in 1827 to 5,671 (total 6,888) in 1897. Among the community's illustrious rabbis were Yitzhak Meir Fraenkel-Teomim and Yosef ha-Levi Ettinger. In the 19th cent., C. became an important hasidic center after R. Avraham David Orbach settled there, with numerous *shtiblekh* in operation. The Zionists became active in the late 19th cent. At the outset of WWI, the Jews suffered from the depredations of Russian soldiers. The community later cared for 1,100 refugees under the Austrian occupation (1915–18). During the 1920s, Orthodox circles controlled community affairs but in 1931 a Zionist became chairman of the community council. In the 1920s, Jews, who consti-

tuted about 80% of the total, also dominated the municipal council but were subsequently pushed out because of new regulations. Mizrachi (with 500 members), the Yiddishists, and Agudat Israel ran their own schools. In the 1930s, Betar became the biggest youth movement with 200 members. Hundreds of Jews fled east on the approach of the Germans in Sept. 1939. Within a few days of the occupation, 30 community leaders were burned alive in the *beit midrash*. Afterwards a *Judenrat* was appointed and a regime of forced labor and "contributions" instituted. In April 1941, a ghetto was established and within a few months 104 were dead of typhoid fever. Refugees increased the pop. to about 9,000 in June 1942. In summer 1942, 1,200 young Jews were sent to the Skarzysko-Kamienna labor camp. Additional refugees brought the J. pop. up to 11,000 when deportations commenced on 5 Oct. 1942. About 500 Jews were murdered during the *Aktion* and 8,500 marched nearly 30 miles to Chencini with hundreds shot on the way by German and Ukrainian guards. After four days without food or water, they were loaded onto railway cars and transported to the Treblinka death camp. The 500 surviving Jews, including many who had escaped deportation but had returned to the ghetto, were rounded up on 5 Nov. and sent to labor camps. Forty survivors returned to C. after the war, but acts of violence and the murder of two Jews led most to leave in 1945.

CHOCIESZOW   Volhynia dist., Poland, today Ukraine. Jews numbered 20 families in the 1930s. In the Holocaust they were expelled to the Ratno ghetto.

CHOCIMIERZ   Stanislawow dist., Poland, today Ukraine. The J. pop. in 1921 was 160. The Jews were probably expelled to Tlumacz for liquidation in April-May 1942.

CHODECZ   Warsaw dist., Poland. Jews probably settled in the first half of 19th cent. and maintained a pop. of around 450 (25% of the total) until after WWI. The Germans arrived in early Sept. 1939. Nearly all J. men were sent to forced labor camps in the Poznan dist. during 1940; the rest were expelled to the Lodz ghetto in Sept. 1941. Most fell victim to starvation and disease.

CHODEL   Lublin dist., Poland. Jews first settled in the mid-19th cent. and numbered 699 (total 1,439) in

1897. Most of their homes along with the synagogue were destroyed in WWI. In WWII, refugees increased the J. pop. from 770 in 1939 to 1,644 in mid-1941. Hundreds died under the harsh conditions of the occupation. In May 1942, the Germans murdered hundreds in a mass *Aktion* with the remaining Jews sent to Opole and then to the Sobibor death camp. In Sept., the last remnants of C. where deported to the Belzec death camp.

CHODOROW   Lwow dist., Poland, today Ukraine. The J. community dates from the 17th cent., with a richly decorated wooden synagogue built in 1642 that was destined to survive almost miraculously the town's many devastating fires and earn a legendary reputation. The coming of the railroad under Austrian rule boosted the economy and Jews exercised considerable influence in the municipal council, with a J. mayor elected in 1913. The J. pop. almost doubled up to WWI from an 1880 figure of 1,049 (40% of the total), but dropped to 1,230 in 1921 after the Russians burned the town during the war. Zionist activity and influence was extensive between the World Wars. While most children were enrolled in Polish schools, there was also a Hebrew school for 50–120 pupils and a *talmud torah*. The German occupation of 30 June 1941 initiated a regime of persecution. The synagogue was burned down, Jews were put to forced labor, beaten, and sometimes murdered. The first *Aktion* took place in early Sept. 1942. The sick and weak were killed immediately and between 1,100 and 1,500 deported to the Belzec death camp. Two weeks later another 350 Jews were deported to Belzec via Stryj. Those remaining were shot near the local sugar plant in Feb. or March 1943.

CHODZIEZH   Poznan dist., Poland. A J. community was present in the 16th cent. In the early 18th cent, J. refugees in the cloth trade arrived from Leszno after a fire there. The well-to-do class was encouraged by Frederick the Great after the annexation to Prussia in 1772. The J. cloth merchants traveled as far as Moscow and the Turkish border. The J. pop. grew to 1,062 (total 2,925) in 1837, when a new synagogue was built. Emigration reduced the J. pop. steadily to 92 in 1921. The last 19 Jews were expelled to Wloszczowa in Nov. 1939 and shared the fate of the local Jews there

CHOJNICE   Pomerania dist., Poland. Jews were in-

vited to settle under protected status by Frederick the Great and numbered 80 families in 1813. A small wooden synagogue was built in 1809 and a J. elementary school was founded in 1828. A new synagogue was erected in 1869. By 1885 the J. pop. stood at 563 (total 5,029). Jews contributed significantly to the economic development of the town, particularly in trade and the textile and food industries. Violent anti-J. riots lasting eight days broke out in 1881. In 1884 the synagogue was burned and new rioting occurred in 1900 over a blood libel. Emigration to the big German cities increased in the late 19th cent., reducing the J. pop. to 111 in 1921 and 58 in 1931. The few Jews remaining in Sept. 1939 were expelled by the Germans to General Gouvernement territory.

CHOLOJOW Tarnopol dist., Poland, today Ukraine. J. families were present in the early 18th cent. The J. pop. grew to 1,139 by 1900 (total 3,965) but fell to 793 after WWI in the wake of Cossack depredations, epidemics, and flight. The community was largely dominated by its hasidic courts, with the Zionists only becoming active between the World Wars. With the German occupation of 24 June 1941, Jews were seized for forced labor. On 15 Sept., they were assembled in the square and led out of the town to be shot beside a common grave. Further roundups by Germans and Ukrainians eliminated the remaining Jews.

CHOMALOVO (Hung. Csomanyfalva; Yid. Chemalif) Carpatho-Russia, Czechoslovakia, today Ukraine. Jews probably settled in the first quarter of the 19th cent. Their pop. was 35 in 1830 and 170 (total 1,224) in 1880. Most earned their livelihoods in trade, crafts, and agriculture. In 1921, the J. pop. was 132, rising to 202 in 1941. Following the Hungarian occupation in March 1939, Jews were drafted into forced labor battalions. In Aug. 1941, a few J. families without Hungarian citizenship were expelled to Kamenets-Podolski and murdered. The rest were deported to Auschwitz in late May 1944.

CHOMSK Polesie dist., Poland, today Belarus. The J. settlement began in the early 17th cent. From the mid-17th cent. it frequently hosted meetings of the Council of the Land of Lithuania, but remained a backwater when bypassed by the railroad and new roads. Its pop. stood at 1,048 (total 1,678) in 1921 with the Zionists and the Bund becoming active. On 3 Aug. 1941 the Jews were brought out in groups to freshly dug pits by the German SS and murdered.

CHOMUTOV Bohemia (Sudetenland), Czechoslovakia, today Czech Republic. Jews were martyred in 1421 resisting forced conversions by the conquering Hussites. About 100 J. families received expulsion orders in 1517 and only after 1848 was a new community established, with Jews contributing to the city's economic life and starting a Zionist society in 1904. Their pop. was 562 (5.6% of the total) in 1880 and 444 in 1930. All left during the Sudetenland crisis of 1938.

CHONGAR Zaporozhe dist., Ukraine. Jews settled with the founding of the town in 1922. In 1927, about 430 J. families resided there alongside 370 non-J. families. The number of J. families dropped to 376 in 1930. Most of the Jews worked in agriculture in a few neighboring J. kolkhozes and in the salt industry. C. had a J. council (soviet) and a J. school. In the 1930s, pressure was applied to get the Jews to leave the town. The Germans captured C. on 15 Aug. 1941. In early 1942, 18 Jews from C., half of them children, were murdered at the Royter Shtern ("Red Star") kolkhoz.

CHOPOVICHI Zhitomir dist., Ukraine. The J. pop. was 919 in 1897 and 1,533 (total 9,369) in 1926. The Germans captured the city on 10 Aug. 1941. In late Aug., 165 local Jews were murdered on the road to Korosten.

CHOROSTKOW Tarnopol dist., Poland, today Ukraine. Jews were invited to settle as tradesmen with residence rights in the mid-18th cent. and maintained an organized community from the end of the cent. Under Austrian rule, fear of legislation that would set a minimum marital age of 24 for men led to a spate of barely pubescent marriages in the 1860s. Devastating fires struck the town in 1862 and 1869 and heavy taxes continued to oppress the community, but economic conditions remained stable. Despite this, there was a trickle of emigration reducing the pop. by about 10% from an 1880 high of 2,130 (total 5,623). Economic conditions took a turn for the worse between the World Wars. Government policy and stiff competition from the Polish cooperatives undermined J. liveihoods as Jews lost their traditional monopolies in the salt, tobacco, and alcoholic beverage

(Sadagora, Makarov, Skvira). In 1910, a *talmud torah* and three private J. schools were active. In the disturbances of 1905, 12 J. self-defense fighters were killed when they went to Zhitomir to help the Jews there. In the late 1920s, under the Soviets, about half the Jews were unemployed. In the 1930s, the Soviets opened a number of factories and a J. elementary school was operating. The J. pop fell to 2,506 in 1939. The Germans captured C. on 7 July 1941. The Jews were transferred to an open ghetto, ordered to wear the yellow star, and subjected to forced labor. In Aug., 68 were murdered, as were the rabbi and two J. women on 8 Sept. On 20 Sept., 1,500 Jews were taken to a park in the town and executed with the active participation of Ukrainian police. The skilled J. workers who were temporarily spared were executed later.

CHUDOVO Leningrad dist., Russia. Jews probably settled around the turn of the 19th cent. Their pop. was 120 in 1926 and 75 (total 12,259) in 1939. The Germans arrived on 20 Aug. 1941 and on 17 Sept. murdered the few Jews who had neither fled nor been evacuated.

CHUGUYEV Kharkov dist., Ukraine. Jews numbered 187 in 1897 and 277 (total 18,071) in 1939. The Germans arrived on 29 Oct. 1941 and murdered 32 Jews in Jan.–Feb. 1942.

CHUROVICHI Oriol dist., Russia. Jews probably settled in the mid-19th cent., numbering 402 (total 3,611) in 1897 and 227 in 1926 under the Soviets. The Germans arrived on 24 Aug. 1941, murdering about 370 Jews from C. and its environs, many near Klimovo.

CHUST (Hung. Huszt) Carpatho-Russia, Czechoslovakia, today Ukraine. Jews are first mentioned in the late 17th cent. Two J. families were living there in 1727. In the early 19th cent., the community was given the right to choose a rabbi. The first was R. Yaakov from Zydaczow. The J. pop. was 132 in 1830 and 1,062 (total 6,228) in 1880. In the mid-19th cent., when Shemuel Klein was rabbi, a widely renowned yeshiva was founded, with 400 students in the period of R. Moshe Grinwald. In 1921, under the Czechoslovakians, when C. became a county seat, the J. pop. rose to 3,391. In 1941 it was 6,023 (total 21,118). In addition to the yeshiva, the community maintained a

talmud torah, an elementary school, and a number of *hadarim*. Various J. political parties were active, such as Agudat Israel, those of the Zionist organizations and especially the youth groups, and the J. National Party, which represented the community in the municipal council. Most of the city's business establishments and workshops were in J. hands. Jews also owned three banks, factories, and flour mills. A number of Jews belonged to the professional class and the community included seven doctors, three pharmacists, and some administrative officials. The Hungarians occupied the city in March 1939. Jews were gradually cut off from their sources of livelihood and in 1940–41 hundreds were drafted into labor battalions, some being sent to the eastern front, where most were killed. In late July 1941, hundreds lacking Hungarian citizenship were expelled to the German-occupied Ukraine and murdered. When the Germans took over the city in March 1944, 5,351 Jews were present. A ghetto and *Judenrat* were set up with another 5,000 Jews from the area being brought to the ghetto. In late May and early June, the Jews there were deported to Auschwitz in four transports, most to perish. A few dozen Jews, volunteering for the Czechoslovakian army created in the Soviet Union, fought against the Nazis on the eastern front.

CHYROW Lwow dist., Poland, today Ukraine. Jews were apparently among the founders of the town in the first half of the 16th cent. Up to WWI the community was dominated by its well-to-do families under the spiritual aegis of Hasidism, with the Zionists coming to the fore afterwards. The J. pop. leveled off at around 1,000 from the late 19th cent. (35–40% of the total). The community was probably liquidated in July 1942.

CIACOVA (Hung. Csak) S. Transylvania dist., Rumania. One of the oldest J. communities in the district, C. was founded in 1780. The J. pop. in 1930 stood at 64 (2% of the total). On 24 June 1941, J. property was confiscated and the J. pop was deported to Timisoara.

CICAROVCE (Hung. Csicser) Slovakia, Czechoslovakia, today Republic of Slovakia. Jews probably settled in the early 18th cent, founding an independent community in the mid-19th cent. and reaching a peak pop. of 121 (total 1,270) in 1880. In mid-May 1944, the 50 remaining Jews were deported to Auschwitz via Uzhorod.

CIECHANOW Warsaw dist., Poland. Jews were continuously present in C. from the mid-15th cent. to WWII, employed at first mainly in moneylending and the lumber trade. In the aftermath of the mid-17th cent. Swedish war about 50 J. families were massacred by troops of the Polish commander Stefan Czarniecki. The Jews were permitted to rebuild their community by royal decree and licensed to deal in alcoholic beverages. Until the mid-18th cent. a number of nearby communities were attached to it (Makow, Mlawa, Noszyce, Plonsk). During the 19th cent. the J. pop. more than tripled to 4,056 in 1897 (total 9,627). Jews were active as wholesalers of farm produce and many tailors and furriers did piecework for textile factories in the big cities. In addition to its synagogue the community had numerous hasidic prayer houses (Gur, Aleksandrow). R. Avraham Landau (Czechanower) founded a yeshiva and had many hasidic followers as rabbi of the community until his death in 1875. The first Zionist groups were organized in 1894. The Bund and Po'alei Zion became active in the early 20th cent., when the community's first public library and drama circle were founded. At the outset of WWI, the Jews suffered from Cossack depredations and during the subsequent German occupation they endured food shortages and an economic standstill; however, public life continued

Jewish stores, Chust, Czechoslovakia, 1936

total). In Oct. 1941, the Jews of C. were deported to Bogdanovka in Transnistria and killed there.

CINCAU Bukovina, Rumania, today Ukraine. The Jews of C. were a branch of the Zastavna community. The J. pop. in 1930 was 58. In June 1941 the Jews were transferred to Ocna, where most died. The rest were deported to Transnistria.

CIORNOHUZI (Chernohauz) Bukovina, Rumania. The Jews belonged to the Vijnita community and had no independent institutions. The J. pop. in 1933 was 15 families. In June 1941, the local pop. murdered some Jews and the rest were deported to Transnistria. Few returned.

CIRC Slovakia, Czechoslovakia, today Republic of Slovakia. The community began to grow in the late 18th cent. with the arrival of J. refugees from Galicia, who gave it a hasidic East European character which was not typical of J. life in Slovakia. A synagogue was opened in the mid-19th cent. and R. Mordekhai Lichtenstein founded a yeshiva in the early 20th cent. that operated until 1942. The J. pop. reached a peak of 137 (total 1,084) in 1869 and then declined steadily to 59 in 1940. The Jews were deported to the death camps of the east in spring 1942.

CIRESI Bukovina, Rumania, today Ukraine. Jews lived here from the late 19th cent. The J. pop. in 1930 was 106. In 1941, the local Ukrainian pop. cruelly murdered almost all the Jews. The few survivors were deported to Transnistria.

CISNA Lwow dist., Poland, today Ukraine. Jews numbered 150 in 1939. They were expelled by the Germans to Lesko on 20 June 1942 and from there to the Zaslawie concentration camp in Sept. for extermination.

CIUDEI (also Ciudeiu) Bukovina, Rumania, today Ukraine. A J. community existed in 1891. The Jews engaged in trading lumber and cattle. The J. pop. in 1930 was 568. In June 1940, the Soviets destroyed the synagogue built in the mid-19th cent. On 4 July 1941, the Rumanian army murdered 450 Jews and shot the rest two days later.

CIULENI (Hung. Incsel) S. Transylvania dist., Ru-

mania. Jews first settled in the early 18th cent., and were attached to the Huedin community. The J. pop. in 1930 was 160 (15% of the total). In 1940, the Jews were transferred to the interior of Rumania and all traces of them were lost.

CLERMONT-FERRAND Puy-de-Dome dist., France. A J. presence in C. is recorded in the fifth cent. In 576, the synagogue was destroyed and 500 Jews were forced to accept baptism. The remainder fled to Marseilles. A new community was formed, at the latest, during the tenth century. Expelled from C., the Jews moved to Montferrand, where they stayed until the general expulsion from France in 1394. Immigrants from southern France, Turkey, and Alsace established a new community at the end of the 18th cent. A synagogue was established in 1862. By 1901, the community, the site of the regional rabbinate, numbered 25–30 families and belonged to the consistory of Lyons until 1905. In 1941, 3,000 Jews lived in the whole department of Puy-de-Dome. The majority of the 1,200 Jews who lived in C., the capital, were refugees from the north. Situated in the Free Zone, refugees continued to arrive and it is estimated that their numbers soon reached 8,500. From summer 1942 they were forced by the police to leave. The University of Strasbourg, which was located in C. itself, was severely criticized for ignoring regulations limiting the number of J. students to 3% of the student body and for refusing to hand over lists of students to the police. Between Nov. 1943 and March 1944, 119 Jews were deported or shot. In 1964, there were 800 Jews living in C.

CLOPPENBURG Oldenburg, Germany. Jews established a community numbering around 30 (1816–1925) which included members in Friesoythe and Loeningen (1863). Mostly engaged in the cattle trade, they opened a new synagogue in 1866. By 1933, their numbers had grown to 45. Nazi persecution, culminating in the synagogue's destruction on *Kristallnacht* (9–10 Nov. 1938), aroused some local non-J. protests. About 20 Jews emigrated to England, South Africa, and the U.S. At least 19 (including four who had taken refuge in Holland) died in Nazi camps.

CLUJ DISTRICT Hungary. Jews first settled in the towns and villages of this district in the 19th cent. The entire J. pop. was deported to Auschwitz in summer 1944.

Aghiresu (Hung. Apahida). The J. pop. was 50 in 1920 and 56 during the Holocaust period (total 1,802). All were ultra-Orthodox.
Bontida (Hung. Bonczida). The first Jews settled in the 18th cent. The J. pop. was 31 in 1920 and 40 during the Holocaust period (total 2,290).
Borsa-Cluj (Hung. Kolozsborsa). The J. pop. was 44 in 1920 and 57 during the Holocaust period with 256 Jews in surrounding villages.
Ciucea (Hung. Csucsa). During the Holocaust the J. pop. was 134 (total 1,777).
Gilau (Hung. Gyalu) The J. pop. was 89 in 1920 and 161 during the Holocaust period (total 3,330) with 60 Jews in surrounding villages.
Huedin (Hung. Banffyhunyad) Jews first settled in the mid-19th cent. A synagogue was consecrated in 1852 and a yeshiva opened. The J. pop. was 260 in 1920 and 960 during the Holocaust. In 1947, 345 Jews lived there, most of whom left. There were 28 Jews in the surrounding villages.
Panticeu (Hung. Pancelcseh). The J. pop. was 69 in 1920 and 91 during the Holocaust (total 1,474).
Sanmihaiul de Campie (Hung. Mezoszentmihaly). During the Holocaust the J. pop. was 72 (total 1,151).
Zimboru (Hung. Kolozs-Zsombor). During the Holocaust the J. pop. was 87 (total 1,146).

CLUJ-NAPOCA (Hung. Kolozsvar; Ger. Klausenburg) N. Transylvania, Rumania. Sephardi traders lived here from the early 17th cent. but it was only in the early 19th cent. that a J. community was organized and the first temporary synagogue set up in 1818. R. Moshe Shemuel Glasner, who served the community as rabbi in 1877–1923, openly supported Herzl and the establishment of the Zionist movement in Transyl-

Jewish boy scouts at the Hebrew high school in Cluj, Rumania, 1922 (Abasma Archives, Tel Yitzhak/photo courtesy of Yad Vashem, The Holocaust Martyrs' and Heroes' Remembrance Authority, Jerusalem)

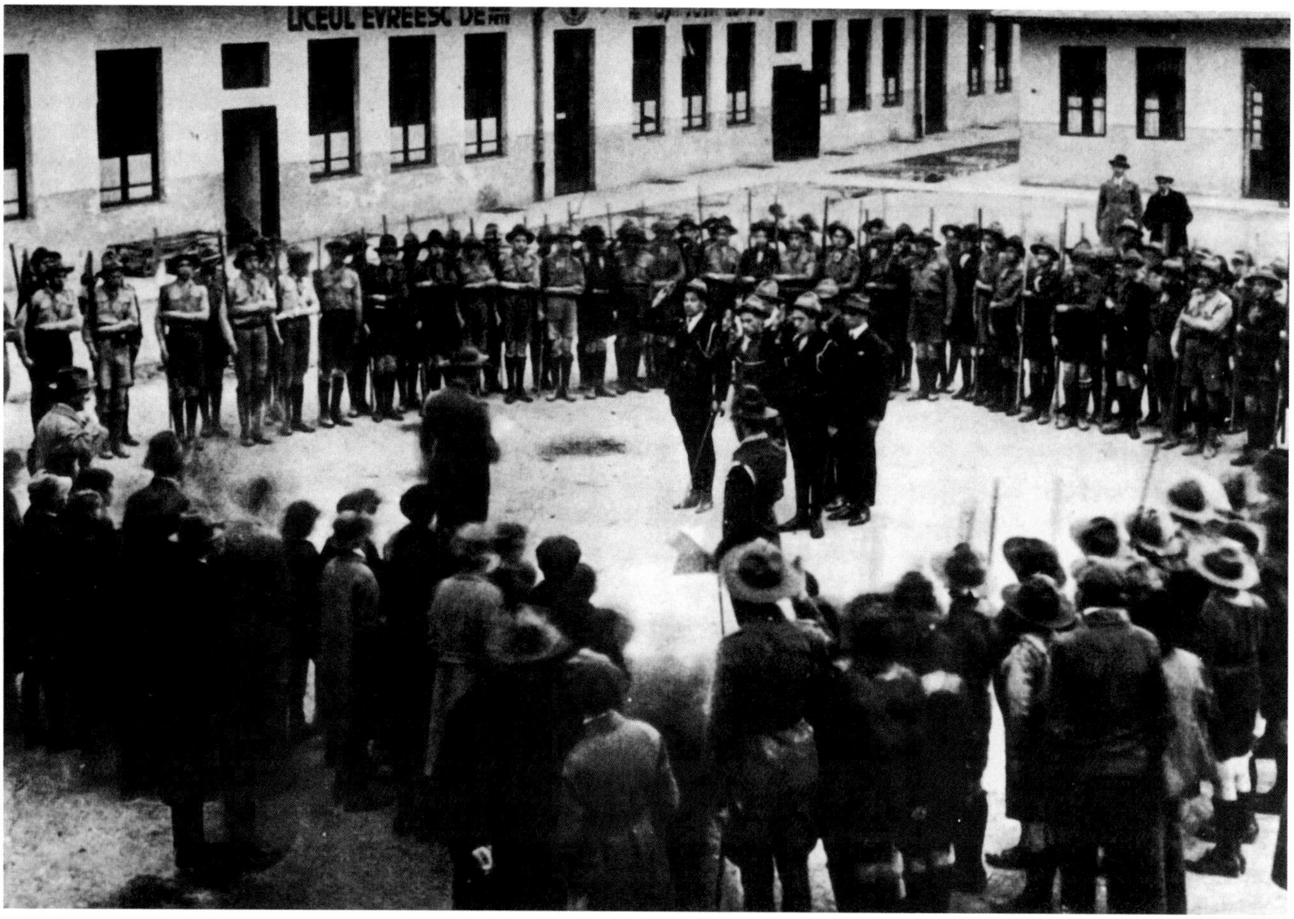
LICEUL EVREESC DE

vania. In 1881 a group of intellectuals broke away from the Orthodox community and set up a Neologist congregation, consecrated its synagogue in 1887, and appointed its own rabbis, among them Dr. Matyas Eisler (1891–1930), who wrote the history of the J. community of Transylvania. The J. pop. in 1891 was 2,414 (7.4% of the total). A Zionist organization began to operate in Nov.–Dec. 1918, publishing the Hungarian-language weekly (later daily) *Uj Kelet*. The leaders of the Zionist movement, Dr. Yosef Fischer, Dr. Theodor Fischer, and Dr. Erno Marton (1896–1960; editor of *Uj Kelet*), represented Transylvanian Jewry in the Rumanian parliament in Bucharest. The national headquarters of the J. National Fund and Keren Hayesod were opened there. C. became the center in Transylvania of all activity of the Zionist youth and adult movements. Jews were active in the Hungarian party and held leading positions in the underground Communist movement. J. representatives served on the municipal council and Dr. Marton was elected deputy mayor. Antisemitic manifestations were rife after C. was incorporated into Rumania in 1920. Jews were expelled from government positions and from the university. In 1927 antisemitic students devastated the synagogue and the *Uj Kelet* printing press and its editorial offices. A J. hospital was opened in 1927 which later trained J. medical students ousted from the university. B'nai B'rith set up its Transylvanian headquarters in C. In 1918 a hasidic-oriented group of 100 broke away from the Orthodox community and set up the "Sephardi Community" under the influence of the Satmar Rabbi, R. Yoel Teitelbaum. The Orthodox community opened an elementary school in 1870 and the Neologist community's school opened in 1904. Both functioned until the Holocaust. The Tarbut organization was established to fund the J. high school (separate premises for boys and for girls) which existed from 1920 to 1927. J. self-defense units were organized to prevent attacks during the antisemitic Goga-Cuza regime in 1937.

The Hungarian army entered C. on 11 Sept. 1940 and promulgated decrees restricting the economic activities of the Jews. The newspaper was closed down. J. pupils banned from government high schools attended the J. high school opened in Oct. 1940 which functioned till 1944. In July 1941, hundreds of J. families who did not possess Hungarian citizenship were expelled to Galicia and most were murdered in Kamenets-Podolski; in summer 1942, 300 military-age Jews were drafted into labor battalions and sent across the eastern border. Further groups were drafted and the majority died. Some Zionist youth succeed in escaping through Rumania to Palestine. When the Germans entered C. in March 1944, the Gestapo set up a *Judenrat* headed by Dr. Fischer of the Neologist community. The J. community was forced into a ghetto on 2 May 1944. Together with Jews from nearby Szamosujvar and neighboring villages, the ghetto encompassed 18,000 inhabitants. Jews were tortured until they revealed the whereabouts of their hidden jewelry and other property. Three weeks after the opening of the ghetto typhus broke out and many died through lack of medication. From 29 May 1944 to 13 June, the J. pop. was deported to Auschwitz. On 10 July 1944, 388 Jews were transferred to Budapest to join other Hungarian Jews on the Rescue Committee train to Switzerland. After the war, survivors began to return and the community numbered 6,500 in 1947, but the majority left for Israel and other countries. By 1990, only 750 remained.

CMIELOW Kielce dist., Poland. Jews settled in the mid-17th cent. They numbered 232 in 1857 and 664 (total 2,468) in 1921. The Zionists were active between the World Wars, while antisemitism intensified in the 1930s. Nearly 500 Jews were present when the Germans arrived in Sept. 1939. Their property was confiscated and "contributions" were exacted from the community. On 1 June 1942, they were confined to a ghetto and in Oct. 1942, 900 including refugees were deported to the Treblinka death camp. In Jan. 1943, a prison camp was established in C. for those found in hiding. The exact date of their deportation to the Treblinka death camp is unknown.

COBURG Upper Franconia, Germany. Jews were present in the mid-13th cent. and inhabited a J. quarter with a synagogue and other facilities. The community was destroyed in the Black Death persecutions of 1348–49 and renewed by survivors soon after. The Jews engaged mainly in lending and changing money. In 1422 they were forced to wear a special badge and in 1447 the synagogue was converted into a church and the cemetery impounded. The Jews were expelled shortly thereafter. The modern community dates from the early 19th cent. and grew to 240 in 1895 (total 18,868). In 1872 a Catholic church built in 1473 was given to the community for its synagogue. During the Weimar Republic, C. was a hotbed of Naz-

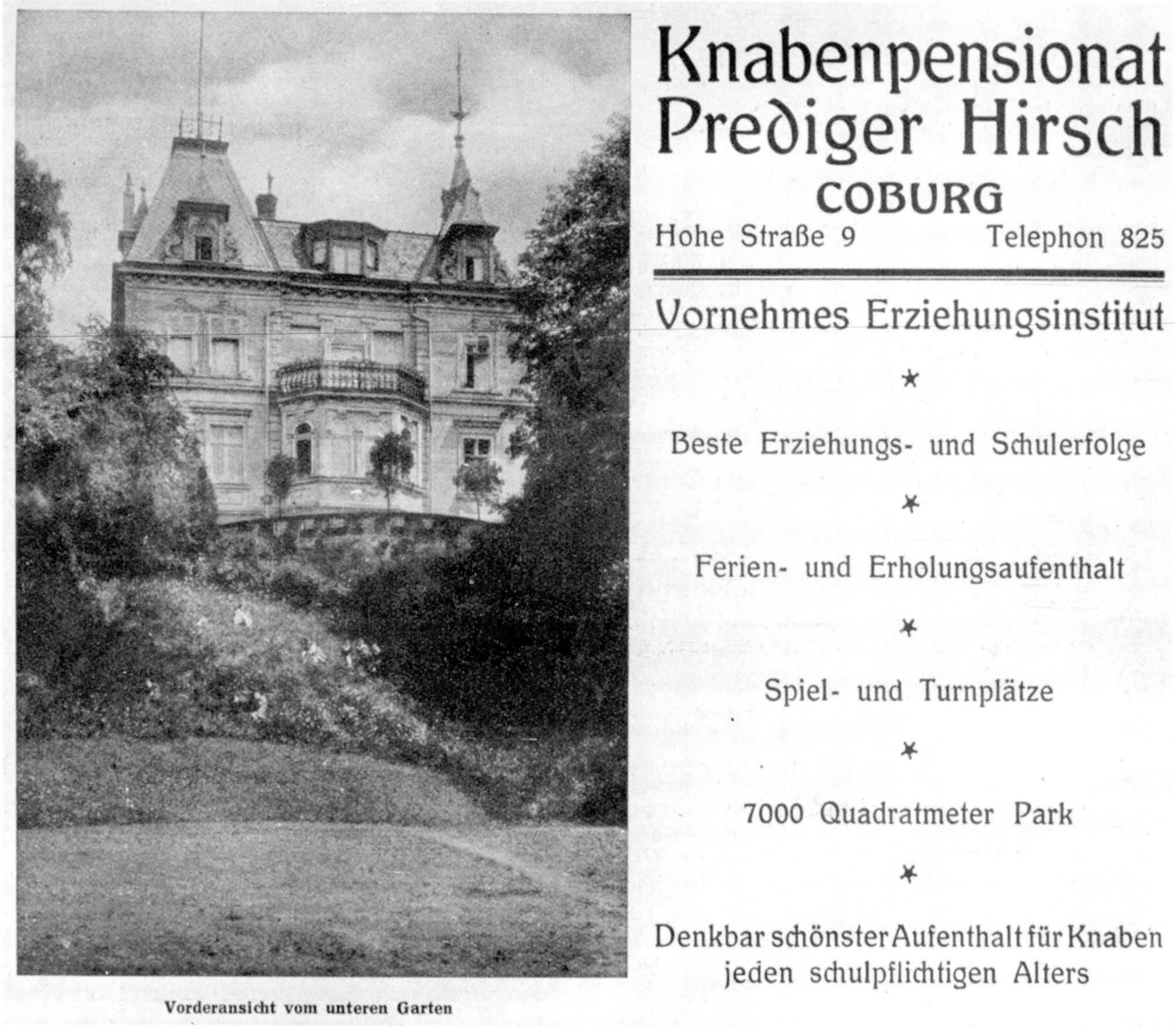
Knabenpensionat
Prediger Hirsch
COBURG
Hohe Straße 9 Telephon 825
Vornehmes Erziehungsinstitut
Beste Erziehungs- und Schulerfolge
Ferien- und Erholungsaufenthalt
Spiel- und Turnplätze
7000 Quadratmeter Park
Denkbar schönster Aufenthalt für Knaben
jeden schulpflichtigen Alters
Vorderansicht vom unteren Garten

Hirsch Boarding School, Coburg, Germany, 1927

ism, with Hitler himself leading marches there in 1922 and 1932. Throughout this period, the Jews operated large factories and business establishments, especially in the clothing industry. When the Nazis came to power in 1933, the J. pop. was 233. Forty of the community's leading figures were arrested and brutally beaten and Jews were banned from various public places. The synagogue was also closed down. On *Kristallnacht* (9–10 Nov. 1938), J. homes and stores were destroyed. By 1942, 85 Jews managed to emigrate and 61 left for other German cities. Those remaining were confined to two buildings and expelled in three groups: to the Riga ghetto on 27 Nov. 1941, to Izbica in the Lublin dist. of Poland on 25 April 1942, and to the Theresienstadt ghetto on 9 Sept. 1942.

COCHEM A. D. MOSEL Rhineland, Germany. A J. community existed in the 13th cent. Seventeen Jews were murdered in the Oberwesel blood libel of 1287. Jews were also victimized in the Armleder massacres of 1336–39 and the community was destroyed in the Black Death persecutions of 1348–49. A permanent J. settlement existed in the early 19th cent., reaching a pop. of 42 in 1808 and a peak of 114 in 1895 before dropping to 49 in 1932. A synagogue was built in 1861. Most Jews left in the Nazi era. The last three

were deported to the Theresienstadt ghetto in June 1942. At least nine Jews perished in the Holocaust.

CODAIESTI Moldavia dist., Rumania. Jews founded C. in the mid-19th cent. and in 1899 the J. pop. stood at 560, dropping to 415 in 1930 (21% of the total). A J. elementary school existed on the eve of WWII. At the outbreak of the Soviet-Rumanian war (June 1941), the J. women were expelled to Vaslui and the men to the Targu-Jiu internment camp. The latter were sent to forced labor in Vaslui and later to the labor camp at Doaga. About half the J. pop. returned after the war.

COESFELD Westphalia, Germany. Jews were present from the late 13th cent. The small community was destroyed in the Black Death persecutions of 1348–49. Jews are again mentioned in the 17th cent. and eight families were living there in the late 18th cent. A synagogue was erected in 1810 and 26 children were being taught by a J. teacher in 1818. The J. pop. reached a peak of 114 in 1849 and a new synagogue was built in 1884. In June 1933, 57 Jews remained (total 12,934). In the first years of Nazi rule, 20 left the city. Thirty-five remained on the eve of *Kristallnacht* (9–10 Nov. 1938), when local residents wrecked the synagogue and J. homes and stores and beat Jews. Another 16 emigrated in 1939. The 19 who remained were confined to a few houses. On 10 Dec. 1941, they were brought to Muenster and from there deported to the Riga ghetto; 16 of this group are known to have died.

COEVORDEN Drenthe dist., Holland. The J. presence dates from the late 17th cent. From the 1760s the community began to grow rapidly and its development continued throughout the 19th and early 20th centuries. The J. pop. in 1883 was 247. A Zionist youth movement was active in the 1930s. The J. pop. in 1941 was 139 (total 7,279). At the time of the deportations of Oct. 1942 the police chief warned the Jews and obtained ships for their escape. However, his counsel was rejected and consequently 91 were deported to Westerbork. Only 14 were saved.

COLMAR Haut-Rhin dist., France. The J. presence in C. dates from the middle of the 13th cent. In 1279 fire destroyed the synagogue. In 1285 the Jews were expelled and R. Meir of Rothenburg was taken into captivity. Emperor Rudolph of Habsburg demanded an enormous ransom, but the rabbi refused to let his people pay the ransom and he died in captivity. Later the J. community in C. provided refuge for the Jews persecuted in Rouffach, Mutzig, and other localities and also during the Armleder persecutions in 1336–39. During the Black Death persecutions, the Jews of C. were condemned to death and they were burned at the stake in 1349 at a site outside the city called "Judenloch." The Jews resettled in C. in 1385 and numbered at least 29 adults (possibly families) in 1392. Later their number decreased, and they were expelled in 1512. C. was annexed to France in 1681, but Jews were not permitted to settle there. A few Jews were allowed to reside in C. in the 18th cent. After the French Revolution, the Jews were officially granted permits to reside in C., which became in 1808 the seat of a consistory with 25 dependent communities and in 1823, the seat of the chief rabbinate of Alsace (Haut-Rhin). A synagogue was built in 1843. By 1851, 849 Jews resided in C. In 1885, the community numbered 3,060 members, decreasing in 1895 to 2,728. This downward trend continued, so that in 1931 the community numbered only 1,662 members. On the eve of WWII, there were 1,140 Jews in C. The Germans expelled them to the south of France and the synagogue was almost completely destroyed. After the war, the survivors rebuilt the community and set up communal institutions. In 1964 the community numbered 800 Jews.

COLOGNE (Ger. Koeln) Rhineland, Germany. Two decrees of Constantine from 321 and 331 indicate J. settlement in Germany during Roman times. The first revoked the Jews' exemption from serving on the city council and the second exempted community officials from the obligations of the lower-class citizens. For the next 700 years there is no evidence of a J. presence in C. A prosperous J. community reemerged in the High Middle Ages, the growing importance of C. as a major trading center attracting to it an increasing number of Jews. There was a J. quarter in 1075, and by the 1090s, the community numbered some 1,000 members. After suffering death and destruction at the time of the First Crusade (1096), the community was reestablished and continued uninterruptedly for some 250 years. It maintained a synagogue and a cemetery (both dating from before 1096), a separate synagogue building for the women (*Frauenschule*), a *mikve*, bak-

ery, hospice, and community center. The archbishops of C. and the town council granted the Jews a number of rights, including the right to bear arms. After the construction of the city wall in 1106, they were entrusted with the defense of one of the city's gates, the so-called *Porta Judaeorum* (the Gate of the Jews). Jews were also allowed to own houses, the number of J.-owned houses rising from about 30 in 1135 to 75 in 1340. At the head of the J. community stood a so-called *episcopus Judaeorum* (bishop of the Jews) and a council of possibly 12 members. Jurisdiction over internal matters was in the hands of a rabbinical court, except in the severest cases which were left to the archbishop. In 1331, rabbinical jurisdiction was even extended to financial claims against Jews, meaning that Christian plaintiffs, including clergymen, could be summoned to appear in the rabbinical court. Several well-known rabbis were associated with the C. community. Among them were R. Eliezer ben Yoel ha-Levi (c. 1160–1235) and R. Asher ben Yehiel (ha-Rosh, c. 1250–1327) and his son R. Yaakov ben Asher (c. 1269–1343), author of the influential *Arba'a Turim*, who were active in C. before their emigration to Spain. In the first half of the 14th cent. the position of the Jews in C. deteriorated. Goldsmiths refused to work for them and walls were erected around the J. quarter. In the 1320s, the streets leading to it were closed by gates, which were locked at night. In the Black Death persecutions of 1348–49, the community was destroyed. Although reestablished in 1372, the Jews were soon faced with new restrictions, such as special dress regulations and a ban on the employment of Christian wet-nurses. From 1393 on, the city unwillingly renewed the community's letter of protection but by 1424 all Jews had to leave. Their buildings were confiscated and the synagogue was turned into a chapel. Jews were not allowed to settle in C. for the next 400 years. Even traders, physicians, and court bankers, who could occasionally enter the city, were not generally permitted to stay overnight. A large group of those expelled founded a community in neighboring Deutz, while others joined the community at Muelheim/Rhine. Both communities used the old C. cemetery, until a new cemetery was established in Deutz in 1695. Following the French occupation of the Rhineland in 1794, residence restrictions were removed, and in 1798, the first J. family settled in C. The position of the town as the Rhineland's major trade center once again attracted Jews, and the com-

munity, founded officially in 1801, grew steadily in spite of the "Infamous Decree" of 1808 restricting J. rights and the reactionary backlash following annexation to Prussia in 1815. The J. pop. grew from 211 in 1815 to 615 in 1840, reaching 2,322 in 1861. Already by 1850, C. was the fifth largest J. community in Germany. From the outset, the C. community, which counted among its first members some of the wealthiest J. residents from Bonn and Muelheim, was relatively affluent. Particularly noteworthy is the presence of the Oppenheim family in C. The bank of Solomon Oppenheim (1772–1828), formerly the archbishop's court banker in Bonn, was, in 1810, the second largest in C. Oppenheim was elected in 1822 to the local chamber of commerce, the first Jew to hold a public office in the town. Under his son Abraham (1804–78), the bank played a pioneering role in promoting the construction of railways in the Rhineland. With the dawning of the era of liberalism in the 1840s, the Oppenheims, together with other Jews, became increasingly involved in political life. In 1841, Abraham Oppenheim and his brother Simon presented King Frederick William IV with a petition concerning the legal status of the Jews. The Oppenheims also gave financial support to the liberal paper *Rheinische Zeitung*, which was edited by Moses Hess (1812–75), whose father, David, was chairman of the J. community. Abraham Oppenheim became in 1846 the first Jew to be elected to the city council. Despite its apparent size and wealth, the community, which in matters of taxation and religious leadership was subordinate to the Krefeld and later to the Bonn consistory, developed in the first decades only the most basic communal institutions: a synagogue (dedicated 1804; closed 1853–54); two welfare associations (c. 1820); and an elementary school (1830s), with a separate section for boys and girls. The dead were buried at the Deutz cemetery (a cemetery in C. itself being established only in 1918). The first rabbi, Dr. Israel Schwarz, was only appointed in 1857. In 1861, the community became a public corporation and a few months later dedicated a magnificent synagogue at the site of the old building in the Glockengasse. In the last four decades of the 19th cent., the number of Jews more than quadrupled, reaching 9,745 in 1900; 16,093 in 1925; and a peak of 19,250 in 1931. About 4,000 Jews or one-fourth of the J. pop. in the 1920s were emigrants from Eastern Europe. The community incorporated the neighboring communities of Ehrenfeld (1913), Deutz (1927), and

forced labor or service on the eastern front, where most died. The rest were deported to Auschwitz in the second half of May 1944.

COPALNIC MANASTUR (Hung. Kapolnokmonostor) N. Transylvania dist., Rumania. A J. community existed here in the 1820s. R. Yekutiel Shwartz and his son R. Binyamin Ze'ev Shwartz are quoted in the Responsa literature of Hungary and Transylvania. The J. pop. in 1930 was 319 (26% of the total). In May 1944 the J. pop. was transferred to the Satu Mare ghetto and in June deported to Auschwitz. After the war over 100 Jews returned and by the 1960s the majority had left for Israel.

COPENHAGEN capital of Denmark. The J. community was established in 1657, but Jews resided in the kingdom before that. With J. mintmasters, financiers, jewelers, and physicians arriving and linked to the court, a united Sephardi–Ashkenazi community was subsequently established in 1684 by King Christian V. A burial site dates back to 1693. After 1726, the criteria for citizenship in C. were a minimum of capital, the means to build a house, or the establishment of a workshop or factory. From the middle of the 18th cent., the community obtained dispensations in cases where newcomers wished to marry into established families. These newcomers, mostly from Altona and Hamburg, were required to pay a small tax only. Under these circumstances, the community grew from 19 in 1682 to about 1,200 by 1784. Jews also settled in the provincial towns, such as Frederica. They were mainly engaged in moneylending, mortgage transactions, and the secondhand clothing trade. During the second half of the 18th cent., with the growth of the Danish merchant fleet and colonial trade, several important J. trading houses were founded. In 1747, Jews were required to take a special public oath accompanied by degrading rituals. The last traces of the oath were abolished only in 1864. By 1788, the Jews were allowed entry into craft guilds and in 1799 into high schools. During the great fire of 1795, the Ashkenazi synagogue, which had been consecrated in 1766, was destroyed. In 1805, a school for poor J. boys was opened; a similar girls' school was opened in 1810. In 1809, the Jews of Denmark became liable for military service. In 1814, King Frederik granted civil rights to the Jews, but they were barred from the political arena. Danish Jews were required to conduct religious

studies in Danish and also to preach in that language. The Great Synagogue of C., completed in 1833, became the seat of the chief rabbinate. In 1849, King Frederik VII granted full citizenship to Danish Jews. A second cemetery was consecrated in 1886. In the mid-19th cent., there were about 4,200 Jews living in Denmark, but the number declined to 3,500 in 1901. Between 1901 and 1921, the arrival of J. refugees from Russia bolstered the community. In 1902, the Zionist movement was introduced into the country. During WWI, World Zionist Congress headquarters operated from C. J. periodicals appeared in Danish from 1907 and a Yiddish daily appeared during WWI. The J. pop. in Denmark in 1921 was an estimated 6,000. Before Hitler came to power in Germany in 1933, Denmark had about 8,000 Jews. It was then that Benjamin Slor, a prominent Zionist, proposed that the Zionists use Denmark as a model for agricultural development. He was instrumental in establishing training farms for pioneers from Germany and Eastern Europe. Of the 1,400 Jews trained there, 1,000 reached Palestine before the German occupation of Denmark. With the advent of Nazism, Jews from Germany, Austria, and Czechoslovakia also found sanctuary in Denmark in the period before the German occupation. From these approximately 4,500 refugees, two-thirds left for other countries prior to the occupation.

Denmark was occupied on 9 April 1940. On 29 Aug. 1943, the Danish government resigned and Von Hanneken, the German supreme commander, took over. However, administrative departments remained in the hands of Danish officials. In Sept. 1943, martial law was declared in Denmark, and then, with a German roundup of Jews imminent, a rescue organization sprang up overnight. In Sept. 1943, Jews heard the dreadful news about the coming arrests while in the synagogues, where they had gathered to commemorate the J. New Year. It was planned to arrest the Jews between 1 and 2 Oct. A spontaneous popular movement developed into an organized effort by the Danish resistance movement. Within a few days, several organizations were created to rescue the Jews and a ten-member central committee was formed. About 90% of the J. pop. was spirited away to safety in neutral Sweden. In three weeks, Danish sea captains and fishermen secretly transported to Sweden 5,191 Jews, 1,301 part Jews, and 686 Christians married to Jews. The operation was referred to as a "little Dunkirk." Though many Jews were rescued during the night of 1–2 Oct. 1943

and subsequently, 475 were sent to the Theresienstadt ghetto in Bohemia, where they remained until spring 1945; 49 lost their lives there. In 1962, the J. pop. was about 6,500, residing mainly in C. In 1968, 2,500 refugees from Poland, victims of a Communist Party witch hunt, settled in the C. area. At the end of 1968, the J. pop. of Denmark was 6,000–7,000 with only 1% living outside C.

COPOU-TARG   Iasi dist., Rumania. The Jews were attached to the Iasi community but from 1870 had their own synagogue and *talmud torah*. In 1888, the J. pop. came to 185. In June 1941, at the outbreak of the Soviet-Rumanian war, the J. pop. of 182 was transferred to Iasi, where many were killed in pogroms there.

CORABIA   Walachia dist., Rumania. Jews first settled in the late 19th cent. and mainly traded in the export of wheat. Synagogues existed for the Sephardi and Ashkenazi communities. The J. pop. in 1899 came to 100, dropping to 63 in 1930. By 1942, all the Jews had fled to Caracal. The Jews never returned after the war.

CORBEIL   (Corbell-Essones) Essonne dist., France. The J. presence dates back to the second half of the 12th cent. at least. The Jews were expelled in 1180 but are mentioned again in the beginning of the 13th cent. C. was famous for its *yeshivot*. Among its scholars were the tosafist Yehuda of C., Yaakov the Saint, Shimshon of C., and others. The Jews were expelled in 1306 with the other Jews of the kingdom but returned in 1315. The community ceased to exist in 1321. During WWII, at the beginning of the German occupation of France (1941), 13 J. families were registered in C.

CORFU   (Kerkyra, Kerkira) Ionian Islands, Greece. In the Middle Ages a community of Romaniot Jews from the Balkan peninsula was formed in C. Under Venetian rule (from 1386) the Jews were subject to prejudicial enactments, but also enjoyed various rights, economic stability, and political security. In the late 14th cent., Jews from southern Italy settled in C. and in the late 15th cent. a number of Jews exiled from Spain, Portugal, and Sicily settled there. In 1522, there were about 200 J. families in C., mostly Romaniot. In the 16th cent., the Italian congregation developed, and from 1540–41 included exiles from Naples.

The Jewish quarter of Corfu, Greece (Netta Gatian/photo courtesy of Yad Vashem, The Holocaust Martyrs' and Heroes' Remembrance Authority, Jerusalem)

Among them was Yitzhak Abravanel, who wrote his commentary on the book of Isaiah there before moving to Venice. There were three synagogues at that time. In 1622, the Jews were ordered to live in a ghetto and received protection from the authorities. By this time the Italian community predominated over the Romaniot community in size and organization. However, the Romaniot community preserved the Greek tradition over the centuries, which became known as the Corfu Rite (*Minhag Corfu*). Friction between the two prevailed, although they cooperated in the redemption of captives. Most Jews were engaged in trade, many focusing on the citron (*etrog*) trade. Many joined the Venetian struggles against the Turkish invaders in the 16th and 18th cents. In 1797–99 and in 1806–15, C. came under French occupation. During this time the Jews en-

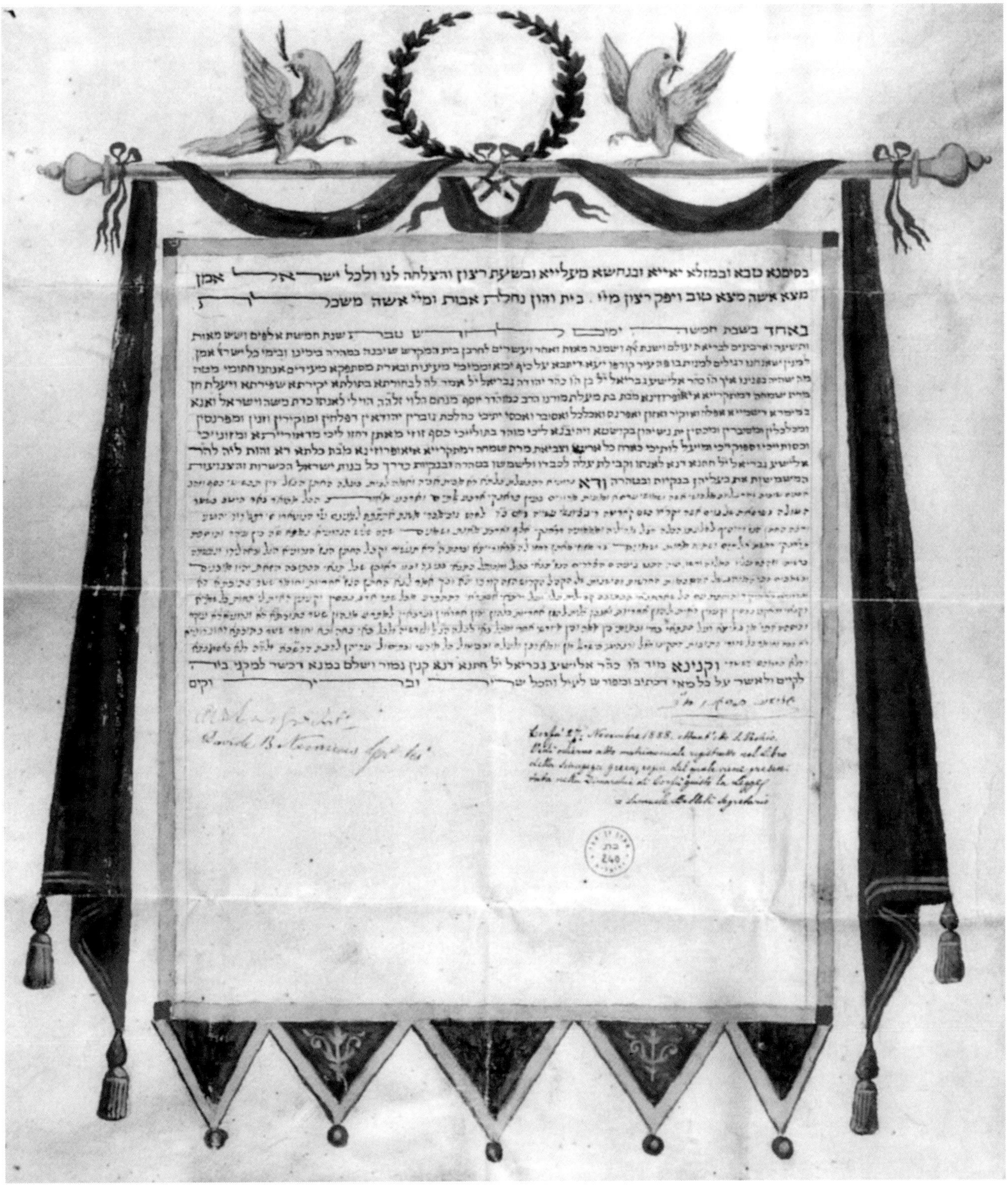
בסימנא טבא ובמזלא יאייא ובנחשא מעלייא ובשעת רצון והצלחה לנו ולכל ישראל אמן
מצא אשה מצא טוב ויפק רצון מה׳ . בית והון נחלת אבות ומה׳ אשה משכלת

*Marriage contract (*Kettubah*), Corfu, Greece (Collection Ben Zvi Institute/photo courtesy of Yad Vashem, The Holocaust Martyrs' and Heroes' Remembrance Authority, Jerusalem)*

joyed equal civil rights. In the early 19th cent., the J. pop. grew with an influx of Jews from Italy and the Ottoman Empire. The J. pop. in 1802 was 1,229 (total 45,000). Under British rule (1815–64), the Jews were deprived of their civil rights and subjected to antisemitic propaganda that culminated in a blood libel in 1856. In the 1820s and 1830s, many Romaniot Jews fleeing the violent Greek struggle for independence arrived in C. During this period, J. education on the island was modernized and traditional studies were expanded to include science, Greek, and Italian alongside Hebrew. In 1863, C. was annexed to Greece. That year the J. pop. peaked at 6,000 (total 64,974). Under Greek rule the Jews received full civil rights. Many entered the free professions and some participated in municipal politics, with a Jew serving as deputy mayor and others on the municipal council. A Hebrew press operated intermittently between 1853 and 1896. After 1875 a J. girls' school for the poor was opened and a J. elementary school was established in 1887. Despite the Jews' patriotism, their newfound achievements triggered anti-J. sentiment amongst the Greeks and a blood libel took place in April 1891, when a Jew was accused of murdering a Christian girl. Thousands of Greeks rioted for a month in the J. quarter with knives, stones, and bayonets. A curfew on the J. quarter to protect its inhabitants led to hunger, illness, and many deaths. European governments became involved in the affair and a long trial was held in Patras. In following years, anti-J. sentiment arose on the eve of Easter, when the Jews would confine themselves to their homes. J. communities, organizations, and philanthropists worldwide sent donations and aid to the riot victims, including the Alliance Israelite and the Hirsch and Rothschild families. About this time, in 1875, the *etrog* or citron trade plummeted when R. Yitzhak Elhanan Spektor of Kovno judged the crops unfit for ritual use. As the J. security and financial standing were undermined, about one-quarter of the J. pop. left C. for other countries and towns. In the early 20th cent., many Jews were poor and the community's school was closed down. In 1906 a Zionist organization, the second in Greece, was established in C. Attempts to provoke blood libels again in 1915, 1918, and 1922 led many Jews to emigrate to Palestine. By 1923 the community numbered only about 3,000 Jews. Nevertheless, in 1928 C., with 1,832 Jews (total 102,552), was the fourth largest community in Greece after Salonika, Kavala, and Jan-

ina. Many Zionist activists emigrated in the 1930s and the Zionist organization consequently closed down. In the early 1930s C.'s economy improved, also to the Jews' benefit.

Prior to the Holocaust, the J. community numbered 1,880 (total 108,345), two-thirds of whom belonged to the Italian community and one-third to the Greek. The Italian community had three synagogues and the Greek community had one. The Italians occupied C. in April 1941, after heavy bombing that led a number of Jews to flee. Under the Italians, the Jews were relatively safe and refugees from German-occupied areas of Greece arrived there. In Sept. 1943 the Germans bombed C., destroying many J. homes and the three Italian synagogues. As C. came under German control, intricate plans were made for the deportation of its Jews to Polish death camps. In May 1944, pursuit, oppression, and humiliation of the Jews began. On 24 May, six ships arrived at C.'s port, but as the Greek security police did not cooperate in assisting the deportations, the Germans were unable to board the Jews on the ships. On 9 June, all the Jews were rounded up – including the children, elderly, and sick – and were held in a fortress. They numbered about 1,800. About 200, mainly women, managed to hide in island monasteries and villages. The possessions of the Jews were now confiscated and their homes plundered. Over the following week the Jews were taken in three transports to Athens, via Patras. They were then conveyed, beginning on 20 June, by a freight train to Auschwitz; several died on the way. Only a few survived the death camp. Several J. families from C. went into hiding and survived. A few survivors returned to C. after the war and were joined by about 120 from other areas. Thus the community was revived but remained small. The J. pop. was 125 in 1948 and 85 in 1958, rising to 104 in 1959.

COSEL (Pol. Kozle) Upper Silesia, Germany, today Poland. Small-scale J. settlement began in 1373. In 1563, J. settlement in C. and the surrounding area was banned. Only in the 18th cent. were Jews again permitted to settle. Their number rose from two in 1750 to 112 in 1782. The community maintained a synagogue (from 1884), J. school (1820), and cemetery. It reached a peak pop. of 236 in 1880, earning its livelihood from leaseholds and the wholesale trade in cattle and grain. Emigration to the big cities reduced the J. pop. to 119 in 1910 and 84 in 1930. The Nazi racial laws were not enforced until July 1937 owing

to the extension of the League of Nations' minority rights convention to the Jews of the area. J. children were subsequently removed from the local public school and transferred to the regional J. school in Ratibor. The synagogue was set on fire on *Kristallnacht* (9–10 Nov. 1938), and in 1939, 24 Jews remained. In June 1942, the Jews were deported to Poland together with the Jews of Gleiwitz. Eight remained on 19 Nov. 1942.

COSMENI (Cozmeni or Cotmani; Ger. Kotzman, Rus. Kucmeh) Bukovina, Rumania, today Ukraine. A J. community existed in the late 19th cent. The J. pop. in 1930 was 647. From 1926 to 1936, R. Barukh Hager of the Vizhnitz hasidic dynasty served as rabbi. In June 1941, 27 leaders of the community were shot by the Germans and in Oct., 560 Jews were deported to Transnistria.

COSTESTI Bukovina, Rumania, today Ukraine. Jews settled in the late 19th cent. and engaged in commerce and agriculture. The J. pop. in 1930 was 274. In June 1941, 420 Jews were taken to an open field and shot.

COTTBUS Brandenburg, Germany. Evidence of a J. presence in C. dates back to 1448. This early community was subjected to the two general expulsions of all Jews from the Brandenburg province in 1510 and in 1573. A permanent settlement was started in 1740. A prayer room was set up in 1811 and a burial ground purchased in 1814. In the 1850s, when the J. pop. numbered about 45 individuals, an official synagogue community was set up which adopted Liberal Judaism. The J. pop. was 354 in 1880 and 396 in 1910. A larger synagogue was dedicated in 1902 and a new cemetery opened in 1918. When the Nazis came to power in 1933, there were 450 Jews in C. In 1938–39, a pioneer training farm was run at nearby Echow. The expulsion of the Polish Jews from Germany at the end of Oct. 1938 affected 31 Jews in C. On *Kristallnacht* (9–10 Nov. 1938), the synagogue was burned down, J. shops and apartments were demolished, and the old cemetery was desecrated. Thirty people were arrested and deported to the Sachsenhausen concentration camp. Two died shortly after their release in Dec. 1938 as a result of the maltreatment they suffered. By May 1939, 142 Jews and 79 persons of partial J. origin (*Mischlinge*) were still living in C. The Jews

were assigned to "J. houses" and compelled to do forced labor. At the end of 1940 or in 1941, deportations began to various locations in Eastern Europe, including the Warsaw ghetto (April 1942) and the Theresienstadt ghetto (24 Aug. 1942). By Oct. 1942, there were only 29 Jews in C., most married to non-Jews. The men were taken to forced labor camps in 1943–44. At the end of the war, there were only 13 Jews left in C.

COURBEVOIE Seine dist., France. According to the census of 1941, there were 386 Jews listed as residing in C. In July 1942, 34 were arrested.

CRACIUNESTI (Hung. Karacsonfalva, previously Tiszakaracsonfalva; Yid. Kretschinev) N. Transylvania dist., Rumania. Jews first settled in the early 18th cent. and engaged in the lumber trade. The community declined after WWI. The J. pop. in 1930 was 889 (48% of the total). In summer 1941 some Jews who did not have Hungarian citizenship were expelled to Galicia and were murdered by the Nazis in Kamenets-Podolski. In 1942 Jews aged 20–42 were drafted into labor battalions, mainly in the Ukraine, where they died. In April 1944 the J. pop. was transferred to the Sighet ghetto and then deported to Auschwitz.

CRACOW (Pol. Krakow) Cracow dist., Poland. A permanent J. settlement is known from the early 14th cent. but Jews were probably present much earlier. The first J. settlers apparently came from Czechoslovakia and lived in their own quarter around a small square near the city wall, with a J. cemetery outside. In 1334, King Casimir the Great confirmed the general privilege granted to the Jews of Greater Poland in 1264 guaranteeing them freedom of trade and residence and the right to lend money against mortgaged property, their major occupation in the 14th cent. The few tradesmen among the Jews mainly served the community. A number of the J. moneylenders conducted business on a large scale, including loans to the king. One named Levko was court banker to Casimir and in 1368 was given administrative control of the treasury and won the salt mine concession in Wieliczka and Bochnia. The location of a university within the J. quarter in 1400 led to constant friction with the students, fed by clerical anti-J. agitation. In 1407, rioting townsmen killed a large number of Jews and destroyed J. homes and property. Another outbreak of violence in 1423

The Rema synagogue in the Jewish quarter of Cracow, Poland

was instigated by members of the municipal council. Due to clerical prompting the king restricted loan pledges to the Jews to valuables (in place of property), thus severely limiting the scope of J. business. Further agitation caused the king to rescind J. privileges in all Poland in 1454. Shortly afterwards Jews were again attacked following a fire in the city. In 1463 Crusaders attacked the Jews in C., killing 30 and looting the J. quarter. Under unremitting pressure, Jews were forced to sell off public property, leave their homes, and "voluntarily" undertake to abstain from trading and pursuing their crafts in the city. New riots followed a fire in 1494 and this time the king was induced to expel the Jews from the city, permitting them to settle in adjacent Kazimierz, which became the seat of Cracow Jewry for the next 400 years. The refugees joined an organized J. community there. The magnificent Gothic synagogue (the older Stara synagogue) traditionally dates from the 15th cent. (It still stands and since WWII has been used as a J. museum.) Refugees

from Czechoslovakia along with settlers from Germany and Italy arrived in the first half of the 16th cent., bringing the J. pop. up to 2,100 in the second half of the cent. and 4,500 in the first half of the 17th cent. despite frequent debilitating epidemics and fires. Many arrived from the Ukraine and Rzeszow in the wake of the Chmielnicki massacres of 1648–49. In 1583 the Jews received permission from the king to expand the J. quarter but because of local opposition and rioting the decision was only implemented in 1608, fixing the boundaries of the J. residential area until the First Partition of Poland in 1772. J. trade remained confined to the J. quarter even after the lifting of restrictions for all of Poland in 1532 by King Sigismund I. Only in 1576 were they allowed to rent stores and warehouses throughout the city, though in 1587 the city council again rescinded this privilege and subsequently even restricted their right to buy food freely. At the same time, the Christian (Czech) guilds waged war against J. artisans. Nonetheless the Jews managed

After morning prayers, Cracow, Poland, 1937

to engage in all the crafts and also formed a society of prosperous jewelers. Jews were also bankers, leaseholders, and merchants. Prominent in all these endeavors were such Czech Jews as Avraham Franczek, the Fischel family, and Yisrael Isserles, father of the famous rabbinic authority Moshe Isserles (the "Rema"; 1525 or 1530–72). Shelomo Ashkenazi of Modena, Italy, ran his affairs in C. in 1541–1564 and afterwards became court banker to the Turkish sultan. In the 17th cent., R. Yitzhak Jekeles and Wolf (Boscian) Popper founded commercial dynasties. In this period the J. settlement was one of the largest in Poland and was in effect divided into a Polish and Czech community. Because of the friction between the two, the famous halakhist R. Yaakov Pollack, founder of the talmudic

method of *hillukim* ("fine distinctions") that spread through Poland, was deposed from his rabbinical chair in 1508 and only allowed to run his yeshiva. Subsequent yeshiva heads were such illustrious rabbis as Moshe Isserles, best known for his glosses on the *Shulhan Arukh* (the Rema synagogue built by his father is still in use), Meir ben Gedalya of Lublin, Yoel Sirkes, and Yom Tov Lippman Heller, who also served as rabbi from 1644 until his death in 1654. Hebrew printing presses were in operation from 1530. Yitzhak of Prossnitz and his sons published about 200 books in 1569–1626, including the Babylonian and Jerusalem Talmuds. The Meisels family took over the firm's equipment and was active in 1630–70. The community's prosperity was curtailed by the Swedish

invasion of 1655, when the conquering army was given three days of license to murder and pillage after breaking through the city walls. About 2,500 Jews were killed and the community was subsequently forced to quarter the Swedish soldiers and pay heavy tributes. Jews were attacked by the local pop. as well during the war years and the community was further decimated by plague (1,100 dying in 1677). A long period of economic depression now set in. J. tradesmen came under pressure from the guilds, with the old 15th cent. restrictions again invoked and finally sanctioned by King Augustus II in 1761. Throughout the period, however, owing largely to the importance of the Jews to the royal house as sources of tax revenues, credit, and loans, the community maintained an important economic position. J. merchants and moneylenders became royal factors and the bigger ones were rewarded with public and private concessions (salt mines, distilleries, taxes). However, the overall decline of the community undermined its position as a provincial center and caused smaller communities to break away from under its aegis, most becoming independent by the mid-17th cent. The turmoil of the period also had spiritual repercussions as messianic yearnings came to the fore and the Kabbalah attracted students. Prominent among the kabbalists was the yeshiva head R. Natan Shapiro (d. 1633) and his successor Berahiyya-Barukh Shapiro, who sailed to Constantinople with a number of disciples to receive Shabbetai Zvi. However, in the famous dispute surrounding the supposed Shabbatean leanings of R. Yonatan Eybeschuetz (d. 1764), a native of the city, the community placed a ban on his antagonist R. Yaakov Emden. In the period preceding the First Partition, the community suffered at the hands of the Polish and Russian armies, who exacted tributes and pillaged J. property. After the Partition in 1772, Kazimierz, with its community of 4,000 Jews, came under Austrian rule while C., with its many J. stores and workshops, remained under the Poles. Consequently, 258 J. businesses were transferred to the Christian sections of Kazimierz under agreements signed with the municipal council; 92 remained in C. In 1795 (Third Partition of Poland), C. as well came under Austrian rule and all the Jews now were affected by the 1789 "Edict of Tolerance" (*Toleranzpatent*) of Emperor Joseph II, whose declared aim of "modernizing" the Jews was interlaced with economic restrictions and discriminatory taxes. In 1802, the Austrian authorities yielded to local pressure and ordered the remaining J. businesses out of C. In 1809, as an outcome of the Franco-Austrian peace treaty, C. became part of the Grand Duchy of Warsaw, whose liberal constitution was never applied to the Jews. In 1815, after the Congress of Vienna, the C. Republic was established, embracing 244 villages with a pop. of 23,000 in a 20 sq. mile (52 sq. km) area. Here, too, the old restrictions against the Jews remained in force while Jews were also excluded from operating distilleries, an important source of income. J. autonomy was seriously affected when the old community council was replaced by a Committee for J. Affairs headed by a Christian and with its finances handled by the municipal treasurer. Laws regulating J. marriage were also passed and in 1840 the Senate ordered the *heder* and *talmud torah* system closed down in an effort to get J. children to attend public schools. Thus Jews were obliged to fabricate documents to qualify for marriage and educate their children clandestinely. In this period the J. pop. nearly doubled, from 7,252 in 1818 to 13,080 in 1843. Despite restrictions, the Jews found

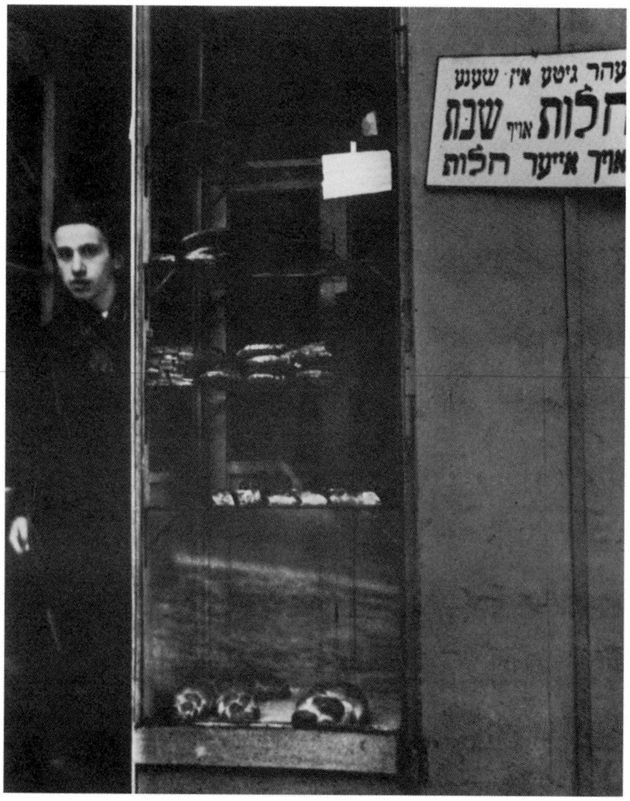
גיטע און שענע
אויף שבת
אייער חלות

Jewish bakery in Kazimierz suburb of Cracow, Poland, 1937. The sign reads: "Very Good and Beautiful Challahs for the Sabbath. Egg Challahs Too"

ways to exploit the opportunities made available by C.'s status as a free city and the laying of a railway line to Vienna in 1844. They were among its first industrialists, setting up brickyards and porcelain and liqueur factories. Most trade remained in J. hands, though many Jews were reduced to peddling, where government control was relaxed. A few were prominent bookdealers and the number of J. artisans also increased. The growing professional and educated class tended to adopt modern dress and European ways and in 1840 opened a Reform temple in a private house (transferred to its own building in 1862). About 500 Jews, including the influential rabbi of the community, Dov Berush Meisels, participated in the Polish rebellion against Austria in 1846. Under renewed Austrian rule from 1846, the rate of growth of the community slowed down, the pop. reaching 20,269 (total 66,096) in 1880, with emigration to Western Europe and America subsequently stepped up and the proportion of Jews in the general pop. declining as outlying villages and suburbs were incorporated into the city. In addition, 379 Jews converted in the 1887–1900 period. Industrial development was slow though a home textile industry developed. Most Jews now owned small stores or stalls. In 1905, 70 of the city's 114 lawyers were Jews and a number of doctors held chairs at the university. The community operated numerous mutual aid and loan societies and charitable organizations. A branch of the Alliance Israelite was opened in 1880 as well as a vocational school sponsored by Baron Hirsch. In 1870 the J. hospital was expanded to 80 beds and an old age home was opened in 1879. Most of the community remained Orthodox, with Hasidism (Zanz, Radomsk, Blazow, Belz) infusing its life. The "enlightened" minority concentrated around the temple and its preacher. The moderates were pro-German, and the extremists with their Polish assimilationist tendencies gathered in the Shomer Israel society. Though Orthodox and Haskala circles were bitterly at odds with one another, they were united in their opposition to the Zionists, who began their activities in 1883 and included women's and youth groups. Other Jews were attracted to the Social Democrats. J. education expanded, with a *talmud torah* for 400 children beginning a process of modernization in 1879 and two Hebrew elementary schools founded in 1905–14. In 1902, J. students set up an open university. Libraries, social clubs, and a popular Yiddish theater all operated as well. J. life was seriously disrupted by WWI.

Despite the city's distance from the front, disease, food shortages, inflation, and economic standstill plagued the community. With the disintegration of Austrian rule, peasant disturbances multiplied and the Jews set up a self-defense group with 250 regulars and many more in reserve. In late 1918, the Polish General Haller arrived and his soldiers, accompanied by a local Polish mob, broke into the J. quarters and fought a pitched battle with the J. defenders, after which the Jews were permanently disarmed by the authorities. Economic recovery was slow under Polish rule in the face of anti-J. boycotts, discriminatory government measures, and the loss of Austrian markets. The J. pop. rose from 32,321 in 1910 to 45,229 in 1921 and 55,515 (total 215,963) in 1931. Three-quarters of the Jews earned their livings in trade, crafts, and manufacturing and over half of J. production was concentrated in the clothing industry. In 1938, Jews owned 45% (577 in number) of the big and medium-sized factories in the city and 63% (3,413) of its workshops. Among the doctors and lawyers, 61% were Jews. Immediately after WWI a clinic treating 30,000 patients a year was opened with assistance from the Joint Distribution Committee and the J. orphanage sheltered 100 children. The Orthodox-assimilationist alliance controlled the community council in the 1920s while Jews, though underrepresented, served as deputy mayors on the city council. Zionist activity revived between the World Wars. The General Zionists were the largest group and among the many youth movements Bnei Akiva reached a membership of nearly 1,000 in 1939. Agudat Israel was active in community institutions and the Bund found support among J. workers in the trade unions. Jews were also active in the illegal Communist Party. Yehoshua Thon represented the city and Western Galicia in the Polish Sejm in 1919–35. The prewar Hebrew school was converted into an elementary and bilingual secondary school, the former with an enrollment of 507 in 1937–38, the latter with 825. Mizrachi also operated primary and secondary schools and a J. business school had 400 students in 1936–39. A vocational school for girls had 200 students in 1930, when it was joined by a school for boys. In 1930–31. 1,857 Jews (23.8% of the student body) studied at the local university, though the *numerus clausus* was applied in a number of faculties, such as medicine and pharmacy, where few Jews were admitted. In the public school system as well, where most J. children studied, antisemitism was com-

Bnei Akiva activists in Cracow. First and second from left: Gusta (Justyna) and Shimon (Simek) Draenger, editor-in-chief of the Akiva Chronicles, *Cracow, Poland, 1940 (Photo courtesy of Draenger family)*

mon and throughout the 1930s it intensified in daily life, with Jews sometimes attacked physically in the streets.

Many fled to the east on the approach of the Germans in Sept. 1939 and were among the refugees exiled by the Soviets from Eastern Galicia to the interior of Russia in 1940. About 300 fighting with the Polish army were taken prisoner by the Germans and released in early 1940. During Sept. 1939 many J. refugees reached the city. The *Wehrmacht* immediately instituted a regime of forced labor, robbery, and persecution. J. businesses were "Aryanized" and J. property was confiscated. In Dec., all J. schools were closed down and J. children expelled from the public schools. The synagogues were closed as well and ritual slaughter was prohibited. Jews were banned from public places and restricted in their movement. To deal with the many J. refugees, the *Judenrat* set up soup kitchens, serving over three million meals up to Sept. 1940 and distributing clothing to 9,000 people as well as free medicines. An estimated 70,000 Jews were present in C. and its suburbs in Nov. 1939 as opposed to 56,000 on the eve of the war. In May 1940 the Germans announced their intention to reduce the J. pop. to 15,000 essential workers through "voluntary" evacuation. Many chose to seek shelter in neighboring villages, but by Oct. 1940 only 32,000 had left. Eight thousand more without work permits were expelled to the Lublin dist. of Poland and other localities between Nov. 1940 and April 1941. Those remaining suffered during the winter from disease, hunger, and the cold. A ghetto was sealed off in the southern part of the city in March 1941, holding over 12,000 Jews as many more chose to leave the city. Many in the ghetto were reduced to living in warehouses, cellars, attics, and hallways. Epidemics broke out, raising the mortality rate to 13 times its prewar level. In Nov. 1941, 2,000 Jews without permits were expelled to the Lublin dist. At the same time, about 6,500 Jews from the surrounding villages were transferred to the ghetto, so that together with the 1,318 Jews in the orphanage and old age home, its pop. rose to above 18,000. In the winter of 1941–42 the ghetto post office was closed, thus severing all contact with the outside world. Thousands of Jews worked for German industry while others worked in local workshops set up by

completed their occupation of Greece with the conquest of C. (May 1941). No special restrictions were placed on the Jews, who numbered 320. A few families fled but the rest (except for some youths) were arrested on 20 May 1944 and placed on a ship destined for a death camp. The ship, named the *Tanais* or *Danae*, containing about 265 Jews, 400 Greek hostages. and 300 Italian prisoners of war, was torpedoed on 9 June by a British submarine and all aboard perished. It is still unknown whether the British were aware of the ship's human cargo.

CRISTUR (Hung. Szekelykeresztur) N. Transylvania dist., Rumania. A J. community was founded in the 1880s. The J. pop. in 1930 was 155 (4% of the total). In 1941, some Jews who did not have Hungarian citizenship were expelled and murdered in Kamenets-Podolski. In May 1944 the J. pop. was transferred to the Sfantul Gheorghe ghetto and in June deported to Auschwitz.

CRONHEIM Middle Franconia, Germany. The Jews were expelled in 1630 and after 1650 formed a community under the protection of the prince-bishop, Marquart II of Eichstaett. A new synagogue was built in 1816 and the J. pop. reached 197 in 1837 (total 500) but thereafter declined. In 1933, 35 Jews remained. The synagogue was sold on 1 Nov. 1938 after the interior had been wrecked ten days earlier. All the Jews had left by that time, many to the U.S.; the last eight were expelled to Augsburg in Oct. 1938 and perished in the Holocaust.

CROSSEN (Pol. Krosno Odrzanskie) Brandenburg, Germany, today Poland. The J. community maintained a synagogue (1851) and a cemetery. The J. pop. was 176 in 1880. When the Nazis came to power in 1933, there were only 67 Jews in C. On *Kristallnacht* (9–10 Nov. 1938), the synagogue was burned down. By May 1939, there were 24 Jews and eight persons of mixed J. origin (*Mischlinge*) in C. Probably the Jews who did not manage to emigrate were deported to the east, with the exception of two women married to non-Jews who were still living in the town in Nov. 1944.

CRUMSTADT Hesse, Germany. The community numbered 84 (6.2% of the total) in 1880. Most Jews left before 1939, often emigrating to the U.S. Some

German townsfolk objected to *Kristallnacht* (9–10 Nov. 1938), which resulted in the synagogue's demolition. The last Jews were deported in 1942.

CSABRENDEK Zala dist., Hungary. Jews settled in the mid-18th cent., reaching a pop. of 583 in 1869, when they formed a Neologist congregation. A synagogue was built in 1782 and a J. public school opened in 1859. Many earned their living producing and marketing lime. Gradually residents left for the big cities and the J. pop. dropped to 107 in 1930 and 57 in 1941. All were deported to Auschwitz after being brought to Zalaegerszeg in mid-May 1944.

CSANY Heves dist., Hungary. Jews settled in the first half of the 19th cent. and numbered 63 in 1930. The community defined itself as Neologist and a synagogue was built in 1891. In 1942, the men were sent to forced labor in the Ukraine where many died. The rest were brought to the Hatvan ghetto in the beginning of June 1944 and deported to Auschwitz on 8 June.

CSENGER Szatmar dist., Hungary. Jews settled in the late 18th cent., at the invitation of Count Karlyi. A synagogue was consecrated in 1820 and a J. school was opened in 1896. R. Avraham Jungreisz, who officiated in 1874–1904, founded a popular yeshiva. The J. pop. was 630 in 1910 and 538 in 1941. Mizrachi was active in the 1930s. The 1939 racial laws undermined J. livelihoods. In April 1944, the Jews were expelled to Mateszalka. The able-bodied were sent to work in Kassa and the rest were deported to Auschwitz from 19 May to 5 June 1944.

CSEPEL Pest–Pilis–Solt–Kiskun dist., Hungary. Jews settled after 1893, when Manfred Weisz opened his metal-working factories, becoming the major employer of Jews. The J. pop. rose from 260 in 1910 to 902 (2% of the total) in 1941. In 1943, J. males were sent on forced labor. On 10 May 1944, the remaining Jews were confined, together with 3,000 Jews from the area, to a ghetto near Weisz's factories and on 30 June 1944, all were deported to Auschwitz. Eighty survivors reestablished the community.

CSEPREG Sopron dist., Hungary. A J. quarter is mentioned in 1492 but few Jews were present after the expulsion of 1526 until the late 18th cent. The community organized itself in 1860, building a synagogue

that same year. At first defining itself as Status Quo, the community subsequently became Neologist and then, in 1925, Orthodox. In 1930 the J. pop. was 61. In the beginning of July 1944, the Jews were deported to Auschwitz via Sarvar.

CSOMOR Pest–Pilis–Solt–Kiskun dist., Hungary. The J. pop. stood at 77 in 1930. The Jews were rounded up on 28 June 1944 and then deported to Auschwitz in July.

CSONGRAD Csongrad dist., Hungary. Jews settled in the late 18th cent., becoming prominent wine growers and sellers. They also founded most of the city's banks and initiated the construction of a hospital. The community organized in 1800 and a synagogue was built in 1854. The community defined itself as Neologist in 1869. Its pop. rose to a peak of 415 (1.7% of the total) in 1910, dropping to 286 in 1941. During the White Terror, a bomb at a J. event killed three and injured 40. At the end of June 1944, the Jews were expelled to Szeged and from there deported to Auschwitz and Austria. Survivors renewed the community but it gradually disintegrated over the years.

CSORNA Sopron dist., Hungary. Jews settled in the late 18th cent., founding a school and synagogue in 1854 and maintaining a 6,000-volume library. The J. pop. was 512 in 1880 and 795 in 1930. In May 1944, the Jews were confined in a ghetto; on 18 June, they were taken to the Sopron ghetto; and on 5 July they were deported to Auschwitz. Survivors reestablished the community.

CSURGO Zala dist., Hungary. The J. community organized in the early 19th cent., erecting a synagogue in 1840 and opening a school in 1850. Defining itself as Neologist, the community numbered 276 in 1880 and 229 in 1930. During the White Terror disturbances, seven Jews from C. were shot to death. In May 1944, the Jews were brought to Barcs and from there deported on 6 July to Auschwitz.

CUHEA (Hung. Izakonyha) N. Transylvania dist., Rumania. Jews first settled in the early 18th cent. Most of the Jews were poor and engaged in agriculture. R. Pinhas Shapira had a hasidic court in C. The J. pop. in 1930 was 321 (15% of the total). In April 1944 the J.

pop. was transferred to the Viseul de Sus ghetto and then deported to Auschwitz. Thirty survivors returned after the war but most left for Israel.

CULEMBORG (Kuilenburg) Gelderland dist., Holland. The earliest mention of Jews is from the late 17th cent. A community was organized in the mid-18th cent. and grew rapidly in the early 19th cent., peaking at 193 in 1869 (total 6,215). A number of social welfare organizations were operating by the late 19th cent., including a branch of the Alliance Israelite (1888-1905). The most important field of occupation among the Jews was trade in manufactured textile goods. They were active in the general culture and politics of C. From the mid-19th cent. a J. school operated. The community began to dwindle in the 1880s. The J. pop. in 1941 was 54 (total 9,738). The Jews were deported in the Holocaust; four survived the deportations and ten in hiding.

CURTICI (Hung. Kurtos) S. Transylvania dist., Rumania. A J. community existed here in 1863 and was attached to the community in Arad. The J. pop. was 97 (1% of the total) in 1930. On 24 July 1941, the J. pop. was expelled to Arad.

CURUG Vojvodina dist., Yugoslavia. The Jews of this community, established in the early 20th cent., numbered 75 in 1931 (total pop. 10,483). In Jan. 1942 they were concentrated in storehouses where they died of hunger, torture, and shooting.

CUYK Noord-Brabant dist., Holland. A community existed from the 18th cent. The J. pop. was 17 in 1941 (total 4,445). Seven survived the Holocaust in hiding; the rest were deported and perished.

CUXHAVEN Hamburg, Germany. C. sprang from a mid-18th cent. settlement at Ritzebuettel, at the mouth of the Elbe River. In 1797, the Jews here established a community, dedicated a synagogue in 1816, and by 1820 numbered 108 (over 2% of the total). Calls to end J. business competition (1752-1828) were rejected by the local authorities. Following emancipation in 1849, many Jews emigrated and their number dwindled to 29 in 1880. In 1907, a naval base, seaside hotels, and a fishing industry led to the development of C. as a new German seaport. Local antisemitism restricted the growth of the J. pop., which again declined –

Election rally, Czenstochowa, Poland (YIVO Archive, New York, Gustav Eisner Collection/photo courtesy of Beth Hatefutsoth, Tel Aviv)

banned from the religious article trade, they went over to toy manufacturing. By 1895, Jews owned 14 of C.'s 23 larger factories, employing 3,030 workers. Among them were a printing and lithography plant, an iron foundry, and textile, paper, and cable factories. Afterwards Jews founded a hat factory employing 450 and another textile plant with 1,150 workers. No more than 200 Jews worked in these factories, most preferring self-employment and refusing to work on the Sabbath. In 1898, 1,938 J. craftsmen were registered in the city as the J. pop. rose from 1,141 in 1827 to 11,764 (total 39,869) in 1897. In the late 19th cent., thousands of Orthodox Jews began to settle from the neighboring villages and in the course of time came to share power in the community with the Zionists, who became active in the early 20th cent. By 1908 the J. pop. was 22,024 (total 69,525). In 1894, Nahum Asch became rabbi, serving for 42 years as a pillar of the community and working to promote good relations with the Polish pop. The community maintained six hasidic courts and a number of *shtiblekh* in the city. Among the large hasidic groups were the followers of R. Nahman of Bratslav. In 1906, the cantor (*hazzan*) and composer

Avraham Baer Birnbaum opened a school for cantorial music, the first of its kind in the world. Throughout the 19th cent., the community maintained mutual aid and charity organizations. In 1899, a roof organization for charity services, called *Dobroczynnosc*, was created. In addition to furnishing food, clothing, medical aid, and fuel to the needy, it operated an old age home. In 1913, it dedicated a J. hospital with 50 beds and two operating rooms. J. schools were in operation from the second half of the 19th cent. On the eve of WWI, 5,000 children were studying in five J. elementary schools, three *talmud torah* schools, and two or three vocational schools. Another 4,000 children were enrolled in the *heder* system. Most Jews barely eked out a living, with half the J. pop. exempt from community taxes. During the 1890s, strikes began to break out in the factories and many Jews, attracted to the socialist camp as well as to the Zionists, played an active role in the revolutionary events of 1904–06. By 1905, the Bund had 200 members. Prewar cultural life revolved around the Lyre Society for Literature and Music, founded in 1908, where a spirit of assimilation prevailed. A sports club founded in 1915 had 500 members. In the late

19th cent., antisemitism came to the fore. A pogrom organized in Aug. 1902 involved wild rioting, the injury of many Jews, and the destruction of 120 J. stores. Under the German occupation in WWI, economic life came to a virtual standstill and 1,942 residents of the city died of starvation and disease. At the same time, political life revived and Jews enjoyed new educational opportunities. In 1921, 2,730 Jews were employed in J. workshops and factories, most in the garment industry. Although newly established J. factories produced baby carriages, roller skates, and bicycle parts and J. banks proliferated, most of the period was characterized by economic hardship. In 1931, the J. pop. was 25,588 (total 117,179). A ramified system of welfare services continued to operate, augmented by the TOZ public health organization, which treated 15,000 Jews a year, provided meals to schoolchildren, and ran camps. With the rise of a J. proletariat in the city, J. left-wing parties became prominent. The Bund was active in workers' organizations as well as in the community, operating women's, children's, and sports auxiliaries. Another major force were the J. trade unions with their 5,000 members, 3,000 of them garment workers. The first Zionist youth movement in the city was Hashomer Hatzair, founded in 1914. In 1927, it began operating a pioneer training farm. Ha-No'ar ha-Tziyyoni had 200 members in 1935. The Revisionists had 300 members in 1933 and Mizrachi was also active. Agudat Israel had its own youth movement and operated a Beth Jacob school for girls and a commercial bank. The educational system expanded to include six kindergartens for 430 children; eight elementary schools enrolling 2,100; two secondary schools (500); a vocational school (120) offering day and night classes; and an ORT school for electricians and welders (from 1938). One of the secondary schools was headed by the historian Meir Balaban, who expanded Hebrew studies. *Heder* students continued their studies in the city's *yeshivot*, the most notable being the Keter Torah yeshiva. The community had two synagogues, three *battei midrash*, 16 *shtiblekh*, and over a hundred other prayer houses. It also had numerous libraries and extensive cultural activity, including a permanent J. theater. A Maccabi contingent was sent to the Second Maccabiah Games in Tel Aviv in 1935. During the period, about 20 J. periodicals were published in C. Antisemitic outbursts continued between the World Wars. Pogroms were periodically staged and in the 1930s the anti-J. boycott caused many Jews to liquidate their businesses. In 1937, rampaging Endecja hoodlums injured dozens of Jews, destroyed a J. school, and seriously damaged 13 J. homes, 37 J. stores, and the two synagogues.

The Germans captured C. on 3 Sept. 1939, indiscriminately killing 300–500 civilians, including Jews. On 26 Oct., C. was incorporated into General Gouvernement territory and thus cut off from its economic hinterland—the mining and industrial regions of Silesia and Lodz. A reign of terror was instituted against the Jews, with men, women, and children seized in the streets for forced labor and abused, beaten, and robbed. Already in Sept. the old synagogue was destroyed with the aid of a Polish mob. On 25 Dec., hundreds of German police and *Volksdeutsche* went on another rampage, breaking 1,000 windows in J. homes and burning down the second synagogue. In Jan. 1940, thousands of Jews were brought to one of the city squares and searched for valuables; women were taken to a nearby building and raped. Jews were thrown out of their homes and J. factories and business premises expropriated. Large tributes were also exacted from the community. A *Judenrat* was in operation from 13 Sept. 1939. By the end of 1940 it employed 676 workers in 17 departments. All J. males aged 12–16 were registered for forced labor. The daily average of those taken rose from 2,624 in 1940 to 7,597 in 1942. In June 1940, 300 J. men aged 18–35 were sent to the nearby Przyrow labor camp and in Aug., 910 of the young were sent to the Czieszanow labor camp via Lublin., where many died from physical abuse or disease. The *Judenrat* was able to arrange for 2,000 business licenses for J. artisans and opened a carpentry shop to fill German orders (and illegally teach the trade to youngsters). Six soup kitchens were in operation, providing 392,086 meals in Oct.–Dec. 1940. In the first half of 1940, 13,157 Jews (3,570 families), including 1,438 refugees, received regular financial assistance and in April 1940, nearly 20,000 received assistance for the Passover holidays. The *Judenrat* was responsible for the old age home (188 residents) and the orphanage (150); opened a second hospital; and arranged housing for 4,722 Jews. A J. police force with 250 men by 1942 was charged with keeping order. The TOZ organization, with its 31 doctors, offered extensive health care, treating the victims of forced labor after beatings and exposure to the cold, inoculating 17,125 Jews against typhus, and feeding 2,000 children in day care centers. In April 1941, the Jews were ordered into a ghetto that included about

10,000 refugees from Lodz, Radomsko, Warsaw, Cracow, Plock, and other places. Many died of starvation and exposure in the harsh winter of 1941–42. About 19,000 or half the residents of the ghetto, were registered with the *Judenrat* as requiring relief. During the period, members of the J. political parties and youth movements continued to meet clandestinely with the Tarbut educational network operating schoolrooms. The Zionists and the Bund also organized cultural activities and the first efforts were made to unite the underground groups. The Orthodox also defied German bans and continued to pray and study in small groups. In Sept. 1942, Ukrainian and Latvian police arrived in the city, presaging an *Aktion*. Though the Germans declared Yom Kippur a holiday and authorized public prayer in order to catch the Jews off guard, many reported at their places of work and tried to get their families out of the ghetto. On 22 Sept., the Jews were herded together and selections made. About 7,000 were then deported to the Treblinka death camp. A few hundred were murdered during the course of the day. Five additional *Aktion*s followed in late Sept. and early Nov. In each, about 6,000 Jews were transported to Treblinka. In the city itself, up to 2,000 Jews were murdered, including the residents of the old age home and 13 newly delivered mothers with their infants. Other new mothers were lured out of hiding by a promise of amnesty, only to be deported to Treblinka as well. During the *Aktions*, the able-bodied were sent to ten temporary labor camps inside the city, including those at the Hassag factories. On 1 Nov. a "small ghetto" was set up for the remaining 5,185 "legal" Jews. Hundreds more filtered in illegally. Their numbers were reduced steadily through executions, expulsions, and flight. The *Judenrat* operated a day care center for the ghetto's 120 children, ostensibly tolerated by the Germans but again used as a lure for those in hiding. All but 18 of the children were deported to the Treblinka death camp on 4 Jan. 1943; the rest were murdered on 30 March. An atmosphere of fatalism prevailed in the ghetto, leading to a relaxation of moral standards among many. In Dec. 1942, the J. underground groups united and affiliated themselves to the J. Fighting Organization (ZOB). They maintained close contacts with Warsaw and the heads of the underground there, such as Anielewicz, Wilner, Kaplan, and others, visited C. The underground, with a membership of 300, was divided into cells of five and comanded by Moshe (Moitek) Zylberberg. On 4 Jan. 1943, in the first instance of armed resistance, two were killed and others executed or deported. Within the city, the underground engaged in sabotage in the German factories, manufactured explosives, and dug out bunkers and tunnels. They also stepped up efforts to obtain arms. On 20 March 1943, the Germans executed 127 Jews at the J. cemetery, mainly from the professional class. On 25 June, as a final *Aktion* commenced in the ghetto, some members of the J. underground were able to escape to the forests while others were killed fighting. After selections, hundreds were murdered and the rest deported to the Treblinka death camp, leaving about 4,000 Jews who worked in the Hassag factories, including their families. On 19 July 1943, 400 of them were executed at the J. cemetery. In the second half of 1943, 5,000–6,000 Jews from Lodz, Plaszow, and Skarzysko-Kamienna were brought to the factories. At the approach of the Red Army in Jan. 1945, many were sent to German concentration camps; 5,200 were liberated by the Soviets, including 1,518 of C.'s Jews. A group of 23 Jews under the command of Barukh Gvirtzman and Yehuda Glickstein engaged in effective partisan action in the Koniecepol area. Many were murdered by Polish Armia Krajowa partisans. Another group operated in the Zloty Potok forest until wiped out by the Germans. At Treblinka, surviving Jews from C. participated in the uprising of 2 Aug. 1943. After the liberation of C., a community numbering 2,167 in June 1946 was reestablished but many left in the face of Polish antisemitism and by 1962 just 200 remained. Yad Vashem honored several Poles from C. as Righteous among the Nations, while many Germans were subsequently tried for committing war crimes against the Jews of C.

CZEREMOSZNO Volhynia dist., Poland, today Ukraine. The J. pop. in 1921 was 102 (total 681). The Jews were probably brought to Powursk for liquidation in the Holocaust.

CZERNELICA Stanislawow dist., Poland, today Ukraine. The J. community existed from the early 18th cent. with a pop. of 662 (total 2,917) in 1880. There was strong Zionist activity between the World Wars. The Jews were expelled to Horodenka by the Germans in Aug. 1942 for deportation to the Belzec death camp.

CZERNIANY Polesie dist., Poland, today Belarus. The J. pop. in 1921 was 105 (total 704). The Jews

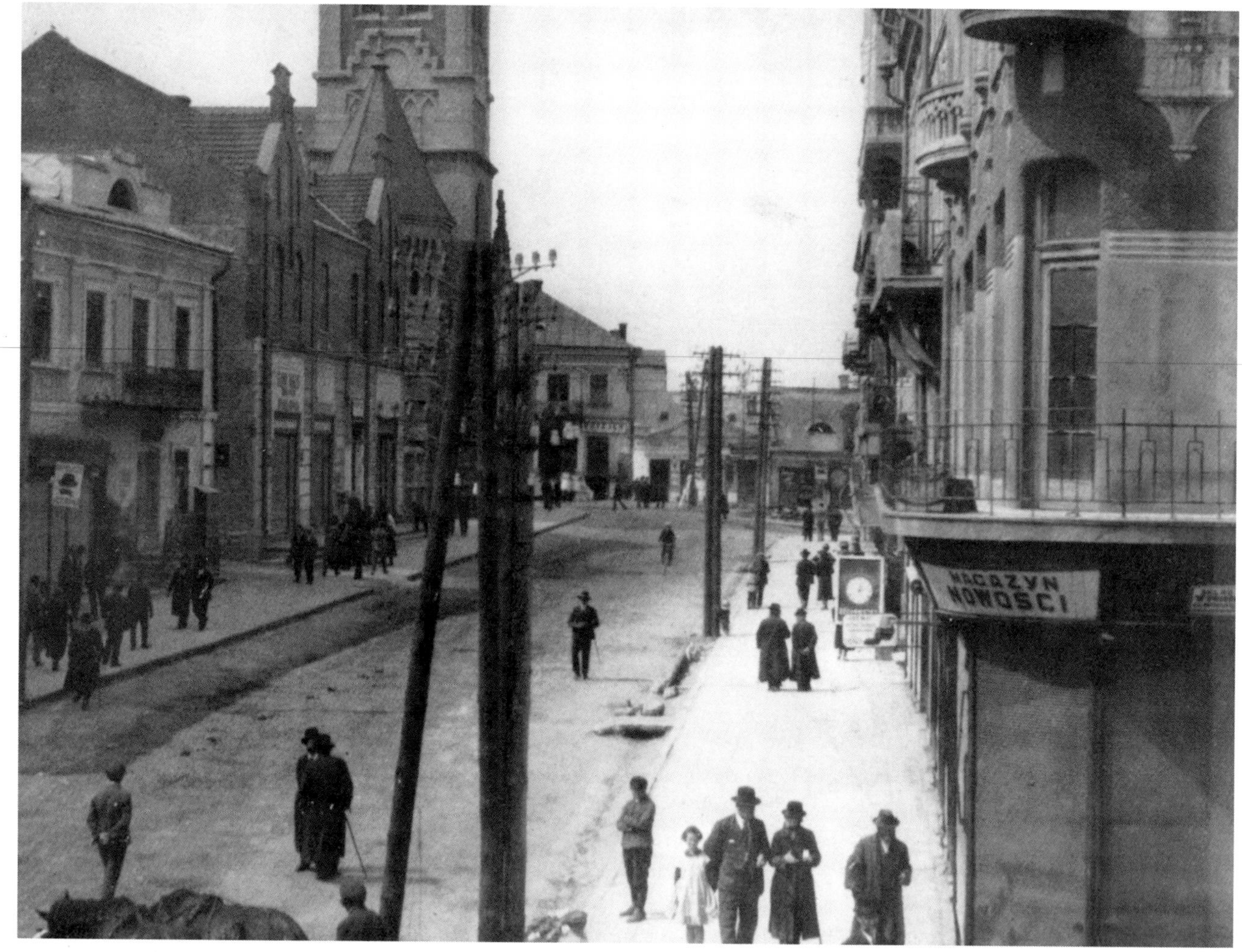
MAGAZYN
NOWOSCI

The main street of Czortkow, Poland

were probably murdered by the Ukrainians in June 1941, prior to the arrival of the Germans.

CZERNIATYN Stanislawow dist., Poland, today Ukraine. The J. pop. in 1921 was 105. The Jews were possibly expelled to Horodenka for liquidation in April 1942.

CZERNIEJOW Stanislawow dist., Poland, today Ukraine. In 1921 the J. pop. stood at 336 (total 2,432), most engaged in farming,. The Jews were probably expelled to Stanislawow in the fall of 1942 and were either shot at the Rodolf Mill or sent to the Belzec death camp.

CZERWIN Bialystok, Poland. An independent community existed in the late 19th cent., numbering 218 (total 362) in 1921. The Jews were expelled by the Germans shortly after their arrival in Sept. 1939.

CZOLHANY Stanislawow dist., Poland, today Ukraine. The J. pop. in 1921 was 124. The Jews were probably expelled to Bolechow for liquidation in Aug. 1942.

CZORTKOW Tarnopol dist., Poland, today Ukraine. The 17th cent. community of around 50 families was wiped out in the Chmielnicki massacres of 1648–49. In 1772 the Jews were accorded extensive residence and trade privileges but the heavy taxes of the Austrian government caused their economic situation to worsen. In 1880 the J. pop. reached 2,214 (total 3,524) and continued to grow despite emigration to the U.S., reaching 3,314 in 1921. In the same period

light industry expanded, employing a large number of Jews. In 1860, R. David Moshe Friedmann, son of Yisrael of Ruzhin, established his hasidic court there, coming into bitter conflict with the progressive incumbent rabbi, Yeshayahu Meir Kahana Shapira, who was a leading spirit in the development of mutual aid in the town and whose followers became its first Zionists when the movement was founded there in 1897. A Bund group was formed after the 1905 revolution by J. refugees arriving from Russia. From the beginning of WWI, Jews served traditionally as mayor or deputy mayor of the town. Under the Russian occupation, 5,000 refugees flooded into the town and epidemics claimed many J. lives (35% of the refugees and 20% of local Jews). An orphanage accommodating 60 war orphans was set up. Subsequently the Jews suffered under the West Ukrainian Republic in 1918–19 and at the hands of conquering Polish soldiers. The war left the Jews in dire economic straits, requiring aid from former townsmen in the U.S. Most community council members were Zionists, who dominated the cultural and social life of the town. Antisemitism intensified in the 1930s as the J. pop. reached 5,869 in 1935 (total 19,089). The arrival of the Soviets on 17 Sept. 1939 brought J. communal and political life to an end, while the property of wealthy merchants was nationalized and craftsmen were organized into cooperatives. Many of the young joined the Red Army on its withdrawal. The Germans took the town on 6 June 1941. On 10 July, local Ukrainians staged a pogrom with German assistance, murdering 300 Jews for alleged collaboration with the Soviets. On 28 July, another 150 Jews were executed by the Germans in the nearby Black Forest. A *Judenrat* was set up to regulate the supply of forced labor. On 15 Oct., a further 200 Jews, mostly from the professional class, were murdered in the Black Forest. In the winter of 1941–42 hunger and disease claimed many victims. A ghetto was established in April 1942, crowding as many as 20 people into a room as refugees arrived as well. On 27 Aug. a mass *Aktion* dispatched about 2,000 Jews to the Belzec death camp after the Germans weeded out skilled workers and murdered 600 of the sick, aged, and young. Another 500 were sent to Belzec on 5 Oct. On 15 Dec., 530 of the skilled workers were confined to a labor camp, their ranks and mostly their families being thinned out in periodic executions. An underground was organized in the ghetto where – as in the neighboring forests – there was resistance to the Germans and their collaborators. On 23 June 1943, the labor camp was liquidated, as was the ghetto in Sept. About 100 Jews survived the war in hiding and in the labor camps.

CZORTOWIEC   Stanislawow dist., Poland, today Ukraine. In 1921 the J. pop. reached 317 (total 4,723), around a fifth engaged in farming. Most were expelled to Horodenka in the summer of 1942 for deportation to the Belzec death camp.

CZUDEC   Lwow dist., Poland, today Ukraine. An organized community existed from the late 18th cent., reaching a peak pop. of 410 in 1900 (33% of the total). The Zionists were active from the late 1920s. Occasional violent antisemitism marked the period between the World Wars. In June 1942 the Germans expelled the Jews to the Rzeszow ghetto, from where most were deported to the Belzec death camp in July.

CZYZEWO   Bialystok dist., Poland. Jews, among C.'s founders (18th cent.), constituted the majority of the inhabitants. Income came initially from leasing rights to inns, milk and grain marketing, etc. After a railway was built near C. (1854), the J. community developed further. Many C. Jews were craftsmen or carters, a few were wealthy grain traders or flour mill owners. At the end of the 19th cent., Hasidism grew. As the Russians retreated in WWI, the Jews suffered murder, pillage, and arson. The J. pop. between 1897–1921 was static at 1,595 (out of about 1,800). Between the World Wars taxes were heavy, antisemitism increased, and J. stores and goods were boycotted. Pogroms took place. The Zionists gained influence in the community. Among the educational institutions were a government school for Jews, a modern *heder*, and an Agudat Israel girls' school. In WWII, the Soviets occupied C. until June 1941, when the Germans entered. They established a *Judenrat*. In Aug. 1941, after separating 100 able-bodied men, some 1,750 men, women, and children were shot to death in a nearby forest. The laborers lived in a ghetto until its closure in Nov. 1942, when they were transferred to Zamborow and then to Auschwitz in Jan. 1943.

D

DABEIKIAI (Yid. Dabaik) Utena dist., Lithuania. The J. community began in the 17th cent. During WWI the Russians forced the Jews into Russia and destroyed the *beit midrash*. After the war, economic conditions forced many to emigrate. The J. pop. in 1923 was 175 (55% of the total). After Germany's invasion in June 1941, three of the ten J. families remaining in G. fled. The others were killed on 29 Sept. 1941 in Utena.

DABER (Pol. Dobra) Pomerania, Germany, today Poland. Jews lived in D. since 1700. The community remained small, numbering 82 individuals in 1849. In the 1920s, it became affiliated to the Naugard community. When the Nazis came to power in 1933, the J. pop. numbered 25. By May 1938, most were probably still living in the town since three J. businesses were still operating. It may be assumed that those who did not manage to move abroad were deported to the east. In Oct. 1942, only two Jews were left in D., probably protected by marriage to non-Jews.

DAGDA Latgale dist., Latvia. The community was founded in the 1820s by Jews from the nearby village of Dishovka. J. tradesmen enjoyed a measure of prosperity and the J. pop. rose to 1,026 in 1897 (total 1,516). Thereafter a steady stream of emigration reduced the J. pop. while others left for the interior of Russia in WWI, leaving 727 Jews in D. in 1920. After the war the new border with Russia cut D. off from its agricultural hinterland and affected J. livelihoods, necessitating aid from the Joint Distribution Committee. By the mid-1920s the economic situation stabilized, with 85 of the town's 89 stores in J. hands. Two of the community's three synagogues belonged to Hasidim and the third and largest to the *Mitnaggedim*. The Zionists were also active. Under Soviet rule

(1940–41) J. community life came to an end. About 60 Jews were able to flee to the Soviet Union prior to the arrival of the Germans in July 1941. A Latvian "self-defense" group operating with German blessings initiated a regime of murder and rape. The remaining Jews were expelled to the Daugavpils (Dvinsk) ghetto at the end of July and within a few days executed in the Pogulianka forest along with Jews from other provincial towns.

DAHN Palatinate, Germany. A J. community existed in the 19th cent., the J. pop. numbering 134 in 1848 and 85 in 1875. All were engaged in trade and light industry. The community maintained a synagogue (renovated 1871–72) and elementary school. In June 1933, about four months after the Nazi assumption of power, the J. pop. numbered 50. Emigration abroad and to other German cities in the Nazi period reduced the J. pop. to eight in 1939. These were evacuated on 1 Sept. 1939 with the rest of the inhabitants owing to the town's proximity to the French border. Some were undoubtedly included in subsequent deportations.

DALESZYCE Kielce dist., Poland. The J. community numbered 131 (total 1,458) in 1857, 306 in 1921, and about 200 on the eve of WWII. After three years of German rule, the Jews were transferred to the Bodzentyn ghetto in Sept. 1942 and from there deported to the Treblinka death camp.

DAMBACH-LA-VILLE Bas-Rhin dist., France. The J. presence dates from the 16th cent. A cent. later D. was regarded as the site of an important J. community. In 1784 it consisted of 120 members. By 1865, the J. pop. was 315. It established a synagogue in 1867. The community dwindled to 65 members in 1936. During WWII, they were expelled by the

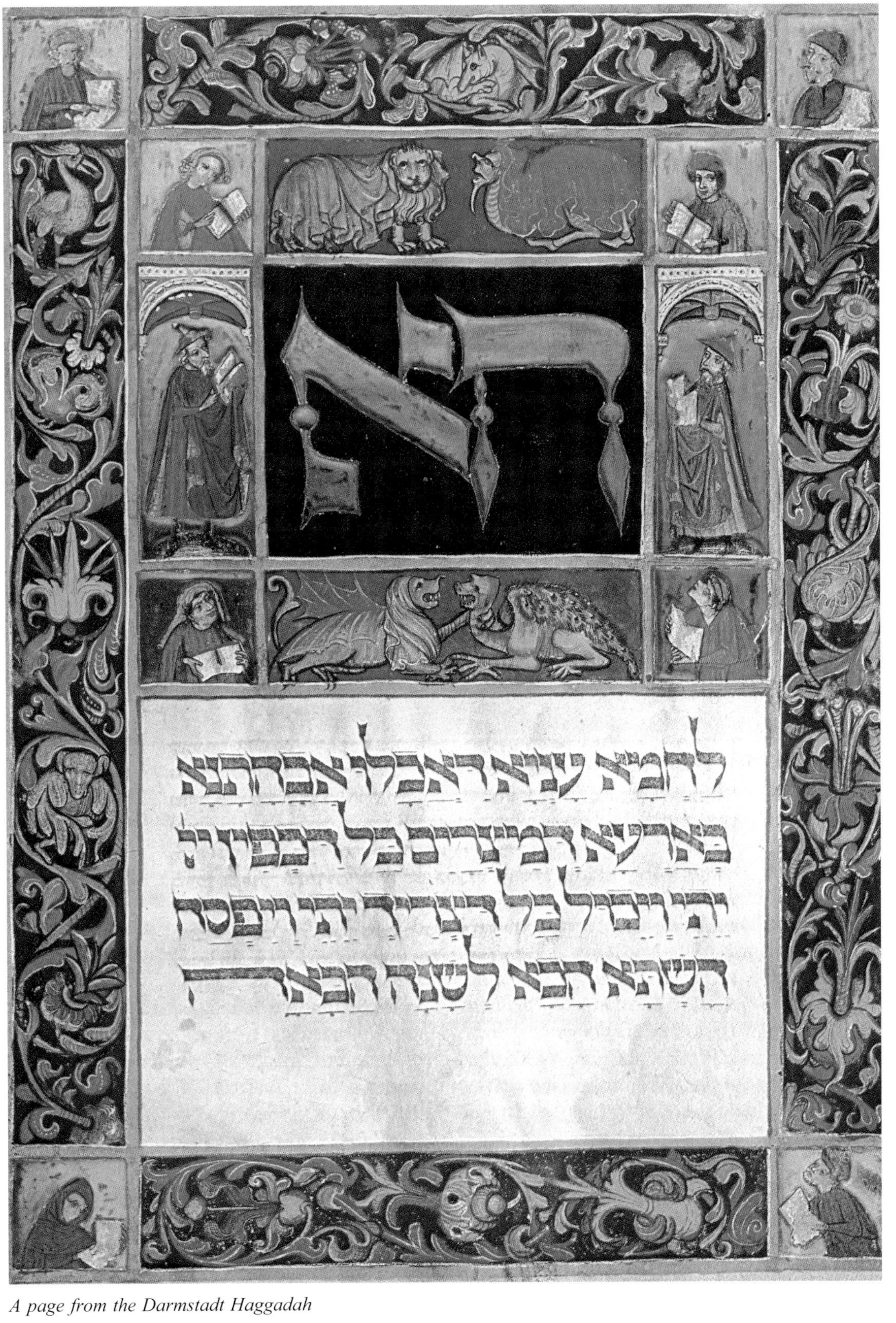
הא
לחמא עניא דאכלו אבהתנא
בארעא דמצרים כל דכפין יי
תי ויכול כל דצריך יתי ויפסח
השתא הכא לשנה הבאה

A page from the Darmstadt Haggadah

and the *aliya* of no fewer than 200 Jews through its Palestine Office (1933–36). Modern Hebrew was also taught at the Orthodox day school, and various movements provided educational, social, sports, and other activities for the young. On *Kristallnacht* (9–10 Nov. 1938), a group of SA troops destroyed the Orthodox synagogue's interior and facade, but kept the blaze under control so as to avoid damaging adjacent property. Most of the 28 Torah scrolls (previously hidden on the rabbi's instructions) remained intact. The Liberal synagogue was burned to the ground, however, and all of its precious Torah scrolls—including two dozen that belonged to smaller communities—were reduced to ashes. J. homes and property were vandalized; two of the 169 men imprisoned at the Buchenwald concentration camp died there; and the city council made a point of charging both congregations for the removal of debris. After *Kristallnacht* there was a final surge of emigration and *aliya*. By then, an amalgamation of the Liberal and Orthodox communities had taken place, excluding worship and interment. From Dec. 1940, the remaining Jews were deported, about 380 being sent to the Theresienstadt ghetto, Auschwitz, and other death camps in 1942–43. After WWII the community was reestablished, numbering about 130 in early 1990s.

DARSUNISKIS (Yid. Darshunishok) Troki dist., Lithuania. The J. pop. in 1923 was 120 (15% of the total). After Germany's invasion in June 1941 the Jews, together with those of neighboring communities, were kept in a ghetto and taken to forced labor. All the Jews were killed in Aug. and Sept. 1941 by Lithuanians.

DARUVAR Croatia, Yugoslavia, today Republic of Croatia. Jews first settled in D. in the 18th cent. In the 1920s, Zionist activism developed. The J. pop. in 1940 was 205 (total 5,757). In May–Aug. 1941 most of the Jews were taken to their deaths in Croatian camps, Jasenovac, and Auschwitz; 146 were killed. Six partisans fell in fighting.

DASHEV Vinnitsa dist., Ukraine. The J. pop. was 406 in 1765 and 2,911 (total 5,623) in 1880. In late Nov. 1917, many Jews were beaten and robbed in a pogrom. In the Soviet period, the J. pop. fell to 2,168 in 1926 and 967 in 1939. A J. council and J. elementary school were operating and a number of families

worked in a J. kolkhoz. Upon their arrival on 25 July 1941, the Germans murdered about 100 Jews from D. and its environs. In mid-Nov. they executed another 814 near the village of Polivye.

DASHOVKA Mogilev dist., Belorussia. The J. pop. was 392 (total 1,228) in 1897. In the Soviet period, a J. kolkhoz was founded in 1925, with 19 J. families working there in 1930. Another kolkhoz, founded in 1928, accommodated 49 J. families. The Germans occupied the town in July 1941, apparently expelling the Jews to Mogilev, where they were murdered in one of the *Aktions*.

DATTELN Westphalia, Germany. In 1814, two J. families settled in D. and the J. pop. reached its peak in 1900 with 56. The community had a prayer room from its early days and in 1929 dedicated a synagogue. In 1933 the community numbered 33. In 1937 only 21 remained. On *Kristallnacht* (9–10 Nov. 1938), J. homes were attacked (the synagogue had already been sold beforehand). On 25 Jan. 1942, the 11 remaining Jews were deported to the Riga ghetto. All perished.

DAUBORN Hesse–Nassau, Germany. In 1750, Jews from D. and from three neighboring villages—Heringen, Kirberg, and Mensfelden—established a community with synagogues in Kirberg (1744) and Heringen (1846). They numbered 130 altogether in 1843, but only 49 in 1933, thereafter falling victim to Nazi terror. By 1939 all the Jews had left.

DAUGAI (Yid. Doig) Alytus dist., Lithuania. D.'s first Jews arrived in the 16th cent, while the J. community was founded at the end of the 18th cent. The J. pop. in 1897 was 511 (40% of the total). A fire in 1905 destroyed most of the city. The economic situation forced the emigration of many, who then sent money back to their remaining relatives. The Zionist movement won widespread support. Between the World Wars antisemitism caused further emigration. The J. pop. in 1936 was 396 (33% of the total). After the German conquest in June 1941, a group of suspected Communists, mostly Jews, was arrested and shot. After another group of Jews was shot, most of D.'s remaining Jews were taken to the Vidzgiris forest, where they were ordered to strip. They were shot and then buried in mass graves that had been previously prepared.

DAUGAVPILS (Ger. Duenaburg; Rus. and Yid. Dvinsk) Latgale dist., Latvia. The J. community was founded between 1750–60, toward the end of the period of Polish rule. Under the Russians, the J. pop. grew to 1,559 in 1815 (57% of the total). With the expansion of the city's fortifications in 1812, Jews were forced to move to a suburb over a mile away (afterwards named Altstadt) and later also to a new quarter along the Dvina River which became D.'s commercial center. In 1823, the J. pop. was augmented by Jews expelled from villages in the Vitebsk province as well as other Jews attracted by the expanding economy. The community became one of the most important in northwest Russia, with its pop. growing to 11,000 in 1863 and 32,369 (total 69,675) in 1897. With construction work constantly underway around the city's fortress, J. building contractors settled and in the 1860s, when the city became an important railway junction, J. merchants began to arrive. Jews were especially active in the lumber industry, exploiting the Dvina River to move logs down to Riga for export. In the 1870s and 1880s, Jews opened a number of big factories: the Zaks match factory employing 600–800 mostly J.

girls aged 12–14; sawmills; hide-processing plants; distilleries; five cigarette factories; three button factories; and numerous sewing shops supplying the army. Among the leading building contractors was Meshullam Feivel Friedland, who funded the construction of a J. hospital in the 1860s, one of the first of its kind in Russia. Among the J. gainfully employed, a third were artisans; many others were carters and porters, peddlers and stallkeepers, maids and laundresses, and teachers. Though the army remained a source of income for as much as half the city's residents, an economic recession in the 1880s and 1890s affected many, with 1,998 J. families (a third of the total) on relief in 1897. Emigration to the U.S. increased in this period, reaching 754 in 1909. A mutual aid and loan society founded in 1883 for sales personnel became a leading force in the community, fighting for better working conditions, sponsoring cultural events and setting up a library as well as building a synagogue for its members. In the late 19th cent., rivalry between Hasidim and *Mitnaggedim* led to a split in community institutions and separate rabbis. Efforts were made to unite the rabbinical seat in 1888 under R. Meir Simha ha-

Jewish school, Daugavpils (Dvinsk), Latvia

Kohen (1843–1926), one of the great talmudic scholars of the age, but when the attempt failed, R. Yosef Rozin (1848–1936; "the Rogachover"), of equal stature, was brought from Warsaw to officiate for the Hasidim. A Great Synagogue whose construction commenced in 1865 with funds from the Friedland family was only completed in 1894 after work had been stopped by the city (with its height approaching that of the nearby church) and because of community disputes over its control. Three *talmud torah* schools served the children of the community and a yeshiva for 100–120 students was founded in the late 19th cent. The first secular J. school (for girls) was opened in 1861 and a vocational school for girls enrolling 200 was started in 1902. A vocational school for boys was founded in 1887 and by 1902 was the fourth largest in Russia for Jews. The first Yiddish school was opened in 1913. The Zionists became active with an Ohev Zion society founded in 1883 and other groups following. D. became one of the centers of the Bund, which took the lead in labor agitation and revolutionary activities. In 1898 it organized a successful six-month strike against the Zaks factory which became a milestone in the city's labor relations. In 1904 the Bund had over 1,000 members. During this period, J. self-defense groups were instrumental in averting pogroms. Further economic expansion brought the J. pop. up to 55,680 (50% of the total) in 1914. On the eve of WWI, 301 of the city's 400 workshops were J.-owned and 32 J. factories employed 1,942 Jews. The three button factories, the only ones in the Vitebsk province, now employed 475, mostly J. women. In 1915 thousands of J. refugees arrived from Lithuania and Courland and were cared for by the community. Flight and organized evacuation in the face of aerial bombardments and the nearness of fighting reduced the J. pop. to 20,000 in 1917 and 10,000 in 1918 as the city was virtually destroyed. Between the World Wars, the J. pop. leveled off at about 11,000 (25–30% of the total), cut off from its prewar commercial partners in Poland, Lithuania, and the Soviet Union and substantially supported by the Joint Distribution Committee. With many Jews reduced to petty trade, a large number emigrated to the U.S. and South Africa. In 1926, 200 more J. families suffered when a fire destroyed their wooden stalls in the marketplace. The deterioration in the situation of the Jews was further exacerbated by the general economic crisis and government policy favoring Latvians over minorities. Jews, nonetheless, maintained their traditional com-

mercial role, with 80% of the city's larger stores in their hands and virtual monopolies in the trade in textiles, footwear, hides, tobacco, steel, and grain. The community, too, maintained its traditional institutions, including the hospital, an orphanage for 300 children, an old age home with 60–80 residents, a *talmud torah*, and large-scale welfare services. Two Yiddish schools and two Hebrew schools operated in the 1930s, augmented by an Agudat Yisrael school and a J. high school. The J. vocational school was run by ORT and in its 50-year existence until closing in 1937 had over 1,000 graduates. ORT also helped open a vocational school for girls. The Bund remained the leading J. political party through the 1920s but the Zionists gained increasing influence. Hehalutz set up a pioneer training farm and later Hashomer Hatzair became the largest youth movement in the city, many of its members settling in kibbutzim as an estimated 1,200–1,400 Jews left for Palestine during the period. J. self-defense groups continued to operate in the face of antisemitic outbursts as gangs of Latvian nationalists arrived from Riga at Christmas time.

The Soviets arrived in June 1940, nationalizing J. businesses and shutting down community life as well as sovietizing the J. educational system. Many young Jews went to work in the now government-operated factories while in many cases former owners stayed on as managers. Before evacuating the city in June 1941, the Soviets exiled large numbers of J. business and political leaders to Siberia. The Germans captured D. on 26 June 1941 after heavy bombardments and subsequent fires left over 2,000 homes and business premises destroyed. Thousands of Jews were arrested and forced to engage in hard labor without food or water and subjected to beatings by Latvian guards. After a week, systematic execution of the prisoners commenced, claiming 1,150 victims by 16 July. At the end of July, the entire J. pop. was transferred to the abandoned Latvian cavalry barracks. Most of the 14,000 to 16,000 Jews, including thousands from the surrounding towns, were packed into the stables occupying the ground floor. Many were left without a roof over their heads. The old and sick were first taken out and murdered. Immediately afterwards, thousands more from among the refugees were led to the surrounding forests on the pretext of relocation and slaughtered. The local pop. was decimated in two more *Aktions*. On 8–9 Aug., unessential workers and the unfit together with their families and 400 orphans were executed. Ten

days later a broader selection was made and thousands more were slaughtered. Victims in the two *Aktions* were taken to the Pogulanka resort area and Peski, where they were ordered to undress and lie down in long ditches. They were then executed. Infants were beaten to death with rifle butts or shot with pistols. The death toll between 17 July and 21 Aug. was 9,012. About 7,000 Jews remained alive. Most were put to work for the German army until the next *Aktion* on 7-9 Nov. 1941, when even the families of essential workers were taken to Pogulanka and slaughtered. This time 3,000-5,000 were executed, including nearly 1,000 children. The final liquidation of the ghetto commenced on 17 May 1942, when 500 Jews were murdered, the sick and infants in their beds, the others at Pogulanka. The few hundred who remained were mostly preferred workers living at their places of employment. Efforts to flee the city were made after the big *Aktion* of Nov. 1941, at first to Braslav 25 miles away where mass murders had not yet commenced and later to the forests to join up with partisan units. Few of the latter attempts succeeded. Of those reaching Braslav, most were murdered in the *Aktions* there in summer 1942. The remnant of D.'s Jews was sent to the Riga ghetto in Oct. 1943 and afterwards confined in the Kaiserwald concentration camp. When the Red Army liberated D. on 27 July 1944, it found 20 Jews there. By 1946, over 2,000 Jews had gathered, arriving from the Soviet Union and other places of survival and forming an organized community; over the years, most left for Riga.

DAUGIELISZKI Vilna dist., Poland, today Belarus. Jews first settled in the late 18th cent. and engaged mainly in crafts. The laying of a railroad line in 1862 provided Jews with jobs but on its completion a process of emigration set in. The J. pop. dropped from 300 in 1907 to 175 in 1930 (total 350) after the destructiveness of WWI and the economic hardships that followed. Between the World Wars, nearly half the Jews were peddlers and the rest shopkeepers and artisans. Many of the young fled with the Soviets on the approach of the Germans in June 1941 and later served with the Red Army. Under the German-appointed Lithuanian mayor, a number of Jews were murdered and the rest confined to a ghetto. On 27 Sept. 1941 the Jews were sent to the Poligon transit camp. On 9 Oct. 1941, 190 were executed nearby

DAVIDESTI Bukovina, Rumania, today Ukraine.

Jews settled in the 19th cent. The J. pop. in 1930 was 48. In July 1941, the J. pop was deported to Transnistria. Few survived.

DAVIDOVKA Polesie dist., Belorussia. D. was founded as a J. farm settlement in 1847 and had a pop. of 168 in 1898. In the mid-1920s, under the Soviets, the J. pop. was about 450, with 60% occupied as workers and artisans and only 25% engaged in agriculture. A local J. school had 105 students in 1925 and a J. rural council was established the same year. D. was captured by the Germans in July 1941. On 8 Feb 1942, they murdered 129 Jews.

DAWIDGRODEK Polesie dist., Poland, today Belarus. The J. settlement was founded in the 1650s and grew to 3,087 (total 7,815) in 1897. Most of the wholesale trade was in J. hands, benefiting from the town's lively river traffic. Zionist activity commenced in the late 19th cent. while a Bund group was founded in 1905 and the Territorialist Socialists organized J. self-defense. In 1921 the J. pop. stood at 2,832 (total 9,851). Between the World Wars, a Tarbut school became prominent, with 400 students in 1934. Its director, Avraham Olshanski, founded a nationwide Hebrew-speaking movement called Benei Yehuda. Jews continued to dominate trade as well as the crafts and were active in the major lumber industry. Under the Soviets (Sept. 1939-July 1941) instruction in Yiddish and a Soviet curriculum were introduced into the Tarbut school. Under the Germans, J. males over 14 were murdered outside the town by the SS on 10 Aug. 1941. The women and children were expelled and tried to settle in other towns but only a few hundred succeeded. Most returned and in Sept. 1942, numbering 1,263 with just 30 men, they were also executed; of the 100 or so who escaped, some joined the partisans.

DEBELJACA Vojvodina dist., Yugoslavia. A J. community was established in the 1880s and liquidated in the Holocaust. There were 225 Jews in 1931 (total 6,010).

DEBRECEN Hajdu dist., Hungary. Jews first settled in 1840 and by 1848 numbered 118. They were only allowed to purchase real estate in 1863. In the subsequent period of prosperity, Jews led the way in commerce and industry, comprising 70-80% of the professional class. By 1920, numbering 10,170 (10% of the

total), up from 3,089 in 1880, they owned nearly half the large estates in the area. From the early 20th cent., the community was divided into Orthodox and Status Quo congregations. The first synagogue was built in 1852 and the magnificent Great Synagogue in 1897. Another three synagogues were built in the early 1920s. The first J. school was opened in 1886, enrolling 615 by 1900. A girls' school founded in 1906 was attended by 200–250 students. A J. high school, started in the 1920s when local schools were closed to Jews, graduated 500 until 1944. Many high school teachers promoted Hebrew and Zionism, whose influence spread between the World Wars. Antisemitism intensified in the early 1920s, led by students at the newly founded local university, and again after the Nazi rise to power in 1933. The racial laws of 1938 undermined J. livelihoods and in 1940–41 forced labor became widespread. The J. pop. in 1941 was 9,142. In fall 1941, Jews of Galician or Polish origin were expelled, many murdered on reaching Kamenets-Podolski (Ukraine). In 1942, Jews were drafted into labor battalions and sent to the Ukraine, where many died in the minefields. With the German invasion in 1944, the Jews were confined to a ghetto in May and at the end of June deported to Auschwitz and Austria. Small groups of the young, mainly from the J. high school, managed to evade the deportations, escaping to Budapest, where they joined the underground. Some of the local Zionists joined the Rescue Committee (Kasztner) train to Switzerland. As the Germans attempted to evacuate the Austrian camps on the approach of the Red Army, many Jews were murdered, but most survived. Those who returned to D. after the war formed the largest J. community in the region, numbering 4,640 in 1946 and 1,200 in 1970. About 400 settled in Israel.

DECIN Bohemia (Sudetenland), Czechoslovakia. The Jews present in the first half of the 16th cent. were apparently later expelled. The community was reestablished only in the mid-19th cent. A synagogue was opened in 1907 as the J. pop. grew steadily from 162 in 1887 to 515 (total 35,513) in 1930. In WWI, 1,100 Jews found refuge in D. with the assistance of the J. community. The Zionists were active after WWI. Most Jews left D. in 1933–38. After WWII, J. refugees, some of them demobilized soldiers and most from Carpatho-Russia, formed a new community, reaching a pop. of 610 in 1948. Most left in two waves of emigration, in 1948 and 1969.

DECS Tolna dist., Hungary. Jews settled in the mid-19th cent., mostly selling groceries and farm produce. In 1930, they numbered 56. The remaining 48, who had not been sent to forced labor, were deported to Auschwitz via Tolna on 4–6 July 1944.

DEDA N. Transylvania dist., Rumania. Jews settled in the early 19th cent. The J. pop. in 1920 was 185 (7% of the total). In May 1944 the community was transferred to the Reghin ghetto and in June deported to Auschwitz.

DEDEMSVAART (Avereest) Overijssel dist., Holland. Jews settled from 1820. The J. pop. was 85 in 1911 and 43 in 1941 (total 10,393). In 1943 most were deported to Poland. A few survived in hiding.

DEDKOVITCHY Zhitomir dist., Ukraine. J. settlement began in the late 18th cent. Four Jews were present in 1778. In 1897 the J. pop. was 276 (total 2,511) but by 1926 it fell to 103. In 1939 most of the 206 Jews in the Narodichi region lived in D. After they occupied the town in mid-Aug. 1941, the Germans murdered those Jews who had neither fled nor been evacuated.

DEGGENDORF (in J. sources, Takendorf) Lower Bavaria, Germany. The J. settlement dates from the early 14th cent. In Sept. 1338, all the Jews were burned alive in their ghetto by the local pop. The massacre and its approval by Duke Heinrich XIV sparked an orgy of violence against the Jews throughout Bavaria and Austria. A handful of Jews lived in D. from the 1870s, attached to the Straubing community.

DEISEL Hesse–Nassau, Germany. Jews from D., Trendelburg, and four other villages maintained a community numbering 134 in 1850. By 1933 it had dwindled to 14 and all the Jews left, mostly emigrating, before 1938.

DEJ (Hung. Des) N. Transylvania dist., Rumania. Jews first settled in 1834. In 1850 three J. soldiers in the Russian army encamped in D. defected, took on new names, and set up families. One later became chairman of the community council. In 1909 a synagogue was consecrated, and was considered to be one of the finest in Transylvania. R. Mendel Panet, who was appointed rabbi of the congregation in

gration as the economy declined. From the first half of the 19th cent. the community identified with Ropczyce (Ropshits) Hasidism. The Zionists became active in 1894. Shortly after the outbreak of WWI, Cossacks entered the town and went on a week-long rampage, beating J. men, raping women, and pillaging property. All the Jews fled when the Austrians withdrew after retaking the town for a few days. Around 600 never returned, reducing the J. pop. to 1,564 (total 3,922) in 1921. A pogrom was averted in Nov.–Dec. 1918 when the Zionist Va'ad Le'ummi bribed the municpal police and organized itself for self-defense with 100 bayonets supplied from a local J. workshop. Economic decline marked the years between the World Wars. The Germans occupied the city on 8 Sept. 1939 and soon

instituted a regime of forced labor and extortion, enclosing the Jews in a ghetto early in 1941. Refugees brought the pop. up to 4,000 in June 1942 and in a large-scale *Aktion* at the end of the month, 2,000 were dispatched to the Belzec death camp, after a selection left 200 dead and other groups earmarked for labor camps. Selections continued among the 600 Jews left behind and the hundreds of refugees pouring in as the ghetto itself became a labor camp. The last Jews were transferred to other camps in April 1943.

DEMBLIN-IRENA (Yid. Modzhitz) Lublin dist., Poland. The community grew with the economic development of the town in the first half of the 19th cent. and numbered 2,271 (total 4,063) in 1897.

White Russian general being greeted by Jews with bread and water after capturing Demblin from the Bolsheviks, Poland, 1920 (YIVO Archive, New York/photo courtesy of Beth Hatefutsoth, Tel Aviv)

Many Jews earned their livelihoods by supplying the garrison at the local fortress as well as from employment in the steel and tourist industries. D. became famous as a hasidic center after R. Yisrael Taub established in 1889 the Modzhitz dynasty, known for its concept of music as a basis for prayer and work. Gur Hasidism was also prominent. Community life centered around the hasidic courts and *shtiblekh*. Unlike other communities in the area, D. failed to develop modern political or cultural institutions. Following WWI, the Jews suffered from the depredations of General Haller's Polish troops and in 1919, four J. children were murdered. In 1921, the J. pop. was 2,702. Between the World Wars, the Zionists, Agudat Israel, and the Bund became active, with most Jews living in straitened economic circumstances. Antisemitism intensified in the 1930s, with violent outbursts in 1936–37. The Germans captured the town on 20 Sept. 1939, imposing tributes and setting up a *Judenrat* and a forced labor regime which put 400 Jews to work building an airfield in summer 1940. In Nov. 1940, a ghetto was established and in 1941–42 five labor camps began operating. On 6 May 1942, 2,500 Jews were deported to the Sobibor death camp. Within 12 days 2,200 refugees from Slovakia were added to the 1,000 Jews remaining in the ghetto. The last 2,500 Jews were deported to Treblinka on 15 Oct. 1942. The 1,000 Jews in the airfield labor camp were sent to the Czenstochowa camp in July 1944 after many were executed.

DEMECSER Szabolcs dist., Hungary. Jews settled c. 1770, most engaging in the grain trade. Others were farmers, artisans, and factory workers. They numbered 148 in 1880 and 368 in 1930. In 1941, 80 Jews were seized for forced labor On 17 May 1944, all were transferred to Auschwitz via Nyiregyhaza and Varjulapos.

DEMIDOV (until 1918, Pereche) Smolensk dist., Russia. Jews settled in the mid-19th cent. and numbered 337 (total 5,688) in 1897. In the Soviet period, their pop. rose to 416 in 1926 and then dropped to 206 in 1939. The Germans occupied D. on 13 July 1941, murdering the few Jews still there who had not fled or been evacuated.

DEMIDOWKA Volhynia dist., Poland, today Ukraine. Jews were probably present from the late 18th cent. and constituted the entire pop. of 679 in 1897 and 595 of a total 1,283 in 1921. The Germans entered the town on 22 June 1941 and with Ukrainian collusion instituted a regime of severe persecution. A *Judenrat* was established. The Jews were put to forced labor on farms and peat bogs. In late 1941 they were confined to a ghetto. After a week in detention without food, all were trucked to waiting pits on 8 Oct. 1942, and murdered.

DEMMELSDORF Upper Franconia, Germany. Jews were present in 1670. In 1739 their residence was limited to six families. A synagogue was erected in 1748 and a J. public school opened in 1827. In 1812 the J. pop. reached a peak of 136 (total 217), thereafter declining steadily to 42 in 1933 (total 172). Sixteen Jews are known to have emigrated in the Nazi era. On *Kristallnacht* (9–10 Nov. 1938), the synagogue was vandalized (and subsequently razed) and Jews were beaten. The last 14 were deported to Izbica in the Lublin dist. (Poland) via Bamberg in April 1942.

DEMYCZE Stanislawow dist., Poland, today Ukraine. The J. pop. in 1921 was 443. The Jews were probably murdered locally in Dec. 1941 or sent to the Belzec death camp.

DEN BOSCH (also 's-Hertogenbosch) Noord-Brabant dist., Holland. A J. presence was noted in the 13th–14th cents. Despite limitations on J. settlement and communal organization (such as public prayer) in the 17th and 18th cents., Jews settled in D. B. After emancipation (1796) they were granted full rights of settlement and communal activity. In 1814 D. B. became the seat of the Noord-Brabant chief rabbi (united with the chief rabbinate of Limburg in 1907). At the end of the 19th cent. there were religious and welfare organizations, a branch of the Alliance Israelite, and a school. The J. pop. in 1901 was 428. In the 1930s, Zionist youth activity began. In 1941 there were over 60 refugees in D. B. The J. pop. in 1941 was 480 (total 49,524). In Aug. J. men were taken to labor camps. D. B. later became a transit center for the deportation of the Noord-Brabant Jews (via nearby Vught). Deportations began in Aug. 1942 and ended in April 1943. In all, 317 were deported to the east; 13 survived the camps while 133 others survived in hiding. A small community was reestablished after the war.

DEN HELDER   Noord-Holland dist., Holland. J. settlement began in the late 18th cent. An active community developed in the 19th cent. The J. pop. in 1883 was 400 and in 1941 it was 123 (total 27,951). The Jews were transferred in 1942 to Amsterdam and then deported. Only some 30 survived in hiding.

DENEKAMP   Overijssel dist., Holland. J. settlement began in the 17th cent. and in 1860, 92 Jews were living there. An independent community was officially recognized in 1913. The J. pop. in 1941 was 58 (total 7,348). All but two Jews who hid were deported in the Holocaust.

DENKOW   Kielce dist., Poland. Jews may have been present in the 16th cent. In 1921, they numbered 260 (total 2,267), most living in penury and subjected to physical attack as antisemitism intensified in the 1930s. In the 1930s, young people expressed their Zionism by establishing branches of Betar and Ha-Shomer ha-Dati. With their arrival in Sept. 1939, the Germans exacted exorbitant tributes from the community. In July 1941, 150 refugees from Konin joined the 400 Jews of D. and in June 1942 all were confined to a ghetto except for a group sent to the nearby labor camp. On 13 Oct. 1942, 500 were deported to the Treblinka death camp. D. then became a concentration point for Jews en route to the death camps.

DERAZHNO   Volhynia dist., Poland, today Ukraine. A small community existed from the 17th century, increasing to 770 (half the total) in 1897. Growing antisemitism saw the burning of 30 J. homes in 1936. Russian rule in 1939–41 put and end to J public life. The Germans arrived on 28 June 1941, murdering a group of J. men, establishing a *Judenrat*, and setting up a ghetto in Oct. All were murdered beside open pits on 22 Aug. 1942.

DERAZHNYA   Kamenets-Podolski dist., Ukraine. The J. community dates from the 18th cent. In 1734 it suffered a Haidamak attack. The J. pop. was 316 in 1784 and 3,333 (68% of the total) in 1897. A J. girls' school with an enrollment of 140 and a J. library were operating in the early 20th cent. Pogroms were staged against the Jews on 1 Dec. 1917 and in June 1919. In the 1920s and 1930s, a J. council, a kolkhoz, and a court in Yiddish were active. A J. elementary school founded in 1923 added higher grades in the 1930s and was attended by 336 students, representing 90% of the town's school-age children. In 1939, the J. pop. was 2,651. The Germans captured the town on 11 July 1941 and set up a ghetto surrounded by a barbed wire fence where 3,647 Jews were confined. Exorbitant tributes were exacted; gold, silver, and foreign currency were confiscated. In Sept. 1942, 4,080 Jews were executed – 3,800 from D. and its environs and 280 from the Volkovintsy dist. Two hundred skilled J. workers from D. were murdered at Letichev in 1942.

DERECSKE   Bihar dist., Hungary. Jews settled in the early 19th cent., mainly selling farm produce. A few grew medicinal plants. The first synagogue was consecrated in 1851; a J. school was opened in 1887. The J. pop. was 355 in 1869 and 523 (5% of the total) in 1941. At the end of June 1944, the Jews were deported to Auschwitz via Nagyvarad. Fifty survivors tried to reestablish the community after the war, but soon left.

DERECZYN   Nowogrodek dist., Poland, today Belarus. Jews are first mentioned in 1550. Their pop. grew to 1,887 (total 2,663) in 1897. The community maintained a large stone synagogue and two *battei midrash* as well as a number of *shtiblekh*, the most prominent serving the Lubavich Hasidim. Among the community's outstanding personalities were R. Yehezkel Feivel (the *maggid* of D.), who began his career in the town in 1773 at the age of 18, and R. Mordekhai Gimpel, who was active in Hovevei Zion in the 1880s. After WWI, with the J. pop. declining to 1,346 in 1921, Zionist activity intensified and some emigrated to Palestine as well as to Argentina. A Hebrew school founded in 1918 later joined the Tarbut network. Under Soviet rule in 1939–41, Jews found employment in the cooperative system. The Germans captured D. on 27 June 1941, instituting a regime of forced labor. A ghetto was established in Jan. 1942 and filled with refugees. In March 1942 a few hundred Jews were expelled to Pozowice; 200–250 of them were executed in late April. Another 100 of D.'s Jews were murdered by the Germans in June. On 23 July, the remaining 2,500 Jews in the ghetto were executed. A group of 250–300 who had escaped reached the family camp of Dr. Y. Atlas, a partisan commander, and the partisan units commanded by Boris Bulat and Pawel Bulak. Seventy fell in battle.

DEREWNO   Nowogrodek dist., Poland, today Bela-

rus. Jews probably settled in the late 18th cent. Most were peddlers trading in the surrounding villages or on weekly market days. In 1897 they numbered 350 (total 851). J. trade declined in the economic crisis and antisemitic atmosphere of the post-WWI years. The J. pop. in 1939 was 50–60 families. The Germans murdered 35 Jews on their arrival in late June 1941. The rest were expelled to the Rubiezhowicze ghetto in the fall and from there dispersed to other places, most being murdered in summer 1942.

DERNA Cyrenaica dist., Libya. Spanish exiles apparently settled in the 16th cent. and there is evidence of a J. community in the 18th cent. In the late 19th and early 20th cent., the J. pop. was 80–150 (total 6,000). Jews found employment as peddlers and sold cosmetics and perfume to Moslem women. The pride of the community was a Torah scroll said to date from the time of Ezra the Scribe and miraculously rescued from the sea. After the Italian occupation in 1911, the presence of Italian army units stimulated commerce. Jews opened stores, selling food and haberdashery products, while J. tailors bought up hides and wool from Bedouin tribesmen to produce garments for their customers. Jews also dealt extensively with the Italian banks in the city. R. Reuven Serusi, son of R. Moshe Serusi, chief rabbi of Tripoli, was chief rabbi of D. from 1889 until his death in 1937. He was responsible for the *talmud torah* where J. children studied in the afternoons after attending the Italian elementary school in the morning. Zionist activity commenced in 1922 with the founding of the Palestina Society, which confined itself to the study of Hebrew and the collection of funds for Keren Kayemet. In 1938, Italy's racial laws were published, preventing J. children past the fourth grade from continuing at Italian schools. Jews were dismissed from the public service while J. businessmen were forced to keep their businesses open on the Sabbath. In the atmosphere of uncertainty, many fled to the nearby village of Beda Litoria and to Tripoli. Most were expelled to the Jado camp in May–Oct. 1942, where the able-bodied were subjected to forced labor. The legendary Torah scroll was taken there as well. After the British liberated D. on 24 Jan. 1943, the Jews returned to find their homes and stores looted. Many left for Benghazi and Tripoli to seek work. After the J. soldiers with the British army left, Hebrew classes ceased and community life declined. Relations with the Arab pop. also deteriorated against the back-

ground of Israel's independence. In 1947 the J. pop. was about 500, about half receiving aid from the Joint Distribution Committee. Most Jews began leaving clandestinely for Tripoli and from there made their way to Israel.

DERVENTA Bosnia-Hercegovina, Yugoslavia, today Republic of Bosnia. Jews settled there during the 19th cent. From 1919 the community was actively Zionist. There were 150 Jews in 1931 (total 6,654). In 1939, 100 J. refugees from Germany and Austria were absorbed by the community. In 1942 they, together with the Jews of D., perished in the Jasenovac death camp.

DESSAU Anhalt, Germany. A continuous J. settlement started in D. only in 1672. The J. pop. grew quickly, numbering 25 families in 1685 and peaking in 1818 at 807 individuals (about 9% of the total). A cemetery was established in 1674 and a synagogue in 1687, one of the first to be built in central Germany. Moses Benjamin Wulff, banker at the court of Anhalt in 1686–1729, opened a Hebrew printing press in 1694. With branches in several towns, the press operated until 1744. David Fraenkel served as rabbi in D. (1737–43), where he opened a *beit midrash* and initiated a new printing of Maimonides' works. These first signs of the Haskala movement in D. left their imprint on the Enlightenment philosopher Moses Mendelssohn (1729–86), who was born in D. The progressive J. Gymnasio for teachers and rabbis, founded in 1786, was opposed by community members, but the Juedische Freischule (1799–1848), which was committed to Mendelssohn's ideas, became a renowned institute, and in 1825 the Gymnasio, now a seminary for teachers, was merged with it. The D. community became one of the earliest Reform communities. Ludwig Philippson (1811–89), one of the future leaders of German J. Liberalism, was born here. From 1806 to 1848 *Sulamith*, the first J. periodical to appear in the German language and script, was published here. Although the community had shrunk by 1895 to 458 members, it dedicated in 1908 a new and magnificent synagogue financed by the Cohn-Oppenheim Foundation. Several community members were elected members of the Anhalt parliament and Moritz von Cohn (1812–1900) served as court banker. Zionism began to develop among the youth in the 1920s. By 1933, the J. pop. in D. numbered 360. On *Kristallnacht* (9–

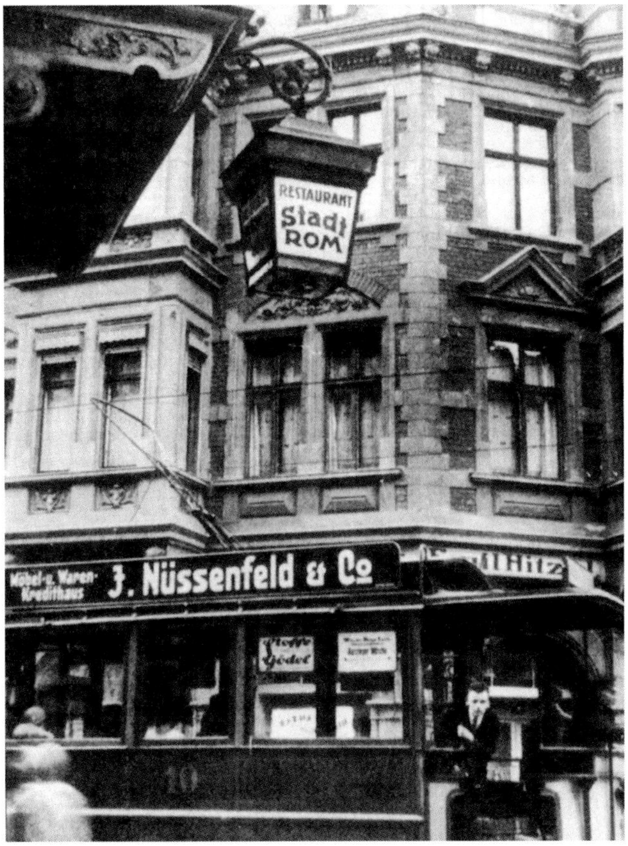
RESTAURANT
Stadt
ROM
J. Nüssenfeld & Co
An advertisement on a bus for a Jewish textile firm (J. Nuessenfeld), Dessau, Germany, 1929

10 Nov. 1938) the synagogue was set on fire, stores and homes were looted, and the J. men were taken off to the Buchenwald concentration camp. Of the 121 Jews who were still in D. in 1939, most were deported and perished.

DETA (Hung. Detta) S. Transylvania dist., Rumania. A J. community was organized in 1858 and a synagogue built. At the beginning of the 20th cent., the J. pop. numbered over 100, declining to less than 50 by the end of the 1930s. At the outbreak of WWII, the Jews were transferred to Timisoara.

DETMOLD Lippe, Germany. A Jew was first permitted to settle there in 1500. Those who arrived in 1599–1612 included Natan Melrich, whose granddaughter, Glueckel of Hameln, published her famous memoirs of German-J. life in the 17th–18th cents. Banished in 1614, the protected Jews (*Schutzjuden*) who returned in 1698 established a growing community and engaged in various trades. Having obtained the post of court factor (1718), Josef Isaak gained control of the tobacco industry but fell under suspicion. He was imprisoned and after an antisemitic show trial in 1737, he lost all his wealth. The J. community extended its burial ground in 1726, acquired new premises for a synagogue in 1742, and appointed a district rabbi in 1776. The D. community was the first in Lippe to embrace Reform Judaism in 1829, introducing prayers in German, a mixed choir, and confirmation for girls. Leopold Zunz (1794–1886), one of the architects of the scientific and critical study of Judaism (*Juedische Wissenschaft*), was the most famous Jew born there. A J. school opened in 1808 had no more than 50 pupils since most children left at 13 or attended non-J. schools. From 117 in 1803, the community grew to 240 (2% of the total) in 1895, but no rabbi was appointed after 1876. Jews financed apprenticeship schemes and contributed to the city's industrialization. Accommodating 242 worshipers, the new Liberal synagogue was dedicated on 20 July 1907. The periodical *Detmolder Volksblatt* adopted a vicious anti-J. line after WWI, and members of the Central Union (C.V.) and the J. War Veterans Association took counteraction. Prince Friedrich of Schaumburg-Lippe referred to the "menace of international Jewry" (1932); Hitler addressed 16 rallies in the neighborhood during his 1933 election campaign. A teacher was the first Jew to be dismissed when Hitler came to power. One of those who forced him to resign was Lippe's auxiliary police chief, Juergen Stroop, who (as an SS major general) completed the Warsaw ghetto's destruction in 1943. Felix Fechenbach, J. editor of the Social Democratic newspaper and a Zionist, was "shot while trying to escape" en route to the Dachau concentration camp in Aug. 1933. Nazis burned the synagogue on *Kristallnacht* (9–10 Nov. 1938), and some Jews were dispatched to the Buchenwald concentration camp. How many reached safe havens is not clear. Eighty Jews from D. were transported to Nazi death camps (1941–42). After WWII, Holocaust survivors established a community which had dwindled to ten by 1970. Rebuilt in 1979, the former synagogue is now preserved as a memorial.

DETTELBACH Lower Franconia, Germany. Jews are first mentioned in 1675. In the 19th cent. they mainly engaged in the wine trade. In 1837 the community numbered 130 (total 2,445). A synagogue was built in 1862. The J. public school was closed

down in 1924. In 1933 the J. pop. was 39. In the 1933–41 period, 18 left the town, 15 of them emigrating from Germany. Another 12 were deported to Izbica in the Lublin dist. (Poland) via Wuerzburg on 25 April 1942 and the last 11 to the Theresienstadt ghetto on 23 Sept. 1942.

DETTENSEE Hohenzollern, Germany. A quota of 23 families was present from 1720 to the 1830s under letters of protection, eking out a living as peddlers and as traders in horses and cattle, hides, and copperware. A synagogue was opened in 1820, a cemetery in 1830, and a J. public school in 1826. The J. pop. dropped from 173 in 1830 to 48 in 1898 through emigration. The two Jews remaining in 1933 were attached to the Haigerloch community.

DETVA Slovakia, Czechoslovakia, today Republic of Slovakia. Jews settled in the mid-19th cent., founding a Neologist congregation and reaching a peak pop. of 140 (total 10,320) in 1880. In the early 20th cent., the young began to leave, reducing the J. pop. to 48 by 1940. Jews owned sawmills and clothing and grocery stores. In the Slovakian state (from March 1939), their businesses were closed and on 9 June 1942 they were deported to the Lublin dist. of Poland via Zwolen. The young men were sent to the Majdanek concentration camp, the others to the Sobibor death camp.

DEUTSCH EYLAU (Pol. Ilawa) East Prussia, Germany, today Poland. The J. community numbered 15 families in 1722. In 1831, the J. pop. came to 111; about 165 in 1846; and 60 in 1895. In 1925, the pop. grew again (to 110) due to immigration from areas which came under Polish sovereignty after WWI. The community maintained a synagogue and a cemetery. When the Nazis assumed power in 1933, about 100 Jews were living in D., dropping to 37 by summer 1936. The community sold the synagogue, which was turned into a brewery. By May 1939, only eight Jews were still living in D. No further information about their fate under Nazi rule is available.

DEUTSCHKREUTZ Burgenland, Austria. The community was one of the Seven Communities (*Sheva Kehillot*) in Burgenland. Jews first settled in 1478. In the 16th and 17th cents., they occupied a ghetto which in 1664 came under the protection of Prince Esterhazy. During this period, a J. cemetery was established. In 1747 a synagogue was inaugurated, but a large fire destroyed the ghetto almost completely, including the synagogue. From 1763 until the 1920s, a J. elementary school was functioning. In the second half of the 19th cent., a yeshiva under the auspices of R. Menahem Katz-Wannfried became well known all over Europe. In 1834, a new synagogue was built. Jews were engaged mainly in the textile and grain trade. The composer Karl Goldmark (1830–1914) was born in D. In 1729, the J. pop. stood at 222, rising to 1,230 in 1880 (of a total 3,254) and declining to 764 in 1911. When Burgenland became part of Austria in 1921, the number of Jews declined once again to 433 (12.2% of the total). From 1931 until 1938, several Jews served on the city council. On the day of the *Anschluss* (13 March 1938), J. houses were damaged and confiscated shortly afterwards. In April 1938, all Jews were expelled from D. Some were able to escape; the rest were sent to Vienna and then in June 1942 to the east. By the beginning of May, there were no Jews living in D. In Feb. 1941, the synagogue was blown up.

DEUTSCH-KRONE (Pol. Walcz) Posen–West Prussia, Germany, today Poland. The first authenticated report about Jews, who were only allowed to live in parts of the town along the lake shore, is dated 1623. By 1698, the J. settlement already comprised 37 houses and a synagogue. The community continued to grow, numbering about 240 individuals in 1774 and 564 in 1831 (20% of the local pop.). In the first half of the 19th cent., the community established a synagogue, an elementary school (1842), and a cemetery. The J. pop. reached a peak of 647 in 1871, dropping to 337 individuals in 1913 and 225 in 1925. The school was closed in 1912. On the eve of the Nazi assumption of power in 1933, some 250 Jews were living in the town. While most of the larger J. businesses were "Aryanized" by 1936, J. peddlers in the vicinity were still earning well and horse traders were also able to make a living. On *Kristallnacht* (9–10 Nov. 1938), the synagogue was destroyed, J. businesses were demolished, and the men were taken off to the Sachsenhausen concentration camp. By May 1939, 57 Jews were left in D. Of these, those still present in March 1940 were interned in the Buergergarten camp near Schneidemuehl and then deported to the east shortly afterwards.

organized community was formed in the later 18th cent. The J. pop. grew to a peak of 225 in 1842 (20% of the total) and played a central role in the town's economy, with not a few working the land. After emancipation, the J. pop. began to dwindle (many going to nearby Strasbourg), falling to 26 in 1933. By 1938, all J. businesses were liquidated and nine Jews had emigrated. On *Kristallnacht* (9–10 Nov. 1938), the synagogue was vandalized and all J. men were sent to the Dachau concentration camp. Of those remaining, 11 were deported to the Gurs concentration camp on 22 Oct. 1940.

DIESPECK Middle Franconia, Germany. The 18th cent. community had a synagogue as well as a cemetery serving neighboring settlements. It numbered 270 (total pop. 820) in 1837 and was attached to Neustadt an der Aisch in 1933. The three remaining Jews left by 1937.

DIETZENBACH Hesse, Germany. Numbering 28 at its height (1861–1910), the community had no synagogue but worshiped in Dreieichenhain. Although the village was anti-Nazi until 1933, all the Jews left by Sept. 1938, some emigrating to the U.S.

DIEUZE Moselle dist., France. There was a small J. community from the mid-18th cent. Three Jews participated in the 1886 municipal elections. A new synagogue was inaugurated in 1907. Between the World Wars, the community contributed to helping Jews in Eastern Europe. During WWII, the cemetery was looted and the Germans burnt down the synagogue. The synagogue was rebuilt after liberation. In 1965, the community numbered 40 members.

DIEZ Hesse–Nassau, Germany. Annihilated in the Black Death persecutions of 1348–49, the J. community was reestablished 300 years later, opening a synagogue in 1706. A new synagogue was built in 1863 and a J. boys' home, funded by wealthy German Jews, was maintained (1888–1935). The community, numbering 130 (3% of the total) in 1895, declined after WWI. On *Kristallnacht* (9–10 Nov. 1938), the synagogue was damaged by fire. Only one of the 68 Jews living there in 1933 still remained in 1940.

DIHTINETI Bukovina, Rumania, today Ukraine. The local Jews became part of the Putila community.

The J. pop. in 1930 was 56. In fall 1941, the Jews were deported to Transnistria. Eight families returned after the war.

DIJON Cote d'Or dist., France. The J. presence in D. dates to the 12th cent. In the 14th cent., the Jews of D. were expelled several times, until the general expulsion edict of Charles VI in 1394. The modern community was established after the French Revolution, in the last decade of the 18th cent. In 1803, there were about 50 J. families in D., most from Alsace. In 1869, the community included 100 families. In 1879. there were 550 Jews in D. and a synagogue was inaugurated. On the eve of WWII, 150 J. families were listed as residing in D. During the occupation, there was an influx of refugees from Alsace to D. The Germans used the synagogue as a warehouse. On 25 and 26 Feb. 1942 (possibly the 26th and 27th), 22 Jews from D. were arrested and deported to the Drancy concentration camp. On 9 Feb. 1944, 92 Jews were deported. Only two returned. During the occupation, some Jews managed to escape to the south or to Switzerland, with the help of local French residents. The Red Cross was very active in rescuing J. children. Fewer than 70 families survived deportation. After the war, the synagogue was restored. In 1964, there were 1,000 Jews in D., many of them from North Africa.

DILLICH (now part of Borken), Hesse–Nassau, Germany. Established around 1740, the J. community numbered 48 (9% of the total) in 1885. The remaining 16 Jews left by 1938.

DILLINGEN Saar, Germany. There is evidence from the mid-18th cent. of a J. cemetery. A settlement developed in 1800, numbering 46 Jews by 1900. In the mid-19th cent. the Jews attended services in Diefflen, but later had their own *minyan* in a private home. From the turn of the cent., the J. pop. increased because of the town's industrial development, and in 1925 it was 140. In 1924 a synagogue was consecrated, and in 1929 D. became an independent community. When the German Reich annexed the Saarland in March 1935, about half of the 113 Jews in D. emigrated, mainly abroad. The community was disbanded at the end of 1935. On *Kristallnacht* (9–10 Nov. 1938), the synagogue was burned down and the remaining 14 Jews were maltreated and their homes wrecked. In 1939, there were still three Jews in D. At least 28

Jews perished in the Nazis camps, including those who sought a haven in neighboring countries the Nazis later occupied.

DIMER Kiev dist., Ukraine. Jews numbered 52 in 1765 and 984 in 1897. A. J. agricultural colony was located nearby. In Sept. 1919 Cossacks looted J. homes and stores after failing to receive all of a tribute they demanded. In 1939, under the Soviets, the J. pop. was 153. The Germans occupied D. on 25 Aug. 1941 and within a few days sent the Jews to Gestapo headquarters in Kiev, where they were executed.

DINKELSBUEHL Middle Franconia, Germany. Jews were victims of the Rindfleisch massacres of 1298, maintaining a community until expelled in 1400. Jews arriving in D. during the Thirty Years War (1618–48) were expelled in 1648. The community formed in the late 19th cent. numbered 49 (total 5,286) in 1880. Of the 64 Jews present in 1933, 17 emigrated and 28 left for other German cities before Nov. 1938. The last 18 were expelled shortly after *Kristallnacht* (9–10 Nov. 1938).

DINSLAKEN Rhineland, Germany. Jews were present in the 14th cent., their settlement being interrupted by the destruction of the community during the Black Death persecutions of 1348-49. Between 1516–30, Wilhelm the Jew, perhaps as a convert, served as *Rentmeister* to the Count of Cleves. Jews are again mentioned in the late 17th cent., their number rising from ten families in 1809 to 167 in 1880 and reaching a peak of 388 in 1895. A synagogue was consecrated in 1813 and a J. elementary school began operating in 1824. In 1854, D. was established as an affiliated community to the Duisburg regional community and in 1877 became independent. A J. orphanage was opened in 1885, eventually housing 38 children in 1930 and serving as a social center for the community. In June 1933, four months after the Nazi assumption of power, the J. pop. numbered 208 and by the beginning of 1938 it dropped to 146. In Oct., six Jews with Polish citizenship were expelled to the Polish border. On *Kristallnacht* (9–10 Nov. 1938), the J. orphanage was destroyed and the synagogue and some adjoining J. homes were set on fire. J. men were sent to the Dachau concentration camp after severe beatings. The J. orphans and the staff moved to Cologne (from where they reached Holland in Feb. 1939.) Many Jews emigrated or moved to cities in the Ruhr region. In May 1939, 37 Jews lived in D. Those who remained during the war were deported in 1941–42 to the death camps of Eastern Europe. In all, the Nazis murdered 77 Jews, including orphans deported from Holland.

DINXPERLO Gelderland dist., Holland. Jews settled in the 18th cent. and numbered 59 in 1854. The J. pop. in 1941 was 84 (total 3,948). The Jews were deported in the Holocaust; only four survived.

DIOSEK Slovakia, Czechoslovakia, today Republic of Slovakia. Jews probably settled in the early 18th cent. but were soon expelled and did not return until the 1830s. The community maintained a synagogue and elementary school and reached a peak pop. of 220 (total 2,997) in 1910. Many Jews worked in a large sugar refinery. Both the Zionists and Agudat Israel were active between the World Wars. Persecution commenced with the annexation of D. to Hungary in Nov. 1938. Dozens of J. men were drafted into forced labor brigades in 1941. In June 1944, after the German occupation, the remaining 90 Jews were sent to Galanta and from there, on 12 June, to Auschwitz.

DIOSGYOR Borsod dist., Hungary. Jews are first mentioned in the early 18th cent. The J. pop. peaked at 441 (2.6% of the total) in 1910, declining to 222 by 1941. Hungary's racial laws of 1938 undermined J. livelihoods. From 1940, many J. men, seized for forced labor to work in the area's coal, steel, and copper mines, succeeded in escaping and joining the partisans. In June 1944, the Jews were transferred to Miskolc and on 12 June deported to Auschwitz.

DITRAU (Hung. Ditro) N. Transylvania dist., Rumania. Jews settled in the mid-19th cent. The J. pop. in 1920 was 213 (3% of the total). In May 1944 the Jews were transferred to the Sfantul Gheorghe ghetto and in June deported to Auschwitz.

DITTLOFSRODA Lower Franconia, Germany. The J. pop. numbered 68 in 1816 (total 383), declining immediately thereafter mainly through emigration to the U.S. (including 18 in 1830-54). A synagogue was built in 1795. Seventeen Jews were present in the Nazi era; 13 left in 1936-39, 11 for other German cities. The last two were deported to the Theresienstadt ghetto in Sept. 1942.

DJAKOVO Croatia, Yugoslavia, today Republic of Croatia. A. J. community was established in 1852. The Hebrew invitation to the First Zionist Congress was printed there, at the initiative of Marcus Ehrenpreis, Herzl's close collaborator, who was rabbi in D. from 1896 until 1900, when he was appointed chief rabbi of Bulgaria. Cultural, religious, and Zionist activities peaked early in the 20th cent. The J. pop. in 1931 was 329 (total 7,339). In 1941 the Jews were concentrated in a camp in D., where some died. The rest were taken to the Jasenovac death camp in 1942. None survived.

DJERBA Djerba dist., Tunisia. A number of traditions surround the ancient origins of the island community. The most popular maintains that J. priests fleeing from Jerusalem settled in D. after the destruction of the First Temple in 586 B.C.E. It is said that they brought a door and some stones from the Temple which were used to build the al-Ghariba synagogue, which became a place of pilgrimage for North African Jews. Other traditions place the first settlers in the time of David or Solomon or the destruction of the Second Temple. In any case, the settlement was apparently one of the chain of J. colonies founded on the North African coast in Roman times. Jews are first mentioned as merchants in the 11th cent. and as prisoners of the Normans in 1135–36 after the latter captured the island. In the 12th cent., Jews from Tripoli found a haven there in the wake of the disturbances in their city, thus initiating a long-standing connection between the two communities. In the 11th and 12th cents., the Jews of D. constituted a well-established community engaging in the trans-Sahara trade. Maimonides noted their strict observance of the laws of purity and their mediocrity as religious scholars. The Almohads destroyed the community in 1149. Jews returned to the island in the early 13th cent. Jews from D. are also mentioned in 1239 as residing in Palermo. In the 16th cent., the Jews occupied two settlements on the island, known as al-Hara al-Kabira ("the Big Quarter") and al-Hara al-Saghira ("the Small Quarter"). They wore distinctive dress – blue or violet gowns down to their knees and yellow turbans – and were ruled by the discriminatory Moslem *Dhimmi* laws. In the 18th cent., D. became an important center of J. learning, competing for primacy with Tunis. Its renaissance is associated with the arrival of R. Aharon Peretz (d. 1766) from Morocco. Another factor was the Shab-

Al-Ghariba synagogue, Djerba, Tunisia, 1930 (Beth Hatefutsoth Photo Archive, Tel Aviv/courtesy of Gaston Cohen-Solal, Marseilles)

batean movement, which served to strengthen the link of North African Jewry to Eretz Israel. Most of the synagogues in the Hara Kabira were built in this period. The island came to be called the Jerusalem of Africa due to its rabbinical court and a number of *yeshivot* in operation under the guidance of local rabbis and sages. The two J. communities identified themselves with the east and west, respectively, in their rivalry – the Hara Saghira with Eretz Israel and the Hara Kabira with Spain and Morocco. Each could boast a number of satellite communities on the mainland: Ben Gardane, Medenine, and Zarzis (Hara Kabira) and Tataouine (Hara Saghira). There were also communities of D. Jews residing in Gabes and Sfax. Jews owned grocery stores and numerous workshops, being particularly known for their jewelry and prayer shawls. Jews also operated three flour mills. At the turn of the 18th cent., Leghornian (*Gorni* or *Grana*) Jews founded a small J. community in the Moslem set-

tlement of Houmt-Souk on the island. The leading J. family there were the Parientes, with Giuseppe Pariente serving as Italian consul in the city. Relations with the Moslem pop., mostly semi-nomadic Berbers, were largely based on economic coexistence. Occasional disturbances were the result of economic competition or Bedouin attacks. In such an attack in 1864, against the background of the bey's constitutional reforms, Bedouin tribesmen raped J. women, beat the men, pillaged J. property, and desecrated the synagogues in a five-day rampage. In 1876, a number of cases of murder were reported. The establishment of the French Protectorate in 1881 brought far-reaching changes, turning the island into a commercial and administrative center. A modern new quarter sprang up in Houmt-Souk with stores, hotels, and cafes. The J. pop. was also growing, reaching about 3,000 before WWI and about 4,000 between the World Wars. The two original J. quarters, however, retained their traditional aspect, with public baker's ovens to keep Sabbath meals warm, a special Passover bakery, private ritual baths and wine presses. Charms were affixed to door posts to ward off the evil eye and the resistance to western influence continued unabated. The French period also brought about a reversal of economic roles. The Berbers took over outside trade while the Jews confined themselves to island commerce. Jews of the Hara Saghira specialized in woolens and in jewelry and luxury items while tradesmen in the Hara Kabira were more varied. A specialty of J. tanners was the manufacture of the leather watering buckets used by farmers for irrigation while J. metalworkers specialized in Arab coffee pots (*tanakji*). In the wool industry, Jews and Moslems cooperated in producing the finished product: the Moslems spinning and weaving and the Jews dyeing the wool. J. livelihoods were seriously affected by French decrees banning the commercial distillation of date beverages, a J. trade, and restricting the stamping of metal products to Tunis. Community income was derived mainly from the 25% meat tax. Additional taxes were levied on wine and property. A poll tax was paid to the bey. The educational system remained strictly traditional, with great efforts made to keep out the Alliance Israelite Universelle with their schools. Children could study for ten years and attend the city's renowned *yeshivot*, whose reputation grew as other communities fell by the wayside of modernity. In D., rabbis ruled supreme as the ultimate arbiters in public and private

life in a kind of theocratic republic. Among the illustrious rabbis were Sasi Matuk Kohen Yehonatan (1831–1905), who produced important Mishna commentaries and Responsa and placed a ban on the Alliance; Mordekhai Khamus ha-Kohen (1886–1974), author of the Responsa collection *Gedolat Mordekhai* and chief rabbi in 1915–35; and Moshe Khalfon ha-Kohen (1874–1950), the outstanding rabbinical figure of his generation (chief rabbi in 1935–50) and the most admired leader of the modern community of D. He was an ardent Zionist and his four-volume *Brit Kehuna*, a collection of local regulations and customs, was halakhically authoritative in the community. D. was also known for its Hebrew printing presses, producing 500 local works in the first half of the 20th cent. Zionist activity commenced with the founding of the Ateret Zion society in 1919. Its members concerned themselves with raising money for Palestine and eagerly followed events in the Holy Land through a wide range of periodicals. Relations with the Arabs deteriorated with the onset of WWII and from mid-1942, J. merchants suffered from the racial laws of the Vichy regime, particularly insofar as they concerned the "Aryanization" of J. property. German and Italian troops arrived in Jan. 1943. Though no organized effort was made to persecute the Jews, goods were confiscated, rabbis were humiliated, and under a threat of mass execution, a large quantity of gold was extorted from the community. The English occupied the island shortly thereafter and the community gradually began to recover with the assistance of the Joint Distribution Committee and OZE. After WWII, another radical change occurred in the occupational structure of the community as 60% of breadwinners became jewelers and 30% remained tailors or worked in the wool industry. Children continued to study at the *talmud torah* (numbering about 350 boys) while 300 boys and girls studied modern Hebrew and academic subjects at a Daber Ivrit school in the afternoons. Zionist activity revived and expanded, remaining in the framework of the Ateret Zion movement. Branches were opened in the satellite communities. In 1946, the Hagana organization started a pioneer training farm 4 miles outside the Hara Kabira. Its members were among the founders of Moshav Berekhya near Ashkelon in Israel. Relations with the Arabs deteriorated further in 1947 in connection with Israel's struggle for independence. Arabs tried to attack the J. training farm and boycotted J. tradesmen. Pressure to emigrate in-

creased, with about 75% of the Jews finally leaving for Israel. In the 1990s, about 800 remained in D., preserving their traditions and the use of the Hebrew language.

DLUGOSIODLO   Bialystok dist., Poland. Jews first settled there at the beginning of the 19th cent. By the end of the cent. there were 800 Jews (total 1,249). Antisemitism in the 1930s restricted trade and led to small-scale violence. In 1931, the community council had six Zionist and two Agudat Israel representatives. On 5 Oct. 1939, the Germans ordered all Jews to leave for the east. Those who tried to hide were shot. Most reached Bialystok, but only a few survived the Holocaust.

DMITREVKA   Chernigov dist., Ukraine. The J. pop. was 438 (total 644) in 1897 and 195 (total 4,138) in 1939. The Germans entered D. on 14 Sept. 1941. On 23 Sept. they murdered 15 Jews. Subsequently, they randomly seized and murdered J. children.

DMITRIEV-LGOVSKYI   Kursk dist., Russia. Jews probably settled in the late 19th cent. numbering 104 (total 6,403) in 1897. In 1903, they were given permission to open a prayer house. The J. pop. rose to 180 in 1926. The Germans arrived on 8 Oct. 1941, robbing the few Jews who had neither fled nor been evacuated. They moved them into a single house under a forced labor regime before murdering them.

DMITROVSK-ORLOVSKI   Oriol dist., Russia. Jews settled in the mid-19th cent., numbering 72 (total 5,291) in 1897 and 21 in 1926. The Germans, after their arrival on 2 Oct. 1941, murdered the few Jews who had neither fled nor been evacuated.

DNEPRODZERZHINSK   (until 1936, Kamenskoye) Dnepropetrovsk dist., Ukraine. J. settlement commenced in the late 19th cent. with the development of the local steel industry and reached a pop. of 852 (total 16,878) in 1897. In 1931, under the Soviets, 360 J. students (total 4,000) attended the local industri-

Orthodox children exercising, Dlugosiodlo, Poland

al school, 230 of them in classes with Yiddish as the language of instruction. In 1939, the J. pop. was 4,900 (total 148,000). The Germans captured the city on 22 Aug. 1941 and on the same day murdered 206 residents, apparently all Jews. Another few hundred Jews, including 96 children, were murdered at the end of the month.

DNEPROPETROVSK (until 1926, Yekaterinoslav) Dnepropetrovsk dist., Ukraine. J. settlement commenced in the late 18th cent. In 1805, the J. pop. was 376 and by 1853 the community had a synagogue built of stone. A pogrom was staged on 20–21 July 1881. J. self-defense units foiled another attempt by rioting Ukrainians during Easter 1901. By 1897, the J. pop. had risen to 41,240 (total 112,000). Most Jews engaged in petty trade (particularly in farm produce) and tailoring. In July and Oct. 1905, there was a new outbreak of pogroms, with 65 Jews killed and twice as many injured. About 50 J. homes were burned and

looted. In the 1920s, a few dozen J. educational institutions were operating, including three *talmudei torah, yeshivot,* and secular schools for boys and girls. From the late 19th cent. until the Oct. 1917 Revolution, D. was an important Zionist center and M. Ussishkin (in 1891–1906) and Shmarya Levin were active there. Further pogroms occurred in fall 1917, early 1918, and Aug. 1919. In the mid-1920s, under Soviet rule, five J. schools, numbering 1,200–1,500 students, were still open. Apparently just two remained in 1936, one of them a secondary school. A technical school was founded in 1924 with an enrollment of 100 children in 1926. Two J. schools had boarding facilities for 240 children. A central J. library was still open in the late 1920s and in 1931 a theater for J. working youth was set up. In 1926, a section in the law courts with deliberations in Yiddish was inaugurated. Many Jews worked in the numerous factories in the city, including 1,500–5,000 in the Petrovski steel works and 1,085 in the Lenin factory. Among the notable figures born in

Drafting class in a Dnepropetrovsk factory, Ukraine, 1932 (State Central Photos and Film Archives, Kiev/photo courtesy of Yad Vashem, The Holocaust Martyrs' and Heroes' Remembrance Authority, Jerusalem)

in 1939 ended J. community life. The Germans took the city on 28 June 1941. A reign of terror was instituted with the Ukrainians given a free hand to pillage and intimidate the J. pop. The Great Synagogue burned to the ground along with other houses of prayer and study. Fifty young Jews were murdered at the town's abandoned salt mine. In the *Aktion* of 29 July 1942 all but the able-bodied were deported to the Belzec death camp. The others were put to forced labor. The 500 Jews remaining in D. were executed on 24 Nov. 1942 at the Lichtman sawmills.

DOBROMYSL   Vitebsk dist., Belorussia. The J. pop. was 272 (total 332) in 1880 and 371 in 1923 under the Soviets. A kolkhoz founded in 1930 supported 12 J. families. The Germans arrived in July 1941 and soon afterwards concentrated all the Jews in a single building. In Feb. 1942, they were all murdered, together with a number of Jews from Vitebsk, beside a big pit on the way to Liozno, making a total of nearly 80 dead.

DOBROTWOR   Tarnopol dist., Poland, today Ukraine. A small J. community existed from the second half of the 16th cent. but never developed significantly, reaching a pop. of 383 (total 3,314) in 1900 and dropping to 216 between the World Wars. The community was expelled and liquidated by the Germans probably in Sept. or Oct. 1942.

DOBROVELYTCHKOVKA   (until 1883, Revutskoye) Odessa dist., Ukraine. J. settlement commenced in the first half of the 19th cent. In 1897, the J. pop. was 1,718 (total 2,849). In the early 1920s, under the Soviets, a J. elementary school was started. In 1939, 366 Jews remained. The Germans arrived on 1 Aug. 1941, murdering 185 local Jews and 209 from the surrounding area. On 22 Dec. 1942, eight children from the local children's home were murdered.

DOBRUSH   Gomel dist., Belorussia. The J. pop. was 372 in 1926 and 441 (total 13,815) in 1939. The Germans arrived on 21 Aug. 1941. In Oct., the Jews were incarcerated in two shacks at a tractor garage under conditions of overcrowding and starvation. On 21 Nov., they were executed beside freshly dug pits. The last 70 Jews in the city were executed on 5 April 1942.

DOBRUSHINO   Crimea, Russia, today Ukraine. D.

was founded as a J. agricultural settlement in the 1920s and numbered 230 Jews in 1932. A large J. kolkhoz was under the jurisdiction of the local rural council (soviet). The Germans arrived in late Oct. 1941, murdering 18 Jews at the kolkhoz on 13 Feb. 1942 and another 15 on 19 March. In all, 45 Jews were murdered during the Nazi occupation. A few dozen J. families returned to the kolkhoz after the war. They comprised 60% of its pop. and in 1947 a J. served as its chairman. Apparently the Jews left at about this time.

DOBRUSKA   Bohemia, Czechoslovakia. Jews are mentioned in the first half of the 16th cent. All their homes and the synagogue were destroyed in an 1806 fire. The J. pop. was 39 in 1930 (1% of the total). In Dec. 1942 the Jews were deported to the Theresienstadt ghetto via Hradec Kralove. Almost all were sent to Auschwitz in 1943.

DOBRZYN NAD DRWENCA   Warsaw dist., Poland. Jews are first mentioned in the 17th cent. and in 1783 were confined to a special quarter. J. commercial life centered around market days and big fairs a few times a year. The J. pop. stood at 1,938 (total 3,734) in 1897. Many of the young emigrated abroad, later supporting those left behind. The Zionists became active in the late 19th cent. and after WWI were represented by numerous groups, including Hehalutz, which sent many of its members to Palestine after agricultural training on a local J. farm. The Bund and Agudat Israel were also active, the latter founding schools for boys and girls (Beth Jacob). A modern J. elementary school was opened in the early 1920s. The Germans arrived on 3 Sept. 1939. On 10 Nov. all the Jews were expelled from D., most to Plonsk and a few to Warsaw, sharing the fate of the Jews there.

DOBRZYN NAD WISLA   Warsaw dist., Poland. An organized community existed from the second half of the 17th cent. Most lived in straitened economic circumstances, reducing the J. pop. through emigration from 1,816 in 1808 to 927 (total 2,485) in 1897. After WWI the Zionists became active while Agudat Israel controlled the community council, maintaining the *heder* system and a yeshiva. The Germans took the city in early Sept. 1939. In early Oct. all the Jews were expelled from the city. Details of their fate are not known.

DOBSINA Slovakia, Czechoslovakia, today Republic of Slovakia. Jews from Roznava first settled after 1848. A synagogue was erected in 1900. The J. pop. grew to 110 in 1910 and a peak of 186 (total 4,622) in 1921. Jews engaged mainly in trade but also owned a few large wood-processing factories. The Zionists became active in the 1920s. In 1940, the J. pop. was 147. Persecution commenced with the establishment of the Slovakian state in March 1939, under the instigation of local German Nazis. J. children were expelled from the public schools and J. businessmen were forced out of their businesses. In March and April 1942, 59 young J. men and women were sent to Novaky and Poprad, respectively. Families followed, en route to Auschwitz. Attempts to flee to Hungary were unsuccessful.

DOESBURG Gelderland dist., Holland. Jews first lived there in the Middle Ages. Settlement was renewed in the 17th cent. and a community, primarily poor, was established. The J. pop. was 47 in 1860 (total 3,995) and 25 in 1941 (total 5,097). In Oct. 1941, three Jews were deported to Mauthausen. In 1942–43, ten were sent to the Westerbork and Vught camps. Eight Jews survived in hiding.

DOETINCHEM Gelderland dist., Holland. Jews first settled in D. in the 17th cent. Despite its poverty from the early 19th cent., the community steadfastly supported its J. education. By 1901 there were 208 members in the community and 188 in 1938. In Oct. and Nov. 1942, 73 Jews were arrested and deported. The remaining Jews were deported to camps in April 1943. In all, 150 perished in camps while about 30 survived, mostly in hiding. A small community was reestablished after the war.

DOKSZYCE Vilna dist., Poland, today Belarus. A community of 210 taxpayers was present in 1766. Many leased fields and forest land and dealt in lumber, flax, grain, fur, and pig bristles for brushmaking. Trade in the early 19th cent. extended to the cities of Russia and Congress Poland and even Leipzig. During the 19th cent., Jews expanded into crafts and farming as their pop. grew to 2,762 (total 3,642) in 1897. Most were Habad Hasidim. After WWI J. merchants lost many of their markets and heavy taxes undermined the livelihoods of J. artisans. The J. pop. in 1925 was 3,000. From 1935, economic conditions deteriorated further in the face of economic boycotts and occasional violence in the local market. A Tarbut school founded in 1924 enrolled 150 children and was a focus of Zionist and cultural activity. The Germans arrived on 22 June 1941 and on 30 Sept. confined the Jews to a ghetto. The ghetto was liquidated in spring 1942. During Passover 65 Jews were executed outside the town, 350 at the J. cemetery a month later, and the rest in an *Aktion* commencing on 29 May and lasting 17 days. In all, more than 3,000 were murdered.

DOLGESHEIM Hesse, Germany. The community, numbering 54 (6.9% of the total) in 1861, dwindled to 11 in 1933. By Sept. 1939 Nazi violence had forced all Jews to leave.

DOLHE PODBUSKIE Lwow dist., Poland, today Ukraine. The J. pop. in 1921 was 144. Those Jews not murdered earlier were deported to the Belzec death camp in summer–fall 1942.

DOLHINOW Vilna dist., Poland, today Belarus. Jews probably arrived in the first half of the 16th cent. and formed an organized community in the 17th, numbering 485 in 1667. In the 19th cent. Jews continued to earn their livelihoods from leaseholdings but also expanded into the wholesale trade, exporting grain, flax, and fruit through Danzig. In 1881 and 1886 J. homes and shops were attacked in anti-J. rioting. Poverty and persecution led many to emigrate to the U.S., Canada, and South Africa. In 1897 the J. pop. stood at 2,259 (total 3,552). The Jews suffered further depredations in WWI and their economy suffered in its aftermath with the loss of the agricultural hinterland to the Soviet Union, though a lively smuggling trade developed across the border. The J. pop. in 1925 was 2,500. Most children studied at the Tarbut school founded in the 1920s and the Zionist youth movements were active. Under Soviet rule (Sept. 1939–June 1941), the Jews accommodated themselves to a state-run economy. The Germans began arriving in late June 1941. Jews suffered from a series of discriminatory orders. A *Judenrat* was appointed to supply forced labor and meet extortionate demands. On 28 March 1942, 1,500 Jews were gunned down in the market square and the rest confined to a ghetto. On 5 May another 1,200 were executed. The 300 skilled workers left alive were murdered on 22 May. Some escaped to the forest and joined the partisans.

DOLINA Stanislawow dist., Poland, today Ukraine. The permanent J. settlement dates from the 17th cent. The Austrian occupation (1772–1868) brought disabilities and heavy taxation, though there was some improvment of economic conditions with the granting of equal rights and the coming of the railroad. Many left for the U.S. around the turn of the century. J. life was strongly influenced by Hasidism, with the Zionists making inroads from the late 19th cent. The J. pop. reached a peak of 2,654 in 1900 (total 9,110), dropping to 2,014 in 1921. The town was under the Soviets (Sept. 1939–June 1941), the Hungarians (2 July 1941), and then the Germans, who instituted a *Judenrat* and a regime of forced labor and extortion. At the end of July 1942, after Jews from the surrounding settlements were concentrated there, around 3,000 were executed beside mass graves at the local cemetery. Some 50 Jews were in the Babi partisan unit, but only five survived, as well as a few who hid in the forests.

DOLNI KOUNICE Moravia, Czechoslovakia. Jews probably settled in the late 14th cent. A large community evolved, with a J. quarter probably established in the latter part of the 15th cent. At the time, Jews uncharacteristically owned vineyards and wine presses. Swedish soldiers destroyed the city in 1645, during the Thirty Years War (1618–48). Subsequently J. settlement was renewed in another part of the city, with a synagogue consecrated in 1652. Fire, plague, and foreign invasion struck the community from the 17th cent. to the 19th cent. The J. pop. reached a peak of 649 in 1850 and then declined steadily to 53 (total 3,130) in 1930 as many left for such cities as Brno and Vienna. D. was the birthplace of Bruno Kreisky (1911–90), who served as chancellor of Austria (1970–83). The Nazis banned public prayer and closed the synagogue in 1940. The 57 Jews in the city were deported to the Theresienstadt ghetto on 14 March 1942 and from there to the death camps of the east.

DOLNJA LENDAVA Slovenia, Yugoslavia, today Republic of Slovenia. At the end of the 18th cent., Jews settled in D. and an organized community was established at the beginning of the 19th cent. In 1940 the Jews numbered 155 (total 3,000). Under the Hungarians (1941–44), 183 young Jews fell in labor battalions on the Ukrainian front and as partisans. After the German takeover, the Jews of D. were sent to Auschwitz, where nearly all perished.

DOLNY KUBIN Slovakia, Czechoslovakia, today Republic of Slovakia. Jews probably settled in the early 18th cent. and were mostly shopkeepers. The synagogue, built in 1775, burned down in 1893 and was replaced by a new one. In 1870, 40 families split off and formed a Liberal congregation but the two were reunited in 1886 under the Status Quo banner. The community reached a peak pop. of 431 (total 1,552) in 1880. In the 1890s the community maintained a J. elementary school and *talmud torah*, the former attracting non-J. children as well. A Zionist society, one of the first in Hungary, was founded in 1897. Dr. Ludwig Yomtov Bato (1886–1974) later became one of the leaders of Hungarian Zionism. Hashomer Hatzair became active after WWI. In the Czechoslovakian Republic, Jews held public positions and owned 37 business establishments and 17 workshops and factories. In 1940, their pop. was 245. In 1941, most of their businesses were closed down by the authorities and in spring and summer 1942, 94 families (75% of the total) were deported to the east. Most of those who remained behind managed to flee during the Slovakian national uprising in 1944.

DOLNY STAL (Hung. Alistal) Slovakia, Czechoslovakia, today Republic of Slovakia. Jews settled in the late Middle Ages, later abandoning the town and only returning c. 1740. They reached a peak pop. of 115 (total 1,089) in 1880, opening an elementary school for over 60 children from the area. In 1930, 32 Jews remained. Including the outlying settlements, the congregation numbered 130 when the Germans arrived in March 1944. All were sent to Komarno and on 13 June deported to Auschwitz.

DOLZKA Stanislawow dist., Poland, today Ukraine. The J. pop. in 1921 was 141. The Jews were possibly expelled to Bolechow for liquidation in Aug. 1942.

DOMACZEWO Polesie dist., Poland, today Belarus. The J. settlement dates from the late 18th cent., growing to 1,057 in 1897 and 1,337 (total 1,504) in 1921 after much suffering in WWI. Hasidim worshiped at five of the town's eight synagogues. Summer tourism augmented J. incomes. The Germans arrived on 22 June 1941 and established a *Judenrat*. On 1 Nov. the Jews were confined to a ghetto under a regime of forced labor and sporadic killing; all were executed on 20 Sept. 1942.

DOMANEVKA   Odessa dist., Ukraine. The J. pop. was 903 (total 1,145) in 1897 and 369 in 1939. The Germans captured the town on 5 Aug. 1941. Twenty-four Jews were murdered on 29 Aug. After D. was annexed to Transnistria in Sept., tens of thousands of Jews from Moldavia and Odessa were expelled to D. and to the camps in the area. From late Dec. to mid-Jan. 1942, as many as 52,000 Jews were murdered. At the nearby Akmechetka camp, only 150 of the total 4,000 Jews from Odessa remained alive on liberation day. A similar situation prevailed at the other camps.

DOMANOVO   Mogilev dist., Belorussia. D. was founded as a J. colony in 1848 with a pop. of 15 families. In 1898, the Jews numbered 119 and owned 260 acres of land. Most worked on the Berezina River and in the neighboring forests as the settlement became a summer resort thanks to its magnificent scenery. The Germans occupied D. in early July 1941, murdering the few remaining Jews.

DOMARADZ   Lwow dist., Poland. Jews are first mentioned in 1808 and numbered 123 in 1921 (total 3,386). From Sept. 1939 the Germans enforced a regime of persecution and expelled them to Jasienica Rosielna in July 1942.

DOMAZLICE   Bohemia, Czechoslovakia. Jews settled after the 1848 revolution, consecrating a synagogue in the 1880s and reaching a pop. of 153 in 1890, which dropped to 69 (total 9,068) in 1930. The synagogue was destroyed in 1939 or 1940. In Nov. 1942 the Jews were deported to the Theresienstadt ghetto. In Jan. and Sept. 1943, they were sent on to Auschwitz. Few survived.

DOMBIE   Lodz dist., Poland. Jews lived here from the 18th cent. and the community grew with the development of the textile industry. From the early 20th cent., Agudat Israel and the Bund were active. In summer 1940, the Germans established a ghetto. On 14–17 Dec. 1941 the 1,000 Jews of D. were deported to the Chelmno death camp.

DOMBOVAR   Tolna dist., Hungary. Jews settled in the first half of the 18th cent. The first synagogue was built in the early 19th cent. on land donated by Prince Esterhazy. Many Jews were attracted to D. after the railroad arrived in 1870. The J. pop. grew from 350 in 1868 to 722 in 1930. In late April 1944, a ghetto was established, containing 1,100 Jews including those from the surrounding settlements. All were deported to Auschwitz at the beginning of July. Some 120 survivors from D. and the area reestablished the J. community after the war. By 1956, only a few Jews remained.

DOMBRAD   Szabolcs dist., Hungary. Jews, first mentioned in 1770, mostly engaged in petty trade, in farming, and in marketing local farm produce. Jews also operated a distillery, flour mill, sawmill, and a factory for processing medicinal plants. In 1930, the J. pop. was 234. Zionist activities were blocked by the authorities and hasidic groups. A J. defense group in 1935 stopped attacks by local farmers. The racial laws of 1938 destroyed J. livelihoods. The Jews were deported to Auschwitz via Kisvarda on 29–31 May 1944.

DOMBROWA   Bialystok dist., Poland. Jews appeared in the first half of the 18th cent. The J. pop. grew to 1,499 (total 1,988) in 1897. Most were *Mitnaggedim* and sent their children to the Sokolka yeshiva 20 miles away. Many had auxiliary farms. While Jews owned more than half the town's 82 workshops and most of its 76 stores, their economic situation was precarious in the face of the general economic crisis between the World Wars. The J. pop. in 1939 was 2,350. Half the town was destroyed in the German-Soviet fighting of June 1941. The Germans burned down the rest when they captured the town. In July many young Jews were led away to an unknown destination. The 600 Jews remaining in the ruins of the town were put to forced labor. In May 1942 the old were expelled to the Suchowola ghetto and on 2 Nov. 1942 the rest were sent to the Kelbasin transit camp near Grodno, from where they were deported to the Treblinka death camp on 14 Dec.

DOMBROWA GORNICZA   Kielce dist., Poland. Jews began settling in 1828 when they were hired as miners in the area. Others made their livings supplying the mineworkers with their needs. The J. pop. grew to 2,554 in 1896. In 1910, a cemetery was opened and in 1916 a synagogue was completed as the community achieved independence from Bendzin. R. Alter Moshe-Aharon Levi became its rabbi until his death in 1933. After WWI, the community continued to

grow with the J. pop. numbering 4,304 in 1921 and 5,150 (total 36,942) in 1931. About 40% of the Jews worked in the garment trade. During the 1920s, four J. banks were founded and about 300 Jews were members of a merchant association. In the early 1920s, Mizrachi was the largest Zionist organization in the city, founding the first J. school there. In the 1930s, Hashomer Hatzair was the largest youth movement. Hehalutz ran a pioneer training facility that had 70 members in 1933. Community institutions were under the influence of Orthodox circles. In 1936–37, antisemitism intensified as a consequence of Endejca agitation. The Germans arrived on 3 Sept. 1939, setting up a *Judenrat* in Nov. and taking over most J. businesses by March 1940. Refugees from Austria, Czechoslovakia, and Silesia brought the J. pop. up to 6,300 in early 1940 as Jews were mobilized for forced labor and hundreds sent to labor camps in Germany. Another 2,000 were employed in shops supplying the German army. In May 1942, 700 Jews were deported to Auschwitz. Another 1,500 were sent there on 12 Aug. Those Jews left behind to work were confined in a ghetto. In fall 1942, 650 were sent to the Skarzysko-Kamienna labor camp and the last 1,000 were transferred to the Srodula ghetto in Sosnowiec and from there deported to Auschwitz. About 300 survived the labor camps.

DOMBROWICA Volhynia dist., Poland, today Ukraine. A J. settlement already existed in the early 16th cent. and in the 17th the small community was attached to Pinsk. In the mid-18th cent. it was accorded wide-ranging privileges by the town's proprietor and by 1897 reached a pop. of 2,868 (total 6,006) with most stores and factories in J. hands. Stolin-Karlin Hasidism predominated with the Zionists and Bund socialists becoming active in the early 20th cent. Up to the Oct. 1917 Revolution the community benefited economically from the presence of Russian Army headquarters in the town but in the subsequent chaos suffered grievously until the stabilization of Polish rule in the 1920s. Between the World Wars, Jews controlled 98% of petty trade and most crafts. The Tarbut school reached an enrollment of 280 and Zionist activity expanded to include youth movements like Hehalutz, which operated a labor-training group for 300 youngsters. The J. pop. in 1937 was 3,225. About 200 of the young left for Kiev as the Red Army retreated in June 1941. The German occupation of 6 July was followed by a Ukrainian pogrom. A *Judenrat* was appointed, and a ghetto crowding together 4,327 Jews including refugees was set up in March 1942. As the community was being marched to the railroad station in the *Aktion* of 26 Aug 1942, 1,500 fled in panic when the sound of gunfire was heard. Two hundred were shot and killed; 800 were brought to Wysock to meet their end; and 500 escaped to the forest, of whom 50 survived the war. The remaining Jews were taken to Sarny, where they perished. Some managed to escape. Another 50 of those who fled before the *Aktion* survived as partisans.

DOMBROWICE Warsaw dist., Poland. This community began in the mid-18th cent. In June 1940, the 150 Jews were transferred to the ghetto in Kutno.

DOMROWA TARNOWSKA Cracow dist., Poland. Jews lived there from the late 16th cent. and formed an organized community a century later. Under Austrian rule from 1772, economic conditions worsened and many Jews were reduced to poverty, being the first to succumb to the cholera epidemic of 1855. Cholera again struck in 1873 and in its wake a small J. hospital was established. In the same period the hasidic Unger dynasty established its court there, boosting the pop. to 2,418 by 1900 (80% of the total). Zionism became active from 1893 and in the same year a Baron Hirsch school was set up. By 1908 it had 150 students, and the local yeshiva 60. WWI claimed further epidemic victims and rampaging peasants struck at the Jews in 1918 and 1919. All this served to reduce the J. pop. to 2,100 in 1921 with economic hardship increasing from year to year. The Germans entered the town on 8 Sept. 1939, murdering a number of Jews before instituting a regime of forced labor. A large influx of refugees swelled the number of Jews; 3,100 remained after 1,500 were sent to the Pustkow labor camp in March 1942. Sporadic killings commenced early in 1942 and on 19 June another 50 were murdered in the process of deporting 450 Jews to the Belzec death camp. On 22 July, the Jews were sealed into a ghetto and in the same month another 1,800 were deported to the Belzec death camp and 100 murdered. Almost all the rest were deported in Sept. and Oct.

DOMSOD Pest dist., Hungary. Jews were present in the early 19th cent. and numbered 94 in 1930. On 7–8 July 1944, they were deported to Auschwitz via Csepel.

DONETSKO-AMVROSIEVKA   Stalino dist., Ukraine. The J. pop. in 1939 was 128 (total 15,001). The Germans captured D. on 22 March 1942. The Germans are known to have murdered three Jews from D. and eight from nearby villages.

DONJI MIHOLJAC   Croatia, Yugoslavia, today Republic of Croatia. Jews first settled in the 19th cent. The J. pop. in 1940 was 173 (total 6,000). The community perished in the Holocaust.

DORDRECHT   Zuid-Holland dist., Holland. J. settlement began in the late 17th cent. and in the early 18th cent. a community was organized. It suffered poverty from the outset, although a slight improvement was felt in the 19th cent. In 1856 a community center was inaugurated and included a synagogue, a school, and rooms for other activities. The J. pop. in 1860 was 372. Welfare organizations were active in the 19th and 20th cents. In 1938 there were 300 community members. Of the 290 Jews deported from Aug. 1942, five survived, while 50 others survived in hiding. A small community was reestablished after the war.

DORMAGEN   Rhineland, Germany. Continuous J. settlement dates back to 1655 with the community reaching an average pop. of 47 in the second half of the 19th cent. The community maintained a synagogue and opened a cemetery in 1862. In 1930, the J. pop. reached a peak of 51, dropping to 42 in June 1933 after the Nazis came to power. On *Kristallnacht* (9–10 Nov. 1938), the SS pillaged four J. homes and stores. In 1941, the last 12 Jews were deported to the Lodz and Riga ghettoes.

DORNESTI   Bukovina, Rumania. J. traders settled in 1774. During WWI, Jews were evacuated with the rest of the pop. The J. pop. in 1930 was 84. In June 1941, the J. pop. was moved to Radauti and then deported to Transnistria.

DORNHEIM (I)   Hesse, Germany. The community, established by livestock traders in the 18th cent., numbered 85 (7.7% of the total) in 1861. A new synagogue was opened two years later, but the community declined. On *Kristallnacht* SS stormtroopers and villagers looted J. homes and demolished the synagogue. Of the 35 Jews living there in 1933, 21 emi-

grated to the U.S. and England; nine others were eventually deported.

DORNHEIM (II)   (in J. sources, Tarnim) Middle Franconia, Germany. A small community existed from at least the 16th cent., numbering 62 in 1867 (total 450). The three Jews in D. in 1941 were expelled to the Riga ghetto via Nuremberg on 29 Nov.

DORNUM   Hanover, Germany. By 1723, the J. community had an old burial ground and in 1841 a synagogue. The community numbered 63 (7% of the total) in 1861, and included members from neighboring villages in East Friesland. Mostly poor tradesmen, the Jews could not hold regular Sabbath services and the Emden rabbinate complained about their unsupervised ritual slaughtering (*shehitah*) practices. Numbering 85 at its height in 1905, the community ran a school attended by 28 children in 1908. Their numbers dwindled after WWI. After the Nazi rise to power in 1933, most of D.'s 52 Jews left, about 24 emigrating abroad, primarily to Scandinavia, the Americas, and Palestine. In June 1938, three J. citizens were arrested and transported to the Buchenwald concentration camp, where one died. Although in Oct. 1938, the 15 remaining Jews disposed of the synagogue, the building was nevertheless plundered on *Kristallnacht* (9–10 Nov. 1938), and the Torah scrolls set on fire. J. men were arrested and incarcerated in Sachsenhausen. By March 1940, there were no Jews left in D.; 24 perished in Nazi camps and ghettoes.

DOROGOBUZH   Smolensk dist., Russia. Jews are first mentioned in 1648. Their pop. was 231 (total 4,850) in 1926 and 122 in 1939. The Germans occupied D. from 5 Oct. 1941 to mid-Feb. 1942 and again, for a longer period, from 7 July 1942, this time murdering the few Jews who had not fled or been evacuated.

DOROHOI   Moldavia dist., Rumania. Jews settled in the late 18th cent. In 1881, the Jews expelled from the nearby villages came to D. and the J. pop. doubled from 3,031 in 1859 to 6,804 in 1899 (54% of the total). The Great Synagogue was built in 1825. The community built a school in 1898 that was attended by 164 pupils. In 1899, there were 357 J. merchants and only 29 Rumanian merchants in D. In 1902, of the 297 artisans, 231 were Jews. Zionist activity

Synagogue built by Jewish farmers in the 1880s, Dorohoi, Rumania (1985 photo) (Beth Hatefutsoth Photo Archive, Tel Aviv/courtesy of Yale Strom, U.S.A.)

began in 1893. In March 1907, peasants incited by priests and teachers plundered the houses of 333 J. families. In Jan. 1917, the local commander of the Rumanian forces ordered all Jews to report for work to construct barracks for his soldiers; those who failed to do so were whipped. The economic situation of the Jews between the World Wars was at its lowest ebb. The community opened a nursery school immediately after WWI; continued to run the J. school; and opened a hospital in 1920 and a home for the aged in 1926. On 1 July 1940, Rumanian soldiers attending the funeral of a J. comrade were shot at the graveside by soldiers of another unit, who then murdered J. civilians. The troops plundered the J. quarter, and in the ensuing pogrom 200 Jews were killed. In June 1941, 300 D. Jews were charged with being Communists and taken to concentration camps in Targu–Jiu and Craiova. On 7–8 Nov., the 6,000 J. refugees from Darabani, Ra-

dauti, Saveni, and Mihaileni brought to D. in June were deported to Transnistria. The deportation of the J. pop. began on 12 Nov. 1941, in two groups of 2,500–3,000. They were brought to Ataki and ferried across the Dniester River, marched to Mogilev, and then sent to camps in the district. On 7 June 1942, 450 returnees from labor battalions were deported to the Cariera-de-Piatra camp in Transnistria. At the end of Dec. 1943, 2,000 of the 3,074 J. deportees were returned to D. They suffered under the antisemitic regime until Soviet forces entered in April 1944. In 1947, 7,600 lived in D. but almost all later left for Israel. A small community existed in the mid-1990s.

DOROSAUTI Bukovina, Rumania. The Jews were attached to the Zastavna community and prayed in the Vasilau synagogue. The J. pop. in 1930 was 58. In June 1941 the Jews were transferred to Ocna,

where most died. The rest were deported to Transnistria. Few survived.

DORSTEN Rhineland, Germany. J. settlement in D. started in the 18th cent. In 1800 there were 4–6 families. The J. community, comprising also Jews from the surrounding area, peaked at 100 in 1861. It maintained a synagogue (from 1861 at least) and a cemetery (1828). In 1910, the Jews of Bottrop, Gladbeck, Buer and Horst set up their own communities. Later when they had more members than D. they broke away. In June 1933, about four months after the Nazis assumed power, 48 Jews were living in D. On *Kristallnacht* (9–10 Nov. 1938), the synagogue was wrecked, the cemetery was devastated, and J. businesses and homes were looted and vandalized. The 12 Jews who did not manage to emigrate were forced to move into two "J. houses" and were deported on 24 Jan. 1942.

DORSTFELD Westphalia, Germany. Jews are first mentioned in 1731. The J. pop. grew to 69 individuals in 1880 and a peak of 93 in 1842. A small synagogue was erected in the first half of the 19th cent., a new cemetery was opened in 1861, and a J. elementary school was started in 1886 (operating until 1909). The J. pop. dropped to 59 in 1912. On *Kristallnacht* (9–10 Nov. 1938), the synagogue was damaged. The local Jews shared the fate of those of Dortmund, which had incorporated Dorstfeld in 1914.

DORTMUND Westphalia, Germany. Transient J. merchants were present in the late 11th cent, but permanent J. settlement only began in the early 13th cent. By mid-cent., there was an organized community with a synagogue. A cemetery was opened outside the city walls in 1336. Jews engaged in moneylending and were, for the most part, under the protection of the Counts of the Mark, though the Emperor, the Archbishop of Cologne, and the municipality all vied for the right to tax them. In 1350, during the Black Death persecutions, the Jews were accused of poisoning wells, arrested, and expelled under an agreement between the Count of the Mark and the municipality to divide up their property. Some died in the course of the events. In 1372, the Jews were invited to return, so that the municipality might again benefit from their financial services. Ten protected J. families were present by 1380 with Shimshon ben Shemuel of Dueren as their rabbi. The J. pop. dropped with the decline

of the city as a political and economic force and by the mid-15th cent. no Jews remained. Residence rights were again accorded in 1543, but in 1596 the Jews were expelled, effectively ending J. settlement until the modern era. Only after equal rights were accorded to the Jews in the Grand Duchy of Berg in 1808 were residence restrictions lifted and merchants and peddlers living in nearby villages allowed to settle. In 1846, they comprised 38 families, living in straitened economic circumstances. In the mid-19th cent., with the accelerated economic and demographic development of the city, the situation of the community improved and its pop. began to expand rapidly, reaching a figure of 1,924 (total 142,733) in 1900. A synagogue was built in the mid-19th cent.; an organ introduced in 1870 testified to the Liberal character of the congregation. A new synagogue, one of the most beautiful in Germany and with a seating capacity of 1,200, was consecrated in 1900. A J. elementary school was founded in 1840. In 1871, it had over 100 students and 220 in 1910, when it became part of the public school system. Religious classes were provided for children attending non-J. schools and a *talmud torah* with an enrollment of 50 was opened in 1916 under Orthodox auspices. Agudat Israel became active in 1914. The Zionist group active in 1899 was the earliest in Westphalia. In 1907, 62% of the Jews were engaged in trade and transport services; 23% in crafts and industry; and 5.2% belonged to the free professions. Jews took an active part in public life following emancipation, with three serving on the municipal council in 1910 and one serving as chairman of the local medical society. In the late 19th cent., D. became a focus of antisemitic propaganda in Westphalia. The antisemitic *Westfaelische Reform* was published there from 1882, attacking J. merchants and instigating occasional mob violence. In the Reichstag elections of 1890, the antisemites won 3% of the vote, but practically disappeared by the end of the century. Antisemitic outbursts were renewed after WWI against a background of economic crisis. During WWI, many East European Jews settled in D., representing a third of the J. pop. in 1925, which had now grown to 3,820. The old pop. comprised the middle class, mostly businessmen, but with some professionals, musicians, theater people, and artisans. The East European Jews constituted the lower class, living in rundown neighborhoods and earning meager livelihoods in petty trade, peddling, and crafts. It was they who strengthened the city's Or-

Synagogue built in 1900, Dortmund, Germany (Beth Hatefutsoth Photo Archive, Tel Aviv)

thodox circles as well as the Zionist movement. Hebrew courses were offered from 1921 under Zionist auspices. The struggle for representation between the East European and German Jews created a public furor echoed in the J. press throughout Germany, with the old guard accusing the Zionists of endangering the "patriotic German character" of the community. The community maintained extensive social and welfare services, including a soup kitchen providing schoolchildren with a warm cup of milk each day and women's organizations sending needy children to summer camps. An orchestra and choir were active and the community published a bulletin. Within the city, Jews belonged to professional associations and sports and hiking clubs.

In June 1933, four months after the Nazis came to power, the J. pop. numbered 4,108 (total 540,875). The new regime undertook a Nazification campaign in the municipality, eliminating Jews and opposition forces. During 1933, 217 Jews were arrested, including a few from other communities in the district. Many fell victim to unorganized acts of violence and harassment by individuals. The economic boycott against the Jews was rigorously enforced with municipal institutions breaking off commercial ties with the Jews and shoppers staying away from J. stores. Agitation against J. businessmen was intensified in summer 1935, with boycott watches in front of J. stores and windows occasionally smashed. Anti-J. demonstrations were accompanied by signs labeling the Jews as traitors, murderers, warmongers, and defilers of women. The community strove to sustain its members, organizing cultural and educational activities. The J. Cultural Association offered lectures in J. subjects and produced plays and concerts; the community bulletin published articles on Palestine and J. history. The community also offered practical vocational training and courses in Hebrew and English. In 1934, the Palestine Office

opened a local branch and, together with Hehalutz, organized emigration to Palestine. Welfare services brought financial relief to 800 Jews while the J. school, which also offered vocational training, accommodated 356 children in 1934 and 258 in Feb. 1938. In July 1938, the municipality instituted proceedings to dismantle the Great Synagogue, a process which began on 3 Oct. 1938, more than a month before *Kristallnacht* (9–10 Nov. 1938). By Aug. 1938, the community was reduced to 2,600, with 500 business establishments still operating. By Oct. the number of J. businesses had been reduced by a further 144 and 600 Jews with Polish citizenship were expelled from the city. On *Kristallnacht*, J. homes and stores were wrecked along with the community center and wealthy Jews were forced to make "contributions" to their tormentors. Through 16 Nov., 600 Jews were arrested, most being sent to the Sachsenhausen concentration camp. Seventeen died there and others were released after meeting extortionate demands. Another 500 Jews fled the city after *Kristallnacht*, leaving 1,444 in May 1939. By Sept. 1939, just 63 houses remained in J. hands and by late 1939, just 80 business establishments. With another 200 Jews managing to leave after the outbreak of war, 1,222 remained in June 1941. These were left without rights, property, homes, or income. They were not allowed to use public shelters, radios, telephones, or even the streets without authorization. Gradually they were confined to "J. houses." D. was a district concentration point for deportations to the east. Between 1942 and 1945, there were eight transports, each containing about 5,000 Jews, including the Jews of D. On 27 April 1942, the largest group of Jews from D., numbering 700–800, was deported to Zamosc in the Lublin dist. (Poland) and from there sent to the Belzec death camp. On 29 July 1942, 331 elderly people were deported. After the war, 40–50 survivors, mostly from the Theresienstadt ghetto, formed a new community, which grew to 420 in 1962, making it the largest in Westphalia. In the 1990s, Jews arriving from the former Soviet bloc created a community of 1,310 in 1993.

DOTNUVA   Kedainiai dist., Lithuania. The J. community began in the 18th cent. The J. pop. in 1897 was 233 (38% of the total) and 120 in 1939. During WWI, D.'s 120 J. families were exiled to the Russian interior; only some returned. After the German invasion in June 1941, Jews were forced to do hard labor. In

Aug. they were all detained in a monastery near the town of Krakes and murdered on 2 Sept. 1941.

DOUAI   Nord dist., France. The community was founded in 1825. By the 20th cent. the community was composed of Jews of French origin as well as immigrants from Central Europe and Turkey. In the 1936 census, 62 Jews were listed in D. During WWII, the Nord and Pas de Calais districts were under the jurisdiction of the military commander of Belgium and on 13 June 1942, it was decreed that the Jews of these districts must wear the yellow badge. Shortly afterwards, they were ordered to register and a list of of J. shops and businesses was drawn up for "Aryanization." Arrests began in Sept. 1942. The Jews were transported to Auschwitz via Malines. In 1962 the community was reestablished following the influx of Jews from North Africa, and in 1964 it included 240 members.

DOVBISH   (in 1925–44, Markhlevsk) Zhitomir dist., Ukraine. Fewer than 500 Jews were present in the late 19th cent. In 1925, D. became the capital of a Polish autonomous region (abrogated in 1935) whose J. pop. of 1,319 constituted 3% of the total. In 1939, the J. pop. was 513 (total 4,296). The Germans captured D. on 10 July 1941, presumably murdering most of the Jews.

DOVHE   (Hung. Dolha) Carpatho-Russia, Czechoslovakia, today Ukraine. Jews probably settled in the late 18th cent. Their pop. was 22 in 1830 and 113 (total 1,315) in 1880. A yeshiva with 50 students operated during the 19th cent. The J. pop. grew to 462 in 1921 under Czechoslovakian rule and to 531 in 1941. A number of J. families earned their livelihoods in agriculture and at a local steel-rolling plant. Following the arrival of the Hungarians in March 1939, Jews were forced out of work. In 1941, dozens were drafted into labor battalions, many dying on the eastern front. In Aug. 1941, five J. families without Hungarian citizenship were expelled to Kamenets-Podolski. The rest were deported to Auschwitz on 25 May 1944.

DOWGIELISZKI   Vilna dist., Poland, today Lithuania. The J. pop. was 48 in 1898. In Oct. 1941, the Jews were expelled by the Germans to the Radun ghetto. In the *Aktion* of 10 May 1942, about 1,000 were killed. Many who escaped to the forest were killed by Polish partisans or handed over to the Nazis by informers.

Others joined a Soviet partisan unit operating in the area. On 7 or 8 June, the remaining Jews in the ghetto, primarily artisans, were transferred to the Szczuczyn ghetto. Where they were sent afterwards is unknown.

DRACINETI Bukovina, Rumania, today Ukraine. The Jews were attached to the Stanestii community and had no independent institutions. The J. pop. in 1930 was 232. In July 1941, Rumanian soldiers murdered 120 Jews; the remainder were deported to Transnistria, where most died.

DRAGOMIRESTI (Hung. Dragomerfalva) N. Transylvania dist., Rumania. Among the first Jews to settle in 1780 was R. Shemuel Stern, of the Kosov hasidic sect., followed by Hasidim from Galicia who worked in Stern's lumber mills. The J. pop. in 1920 was 756 (28% of the total). After N. Transylvania was annexed to Hungary in 1940, Jews aged 20–40 were drafted into labor battalions in the Ukraine. On 15 April 1944, 2,000 Jews, including those from the surrounding villages, were ghettoized. On 15 May males aged 12–60 were taken on foot and the women, children, and aged in wagons, 17 miles to the Viseul de Sus railway station where they were deported to Auschwitz.

DRAGUIGNAN Var dist., France. Towards the end of the 13th cent. there was a J. community in D. In the middle of the 14th cent., it consisted of 200–250 members, their numbers increasing in the next cent. Nevertheless, in 1489, the Jews of D. were the first victims of the edict of expulsion from Provence. Five were baptized to avoid expulsion. During WWII, about 12 families were living in D. After the war the community was revived by North African Jews, who numbered approximately 100 in 1968.

DRAGUSENI Moldavia dist., Rumania. Jews settled in 1831 and in 1898 constituted all the storekeepers and artisans in the town. The J. pop. in 1910 was 238 (16% of the total). In June 1941, the J. community was expelled to Galati.

DRAHOVO (Hung. Kovesliget) Carpatho-Russia, Czechoslovakia, today Ukraine. J. settlement probably began in the early 18th cent. Two J. families were present in 1735. In 1830, the J. pop. reached 130 and 328 in 1880. From the mid-19th cent., the com-munity operated a wide range of welfare and charity organizations. Most Jews were employed in trade (19), crafts (25), and farming. Jews also owned two flour mills and a sawmill. In the period of the Czechoslovakian Republic, the J. pop. rose to 725 in 1930 and 1,081 in 1941, with the Hungarians arriving in March 1939. Many young Jews were organized in such Zionist groups as Betar and Hehalutz. The Hungarians drafted dozens of Jews into labor battalions, some for forced labor, some for service on the eastern front. In Aug. 1941, a few dozen J. families without Hungarian citizenship were expelled to Kamenets-Podolski, where they were murdered. The remaining 450 Jews were deported to Auschwitz in the second half of May 1944. A few dozen survivors from D. and its environs returned after the war, most leaving for Israel with the beginning of *aliya* from the Soviet Union in the late 1980s.

DRAMA Drama dist., Greece. Benjamin of Tudela found 140 Jews there in the 12th cent. In the 17th cent., a small community existed and at the end of the 19th cent. there were 150 Jews. The J. pop. in 1912 was 600. Although a J. school already existed, a new school replaced it in 1925. By then a number of welfare and Zionist organizations operated. When the Bulgarians arrived in spring 1941, the J. pop. stood at 1,200. Most Jews refused the Bulgarian offer of citizenship and were subsequently persecuted as if they were Greeks. About one-quarter fled to southern Greece and some youths were taken to forced labor in Bulgaria. On 4 March 1943, all the Jews were arrested and transferred to a transit camp in Bulgaria, with no possessions and very little clothing. After two weeks they were conveyed into German hands and loaded on ships. One ship, carrying J. men, sank in the Danube; three others reached Vienna between 25–31 March. From there the Jews were transferred to the gas chambers of the Treblinka death camp. Of 780 Jews, only a few, primarily those sent to forced labor, survived the Holocaust.

DRAMBURG (Pol. Drawsko Pomorskie) Pomerania, Germany, today Poland. The first Jews arrived in D. between 1735 and 1740. The community numbered 186 in 1861 and maintained a synagogue, built in 1839, and a cemetery. When the Nazis came to power in 1933, the community numbered 24 members. The synagogue was sold in 1935 and subsequently

Jewish textile merchants in the market, Drama, Greece, WWI (Beth Hatefutsoth Photo Archive, Tel Aviv/courtesy of Polska Akademia Nauk, Warsaw)

pulled down. By May 1938, nine J. businesses were still open, but the process of their "Aryanization" or liquidation had already begun. It may be assumed that those Jews who did not manage to emigrate abroad where deported to the east. By Oct. 1942, only two Jews were left in D., probably protected by marriage to non-Jews.

DRANCENI Moldavia dist., Rumania. Jews settled here in the mid-19th cent. The J. pop. in 1939 was 318 (9% of the total). In June 1941, all the Jews were expelled to Husi.

DRANSFELD Hanover, Germany. Jews were apparently present for awhile in the 14th cent. but only returned in the late 17th cent. There were only a few there in 1689. In 1846 their number was 96; in 1864, 111. A synagogue was erected in 1836 and the Jews of neighboring Guentersen joined the congregation in 1861. The cemetery, which became community property in 1853, was twice desecrated, in 1924 and 1931. In 1933, the J. pop. was 40. The contents of the synagogue were burned on *Kristallnacht* (9–10 Nov. 1938). With emigration intensifying during the Nazi period, only 17 Jews remained in 1939. Ten are known to have been deported to the death camps of the east. Another two committed suicide in the face of Nazi persecution.

DRESDEN Saxony, Germany. Jews living in D. probably received a site to erect a synagogue around 1300. After the Black Death persecutions (1348–49), the first reference to Jews is not until 1375. Although in the 14th and 15th cents. there were "J. houses" in two streets, which also included a synagogue and probably a *mikve*, there was no ghetto. The community also maintained a cemetery. The community was persecuted again in 1430, and it was not until after

bor, including eviction from coveted apartments. In July a *Judenrat* was appointed. On 30 Nov. 1941, 300 Jews were executed in the nearby Bronica forest. Hundreds more died from hunger and disease in the severe winter of 1941–42. To avoid the labor camps, the *Judenrat* organized workshops to provide essential goods. Another 1,600 Jews were employed in the oil industry. At the end of March 1942, 2,000 Jews were deported to the Belzec death camp. The second mass *Aktion* commenced on 8 Aug. as German and Ukrainian police rounded up Jews from their homes, murdering 600 in the process while sending another 2,500 to Belzec. A ghetto was established in Sept. for the remaining 9,000 Jews (including 1,000 from the surrounding villages). In a third *Aktion* (23–24 Oct. 1942), a further 2,300 Jews were deported to Belzec and 200 hospital patients murdered. Deportations continued through Nov. and on 15 Feb. 1943 the ghetto was combed for additional Jews, with 450, including 300 women, brought to the Bronica forest for execution, leaving mainly essential workers behind in labor camps. Of these, 800 were murdered in the forest in March 1943. The last Jews in the ghetto were rounded up and murdered toward the end of May and the labor camps were gradually liquidated over the following 12 months in the Bronica killing grounds, the last Jews being sent to the Plaszow concentration camp in April 1944. During the *Aktions* in the city and the camps there were cases of resistance by groups and individuals. With the arrival of the Soviet Army in Aug. 1944, about 400 Jews gathered in the city. Most subsequently emigrated.

DROMERSHEIM Hesse, Germany. The community, numbering 42 (3.6% of the total) in 1861, had dwindled to 12 by 1933. The remaining Jews left after *Kristallnacht* (9–10 Nov. 1938).

DROSSEN (Pol. Osno Lubuskie) Brandenburg, Germany, today Poland. Evidence of Jews in D. dates from 1430 and 1690, but a permanent J. settlement is documented only from the beginning of the 19th cent. The community maintained a synagogue and a cemetery and numbered 84 Jews in 1855. When the Nazis came to power in 1933, there were 28 Jews in D. On *Kristallnacht* (9–10 Nov. 1938), the apartments of the remaining Jews and two J.-owned businesses were damaged. Five Jews were arrested. No further information about the community's fate is available.

DROVE Rhineland, Germany. Jews are mentioned in 1663. The community was affiliated to Dueren and during the 19th century had 35–65 members. In 1930 the J. pop. was 36. On *Kristallnacht* (9–10 Nov. 1938), the synagogue (consecrated in 1865) was set on fire. In all, 26 Jews perished in the Holocaust along with another 11 from neighboring Nideggen.

DRUJA Vilna dist., Poland, today Belarus. Jews settled in the late 16th cent. and numbered 1,306 in 1766. In the late 18th cent. the community built one of the most beautiful synagogues in Lithuania. The community also had two *battei midrash*, a *talmud torah*, a *mikve*, and a cemetery. Jews were a dominant force in the town's commerce, numbering 3,006 (total 4,742) in 1897. Under Haskala influence the first J. school with Russian as the language of instruction was founded in 1889, enrolling 150 children. After an interruption during WWI, J. merchants resumed their trade in flax, lumber, grain, hides, and geese and smaller tradesmen recovered with loans from community financial institutions. Jews also owned 18 farms. In 1925 the J. pop. was 1,800. The Bund-dominated Yiddish school (*Folksshul*) was the center of the community's cultural life, operating a drama circle and adult education classes, though many of its graduates joined Hehalutz. Under the German occupation from June 1941, the Jews were subjected to forced labor and extortionate "contributions." In April 1942 they were confined to two ghettoes, for workers and non-workers. On 2 July, all were executed in the woods near the J. cemetery.

DRUJSK Vilna dist., Poland, today Belarus. Jews arrived as the village's first settlers in the 1870s, receiving land for cultivation. In 1897 their number reached 515. In the 1930s, Jews were operating 44 farms on 850 acres of land and the cheese produced in their dairy cooperative was known throughout Poland for its superior quality. Some were also lumber merchants sending logs down the Dvina and Droika Rivers and some opened stores serving the border garrison. A Horev Hebrew school was opened in 1931 and most of the young were members of Hehalutz or Betar. The J. pop. in 1931 was 412. On the approach of the Germans in June 1941, local peasants pillaged J. homes. The Germans seized Jews for forced labor, murdered at least 150, and confiscated livestock and farm implements. In Feb. 1942, over 1,000 Jews in-

cluding refugees were expelled to the Widze ghetto. From there they were dispersed among various camps and subsequently executed.

DRUSKIENIKI Bialystok dist., Poland, today Lithuania. J. settlement probably commenced in the mid-19th cent. With D.'s development as a health resort, a J. hospital was built serving numerous J. communities in the area. In 1887 the second congress of Hovevei Zion convened there. In 1897 the J. pop. reached 636 (total 1,280). After WWI, when the J. pop. was 294, a CYSHO Yiddish school was opened, becoming a center of cultural activity. The Germans took D. in late June 1941, transferring the J. pop. of 800 to shacks on the outskirts of town. In Aug. 1942 they were expelled to the Kelbasin transit camp and from there deported to the Treblinka death camp.

DRUSZKOPOL Volhynia dist., Poland, today Ukraine. J. settlement began in the second half of the 17th cent. The town's border location after the Second Partition of Poland (1793), with its customs house and Russian army barracks, stimulated the economy, promoting trade with Austrian Galicia and the spread to D. of Belz-Olesk Hasidism, which later came into bitter conflict with Turzysk Hasidism. The J. pop. stood at 870 (total 1,340) in 1897. The Jews suffered under both the Cossacks and Austrians in WWI. Under the German occupation from 22 June 1941, the Jews were put to forced labor and a *Judenrat* was established. All 900 of D.'s Jews were brought to the Horochow ghetto in Oct. 1941 and murdered with the local pop. on 8 Sept. 1942.

DRUZHKOVA Stalino dist., Ukraine. The J. pop. in 1939 was 433 (total 31,781). The Germans captured the city on 22 Oct. 1941. Probably in April 1942, 135 J. families were murdered—the children poisoned and the adults electrocuted.

DRZEWICA Lodz dist., Poland. At the end of the 19th cent., German Jews were involved in the sale of the products of the Gerlach metal factory founded here. The majority of the community were Gur Hasidim, who dominated the community council. In 1939, the 780 Jews (61% of the total) increased three-fold due to the influx of refugees. On 22–23 Oct. 1942 the inhabitants of the ghetto were sent to the Treblinka death camp.

DUBECZNO (I) Volhynia dist., Poland, today Ukraine. The J. pop. of 20 families was probably liquidated after transfer to the Ratno ghetto.

DUBECZNO (II) Lublin dist., Poland. Jews settled in the late 18th cent., maintaining an independent community from the end of the 19th cent. and numbering 400 (total 1,498) in 1921. On 1 Sept. 1939, there were only five Jews in D. but in 1941 about 100 refugees arrived from the Warthegau district. Many were sent to labor camps. The rest were expelled to the Wlodawa ghetto in June 1942 and in Nov. 1942 deported to the Sobibor death camp.

DUBIECKO (Yid. Dubatsk) Lwow dist., Poland. Jews are recorded from 1622 and from the early 18th cent. constituted a growing community, reaching a peak pop. of nearly 977 (over half the total) in 1900, with most trade in J. hands. Emigration, WWI, and a destructive fire in 1927 curtailed further growth. Until the period between the World Wars, a zealously traditional hasidic milieu (Blazow-Dynow) prevented the spread of Zionism and "enlightened" ideas with children avoiding compulsory state education. On the approach of the Germans in Sept. 1939, many young Jews fled toward the Rumanian border. After the Germans arrived (8 Sept.), 13 young Jews were murdered and the synagogue was burned down. In Nov., all were expelled to Soviet-held territory, many reaching Lwow and subsequently being exiled to the interior of Russia.

DUBIENKA Lublin dist., Poland. A J. settlement existed by the late 16th cent. In the 18th cent., Jews were prominent in the grain trade along the Bug River as well as in running numerous inns and distilleries. Their pop. rose to 1,427 in 1861 and 2,343 (total 5,163) in 1897. After WWI, economic conditions deteriorated and many young people emigrated. The German occupation of Sept. 1939 introduced a regime of persecution and extortion. In Dec. 1939, able-bodied men were expelled across the Bug River to Soviet-held territory after a march that left half of them dead. Refugees increased the J. pop. to 2,907 in May 1942. All but 200 skilled workers were deported to the Sobibor death camp on 2 June 1942. The rest died of starvation or were murdered.

DUBINGIAI (Yid. Dubinik) Ukmerge dist., Lithuania. A J. community was established here in the 19th

cent., but many emigrated due to the economic situation. The J. pop. in 1897 was 280; in 1940, 80. After Germany's invasion in June 1941, Lithuanian nationalists killed the remaining Jews in several waves.

DUBINOVO Vilna dist., Poland, today Belarus. D. was a J. agricultural colony founded in 1848 on 1,350 acres of land distributed by Czar Nicholas I. Jews grew cereal crops, peas, and potatoes, owned some livestock, and supplemented their incomes with crafts. After WWI, when the community numbered about 90 families, a dairy was set up to market cheese and butter. Drought and the economic crisis undermined the community in the 1930s. Soon after their arrival, on 19 July 1941, the Germans executed 20 Jews in a nearby field. The rest were expelled in March 1942 to the Widze ghetto, where they shared the fate of the local J. inhabitants.

DUBNICA Slovakia, Czechoslovakia, today Republic of Slovakia. Jews settled in the early 18th cent. under the protection of Count Illehazy, building a synagogue c. 1830 and forming a Neologist congregation after the split in 1869. The J. pop. grew from 36 in 1828 to 114 (total 1,735) and then declined steadily to 64 in 1940. Jews owned a brickyard, sawmill, and flour mill. The young joined Hashomer Hatzair. Most Jews were deported to the Lublin dist. (Poland) on 8 June 1942 and perished.

DUBNO Volhynia dist., Poland, today Ukraine. Jews began to settle in the early 16th cent. and numbered around 2,000 at the time of the Chmielnicki massacres of 1648–49. Between 1,100 and 1,500 were murdered by the Cossacks in 1648 after being denied refuge in the local fortress. Within a short time the community was once again among the most important in the region, with representation on the Council of the Four Lands. Economic prosperity continued through the 18th cent., allowing a large stone synagogue to be built in 1782–84. A Hebrew printing press was set up in 1794 and operated for 30 years. Among the city's prominent figures was R. Yaakov Kranz (1741–1804), known as the Maggid of Dubno, the most famous J. preacher in Lithuania in the 18th cent. Under Russian rule, economic decline set in, though the J. pop. rose to 7,108 (total 14,257) in 1897. Two fires, in 1878 and 1895, caused great damage and necessitated outside help to rehabilitate the community. The

Synagogue in Dubno, Poland

Hovevei Zion movement held yearly meetings in D. from 1893 and a number of Haskala Jews were active there. After the Feb. 1917 Revolution, J. public life flourished, but in the chaos of civil war, 18 Jews were murdered in a pogrom staged by Cossack soldiers in March 1918. Between the World Wars, Jews also engaged in light industry and were prominent as exporters of hops and grains. About 85% of petty trade was in J. hands. The community ran a hospital, orphanage, and old age home, while a Tarbut school reached an enrollment of 400 and a private J. high school another 120. All the Zionist parties were active as well as many of the youth movements. The Germans entered D. on 25 June 1941. On 30 June, 23 Jews were taken outside the city and murdered and on 22 July, another 80 were killed at the J. cemetery. A *Judenrat* was established on 3 Aug. On 21 Aug. 1941, 1,075 mostly J. men were executed at the cemetery. In March 1942, Ukrainian peasants were invited by the Germans to "clean out" J. homes. A ghetto was set up on 2 April 1942 under a continuing regime of forced labor. All but skilled workers and their families were executed on 26–27 May, leaving 4,500 in the ghetto including workers

from surrounding settlements. These were murdered on 5 Oct. 1942. Around 400 Jews survived the war – 120 in hiding and the others in the USSR.

DUBOSSARY Moldavia, today Republic of Moldova. J. settlement commenced in the late 18th cent. In 1882, two Jews were killed and six injured in antisemitic disturbances. A blood libel in 1903 nearly led to another pogrom and Jews were also persecuted in the civil war of 1918–21. The existence of J. self-defense groups prevented loss of life. Thousands of J. refugees passed through D. in 1920–22. The J. pop. was 5,220 (total 12,089) in 1897, dropping in the Soviet period to 3,630 (total 4,530) in 1926 and 2,198 in 1939. German and Rumanian forces captured D. in mid-July 1941. Almost all Jews in the dist., numbering about 6,000, were concentrated there, including refugees from Bessarabia. A ghetto was set up on a few streets in the suburbs. Mass executions commenced on 12 Sept. 1941. By the end of the month, nearly all the Jews were dead and buried in mass graves. A partisan unit led by Yankel Gronitzky of D. operated from the beginning of the occupation, blowing up a bridge on the Dniester River as well as the local power station. In Dec. 1942, ten J. accountants and ten doctors and pharmacists were brought to D. to serve the Rumanian authorities while held as prisoners. In Sept. 1943, a few thousand Jews expelled from Transnistria were brought to D. to repair the road to Grigoriopol. Many perished under the inhuman conditions.

DUBOVE (Hung. Dombo; Yid. Dibeve) Carpatho-Russia, Czechoslovakia, today Ukraine. J. settlement began in the first half of the 19th cent. In 1880, the J. pop. was 347 (total 2,271), increasing to 737 in 1921. Both the Zionist and Orthodox youth organizations were active in the community. The Hungarians arrived in March 1939. In late July or early Aug. 1941, they expelled a few dozen J. families without Hungarian citizenship to Kamenets-Podolski, where they were murdered. In 1941, the J. pop. was 984 (total 6,003). In late May 1944, the remaining Jews were deported to Auschwitz. A few who escaped to the forests joined the partisans.

DUBOVO Kiev dist., Ukraine. Jews numbered 1,104 in 1897. On 17 June 1919, the Sokolowski gangs attacked and murdered Jews and looted homes

and stores. In 1926, under the Soviets, only 57 Jews remained. Those there when the Germans occupied the town in WWII were murdered.

DUBOVOYE Tula dist., Russia. After occupying D. in Oct. 1941, the Germans murdered in Nov. 25–30 Jews from among the few dozen they had concentrated there from the neighboring villages.

DUBROVKA Oriol dist., Russia. Jews settled in the late 19th cent. Their pop. was 542 in 1926 and 360 (total 4,170) in 1939. A J. school was in operation in the mid-1920s. The Germans occupied the town on 10 Aug. 1941. In Dec., they burned 12 Jews alive in the local blacksmith's shop. Another 55 were murdered at different times.

DUBROVNIK (Ital. Ragusa) Croatia, Yugoslavia, today Republic of Croatia. Jews first settled in the Middle Ages. The arrival of J. refugees from Spain and Portugal triggered a blood libel in 1502 and a call for expulsion in 1515. J. trade in the region led to resettlement in the 1530s, although the Jews were deprived of civil rights. Throughout the 16th cent. D.'s economy thrived on commerce, in which many Jews participated, often trading with Jews of other European countries. In the early 17th cent. there was a Catholic attempt to isolate the Jews by limiting their movement, trade, and actions. Another blood libel took place in 1622 and at the same time the au-

Redemption of Firstborn ceremony (pidyon ha-ben), Dubrovnik, Yugoslavia, 17th cent. parchment (Yitzhak Einhorn Collection, Tel Aviv/photo courtesy of Beth Hatefutsoth, Tel Aviv)

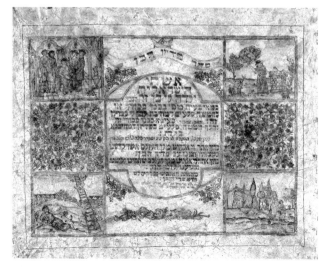

thorities published anti-J. propaganda and demanded that the Jews be closed within a ghetto. This led many Jews to leave D. for other towns, but by 1633 ghettoization was not enforced and Jews were permitted to return. D.'s trade then suffered a decline, which affected the J. community. Along with the rest of D., the Jews were severely hit during the earthquake of 1667. The Catholic Church continued its campaign against the Jews, periodically calling for enforced ghettoization and J. dress codes. In the mid-17th cent. the location and organization of the J. ghetto was secured and the synagogue established. By the end of the cent., the Jews received civil rights, owing to their role in the local society and economy. During the 18th cent. the J. community grew even stronger, larger, and more organized. However, the Jews were still prohibited from purchasing real estate and were urged by the authorities to concentrate themselves within the confines of the enlarged ghetto (although the majority already lived outside the ghetto). J. movement in and out of the ghetto was also limited (sometimes encouraged by the Jews themselves, to avoid assimilation and provocation). The Catholic Church still continued its efforts to isolate the Jews, confiscating Talmudic texts and fining those who withheld them. In this period, until the last decade of the 18th cent., D. experienced economic prosperity, trading notably with the Balkans and the Levant. The D. Jews were active in this trade because of their connections with Jews of other cities. D. came under French rule in 1808 and the Jews were then granted full civil rights. The ghetto was abolished at that time, and the number of Jews living outside it was increasing. During French rule, almost all commerce was terminated, affecting J. activity in the economy. Under Austrian rule, from 1814, the Jews were again promised equal rights. However, restrictions were imposed on J. trade, real estate, and employment of Christians. These restrictions were withdrawn by 1860. In 1830, the number of Jews in D. peaked at 260, including Jews of the surrounding areas (total over 6,000). The community of D. proper, however, became very small, numbering only 121 in 1857, and suffered economic difficulties. The Catholic anti-J. restrictions were canceled, however, in the late 19th cent. D. became part of Yugoslavia in 1914–41. In the first half of the 20th cent. the D. community lacked sufficient funds for its synagogue, teacher, and refugees from Central Europe. Prior to WWII, the J. com-

munity of D. numbered 1,600 persons (including refugees), of whom only 87 were residents of D. itself. Despite its few members, the community was culturally active and operated an organization for J. culture (until 1929).

In the 1940s, antisemitism increased in Yugoslavia, but it did not find violent expression in D. until the town became part of independent Croatia in mid-1941. From June 1941 the Jews were victims of discrimination, their possessions confiscated, and their movements limited. Some were taken to the Jasenovac death camp that month. Despite their own hardships and poverty, the Jews of D. extended assistance to refugees of other towns. In the fall of 1941 the Jews' security was somewhat improved as D. came under Italian rule. However, under German and Italian Fascist pressure, the Italians began to concentrate the Jews of D. in camps at the end of 1942; at this point the J. community of D. was no longer operative. In May–June 1943, D.'s Jews, along with Jews of other towns, were sent to a camp on the Island of Rab, where living conditions were particularly harsh. With the fall of Italy in Sept. 1943, many of the inmates joined the fight against the Fascist forces. Others moved to areas under Allied control, some of whom died in German raids. Only 180–200 Jews remained on Rab Island; they were taken by the Germans to Auschwitz in March 1944 and all died there. A few Jews of D. survived the Holocaust and some returned to D. The synagogue, dating in its present form from the 17th cent., is one of the oldest in Europe still in use, albeit irregularly. Its Torah scrolls (successfully hidden in WWII) may originate in pre-expulsion Spain.

DUBROVNO   Vitebsk dist., Belorussia. Jews settled in the early 18th cent. In 1766, the J. pop. of D. and its environs was 801 and in 1897 the J. pop. came to 4,364 (total 7,974). A J. printing press was started in 1802. Most Jews engaged in trade and crafts, the manufacture of prayer shawls for Russian Jews occupying a prominent place. In the Soviet period, a J. elementary school was in operation until the mid-1930s. In 1939, the J. pop. was 2,119. The Germans occupied D. on 16 July 1941. In the fall, all the Jews were concentrated in a ghetto and 1,500 were executed in Dec. The 300 skilled workers and their families whom the Germans let live were murdered in Feb. 1942.

Celebration of completion of writing of Torah scroll, Dubrovno, Belorussia (A. Litwin/photo courtesy of Yad Vashem, The Holocaust Martyrs' and Heroes' Remembrance Authority, Jerusalem)

DUBROWA Nowogrodek dist., Poland, today Belarus. D. was founded as a J. agricultural colony in 1848 and numbered 25 families between the World Wars. All were expelled by the Germans to Rozhanka in June 1941 and from there to the Szczuczyn ghetto in Oct., sharing the fate of local Jews.

DUCHCOV Bohemia (Sudetenland), Czechoslovakia. Jews are mentioned at the turn of the 14th cent. and were most likely expelled before 1527, reestablishing the community only after the 1848 revolution. Their pop. reached a peak of 233 (total 12,001) in 1900 and then dropped to 111 in 1930. The Zionists were active in the Czechoslovakian Republic. Most Jews left the city shortly before the Munich Agreement of Sept. 1938, about a third emigrating with many reaching Palestine. Some joinied the British or Free Czechoslovakian armies to fight against the Nazis.

DUDERGOF Leningrad dist., Russia. Jews probably settled in the early 20th cent. and numbered 120 (total 2,712) in 1939, when the settlement was called Nagornoye and was part of the city of Krasnoye Selo. Jews who had not fled or been evacuated were murdered after the German occupation of mid-Jan. 1942.

DUDERSTADT Hanover, Germany. There is evidence of Jews in D. as early as the beginning of the 14th cent. By the mid-15th cent., the community numbered about 12 families. This community apparently came to an end when the last Jews left D. at the beginning of the 16th cent. In 1812, Jews returned to the town, but their number did not exceed five families. From 1867-68, the J. pop. began to rise, peaking at 84 in 1885. In 1898, a new synagogue was dedicated; a J. cemetery was established before 1870. When the Nazis came to power in 1933, there were about 30 Jews in D. On *Kristallnacht* (9–10 Nov. 1938), the synagogue was burned down, J. men were arrested, and J.-owned stores were looted. By May 1939, there were only six Jews in D. Five were forced to move to a "J. house." They were deported in spring 1942.

DUEDELSHEIM Hesse, Germany. Established before 1722, the community numbered 136 (11.6% of the total) in 1861 and originally included Jews from neighboring Rohrbach, Glauberg, and Stockheim. They mostly dealt in livestock. Numbering 72 in 1933, the community was dissolved in 1934, when Jews began emigrating to the U.S. and South Africa. On *Kristallnacht* the synagogue and J. homes were vandalized, and the remaining Jews then left.

DUELKEN Rhineland, Germany. Jews were present in the first half of the 14th century. A synagogue was consecrated c. 1659 and a cemetery was opened in 1781. In the 19th and 20th cents., the J. pop. maintained a level of 70–95. A J. elementary school operated between 1888 and 1923. In June 1933, about four months after the Nazi assumption of power, the J. pop. was 60. Under the Nazis, over half emigrated and at least 20 were deported, including 13 to the Riga ghetto on 10–12 Dec. 1941, with most perishing there.

DUELMEN Westphalia, Germany. Jews are first mentioned in 1554. The J. pop. of three families in 1667 rose to 52 individuals in 1816 and a peak of about 120 individuals in the 1870s. A synagogue was consecrated in 1801 and a new one in 1864. The J. elementary school opened in the same building became a J. public school in 1862. A new cemetery was opened

the Dachau concentration camp, including R. Eschelbacher, who emigrated to England several months after his release at the beginning of 1939. The community, which had been compelled to sell the synagogue in 1939, was charged with the cost of demolishing its ruins. In May 1939, there were 1,831 Jews in D., two–thirds less than in 1933. By 1941, there were only 1,400 Jews left in the city. At this point, the school closed and deportations began. In Nov. and Dec. 1941, there were deportations to the Minsk, Lodz, and Riga ghettoes, and in July 1942 to the Theresienstadt ghetto. In these four transports, a total of 2,487 Jews from D. and the surrounding area were deported. Before the Dec. 1941 deportation, Siegfried Falk, a banker and community president after *Kristallnacht*, and his wife committed suicide. No figures are available for the number of Jews in the deportations which took place in March–April and July 1943 to the Lublin, dist. (Poland) and in Feb. 1945 to Theresienstadt. Nor are there figures available regarding those who emigrated. While R. Eschelbacher estimated that 600 Jews had moved away by Sept. 1933 alone, it is known that of the slightly more than 5,000 community members in 1933, only about 1,500 survived, i.e. many D. Jews who had emigrated to other towns or neighboring countries also fell into Nazi hands and perished. At the time of liberation there were 57 Jews living in D. Their number soon increased to 350, stabilizing at 1,500 in 1968. The new community, which was founded in 1945, consecrated a new synagogue in 1958. Since 1993, as a result of the high proportion of young Russian Jews, a J. elementary school has once again been established.

DUISBURG Rhineland, Germany. A small J. community apparently existed in D. in the 12th cent. The community was completely destroyed in the Black Death persecutions of 1348–49. Due to the subsequent residence ban, few Jews were present until 1719. During the 18th cent., there were never more than three extended J. families in the city. In addition, as many as 21 Jews studied at D. University in the course of the cent. Living conditions were difficult as a result of the economic collapse throughout the Prussian Lower Rhineland, particularly in the Duchy of Cleves, and the heavy taxation to which the Jews were subjected. A synagogue was dedicated in 1793. Although in 1806, under Napoleon, the Jews were accorded civil rights, replacing the old letters of protection, J. commerce

was in fact restricted by Napoleon himself. With the return of Prussian rule, anti-J. discrimination was reinstated. Antisemitic outbursts occurred in the Hep! Hep! riots of 1819 and in 1885, with the general flare-up of antisemitic agitation in Germany. The J. pop., which grew from 70 in 1827 to 307 in 1880 and 1,554 in 1910, never exceeded 1% of the general pop. In the first half of the 19th cent., most new J. settlers arrived from neighboring towns and villages; by the end of the cent., most came from Poland. Economic conditions for the Jews improved somewhat in the early 19th cent. Most engaged in petty trade and peddling. Some were butchers or dealt in cattle and hides; others entered light industry. The Samuel Meir & Levi Co. manufactured cotton goods and Philip Politz contributed to the development of the modern steamship and railway services vital to the region's industry and mining. On the whole, however, the community remained poor. A new synagogue was consecrated in 1828 and another in 1875. The local cemetery was opened in 1823 and a private J. school began to operate in 1824 under Prussia's compulsory education law. After years of sporadic operation, it was finally closed in 1876. Also according to Prussian law, D. became the seat of a regional congregation in 1854, with the communities of Ruhrort, Holten, and Dinslaken attached to it as well as the Jews of Goetterswickerhamm, Gahlen, and Sterkrade. The congregation was dismantled in 1877. In 1905, the city became Greater D., uniting D. and Ruhrort. A new J. school opened in 1927 to serve both communities. The community's first and only rabbi, Dr. Mannes Neumark of Poznan, was appointed in 1904 and served until the Nazi era. The Zionists became active in 1903. There was a constant struggle between the Zionists and Liberal, non-Zionist, and anti-Zionist circles with most identifying with the Central Union (C.V.), which opened its offices in the city in 1909. The Zionists were able to get the upper hand in the 1909 community elections through a coalition of East European voters. The Zionists again defeated the Liberals in 1912, with the Liberal rabbi Dr. Neumark now the chairman of the Central Union. The first J. youth group (Juedischer Jugendbund) was founded in 1906 with the declared aim of preparing the young for the fight against antisemitism. During WWI, many Jews arrived from Poland as laborers as part of "Operation Hindenburg," bringing the number of East European Jews in Greater D. up to 1,500 in 1920. Many subsequently left but some remained, ab-

sorbed into the commercial economy. By 1925, the J. pop. of the city was 2,080. Mostly Orthodox, the East European Jews had their own synagogue and in 1926 opened a *talmud torah* financed by Agudat Israel. Most Jews engaged in trade, a few operated big department stores, while others were butchers and artisans. A few belonged to the professional class (doctors, lawyers, engineers). During the Weimar period, there were about 30 community and social organizations, some of a political and cultural nature, others providing extensive charitable and welfare services. The Central Union continued to promote the idea of being German while remaining J. as did the J. War Veterans Association, which had a membership of 100. Hehalutz began operating in 1925 but only became a significant force after 1933. WIZO and Tze'irei Mizrachi were also active in the late 1920s. The most important youth group in the city was Habonim, which attracted many of the East European Jews in the city and offered Hebrew instruction and promoted pioneer settlement in Palestine. Also associated with the East European Jews were the left-wing Zionist political parties—Po'alei Zion and Ha-Po'el ha-Tza'ir, which united in 1932. The newly opened J. school reached an enrollment of 240 in 1929–30, with Hebrew and J. history taught. Antisemitism continued to be a force during the period, intensifying after the Nazi successes at the polls.

The J. pop. of D. (including the independent communities of Hamborn and Ruhrort) was 2,560 (total 440,419) in 1933. Anti-J. agitation commenced before the official 1 April Boycott Day. J. merchants, particularly East Europeans, were accused of Communist ties and attacked. J. judges, lawyers, and doctors were gradually pushed out of their professions. Municipal workers were threatened with dismissal if they patronized J. stores and J. butchers were denied the use of the municipal slaughterhouse. A number of East European families were expelled from the city in 1933. By March 1936, 536 Jews had emigrated, 174 of them to Palestine. In July 1937, the communities of D. (with 902 Jews remaining), Hamborn (348), and Ruhrort (155) were united. The Central Union ceased its operations in Nov. 1937 but the Zionists intensified theirs as *aliya* became a means of escape from Nazi Germany. Many young made their way to Palestine through Hehalutz despite difficulties in obtaining permits. In the 1934–38 period, an average of 185 students attended the J. school. An additional class for 14–16-year-olds was opened in 1935 to prepare them for emigration. Pupils

were taught Hebrew and English, bookkeeping, and technical drawing while girls studied homemaking and handicrafts. Others studied at the Yavne school in Cologne, the only J. secondary school in the Rhineland and Westphalia. The D. school closed down in June 1942. J. cultural life was maintained through the J. Cultural Association (Juedischer Kulturbund), which staged three performances a month in the city and arranged lectures. The social and economic isolation of the Jews continued with the passage of the Nuremberg Laws in Aug. 1935. Jews were dismissed from their jobs and pressured into liquidating their businesses. In Nov. 1935, 89 J. business establishments were still operating in the city. In Oct. 1938, 140 Jews with Polish citizenship were expelled to the Polish border. On *Kristallnacht* (9–10 Nov. 1938), the synagogue was set on fire; 40 J. homes and 25 J. stores were destroyed; the furnishings in the community center and J. school were vandalized; Jews were beaten; and 23 were sent to the Dachau concentration camp. Efforts were still made to escape. In early Dec. 1938, a group of children was brought to Holland in a *Kindertransport*. Some later reached England and thus survived the war. In May 1939, the J. pop. of D. (including Hamborn and Ruhrort) numbered 809. The remaining Jews were crowded into 11 "J. houses." Between 1941–42 they were deported to the ghettoes and to the death camps. The transport to the Riga ghetto on 11 Dec. 1941 involved a journey of 61 hours in subfreezing weather without food. Of those earmarked for the ghetto there, just 3% survived. On 25 July 1942, 127 local Jews were sent to Theresienstadt in a transport of 980 from the region. Few remained in the city after that date. Dr. Kaufmann, the last community head, was kept behind "to liquidate the last traces of J. property." He was arrested on 23 June 1943 and murdered with his wife at Auschwitz.

DUISBURG-MEIDERICH Rhineland, Germany. J. settlement dates from the first half of the 18th cent. and was renewed after a lapse of 50 years in the 1830s. In 1877, the J. pop. was 39. The community was affiliated to Duisburg-Ruhrort. In the Nazi era, 16 J. businesses were still operating in late 1935. Local Jews shared the fate of the Jews of neighboring Duisburg and Ruhrort.

DUISBURG-RUHRORT Rhineland, Germany. Small numbers of Jews were present in the late 16th and in the 17th cents. The J. pop. grew from 34 individuals in 1798 to 181 Jews in 1880, reaching its

peak in 1910 with 520. The quick growth from the end of the 19th century on was a result of the influx of East European Jews who found employment in the flourishing steel and mining industries. The community established two synagogues (1825, 1841) and two cemeteries (1708, 1893). On the eve of the Nazi assumption of power in 1933, the J. pop. had dropped to about 400 and by 1936 only about 200 remained. In 1937, the community, as well as the Hamborn community, was united with the Duisburg community. On *Kristallnacht* (9–10 Nov. 1938), the synagogue was set on fire and J. men were sent to the Dachau concentration camp. Subsequently the last J. businesses were liquidated and in Sept. 1939 the remaining Jews were confined to "J. houses." They shared the fate of the Jews of Duisburg.

DUKHOVSHCHINA   Smolensk dist., Russia. Jews probably settled in the mid-19th cent. Their pop. was 195 (total 2,906) in 1926 and 102 in 1939. The Ger-

mans arrived on 15 July 1941 and in summer 1942 murdered the few remaining Jews who had not fled or been evacuated.

DUKLA   Lwow dist., Poland. The permanent J. settlement dates from the 16th cent. and came to be one of the largest and most important of the region and a respected member of the Council of Lesser Poland, boasting a long line of illustrious rabbis. With its economic prosperity linked to the Hungarian wine and cattle trade, the J. community flourished in the first half of the 19th cent., numbering 2,539 in 1900 (80% of the total). By that time Rymanow and Zanz Hasidism set the tone among the Jews, but new ideas also made inroads. The Baron Hirsch school founded in 1895 had 140 students in 1908 and Zionist activity commenced in 1906. Between the World Wars the community declined economically and was now supported by the Joint Distribution Committee. With the approach of

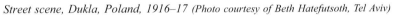

Street scene, Dukla, Poland, 1916–17 (Photo courtesy of Beth Hatefutsoth, Tel Aviv)

the Germans on 8 Sept. 1939, some Jews fled east. The Germans initiated a regime of forced labor and persecution. Many were expelled to Soviet-held territory shortly thereafter. The rest, with the addition of refugees, fell victim to the *Aktion* of 10 Aug. 1942. The old and sick were executed and the fit confined to the local labor camp until their liquidation in Dec. 1942. The rest were deported to the Belzec death camp. About 150 survived – 100 in the Soviet Union

DUKORA Minsk dist., Belorussia. Jews probably settled in the first half of the 18th cent. Their pop. was 462 in 1766, falling to 67 in 1811 and rising again to 604 (total 1,358) in 1897. In 1923, under the Soviets, the J. pop. was 501. A number of families founded a J. kolkhoz in the mid-1920s and a J. school was in operation in 1931. Following the German occupation in late June 1941, the Jews were confined in a ghetto. Over 300 were murdered toward the end of Oct.

DUKSZTY Vilna dist., Poland, today Belarus. Jews began arriving after the laying of the Petersburg–Warsaw railroad line in 1863 and numbered about 600 in 1897. J. lumber merchants set up sawmills and woodworking factories to produce railroad ties and paper products. J. flax merchants became big enough to necessitate the employment of others to clean, package, and transport the raw material. In an atmosphere of general prosperity, Jews later opened stores around the railway station as well as restaurants and overnight sleeping facilities. In the post-WWI economic crisis J. livelihoods were undermined. The Zionists and the Bund contended for influence in the community, operating Tarbut (Hebrew) and CYSHO (Yiddish) schools. The J. pop. in 1925 was 643. The arrival of the Germans in June 1941 unleashed Lithuanian attacks against the Jews, after which they were put to work laying a railroad line. On 27 Aug. 1941 they were led to the forest and shot down as they fled from the awaiting mass graves.

DUMBRAVENI (I) Bessarabia, Rumania, today Republic of Moldova. This settlement was founded in 1836 by Jews who engaged in agriculture. A community school was opened in 1900 by the ICA. The economic situation of the Jews declined after WWI. Zionist activity began with the organization of Young Zionist and General Zionist groups and pioneers im-

migrated to Eretz Israel at the end of the 19th cent. Members of this community were among the early settlers of Kefar Yehoshua and the immigration of pioneers continued up to the outbreak of WWII. The J. pop. in 1930 was 1,198 (87% of the total). Under the Soviet regime, the property of wealthy Jews was confiscated. With the return of the Rumanian army in July 1941, J. property was plundered and the J. pop. was forced to leave. Most went eastward in order to cross the Dniester River while others went to the west where German soldiers murdered most of them. The remainder were deported by the Rumanians to Transnistria, where they were killed or died from hunger and disease.

DUMBRAVENI (II) (Hung. Erzsebetvaros; Ger. Elisabethstadt) S. Transylvania dist., Rumania. Jews first settled in 1848 and a synagogue was founded in the late 19th cent. The J. pop., which came to 146 in 1920, declined following WWI, to 90 in 1930. Habonim established a branch between the World Wars. On 10 July 1941, the J. pop was transferred to Blaj, but returned at the end of the year. By the end of 1950, the community had ceased to exist.

DUNAFOLDVAR Tolna dist., Hungary. The J. community dates from 1840, numbering 673 (5% of the total) in 1880 and 355 in 1941. Most were merchants. A school was opened in 1853 and a synagogue consecrated in 1856. In May 1944, a ghetto was established for the area and all were deported on 4–6 July to Auschwitz. The community was reorganized after the war, but only a few Jews remained.

DUNAHARASZTI Pest-Pilis-Solt-Kiskun dist. Hungary. Jews settled in 1840, despite opposition from residents who were of German origin and who remained highly antisemitic down through the years. They formed a Neologist congregation in 1885, building a synagogue in 1888 and reaching a pop. of 151 in 1930 (2% of the total). In WWII, the 112 remaining Jews were sent to Auschwitz via Bekesmegyer in the final deportation from Hungary on 8 July 1944.

DUNAJOW Tarnopol dist., Poland, today Ukraine. Though Jews were present from the 17th cent. the community never developed greatly, reaching 338 members in 1900 (total 2,350) and dropping to 95 after the destruction of the town in WWI. In Jan. 1942,

there were 321 Jews, including refugees; all were deported in Sept. 1942.

DUNAJSKA STREDA (Hung. Dunaszerdahely; Yid. Sezdahely) Slovakia, Czechoslovakia. Jews were present in the early 18th cent., if not earlier. In 1739 Count Palffy granted them communal autonomy and wide-ranging rights. A synagogue was probably erected in 1787. In 1828, the J. pop. was 982 (57% of the total), helping make D. a regional center. Fifty settlements were attached to its rabbinate. A Great Synagogue was completed in 1865, accommodating 800 worshipers. A school combining religious and secular studies was opened in 1848. Following a spate of antisemitic agitation, the J. quarter was set on fire in 1887, leaving about 80 families homeless. Under R. Yehuda Asad (1852–66), the local yeshiva flourished, reaching an enrollment of 150–200. A second yeshiva was set up when part of the community broke away and founded an Adat Yisrael congregation in 1927. The J. pop. grew to 1,874 in 1880 and 2,501 in 1921. Both the Zionists and Adat Yisrael struck roots in the community before WWI and expanded their activities in its aftermath. Orthodox girls were organized in the Beth Jacob movement and Mizrachi and WIZO were prominent among the Zionists. Aside from the two *yeshivot*, with a combined attendance of 350 in the 1930s, and the J. school with an enrollment of 450 in the late 1930s, the community maintained three synagogues, two *battei midrash* a *talmud torah*, an old age home, and a *matza* bakery. A J. newspaper, the *Juedischer Herold*, was published in the 1920s and 1930s. Half the members of the local council were Jews and Jews owned 184 business establishments, 53 workshops, and eight factories. In 1940, the J. pop. was 2,645 (total 6,584). After the annexation to Hungary in Nov. 1938, J. stores were looted in riots. Anti-J. violence continued after the German occupation in March 1944. J. property was confiscated and Jews seized for forced labor. A ghetto was set up on 10 May, with Jews from 70 settlements brought there. On 15 June, 2,970 Jews were deported to Auschwitz. Most of the postwar community of 650 emigrated to Israel and other countries in 1949. There were about 20 families in 1990.

DUNAKISZL Pest dist., Hungary. J. pop. (1930) 100. The Jews were brought to Monor and deported on 8 July 1944 to Auschwitz.

DUNAPATAJ Pest–Pilis–Solt–Kiskun dist., Hungary. Jews arrived in the early 19th cent, opening a school by 1830 and building a synagogue in 1879. They numbered 126 in 1930. Eighteen perished under forced labor in 1942 and the rest were deported to Auschwitz via Kalocsa at the end of June 1944.

DUNAPENTELE Fejer dist., Hungary. Jews were present in the Roman period. A modern community of 20 families dates from the early 19th cent. A synagogue was built in 1836 and a school opened in 1855. The 80 Jews of D. were deported to Auschwitz on 18 June 1944..

DUNAVECSE Pest–Pilis–Solt–Kiskun dist., Hungary. Jews settled in the first half of the 19th cent., selling local farm produce in Budapest. A synagogue was established in 1890. The Jews numbered 94 in 1930. On 17 June 1944, they were deported to Auschwitz via Kalocsa.

DUNDAGA Courland dist., Latvia. J. pop. (1935) 15 (total 361). The Jews were murdered in the second half of 1941 under the German occupation.

DUNILOWICZE Vilna dist., Poland, today Belarus. A J. community is known from the early 19th cent., growing to 1,553 in 1897 (total 1,810) and living in straitened economic circumstances. With the renewal of commerce after WWI, when the J. pop. dropped to 685, Jews opened stores in the marketplace, but high taxes and the competition of the Polish cooperatives prevented recovery. Many were saved from starvation by their auxiliary farms. A Yiddish school opened in 1924 became the center of the community's cultural life, running a drama circle, adult education classes, and a library. Zionist youth were represented by Hehalutz Hatzair and Hashomer Hatzair. The Germans captured the town on 25 June 1941. Local antisemites and *Volksdeutsche* immediately began pillaging J. homes. A ghetto was set up in Jan. 1942, crowding 900 Jews into a single street. They were put to work in a sawmill, in tobacco fields, and digging a canal, at a daily wage of 4 oz of bread. On 22–23 Nov. 1942, the ghetto was liquidated as the Jews were searched out and murdered in a final *Aktion*.

DUNINO Smolensk dist., Russia. D. was founded as a J. colony in 1848. In 1898, the J. pop. was 169, rising

to about 400 in 1923 under Soviet rule. After their arrival around the end of Aug. 1941, the Germans murdered the few remaining Jews who had not fled or been evacuated.

DUNKERQUE (Dunkirk) Nord dist., France. The J. community was established in the first half of the 19th cent. consecrating a synagogue in 1922. In WWII, the Nord/Pas de Calais districts were under the jurisdiction of the military commander of Belgium. During the course of fighting around D. in 1940, the synagogue was destroyed and then rebuilt after liberation. In 1965, the community numbered 100 members.

DUPPIGHEIM Bas-Rhin dist., France. In 1781, there were 86 Jews living in D. (total pop. 584). The local synagogue was inaugurated in 1877. On the eve of WWII, 59 Jews were listed as living there. During the war, they were expelled by the Germans to the south of France, and the synagogue was completely destroyed. Six were deported.

DURBE Courland dist., Latvia The J. pop. in 1935 was 8 (total 525), down from 30 in 1920. The Jews were murdered by the end of 1941 under the German occupation.

DURLACH Baden, Germany. The 14th cent. community was wiped out in the Black Death persecutions of 1348–49. A few families lived there in subsequent centuries. In 1895 the community was attached to Groetzingen and in 1933 it numbered 57 Jews (total 18,658). Many emigrated in the Nazi era. At least five perished in the camps.

DURMENACH Haut-Rhin dist., France. The J. community numbered 73 families (340 persons) in 1784. The local synagogue was inaugurated in 1803. During the 19th cent., the J. pop. numbered 640 members, forming a majority in D. Prior to WWII, the J. pop. decreased and only 61 Jews were recorded in D. The Germans expelled all from their homes to the south of France. In 1965, the community numbered 15 members.

The People's Bank, Dusetos, Lithuania

DUSETOS (also Dusetai; Yid. Dusiat) Zarasai dist., Lithuania. The J. community began in the 16th cent. and constituted the majority of the total until the Holocaust. The J. pop. in 1897 was 1,158 (91% of the total). A fire broke out on Easter Day 1905 which damaged both J. and non-J. property. The non-Jews blamed the Jews and a pogrom broke out in which J. businesses and homes were destroyed and one Jew was killed. Another fire in 1910 burned almost all the J. houses in D and resulted in many Jews emigrating. The J. pop. in 1923 was 704 (60% of the total). In the 1930s the local branch of Verslas, the Lithuanian merchants association, incited tension between the Lithuanians and Jews. The J. community maintained two synagogues, aid societies, a Hebrew school, and Zionist organizations. With the withdrawal of the Red Army in June 1941, armed Lithuanian nationalists took over the town and persecuted the Jews. When the Germans arrived, they confined the Jews in a makeshift ghetto. On 26 Aug. 1941 all the Jews were taken to the Deuguciai forest and killed.

DUSINA (Hung. Zajgo) Carpatho-Russia, Czechoslovakia, today Ukraine. Jews probably settled in the early 19th cent. Eight Jews were present in 1830 and 52 (total 536) in 1880. The number of Jews rose to 123 in 1921 under Czechoslovakian rule and to 176 in 1941. The Hungarians occupied the town in March 1939, drafting a few dozen Jews into labor battalions. In July 1941, they expelled a number of J. families without Hungarian citizenship to Kamenets-Podolski, where they were murdered. The rest of the Jews were deported to Auschwitz in mid-May 1944.

DUTTLENHEIM Bas-Rhin dist., France. The local synagogue was inaugurated in 1860. In 1936, there were 65 Jews listed in the town. During WWII, they were expelled by the Germans to the south of France. The community disappeared after 1945.

DVORY NAD ZITAVOU (Hung. Udvard) Slovakia, Czechoslovakia. Jews were apparently present in small numbers in the early 18th cent. They are not mentioned in the late 18th cent. They reestablished the community only in the 1820s. By 1880, their pop. was 219 (total 4,035), declining in the 20th cent. as the young left for the big cities. The Zionists and Agudat Israel were active after WWI. In 1941, the J. pop. was 88. Under Hungarian rule, dozens of Jews

were seized for forced labor and on 15 June 1944 they were deported by the Germans to the Auschwitz concentration camp after being expelled to the Nove Zamky ghetto in May.

DVUR KRALOVE NAD LABEM Bohemia (Sudetenland), Czechoslovakia. Jews are first mentioned in 1838, trading in salt and tobacco and later becoming cloth manufacturers. In 1890 the community became independent and a synagogue was opened. The pop. was 332 in 1910 and 182 (total 16,585) in 1930, with Czech culture replacing the previous German orientation. After the annexation of the Sudetenland to Germany in Sept. 1938, J. refugees arrived in the city. On 17 Dec. 1942, 92 Jews were deported to the Theresienstadt ghetto via Hradec Kralove. Another 23 were dispatched to Theresienstadt on a different transport. None returned.

DWINGELO Drenthe dist., Holland. J. settlement began in the 18th cent. and numbered 71 in 1860. The J. pop. in 1941 was 11 (total 3,227). Nine were deported and perished in the Holocaust.

DWORZEC Nowogrodek dist., Poland, today Belarus. Jews are first mentioned in 1566. The community's main growth occurred in the late 19th cent., reaching a pop. of 868 (total 1,366) in 1897 and then declining to 388 in 1921 under conditions of economic hardship. The Germans entered the town on 26 June 1941 and in Dec. confined the Jews to a ghetto whose pop. rose by May 1942 to 3,000 including the attached labor camp where Jews were sent from Zdzieciol, Lubycza, Delatycze, and Rubiezhowicze. On 28 Dec. 1942, the Jews were brought to Nowojelnia and executed beside open pits. During the entire period, as many as 500 fled to the forests, but most were murdered there and only some managed to join the partisans, mostly the Atlas and Bielski J. units.

DYNOW Lwow dist., Poland. Jews are first noted in 1552. The court of the D. hasidic dynasty founded by R. Tzevi Elimelekh Shapira (after 1825) propped up the traditional J. economy, while a few wealthy merchants dealt in grain and lumber. A great circular synagogue decorated with oil paintings was built in the 18th cent. By 1880 the J. pop. stood at 1,241 (total 2,784). Most of the Jews left D. for Czechoslovakia, Hungary, and Austria at the outbreak of WWI,

returning four years later to find the town virtually destroyed. Pogroms and antisemitic incidents followed. Between the World Wars, Jews became active in light industry, producing soft drinks, jam, and pegs that were marketed throughout Poland. In addition to joining Zionist youth groups a number of the young were attracted to the illegal Communist Party. With the approach of the Germans, large numbers of refugees reached the town. On 15 Sept. 1939, an SS unit arrived and rounded up 300 men and shot them in the forest. The Great Synagogue was burned to the ground on the same day. The rest of the Jews were expelled to Soviet-held territory. Some were exiled to Siberia, others found their deaths in Lwow and Przemsyl, and the few who returned to D. ended their days in the Brzozow ghetto. Some 200–250 survived the war, most in the Soviet Union.

DYWIN Polesie dist., Poland, today Belarus. Jews formed an organized community with wide-ranging rights from the late 16th cent., numbering 1,094 in 1897 (total 3,737). A great fire in 1892 destroyed most homes and economic decline led to emigration, leaving 786 Jews in 1921. The Germans arrived early in WWII and established an open ghetto. They murdered 1,000, including refugees, in late summer 1942.

DZERZHINSK (I) (until 1932, Koidanovo) Minsk dist., Belorussia. A J. community of 560 poll tax payers was already present in 1765. Its pop. grew to 3,156 (total 4,744) in 1897. Retreating Polish soldiers staged a pogrom on 10–12 July 1920, extensively damaging the property of 400 J. families. In 1924, under Soviet rule, an J. elementary school was opened, named for the J. poet Avraham Reisen (1876–1953), a native of the town. In the mid-1920s, about 30 families (150 Jews) were employed in agriculture. In 1939, the J. pop. was 1,314. The Germans occupied the town on 28 June 1941, murdering 1,000 Jews and Communists on 20 or 21 Oct. On March 1942, about 1,300 Jews, probably from Minsk, were murdered at D.'s railway station. In all 15,000 inhabitants of the region, including many Jews, were murdered during the war, most near the village of Ryzhavka.

DZERZHINSK (II) (until 1936, Shcherbinovka) Stalino dist., Ukraine. J. settlement began in the early 20th cent. In 1939, the J. pop. was 278 (total 31,750). The Jews who had neither fled nor been evacuated, perished under the German occupation initiated on 22 Oct. 1941.

DZHANKOY Crimea, Russia, today Ukraine. Jews settled in the 19th cent., numbering 109 (total 957) in 1897. In 1924, under the Soviets, the region was designated for J. agricultural settlement with D. as its center. In 1939, the J. pop. of the town reached 1,397 (total 19,581). A national J. region was established with seven J. rural councils (soviets) responsible for thousands of J. farmers. In 1932, 704 J. families (about 3,500 people) were living in 14 J. farm settlements in the county (comprising about 14% of the total) and working over 80,000 acres of land. A J. school was in operation in the town and most of the J. farm settlements also had their own J. schools. The Joint Distribution Committee supported a hospital which was apparently in operation in the mid-1920s. The Germans occupied D. on 31 Oct. 1941. In the first half of Dec., they murdered 15 Jews at one of the kolkhozes. In mid-Dec., they herded hundreds of Jews into the local cheese factory and on 30 Dec., at the J. cemetery, they murdered 443 from D. and from the kolkhozes. A few thousand Soviet citizens, probably most of them Jews from D. and its environs, were murdered in Jan.–Feb. 1942. Hundreds of Jews from the kolkhozes were murdered in gas vans.

DZHURCHI (from 1944, Pervomayskoye) Crimea, Russia, today Ukraine. Jews probably settled in the 1920s. Some were farmers. With the creation of a J. county in Larindorf and the decline of Fraydorf, D. attained the status of a regional center. In 1939, its J. pop. was 140 (total 878). Some Jews apparently succeeded in fleeing to the interior of the Soviet Union before the Germans arrived in late Oct. 1941. The few who remained were probably murdered in Nov. or Dec. Some survivors returned after the war. Although a Jew became chairman of the settlement, the Jews left after awhile.

DZIALOSHYN (Yid. Zaleshin) Lodz dist., Poland. Jews first settled early in the 17th cent. and by the 18th cent. D. was the largest J. community in the Wielun district (846 Jews in 1793). In the 19th cent., Jews were involved in textile trading between Poland and the Prussian-dominated areas and Galicia. Some became wealthy but by the end of the cent. the situation of the Jews deteriorated when D. ceased to be a center

of the wool trade. Matters became worse and in Jan. 1937 there was a pogrom. In Sept. 1939 the town was destroyed by bombing and most of the 2,000 Jews in D. fled to nearby Pajeczno and shared the fate of that community.

DZIALOSZYCE   Kielce dist., Poland. Jews were probably present in the 14th cent. and constituted a majority by the mid-18th cent., making D. a center of trade and crafts for the large peasant pop. in the area. J. prosperity was reflected in the construction of a hospital in 1861 as well as a Great Synagogue and new *talmud torah* in the late 1870s. The J. pop. was 2,514 in 1856 and 6,446 (total 7,688) in 1910. The Stashevsky family provided the community with rabbis for three generations from the mid-19th cent. Most Jews were Hasidim and opposed to progress and change. Because of their opposition, the Zionists only set up their first group in 1911. Zionist activity intensified after the publication of the Balfour Declaration in 1917 and continued between the World Wars. Mizrachi became active in 1919 and founded a Yavne elementary school in 1927. The Jews were the dominant factor in the economic life of D. J. trade unions were under the influence of the Bund, Po'alei Zion, and the Communists. The Germans captured D. on 7–8 Sept. 1939, expropriating J. property and setting up a *Judenrat*. The relatively quiet conditions in D. drew large numbers of J. refugees, nearly doubling D.'s pop. to 12,000 in 1941. Overcrowding led to typhoid and dysentery epidemics. A group of Zionist youngsters opened a day-care center for the refugee children and a soup kitchen, providing 170,000 meals through April 1941. Many were sent to labor camps. The liquidation of the community commenced on 2 Sept. 1942 when 15,000 Jews were brought to Michow and then deported to the Belzec death camp, after 800 were selected for the labor camps. Those unfit to journey to Michow, numbering 1,200–2,000, were herded into open pits at the J. cemetery and murdered. A few hundred escaped.

DZIEDZICE   Silesia dist., Poland. After the lifting of residence restrictions in 1860 under the Austrians, Jews settled and uncharacteristically maintained a secular way of life. Only two of 50 J. stores closed on the Sabbath in the 1930s, when the J. pop. had reached around 400. With Zionism the leading force, D. became the only J. settlement in Poland where the community council financed free Hebrew-language instruc-

tion. Most fled on the eve of the war in Aug. 1939. The last Jews were deported by the Germans to death camps in 1942.

DZIEWIENISZKI   Vilna dist., Poland, today Belarus. The J. community formed in the 18th cent. and despite mass emigration grew in the 19th after the expulsion of Jews from the surrounding villages. In 1897 the J. pop. reached 1,225 (total 1,897), of whom 277 were artisans. Economic life came to a standstill in WWI, with forced labor and food shortages accompanying the German occupation of 1915–18 and subsequent persecution by General Haller's Polish troops. J. livelihoods suffered further between the World Wars from the competition of the Polish cooperatives and the general economic crisis. Zionist influence was dominant in the community. A Tarbut school was founded in 1922 and graduates of the youth movements made their way to Palestine. After two years of Soviet rule, the Germans captured the town on 24 June 1941. In Jan. 1942 the Jews were transferred to the neighboring town of Woronowo. Within ten days, 28 elderly Jews were murdered. On 11 May 1942, some 5,000 of the Jews gathered in Woronowo were led into the forest and shot in the back as they were forced into mass graves. The skilled workers were sent to the Lida ghetto where a labor camp with 4,000 Jews was organized. About 120 were active in a J. underground. Eliyahu Blecher of D. succeeded in guiding 241 Jews to the partisans in the forest in four separate trips. The ghetto was liquidated on 18 Sept. 1943.

DZIKOW STARY   Lwow dist., Poland, today Ukraine. The J. community grew to about 500 in the 19th cent. around the hasidic court connected with the Ropczyce (Ropshits) dynasty. With its decline, between the World Wars, the J. pop. fell to 360 (total 2,317). The Soviets held D. for two weeks and most of the Jews left with them. German occupation came in Oct. 1939 and in June 1940 a labor camp which functioned until Aug. 1942 was set up for thousands of Jews. As many as 100 may have survived the war.

DZISNA   Vilna dist., Poland, today Belarus. Jews are assumed to have arrived from Western Europe in the 16th cent. A J. settlement is known from the later 18th cent., reaching a pop. of 412 in 1797, many of whom engaged in the wholesale trade (flax, lumber, hides, grain). Most Jews were Habad Hasidim. They

came into conflict with Haskala proponents in the 1880s. By 1897, the J. pop. stood at 4,716 (total 6,756). Cut off from their Russian markets, J. merchants suffered the most in the post-WWI economic crisis as the J. pop. fell to around 3,000. The repair of the railroad enabled the shipment of farm produce to the cities of Poland and many J. stores were able to reopen in the general recovery. Most children studied at the Bund-sponsored CYSHO Yiddish school, which enrolled 180 in 1929–30. The young were active in the Zionist youth movements, with many of their graduates reaching Palestine. After two years of Soviet rule, the Germans captured the town on 2 July 1941. On 14 July, ten Jews were arbitrarily executed. On 3 Aug. the Jews were herded into a ghetto and put to forced labor. On 14 July 1942 the Germans and local police surrounded the ghetto and opened indiscriminate machinegun fire, killing 2,000–3,000 as Jews fought back with whatever came to hand. Few escaped.

DZIULINKA   Vinnitsa dist., Ukraine. Jews settled in the 1770s and included ten who were paying a poll tax in 1784. In 1939, the J. pop. was 212 (total 4,527). The Germans occupied D. on 29 July 1941 and on 2 April 1942 murdered all the Jews outside the town.

DZIUNKOV   Vinnitsa dist., Ukraine. The J. pop. was 137 in 1765 and 1,137 (total 4,314) in 1897, dropping again to 365 in 1926. The Germans captured D. in late July 1941 and murdered the Jews in *Aktions* occurring in late Oct. 1941 and during 1942.

DZURIN   Vinnitsa dist., Ukraine. Jews numbered 84 in 1765 and 1,585 (total 4,656) in 1897. Anton Denikin's White Army troops attacked the Jews of D. in Dec. 1919. A J. council (soviet) and J. elementary school were set up in the Soviet period. In 1924, a J. kolkhoz was founded, supporting 50–60 J. families. Dozens of other J. families earned their livelihoods in a local sugar refinery. In 1939, the J. pop. was 1,027.

The Germans captured the town on 22 July 1941, placing it under the administration of the Rumanians, who established a ghetto run by a *Judenrat* and J. police. Thousand of Jews from Bessarabia and Bukovina were expelled to D. Many died of starvation or disease. In all, 500 perished among the refugees and local Jews.

DZURKOW   Stanislawow dist., Poland, today Ukraine. The J. pop. in 1921 was 100. The Jews were probably murdered locally or expelled to Kolomyja for liquidation in April 1942.

DZWINIACZ GORNY   Lwow dist., Poland, today Ukraine. Around 30 J. families (less than 10% of the total) were living mainly as farmers between the World Wars. In Sept. 1939 they found themselves in the Soviet border zone and were transferred to Malynsk in the Rovno dist., where they shared the fate of local Jews in 1942.

DZWINOGROD   Lwow dist., Poland, today Ukraine. The J. pop. in 1921 was 116. The Jews were probably expelled to Bobrka for liquidation in the second half of 1942.

DZYGOVKA   Vinnitsa dist., Ukraine. Jews numbered 17 in 1765 and 2,187 (total 7,194) in 1897. The majority of stores were in J. hands and most artisans in D. were Jews. In early Dec. 1917, the Jews were attacked in a pogrom. During the Soviet period, many Jews worked in the local sugar refinery and in the 1930s a few dozen families were employed in a J. kolkhoz. A J. elementary school was in operation from the mid-1920s and expanded to include a few higher grades in the late 1930s. In 1939, the J. pop. was 858. The Germans captured D. on 18 July 1941, murdering a large number of Jews in Aug. The remainder were confined to a ghetto with Jews expelled from Bessarabia and Bukovina after D. was attached to Rumanian Transnistria in Sept. 1941. On 1 Sept. 1943, 105 Jews still remained there.

life and some Yiddish terms entered local parlance. The community in E. was established in 1864, when a new and larger synagogue was opened. The J. pop. declined from 96 (6.1% of the total) in 1880 to 56 (3.5%) in 1933. On *Kristallnacht* (9–10 Nov. 1938), the synagogue's interior was destroyed and J. homes were vandalized. By 1939 only a few Jews remained.

ECKARTSHAUSEN   Hesse, Germany. Numbering 30 (4.5% of the total) in 1861, this small community had its own synagogue and cemetery. By 1939 all the Jews had emigrated.

EDELENY   Borsod dist., Hungary. Jews are first mentioned in 1736 and numbered 129 in 1880, maintaining a synagogue, school, and yeshiva. In May 1944, the town's 250 Jews were confined in a ghetto with 130 Jews from neighboring villages. On 12–15 June 1944, they were deported to Auschwitz via Miskolc.

EDELFINGEN   Wuerttemberg, Germany. Jews are mentioned in 1348–49 in connection with the Black Death persecutions when all were apparently murdered. A small community was in existence in the late 16th cent. Unlike other villages it maintained its pop. in the 19th cent. (170 of a total 1,151 in 1895). Many were butchers employed in a big slaughterhouse or smaller butcher shops. There was a kosher hotel. Relations with the local pop. deteriorated under Nazi rule, with an outburst of violence on *Kristallnacht* (9–10 Nov. 1938). Sixty-three of the town's Jews emigrated from Germany between 1933 and 1941; the remaining 20 were expelled.

EDENKOBEN   Palatinate, Germany. Jews were continuously present in E. from at least 1660. A synagogue was erected in 1780–81; a new one was consecrated in 1827; and a J. school operated from 1830 to the Weimar years. The congregation was one of the first to reveal clear-cut Reform tendencies, introducing German-language prayers and an organ into the synagogue. The J. pop. reached a peak of 190 in 1847, declining to 120 (total 5,232) in 1900. In June 1933, about four months after the Nazi rise to power, the J. pop. numbered 66. With the Nazis receiving over 50% of the vote in the 1932 elections, official antisemitism was enthusiastically augmented by partisan violence against the Jews. As part of the anti-J. boycott, eight

J. wine merchants were banned from the trade and business contacts with Jews were severely circumscribed. Twelve Jews left the town by Feb. 1935. In 1937–39, 20 left for the U.S. On *Kristallnacht* (9–10 Nov. 1938), the windows of J. homes and stores were smashed and all J. men arrested. Subsequently the electricity and water to J. homes were cut off and women and children warned not to leave their houses. On 22 Oct. 1940, 14 of the last 16 Jews in E. were deported to the Gurs concentration camp. Some of these were sent afterwards to camps in the east where they perished.

EDESSA   Pella dist., Greece. In 1928 there were four Jews in E. among 12 in the whole district. In 1940 there were 132 in the dist. and only two remained in 1951.

EDINETI   (Yid. Yedinitz) Bessarabia, Rumania, today Republic of Moldova. The first settlers in E. were Jews (in 1820). By 1878 there were eight prayer houses. An attempted pogrom in 1887 was thwarted. The J. pop. in 1897 was 7,379 (72% of the total). Near the end of WWI, the Jews were robbed and their property plundered. When the Rumanian army entered E. in March 1918, there were widespread antisemitic actions which continued in the 1920s, especially by students at the theological college. Between the World Wars Jews played a leading role in marketing agricultural produce. In 1935–36 a workers' union was established, the majority of whose members were Jews. In addition to the *talmud torah*, eight *hadarim* functioned; instruction in some was in Hebrew. There were three J. elementary schools and a J. high school. Zionist activity was extensive, with most of the organizations and youth movements represented. The J. pop. in 1930 was 5,341 (90% of the total). Jews were persecuted during the Goga-Cuza regime (1937) when all J. institutions were outlawed and the J. mayor deposed. Under the Soviets (1940), Jews were forced to forfeit their property, synagogues were turned into storehouses, and wealthy Jews and Zionists were expelled to Siberia. When Rumanian and German soldiers took the city from Soviet forces on 2 July 1941, they plundered J. property and within two weeks killed 1,000 Jews. The J. pop. was expelled to Atachi, Rezina, and Secureni. Some succeeded in escaping across the Dnieper River to Russia but the majority shared the fate of most of the J. communities

where they took refuge. A transit camp was set up in E. in Aug. 1941 for Jews from Bukovina and Bessarabia. Conditions were atrocious and the internees slept in stables, in cowsheds, and even in the open. There was no food and up to 100 persons died daily from starvation and exhaustion. Groups of several hundred were sent to work on roads. A total of 23,000 Jews were eventually housed in this camp. In Nov. 1941, the camp was dismantled and the Jews sent to Marculesti, Bessarabia, and to Atachi and Mogilev, many dying on the way.

EGELSBACH Hesse, Germany. This Orthodox community numbered over 90 (3.2% of the total) in 1905, declining to 60 in 1933. The Nazi boycott campaign drove Jews from the town and by Dec. 1938, after *Kristallnacht* (9-10 Nov. 1938), the remaining 44 had left — some emigrating to the U.S. and Palestine.

EGENHAUSEN Middle Franconia, Germany. J. settlement began in 1715 and numbered 79 (total 383) in 1880. The four Jews remaining under Nazi rule left E. by 1939.

EGER Heves dist., Hungary. Jews were already present by the early 15th cent. After the Ottoman conquest in 1569, many Turkish Jews settled in E., leaving in 1687 with the end of Turkish rule. A new community was formed in the late 18th cent. at the urging of the local bishop, who wished to encourage economic growth. The pop. grew to 2,396 (10.7% of the total) in 1890, dropping to 1,787 at the beginning of WWII. A synagogue was consecrated in 1851 and by 1885 numerous small J. communities were affiliated with the congregation. In 1878, the community split into two separate communities, Orthodox and Status Quo. The community's first rabbi was Yosef Tzevi Weisz (1840-79), grandfather of Stephen Wise, the American Reform and Zionist leader. Two J. schools existed in E. Between the World Wars, the community continued to flourish and Zionist activity intensified. The publication of the Hungarian racial laws of 1940 seriously undermined the economic position of the Jews. In 1942, J. males aged 18-42 were drafted into labor battalions and sent to the Russian front where most perished. In June 1944, the town's 1,800 Jews were confined in a ghetto. The local bishop, Czapik Gyula, forbade parish priests to assist extremist groups. Eight J. women were saved by working in the bishop's kitchen.

R. Yohanan Sofer, Eger, Hungary

On 8 June the Jews were deported to Auschwitz. The postwar community numbered 300 in 1959.

EGLAINE (Yalovka) Courland dist., Latvia. The J. pop. in 1935 was 25 (total 511). The Jews were murdered by the Germans shortly after their occupation of late June–early July 1941.

EGYEK Hajdu dist., Hungary. Jews settled in the mid-18th cent. Most were small merchants. There were a few artisans. The community only succeeded in building a synagogue in 1905. The pop. numbered 123 in 1930. In 1941, J. males were seized for forced labor and on 1 July 1944 the Jews were deported to Auschwitz via Debrecen.

EHRENBREITSTEIN Rhineland, Germany. A synagogue was erected in 1802 and the J. pop. reached 82 in 1836. In 1925, 19 Jews remained. Seven were deported to the east in 1942.

EIBELSTADT Lower Franconia, Germany. A J. settlement existed from 1583 under the emperor's protection, with a synagogue erected in 1610 and a pop. of 101 in 1630. The community ended in 1655 when the last Jews were expelled.

EIBERGEN Gelderland dist., Holland. Jews were

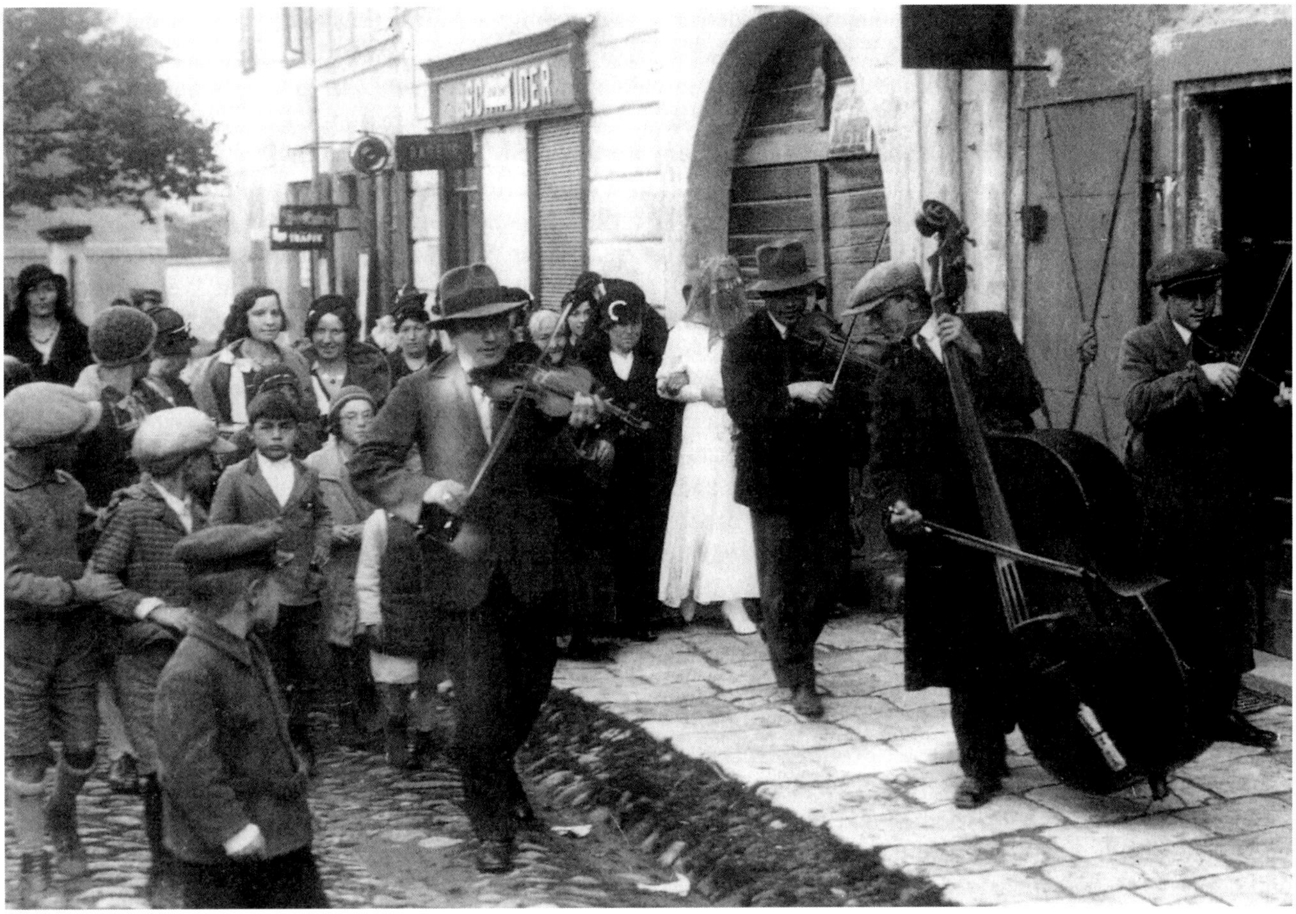
SCHNEIDER

Wedding procession with klezmerim *in streets of Eisenstadt, Austria, 1934 (Amt der Burgenlandischen Landesregierung, Eisenstadt/photo courtesy of Yad Vashem, The Holocaust Martyrs' and Heroes' Remembrance Authority, Jerusalem)*

Jews were physically attacked. In 1936, a Jew was arrested and accused of "racial defilement" (*Rassenschande*). On *Kristallnacht* (9–10 Nov. 1938), the synagogue was not burned down, probably because it was part of a row of houses, but the interior was destroyed. J. apartments and shops (ten out of 23 were still in J. hands) were destroyed, and the cemetery was desecrated. Four men were arrested and taken to the Buchenwald concentration camp. Soon after the rioting, the last J. stores were "Aryanized." In 1939, the synagogue was sold and the community was affiliated with the Halle community. There were only 30 Jews in E. in Oct. 1939. In 1941, the 17 remaining Jews were billeted in a "J. house" and compelled to carry out forced labor, irrespective of age and health. All but four, who were probably protected by marriage to non-Jews, were deported, most of them in Sept. 1942 to the Theresienstadt ghetto.

EITERFELD Hesse-Nassau, Germany. The J. community, numbering 105 (18% of the total) in 1885, maintained an elementary school (1861–1933) and absorbed the last Jews in Buchenau and Erdmannrode, shouldering the burden of their debts (1928). The once larger Erdmannrode community – numbering 129 in 1861 – dwindled to one family in 1927. Owing to Nazi persecution, E.'s expanded community disbanded ten years later and by Nov. 1938 most of the Jews had left.

EJSZYSZKI Nowogrodek dist., Poland, today Belarus. Karaite Jews probably settled in the 12th cent. with Rabbanite Jews following in the 13th cent. The J. pop. grew from 661 in 1847 to 2,376 (total 3,196) in 1897, with J. livelihoods centered around market days and the yearly fairs. Most of the town's stores were J.-owned and about a third of the Jews were artisans.

Some had auxiliary farms and a number of wealthy merchants dealt in horses and cattle. After a devastating fire in 1895 destroyed many J. homes, some emigrated. The community was known for its ardent talmudic scholars and its large yeshiva. Haskala and Zionism made inroads in the late 19th cent. despite strong Orthodox opposition. The Zionist groups intensified their activities after WWI, sending many of their pioneers to Palestine. The J. pop. in 1925 was 2,800. In 1929–30 about 100 children studied at a religious Hebrew school. Jews suffered from antisemitic violence and economic boycotts in the 1930s. After annexation to the Soviet Union in June 1940, a number of Zionist activists were exiled and Yiddish was substituted for Hebrew as the language of instruction in the J. school. The Germans arrived on 22 June 1941, seizing Jews for forced labor and setting up a *Judenrat* as a means of implementing their extortionate demands. Under brutal Lithuanian police, Jews were periodically tormented. On 24 Sept. 1941, 4,000 Jews, including 900 refugees from Olkieniki, were led to the J. cemetery and executed. Most of the 490 who fled were hunted down and murdered. A few joined the partisans and were among the 300 Jews murdered by the Polish Armia Krajowa underground in Oct. 1944.

ELBING (Pol. Elblag) East Prussia, Germany, today Poland. The E. community was one of the oldest J. communities of East Prussia, the first Jew being allowed to settle there in 1783. The J. pop. grew to 33 families in 1812 and 549 individuals in 1880, declining to 445 in 1905. In 1925, numbers were still at 434, as the movement of many Jews to bigger towns was offset by the arrival of newcomers from the territories that came under Polish sovereignty after WWI. The community became Reform in the second half of the 19th cent. It maintained a synagogue from 1824, a cemetery from 1812, and employed rabbis continuously from 1875 on. In the early 20th cent., the Association of East Prussian Communities established an office for the care of poor J. immigrants from Eastern Europe. As early as 1844, a Jew was elected a member of the city council. The J.-owned Loeser & Wolff cigar factory, founded in 1874, was one of the leading industrial concerns in eastern Germany, employing more than 4,000 workers in 1926. When the Nazis came to power, about 460 Jews were living in E. Many left for other German towns or emigrated. In 1933, there were 367 Jews and 207 by Aug. 1936. The community

organized a wide range of cultural and language courses for those who remained. By May 1939, there were only 53 Jews remaining in E. It may be assumed that those who failed to emigrate were deported, with the exception of seven persons who were still living in the town in Nov. 1942 and probably protected by marriage to a non-J. partner.

ELBURG Gelderland dist., Holland. Jews first settled there in 1700. The J. pop. in 1859 was 115. There were 34 Jews in 1938. Most managed to hide during WWII; 19 were deported to Poland, only one of whom returned.

ELDAGSEN Hanover, Germany. Jews began to settle in E. in the second decade of the 18th cent. The community built a synagogue in 1868 and operated an elementary school. It numbered 55–57 (over 2% of the total) in 1880–1933. Jakob Goldschmidt (1882–1955), a native of E., became an important banker in the Weimar period. During the early Nazi years, most Jews left, and by Oct. 1938, only 16 remained. On *Kristallnacht* (9–10 Nov. 1938), the synagogue was destroyed and five Jews were arrested. A total of 44 Jews emigrated, 25 to the U.S.; at least six perished in the Holocaust.

EL-HAMMA Gabes dist., Tunisia. The J. settlement was probably founded in the tenth cent. It was destroyed in 1150 in the Almohad disturbances. According to tradition, settlement was renewed in the 16th cent. but a community is only known from the late 18th cent. The Jews seem to have arrived from Gabes and Djerba, settling in their own quarter and building a synagogue in the mid-19th cent. Under the French Protectorate in the late 19th cent., many from Gabes settled in E., turning it into a suburb of Gabes. The J. pop. grew to 452 in 1921 (of a total 5,364, not including Europeans). Most Jews moved to the new al-Medina quarter, which became the commercial and administrative center of the settlement. They built a synagogue named for the kabbalist R. Yosef al-Maghrebi, said to have been a student of Yitzhak Luria (Ha-Ari) in Safed in the 16th cent. The grave of al-Maghrebi in E., associated with miraculous occurrences, became a place of pilgrimage on Hanukkah. A second, luxurious synagogue was built in 1936. For generations, the Damari family provided the community with its rabbis and community leaders. Eliyahu Hai Damari was chief

Nov. 1938), SA men destroyed the synagogue's interior and Nazis looted J. property (especially wine cellars) throughout the region. Of the 37 Jews left in E., 12 emigrated and 18 moved elsewhere; all those remaining in the area were deported by 1941.

EMBKEN Rhineland, Germany. The first Jew settled in E. in 1783 and in 1812 there were already 19 Jews in the village, working mostly as cattle dealers. In 1885, the J. pop. peaked at 59, constituting 10% of the total. The community maintained a synagogue from 1869 and a cemetery from 1884. By 1930, the community had declined to 43 Jews. Most left after the Nazi rise to power in 1933. On *Kristallnacht* (9–10 Nov. 1938), the synagogue was destroyed. After the outbreak of war, the last seven Jews were deported to the east. At least eight Jews from E. perished in the Holocaust.

EMDEN Hanover, Germany. Political and economic factors motivated the city's decision to permit J. settlement in the mid–16th cent. The first Jews to arrive were *Hochdeutsch* Ashkenazim (1571); former Portuguese Marranos came later but most had moved elsewhere by 1712. Thanks to relatively favorable conditions, the community prospered and grew from 16 to 98 families (1613–1741), becoming one of the largest in northwestern Germany. However, during the years of Prussian rule (1744–1807), it was also one of the most disadvantaged. Many Jews earned their livelihood from the cattle trade, in which they eventually attained predominance. Three *parnasim* headed the E. community, which acquired a synagogue and a cemetery and established a burial society in the 17th cent. Communal regulations were drawn up in 1780. From its inception, the community engaged a rabbi: the first, Moshe Uri ha-Levi, known also as Philips Joost (1540–1620), helped Portuguese Jews set up a congregation in Amsterdam. Yaakov Emden, the son of "Hakham Tzevi" Ashkenazi, also occupied the rabbinate (1728–33) before returning to his native Altona. During the Napoleonic era, when Jews were emancipated under French rule (1808), the city's J. pop. numbered 500. Although the Hanoverian government reintroduced various discriminatory measures after Napoleon's downfall, the J. pop. increased to 802 (nearly 7% of the total) in 1828. In 1836, the syna-

Synagogue in Emden, Germany

gogue was rebuilt. An edict that transferred to E. the prerogatives of the Jews from the nearby town of Aurich, also led to Avraham Loewenstamm's installation as chief rabbi of East Friesland (1827–39). His religious traditionalism, displayed in the prohibition of organ music, characterized future leaders of the community. An attempt by Aurich Jews to regain control of the (provincial) rabbinate was the main reason for a delay in the appointment of Shimshon Rafael Hirsch as Loewenstamm's successor (1841–47). Hirsch, the architect of Neo-Orthodoxy, wore clerical dress, preached in German, and launched a campaign for J. civil rights. He vastly improved the education of girls as well as boys, obtaining state aid for the J. elementary school. New railroads, canals, and harbor extensions marked the city's growth after 1848, when Jews first became active in municipal and commercial affairs. The National Liberal Party administration fostered religious harmony and denounced antisemitism. Jakob Pels, a communal leader for over 50 years, served as deputy chairman of the city council in 1905, when the J. pop. numbered around 900 (4% of the total). Few members of the community were attracted by Liberal Judaism or married out of the faith, but a drift toward assimilation alarmed successive chief rabbis. Paul Buchholz (1874–93) attacked "religious indifferentism"; Jonas Loeb (1894–1911) established a *talmud torah* so as to counteract this "pernicious spirit of the age"; and Moses Hoffmann (1913–21) took a firm stand against mixed choirs. Until the Nazi era, however, most parents sent their children to the J. elementary school and many refused to give them a high school education. The chief rabbinate's authority extended to Stade, near Hamburg, and to 25 communities in the Aurich and Osnabrueck districts (1893). The community maintained an extensive welfare system, an old age home, an orphanage, women's groups, a cultural society, and youth clubs. During the Weimar period, the J. pop. dwindled – to 700 (2%) in 1925. The German Zionist Organization's branch was established as early as 1901. Youngsters from more assimilated homes joined the Blau–Weiss movement and some who were trained at *hakhsharot* emigrated to Palestine. Religious Zionism had a keen advocate in Samuel Blum, the last chief rabbi (1922–39), and voters favored Mizrachi in elections to the 16th Zionist Congress (1929). Members of the J. War Veterans Association and the Central Union (C.V.) were active in combating antisemitism. Thereafter, in Reichstag elections, the Nazi vote skyrocketed from 2% (1928) to 37% (1932).

In 1933, the J. pop. numbered 581. After Hitler's appointment as chancellor, the windows of J. stores were smashed on 28 March 1933 in anticipation of Boycott Day (1 April). Newspapers, broadcasts, and parades heightened the anti-J. atmosphere, which aroused horror abroad. Chief Rabbi Blum, forced to condemn "exaggerated reports" of Nazi persecution, worked hard to maintain communal and religious life. After the banning of *shehita*, a temporary arrangement was made to import kosher meat from Holland. Nazi attempts to enforce the economic boycott sometimes ran into local opposition. When SA stormtroopers provoked a riot in E. (May 1935), two were actually arrested by the police. Until 1937, the leading J. cattle traders remained in business, thanks to German dealers who trusted them and ignored the boycott. Approximately 25% of the remaining Jews left E. between 1933 and 1938: 130 emigrated while 50 moved to other German cities. Those who made the mistake of settling in Holland were mostly deported after the German occupation. On *Kristallnacht* (9–10 Nov. 1938), organized by SA and SS men, Nazis burned down the synagogue and shot or tortured Jews. A few courageous Germans handed food parcels to J. men being dispatched to the Sachsenhausen concentration camp. Emigration both inside and outside Germany was accelerated after the pogrom, with at least 13 making it to safe havens in England (3), Palestine (3), Argentina (2), New York (1), and the Dominican Republic (4). The community shrank from 430 (Sept. 1938) to 320 (Nov. 1939). By mid-1940 it had ceased to exist, the last 150 Jews being deported to the east on 23 Oct. 1941. At least 465 Jews from E. perished and only 13 survived the Holocaust.

EMES Nikolaiev dist., Ukraine. E. was founded as a J. colony and in the Soviet period it had a J. rural council (soviet) and a J. elementary school with 98 students in 1931 (25 of them as boarders from outside E.). The big J. Iskra kolkhoz was attached to the council, numbering 65 J. families (most from Ukrainian towns) in 1937. The Germans captured E. in late Aug. 1941, murdering 160 Jews in the area, including 112 from E.

EMILCHINO Zhitomir dist., Ukraine. Jews settled in the early 19th cent. and numbered 1,049 (total 2,477) in 1897. On the eve of Passover 1919 the Pet-

lyura gangs went on a rampage of murder, rape, and robbery that left ten Jews dead. In 1939, the J. pop. stood at 1,115. A J. elementary school was in operation. The Germans captured E. on 2 July 1941. Some Jews fled. The Germans murdered 507 people in the area.

EMMEN Drenthe dist., Holland. An independent J. community developed in the second half of the 19th cent. and numbered 64 in 1860. The J. pop. in 1941 was 180 (total 49,327). In 1942, over 140 Jews were deported to Poland and perished. Some 30 survived in hiding. A small community was constituted after the war.

EMMENDINGEN Baden, Germany. Jews were present in the mid-16th cent. and after expulsion in the early 17th a few returned after the Thirty Years War (1618–48). None seem to have been living there at the end of the cent. A new settlement was established in 1716 through the efforts of the Court Jew Josef Guenzburger. A cemetery, the oldest in Upper Baden, was opened in 1717 and a synagogue was dedicated in 1723. In 1801 the J. pop. reached 158 and in 1875 a peak of 406 (total 3,487). In 1830–72 a J. elementary school was in operation. Jews continued to earn their livelihood mainly from the cattle trade and at the outset of the 20th cent., 65% were so engaged. In the same period the Wertheimer distillery became the largest in the state. The J. pop. dropping somewhat after 1925 with an exodus to the big cities, totaled 296 in 1933, including new settlers fleeing the Nazi persecutions. By Oct. 1938, 147 had left, 100 of them emigrating. Another 111 (86 emigrating) left after *Kristallnacht* (9–10 Nov. 1938), when the synagogue and two cemeteries were wrecked and Jews were taken to the Dachau concentration camp. The last 66 Jews were deported to the Gurs concentration camp in Oct. 1940, while 19 Jews who had previously left the city were also deported from their places of refuge. In all, 23 survived the camps. In addition, the Germans murdered 25–30 patients at the local J. insane asylum.

EMMERICH Rhineland, Germany. There is evidence of an occasional J. presence in the Middle Ages. A modern J. settlement developed from the end of the 16th cent. The J. pop. stood at seven families in 1701. There were 35 individuals in 1801 and 158 in 1880. A synagogue was in use before 1667. The congregation's Liberal tendencies were reflected in the introduction in the synagogue of a harmonium, a mixed choir, and mixed seating. In June 1933, about four months after the Nazi rise to power, 86 Jews remained. The synagogue was sold in Aug. 1938. On *Kristallnacht* (9–10 Nov. 1938), SA men destroyed J. homes and stores and J. men were arrested. In May 1939, the J. pop. was reduced to 32, and on 22 July 1942, the last six Jews were deported to the Theresienstadt ghetto.

EMOD Borsod dist., Hungary. Jews settled in the first half of the 19th cent., numbering 123 in 1880 and 72 in 1930. In WWII, most were sent to labor camps; the rest were deported to Auschwitz via Miskolc on 1 July 1944.

EMS, BAD see BAD EMS.

ENCS Abauj–Torna dist., Hungary. Jews settled in about the mid-19th cent. and numbered 140 in 1896 and 272 in 1930. A synagogue was erected in 1921 and the community maintained a J. school, yeshiva, *talmud torah*, and library. In spring 1944, the Jews were sent to the Kasza ghetto, and from there on 12–15 June to Auschwitz.

ENCSENCS Szabolcs dist., Hungary. Jews are first mentioned in 1747, numbering 77 in 1880 and 62 in 1930. They enjoyed good relations with their neighbors. At the end of April 1944, they were sent to the Nyirjes concentration camp, and were deported to Auschwitz on 29 May–6 June.

ENDINGEN Baden, Germany. Medieval J. communities ended in the Black Death persecutions of 1348–49 and in expulsion in 1462 following the execution of the rabbi and his brothers on charges of killing a Christian family. A community of 43 existed in 1888 (total 2,705). The five remaining Jews were attached to the Eichstetten community in 1933 and dispersed. In 1965 the medieval blood libel was investigated, the Jews pronounced innocent, and the remains of the dead family, which had been worshiped as martyrs, removed from the Catholic church.

ENDROD Bekes dist., Hungary. Jews numbered 182 in 1880 and 65 in 1940. They were deported to Auschwitz on 26 June 1944 via Bekescsaba.

ENFIDAVILLE Sousse dist., Tunisia. A small J. community originated in the 1920s (49 Jews), reaching 75 by 1936 and 105 in 1946. Jews owned textile shops. During the 1920s, the community built a small synagogue. Relations with the Muslims were poor and deteriorated in the 1930s with the establishment of the nationalistic Neo-Dustur organization. During WWII, a small Italian-supervised work camp existed nearby for J. prisoners. The lax supervision enabled many to escape. After the war most Jews left E. for Tunis and Sousse.

ENGHIEN-LES-BAINS Val-d'Oise dist., France. The synagogue was inaugurated in 1889. Sephardi and Ashkenazi Jews actively participated in the joint religious organization of the community. In 1932, a separate chapel for Sephardi Jews was inaugurated. The synagogue was also renovated. During WWII, according to the 1941 census, there were 129 families (289 individuals) listed in the community. Sixty local Jews were deported to the Drancy concentration camp in Nov. 1942. On Yom Kippur (10 Oct.) 1943, the Gestapo arrested 35 Jews at the local synagogue.

ENKHUIZEN Noord-Holland dist., Holland. Jews lived in E. from the 17th cent. In the 18th cent. a community flourished, numbering 48 in 1901. In April 1943, 52 of E.'s 54 Jews (total pop. 10,000) managed to hide and escape deportation and death.

ENSCHEDE Overijssel dist., Holland. The J. presence dates back to the mid-17th cent. In the 19th cent. the community became more organized and a synagogue was consecrated in 1834. By 1892 there were 527 Jews (total 23,000). The community grew rapidly in the 20th cent. and a large synagogue – considered one of the most beautiful in Western Europe – was consecrated in 1928. Zionist activity developed between the World Wars. In the 1930s, 561 German-J. refugees arrived. In 1941 there were 1,310 Jews (total 92,895). In Sept. 1941 some 100 were arrested and sent to their deaths in the Mauthausen concentration camp. From Oct. 1942 more were arrested and deported to the Westerbork transit camp. In all, some 800 were deported, only a few of whom survived. About 550 survived in hiding, thanks to the initiative of the local J. council and with the assistance of Christian clergy, local officials, and other sympathizers. The community was reestablished after the war and became the leading J. center in eastern Holland.

ENYING Veszprem dist., Hungary. Jews arrived in the first half of the 19th cent., erecting a synagogue in 1870 and opening a J. school in 1883. Several were murdered during the White Terror of 1919–21. The J. pop. was 178 in 1930. A Zionist youth group offered Hebrew lessons and J. cultural activities. At the end of June 1944, the Jews were deported to Auschwitz via the Veszprem ghetto.

EPERNAY Marne dist., France. During the Middle Ages the Jews occupied three streets in E. The community ceased to exist after the expulsion edicts issued in France in the 14th cent. (1306 and 1394). It revived after the 1870 Franco-Prussian war when Jews from Alsace-Lorraine settled in E. In 1890, the local synagogue was inaugurated. During WWI, in spring 1918, the synagogue was virtually destroyed in the bombardment; it was newly inaugurated only in 1925. On the eve of WWII, the community consisted of about 40 families. Most Jews left before the Germans entered E. on 10 June 1940. The German forces destroyed the synagogue. Arrests began in 1942. First J. refugees from abroad were arrested, but later no distinction was made between local Jews and foreign nationals. By 1944, there were only two Jews left in E. In 1969, the community numbered fewer than 200.

EPINAL Vosges dist., France. The community was established in the first half of the 19th cent. under R. Moise Durckheim, the father of Emil Durckheim, the celebrated sociologist (1858–1947). The synagogue was inaugurated in 1864. After the Franco-Prussian war in 1870, the J. pop. grew due to an influx of refugees from Alsace. In 1886, the community consisted of 350 members, increasing to 390 in 1900. In the 1920s, a local J. youth society was organized. During WWII, the census of 20 June 1942 listed 142 Jews. Most left for the south. The remaining Jews in E. were arrested and deported on 9 March 1943 and 9 March 1944. The Nazis burned the synagogue in 1940. It was reconstructed in 1958. In the 1960s, the community consisted of 240 members.

EPPELSHEIM Hesse, Germany. The community, numbering 70 (5% of the total) in 1828, disbanded in 1935 and by Aug. 1939 no Jews remained.

EPPERTSHAUSEN Hesse, Germany. The community, numbering 63 (7.3% of the total) in 1828, later declined. The Nazis received only 5% of local votes in July 1932, but all the Jews (numbering 28 in 1933) fled after *Kristallnacht* (9–10 Nov. 1938).

EPPINGEN Baden, Germany. The J. settlement was founded in the first half of the 14th cent. and destroyed in the Black Death persecutions of 1348–49. Settlement was renewed in 1381 and a limited J. presence was maintained over the next few centuries. A cemetery was opened in 1738 and a synagogue built in 1772 while a J. elementary school was established in 1835 and a new synagogue dedicated in 1873. The J. pop. reached 222 in 1842 (7% of the total), with most Jews trading in cattle and tobacco. It declined to 124 in 1900 and 60 in 1933. Under Nazi rule, emigration accelerated, with 39 of the 53 Jews who left the town moving in 1937–39, including 20 who emigrated from Germany. The synagogue was burned on *Kristallnacht* (9–10 Nov. 1938). The last four Jews were deported to the Gurs concentration camp on 22 Oct. 1940.

ERBENDORF Upper Palatinate, Germany. The J. pop. in 1933 was 23 (total 1,782); 16 emigrated in 1933–39, four left for other German cities, and three were expelled to Piaski near Lublin in April 1942.

ERBESBUEDESHEIM Hesse, Germany. Numbering only 39 (4.7% of the total) in 1880, the community had its own synagogue and burial ground. Only eight Jews remained in 1933; practically all left by 1939.

ERCSI Fejer dist., Hungary. Jews are mentioned in 1778. In 1880, they founded Hungary's largest sugar refinery. A J. school existed in E. In 1930, the J. pop. was 140. All were deported to Auschwitz via Szekesfehervar on 18 June 1944.

ERD Fejer dist., Hungary. Jews settled under the Turks. In 1940, they numbered 180. All were deported by the Germans to Auschwitz on 5 June 1944 via Szekesfehervar.

ERDOBENYE Zemplen dist., Hungary. Jews settled in the early 18th cent., achieving fame as winegrowers. The J. pop. was 332 in 1880 and 153 in 1930. On 25 May–3 June 1944, the Jews were deported by the Germans to Auschwitz via Satoraljaujhely.

ERFELDEN Hesse, Germany. Twenty-five Jews were living there in 1828, but the community was not established until 1875, when it numbered around 50 (6% of the total). Most Jews left before 1937.

ERFURT Saxony, Germany. There was J. settlement in E. from the second half of the 12th century. The flourishing community maintained two synagogues, a *mikve*, a cemetery, a yeshiva, and several famous rabbis. From the mid-14th cent. the synods of the rabbis of Thuringia and Saxony took place in E. and members of the community were *shofar* makers for all Germany. During the Black Death persecutions of 1348–49, rioters murdered 100 out of 976 Jews. Many others committed suicide, by setting fire to their own houses. In 1453–54, the Jews were forced to leave the town, and it was not until 1768 that they were again allowed to trade and live temporarily in E. The modern J. settlement was established at the beginning of the 19th cent. A synagogue and cemetery were established and the community grew to 191 members in 1853; to 479 in 1860; and to 782 in 1900. The community maintained a religious school from about 1860 and a cemetery from 1873. A synagogue was established in 1884. There were also several welfare associations, a local branch of the Central Union (C.V.), and a J. History and Literature Society (1928). Jews played an important role in the city's economic development, by setting up clothing, wool, shoe, and malt factories. There were also numerous J. lawyers and physicians. Three Jews were members of the city council. Willy Muenzenberg (1889–1941), a Communist member of the Reichstag (1924–33), was born in E. In the 1920s, systematic antisemitic propaganda inspired attacks on Jews and their property. In 1933, the J. pop. of E. was 831 (0.6% of the total) and included a large number of immigrants from Eastern Europe. In April 1933, J. stores were boycotted and in July, two J. Communists were murdered. Emigration began and by 1936 the J. pop. dropped to 660. From 1937, the 100 stores and businesses still remaining in J. hands were subject to an extensive boycott. Some 100 Jews with non-German citizenship were deported to Poland in Oct. 1938. On *Kristallnacht* (9–10 Nov. 1938), the synagogue was set on fire and the chapel at the cemetery destroyed. The Nazis arrested and maltreated 197 Jews with ten men requiring hospitalization. Others were interned in the Buchenwald concentration camp. In Sept. 1941, 188 Jews still lived in E. In

four transports to the east, between May 1942 and Jan. 1944, 152 were deported, with four individuals committing suicide beforehand. Of those left in E. – probably owing to marriage to non-Jews – 18 were deported to the Theresienstadt ghetto in Jan. 1945. In 1946, a new J. community was established with 120 members. In the early 1950s, this was the largest community after Berlin in East Germany (GDR). A new synagogue was consecrated in 1952, but in 1988, the community had just 30 members.

ERKELENZ Rhineland, Germany. Four Jews were present in 1346. All were massacred in the Black Death persecutions of 1348–49 and only in the mid-19th cent. did Jews settle again. In 1855, they numbered six. In 1862, a synagogue was opened in a rented house and in 1865 a J. cemetery was consecrated. The synagogue was moved to a community building in 1869. In 1905, the J. pop. peaked at 83. By then, Jews owned all the large stores in E. dealing in textiles and fruit. In June 1933 the J. pop. was 52. On *Kristall-*

nacht (9–10 Nov. 1938), the synagogue was vandalized along with J. homes and stores. J. men were sent to the Sachsenhausen concentration camp. By May 1939, 31 Jews were left, several of them still managing to emigrate. In April 1941, 15 Jews were moved to a "J. house" in Hetzerath. Most were deported to Izbica in the Lublin dist. (Poland) in 1943; a few were sent to forced labor camps.

ERLANGEN Middle Franconia, Germany. Jews are first mentioned in 1432 and were expelled in 1515 in the general expulsion from the principality. Jews studied at E. University from the early 19th cent. and later taught there, with the physician Jakob Herz (d. 1871) becoming the first J. professor in Bavaria in 1863. However, the modern community was only organized in 1873, numbering 239 in 1890 (of a total 17,559) and 130 in 1933. Under Nazi rule, Jews suffered from the economic boycott and on *Kristallnacht* (9–10 Nov. 1938), all who remained were arrested. The men were held in the Nuremberg prison for six weeks.

Jews in detention during Kristallnacht, *Erlangen, Germany (Bildarchiv Preussischer Kulturbesitz/photo courtesy of Yad Vashem, The Holocaust Martyrs' and Heroes' Remembrance Authority, Jerusalem)*

looted and vandalized J. property; and, after being paraded through the street, J. men were imprisoned in concentration camps. Of the 535 Jews registered there after 1933, 222 emigrated (chiefly to the U.S., Latin America, and Palestine); the last 190 were deported in 1941–42. After WWII, most of the J. Displaced Persons housed in a local United Nations Relief and Rehabilitation Administration (UNRRA) camp emigrated to Israel.

ESCHWEILER Rhineland, Germany. Jews are first mentioned in 1750. The J. pop. grew to 30 individuals in 1806 and reached a peak of 166 in 1885. A J. elementary school was opened in 1858 and a synagogue was consecrated in 1891. A cemetery is mentioned already in 1820. Community institutions maintained an Orthodox character. A Zionist association was active already in 1911, whereas a branch of the Central Union (C.V.) was opened only in 1922. In June 1933, about four months after the Nazi assumption of power, 107 Jews were living in E., and 92 in 1936. On *Kristallnacht* (9–10 Nov. 1938), SA troops set the synagogue on fire, J. stores were wrecked, and J. men were sent to the Oranienburg concentration camp. Forty Jews subsequently left the city. Out of a total of about 70 who left in the 1933–41 period, half relocated in Germany, 13 reached Palestine, and 20 crossed the sea. The last 20 Jews were deported to ghettoes in the east: 15 on 22 March 1942; two on 15 June; and three on 25 July.

ESENS Hanover, Germany. East Friesland's ruling house allowed Jews from Emden to settle there in 1637, and by 1702 they had a prayer house and a burial ground. Numbering 87 in 1744 and 124 (6% of the total) in 1840, the community also drew members from Westeraccumersiel and other small villages. The community, affiliated with the Emden rabbinate, maintained a religious school from 1680 to 1927, dedicated a synagogue in 1828, and built a new community center in 1899. J. town councilors were elected after WWI. After Hitler's accession to power in 1933, the economic boycott—directed mainly against J. cattle dealers—forced more than half of the 82 Jews to leave before Nov. 1938. On *Kristallnacht* (9–10 Nov. 1938), local Nazis burned the synagogue and dispatched all J. men to the Sachsenhausen concentration camp. More than 50 Jews from E. managed to emigrate, primarily to Argentina and the

U.S. At least 40 perished in Nazi camps (20 in Auschwitz).

ESSEN Rhineland, Germany. Jews are first mentioned in 1291, living under the protection of the local monastery. They were expelled from the city during the Black Death persecutions of 1348–49 following a well-poisoning libel. By the end of the cent., they had resettled, all living around a single court (*Judenhof*) and earning their livelihoods as moneylenders. Over the next few hundred years, they continued to live under letters of protection issued by the mother superiors of the monastery. With the exception of the 1545–78 period, they were able to remain on monastery land even when expelled from within the city limits (as in 1437, 1495, and 1648). In 1578, the J. settlement was renewed by the Gottschalk family, whose descendants resided in the city until the Nazi era. Under French rule in the early 19th cent., the Jews were accorded equal rights. They subsequently participated in the revolutionary events of 1848 and gained the support of the municipal council in their struggle for emancipation. The city's liberal atmosphere and industrial development attracted large numbers of Jews, mainly from Westphalia. The J. pop. thus grew from 222 in 1836 to 832 in 1871 and 1,500 (total 103,010) in 1895. Jews came to occupy key positions in the city's public, cultural, and economic life. When the gates of the local university were thrown open, many were able to study medicine, law, and engineering. In trade, the Jews were prominent in the clothing industry but also ran banks and department and furniture stores. Wealthy Jews were philanthropists and patrons of the arts and Jews sat on the municipal council. Toward the end of the 19th cent., the composition of the J. pop. began to change as East European Jews arrived in the city. They engaged in petty trade and peddling or worked in industry or the mines. Their appearance and ways made them a ready target for local antisemites and within the J. community itself created a large social gap. By 1805, a synagogue was in use. A new one in the Moorish style was consecrated in 1870. In 1913, a magnificent edifice seating 1,400 was completed, one of the most beautiful synagogues in Germany. Towered and domed, it was styled after the Temple in Jerusalem. A J. school was founded in 1830, reaching an enrollment of 264 in 1915. The educator Moses Blumenfeld (1821–1902) became its guiding spirit and a leading figure in the city. Dr. Salomon Samuel became rabbi

Synagogue in Essen, Germany

in 1894, serving 38 years. The community maintained extensive social and welfare services. Central Union (C.V.) and Hilfsverein branches were opened in 1903. The Zionists became active in 1904 and Agudat Israel in 1914. The J. pop. continued to grow, reaching 2,773 in 1910 and 4,504 in 1925 (total 629,564). In the latter year, there were 1,173 Jews of East European origin, constituting a reservoir of Zionist support and religious Orthodoxy. Among the Zionist groups were Mizrachi and Ha-Po'el ha-Tza'ir. In the Weimar period, over half the Jews were still engaged in trade. The Ha-Ko'ah sports organization had a membership of 800 in 1925, making it the largest J. sports club in western Germany.

Antisemitism intensified in the 1920s, with efforts at boycotts, incidents of vandalism and violence, and even a blood libel. In the March 1933 Reichstag elections, the Nazis received a third of the local vote. Arrests, beatings, and murders followed. Jews were sent to the Oranienburg concentration camp while anti-J. riots broke out in the city's cattle market. J. butchers were excluded from the municipal slaughterhouse; J. civil servants were dismissed; J. doctors and lawyers lost their means of livelihood; and Jews were disqualified as municipal suppliers. Jews were also fired from their jobs in the private sector, including those working for the Krupp Co., among them Prof. Benno Strauss (1873–1944), inventor of stainless steel. By 1938, 80% of J. businesses had been "Aryanized." Emigration was stepped up, mainly among the young and East European Jews, many leaving for Palestine. The community geared itself to the new situation, maintaining cultural and social services and setting up bodies to prepare its members for emigration through vocational retraining and foreign language courses (Hebrew, English, etc.). The Central Union maintained its regional office for the Rhineland and Westphalia in E., offering legal and economic services. For the Zionists, WIZO,

The last family of six Jews was deported to the Gurs concentration camp in Oct. 1940.

ETTLINGEN   Baden, Germany. A J. settlement existed in the early 14th cent. It was destroyed in the Black Death persecutions of 1348–49 and renewed in 1526. The community was expelled in 1584 as part of the general expulsions in Baden and again in 1614. Few Jews lived there between the Thirty Years War (1618–48) and the early 18th cent. and a few dozen (1% of the total) during the 19th cent. A small synagogue was built in 1849 and a larger one in 1889. Jews ran a big paper factory. In 1910 the J. pop. reached 75, with 48 remaining in 1933 and 31 joining the community later. Of the former, 16 emigrated, six left for other German cities, and 14 were expelled (seven to the Gurs concentration camp and seven to Poland). Of the latter, eight emigrated and 21 left for other German cities. The synagogue was burned down on *Kristallnacht* (9–10 Nov. 1938).

EUBIGHEIM   Baden, Germany. Jews were allowed to settle after the Thirty Years War (1618–48) to rebuild the village. Their numbers increased in the 17th and 18th cents. with an influx of Jews expelled from Wuerzburg. A synagogue was built in 1850 and a cemetery was consecrated in the 1880s. The J. pop. reached a peak of 96 in 1887 (15% of the total) and thereafter declined steadily to 39 in 1933. By July 1938, 23 had emigrated to the U.S. as did the last five in Feb. 1939. Two were trapped in Holland and sent to Auschwitz.

EUERBACH   Lower Franconia, Germany. A J. community existed in the early 17th cent. and numbered 68 in 1816 (total 463). Few Jews remained in the 20th cent. The cemetery was destroyed by Hitler Youth in Nov. 1938 and the four J. women remaining in E. in 1942 were deported to Izbica in the Lublin dist. (Poland) and to the Theresienstadt ghetto.

EUSKIRCHEN   Rhineland, Germany. Jews were living on their own street in 1349; they were murdered in the same year during the Black Death persecutions. In 1420, they were again present there. In the 17th cent., the princes of the Palatinate allotted letters of protection to three to five J. families. Jews were employed primarily as butchers; two were moneylenders. In 1784, a J. merchant ran a lottery. In the early 19th cent., with the development of the local cloth industry under the Prussians, Jews opened knitting mills. By 1847, six of the 15 J. breadwinners were employed in the cloth industry and five were butchers. By the end of the 19th cent., the city mills were filling a third of the Prussian army's cloth orders. However, J. prominence in the trade came to an end when the local Wolf family set up its mills in Belgium in the same period. The J. pop. rose from 50 in 1825 to 153 in 1875 and 255 (total 12,776) in 1911. In 1906, 13 of the city's 14 livestock dealers were Jews as well as nine of its 35 butchers. Jews were active in the social and political life of the city. Six Jews fought in the Franco-Prussian war of 1870–71 and in 1887, there was a J. assemblyman in the city for the first time. In 1847, E. became the seat of a regional congregation with the communities of Weilerswist, Wisskirchen, Lommersum, and Grossbuellesheim attached to it. A synagogue – the first in the region – was consecrated in 1856. In 1886, it burned down; a new one was built in 1887. A J. elementary school was attended by 34–43 children in the 1874–1913 period. The community remained Orthodox. Ezra, the Agudat Israel youth movement, was active in 1909. Four J. families of Polish origin arrived in the city in 1919–20, establishing themselves as successful shopkeepers within ten years. A Central Union (C.V.) branch with 60 members was opened in 1920. In 1933, the J. pop. was 231. In 1934, under the Nazis, four J. businesses were forced to close down and J. livestock dealers began losing their customers. Another five J. businesses closed in 1935 and two more were "Aryanized" in 1936. In the latter year, the last J. student was expelled from the local boys' secondary school. Eight Jews of Polish origin were expelled from the city in late Oct. 1938. In the first ten months of 1939, 16 additional J. business establishments were liquidated. Throughout the period, J. life was maintained in the community, owing largely to the activities of the Zionists, who organized lectures and study groups in J. and Zionist history. Both Hehalutz and B'rit ha-No'ar were active. In the 1933–38 period, 103 Jews left the city. On *Kristallnacht* (9–10 Nov. 1938), the synagogue was set on fire, the J. cemetery was desecrated, and J. stores were destroyed. Remaining J. property was sold off in the following months and the last eight J. businesses were liquidated in June 1939. Jews were mobilized for forced labor, doing farm and road work. In May 1941, 87 Jews remained. These were moved to eight "J. houses." A total of 178 Jews left

the city in the Nazi era (with 60 arriving from other places), including 17 for Holland, 13 for England, 12 for Rhodesia, and six for Palestine. Ninety-five of the emigrants moved to other German cities, including 56 to Cologne. The deportation of those who remained began in summer 1942 when 42 were transported to the Theresienstadt ghetto via Cologne on 14–15 June. Another 33 were deported on 6 or 7 July, seven more on 19 July, and the last five on an unknown date. In addition, 14 local Jews were deported from other German cities, seven from Holland, and one from Belgium. In all, 112 perished.

EYDTKUHNEN (Rus. Chernyshevskoye) East Prussia, Germany, today Russia. The J. community numbered 347 in 1880. It maintained a synagogue built in 1870 and a cemetery. Since E. was one of the main border crossing points through which the masses of East European emigrants passed on their way westward from the 1880s to the eve of WWI, the Association of East Prussian Communities established an office here for the care of poor J. emigrants. A considerable number of community members were themselves immigrants from Eastern Europe and at times threatened by expulsion. On the eve of WWI, the J. pop. had already dropped to about 200, and by 1925 the community comprised only about 120 individuals. The synagogue was destroyed on *Kristallnacht* (9–10 Nov. 1938). No information is available about the fate of the Jews under Nazi rule.

Marcus Koplanski and his family, Eydtkuhnen, East Prussia, Germany, 1931 (Beth Hatefutsoth Photo Archive, Tel Aviv/courtesy of Ya'acov Hinden, Israel)

F

FABIANHAZA Szatmar dist., Hungary. Jews settled c. 1800. Most were artisans or traded in farm produce. They numbered 156 in 1900 and 86 in 1930. The community maintained a synagogue, yeshiva, and *talmud torah*. In April 1944, the Jews were expelled to Mateszalka, which held 18,000 Jews from the area. In late May, deportations to Auschwitz began.

FAGARAS (Hung. Fogaras) S. Transylvania dist., Rumania. A J. community was established in 1827 and by the mid-19th cent. was the largest in S. Transylvania. The first rabbi, Yehuda Silbermann (1855-63), kept a diary of communal events (still extant and referred to as the "Fagaras Diary") that served as a source for the history of Transylvanian Jewry. In 1869, the F. community joined the Neologist association. A J. school opened in the 1860s. The J. pop. in 1856 came to 286, rising to 390 (5% of the total) in 1930. During WWII, the local German pop., together with Iron Guard Legionnaires, attacked Jews and plundered their property. Sixty Jews were sent to forced labor. After the liberation many left for larger cities or immigrated to Palestine.

FAGET (Hung. Facsad; previously Facsed), S. Transylvania dist., Rumania. Sephardi and Ashkenazi Jews, both from Moravia, first settled in the mid-18th cent., organizing a community which defined itself as Neologist in the 19th cent. A synagogue was consecrated in 1897. Community members were particularly wealthy and were active in local politics. The J. pop. in 1930 was 89 (3% of the total). In Sept. 1940, the Iron Guard confiscated J. property and the men were sent to the Targu-Jiu labor camp. The Jews left after the war.

FALCIU Moldavia dist., Rumania. Jews first settled in the mid-18th cent. In the 1907 revolt, peasants destroyed the homes and stores of 64 J. families. After WWI, Jews from Bessarabia settled and traded in produce. Zionist activities were organized by the community council. From a peak of 220 in 1899, the J. pop. dropped to 154 (3% of the total) in 1930. In Aug. 1940, Jews began fleeing the persecution of Iron Guard Legionnaires and by Nov. no Jews remained. Those who fled to Bessarabia were murdered in summer 1941 when the area was reconquered by the Germans and Rumanians.

FALENICA Warsaw dist., Poland. Jews arrived there in the 1880s, founded a community around 1900, and — as the resort town expanded — their number grew to 1,108 (63% of the total) in 1921. Avraham Moshe Kalish of Warka established a hasidic court there. Agudat Israel, the Bund, and Zionist parties were active. By 1939 the J. pop. had reached 2,000. Following the German occupation (19 Sept. 1939), a *Judenrat* was set up, conditions worsening after the invasion of Russia (June 1941). The ghetto, into which 6,500 Jews had been packed, was liquidated (18 Aug. 1942) and most of its inhabitants were deported to the Treblinka death camp. A few were hidden by Polish neighbors or joined the partisans.

FALESTI Bessarabia, Rumania, today Republic of Moldova. Jews first settled in the late 18th cent. In 1918 they were granted land for agriculture. The J. pop. in 1930 was 3,258 (51% of the total). The community had seven synagogues and the Great Synagogue was considered to be especially beautiful. Gordonia, the leading Zionist youth movement in F., closed its doors in 1937. Under Soviet rule (1940-41), Zionist leaders and wealthy Jews were sent to Siberia. On 21 June 1941, Jews were killed in the Ger-

man bombardment. Those who fled across the Dniester River were caught in air raids or shot by advancing German troops or the local peasants. The Rumanian troops and peasants killed and robbed Jews and ghettoized the remainder. The aged and children were murdered in the vicinity of Odessa. Another group was marched to Transnistria, where most died.

FALKENBERG Hesse–Nassau, Germany. Established before 1750, the J. community opened a regional elementary school (transferred to Homberg in 1909), had members in the village of Hebel, and numbered 84 (19% of the total) in 1871. On *Kristallnacht* (9–10 Nov. 1938), the synagogue was destroyed. Of the 27 Jews who lived there in 1933, eight emigrated; at least eight more perished in the Holocaust.

FALKENBURG (Pol. Zlocieniec) Pomerania, Germany, today Poland. A Jew was present in 1720 but a community only developed in the 19th cent., consecrating a synagogue in 1841. There were 121 members in 1880. In 1881, riots in Pomerania, sparked by an arson attack on the Neustettin synagogue, led to attacks against J. property. When the Nazis came to power in 1933, the community numbered 12 tax-paying members. On *Kristallnacht* (9–10 Nov. 1938), the synagogue was burned down. Jews who did not manage to escape abroad were probably deported to the east. By Oct. 1942, there was only one Jew still living in F., probably protected by marriage to a non-Jew. Rudolf Katz, whose family came from F., served as West German minister of justice and vice-president of the Federal Constitutional Court.

FALKENSTEIN (I) Hesse–Nassau, Germany. Jews lived in F. before they were expelled during the Black Death persecutions of 1348–49. From the 15th cent. on there was intermittent settlement of Jews which became permanent in the 18th cent. The community maintained a cemetery from 1754 and its synagogue also served the neighboring community of Koenigstein, to which it was affiliated. The Jews in F. numbered 23 in 1843, 31 in 1871, and 15 on the eve of the Nazi rise to power. They shared the fate of their brethren in Koenigstein.

FALKENSTEIN (II) Saxony, Germany. A small J. settlement existed in the 19th cent., numbering 15 individuals in 1903. The community, which was affiliated

Synagogue in Falkenstein (Hesse-Nossau), Germany

to the Plauen community, grew due to immigration of Jews from the Austro-Hungarian territories. The Orthodox Jews in the community maintained their own prayer room for several years. In 1933, the community numbered 102. When the Nazis murdered a young Jew after 1933, 20 Jews immediately left the town. In Oct. 1938, 20 Jews of non-German citizenship were deported to Poland. After the *Kristallnacht* riots (9–10 Nov. 1938), several Jews still managed to emigrate. Of the 13 Jews still living in F. in 1939, most were probably deported in 1941. Two Jews married to non-Jews survived.

FALTICENI Moldavia dist., Rumania. Jews founded F. under a privilege granted in 1780 by Prince Constantin Moruzi. This was the first town in Rumania founded by Jews under privileges granted by princes. Moruzi was so satisfied with his J. settlers that he granted Jews in other small towns similar privileges. Jews exported lumber and hides but the majority were artisans. A J. hospital was founded in 1857. Eleven synagogues functioned in F., including separate ones for members of different trades. Despite objections from Orthodox circles, a J. school was opened in 1866, but closed after two years. A *talmud torah* (opened in 1874) had 300 pupils in 1896. Another J. school was opened in 1897 (after the authorities closed all the *hadarim*) with 350 pupils. The J. pop. in 1899 was 5,499 (57% of the total). A school for girls opened in 1899 with 168 pupils. Zionist activity began at the turn of the century. Jews suffered greatly during the economic crisis after WWI and many left. Antisemitsm was widespread between the World Wars and in 1936

the Iron Guard ransacked J. stores. In 1941, the Germans sent 1,000 J. males (including those brought there from Lespezi and Liteni) to forced labor in Bessarabia. Many Jews made their way to Palestine, with some drowning on the ill-fated ship *Struma*. Others were drafted into labor battalions and sent to distant sites. With the approach of the Soviet army in 1944, the entire pop. was evacuated with most of the Jews fleeing to Botosani and Suceava. Only 3,700 returned. They found their property had been stolen. After considerable difficulty, the Jews succeeded in rehabilitating the community and its various institutions.

FANCIKOVO (Hung. Fancsika) Carpatho-Russia, Czechoslovakia, today Ukraine. J. settlement commenced in the early 19th cent. The J. pop. was 104 in 1830 and 124 in 1880, then declined to 114 (total 882) in 1921 and 96 in 1941. The Hungarians occupied F. in Nov. 1938 and in 1941 drafted several Jews into forced labor battalions. In Aug. 1941, a few families were expelled to the German-occupied Ukraine and

murdered. The rest were deported to Auschwitz in the second half of May 1944.

FARAD Sopron dist., Hungary. Permanent J. settlement commenced in the 18th cent., reaching a peak pop. of 146 in 1831 and dwindling to a few dozen by the early 20th cent. A synagogue was established in 1810. The nine remaining families were confined to the Csorna ghetto in May 1944 and deported to Auschwitz on 5 July.

FARKASD Slovakia, Czechoslovakia, today Republic of Slovakia. Jews probably settled in the 1830s, consecrating a cemetery in the 1880s and a synagogue at the end of the cent. The community also maintained a J. school combining secular and religious studies. The J. pop. was 177 (total 5,289) in 1900 and 147 in 1941. Between the World Wars, Jews owned a dozen grocery and general stores and seven taverns. The Zionists, Agudat Israel, and the J. National Party were all active. After the annexation to Hungary in Nov. 1938,

Funeral procession for Jewish victims of White Terror pogrom under General Denikin, Fastow, Ukraine

Jews were persecuted and seized for forced labor. On 10 May 1944, 111 Jews from F. and its environs were deported to Auschwitz via Shale and Nove Zamky.

FARSALA (Pharsala) Thessaly Greece. A small J. settlement in the mid-19th cent., F. numbered only three Jews in 1928. After WWII, the sole surviving Jew from F. stated that there had been 25 J. families there prior to the Holocaust.

FASTOW Kiev dist., Ukraine. The J. pop. was 381 in 1765 and 5,595 in 1897. In the late 18th cent., J. property was pillaged and destroyed in Haidamak attacks. In the 19th cent., many Jews engaged in crafts and in farming. Three J. agricultural colonies were founded nearby: Kadlovitskaya, Chervonnaya, and Obershovaya. In Sept. 1919, Anton Denikin's White Army soldiers murdered 1,000 Jews, raped women, and looted property. The three J. colonies were totally destroyed but in the Soviet period, they were rebuilt and many Jews went back to living and working in them. In 1926, 80% of local artisans were Jews and in 1939 the J. pop. was 2,149. The Germans occupied F. on 20 July 1941, murdering 262 Jews in Aug. A few days later, another 50 were executed. By the end of the year most F. Jews were dead.

FAULQUEMONT Moselle dist., France. Until the Napoleonic era, Jews were forbidden to reside here. The local synagogue was inaugurated in 1900. In 1940, the Germans destroyed the synagogue and the cemetery was damaged. After liberation, the synagogue was reconstructed. In 1965, there were 50 Jews living in F.

FECHENBACH Lower Franconia, Germany. Jews were present in the early 18th cent. and numbered 70 in 1837 (total 850). In 1933, 11 remained, nine of them leaving in 1937 for other German cities.

FEDOROVKA Tula dist., Russia. The Germans occupied F. in Oct. 1941, pillaging property on 7 Dec. and afterwards murdering a few dozen Jews from F. and the surrounding villages.

FEGERSHEIM Bas-Rhin dist., France. In 1784, the J. community comprised 175 members. By 1807, it increased to 262 and in 1844 to 475 members. Afterwards the community dwindled. The local synagogue was inaugurated in 1850. In 1885, the community numbered 337 members. In 1926, the J. pop. was 126 and in 1931 it was 83. During WWII, the Germans expelled all to the south of France. In 1965, eight Jews were living in F.

FEGYVERNEK Jasz–Nagykun–Szolnok dist., Hungary. Jews settled in the first half of the 19th cent., forming a Neologist congregation in 1869 and maintaining a synagogue and school. The J. pop. of 237 in 1880 began dropping after WWI, reaching 85 in 1930 owing to emigration to the big cities and a declining birthrate. White Terror gangs took over F. in 1920, robbing and beating Jews. In 1941, government orders halted the activities of a small group of Zionists. In the beginning of June 1944, the Jews were brought to Szolnok, from where they were deported on 26 June 1944 to Auschwitz. Thirty survivors reestablished the community, but most left for Israel after 1948.

FEHERGYARMAT Szatmar dist., Hungary. Jews arrived in the late 18th cent., marketing local farm produce and making F. a commercial center for 42 surrounding settlements. The economic ascendancy of the Jews over the nobility was a source of antisemitic hatred. The Orthodox congregation exercised jurisdiction over numerous smaller communities and maintained a synagogue, *beit midrash*, and J. school. The J. pop. was 455 in 1900 and 679 in 1930, with Jews severely abused in the White Terror following WWI. Many left at this time for Canada and the U.S. On 17 April 1944, the Jews were expelled to Mateszalka and from 19 May to June 5 deported to Auschwitz. Of the 84 survivors who reestablished the community, 23 left for Israel in 1948. By 1962, there were no Jews left in F.

FELEDINCE (Hung. Feled) Slovakia, Czechoslovakia, today Republic of Slovakia. Jews settled in the mid-19th cent. and numbered about 70 in the 20th cent. (5% of the total). A synagogue was built in 1926. Persecution commenced with the annexation of F. to Hungary in Nov. 1938 as Jews were pushed out of work and mobilized for forced labor. In May 1944, after the Germans arrived, the Jews were sent to the Rimavska Sobota ghetto and from there to Miskolc and on to Auschwitz in June.

FELLHEIM Swabia, Germany. Five J. families were among the settlers who rebuilt the village in

Jews remained. On *Kristallnacht* (9–10 Nov. 1938), the synagogue and three J. stores were destroyed. No information on the fate of the community in WWII is available. Presumably those who did not emigrate to safety perished after deportation.

FEUCHTWANGEN (in J. sources, Vahtvank) Middle Franconia, Germany. Jews were present in the second half of the 13th cent. The community was destroyed in the Black Death persecutions of 1348–49 and reestablished soon after. In the early 17th cent., F. was the temporary seat of the chief rabbinate of the Ansbach principality and the home of one of its most prosperous J. communities. A new synagogue was erected in 1833 and the J. pop. rose to 170 in 1867 (total 2,345). Thereafter it declined steadily to 39 in 1933. By May 1938 all had left the town, most to other German cities. On *Kristallnacht* (9–10 Nov. 1938), the synagogue was burned to the ground.

FEUDENHEIM Baden, Germany. The J. pop. in 1860 was 125, and the community maintained a synagogue and elementary school. The synagogue was de-

Street in the Jewish ghetto, Feuchtwangen, Germany, 1926

stroyed on *Kristallnacht* (9–10 Nov. 1938). The last 14 Jews were deported by the Germans to the Gurs concentration camp on 22 Oct. 1940.

FILAKOVO (Hung. Fulek) Slovakia, Czechoslovakia, today Republic of Slovakia. Jews probably settled in the 1830s. The community was officially recognized in 1872, becoming the seat of a regional rabbinate with about 30 settlements attached to it. The historian R. Dr. Shemuel (Alexander) Buechler (1869–1944) was born in F. The J. pop. rose to 165 (total 1,692) in 1869 and then maintained a level of 200–250 in the 20th cent. Most of the town's business establishments were in J. hands. Agudat Israel became active in 1913 and the Zionists began to operate after WWI, with Bnei Akiva attracting dozens of youngsters in the 1930s. After the annexation of Slovakia to Hungary in Nov. 1938, Jews were mobilized for forced labor. When the Germans arrived in March 1944, there were 154 Jews remaining in F. They were confined in a ghetto in late May and on 13 June deported to Auschwitz.

FILEA (Hung. Fulehaz) N. Transylvania dist., Rumania. Jews settled around the early 19th cent. The J. pop. in 1930 was 106 (5% of the total). In May 1944, the community was transferred to the Reghin ghetto and in June deported to Auschwitz.

FILIPEC (Hung. Fulopfalva) Carpatho-Russia, Czechoslovakia, today Ukraine. J. refugees from Galicia settled in the early 19th cent. In 1830, the J. pop. was 38, rising to 78 (total 595) in 1880. A few Jews were farmers and one owned a flour mill. The J. pop. was 124 in 1921 and 110 in 1941. Following the Hungarian occupation in March 1939, J. men were drafted into forced labor battalions. In Aug. 1941, a number of J. families without Hungarian citizenship were expelled to Kamenets-Podolski and murdered. The rest were deported to Auschwitz in the second half of May 1944.

FILIPOW Bialystok dist., Poland. Jews settled in the 18th cent., reaching a pop. of 856 (total 2,457) in 1857. A synagogue and cemetery were consecrated in the mid-19th cent. The J. pop. dropped to 280 in 1921. All Jews were expelled by the Germans around early Nov. 1939, most reaching Lithuania or the Soviet Union. Few survived the Holocaust.

FIRLEJ Lublin dist., Poland. Jews were among the town's first residents in the 16th cent. and were granted a privilege of unlimited residence in 1664. However, until the 19th cent. the community did not grow. In 1921, the J. pop. was 180 (total 1,150). When the Germans arrived on 15 Sept. 1939, the pop. stood at 167. The Germans instituted a regime of forced labor and extortion. In April 1942, a ghetto was established, crowded with refugees. In Oct. 1942, all were sent to Lubartow for deportation to the Belzec and Sobibor death camps. Fifty young Jews escaped from Lubartow to the forest and engaged in effective partisan activity in the forests between Lublin and Parczew.

FISCHACH Swabia, Germany. A J. settlement existed in the last quarter of the 16th cent., augmented by Jews expelled from the Burgau margravate in 1617. A synagogue was built in 1739 and in 1867 the community numbered 284 (total 720). R. Shimon Simha Bamberger served as the community's last rabbi (1856–82), after which it came under the auspices of the Ischenhausen district rabbinate. In 1933, 127 Jews remained. Among the organizations active were the Central Union (C.V.), Zionist Organization, Agudat Israel, and the Hilfsverein. On 10 Nov. 1938, 15 Jews were sent to the Dachau concentration camp. Only 40 left (35 emigrating) until 1940. The synagogue was converted into a sports arena shortly after *Kristallnacht* (9–10 Nov. 1938), and the last 65 Jews were deported in 1942: 56 to Piaski (Poland) via Munich on 3 April and nine to the Theresienstadt ghetto on 10 Aug.

Document securing synagogue land in 1730 under the name of Simon Muendle Burgau, Fischach, Germany

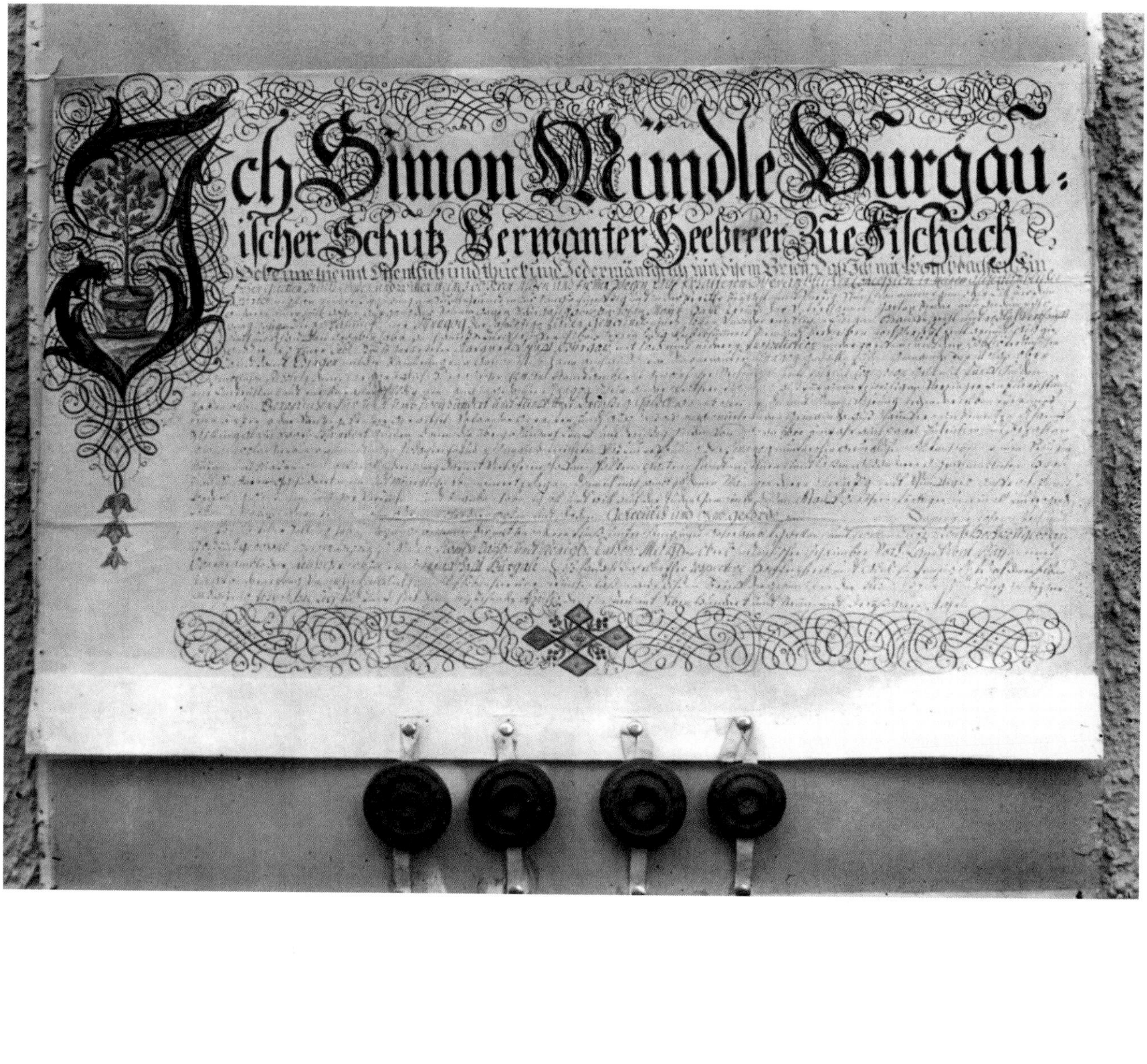
Ich Simon Mündle Burgau:
ischer Schutz Verwanter Heebrerr Zue Fischach

FISCHBORN Hesse–Nassau, Germany. Established in 1823, the community numbered 62 (14% of the total) in 1861, built a synagogue in 1868, and drew members from Kirchbracht and Mauswinkel. Most of the 20 Jews who remained in 1933 went to Frankfurt (1939–40); 11 perished in the Holocaust.

FLACHT Hesse–Nassau, Germany. Despite repeated efforts (1848–1914), Jews from Oberneisen, Niederneisen, and F. only managed to establish an independent community after WWI. Excluding members in Hanstaetten (14), they numbered 35 in 1925 and dedicated a new synagogue three years later. No more than a dozen remained on *Kristallnacht* (9–10 Nov. 1938), when the synagogue was destroyed. Eighteen perished in the Holocaust.

FLAMERSHEIM Rhineland, Germany. With the region regarded as a place of refuge, two J. families arrived in 1659. A cemetery was opened in 1828 and a synagogue in 1878. The J. pop. reached a peak of 100 (total 905) in 1900, dropping to 62 in 1932. On *Kristallnacht* (9–10 Nov. 1938), the synagogue was destroyed. Twenty-two Jews were deported to the east; 12 are known to have died.

FLATOW (Pol. Zlotow) Posen–West Prussia, Germany, today Poland. Jews are first mentioned in 1564. During the Swedish invasion (1655–57), the Poles executed a number of Jews on trumped-up charges of collaboration with the enemy. Many of the 107 Jews lost their homes in the wake of a fire in 1674, but in 1690 they managed to establish a synagogue and a cemetery. By 1774, the Jews constituted 55% of the pop. in F. In 1846, they were 22% of the pop. and numbered 564. In 1854, the J. pop. was 609; in 1880, 524. In the following decades, the community steadily declined due to various factors including extreme antisemitism. On the eve of the Nazi assumption of power in 1933, there were 186 Jews living in F., most engaged in trade. They suffered greatly from the April 1933 boycott. On *Kristallnacht* (9–10 Nov. 1938), the synagogue was destroyed, J. businesses were demolished, and the men were taken to the Sachsenhausen concentration camp. Those remaining after the outbreak of war were interned by the Nazis in March 1940 in the Buergergarten camp near Schneidemuehl. They were deported to the east shortly afterwards.

FLEHINGEN Baden, Germany. Jews are first mentioned in 1548 and were among the new settlers after the village was destroyed in the Thirty Years War (1618–48). In the Nine Years War (1689–1697), a single Jew remained in the village on the approach of the French. The community grew to a peak of 160 in 1827 (total 1,143). The 16th cent. J. cemetery served the surrounding communities for hundreds of years and in 1874 a synagogue was constructed. A. J. elementary school was opened in 1841. Anti-J. riots broke out during the 1848 revolution. In 1933, 59 Jews remained. By 1938, all J. businesses had been liquidated. At least 40 Jews emigrated. The synagogue was burned down on *Kristallnacht* (9–10 Nov. 1938), and 18 Jews were deported, all but one perishing, including 11 in Auschwitz.

FLENSBURG Schleswig–Holstein, Germany. Fifteen Jews were living there in 1835 and at its peak in 1900, the community numbered 89 Jews, dropping to 61 in 1925 and 44 in 1933. The community dedicated a synagogue in the 1870s. The Zionists became active in 1900. A teacher provided religious instruction for the community's 15 J. children. It was, however, too poor to acquire its own cemetery. After the Nazi rise to power, the Zionists set up a Hehalutz training center at the Wolff family estate on the outskirts of the town. Mostly recruited from Liberal families in other parts of Germany, the 46 youngsters had no contact with local Jews until *Kristallnacht* (9–10 Nov. 1938), when they were attacked and J. property in F. and at the training center was destroyed. Only three Jews remained in F. by May 1939; some center trainees succeeded in arriving in Palestine.

FLIEDEN Hesse–Nassau, Germany. Dating from the 16th cent., the community was expelled in 1671 but revived and grew to 25 families in 1790. The Jews opened a school in 1878 and a new synagogue in 1885. They numbered 86 (6% of the total) in 1895 and 63 in 1933. Religiously Orthodox, they maintained good relations with their anti-Nazi Catholic neighbors. By May 1938, however, 55 Jews had left (24 emigrating). One elderly couple remained after the synagogue was vandalized on *Kristallnacht* (9–10 Nov. 1938); they were sent to a Nazi death camp in 1942.

FLOERSHEIM Hesse–Nassau, Germany. Jews settled there in the early 17th cent. and their synagogue

(dating from 1718) was the oldest in Nassau. Numbering 114 in 1842, the community declined to 45 (1% of the total) in 1905. Under the Weimar Republic, it drew members from neighboring villages and was affiliated with the rabbinate of Wiesbaden. Thirty Jews remained on *Kristallnacht* (9–10 Nov. 1938), when the synagogue was vandalized by SS troops from Ruesselsheim. Of the 45 Jews who left after 1933, 21 emigrated; ten perished in Nazi death camps.

FLONHEIM Hesse, Germany. Jews were living there by 1650, the community numbering 110 (6% of the total) in 1861 and 51 (3%) in 1933. Nazis looted J. homes and vandalized the synagogue on *Kristallnacht* (9–10 Nov. 1938), after which most of the remaining Jews emigrated.

FLORENCE (Ital. Firenze) Tuscany, Italy. Until the 13th cent., there is no evidence of a J. presence in F. In 1430, moneylenders were officially invited to reside in F. Communal life was organized in 1437. Families from Pisa, Tivoli, and Fano constituted the nucleus of the community. From 1439, the Jews had to wear the distinctive J. badge. The local pop. often demonstrated hostility towards the Jews. There were anti-J. demonstrations as well as pressure to expel them. Their protectors were the Medici family, which highly esteemed J. scholars and writers. In 1551, Cosimo I invited Levantine Jews to settle in F. in order to promote trade with the Levant. Various communal bodies developed for promoting mutual aid and education. The Italian and Levantine communities united in 1688, but their synagogues practiced different religious rites. In 1553, Cosimo I consented to the burning of the Talmud. Under Pius V, in 1567, the J. badge was introduced and in 1571, a ghetto was established, inhabited by 500 Jews. Engaged at first mainly in moneylending, the Jews of F. dealt later in textiles and precious stones.

Purim celebrations in the Florence ghetto, Italy, 1886 (Alinari, Italy/photo courtesy of Beth Hatefutsoth, Tel Aviv)

Members of the Levantine community were especially involved in international commerce. A Hebrew printing press operated in F. between 1734–36. By the second half of the 18th cent., Grand Duke Leopold conferred certain civil rights upon the Jews. Emancipation came with Napoleon's army in 1799. With the return of the Grand Dukes in 1814, the Jews continued to enjoy various rights. In 1828, a congress of the representatives of all Italian Jews was convened in F. Leopold II granted equality in 1848, but full civil rights were conferred upon the Jews of F. when Tuscany was incorporated into the Kingdom of Sardinia in 1859 and, two years later, into the Kingdom of Italy. In 1867, a second congress of J. communities was held in F. In 1873, the community numbered 1,460 members, growing to 2,400 in 1886. In 1875, the Istituto Convitto Campagnano school was established. The Great Temple, practicing the Sephardi rite, was inaugurated in 1882 and in 1899 the Rabbinical Seminary was transferred from Rome to F. Headed from 1888 by R. Shemuel Hirsch Margulies, the Seminary became a center of J. learning. Among its graduates were the renowned rabbis Raffaello della Pergola, Gustavo

Calo, Dario Disegni, Angelo Sacerdoti, Elia S. Artom, Gustavo Castelbolognesi, Aldo and Armando Sorani, and David Prato. By 1901, the community numbered 3,000 Jews. J. publications appearing in F. included *Rivista Israelitica* (1904–15); *Setimana Israelitica* (1910–15); *Israel* (from 1916), and *Rassegna Mensile di Israel* (from 1925). The last two were later issued in Rome. In 1908, a group of Margulies' disciples established the Pro Cultura Association. In the 1920s, the Zionists were active and a Zionist publication, *Cumune Ebraico*, was founded in F. in 1920. According to the 1930 law reforming the J. communities in Italy, F. was one of the 26 communities legally recognized by the Italian government. Its district included the communities of Siena, Arezzo, Prato (comprising 30 Jews in 1936), and Pistoia (18 Jews in 1925). In 1936, under R. Eugenio S. Artom, the community numbered 3,200 members. During WWII, on 6–7 Nov. 1943, the first group of about 200 local and foreign Jews was deported to Auschwitz. No one from this group survived the war. On 26 Nov. a second group was arrested and deported. On 6 June 1944, 16 Jews from the old age home were deported. The synagogue was vandalized.

Praying in a synagogue, Florence, Italy

A total of 248 local Jews were deported; eight were shot; four were baptized, and 34 foreign Jews were arrested in F. Four local Jews died heroically during underground activities. Only 13 survivors returned from the camps. After liberation, communal life gradually was reestablished. In 1948, the community numbered 1,500 members, reduced to 1,250 by 1970.

FLORINA Macedonia, Greece. A Sephardi community existed in F. in the 17th and 18th cents. J. settlement was renewed during the Balkan wars and WWI by Jews from Bitola (Monastir in Yugoslavia). The community, consisting of 100 families, was organized in 1914. A J. school was established in 1917 and a Zionist organization was then active. In 1921–22, when antisemitic outbreaks followed a government decision to change market day from Saturday to Wednesday, it was soon returned to Saturday. Fearing increased antisemitism and compelled to work on the Sabbath or suffer poverty, many Jews left F., mostly for Bitola. In 1925, 1926, and 1927 the Jews were victims of blood libels. By 1929, the community had dwindled to 293 members (total 10,585), rising to

about 400 by 1940. During WWII, many joined the Greek forces against the Italian invaders. In spring 1941, the Germans occupied F. and J. youths were sent to forced labor. In early 1943, a number of Jews joined the partisans and 60–70 fled to the surrounding hills and villages. On 30 April 1943, 372 Jews were arrested and deported to the Birkenau (Auschwitz) death camp via Salonika. After the war, 64 Jews returned to F. but by 1959 only seven remained.

FLOSS Upper Palatinate, Germany. Four J. families received residence rights in 1684, joined later by Jews from Bohemia, all settling in a quarter (*Judenberg*) outside the town. A synagogue was erected in 1722 and in 1744 the Jews received extensive trade privileges together with the Jews of Salzbach. In 1812, a J. public school was opened. In 1836 there were 40 J. stores in the *Judenberg*, mostly selling wool and cloth, and in 1840 the J. pop. reached 391 (total 1,914), dropping at mid.-cent. when 70 Jews emigrated to the U.S. This last ghetto in Germany was only opened in 1870. By 1933, only 19 were left in F. In 1937 the J. cemetery was desecrated and on *Kristallnacht* (9–10

Synagogue in Floss, Germany, before wwii

FORRO Abauj–Torna dist., Hungary. Jews settled in the early 19th cent., numbering 83 in 1880 and 57 in 1930, with many leaving as a result of the hostile atmosphere. They were deported to Auschwitz via Kassa between 14 May–2 June 1944.

FORST Brandenburg, Germany. A J. settlement dating from the beginning of the 16th cent. ended with expulsion in the 1530s. A permanent settlement started up in 1821. The 56 Jews in F. in 1880 belonged to the Guben community. In 1894, an independent district community, including neighboring localities, was organized. A prayer room and a cemetery were established and a preacher employed. In 1905, the community numbered 148, many of Polish origin. A synagogue was dedicated in 1914. In 1920, a massive antisemitic campaign was launched. When the Nazis came to power in 1933, there were 200 Jews in F. The community intensified its Zionist activities, setting up a local branch in 1933. By autumn 1938, Jews no longer owned any important businesses. At the end of Oct., at least 19 Jews were included in the deportation of the Jews of Polish citizenship. On *Kristallnacht* (9–10 Nov. 1938), the synagogue was not burned down since the fire would have put the neighboring houses at risk, but its interior furnishings were destroyed and most of the ritual objects burned. J. apartments were damaged and 31 men were arrested, of whom 22 were deported to the Sachsenhausen concentration camp. By 1939, the J. pop. had lost about 75% of its 1932 members and numbered about 50 individuals. It may be assumed that those who did not succeed in emigrating were deported to the east with the exception of two Jews who were married to non-Jews.

FORTH Middle Franconia, Germany. Jews were present in the late 16th cent. A new synagogue was built in 1754 and the J. pop. numbered 151 in 1867 (total 579). In 1933, 31 remained. Up to Oct. 1938 23 left, 17 of them to Nuremberg. The last four Jews escaped from F. on *Kristallnacht* (9–10 Nov. 1938).

FOUSSEMAGNE Belfort dist., France. The local synagogue dates from 1864. In 1901, the community was under the jurisdiction of the Epinal consistory. Prior to WWII, there were 194 Jews living in F. During WWII, the Germans expelled them to the south of France.

FRAENKISCH–CRUMBACH Hesse, Germany. Jews lived there from the early 18th cent. and numbered 105 (2% of the total) in 1871, declining to 52 (3%) in 1933. Between Jan. 1933 and Dec. 1939 all the Jews left, at least half emigrating to the U.S. and Latin America.

FRAMERSHEIM Hesse, Germany. Established around 1750, the community numbered 105 (7% of the total) in 1861. Only 13 remained on *Kristallnacht* (9–10 Nov. 1938), when J. property (including the synagogue) was destroyed. By 1940 seven of these Jews had emigrated.

FRAMPOL Lublin dist., Poland. Cossack incursions in the 1650s destroyed a small early 17th cent J. settlement. Jews were again present in the 18th cent. and in the 19th cent. operated textile and hide-processing plants while others supplied the local garrison. The J. pop. grew to 659 in 1857 and 1,465 (total 2,720) in 1921. Many left for the U.S. as economic conditions deteriorated between the World Wars. The Zionists, active since the early 20th cent., expanded their activities. Many fled to neighboring villages in the German bombardments of Sept. 1939 which virtually destroyed the town. In summer 1942, when the J. pop. reached 1,200 including refugees, the *Judenrat* encouraged many to flee because of rumors of a planned *Aktion*. The many reaching Goraj were sent back to P. along with the local Jews in Oct. 1942 and deported to the Belzec death camp in Nov.

FRANKENAU Hesse–Nassau, Germany. Jews lived there from the 17th cent. and dedicated a new synagogue in 1865. They numbered 61 (6% of the total) in 1871 and 65 in 1933. The community disbanded in 1938; by March 1939 all the Jews had left.

FRANKENBERG Hesse–Nassau, Germany. Although Jews lived there in medieval times, the community dated from the 17th cent. It maintained an elementary school from 1828 to 1939 and a synagogue was established in 1838. The community numbered 133 (4% of the total) in 1905. Zionism gained support after 1933. On *Kristallnacht* (9–10 Nov. 1938), both the synagogue and a J. teacher fell victim to the pogrom. Of the 101 Jews registered in 1933, 57 emigrated (mostly to the U.S.); others were sent to Nazi death camps in 1942.

FRANKENSTEIN (Pol. Zabkowice Slaskie) Lower Silesia, Germany, today Poland. J. settlement commenced in the late 14th cent. at the latest, with a Street of the Jews first mentioned in 1403. During the 15th cent., the Jews were expelled. J. settlement was renewed in the early 18th cent. The J. pop. was 129 in 1845 and 99 in 1898. Twelve families remained in 1925. The community maintained a synagogue and two cemeteries (dating back to 1815 and 1878). The J. pop. was 47 on the eve of the Nazi rise to power, dropping to 20 in 1937. On *Kristallnacht* (9–10 Nov. 1938), rioters destroyed the prayer house, a J.-owned brush factory, and an office. Eleven Jews remained in 1939 and one intermarried Jew in Nov. 1942. No further information on the fate of the Jews in WWII is available. Presumably those who failed to emigrate to safety perished after deportation.

FRANKENTHAL Palatinate, Germany. Jews in small numbers were present as temporary residents from at least 1586. Eight families were there in 1785 and in 1798, under French rule, a Jew had become a member of the municipal council. Until the mid-19th cent., religious orthodoxy prevailed in the community and from 1828 F. was the seat of the regional rabbinate. In the late 19th cent., the Liberal rabbi Dr. Salvendi introduced an organ and choir into the synagogue (consecrated in 1885). A J. school was functioning in 1841. The J. pop. rose from 144 in 1827 to 371 (total 16,899) in 1900. The Zionists became active in 1907. In the Weimar period, Jews participated in public life, continuing to serve on the municipal council and other public bodies. Jews were active in the textile and clothing trade and owned numerous stores. In 1933, 266 Jews remained. The Tietz department store and the large Schweitzer & Wertheimer establishment were almost immediately "sold" and by 1937, almost all other J. businesses had been liquidated or "Aryanized." Jews were severely persecuted and sporadically arrested throughout the period. On *Kristallnacht* (9–10 Nov. 1938), the synagogue was set on fire, 16 J. homes and stores were destroyed, and J. men were sent to the Dachau concentration camp. In all, 72 Jews managed to emigrate from Germany, including 15 to the U.S., 14 to France, and ten to Palestine; 137 moved to other German cities. The last 39 Jews were deported to the Gurs concentration camp in Oct. 1940.

FRANKENWINHEIM Lower Franconia, Germany.

Ark of the Law in the Frankenwinheim synagogue, Germany, 1931

Jews are known from the second half of the 18th cent. and numbered 100 in 1837 (total 546) with a synagogue and public school. In 1933, 54 Jews remained. Anti-J. riots broke out in Oct. 1938 in a well-poisoning libel and on *Kristallnacht* (9–10 Nov. 1938). J. women were forced to burn the religious articles taken out of the synagogue. J. homes were also destroyed and valuables stolen. Five men were imprisoned in the Buchenwald concentration camp. Twenty-two Jews emigrated in 1938–41 and 20 left for other German cities in 1935–1940. Of the remaining Jews, 13 were deported to Izbica in the Lublin dist. (Poland) via Wuerzburg on 24 April 1942.

FRANKERSHAUSEN Hesse–Nassau, Germany. Jews lived there from the 17th cent., many bearing the surname Plaut. They opened a synagogue in 1855 and numbered 96 (10% of the total) in 1861 and 33 in 1933. Only 14 Jews remained on *Kristallnacht* (9–10 Nov. 1938). By 1941 all had left.

Falk (1741–56). Other famous rabbis, who were born and bred in F., included Meir ben Yaakov ha-Kohen ("Maharam") Schiff (1605–41); Natan ha-Kohen Adler (1742–1800); David Tevele Schiff, chief rabbi of London's Great Synagogue (1765–92); and Moshe Schreiber ("Hatam Sofer"; 1762–1839), rabbi of Pressburg and head of its famous yeshiva. The Rothschild family took its name from the red shield (*Zum roten Schild*) hung outside Yitzhak Elhanan's house (1567) and emerged from obscurity when Mayer Amschel Rothschild (1744–1812), a dealer in old coins, began supplying the future landgrave with rare items. From 1769, as a trustworthy advisor, Mayer Amschel helped to enrich William IX of Hesse-Kassel and established a private bank. His five sons later ran commercial branches in Vienna, London, Naples, and Paris. During the Napoleonic era they also managed to preserve the exiled landgrave's fortune through shrewd transactions on the London stock exchange.

Under French rule (1798–1813), J. disabilities were steadily removed. Salomon Trier was a rabbinical delegate to the Paris Sanhedrin (1807); 447 families acquired citizenship (1808); and a decree signed by the Grand Duke (28 Dec. 1811) – in return for a payment of 440,000 guilders – abolished ghetto restrictions and bestowed equal rights for the Jews, who then numbered 3,117 (7% of the total). Educational reforms provoked bitter opposition among the established leadership, which objected to the introduction of a secular curriculum. However, the Philanthropin school (1804), which strongly favored educational reforms, already functioned in 1822 under the auspices of the community. In the years following the reactionary Congress of Vienna (1814–15), the rights gained by the Jews during the French period were gradually whittled away by the city senate. During the Hep! Hep! riots, which spread to F. in Aug. 1819, a mob that invaded the J. quarter created havoc, targeting the Rothschild home and injuring a number of Jews. The F. senate called in Austrian troops and, after condemning the disturbances, advised Jews to refrain from "behavior that might justify Christian complaints." In 1824, the senate granted J. residents a third-class form of citizenship excluding them from public office but allowing them to practice law. The removal of J. disabilities speeded up when F. joined the German customs union (*Zollverein*) which gave more commercial importance to the city after 1835. Many Jews participated in the struggle for political reform and a constitution that

would guarantee their civil liberties. Ludwig Boerne (1786–1837), a leading radical, moved to Paris after the July revolution of 1830. Gabriel Riesser, the foremost champion of J. emancipation, lived near F. – in Bockenheim – for some years (1836–40). Numbering 4,737 (8% of the total) in 1847, F. Jews maintained seven synagogues, about a dozen *minyanim*, and various welfare organizations, but Salomon Trier, the last chief rabbi (1817–44), headed a declining yeshiva. From 1825, the election of communal leaders and even religious decisions needed the F. senate's approval and J. radicals used their influence with the senate to introduce other changes. In May 1839, reformers won a sweeping victory in the communal elections. Theodor Creizenach and other extremists denounced in 1842 circumcision, the dietary laws, and anything else that kept Jews and gentiles apart. At the second Reform synod, held in F. in 1845 R. Leopold Stein backed Zacharias Frankel's demand for the retention of Hebrew in worship, but accepted the will of the majority. His own reforms included a triennial cycle of weekly Torah readings and the abolition of prayers for the renewal of sacrifices. During the 1848 revolution, most Jews, associating political with religious liberalism, pinned their hopes on the revolution: Gabriel Riesser became deputy chairman of the F. National Assembly; Martin Eduard von Simson, a baptized Koenigsberg lawyer, served as its chairman and led a delegation which offered the German crown to King Frederick William IV of Prussia. Shortly after the National Assembly promulgated the "Basic Laws of the German People," an enactment recognizing Jews as equal citizens was unanimously adopted by the senate (20 Feb. 1849). With the revolution's collapse and the triumph of reactionary forces in Germany and Austria, these measures were repealed. In F., however, new elections brought the Liberals to power once again in Sept. 1853. J. rights were partly restored and, following pressure in the senate and a referendum, a law granting equal civil rights to Jews entered the statute books on 7 Oct. 1864. In 1863, Abraham Geiger, the locally born architect of German Liberal Judaism, replaced Stein as communal rabbi (1863–70). Meanwhile the ascendancy of the reformists within the community had been challenged by a traditionalist campaign planned by a weekday Talmud study group, to which young Wilhelm Karl von Rothschild (1828–1901), nicknamed "Baron Willy," lent his enthusiastic support. In 1850, the traditionalists, who had obtained the senate's permission to con-

stitute themselves as an independent Orthodox congregation (*Israelitische Religionsgesellschaft*), invited Shimshon Rafael Hirsch to serve as their Rabbi. Hirsch (1808–88), the founder of J. Neo-Orthodoxy, transformed the *Religionsgesellschaft* into a synagogue community (Adass Jeshurun) with regular worship, Sabbath sermons in the German language, and a trained male choir. By 1860 it had a membership of 250 families, who still belonged to the main community. The J. pop. grew from 5,730 (9% of the total) in 1858 to 8,238 (over 10%) in 1867, mainly through immigration from rural Hesse. After the foundation of the Second German Reich in 1871, the number of Jews increased from 11,887 (or nearly 12% of the total) in 1875 to 26,228 (6%) in 1910, with a rising proportion of Jews from Eastern Europe (*Ostjuden*). The J. quarter was finally demolished in 1874 and renamed Boernestrasse and Boerneplatz (1884). Jews played a prominent role in the economic and political life of the city.

Leopold Sonnemann (1831–1909), owner and editor of the *Frankfurter Zeitung* from 1866, served as chairman of the city council for nearly 20 years and as a member of the Reichstag (from 1871). During the years 1867–90 (virtually without a break), Jews represented F. in the Reichstag – an achievement that no other German city could match. Campaigners for women's rights included Henriette Fuerth, a leading Social Democrat, and Bertha Pappenheim, cofounder of the League of J. Women. Despite abiding social discrimination and the growth of new political antisemitism, Jews made a major contribution to the cultural and scientific progress of the city. A public library was endowed by the Rothschilds and Charles Hallgarten (1838–1908), a philanthropist who had lived in the U.S., donated hundreds of volumes (including an entire collection on J. liturgical music). Jews were involved in the new F. University's establishment in 1914; they supported the teaching of modern languages, history, law, and

The Otto Frank family, Frankfurt am Main, Germany, 1927 (Anna Frank Stichting/photo courtesy of Yad Vashem, The Holocaust Martyrs' and Heroes' Remembrance Authority, Jerusalem)

economics; and Jacob Schiff, the F.-born American philanthropist, helped to fund a chair in semitic philology. When a campaign was launched against the "J. University," leaders of the Central Union (C.V.), the J. self-defense organization which opened its F. branch in 1907, derided weak-kneed J. benefactors as well as the antisemitic propagandists. To allay J. fears, a clause in the constitution guaranteed that religion would have no influence on academic appointments. Berthold Freudenthal served as the university's first rector and dean of its law faculty; Paul Ehrlich (1854–1918), the Nobel Prize laureate (1908), headed an institute of chemotherapy bearing his name. Many other prominent J. scholars taught there down to the Nazi era. In July 1876, a Law of Secession, advocated by Hirsch and supported by Eduard Lasker, who represented F. in the Prussian Landtag, was passed, enabling Jews to leave their community on religious grounds and to establish or join another. However, contrary to Hirsch's initial expectations, many of his traditionalist followers preferred to reach a compromise agreement with the Liberal majority, providing for separate Orthodox membership, facilities, and rabbinical authority. This transformed the "old" community into a united community (*Einheitsgemeinde*) in which Orthodox Jews and Liberals maintained a form of coexistence. Hirsch and his adherents, for their part, seceded from the main community, constituting themselves as a secessionist community (*Austrittsgemeinde*) which became a model for similar communities. The new majestic synagogue of Adass Jeshurun, dedicated in 1907, had 1,600 seats and was the largest in F. Hostility toward communal Orthodox rabbis intensified under Salomon Breuer (1850–1926), Hirsch's son-in-law and successor. Shortly after its establishment in 1897, the German Zionist Organization opened a branch in F. Like the industrialist Fritz Sondheimer and Jakob Goitein, a delegate to the First Zionist Congress, those heading the movement were identified with communal Orthodoxy and leaned toward a religious Zionist (Mizrachi) outlook. Zionist membership increased to 600 by WWI, Jews from Eastern Europe comprising the rank and file. Thousands of F. Jews, volunteered to serve at the front during the war; 467 died in action. Under the Weimar Republic, Ludwig Landmann (1868–1945) was elected burgomaster on the Democratic Party ticket in Oct. 1924, retaining his office until March 1933. Heinrich Simon published the *Frankfurter Zeitung*; Ludwig Fulda, a Philanthropin graduate, won fame with his social dramas and comedies; Hans Feibusch and Samson Schames were leading artists; Benno Elkan designed the city's war memorial (1919). Jews also established in 1923 the university's Institute for Social Research, which tried to combine the ideas of Marx and Freud. Its first director, Karl Gruenberg, was succeeded by Max Horkheimer. Erich Fromm and Theodor Adorno taught there, as did Herbert Marcuse. Other members of the university staff included the Zionist philosopher Martin Buber (1878–1965); Franz Oppenheimer, an architect of the kibbutz; and Max Wertheimer, the founder of Gestalt psychology. At its height, in 1925, the J. community numbered 29,658 (over 5% of the total). To spread J. enlightenment among the non-Orthodox, a "popular university" was established in 1920 with Franz Rosenzweig (1886–1929), author of *The Star of Redemption*, as its first director. He made the Freies Juedisches Lehrhaus ("Free J. House of Learning") a center that enabled adults to master Hebrew and study classic J. texts through an active learning experience. Although the Lehrhaus closed after his death, it gave rise to similar institutions throughout Germany and to the development of local interest in J. history and culture. A J. museum opened in March 1922. All the principal German J. organizations had branches in F. Agudat Israel and the Zionists fostered J. settlement in Palestine; the J. War Veterans Association boasted a membership of 1,000 in 1928 and fought antisemitism while stressing its German patriotism; the Association of National German Jews (1921) displayed a pathological animosity toward East European Jews. There were Orthodox, Zionist, and Liberal youth movements, as well as Zionist and non-Zionist sports clubs. Women's organizations helped to relieve J. economic distress, providing food, shelter, and advice about employment. A fully representative J. welfare bureau was also established. The economic recession of 1929 fostered antisemitic propaganda: Jews were said to control 35% of the city's business, owning a wide variety of commercial enterprises together with most banks and department stores. In Reichstag elections, the local Nazi vote soared from under 5% (May 1928) to almost 39% (July 1932). Stormtroopers fought their left-wing opponents, insulted Jews, and defaced J. property. The German Zionist Organization's 24th conference, held in F. in Sept. 1932, was therefore overshadowed by the menace of Nazism.

The Boerneplatz Synagogue in Frankfurt am Main, Germany

On 12 March 1933, some six weeks after Hitler's rise to power, Ludwig Landmann was forced to resign and a Nazi replaced him as burgomaster. Leading opponents of the regime (including many Jews) were arrested and sent to concentration camps. "Non-Aryan" officials and university professors were dismissed, their exodus from the Reich began, and Nazi Party circles carefully orchestrated an economic boycott against J.-owned factories, department stores, shops and kiosks, theaters and cinemas as well as against J. lawyers, physicians, artists, actors, singers, musicians, writers, and journalists. As this campaign intensified, the community published a dignified statement in the *Frankfurter Zeitung* and the *Gemeindeblatt* emphasizing its ancient history and unshakable religious faith. On the morning of Boycott Day (1 April), SA and SS men in uniform picketed J. stores and offices, displaying and chanting antisemitic slogans. In the following months, J. teachers and judges were fired and, by Oct., one-third of the university's teaching staff had

been dismissed. A local Nazi business association ran an aggressive campaign to eliminate J. competitors, resulting in the closure of several hundred firms in 1934, the expulsion of Jews from the cattle trade in 1935, wholesale unemployment, and a massive flight of capital. Jews were increasingly treated as pariahs. Schoolchildren, forced to endure insults from their teachers and classmates, were eventually limited to two city schools along with four J. teachers retained by the municipality. A law establishing the Reich Chamber of Culture, which made Propaganda Minister Josef Goebbels the arbiter of German cultural life, inevitably restricted Jews to a ghetto existence. The city's opera house, theaters, and museums had difficulty continuing without their J. directors, performers, and subscribers; the independent New Theater, refusing to accept Nazi dictates, closed only in Feb. 1935. Most sports clubs expelled Jews and, over a period of four years (1934–38), only the J. War Veterans' Schild and Maccabi's Bar Kokhba clubs had (limited) access to

municipal facilities and permission to compete with "Aryan" teams. Any reminder of J. contributions to the city in former times was eliminated: after the removal of the Heine monument for storage, every street or square bearing a "J." designation was renamed in 1935–36. According to the June 1933 census, there were 26,158 Jews in F. (less than 5% of the total) and about four–fifths belonged to the main community. As younger Jews emigrated, the birthrate declined steeply and the number of those abandoning or reverting to Judaism fluctuated. Widows and elderly couples feeling insecure in rural communities swelled the J. pop., but an even greater number of Jews left (16,359 between Jan. 1933 and Sept. 1938) and about 50% emigrated. Under the pressure of intensified Nazi persecution, the Liberals agreed to a power-sharing arrangement with the Zionists, who had gained much ground after the Nazi takeover. Although cooperation with the Adass Jeshurun leadership was harder to

achieve, the April 1933 law banning ritual J. slaughter, (*shehita*) resulted in a joint endeavor to import kosher meat and poultry until this was also forbidden (1936). Almost a fifth of F. Jews became dependent on public relief. J. aid agencies supplied food, clothing, and fuel. There was a lack of space in J. hospitals and old age homes. More kindergartens were needed to help working mothers and the communal soup kitchen provided 278,192 meals in 1935–36. A winter relief charity was organized on a huge scale, involving all 11,000 members of the general and secessionist communities, nine emergency campaigns, and 450 volunteers collecting money from house to house. The number of Jews drawing benefits rose to 4,765 (1936–37). They received food and clothing vouchers, fuel, and other essentials, but the whole enterprise came to an end in 1939. Zionism attracted increasing interest and support after Jews were excluded from normal German life. Zionist parties and organizations had a growing mem-

The metalworking school in Frankfurt am Main, Germany, before WWII

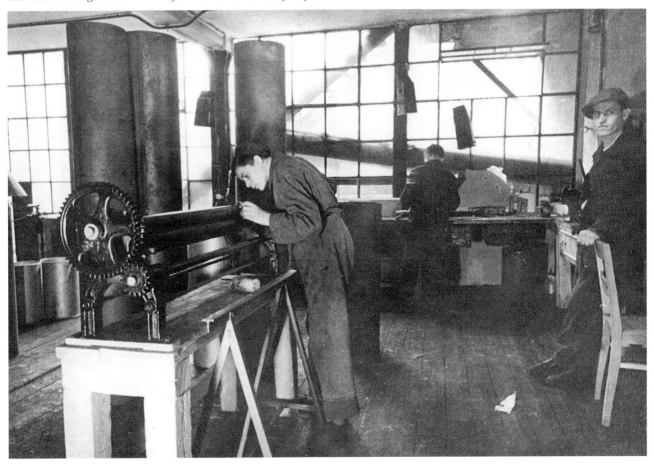

bership; Hebrew classes and Oneg Shabbat gatherings took place; training farms prepared youngsters for work on a kibbutz; and *aliya* arrangements were made through the local Palestine Office, which had to extend its working day. Vocational training schemes for the young and retraining schemes for adults helped to reduce J. unemployment. Emphasis was laid on "productive" (agricultural or technical) work and on the study of foreign languages – courses now taught by the Philanthropin and S. R. Hirsch elementary and high schools, which had an enrollment of over 2,000 in 1935–36. A branch of the new J. Cultural Association (Juedischer Kulturbund), with 1,300 members and a program covering art, music, and theater, was established in May 1934. The "J. House of Learning" (*Juedisches Lehrhaus*) was revived in Nov. 1933. It managed to operate in spite of Nazi watchdogs, and celebrated the 800th anniversary of Maimonides' birth in Jan. 1935. The leading J. sports clubs, Bar Kokhba and Schild, each had about 1,500 members at the end of 1935, when Schild opened the world's only iceskating rink used exclusively by Jews. Bar Kokhba organized a major sports event in F. and trained for the Second Maccabiah. After a relatively "quiet" period during 1936-1937, anti-J. activity picked up again in 1938. On 28 Oct., 2,000 "stateless" East European Jews were expelled from F. and driven to the Polish border, where they were turned back. Upon their unexpected return to F. on 31 Oct., the deportees became the responsibility of communal workers. The *Kristallnacht* pogrom began in F. early on the morning of 10 Nov., when stormtroopers looted and set fire to the Adass Jeshurun (Friedberger Anlage) synagogue; 40 Torah scrolls were destroyed in the blaze. The "old" community's three imposing synagogues, Orthodox and Liberal, also went up in flames. Others were vandalized and burned later in the day. Stormtroopers broke into J. homes and stores, looting goods, smashing windows, and attacking any Jew whom they met. Rioters invaded the communal offices and pillaged the J. museum, but the burgomaster ensured that historically valuable archives were rescued. Police had orders not to intervene as fires raged. Streets were littered with broken glass, and acts of violence continued. According to the *Frankfurter Volksblatt* (11 Nov.), these disturbances were "a popular, spontaneous reaction to World Jewry's campaign of [anti-German] incitement." Mass arrests of J. men aged 16–50 took place and only at the British consulate were holders of foreign passports given shelter. Those de-

tained had to endure infinitely more brutal treatment when stormtroopers relieved the police guards (11–12 Nov.). Compelled to surrender money and valuables, the 2,621 Jews were paraded before a hostile mob and dispatched to the Buchenwald concentration camp. Several died shortly after their release from imprisonment. The number of J. emigrants (618 in Nov. 1938) rose to 8,500 between April 1939 and March 1940. They often had to leave with one suitcase. The outbreak of WWII (1 Sept. 1939) made safe havens difficult to find. In May 1939, 14,191 "Jews by race" still lived in F. The main and separatist communities were amalgamated, with an Orthodox rabbi and a Liberal preacher, and services took place in the S. R. Hirsch school. Between the *Kristallnacht* pogrom and the beginning of deportations, life for Jews became increasingly more intolerable. Jews were forbidden to use public telephones, buy newspapers, visit places of entertainment, or even walk in the street. They were evacuated from their homes to make room for "Aryan" families and confined to special "J. houses." In Sept. 1941, all Jews over the age of six were obliged to wear a yellow star with the word *Jude* inscribed in black Hebrew-style lettering. More than 700 committed suicide. Relief and welfare work continued until the community's official liquidation on 6 Nov. 1942. Between 19 Oct. 1941 and 8 Jan. 1944, a total of 9,415 Jews (non-residents included) were deported – 6,332 for "resettlement" (mainly in Poland) and 3,083 to the Theresienstadt ghetto. On 1 July 1944, only 428 Jews remained, most of them individuals living in "privileged" mixed marriage with non-J. spouses. Even these were subject to last-minute deportation on 14 Feb. 1945. When Allied troops entered the city on 29 March 1945 few Jews were still alive and most of those who returned (including 360 Theresienstadt survivors) had never belonged to a synagogue. J. Displaced Persons from Eastern Europe, housed at the Zeilstein camp near Hoechst, organized a separate community, which grew to 3,500 in 1948. Although most emigrated to Israel, a few hundred remained and left their impress on F. Jewry. The Westend synagogue was renovated and rededicated in 1950. Services adhered to Orthodox tradition and Isaak Lichtigfeld, a one-time student at the Breuer yeshiva, headed the communal and district rabbinate (1954–67). Numbering 5,300 in 1996, the F. community was the most populous in Germany after Berlin. It had five synagogues, two old age homes, community and youth centers, and

1895 and 112 in 1910. When the Nazis came to power in 1933, there were 54 Jews in F. A J. actor at the Freiberg Theater lost his position in 1933. Nothing is known about what happened to the Jews of F. during the Nazi period other than that at least 18, living in so-called mixed marriages, or *Mischlinge*, were mobilized for forced labor towards the end of the war in the Todt Organization in Osterode. In 1944–45, J. women from the concentration camps were brought to F. to work in the armaments industry.

FREIBURG   Baden, Germany. Jews are first mentioned in 1230 but probably traded there in the 12th cent. In 1326 they numbered eight families, engaged in moneylending and controlling the grain trade. Most were burned alive over a well-poisoning libel during the Black Death persecutions of 1348–49. Those spared – 12 wealthy Jews, pregnant women, and children – were expelled, with the children baptized and J. property expropriated. Jews were present again in the second half of the cent. under a letter of protection but conditions worsened as a "Jew Law" published in 1394 introduced new disabilities. The Jews were again expelled in 1401 and for a final time in 1424. During the Thirty Years War (1618–48), J. army suppliers set up offices in F. and with the liberalization that followed annexation to Baden in 1805 Jews gradually began settling again. After emancipation in 1862 there was a large-scale influx of Jews to the city from the surrounding countryside. The J. pop. grew from 333 in 1871 to 1,013 in 1900 and 1,320 in 1910 (total 83,324). Jews became active in banking and industry and became part of the city's economic and intellectual elite. A magnificent synagogue was dedicated in 1870, its Reform service accompanied by an organ. In 1873, a cemetery was opened and in 1874 a J. orphanage. F. became the seat of the district rabbinate in 1885. Its first chief rabbi, Adolf Lewin (1843–1910), was also the first historian of the Jews of Baden. In 1895 a separate Orthodox congregation was formed and in the early 20th cent. traditional forces began to gain ascendancy over the Liberals. Jews were first admitted to F. University toward the end of the 18th cent. and despite unrelenting antisemitism ultimately grew to comprise 10% of the student body, the majority in the medical faculty. The Zionist leader and first president of Israel, Chaim Weizmann, obtained his doctorate in chemistry there in 1899. After WWI, Jews continued to play a leading economic role in the city, ensconced in its upper middle class as professionals and businessmen and running ten factories, a bank, and the big Knopf department store with its branches throughout south Germany. The community itself operated extensive social and cultural services with an active Zionist movement. In 1933, there were 1,138 Jews in the city. Anti-J. measures were immediately instituted and at the university all 21 J. professors and lecturers were dismissed in 1933–35. These included Hans Adolf Krebs, who moved to England and won the Nobel Prize for Medicine in 1953. In the same period the number of J. students was reduced from 183 to 54. Most J. businesses were liquidated by Nov. 1938. The community responded by providing financial support, organizing job placement and vocational retraining services, and, to aid emigration, offering courses in English and Hebrew. On 28 Oct. 1938, Jews of Polish origin were expelled to the Polish border. On *Kristallnacht* (9–10 Nov. 1938), the synagogue was blown up by SS and SA stormtroopers and 100 J. men were sent to the Dachau concentration camp for prolonged detention, two perishing there. During the Nazi era, 657 Jews managed to emigrate, including about 200 to the U.S., 100 to Palestine, 100 to France, 70 to Switzerland, and 70 to England; about 30 of the emigrants were subsequently arrested under the German occupation and deported to their deaths. Another 350 were deported from F. to the Gurs concentration camp on 22 Oct. 1940; of these, 273 perished. Of the 41 Jews remaining in F., about 30 were sent to the Theresienstadt ghetto on 23 Aug. 1942. During the war a Catholic organization headed by Gertrud Luckner worked to save J. lives. She was recognized by Yad Vashem as one of the Righteous among the Nations. A new J. community was formed in F. after the war by former residents and East European refugees. In 1977 it numbered 381.

FREIENWALDE   (Pol. Chociewel) Pomerania, Germany, today Poland. There was a Jew living in F. in 1705, and in 1728 there were three J. families. The community numbered 60 members in 1880 and maintained a synagogue and a cemetery. When the Nazis came to power in 1933, the J. community had 33 members. The cemetery was desecrated in 1938. Those Jews who did not leave F. before the outbreak of WWII were probably deported to the east. By Oct. 1942 there was just one Jew still living in the town, possibly protected by marriage to a non-Jew.

FREIENWALDE AN DER ODER, BAD   Branden-burg, Germany. Evidence of a Jew in F. dates from 1674. By 1812, there were 25 family heads. In 1880, the J. pop. was 82. The community maintained a cemetery (end of the 17th cent.) and a synagogue (about 1820). A harmonium introduced in the synagogue in 1912 indicated the Liberal orientation of the community. Prosperous Berlin Jews enjoyed frequenting the local spa. When the Nazis came to power in 1933, there were ten J. families living in the town. In Aug. 1935, placards were put up at the local railway station announcing that Jews were not wanted in F. On *Kristallnacht* (9–10 Nov. 1938), the synagogue was set on fire. By May 1939, there were 11 Jews and 17 persons of partial J. origin (*Mischlinge*) in F. Nearly all the Jews managed to flee abroad or to Berlin before the beginning of the deportations. No further information about their fate is available. By Oct. 1942, only one Jew, probably protected by marriage to a non-Jew, was registered as living in F.

FREISING   Upper Bavaria Germany. Jews were possibly present in the 13th–14th cent. In 1910, 26 were living there (total 14,946) and in 1933, 16, of whom 14 left by 1939, 11 of them to Munich.

FREISTETT   Baden, Germany. A J. settlement existed from the 17th cent., with Jews permitted to operate stalls from mid-cent. In the 19th cent., Jews traded in cattle, textiles, foodstuffs, and tobacco as their pop. stabilized at around 80 in the second half of the cent. (about 4% of the total). In 1933, 33 remained. Under the economic boycott in the Nazi era, they were forced to liquidate their businesses and 23 emigrated, 17 of them to France; another five left for other German cities and were ultimately deported to the camps.

FREREN   Hanover, Germany. Jews lived there in 1724, numbering 15 by 1836. Their prayer house served the F.-Fuerstenau district community established in 1913. Lingen Jews, who formed an independent community numbering 63 in 1922, sent their children to the F. religious school. Despite Nazi boycott measures and terror, there were still 23 J. residents in 1938. On *Kristallnacht* (9–10 Nov. 1938), Nazis looted and destroyed J. property, including the interior of the prayer house. Jews were driven through the streets on cattle trucks and local J. cemeteries were desecrated. No more than four or five Jews managed to reach safe havens; nine perished in Auschwitz and five in Sobibor. Only three of those deported survived the Holocaust.

FREUDENBERG   Baden, Germany. The first J. community was destroyed in the Rindfleisch massacres of 1298. A new settlement was founded in 1442. Under local pressure, a series of disabilities was imposed on the Jews in the late 17th cent. The J. pop. reached 81 (around 4% of the total) in 1865. At the end of the cent. over half the Jews were cattle traders or shopkeepers. By 1933, 15 remained. After *Kristallnacht* (9–10 Nov. 1938), when the synagogue was vandalized, the three J. textile establishments in F. were transferred to "Aryans." One family of four left for Berlin and perished in the east in 1942; two children reached France and subsequently the U.S.; the last six Jews in F. were deported to the Gurs concentration camp on 22 Oct. 1940.

FREUDENBURG   Rhineland, Germany. J. institutions began developing in the late 18th cent., with a synagogue erected in 1785. A J. school was in operation in 1830. In 1905, the J. pop. reached a peak of 69 (total 1,154); 44 remained in 1933. Under the Nazis, the Jews were subjected to particularly severe persecution, with anti-J. riots staged in 1935. Subsequently, many Jews fled to the Saar region, Luxembourg, and France. On *Kristallnacht* (9–10 Nov. 1938), the synagogue was partially destroyed. Six local Jews perished in the Holocaust.

FREUDENTAL   Wuerttemberg, Germany. As part of the Duchy of Wuerttemberg, Jews in the 18th cent. lived in F. under a liberal letter of protection according extensive privileges and serving as a model for other such charters (freedom of worship and movement, use of town's natural resources, exemption from military service and quartering of soldiers, etc.). The community erected its first synagogue in 1770 and by 1800 was one of the few in Wuerttemberg to reach 45% of the total pop. In 1855 the J. pop. stood at 364 but thereafter declined sharply owing to emigration. Many engaged in the cattle trade and belonged to the town's wealthy class. A J. school was founded about 1816. Good relations generally prevailed with the local pop. In 1933, 50 Jews remained (with another seven joining the community later), subjected from the outset of Nazi rule to anti-J. propaganda. On *Kris-*

FRONHAUSEN   Hesse–Nassau, Germany. The Jews of Lohra, Roth, and F. maintained one community which, for practical reasons, was based in F. after 1878. Numbering 44 (4% of the total) in 1895 and 19 in 1934, the community survived until 1941–42, when the last Jews were sent to Nazi death camps.

FRUMUSICA   Moldavia dist., Rumania. In 1832, there were 82 Jews in F. and seven Christians. In 1894 a branch of Hovevei Zion functioned with 100 members and in 1910, 128 pupils attended the J. school. Peasant riots in 1907 led 200 Jews to temporarily flee the city. Two synagogues existed between the World Wars. The J. pop. in 1910 was 596, rising in 1930 to 634 (66% of the total). In June 1941, the Jews were transferred to Botosani. Those suspected of Communism were sent to the Targu-Jiu detention camp. After the war, about one-third of the J. community returned.

FRUNZOVKA   (until 1927, Zaharovka) Odessa dist., Ukraine. The J. pop. in 1897 was 1,732 (total 3,574), many engaged in agriculture. A J. colony was founded nearby in 1923 under the Soviets and in 1927 included 25 families from Rashkov and a few from F. A J. elementary school was founded in F. in 1923, reaching an enrollment of 219. In 1939, the J. pop. was 520. The Germans captured F. on 3 Aug. 1941 and murdered 56 Jews on 4 Oct. Another 21 were murdered at the nearby village of Pavlovka on 21 Sept. The Germans killed 97 people in the area, probably all Jews.

FRYDEK-MISTEK   Moravia, Czechoslovakia. Two communities were formed in the two towns in the latter half of the 19th cent. A joint synagogue was consecrated in 1865 and a cemetery in 1882 in F. A J. school was started in 1864. Jews pioneered the textile industry and Herzl's daughter, Trude, married a local factory owner's son. The two community's were amalgamated in 1890, when F.'s J. pop. was 262 and M.'s 227. A new synagogue was built in 1896. The combined J. pop. was 468 in 1930 (total 22,000). There was a Jew serving on the municipal council. Many Jews were sent to the Nisko camp in Poland in Oct. 1939, afterwards returning. Over 280 Jews were finally deported, most to the Theresienstadt ghetto on 18 Sept. 1942 and from there on to the Treblinka death camp.

FRYSZTAK   Lwow dist., Poland. The organized J community dates from the mid-17th cent. and constituted a majority of the pop. from the outset. All trade and crafts were in J. hands as well as the town's single industrial facility, a steam-operated sawmill. The J. pop. stood at 820 (total 1,344) in 1880 and 1,010 in 1921. In the peasant riots of 1898, Jews were beaten and homes and stores looted, but after WWI fairly harmonious relations prevailed. Traditional circles zealously suppressed all Zionist activity until the 1930s. The Germans took the town on 8 Sept. 1939 and appointed a *Judenrat*. A week later, on Rosh Hashanah, Jews were murdered at prayer and religious books burned by the *Wehrmacht*. Forced labor and persecution ensued. From early 1941 until the fall, a labor camp housing mostly Warsaw Jews operated in F. A ghetto was established in June 1942. On 12 July local Jews were among the 260 murdered in the area by the Gestapo and on 16 Aug. the liquidation of the ghetto commenced with most being transported to Jaslo for immediate deportation to the Belzec death camp. Many were sheltered by Christian families and 35 formed an armed group. Few survived.

FUERFELD   Hesse, Germany. Jews lived there from the beginning of the 19th cent. and numbered 145 (12% of the total) in 1861, with members in nearby Frei-Laubersheim. The community's synagogue was consecrated in 1895. By 1940, the remaining Jews had left, one-half (30) emigrating, mostly to the U.S.

FUERSTENAU (I)   Westphalia, Germany. A protected Jew is mentioned in 1683. A few were there in the late 18th cent., their number rising to five families in the early 19th cent and a peak of 12 (56 Jews, or 5.5% of the total) in 1846. The community maintained a prayer house in a rented facility and a cemetery from at least 1773. A synagogue was erected in 1854. The J. pop. dropped to 31 in 1871 and 20–22 in the 1905–33 period. On *Kristallnacht* (9–10 Nov. 1938), the synagogue was set on fire. Eighteen Jews remained at the outbreak of war. They were all deported to the camps, where most perished.

FUERSTENAU (II)   Hanover, Germany. Jews living there and in four other towns—Freren, Lengerich, Lingen, and Thuine—established a district community numbering 45 in 1844. It maintained a religious school and prayer houses in F. and Freren, but Lingen became

independent in 1873. Of the 48 F. Jews (nearly 2% of the total) registered in 1933, 30 left before *Kristallnacht* (9–10 Nov. 1938), when the prayer house was burned down. Two families emigrated to the U.S. in 1939, but at least 12 other Jews died in Nazi camps.

FUERSTENWALDE Brandenburg, Germany. Evidence of a J. presence dates back to 1379 and an account of a Jew being burned to death. A J. settlement developed in the 18th cent. and numbered four J. families in 1743. Two J. cemeteries were set up in 1795 and 1829. In the mid-19th cent., the 27 Jews of F. had no prayer room of their own and had to join the congregation of Frankfurt an der Oder. In the 1870s, the local Jews established a synagogue. In 1880, the J. pop. was 145 and an independent community was organized in 1886. In 1873, the first J. deaf-mute school in Germany was set up in F. and in 1884, the J. Deaf-Mute Society for all Germany was founded in the town. When the Nazis came to power in 1933,

Feeding chickens on a farm in Fuerstenwalde, Germany, 1934 (Juedisches Museum im Stadtmuseum, Berlin/photo courtesy of Yad Vashem, The Holocaust Martyrs' and Heroes' Remembrance Authority, Jerusalem)

the J. community numbered 150. Two agricultural training centers for preparing young people for immigration to Palestine were set up near F. On the Neuendorf estate there were 120–200 trainees, and at the Winkel estate in Spreenhagen there were 30–40 places. On *Kristallnacht* (9–10 Nov. 1938), the synagogue was burned down; the cemetery desecrated and its mortuary destroyed; J. businesses were destroyed and looted; and Jews were beaten up. By May 1939, only 37 Jews and 30 persons of partial J. origin (*Mischlinge*) were still living in the town. It may be assumed that those Jews who did not manage to emigrate were deported to the east. Six Jews, probably protected by marriage to non-Jews, remained in F. The trainees from the two agricultural centers were probably deported by summer 1943.

FUERTH Middle Franconia, Germany. The Jews present in the 15th cent. were apparently expelled and a new community was founded in the first half of the 16th under the protection of the margrave George the Pious. The proximity of the settlement to the commercial center of Nuremberg and the rivalry between the Protestant nobility of Ansbach and the Catholic bishops of Bamberg enabled the development of the J. community, which became the largest in Bavaria and one of the most important in Germany. In 1537 Mikhal Derenburg, one of the leading J. financiers of the time, settled there and many arrived after the expulsion from Ansbach in 1560. The Jews of F. were restricted primarily to moneylending and citizenship in the town was denied to them. A synagogue (the "Altschul") was built in 1617 when the J. pop. stood at around 1,500. The Jews fled temporarily in the Thirty Years War (1618–1648) after Croatian mercenaries attacked the Jews in 1634. After the war the community continued its growth under the protection of the bishop of Bamberg and founded the first J. hospital in Germany. Many refugees arrived from Vienna in 1670 after the expulsion there, including members of the well-known Fraenkel family. Shemuel Baermann Fraenkel served as rabbi in 1700–08 and was head of the yeshiva, where most of Germany's rabbis studied in the 17th and 18th cent. At the end of the 17th cent. F. had five synagogues and its prayer rite spread throughout most of south Germany and was a direct continuation of the medieval Nuremberg rite. Numerous J. printing presses also operated in F. from the late 17th cent. In this period, the J. community enjoyed

Street in the historical Jewish ghetto of Fuerth, Germany, 1927

a unique legal status in Germany, including civil rights and broad autonomy. In 1763 the community founded the first J. orphanage in Germany and the only one in Bavaria. Jews were active as court agents and army suppliers and pioneered local industry, setting up the first factories for the manufacture of eyeglasses, mirrors, pencils, etc. They were also the first Jews in Bavaria to enter the professions and serve in state institutions. Dr. Gruensfeld of F. was the first J. lawyer in Bavaria (1843), David Morgenstern the first J. deputy in the Bavarian Landtag (1849), and Shelomo Berolzheimer the first judge (1863). In 1880 the J. pop. reached a peak of 3,330 (total 31,063). Orthodox opposition to the spirit of religious reform inspired by the emancipation led to the founding of a tradition-oriented J. public school which received government recognition in 1899. With the completion of the emancipation in Germany and the growth of new J. pop. centers, F. lost its special position and its J. pop. began to decline, numbering 2,504 in 1925 and 1,990 in 1933 (total 77,135). In 1933 the community operated seven synagogues, a community center with a big library, numerous welfare agencies, and branches of national organizations like the Central Union (C.V.), the J. Cultural Association (Juedischer Kulturbund), the Zionist Organization with the Hehalutz youth movement, and Agudat Israel. Jews owned 220 of the city's 720 business establishments, including 50% of its wholesale outlets. Among the city's natives was the well-known Feuchtwanger banking family.

Already in 1933 there were frequent antisemitic outbursts, with mass arrests and beatings by the SA. In Oct. 1938, all Jews without citizenship papers (i.e., East Europeans) were expelled from F. On *Kristallnacht* (9–10 Nov. 1938), most community buildings were destroyed by the SA along with J. stores. The Jews were dragged out of their beds in the middle of the night and held in the city square; 150 of the men were then sent to the Dachau concentration camp after severe beatings. Between 1933 and 1941, 1,400 Jews managed to leave F., many to the U.S. and Shanghai. Among them was Henry Kissinger, future U.S. secre-

tary of state. The liquidation of the community commenced on 28 Nov. 1941 when 83 Jews were deported to the Riga ghetto. Another 224, almost all the remaining Jews under the age of 65, were sent to Izbica in the Lublin dist. (Poland) on 24 March 1942. On 10 Sept. 1942, 153 of the sick and old and the children at the orphanage were expelled to Theresienstadt. In all, 504 Jews were deported through the end of 1943. After the war about 40 Jews returned, forming a new community that numbered 200 in 1970.

FULDA Hesse–Nassau, Germany. Although Jews may have lived there in the ninth cent., their pop. only became substantial after the First Crusade (1096). A blood libel in 1235 led to the martyrdom of 32 Jews, and nearly 200 perished during the Black Death persecutions of 1348–49. Reestablished in 1367, the community established a synagogue in the J. quarter (*Judengasse*) in 1423 and, despite heavy taxation and restrictions, grew to number 77 families by 1653. F. became the seat of a regional religious court, (*beit din*), one of five in Germany. Its chief rabbis, who also headed the yeshiva, included Eliyahu Loanz (1604–09) and Meir ben Yaakov ha-Kohen Schiff (the "Maharam"; 1622–40), a leading talmudist who was appointed at the age of 17. Although 2,000 Jews were expelled from the diocese in 1671, some returned shortly afterward and eventually opened one of the first German J. schools in 1784. French occupation authorities compelled them to adopt surnames in 1812, but they only obtained civil rights in 1833. Abandoning their former occupations, the Jews became department store owners, textile and paint manufacturers, lawyers, and physicians. Catholics in F. discountenanced the rise of political antisemitism and the community built a larger synagogue in 1859 to accommodate new members from rural areas, growing from 237 (3% of the total) in 1802 to 861 (4%) in 1905. As district rabbi (1877–1919), Dr. Michael Cahn transformed Orthodox F. Jewry into a bastion of Agudat Israel, denouncing both Liberal Judaism and Zionism (including Mizrachi). Thanks to his initiative, phylacteries (*tefillin*) "made in F." were prized throughout Europe. In response to the Tiszaeszlar blood libel in 1882 F.'s Catholic bishop circulated a declaration refuting the charge. East European refugees founded a congregation of their own during WWI, but soon became an integral part of the community. During the Weimar Republic era, branches of the Central Union (C.V.), J. War Veterans

Association, and B'nai B'rith were established. Leo Cahn succeeded his father as rabbi (1919–38) and at its height the community numbered 1,137 in 1925. The synagogue was further enlarged and with the aid of Kalman Kahana, a rabbi from Brody, Barukh Kunstadt reestablished a yeshiva. While the older generation remained anti-Zionist until 1933, members of the Blau-Weiss youth movement left for Palestine in the 1920s. Around that time a training farm (*hakhshara*) was established by the religious Zionist Bahad movement in Rodges, and its philosophy had a great attraction for Orthodox youth in neighboring F. A larger training farm at Geringshof survived until 1938. Most of the graduates of these farms emigrated to Palestine, where they helped found religious kibbutzim such as Yavne and Tirat Tzevi.

The Catholic Center Party in F., which many Jews supported, retained an absolute majority (51.5% as against the Nazis' 27%) in March 1933, when Hitler was already chancellor. Nazi terror silenced the free press and deprived Jews of their livelihood. Even the rabbi's sermons were monitored by Gestapo agents. On *Kristallnacht* (9–10 Nov. 1938), the synagogue (with its ancient *Memorbuch* dating from 1550) was burned to ashes. One J. girl was raped and the men were sent to the Buchenwald or Dachau concentration camp. Of 1,058 Jews registered in F. at the beginning of 1933, 935 emigrated (195 to Palestine); virtually all the remainder were deported: 132 to the Riga ghetto (Dec. 1941); 36 to the Lublin dist. (May 1942); and 76 to the Theresienstadt ghetto (Sept. 1942). Among those who moved to Palestine, R. Barukh Kunstadt established the Kol Torah Yeshiva in Jerusalem while Dr. Kalman Kahana, a founder of Kibbutz Hafetz Hayyim, later served as Israel's deputy minister of education (1962–69).

FULESD Szatmar dist., Hungary. Jews settled in the late 18th cent. Mostly engaged in farming, they numbered 50 in 1930. In late May 1944, they were sent to Mateszalka where 17,000 Jews from the district were being held, and then deported to Auschwitz.

FULUPSZALLAS Pest–Pilis–Solt–Kiskun dist., Hungary. Jews arrived c. 1830, erecting a synagogue in 1880. They numbered 60 in 1880 and 83 in 1930. After suffering in the post-WWI White Terror and under Hungary's racial laws of 1938, when the young men were taken to forced labor, the remaining

80 Jews were deported to Auschwitz via Kiskoros and Kecskemet on 23 June 1944.

FUZESABONY Heves dist., Hungary. Because of the opposition of the Catholic Church, Jews were only allowed to settle in F. in the late 19th cent. They numbered 197 in 1880 and 230 in 1930. A synagogue was erected in 1910. The community refused to allow Zionist activity to take place. Following the 1938 racial laws, rich Jews were sent to internment camps and the situation of the community deteriorated to the extent that most were on welfare. In 1942, 15 young men were sent to forced labor. In May 1944, the remaining Jews were expelled to Bagolyuk with 2,000 other Jews from the area. By 8 June, all had been deported to Auschwitz. Survivors reestablished the community, but by 1964 only eight Jews remained in F.

FUZESGYARMAT Bekes dist., Hungary. Jews settled in the late 19th cent., numbering 171 in 1880 and 217 in 1930. In 1942, most of the men were sent to forced labor. In mid-June 1944, the remaining Jews were expelled to Bekescsaba and on 25 June deported to Austria, where most survived the war. The survivors reestablished the community, but most soon left, primarily to Israel.

G

GABES (also Qabis) Gabes dist., Tunisia. Jews are first mentioned in the ninth cent., when a large community apparently existed and the *gaon* Avraham al-Qabisi made his home there. Jews continued to live in G. under the Fatimids and Zeirids in the 10th–12th cents., maintaining close connections with the *geonim* of Babylonia. Most lived in a crowded J. quarter within the city walls and engaged in financially sophisticated land transactions involving credit, organized bookkeeping, agents, and arbitration by local courts. Others farmed their own land, using advanced irrigation systems, and some played an important role in Mediterranean and trans-Sahara commerce as moneychangers. J. artisans were prominent as blacksmiths and builders. During the entire period, the dynastic Ibn Jama family provided the community with halakhic authorities. By the early 11th cent., G. had a large and important *beit midrash*. Many scholars from Kairouan arrived in the mid-11th cent., fleeing Bedouin depredations in the interior of the country. The community was destroyed in the Almohad invasion of 1159. Its slow recovery probably commenced in the 13th–14th cents. under the Hafsids but nothing is known about the community until the late 18th cent. According to tradition, the modern community was founded by Jews from Djerba and from Leghorn in Italy in the early 18th cent. Jews inhabited the two ancient settlements—Menzel and Djara—within the city walls. Most stores and workshops were in J. hands. Unlike their countrymen in Tunis, the Leghornian Jews assimilated to local J. life. The wealthier merchants engaged particularly in the trans-Sahara trade in the *alafa* plant used to manufacture paper and exported especially to England. They also dealt in sea sponges, fish, dates, and farm produce. The monopolization of trade by the Jews, some of them as privileged foreign nationals, created a degree of tension with the local Moslem pop. Violent anti-J. incidents occurred in 1864 and again in 1881 during the revolt against French rule. Many Jews fled with the European residents, some to Djerba and others to Matmata and as far away as Tunis. Four Jews were killed and J. homes were burned together with the Menzel synagogue. The stability of the French Protectorate, bringing improved security and better economic conditions, attracted many Jews to the city from the rural periphery of southern Tunisia. Jews began moving to the new Djara quarter outside the city walls. Here a market and city square were built and community institutions were transferred to the new neighborhood. A number of westernized Jews moved to a fourth, European quarter which was soon built on the seashore. In 1899, a single community council was established for all the quarters, though activity continued on a neighborhood level. The council was styled the J. Relief Fund (Caisse de Secours et de Bienfaisance) as in the rest of Tunisia and charged with charity work and synagogue maintenance. The community had a number of illustrious rabbis, including Moshe Idan (1842–94), who founded a *beit midrash*; Yitzhak Hai Bokhovza, who served in 1920–26 and was later chief rabbi of Tripoli; and Hayyim Houri (1926–56), the community's dominant figure for three decades. He was a staunch opponent of the French influence in education and at the same time encouraged ties with Palestine. Among his best-known works are *Benei Moshe*, *Derekh Hayyim*, and *Matza Hayyim*. J. children attended French public schools and a *talmud torah*. The central synagogue was located in the new Djara quarter. Most Jews remained traditional in outlook. Zionist activity commenced in 1921 with the founding of a Herzl-Zion society. Betar was active in 1936–39 with 60 members. Between the World Wars, the J. pop. was around 2,500 (15–18% of the total), up from 1,271 in 1909. With the outbreak of WWII,

emancipation in 1862. In 1870, Leopold Guggenheim became the first Jew in Germany to head a municipal council. In 1827, G. became the seat of the district rabbinate. A synagogue was built in 1836, a 26-bed hospital in 1892, and an old age home in 1898. A J. elementary school was opened in 1815 and a school of commerce in 1890. In the 19th cent. Jews spread into crafts and the professions and enjoyed a measure of prosperity for the first time. With the development of industry, many became traveling salesmen, representing German firms in nearby Switzerland. In 1858, the J. pop. reached a peak of 996 (half the total), dropping to 663 in 1900. A number of J. families of East European origin were well integrated in the community. As Nazi rule progressed and the economic boycott was tightened, Jews were forced to liquidate their businesses. In 1938, J. community life was terminated as all J. organizations were officially closed down. In Oct. 1938, Jews of Polish origin were expelled to the Polish border and on *Kristallnacht* (9–10 Nov. 1938), the synagogue was vandalized and 12 Jews were sent to the Dachau concentration camp. Emigration abroad and to other German cities reduced the J. pop. from 314 in 1933 to 75 in 1940, with another 90 in the old age home and 13 in the J. hospital. All were deported in Oct.–Nov. 1940. Of the total, 47 perished in the Gurs concentration camp, 18 in other French concentration camps, and 37 in Auschwitz; 57 survived the Holocaust. Of the 17 Jews in the attached community of Donaueschingen, founded in the 17th cent., 16 managed to emigrate.

GAIVORON Odessa dist., Ukraine. The J. pop. in 1939 was 841 (total 9,256). The Germans captured G. on 29 July 1941 and on 16–18 Feb 1942, they killed 211 people. Most were probably Jews.

GAJARY Slovakia, Czechoslovakia, today Republic of Slovakia. Jews are mentioned in the 17th cent. In 1755, their pop. reached 20 families, most engaged in crafts. In 1828, their pop. was 180 (total 2,852). A synagogue was erected in the late 18th cent. and a J. elementary school was opened by the mid-19th cent. Between the World Wars, Jews prospered as shopkeepers and artisans. In 1940, 36 remained, under direct German rule, and consequently endured severe persecution. In 1942, refugees increased the J. pop. to 55 (18 families). They were deported to the death camps of the east in the spring.

GALANTA Slovakia, Czechoslovakia, today Republic of Slovakia. Jews settled under the protection of Count Esterhazy at the turn of the 17th cent., numbering 69 in 1728 and enjoying religious and economic freedom. A school and synagogue were opened in the 18th cent. A large yeshiva gave G. a reputation as a center of J. learning. The congregation split in 1891 over the appointment of a new rabbi. One congregation was subsequently served by R. Yosef Tzevi Duschinsky (1895–1921), a great Hungarian scholar and head of one of its largest and best-known *yeshivot*. A splendid new synagogue was erected in 1899 as the J. pop. grew from 559 in 1828 to 937 (total 2,976) in 1900. Jews leased estates and founded factories (enamel, meat products, a flour mill, and a brickyard). The Zionists were active from the early 1920s, particularly Mizrachi. Agudat Israel was operating prior to WWI. Jews were active in public life, with nine serving on the local council. Jews owned 115 of the town's 130 business establishments. Another 40 Jews were artisans. In 1941 the J. pop. was 1,216. Persecution began with the annexation of G. to Hungary in Nov. 1938. Over 200 Jews were seized for the forced labor battalions. On 4 June 1944, after the German occupation, the Jews were herded into a ghetto, including 600 Jews from surrounding villages. From there they were sent to Komarno and on 13 June they were deported to Auschwitz. About 1,800 Jews from the area perished in the Holocaust. Most of the survivors emigrated to Israel in 1948–49.

GALATI Moldavia dist., Rumania. Jews first settled in the late 16th cent. and suffered from antisemitic persecution throughout their history here. An official J. community was established in 1812. Divisions within the community began to develop when individual professional trade organizations opened synagogues, appointed their own rabbis, and collected dues. A J. hospital, which became the largest hospital in Moldavia, was opened in 1834 (rebuilt in 1899). A short while later an old age home began to function. B'nai B'rith opened a lodge in 1873 that supported the community's welfare and educational institutions. In 1896, 773 pupils attended the two J. schools. A commercial school, opened in 1898, became a high school in 1919. During the 19th cent., local and visiting Greeks continually attacked the Jews. In 1859, Jews were victims of a blood libel, with several murdered and the synagogue destroyed. The international com-

Sewing class in B'nai B'rith vocational school, Galati, Rumania, 1920s (Moshe Ussokin, Jerusalem/photo courtesy of Yad Vashem, The Holocaust Martyrs' and Heroes' Remembrance Authority, Jerusalem)

munity, especially France and Baron Rothschild, were instrumental in stopping the riots. From 1881, the Zionist organizations were a dominating force in the community and G. became the center in Rumania of the Zionist movement. The first convention of Hovevei Zion took place here in 1894. The J. pop. in 1899 stood at 13,992 (21% of the total). G. was a center of J. and Zionist journalism in Yiddish, German, and Rumanian. The Zionist Federation's journal *Hatikva*, appearing in 1915–19, made an impact on J. cultural life throughout Rumania. The artist Reuven Rubin was born in G. as was Abba Bardichev, one of the J. parachutists from Palestine during WWII, after whom the kibbutz Alonei Abba was named. In 1919, the Rumanian authorities granted citizenship to 1,600 heads of J. families, another 1,700 in 1923, and 800 from Bessarabia. After WWI and up to 1921, 11,000 refugees from the pogroms in the Ukraine passed through G. on their way to Palestine. G. was also a pioneer training center. Prior to WWII, 22 synagogues were functioning, two schools for boys, one for girls, and a high school. Antisemitic manifestations were widespread during the 1920s and

1930s. In 1935, the city council stopped all grants to the J. community and in 1938, J. lawyers were ousted from the lawyers association. The Iron Guard Legionnaires imposed restrictions on Jews from Sept. 1940. Merchants were forced to hand over their shops, and J. schools closed. In June 1941, 3,700 J. men over 18 were taken to a camp in nearby Filesti and forced to work under extremely harsh conditions. Some Jews, charged with Communism, were interned in Targu-Jiu; others were expelled to Transnistria. The J. pop. in 1941 stood at 13,511 (14% of the total). During the war, the J. community provided assistance to the increasing numbers of impoverished members and refugees. In Aug. 1944, after the armistice, the Germans burned down J. neighborhoods as well as the Great Synagogue and other institutions. After the war the community increased its activities, providing for refugees and those returning from the labor battalions.

GALGAU (Hung. Galgo) N. Transylvania dist., Rumania. Jews settled in the early 19th cent. The J. pop. in 1920 was 131 (19% of the total). On 4 May 1944 the

community was transferred to the Dej ghetto and then deported to Auschwitz.

GAMBACH Hesse, Germany. The modern community dates from 1705 and 200 years later, in 1905, it numbered 78 (5% of the total). On *Kristallnacht* (9–10 Nov. 1938), villagers helped destroy the synagogue. Of the 56 Jews living there in 1933, 16 emigrated (nearly all to Argentina); the last 18 were deported in 1942.

GANDERSHEIM Brunswick, Germany. Jews lived there in medieval times (1252–1447) but eventually disappeared. Established by 1785, the community grew to 44 in 1880. Jews attended the private synagogue of the Bremer banking family from 1853 to 1900. Having dwindled to 20 in 1909 and ten in 1931, the J. pop. became affiliated with Seesen's community. By WWII, seven Jews had emigrated; the last two perished in the Riga ghetto in 1941.

GANGELT Rhineland, Germany. Jews numbered 63 (total 2,495) in 1871 and 35 in 1925. The community maintained a cemetery and a synagogue which was destroyed on *Kristallnacht* (9–10 Nov. 1938). Nine Jews perished in the Holocaust.

GANICE (Hung. Ganya) Carpatho-Russia, Czechoslovakia, today Ukraine. J. settlement probably began in the late 18th cent. The J. pop. was 365 (total 1,538) in 1880 and 674 in 1921. A number of J. families engaged in agriculture. Of the youth groups, the most active were the Orthodox, such as Pirhei Agudat Israel. The Hungarians occupied G. in March 1939 and in 1940–41 drafted dozens of Jews into labor battalions, some for forced labor, some for service on the eastern front, where many perished. In 1941, the J. pop. was 730. In late July, dozens of J. families without Hungarian citizenship were expelled to German-occupied territory in the Ukraine, where they were murdered. About 500 Jews were deported to Auschwitz in the second half of May 1944.

GARBATKA Kielce dist., Poland. The J. pop. was 111 (total 1,739) in 1921. After the German occupation of Sept. 1939, a few hundred refugees arrived. The young were sent to the Pionki labor camp and 100 Jews were murdered outside the village in July 1942. The few remaining Jews were transferred to the Gnie-

woszow ghetto and then deported to the Treblinka death camp.

GARDELEGEN Saxony, Germany. Jews were living in G. already in 1344. Expulsions took place in 1510 after the Host Desecration trial in Berlin, in which three local Jews were involved. The Jews were again expelled in 1565. In the 18th cent., J. settlement was renewed. By the 1860s, the community numbered 40 individuals. About 1880, a cemetery was established. A private building was used as a synagogue, but after 1914, services were held only in rented rooms. Most Jews traded in beer hops. In 1933, there were beer about 40 Jews living in G. On *Kristallnacht* (9–10 Nov. 1938), shops were wrecked and the men were taken to the Buchenwald concentration camp. Prior to the outbreak of WWII, three families and a number of young people managed to escape abroad. The remaining Jews, probably about 15 people, were moved in Aug. 1941 to a six-room house outside the town. Some died there, probably committing suicide. The others were deported in April and Nov. 1942 to the east. Only one survived.

GARGZDAI (Yid. Gorzd) Kretinga dist., Lithuania. Jews first settled in the 15th cent. In 1639, King Wladyslaw IV granted Jews a letter of privileges, later reconfirmed by King Augustus III in 1742. The J. pop. in 1897 was 1,455 (59% of the total). Most Jews were lumber exporters or horse traders. When pogroms were staged most of the Jews fled to Germany, returning when it was safe. During WWI, Germany brought in J. refugees from Poland for forced labor. Many remained in G. after the war. About 80% of the J. breadwinners worked in the nearby big city of Memel, until the annexation in 1939. Then Jews stopped working there and their economic situation declined. The community's two schools, one Hebrew and one Yiddish, were recognized by the Lithuanian government. Most Zionist parties were represented in G. After Germany's invasion in June 1941, the Gestapo detained all of G.'s Jews. The men were forced to deepen an antitank ditch, later used as their mass grave. The J. women and children were forced to reside in empty barns without food, the women being put to forced labor. In Sept. they were taken to the Vezaitine forest and murdered by Lithuanians.

GARLELE-GAZARIEI Moldavia dist., Rumania.

In the early 19th cent. Jews provided supplies to the workers at the J.-owned oil refineries, the first in Rumania. The J. pop. in 1930 was 179 (4% of the total). In June 1941, the 92 Jews there were expelled to Moinesti and on 15 July 1941 to Bacau.

GARLIAVA (Yid. Gudleve), Kaunas dist., Lithuania. Jews were among the town's first settlers at the beginning of the 19th cent. The J. pop. in 1897 was 469 (49% of the total). By WWII the J. pop. was about 70 families. After the German invasion of 1941, the J. men were forced to dig a large pit. They were then pushed into it and shot. G.'s J. women and children were also shot there at a later stage.

GARTZ AN DER ODER Pomerania, Germany. Jews are first mentioned in G. in 1481, but modern J. settlement started only after 1812, growing to 114 individuals in 1861. The community maintained a synagogue (consecrated in 1862) and a cemetery. When the Nazis came to power in 1933, only 26 Jews were still living in the town. No information about their fate under Nazi rule is available.

GARWOLIN Lublin dist., Poland. A J. community existed by the 17th cent., expanding significantly in the 19th cent and reaching a pop. of 2,182 (total 4,591) in 1897, with J. tradesmen prospering from the lively trade on the weekly market day and at the monthly fair. Others benefited as suppliers and building contractors from the presence of a Russian army garrison. In 1860, an impressive synagogue was erected, noted for its high windows and decorative stone facade. Despite the competition of a Polish farmers' marketing cooperative and attacks on J. peddlers at the turn of the 19th cent., the community continued to grow, reaching 2,424 (total 5082) in 1921. Most of the Jews were Radzymin Hasidim, but there were also followers of Gur

Sanatorska St., Garwolin, Poland

and Aleksandrow. The first Zionist group formed in the early 20th cent. Most of the Zionist parties and youth movements were active between the World Wars, contending with Agudat Israel for leadership of the community and promoting extensive cultural activity. During this period, the Joint Distribution Committee helped the community cope with the deteriorating economy in the face of discriminatory government policies and the anti-J. boycotts of the mid-1930s. During the German bombardments of Sept. 1939, 40 Jews were killed and many were injured. Many left the destroyed town. Most of the 200 who remained, about 40 families, were removed to Parysow in May 1940 and shared the fate of the local Jews.

GARZWEILER Rhineland, Germany. Jews are first mentioned in 1703. Construction of a synagogue was approved in 1756 and the J. pop. rose to 74 in 1850. Twenty-two Jews remained in 1932. Nine perished in the Holocaust.

GASPRA Crimea, Russia, today Ukraine. Jews were only granted formal residence rights in 1903, though they were probably present for some time before that. In 1939, their pop. was 46 (total 2,130). The Germans occupied G. on 8 Nov. 1941 and in Dec. murdered the few Jews who had neither fled nor been evacuated.

GAU-ALGESHEIM Hesse, Germany. Annihilated in the Black Death persecutions of 1348–49, the community was reestablished 350 years later and numbered 66 (2% of the total) in 1880. The Jews, mainly livestock traders, played an active role in civic affairs and the local theater. By 1939, no Jews remained in the town: some emigrated to the U.S., others were eventually deported. A memorial was unveiled there in 1986.

GAU-ODERNHEIM Hesse, Germany. Established by protected Jews *(Schutzjuden)* in the 14th cent., the community numbered 106 (6% of the total) by 1880. Of the 40 Jews living there after the Nazis came to power, 27 emigrated and 11 were eventually deported.

GAUKOENIGSHOFEN Lower Franconia, Germany. The 17th cent. J. settlers formed a community with their own rabbi in the early 18th cent. The Court Jew Baron Jakob von Hirsch, grandfather of the philanthropist Maurice de Hirsch and founder of the family fortune as well as the first J. estate owner in Bavaria, was born there in 1765. The Jews maintained a stable pop. (90–100) throughout the 19th cent. In 1933, 54 remained. Fifteen emigrated after *Kristallnacht* (9–10 Nov. 1938), when the synagogue was vandalized along with J. homes and business premises and J. landowners were forced to sell their property at a fraction of its value. Of those remaining, 25 were deported to Izbica in the Lublin dist. (Poland) via Wuerzburg on 25 April 1942. The six Jews of the attached community of Acholshausen (57 Jews in 1814) were similarly dispersed.

GAVA Szabolcs dist., Hungary. Jews are mentioned in 1770, attracted by estate owners eager to market their produce. They numbered 274 in 1880 and 186 in 1930. Most able-bodied men were sent to different parts of Hungary and then to the Ukraine in 1942 for forced labor. The rest were deported to Auschwitz via Nyiregyhaza on 17 May 1944.

GAYCHUR (from 1946, Ternovatoye) Zaporozhe dist., Ukraine. A number of Jews settled after the coming of the railroad to G. in the late 1890s. The few Jews who remained in WWII were murdered by the Germans after their arrival on 6 Oct. 1941, probably at the end of the year.

GAYSIN (Yid. Haysin) Vinnitsa dist., Ukraine. Jews numbered 62 in 1765 and 4,321 (total 9,374) in 1897. In the Russian civil war (1918–21), the Jews were attacked four times and on 12 May 1919, 390 were murdered. In the Soviet period, a J. law court, elementary school, and teachers' college operated, but the pride of the community was the medical college opened in 1929. A few dozen J. families worked in a kolkhoz. In 1939, the J. pop. was 4,109. The Germans captured the city on 25 July 1941. The Jews were immediately concentrated in a ghetto. Most were murdered in an *Aktion* on 16–17 Sept. Another 230 were executed on 14 Oct. In early Nov. 1942, 1,000 Jews expelled to G. from Transnistria were murdered. A total of 3,951 Jews were murdered in the area.

GBELY Slovakia, Czechoslovakia, today Republic of Slovakia. The J. community numbered 183 in 1869, maintaining a synagogue and cemetery. In 1920, 30 Jews remained.

Jewish labor union representatives on municipal council, Gaysin, Ukraine, 1924 (The Central Archive for the History of the Jewish People, Jerusalem/photo courtesy of Yad Vashem, The Holocaust Martyrs' and Heroes' Remembrance Authority, Jerusalem)

GDANSK   (Ger. Danzig) Pomerania dist., Poland. J. merchants were active in the city from the mid-15th cent. despite the ban imposed by the Teutonic Order. They continued to trade without permanent residence rights under Polish rule, exporting grain and lumber through the big port. Jews were able to settle in nearby settlements like Altschottland, where a synagogue and hospital were founded in 1777. Few lived in the city itself in the first years of Prussian rule. Their numbers increased in the early 19th cent. and Jews from the Russian Empire arrived after mid.-cent., forming their own community of about 300. The five separate congregations in the environs of G. – Schottland, Langfuhr, Weinberg, Mattenbunden, and Breitegasse – united in 1883. The community was served from 1837 by R. Yisrael Lipschuetz, known for his *Tiferet Yisrael* commentary on the Mishna. From the mid-19th cent., the Jews of G. were active in the struggle for emancipation and participated in public and cultural life. Their protests modified the expulsion order from G. issued against Russian Jews in 1885, limiting it to include only the poor, whom the community helped emigrate to the U.S. Despite differences, reflecting their historical and cultural origins, Orthodox and Liberals were able to build a common synagogue in 1887. Greater resistance was shown to the Zionists, with the community subscribing to the 1897 declaration by the rabbis of Germany that Zionism was a danger to the Jews because it exacerbated antisemitism. By 1910, the community numbered 2,717. Most Jews belonged to the middle class, thriving in a city known for its liberalism. After WWI, G. became a free city under League of Nations auspices, thus opening the door to East European immigration, which swelled the J. pop. to 9,239 in 1924 and 12,000 in 1937. The newcomers were fully integrated in public and economic life, serving in the senate and judiciary and opening department stores, banks, and

Synagogue in Gdansk (Danzig), Poland

amber- and tobacco-processing plants. In 1925, Jews constituted a third of the city's lawyers and even a higher percentage of its doctors and dentists. However, J. artisans in traditional occupations like tanning, tailoring, and carpentry faced stiff Polish competition and discriminatory government policy. From the 1930s, with the Nazi Party gaining a majority in the local senate, antisemitism increased dramatically, disillusioning many of the liberals and assimilationists among the Jews and driving them into the camp of the Zionists, whose activities expanded greatly after WWI. J. complaints to the League of Nations and the local courts about official discrimination were of little avail. On 20–23 Oct. 1937, after a virulent Nazi propaganda campaign, a pogrom was staged with heavy damage to J. homes and businesses. In Sept. 1938 the licenses of J. doctors were revoked and on 13 Dec. local Nazis staged their own *Kristallnacht*. While the synagogue was damaged, its contents were saved and sent for safekeeping to the J. Theological Seminary in New York. With all J. children in a separate J. school after being forced out of the public schools by Hitler Youth harassment, preparations

were made there for emigration to Palestine through Youth Aliya by including classes in agriculture. Vocational training was also organized among adults, with 700 participating in 1938. By Sept. 1939, 1,666 Jews remained in the city (total pop. 449,990). Additional efforts were made to emigrate, the last group sailing for Palestine on the *Patria*, which was subsequently sunk by the British in Haifa port. Of the 600 Jews in the city in early 1941, 395 were expelled to General Gouvernement territory in Feb. and the 200 residents of the J. old age home were deported to the Theresienstadt ghetto. A community was reestablished after the war.

GDOV Leningrad dist., Russia. Jews probably settled in the mid-19th cent. Their pop. was 69 (total 2,106) in 1897. In the Soviet period, their pop. stood at 86 in 1926 and 36 in 1939. Those Jews who had not fled or been evacuated were murdered after the German occupation of 19 July 1941.

GDOW Cracow dist., Poland. The J. pop. numbered 376 in 1880 and 245 (total 1,753) in 1921. In 1918 and 1919, local peasants and demobilized soldiers went on a rampage, beating Jews and pillaging their property. The Germans established a *Judenrat* at the end of 1939 and instituted a regime of terror and extortion. The community was liquidated in Aug. 1942, when the J. pop. was expelled to Wieliczka in time for the *Aktion* of 28 Aug. that sent most to the Belzec death camp.

GDYNIA Pomerania dist., Poland. A few dozen Jews were living in G. in 1921. Many arrived from former Congress Poland and Galicia in the late 1920s, attracted by the thriving port and general development of the city. In the mid-1930s the community was the largest in the region with a J. pop. of 700 (total 40,000). Many left on the eve of WWII. The Germans arrested a large number of Jews on their arrival in Sept. 1939, executing them in the nearby village of Wisznice. Another 98 were sent to the Stutthof concentration camp near Gdansk. Twenty-seven J. families escaped to the Guzcino forests but were turned in by local residents in May 1940 and sent on to Auschwitz, 13 surviving the Holocaust. The Jews remaining in G. were expelled to General Gouvernement territory and perished.

GEBE Szatmar dist., Hungary. Jews settled in the

first half of the 19th cent., marketing mostly rice and tobacco grown by peasants. A synagogue was established in 1840. The J. pop. was 250 in 1880 and 137 in 1930. All were deported to Auschwitz via Mateszalka in early June 1944.

GEDERN Hesse, Germany. Established before 1700, the community numbered 183 (9% of the total) in 1861. The Jews, primarily earning their living as livestock dealers, were religiously Liberal but affiliated with the Orthodox rabbinate of Giessen. From 13 March 1933, the Nazi boycott and vicious assaults drove Jews to leave the town. As a result of severe persecution, none remained by April 1937; 15 emigrated and 105 moved to other parts of Germany.

GEERTRUIDENBERG Noord-Brabant dist., Holland. The J. presence stabilized from the second half of the 18th cent. A community was organized around 1810 and numbered 21 in 1860. The J. pop. in 1941 was 14 (total 3,008). All but three who hid were deported and perished in the Holocaust.

GEGENY Szabolcs dist., Hungary. Jews are first mentioned in 1770, numbering 78 in 1880 and 103 in 1930. The premises of the well-known Goldstein trading firm were burned in the post-WWI White Terror and J. stores were looted. Local authorities tried to soften the impact of the 1938 racial laws. In late May 1944, the Jews were deported to Auschwitz via Nyiregyhaza.

GEHAUS Thuringia, Germany. Jews settled in G. in the early 18th cent. A J. cemetery existed from 1730, a synagogue from 1884. The J. pop. reached a peak at 50 in 1900, when a J. community was founded. In 1932–33, the J. pop. numbered 40, including Jews from the affiliated communities of Dermbach and Unteralba. When the Nazis came to power in 1933, 11 Jews managed to emigrate. On *Kristallnacht* (9–10 Nov. 1938), the synagogue and J. stores were vandalized. The cemetery was also desecrated. The head of the J. community was executed in Erfurt for alleged espionage. The remaining three to four Jews were deported. Altogether, 14 Jews from G. perished in the Holocaust.

GEILENKIRCHEN Rhineland, Germany. Five J. families are known from the mid-18th cent. In 1861,

G. became the seat of a dist. congregation with the communities of Gangelt, Waldenberg, Schwanenberg, Heinsberg, and Erkelenz attached to it. A synagogue was erected in 1869. The J. pop. rose from 56 in 1808 to a peak of 171 (total 4,426) in 1905. In 1932, 125 Jews remained. About ten emigrated in 1933. By 1939 many had left for other German cities, such as Cologne and Duesseldorf, while others reached Holland or went overseas. On *Kristallnacht* (9–10 Nov. 1938), the synagogue was set on fire. The last Jews were expelled to Dueren and Aachen in Dec. 1938. After being confined to a few crowded apartments under a regime of forced labor, they were deported in 1941 and 1942 to Auschwitz, Majdanek, Sobibor, and the Theresienstadt ghetto.

GEINSHEIM Palatinate, Germany. The J. pop. was 31 in the early 19th cent. and 55 in 1821. In 1848, the J. pop. reached a peak of 94 (18 families), with 13 breadwinners engaged in trade, two in farming, and three working as farmer-merchants. A synagogue was erected in the second half of the 19th cent. The J. pop. dropped to 75 (total 1,502) in 1875, 46 in 1900, and 30 in 1932. Fifteen Jews remained in May 1939. Half left the village and the last seven were deported to the Gurs concentration camp on 22 Oct. 1942, six perishing.

GEISIG Hesse–Nassau, Germany. Numbering 24 (7% of the total) in 1871, the Jews only established an independent community around 1890. By Dec. 1939 it had ceased to exist.

GEISTINGEN Rhineland, Germany. Three J. livestock dealers and their families were living in G. in 1791. In 1845 the community numbered 16 families (83 Jews). The Orthodox community maintained facilities for ritual slaughter and purification along with a cemetery (opened in 1860) and a synagogue (1862). In 1933, the J. pop. was 50. The cemetery was desecrated in the Nazi period and the synagogue was razed on *Kristallnacht* (9–10 Nov. 1938). Most Jews left; those who remained were deported to the east in late 1941 and summer 1942.

GELDERN Rhineland, Germany. The J. community was one of the oldest in the Lower Rhineland. In 1096, during the First Crusade, the Jews were forcibly converted. Jews are also known from the 13th and 14th

cents., but none were present by the late 15th. A small community existed in the early 19th cent. With the coming of the railroad in 1860, Jews consolidated their economic position, starting cattle and textile businesses. Their pop. reached a peak of 164 in 1863 and then declined steadily to 57 (total 7,066) in 1933. A cemetery was opened in 1860; a synagogue and J. elementary school were inaugurated in 1875. The synagogue was set on fire on *Kristallnacht* (9–10 Nov. 1938), while J. homes and stores were damaged. About half the Jews left the town, most to Holland and other German cities. The last 12 Jews were deported to the east in June and July 1942. Seventeen perished in the Holocaust, along with another five from the attached community of Straelen.

GELNHAUSEN Hesse–Nassau, Germany. Jews lived there in 1242. In 1337 they were paying an annual tax on their synagogue. During the Black Death persecutions of 1348–49 they were massacred. Other Jews who settled in the town were expelled in 1576 but returned and built a new synagogue in 1601, which they restored after the Thirty Years War (1618–48) and later enlarged (1735–40). Despite hostile measures (such as confinement to a ghetto), they numbered 33 families in 1734. Originally restricted to moneylending, the Jews became traders and later entered the professions. Numbering 261 (7% of the total) in 1835, they opened a religious school in 1836 to counteract Protestant teaching, established a J. lending library in 1894, and were affiliated with the rabbinate of Hanau. An anti-J. boycott campaign was launched even before the Nazis came to power in 1933 and 72 of the 218 Jews fled by Nov. 1933. They disposed of their synagogue in July 1938 and, after the last Jew's departure (1 Oct.), G. was proclaimed "free of Jews" (*judenrein*). At least nine former J. residents perished in Auschwitz. The synagogue was renovated in 1986 and transformed into a cultural center, with a permanent exhibition devoted to local J. history.

GELNICA (Hung. Golnicbanya) Slovakia, Czechoslovakia, today Republic of Slovakia. Jews arrived in the 1850s but the opposition of the local German pop. kept their number low until the 20th cent. In 1930 they reached a peak pop. of 274 (total 3,975). A yeshiva with 80 students was opened in the 1920s. Mizrachi and Agudat Israel were active between the

World Wars. Jews owned 14 business establishments and nine workshops. In 1940, 231 Jews remained. With the outbreak of war, local Germans destroyed the synagogue and J. school and desecrated the J. cemetery. In 1941, Jews were forced out of their businesses and in early April 1942, young J. men and women were deported to the Majdanek concentration camp and to Auschwitz, respectively. Families were sent to the death camps of the east in April and May and on 9 Sept. 1944, local Germans murdered another 11 Jews during the Slovakian national uprising.

GELSENKIRCHEN Westphalia, Germany. Jews settled in the early 18th cent., their number remaining small until the early 19th cent., when the community began to grow steadily. Most engaged in trade. The Jews of G. were attached to the Wattenscheid congregation. In the first half of the 19th cent., they were active in the social life of the town, joining the volunteer firemen and the marksmen's club. In 1874, they formed an independent regional congregation with other communities attached to it (Braubauerschaft, Schalke, Bulmke, Hessler, Huellen). The local J. school, which became a public school in 1884, reached an enrollment of 140 in 1908. A synagogue with an organ and mixed choir was consecrated in 1885 as the congregation became Liberal. From about 1860 on, three Orthodox congregations were also functioning, including one comprised of Polish Jews. In the late 19th and early 20th cents., the community began to grow rapidly, its pop. increasing from 96 in 1871 to 648 in 1896 and 1,352 (total 176,093) in 1915, making it the second largest in Westphalia. About two-thirds were still engaged in trade. Although antisemitic tendencies were manifest from the 1880s, Jews were holding public positions by the early 20th cent. The community maintained numerous charitable organizations. In 1914, Dr. Siegfried Galliner became rabbi, serving the community until WWII. Zionist influence increased in the 1920s as the community reached a peak pop. of about 1,700. A new synagogue was completed in 1932. The start of Nazi rule in 1933 was accompanied by anti-J. violence and unremitting persecution. Under Nazi pressure, many local residents ceased to associate with Jews while public servants were explicitly prohibited from patronizing J. businesses. Nonetheless, many continued to buy from Jews and there were 160 J. business establishments still open in

Aug. 1938. Until the official ban in Oct. 1938, J. doctors continued practicing. In that same month, Jews of Polish origin were expelled from the city. Community life continued to flourish throughout the period. R. Galliner set up a school for adult education (*Lehrhaus*) in early 1935 with courses on Zionist subjects and Hebrew language study. The community also offered courses in Hebrew and English and the Rhineland–Ruhr J. Cultural Association offered theater performances. In the 1933–38 period, the J. pop. dropped from about 1,600 to 1,000 while the number of students in the J. school fell from 160 to 60 between 1937 and 1939. On *Kristallnacht* (9–10 Nov. 1938), the synagogue was set on fire, J. homes and stores were wrecked, and Jews were beaten and arrested. Some were sent to the Sachsenhausen concentration camp, where 13 died. In 1939, R. Galliner emigrated to England. The remaining Jews were subjected to forced labor seven days a week, working 10–12 hours a day in underground building sites and coal mines. In early 1942, 500 Jews remained. On 27 Jan., 350 were deported to the Riga ghetto. The last Jews, mainly the sick and old, were deported in two additional transports: 40 to Warsaw on 31 March 1942 and 90 to the Theresienstadt ghetto on 27 July. A total of 574 Jews perished in the Holocaust, including the Jews of Buer and Horst. After the war, 45 survivors reestablished the community. A community center with a synagogue was erected in 1958. In 1993 the J. pop. of G. was 157.

GELVONAI (Yid. Gelvan) Ukmerge dist., Lithuania. Jews began settling here in the 17th cent. The J. pop. in 1914 was about 90 families (90% of the total). Before WWI the community prospered and the Jews had close trade connections with Vilna. After WWI these links were cut off and the economy deteriorated. Many Jews emigrated, some to Palestine. When Germany invaded the USSR in June 1941, Lithuanian nationalists began persecuting Jews. In July, all Jews were taken to a marsh far from town and the men tortured. Upon their return, they found their homes had been looted. The local priest intervened and the stolen property was returned. On 5 Sept. 1941, all Jews were taken to the Pivonija forest and murdered.

GEMEN Westphalia, Germany. Jews are mentioned in 1567 but a community of 30–40 Jews (2–3% of the total) was only formed in the 20th cent. In the mid-19th

cent., when three families of J. peddlers were living there, G. was attached to the Borken regional congregation. A synagogue was consecrated in 1912 as the community remained Orthodox. Community chairman Oskar Loewenstein was among the founders in 1896 of the Association for the Safeguarding of Traditional Judaism in Westphalia. The communities of Weseke and Ramsdorf were attached to the G. congregation. In 1935, Austrian SA forces stationed nearby attacked Jews in the synagogue. On *Kristallnacht* (9–10 Nov. 1938), the synagogue was set on fire and four J. homes were damaged. J. men were arrested. In 1938, 17 Jews left the town; another 15 left in 1939. Twenty-six Jews are known to have perished in the Holocaust. Eleven Jews from Weseke were deported to the Riga ghetto on 13 Dec. 1941 and 13 perished in the Holocaust.

GEMMINGEN Baden, Germany. The first Jews may have settled after the Thirty Years War (1618–48) but their presence is only known for certain from the 18th cent. A J. elementary school was opened in the 1830s and a synagogue was erected in 1882. The J. pop. reached a peak of 252 in 1871, dropping to 105 in 1910 (total 1,235) and 47 in 1933. On *Kristallnacht* (9–10 Nov. 1938), the synagogue was vandalized. In 1934–39, 21 Jews emigrated from Germany (13 to the U.S., six to South America), while 26 left for other German cities, six of them being ultimately sent to the camps, as were five directly from G. to the Gurs concentration camp on 22 Oct. 1940.

GEMUEND Rhineland, Germany. Jews were present from the early 18th cent. and in the early 19th cent. numbered 30–45. They earned their livelihoods as petty traders, butchers, and moneylenders. In 1871, the J. pop. reached a peak of 71 (total 1,499), subsequently dropping to 50 in 1910 and 28 in 1932. The last community leader perished in Auschwitz; the fate of the remaining Jews in the Nazi era is not known. The synagogue founded in 1874 was burned on *Kristallnacht* (9–10 Nov. 1938). The J. cemetery, dating from 1860, was desecrated in 1958.

GEMUENDEN Lower Franconia, Germany. The medieval J. community was destroyed in the Rindfleisch massacres of 1298. Jews appeared in the mid-17th cent. and maintained a presence throughout the 18th and 19th cents., numbering 100 in 1900 (total

GERA Thuringia, Germany. There is evidence of sporadic settlement as well as expulsion of Jews from G. since the 14th cent. A synagogue is known to have existed in 1502. A sizable J. pop. began to develop only in the late 19th cent., increasing rapidly owing to the influx of Jews from Eastern Europe. A J. community was formally founded in 1885 and in 1895, there were 90 Jews in G., engaged mostly in commerce. Hermann Tietz and his nephew Oskar Tietz, who came to G. in 1882, were the founders of a chain of department stores all over Germany. The J. pop. grew from 150 in 1900 to 519 in 1925 (0.6% of the total). With the Nazi rise to power in 1933, many Jews emigrated and the J. pop. dropped to 378. Forced "Aryanization" of J. businesses began here as early as 1933 and in 1934 the Tietz concern was forced to sell out. In Oct. 1938, all Jews who had Polish citizenship were deported to Poland. On *Kristallnacht* (9–10 Nov. 1938), the two synagogues in G. were vandalized and one destroyed, 36 J. men were arrested, and the J. shops were closed down. In 1939, only 77 Jews remained in G. They were deported to death camps during the war.

GERGELYIUGORNYA Bereg dist., Hungary. A small Orthodox community was organized in the 19th cent., numbering 175 in 1930. The Jews were deported to Auschwitz via Beregszasz on 20 May 1944.

GERMANOWKA Kiev dist., Ukraine. Jews numbered ten in 1775 and 1,049 (total 3,628) in 1897. A *talmud torah* was opened in 1909. On 29 Aug. and 28 Sept. 1919, the Jews were attacked in riots. In 1926, under the Soviets, they numbered 62. Most were murdered during the German occupation in WWII.

GERMERSHEIM Palatinate, Germany. Jews were present in the free city of G. in the Middle Ages. On 26 April 1343, they were burned at the stake following a blood libel. The community was again destroyed in the Black Death persecutions of 1348–49. Jews were once more present in 1390 but from then until the early 19th cent. there is no information about Jews in the city. In 1804, the J. pop. was seven, growing to 28 in 1840 and 93 in 1848. Of the 21 family heads in the latter year, 13 were merchants, five farmers, and three artisans. In 1875, the J. pop. was 134 (total 6,455). A synagogue was consecrated in 1838; a women's society was founded in 1846; and a new *mikve* was opened in 1848. The synagogue was completely renovated in 1863 and a teacher's apartment and a classroom for a J. elementary school were set up in the upper story (the school closed in 1887). The existence of an organ in the synagogue in the early 20th cent. indicated the Reform tendencies of the congregation. A relief organization operated in 1909. The J. pop. dropped to 58 in 1900 and 38 in 1932. Seven Jews remained in 1939. These were deported to the Gurs concentration camp on 22 Oct. 1940, five perishing there. During the Nazi era, the Germans took over the synagogue, which became a private residence after the war.

GERNSBACH Baden, Germany. Jews first settled in 1683, concentrating in a J. quarter in the old city and later in a suburb outside the town walls. From the early 19th cent. to the Nazi era the Jews maintained a pop. of around 60 (2.5% of the total). A new synagogue was erected in 1860. A number of smaller communities were attached to G., including Hoerden with its 14 Jews. Of G.'s 54 Jews (1933), 29 emigrated in the Nazi era, mostly to the U.S., and 12 left for other German cities. On *Kristallnacht* (9–10 Nov. 1938), the synagogue was burned, J. homes and businesses were heavily damaged, and 20 Jews were sent to the Dachau concentration camp. The last nine Jews were deported to the Gurs concentration camp on 22 Oct. 1940. Of the Jews in Hoerden, eight emigrated and four were deported to Gurs.

GERNSHEIM Hesse, Germany. Founded in the late 18th cent., the community numbered 96 (3% of the total) in 1880. By 1933 it had dwindled to 27 and four years later its Torah scrolls were moved to Darmstadt. On *Kristallnacht* (9–10 Nov. 1938), the remaining 19 Jews were beaten, stripped naked, and pelted with stones. A memorial to those who perished in the Holocaust was erected by the town council in 1985.

GERODA Lower Franconia, Germany. The J. community numbered 63 in 1880 (total 691) and 43 in 1933, mostly engaged in farming. The community maintained a synagogue, rebuilt in 1907, and a cemetery, consecrated in 1910, which served other communities as well. On *Kristallnacht* (9–10 Nov. 1938), Jews were severely beaten and two were murdered in the Dachau concentration camp and the synagogue was

Ark of the Law from 1580 in the Geroda synagogue, Germany

wrecked. In all, 29 Jews managed to leave G. in 1936–41, ten emigrating from Germany. The rest were sent to the Dachau and Buchenwald concentration camps, Izbica in the Lublin dist. (Poland), and the Theresienstadt ghetto in 1941–42.

GEROLDSHAUSEN Lower Franconia, Germany. Jews numbered 50 in 1814 (total 233) and nine in 1933. Four emigrated to the U.S. in 1940–41 and the last two were deported to Izbica in the Lublin dist. (Poland) via Wuerzburg on 25 April 1942.

GEROLSTEIN Rhineland, Germany. A few Jews were present before the Black Death persecutions of 1348–49. In 1719, two protected Jews received residence rights. In the second half of the 19th cent., the J. pop. still numbered only 14–25, growing to 45 in 1911 and 61 (total 2,740) in 1925. A cemetery was opened in 1894. In 1936, 34 Jews remained and 19 in 1937. After the outbreak of war, there were eight Jews remaining. All were deported to the east.

GEROLZHOFEN Lower Franconia, Germany. Jews were victims of the Rindfleisch massacres of 1298. The modern community dates from the first half of the 17th cent., with a cemetery consecrated in 1639 serving seven other communities as well. A new synagogue was built in 1874. The J. pop. reached a peak of 148 in 1900 (total 2,163) and numbered 125 in 1933. On *Kristallnacht* (9–10 Nov. 1938), Jews were beaten and arrested and their homes wrecked along with the synagogue. In 1933–41, 61 Jews emigrated from Germany, 39 of them to the U.S. Another 35 left for other German cities. On 25 April 1942, 19 Jews were deported to Izbica near Lublin via Wuerzburg; another six were sent to the Theresienstadt ghetto in Sept.

GERRESHEIM Rhineland, Germany. In the mid-18th cent., there were 29 Jews living in G. From 1840, the community was affiliated to the Duesseldorf community. The community maintained a synagogue, consecrated in 1875 but sold in 1917, and two cemeteries, one from mid-18th cent. and the other from 1899. The Orthodox Duesseldorf Adass Jisroel breakaway community acquired burial rights in G. in 1925 and conducted funerals there up to 1938. In 1933, there were about 100 Jews living in G. During the boycott in April 1933, SA troops rounded up and abused Jews. On *Kristallnacht* (9–10 Nov. 1938), several J. homes were wrecked and the books of a lending library belonging to a Jew were thrown into the street and burned. Three Jews barely escaped being murdered. Altogether 25 Jews managed to escape to other countries. At least two Jews committed suicide before deportation and 40 perished in the Nazi camps.

GERSFELD Hesse–Nassau, Germany. Established around 1750, the community numbered 119 (8% of the total) in 1871. A new synagogue (its third) was built after a disastrous fire in 1886. Jews played a major role in commerce and were elected to the town council. Nazi violence and boycott measures reduced their number from 114 (7%) in 1933 to 20 on *Kristallnacht* (9–10 Nov. 1938), when the synagogue was destroyed. At least 39 Jews emigrated (15 to Palestine). Some of the 56 who moved to other German towns later perished in death camps. J. survivors of the Buchenwald concentration camp, housed in G. after WWII, mostly left for Israel in 1948.

Zionist activity began in 1925. When the Hungarians entered N. Transylvania in Sept. 1940 the situation of the Jews declined, and in 1942 several score were expelled to Kamenets-Podolski where they were killed by Hungarian soldiers. Community leaders were sent to concentration camps in western Hungary. In May 1944 the J. community was transferred to the Sfantul Gheorghe ghetto and in June deported to Auschwitz. An attempt to rehabilitate the community after the war was shortlived.

GHERLA (Hung. Szamosujvar) N. Transylvania dist., Rumania. Jews settled in the early 19th cent. In 1903 a synagogue seating several hundred was built. The J. pop. in 1920 was 1,041 (16% of the total). In the 1920s the yeshiva had 50 students. R. Barukh Rubin had a hasidic court in G. Jews were elected to the city council and a Zionist, Adolph Goldstein, was council secretary for many years. Zionist activity began in 1919 when a local branch of the National Association of Transylvanian Zionists was set up. Youth movements and women's Zionist organizations were established. The situation of the Jews declined when the Hungarians took control in 1940. In June 1942, 424 Jews of the district aged 21–42 (including 20 from G.) were conscripted for labor battalions and sent to the Ukraine, where most died. The situation deteriorated further with the conquest of G. by the Germans on 19 March 1944 and the introduction of new restrictions and the boycott of businesses. About 1,400 Jews, including 500 from surrounding villages, were ghettoized on 2 May 1944. On 17 May all the inmates were transferred to the Cluj ghetto and on 26 May deported to Auschwitz. In 1945, 158 survivors returned, but all left over the years.

GHIMES-FAGET (Hung. Gyimesbukk) N. Transylvania dist., Rumania. Jews settled in the mid-19th cent. At the end of the cent. they were persecuted by the local pop. The J. pop. in 1930 was 224 (4% of the total). In summer 1941 all the Jews were expelled and dispersed throughout the country.

GIDLE (Gidjel) Lodz dist., Poland. Jews were involved in agriculture and services to Christian pilgrims. R. Herschel of Gidle lived here, and Hasidim visited the sage's tomb in Plawno. The J. pop. in 1921 was 192. On 6 Oct. 1942, the 600 Jews of Gidle and Plawno were murdered.

GIEBELSTADT Lower Franconia, Germany. A community is known from the mid-18th cent. and a synagogue was consecrated in 1799. The J. pop. reached 103 in 1814 (total 597) and declined steadily thereafter to 38 in 1933. Twenty-four Jews left in 1933–38, 16 of them emigrating from Germany. On *Kristallnacht* (9–10 Nov. 1938), the synagogue and J. homes were wrecked by the SA and SS. The last five Jews were deported to Izbica in the Lublin dist. (Poland) via Wuerzburg on 25 April 1942.

GIEDRAICIAI (Yid. Gedrevitsh) Ukmerge dist., Lithuania. The J. community dates to the beginning of the 19th cent. Between the World Wars, its adults and youth were involved in Zionist activities. The J. pop. in 1939 was 200 (36% of the total). Under the Soviets (1940–41), Zionist and Hebrew activities were stopped. After Germany's invasion in 1941, Lithuanians killed several dozen Jews. Others were murdered prior to the mass murder of about 100 Jews in the Vaitkiskiu Dvaras forest or Pivonija in Sept.

GIELNIOW Lodz dist., Poland. The J. pop. in 1857 was 124. During WWII the community increased to 250, all of whom were deported to the Treblinka death camp on 24 Oct. 1942.

GIESENKIRCHEN Rhineland, Germany. Protected Jews are known from 1737. A single congregation was formed with Schelsen (pop. 60, or 3% of the total, in 1801), becoming part of the Moenchengladbach regional congregation in 1854 and a satellite of Rheydt in 1890. Ten Jews remained in 1924–25 and one family in 1938. The parents were deported to the Lodz ghetto in Dec. 1938; the two daughters emigrated.

GIESSEN Hesse, Germany. Jews lived there from the mid-13th cent., but their community was annihilated in the Black Death persecutions of 1348–49. After returning early in the 15th cent., Jews were banished in 1662. The community was reorganized in 1720–25, and Jews helped G. become a center of the livestock trade. When Abraham Alexander Wolff left to become chief rabbi of Denmark in 1828, he was succeeded by Benedikt Samuel Levi, a champion of J. rights, whose rabbinical career spanned 69 years (1828–96). During his time an organ and choir were introduced into the synagogue, representing the Liberal orientation of the community. G. replaced Friedberg

as the seat of Upper Hesse's chief rabbinate in 1842 and another synagogue was constructed between 1867–91. Hermann Levi, Benedikt's son, won fame as a conductor (especially of Wagner's operas). Orthodox secessionists later founded a separate community (*Austrittsgemeinde*) in 1887, chose a different rabbi, and built their own synagogue in 1899. Leo Hirschfeld served as their regional chief rabbi (1895–1933). The city's J. pop. grew from 384 in 1871 to 1,035 (over 3% of the total) in 1910 and Jews were elected to the city council, the chamber of commerce, and the state assembly (Landtag). Although Jews were barred from teaching posts at the University of G. until 1873, they constituted 10% of the faculty members during the Weimar Rebublic. Scholars in different fields — Margarete Bieber (art history and archeology), Fritz Heichelheim (ancient history), Kurt Koffka and Erich Stein (psychology), Richard Laqueur (classical literature), Samuel Bialoblocki and Yisrael Rabin (Judaica) — were among those who taught there before the Nazi era. Relations between the Liberal and Orthodox communities improved after WWI, both groups working together in local branches of the Central Union (C.V.), the J. War Veterans Association and German Zionist Organization, and several youth movements. Jews played a leading role in cultural and professional life during the Weimar Republic. Many festive events took place in the community center and a large number of students at the university promoted Zionism. Among the first graduates to leave for Palestine were Adolf Reifenberg, a Hebrew University agronomist from 1924 and an expert on ancient J. coins; Moshe Smoira, first president of Israel's Supreme Court (1948–54); and the archeologist Benjamin (Maisler) Mazar, who later became president of the Hebrew University (1953–61). Antisemitism was prevalent in G. long before the Nazi era. As elsewhere in Germany when Hitler came to power in 1933, anti-J. violence mounted day by day as the Nazi boycott was imposed (1 April). A book-burning ceremony took place on 8 May, and the last "non-Aryan" teachers were dismissed from the university on 20 July. Communal and Zionist workers fostered *aliya* while maintaining a semblance of J. life. The Liberal and Orthodox communities amalgamated shortly before *Kristallnacht* (9–10 Nov. 1938), when both synagogues were destroyed in a general pogrom. Of the 1,265 Jews living in G. and its vicinity in 1933, 730 had emigrated or moved elsewhere by the end of 1938. The community (swelled by refugees) vanished when the last remaining Jews were deported in Sept. 1942. On 2 March 1943, G. was declared "free of Jews" (*judenrein*). According to an official estimate, 465 Jews emigrated during the Nazi period, (185 to Palestine and 176 to the U.S.); 346 perished in death camps. The fate of another 530 is uncertain. Mainly comprising students and former Displaced Persons, the J. community established after WWII numbered 200 in 1998.

GILGENBURG (Pol. Dabrowno) East Prussia, Germany, today Poland. The J. community numbered 119 Jews in 1880, but gradually declined in the first decades of the 20th cent. to about 52 in 1925. It maintained a synagogue and a cemetery. When the Nazis assumed power, 47 Jews were living in G. Many left during the first years of Nazi rule. In 1937 the synagogue was sold and the community dissolved. No further information about the fate of the Jews of G. under Nazi rule is available.

GILSERBERG Hesse–Nassau, Germany. Established around 1830, the community numbered 71 (15% of the total) in 1895 and 35 (6%) in 1933. Torah scrolls previously moved to Kassel were destroyed on *Kristallnacht* (9–10 Nov. 1938). By Dec. 1939, all the Jews had left, mostly emigrating, 17 to the U.S.

GIMBSHEIM Hesse, Germany. Although Jews first arrived there in the 17th cent., an independent community was not established until 1875, numbering 72 (3% of the total) in 1900. It then declined, and by Dec. 1939 all the Jews had left.

GINDORF Rhineland, Germany. A small J. settlement existed in the second half of the 18th cent. Antisemitic outbursts followed blood libels in the area in 1834 and 1892 (the latter in Xanten). In 1885, the J. pop. was 71 (total 1,071), dropping to about 30 in 1933. The synagogue, dating back to 1834, was destroyed on *Kristallnacht* (9–10 Nov. 1938). Most Jews left the village before the outbreak of war, the last two being deported in 1942.

GIRALTOVCE (Hung. Giralt) Slovakia, Czechoslovakia, today Republic of Slovakia. The community was a satellite of Hanusovce and became organized around the mid-19th cent. when a synagogue was

built, uncharacteristically, next to the cemetery for want of an alternate site. The J. pop. rose from 104 (total 760) in 1880 to 265 in 1930. The Zionists became active in the 1920s, with Mizrachi the leading movement and Hashomer Hatzair running a pioneer training farm in the 1930s. Most of the town's businesses were in J. hands, including 24 commercial establishments, four workshops, a sawmill, a flour mill, and a distillery. In 1941, in the Slovakian state, Jews were forced out of their businesses and on 21 March 1942, 100 young J. men and women were rounded up for deportation to the Majdanek and Auschwitz concentration camps, respectively. Families were deported to the Rejowiec ghetto in the Lublin dist. of Poland on 24 and 26 May. Over 80% of the town's Jews were sent to the death camps in 1942. Another 44 were evacuated to western Slovakia in mid-May 1944.

GIRKALNIS (Yid. Girtegole) Raseiniai dist., Lithuania. The J. pop. was 530 in 1897 (82% of the total) and 27 families in 1939. After Germany's invasion in June 1941, Lithuanian nationalists trampled and danced on the community's Torah scrolls and seriously injured the rabbi. All 120 Jews were then detained for a week without food, dragged half a mile, ordered to strip, and shot.

GIULESTI (Hung. Maragyulafalva) N. Transylvania dist., Rumania. Jews settled in the early 18th cent. The J. pop. in 1920 was 207 (10% of the total). In April 1944 the Jews were transferred to the Berbesti ghetto and then deported to Auschwitz.

GIURGIU Walachia dist., Rumania. Sephardi J. merchants came to G. from the Balkans in the 1820s and Ashkenazi Jews settled later, which led to communal disputes. A Zionist group was formed in 1899 with 70 members and a joint J. school opened in 1878, with 60 pupils in 1910. The J. pop. in 1910 was 533 (4% of the total). Jews were forced to forfeit their property to the Iron Guard in 1941 and at least half of the 113 Jews living there in 1941 left. A community existed after the war.

GLADBECK Westphalia, Germany. The first Jews settled in 1822 and 1837 but the community only began to develop in the late 19th cent. with the economic development of the city. Jews supplied essential goods to the miners and industrial workers of G. Their

pop. rose to 97 in 1910 and 264 (total 60,043) in 1925 as J. workers from Galicia began arriving. They soon constituted a majority among the Jews. In 1928, a blood libel was leveled against the Jews and in 1929 the cemetery was desecrated. In 1933, the Nazis severely persecuted the 224 Jews who remained and the municipality imposed a long list of restrictions upon them. Consequently, dozens of Jews left the city. In late Oct. 1938, 25 Jews of East European origin were expelled. On *Kristallnacht* (9–10 Nov. 1938), J. homes and stores were damaged and Jews were beaten and arrested. Emigration was again stepped up and in May 1939, only 20 Jews remained. It is not known how many of these survived.

GLADENBACH Hesse–Nassau, Germany. Established before 1770, the community numbered 160 (13% of the total) in 1861 and 184 (12%) in 1905. A new synagogue was dedicated in 1891. Although antisemitic propaganda increased from 1885, Jews were elected to the village council. Affiliated with the rabbinate of Marburg and numbering 103 (6%) in 1933, the community fell victim to Nazi aggression. By Nov. 1938, only 11 elderly Jews remained. The synagogue, partly destroyed on *Kristallnacht* (9–10 Nov. 1938), was demolished three months later. By mid-1940 all the Jews had left.

GLATZ (Pol. Klodzko) Lower Silesia, Germany, today Poland. Jews are first mentioned in 1300. A synagogue, cemetery, and J. education are mentioned in 1384. All the Jews were expelled in 1492 on charges of "fraud and desecration." Undisturbed J. settlement only resumed in 1812. In 1840, the J. pop. was 60, most engaged in trade, and 251 in 1880. The community maintained two cemeteries and two synagogues (from 1821 and 1823) until a new Reform synagogue was built in 1884–85. The J. pop. was 183 in 1900 and 106 in 1933. Many emigrated in the 1933–36 period, leaving 62 Jews in G. in 1937. On *Kristallnacht* (9–10 Nov. 1938), the synagogue was set on fire and J. stores were destroyed. Twenty-six Jews remained in 1939 and three intermarried Jews in Nov. 1942. The fate of the community in WWII is unknown. Presumably those Jews who did not emigrate in time were deported and perished.

GLAUBERG Hesse, Germany. Members of this small community, numbering 30 (about 5% of the

total) in 1900, earned a livelihood from trade and agriculture. Having disposed of their synagogue, the last Jews moved elsewhere before Aug. 1938.

GLEHN Rhineland, Germany. Two families were present in 1716, the J. pop. growing to a peak of 74 (total 2,446) in 1871 and then dropping to 30 in 1925. The synagogue was vandalized on *Kristallnacht* (9–10 Nov. 1938).

GLEICHERWIESEN Thuringia, Germany. Jews first settled here in 1680 and a synagogue was dedicated in 1787. In 1818, there were 139 Jews (26 families) in G., with 233 in 1875 and 46 in 1925. Following the Nazi assumption of power in 1933, most of the 26 Jews remaining sold their belongings and left. On *Kristallnacht* (9–10 Nov. 1938), the synagogue's interior was ransacked and the building partly destroyed. J. stores and homes and the cemetery were vandalized and J. men were arrested and deported to the Buchenwald concentration camp. At least six Jews were deported to their deaths in 1942. No further information is available about those who failed to emigrate to safe havens overseas.

GLEIWITZ (Pol. Gliwice) Upper Silesia, Germany, today Poland. Jews were probably present in the 14th cent. In 1587, under the Hapsburgs, they were expelled from the city. The community was only renewed in 1715, reaching a pop. of 62 in 1793, including a number of landowners. The J. pop. then rose to 180 in 1812 and 2,009 (16.5% of the total) in 1867. The first synagogue was consecrated in 1812. In the same year the community enjoyed the services of a rabbi. A new and larger synagogue was built in 1860–61. In 1856 a J. elementary school was opened. Between the World Wars, the community maintained an old age home, orphanage, soup kitchen, Hebrew classes, and a kindergarten. The synagogue was Orthodox and the community also provided welfare services for the sick and needy. Also operating were organizations like the J. War Veterans Association, the Ha-Ko'ah and Bar Kokhba sports clubs, and four Zionist groups. Many were also active in the Social Democrat and Communist parties. Jews earned their livelihoods in trade, with some operating small factories and flour mills. The J. workforce also included 12 doctors and 14 lawyers. In 1932, the J. pop. was 1,845 with 20 smaller communities attached to the congregation. Even though

the Jews were protected from the Nazi racial laws by the League of Nations' minority rights convention, nonetheless the community was persecuted in the early years of Nazi rule, particularly in 1933, several years before the laws came into full force on 16 July 1937. It is therefore not surprising that the J. pop. dropped to 1,443 in this period. The institution of discriminatory measures in 1937 was accompanied by widespread disturbances. On *Kristallnacht* (9–10 Nov. 1938), rioters set the synagogue on fire and destroyed 40 J. stores. Hundreds of Jews were locked into a building owned by the community and the next day, 235 were sent to the Buchenwald concentration camp where at least six perished. Many emigrated to South Africa and Latin America in the late 1930s. Deportations to General Gouvernement concentration camps commenced in May 1942. Five transports left G. in June 1942, leaving behind 40 intermarried Jews. During this period, a number of Jews committed suicide.

GLEMBOKIE Vilna dist., Poland, today Belarus. Jews first settled in the 18th cent, numbering 755 in 1776. They exported lumber, farm produce, and bristles to various cities in Russia and Poland and purchased textiles and colonial imports from Leipzig as the town became a regional trade center. Jews owned flour mills, sawmills, and hide-processing shops. By the late 19th cent. there were ten prayer houses and a Great Synagogue in the town, with the majority identifying with Habad Hasidism. In 1897 the J. pop. reached 3,917 (total 5,564). Hebrew and Yiddish schools were opened in 1909. After WWI, J. commerce revived on a smaller scale. Most Jews had small auxiliary farms. The J. pop. in 1925 was 4,000. A Tarbut high school was opened in 1927 and Hehalutz was the dominant Zionist organization, operating pioneer training facilities. Most Jews adapted themselves to the Soviet regime of 1939–41. The Germans took the town on 2 July 1941. A *Judenrat* was set up and on 22 Oct. 1941 the Jews were ordered into a ghetto. In Dec., 110 Jews were executed in the forest and in April 1942 another 800 were murdered outside the town. The ghetto was then divided into working and nonworking sections. On 19 July, 2,500 Jews from the latter were murdered in the forest. Remnants from 42 other communities replaced them. On 20 Aug. 1943, the Germans set the ghetto on fire in a final *Aktion* that left 5,000 dead. Of the many who fled and joined the partisans throughout the period, about 100 survived.

GLINIANY (Yid. Glina) Tarnopol dist., Poland, today Ukraine. Jews are first noted from 1474 as leaseholders. A number of Jews were killed in the Chmielnicki massacres of 1648–49. At the beginning of the 18th cent. a fortresslike synagogue was built to replace the old wooden one. Shabbateanism and the Frankist movement found many followers in the community. In the mid-19th cent a hasidic court was established by Yehiel Mikhl Moskovitz, great-grandson of Yehiel-Mikhl of Zloczow. Austrian rule brought heavy taxation. The wealthy traded in agricultural commodities. In 1895, a Baron Hirsch school was opened and among its teachers was the historian Meir Balaban. In 1909 a Hebrew school was founded. By 1910, the pop. had grown to 2,418 (total 5,344), but most Jews fled the town at the beginning of WWI, with the local pop. pillaging and burning their homes. Between the World Wars, the diminished community suffered additionally from Polish and Ukrainian economic competition as well as rising antisemitism. J. public life, under increasing Zionist domination, came to an end with the Soviet annexation in Sept. 1939. The arrival of the Germans on 1 July 1941 initiated a regime of persecution in collusion with the local Ukrainian pop., who attacked Jews and pillaged their homes. In July and Aug., the J. badge was imposed, a *Judenrat* formed, and a heavy fine exacted. Most of the Jews were expelled to the Przemyslany ghetto at the end of Nov. 1942 and from there deported to the Belzec death camp on 3 Dec. 1942. From summer 1942, dozens of G.'s Jews fled to the forests; most were killed by Ukrainian peasants; some joined partisan groups.

GLINKA Smolensk dist., Russia. Jews probably arrived in the mid- or late 19th cent. In 1919, a few were killed and J. homes seriously damaged in a pogrom. In 1939, the J. pop. was 41 (total 653). The Germans arrived in July 1941, murdering 11 Jews at the nearby village of Synyiaki in Dec. 1941 and 65 Jews from the area in Jan. 1942.

GLINKI Volhynia dist., Poland, today Ukraine. The J. pop. in 1921 was 317 (total 1,134). It was probably liquidated by the Germans after transfer to the Rowne ghetto.

GLINNOVE Moldavia dist., Ukraine, today Republic of Moldova. The J. pop. in 1939 was 221 (total 7,308). German and Rumanian forces captured the city in early 1941. Local Jews shared the fate of the other Jews in the region.

GLINSKO Lwow dist., Poland, today Ukraine. The J. pop. in 1921 was 124. The Jews were possibly deported to the Belzec death camp in Nov. 1942, via Zolkiew or directly.

GLOD N. Transylvania dist., Rumania. A J. community was organized in the early 19th cent. The J. pop. in 1920 was 225 (23% of the total). From Sept. 1940 the situation of the Jews deteriorated. In April 1944 they were transferred to the Dragomiresti ghetto and then deported to Auschwitz.

GLOGAU (Pol. Glogow) Lower Silesia, Germany, today Poland. Jews are mentioned in 1280 as residents of a separate street and maintaining a synagogue and cemetery. The general expulsion order of 1484 was not enforced in G. and Jews continued to live there in the 15th–16th cents. In 1582, when all the Jews of Silesia and Bohemia were expelled, the Jews of G. and Zuelz (Upper Silesia) were the only two communities allowed to remain. The community grew rapidly and in the 17th cent. consecrated three new cemeteries. In 1636, a synagogue and a new J. residential quarter were dedicated. The J. pop. grew from 1,564 in 1725 to 1,644 in 1756 and nearly 2,000 in 1790. Subsequently it declined, to 716 in 1900; 700 in 1931; and 503 on the eve of the Nazi rise to power in 1933. The community maintained two synagogues and various organizations, including a sports club and a B'nai B'rith lodge. A Zionist study group was founded in March 1933 and a J. War Veterans Association youth group was started in July. By 1936, the J. pop. had dropped to 307. On *Kristallnacht* (9–10 Nov. 1938), the synagogue and J. stores were burned. Many emigrated in 1939; 120 Jews remained. After the deportations to the Theresienstadt ghetto and General Gouvernement territory from March 1942, six intermarried Jews remained in Nov. 1942.

GLOGOW Lwow dist., Poland. Jews apparently settled in the late 17th cent., reaching a pop. of 1,201 (total 2,831) in 1880 but declining to 648 in 1921 in the wake of emigration and the rigors of WWI, including attacks against Jews in 1918 and 1919. Despite economic hardship between the World Wars, public and cultural life flourished under the dominance of

Synagogue in Glogau, Germany

the Zionists. Sporadic killing accompanied the German conquest in WWII. The community was liquidated when the Jews were expelled to Rzeszow in June 1942 and a month later deported to the Belzec death camp.

GLOWACZOW   Kielce dist., Poland. Jews settled in the mid-16th cent., becoming a majority with a pop. of 1,109 in 1897 and 1,411 in 1921. After three years of German occupation in WWII, they were expelled to the Kozienice ghetto in Sept. 1942 and from there deported to the Treblinka death camp.

GLOWNO   Lodz dist., Poland. From the second half of the 18th cent., Jews constituted a majority of the inhabitants (61% in 1793–94, 59% in 1921). In 1848 they suffered from a cholera epidemic, and a fire destroyed community buildings. Six representatives of five J. parties were elected to the 12-member town council in 1924. In 1927 a unified J. national party contested the municipal elections. Almost all Zionist organiza-

tions were represented. By April 1940, when the ghetto was organized, some 2,700 refugees from areas of Poland annexed to the Reich (the Warthegau) had arrived and were housed together with the 2,100 members of the community. Glowno, annexed to the General Gouvernement, was situated on the border between the two administrative districts. At first, thanks to bribery, Jews were given free access to the city and thus were able to continue to work, to smuggle food, and to trade on the black market. In Feb. 1941, the majority of G.'s Jews were expelled from the town and deported to Warsaw.

GLUKHOV   Sumy dist., Ukraine. Jews are mentioned in the 1720s. In 1897, the J. pop. was 3,853 (26% of the total). On 7 March 1918, Red Army soldiers killed over 100 Jews in a pogrom. Between the World Wars, the J. pop. dropped to 1,501. The Germans captured G. on 7 Sept. 1941. On 30 Dec. 1941, they murdered 105 Jews and in Nov. 1942 another 700, including some from the surrounding area.

consecrated in 1868. The congregation belonged to the Reform movement and its members played a leading role in the city's industrial development, especially in textiles. However, from the 1890s, the J. pop. began to decline, numbering 612 in 1912 and 567 in 1925. Among the organizations active in the community were the Central Union (C.V.), the Zionist movement, and the J. War Veterans Association. In 1933, the J. pop. was 376 (total 94,182). In March 1933, the J. chairman of the local transport union was forced to resign and in May it was taken over by the Nazi Party. Thirty-seven Jews, including two judges and five lawyers, were arrested on Boycott Day (1 April 1933). In 1935, after the introduction of the Nazi racial laws, a local Jew was harassed for "racial defilement." He was arrested a second time and murdered in a Breslau prison in Oct. 1935. The J. pop. continued to dwindle, from 285 in 1934 to 207 in fall 1938. On *Kristallnacht* (9–10 Nov. 1938), J. homes and stores were destroyed, the synagogue was partially burned, and 24 Jews were sent to concentration camps. The "Aryanization" of J. businesses was completed on 9 Aug. 1939, when a sock factory was seized from its J. owner. The J. pop. was now 131. On the outbreak of war, the Jews were moved to "J. houses" and on 10 Dec. 1941, the Nazis began transferring local Jews to the nearby Tormersdorf camp, where they were put to forced labor until deported to Auschwitz and the Theresienstadt ghetto in fall 1942. In Oct. 1942, 33 Jews, apparently intermarried, remained,.

GOETTINGEN   Hanover, Germany. The first evidence of a protected Jew (*Schutzjude*) dates from 1289. The medieval community numbered 11–14 families between 1370–1460. About 1460, the community came to an end as the town did not extend the Jews' letters of protection. A community arose again in the 17th cent. and by 1790 included 11 families. The community maintained a cemetery from its early days and in 1783 a synagogue was dedicated. As a result of the influx of East European Jews, there were 638 Jews in 1895. That year, the Liberal community installed an organ and refused to build a *mikve*. This caused the Orthodox to break away and set up their own prayer room. In the Weimar period, a number of J. professors, including Nobel Prize laureates, taught at the University of G. The cemetery was descrated in 1928 and the synagogue in 1931. The administrator of the community suffered severe injuries at the hands of Nazis in

1932. In 1933, there were 410 Jews living in G. On Boycott Day (1 April 1933), the windows of all J. businesses were smashed. In 1934, Jews were physically attacked. The community's cultural and Zionist activities intensified. On *Kristallnacht* (9–10 Nov. 1938), the synagogue was burned down, J. stores and homes were wrecked, and several Jews were maltreated and imprisoned. Those who did not manage to emigrate were billeted in "J. houses." In March and June 1942, 150 individuals were deported. In all, at least 267 Jews from G. were murdered under Nazi rule, including many who had moved to other German towns or to neighboring countries.

GOLANCZ   Poznan dist., Poland. Jews first settled in 1766 under a charter of privileges and by the time of Prussian rule in 1772 formed an organized community, with most engaged in petty trade and peddling. In the 19th cent. they opened stores and workshops and many of the young people entered the professions and left the town as the J. pop. fell from 243 in 1871 (total 1,281) to 87 in 1911 and 23 in 1939. All were expelled by the Germans to General Gouvernement territory shortly after the occupation.

GOLAYA PRISTAN   Nikolaiev dist., Ukraine. Jews probably settled in the early 19th cent. and numbered 667 (total 6,143) in 1897 and 276 in 1939 under the Soviets. The Germans arrived on 13 Sept. 1941 and on 12 Oct. murdered about 150 Jews. In all, the Germans murdered 430 inhabitants of the region, most of them apparently Jews.

GOLCUV JENIKOV   Bohemia, Czechoslovakia. Jews were probably present in the late 16th cent. After a series of devastating fires in the town, a new synagogue was built in 1870. The community was one of the most important in Bohemia during the 18th–19th cents., with a pop. of 613 (28% of the total) in 1842. Isaac Mayer Wise, founder of the Reform movement in the U.S., studied at the local yeshiva from 1835. A J. school established in 1797 operated throughout the 19th cent. until it was closed in 1907. In 1930, the J. pop. was 79 after dropping steadily from the late 19th cent. A few Jews emigrated in WWII. The rest were deported to the Theresienstadt ghetto in 1942 and from their to the death camps of Poland.

GOLDAP   East Prussia, Germany, today Poland. The

J. pop. was 60 in 1843, 84 in 1880, and 58 in 1905. The first cemetery dates back to the beginning of the 19th cent. and a synagogue was established in mid-cent. In the 1920s, the community could no longer employ its own community official. When the Nazis assumed power in 1933, there were 48 Jews in G. The synagogue was destroyed on *Kristallnacht* (9–10 Nov. 1938). By May 1939, the J. pop. numbered 19. No further information about their fate under Nazi rule is available.

GOLDBACH Lower Franconia, Germany. Jews may have been present in the 14th cent. An organized community is mentioned in the early 18th cent., growing to 72 in 1890 (total 1,668). In 1933, 38 remained. On *Kristallnacht* (9–10 Nov. 1938), the synagogue and J. homes were vandalized. Of the 24 Jews remaining in 1942, 16 were deported to Izbica in the Lublin dist. (Poland) via Wuerzburg on 25 April and five to the Theresienstadt ghetto in Sept. 1942.

GOLINA Lodz dist., Poland. Jews lived here in the early 18th cent. after the ban on J. settlement was lifted. The J. pop. in 1897 was 679 (38% of the total). In July 1940 the Jews were expelled to Zagorow and other ghettoes and shared the fate of the local Jews.

GOLLNOW (Pol. Goleniow) Pomerania, Germany, today Poland. In 1782, there were 62 Jews living in G. and 165 in 1840. A synagogue and a cemetery were established. When the Nazis came to power in 1933, the community numbered 73. The last four J. businesses were "Aryanized" in 1938. By May 1939, there were 45 Jews and 17 persons of partial J. origin (*Mischlinge*) in the town. On 12–13 Feb. 1940, the remaining Jews were deported to the Lublin dist. (Poland) together with the Jews of Stettin and most perished.

GOLOGORY Tarnopol dist., Poland, today Ukraine. Jews are first mentioned in 1470, with a synagogue built at the beginning of the 17th cent. The number of Jews reached a peak of 1,216 (total 2,766) in 1880 but declined by 60% after WWI and the attacks of Russian troops, who murdered over a 100 and burned most of their homes. The small community of around 575 was expelled to Zloczow in Nov. 1942 and shared the fate of the local Jews.

GOLOSKOV Odessa dist., Ukraine. The J. pop. was 1,272 in 1897 and 1,572 (total 4,887) in 1926. On 1 Feb. 1907, Ukrainian rioters overturned and burned J. stalls in the market. In the 1920s, under the Soviets, about 90 J. families worked in agriculture in a J. kolkhoz and another 90 Jews belonged to artisan cooperatives. A J. council (soviet) was active and from 1923 a J. elementary school with 70–200 students was operating. R. Hayyim Shapiro was still officiating in the community in the late 1920s. G. was the birthplace of the Yiddish poet and novelist Leib Kvitko (1890–1952). The Germans took the town on 4 Aug. 1941 and immediately murdered 241 Jews, including 79 children, on the banks of the South Bug River.

GOLOVANEVSK Odessa dist., Ukraine. Jews settled in the mid-18th cent. and numbered 456 in 1790 and 4,320 (total 8,148) in 1897. In 1910, a private J. boys' school was opened. On 4 Aug. 1919, the Petlyura gangs murdered 200 Jews. J. self-defense forces killed several attackers. During the Soviet period, many J. families (72 in 1924) engaged in agriculture. A J. elementary school was still open in the late 1930s. The J. pop. dropped to 1,393 in 1939. The Germans captured the town on 1 Aug. 1941 and immediately shot 100 Jews. In Sept., the Germans and the Ukrainian police murdered another 776 Jews. Young J. girls were first raped and infants were hurled alive into pits. On 3 Jan. 1942, Ukrainian police murdered 36 children aged 4–9 from the nearby Lipovensky children's home. A month later, the Germans murdered another 168 Jews, among them 49 children.

GOLOVCHIN Mogilev dist., Belorussia. The J. pop. was 280 in 1765 and 433 in 1897. Jews earned their livelihoods in petty trade and crafts. In 1923, under the Soviets, the J. pop. was 378 (total 1,395), with 49 families employed in agriculture in 1924–25. The Germans arrived in Aug. 1941, murdering the Jews in late summer 1942.

GOLUB-DOBRZYN Pomerania, Poland. Jews established a flourishing community on the east bank of the Drawanicze River dividing the town. They suffered greatly in the Swedish wars of the mid-17th cent. but recovered quickly and numbered 795 in 1765. After the First Partition of Poland in 1772, J. settlement was also permitted on the west bank under Prussian rule while the east bank came under Russian rule. In the former area, Jews became well established, trading

in textiles, wool, furs, and grain and reaching a peak pop. of 702 in 1857 (total 2,452) before the process of emigration to the German cities set in among the young. A large synagogue was built in the late 18th cent. and a J. elementary school under government supervision was opened in the first half of the 19th. The Jews of D. (the east bank) were mainly petty traders and numbered 1,610 in 1857. Small Zionist and Bund groups became active at the turn of the cent. Most Jews fled to G. in WWI in the face of Russian persecution. Under Polish rule after WWI, the two communities united as emigration continued and Zionist activity intensified, as did antisemitism. Throughout the period, cultural activity was widespread. In 1937, 189 Jews remained. Most were expelled to General Gouvernement territory after the German occupation of Sept. 1939.

GOLUBOVKA Voroshilovgrad dist., Ukraine. The J. pop. in 1939 was 166 (total 26,590). After their arrival on 17 July 1942, the Germans murdered the Jews of G.

GOMBIN Warsaw dist., Poland. J. residents are mentioned from the 16th cent. but only in the early 18th, with the recovery of the town from the Swedish invasion (1655), did J. community life take root. The J. pop. grew to 2,539, or half the total, by the end of the 19th cent. Between the World Wars, the Jews suffered economic hardship, compounded by the Polish boycott against them. Nevertheless, social and cultural life flourished with the entire range of Zionist organizations represented as well as Agudat Israel and the Bund. Under the Nazi occupation from 7 Sept. 1939, Jews were persecuted severely and sent to forced labor camps. At the beginning of 1940 they were herded into a ghetto. The ghetto was destroyed in May 1942 and its inhabitants were sent to Chelmno. Of the 180 or so who survived the war, most emigrated to Israel.

GOMEL (I) Vitebsk dist., Belorussia. The J. pop. was 129 (total 140) in 1920. In 1925, 22 of the 49 J. families in the village engaged in agriculture. The Germans occupied G. in Aug. 1941. In Oct. they murdered 18 Jews and in Jan. 1942, the remaining 80.

GOMEL (II) Gomel dist., Belorussia. Jews arrived in the 16th cent. and an organized community was already in existence in 1639. About 2,000 Jews were murdered during the Chmielnicki massacres of 1648–49. Most of the Jews who converted to save themselves returned to the faith when Polish rule was reestablished in 1665. In 1765, the J. pop. was 658. The first synagogue was erected in the 18th cent. In the 19th cent., Habad Hasidism became influential in the community, primarily through R. Yitzhak, who was an intimate of Shneur Zalman of Lyady. In 1897, the J. pop. was 20,385 (total 36,775). On 1 Sept. 1903, ten Jews were murdered, many were injured, and J. property was damaged in a pogrom, but J. self-defense forces under the command of Yehezkel Henkin prevented the violence from spreading. Thirty-six of the J. defenders were brought to trial together with the rioters but were exonerated. Most self-defense members emigrated to Eretz Israel in 1904, with Henkin becoming a founder of the Hashomer ("Watchman") association. The Zionist Organization and numerous cells of the Bund were active in the city. In 1917, the community maintained 17 synagogues and 13 *battei midrash*. Only two stayed open until 1941. Many Zionist groups were active in the 1917–26 period: Tze'irei Tziyyon, Kadima, Hehalutz, the Socialist Zionists, etc. The Zionists set up two Hebrew kindergartens, a Tarbut secondary school, and a library. In 1923, under the Soviets, an artisan association was founded; 90% of its members were Jews. By 1926, the J. pop. was 37,745 (total 86,393). Among J. breadwinners, 3,482 were factory hands; 4,057 white-collar workers; 3,235 artisans; and 5,046 farmers. In 1930, eight J. kolkhozes were founded near the city, employing 400 J. families (1,889 people) on 21,000 acres of land. A J. section was opened at the local law courts. In 1926, six J. schools and two J. kindergartens were operating. A J. dept. was opened at the district Communist Party school located in G. A Yiddish-language teachers' seminary was active in the early 1920s but was transferred to Smolensk in 1929. In 1939, the J. pop. was 40,880. The Germans captured the city on 19 Aug. 1941. Many Jews succeeded in escaping to the interior of the Soviet Union. Those who remained were herded into four ghettoes under conditions of overcrowding and starvation. Their property was confiscated and they were put to hard labor. Three labor camps were also set up in the city: Manastyrsk (holding 800 Jews), Novo Lubieisk (500), and Novaya Belitsa (200). In Oct. 1941, 2,365 Jews from the camps and ghettoes were executed in retaliation for supporting

the partisans. By Dec., 4,000 Jews had been murdered at the antitank ditches outside the city. Women and children were gassed to death.

GONC Abauj–Torna dist., Hungary. Jews from Carpathia arrived in the late 18th cent. The first synagogue was built in 1828. The J. pop. rose to 307 in 1880, declining to 200 in 1941. The Zionists were active between the World Wars. Thirty Jews were sent as forced laborers in 1942 to the Ukraine, where most perished. The rest were deported to Auschwitz from Kassa on 12–17 June 1944.

GONCRUSZKA Abauj–Torna dist., Hungary. Jews probably settled in the late 18th cent. and numbered 247 in 1840, 142 in 1880, and 38 in 1941. They were deported to Auschwitz via Kassa on 14 May–2 June 1944.

GONIONDZ Bialystok dist., Poland, today Belarus. Jews were present in the 17th–18th cent. despite the residence ban in force until Prussian rule in 1795. In 1800 the J. pop. was 498, growing to 2,056 (total 3,436) in 1897. J. merchants were the first in the area to engage in the export-import trade, dealing in cloth, wood products, chemicals, and plows. Under Russian rule after 1807, Jews were employed in the rebuilding of the Osowietz fortress and supplied the garrison with goods and services. J. merchants were active in the grain and lumber trade and Jews ran seven big flour mills and a big sawmill. Hovevei Zion sent 21 Jews to Eretz Israel in the late 19th cent., most to Petah Tikva. Two big fires in 1906 and 1911 left many Jews homeless. In WWI the Jews were expelled to Bialystok by the Russian army, returning under the German occupation to a regime of forced labor. In 1921, 1,135 remained. Hebrew and Yiddish elementary schools were opened, with the Zionists becoming the dominant force in the community. The Germans arrived on 26 June 1941 after two years of Soviet rule. The town's 900 Jews were subjected to a reign of terror. By Nov. 1942, the Germans and their Polish collaborators had murdered 217 Jews. On 2 Nov., the rest were brought to the Bogosze transit camp, where 7,000 Jews were being held, and on 3 Jan. 1943 they were deported to the Treblinka death camp.

GOOR Overijssel dist., Holland. Jews were present in G. and neighboring Diepenheim and Markelo in the 14th cent. Settlement stabilized from the 17th cent. The communities were united in 1821 and their combined pop. in 1860 was 131. The J. pop. in 1941 was 60 (total 11,948). In Aug. 1941 Nazis killed a Jew; 16 then went into hiding; the rest were deported and perished.

GORAJ Lublin dist., Poland. Jews are first mentioned in 1626 but may have been present earlier. Recovering from the Chmielnicki massacres of 1648–49, the community resumed its position as one of the most important in the area. In the 19th cent., Jews traded in lumber and opened small pottery and textile factories. They numbered 563 in 1827 and 394 (total 2,331) in 1921. Despite economic hardship between the World Wars, requiring the assistance of the Joint Distribution Committee and of U.S. Jews, Zionist activity flourished, though Agudat Israel controlled the community council. Under the German occupation from Sept. 1939, J. refugees from nearby Frampol and Bilgorai arrived, but left following an outbreak of typhus. In Oct. 1942, J. homes were burned and the J. pop. was transferred to Frampol. In Nov. all were deported to the Belzec death camp.

GORA KALWARIA (Yid. Gur) Warsaw dist., Poland. The J. community was formed under Prussian rule from 1795, growing to 500 in 1827 and 2,019 in 1897 and comprising a majority of the general pop. Most Jews engaged in petty trade and crafts while the Christian pop. mainly farmed. Jews also entered light industry, manufacturing prayer shawls and candles. A J. elementary school was founded in 1850. In 1859, R. Yitzhak Meir Alter (Rothenberg) (1789–

R. Avraham Mordekhai Alter, Gora Kalwaria, Poland

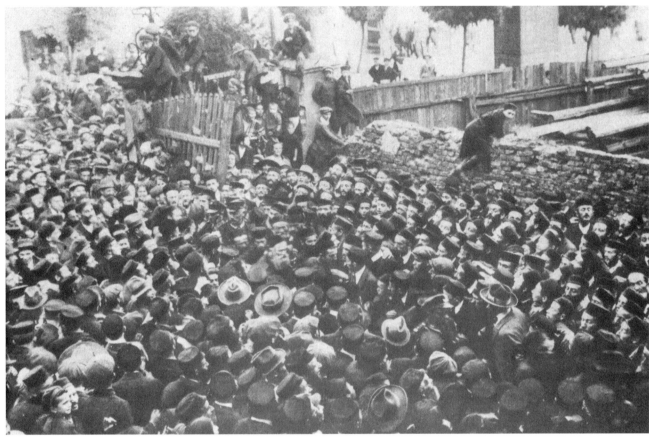

Wedding celebration for the Gerer (Gur) Rebbe's son, Gora Kalwaria, Poland

1866) settled in G., founding the Gur dynasty and making the town one of the most important hasidic centers in Poland. He was succeeded by his grandson, R. Yehuda Aryeh Leib Alter (1847–1905), as the authority of Gur Hasidism spread to other communities and tens of thousands of followers streamed to the rabbi's court, boosting the local economy significantly as boarding houses and restaurants proliferated. R. Yehuda Leib was a staunch opponent of Zionism and one of the founders of Agudat Israel. In 1900 a fire left hundreds of Jews homeless and in WWI J. commerce came to a standstill under the German occupation (1915–18). Between the World Wars, when the J. pop. maintained a level of about 3,000, R. Avraham Mordekhai Alter (1866–1948), who succeeded his father as Gur Rabbi, became a leader of Polish Jewry as well as the spiritual father of Agudat Israel. Gur Hasidism continued to grow, making G. the largest hasidic center in the world. The great *beit midrash* dedicated in 1909 held 3,000 people and Agudat Israel sponsored a Beth Jacob school for 300 girls. Zionist activity also ex-

panded along with its youth movements. Throughout the period, Polish antisemitism intensified, with occasional outbursts of violence. The Germans captured the city on 8 Sept. 1939, immediately subjecting the Jews to severe persecution. A *Judenrat* was set up on 15 Jan. 1940, charged with supplying forced labor and meeting extortionate demands. In Feb. 1940 the Jews of G. and surrounding villages were transferred to a ghetto. On 25 Feb. 1941, 1,600 were expelled to the Warsaw ghetto, and 1,349 the following day. A few hundred died in the Warsaw ghetto in the course of the year, stricken by starvation and disease. The rest were sent to the death camps in the big *Aktion* of Aug. 1942. The Gur Rabbi escaped from G. soon after the German occupation and hid out in Warsaw for awhile before obtaining an Italian visa and reaching Palestine via Trieste in 1940. Israel subsequently became the world center of Gur Hasidism.

GORA WISNIOWA Lodz dist. Poland. In 1921, 56 Jews lived in this summer resort and made their living

from services to vacationers. In the 1930s they suffered harassment and in Oct. 1939 the small community was expelled to Rokycany.

GORBOPINCEHELY   Tolna dist., Hungary. Jews arrived in the first half of the 18th cent., numbering 273 in 1880 and 147 in 1941. They were severely persecuted in the post-WWI White Terror and on 5 July 1944 were deported to Auschwitz via Bonyhad and Pecs. Twenty-two survivors returned to reestablish the community but soon left.

GORINCHEM   (Gorcum, Gorkum, Gorkom) Zuid-Holland dist., Holland. J. settlement began towards the end of the 18th cent. A community was organized around 1800 and numbered 212 in 1911 but it dwindled to 85 in 1940. Fifteen Jews survived the Holocaust in hiding; the rest were deported and perished.

GORIZIA   Italy. G. was part of the Austrian Empire until 1918. The J. presence in G. dates back to 1348. The Jews were mainly engaged in moneylending. In 1648, the Jews were confined in a ghetto. In 1777, the J. community of G. absorbed the Jews expelled from Venetian towns. During the reign of Joseph II, the local Jews were tolerated and the community flourished. The J. community numbered 270 in 1788. Among its renowned rabbis and public figures were R. Abramo Vitta Reggio and his son Isacco Samuele; the linguist Graziadio Isaia Ascoli; and Giuseppe Lazzaro Morpurgo, founder of the Assicurazioni Generali. In 1910, there were 236 Jews in G. but only 48 were living in the old J. ghetto. They were active in commerce and the professions. After WWI, the community was reorganized and a Zionist group was established. According to the 1930 law reforming the J. communities, G. was declared one of the 26 districts legally recognized by the Italian government. Attached to the community were those of S. Daniele del Fruili (five Jews in 1936) and Udine (60 Jews in 1936). In 1933, the community consisted of 200. Their spiritual leader was R. Prof. Abraham Schreiber, who attracted a number of disciples around him. The Koschitzky and Mayer families operated the local *matza* factory. In the mid-1930s, a new synagogue was inaugurated, named after Abramo Vitta Reggio. G. became a haven for J. fugitives from Germany. According to the 1938 census, there were 239 Jews listed in G. After the promulgation of the racial laws, several old

and powerful families left the city. In 1940, a street named after a J. family, Ascoli, had its name changed. In autumn 1942, forced labor was instituted in G. After the armistice of Sept. 1943, most Jews left G. On 23 Nov. 1943, the Germans arrested 45 local Jews They were taken to Risiera di S. Sabba and from there, on 6–7 Dec., they were deported to Auschwitz. Two joined the underground and died in battle. After the war, 30 Jews remained in G. From 1959, the community was attached to that of Trieste.

GORKAYA   Zaporozhe dist., Ukraine. Jews from the Vitebsk and Mogilev regions founded G. as a J. colony in 1850. The J. pop. was 488 in 1858. During the May 1881 pogroms, peasants from the neighboring village of Torkanivski protected the Jews of G. During the Russian civil war (1918–21), rioters murdered nearly half the town's Jews. After the German occupation of early Oct. 1941, the few Jews who had neither fled nor been evacuated were presumably murdered as well.

GORKI   Mogilev dist., Belorussia. An organized J. community that existed in 1643 came to an end after the Chmielnicki massacres of 1648–49 and Czar Alexius's campaign in Belorussia in 1654. The J. settlement was renewed in 1699 and in 1766 numbered 511. In 1810, the town's proprietors expelled the Jews although a few families remained. With renewed settlement, the J. pop. rose to 3,029 (total 6,735) in 1897. In 1904, anti-J. riots caused considerable damage to J. property but no loss of life. Further rioting occurred in 1920 when the Polish army withdrew from the region. In the Soviet period, a J. elementary school was in operation and a dept. of J. agricultural history was inaugurated at the local academy of agriculture. In 1939, the J. pop. was 2,031. The Germans captured the town on 12 July 1941, establishing a ghetto for the Jews of G. and the surrounding area. On 6 Oct. they executed 2,000 in the vicinity of Mt. Mstislavskaia.

GORLICE   Cracow dist., Poland. An independent community existed from the early 19th cent. Some engaged in trade with Hungary, exporting linen and furs and importing wines and agricultural produce. A few ran oil refineries, but most eked out a living as carters and peddlers. A fire in 1874 caused much suffering and only the organization of a self-defense group averted a pogrom. More disturbances occurred in 1898 when homes were destroyed and property was pillaged.

Selling barrels, Gorlice, Poland

The J. pop. then stood at around 3,000 (half the total), continuing to grow somewhat until WWI but declining to 2,300 in 1921. Competition from the Polish cooperatives and anti-J. boycotts undermined the livelihoods of J. tradesmen between the World Wars. Jews dealt in cloth, grain, flour, and a wide range of agricultural produce; some were in lumber and oil and others were active in light industry. G. was predominantly hasidic, associating itself mainly with the Sieniawa and Bobow dynasty of Zanz but there were also Belz, Sadagora, and Dzykow representatives. Agudat Israel was active alongside the Zionist movement, which operated a training farm common to its various youth groups. With refugees arriving in the wake of the German occupation on 7 Sept. 1939, the pop. swelled to 4,000 in fall 1940. In Oct. 1941 the Jews were packed into a ghetto, 10–15 to a room; many were struck down by disease, others by sporadic killing at the hands of the Gestapo. On 14 Aug. 1942, 700 of the old and sick were murdered together with children in the forest.

Hundreds of the able-bodied continued to be sent to the Plaszow concentration camp near Cracow. Most of the others were deported to the Belzec death camp in the course of the following year.

GORLOVKA Stalino dist., Ukraine. Jews apparently began arriving only in the 20th cent., primarily in the Soviet period, when the city became a regional center for the chemical, machine, and metal industries. In 1939, the J. pop. was 2,339 (total 109,308). The Germans captured G. on 29 Oct. 1941. In Feb. 1942, 369 Jews were executed in G. and in Makeyevka. In April 1942, nearly 500 Jews from Ordzhonikidze were murdered in G. There were probably Jews among the 14,000 people who were murdered at the Uzlovaya coal mine.

GORNIKI (Horniki) Volhynia dist., Poland, today Ukraine. The J. pop. in 1921 was 52 (total 1,096). In the 1930s, there were 20 families.

Jewish self-defense group, Gorodyshche, Ukraine

GORNOSTIPOL   Kiev dist., Ukraine. Jews numbered 57 in 1765 and 1,888 (total 3,286) in 1897. In
1919, the Petlyura gangs murdered Jews and pillaged
their property. In 1939, under the Soviets, the J. pop.
was 573. The Germans arrived on 22 Aug. 1941, exacting large tributes from the community. On 7 Nov.,
230 J. men, women, and children were executed outside the town.

GORODETS   Gomel dist., Belorussia. The J. pop.
was 434 in 1847 and 512 in 1897. In 1926, under
the Soviets, the J. pop. rose to 607 (69% of the
total). Thirty-five J. artisans were organized in cooperatives and another 29 owned their own workshops.
Four J. kolkhozes supporting 70 families were founded
in 1925–27. The Germans occupied G. on 9 July 1941.
Many Jews managed to flee to the interior of the Soviet
Union. In Sept., those who were left behind, 200 local
Jews and 400 J. refugees from Bobruisk and other settlements, were incarcerated in a large building. They

were held there for a month under conditions of overcrowding, starvation, and abuse. Finally, in Oct., they
were brought to the Brogtsev camp and on 6 Nov.
they were executed nearby. Those still alive were murdered in Feb. 1942.

GORODOK (I)   Vitebsk dist., Belorussia. The J.
community is first mentioned in the mid-18th cent.
In 1805, two Jews were running a hide-processing
plant. In 1897, the J. pop. was 3,413 (two-thirds of
the total). In the early 20th cent., the community
maintained ten synagogues, all belonging to the Hasidim. Jews earned their livelihoods in commerce and
light industry. In the Soviet period, a J. elementary
school was in operation and in 1939 the J. pop. was
1,584. The Germans occupied G. on 9 July 1941. The
Jews were held outside the town in the open air along
with other Jews from the area. Over the next few
months they were murdered. A major *Aktion* in
Aug. resulted in the murder of 2,000. On 14 Oct.

the ghetto was liquidated and the remaining Jews killed.

GORODOK (II) Kamenets-Podolski dist., Ukraine. Jews settled in 1630 and were attacked in the Chmielnicki massacres of 1648–49. In 1765, their pop. was 645. In the 19th cent., Jews played an active role in the industrial and commercial development of the town as it became a district center. In 1897 the J. pop. stood at 3,194 (37% of the total), dropping to 2,329 in 1939. The Germans captured G. on 8 July 1941. Most of the Jews were executed at Yarmolintsy in fall 1942 together with other Jews from the region. Another 87 were murdered in Dec. 1942 and 16 more in Jan. 1943.

GORODYSHCHE Kiev dist., Ukraine. Jews numbered 3,124 (total 14,641) in 1897 and 570 under the Soviets in 1939. The Germans captured G. on 1 Aug. 1941, instituting a regime of forced labor and executions. On 2 April 1942, the remaining Jews in G. and its environs—mostly the elderly, women, and children—were executed beside freshly dug pits.

GORREDIJK (Gordijk, Gordyk, Gerdyk) Friesland dist., Holland. J. settlement began in the second half of the 18th cent. A community was organized from 1800 and included Jews of neighboring villages. In 1860, 42 Jews (7% of the total) lived in G. A branch of the Alliance Israelite was opened at the end of the 19th cent. The community's numbers dwindled in the 20th cent. The J. pop. in 1940 was 11. In Aug.–Oct. 1942, 22 Jews were deported. Most perished in Auschwitz or the Sobibor death camp; two survived in hiding.

GORVAL Gomel dist., Belorussia. The J. pop. was 104 in 1789 and 832 (total 2,146) in 1897. Most Jews engaged in petty trade; a few were wholesalers. In 1925, 19 J. families moved to the Crimea. In 1930, 95 J. families worked at nearby kolkhozes. Shortly after their arrival in the area in Sept. 1941, the Germans murdered all the Jews.

GORY Mogilev dist., Belorussia. The J. pop. was 577 (34% of the total) in 1897 and 355 in 1926, when a J. school was opened with an enrollment of 30 in 1927. In 1929 a J. kolkhoz for 32 families was started. The Germans occupied the town in early July 1941, immediately murdering two Jews. In Oct. 1941, the Nazis executed the town's 200 remaining Jews at a nearby factory.

GORZKOW Lublin dist., Poland. Jews are first mentioned in the early 19th cent., maintaining a community that never exceeded 100 families and was affiliated with Krasnystaw. Under the German occupation, commencing Sept. 1939, normal life continued until 1942 but for the establishment of a *Judenrat*, a regime of forced labor, and demands for tributes. Groups of workers were deported to the Belzec death camp in 1940 and 1942. In Nov. 1942 all the Jews in G. were transferred to the Izbica ghetto in the Lublin dist. (Poland), and by the beginning of 1943 they were deported to Belzec.

GOSLAR Hanover, Germany. Favorable conditions induced Jews to settle there in the mid-13th cent. and around 1335 there was a J. community numbering 80–100 (almost 3% of the total). Though defended by the town council and sheltered from the Black Death massacres (1348–49), the Jews ceased to live in G. around 1450. After its revival in 1610, the community built a synagogue in 1693 (replaced in 1802) in the face of Lutheran hostility. It numbered 63 (total 14,866) in 1895, dwindling to 38 in 1933. Nazis vandalized the synagogue on *Kristallnacht* (9–10 Nov. 1938) and brutally attacked the Jews. How many emigrated is uncertain; 22 Jews from G. perished, mostly in Warsaw or the Theresienstadt ghetto. Only four survived the Holocaust.

GOSSMANNSDORF A. MAIN (in J. sources, Gassdarf) Lower Franconia, Germany. A J. community is known from the mid-17th cent., including Jews expelled from Eibelstadt. A synagogue was built in 1765 and the J pop. reached 75 in 1867 (total 723). In 1933, seven were left. On *Kristallnacht* (9–10 Nov. 1938), the synagogue and J. homes were vandalized and the two family heads taken to the Dachau concentration camp. The last two Jews were deported to Izbica in the Lublin dist. (Poland) in April 1942.

GOSTINI (Dankere; Yid. Glazmanke) Zemgale (Courland) dist., Latvia. Jews settled in the first half of the 19th cent. and reached a peak pop. of 1,064 (total 2,328) in 1897. In 1905 the Bund was at the center of local revolutionary activity. In WWI the majority

of the Jews left the town, most spending the war years in Varaklani. In 1920, the J. pop. was 544 (total 878), with the Joint Distribution Committee extending aid to repair war-damaged homes and rehabilitate the J. economy. By 1935, Jews owned 43 of the 52 largest stores in the town. The Zionists were the main political force in the community. A yeshiva was founded in 1927 on the initiative of Habad Hasidim from Riga. Under Soviet rule (1940–41), J. businesses were nationalized and J. public life came to an end. Most of the Jews were murdered by the Germans in Aug. 1941.

GOSTOMYL Kiev dist., Ukraine. Jews settled in the early 18th cent. and numbered 916 in 1897. J. homes and stores were looted and burned in a pogrom on 20 Oct. 1905 and again pillaged in Sept. 1919, when J. lives were also lost. In 1939, under the Soviets, the J. pop. was 169. The Germans captured G. on 19 Aug. 1941 and murdered the Jews shortly afterwards.

GOSTYNIN Warsaw dist., Poland. Jews lived in G. from the latter part of the 15th cent. J. residence was restricted to a special quarter in 1823–62. Subsequently many worked in the building trades and some as suppliers to the army. Until the early 20th cent., when the J. pop. numbered 1,831 (total 6,747), the community maintained a traditional religious orientation. Afterwards the Bund and Po'alei Zion organizations were active and some Jews were attracted to Polish Social Democrat circles. Self-defense groups were organized in the aftermath of the revolutionary events of 1905–06 and the anti-J. riots they produced. The German occupation in WWI brought much suffering, which was not alleviated with the coming of Polish independence. Nazi persecution began immediately with the occupation of the town in the beginning of Sept. 1939. A ghetto was set up in 1940. The able-bodied were taken to forced labor camps and the ghetto was liquidated in April 1942, its inhabitants being sent to the Chelmno death camp.

GOSZCZYN Warsaw dist., Poland. Jews first settled in the late 18th cent., engaging mainly in leasing estates and supplying consumer goods to the proprietors. The J. pop. rose to 185 in 1921 (total 1,237), with livelihoods affected by the call to desist from leas-

The ghetto gate, Gostynin, Poland

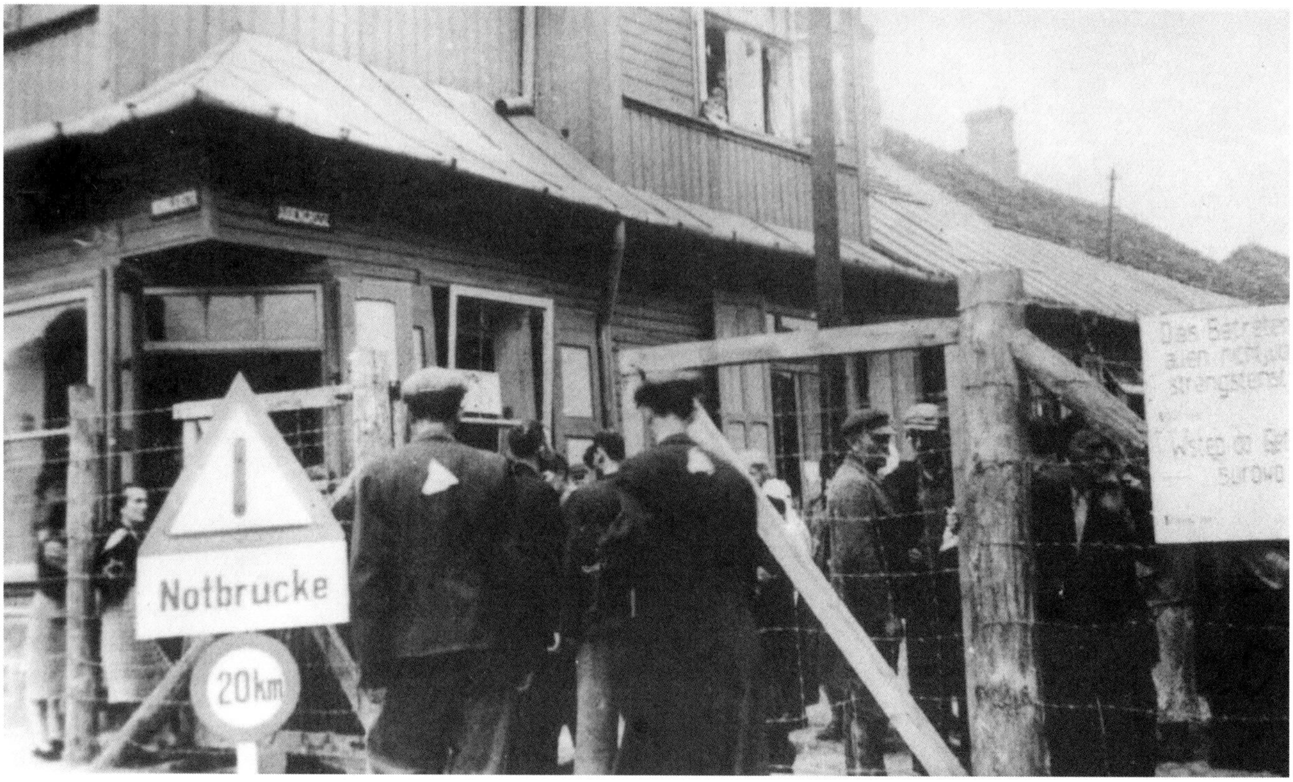
Notbrucke
20km

ing orchards to the Jews and the creation of a peasant dairy marketing cooperative. All the Jews were expelled by the Germans to the Warsaw ghetto in Feb. 1941 and shared its fate.

GOTHA   Thuringia, Germany. Jews lived there at the turn of the 12th and 13th cents. and possibly earlier. Until the 16th cent. the history of the local J. community was marked by successive expulsions and returns. Following the last expulsion in 1543, Jews were not allowed to return to G. until 8 June 1768. The J. pop. began to increase following emancipation of the Jews of the Duchy of Saxony-Coburg-Gotha in 1852. They numbered 27 in 1864; 119. in 1875; 296 in 1900; and 372 in 1910 (total 39,553). Antisemitism and Nazi incitement were widespread in G. even before 1933. In Feb. 1931, the majority of the city council voted to prohibit ritual kosher slaughter. The Nazi takeover in 1933 accelerated emigration, reducing the size of the community from 350 in 1932 to 264 according to the June 1933 census. The local Nazi newspaper conducted a vicious antisemitic campaign, publishing in Sept. 1935 a list of 147 adult Jews "with whom we may no longer associate." Jews wishing to emigrate were assisted by a counseling center at the Confessor's Church headed by the evangelical priests Gerhard Bauer and Werner Sylten (the latter recognized posthumously as one of the Righteous among the Nations). On *Kristallnacht* (9–10 Nov. 1938), the synagogue was burned down; J. shops were vandalized and pillaged; and 38 Jews were deported to the Buchenwald concentration camp. In 1939, only 80 Jews were left in G. and 39 in 1940–41. Probably in Sept. 1942, 28 Jews were deported. To escape deportation at least seven Jews in G. committed suicide.

Synagogue in Gotha, Germany

GOUDA   Zuid-Holland dist., Holland. A number of Jews lived in G. at the end of the 18th cent. During the 19th cent. the community became well organized and established religious, social, and educational organizations. The J. pop. in 1883 was 390. A Zionist agricultural training farm was founded in 1910. In 1940, 257 refugees from the coastal areas arrived. The J. pop. in 1941 was 521 (total 34,311). In Aug.–Nov. 1942, dozens of Jews were taken to Amsterdam. The workers and patients of the community's old age home were sent to the Westerbork transit camp in April 1943. The rest of the Jews went to the Vught camp. Some 40 survived the Holocaust.

GOWARCHOW   Lodz dist., Poland. By 1827, 457 Jews were living here and the community was affluent. At the end of WWI, a pogrom broke out when the Jews were blamed for the desecration of Polish dead bodies. Antisemitism again increased in the late 1920s and 1930s. Between 1939 and 1942, the 450-member community swelled to over 1,000 with the arrival of refugees; all were deported to the Treblinka death camp.

GOWOROWO   Bialystok dist., Poland. Jews were living here in the 18th cent. and maintained an independent community growing to 1,844 members at the end of the 19th cent. (of a total 2,139). During WWI they suffered under the Russian and German occupations but were able to recover with the help of mutual aid societies and money from abroad. The community was dominated by Agudat Israel, but the Zionists and the Bund were also active. The Germans occupied G. on 8 Sept. 1939. The Germans expelled all the Jews (around 2,000) into Soviet Poland in 1939 after their homes and the synagogue were razed. Most perished when they again fell into German hands in 1941.

GOZHKOWICE   Lodz dist., Poland. Jews lived here from the mid-19th cent. and numbered 273 in 1897. Between the World Wars, some were involved in the lumber trade, among them, Gershon Winter, who was called "King of Poland's Forests." When the Germans entered G. in 1939, the 650 Jews swelled to 1,500, including refugees who were housed in the synagogue. In Oct. 1942, they were transported to the Treblinka death camp.

GRABEN   Baden, Germany. Jews settled in the early 18th cent. and reached a pop. of 49 in 1887 (2% of the total), operating a distillery and cigarette factory. Ten of the 22 Jews present in 1933 left by 1938 and most of the others after *Kristallnacht* (9–10 Nov. 1938). The last three were sent to the Gurs concentration camp on 22 Oct. 1940.

GRABOW   Lodz dist., Poland. The first Jews settled here in 1764, and in the 19th cent. their numbers increased (640 in 1897; 61% of the total). They suffered severely from a boycott in the 1930s. By early 1941, refugees had increased the J. pop. to 1,240. In Apr. 1942, they were deported to Chelmno.

GRABOWIEC (I)   Stanislawow dist., Poland, today Ukraine. The small J. farming community originated perhaps in the 16th cent. and numbered 105 (total pop. 1,536) in 1921. The Jews were either liquidated by the Ukrainians after the Soviet departure in June 1941 or fell victim to the Germans in Sept.–Oct. 1942.

GRABOWIEC (II)   Lublin dist., Poland. Jews are mentioned in the first half of the 17th cent. and increased steadily from the mid-18th cent., numbering 1,717 (total 3,362) in 1897. The community was hasidic, with courts and *shtiblekh* identified with the Husyatin, Kozmin, Belz, Ruzhany, and other dynasties. Zionist influence spread between the World Wars. A Hebrew elementary school was founded in 1933 and a Yavne school in 1938. Many of the approximately 200 Jews who fled with the Red Army in Oct. 1939 subsequently joined the partisans, while others survived in the USSR. When the Germans arrived, a *Judenrat* and ghetto were soon set up for the 2,000 Jews who remained. On 8 June 1942, a selection was carried out. The sick were murdered immediately, 800 returned to forced labor, and 1,200 were deported to the Sobibor death camp. The last Jews were sent there in Oct. 1942.

GRABOW NAD PROSNA   Poznan dist., Poland. Jews were present from the 16th cent. but a community was only established in the 18th. The J. pop. rose to 170 (total 1,485) in 1840 and thereafter declined steadily through emigration to 59 in 1921. Those remaining were presumably expelled by the Germans to General Gouvernement territory shortly after their arrival in Sept. 1939.

GRADIZHSK Poltava dist., Ukraine. Jews settled in the early 19th cent. and numbered 1,112 (total 9,486) in 1897. In the Soviet period, there was a school for J. children, but only one grade was taught. By 1939, the J. pop. had dropped to 145. The Germans murdered 86 Jews after occupying the town on 13 Sept. 1939.

GRAEFENHAUSEN Hesse, Germany. The community, numbering 67 (7% of the total) in 1861, was augmented by Jews from Weiterstadt and Wixhausen in 1893, but slowly declined. On *Kristallnacht* (9–10 Nov. 1938), SA troops from the Darmstadt area came to G. and vandalized J. property. By 1940, 13 of the remaining 22 Jews had emigrated; the rest were eventually deported.

GRAJEWO Bialystok dist., Poland. Jews were present in the second half of the 17th cent. but only formed an organized community in the late 18th cent., growing to 1,459 (total 1,917) in 1857. Jews operated a number of factories (rubber and building products, bone grinding), flour mills, and distilleries. Many owned stores, particularly groceries, and J. craftsmen had stalls in the market to sell their wares. Most were poor and lived in substandard housing. Almost all their homes were destroyed in an 1886 fire. Haskala made inroads in the late 19th cent., led by the writer and educator Avraham Mordekhai Fiorka, who founded a modern *heder* and published a children's literary magazine in Hebrew. A beginner's Hebrew school was founded in the early 20th cent. G. was a bastion of the *Mitnaggedim* but its leading rabbis, Eliyahu Aharon Milkowski, future head of the Tel Aviv *beit din* (from 1892), and Moshe Avigdor Amiel, future chief rabbi of Antwerp and Tel Aviv (from 1913), were open to modern ideas. Hovevei Zion became active in 1886 and the Bund in 1902. The J. pop. was 2,834 in 1921 (total 7,346) with economic conditions deteriorating as Jews were cut off from their Russian and German markets and faced stiff competition from the Polish cooperatives. The Zionists expanded their activity, particularly in the youth movements. Agudat Israel, founded in 1921, embraced 200 families, most of them Gur Hasidim, and set up a Beth Jacob school for 150 girls in 1924. Under the Soviet occupation of Sept. 1939–June 1941, J. businesses were nationalized and most Jews found employment within the Soviet bureaucracy or cooperative system. The Germans arrived on 22 June and instituted a reign of terror, aided by local Poles. In Aug 1941, 1,600–2,000 Jews were confined to a ghetto, able to maintain a semblance of normal life until Nov. 1942, when all were sent to the Bogosza camp. Most were deported to the Treblinka death camp in Dec. and the rest to Auschwitz in Jan.

GRANICA (I) Kielce dist. (Bendzin prov.) Poland. Jews arrived from Bendzin in 1850. Most were Hasidim. With increasing movement to larger cities, 30 J. families remained in the 1930s. They were probably transferred to the Bendzin and Sosnowiec ghettoes in 1940–41 and deported to Auschwitz in 1942.

GRANICA (II) Kielce dist. (Kozienice prov.) Poland. J. settlement began in the early 19th cent. The J. pop. was 839 in 1827 and 651 in 1921 (total 1,030). After being transferred to the Gniewoszow ghetto, which was established in 1942, the Jews were deported to the Treblinka death camp on 29 Sept. 1942.

GRANOV Vinnitsa dist., Ukraine. The J. pop. was 662 in 1765 and 753 (total 6,850) in 1897. It dropped to 161 in 1926 under the Soviets. The Germans occupied the town on 27 July 1941, murdering those Jews who had neither escaped nor been evacuated in summer 1942

GRAVE Noord-Holland dist., Holland. Jews lived there from the Middle Ages. A community was established in the 19th cent. and numbered 55 in 1843. In the Holocaust, the remaining five Jews (total 2,395) were deported and perished.

GRAZ Steiermark, Austria. Jews first settled in 1261. By 1300, there were about 150 Jews in G., occupying a J. quarter and engaged in moneylending. They were expelled from G. in 1438–39, but allowed to resettle ten years later. In 1863 G. was recognized as an independent community. In 1865, a J. cemetery was established and in 1890 a splendid synagogue with a school and administration building was inaugurated. Jews engaged in trade and were represented in the professional class as university professors, doctors, and lawyers. They were also active in public life and served on the city council. In 1897, a Zionist student movement, Charitas, was founded at the University of G. In 1914–15 the Zionists were strengthened when about 1,000 Jews from the east (*Ostjuden*) settled in the G. area. In 1930 there was an active Zionist

Synagogue in Graz, Austria

youth movement with its own house organized along kibbutz lines in order to prepare members for emigration to Palestine. By 1923, the J. pop. reached a peak of 2,000 (of a total 153,000). On the eve of the German occupation, the J. pop. stood at 1,720. Until 1938, antisemitism was marked in G. though not violent. In the beginning of March 1938, some Jews were expelled from their homes and their property was destroyed. Immediately after the *Anschluss* (13 March 1938), Polish Jews living in G. were compelled to leave for Poland. By the end of 1938, almost all J. property was confiscated and J. shops "Aryanized." On *Kristallnacht* (9–10 Nov. 1938), the synagogue and the chapel at the cemetery were burned down completely. Men, women, and children were evicted from their homes and forced to sleep in the woods. In the morning, the men were arrested and sent to the Dachau concentration camp where some were beaten to death. They were only released in April 1939. Of the 1,599 Jews living in G. on *Kristallnacht*, 417 managed to emigrate to Palestine,

America, England, and the Dominican Republic. Some illegally crossed into Yugoslavia, France, and Italy. In June 1939, 300 Jews were still living in G. By 1941, most were deported to Vienna and then to the death camps in the east where all perished.

GREBENAU Hesse, Germany. One of the oldest and (proportionately) largest in Hesse, this community numbered 186 (27% of the total) in 1861. Its state-funded J. school (1839–1929) was also attended by Christians. G. became a Nazi stronghold and on 6 Nov. 1938, shortly before *Kristallnacht* (9–10 Nov. 1938), local youths set fire to the synagogue. Of the 60 Jews living there after 1933, 23 emigrated. By Oct. 1939 there were no Jews in G.

GREBENKI Kiev dist., Ukraine. The Jews of G., together with those from the neighboring village of Salinovki, numbered 551 in 1897. J. lives were lost in a pogrom staged by Anton Denikin's White Army soldiers in March 1918. In 1939, the J. pop. was 84. The Germans occupied G. on 19 July 1941 and executed all the Jews there on 25 Aug. The children were cast into the pits while still alive.

GREBENSTEIN Hesse-Nassau, Germany. In nearby Immenhausen Jews fell victim to the Black Death persecutions of 1348–49 and a community was not established in G. until the 18th cent. It numbered 105 (4% of the total) in 1835. The Jews maintained an elementary school (1831–1911) and dedicated a new synagogue in 1895. Affiliated with Kassel's rabbinate, the community dwindled to 50 in 1932 and the last ten Jews disposed of their synagogue before *Kristallnacht* (9–10 Nov. 1938). A few emigrated, but 34 of those who remained in Germany perished during the Holocaust.

GREIFENBERG (Pol. Gryfice) Pomerania, Germany, today Poland. A J. resident is mentioned in 1692, and in 1752 there was a J. settlement of seven families. In 1880, the community numbered 146 members and maintained a synagogue and a cemetery. When the Nazis came to power in 1933, there were still 68 Jews living in G. By May 1939, there were 22 Jews and five persons of partial J. origin (*Mischlinge*). No information about their fate is available.

GREIFENHAGEN (Pol. Gryfino) Pomerania, Ger-

The Grebenstein Synagogue, Germany

many, today Poland. The first evidence of a J. presence dates from 1481, but a permanent settlement began only in 1705 with four families. The J. pop. numbered 205 in 1861 and gradually declined in the following years. The community maintained a synagogue and a cemetery which was desecrated in 1928. When the Nazis came to power in 1933, there were 35 Jews in G. The three families who remained in the town on *Kristallnacht* (9–10 Nov. 1938) were imprisoned in a railway car outside the town. On 12–13 Feb. 1940, the remaining Jews were deported to Lublin with the transport from Stettin and most perished.

GREIFSWALD   Pomerania, Germany. There is evidence of J. presence in G. as early as the middle of the 13th cent. and the first half of the 14th cent. The modern settlement developed in the 19th cent. and numbered 11 Jews in 1816 and 167 in 1880. Originally affiliated to the Stralsund community, the local Jews set up their own community in 1871 after establishing a prayer room and a cemetery in 1860. There was a

university in G. and a small number of J. students lived in the town. When the Nazis came to power in 1933, the community numbered 46. In 1935 a Jew was driven through the streets on so-called racial defilement (*Rassenschande*) charges. On *Kristallnacht* (9–10 Nov. 1938), J. businesses were wrecked. By May 1939, there were only 14 Jews and 11 persons of partial J. origin (*Mischlinge*) in G. The remaining Jews, at least four, were deported to the Lublin dist. (Poland) with the Jews of Stettin on 12–13 Feb. 1940 and most perished.

GREMBOW   Lwow dist., Poland. The J. pop. in 1921 was 172 (total 5,080). A pogrom shook the community in 1918 and in 1919 commercial licenses were revoked by the Polish authorities. The German regime of persecution culminated in the expulsion of the community, apparently to Tarnobrzeg, on 24 June 1941.

GRENOBLE   Isere dist., France. There are indications of a J. presence from the fourth cent., making

this area probably the first to be settled by Jews in France. In the second half of the 13th cent., a lamentation on the martyrdom of ten local Jews was incorporated into the Bourguignon festival prayer book (*mahzor*). After the Jews were expelled from France in 1306, some were permitted to settle in G. and in the 14th cent., this group developed into an important J. community. In 1348, at the time of the Black Death persecutions, 74 Jews were arrested and later burned at the stake. From 1394 until the French Revolution there were no Jews living in G. In 1717, a group of Jews from Comtat-Venaissin sought to settle in G., but the city parliament was opposed. After the French Revolution a new community emerged in G. Alsatian refugees revived the community in 1871. By 1928, the community, which was composed of fewer than 40 families, established a religious organization. During WWII, first occupied by the Italians and later by the Germans, G. was important as a center of J. shelter and resistance. About 30,000 Jews found refuge in G., from which it was relatively easy to escape to Switzerland. In 1941 there were 250 J. families in the city. In the fall of 1942 the headquarters of the Mouvement de Jeunesse Socialiste (MJS) moved from Montpellier to G. The Gestapo became especially active from 1943 and the Forcat factory became a center for roundups of Jews and refugees. In 1943 Yitzhak Schneersohn clandestinely created the Centre de Documentation Juive Contemporaine in G. G. had a secret synagogue at the La Brise Neige Catholic orphanage. After the war, the community numbered about 250 families, mostly refugees from Central Europe. By 1969, the J. pop. was 5,000, previously immigrants from North Africa.

GRENZHAUSEN Hesse–Nassau, Germany. The community, numbering 86 (5% of the total) in 1885, built a new synagogue in 1900 but dwindled to 25 in 1933. Though no longer in J. possession, the synagogue was burned on *Kristallnacht* (9–10 Nov. 1938). Jews who did not emigrate perished in the Holocaust.

GRESK Minsk dist., Belorussia. J. settlement probably commenced in the first half of the 19th cent. In 1897, the J. pop. was 207 (total 1,674). In 1930, under the Soviets, 12 families earned their livelihoods in a kolkhoz and a J. school (apparently with two grades) was still operating in 1931. In 1939, the J.

pop. was 149. The Jews still there in 1941 were apparently murdered immediately after the German occupation of 27 June.

GREVENBROICH Rhineland, Germany. Jews are known from the late 14th cent. The Gottschalk and Alexander families founded a permanent settlement in 1621 under letters of protection. A synagogue was opened at mid-cent. Jews traded in livestock and farm produce and engaged in moneylending and land brokerage. In 1786, with nine families, they constituted a tenth of the total pop. In accordance with Prussian law, G. became the seat of a dist. congregation for 367 Jews after 1848. A new synagogue was completed in 1858 and a J. elementary school was opened in 1859 (closing in 1866 when the teacher retired). The J. pop. reached a peak of 130 (total 1,498) in 1895. Jews owned a number of large business establishments (grain, textiles, etc.) and participated in public life. A spate of antisemitic incidents, mostly initiated by factory workers in the area, followed an 1892 blood libel. In mid-1933, 61 Jews remained, with a number of attached communities (Hemmerden, Gustorf, Huelchrath, Frimmersdorf, Wevelinghoven, Kapellen). Of the 61 Jews who left the town in the Nazi era, 23 moved to other localities in Germany and 14 emigrated to Palestine. At least 14 perished in the Holocaust.

GRIEDEL Hesse, Germany. First mentioned in 1596, the community numbered 70 (8% of the total) in 1861, dwindling to 28 in 1933. Local support for the Nazis grew and most of the Jews left before *Kristallnacht* (9–10 Nov. 1938), when their synagogue was destroyed. By May 1940 none remained.

GRIESHEIM Hesse, Germany. A mere handful of Jews lived there from the 17th cent. Numbering 174 (5% of the total) in 1861, the community played a major role in G.'s development. While the Nazis won only 11% of the 1930 Reichstag vote, in the July 1932 elections they reached 32%. Persecution of local Jews began in March 1933. On *Kristallnacht* (9–10 Nov. 1938), SA troops from Darmstadt vandalized the synagogue and townspeople destroyed J. property. After 1933, more than half the remaining 62 Jews emigrated, the rest settling elsewhere in Germany.

GRIGORIOPOL Moldavia dist., Ukraine, today

Republic of Moldova. Jews probably settled with the founding of the town in the late 18th cent. The J. pop. was 832 in 1897 and in the Soviet period 796 (total 8,876) in 1926 and 562 in 1939. G. was captured by German and Rumanian forces in the beginning of Aug. 1941. In Sept.–Oct. 1941, the Jews were beaten and expelled to neighboring Dubossary, where they were executed.

GRIJPSKERK Groningen dist., Holland. A community existed from the second half of the 19th cent. and in 1860, 57 Jews lived in G. and neighboring Ezinge. In 1941, 14 Jews were there; all but one were deported in the Holocaust.

GRINKISKIS (Yid. Grinkishok) Kedainiai dist., Lithuania. A J. community existed in the 17th cent. Economic conditions from the end of the 19th cent. until WWII resulted in J. emigration. The J. pop. was 235 in 1923 (24% of the total). On 2 Sept. 1941 Lithuanian nationalists killed the remaining 20 J. families after taking them to Krakes.

GRISKABUDIS (Yid. Grishkabud) Sakiai dist., Lithuania. There were Jews here in the 18th cent. The J. pop. in 1923 was 92 (12% of the total). Most Jews emigrated to the U.S. because of economic conditions. All of G.'s eight remaining J. families were killed in Sikiai on 13 Sept. 1941.

GRITSEV (Yid. Ritsov) Kamenets-Podolski dist., Ukraine. The J. pop. was 1,194 in 1847, dropping to 979 (97% of the total) in 1897. Jews were attacked in a pogrom on 21 Sept. 1917. In 1939, their pop. was 1,095. The Germans captured the town on 5 July 1941, twice murdering hostages at the outset of the occupation. A ghetto surrounded by a barbed wire fence was established in early Aug. 1941. In the same month, 286 J. men were executed. A second *Aktion* took place in Oct. In June 1942, the Jews were transferred to the Staro-Konstantinov ghetto, where they were murdered. In all, 1,900 Jews from G. and its environs were killed. One group of Jews managed to escape from the ghetto and join the partisans.

GRIVA Zemgale (Courland) dist., Latvia. Jews from the neighboring villages settled in the 19th cent. Despite a severe epidemic in the 1890s and flooding of the Dvina River in 1903 which claimed 200 mostly J. lives, the J. pop. continued to climb to a peak of 5,205 (total 12,240) in 1910. Many worked in the big factories across the river in Daugavpils (Dvinsk). The community had four synagogues, a *talmud torah*, and a yeshiva. R. Avraham Yitzhak Kook (1865–1935), the future chief rabbi of Palestine, was born and raised there. In WWI the town was almost totally destroyed and most Jews fled. Most settled in Daugavpils and Riga after WWI. The local J. pop. reached 234 in 1935 (total 5,546). The Germans arrived in June 1941 and after murdering a number of Jews expelled the rest to the Daugavpils ghetto at the end of July to share the fate of the Jews there.

GROBINA Kurzeme (Courland) dist., Latvia. An organized community existed in the early 19th cent. The J. pop. numbered 677 in 1861 and 258 in 1910 (total 1,359). The pop. dropped because of resettlement in Kherson in S. Russia, a cholera epidemic in 1848, and abandonment of the town by many for the more prosperous Liepaja in the late 19th cent. A unique school, combining traditional yeshiva studies with Musar and general subjects, operated in 1879–86. Despite declining numbers (95 in 1935) the Jews were prominent in the town's economy, owning two factories and 15 of its 58 business establishments. All Jews were murdered by the Germans in late 1941.

GRODEK JAGIELLONSKI (Yid. Greiding) Lwow dist., Poland, today Ukraine. Jews were present from at least 1445 and continued in the 16th cent. despite residence restrictions. A J. quarter was authorized in the mid-17th cent. on castle land and the community began to develop. In the 18th and 19th cents. most Jews were active in trade. A *beit midrash* and yeshiva were added to the luxurious synagogue with its famous collection of books as the J. pop. grew to 3,866 by 1910 (nearly a third of the total). Belz Hasidism became rooted in the town and offered unrelenting resistance to Haskala and Zionism. J. trade underwent a serious crisis in the early years of the 20th cent., reducing many to peddling. Recovery after WWI was hampered by Ukrainian and Polish antisemitic activity and competition. Both the Zionists and Agudat Israel gained strength in public life. In Sept. 1939 G. was occupied by the Soviets. With the arrival of the Germans on 29 June 1941, the Ukrainians robbed J. property. A *Judenrat* was organized and forced labor instituted. An *Aktion* on 7 May 1942 sent hundreds more to the labor

camps and purchase of food from the peasants was forbidden. On 13 Aug. nearly half the pop. was deported to the Belzec death camp or murdered on the spot. On 26 Dec., 1,300 Jews were taken out of the ghetto and shot. The rest were killed in the following month. The labor camps were liquidated in May 1943. Just 20 Jews appeared when the Russians liberated the town on 25 July 1944.

GRODEK SOKOLSKI Bialystok dist., Poland, today Belarus. J. settlement commenced in the late 17th cent., amounting to 24 families in 1789. From the mid-19th cent., J.-owned textile factories became the major source of J. employment. Industrialization was accelerated by the laying of a railroad line in 1886. Most had small auxiliary farms. *Mitnaggedim* were in the majority while the Hasidim ran two *shtiblekh*. A Hovevei Zion society was founded in 1898 as the J. pop. rose to 2,513 (total 2,963). The Bund was also active. Many fled from the Cossacks at the outset of WWI and under the German occupation of 1915-18 the Jews suffered from food shortages, heavy taxes, and a regime of forced labor. In 1921, 1,508 Jews remained as the community recovered with support from the Joint Distribution Committee. Except at the height of the season, few Jews worked in the textile factories because of the low wages. Most earned their livelihoods as tradesmen under a heavy tax burden that stimulated further emigration. Zionist influence increased. A CYSHO Yiddish school, much esteemed in the community, was closed down by the Polish authorities in 1928 for alleged Communist activity. A Tarbut school operated from 1925. With the arrival of the Germans on 26 June 1941, a *Judenrat* was set up and the Jews were put to forced labor. A ghetto was established in 1942. On 29 Oct. 1942 the town's 1,500 Jews were transferred to the abandoned cavalry barracks near Bialystok and from there deported to the Treblinka death camp on 29 Nov.

GRODEK WILENSKI Vilna dist., Poland, today Belarus. Jews are presumed to have settled in the early 19th cent. and numbered 1,230 (total 1,603) in 1897. They owned most of the town's stores and had auxiliary farms next to their houses. Heavy taxes after WWI brought many J. tradesmen to the point of penury. The J. pop. in 1921 was 990. Agudat Israel strongly opposed the Zionists, winning the elections to the community council in 1928, but most children

studied in a Tarbut Hebrew school. After two years of Soviet rule, the Germans entered the town in June 1941. A *Judenrat* was appointed and Jews were put to forced labor. A ghetto was established on 13 March 1942. Two hundred Jews were sent to the Krasne labor camp in May and 400 more on 11 July, when the other 900 Jews of G. were executed outside the city. The Krasne ghetto and labor camp were liquidated in March 1943.

GRODNO (Yid. Horodno) Bialystok dist., Poland, today Belarus. The J. community was one of the oldest in the the Grand Duchy of Lithuania. Jews arrived in the late 12th cent. from the Grand Duchy of Kiev and from Western Europe in flight from the depredations of the Crusades. By the late 14th cent., the community had a synagogue and cemetery. In 1495 the Jews were expelled but returned in 1503 and conducted a long struggle to regain sequestered property. In the 16th–17th cents. it was one of the three leading communities in the Lithuanian Council. In the 17th cent., the Jews faced various restrictions and Jesuit persecu-

The Vin family at Grodno cemetery, Poland, 1916 (Shlomo Gafni, Private Collection)

satzkommando 9 reported the execution of 96 Jews from G. and from Lida. According to another report, at least 100 J. "intellectuals" were rounded up and murdered in the city. Jews were banned from walking on the sidewalk, using public transportation, or going to places of entertainment. A *Judenrat* was set up and a regime of forced labor and extortion instituted. Jews were evicted from houses on the city's main streets. At the same time, German soldiers broke into J. homes and stole whatever took their fancy. Jews were put to work cleaning streets and army barracks and repairing roads while skilled workers continued working under special permits at 60% of ordinary wages. On 1 Nov. 1941, the Jews were separated in two closed ghettoes. The first ghetto was located in the center of the old city near the local fortress and crowded together 15,000 Jews classified as "productive." The second, 1.5 miles (2.5 km) away, held 10,000 in a larger area. To alleviate suffering the *Judenrat* set up 13 departments, employing 850 public workers. The first priority was the supply of food. In the first ghetto, 3,000 meals a day were distributed and in both ghettoes vegetable gardens were planted. J. tailors and shoemakers in German workshops supplied the Germans with clothing; ghetto workshops and small factories provided a wide range of goods. In Nov. 1942, at least 4,000 Jews from the second ghetto were deported to Auschwitz in two transports. Another 4,000 managed to reach the first ghetto, but in late Nov. deportations commenced from there as well, with 4,000 sent to the death camps via Kelbasin. The Kelbasin transit camp was located 3 miles (5 km) from G. and held 35,000–38,000 Jews under inhuman conditions. The Jews were housed in long dugouts and subjected to arbitrary beatings and executions. About 70 a day died of disease. Six hundred Jews were able to hide out and avoid deportation. Others attacked their guards when they arrived at the Treblinka death camp from Kelbasin. In late Dec., when it was decided to liquidate the transit camp, the 3,000 Jews there, including some from G., were sent back to the first ghetto. In Jan 1943, 11,650 were deported directly to Auschwitz, 9,851 being gassed immediately and 1,799 selected out for forced labor. About 5,000 Jews, half skilled workers, half "illegals," remained in the ghetto. In Feb., roundups continued and two more transports with 4,000 Jews left for Treblinka. On 12 March the remaining 1,000 Jews were transferred to the Bialystok ghetto after 30 hospital patients were murdered. From 1942, G. served as an underground communications center in the Vilna–Bialystok–Warsaw resistance configuration. Bela Hazzan of Deror–Hehalutz Hatzair, using forged Aryan papers, served as a link between the ghettoes from a rented apartment in G. With Mordekhai Tenenbaum she tried to persuade the *Judenrat* to take part in an uprising but only succeeded in impressing the young. About 100 of them began gathering weapons, but all efforts to act effectively failed. A few dozen managed to join the partisans; most of the others went to Bialystok, losing their lives fighting in the Aug. 1943 uprising. On the liberation of the city by the Red Army on 14 July 1944, about 250 survivors gathered there. Most subsequently emigrated, to Palestine, the U.S., Latin America, and even Russia. In the course of time, a new community of around 1,000 Jews developed.

GRODZIANKA   Mogilev dist., Belorussia. The J. pop. was 150 (total 1,247) in 1939, with most employed at a large wood factory. The Germans arrived in late June 1941 and on 15 Aug. executed a group of 45 J. men and another mixed group of 43 Jews and Belorussians. In a second *Aktion* in Oct. 1942, 92 Jews were murdered.

GRODZIEC   Kielce dist., Poland. Jews first arrived in the mid-19th cent., numbering 200 (total 700) between the World Wars. Their number rose to 283 with the arrival of Silesian refugees in WWII. In June 1942, all were expelled to the Bendzin and Sosnowiec ghettoes and from there deported to Auschwitz in fall 1942 and spring 1943.

GRODZISK   Warsaw dist., Poland. Jews probably settled in the late 17th cent., permitted to build houses and pursue their livelihoods freely by estate owners eager to develop the town. Jews constituted a majority of the total pop. until WWI, increasing to 2,154 in 1897. Pioneering local industry, J. manufacturers specialized in socks and berets while a ribbon factory supplied the clothing industry in all of Poland and beyond. A large synagogue was built in 1860 and a new *beit midrash* in 1901. The Shapiro family, descendants of the famous preacher (*maggid*) R. Yisrael of Kozienice, established a local hasidic dynasty. R. Elimelekh Shapiro presided over his court from 1849 to 1892. Many Jews left under the Russian occupation in WWI, diminishing the city's industrial resources. Emigration continued after the war, many reaching Palestine, as economic

conditions further deteriorated. All Zionist parties were active, as were Agudat Israel and the Bund. By 1936 only five of the city's 20 factories were in J. hands and large numbers were reduced to keeping stalls in the market. The Zionists with their youth movements intensified their activity. A scion of the Shapiro family, R. Yeshayahu, encouraged *aliya* among the Hasidim and became a founder of Ha-Po'el ha-Mizrachi in Palestine and established the G. dynasty there. In the wake of the German occupation of 10 Sept. 1939, refugees swelled the J. pop. to 6,000 (from 3,587 in 1936). All were expelled to the Warsaw ghetto in Feb. 1941 and subsequently murdered in the Treblinka death camp.

GRODZISKO DOLNE Lwow dist., Poland. Jews were among the town's first settlers in the second half of 18th cent. A flu epidemic claimed many lives in 1918 and later in the year peasants staged a pogrom destroying much property. The J. pop. in 1921 was 367 (total 589). Economic conditions in the poorly developed town continued to decline between the World Wars. Severe persecution followed the German occupation in WWII. The Jews were expelled into Soviet-held E. Galicia after fall 1939. Most of the 30–40 families who returned were presumably deported in July-Aug. 1942.

GRODZISK WIELKOPOLSKI Poznan dist., Poland. Jews first settled in the late 16th cent. and by 1663 numbered 374. J. merchants maintained commercial relations mainly with the nobility, dealing in wool, cloth, and alcoholic beverages. In 1749 the Jews received a charter according them extensive trade rights with free access to the marketplace and the right to practice various crafts. Among the community's rabbis was Eliyahu Gutmacher (1795–1874), who was a precursor of Zionism and attracted thousands of followers. Under Prussian rule from 1793, the Jews prospered and became active in public life, reaching a pop. of 793 (total 3,587) in 1875. However, in the latter half of the 19th cent. emigration to the big German cities increased, reducing the J. pop. to 50 in Sept. 1939. Most fled on the approach of the Germans; 13 were expelled to General Gouvernement territory.

GROENLO (Groenloo, Grol) Gelderland dist., Holland. J. settlement began in the second half of the 17th cent. A community was organized in the late 18th cent.

and included Jews from nearby Lichtenvoorde. It numbered 119 in 1860 (7% of the total) and 105 in 1938. In 1942, 58 Jews were deported and perished. A few more, found hiding, were deported in April 1943; 25 survived the Holocaust in hiding.

GROETZINGEN Baden, Germany. Jews settled temporarily in the 16th cent., establishing a permanent settlement only after the Thirty Years War (1618–48). In the late 18th cent., Jews—who until then had dealt in livestock, agricultural produce, and moneylending—engaged in more "productive" occupations in keeping with government policy, opening factories for the manufacture of organic dyestuffs and cooking oil. A synagogue was consecrated in 1799 and the J. pop. grew to a peak of 152 in 1844. In 1848, anti-J. riots broke out. From the second half of the 19th cent. the J. pop. declined steadily through emigration, numbering 72 in 1900 (total 2,226) and 20 in 1933, when the Nazis came to power. No Jews left until 1938 since the community continued to maintain ordinary life. Seven subsequently left when the synagogue was burned down by the SA on *Kristallnacht* (9–10 Nov. 1938); 12 were deported to the Gurs concentration camp on 22 Oct. 1940.

GROJEC (Yid. Gritze) Warsaw dist., Poland. An organized community dates from the 18th cent. A wooden synagogue whose interior was beautifully designed by the well-known artisan David Friedland was erected in the mid-19th cent. G. became a center of Kozienice Hasidim after the preacher (*maggid*) R. Yisrael resided there for awhile. Aleksandrow Hasidism was rooted there as well, thanks to R. Shraga Feivel Danziger (d. 1849), who was rabbi of G. and whose son R. Yehiel founded the dynasty. The J. pop. rose to 3,723 (total 5,866) in 1897 and 4,922 in 1921. The economic stagnation and antisemitism of the postwar period struck the community hard, with many emigrating to the U.S. The Germans arrived on 8 Sept. 1939, burning the synagogue and instituting a regime of forced labor and extortion. A *Judenrat* was set up in Nov. and in July 1940 the city's 5,850 Jews (including 447 refugees from western Poland) were confined to a ghetto. A thousand fled to Bialobrzegi, either to be murdered there or deported to the Treblinka death camp in fall 1942. The ghetto was liquidated on 28 Feb. 1942, when most were sent to the Warsaw ghetto; 250 workers left behind were executed on 4 June 1943;

and most of another 83 sent to a labor camp in Smolensk were also murdered.

GROKHOLICE   Lodz dist., Poland. Jews settled here early in the 18th cent. The J. pop. in 1857 was 151. At the end of 1941 its 51 members were deported to Belkhatow and in Aug. 1942 to Chelmno.

GROMBACH   Baden, Germany. Jews settled temporarily during the Thirty Years War (1618–48), founding a permanent settlement in the 18th cent. that numbered 40–50 Jews throughout the 19th cent. (about 6% of the total). The number dropped to 20 by 1933, with the Jews gradually forced to liquidate their businesses under the economic boycott. Eight left for other cities in southern German, in 1933–39. The synagogue was burned on *Kristallnacht* (9–10 Nov. 1938), and seven of the last eight Jews were deported to the Gurs concentration camp on 22 Oct. 1940.

GROMNIK   Cracow dist., Poland. Jews were living there in the mid-19th cent. and in 1921 numbered 140 (total 1,249). The Germans took G. in Sept. 1939, imposing a regime of forced labor and impounding J. farms. Most Jews were presumably expelled in summer 1942 and deported to their deaths.

GROMOKLEYA   Kirovograd, Ukraine. G. was founded as a J. colony in the mid-19th cent. Its pop. declined from 330 in 1879 to 270–280 (70 families) in the 1920s under Soviet rule. A J. kolkhoz was apparently founded in the late 1920s and a J. elementary school was functioning in the early 1930s. The few Jews who remained at the time of the German occupation in Aug. 1941 were murdered in late 1941 or early 1942.

GRONAU   Westphalia, Germany. One J. family was present at the turn of the 17th cent. and a small permanent community developed in the 19th, reaching a pop. of 70. It engaged in petty trade and butchering. The Orthodox congregation consecrated a synagogue in 1926. Forty Jews remained in 1933 when the Nazis came to power, 23 leaving by late 1938. The synagogue was wrecked on *Kristallnacht* (9–10 Nov. 1938), as were J. homes and stores. Another 15 Jews subsequently emigrated. Among those who left, 26 reached Holland and nine Palestine. Four elderly Jews were deported to the Riga and Minsk ghettoes, where they perished.

GRONINGEN   Groningen dist., Holland. J. settlement began in the mid-16th cent. and organized community activity in the 1740s. A synagogue was inaugurated in 1756. The Jews received equal civil rights in 1796. The community was split from 1848 over differences about the prayer service and the introduction of a choir. The strictly Orthodox seceded in 1852 to found their own congregations. Only in 1881 was unity reattained. A number of welfare and social organizations were established, as well as a branch of the Alliance Israelite. J. education was unified in 1815 with the founding of the Tiphereth Bachurim school, which initially taught secular as well as religious subjects. A number of Jews made their mark on the development of G. – in industry, business, and education. The J. pop. in 1860 was 1,517 (total 35,502). The community continued to increase in size and affluence from the beginning of the 20th cent. until the Holocaust. A new synagogue was inaugurated in 1903. Zionism was introduced early in the cent. and included youth movements. It caused a rift in the community in 1909 when the anti-Zionist chief rabbi of G. differed with Zionist community leaders. A branch of Agudat Israel was also organized in that period. German refugees arrived in the 1930s and early 1940s, numbering 250 by 1941. In 1940 the Jews were dismissed from public positions and in 1941 J. students were expelled from the general schools and the University of G. In 1941 a branch of the Central J. Committee serving the entire district was opened in G. The J. pop. in 1938 was 1,173. Deportations began in Aug. 1942; most were sent to the Westerbork transit camp. In Feb. 1943, a Jew found hiding shot an SS member. In retaliation 189 J. council workers from G. and the region were deported. Only a few G. Jews went into hiding; 120 returned after the war and a community was refounded.

GROSS-BIEBERAU   Hesse, Germany. The community declined from 87 (5% of the total) in 1900 to 43 in 1933. Though Orthodox, it was affiliated with Darmstadt's Liberal rabbinate. The synagogue, no longer J. property, was burned down on *Kristallnacht* (9–10 Nov. 1938). The remaining Jews left by 1939.

GROSSEICHHOLZHEIM   Baden, Germany. Jews first appeared in 1716 and after suffering considerable persecution maintained a pop. of around 100 (12% of the total) throughout the 19th cent. A synagogue was completed in 1887. By 1933 the J. pop. had dropped

to 51 through emigration and the exodus to the big cities. Under the Nazis, J. livelihoods were gradually eroded and by 1936, 22 Jews had emigrated (ten to Argentina, seven to the U.S) and four left for other German cities. On *Kristallnacht* (9–10 Nov. 1938), the synagogue was vandalized. The last 16 Jews were deported to the Gurs concentration camp on 22 Oct. 1940.

GROSSEN-BUSECK   Hesse, Germany. Established before 1739, the community numbered 120 in 1828, but had already declined to 74 (4% of the total) in 1895. Religious facilities were shared with the Jews of Alten-Buseck, Beuern, and Reiskirchen. On *Kristallnacht* (9–10 Nov. 1938), the synagogue was vandalized and anti-J. violence occurred. Of the 34 Jews still living there in 1933, 13 emigrated and by Nov. 1939 none remained.

GROSSEN-LINDEN   Hesse, Germany. The community numbered 40 (4% of the total) in 1828, its old burial ground (1637) serving Jews throughout the region. By April 1939, the remaining 28 Jews had mostly emigrated to the U.S. or Palestine and their syn-

agogue had become the local SA headquarters. A memorial was erected there on the 50th anniversary of *Kristallnacht* (9–10 Nov. 1938).

GROSS-ENZERSDORF   Lower Austria, Austria. A permanent J. settlement dates from the middle of the 18th cent., reaching a peak pop. of 220 in 1934. In 1865, a synagogue was built and in 1880 a J. cemetery was consecrated. In 1898, the community was recognized as a religious association (*Kultusverein*). Jews earned their livelihood as storekeepers and farmers. They were represented in the professional class as doctors and veterinarians. In 1920, a Maccabi sports club was founded. After the *Anschluss* (13 March 1938), the community was incorporated into the Vienna community. By this time there were 103 Jews living in G. They were forced to move to special houses in Vienna, leaving their property behind. Of the 86 sent to the east, none returned.

GROSS-GERAU   Hesse, Germany. No permanent community was established there until 1738, when the town council authorized the building of a syna-

Synagogue in Gross-Gerau, Germany, 1938

gogue. The community numbered 141 (4% of the total) in 1885. A larger synagogue was opened in 1892 in the town center and – though affiliated with the Liberal rabbinate of Darmstadt – kept to the Orthodox mode of worship. Under the Weimar Republic, Jews attained prominence in civic and commercial life. By 1925, the J. pop. had risen to 161 (3%), but from 30 March 1933 the Nazi boycott campaign subjected Jews to public insult, violence, and ruin, compelling many to leave. On *Kristallnacht* (9–10 Nov. 1938), the synagogue was burned down and 24 Jews were attacked, their homes looted and vandalized. Nearly all of the 140 Jews left after 1933 (more than 30 emigrating), and on 7 Nov. 1940 the town was declared "free of Jews" (*judenrein*). In 1978 a memorial was erected on the site of the destroyed synagogue and in 1984 Yad Vashem awarded the (posthumous) title of Righteous among the Nations to Wilhelm Hamann of G., who helped save the lives of 150 J. children while imprisoned in the Buchenwald concentration camp.

GROSS-KACKSCHEN   (Rus. Sadovo) East Prussia, Germany, today Russia. The J. pop. numbered 205 in 1895 and about 125 on the eve of WWI. Although there was no synagogue building, a community official was employed and religious services were held regularly. No information is available on the fate of the 30 Jews who were living in G. when the Nazis took power.

GROSS-KARBEN   Hesse, Germany. Established in the 17th cent., the community numbered 217 (about 24% of the total) in 1871, had members in nearby Rendel, and was affiliated with the Orthodox rabbinate of Giessen. The Jews dealt in agricultural produce and owned stores, including three kosher butcher shops. On *Kristallnacht* (9–10 Nov. 1938), the synagogue was burned down and a full-scale pogrom took place. Of the 80–100 Jews living there in 1933, about two dozen emigrated and survived; the rest were eventually deported.

GROSS-KROTZENBURG Hesse–Nassau,   Germany. Jews settled there in the 17th cent. and founded a community, dedicating a synagogue in 1826 and maintaining an elementary school (1855–1933). They numbered 161 (about 10% of the total) in 1905 and 137 in 1925. Affiliated with the rabbinate of Hanau, the community also drew members from Gross-Au-

heim. Most Jews left before *Kristallnacht* (9–10 Nov. 1938), when the synagogue's interior was destroyed. Fifty-two emigrated and at least 45 (including "euthanasia" victims) died in the Holocaust.

GROSSLANGHEIM Lower Franconia, Germany. Jews are first mentioned in 1590. The J. pop. was 70 in 1837 (total 1,223) and 18 in the Nazi era. Seven left for other German cities by Nov. 1937 and another six left in the first half of 1939 after the synagogue was wrecked on *Kristallnacht* (9–10 Nov. 1938). The last four were deported to Izbica in the Lublin dist. (Poland) and to the Theresienstadt ghetto in 1942.

GROSSOSTHEIM   (in J. sources, Oistheim) Lower Franconia, Germany. Jews are mentioned in connection with the Rindfleisch massacres of 1298 and again in the early 18th cent. The J. pop. numbered 79 in 1890 (total 2,664) and 28 in 1933. Ten left in 1935–1938 and another eight after *Kristallnacht* (9–10 Nov. 1938), when the synagogue was vandalized. The last five Jews were deported to the Theresienstadt ghetto on 10 Sept. 1942.

GROSS-ROHRHEIM   Hesse, Germany. The community, numbering 78 (5% of the total) in 1861, disbanded in 1933 and no Jews remained there after 1938.

GROSS-STEINHEIM   Hesse, Germany. The community, numbering 38 (3% of the total) in 1828, grew to 88 (4%) in 1900 and was affiliated with the Offenbach rabbinate. By 1933 it had declined to 45, excluding members in nearby Dietesheim (21), Hainstadt (eight), and Klein-Anheim (37). The synagogue was vandalized on *Kristallnacht* (9–10 Nov. 1938) and 35 Jews left (mostly emigrating) by 1939. The remainder were presumably deported in 1942.

GROSS-STREHLITZ   (Pol.   Strzelce   Opolskie) Upper Silesia, Germany, today Poland. There is no evidence of a J. presence before 1812. In 1832, the J. pop. was already 112 and in 1840 it was 140. A synagogue and cemetery were opened in the 1850s. Jews were active in public and social life. They were elected to the municipal council from the 1820s and received support for the community's needy from Christian welfare agencies. The J. school was amalgamated with the city's municipal and Protestant schools in 1874 to create a single school in the mostly Catholic settlement. The

Synagogue and Jewish community center, Grosslangheim, Germany

J. pop. climbed to 509 in 1880. The community maintained a library and numerous institutions, including welfare and youth organizations. A new J. sports club was started in 1933. With the Nazi rise to power in 1933, the J. pop. stood at 114. On *Kristallnacht* (9–10 Nov. 1938), the synagogue was set on fire and five J. stores and a number of J. homes were destroyed. Seventy Jews remained in 1939. Deportations to General Gouvernement territory and the Theresienstadt ghetto commenced on 20 May 1942. On 19 Nov. 1942, there were still ten Jews in G. Their fate is unknown.

GROSSULOVO (from 1945, Velikaya Michaylovka) Odessa dist., Ukraine. The J. pop. was 1,201 (total 2,088) in 1897. In the Soviet period, 224 of a total 669 J. breadwinners were stripped of their rights in the late 1920s. The local *beit midrash* still served as a prayer and religious study house at this time. A J. rural council (soviet) and J. elementary school were active. A few dozen local J. families worked in the nearby J. kolkhoz, which also had a J. elementary school. In 1939, there were 522 Jews here. The Germans captured G. on 7 Aug. 1941 and five days later executed 124 Jews, including 35 children, at the local cemetery.

GROSS-UMSTADT Hesse, Germany. Numbering 69 (2% of the total) in 1861, the community grew to 87 in 1905 and was affiliated with the Orthodox rabbinate of Darmstadt. On *Kristallnacht* (9–10 Nov. 1938), Nazis destroyed the synagogue's interior and conducted a pogrom. Nearly all of the 57 Jews living there in 1933 fled (21 emigrating) before WWII. In 1983 a reconstruction of the synagogue was added to the Hessenpark outdoor museum in Neu Anspach.

GROSS WARTENBERG (Pol. Sycow) Lower Silesia, Germany. A small J. community made up mainly of Polish refugees was present by 1657. In 1739, it

viduals). They earned their living as butchers, horse traders, food merchants, and wax manufacturers. On the eve of WWII, there were 64 Jews listed in the community. Jews began leaving G. in Sept. 1939, the last members of the community leaving in June 1940. The houses, cemetery, and synagogue on Riedgasse were all completely destroyed during the war. The Germans deported 20 community members. Only one survived. The last J. family left G. in 1955.

GRUZDZIAI   (Yid. Gruzd) Siauliai dist., Lithuania. The J. community was founded at the end of the 18th cent. The J. pop. in 1897 was 482 (41% of the total). Many Jews emigrated because of economic conditions. The J. pop. in 1939 was 75 (6% of the total). On 5 Aug. 1941 Lithuanian nationalists killed 50 Jews at the J. cemetery. In Sept. the rest were taken to Zagare and murdered.

GRYBOW   Cracow dist., Poland. A permanent settlement is known from the mid-18th cent. The J. pop. was 596 in 1880 (25% of the total) and 908 in 1910. Zanz Hasidism was dominant, controlling the community council until 1928, but the Zionist movement was also a cultural and educational factor. In 1898, rioting peasants attacked J. distillers and innkeepers in G. and the surrounding villages and in 1918 a pogrom caused much damage to property and even injured young children. Antisemitic agitation continued between the World Wars. Some Jews fled permanently to Soviet-occupied E. Galicia on the approach of the Germans in Sept. 1939. At the end of the year, a *Judenrat* was set up to regulate the supply of forced labor. Thirty Jews were sent to Nowy Soncz on 29 April 1942 and murdered there; ten more were executed in the town. On 16 Aug., the entire pop. was ordered to Nowy Soncz, where they were murdered. The sick and elderly were murdered beforehand.

GRZYMALOW   (Yid. Rimalov) Tarnopol dist., Poland, today Ukraine. The Jews were among the first settlers in the town in the early 18th cent. and maintained a level of 50–60% of the total pop., with a peak of 2,977 in 1890. Jews were active in trade but with the transfer of the county capital from here to Skalat after WWI, a decline set in and the J. pop. dropped to

Street in Gruzdziai, Lithuania, 1927

around 1,500. On the whole, the Jews lived in relative harmony with the Poles and Ukrainians, receiving a third of the seats on the municipal council. Under the Soviets (Sept 1939–June 1941), the J. pop. swelled to around 2,000 with an influx of refugees. Within a few days of the German occupation on 6 July 1941, 350–500 Jews were rounded up and murdered. Those not sent to the labor camps in G. and its environs were expelled to Skalat in Oct. 1942. The camp in G. was burned to the ground on 24 Jan. 1943 with most of the Jews inside. Around 30 survived the war.

GUBEN Brandenburg, Germany. There was a medieval J. community during the 14th cent. and in the first half of the 15th cent. The community was persecuted during the Black Death disturbances of 1348–49. Jews settled again in G. in 1650. In 1834, there were 31 Jews in the village. The community set up a synagogue in 1837 and a cemetery in 1839, and formally organized in 1849. During the second half of the 19th cent. the J. pop. was more than 200. In 1878 a larger synagogue was consecrated. From 1912 to 1924, a Jew served as the town's mayor. When the Nazis came to power in 1933, there were still about 200 Jews living in G. On *Kristallnacht* (9–10 Nov. 1938), the synagogue was destroyed; Torah scrolls were burned; J. businesses were destroyed; and the cemetery was desecrated. J. men were maltreated, arrested, and deported to the Sachsenhausen concentration camp. By 1939, there were 60 Jews in G. Those who did not emigrate were deported to the east. One of the last deportations was of the elderly to the Theresienstadt ghetto in 1942. By Oct. 1942, only ten Jews were still registered as living in G., probably protected by marriage to non-Jews. Some were deported in 1944. In the same year, 300 J. women of Hungarian origin were brought to G. for forced labor in a local factory.

GUDELIAI (Yid. Gudel) Marijampole dist., Lithuania. The J. pop. in 1923 was 193, but fell to less than half of that by WWII. Lithuanians killed all the Jews in the Azuolo Buda forest on 23 July 1941.

GUDENSBERG Hesse–Nassau, Germany. Established in the 18th cent., the community built a synagogue in 1843, maintained an elementary school from 1825 to 1934, and grew to 194 (10% of the total) in 1871. Many Jews raised cattle or poultry and owned farms. Israel Meyer Japhet (1818–92)

taught there prior to becoming in 1853 musical director of the Orthodox Adass Jeshurun congregation in Frankfurt, Mordecai Wetzlar, who served as district rabbi (1830–75), founded a yeshiva attended by Yitzhak Ruelf (1831–1902), the rabbi of Memel and pioneer German Zionist. Affiliated with Kassel's rabbinate, the community numbered 118 in 1925. By May 1938, however, all the Jews had left and G. was proclaimed "free of Jews" (*judenrein*).

GUEBWILLER (Ballon de or Grand Ballon; Ger. Grosser Belchen or Sulzer Belchen) Haut-Rhin dist., France. After the Black Death persecutions of 1348–49, the community ceased to exist until the beginning of the 17th cent. In 1865, there were 80 Jews in G. The synagogue was consecrated in 1872. In 1885, the community consisted of 1,512 members, dwindling to 973 in 1905 and to 470 in 1931. During WWII, the Germans expelled 126 Jews still in G. to the south of France, with the rest of Alsace-Lorraine Jews.

GUELZOW (Pol. Golczewo) Pomerania, Germany, today Poland. A Jew is first mentioned in 1705. The J. community remained small, numbering four families in 1752 and 48 individuals in 1905. It maintained a prayer room and a cemetery. When the Nazis came to power in 1933, there were 25 Jews in G. By May 1938 there were still two J. businesses operating. No further information about the fate of the Jews under Nazi rule is available.

GUERZENICH Rhineland, Germany. Jews are mentioned in the first half of the 18th cent. and reached a peak pop. of about 58 in 1871–94. A new synagogue was dedicated in 1906. The community was affiliated to Dueren. In 1928, the J. pop. numbered 29. On *Kristallnacht* (9–10 Nov. 1938), the synagogue was destroyed. Those who did not make it in time to a safe haven perished.

GUESSING Burgenland, Austria. J. settlement dates back 400 years. A burial society was founded in 1770. In 1840, a synagogue was inaugurated. Jews were engaged in trade and crafts. By 1840, the J. pop. stood at 527, declining to 108 in 1914. In May 1938, 138 Jews were living in G. They were expelled in the following months. Some emigrated or succeeded in escaping. Others were sent to Vienna and from there to the east.

opened and a new synagogue was dedicated in 1883. In 1890 the J. pop. was 291 (total 3,853). In the 1920s G. was one of the hotbeds of Bavarian antisemitism. In 1928 windows were smashed in the synagogue and in 1929 the cemetery was desecrated. The number of Jews in 1933 was 184. The Zionist Organization, Central Union (C.V.), and Agudat Israel were active. Jews were already being attacked in the streets in early 1933 and in 1934 a full-scale pogrom was staged under SA auspices with the participation of 1,000–1,500 townsmen. Jews were severely beaten and 35 were arrested. Two weeks later windows were smashed in J. homes and stores. By 1938 over two-thirds of the town's Jews had left. The rest left shortly after *Kristallnacht* (9–10 Nov. 1938), when rioters damaged the synagogue and wrecked J. homes. In all, 52 emigrated, including 22 to the U.S. and 18 to Palestine, and 116 left for other German cities. Seven were sent to the Dachau concentration camp.

GURAHONT (Hung., Honczto) S. Transylvania dist., Rumania. Jews first settled in the early 19th cent. and an organized community existed from the end of WWI. The J. pop. in 1930 was 92 (8% of the total). In 1942 the Jews were expelled to Arad. The Jews never returned to G.

GURA-HUMORULUI Bukovina, Rumania. The first Jews who settled in 1835 provided supplies for the Austrian military forces encamped there. Jews were artisans and engaged in the lumber industry. All the Jews of G. were Wiznitzer Hasidim. Zionist activity began in 1908, and in 1933 a training farm was opened for pioneers from Bessarabia. J. stores were plundered when the Russian army entered G. in Jan. 1915, Jews suffered again when the Rumanian army arrived on 10 Nov. 1918. The J. pop. in 1930 was 1,951 (31% of the total). In 1940, a J. elementary and high school were opened after J. pupils were expelled from government schools. In June 1941, 800 J. refugees expelled from the surrounding towns and villages were housed by the community. On 10 Oct. 1941, the J. pop. (2,900) was deported to Transnistria, but on 14 March 1944, 1,500 were allowed to return. They found their houses wrecked and a hostile local pop.

GUR-PUTILEI Bukovina, Rumania, today Ukraine. The Jews were attached to the Putilei community and had no independent institutions. The J. pop. in 1930

was 115. In 1941 all the Jews were deported to Transnistria. Few survived.

GURZUF Crimea, Russia. Jews were granted formal residence rights only in 1903 but some were apparently present before that time. In 1939 the J. pop. was 89 (total 6,117). The Germans occupied G. on 8 Nov. 1941 and in Dec. murdered the few Jews who had neither fled nor been evacuated.

GUSINO Smolensk dist., Russia. Jews probably settled in the late 19th cent. and numbered 427 (total 706) in 1926. A J. kolkhoz was in existence until June 1941. The Germans arrived in July 1941, confining the Jews to a ghetto camp and murdering 278, including Jews from the surrounding area, on 6 Feb. 1942.

GUSTORF Rhineland, Germany. Jews are first mentioned in 1721, numbering 19 in 1871 and 12 in 1905. They were affiliated to the Grevenbroich community. Nine Jews are known to have perished in the Holocaust.

GUSYATIN Kamenets-Podolski dist., Ukraine. Jews are first mentioned in 1578. In 1704, soldiers pillaged their property. In 1765 they numbered 1,444. Most remained in Poland after the First Partition in 1772. In 1897, the J. pop. was 1,153 (41% of the total). In 1923, after the pogroms of the Russian civil war, 546 remained. Those still there during the German occupation of WWII shared the fate of all the Jews in the area. (see also HUSIATYN.)

GUTA Slovakia, Czechoslovakia, today Republic of Slovakia. Jews probably settled in the early 18th cent., returning in the mid-19th cent. after being expelled in the mid-18th cent. Their number grew to 124 in 1880 and 230 (total 8,906) in 1910. The community maintained an elementary school, *talmud torah*, and kindergarten. Agudat Israel ran a big branch after WWI and the Zionists, including Betar and Maccabi, became active in the 1930s. By 1941, the J. pop. was 372. Under Hungarian rule, J. livelihoods were undermined and Jews were seized for forced labor. In mid-June 1944, the Jews were deported to Auschwitz.

GUTTENTAG (Pol. Dobrodzien) Upper Silesia, Germany, today Poland. Jews settled in the 17th cent. and numbered 120 in 1787. They engaged in petty

trade, crafts, and also agriculture. A prayer house was in use in 1781. The J. pop. grew to 280 in 1861 and a J. elementary school was founded in 1868. With the decline of local industry, the J. pop. also fell, reaching 47 in 1925. The Nazi racial laws were not applied until July 1937 since the Jews were under the protection of the League of Nations' minority rights convention. Their subsequent implementation was accompanied by antisemitic disturbances. On *Kristallnacht* (9–10 Nov. 1938), the prayer house was set on fire. In 1939, 14 Jews remained, all probably deported to their deaths. On 19 Nov. 1942, there were reports of one J. still in G.

GUTTSTADT (Pol. Dobre Miasto) East Prussia, Germany, today Poland. Jews were allowed to trade at the local fairs in 1802. In 1814 three J. families were permitted to settle permanently. In 1847, the J. pop. was 120 individuals and 243 in 1871. The community had a cemetery in 1814 and a synagogue in 1855. In 1869, four Jews served as members of the city council. In 1905, the J. pop. came to 149, dropping to 93 in 1926. In June 1933, about four months after

the Nazis assumed power, there were still about 90 Jews living in G. On *Kristallnacht* (9–10 Nov. 1938), the synagogue was burned down. By Oct. 1942, only one J. resident was left, probably protected by marriage to a non-J. partner. It may be assumed that those who did not manage to emigrate were deported.

GUXHAGEN Hesse–Nassau, Germany. Founded around 1809, the community built a synagogue in 1843, maintained a school (1823–1936), and numbered 170 (12% of the total) in 1905. Affiliated with the rabbinate of Kassel, its members established a branch of the J. War Veterans Association in 1925 and were noted for their strict religious orthodoxy. Of the 158 Jews living there in 1933, only 82 remained on *Kristallnacht* (9–10 Nov. 1938), when SA troops vandalized the synagogue and organized a pogrom. The last 39 Jews were sent to death camps and to the Theresienstadt ghetto in 1941–42.

GWOZDZIEC Stanislawow dist., Poland, today Ukraine. Jews are first recorded in 1635, with the community's splendid synagogue (which burned

Synagogue in Gwozdziec, Poland

down in WWI) dating to 1640. The J. pop. in 1900 was 1,663. (66% of the total). Traditional life with a hasidic emphasis persisted throughout the 19th cent. The economic situation of the Jews deteriorated between the World Wars as a result of organized Ukrainian competition. In WWII, Soviet rule (Sept. 1939–June 1941) destroyed communal life and much private enterprise. The relatively quiet Hungarian occupation in June–fall 1941 was replaced by the German regime, which brought immediate ghettoization. On 12 April 1942, about half the Jews were rounded up. They were shot in the nearby forest or murdered in the streets; others suffocated in the smoke and flames of the incinerated buildings. On 24 April the remaining Jews were expelled to Kolomyja, but many escaped to other ghettoes or even to labor camps. In the end, few survived the final deportations to the Belzec death camp.

GYMNICH Rhineland, Germany. Three protected J. families were present in 1730. In the first half of the 19th cent., the J. pop. was 40–50 and grew to 112 in 1860. The community maintained a synagogue and cemetery (both opened early in the cent.). In 1933, the J. pop. was 33, dropping to 22 with the outbreak of war in 1939. The synagogue, which was seriously damaged on *Kristallnacht* (9–10 Nov. 1938), served as a "J. house" from 1941 for the 14 remaining Jews of G. and Lechenich, all of whom were deported to the east in July 1942. A total of 22 local Jews perished in the Holocaust.

GYOMA Bekes dist., Hungary. Jews settled in the first half of the 19th cent. A nationally known printing press, established by Isador Kner in 1880, employed 50 workers in 1929. A J. public school was opened in 1858 and a synagogue in 1869. The J. pop. was 305 (3% of the total) in 1869 and 129 in 1941. In 1940, the men were sent to forced labor and in May 1944, the remaining Jews were enclosed in a ghetto and forced to raise silk worms. They were deported to Austria and Auschwitz via Szolnok on 29 June. Eighty-six returned after the war but soon dispersed.

GYOMORE Pest–Pilis–Solt–Kiskun dist., Hungary. Jews settled in the early 18th cent. A synagogue was erected in 1840, when the J. pop. was 242. In 1941 the J. pop. was 180. On 15 June 1944 the Jews were deported to Auschwitz after being detained in Magyarovar and Gyor.

GYOMRO Pest–Pilis–Solt–Kiskun dist., Hungary. Jews settled in the early 18th cent., forming a Neologist congregation in 1869 and reaching a peak pop. of 175 in 1930. In 1941, the young men were sent to local labor camps while the older men were sent to White Russia and the Ukraine, where most died. On 25–27 June 1944, those who remained were deported to Auschwitz via Nagykata.

GYON Pest–Pilis–Solt–Kiskun dist., Hungary. Jews numbered 220 in 1851 and 53 in 1930. They were deported to Auschwitz via Lajosmizse and Monac on 8 July 1944.

GYONGYOS (Yid. Gondish) Heves dist., Hungary. Jews settled here with the Turkish conquest in the 15th cent. Most were of Sephardic origin. They left with the Turks when the city was destroyed, only returning in the early 18th cent. Jews excelled as winegrowers and were officially awarded the right to sell without customs or tax throughout Hungary. The Jews of G. played a vital role in developing the region economically. The first synagogue was consecrated in 1813 and a J. school was established in 1839. The J. community was one of the largest in Hungary. The J. pop. numbered 2,000–2,200 from the 1860s through WWII (10–12% of the total). Between the World Wars, Hashomer Hatzair was active. Following the German occupation of spring 1944, the Jews were subjected to a reign of terror with the participation of Hungarian Fascists. In May, they were confined to a ghetto under a regime of forced labor and at the end of June deported to Auschwitz. After the war, 300 returned, mainly from the labor camps; most left in 1956.

GYONK Tolna dist., Hungary. Jews settled in the early 18th cent. An important yeshiva was founded by R. Moshe Kanizsa, who officiated in 1823–33. A synagogue was consecrated in 1836. R. Amram Fischer, an outstanding Torah scholar, served from 1878. The J. pop. was 100 in 1890 and 70 in 1941. The Jews were deported to Auschwitz from Pecs on 5 July 1944

GYOR Gyor–Moson dist., Hungary. Jews are first mentioned in the 15th cent. In the 16th cent., they lived under the protection of the military commander of the local fortress. From 1669 on they were denied permanent residence in the town and in 1748 forced

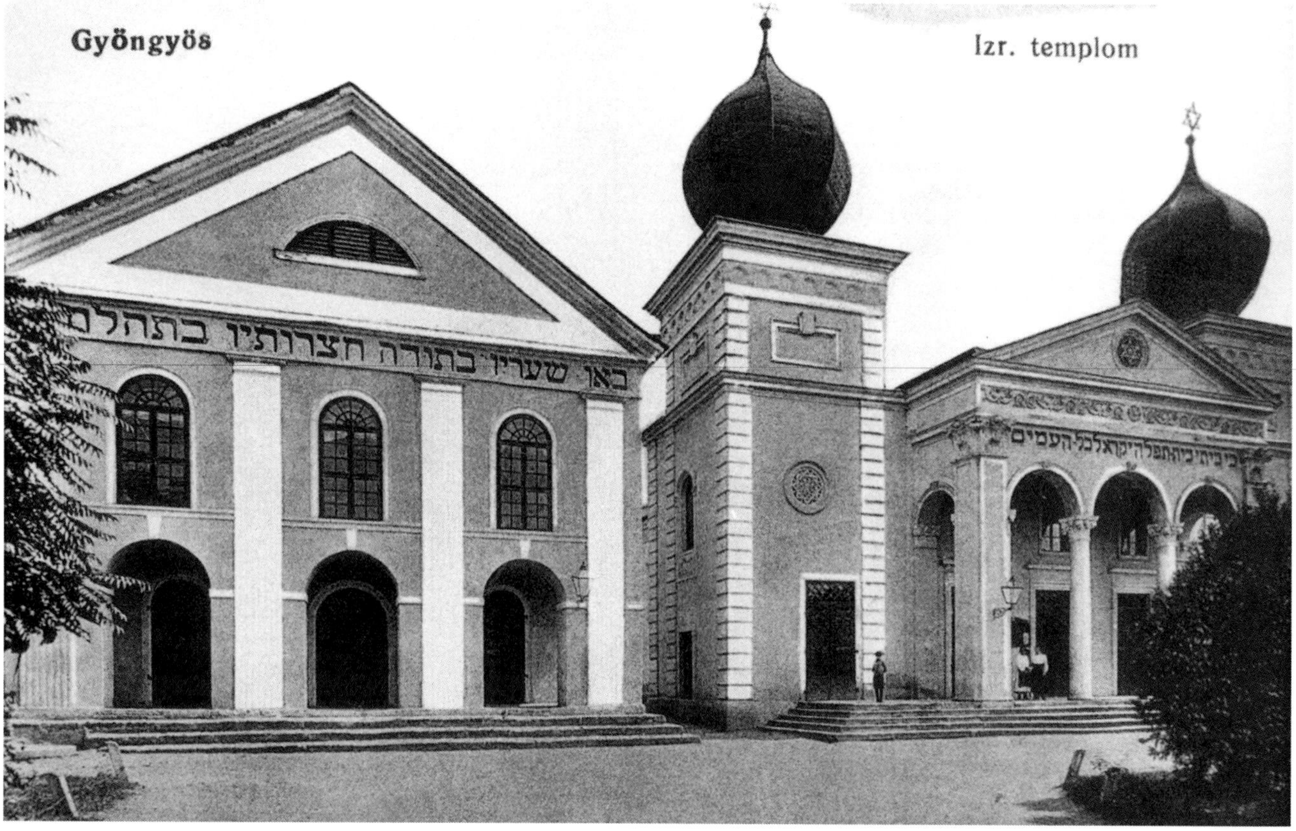
Gyöngyös
Izr. templom
באו שעריו בתודה חצרותיו בתהלה

Synagogue in Gyongyos, Hungary, before WWII

to reside on the nearby island of Gyor-Sigat. In 1791, 30 J. families from the island were permitted to live in G. In 1840, residence was allowed in exchange for heavy tax payments. In the second half of the 19th cent., Jews were prominent as exporters in the burgeoning grain trade with Serbia, Rumania, and Bulgaria. Many also started factories (alcohol, matches, farm implements, candy) and brickyards and flour mills. A separate Orthodox community was formed in 1871. A J. school was founded in 1851, enrolling 222 children by 1858. The J. pop. grew from 3,051 in 1869 to a peak of 5,904 (12% of the total) in 1920. In 1941, 4,688 remained. In May 1944, the Jews were confined in a ghetto on the island. On 7 June, they were brought to a temporary camp near the city with other Jews from the neighborhood and on 11 June sent to Kassa en route to Auschwitz. After the war, several hundred returned to renew the community, but only a few remained after 1956.

GYORASSZONYFA Gyor-Moson dist., Hungary. Jews settled in 1810 and marketed produce from nearby estates. They numbered 273 in 1840 and 12 in 1941. They were deported to Auschwitz via Gyor on 11 June 1944.

GYORSZENTMARTON Gyor-Moson dist., Hungary. Jews settled in the mid-19th cent., establishing a synagogue in 1882 and a school in 1880. In 1931, they numbered 94. Despite the German occupation, a ghetto was never established in G. and the Jews remained relatively free until all were deported to Auschwitz via Gyor on 11 June 1944.

GYULA Bekes dist., Hungary. Jews settled in the mid-19th cent. They set up a flour mill and factories to produce matches, alcoholic beverages, and knitwear. They reached a peak pop. of 921 (4% of the total) in 1910, declining to 510 by 1941. In 1869, they formed a Neologist congregation and in 1873 erected a synagogue. Between the World Wars, the Zionists were influential among the young. J. males were seized for forced labor on 15 May 1944 and transferred to Germany on 15 Oct. The rest were deported to Auschwitz

via Bekescsaba on 29 June 1944. Survivors reestablished the community but left in 1956.

GYULAHAZA   Szabolcs dist., Hungary. Jews are mentioned in 1747, numbering 168 in 1860 and 79 in 1930. Most were wheat and potato merchants. Anti-J. violence commenced in 1940. On 28–31 May 1944, the Jews were deported to Auschwitz via Kisvarda.

GYURE   Szabolcs dist., Hungary. Jews are mentioned in 1770, numbering 150 in 1880 and 122 in 1930 after severe persecution during the Rumanian oc-

cupation of WWI and then the White Terror. On 25–27 May 1944, they were deported to Auschwitz via Kisvarda.

GZHATSK   Smolensk dist., Russia. Jews probably settled in the mid-19th cent. and numbered 152 (total 6,324) in 1897. In 1901, they received permission to operate a prayer house. In the Soviet period, the J. pop. reached 276 in 1926 and then dropped to 181 in 1939. After the German occupation of 9 Oct. 1941, the few who remained and had not fled or been evacuated were murdered.

H

HAAKSBERGEN Overijssel dist., Holland. J. settlement began in the late 17th cent. The J. pop. was 70 in 1892 and 56 in 1941 (total 10,047). In 1943, 18 Jews were deported and perished. The rest survived in hiding.

HAAPSALU Estonia. Between the World Wars a handful of Jews remained in the 19th cent. settlement with others frequenting the resort town in summer. All fled to the Soviet Union in summer 1941.

HAARLEM Noord-Holland dist., Holland. Jews lived in H. sporadically during the Middle Ages. In 1605 three Jews received rights to settle with their fam-

Jozef Mickey van Coevorden, jazz musician from Haarlem, Holland, who hid out from the Nazis until 1944, when he was betrayed by an informer and sent to Auschwitz

ilies and to practice Judaism freely. In the first half of the 18th cent., Ashkenazi Jews settled. Many restrictions on their professional practices were lifted, and organized community activity began. A synagogue was consecrated in 1765 and a larger one was built in 1841. In the latter 18th cent., a Portuguese community was established and a synagogue was founded in 1780. A community building, including a school, was built in 1888. Various welfare organizations and a branch of the Alliance Israelite were established during the 19th cent. There were 688 members in the community in 1883. From the end of the cent., the community grew significantly and expanded its activities. Zionism was introduced in the early 20th cent. and quickly dominated the community. In 1936 H. became the seat of the Noord-Holland chief rabbinate. By May 1938 there were 180 German refugees in H. In 1940, after the German invasion, the refugees were ordered to leave. Restrictions on J. movement were imposed. The J. pop. in 1941 was 1,623 with 341 in nearby Bloemendaal and 234 in Heemstede. Deportations took place from Aug. 1942 until Feb. 1943. In Feb. 1943 three community leaders were executed. In all, some 1,000 were deported, while hundreds were hidden. Only ten returned from the camps. After the war the community was reconstituted.

HABITZHEIM Hesse, Germany. Established around 1800, the community numbered 78 (7% of the total) in 1861 but declined. Twelve Jews emigrated between 1933 and 1939; seven others were deported in 1942.

HABURA Slovakia, Czechoslovakia, today Republic of Slovakia. The J. pop. was 135 in 1880 with a synagogue and cemetery in use. In 1930, 41 Jews remained in H.

HACHENBURG Hesse–Nassau, Germany. Established in the late 18th cent., the community numbered 73 in 1843 and 124 (7% of the total) in 1905. It also drew members from seven other townships, but constant arguments delayed the building of a synagogue until 1897. Affiliated with the rabbinate of Bad Ems, the community provided H. with eight of its nine cattle traders after WWI. Nazi boycott measures reduced the J. pop. to 28 on *Kristallnacht* (9–10 Nov. 1938), when SA troops organized a pogrom. By 1 March 1940, all the Jews had left with half of the 40 emigrants going to

the U.S.; 36 who remained on German soil perished in the Holocaust.

HADAMAR Hesse–Nassau, Germany. Established in the 17th cent., the J. community built a synagogue in 1841 and numbered 100 (5% of the total) in 1842. Salomon Wormser, the dist. rabbi (1852–60), tried to promote Reform Judaism but met with strong opposition. Numbering 80 (3%) in 1925, the community also had members in Hausen and Langendernbach. On *Kristallnacht* (9–10 Nov. 1938), the synagogue's interior was destroyed. Of the 68 Jews who lived there in 1933, 29 left (17 emigrating), four committed suicide, and 27 were deported (1942). The psychiatric hospital in H. was turned into a Nazi "euthanasia" center housing a gas chamber and crematoria which was used in Jan.–Aug. 1941 to eliminate 10,000 mentally ill, retarded, or incurable people – some of them Jews, including the children of mixed marriages.

HADJEB EL-AYOUN Kairouan dist., Tunisia. A tailor, Yehoshua Maimon, arriving alone from Gabes in 1905 with only his sewing machine, was the community's founder. He was later joined by his family. Additional families, attracted by his success, came ten years later. After WWI, the community continued to grow, with Jews earning their livelihood from the health resort centered around the local sulfur springs as well as from tailoring, the principal occupation. The J. pop. reached a peak of 140 (total 1,144) in 1931. The prosperous Maimon family represented the concessionaires of the *alafa* (paper plant) export trade. It also owned the town's only bakery, an oil press, one of the town's two inns, and 35 acres of cultivated land along with livestock. Most Jews lived in rented three-room apartments. They spoke the local Arabic dialect rather than Judeo-Arabic while the older generation could speak in biblical Hebrew. Maimon and his two sons served alternately as president of the community. Children attended a French public school and afterwards a *talmud torah*. Relations with the Arabs remained good until WWII. During the war, the Jews suffered from shortages in basic necessities and in late 1942 the Allies bombed the town. Within a few weeks of the German occupation, the Jews left the town, to stay with the Bedouins in the hill country from Dec. 1942 until May 1943. When the Jews returned with the Allies in May 1943, they found their homes and property pillaged by the local Arabs. In

the late 1940s, as the struggle for Arab independence intensified, tensions increased. There was no organized Zionist activity and when Jews began to leave, their chief motivation was religious-messianic. Arab hostility increased after the establishment of Israel, with efforts made to boycott J. stores. As Jews, in the guise of tourists, began to leave the country for Israel via France, the community came to an end in the 1953–55 period.

HAGEN Westphalia, Germany. The first Jews are mentioned in 1722. Some were "protected" Jews while others tried to settle as their servants. In the early 19th cent., Jews were peddlers. The poverty and smallness of the community kept it from employing a full-time teacher for its children. In 1854, H. became the seat of a regional congregation with the communities of Schwelm and Herdecke attached to it. The Jews of H. participated fully in the political and social life of the city. Avraham Levi (d. 1894) was a city assemblyman for 28 years. In 1844, the J. religious school became a J. public school with a full curriculum. The congregation became Liberal during the second half of the 19th cent. The synagogue, built in 1859, lacked a woman's section, though seating was still separate. A choir and organ were later introduced. Numerous organizations offering social and welfare services operated in the community. A branch of the Alliance Israelite Universelle was opened in 1883 with 32 members. The J. pop. grew from 37 in 1816 to 309 in 1875 and 641 (total 143,701) in 1925. Polish Jews began arriving in the early 20th cent. and comprised 30% of the community by 1931. A Zionist group with 39 members was active in 1922. In the Weimar period, 94 J. businesses were listed (according to Nazi compilations), 33 in the clothing trade. Jews continued to occupy key public positions but antisemitism also intensified. In 1933, the J. school had 40 pupils while 73 received religious instruction. A *talmud torah* was also in operation and the Orthodox had their own congregation. In the March 1933 Reichstag elections, the Nazis received 36.8% of the local vote. Anti-J. measures were immediately instituted. J. butchers were banned from the municipal slaughterhouse, J. businesses were boycotted, and J. doctors and lawyers were prevented from practicing. Two J. families of Polish origin were expelled from the city in July and Aug. 1933 and emigrated to Palestine. J. store windows were occasionally smashed and Nazis beat Jews in the

streets. In the 1933–38 period, between 223 and 242 Jews emigrated while 11 moved to other German cities (eight of these later emigrating as well). In late Oct. 1938, 53 Polish Jews were deported; 46 perished in the Holocaust. On *Kristallnacht* (9–10 Nov. 1938), J. homes and stores were destroyed and the synagogue was set on fire. All J. men were arrested and sent to concentration camps, including Sachsenhausen-Oranienburg and Dachau. From Nov. 1938, Jews were mobilized for forced labor, working in subterranean building sites, as porters or as handlers of dangerous materials without protective clothing. Remaining J. property (in all, at least 59 stores) was sold off. Another 56 to 75 Jews emigrated in 1939 and eight more in 1941–42, making a total of about 300. These included 30 to Holland; 16 to Belgium; 21 to France; 74 to the U.S.; 67 to Palestine; and 28 to England. Deportations commenced in 1942, via Dortmund: nine Jews to the Theresienstadt ghetto and 36 to Zamosc (Lublin dist., Poland) on 27–28 April; eight to Auschwitz on 27 July; 26 to Theresienstadt on 29 July (mostly the old); 12 to Auschwitz on 9 March 1943; and two to Theresienstadt on 11 May. A total of 153 Jews perished in the Holocaust. The postwar congregation included numerous communities from the area and numbered 129 in 1947.

HAGENBACH (I) Upper Franconia, Germany. Jews there in the 17th cent. were under the protection of the nobles of the house of Guttenberg. In the 18th cent. they were restricted to the cattle trade. A synagogue was erected in 1727. The J. pop. was around 200 in the early 19th cent. (over half the total) and then declined steadily. Two old couples remained in 1938. These were arrested in Nov. and sent to the Forchheim jail as rioters vandalized their homes and the local synagogue.

HAGENBACH (II) Palatinate, Germany. By the second quarter of the 19th cent, there was an organized J. community with a synagogue, cemetery, school, and *mikve*. In 1848, the J. pop. was 109 (25 families), mostly engaged in trade with just three working as artisans. The J. pop. reached a peak of 151 (8% of the total) in 1875 and then dropped to 137 in 1880; 88 in 1900; and 38 in 1925. In 1878, the J. elementary school moved to a new building. However, the number of students dropped from 27 in 1876 to five in 1910 and the school closed after WWI. In 1933, the J. pop. was 24. All left by Nov. 1938. Four emigrated and

20 remained in Germany. At least nine perished in the Holocaust. The synagogue was burned on *Kristallnacht* (9–10 Nov. 1938), and the J. cemetery was desecrated in 1978.

HAGUE THE ('s-Gravenhage, Den Haag) Zuid-Holland dist., Holland. J. settlement began early in the 17th cent. The Portuguese Jews arrived first and were joined by Ashkenazi Jews in the middle of the cent. It was then that communal activity began. From 1694 the Ashkenazi community prayed separately, building its first synagogue in 1723 (a new one was built in 1844 and another in 1879). The Portuguese community built a fine synagogue in 1726, which served it until the Holocaust. The Portuguese held influential positions in the public sector and established personal friendships with royal figures. Many were well-to-do, such as the members of the Suasso family. Antonio Lopes Suasso was the diplomatic representa-

tive of Charles II of Spain while his son, Francisco Lopes, gave large amounts of money in 1688 to fund William of Orange's move to England prior to his reign there as William III. The Portuguese were also involved and influential in the general culture of H. In the last quarter of the 18th cent., however, Holland suffered an economic and political setback, which affected the community. Many lost their wealth and a few moved to Amsterdam. The community maintained its independence and character, nevertheless, until the Holocaust. The Ashkenazi community grew significantly in the 18th cent. and surpassed the Sephardim in numbers. In stark contrast to the Portuguese wealth and influence, the Ashkenazim were mostly poor. Their occupations were limited as various guilds rejected them for fear of competition. From the early 18th cent., various welfare organizations assisted these poor. Additional organizations and institutions were established in the 19th cent. In the mid-18th

Scout meeting, The Hague, Holland, 1938 (Joods Historisch Musuem, Amsterdam/photo courtesy of Yad Vashem, The Holocaust Martyrs' and Heroes' Remembrance Authority, Jerusalem)

cent., H. became a center of J. culture and maintained a Hebrew printing press until 1781. A J. school functioned from this period until 1920, although the wealthy preferred to have their children tutored privately. With the emancipation of 1796, most Jews wanted to maintain their previous status, when the autonomous J. community had greater power, but a group of intellectuals fought for equal rights for the Jews as a community and as citizens of H. These were achieved slowly over the following years. In 1814, the National Organization of Communities was established and its Committee for J. Affairs was based in H. In the 19th cent. the J. community grew significantly, from 1,800 Jews at its outset to more than 6,000 in 1901 (in a total pop. of over 20,000). Its economic situation slowly improved, although many were still needy. During this century various religious and social organizations were founded, including a branch of the Alliance Israelite. From the end of the 19th cent. until

WWII, the Ashkenazi community almost tripled in size, reaching 17,379 in 1940. The Portuguese then numbered some 200 (total pop. 504,262). Jews established a number of important industries and held influential positions in the public sector. With the growing secularization and assimilation of the community, various organizations emphasizing J. roots and religion were established, including a branch of Agudat Israel in the 1920s. Additional welfare organizations were also founded during this period. H. played a significant role in the Zionist movement. In 1897 a branch of the Zionist Organization was opened there. Jacobus Kann (1872–1944), a banker from H., was the only Dutch Jew present at the First Zionist Congress in Basle (1897). He maintained close ties with Theodor Herzl and David Wolffsohn. Kann perished in the Theresienstadt ghetto during the Holocaust. In 1907 the Eighth Zionist Congress was held in H., which was also the headquarters of the J. National Fund during and imme-

The Sephardi synagogue in The Hague, Holland (Ministry of Education and Culture/photo courtesy of Yad Vashem' The Holocaust Martyrs' and Heroes' Remembrance Authority, Jerusalem)

diately after WWI, when Nehemia de Lieme of H. was its chairman (1919–21). During WWI and in the 1930s, a large number of Jews from Eastern Europe arrived in H. With differing approaches to Zionist ideas, however, friction arose between the Dutch and East European Zionists. Zionist youth groups were active during the 1920s and 1930s and a number of Zionist journals were published. In 1930 Reform Judaism was introduced and a small Reform community developed with 71 members in 1932. By May 1938 there were 1,565 German refugees in H. They were warmly welcomed by the Ashkenazi community and many joined the Reform movement.

Since H. was the seat of the Dutch government, the German government (*Reichskommissariat*) also based its offices there. A wave of J. suicides (some 30 cases) occurred with the German invasion of Holland in May 1940. In Sept. 1940, the Germans ordered the Jews to evacuate the costal regions and some 2,000 left H. Those who remained were subject to anti-J. legislation. J. children were expelled from the general schools and a number of J. schools were opened. At first they were sponsored by the city council, but sponsorship was transferred in Sept. 1942 to the "J. Council." This Council – run by Jews – cooperated with the Germans and prepared lists of J. addresses in preparation for deportations. From 1942 fewer and fewer students remained in the J. schools. In Feb. 1941, five Jews were arrested and deported to death camps. Early in 1942 youths were sent to labor camps in various locations in Holland, while drastic restrictions were placed on J. movement in H. In Aug. 1942 some 1,200 Jews were deported. In Sept. a few were sent to the SS training school in Ellecom. There they were abused and tortured until Nov., when they were transferred to the Westerbork transit camp. Deportations took place continuously in the following months, some to Westerbork and some via Amsterdam. In the first months of 1943, deportations included hospitalized patients, who were forcibly dragged away. In April 1943, the remaining Jews were ordered to report to the Vught and Westerbork camps. The two representatives of the "J. Council" were permitted to remain in H., but they too were deported in July. The H. police generally assisted the Germans. In all some, 15,000 Jews were deported from H. with 2,000 surviving the Holocaust. A few claimed non-J. origins or intermarriage and a small number survived the camps, but most survived in hiding with the assistance of the local pop. The community was reestablished after the war and numbered about 2,000 in 1990.

HAGUENEAU   Bas-Rhin dist., France. Jews were probably present in H. before 1235, when a blood libel was perpetrated against them. The synagogue was built in 1252. In Feb. 1349, the community was destroyed in the Black Death persecutions of 1348–49. In 1354, a new community was founded. The J. cemetery dates from the 16th cent. The synagogue, burned down in 1676 with the rest of the city, was reconstructed in 1683. Down through the years, H. absorbed Jews from the surrounding district as well as from Poland. Among H.'s noted rabbis was Elie Schwab (1721–49). The community numbered 325 members (64 families) in 1784. The synagogue on Rue des Juifs was built in 1821. By 1865 the community consisted of 687 members. In the H. district, there were 2,701 Jews in 1885 and 2,109 in 1905. An orphanage was inaugurated in May 1906. In 1926, there were 1,455 Jews in the district of H. and 1,391 in 1931. R. Meyer Jais, later chief rabbi of Paris, held office in H. in 1933–38. By 1936, there were 113 Jews in H. and 564 in the H. district. During the war, the Germans expelled all to the south of France with the rest of Alsace-Lorraine Jews. Altogether 111 Jews were deported; 148 persons died either from deportations or in the course of the fighting. During the war, the Nazis looted the synagogue. In 1968 the community numbered 300.

HAHNHEIM   Hesse, Germany. The community, numbering 84 (11% of the total) in 1861, also had members in neighboring villages. Of the 17 Jews living there in 1933, only four (who converted) remained after *Kristallnacht* (9–10 Nov. 1938).

HAHOT   Zala dist., Hungary. Jews settled in the mid-18th cent. on a church-owned estate. They constructed a synagogue in 1872, opening a school in 1880, when the J. pop. reached 109. In 1930, 45 Jews remained. All were deported to Auschwitz via Zalaegerszeg on 1 July 1944.

HAIGER   Hesse–Nassau, Germany. A community was established in 1910, when the number of Jews had grown to 30 (1% of the total). As cattle traders, they were deprived of their livelihood under the Nazis and all left (21 emigrating) by July 1940.

HAIGERLOCH Hohenzollern, Germany. Jews are first mentioned in 1343 and were burned to death in the Black Death persecutions of 1348–49. They are again mentioned late in the 15th cent. and by 1570 constituted a well-established settlement. From 1640 until 1837 they lived under various restrictive letters of protection issued by the Hohenzollerns. In 1745, their number was limited to 20 families. Marriage was prohibited and from 1752 they were forced to listen to church sermons. From 1780 they were not allowed to buy houses. The J. pop. grew to 382 in 1852 (about a quarter of the total). A. J. public school operated from 1823 to 1939. Jews sat on the municipal council. In 1933, the J. pop. was 186. On *Kristallnacht* (9–10 Nov. 1938), the synagogue, community center, and school were damaged and ten Jews sent to the Dachau concentration camp. At least 53 Jews managed to emigrate from Germany; most of the others were deported to the east in 1941–42.

HAINGRUENDAU Hesse dist., Germany. This small impoverished community numbered 15 (2% of the total) in 1910, and no Jews remained there after 1936.

HAINSFARTH Swabia, Germany. Jews are mentioned in the 13th cent. and six families with permanent residence rights were present in the 16th cent. A synagogue was erected in 1723 and a J. public school operated from the first half of the 19th cent. The J. pop. declined steadily from 452 (total 1,142) in 1809 to 211 in 1880 and 34 in 1933. Nineteen Jews left in 1938–41. Six were deported to Piaski (Poland) on 3 April 1942 and the last two to the Theresienstadt ghetto on 10 Aug.

HAINSTADT Baden, Germany. Jews were present in the 16th cent. and the small community grew with the addition of refugees from Buchen in the 17th cent. A synagogue was built in 1819 and a J. elementary school was opened around the end of the 1820s. Over half the Jews were cattle traders and Jews also pioneered the local cloth industry. The J. pop. reached a peak of 249 in 1842, subsequently declining steadily through emigration and the exodus to the big cities. In 1933, 38 remained (total 1,084). By early 1938, six had left and in the course of the year another 12 fled. Seven more emigrated after *Kristallnacht* (9–10 Nov. 1938), when the synagogue was vandalized. The last six were deported to the Gurs concentration camp on 22 Oct. 1940.

HAJDUBAGOS Bihar dist., Hungary. Jews arrived in the early 19th cent., never exceeding 50 in number. In the beginning of June 1944, they were deported to Auschwitz via Nagyvarad.

HAJDUBOSZORMENY Hajdu dist., Hungary. Jews settled in 1822, their numbers increasing to 564 in 1880. In 1920, J. refugees from Galicia raised the pop. to 1,001 (3.5% of the total) These joined the hasidic *minyan* started in 1890. The synagogue was built in 1863. During the 1930s, tension arose between the community and the Hasidim. During the 1860s, a J. school was established and the community maintained a *talmud torah* and yeshiva. Jews were prominent as grain merchants and many belonged to the professional class. From 1939, Jews were seized for forced labor. On 27 May 1944, a ghetto was established and on 16 June they were brought to Debrecen. Most were deported on 25–28 June to Auschwitz and others sent to Austria. After the war, 313 returned to revive the community. The Joint Distribution Committee established a cooperative farm here where Zionist youth underwent training. By 1969, only 16 remained.

HAJDUDOROG Hajdu dist., Hungary. Jews probably settled in the early 19th cent., numbering 732 (8.4% of the total) in 1890 and 321 in 1941. The community maintained a synagogue, school, *talmud torah*, and yeshiva. At the end of April 1944, the Jews were concentrated in a ghetto. On 17 June they were deported to Debrecen and from there to Auschwitz and Austria on 25–28 June. After the war, 57 survivors returned. By 1956, most had left.

HAJDUHADHAZ Hajdu dist., Hungary. The J. community formed in the mid-19th cent., numbering 331 in 1880 and 471 (4% of the total) in 1941. Most were farmers at first, later going into trade. A synagogue was erected in 1898 and a J. public school was maintained. In 1942, 50–60 of the young were sent to the Ukraine for forced labor, few surviving. At the end of April 1944, the Jews were enclosed in a ghetto and on 25–28 June deported to Auschwitz and Austria via Debrecen. After the war, 198 Jews returned, but most soon left.

On the way to the ghetto, Hajduboszormeny, Hungary, 1944

HAJDUNANAS   Hajdu dist., Hungary. Jews settled in the first half of the 19th cent. as tradesmen and artisans. The J. pop. rose from 730 in 1869 to 1,147 (6.7% of the total) in 1920. The community maintained a synagogue, yeshiva, and school. The Zionists became active between the World Wars. In 1941, young Jews were sent to the Ukraine for forced labor, many perishing there. On 14 May 1944, the remaining Jews, about 1,000, were confined to a ghetto; on 17 June they were sent to Debrecen and on 25–28 June, they were deported mainly to Auschwitz. About 65–70 families sent to Austria survived and reestablished the community after the war, most leaving by 1960.

HAJDUSAMSON   Hajdu dist., Hungary. Jews arrived in the first half of the 18th cent., reaching a peak pop. of 418 in 1840, then declining steadily to 216 in 1941. After transfer to Debrecen, most were deported to Auschwitz on 25–28 June 1944. Most of those sent to Austria reached the Theresienstadt ghetto in March 1945 and survived the war.

HAJDUSZOBOSZLO   Hajdu dist., Hungary. Jews arrived in the early 19th cent. as hide and horse traders. They numbered 247 in 1869; 554 in 1919 (3.5% of the total); and 490 (3% of the total) in 1941. A synagogue was built in 1862, a school opened in 1885, and another synagogue was consecrated in 1895. In 1925, with the discovery of mineral springs, the Jews became active in the health resort trade. In 1942, young Jews were sent to forced labor in the Ukraine, where most perished. Thirty-two Jews deported to Austria on the arrival of the Germans in March 1944 survived the war. Most of the others were deported to Auschwitz via Debrecen on 15 June while some were sent to Strassburg in Austria. Attempts to reestablish the community after the war failed.

HAJDUSZOVAT   Hajdu dist., Hungary. Jews settled in the first half of the 19th cent., numbering 131 in 1880 and 144 in 1930. A synagogue was consecrated in 1870. The Jews were transferred to Debrecen via Puspokladany and Hajdudorog in May 1944. From

there some were deported to Austria and survived the war. Survivors reestablished the community, but by 1966 only one Jew remained in H.

HAJNOWKA Bialystok dist., Poland. Jews first settled in the late 19th cent. as merchants and shopkeepers. The community numbered 41 in 1921, growing to 600 in 1939. A synagogue was built in 1929. Most children studied at a Hebrew school founded in the 1920s. The largest Zionist youth movement was Betar. The Germans arrived on 24 June 1941. In Aug. the Jews were expelled to the Pruzhany ghetto, the men beaten and tormented in a forced march that left 24 dead. Many died in the ghetto of starvation and disease. The rest were deported to Auschwitz on 31 Jan. 1943.

HALBERSTADT Saxony, Germany. According to tradition, Jews had settled in H. by 1146. The earliest documentary evidence dates only from 1261. In 1364 there was a Jews' village (*Judendorf*) with a synagogue. The Jews were persecuted in 1335 and 1343. They were probably expelled in 1493. It was not until the 17th century that a permanent J. settlement could be established. In 1644, a cemetery plot was leased and in 1661 a synagogue was built. Between 1670 and 1673, Jews who had been expelled from Vienna settled in H., increasing the J. pop. in H. to 698 in 1701. In 1728, there were about 1,000 Jews living in the town, constituting as much as 10% of the pop. and making the community one of the largest in central Germany. Behrend Lehmann (1661–1730) was the most prominent member of the community. A

banker and Court Jew, he had a decisive influence at the courts of Berlin, Hanover, and Dresden. In 1703, he founded a *beit midrash* that included a synagogue and a library where J. scholars could live and study. The institution achieved a great reputation and attracted famous rabbis. The community's new synagogue, dedicated in 1712, was built largely owing to his financial assistance. In 1795 an elementary school was set up. A girls' school was added in 1826. During the 19th cent., many Jews moved to bigger towns, reducing the pop. to 600 in 1885. A new cemetery was established in 1895 and the community maintained a wide range of welfare institutions, including an old age home in 1912. The Auerbach family, which produced most of H.'s rabbis from 1863, determined the community's Orthodox character. Close contact was maintained with Dr. Azriel Hildesheimer (1820–99), a native of H., who founded in 1873 in Berlin an Orthodox rabbinical seminary which subsequently became one of the primary institutions for training Orthodox rabbis in Central Europe. From 1914, a large number of Jews from Eastern Europe settled in H., increasing the pop. to about 1,000. The newcomers strengthened Orthodoxy within the community and H. became the center of Orthodoxy in Germany. In 1920, the Alliance of Torah-True J. Communities in Germany, also called the Halberstaedter Verband, was founded here. Already during the 1920s, Jews were being harassed. In 1933, the community numbered 706 Jews. Physical attacks took place during the first months of the Nazi period and preparations for emigration intensified. An agricultural training center was set up; Hebrew language courses were offered; and a local branch of Mizrachi

Embroidered ribbon for binding Torah scroll, Halberstadt, Germany

was established. In Oct. 1938, about 100 Jews with non-German citizenship were expelled to Poland. On *Kristallnacht* (9–10 Nov. 1938), the synagogue was set on fire, but then extinguished out of fear that other buildings might burn down. The three cemeteries were desecrated and J. stores and homes were looted and wrecked. Forty Jews were arrested and interned in the Buchenwald concentration camp. The synagogue was subsequently pulled down. In 1939, there were only 235 Jews in H. The J. school, which in 1938 still had an enrollment of 55 students, was closed in summer 1941. From April to Nov. 1942, 147 Jews were deported to the east. In 1945–46, only ten Jews were left in the city, all married to non-Jews. Altogether 189 Jews from H. perished under Nazi rule, including Jews who were deported from the towns or the neighboring countries where they had hoped to find shelter.

HALICZ Stanislawow dist., Poland, today Ukraine. Jews are mentioned from the 15th cent. with a small Karaite community also surviving into the 20th cent. (There were 40 Karaite families in 1923, mostly farmers.) The J. community grew significantly in the late 19th cent., reaching a peak of 1,568 (total 4,850) in 1900, but dropping to 582 (15%) in 1921 owing to emigration. The community was hard hit by the Russian occupation and the Ukrainian Petlyura gangs in 1920, with a total of 183 J. houses destroyed during this period. Most families required assistance between the World Wars, with two soup kitchens in operation. The Joint Distribution Committee and the American Relief Committee contributed significantly. There was intense Zionist activity. The community was liquidated by the Germans in 1942 in two *Aktions*, deporting the Jews to Stanislawow and the Belzec death camp.

HALLE Saxony, Germany. The first clear evidence of Jews living in the town dates only from the second half of the 12th cent. They earned their living in the salt and wine trade, and from moneylending in the 14th cent. They lived in a Jews' village (*Judendorf*) within the city walls and maintained a synagogue and a *mikve*. A cemetery outside the city is mentioned only in 1401, but probably existed before 1350. In the 15th cent., the community had a rabbinical court (*beit din*) and a yeshiva. The Jews suffered from several persecutions, particularly those associated with the Black Death (1348–49). In 1493 they were expelled, together with all the

Jews in the archbishopric of Magdeburg. In 1688, the Jews were again allowed to settle in H. and soon established a synagogue. One of the first J. residents, Assur Marx, who later became bookkeeper at the Polish court, received permission (1692–93) to purchase land for a cemetery. He also had an extensive library, which he made available to J. students, who were able to register at the University of H. from 1694 onwards. In the years 1724–1800, 60 J. students were granted a doctorate, among them, Issachar Falkenson Behr in 1772, the first J. poet writing in German. In the 18th cent., the J. pop. was 70 in 1700 and 85 in 1805. By 1864, the number of Jews had increased to 443, reaching 1,397 (0.7% of the total) in 1910. In 1869, a cemetery was consecrated and in 1870 a synagogue. An organ installed in 1901 indicated the Liberal orientation of the community. The community also maintained a religious school and numerous social organizations. In 1927, another synagogue with a community center was consecrated, and in 1929 an additional cemetery. When the Nazis came to power in 1933 there were still about 1,300 Jews living in H. They operated 217 stores and businesses, as well as six banks, three bar-restaurants, and one publishing house. Boycott of these institutions began prior to the official boycott day of 1 April 1933. On the day of the boycott proper, there were mass demonstrations. At least six J. professors and 41 Jews employed in the public services were dismissed. Thirteen lawyers were no longer allowed to practice. In June 1933, the J. pop. was 1,086. Boycott measures intensified from 1935 on. The influence of the Zionists within the community strengthened, and in 1936 they won four out of ten seats in the community council. On *Kristallnacht* (9–10 Nov. 1938), the synagogue, including the community center, was burned down. Of the 150 men who were arrested, 124 were taken to the Buchenwald and Sachsenhausen concentration camps, at least one man dying at the end of 1938 as a result of his detention. In all, 584 Jews from H. managed to emigrate. From Oct. 1939 onwards, the remaining Jews were compelled to perform forced labor. Between 1940–42, 17 Jews committed suicide. By 1942, the Jews were concentrated in seven "J. houses." From there, 262 people were deported to the east; only 43 survived. In July 1944, in H. itself, there were still 92 Jews, most probably protected by marriage to non–Jews. In 1947, a new community was established with 50 members, consecrating a synagogue in 1953. The dwindling

numbers rose in the 1990s because of the influx of Jews from the former Soviet Union.

HALLENBERG Westphalia, Germany. Twenty Jews were present in the early 19th cent., dwindling to fewer than ten at mid-cent. Their numbers rose again to 27–40 later in the cent., peaking at 49 (total 1,202) in 1910. The community maintained a synagogue (renovated in 1923) and was allotted a section of the local cemetery for J. burial in 1900. At the outset of the Nazi era, the J. pop. was 36–39 with 25 still remaining just before *Kristallnacht* (9–10 Nov. 1938), when the synagogue was set on fire, J. homes were vandalized, and ten J. men were detained in the Sachsenhausen concentration camp (until the end of the year). Most Jews subsequently left the town. In all, 15 emigrated in the Nazi period and ten moved to other places in Germany. The last eight were deported to the east in April 1942. At least 11 Jews perished in the Holocaust.

HALMAJ Abauj–Torna dist., Hungary. Jews settled in the early 19th cent. and numbered 58 in 1930. They were deported to Auschwitz via Kassa on 19 May 1944.

HALMEU (Hung. Halmi) N. Transylvania dist., Rumania. Jews from Galicia settled in the early 18th cent. and engaged in winegrowing and agriculture. The J. pop. in 1930 was 1,373 (32% of the total). A J. school was opened in 1934. R. Shalom Klein, a leading rabbi of Transylvania, ran a yeshiva with 120 students. Zionist activity began in 1928. In July 1941, J. families were expelled across the border, and many were taken by the Gestapo to ghettoes in Galicia or murdered in Kamenets-Podolski. In 1942, Jews were drafted into labor battalions in the Ukraine, where most perished. In May 1944 the community was transferred to the Nagyszollos ghetto and then deported to Auschwitz.

HALSDORF Hesse–Nassau, Germany. The community opened a regional synagogue in 1856 and numbered 51 (11% of the total) in 1871, declining to 37 (6%) in 1933. Affiliated with the Marburg rabbinate, it also had members in Wohra and Josbach. By Feb. 1941, no Jews remained in H., most (20) having emigrated to the U.S. Josbach's last five Jews perished in the Holocaust.

HALTERN Westphalia, Germany. Two Jews received residence rights from the Bishop of Muenster in 1586. A synagogue was consecrated in the early 19th cent. About ten J. families, mainly engaged in trade, lived in the town throughout most of the 19th cent. In 1925, 40 Jews remained and in 1933, 14 (total 9,696). On *Kristallnacht* (9–10 Nov. 1938), the synagogue, cemetery, and J. homes and stores were vandalized. The last five Jews were deported in Jan. 1942. Ten perished in the Holocaust.

HAMBORN Rhineland, Germany. J. settlement began in 1893 and expanded with the city's industrial development. By 1910, the J. pop. was 345 (total 101,703), about a quarter from Eastern Europe. A Central Union (C.V.) branch was opened in 1910. Most community members joined the J. Historical and Literary Society when it started in 1911. East European immigration increased during WWI as the German authorities sought to import industrial workers in place of those at the front. By 1925, 476 of the community's 818 Jews were of East European origin, though from 1927 they increasingly emigrated to the U.S. The Zionists became active in 1919. Ha-Po'el ha-Tza'ir started a branch in the same year and the rival Social-Zionist Po'alei Zion in 1925. (They amalgamated in 1932.) The Bar Kokhba and Maccabi organizations were also active. In 1929, 70 J. stores were operating in the city (clothing, shoes, furniture). At the outset of Nazi rule in 1933, the windows of J. stores were repeatedly smashed and Jews were attacked. SA men shot one Jew to death in the street. By 1937, the J. pop. had dropped to 348. All J. stores were liquidated by late 1938 along with 17 or 18 J. workshops. Though the community sold the synagogue on 1 Nov. 1938, it was nevertheless set on fire on *Kristallnacht* (9–10 Nov. 1938). J. homes and stores were then destroyed and Jews mercilessly beaten; 150 were sent to the Buchenwald and Dachau concentration camps. Those remaining were deported together with the Jews of Duisburg to the death camps of Eastern Europe.

HAMBURG Free Hanseatic city, Germany. The first Jews arrived from Portugal in 1575, conceivably as forced converts (*anusim*) and as part of the wave of exiled Jews dispersing throughout Europe. As supposed Catholics, they were allowed to settle in the town, which at the time was still closed to Jews. Among them was Rodrigo de Castro (1550–1627), who

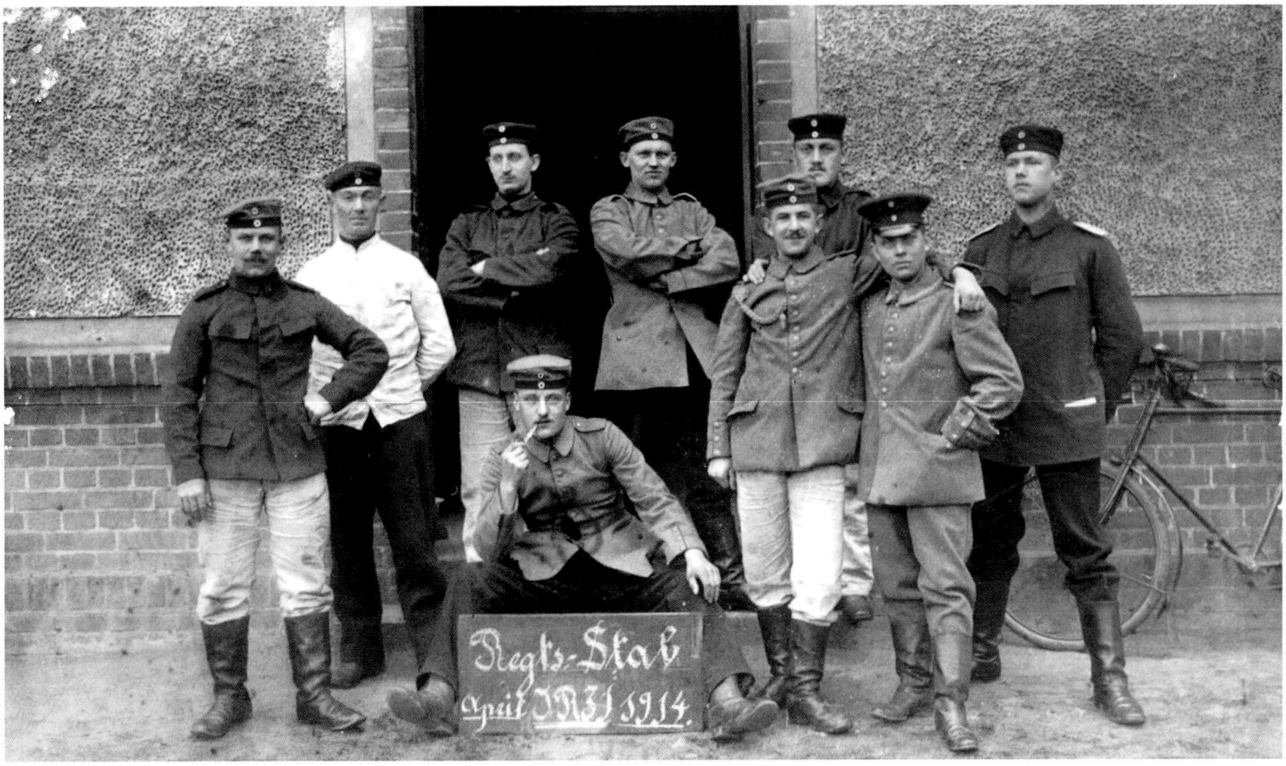
Regts-Stab

Jews in the German army in WWI*, Hamburg, Germany*

achieved prominence combating the plague in H. in 1596 and as a court physician. Another group of Portuguese Jews arrived in 1601, and only two years later were mentioned for the first time as Jews. They were accorded residence rights against the payment of a special tax and allowed to bury their dead in neighboring Altona, whose J. cemetery served the community from 1611 until the late 19th cent. Intolerance and anti-J. agitation intensified in the mid-17th cent. The insecurity of the community created fertile ground for the spread of Shabbateanism and messianic expectations. A new decree promulgated in 1650 granted the Portuguese Jews freedom of public worship though limiting the number of congregants to 15 families. Jews contributed significantly to the economic development of the city, particularly in furthering the links of the Hanseatic League with Spain and Portugal and their overseas colonies. As early as the late 16th cent., the Ximenes and Alvares families were trading with Brazil, while other Jews exploited family and community ties overseas. Jews were also active in shipping and shipbuilding and as jewelers and confectioners. They played a key role in the development of the banking system of the town, 30 Jews (out of 560) acting as co-founders of the Bank of Hamburg in 1619. Local Jews represented foreign governments in H. and served as suppliers to the Scandinavian courts and as commercial agents. Among the prominent physicians were also Immanuel Rosales (1588–1662), who studied astronomy with Galileo, and Shemuel da Silva (1571–1631). Yosef Shelomo Delmedigo was also active in H. for awhile. Hebrew printing presses are known from the late 16th cent. The Ashkenazi community dates from at least the early 17th cent, the first *Hochdeutsche Juden*, as they were called, coming from Altona, especially to seek shelter during the Thirty Years War (1618-48). In 1649 the Altona refugees were expelled from the city but continued to work there and returned again in the face of Swedish incursions. A fascinating mirror of the times is provided in the famous memoirs of Glueckel of Hameln (1646–1724). After the death of her first husband, Glueckel, who was born in Hamburg and lived there for many years, started writing her memoirs for the edification of the 14 children she bore him. Like the Portuguese Jews, the Ashkenazim were active in trade, though mostly in Germany itself, dealing in gold, precious stones, tobacco, and wool as well as in moneylending. Some were peddlers and

among them were court suppliers like Meyer Marx. The hostility of the monopolistic guilds, who refused to admit Jews, and often resorted to harassment, intensified the sense of insecurity. New laws in 1710 regulated J. life for the next 100 years, defining restrictions and rights with reference to commerce, worship, and judicial authority and more or less equalizing the status of the Ashkenazi Jews to that of the Portuguese. About 50 years later the senate designated 14 streets in the New City (Neustadt) for J. residence and six in the Old City (Altstadt). In the mid-18th cent., the Ashkenazi community began to surpass the Portuguese community in wealth and influence. At this time there were 858 J. taxpayers registered in 68 occupations, including 278 merchants, 28 teachers, and 20 scholars. Jews were particularly active in industry, including large cotton-printing plants with up to 500 workers and metal-refining plants. Local hostility continued to be a factor in the community's life but there were occasional violent outbursts directed against the Jews, often brought on by economic crisis. In 1730, thousands of seamen and shopkeepers attacked Jews in streets and homes, causing mass flight to Altona, Wandsbek, and neighboring villages. The unrest only ceased when the city senate sent in forces and threatened to impose severe punishments. The Portuguese Jews, organized as the Beth Israel congregation from the mid-17th cent., were authorized to erect a synagogue in 1668 by the mayor of H. With decline setting in during the 18th cent., the Portuguese synagogue was no longer used after the 1830s. The Ashkenazi community, which stood under the tutelage of the Portuguese community until the mid 17th cent., consecrated its first synagogue in 1654. A new synagogue was consecrated in 1790, serving the community until 1906. In 1671 the three communities of H., Altona, and Wandsbek united into a single congregation, AHW, with Altona as its seat. With the influence of Haskala making itself felt in the 19th cent. the Jews of H. now turned to the struggle for Emancipation. Though equal rights were accorded to the Jews under French law in the Napoleonic era, these were severely modified by the Infamous Decree (1808), which imposed further economic restrictions and limited their freedom of movement. In the case of H., the Decree was soon reversed and Jews were appointed for the first time to public office. The French also dismantled the united congregation of the three neighboring cities into its constituent communities after 140 years of unification. Throughout the period the Jews lived under economic duress, as a result of Napoleon's continental blockade and various war measures, including the temporary expulsion of 3,000 Jews, exacerbating the situation. Subsequently, despite petitions to the Congress of Vienna, the Jew Laws of 1710 were again invoked. Gabriel Riesser, founding editor of *Der Jude*, was in the forefront of the J. struggle for equal rights. Deliberations on the subject in the local senate in 1834 led to anti-J. riots but in 1842, after a devastating fire, property-holding restrictions were lifted by the senate in the hope that Jews would contribute to the rehabilitation of stricken areas of H. By 1852, about 600 Jews had also been granted citizenship in the city. In 1859, nine Jews were elected to H's. 84-member parliament. Further legislation, which came into force in Sept. 1860, stipulated full re-

Exterior and interior of Central Synagogue at Bornplatz in Hamburg, Germany, before wwii

wrecked and looted. Ten Jews were deported to the Buchenwald concentration camp where two died because of maltreatment. By Oct. 1939, the J. pop. had shrunk further to 44. Those who failed to emigrate and were not protected by marriage to non-J. partners were deported in 1942, 13 of them to the Theresienstadt ghetto. Many Jews who had moved to bigger towns or to the Netherlands were deported also. Altogether 101 Jews from H. perished under Nazi rule.

HAMM Westphalia, Germany. Jews were present in the late 13th cent. Two were killed in 1287-88 and the entire community was murdered or expelled during the Black Death persecutions of 1348-49. Those who were immolated were described as going readily to the pyre rather than consenting to conversion. Jews were again present in 1370 and a number were accorded letters of protection in 1408. From 1604, the Jews maintained a permanent settlement. A prayer house was in existence from the 17th cent. and a J. religious school was operating in 1722. With the creation of the Grand Duchy of Berg by the French in 1806, the Jews received equal rights. In 1846, 13 of 20 J. breadwinners engaged in trade. A Jew founded an investment bank in 1855. Jews were active in public life, serving on the municipal council. In 1846, the J. religious school became a J. elementary school and in 1868 a synagogue was consecrated. The school reached a peak enrollment of 64 in 1885 as the J. pop. rose to 255 (total 22,520). By 1911, the J. pop. stood at 402, dropping to 333 in 1919 but then rising again to 410 in 1933. In the Weimar period, Jews engaged in crafts as well as trade. With the city serving as the seat of the state supreme court, eight local J. lawyers were authorized to appear there. Among the commercial establishments was the Alsberg department store, employing 200 workers and operating branches in other cities as well. In 1919, J. store windows were smashed in anti-J. riots. About this time, a number of J. families from Eastern Europe settled in the city, opening shops or finding employment as blue-collar workers. In the March 1933 elections, the Nazis received 38.1% of the local vote. Persecution commenced immediately and J. livelihoods were undermined through economic boycotts and job dismissals. The Alsberg department store was "Aryanized" in July 1936 through a forced sale to Franz Fahning GmbH. Fourteen Jews emigrated to Palestine in 1933 and 75 left the city in 1934, with another 20 arriving. Zionist activity was stepped up

with a Hehalutz office opening in 1934. In 1938, just 22 stores remained in J. hands. A total of 173 Jews left H. in 1933-37, including 38 to Palestine, 20 to Holland, and 18 to the U.S. On *Kristallnacht* (9-10 Nov. 1938), the synagogue was partially burned and then totally wrecked along with the J. community center, homes, and stores. SS forces and Hitler Youth beat and tormented Jews with particular brutality and 15 men were sent to the Oranienburg-Sachsenhausen concentration camp. In late 1940, the last Jews in H. were moved to five or six "J. houses." In Nov. 1941, 78 were transferred to a shanty camp in the city after another 147 left from 1938. Of the latter, 46 moved to other German cities and 39 left for the U.S. Deportations began on 27 April 1942, when 72 Jews were transported to Zamosc in the Lublin dist. (Poland) via Dortmund. Another 24 elderly Jews were deported to the Theresienstadt ghetto on 27 July. At least 131 local Jews perished in the Holocaust, including 37 in Zamosc, 36 in Theresienstadt, and 22 in Auschwitz.

HAMM A.D. SIEG Rhineland, Germany. Jews are first mentioned in 1663 and lived in H. under letters of protection through the 18th cent., engaging in trade despite the opposition of local merchants and artisans. Notwithstanding the liberal atmosphere in the Napoleonic era, numerous restrictions were applied to the Jews throughout the Duchy of Nassau (against purchasing houses, marrying without official authorization, etc.). In helping make the town a center of the cattle trade in the late 19th cent., J. merchants contributed to its economic development. The J. pop. rose from 39 in 1817 to a peak of 145 (total 1,362) in 1903. In the latter year, 19 Jews were cattle dealers and three were butchers. Jews were active in local life, belonging to the popular markmen's and gymnastics clubs. A synagogue was consecrated in 1824 and a number of communities were subsequently attached to the congregation (Dattenfeld, Rosbach, Schladern, Wissen, Betzdorf, Kirchen). A new synagogue was completed in 1894. In the 1920s, H. became a Nazi stronghold and when the Nazis came to power in 1933, the generally good relations between the Jews and the local pop. began to deteriorate as the economic boycott was enforced. In 1933, 50 Jews remained, with the J. pop. rising to 93 in 1936. In early Oct. 1938, windows of J. houses were smashed. On *Kristallnacht* (9-10 Nov. 1938), the synagogue was set on fire and J. homes and stores were wrecked along with the J. cemetery.

Jews were detained at the Dachau concentration camp for six weeks. Of the 50 Jews present in 1933, 37 moved to other German cities, most between April and Nov. 1938. They ultimately perished in the concentration camps.

HAMMAM EL-LIF Tunis dist., Tunisia. The J. settlement apparently dates from the Phoenician period. The J. pop. increased following the destruction of the Second Temple and the expulsions ordered by Titus. The settlement apparently ended under the anti-J. measures of the Byzantine emperor Justinian I in 533. It was renewed under Moslem rule in the 8th–11th cents., but destroyed by the Almohads in the 12th cent. The modern settlement began to develop with the growth of the J. community in Tunis (12 miles away) in the 18th cent. and particularly after the bey's reforms in 1857 gave the Jews equal rights. Nissim Shamama, the bey's finance minister and the *qa'id* (head of the J. community) in Tunis, built a yeshiva and *beit midrash* in H. in 1865. The J. pop. rose to 345 in 1921 and 543 (total 6,700) in 1936 as Jews from Tunis moved there, commuting to work in the

capital, which was three-quarters of an hour away by train. Some Jews joined the professional class as doctors and lawyers or entered the French civil service. Children studied at the local French elementary school and continued their studies in Tunis. The Zionists were active between the World Wars and Betar established a branch there in the 1930s. Most of the community identified with French culture. In WWII, the Jews suffered under the racial laws of the Vichy regime and from widespread Arab looting. As H. was the residence of the bey, the Germans agreed to refrain from harming it and thus the Jews were spared excessive persecution under the German occupation. The city was liberated on 10 May 1943. After the war, the Joint Distribution Committee and OZE helped the community recover and Zionist activity intensified. Dozens left for Israel after the establishment of the state but most left in the late 1950s after Tunisian independence, half to France, half to Israel.

HAMMAMET Grombalia dist., Tunisia. A J. settlement apparently existed in the 10th–11th cents. and ended in the late 13th cent. when H. was declared a

Ha-Gedud—young Zionist pioneers and students from the Lycee Carnot, Hammam el-Lif, Tunisia

holy city of Islam and the Jews were expelled. Jews settled again in the 20th cent., exporting fruit and vegetables to Tunis. They also became active in the olive oil and wool-spinning industries. A forced labor camp for over 200 Jews, building German coastal fortifications around Cape Bon, was located there in WWII. Many escaped through the laxness of the Italian guards. The J. pop. was 11 in 1936 and 47 in 1946 (total 7,778).

HAMMELBURG   Lower Franconia, Germany. The community was one of the oldest in Bavaria, with Jews continuously present from at least the late 13th cent. During disturbances in 1298, 1336, and 1349 they suffered from persecution and in 1560 from the institution of residence and trade restrictions. A synagogue and cemetery were consecrated during this period. Further persecution was endured during the Thirty Years War (1618–48) and in 1671 the community was expelled for a few years, but it maintained its wealth and importance throughout. A new synagogue was built in 1770. The J. pop. reached a peak of 172 in 1890 (total 2,889). In 1933, 79 remained, engaged mainly in the cattle and cloth trade. Under Nazi rule, J. livelihoods were undermined by the economic boycott and in 1938 all the Jews were forced to sell off their property at a fraction of its value while public prayer and the use of the J. cemetery were banned. On *Kristallnacht* (9–10 Nov. 1938), the synagogue and J. homes were vandalized. All the Jews but two in mixed marriages left H. in 1933–39, 31 of them emigrating (including 17 to the U.S.).

HAMMERSTEIN (Polish Czarne) Posen–West Prussia, Germany, today Poland. The J. pop. of H. numbered 142 in 1831 and 195 in 1880. The community maintained a synagogue and a cemetery. In 1881, antisemitic riots in Pomerania and West Prussia led to attacks against Jews and their property. On the eve of the Nazi assumption of power, there were 55 Jews in H. On *Kristallnacht* (9–10 Nov. 1938), the synagogue was destroyed and J. businesses were demolished. Those J. residents who did not emigrate were arrested in March 1940 and interned in the Buergergarten camp near Schneidemuehl. They were then deported to the east where most perished.

HANAU   Hesse–Nassau, Germany. After Jews living there perished in the Black Death persecutions of 1348–49, no community existed until 1600, when J. families were invited to help develop trade and industry. By 1608, the Jews had a synagogue and numbered 159, growing to 540 (over 4% of the total) in 1822. Their principal rabbis were Eliyahu Loanz (1609–15), Gershon Ashkenazi (1642–46), Moshe Broda (1704–18), and Tuvia Sontheim (1795–1830), who founded a yeshiva. Hebrew books were printed by Yaakov Hena (1606–30) and the Christian Hebraist H. J. van Bashuysen (1708–45). In the Napoleonic era, Louise Grafemus (Esther Manuel) – who joined the Prussian army disguised as a man (1813) – was awarded the Iron Cross and became a German-J. heroine. The grammarian Solomon Hanau (1687–1746) and the famous artist Moritz Oppenheim (1800–82) were also born in H. The community attained its maximum size in 1905, numbering 654 (2% of the total). During the Weimar Republic, Jews were active in civic affairs and politics. They played a leading role in the diamond and gem industry and owned factories, banks, textile firms, and a Woolworth department store. As a result of the Nazi boycott, however, Jews were dismissed from public office and their businesses collapsed. Emigration and Zionist activity increased. A murderous pogrom occurred on *Kristallnacht* (9–10 Nov. 1938), when the synagogue was burned down, and the community shrank from 477 in 1933 to 82 in June 1939. A transport of 75 Jews left H. for Nazi death camps in 1942. Only half-Jews and those married to "Aryans" remained; most were deported to the Theresienstadt ghetto in Feb. 1945 and survived.

HANCEWICZE   Polesie dist., Poland, today Belarus. Jews were only allowed to settle from 1903. With the development of the lumber industry, in which 10% were employed, the J. pop. reached 485 in 1921 (total 1,015). There was extensive Zionist activity between the World Wars and a Tarbut school was opened. Under the Soviets (from 18 Sept. 1939) J. enterprises were nationalized and cultural activities stopped. The J. pop. in 1941 was about 3,000. The Germans arrived on 29 June 1941 and a day later hooligans staged a pogrom, murdering 16 Jews. On 13 Aug., the J. men were executed outside the town; two days later the women and children were murdered, making H. the first J. community in Belorussia to be liquidated.

HANDLOVA   Slovakia, Czechoslovakia, today Republic of Slovakia. Jews settled in the 1870s despite

local opposition. They constituted an independent, Status Quo congregation only in 1928, but became Orthodox in 1938. Between the World Wars, the J. pop. was about 90. Most of the young were members of the Maccabi sports club and Zionist youth movements in neighboring Prievidza. In the Slovakian state, the German minority attacked the Jews, who were forced out of their businesses. In spring 1942, they were deported to the death camps via Novaky.

HANESTI Moldavia dist., Rumania. Jews settled here in the mid-19th cent. The J. pop. in 1899 was 156 (3% of the total). The J. community developed slowly because of antisemitism. In June 1941, the few remaining Jews were expelled to Dorohoi and then to Transnistria.

HANNOVERSCH MUENDEN Hanover, Germany. A medieval J. settlement existed from the end of the 14th cent. to the end of the 15th cent. A modern community dates from the second half of the 17th cent., numbering 41 members in 1702 and a peak of at 143 in 1885. The community established a synagogue in 1834 and subsequently two cemeteries (1673, 1932). By 1933, 84 Jews were living in H. Up to *Kristallnacht* (9–10 Nov. 1938), Nazi terror led to a suicide and to a murder. During this period 41 Jews left the town. On *Kristallnacht*, the synagogue was burned down and 22 men were arrested and detained in prison in Goettingen. Although 16 Jews had moved away by summer 1941, others had taken their place and by summer 1941, there were still 22 Jews in H. They were deported in 1942.

HANOVER Hanover (prov.), Germany. Evidence indicates that there were Jews in H. from the 13th cent. The settlement probably suffered during the Black Death persecutions of 1348–49. In the Old Town, there was a small number of Jews from 1371. A larger settlement developed in the New Town under the protection of the prince, numbering 17 families by 1585. A cemetery established in 1550 was in use for the next 300 years. Anti-J. riots occurred in 1588 and the synagogue in the New Town was closed in 1589. The H. Jews were expelled in 1591. The Old Town remained closed to Jews for about 250 years, but Jews were allowed to settle in the New Town in 1607–08. In 1724, there were 16 families and in 1798, 91. Towards the end of the 17th cent., community member

Leffmann Behrens served as Court Jew at the Hanover court. In 1703–04, the community established a synagogue and from that time on, the state rabbi (the state rabbinate being established in 1687) was required to live in H. In 1762, a burial society (*hevra kaddisha*) was founded, serving for awhile as a framework for daily Torah study. Towards the end of the 18th cent. the Haskala movement found its first supporters among H. Jews. Meyer Michael David, a friend of Moses Mendelssohn, founded in 1794 a "free school," where subjects of a general nature were taught in addition to J. studies. Most community members rejected Reform. A modern synagogue was dedicated only in 1827 and Rabbi Dr. Nathan Marcus Adler (1830–45) began to introduce moderate reforms. In the 19th cent., as Jews gradually gained civil rights in the Kingdom of Hanover, they began to settle also in the Old Town of H. The J. community numbered 1,371 in 1864; 4,540 in 1900; and 5,521 in 1925. The community also included 1,300 members of East European origin. While most Jews were engaged in trade the number of those in the liberal professions grew and Jews established private banks and industrial concerns. Many community members, particularly those from Eastern Europe, suffered from poverty. The East European sector of the community included many peddlers and day laborers. Already in 1848, a number of Jews were active in different political organizations, and in 1859 the first Jew was elected to the city council. The wealthy bankers, businessmen, and manufacturers were welcomed as members in respected economic and social organizations. In the 20th cent., a number of J. families kept open house for artists and were involved, for example, in supporting the progressive Kestner Society for Modern Art, founded in 1916. Prominent Jews born in H. include the economist Cora Berliner (1890–1942), who worked for the Berlin community until her deportation to the east, and the writer and philosopher Hannah Arendt (1906–75). A new cemetery was established in 1864 and in 1870 the community dedicated a new and imposing synagogue, designed by the city's celebrated J. architect, Edwin Oppler. There were two educational institutes closely linked to the community: a seminary for J. teachers (opened in 1848), which R. Adler had initiated, and the Hebrew Educational Institution (founded in 1893 and renamed the Hebrew Horticultural School in 1919). Located in the nearby village of Ahlem, this school, the first of its type in Germany, provided both elementary schooling and also training in

Ha-Ko'ah athletes, Hanover, Germany

gardening, crafts, and domestic science for J. youth from all over the country. The community maintained an orphanage (1859), a hospital combined with an old age home (1901), and several welfare associations. A branch of the Central Union (C.V.) was active along with a small Zionist local branch (1901) and several youth organizations. In the Weimar period, the community's financial situation deteriorated and it was forced to close the teachers' seminary and the orphanage. However, a new orphanage and a kindergarten were opened in 1925. Immigrants from Eastern Europe had no voting rights in the community and they maintained their own prayer room and associations. Towards the end of the 19th cent., several academic associations and sports clubs refused to accept Jews. After WWI, antisemitic propaganda became more frequent and agitation degenerated into attacks on individuals as well as community facilities such as the synagogue in 1927, 1930, and 1931. From 1924, lectures at the H. Technical

University by the prominent J. philosopher Prof. Theodor Lessing were subject to continual disruptions. When students actually attacked him in 1926, Lessing's university activities were restricted to research.

In June 1933, about four months after the Nazis came to power, there were 4,839 Jews living in H. In Aug. 1933, Nazis murdered Prof. Lessing, who had escaped from Germany to Marienbad. The anti-J. boycott measures started even before the official boycott on 1 April 1933, when the Karstadt Department Store fired all its J. employees. In May 1933, anti-J. rioting took place and J. stores were attacked and looted. Several J. businesses, which were in any case struggling with the consequences of the Depression, went bankrupt. The attacks on J. stores continued into 1934. By the end of 1938, 552 J. stores, businesses, and legal and medical practices which the Nazis had listed in 1935 no longer existed. The community tried to counter its growing social isolation with a more intense cultural

The New Synagogue, Hanover, Germany, 1938 (Deutsch-Israelische Gesellschaft/photo courtesy of Yad Vashem, The Holocaust Martyrs' and Heroes' Remembrance Authority, Jerusalem)

life. The Zionist associations attracted growing interest and in the spring of 1933 the Hebrew Horticultural School in Ahlem began retraining businessmen and academics for emigration to Palestine. In May 1935, a J. elementary school was set up, with four teachers and 85 pupils. A reform of the community's standing orders in June 1936 put an end to the exclusion of East European Jews, and efforts were made to achieve harmony between all groups and interests. At the end of Oct. 1938, 484 Jews of non-German citizenship were deported to Poland. On *Kristallnacht* (9–10 Nov. 1938), the synagogue was set on fire; the mortuary at the cemetery was burned down; the prayer room was wrecked; and the *mikve* was desecrated. In addition, 94 J. stores and 27 J. homes were vandalized and looted and cars and motorbikes were requisitioned. Male Jews, 334 in all, were arrested and taken to the Buchenwald concentration camp, where many were

cruelly maltreated. Other Jews were conscripted for forced labor immediately after the pogrom. Prior to *Kristallnacht* over 1,000 Jews left H.; after the pogrom another mass exodus took place. In Dec. 1938, 100 Jews left the city, followed by another 750 in the course of 1939. In June 1939, another group of Jews of non-German citizenship was deported to Poland, while others were seized and taken to Buchenwald as enemy aliens. In 1940–41, another 92 Jews managed to escape abroad. There were plans to concentrate the remaining Jews in a shanty town outside the city, but eventually, in a lightning operation carried out on 3–4 Sept. 1941, they were billeted in 15 "J. houses" belonging to the community or private individuals. Over 1,200 Jews were forced to leave their homes in just a few hours, only allowed to take the barest necessities. Their property was auctioned off. The Gestapo constantly turned up at the "J. houses" and abused the in-

mates. The deportations which took place in Dec. 1941 and March and July 1942 reduced the J. pop. in H. to some 300 Jews. In mid-1942, the J. hospital was taken over by the municipality and the Ahlem Hebrew Horticultural School was forced to stop its teaching activities. Deportations continued in the following years, culminating in Feb. 1945 in the deportation of Jews married to gentiles. At least 2,200 Jews from H. were murdered under Nazi rule. Around 100 Jews survived within the city itself. The postwar community split into two groups: German Jews and East European Jews. Conflict broke out again with the arrival of Jews from the former USSR in the 1990s. The community, with a membership in 1998 of around 3,000, maintains a variety of institutions and serves as the seat of the state rabbinate.

HANUSOVCE (Hung. Hanusfalva) Slovakia, Czechoslovakia, today Republic of Slovakia. Jews are first mentioned in 1735. The community built a small wooden synagogue in the early 19th cent. and a Great Synagogue in the mid-19th cent. Hasidim settled during the cent. as the J. pop. grew to a peak of 338 (total 1,563) in 1869. R. Eliezer Hayyim Deutsch served as rabbi (1877–97) and ran the local yeshiva. It became well known and reached an enrollment of over 100 after WWI under R. Yoav Adler. Most Jews identified with Agudat Israel. The Zionists confined themselves mostly to fundraising until the youth movements became active in the 1930s. Jews engaged mainly in petty trade and owned most of the stores in the town. In 1940, 299 remained. In the Slovakian state, they were persecuted and attacked; children were expelled from the public schools, leading to the establishment of a J. school in 1940; and businesses were closed or "Aryanized." On 27 March 1942, 63 J. girls were deported to Auschwitz via Poprad. Young men were sent to the Majdanek concentration camp in early April and 300 Jews from H. and its environs were transported to the Rejowiec ghetto in the Lublin dist. (Poland) on 24 May. Most perished. Eleven fought in the Slovakian national uprising in fall 1944.

HARBURG Swabia, Germany. Jews were victims of the Black Death persecutions of 1348–49. A new community was founded in 1671 by 11 Jews expelled from Hoechstaedt. Jews from Monheim arrived in 1741 after the expulsions from the principality of Pfalz-Neuburg. A synagogue was dedicated in 1754. In the 18th cent.

Jews engaged in moneylending and traded in horses and cattle, jewelry, and wine. In 1834 the J. pop. was 360, with 40 children in a J. public school in 1857. The J. pop. subsequently declined through emigration to the big cities, numbering 171 in 1867 (total 1,304) and 13 in 1933. Another ten left by 1939 (six to Palestine).

HARBURG-WILHELMSBURG Hanover (today part of Hamburg), Germany. Two Jews were recorded as receiving letters of protection in H. in 1610. The Jews living here in the 17th cent. and 18th cent. developed only rudimentary community structures. In 1855, there were 109 Jews living in H.; 223 in 1885; and 351 in 1905. A synagogue was consecrated in 1862. Organized religious instruction was provided from 1885. In 1899 and 1928, the cemetery was desecrated. When the Nazis came to power in 1933, there were 315 Jews in H. As early as 1933, a Jew was taken into "protective" custody because of "racial defilement" (sexual relations with an "Aryan"), and another Jew was sentenced in 1936 to six weeks' imprisonment for "statements hostile to the state." In 1934 the synagogue's windows were smashed and in 1935 J. businesses suffered as boycott measures intensified. The community intensified its internal cultural life and the Central Union (C.V.) and the Zionist Organization became very active. By 1936, the J. pop. was 192. On 1 Jan. 1938, the community merged with the Hamburg, Altona, and Wandsbek communities to form the "J. Religious Association of Hamburg." On *Kristallnacht* (9–10 Nov. 1938), the synagogue was burned down and the mortuary at the cemetery was wrecked. Jews from H. were included in the transports which began in the Hamburg area in 1941–42.

HARDENBERG Overijssel dist., Holland. Jews first settled in H. in the early 18th cent. but an organized community was established only after 1821 and numbered 105 in 1883. The J. pop. in 1941 was 39 (total 17,986). In Aug. 1942, eight Jews were sent to a labor camp and in April 1943, 15 were sent to the Vught transit camp. Three survived; the fate of the rest is unknown.

HARDERWIJK Gelderland dist., Holland. Jews first lived in H. in the 17th cent. and organized community life began in 1759, when they were permitted to hold public prayer. A synagogue was built in 1817 and served the community until the Holocaust. Its

numbers decreased towards the end of the cent. when many moved to western Holland or nearby Ermelo. There were 167 Jews in 1883 but only 70 in 1901. The J. pop. in 1941 was 41 (total 9,860) with 107 in Ermelo. The Jews of H. were deported and killed in the Holocaust; 11 survived in hiding.

HARDHEIM   Baden, Germany. A J. settlement existed in the early 14th cent. and was destroyed in the Black Death persecutions of 1348–49. The settlement was renewed by Jews from Swabia in 1690 and subsequently lived under the harsh rule of the bishops of Wuerzburg. After emancipation in 1862, the Jews became more fully integrated in the town's social and economic life and served in its public administration. The J. pop. grew to 158 in 1880 (total 2,345) and then declined steadily to 55 in 1933. Jews still owned a number of stores and factories (hide processing, soap, pumps) and community life, especially Zionist activity, continued under the Nazis. Twenty-three Jews left in 1933–38, most emigrating. Another ten left for the U.S. after *Kristallnacht* (9–10 Nov. 1938). The last 17 were deported to the Gurs concentration camp on 22 Oct. 1940.

HAREN   Hanover, Germany. In 1842, 35 Jews lived in H.. Affiliated with the rabbinate of Emden, their number grew to 40 (about 2% of the total) in 1909, when a new Orthodox synagogue was dedicated. Nine of the 28 Jews registered in 1933 left H. before *Kristallnacht* (9–10 Nov. 1938), when SA troops destroyed the synagogue after burning down others in Meppen, Lathen, and Werlte. J. men were arrested, tortured, and dispatched to the Sachsenhausen concentration camp. By 1940, a total of 16 Jews had left (six emigrating); another 15 perished in the Holocaust.

HARLAU   Moldavia dist., Rumania. Jews settled here in the late 15th cent. They organized as a guild in 1751 and were recognized as a community in 1834. Zionist activity began in 1883. The J. pop. in 1899 was 2,718 (59% of the total). Antisemitism caused about half the J. pop. to leave H. during 1899–1900, but in 1907 Jews moved there from surrounding villages. Between the World Wars Jews were active in municipal politics and in 1930, the rabbi and seven others were elected to the council. During the Antonescu regime, Jews were terrorized and their property requisitioned. Jews were prohibited

from praying in the synagogues and the schools were closed. From May 1942, Jews were sent to forced labor in Bessarabia. In spring 1944, the Russians captured the city, forestalling a massacre by the retreating Germans. After the war J. life returned to normal.

HARLINGEN   Friesland dist., Holland. J. settlement began in the 17th cent. An organized community was established in the 1760s and developed rapidly in the 19th cent., numbering 382 in 1883. A small J. school and various organizations were founded, including a branch of the Alliance Israelite. In the 20th cent. many left for larger towns. The J. pop. in 1941 was 52 (total 10,279). In Aug. 1942, most of the men were sent to labor camps and later to the Westerbork transit camp. In March 1943 the last of H.'s Jews were deported. All perished.

HARMUTHSACHSEN   Hesse–Nassau, Germany. Established in the 18th cent., the community opened a synagogue in 1833 and numbered 130 (25% of the total) in 1861. It was affiliated with Kassel's rabbinate. Most of the remaining 30 Jews had left by 1937, when the community disbanded. At least five perished in the Holocaust.

HARSANY   Borsod dist., Hungary. Jews settled in the first half of the 18th cent., numbering 107 in 1880 and 56 in 1930. They were brought to Miskolc in April 1944 and deported to Auschwitz on 10 June.

HASELUENNE   Hanover, Germany. Established in the 18th cent., this district community maintained a prayer house in 1844 and had members in Bakerde, Herzlake, and Holte. The J. pop. declined from 40 in 1895 to about 30 in 1933. After *Kristallnacht* (9–10 Nov. 1938) and the burning of a Torah scroll, one family emigrated to Canada in 1939. The last 19 Jews perished in Nazi camps.

HASLACH   Baden, Germany. The medieval J. community was destroyed in the Black Death persecutions of 1348–49. The J. pop. in 1900 was 43. Of the eight Jews left in 1939, one family reached the U.S., another perished after deportation to the Gurs concentration camp, and one Jew survived the Theresienstadt ghetto.

HASSELT   Overijssel dist., Holland. Jews lived in H. in the 16th cent. but regular settlement began in the

new community was formed in 1701, limited to ten families under various letters of protection. The Kaulla banking family became court agents to the Duke of Wuerttemberg in 1770. There were disturbances in 1848 with antisemitic overtones. After annexation to Prussia in 1850, the status of the Jews improved, though full civil rights were granted only in 1901. Jews became pioneers in local industry, introducing the first steam engine in Hohenzollern. The J. pop. reached a peak of 809 (total 3,389) in 1843. A magnificent synagogue in the arched classical style was consecrated in 1775 and a J. public school was opened in 1825. From the mid-19th cent., the J. pop. dropped, to 340 in 1880 and 101 in 1933. On *Kristallnacht* (9–10 Nov. 1938), the synagogue was damaged and most J. men sent to the Dachau concentration camp for a month. Subsequently a number of Jews were evicted from their homes. Fifty-three managed to emigrate, mostly to the U.S.; 32 were deported to the east in 1941–42, all but one perishing.

HECHTSHEIM   Hesse, Germany. A synagogue was built there in 1841. The community, numbering 97 (about 3% of the total) in 1900, dwindled to 30 Jews in 1933 and to one only in Dec. 1938.

HECI-LESPEZI   Moldavia dist., Rumania. In the mid-19th cent., L. Meierhofer, a Jew, bought the estate on which H. was situated. The J. pop. in 1899 was 1,427 (17% of the total). At the outbreak of the Russo-Rumanian war in June 1941, the J. pop was expelled to Falticeni and Botosani.

HEDDERNHEIM   Hesse–Nassau, Germany. J. scholars lived there from the 16th cent., when the printer Hayyim Schwarz (Shahor) published various works (1545–47). During the Thirty Years War (1618–48), many Jews took refuge in nearby Frankfurt in 1626. Those who remained, chiefly traders and peddlers, dedicated a synagogue in 1760 and appointed a rabbi, Mendel Lilg (d. 1790). The community prospered and became the largest in Nassau, growing to 354 (24% of the total) in 1840. After wealthier Jews (e.g., the Erlanger banking family) moved to Frankfurt, the J. pop. declined to 62 (1%) in 1905. After H. became part of Frankfurt in 1910, the community still remained independent and affiliated with Wiesbaden's rabbinate. On *Kristallnacht* (9–10 Nov. 1938), the synagogue (containing ancient Torah scrolls) was vandal-

ized; Jews who did not emigrate mostly perished in the Holocaust.

HEERENBERG, 'S-   Gelderland dist., Holland. Jews lived there in the Middle Ages but modern settlement dates from the 18th cent. There were 83 Jews living in H. in 1860. The J. pop. in 1941 was 37 (total 11,673). In the Holocaust, 22 were deported and perished; six survived in hiding.

HEERLEN   Limburg dist., Holland. The J. settlement dates from the early 18th cent. and numbered 80 in 1879. By May 1938 there were 125 refugees from Germany in H. The community numbered some 160 in 1940 (total 50,498). About 100 perished in the Holocaust. A small community was established after the war.

HEHLEN   Brunswick (today part of Bodenwerder), Germany. Dating from 1766, the J. community numbered 53 (6% of the total) in 1829 and maintained a prayer house. The pop. declined and by WWI there were only 33 Jews living in H., all members of the Bach family. On *Kristallnacht* (9–10 Nov. 1938), the family's business premises were looted and "Aryanized." By March 1940, the entire family had succeeded in emigrating.

HEIDELBERG   Baden, Germany. A. J. community with a synagogue and cemetery existed in the early 14th cent. and was destroyed in the Black Death persecutions of 1348–49, with all J. property expropriated by Elector Rupert I. A new community was established within a number of years. Jews traded in cattle and operated stalls in the municipal market as well as engaging in brokerage and moneylending. In 1390 they were expelled by Rupert II together with all the Jews of the Palatinate. Few Jews lived in H. up to the late 17th cent. The Oppenheimer family arrived around 1660, with the well-known Court Jew Joseph Suess Oppenheimer born there in 1698. By 1743, 12 J. families were present as the community continued to expand despite local opposition. In 1724, Jews were admitted to H. University for the first time and maintained a student body of 19 throughout the cent. With the annexation of H. to Baden, legal restrictions affecting Jews were gradually removed and full civil rights were granted. Nonetheless, anti-J. feeling persisted and Jews were attacked in the Hep! Hep! riots of 1819

Synagogue in Heidelberg, Germany, 1913

and the revolutionary disturbances of 1848. The J. pop. grew to 445 in 1852 and 927 in 1900 (total 53,144) as Jews shifted to the professional class and became active in industry and banking and a progressive and well-educated community emerged in the university town, raising the banners of assimilation and religious reform. The leader of Reform in H. and Baden was Karl Rehfuss (1792–1842), who taught at the University and founded a J. elementary school in 1821. He was supported by R. Shelomo Fuerst (1792–1870), who was appointed chief rabbi with jurisdiction over 20 communities when H. became the seat of the district rabbinate in 1827. R. Fuerst adopted a Reform prayer book and introduced an organ into the synagogue in 1854. In 1876 a new synagogue and cemetery were consecrated and in 1894 Baden's first B'nai B'rith lodge was opened. During the 19th. cent., the number of J. students at the University grew, reaching a peak of 76 in the 1884–88 period. Many came from Czarist Russia, including the Hebrew poet Shaul Tchernichowsky (1875–1943) and the historian Yosef Klausner

(1874–1958), while among J. lecturers and researchers a number chose to convert to advance their academic careers as the University remained a hotbed of antisemitism. Hermann (Tzevi Hirsch) Schapira (1848–1948), one of the early leaders of Hovevei Zion and originator of the idea of the Hebrew University and the J. National Fund, came to study there in 1878. J. students from Russia initiated Zionist activity after the First Zionist Congress in 1897. During WWI and after, J. refugees from Poland and E. Galicia settled in H., founding their own congregation. The J. pop. reached a maximum of 1,421 in 1925, dropping to 1,102 in 1933, with Jews remaining a leading force in the local economy, operating furniture and cigarette factories and large wholesale establishments. Most national organizations were represented there, including the Zionist youth movements. At the outset of Nazi rule, 34 J. professors were dismissed from the University and by 1935 one J. student remained in addition to those from mixed marriages. J. children were isolated in separate classrooms in the public school, and by the end of 1938 J. businesses had been completely "Aryanized." On *Kristallnacht* (9–10 Nov. 1938), the synagogue was burned by the SS and SA; impounded religious articles and Torah scrolls were subsequently destroyed by university students. J. homes and stores were also heavily damaged and 150 Jews were detained in the Dachau concentration camp. About 800 H. Jews emigrated from Germany in 1933–1939, including a number who arrived after 1933. Fourteen Jews of Polish origin were expelled to the Polish border in 1938 and 1939. Another 281 were deported to the Gurs concentration camp on 22 Oct. 1940. About 100 were saved from deportation by the Evangelist pastor Hermann Maas, who got them onto a sick list and during the period also arranged to get many Jews out of the country. (He was recognized by Yad Vashem in 1967 as one of the Righteous among the Nations.) On 22 Aug. 1942 a further 111 were deported to the Theresienstadt ghetto. After the war a community numbering 260 in 1948 and about 100 in 1990 was reestablished by concentration camp survivors and former J. residents of H. An autonomous Institute for Higher J. Studies offers academic degrees.

HEIDELSHEIM Baden, Germany. The J. community reached the peak of its development in the mid-19th cent. with a J. pop. of 192 (total 2,307) and a synagogue and elementary school at its disposal. Thereafter

Oil painting of Yom Kippur prayer services in Heidingsfelf synagogue, Bavaria, Germany

it declined sharply to 38 in 1900 and six aged Jews, attached to the Bruchsal community, in 1933.

HEIDENHEIM   Middle Franconia, Germany. Jews were present in the early 18th cent. The grammarian and liturgical scholar Wolf Heidenheim was born there in 1757. A new synagogue was erected in 1853 and the J. pop. stood at 130 (total 1,536) in 1867. After WWI, the majority of Jews were cattle and horse traders. Thirty-one remained in 1933, eight emigrating and 16 leaving for other German cities by 1938. The last six left after the burning of the synagogue on *Kristallnacht* (9–10 Nov. 1938).

HEIDINGSFELD   (in J. sources, Hatzfeld, Hertzfeld) Lower Franconia, Germany. With Worms, Oettingen, and Frankfurt, H. was one of the four J. communities that maintained a virtually continuous existence in Germany from the Middle Ages, living under various letters of protection. Jews from Wuerzburg settled there before the expulsion of 1565 as well as afterwards. In the early 18th cent., H. became the seat of the chief rabbinate of the Wuerzburg region and later of all Lower Franconia, its authority extending over more than a 100 settlements. Among its chief rabbis were Shelomo ben Yitzhak Rothschild (1666–75), founder of the famous banking family. The community was known for its aid to the J. settlement in Eretz Israel. A new synagogue was consecrated in 1780 and a cemetery in 1810. The community attained its peak growth in 1805, becoming the second largest in Bavaria with 600 Jews. In 1819, J. homes were burned in the anti-J. Hep! Hep! riots that spread from Wuerzburg throughout Germany. The J. pop. declined to 273 in 1867 (total 3,242) and 83 in 1925. In 1930 the town was annexed to Wuerzburg and in June 1937 so was

Synagogue built in 1780, Heidingsfeld, Germany

the community. On *Kristallnacht* (9–10 Nov. 1938), the synagogue was burned and J. homes were destroyed.

HEILBRONN (in J. sources, also Heilpronn) Wuerttemberg, Germany. A J. settlement existed in the mid-11th cent. It was largely destroyed in the Rindfleisch massacres of 1298 and again in the Black Death persecutions of 1348–49. Subsequently the community received royal protection. In 1476 the Jews were expelled "perpetually" by the town council. The settlement was renewed in the first half of the 19th cent. and by 1857 included 20 families. Jews owned two textile factories. Another 17 families from the Rhineland joined them after the emancipation of Wuerttemberg Jews in 1861 and an independent community was constituted. In 1867, H. became the seat of the district rabbinate and in 1877 a synagogue was dedicated after a bitter controversy over installing

an organ. A new controversy over cremation split the community in 1910 and resulted in the founding of the Jeshurun Congregation by Orthodox circles with separate community facilities. Jews were fully integrated in public life. They served on the city council and were socially accepted. They were also an important factor in the economic development of H. In addition to textiles, Jews ran cigarette, furniture, shoe, and hide-processing factories. Jews also operated major distilleries that won international prizes at Paris and Vienna. They dominated the horse, cattle, and sheep trade. In 1885 the J. pop. stood at 994 (total 27,758). Antisemitism began to be felt in the Weimar period, though most local residents opposed the National Socialist movement and an attempt was even made on Hitler's life when he appeared in H. in 1926. In 1933, the J. pop was 790 (total 77,569), with ten other communities under the aegis of its rab-

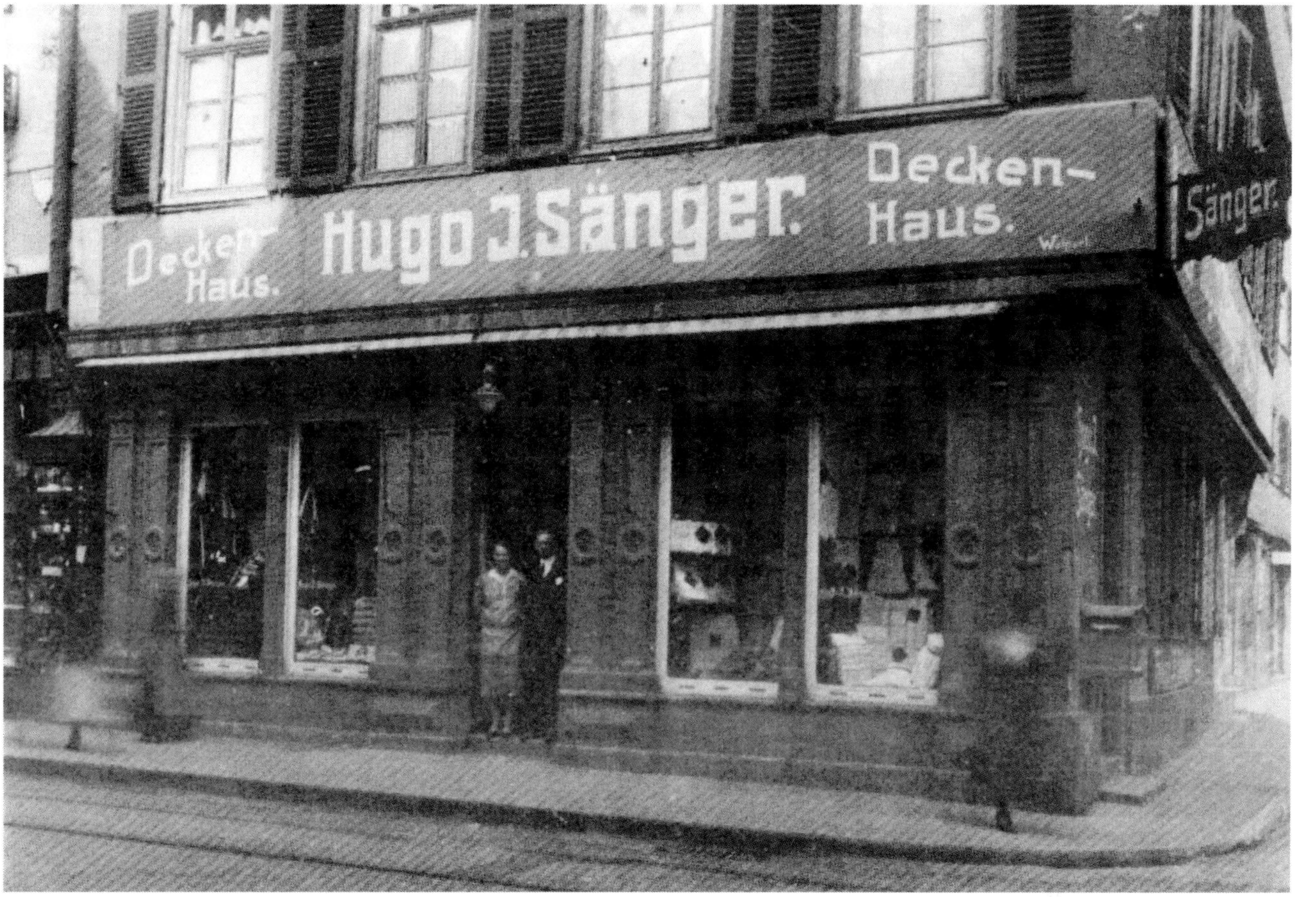
Decken-
Haus.
Hugo J. Sänger
Decken-
Haus.
Sänger

The Mays in front of their store, Heilbronn, Germany, 1918

binate. Among the bodies represented were the Zionist Organization, B'nai B'rith, and ORT. Of the 534 factories and business establishments in H., 149 were in J. hands and Jews were also prominent in the professional class. In the Nazi era, anti-J. propaganda was fostered in the vitriolic local press. Already in 1933, SA units rounded up Jews and beat them and J. children were isolated on separate benches in the public schools. Economic boycotts were instituted and Jews banned in various public places. In response, J. cultural and social life expanded within the community, with the Zionists increasing their activity significantly. In 1936 the community started its own school. On *Kristallnacht* (9–10 Nov. 1938), the synagogue was set on fire and Nazis vandalized the Jeshurun Congregation's prayer house, the cemetery, the community center, and the J. school. J. homes and business establishments were also broken into and destroyed. Subsequently the Nazis impounded J. businesses and homes under their policy of "Aryanization." By Nov. 1938, 353 Jews had emigrated to over 30 countries and by 1941 the number reached 603, including 238 to other countries in Europe, 170 to the U.S., and 105 to Palestine. Those remaining in the city were sent east in a number of stages: 49 to the Riga ghetto on 1 Dec. 1941 (all perishing); 16 to Izbica in the Lublin dist. (Poland) in April 1942; and 52 to the Theresienstadt ghetto in Aug. 1942 by way of Stuttgart. Another 56 were expelled from their various places of refuge throughout Germany and 22 were deported from the European countries where they had found shelter after these areas fell into German hands. After the war a number of Jews returned to H. and one of the J. distilleries was reopened, employing 360 workers and salesmen by 1961.

HEILIGENSTADT Upper Franconia, Germany. A few J. families settled in the 18th cent. under the protection of the nobles of the house of Stauffenberg. The community numbered 68 (total 436) in 1810. In 1902

it was attached to Aufsess and by 1910 no Jews were left.

HEILIGENSTADT-EICHSFELD Saxony, Germany. Jews lived in H. from the first half of the 14th cent. They suffered during the Black Death persecutions of 1348–49 and were finally expelled in 1574. There is evidence of several J. families settling in the city in 1796. The growing community set up a prayer room, a cemetery in 1817, and finally a synagogue in 1872. In 1882, the community numbered 107. In 1933, the number of Jews living in H. was 34. In the first years of Nazi rule there was nearly no emigration. On *Kristallnacht* (9–10 Nov. 1938), the synagogue was set on fire and seven Jews were arrested. Afterwards, 19 Jews managed to emigrate. The remaining 14 Jews were billeted in a "J. house." At least six were deported to the Theresienstadt ghetto. None of the 14 survived the Nazi period.

HEILSBERG (Pol. Lidzbark Warminski) East Prussia, Germany, today Poland. The first evidence of a J. presence dates from 1728. By 1871, the J. pop. was 164. The community maintained a synagogue and a cemetery, which was desecrated in 1932. In June 1933, about four months after the Nazis assumed power, the J. pop. stood at 34. On *Kristallnacht* (9–10 Nov. 1938), the synagogue was burned down and a J. couple shot dead. By May 1939, only ten Jews were left in H. No further information is available about the fate of community members.

HEINEBACH Hesse–Nassau, Germany. Established after 1800, the community opened a synagogue in 1843 and numbered 80 (8% of the total) in 1861. Most Jews earned their livelihood from the cattle trade. By 1933 the community had shrunk to 23 and on the eve of *Kristallnacht* (9–10 Nov. 1938), Nazis desecrated the synagogue. At least 17 Jews perished in the Holocaust.

HEINSBERG Rhineland, Germany. Jews are first mentioned in 1642 and continued to live in H. without a break. In 1806, the J. pop. was 69. A synagogue was consecrated in 1818. Jews were active in local life. In 1840, a Jew was appointed court bailiff, the first to hold a government position in Prussia. The community reached a peak pop. of 104 in 1885. In 1898, a Jew was elected to the municipal council. In 1933, the J. pop.

was 56. In April 1933, a number of Jews were beaten and arrested in Nazi boycott operations. Until Nov. 1938, emigration rates were low. On *Kristallnacht* (9–10 Nov. 1938), the synagogue was vandalized and Torah scrolls and prayer books were torn to pieces. In April 1941, the last Jews were forced to move to an abandoned hide-processing factory along with other Jews in the area. In March 1942, 23 were deported to Izbica in the Lublin dist. (Poland).

HEINSHEIM Baden, Germany. Jews are first mentioned in 1681. A cemetery is known from the early 17th cent., afterwards serving the region and becoming the largest in southern Germany. A synagogue was erected in 1796 and the J. pop. grew to a peak of 118 in 1836. With their economic situation improving, half the Jews traded in cattle in the early 20th cent. In 1933, 24 remained (total pop. 672). Nineteen left the village by the end of 1938. On *Kristallnacht* (9–10 Nov. 1938), the homes of the last five Jews were seriously damaged; two emigrated to the U.S. and three were deported to the Gurs concentration camp on 22 Oct. 1940.

HEJOCSABA Borsod–Gomor dist., Hungary. Jews were present by the mid-17th cent. and numbered 1,280 in 1840. The J. pop. dropped to 337 in 1880 when Jews were allowed to live in Miskolc. A synagogue was established in 1800 and the community maintained a school, *heder*, and *talmud torah*. On 12–15 June 1944, 200 Jews were deported to Auschwitz via Diosgyor and Miskolc. The Nazis spared a few dozen artisans and their families but then on 26 Oct., the families were murdered and the artisans taken to Austria.

HELDENBERGEN Hesse, Germany. The community is thought to have been established in 1500, although records only go back to 1700. Numbering 259 (18% of the total) in 1861, it was affiliated with the Orthodox rabbinate of Darmstadt. Over 40 of the 87 Jews left during the years 1933–35, but 27 were deported in 1942.

HELLSTEIN Hesse–Nassau, Germany. After securing their independence from the nearby community of Birstein, the Jews opened a synagogue in 1868 and numbered 48 (12% of the total) in 1895. Affiliated with Hanau's rabbinate, the community dwindled and

HERGERSHAUSEN   Hesse, Germany. Jews lived there from 1604 and in 1861 numbered 121 (18% of the total). By 1933 the community had dwindled to 31. Most Jews left before *Kristallnacht* (9–10 Nov. 1938); the remainder emigrated to the U.S.

HERLESHAUSEN   Hesse-Nassau, Germany. Even though Jews were living there in 1640, the community did not build a synagogue until 1846 and numbered 129 (12% of the total) in 1871. Nazi boycott measures ruined Jews in the livestock trade and on *Kristallnacht* (9–10 Nov. 1938), the synagogue (enlarged in 1928) was desecrated. Of the town's 86 permanent or temporary J. residents (1933–42), 28 emigrated; an equal number perished in the Holocaust.

HERMANOVICZE   Vilna dist., Poland, today Belarus. Jews were present by the late 19th cent., mostly as vegetable farmers. In 1921 their number reached 209 (total 593), farming now on a smaller scale following the loss of markets and the drop in prices. To earn a living, about 20 opened stores. On the arrival of the Germans in June 1941 the local pop. looted J. property. A *Judenrat* was established and on 10 July the town's 250 Jews were ordered into a ghetto. On 10 Nov. they were expelled to the Szarkowszczyzna ghetto. On 18 July 1942, together with the other ghetto inhabitants, they were slaughtered in panicked flight from an *Aktion* that left 1,200 in the ghetto dead. Remnants reached the Glebokie ghetto and were murdered there on 20 Aug. 1943.

HERMANUV MESTEC   Bohemia (Sudetenland), Czechoslovakia. Jews settled in the early 15th cent., living on their own street and were frequently persecuted for economic reasons. In 1727 they were ordered into a ghetto and in 1760 they built a new synagogue when the old one near the church was destroyed. The J. pop. reached a peak of 721 (about 18% of the total) in 1859, with a J. school started in 1855. Jews pioneered the town's burgeoning shoe and cloth industries late in the cent. In 1939, the J. pop. was about 60. On 3 Dec. 1942, the Jews were deported to the Theresienstadt ghetto and then to Auschwitz.

HERMESKEIL   Rhineland, Germany. Jews settled in the 19th cent. They engaged in trade; sold locally produced nails in nearby cities; dealt in cattle; and served as sources of credit. A community of 17 Jews

existed by 1871, growing to 45 (total 2,795) in 1925. A synagogue and cemetery were opened in the late 19th cent and a religious school was in operation in 1890. The local pop. was generally hostile to the Jews. Antisemitic incidents continued into the Nazi period. In 1936, windows were smashed in five J. homes and stores. On *Kristallnacht* (9–10 Nov. 1938), ten J.-owned buildings were wrecked, Jews were beaten, and the synagogue was set on fire. Most Jews left the city, with 11 remaining in 1938. After *Kristallnacht* those who did not succeed in leaving for Palestine or the U.S. via Trier were deported to the camps.

HERNADNEMETI   Zemplen dist., Hungary. Jews settled in the late 18th cent., mostly as artisans and farmers. They numbered 31 in 1851 and 58 in 1930. The 11 remaining in 1944 were deported to Auschwitz via Satoraljaujhely on 3 June.

HERNADVECSE   Abauj-Torna dist., Hungary. Jews settled in the late 18th cent. and numbered 83 in 1930. Most were merchants. They were deported to Auschwitz via Kassa in late May 1944.

HERNE   Westphalia, Germany. There is evidence of a J. presence in H. from the middle of the 18th cent. but the J. pop. grew only slowly, numbering 75 individuals in 1880. First affiliated to the Bochum community, the Jews of H. set up their own community in 1889, consecrating a new synagogue building in 1911. By then, membership had already started to grow rapidly in the wake of the influx of East European Jews. In 1905 there were 239 Jews living in H. and in 1925 the community reached a peak of 499 individuals. Although the percentage of the East European Jews was about 50% at the time, there was practically no integration of the newcomers. In June 1933, about four months after the Nazis assumed power, there were 467 Jews living in H. Businessmen were attacked on Boycott Day (1 April 1933). In response to the growing economic and social decline, the community stepped up its social aid and cultural life. On *Kristallnacht* (9–10 Nov. 1938), the synagogue was burned down and J. businesses and homes were looted and wrecked. There were still 178 Jews living in H. at this time. Those who did not manage to emigrate were deported in six transports between 1942 and 1943. Thirteen Jews remained in H., probably protected by marriage to non-J. partners. Altogether the Nazis deported a

total of 282 Jews from H. including Jews who had hoped to find shelter in other German cities or in neighboring countries. Most perished.

HERRLINGEN   Wuerttemberg, Germany. The Jews of H., numbering 48 in 1933, formed part of the nearby Ulm community. H. was best known for its J. educational institutions, including a boarding school that maintained J. education in the Nazi era (107 students in 1937) as well as serving as a teachers' training center with such illustrious instructors as Martin Buber. Many students were able to emigrate to Palestine prior to the school's closure in 1939. Subsequently the school building was used as an old age home for Jews from the Wuerttemberg region, the last of whom were deported to the Theresienstadt ghetto in 1942.

HERRLISHEIM   (Ger. Herlishheim) Bas-Rhin dist., France. There were Jews in H. from the first half of the 18th cent. By 1780, there were 15 families (66 persons). In 1936, the local J. community numbered 80 members. In 1940, bombardment destroyed the synagogue. The Jews were expelled to the south of France, with the rest of Alsace-Lorraine Jews.

HERSCHBERG   Palatinate, Germany. The J. pop. reached a peak of 170 in 1848 and then declined steadily to three in 1934. A synagogue was in use in 1815. Three Jews perished in the Holocaust.

HERSFELD, BAD   see BAD HERSFELD.

HERTA   Moldavia dist., Rumania, today Republic of Moldova. Jews founded H. during the early 18th cent. A *talmud torah* opened in 1764. Among the spiritual leaders was R. Eliezer Wolf (1800–52), a Kosover Hasid, subject of many legends. The J. pop. in 1899 was 1,939 (66% of the total). After emancipation (1919), Jews were involved in municipal politics and a Jew served as deputy mayor. On 28 June 1940 H. was annexed to the USSR, J. shops were confiscated and the wealthy ousted from their homes. On 13 June 1941, 38 wealthy families were expelled to Siberia. When Rumania recaptured H. on 5 July 1941, 132 Jews suspected of aiding the Russians were forced to dig mass graves and were shot. All 1,600 Jews were expelled to Edineti in Bessarabia; later they were transferred to Mogilev in Transnistria and then to a number of Rumanian ghettoes.

Chemistry class, Herrlingen, Germany, 1937

HESSDORF   Lower Franconia, Germany. An organized community existed by the latter half of the 18th cent. A synagogue was built in the 1820s when the J. pop. was around 160. Twenty-nine single J. men left in 1830–54, most for the U.S., and the J. pop. fell to 100 in 1900 and 48 in 1933. The synagogue and the homes of the six remaining J. families were wrecked on *Kristallnacht* (9–10 Nov. 1938). Most left by early 1942.

HESSISCH-OLDENDORF   Hesse–Nassau, Germany. The community, numbering 48 (4% of the total) in 1871, built a new synagogue in 1908 which it vacated after the J. pop. had dwindled to 24 in 1925. Owing to Nazi violence, most Jews left by 1939; five were sent to death camps in 1942.

HESSLOCH   Hesse, Germany. Jews lived there from the 15th cent. and numbered 67 (7% of the total) in 1861. Most were engaged in commerce. By 1933, only 30 Jews remained and the (largely Catholic) pop. tended to ignore Nazi boycott regulations. The synagogue was vandalized on *Kristallnacht* (9–10 Nov. 1938), and all the Jews left before WWII. Some emigrated to the U.S., but 15 perished in the Holocaust.

HETINA   (Hung. Tiszaheteny) Carpatho-Russia, Czechoslovakia, today Ukraine. Jews probably settled in the mid-18th cent., with three J. families present in 1768. In 1880, the J. pop. was 59 with a few farming. In 1921, it was 141 (total 520) and 131 in 1941. In the period of Czechoslovakian rule after WWI, Jews served on the local council. In the second half of May 1944, the Jews still there were deported to Auschwitz.

HEUBACH AN DER RHOEN   Hesse–Nassau, Germany. The community opened a synagogue in 1835 and grew to 97 (13% of the total) in 1861. Having shrunk to 31 in 1933, it disbanded and no Jews remained after 1938.

HEUCHELHEIM   Palatinate, Germany. The J. pop. was 48 in 1880. The community was attached to Ingenheim in 1909. In the Nazi period, three Jews were deported to Poland, where they perished.

HEUSENSTAMM   Hesse, Germany. Established before 1650, the community numbered 89 (11% of the total) in 1828–49. Jews from nearby Obertshausen also attended the synagogue, which was badly damaged on *Kristallnacht* (9–10 Nov. 1938). Most of the remaining 26 Jews fled to other German towns and probably died in the Holocaust.

HEVES   Heves dist., Hungary. The J. community, dating from the mid-18th cent., numbered 631 (9% of the total) in 1880 and 331 in 1941. After 1869, a Neologist congregation was formed. A J. school was opened in 1856 and a synagogue in 1867. Many of the young died as forced laborers in the Ukraine in 1940. On 9 May 1944, the 1,500 Jews of the district were sent to the Bagolyuk coal mines and held there until deported to Auschwitz on 8 June. Seventy-three survivors returned to H., but gradually left.

HIDA   (Hung. Hidalmas) N. Transylvania dist., Rumania. An organized J. community existed in the early 19th cent. Many Jews were engaged in apple-growing. The J. pop. in 1920 was 357 (28% of the total). In Sept. 1940 economic restrictions were imposed on the Jews. On 2 June 1944, the J. community was deported to Auschwitz.

HILBRINGEN   Saar, Germany. Jews settled in H. at the beginning of the 18th cent., and in 1833 there were 52 Jews living here. A synagogue was established in 1864 but the community was not big enough to be fully independent and in 1867 it was affiliated with the Merzig synagogue community. By 1895, the number of Jews in H. dropped to 36. When the German Reich annexed the Saar in 1935, there were 31 Jews in H. They took advantage of the emigration laws during the 1935 transition period and emigrated, mostly abroad. In 1936, there were no longer any Jews in H. and that year the synagogue was sold to the town.

HILCHENBACH   Westphalia, Germany. The J. pop. was 11 (total 1,575) in 1870 and 25–28 in 1932–33. The Jews earned their livelihood as merchants, livestock dealers, and butchers and the community maintained a prayer house and a small cemetery (1899). Under the Nazis, 12 Jews emigrated (three to Holland and the rest overseas). Four left for other places in Germany and at least eight were deported to the camps in 1942–43.

HILDBURGHAUSEN   Thuringia, Germany. First mention of Jews there dates from the year 1331, but until the 18th cent. J. settlement was sparse and discontinuous. In 1720, there were 13 J. families in H. and in 1833 the community numbered 123. The community established a synagogue in 1811 and maintained a school (1824–1922). After 1900, a rapid decline set in and by 1930 there were only 33 Jews in H. The synagogue was demolished in 1933 and the new synagogue moved to a private house. In 1938 the first "Aryanization" of J. businesses occurred. On *Kristallnacht* (9–10 Nov. 1938), J. men were arrested, maltreated, and sent to the Buchenwald concentration camp. The last emigrants left in 1939, one family going to the U.S. Those who remained, were deported in 1942 to the Belzec death camp in May and to the Theresienstadt ghetto in Sept. Most never returned.

HILDEN   Rhineland, Germany. The H. community was affiliated to Duesseldorf. The J. pop. was 54 in 1933 and 14 in 1939. On *Kristallnacht* (9–10 Nov. 1938), a J. family was attacked and abused and one elderly man died from his injuries. Altogether, 25 Jews managed to escape abroad and seven were deported and murdered. The latter figure is probably low, because some Jews from H. who had emigrated to nearby countries were subsequently rounded up following the Nazi occupation.

HILDESHEIM   Hanover, Germany. A medieval J. community existed from the first half of the 14th cent. Despite the Black Death persecutions (1348–49), the community continued to function until 1457, when the Jews fled heavy taxation and the city decided not to admit Jews again. Jews returned in the early 16th cent., settling both in H. itself and in neighboring Moritzberg outside the city, where a separate community developed. The main J. settlement in H. continued to grow, reaching about 20 families by the early 17th cent. Religious services were held at the school which was established in 1607. The J. pop. rose to 180–240 members during the second half of the 18th cent. The community was allowed to convert the school building into a synagogue in 1725. The J. pop. was 337 in 1803 and reached a peak of 617 in 1900. A public J. elementary school was opened in 1828, and in 1849 a new synagogue was dedicated. Both the organ and the pulpit with which the syna-

gogue was provided point to the Reform orientation of the community. In the early 20th cent. B'nai B'rith, the Central Union (C.V.), and the Zionist Organization established branches in the town. In June 1933, there were 515 Jews living in H. By the mid-1930s, boycott measures had led to the "Aryanization" of numerous businesses. In the wake of its social insulation, the community intensified its internal cultural life. On *Kristallnacht* (9–10 Nov. 1938), the synagogue was burned down. The school, which had been turned into a community center, was wrecked along with J. businesses and homes. Some 60 men were temporarily placed under arrest. By 1939, 217 Jews were still living in H. Those who failed to emigrate were concentrated in five "J. houses." They were deported in May and July 1942 with the exception of 12 Jews who were protected by marriage to a non-J. partner. In 1997 a J. community was reestablished in H.

HILLESHEIM   Hesse, Germany. Numbering 90 (13% of the total) in 1861, the community declined to 32 (5%) in 1933. By May 1939 all the Jews had left.

HILVERSUM   Noord-Holland dist., Holland. A J. community existed in the second half of the 18th cent. In 1789 a synagogue was inaugurated. In the 19th cent., community activities, including education and welfare, were organized. The J. pop. in 1899 was 535 (total 20,000). The community grew in the 20th cent. and various J. convalescence and children's homes were established in H. and its surroundings. A branch of the Zionist Organization was opened in the early 20th cent. By 1938 there were 67 refugees from Germany in H. and in Sept. some 380 foreign Jews expelled from the coastal regions reached H. The J. pop. in 1940 was 2,000 with 247 in nearby Laren. From Feb. 1941 restrictions were imposed on J. movement. In Sept., the children were dismissed from the general schools. Deportations began in Jan. 1942, most via Amsterdam. Some were sent to forced labor. In March–April 1943, patients from the J. institutions were deported and on 13 April the last of the Jews were deported to death camps via the Vught transit camp. Only the intermarried remained. Some 200 survived the Holocaust and the community was reestablished.

HIMBACH   Hesse, Germany. The community, numbering 38 (8% of the total) in 1900, dwindled to 19 be-

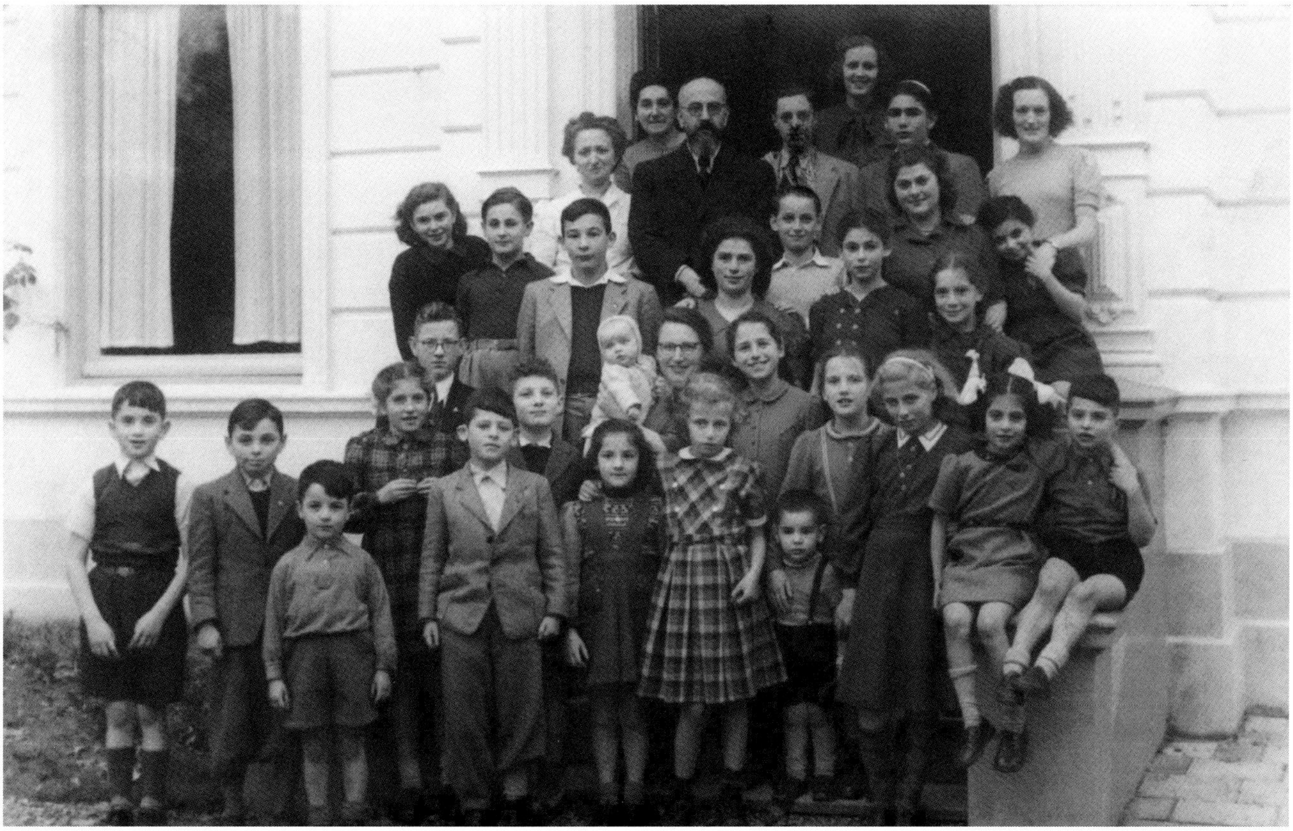

Jewish children from orphanage, Hilversum, Holland, 1946

fore *Kristallnacht* (9–10 Nov. 1938), when the synagogue was destroyed. By May 1939 no Jews remained.

HINDENBURG (Pol. Zabrze) Upper Silesia, Germany, today Poland. J. settlement commenced in the early 19th cent. The community was attached to Beuthen in 1860 and in 1872 recognized as independent. It maintained a synagogue from 1865, an elementary school from 1869, and a cemetery from 1871. In 1871, the J. pop. was 143, rising to 789 in 1895 and 1,027 in 1925. Among the organizations active in the community were the Central Union (C.V.), the Zionist movement, sports clubs, welfare agencies, and B'nai B'rith, which also operated a kindergarten and day care center. Jews traded in cattle and grain. Some owned large stores and others belonged to the professional class. In the Weimar period, there were occasional violent outbursts of antisemitism, including disturbances in Oct. 1922. In 1932, members of the Nazi Party set off of an explosive device in a J. business establishment. The J. pop. reached a peak of 1,200 in 1931. The Nazi racial laws first instituted in 1933 were not applied to local Jews until 16 July 1937 owing to the protection of the League of Nations' minority rights convention. Jews were nonetheless persecuted in other ways during the period. In July 1933, SA forces broke into the synagogue and other antisemitic incidents occurred all through the 1930s. From 1933, Zionists and non-Zionists cooperated in running a counseling service for potential emigrants. Courses in Hebrew were also given. On *Kristallnacht* (9–10 Nov. 1938), the synagogue was set on fire and 350 Jews were arrested; 95 were sent to the Buchenwald concentration camp the next day. Those remaining after the outbreak of WWII were deported to the concentration camps. Thirty-five remained on 8 June 1942 and 16 in Oct. 1944, all but one with a non-J. spouse.

HINTERSTEINAU (now part of Steinau an der Strasse), Hesse-Nassau, Germany. From 13 in 1754, the community grew to 90 (12% of the total) in 1871, but dwindled to eight in 1933. All the Jews left before WWII.

Synagogue in Hindenburg, Germany, before WWII

HIRSCHAID   Upper Franconia, Germany. Jews are known from the second half of the 17th cent., living under the protection of the bishops of Bamberg. The pop. declined after emancipation in the mid-19th cent. (from 83 in 1812 to 51 in 1867) but remained stable thereafter, numbering 64 in 1933 (total 1,713). The J. public school, the last in Upper Franconia, closed in 1924. Emigration in the Nazi era reduced the J. pop. to 43 in 1938. On *Kristallnacht* (9–10 Nov. 1938), the synagogue was burned and the community was dispersed soon after.

HIRSCHBERG IM RIESENGEBIRGE   (Pol. Jelenia Gora) Lower Silesia, Germany. Jews were present in the first half of the 14th cent. but the modern community was only founded in the early 18th cent. The J. pop. was 37 in 1810 and reached a peak of 450 in 1880. Cemeteries were opened in 1820 and 1880 and a synagogue was consecrated in 1853. In 1931, the J. pop. was 184. The first three J. victims of the Nazi regime were three men along with the Christian wife of one of them who were murdered by the SS on the Night of the Long Knives (the Nazi Party purge of 30 June 1934). The victims were arrested along with Communists, clergymen and others suspected of opposition to the regime. In 1937, 146 Jews still remained. On *Kristallnacht* (9–10 Nov. 1938), rioters destroyed the synagogue, part of the cemetery, and J. business premises. Sixty-seven Jews remained in 1939, and nine intermarried Jews after the deportations to the Theresienstadt ghetto and General Gouvernement territory.

HIRSCHHORN   Hesse, Germany. Jews were permitted to settle in 1349. A small community existed in 1744 and by 1828 it numbered 58 (4% of the total). Unable to maintain an independent existence, the community disbanded in 1938 and all but one of the 24 Jews left, most emigrating to the U.S.

HLINIK   (Hung. Vagyagos) Slovakia, Czechoslovakia, today Republic of Slovakia. Jews arrived in the 1730s, building a synagogue c. 1800 and forming a Neologist congregation under the leadership of Leo-

pold Popper. He endowed a new synagogue and a J. school and became president of the Organization of Neologist Communities in Hungary as well as receiving the title of Count von Podyhragya from the emperor. The J. pop. rose to 264 (total 923) in 1880. In 1940, 19 Jews remained. About half were deported in 1942.

HLINITA   Bukovina, Rumania, today Ukraine. Jews settled in the early 19th cent. Between the two World Wars, most Zionist parties were active. The J. pop. in 1930 was 140. In Oct. 1941, the Jews were deported to Transnistria; 15 families survived and emigrated to Palestine.

HLOHOVEC   (Hung. Galgoc; Yid. Frayshtatl) Slovakia, Czechoslovakia, today Republic of Slovakia. Jews are mentioned in 1506. In the late 16th cent., 32 J. families inhabited a Street of the Jews still in existence. They sold wine and farm produce and acted as moneylenders. Many left in the 17th cent. in the face of Turkish incursions. A synagogue was built in the mid-18th cent. Many Jews were tailors in this period and some J. merchants from H. participated in the Leipzig fair. A new synagogue was consecrated in 1832 and a J. elementary school with 130 children was opened in 1855. In 1848, J. homes and stores were looted. The J. pop. rose from 467 in 1828 to 1,160 (total 7,068) in 1869. Immanuel Eisler headed the community. Another synagogue was erected in 1900 with R. Yosef Eliezer Rosenfeld serving the congregation in 1875–1919. The Eisler family helped initiate Zionist activity in H. and in Hungary as a whole after the First Zionist Congress in 1897. J. stores were again looted following WWI. In the Czechoslovakian Republic, Jews served on the municipal council. Jews owned most of the town's 110 business establishments as well as 19 workshops and factories. Most of the young belonged to such Zionist youth movements as Hashomer Hatzair, Bnei Akiva, and Betar. In 1940, the J. pop. was 727. J. Hungarian nationals were expelled in 1938 and 109 Jews were seized for forced labor in 1940. In 1941, Jews were forced out of their businesses. On 29 March 1942, 150 young J. men and women were deported to Novaky and Patronka, respectively. On 25 April, 150 Jews were sent to Sered and on 26 April, 200 were deported to Opole in the Lublin dist. (Poland). In early 1944, 483 Jews remained, including refugees from

Bratislava. The Germans deported many to Auschwitz in Sept. 1944. Most of the postwar community of 125 left for Israel in 1949.

HLUSZA MALA   (Yid. Lishke) Volhynia dist., Poland, today Ukraine. Twenty-five women and children were murdered by the Germans in early 1942 and the rest of the village's 35 J. families were transferred to the Kamien Koszyrski ghetto and killed there in the *Aktions* of 10 Aug. and 2 Nov. 1942.

HLUSZA WIELKA   (Yid. Lishe) Volhynia dist., Poland, today Ukraine. The J. pop. in 1921 was 224. The Jews were transferred to the Kamien Koszyrski ghetto where they were liquidated in the *Aktions* of 10 Aug. and 2 Nov. 1942.

HNIZDYCZOW   Stanislawow dist., Poland, today Ukraine. The J. pop. in 1921 was 100. The Jews were expelled to Stryj for liquidation in Sept. 1942.

HNUSTA   (Hung. Nyustya) Slovakia, Czechoslovakia, today Republic of Slovakia. Jews settled in the mid-19th cent. The community maintained a synagogue and cemetery and reached a peak pop. of 74 (total 2,025) in 1910. In 1940, 48 Jews remained, mostly as shopkeepers. The authorities liquidated their businesses in 1941 and in spring 1942, young J. men and women were deported to Majdanek and Auschwitz, respectively. Most families were sent to the death camps of the Lublin dist. (Poland).

HOCHBERG   Wuerttemberg, Germany. Jews settled in the mid-18th cent. and in 1852 constituted a majority (305 of 490 residents), boasting the first Jew in Wuerttemberg to sit on a municipal council. By 1914 the community had dissolved through emigration. The J. cemetery dating from 1808 remained undisturbed until desecrated by neo-Nazis in 1970–71.

HOCHFELDEN   Bas-Rhin dist., France. The J. community consisted of 71 members in 1784. The synagogue was inaugurated in 1841. By 1865, the J. pop. increased to 257. In 1936, the community numbered 128 members. During WWII, the Germans expelled all, together with the rest of Alsace-Lorraine Jews, to the south of France. Altogether, 22 members of the community were deported. In 1965, only 35 Jews lived in H.

HOCHHEIM AM MAIN Hesse–Nassau, Germany. Jews lived there from the 17th cent., numbered 35 (2% of the total) in 1825, and dedicated a synagogue in 1870. On *Kristallnacht* (9–10 Nov. 1938), it was vandalized and 19 of the 20 Jews registered in 1933 left, ten emigrating before WWII.

HOCHNEUKIRCH Rhineland, Germany. J. peddlers and livestock merchants lived in H. from 1739. The J. pop. was 60–90 in the 19th cent. and 40–55 in the 20th. The community maintained a cemetery, established in 1824, and a synagogue, completed in 1902. It was destroyed on *Kristallnacht* (9–10 Nov. 1938). In all, 27 Jews were deported during the war years.

HOCHSPEYER Palatinate, Germany. Five J. families were present in 1782, mostly trading in cattle. Their number increased to 12 families in 1807 and 13 (72 Jews) in 1848. Subsequently, until WWI, Jews numbered 40–50, dropping to 32 in 1932. A J. elementary school was founded in 1824. After it closed, local children received their religious education from teachers in the neighboring community. A synagogue was in use and in 1930 the community was allotted a section in the local cemetery for J. burial. All but one Jew left the village before *Kristallnacht* (9–10 Nov. 1938). Nine moved to other localities in Germany and 23 emigrated: 17 to the U.S.; four to Argentina; one to France; and one to Palestine. The last Jew of H., an elderly woman, was deported to the Gurs concentration camp in Oct. 1940 and survived the war in an old age home.

HOCKENHEIM Baden, Germany. The first Jews settled in 1510. The community began to grow in the 19th cent. A small synagogue was built in 1833 and a J. elementary school operated in 1820–43. The J. pop. reached a peak of 137 in 1871 (about 3% of the total). Antisemitism increased in the 1890s and in the post-WWI period. In 1933, 52 Jews remained. J. cigarette factories, employing 800 workers, continued to operate until 1938. By that time, ten Jews had emigrated and 13 had left for other German cities. On *Kristallnacht* (9–10 Nov. 1938), the synagogue was burned down by the SA and J. men were detained in the Dachau concentration camp. Another 19 left by the end of 1939. The last six Jews were deported to the Gurs concentration camp on 22 Oct. 1940 while ten of those who had fled to other German cities were also dispatched to the camps.

HODASZ Szatmar dist., Hungary. Jews arrived in the late 19th cent., numbering 279 in 1900 and 167 in 1941. They were deported to Auschwitz via Mateszalka in late May 1944. Sixteen survivors immigrated to Israel.

HODMEZOVASARHELY Csongrad dist., Hungary. Jews settled in the mid-18th cent. under the protection of Count Sandor Karolysi. The community grew despite local hostility, reaching a peak pop. of 1,685 (3% of the total) in 1880. A J. school was founded in 1845 and enrolled 138 children by 1857, when a synagogue was consecrated. In 1869, the community formed a Neologist congregation. At the turn of the century, an organ and choir were introduced into the synagogue and services were conducted in Hungarian. A splendid new synagogue was erected in 1908. Between the World Wars, an increasing tendency toward assimilation was felt, with 48 converting to Christianity in 1938–39. During the White Terror, the Calvinist bishop of Debrecen, Baltazor, intervened on behalf of the Jews in H. In 1930, the J. pop was 1,151. In Oct. 1941, Jews were seized for forced labor and at the end of June 1944 all were transferred to the Szeged ghetto. A day later, some were deported to Auschwitz and the rest sent to the Wiener-Neustadt labor camps in Austria. About 400, mainly from Austria, survived the war and reestablished the community, which steadily dwindled thereafter.

HODOD (Hung. Hadad) N. Transylvania dist., Rumania. Jews settled in the late 18th cent. The J. pop. in 1920 was 128 (7% of the total). In May 1944, the Jews of H. and the surrounding villages were transferred to the Simleul Silvaniei ghetto and in June deported to Auschwitz.

HODONIN Moravia, Czechoslovakia. There was a large J. community from the first half of the 17th cent. In 1693, fire destroyed nearly all J. homes and in 1754, when about 140 J. families were present, 119 J. homes burned down. The Jews were expelled in the 18th cent. after their pop. reached a figure of around 400. In 1798–1848, only 13 J. families received residence rights. A J. elementary school was founded in 1863 as the J. pop. climbed to 433 in 1869 and a

1885–86. A school building was erected in 1906–07. The J. pop. reached a peak of 149 (total 5,836) in 1885. The community became independent in 1908. Despite the rise of antisemitism and the establishment of a Nazi Party branch in the town during the Weimar period, Jews were active socially and politically. Wilhelm Mossbach served on the municipal council from 1924 to 1933. The congregation was Liberal, with J. shopkeepers staying open on the Sabbath and some celebrating Christmas. However, a *mohel* from Hagen and a kosher butcher shop continued to serve the community. In mid-1933, the J. pop. was 81 (total 16,372). Under the Nazis, Jews were expelled from local organizations and J. students from public schools. By Nov. 1938, 34 Jews had left and the synagogue was no longer being used for prayer. The day after *Kristallnacht* (9–10 Nov. 1938), J. homes and stores were destroyed and J. men were sent to concentration camps (Oranienburg, Sachsenhausen, and others). From 1939, Jews were subjected to forced labor in quarries and subterranean construction sites. Up to 1942, another 21 Jews left H. Of the 34 who moved to other German cities, seven later perished in the camps. Nine were deported from H. on 23 or 28 April 1942 and another four on different occasions. All perished.

HOHENSTEIN   (Pol. Olsztynek) East Prussia, Germany, today Poland. There was a small J. settlement of eight in 1831. In 1880, the J. pop. was 111, dropping to 55 in 1925. The community maintained a synagogue and a cemetery established in the first half of the 19th cent. When the Nazis assumed power, only 33 Jews were still living in H. The synagogue was sold in 1935. Those Jews who did not manage to emigrate were deported and perished.

HOLATIN   (Hung. Tarfalu) Carpatho-Russia, Czechoslovakia, today Ukraine. Jews probably settled in the early 19th cent., numbering 43 in 1830 and 58 in 1880. Some Jews farmed small plots of land. The J. pop. rose to 158 in 1921 after the creation of the Czechoslovakian Republic and then fell to 138 (total 970) in 1941. In Aug. 1941, after the annexation of the town to Hungary, a number of J. families without Hungarian citizenship were expelled to Kamenets-Podolski and murdered. The rest of the Jews were deported to Auschwitz in the second half of May 1944.

HOLESOV   Moravia, Czechoslovakia. Jews are mentioned in 1391. Fire destroyed most homes in the mid-16th cent. In the 17th–18th cents. Jews traded mostly in cloth, hides, cotton, wool, and poultry. Heavy taxation under Maria Theresa and a devastating fire in 1745 debilitated the community but in the 18th–19th cents. it was one of the largest and most important in Moravia, its pop. rising from 1,032 in 1794 to 1,764 (about 25% of the total) in 1869. The Jews were active in trade and as artisans. A Reform synagogue was consecrated in 1893. Following anti-J. riots in 1899, many Jews left, their pop. dropping to about 1,200 in 1914 and, after post-WWI rioting, to 273 in 1930. In 1919, the community's J. elementary school, which had been established decades earlier, was closed down. In 1942, 200 J. families from H. and its environs were deported to the Theresienstadt ghetto. Of these, 259 Jews were sent to Uhersky Brod on 23 Jan. 1943. Most were deported to Auschwitz during the year. The Nazis destroyed the new synagogue. After WWII, the J. quarter was restored; a museum of Moravian Jewry was opened; and the grave of R. Shabbetai ben Meir ha-Kohen (the Shakh; 1621–62) became a place of mass pilgrimage from around the world.

HOLIC   Slovakia, Czechoslovakia, today Republic of Slovakia. Jews are first mentioned in 1593 and in the 17th cent. maintained a community under the protection of Count Czobor. H. was closely connected by origin to the nearby town of Hodonin in Moravia. In the 18th cent., the community became one of the largest and most important in Slovakia. In 1736, it came under the protection of the Hapsburg emperors. Heavy taxes subsequently undermined the flourishing J. economy. In 1751, Maria Theresa broadened J. rights in an unprecedented charter of privileges covering the 63 J. families in H. A J. school was opened in 1784 and a synagogue in the baroque style in 1786. The J. pop. reached a peak of 1,316 (total 4,939) in 1869, organized as a Status Quo congregation, and then dropped sharply as the young began to leave. In 1919, the J. pop. was 503. J. homes were looted and vandalized in postwar riots. The Zionists continued their prewar activity and Jews remained prominent in trade, owning 40 of the city's 65 stores in the 1920s. In 1940, 360 Jews remained, soon forced out of their businesses by the Slovakian authorities. In late March 1942, young J. men and women were deported to the Majdanek and Auschwitz concentration camps, respectively.

Families were deported next — 210 Jews to the death camps of Poland on 6 June and dozens of families in July. Altogether, 90% of the Jews were deported in 1942.

HOLLABRUNN   Lower Austria, Austria. Jews first settled in H. at the end of the 17th cent. A J. cemetery was consecrated in 1876 and enlarged in 1909. In 1901, a religious association (*Kultusverein*) and burial society were founded. Jews were engaged in trade. In 1934, there were 420 Jews in H. and 334 in March 1938. Many managed to emigrate. Immediately after the *Anschluss* (13 March 1938) J. shops were looted. In May, J. houses were confiscated. In Sept. 1938, the synagogue was handed over to the municipality, just before Jews were forced to leave for Vienna.

HOLOBUDY   Bialystok dist., Poland. H. was founded as a J. farm settlement in the late 1860s and had a J. pop. of 109 in 1921. In Nov. 1942 all the Jews were executed by the Germans in the Wiszniki forest.

HOLOBY   Volhynia dist., Poland, today Ukraine. The J. pop. in 1921 was 200 (total 1,456). All Jews were brought to the Mielnica ghetto in late 1941 and murdered there on 3 Sept. 1942.

HOLSZANY   Vilna dist., Poland, today Lithuania. Jews probably first settled in the 18th cent., trading in lumber, flax, and pig bristles. Jews also owned a small beer brewery, a flour mill, and hide-processing shops. Most had small auxiliary farms. The Zionist Socialists gained influence after the failure of the 1905 revolution. In WWI the Jews suffered from severe food shortages during the German occupation as well as from the depredations of the Cossacks and General Haller's Polish troops. In 1922 clerical agitation led to a pogrom. Between the World Wars the Jews maintained their prewar pop. of around 1,000 (50% of the total) as heavy taxes added to their economic distress. A modern Hebrew school founded in the face of Orthodox opposition offered a wide range of cultural activity, including a choir, drama circle, and Hebrew library. Hashomer Hatzair prepared many of the young for *aliya*. Under Soviet rule in 1939–41, all J. businesses were nationalized but J. religious life went undisturbed. Under the German occupation, a *Judenrat* and ghetto were set up. About 200 young Jews from the age of

12 were sent to the Zhazhmir labor camp in Lithuania. Another 150 Jews were sent to the Wolozyn ghetto together with the refugees who had congregated in H. and were massacred there in May 1942 along with the local pop. The rest were expelled to the Oszmiana ghetto in Oct. 1942 and were subsequently executed in various localities.

HOLUBICZE   Vilna dist., Poland, today Lithuania. Jews settled in the wake of the May Laws of 1882 and numbered 90 families (of a total 100) in 1931. Many of them were tailors and shoemakers but were reduced to peddling between the World Wars and often saved from starvation by their auxiliary farms. The Germans arbitrarily executed 46 Jews in the market square on their arrival in June 1941. The rest were murdered outside the town in April 1942.

HOLUBINNE   (Hung. Galambos Holubina) Carpatho-Russia, Czechoslovakia. One J. family lived in the town in 1768. The J. pop. grew to 30 in 1830 and 121 (total 775) in 1880. In 1921, under Czechoslovakian rule, it reached 186. Among J. breadwinners were nine tradesmen, six artisans, a few farmers, and a flour mill operator. In 1941, the J. pop. was 209. The Hungarians occupied H. in March 1939, drafting a number of Jews into forced labor battalions. A few J. families without Hungarian citizenship were expelled to Kamenets-Podolski in Aug. 1941 and murdered. The rest of the Jews were deported to Auschwitz in mid-May 1944.

HOLYN   Stanislawow dist., Poland, today Ukraine. The J. pop. in 1921 was 122. The Jews were probably expelled to Kalusz for liquidation in Aug. 1942.

HOLYNKA   Nowogrodek dist., Poland, today Belarus. A number of Jews were present in the mid-16th cent. as leaseholders, tax farmers, and distillers. In 1766, 215 were living there. In 1897 they numbered 339 (total 719), with most working the land. Emigration to South America with ICA aid at the turn of the cent. helped reduce the J. pop. to 224 by 1921. As many as 140 Jews were murdered by the Germans on their arrival in June 1941. The rest were expelled to the Dereczyn ghetto and murdered there or in Slonim in summer 1942.

HOLZAPPEL   Hesse-Nassau, Germany. In 1843,

the Jews of H., Isselbach, and three other villages established a community which numbered 67 in 1905. On *Kristallnacht* (9–10 Nov. 1938), 15 Jews remained in H. (and approximately the same number in Isselbach). At least 12 perished in the Holocaust.

HOLZHAUSEN (Rauisch-Holzhausen) Hesse–Nassau, Germany. Although Jews lived there in 1553, the community was established much later, numbering 78 (12% of the total) in 1861. Yitzhak Ruelf (1831–1902), rabbi of Memel and a pioneer German Zionist, belonged to a local J. family. Under Nazi pressure the community disposed of its synagogue before *Kristallnacht* (9–10 Nov. 1938). The last nine Jews were deported to the Theresienstadt ghetto in 1942.

HOLZHAUSEN AN DER HAIDE Hesse–Nassau, Germany. Numbering 43 (6% of the total) in 1871, the community dwindled to 18 in 1933. All the Jews left by 1940.

HOLZHAUSEN UEBER DER AAR Hesse–Nassau, Germany. Dating from the 16th cent., the community numbered 78 (12% of the total) in 1861. It disbanded in 1938: 14 of the 21 Jews emigrated; four deportees perished in the Theresienstadt ghetto.

HOLZHEIM Hesse, Germany. Jews lived there from 1640 and the community gained official status in 1836. It numbered 52 (4% of the total) in 1880, but thereafter declined. In the late 19th cent. the most extreme antisemitic party won 90% of local votes. Six of the 19 Jews who remained after 1933 managed to emigrate; 11 were deported in 1942.

HOLZMINDEN Brunswick, Germany. There is evidence of Jews in H. in 1557 and in 1600, but a permanent community only dates from about 1690. It grew to 50–60 individuals in 1793 and a peak of 130 members in 1890. A synagogue was established in 1836 and subsequently two cemeteries (1724, 1883). On the eve of the Nazi rise to power in 1933, there were 85 Jews living in H. Already in Feb.–Mar. 1933, Nazis were attacking Jews and their businesses. By Nov. 1938, only 18 Jews remained in the town, of whom eight were arrested on *Kristallnacht* (9–10 Nov. 1938) and deported to the Buchenwald concentration camp. The synagogue was devastated and J. businesses and homes were wrecked and looted. Since emigration continued after Nov. 1938, only two Jews were deported directly from H. to the Theresienstadt ghetto in 1942. However, others were deported from the places where they had hoped to find shelter. In all, at least 38 Jews from H. perished under Nazi rule.

HOMBERG Rhineland, Germany. Fewer than ten Jews lived in H. in the late 19th cent. The community expanded with the growth of the city, reaching a pop. of 87 (total 26,290) in 1925. In June 1933, the J. pop. was 44, with 17 left in May 1939. Eight Jews were deported to the Riga ghetto in Dec. 1941.

HOMBERG AN DER EFZE Hesse–Nassau, Germany. Although Jews lived there from 1679, an independent community was only established in 1909, numbering 36 (1% of the total) in 1925. It had no synagogue and the Jews worshiped in private homes. Most left before 1939; two perished in the Holocaust.

HOMBERG AN DER OHM Hesse, Germany. Founded in 1707, the community grew to 94 (about 6% of the total) in 1895 but dwindled thereafter and ceased to exist in 1937. By 1940 no Jews remained.

HOMBURG Palatinate, Germany. Jews are first mentioned in 1686. In 1791, ten families were present, among them the horse trader Shemuel David, one of the richest men in the principality and a supplier to the court. In 1848, the community reached a peak pop. of 281. Of the 55 family heads, 32 were brokers and 15 livestock dealers. Jews served on the municipal council. The community was officially recognized in 1823. A J. school was opened in the same year, with 45 children attending in 1869. A new synagogue was consecrated in 1862. During the Weimar period, Jews expanded their commercial horizons. In 1921–31, 56 new businesses were opened, including 14 in textiles and 11 in the tobacco industry. J. charities were started and the Zionists and Central Union (C.V.) became active. In mid-1933, 157 Jews remained. By 1935, most Jews had sold or liquidated their businesses, with only four or five families remaining. On *Kristallnacht* (9–10 Nov. 1938), the synagogue was partially burned and the five J. men in the city were sent to the Dachau concentration camp. In all, 135 Jews left H. in 1933–40, 80 emigrating to France and 23 to other German cities. On 22 Oct. 1940, 17 Jews were deported to the Gurs con-

centration camp. A total of 29 perished in the camps, including 16 in Auschwitz.

HOMBURG, BAD see BAD HOMBURG.

HOMBURG AM MAIN Lower Franconia, Germany. The J. pop. grew from 63 in 1815 to 100 in 1883 (total 762) and numbered 36 in 1933. On *Kristallnacht* (9–10 Nov. 1938), the windows of the synagogue were smashed. Twenty-two Jews left H. in 1938–41, ten of them emigrating from Germany. Of the seven remaining in 1942, five were deported to Izbica in the Lublin dist. (Poland) via Wuerzburg on 25 April.

HONNEF, BAD see BAD HONNEF.

HOOF Hesse-Nassau, Germany. The Jews of Breitenbach, Elmshagen, and H. established one community in the 18th cent. Wolf Breidenbach (1751–1829), who grew up there, was a famous champion of J. emancipation. This rural community became the largest in Kassel, enlarging its synagogue in 1854 and numbering 172 (over 16% of the total) in 1861. By 1925 it had declined to 106 (7%). Most Jews emigrated after 1933 and the fate of those who remained is uncertain.

HOOGEVEEN Drenthe dist., Holland. The J. presence dates back to the late 17th cent. A community was organized in 1755, numbering 443 in 1883, but declined to 238 in 1911. The J. pop. in 1941 was 218 (total 17,908). In Oct. 1942, 235 Jews were arrested and sent to Eastern Europe, where they all perished; 22 survived in hiding.

HOOGEZAND-SAPPEMEER Groningen dist., Holland. J. settlement began in the early 18th cent. A community building, including a synagogue and school, was built in 1854. The first female doctor and a leading women's rights activist in Holland was Aletta Jacobs (1854–1929) from Sappemeer. In 1883, 327 Jews were living in H. but their numbers subsequently dwindled. The J. pop. was 132 in 1941 while in nearby Slochteren it was 67. The Jews were deported to Poland in the Holocaust; only 15 survived.

HOORN Noord-Holland dist., Holland. Portuguese Jews began to settle there in 1622 and Ashkenazi Jews in the 18th cent. Organized community activity, including J. education, began in the mid-18th cent.

The J. pop. in 1892 was 306. Many left for Amsterdam in the late 19th cent. In July 1940, 82 German refugees who had come to H. were sent to the Westerbork transit camp. The J. pop. in 1941 was 50 (total 12,988). In April 1942 all the Jews were sent to Amsterdam and were later deported. Five escaped deportation and survived; a few others hid.

HOPPSTAEDTEN Oldenburg, Germany. A J. family was present in 1670. The number of Jews rose to 56 in 1808 and a peak of 212 in 1872. The community had a synagogue consecrated in 1836 and a cemetery. In June 1933, the J. pop. was 74. By Nov. 1938, 20 had emigrated and 19 had moved to other German cities. The synagogue was vandalized on *Kristallnacht* (9–10 Nov. 1938), but the building was not set on fire out of fear of damaging adjacent buildings. Of the five Jews arrested, four were sent to the Dachau concentration camp. By May 1939, 23 Jews were left. The last 16 were deported in 1942.

HORAZDOVICE Bohemia, Czechoslovakia. It is believed that Jews were present from the founding of the city in the 13th cent. In the 16th cent., they dealt mainly in grain and from the early 17th also in livestock. A new synagogue was built after the old one burned in 1868. The J. pop. grew with the coming of the railroad in the late 19th cent. Twelve smaller settlements were attached to the congregation in 1893 and the J. pop. in the area reached 187 in 1921. In 1939, the J. pop. of H. was 196. Under the German occupation, the Jews suffered the fate of the Jews of Prague and the surrounding area. In Oct. 1941, synagogue prayer was banned. Those who did not leave before the end of 1941 were deported to the Theresienstadt ghetto in 1942 and from there to the death camps of Poland. Eighteen survived.

HORB Wuerttemberg, Germany. The 14th cent. community was destroyed in the Black Death persecutions of 1348–49. The J. settlement was renewed in the second half of the 19th cent. and numbered 134 (5% of the total) in 1900. J. merchants controlled factories, business establishments, and a bank and were a dominant factor in the town's commercial life while social relations with the local pop. were satisfactory. In 1933, 100 Jews remained. Windows were broken and the house of prayer desecrated by Hitler Youth on *Kristallnacht* (9–10 Nov. 1938). Sixty Jews managed to

emigrate; 25 were expelled to their deaths in Kiev and the Theresienstadt ghetto and the rest died locally. After the war the richly designed wooden synagogue dating to 1733 was moved from H. to the Staedtisches Museum in Bamberg, which loaned it to the Israel Museum, Jerusalem.

HORBOURG (Ger. Horburg) Haut-Rhin dist., France. In 1723 Duke Leopold Eberhard de Wuerttemberg authorized the first J. family to settle in H. Until 1748, only two to four families lived there, but later the number increased. By 1784, there were 18 families (92 individuals) residing there. A new synagogue was inaugurated in 1837. The community numbered 410 Jews in 1851, dropping over the next 25 years to 299. In 1906, there were 21 children in the local J. school. In 1910, only 134 Jews lived in H. In 1931, the synagogue was renovated and reopened. By 1936, there were 60 Jews in H. During WWII, the Germans expelled all (in 1940) to the south of France together with the rest of Alsace-Lorraine Jews. Eight were deported to Auschwitz. In 1953, only 20 Jews remained in H.

HORGOS Vojvodina dist., Yugoslavia. There were 53 Jews in 1931 (total 9,749). The community perished in the Holocaust.

HORICE Bohemia, Czechoslovakia. Jews first settled in 1637. In 1782 they opened an elementary school and in 1784 they were permitted to purchase houses outside the J. quarter. By 1789, their pop. was 406, dropping to 201 in 1900. In the 19th cent., Jews contributed significantly to the local economy. J. textile plants employed nearly 1,800 workers in 1896 and Jews also manufactured chemicals, rope, alcoholic beverages, and *matza*. In 1930, the J. pop. was 73 (total 8,299). At the outset of WWII, some Jews managed to flee Europe. The rest were assembled in the dist. center of Hradec Kralove in Dec. 1942 and from there, on 17 and 21 Dec., transported to the Theresienstadt ghetto together with the other Jews in the dist. Most were deported to Auschwitz in 1943; few survived.

HORINCOVO (Hung. Herincse) Carpatho-Russia, Czechoslovakia, today Ukraine. J. settlement began in the first half of the 18th cent., with two J. families present in 1746. The J. pop. then rose to 134 in 1830 and 358 in 1880. A number of Jews were farmers and Jews owned a few flour mills. The J. pop. increased to

715 in 1921 under Czechoslovakian rule and to 871 (total 5,397) in 1941. The Zionist youth organizations were active and a few of the young emigrated to Palestine after a period of pioneer training. The Hungarians occupied the town in March 1939 and in 1940–41 drafted about 100 Jews into labor battalions, some for forced labor, some for service on the eastern front, where many died. A number of Jews without Hungarian citizenship, who were rounded up for expulsion in Aug. 1941, eluded the net and were able to return home. The Jews remaining in H. were deported to Auschwitz in late May 1944.

HORN (I) Lippe, Germany. A shortlived J. settlement existed at the beginning of the 16th cent. and another one from the beginning of the 17th cent., until the Jews were expelled from the Lippe dist. in 1614. A new settlement began in 1683. The community remained small, with a peak pop. of 55 in 1890. A synagogue was established in 1859 and a cemetery in 1850. By June 1933, 29 Jews were living in H. On *Kristallnacht* (9–10 Nov. 1938), the synagogue's interior was wrecked and J. businesses and homes were destroyed. A J. woman was injured during the rioting and died. The J. men were abused and taken to the Buchenwald concentration camp; one died soon after his release as a result of his detention. Of the six Jews who were still in H. by May 1939, five were deported in 1942 and one died prior to the deportations.

HORN (II) Lower Austria, Austria. J. settlement began in the 14th cent. In 1338, several Jews were murdered, accused of desecrating the Host. From the beginning of the 17th cent. some Jews were allowed to settle in H. for a short period. The first permanent settlement dates from 1857 and numbered five families. In 1870 a burial society was founded and in 1873 services were held in a private home. A synagogue, which also housed a J. elementary school from 1874, was inaugurated in 1903. By 1880, the J. pop. stood at 89, declining to 52 in 1910 (total 3,059). Jews owned small shops and were artisans. They were represented in the professional class as civil servants and doctors. Although antisemitism was marked in H., it became violent only after the *Anschluss* (13 March 1938). In March 1938 several Jews were arrested. "Aryanization" of J. shops started in May and ended in 1940. By Sept. 1938, 18 Jews had managed to emigrate; the remaining 17 were forced to leave H. and to abandon all their

property. On *Kristallnacht* (9–10 Nov. 1938), J. property was confiscated and the synagogue and some J. houses were looted and severely damaged.

HORNE OZOROVCE   (Hung. Felsoozor) Slovakia, Czechoslovakia, today Republic of Slovakia. Jews were present in the early 18th cent., if not before. Their pop. reached a peak of 201 (total 520) in 1828, declining rapidly in the late 19th cent. through emigration to the cities. With 16 Jews remaining in 1930, the community attached itself to the Banovce congregation. Seven of the eight J. families there in WWII were deported to the death camps in spring 1942.

HORNE SALIBY   (Hung. Felso Szeli) Slovakia, Czechoslovakia, today Republic of Slovakia. Jews appear to have settled in the late 18th cent. and were af-

filiated with the Galanta congregation, organizing a community together with the Jews of Dolne Saliby in about 1840. A synagogue was erected in the mid-19th cent. and a J. elementary school was opened c. 1880. The J. pop. rose to 189 (total 3,473) in 1910. Agudat Israel became active after WWI. Jews traded in farm produce and owned a few factories and farms. In 1941, their pop. was 178. Under Hungarian rule, their livelihoods were undermined and men were seized for forced labor. On 12 June 1944, the Jews were deported to Auschwitz after short stays in Galanta and Nove Zamky.

HOROCHOW   Volhynia dist., Poland, today Ukraine. Jews are recorded from 1536 and were living on a separate street under the local count's jurisdiction from 1601. Trade improved under Russian rule after the

Synagogue and marketplace in Horochow, Poland

Second Partition of Poland (1793) fixed the border nearby. In 1897, the J. pop. reached 2,571 (total 4,699). The town suffered during WWI and the Jews suffered subsequently during the brief rule of the Petlyura forces. With H. a provincial capital under Polish rule from 1920, the economy picked up somewhat, but the Jews remained hard-pressed despite controlling the trade in grain, cattle, and poultry as well as a number of crafts. The community was divided by rival hasidic sects (Olyka, Turzysk, Stolin-Karlin). The Zionists became active in the early 20th cent., with the youth movements operating pioneer training farms between the World Wars. A Hebrew school existed. The Germans took the town on 26 June 1941 and appointed a *Judenrat*. On 12 Aug., an *Einsatzkommando* unit rounded up and murdered 300 Jews in the municipal park with Ukrainian assistance. With the addition of 2,000 refugees, the ghetto set up in Oct. 1941 contained 5,000 Jews. Sporadic killing continued. On 8 Sept. 1942 all were brought to freshly dug pits outside the town and executed.

HORODEC   Polesie dist., Poland, today Belarus. Jews are first mentioned in the mid-16th cent. Through the 19th cent. they operated small factories. They were also active in the food and clothing trade. The Zionists became active in the early 20th cent. In 1897 the J. pop. stood at 648 (total 1,761). In WWI, most fled in the fighting. Finding the town in ruins on their return, they survived by living off abandoned peasant land. At the outset of Polish rule, emigration to Palestine and across the sea increased, reducing the J. pop. to 269. The Germans captured the town on 24 June 1941, imposing a regime of forced labor and in May 1942 sealing the Jews into a ghetto. On 26 July, all were brought to Brona Gora and murdered.

HORODEK   (Grodek) Volhynia dist., Poland, today Ukraine. The J. pop. in 1921 was 62 (total 856). Shortly after a violent Ukrainian local pogrom on 20 July 1941, the Jews were taken to the Maniewicze ghetto to meet their end.

HORODENKA   Stanislawow dist., Poland, today Ukraine. Jews are first recorded in the second half of the 16th cent. but the organized community dates from the early 18th when it had 14 smaller settlements attached to it. H. was a stronghold of the Shabbatean and Frankist movements. Hasidism was also present

in the person of R. Nahman of H., an intimate and pupil of the Ba'al Shem Tov. Under Austrian administration from 1772, the community suffered economic hardship, particularly the J. distilleries, which were subjected to discriminatory policies. After 1848 there was some improvement in economic conditions, with the town's market with its shops and stalls the focus of J. commercial life. Subsequently Jews also entered the dining and lodging trade. At the beginning of the 20th cent. many Jews involved in providing loans to the area's peasants went bankrupt when bank credit was curtailed. Jews also faced stiff competition in trade and crafts from the Poles and Ukrainians. Antisemitism also increased. With the occupation of H. by the Russian army in Sept. 1914, Jews became the target of rape and robbery and nine Jews were hanged. In the early 20th cent, R. Mikhael Hager of the Vizhnitz dynasty resided here. Between the World Wars, too, the community faced severe hardship, having been left with 200 widows, 220 orphans, 450 razed houses, and a pop. dropping to around 3,000 as against over 4,000 (almost 40% of the total) at the turn of the cent. The economic crisis intensified in the 1930s. Zionist activity flourished, with 250 Jews from H. settling in Palestine in the 1919–39 period. With the arrival of the Red Army in 1939, J. communal and political life came to an end, though the town remained one of the East Galician centers of underground activity for the Zionist youth movements. The Hungarian army entered H. on 2 July 1941 and local Ukrainians immediately instituted a regime of persecution and discriminatory measures through the municipal council and the Ukrainian militia. The Germans took over the administration of the town in Sept. In Nov., the Jews were herded into a ghetto and the first *Aktion* took place on 4–5 Dec. 1941, with 2,500 Jews transported out of the town and machinegunned down beside open pits. In a second *Aktion*, on 13 April 1942, 1,400 Jews, including refugees who had fled to H., were deported to the Belzec death camp while another 60 were murdered at the local cemetery. Deportations continued through May and June and the systematic liquidation of the ghetto commenced in July. The last Jews were deported to Belzec or sent to the Janowska labor camp in Lwow on 6 Sept. 1942. Of those who escaped to the forests, some joined partisan groups while around 40 managed to cross the Rumanian border. H. was liberated on 27 March 1944 and the few survivors left for the West.

HORODLO Lublin dist., Poland. The community that formed in the late 16th cent. was destroyed in the 1648–49 Chmielnicki massacres. A new community was established in the first half of the 18th cent. Jews engaged in tax farming and manufactured and sold alcoholic beverages. Most of the community's rabbis were followers of Radzyn Hasidism, but Gur, Trisk (Turzysk), and Belz Hasidism were also represented. The J. pop. was 717 (total 2,112) in 1897 and 994 in 1934. Zionist influence grew after WWI and a Tarbut Hebrew school was founded. The Germans captured H. on 26 Sept. 1939. In spring 1941, they razed the synagogue and turned the J. cemetery into a pasture. In late May–early June 1942, all the Jews were transferred to nearby Uchanie and from there deported to the Sobibor death camp on 10 June after two labor groups were sent to the Stazhin estate and Stawy concentration camp. Those sent to the Stazhin estate were murdered in the fall.

HORODNIA Chernigov dist., Ukraine. Jews settled in the 19th cent., numbering 446 in 1834 and 1,249 (total 4,310) in 1897. Jews were attacked in a pogrom in 1905 and similarly abused by the town's rulers on 23 May 1918. The J. pop. dropped to 731 in 1939. The Germans captured H. on 18 Aug. 1941 after over half the Jews fled. Twenty-one were executed in Sept. as alleged "saboteurs and robbers." On 20 Dec., 75 J. families were brought to the local jail and murdered.

HORODNITSA Zhitomir dist., Ukraine. The J. pop. was 427 in the mid-19th cent. and 1,310 (total 2,314) in 1897. Many Jews were employed in a large porcelain factory as clerks and production workers. In 1939, under the Soviets, the J. pop. was 1,212. The Germans arrived on 10 July 1941. Some Jews managed to flee. During the occupation, 218 people were murdered, most of them apparently Jews.

HORODNO Polesie dist., Poland, today Belarus. The J. pop. in 1921 was 583. Almost all the Jews were killed in the Holocaust.

HORODYSZCZE Nowogrodek dist., Poland, today Belarus. A J. community existed in the early 18th cent., reaching a pop. of 2,108 (total 2,631) in 1897 but dropping to 760 in 1921 after the evacuation of WWI. A fire in 1886 destroyed half the town, including three prayer houses. The Germans entered H. on 27 June 1941.

They murdered all the Jews except skilled workers outside the town on 20 Oct. 1941; the rest were killed a few months later.

HORODZIEJ (Gorodej) Nowogrodek dist., Poland, today Belarus. A small J. settlement existed before the Russian conquest of the late 18th cent. The community grew to 698 (total 754) in 1897 and to 1,137 including refugees in WWII. Under the German occupation, the Jews were placed in a ghetto and subjected to forced labor and an exorbitant tribute. All were murdered outside the town on 18 July 1942.

HOROVICE Bohemia, Czechoslovakia. Jews were present in the 15th cent. Their residence was banned from the early 17th cent. until the mid-19th cent. A synagogue was erected in 1903. The J. pop. was 279 in 1910 and 50 in 1930. The Nazis banned synagogue prayer in Oct. 1941 and in 1942 deported the Jews of H. to the Theresienstadt ghetto together with the Jews of Prague and the surrounding area. From there they were sent to Auschwitz. Few survived.

HORSOVSKY TYN Bohemia (Sudetenland), Czechoslovakia. The original J. community was apparently destroyed in 16th cent. disturbances. It was renewed only in the late 19th cent., reaching a pop. of 99 in 1921. In 1930, the J. pop. was 52. On the annexation of the Sudetenland to the German Reich, the Jews fled. Sixteen J. prisoners were buried in H. after perishing in a death march from one of the Nazi concentration camps.

HORST-EMSCHER Westphalia, Germany. Jews settled following the industrialization of the city in the late 19th cent., seizing the opportunity for trade. With the arrival of East European Jews to work in the coal mines in WWI, the J. pop. grew from 47 in 1910 to 113 (total 24,663) in 1925, with the Zionists gaining majority support. In 1932, 90 Jews remained. The Jews of H. shared the fate of the Jews of Gelsenkichen.

HORSTMAR Westphalia, Germany. Jews were present in the 16th cent. They numbered 19 in 1816 and 65 (total 1,004) in 1905. A synagogue was erected in 1853 and a J. elementary school was opened in 1901 with 18 children attending in 1913. In 1905, the community attached itself to the Orthodox Recklinghausen

rabbinate. In 1933, the J. pop. was 43. By Oct. 1938, many Jews had emigrated. On *Kristallnacht* (9–10 Nov. 1938), the synagogue was destroyed as were J. homes. The last Jews left the town in July 1939.

HORYNGRAD-KRUPA Volhynia dist., Poland, today Ukraine. The Jews numbered 540 (total 1,936) in 1897 and 307 in 1921. With the German occupation, the Ukrainians murdered 25 Jews on 6 July 1941 and 60 the next day. The rest were taken to the Tuczyn ghetto, participating in the revolt of 24–25 Sept. 1942; few survived.

HORYNIEC Lwow dist., Poland, today Ukraine. The J. pop. in 1921 was 120. The 150 Jews present in WWII were expelled to Lubaczow in May 1942.

HOSSZUPALYI Bihar dist., Hungary. Jews arrived in the late 18th cent., numbering 105 in 1880 and 98 in 1930. Jews in H. suffered from the country's racial laws and forced labor in the Carpathian Mountains. When the Germans arrived, they deported the Jews to Auschwitz via Nagyvarad in late May 1944.

HOSTINNE Bohemia (Sudetenland), Czechoslovakia. Jews are first mentioned in the last quarter of the 18th cent. Their pop. was 62 in 1880; 106 in 1910; and 57 in 1930 (1.3% of the total). The Jews fled when the Sudetenland was annexed to the German Reich in Sept. 1938.

HOSZCZA Volhynia dist., Poland, today Ukraine. Jews probably settled in the second half of the 16th cent., growing slowly to a pop. of 884 in 1897 (total 2,091). Zionist activity began early in the 20th cent. In WWI, many Jews left the town and at the end of the war the Jews were victimized by the Petlyura gangs and Polish soldiers. The economic situation improved with the large Polish army camped in the area. A Hebrew school and kindergarten existed. In the German aerial bombardment of 29 June 1941, 165 Jews were killed; ten more were murdered by German soldiers on entering H. on 4 July. The community was liquidated in three *Aktions*: 400 Jews were murdered on 20 May 1942, 350 on 25 Sept., and 123 on 14 Nov.

HOTIN (Pol. Chocim) Bessarabia, Rumania, today

Summer camp for needy children organized by Jews of Hotin, Rumania, 1932

Ukraine. A Karaite community existed in the late 14th cent. and records refer to J. inhabitants in the 18th cent. When the district governor refused permission to lease land in 1866, 80 J. families (some from Falesti and Calarasi) immigrated to Eretz Israel to work land bought with the aid of Baron Rothschild. The location of H. on the Rumanian-Ukrainian border enabled the Jews to trade on both banks of the Dniester River. In the late 19th cent. the community had a hospital and at the beginning of the 20th cent. a synagogue (the first of 26) and a J. school were opened. H. was the first J. community in Bessarabia to organize officially after the Russian Revolution (1917) and was recognized by the authorities in 1929. The Bialik library with books in Hebrew and Yiddish was the largest in Bessarabia. The J. pop. was 5,781 in 1930 (38% of the total). On 13 July 1940, after the entry of the Red Army, Jews were arrested. Zionists, politicians, and government officials were taken to a special camp where most died. A second group, the majority, was taken by train to Siberia and set to work felling trees in the forests. In Oct. they were released to find work and food in the area. In H. the J. community facilities were closed down in 1940 and the remaining Jews were persecuted. In June 1941, 60 J. children and their mothers were killed when the hospital was bombed. Those who succeeded in fleeing the German army by crossing into the Ukraine were later murdered in Kamenets-Podolski. Rumanian forces entered the town on 7 July 1941 and murdered over 2,000 Jews. Some 3,000 Jews, including those from neighboring villages, were marched across the border by German troops and shot. Another 180 Jews who had found hiding places in H. were killed. On 30 July, the remaining Jews were taken on foot to a camp at Secureni where 12,000 Jews of the area were concentrated and later murdered. There were only 300 survivors from H. on liberation. Of these, males up to age 45 were conscripted into the Soviet army; women were sent to work in the coal mines. Few returned after the war and the majority immigrated to Palestine.

HOYA AN DER WESER   Hanover, Germany. J. traders lived there from 1710 and established a community that opened a synagogue in 1833 and an elementary school in 1865. The small neighboring community of Buecken was abandoned in 1866. H. maintained social and charitable institutions. Marcus Lehmann, rabbi of the Orthodox congregation in Mainz

and founder in 1860 of *Der Israelit*, belonged to a prominent local family. Although its synagogue was renovated in 1908, the community had no religious leadership after WWI. In June 1933, nearly four months after the Nazi takeover, 28 Jews were counted in H. Those who had played a leading role in civic and economic affairs fell victim to the Nazi boycott. Communal life revived under external pressure. Branches of the Central Union (C.V.) and J. War Veterans Association were active. On *Kristallnacht* (9–10 Nov. 1938), the synagogue was burned and J. stores were looted. Only six Jews managed to reach safety. Those who had taken refuge in Holland were deported to the Bergen-Belsen concentration camp and the remaining Jews were deported to the Warsaw and Theresienstadt ghettoes in 1942. Four survivors emigrated to the U.S. after WWII.

HRADEC KRALOVE   Bohemia, Czechoslovakia. Jews were present from the founding of the city in 1225 but a community is only known from the late 14th cent. From the mid-15th cent. to the mid-16th cent., they were expelled a number of times. A new community was founded in 1860. A synagogue was consecrated in 1905, when the J. pop. was about 300 (3% of the total). The Zionists were active after WWI. Victor Fishl (Avigdor Dagan) was born in 1912 in H. He served as an aide to Jan Masaryk and was a senior Israeli diplomat. In 1930, there were 425 Jews in H. After the annexation of the Sudetenland to Germany in Sept. 1938, J. refugees arrived and antisemitism intensified as Jews were gradually isolated socially and economically. Eighty converted between 1938 and 1941. About 1,200 Jews from H. and other towns were deported to the Theresienstadt ghetto and the death camps of Poland on 17 and 21 Dec. 1942. Just 16 from H. survived.

HRANICE   Moravia, Czechoslovakia. According to tradition, Jews settled in H. between 1475 and 1553, but a community in a J. quarter is only known from 1644. Its pop. reached 120 families in 1788. In 1857, the J. pop. was 802 with a new synagogue built in 1864; the old J. school (founded in 1770) was expanded in 1865. In 1938, 143 Jews remained. Another 80 arrived after the annexation of the Sudetenland to Nazi Germany in Sept. On 26 June 1942, 202 Jews were deported to the Theresienstadt ghetto via Olomouc and from there to the death camps of Poland.

HRONOV Bohemia, Czechoslovakia. Jews in small numbers were present from the 19th cent. In 1930 their pop. was 65 (1.5% of the total). On 17 Dec. 1942, the Jews were deported to the Theresienstadt ghetto via Hradec Kralove. Most were sent to Auschwitz in 1943. The artist Friedl Dicker-Brandeis, active in Theresienstadt as an educator, was deported in Oct. 1944 to Auschwitz, where he perished.

HROUBOVICE Bohemia, Czechoslovakia. Jews first settled in the early 18th cent. The J. congregation was dissolved in the late 19th cent. Thirty Jews were present in 1930. Those remaining after the German occupation were deported to the Theresienstadt ghetto via Pardubice in Dec. 1942. Most were sent on to Auschwitz in 1943; two survived.

HRUBIESZOW Lublin dist., Poland. Jews are mentioned in the first half of the 15th cent. as tax farmers

Carrying water, Hrubieszow, Poland, 1940

and as merchants doing business in Walachia, Turkey, the Crimea, and Kiev. In 1578, they were granted extensive rights by King Stephen Bathory. Almost completely destroyed during the Chmielnicki massacres of 1648-49, the J. community was soon reestablished, opening a yeshiva and becoming influential in the Council of the Four Lands. In 1736, a fire destroyed the synagogue and 27 J. homes. In the 18th cent., Jews exported farm produce to Danzig (Gdansk) in the Bug–Vistula River trade. In the second half of the 19th cent., they were active in industry, operating two steam-powered flour mills, a beer brewery, a plant for the repair of farm machinery, and a printing press. They also entered the building trades. R. Yosef ben Mordekhai Katznelbogen (d. 1830) of Neskhiz (Nesukhoyezhe), one the leaders of Polish Hasidism, settled in H. in 1818, initiating the construction of a J. shelter for mental patients, a pharmacy, and a hospital, the first medical institution in Poland for Jews and maintained by them. A new synagogue was consecrated in 1874 and an old age home was opened in 1905. Trisk, Kotsk, Gur, Belz, and Ruzhin Hasidim all had their own *shtiblekh* and courts. The J. pop. grew from 2,924 in 1827 to 5,341 (total 9,813) in 1921. Increasing poverty caused many to emigrate to the U.S. and other lands in 1890–1905. In the aftermath of WWI, Jews suffered at the hands of Polish and Ukrainian soldiers. Jews owned several factories (hide processing, soap, metal works) and 333 stores of the 372 in H. but most, despite assistance from the Joint Distribution Committee, suffered from the general economic crisis and heavy taxation which caused hundreds to emigrate, mainly to Argentina and Mexico. In 1931, Jews numbered about 7,000. Zionist influence increased between the World Wars and many of the young left for Palestine, including Yosef Almogi, future minister in the Israeli government and mayor of Haifa. Agudat Israel and the Bund were also active, the latter particularly in the trade unions. Agudat Israel ran a Beth Jacob school for girls and the Zionists opened a Hebrew public school in 1919. Many young people left with the Red Army on 3 Oct. 1939 as the invading German army approached. On 2 Dec. 1939, the Germans led 1,000 Jews (and another 1,100 from Chelm) on a four-day death march to the Bug River, which left 1,500 dead. In early 1940, 6,000 Jews, including refugees from other cities and towns, were crowded into a ghetto and a *Judenrat* was appointed to supply forced labor and

Market day in Hrubieszow, Poland

"contributions." Hundreds more ·refugees arrived from Czenstochowa, Cracow, and Mielec. In May 1942, there were 5,690 Jews in H. In early June, over 3,000 Jews were deported to the Sobibor death camp. The 180 who resisted were murdered at the J. cemetery. The last 2,500 Jews, employed in German factories, were rounded up for deportation to Sobibor on 28 Oct. 1942. Four hundred who resisted were murdered at the J. cemetery and 160 of the young were left behind in a labor camp.

HRUSOVO (Hung. Kortvelyes; Yid. Hrishaf) Carpatho-Russia, Czechoslovakia, today Ukraine. J. settlement probably began in the early 19th cent. though one J. family was present in the first half of the 18th. In 1880, the J. pop. was 59 (total 1,197), increasing during the Czechoslovakian period to 149 in 1921. In the mid-1930s, a Bnei Akiva club and Agudat Israel branch were opened. The Hungarians occupied H. in March 1939 and in 1940-41 drafted a number of Jews into forced labor battalions, sending them to the eastern front. The J. pop. rose to 179 in 1941. In Aug., three

J. families without Hungarian citizenship were expelled to Kamenets-Podolski, where they were murdered. The rest were deported to Auschwitz in late May 1944.

HRUSZOW Lwow dist., Poland, today Ukraine. The J. pop. in 1921 was 164. The Jews were expelled to Lubaczow for liquidation in May 1942.

HUCZKO Lwow dist., Poland, today Ukraine. The J. pop. in 1921 was 202. The Jews were possibly expelled to a neighboring town or murdered locally in July-Aug. 1942.

HUEFFENHARDT Baden, Germany. The J. community was founded after the Thirty Years War (1618-48) but never grew beyond two or three dozen. The Jews earned their living from trade in livestock and farm produce. Seventeen remained in 1933 (total 930) and seven left by Oct. 1938. On *Kristallnacht* (9-10 Nov. 1938), the synagogue was destroyed, J. stores were vandalized, and J. men were detained in the Dachau concentration camp. Another two families

left for the U.S. in 1939 and the last two Jews were deported to the Gurs concentration camp on 22 Oct. 1940 and perished in Auschwitz.

HUELCHRATH Rhineland, Germany. Jews were present from the early 18th cent., numbering 55 in 1871 and consecrating a synagogue in 1875. Most members of the last three J. families in H. perished in the Holocaust.

HUELS Rhineland, Germany. Jews arrived in about the mid-17th cent. Their pop. grew to a peak of 156 (2.7% of the total) in 1871, dropping to 82 in 1906 and 60 in 1925. A J. school operated from 1852 to 1888. On *Kristallnacht* (9–10 Nov. 1938), the synagogue, built in 1883, was burned while J. homes and stores were vandalized. Nine Jews were deported to the Riga ghetto on 11 Dec. 1941 and 12 to the Theresienstadt ghetto on 25 July 1942. All perished.

HUENFELD Hesse–Nassau, Germany. Established in the 18th cent., the community rebuilt its synagogue after a fire in 1886 and numbered 126 (7% of the total) in 1885. A branch of the J. War Veterans Association was established in 1925. Twenty Jews were arrested by the Gestapo in 1935 and the community (numbering 55 in 1933) experienced a reign of terror. On *Kristallnacht* (9–10 Nov. 1938), the synagogue was destroyed. By 1939 only 12 Jews remained, 25 having emigrated. The last 11 Jews were deported to the Theresienstadt ghetto in Sept. 1942.

HUERTH Rhineland, Germany. A small J. settlement existed in the 18th cent. with the pop. trading in cloth and livestock and lending out money. From the early 19th cent. until WWII, it numbered a few dozen Jews. A synagogue was erected in 1856. Under the Nazis, most Jews left by July 1941, the majority to other German cities. Of the remaining Jews, six were deported to the Theresienstadt ghetto on 14 June 1942 and five to the Minsk ghetto on 19 July. All perished.

HUESTEN Westphalia, Germany. Jews are first mentioned in 1675. In 1801, 37 Jews (four families) were living there, with a J. school already in operation. A prayer room was organized in a private home in the mid-19th cent. and a synagogue was constructed in 1903. In 1924, the J. cemetery was desecrated. In 1933, the J. pop. was 112 (total 13,846). Under the Nazis, Jews were thrown out of sports clubs. On *Kristallnacht* (9–10 Nov. 1938), the synagogue was wrecked along with J. homes. The last J. stores were closed down or "Aryanized" in Dec. 1938. In March 1941, the Jews were confined to a quarantine camp and in May 1942 they were dispatched to the Theresienstadt ghetto or other camps in the east.

HUETTENBACH Middle Franconia, Germany. The community was probably founded by Jews expelled from Nuremberg in 1499. From the early 16th cent. until 1780 it was under the protection of the princes of the house of Lochner, developing considerably during the 18th cent. until subjected to heavy taxes and trade restrictions in the 1770s. In 1823 the J. pop. was 378, declining steadily thereafter to 35 in 1933 (total 705). Under the economic boycott of the Nazi era, two-thirds of the Jews left by 1938. The last 12 left after *Kristallnacht* (9–10 Nov. 1938).

HUETTENGESAESS Hesse–Nassau, Germany. The community built a new synagogue in 1842 and numbered 54 (5% of the total) in 1895. None of the 34 Jews living there in 1933 remained in 1938.

HUETTENHEIM Lower Franconia, Germany. The Jews maintained a continuous settlement from the late 16th cent., growing to 173 in 1812 (total 864) and thereafter dropping to 105 in 1867 and 24 in 1933. The J. cemetery, which served four other communities as well, was desecrated in 1935. Fifteen Jews left H. in 1933–37, another four (to the U.S.) in 1939, and the last five were deported to Izbica in the Lublin dist. (Poland) and to the Theresienstadt ghetto in 1942.

HUKLIVY (Hung. Zugo) Carpatho-Russia, Czechoslovakia, today Ukraine. One J. family was present in 1768. In 1880, the J. pop. was 177 (total 968) and included eight shopkeepers, five artisans, a few farmers, and a flour mill operator. The J. pop. was 304 in 1921 and 231 in 1941. After the Hungarian occupation, a number of Jews were drafted into labor battalions, some for forced labor, others for service on the eastern front, where most perished. In late July 1941, a few Jews without Hungarian citizenship were expelled to the German-occupied Ukraine and murdered. The rest were deported to Auschwitz in mid-May 1944.

HULEWICZE Volhynia dist., Poland, today Ukraine. Up to 20 J. families resided there from the mid-17th cent. but none after WWI.

HUMENNE Slovakia, Czechoslovakia, today Republic of Slovakia. Jews were present in the late 17th cent. and possibly earlier. A fine synagogue was erected in 1793 as the community began to expand and prosper, many trading in farm produce. The J. elementary school, opened in 1856, was moved to a new building in 1880 as the J. pop. rose to 1,280 (total 3,810). A yeshiva was founded in the 1880s and after the arrival of Galician refugees in the late 19th cent. a hasidic *beit midrash* and in 1906 a *shtibel* were added. R. Gottlieb Klein (1869–1946), a native of H., became chief rabbi of Sweden and R. Moshe Richtman (1880–1972) was a prominent scholar and Zionist leader. J. homes and stores were looted in post-WWI riots. In 1919, the J. pop. was 1,692 with 28 settlements under the jurisdiction of the local rabbinate. R. Hayyim Yehuda Ehrenreich published the important Orthodox periodical *Otzar Hayyim* until 1938. Jews owned about 90% of the commercial enterprises in the city. Agudat Israel was influential and dozens of Zionist youth movement graduates left for Palestine. Under Slovakian rule in WWII, J. businesses were closed down. In late 1941, the arrival of 120 refugees from Bratislava increased the J. pop. to 2,285. On 25 March 1942, 110 young J. girls were deported to Auschwitz, joined by another 70 on 2 April; 166 young men were sent to the Zilina concentration camp in the same period. Families were deported to Poland in May: over 400 Jews on 8 May and about 1,010 two days later. Most of the remaining 400 were evacuated to western Slovakia on 15 May 1944. Of the postwar community, 390 emigrated to Israel and other countries in 1949 while those remaining, about 150, maintained community life until the late 1970s.

HUMPOLEC Bohemia, Czechoslovakia. Ruins of a synagogue dating from the 13th cent. have been found and Jews are also mentioned in 1385. A synagogue was consecrated in 1762. In 1861, the community opened a J. elementary school. The J. pop. rose to 343 (6.3% of the total) in 1880 and then declined to 89 in 1930. Under the Nazis, most Jews were deported to the Theresienstadt ghetto together with the Jews of Brno and from there to the death camps. Few survived.

HUNCOVCE (Hung. Hunfalu; Yid. Unsdorf) Slovakia, Czechoslovakia, today Republic of Slovakia. H. was a major center of J. learning for 300 years. It was possibly settled by Moravian refugees in the late 16th cent. and later bolstered by refugees from the Chmielnicki massacres of 1648–49. For many years it was the only J. settlement in northern Slovakia. A *talmud torah* was opened in 1787, later becoming a J. elementary school. The first synagogue was built in the 1820s. R. Yehezkel Segal, who officiated at the time, is thought to be the founder of the famous local yeshiva, which, under R. Shemuel Rosenberg in the late 19th cent., reached an enrollment of 350, making it the second largest in Slovakia after the Bratislava yeshiva. The J. pop. grew from 563 in 1787 to 939 (total 2,148) in 1828 but dropped rapidly in the late 19th cent. after residence restrictions were lifted for the Spis dist. In 1919 the J. pop. was 275. After WWI most Jews identified with Agudat Israel. The J. pop. dropped further to 75 in 1940. Persecuted by Nazi supporters and the Slovakian authorities, the Jews were deported to the death camps in spring 1942.

HUNEDOARA (Hung. Vajdahunyad), S. Transylvania dist., Rumania. A J. Orthodox community existed in 1860. The J. pop. in 1930 was 173 (4% of the total). In June 1941, the J. pop was drafted into labor battalions. Communal life was restored after the war.

HUNGEN Hesse, Germany. Jews lived there from the 15th cent. and a community was established in 1700. Numbering 105 (8% of the total) in 1880, it was affiliated with the Orthodox rabbinate of Giessen, but services held in the synagogue (built in 1832) were accompanied by an organ and choir. After WWI, a local branch of the German Zionist Organization was established. In March 1933, some prominent Social Democrats (including a number of Jews) were arrested. The anti-J. boycott won popular support, and on the "Night of the Long Knives" (30 June 1934) SA and SS troops beat Jews attending Sabbath services. On *Kristallnacht* (9–10 Nov. 1938), Nazis vandalized the synagogue's interior and attacked community leaders. Of the 66 Jews living in H. after 1933, at least 29 emigrated (mainly to the U.S. or Palestine) by 1939; more than 20 were deported to the Theresienstadt ghetto in 1942.

HUNINGUE Haut-Rhin dist., France. A small J. community was established in the 19th cent. and a syn-

agogue was inaugurated in 1862. On the eve of WWII, 54 Jews lived in H. During the occupation, the Germans expelled all to the south of France, together with the rest of Alsace-Lorraine Jews. Subsequently there were no Jews in H.

HUSI Moldavia dist., Rumania. Jews settled from the mid-17th cent. An organized J. community existed in 1882. Zionist activity began in 1898. The J. pop. in 1899 was 4,057 (26% of the total, 70% of tradesmen). The community suffered from antisemitism and a blood libel in 1882. In the early 20th cent. and between the World Wars, antisemitism was rife, especially at the high school, from which J. students were expelled. In 1941, 120 Jews were arrested and kept in custody for two months. H. received Jews expelled from surrounding villages and provided them with food and clothing. After the war Jews returning from Transnistria (including 108 orphans) and refugees from north Bukovina settled here.

HUSIATYN Tarnopol dist., Poland, today Ukraine. Jew were among the first settlers in the town in the 16th cent. With the partition of 1772, most of the Jews remained on the Galician-Austrian side of the river dividing H. The town became a trade center and

J. economic life flourished. The economy was given a further boost when H. became a center of the hasidic Husyatin dynasty, with its opulent court enjoying the protection of the local count and attracting thousands of visitors. Refugees from the pogroms in Russia brought new revolutionary and Zionist ideas to H., whose J. pop. numbered 4,197 (two-thirds of the total) in 1890. The town's golden age ended with the Russian occupation of Aug. 1914. Only 29 of 700 J. houses were left unscathed and there was a large-scale exodus of the J. pop. Only 368 Jews remained in H. in 1921 (total 2,104). Despite the decline, communal life was maintained between the World Wars. The Soviet occupation of 1939–41 eliminated almost all private trade. The Germans occupied the town on 6 July 1941 and around 200 Jews, mainly males, were murdered in the same month with the participation of the Ukrainians. The last Jews of H. were expelled to Kopyczynce and Probuzna in March 1942 and shared the fate of the local Jews. (See also GUSYATIN.)

HUSSAKOW Lwow dist., Poland, today Ukraine. Jews are mentioned in H. from the 17th cent. The community grew to 629 in 1900 (40% of the total) but dropped by two-thirds with the sufferings of WWI, all those remaining supported by charitable funds. A pog-

The market in Husiatyn, Poland

rom in the wake of the German occupation (June 1941) claimed many of J. lives. The remaining Jews were deported to the Jaworow ghetto in Nov. 1942.

HUSTOPECE   Moravia (Sudetenland), Czechoslovakia. Jews were probably present in the late 14th cent. and formed a community by 1580. The community established a small synagogue in 1880, a cemetery in 1886, and a school. The J. pop. reached a peak of 260 (7.2% of the total) in 1900 and then dropped to 103 in 1930. On the annexation of the Sudetenland to the German Reich in fall 1938, most Jews left for other places in Bohemia and Moravia. A few also reached England and Palestine. The rest were deported to the Theresienstadt ghetto and subsequently to the death camps of Poland; most perished.

HUTA BRONITSKA   Zhitomir dist., Ukraine. The J. pop. in 1939 was 166 (total 1,412). The Jews were murdered after the German occupation of 13 July 1941.

I

IABLONITA Bukovina, Rumania, today Ukraine. Jews settled in the late 19th cent. and engaged in agriculture and livestock trading. The J. pop. in 1930 was 72. In June 1941, the Jews were transferred to Radauti and in Oct. deported to Transnistria.

IASI Moldavia dist., Rumania. Jews first settled in the late 15th cent. and when I. became the capital of Moldavia (1565) the J. community developed rapidly. The J. Guild (Breasla Jidovilor) was founded in 1622 and served as the central communal institution up to 1834. Jews dominated trade in spirits and wine, especially export to Poland and Walachia. In 1650, Cossacks set I. on fire and massacred Jews. During the late 18th cent., Jews from Galicia and Bukovina joined the community. Jews controlled the trade in agricultural products and cattle, and in the 19th cent. played a central role in most branches of commerce and industry. They replaced Turks and Greeks as bankers and moneychangers. J. craftsmen set up trade unions and each had its own synagogue. During the Greek revolt (1821), hundreds of Jews were massacred. When bubonic and typhus plagues struck in 1824–25 and again in 1829, the J. pop. was expelled to the surrounding hills and 32 children died of the cold. The Jews were expelled again during the cholera epidemic in 1831. Epidemics in 1847–48 took a toll of 3,000 Jews. Under the rule of Mihai Sturza (1834–49) Jews were persecuted by antisemites. During the last decades of the 19th cent., antisemitic manifestations were particularly severe and in 1884, over 140 J. stores were forced to close. The J. pop. in 1899 came to 39,441 (51% of the total). During this period, J. craftsmen constituted over 70% of the total and completely dominated the work force in 20 branches of crafts. The first synagogue was built in 1657–82 and many synagogues were named after the rabbis who served in them. Sephardi rabbis served the community from the end of the 16th cent. and some held the title of *Hakham Bashi* (the title of the chief rabbi in the Ottoman Empire). One of the greatest hasidic rabbis, R. Avraham Yehoshua Heschel of Opta (1755–1825), set up a court in I. In 1837–53, when R. Yosef Landau served as the community's rabbi, I. became a center of talmudic learning. Dr. I. Niemirower

Advertisement for performance of "The Miracle Worker," Iasi, Rumania, 1893 (Beth Hatefutsoth Photo Archive, Tel Aviv/photo courtesy of Yad Vashem, The Holocaust Martyrs' and Heroes' Remembrance Authority, Jerusalem)

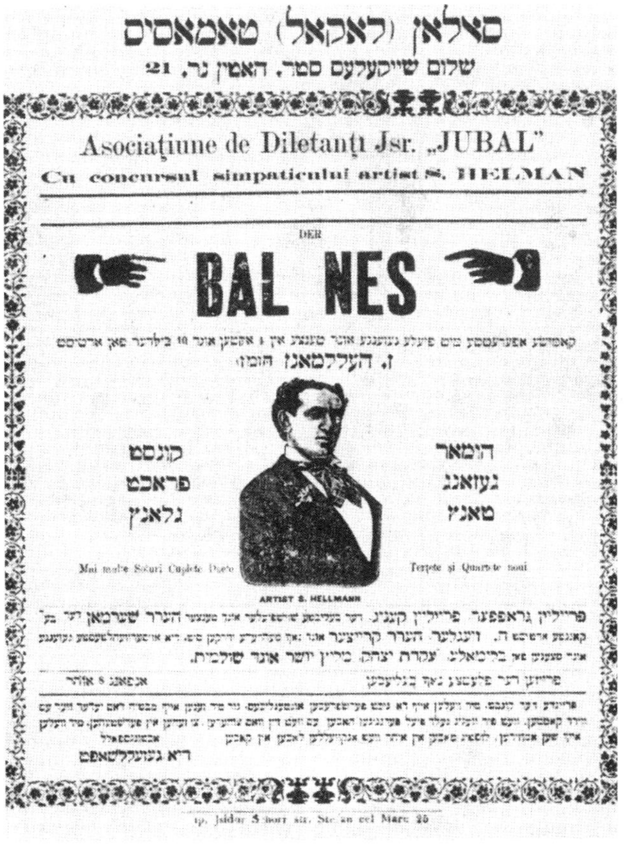
סאלאן (לאקאל) טאמאסים
Asociaţiune de Diletanţi Jsr. „JUBAL"
Cu concursul simpaticului artist S. HELMAN
DER
BAL NES
ARTIST S. HELLMANN

served as rabbi of the modern community in 1896–1911. After WWI, he became the chief rabbi of Rumania. In 1840, 12 *hadarim* were attended by 653 pupils. The first J. school for boys was opened in 1852 and for girls in 1854. Toward the end of the 19th cent., modern J. schools were established. When J. pupils were expelled from government high schools the J. community provided for their education. A J. hospital was opened in 1772 and at first received government support. By the end of the 19th cent. it depended on bequests and donations. In 1894, a clinic at the hospital attended 21,000–22,000 patients while 400–500 mothers gave birth or were under treatment at the J. maternity hospital. A J. orphanage was opened in 1818 and an old age home was founded in 1890. B'nai B'rith was active from the end of the 19th cent. in providing welfare for the poor. The Ohel Shem society disseminated the Hebrew language and culture during 1879–98. In 1878, the poet Naftali Herz Imber (1856–1909) wrote what was to became the J. national anthem, *Hatikva*, with a melody influenced by Rumanian folk music. A branch of the Eretz Israel Settlement movement was founded in 1880 and in 1882 the English Christian Zionist, Sir Laurence Oliphant (1829–88), attended the movement's national convention in I. Zionist groups flourished at the end of the 19th and the beginning of the 20th cents. and a Zionist federation was established in 1910. The Zionists opened a popular university in 1906 which provided courses and lectures by outstanding figures, such as Y.L. Peretz and Nahum Sokolow. A branch of the Union of Rumanian Jews (U.E.P) was opened prior to WWI and played an active role in advocating emancipa-

Banquet honoring Chaim Weizmann (seated seventh from the left), then president of the Zionist Organization, Iasi, Rumania, 1927 (Beth Hatefutsoth Photo Archive, Tel Aviv/photo courtesy of Yad Vashem, The Holocaust Martyrs' and Heroes' Remembrance Authority, Jerusalem)

tion for Jews. I. served as an important center of J. journalism and publishing. In 1842–43, the first Hebrew books in Rumania were printed there. The first Yiddish biweekly appeared from Oct. 1855 to Feb. 1871. Avraham Goldfaden laid the grounds for a Yiddish theater when he produced his plays there in 1876. During WWI, the economic situation of the J. pop. declined radically and over 75% required aid from the community. Between the World Wars, the number of pupils at J. schools declined when government schools were opened to Jews. In 1922, a teachers' seminary was opened with Hebrew as the language of instruction, but was closed a year later. In 1939, the community had one kindergarten, seven boys' and four girls' schools, four *talmudei torah*, and a yeshiva – with a total attendance of 2,250. The J. hospital expanded and in 1932–34 treated 72,462 patients. The old age home was enlarged in 1921. After WWI, the Zionist movement expanded. In 1924, a training center was opened together with Hehalutz in Bessarabia, and during the following decade 700 pioneers trained there prior to immigrating to Palestine. During 1932–40, the J. Party published in Rumanian, Yiddish, and Hebrew a weekly journal, *Tribuna Evreiasca*, with a circulation of 10,000–12,000 copies. Antisemitism at I. University flared up after WWI with the support of the government. In 1922, pogroms broke out led by students and Russian soldiers stationed in I. Attacks on Jews continued throughout the interwar period and J. students ousted from the university set up a self-defense unit. The economic situation of the Jews declined and the number of those requiring aid continued to increase. The J. pop. in 1930 was 35,465 (30% of the total). In 1938, J. lawyers were ousted from the Lawyers' Association and were prohibited from appearing in court.

During the Antonescu regime, the Iron Guard persecuted the Jews, plundered their property, and accused them of being Communist sympathizers. Following

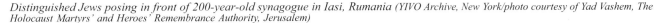

Distinguished Jews posing in front of 200-year-old synagogue in Iasi, Rumania (YIVO Archive, New York/photo courtesy of Yad Vashem, The Holocaust Martyrs' and Heroes' Remembrance Authority, Jerusalem)

an earthquake in 1940, two synagogues were torn down on the pretext that they were endangering the public. Jews appealed to the authorities and with the assistance of bribes succeeded in moderating the damage caused by Iron Guard Legionnaires. On 14 Oct. 1940, thousands of J. pupils and teachers were expelled from government schools and integrated into the J. school system. High schools were opened for boys (400 pupils) and for girls (200). School staff included university lecturers ousted from their posts. J. shops were boycotted and their owners forced to "sell" to the Iron Guard Legionnaires. In Sept. 1940, the Legionnaires closed the pioneer training farm. In June 1941, J. leaders, journalists, and intellectuals were charged as Communists and interned in the Targu-Jiu camp. On 28 June 1941, Rumanian and German soldiers raided J. homes, stole their property, and shot Jews in the streets. Thousands were rounded up and taken to the police station where they were charged with signaling to the Russian forces attacking from the air. In the afternoon, an air raid siren signaled the beginning of a massacre of the imprisoned Jews. All except 2,500 were killed. On 30 June, 2,430 Jews were herded onto a train. On 6 July it arrived at Calarasi with only 1,411 survivors. A second train transported 1,900 Jews to Podul-Iloaei. The 13 mile (20 km) journey took eight hours, during which 1,194 died of suffocation and thirst. It is estimated that during these few days a total of 12,000 Jews were murdered, although no official figures exist. This was the first massacre in Rumania. In spring 1942, the Rumanian parliament subsequently defined the massacre as a war crime. An order drafting J. men aged 18–55 into labor battalions was issued on 1 Aug. 1941 and 4,000 were sent to work sites throughout Rumania. On 6 Aug., the remaining Jews were ordered to move to designated neighborhoods and to wear yellow badges. Numerous Jews charged with defection from the labor battalions were arrested and condemned to death or exiled together with their families to Transnistria. The J. community hosted 4,000 refugees transferred from the surrounding villages. In April 1941, the J. pop. was 33,135. In spring 1943, the newly appointed antisemitic mayor, Constantin Ifrim, ordered the destruction of the 400-year-old J. cemetery with its 27,000 graves. Within 68 days, the area was cleared and all the J. remains were transferred to another J. cemetery. Entire J. neighborhoods were torn down and J. houses were destroyed during Soviet air raids. On 21 Aug. 1944, Soviet forces

entered I. and many Jews returned. After the war, the community was renewed and in 1947 numbered 38,000.

IBANESTI   Moldavia dist., Rumania. The J. pop. in 1930 was 61. In 1940, Rumanian soldiers together with the Iron Guard pillaged J. homes. The Jews were forced to leave for Dorohoi. They were then transported to Transnistria.

IBBENBUEREN   Westphalia, Germany. Jews were possibly present in the late 16th cent. Their pop. reached a peak of 106 in 1840 but subsequently declined steadily to 39 (total 7,266) in 1932. In the 19th cent., Jews were artisans as well as merchants and butchers. A synagogue was in use in 1846; a new one was consecrated in 1913. A J. elementary school was founded in 1838 but closed in 1853. In 1933, 12 J. families were living in I., most earning their livelihoods as cattle dealers and butchers. From 1933 to Oct. 1938, 14 Jews succeeded in emigrating, half to Holland, and 14 left for other German settlements. On *Kristallnacht* (9–10 Nov. 1938), the synagogue was set on fire and J. homes were vandalized. Another 20 Jews subsequently left the town. The last three Jews in I. perished after deportation to the east in 1942.

IBRANY   Szabolcs dist., Hungary. Jews settled in the late 18th cent. and numbered 235 in 1930. Zionism and Hasidism took hold in the community between the World Wars. Jews owned a flour mill, cement factory, dairy, and a factory for drying medicinal herbs. Four families of uncertain citizenship were expelled to Kamenets-Podolski in 1942 and executed. Those who were subjected to forced labor and remained in Hungary were saved. The rest were deported to Auschwitz at the end of May 1944.

ICHENHAUSEN   Swabia, Germany. Jews were present in the mid-16th cent., including the well-known Prague printer Hayyim Schwarz, who had previously resided in Augsburg. While in I. he produced a Pentateuch. In 1550, Jews expelled from Neuburg were allowed to settle there as were, shortly after, Jews from Guenzburg and Thannhausen. Jews were confined to a special quarter (*Judengasse*) until 1618, when King Matthias granted them freedom of movement and trade. A synagogue was consecrated in 1782. Only

Blessing for the new month, Ichenhausen, Germany, 1927

after the Bavarian annexation of 1806 was a Jew allowed to build a house outside the ghetto. In 1811, the J. pop. reached a peak of 893 (of a total 1,978). At mid-cent. over 200 children studied at a J. public school. The J. pop. fell with the commencement of emigration in the 1840s (65 leaving in 1849 alone), mainly to the U.S., France, and Italy. R. Aharon Cohn officiated in the community from 1874 to 1920 and also served as chief rabbi of Swabia. The Jews came to play a central role in the economic development of the town and pioneered the men's clothing industry in Swabia, with over 100 tailors employed in their factories in 1928. In 1933, 309 Jews remained. Under the Nazis, the Central Union (C.V.) was active and most of the youth belonged to the Juedischer Jugendverein and Maccabi. On *Kristallnacht* (9–10 Nov. 1938) the SS and Hitler Youth beat and arrested 80 to 100 Jews, the synagogue was vandalized, and hundreds of tombstones were knocked over in the cemetery. In 1933–41, 168 Jews managed to emigrate from I., 90 of them to the U.S. Another 64 moved to other German cities. Of the 129 present in 1942, 81 were deported to Piaski (Poland) via Munich on 3 April; 32 to the Theresienstadt ghetto on 6 Aug. 1942; and ten to Auschwitz on 8 March 1943.

ICHNIA   Chernigov dist., Ukraine. Jews settled in the mid-19th cent. and numbered 100 families in the 1880s. On 16 Aug. 1881, J. homes and stores were pillaged and destroyed in a pogrom. The J. pop. was 575 (of a total 18,638) in 1917 and 148 in 1939. The Ger-

mans arrived on 14 Sept. 1941. The few remaining Jews who had neither fled nor been evacuated were among the 225 people murdered in the area.

ICLODUL MARE   (Hung. Nagyiklod) N. Transylvania dist., Rumania. An organized J. community existed from the early 18th cent. A synagogue seating several hundred was built in 1834 and still exists. The J. pop. in 1930 was 176 (11% of the total). Aharon Hirsch, among the wealthiest men in Transylvania, owned extensive land in the area, and between the World Wars supported the J. community, as did his brother-in-law, Moshe Tischler, who was awarded a peerage by Emperor Francis Joseph. A yeshiva was opened in 1928 and in addition to rabbinical studies carpentry was taught. In summer 1942, Jews were drafted into labor battalions in the Ukraine, and on 3 May 1944 the entire community was expelled to the Cluj ghetto. On 26 May 1944, the Jews were deported to Auschwitz.

IDAR-OBERSTEIN   Oldenburg, Germany. First mentioned in the 16th cent., the O. community attracted Jews expelled from Rhine towns and, while governed by the margrave of Baden, opened a synagogue in 1784. Numbering 68 in 1808, the Jews of O. and I. established a communal union. When those in I. threatened to secede, Hanau's chief rabbi, Shimshon Felsenstein, reunited the community in 1834. Jews promoted new trades and industries (e.g., footwear, jewelry, textiles), and from 75 in 1865 their num-

ber grew to 151 (nearly 2% of the total) in 1872. Toward the end of the century, the members began to drift away from Orthodoxy. Branches of the Central Union (C.V.), the J. Women's League, and the German Zionist Organization were active before WWI. The J. pop. rose to 192 in 1910. During the Weimar Republic, the community declined to 129 in 1930 and the rate of intermarriage rose. J. cultural and social life intensified during the Nazi period. On *Kristallnacht* (9–10 Nov. 1938) J. men aged 18–60 were detained. Stormtroopers looted and destroyed the synagogue, vandalized J. property, and savagely beat Jews. Emigration accelerated with about 20 leaving for England, 12 for the U.S., eight for Palestine, and six (including a couple from Tiefenstein) for the Far East. Of the 34 Jews who remained in I., one committed suicide and 25 were deported (1940–45). Almost all perished in Auschwitz, the Theresienstadt ghetto, and other Nazi camps.

IDRITSA Kalinin dist., Russia. Jews probably settled in the late 19th cent. In 1939, they numbered 89 (total 4,224). After the Germans occupied the town on 15 July 1941, they murdered the few who had neither fled nor been evacuated.

IDSTEIN Hesse–Nassau, Germany. David Gruenhut was appointed district rabbi in 1709 and the Jews opened a synagogue in 1793. Numbering 75 in 1871 and 112 (3% of the total) in 1923, the community was affiliated with the rabbinate of Wiesbaden. On *Kristallnacht* (9–10 Nov. 1938), the synagogue's interior was destroyed, but most Jews had already emigrated. J. youngsters at the local home for retarded children were subjected to Nazi "euthanasia" in Hadamar.

IECAVA Zemgale (Courland) dist., Latvia. The J. pop. in 1935 was 46 (0.6% of the total). In July 1941, the community was expelled by the Germans to nearby Bauska and two days later murdered in the Weksules (Likbarten) forest with the local Jews.

IERNUT (Hung. Radnot) S. Transylvania dist., Rumania. A. J. community existed here in 1887 and was attached to the Tarnaveni community. The J. pop. in 1930 was 84 (3% of the total). Zionist activity flourished in 1931. After the outbreak of WWII, the J. pop. was transferred to Blaj.

IERNUTENI (Hung. Radnotfaja) N. Transylvania dist., Rumania. The J. pop. in 1920 was 52 (14% of the total). In May 1944 the Jews were transferred to the Reghin ghetto and in June deported to Auschwitz.

IEUD (Hung. Jod) N. Transylvania dist., Rumania. Jews settled in the early 18th cent. The J. pop. in 1920 was 360 (13% of the total), declining in the 1930s. In April 1944, the community was transferred to the Viseul de Sus ghetto and then deported to Auschwitz.

IFFREN (also Yefren) Tripolitania dist., Libya. The J. settlement in the Jebel Nefusa Heights, 110 miles (175 km) southwest of Tripoli, was the oldest in Tripolitania. It originated, according to tradition, when the Arab King Fanjar, who served under Titus at the time of the destruction of the Second Temple, brought J. captives from Eretz Israel to I. Jews fleeing persecution in the coastal towns may also have arrived in the early Christian period (fourth cent.) as well as in the Byzantine period (sixth cent.). Settlement was continuous until the Ottoman period, when many Jews, persecuted by both Berber and Arab tribesmen, fled to Tripoli and the coastal area, leaving behind in I. the three communities of Disir, al-Qsir, and al-M'eaniyim. Jews were mostly itinerant peddlers, selling among other items woven goods made by J. women. Unlike those from the coast, the J. women of I. worked outside the home at weaving, at the local oil and wine presses, and as shepherdesses. J. merchants, dealing in spices, coffee, tea, honey, sugar, and tobacco, served as middlemen in the trade between Tripoli and the mountain region and Central Africa. Because of their role in trade and crafts, including weaponry and medicine, the Jews came to enjoy the protection of local tribes. Each of the three communities of I. kept its own financial accounts. Of the many ancient synagogues, the al-Ghariba synagogue of al-M'eaniyim was said to be endowed with particular holiness. Although local Moslems honored the synagogue as well, this did not prevent them from setting it afire in 1910. Ownership disputes with the Berbers arose over the land where the Disir synagogue, built in 1714, was located. The J. pop. reached a peak of about 1,000 at the beginning of the 20th cent., dropping to 302 (total 14,626) in 1931 as many Jews fled to the coast, particularly to Zuara, during the Arab Revolt of 1915–22. The Jews of I. were untouched by modernization. In spring 1942, the Ital-

ians set up a small detention camp in I. for the Jews of Cyrenaica deported under Mussolini's orders. The largest of the concentration camps, Jado, was located farther away, in the central part of Jebel Nefusa. Of the 2,600 Jews from Cyrenaica held there, nearly 600 perished. After the riots of 1945, most Jews of the three communities of I. left for Gharian, Zuara, and Tripoli in anticipation of their mass *aliya* to Israel.

IGENE   (Ger. Agenhof) Courland dist., Latvia. The J. settlement of 40 families was abandoned during WWI.

IGLIAUKA   Marijampole dist., Lithuania. The J. pop. of 51 was killed off in the Holocaust.

IGNALIN   Vilna dist., Poland, today Belarus. Jews from the surrounding villages settled in I. and formed an organized community by the early 20th cent. The J. pop. grew to 593 (of a total 773) in 1925. Between the World Wars, J. butchers supplied the Polish army and J. merchants dealt in grain, flax, wild berries, and mushrooms. About 70 J. stores, stalls, and workshops operated in the marketplace. Many lost their sources of livelihood in the economic depression of the late 1920s and in the face of competition from government-supported Polish cooperatives and the anti-J. economic boycott. Community activity expanded, with the Zionists and Bund active and Tarbut and CYSHO schools operating. After a two-year Soviet occupation, the Germans arrived on 2 July 1941. Executions followed and 1,200 Jews including refugees were confined to a ghetto. On 27 Sept. 1941 they were brought to a transit camp near Nowo Swienciany and on 7 Oct. over 1,000 were executed.

IGNATOWKA   (Lozishch) Volhynia dist., Poland, today Ukraine. Founded as a J. farm settlement on 700 acres of royal land in 1838, its pop. reached 1,204 in the early 20th cent. Emigration in the WWI period, much of it to ICA settlements in Argentina, reduced it by half. The German occupation of June 1941 was followed by a pogrom carried out by Ukrainians. On 24 Aug. 1942 the community was expelled to Zofjowka and murdered within a few days. Some young Jews joined the Kovpak partisan division

IHRINGEN   Baden, Germany. A few J. families expelled from Ulm were allowed to settle in I. in the early 18th cent. through the efforts of the Court Jew Josef

Guenzburger. A synagogue was completed in 1761. Conditions gradually improved after the annexation to Baden in the early 19th cent., with the community growing to a peak pop. of 263 in 1852 (total 2,336). In 1933, 98 Jews remained. In 1936, J. children were expelled from the local school. On *Kristallnacht* (9–10 Nov. 1938), the synagogue was burned. By 1938, 22 Jews had emigrated and 21 had moved to other German cities; six more left Germany in 1939. By 1940 another 28 had moved to other German cities. The last 12 Jews, all elderly, were expelled to the Gurs concentration camp on 22 Oct. 1940. Two survived the Holocaust.

IKOR   Crimea, Russia, today Ukraine. I. was founded in 1923 by about 40 J. families (202 people) as a J. agricultural settlement within the general framework of J. agricultural settlement in the Crimea. The J. pop. was 636 in 1926 but dropped to 200 in 1932. A J. council (soviet) and elementary school were in operation. The Germans occupied I. in late Oct. 1941. On 24 Dec., a *Sonderkommando 11b* unit murdered 31 Jews. A few dozen J. farmers who survived the Holocaust in the interior of the Soviet Union returned to the settlement after the war but apparently left afterwards.

ILAVA   Slovakia, Czechoslovakia, today Republic of Slovakia. Jews were present in the mid-17th cent. A synagogue was erected in the late 18th cent. and a Status Quo congregation was formed in 1869. A new synagogue was built in 1881 as the J. pop. reached a peak of 190 (total 1,831). The community also maintained a J. elementary school. After WWI the Zionists became active. Jews served on the local council and owned 13 business establishments, 12 workshops, and two factories, including one for wood products employing 200 workers and exporting to England and other countries. In 1940, the J. pop. was 131. In 1941, Jews were forced out of their businesses and in spring 1942 deportations commenced: the young to the Majdanek and Auschwitz concentration camps in late March and early April; families to Auschwitz and other death camps via Zilina in April and June. In all, over 70% of the Jews in the county were deported in 1942. The Germans transported the last Jews to Auschwitz via Sered on 18 Sept. 1944.

ILEANDA MARE   (Hung Nagyilonda) N. Transylvania dist., Rumania. A J. community was established

in the 1830s, and at the end of the 19th cent. nearly all the commerce and small industry of I. and the surroundings were run by Jews. A yeshiva with 30–40 students existed there between the World Wars. Zionist activities began in the 1920s. The J. pop. in 1930 was 308 (26% of the total). In June 1942, 11 Jews were drafted into labor battalions in the Ukraine; only two survived. In May 1944, 900 Jews were expelled to the Dej ghetto and later deported to Auschwitz. The community's rabbi from 1926, R. Josef Paneth, succeeded in escaping deportation together with his family. After the war he served the survivors until the community dispersed in 1950.

ILINO Smolensk dist., Russia. Jews settled in the early 1840s and numbered 21 in 1847, their number rising to 1,105 (of a total 1,415) in 1897. In the Soviet period, their pop. declined to 378 in 1926 and 221 in 1939. In WWII, nine Jews were killed in German air attacks. Following the German occupation of 22 July 1941, the 200 Jews of I. and its environs were confined in a ghetto but escaped death when the town was liberated by the Red Army on 25 Jan. 1942.

ILINTSY (Lints) Vinnitsa dist., Ukraine. J. settlement began in the mid-17th cent. The J. pop. was 386 in 1765 and 4,993 (of a total 10,039) in 1897. In 1909, a private boys' school was in operation. In the Soviet period, many Jews belonged to cooperatives, especially those centered around the food industry as well as tailoring and shoemaking. A local J. council (soviet) was established in the 1920s and a J. school was active until 1937. In 1939, the J. pop. was 2,217 after dropping through internal migration. The Germans entered I. on 23 July 1941, setting up a *Judenrat* and exacting a tribute of gold and silver from the community. In late Aug., the Jews were concentrated in a ghetto. In Nov., Ukrainian police murdered 43 J. men. Together with the Germans, they murdered another 1,000 Jews on 24 April 1942 and on 27–28 May, 700 were executed outside the city. In Dec. 1942, the Germans burned a number of buildings where Jews were hiding and then shot them as they tried to escape. Jews in a labor camp near the town formed the nucleus of a J. partisan company — in the 2nd Stalin Brigade — with 39 of its 124 fighters from I. Another 20 local Jews served in other partisan units in the dist.

ILISESTI Bukovina, Rumania. Jews first settled in the mid-19th cent. All were Hasidim of the Vizhnitz and Sadagora sects. The J. pop. in 1930 was 191. In 1940 the J. pop. was transferred to Suceava and Gura Humorului. After war broke out between Rumania and the USSR, the Jews were deported to Transnistria.

ILJA Vilna dist., Poland, today Belarus. Jews probably arrived in the 17th cent. and formed an organized community with two synagogues (for Hasidim and *Mitnaggedim*) in the 18th cent. In 1809, eight families from among the followers of the Vilna Gaon emigrated to Palestine. Despite the small size of the community (829 Jews in 1897 in a total pop. of 1,431), it maintained a large yeshiva. In the late 19th cent., the influence of Haskala and Zionism spread. Many Jews were employed in a J. glassware factory and some emigrated to America when it closed down temporarily in WWI. A number of wealthy J. merchants dealt in lumber and flax. In WWI most fled on the approach of the Cossacks. When the Jews returned after the war, they found their homes destroyed. Between the World Wars the Jews endured much economic hardship despite the revival of commerce and industry. Hehalutz and Betar sent groups of pioneers to Palestine and a Hebrew school opened in 1922 despite the opposition of Habad Hasidim. With the arrival of the Germans in June 1941, Jews were seized for forced labor while peasants looted J. homes. In Sept. 1941 they were confined to a ghetto. On 15 March 1942, in retaliation for a partisan attack, 770 Jews were taken to a refrigeration plant, ordered to undress, and shot. The remaining 100 skilled J. workers were executed outside the town on 7 June. A few escaped and joined the partisans.

ILK Szatmar dist., Hungary. Jews settled in the late 18th cent., numbering 131 in 1880 and 65 in 1930. In late May 1944, they were sent to Mateszalka and from there to Auschwitz.

ILLEREICHEN-ALTENSTADT Swabia, Germany. Jews first settled after the Thirty Years War (1618–48) but failed to establish a permanent community. A new community was founded in 1719 by Jews expelled from Thannhausen. A synagogue and cemetery were consecrated in that same year. Jews traded in horses and cattle, jewelry, and agricultural produce. A new synagogue was built in 1803 and 57 children were enrolled in the J. public school in 1833. From a peak of 403 in 1834, the J. pop. declined rapidly

through emigration in 1838–54 to the U.S., numbering 46 (total 1,599) in 1933. On *Kristallnacht* (9–10 Nov. 1938), the synagogue was vandalized. Of the Jews remaining in 1942, 13 were deported to Piaski (Poland) via Munich on 3 April and seven to the Theresienstadt ghetto on 4 July 1942.

ILLINGEN   Saar, Germany. Evidence of the first Jew dates from 1717, but Jews were probably already living in I. in the 17th cent. In 1763, there were nine J. families living in I. At its peak in 1910, the community numbered 270. In 1859 a new synagogue was dedicated and in 1895 I. became an independent synagogue community, its school becoming a public J. elementary school (closed in 1933). Between 1926 and 1929, there were three J. representatives on the town council. By March 1935, when the Nazis annexed the Saar, the community numbered 115. Large-scale emigration began and by 1936 only 41 Jews were left. The community was merged with Merzig and Neunkirchen. On *Kristallnacht* (9–10 Nov. 1938), the synagogue was burned down, the cemetery was desecrated, and stores and homes were wrecked. J. men were deported to the Dachau concentration camp. After the Saarbruecken community was disbanded, I. took over the communal care of the region's Jews. On 22 Oct.1940, the town's last 19 Jews were taken to the village of Forbach and from there deported to the Gurs concentration camp, where 15 perished. The Nazis murdered at least 37 Jews from I., including those who had moved elsewhere within Germany as well as those who had emigrated to neighboring countries, seeking safety.

ILMENAU   Thuringia, Germany. Jews probably lived there from the 14th cent. to 1566. There is evidence of J. settlement during the 17th and 18th cents. but a permanent community only developed in the 19th cent. The J. pop. was 54 in 1910 and 80 in 1932. On *Kristallnacht* (9–10 Nov. 1938), the synagogue was vandalized. Six Jews were arrested and two were deported to the Buchenwald concentration camp. No further information is available about the fate of the other Jews in I.

ILNICE   (Hung. Ilonca) Carpatho-Russia, Czechoslovakia, today Ukraine. Jews probably settled in the early 19th cent. In 1880, their pop. was 475 (total 2,872). After the establishment of the Czechoslovakian

Republic, it rose to 759 in 1921 and to 887 in 1941 under the Hungarians. The Hungarians annexed the town in March 1939 and in 1941 drafted dozens of Jews into labor battalions for forced labor or assignments on the eastern front, where many died. In late July 1941, a number of J. families without Hungarian citizenship were expelled to Kamenets-Podolski and murdered. The remaining 800 were deported to Auschwitz in the second half of May 1944.

ILNIK   Lwow dist., Poland, today Ukraine. Between the World Wars the J. community of a few hundred, mostly farmers, constituted 5–10% of the total pop. The Germans arrived in July 1941 and persecution began. Most were deported via Turka to the Belzec death camp in 1942; others were murdered in the forests, some after offering armed resistance.

ILOK   Croatia, Yugoslavia, today Republic of Croatia. A J. community existed from the late 19th cent. until the Holocaust. There were 304 Jews in 1921 (total 5,475) and 310 Jews in 1940. They were killed by the Croatian Ustase.

ILOVAYSK   Stalino dist., Ukraine. The J. pop. in 1939 was 93 (total 15,222). The Germans captured I. on 23 Oct. 1941, setting up two prisoner-of-war camps where over 1,000 were confined and 69 shot, including an unknown number of Jews.

ILUKSTE   Zemgale (Courland) dist., Latvia. Jews began to settle at the end of the 18th cent. The community grew under Russian rule in the 19th cent., reaching a pop. of 1,016 (total 4,100) in 1910. All left in WWI and 71 were present in 1935 (total 1,300). The Jews were transferred to the Daugavpils (Dvinsk) ghetto after the German occupation of June–July 1941 and perished there.

ILUW   (Yid. Ileve) Warsaw dist., Poland. Jews settled there in the mid-18th cent. and by 1921 numbered 374 (about 50% of the total). Under the German occupation from Sept. 1939, the Jews were expelled to nearby ghettoes and sent on to the Warsaw ghetto in Feb. 1941.

ILVA MARE   (Hung. Nagyilva) N. Transylvania dist., Rumania. Jews first settled in the early 19th cent. The J. pop. in 1920 was 140 (4% of the total).

In May 1944 the Jews were transferred to the Bistrita ghetto and in June deported to Auschwitz.

ILVA MICA (Hung. Kisilva) N. Transylvania dist., Rumania. Jews first settled in the early 19th cent. The J. pop. in 1920 was 199 (11% of the total). In May 1944 the Jews were transferred to the Bistrita ghetto and in June deported to Auschwitz.

ILVESHEIM Baden, Germany. Jews were present from the 18th cent. Their pop. grew to 150 in 1825 (total 1,034). With liberalization in the 1850s, Jews from I. enrolled in the medical faculty of Heidelberg University. Many of the young left for other German cities in the 1860s and for the U.S. In 1933, 28 Jews remained, gradually isolated economically and socially. The synagogue was vandalized on *Kristallnacht* (9–10 Nov. 1938) and six Jews were sent to the Dachau concentration camp. By 1939, 17 had left the town, ten for the U.S. The last seven were deported to the Gurs concentration camp on 22 Oct. 1940 and died in the Holocaust.

ILZHA Kielce dist., Poland. Jews settled in the early 19th cent., their pop. growing from 542 in 1861 to 2,069 (total 4,230) in 1897 as Jews helped pioneer the glass and porcelain industry. Jews also owned local flour mills and quarries. After the relocation of the main J. porcelain factory, the J. pop. dropped to 1,545 in 1921. Between the World Wars, the local Tarbut Hebrew school served the region and the Zionist influence was marked. After the German occupation of Sept. 1939, a *Judenrat* and a ghetto were established in July 1941. Its 1,900 residents were deported to the Treblinka death camp in Oct. 1942.

IMBRADAS (Yid. Imbrad) Zarasai dist., Lithuania. The J. pop. in 1923 was 50. All Jews were killed in the Holocaust.

IMSTICOVO (Hung. Misztice; Yid. Mystytchev) Carpatho-Russia, Czechoslovakia. Jews probably settled in the first half of the 19th cent. and numbered 96 (total 1,364) in 1880. In 1921, in the Czechoslovakian Republic, their pop. was 137 and in 1941, under the Hungarians, 125. The Jews were deported to Auschwitz in mid-May 1944.

INDRA Latgale dist., Latvia. The J. pop. in 1935 was 46 (total 294). The Jews were expelled by the Germans to the Daugavpils (Dvinsk) ghetto in late July 1941 and murdered a few days later in the Pogulanka forest.

INDURA Bialystok dist., Poland, today Belarus. Jews are first mentioned in 1539. In 1720, I. was the seat of the Lithuanian Council after it broke away from the Council of the Four Lands. Though dominated by *Mitnaggedim*, the community was an important hasidic center under R. Hayyim Haikel (1772–87), who continued to preside despite a ban on him issued by the J. communities in the province of Grodno in 1781. The J. pop. grew from 1,220 in 1847 to 2,194 (total 2,674) in 1897. The synagogue was rebuilt after a devastating fire in 1882. Haskala made inroads in the late 19th cent. and the Bund became active in the early 20th cent. J. tradesmen mainly traveled from village to village in the neighborhood. Emigration brought the J. pop. down to 1,709 in 1921. Economic conditions deteriorated between the World Wars, with 10–12-year-old children working 14-hour days in sweatshop conditions. Community rabbis included R. Reuven Katz, subsequently rabbi of Petah Tikva. Zionist activity increased. The youth movements organized pioneer training and the Tarbut Hebrew school was the focus of cultural activity. After two years of Soviet rule, the Germans arrived in summer 1941 and soon confined the Jews to a ghetto. In Nov. 1942 they were deported to the Treblinka death camp via the Kelbasin transit camp near Grodno.

INEU (Hung. Borosjeno) S. Transylvania dist., Rumania. A Neologist J. community was founded in 1891. The J. pop. was 136 in 1930 (2% of the total). In Nov. 1940, the Iron Guard Legionnaires confiscated all J. businesses. On 22 June 1941, the J. pop. was transferred to Arad.

INGENHEIM Palatinate, Germany. Jews settled in a local castle belonging to the counts of Gemmingen after the expulsion from Landau in 1347. The 19th cent. community was the largest and most important in the Palatinate with a peak pop. of 578 (a third of the total) in 1848. In 1869, J. merchants included 24 cattle dealers active throughout Germany. Jews also traded in grain and farm produce. A J.-owned cigarette factory set up in 1877 employed 150 people in the 1930s. A synagogue in the Moorish style, the largest

Synagogue in Ingulets, Ukraine

in the Palatinate, was consecrated in 1832 with a J. school attached to it. In 1933, the J. pop. was 90 with three other communities (Goecklingen, Heuchelheim, Klingenmuenster) part of the congregation. In 1938, 57 Jews remained. The synagogue was set on fire on *Kristallnacht* (9–10 Nov. 1938). Most of the remaining Jews left the town. On 22 Oct. 1940, three elderly J. women were deported to southern France, two dying in the Gurs concentration camp and the other in Auschwitz.

INGOLSTADT Upper Bavaria, Germany. Jews fleeing a Munich blood libel (1285) and the Rindfleisch massacres (1298) arrived in the late 13th cent. In 1322 the community of 30 had a synagogue. In the Black Death persecutions of 1348–49 debts to J. moneylenders were canceled and the Jews expelled. Over the next cent., periods of ducal protection alternated with periods of persecution until the final expulsion in 1450. J. merchants only appeared again in 1784 to participate in the fairs. Permanent residence was only

permitted in 1848. From the eve of WWI, the Jews maintained a pop. of around 100 (total 23,745), engaged mainly in the cattle, textile, and oil product trade. The community ended between 1933 and 1939: 70 Jews left for other cities in Germany, mainly Munich; 20 emigrated from the country; and ten died.

INGULETS Dnepropetrovsk dist., Ukraine. I. was founded as a J. colony in 1809 and numbered 90 J. families in 1812. In 1897, the J. pop. was 2,696 (total 2,781). A public school for J. children was operating in 1910. In 1926, a J. agricultural school was founded in Zelene on the opposite bank of the I. River, becoming one of the most important schools of its kind in the Ukraine during the 1930s. In the Soviet period, the J. pop. dropped to 2,160 in 1926 and 226 (total 7,169) in 1939. The Germans captured I. on 13 Aug. 1941. The Jews of I. were murdered together with the 1,400 of the region on 12 July 1942.

INGWILLER (Ger. Ingweiler) Bas-Rhin dist.,

France. The J. presence dates from 1604. At the end of the 17th cent., there were six J. families. In 1784 there were 38 J. families (195 persons). From 1776 they maintained a synagogue. Half of the Jews in I. traded in livestock. In 1805, the J. pop. numbered 400, and peaked at 550 in the middle of the 19th cent. A new synagogue was founded in 1822 and an elementary school in 1836. By the end of the 19th cent. there was a drop in pop. due to emigration. The Germans expelled the 166 Jews in I, to the south of France, together with the rest of Alsace-Lorraine Jews. Twelve Jews were deported to concentration camps. The synagogue was looted and the cemetery was destroyed. In 1969, the community consisted of fewer than 100 persons.

INNSBRUCK   Tyrol, Austria. Jews maintained a continuous presence in I. from the 13th cent. They were engaged in moneylending and trade. During the Black Death persecutions (1348–49), the community suffered but was not destroyed. Under the tolerant reign of Duke Ferdinand II of Tyrol (1618–23) Jews served as flute players and dance masters at his court. In 1714, the city council expelled the Jews. In 1785 there was a small community in I. During the Tyrol revolt against Bavarian-French rule led by Andreas Hofer in 1809, Jews in I. were attacked. The community apparently maintained a Reform synagogue from the 1870s. In 1914 it was recognized as a a religious corporation (*Kultusgemeinde*). In 1930, Elimelekh Rimalt was elected as a Zionist representative on the community council. He served as rabbi of I. until 1938. He subsequently became active politically in Israel, where he served as a government minister from 1969. By 1869, the J. pop. stood at 27, rising to 200 in 1920 and to 317 in 1934 (total 79,250). Jews engaged in trade; there were also some university professors and doctors. Following the Nazi rise to power in Germany in 1933, J. shops in I. were boycotted and many Jews emigrated. Two months after the *Anschluss* (13 March 1938), only 80 Jews were still living in I. In fall 1938, all community facilities were closed. On *Kristallnacht* (9–10 Nov. 1938), J. property was severely damaged, the synagogue was desecrated, and 18 Jews were beaten and arrested. Three were murdered. By the end of 1939, all remaining Jews left for Palestine. A small community was reestablished in 1961.

INOWLODZ   Lodz dist., Poland. Jews first settled here in 1537. At the end of the 19th cent., most of the 324 Jews were employed in services to vacationers. In Aug. 1942 the Germans expelled 500 Jews to the Tomashow-Mazowiecki ghetto.

INOWROCLAW   Poznan dist., Poland. Jews are first mentioned in 1447 and an organized community existed in the 16th cent. The Swedish invasion of 1656 and the subsequent pogrom by the troops of Stefan Czarniecki devastated the community. In 1681 King John Sobieski of Poland renewed the charter (originally given in 1600) granting the Jews internal autonomy and also the right to engage in trade and crafts, including the sale of alcoholic beverages. The annexation of I. to Prussia in 1773 brought new restrictions and disabilities. Jews were prohibited from trading in wool and alcoholic beverages and the old charter was replaced by a new set of regulations dividing the Jews into "productive" and "tolerated" categories with commensurate heavy taxation. A fire destroyed 145 J. homes in 1775 and many Jews left the town. In the 19th cent., after an unpropitious interval (1807–1815) as part of the Grand Duchy of Warsaw, the community waged a struggle for equal rights. Further disaster struck the Jews when a cholera epidemic claimed 120 J. lives in 1831. In the course of Prussian rule, the community underwent a process of Germanization, including the adoption of German names and the language. Economic conditions improved in the second half of the cent. and Jews became active in public life as well. Many entered the professional class as educational opportunities widened, but a flight to the big cities ensued along with emigration. From a peak of 1,917 (total 4,761) in 1837, the J. pop. dropped to 1,157 in 1905 and 252 in 1921, when large numbers left for Germany or the U.S. after I. was included in independent Poland. The 172 Jews remaining at the outset of the German invasion in Sept. 1939 were expelled in Oct.–Dec. to Gniezno and Kroswica and shortly thereafter to Radom in General Gouvernement territory.

INSTERBURG   (Rus. Chernyakhovsk) East Prussia, Germany, today Russia. The first Jew settled in I. in 1834. In 1843, the J. pop. was 41; in 1880, 363; and in 1925, 338. The community established a synagogue in 1865 and subsequently two cemeteries (the first about 1840). I. was a center for regional J. activities and the Association of East Prussian Communities had its central office here, from its foundation in

the Drohiczyn ghetto and liquidated in the *Aktions* of 26 July and 15 Oct. 1942.

JALOWKA Bialystok dist., Poland, today Belarus. Jews probably settled in the late 18th cent. Among J. artisans, carpenters and boilermakers were prominent. Most had auxiliary farms. Although the community stagnated when bypassed by the railroad, its pop. stood at 743 (total 1,311) in 1897. After WWI, many left the town and in 1921, 588 Jews lived there. A Yiddish school was opened between the World Wars and a Zionist youth movement was active. The Germans captured J. in June 1941, instituting a regime of forced labor and extortion. On 2 Nov. 1942, all 600 of the town's Jews along with some refugees were brought to the Wolkowysk transit camp and after a month sent directly to the gas chambers of the Treblinka death camp.

JANINA (Ioannina) Epirus, Greece. Jews first lived in J. some time in the first centuries C.E.. A sizable Romaniot community (dating from the Byzantine period) existed in the 14th cent. Since the Sephardi Jews who arrived following the Spanish and Portuguese expulsions assimilated within it, the J. community remained the largest and oldest Romaniot community in Greece. In 1540, the Sephardi Jews formed their own congregation. Most Jews were engaged in trade. During the Greek revolt of 1821, the Jews saved their own lives by assisting the Turks in suppressing the rebels. In 1824, the Romaniot congregation built a new and magnificent synagogue, which remains intact today, and in 1841 the Sephardi Jews followed suit with an equally grand building. A Sicilian congregation maintained its own synagogue and traditions. The J. pop. in 1856 was 2,400. Two great fires broke out in 1867,

Wedding procession, Janina, Greece, 1908 (Beth Hatefutsoth Photo Archive, Tel Aviv/photo courtesy of Yad Vashem, The Holocaust Martyrs' and Heroes' Remembrance Authority, Jerusalem)

leaving about 840 Jews homeless; some emigrated to Egypt, Eretz Israel, and the U.S. Those who remained were in great distress and pleaded for assistance from communities oversees. In 1872, Greek nationalists rioted against the Jews, accusing them of being Turkish supporters. One Jew was killed and many injured. A number of similar riots took place in the following years. Political upheaval in the first decade of the 20th cent. undermined the security and financial position of the community. Greek nationalists murdered a J. peddler and many Jews did not work for fear of their lives. Large groups emigrated to Bucharest, Alexandria, Istanbul, Eretz Israel, and the U.S. In the meantime, from 1865 an Alliance Israelite committee focused on J. education and in 1904 (when the J. pop. peaked at 4,000) opened a J. school. Two Zionist associations were established in 1905 and 1909. Following the Balkan wars (1912–13), J. came under Greek rule. After WWI, another wave of emigration took place, mostly to the U.S., Turkey, France, and Eretz Israel. In 1928 J. was the third largest J. community in Greece (1,970 Greek-speaking Jews), after Salonika and Kavala. With an increase in antisemitism and an economic crisis in the 1930s, emigration continued. By this time a number of social welfare organizations had been founded, including an old age home. The greatest J. poet writing in Greek, Yosef Eliyia, lived in J. during this period. He translated poems by Yehuda Halevi, Ibn Gabirol, Bialik, and Tchernichowsky from Hebrew into Greek. The J. pop. in 1941 was 1,950. In WWII, many Jews in J. fought against the Italians on the Albanian border. The Jews were not persecuted under the Italian occupation but a number emigrated to Athens and some youths joined the Greek underground movements. In July 1943, the Germans entered J. and in Sept. ordered the Jews to register. Following the advice of a trusted head of the community who believed that the Jews would not be harmed if they acceded to Nazi demands, most Jews remained in J. despite warnings of mass deportations. Only a few fled to the surrounding hills or Athens. Former UN head Kurt Waldheim, part of a German police team operating in J. in 1943, warned that the Jews might endanger the German war effort. On 24 March 1944, the Germans rounded up all the Jews—some 1,870—and deported them to Auschwitz-Birkenau via Trikala and Larissa. Along the way a few managed to escape and joined the partisans, while a number of older deportees died. Only 164 survived the death camps. The community was revived after the war, but remained small.

JANK Szatmar dist., Hungary. Jews settled in the late 18th cent. and numbered 70 in 1930. Most engaged in selling wood and farm crops and transporting goods to local fairs. In late May 1944, they were brought to Mateszalka and then deported to Auschwitz.

JANOSHALMA Bacs-Bodrog dist., Hungary. Jews settled in the early 19th cent. A synagogue was erected in 1860. The J. pop. grew to 273 in 1880 and 359 in 1941. Most were small merchants and artisans; several exported fruit. Many perished in the Ukraine under forced labor during 1942. On 10 May 1944, the Jews were expelled to Bacsalmas and on 25 June they were deported to Auschwitz. Eighty-three survived. A community of 125 Jews was formed after the war, dwindling to 33 by 1962.

JANOSHAZA Vas dist., Hungary. Jews settled in the first half of the 18th cent. Their pop. grew to a peak of 531 in 1880, declining to 380 in 1941. A new synagogue was consecrated in 1897. Jews were subjected to forced labor in 1942, many perishing in the Ukraine. On 4–6 June 1944, the Jews were sent to Sarvar en route to Auschwitz. Fifty survivors reestablished the community, which dwindled to 26 in 1956.

JANOV Vinnitsa dist., Ukraine. Jews numbered 795 in 1765 and 2,088 (total 5,545) in 1897. Three hundred were murdered in a pogrom on 11–15 July 1919. In

Synagogue in Janov, Ukraine

JANOW POLESKI   Polesie dist., Poland, today Belarus. The J. community was formed around the mid-17th cent. under the auspices of the Pinsk community. J. commercial life revolved around the market, where all stores were in J. hands, while the larger merchants exported such products as "Lithuanian" butter. The Lyubeshov Hasidim maintained two rival courts and Karlin Hasidism was also represented. The J. pop. in 1897 was 1,875 (total 3,041). A fire in the 1890s destroyed 50 J. homes and straitened economic circumstances up to WWI led to a steady stream of emigration to the cities of the Ukraine and to the U.S. The Jews remained in the town during the German occupation in WWI (1915–18) and were able to live off abandoned peasant land. Between the World Wars, the businesses of many Jews were concentrated around the new railroad station. A big sawmill employing hundreds of workers was built by J. entrepreneurs. It later served as a training ground for pioneer youth. In 1929, another fire destroyed 75 J. homes and the town was rehabili-tated with the insurance money as well as a government loan. J. commerce expanded, with grain and cattle being exported to Congress Poland and Danzig. Most of the Zionist parties and youth movements were operating by the late 1920s. A Hebrew school existed. In 1939, the J. pop. was about 3,000. Under Russian rule (Sept. 1939–June 1941), Zionist activity ceased and factories were nationalized with 20 wealthy J. families exiled to Asiatic Russia. The Germans arrived on 24 June 1941. On 4 Aug. they rounded up and murdered 420 J. males over the age of 14. A *Judenrat* was then set up. On 11 April 1942, the community was given 24 hours to remove itself to a ghetto, with an allotment of 12 square feet of living space per person and 15–20 to a room. Five hundred or so workers were brought to the sawmill on 23 Sept. 1942 as an *Aktion* commenced against those left behind – mostly women, children, and old people. The Germans set fire to the ghetto to flush out those in hiding. All were killed. Of the 500 at the sawmill, all but 62 skilled

Rahel and Yitzhak Gertman with their children at the dinner table, Janow Poleski, Poland

workers and 37 in hiding were murdered on 25 Sept. The remnant was confined to a smaller ghetto and liquidated in Oct. Of those who escaped, some joined the partisans and others roamed the forests in small, hunted groups; about 100 survived the war.

JANOW SOKOLSKI Bialystok dist., Poland. The first Jews arrived in the early 18th cent. Most shops and stalls in the market built in 1739 belonged to Jews. In 1740 a beautiful synagogue was completed. J. merchants became active in the lumber, grain, and hide trade and Jews opened a hide-processing plant, sawmill, and spinning mill. Israel Davidson (1870–1939), the prominent historian of medieval Hebrew literature, was born in J. By 1897 the J. pop. was 1,797 (total 2,296). The J. pop. dropped to 1,027 in 1921 through emigration. The Germans took the town on 26 June 1941, appointing a *Judenrat* and subjecting the Jews to forced labor. In Aug. they were transferred to a ghetto, many without a place to stay being sent to Suchowola. On 2 Nov. 1942 they were brought to the Kelbasin transit camp near Grodno and from there deported to the Treblinka and Auschwitz death camps.

JANOWIEC (I) Poznan dist., Poland. The 19th cent. community reached a peak pop. of 199 (total 645) in 1871. A synagogue was consecrated in 1894. Of the few Jews remaining in Sept. 1939, three were murdered by the Germans and the rest expelled to General Gouvernement territory.

JANOWIEC (II) Kielce dist., Poland. Jews settled in the mid-16th cent. but fled with the rest of the pop. following the Swedish invasion of 1656. They returned 50 years later. A synagogue established in the 17th cent. was regarded as one of the most elegant in Poland. The J. pop. was 261 (total 1,266) in 1921. In Aug. or Sept. 1942, three years after the German occupation, the Jews were expelled to Zwolen and from there deported to the Treblinka death camp by way of Garbatka.

JARCZOW Lublin dist., Poland. Jews numbered 203 (total 231) in 1863 and 250 between the World Wars. On 22 May 1942, they were deported by the Germans to the Belzec death camp.

JARMI Szatmar dist., Hungary. Jews arrived at the turn of the 18th cent., erecting a synagogue in 1850 and numbering 169 in 1880 and 58 in 1930. In 1942, the men were sent to forced labor and in late May 1944 the remaining Jews were deported to Auschwitz via Mateszalka.

JAROCIN Poznan dist., Poland. The town's proprietor, Jan Radolinski, invited the Jews to settle in the second half of the 18th cent. and an organized community with a wide-ranging charter of privileges was formed. The community grew rapidly under Prussian rule from 1793, opening a synagogue, cemetery, and elementary school and expanding from trade at the local fair to light industry (tobacco, sugar, bricks) and the professions. The J. pop. reached a peak of 557 (total 1,637) in 1840. Emigration from the late 19th cent. reduced the J. pop. to 52 in 1939. On 22 Oct. 1939 the Jews were expelled by the Germans to General Gouvernement territory.

JAROSLAW Lwow dist., Poland. Jews are first

Door of synagogue in Jaroslaw, Poland

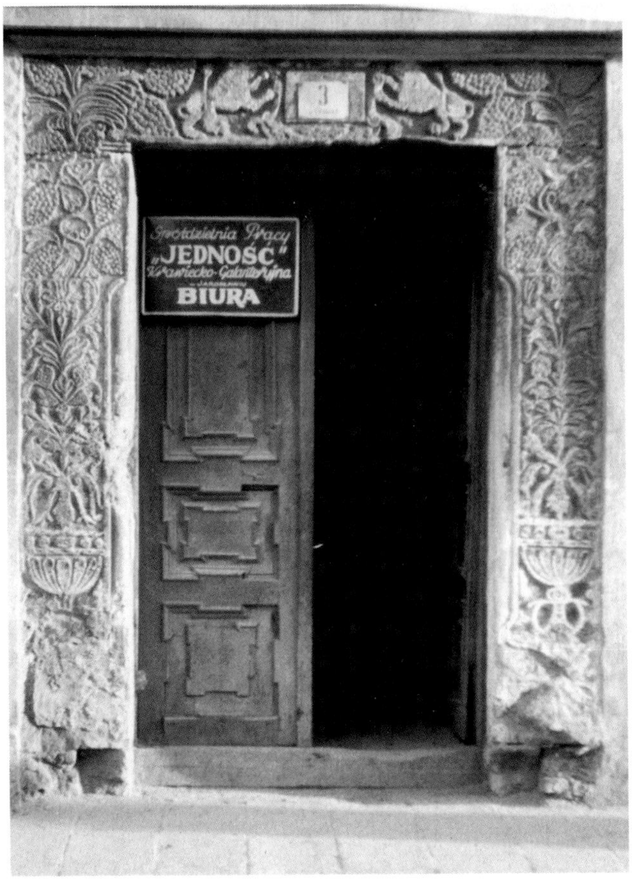
3
Spółdzielnia Pracy
„JEDNOŚĆ"
BIURA

Members of Tze'irei Tziyyon student orchestra, Jaroslaw, Poland, 1905

mentioned in 1464 but were apparently present centuries before. Residence restrictions kept the J. pop. down to a few families until the 17th cent. Most engaged in moneylending. The Jews were able to trade within the town and live outside its walls. By the 1630s a substantial community was in existence despite the ban. Jews leased distilleries and flour mills and operated as tax farmers. With the growth of the community they expanded into trade in hides, grain, and foodstuffs and maintained commercial relations with Danzig. In the 18th cent. the number of J. craftsmen increased, with tailors and butchers prevailing. As J. was an important commercial center, J. brokers also proliferated. From 1680 to 1764, the Council of the Four Lands held most of its meetings there, making the town one of the important centers of Polish Jewry. In 1774 the community was granted independent status. Hasidism gained a foothold at a relatively early stage as did Haskala. The Zionists became active in the 1890s, when the J. pop. stood at 4,820 (total 18,065). Throughout its existence, the community was faced with marked anti-J. feeling. In June 1918, J. property was pillaged in anti-J. riots. Despite this, and despite the depredations of WWI, the J. pop. continued to grow, reaching 6,577 in 1921. Jews also remained dominant in economic life, owning most of the city's factories. In the late 1920s, the economic situation of the Jews deteriorated, necessitating the operation of loan funds and mutual aid societies. The Zionists and their youth movements were active throughout the period while Agudat Israel represented traditional circles. The Germans entered the city in Sept. 1939 and immediately impounded J. property while subjecting 1,000–2,000 Jews a day to forced labor (bridge building and railroad work). On 28 Sept., all the Jews, around 7,000 in number (including refugees), were taken to the Sokol sports field, where they were robbed of their possessions, and then sent across the San River into Soviet-held territory. Most ended up in E. Galicia, mainly in Lwow. The few who remained behind, augmented by refugees, were expelled to Sieniawa in June 1942 and suffered the fate of the local Jews. Many Jews were incarcerated in a local Gestapo jail in 1940–42 and made victims of periodic executions. In Aug. 1942, the local labor camp served as a transit point for around 10,000 Jews on their way to the Belzec death camp. Some survivors returned after the war but soon fled when Polish nationalists murdered several Jews in the area.

JARYCZOW NOWY Lwow dist., Poland, today

Ukraine. The first J. settlement was destroyed in the Tartar invasion of 1578 and a community was reestablished in the early 18th cent. when many Jews specialized in the manufacture of gold- and silver-threaded belts. The pop. grew to 1,608 in 1910 (total 3,186). A great fire in 1872 destroyed many J. homes and in WWI the Russians burned another 200 before withdrawing from the town in May 1915; 140 Jews also died in an epidemic. Hasidism spread in the 19th cent. and Zionism grew influential from the early 20th cent. The J. pop. in 1931 was 976. Of the traditional rabbis, Ze'ev-Wolf Gershtal (d. 1932) was recognized throughout Poland as an authority on the Hebrew calendar. The Germans occupied the town at the beginning of July 1941, imposing a regime of extortion and forced labor along with sporadic acts of violence. All the Jews, including many from the surrounding area, were packed into a ghetto in 1942. The ghetto was liquidated on 15 Jan. 1943, when 2,300–2,500 Jews were taken to the nearby forest and machine-gunned down beside mass graves.

JASIENICA ROSIELNA Lwow dist., Poland. The J. pop. reached a peak of 546 (total 2,302) in 1900. The ghetto set up by the Germans in 1942 also received refugees from nearby places. Two hundred young men were sent to forced labor in Jasliska and the Plaszow camp. On 12 Aug. 1942, the 600 ghetto inhabitants were executed near the town.

JASIENOW POLNY Stanislawow dist., Poland, today Ukraine. The J. pop. in 1921 was 109. The Jews were probably expelled to Horodenka for liquidation in April 1942.

JASINA (Hung. Korosmezo) Carpatho-Russia, Czechoslovakia, today Ukraine. Jews probably settled in the first half of the 18th cent., afterwards abandoning the town and returning in the early 19th cent. The J. pop. was 21 in 1830 and 786 (total 6,391) in 1880. The first rabbi of J. and the small settlements in the area was appointed in 1875. The community also maintained a *talmud torah* and a J. elementary school (founded c. 1900) with instruction in Hungarian. A large new synagogue (apparently built of stone) was erected in 1934. In 1930, in the period of the Czechoslovakian Republic, the J. pop. grew to 1,471. Most J. children attended a Czech state school, receiving their religious education in a *heder* and *talmud torah* main-

tained by the community. Jews owned eight sawmills, where many Jews found employment. A number of Jews were public officials, some in senior positions. Zionist and non-Zionist youth organizations, like Hashomer Hatzair and Tze'irei Agudat Israel, were active. After the Hungarian occupation of March 1939, the Jews were cut off from their sources of livelihood and in 1940–41 many young people were drafted into labor battalions and sent out on forced labor and to the eastern front, where many died. In 1941, the J. pop. was 1,403. In Aug. 1941, about 300 local Jews were expelled to Kamenets-Podolski, where they were murdered together with thousands of other Jews from the area who similarly lacked Hungarian citizenship and who had been held with them in a transit camp in J. In Oct. 1943, several local Jews joined a partisan group formed in the surrounding forests. The Germans took over the town in March 1944 and established a ghetto and *Judenrat*. In May 1944, hundreds of Jews were deported to Auschwitz. A few Jews joined the Czechoslovakian army created in the Soviet Union and fought against the Nazis. A few dozen survivors returned to J. after the war.

JASIONOWKA Bialystok dist., Poland, today Belarus. Jews first settled in the latter 17th cent. The community began to develop after the settlement of Tartar tanners and furriers stimulated J. trade. Jews also exported beer hops to Eastern Prussia and knitted goods to various localities. They became known as master artisans second only to those of Bialystok and Tykocin. In 1897 the J. pop. was 1,154 (total 1,565). Mizrachi was the first Zionist group to become active before WWI. Between the World Wars the community lived under straitened economic circumstances. The J. pop. in 1931 was 1,279. The Germans captured J. on 27 June 1941, immediately carrying out a pogrom with the aid of local antisemites in which 74 Jews were killed. Another 40 alleged Soviet collaborators were imprisoned in Bialystok; all but two (who escaped) were brutally murdered there. With most houses burned down, the Jews were kept in a few buildings under a *Judenrat* responsible for supplying forced labor. A large group, mostly refugees, was expelled to Suchowola in late 1941. On 25 Jan. 1943, 1,600 were rounded up for deportation to the Treblinka death camp. About 400 fled on the way to the railroad station and another 300 jumped out of the trains, but of all these, just 129 survived together with another 100 from previous escapes.

JASLISKA Lwow dist., Poland. The first Jews settled in the early 19th cent. and the community grew to 293 (total 936) in 1900, with Zanz and Sadagora Hasidism represented. The Poles expelled the town's 100 J. families to Rymanow on 1 Sept. 1939 but they returned under the German occupation and passed three relatively quiet years until the community was liquidated in Sept. 1942. The young were deported to the Belzec death camp and the old taken to Dukla and murdered.

JASLO Cracow dist., Poland. Jews are mentioned in the 14th cent. and a community existed in 1565 but subsequent residence restrictions curtailed the settlement until 1860. In 1880 the J. pop. stood at 934, rising to 2,445 in 1921 (25% of the total). Antisemitism was widespread and in 1898 J. stores were looted and a factory was burned down in regional disturbances noted by Theodor Herzl in an article called "Fire in Galicia." In 1906 a magnificent synagogue was completed, winning renown throughout W. Galicia. Communal education and welfare services were organized at the same time as well as the beginnings of Zionist activity. In the traditional religious atmosphere of the community, public school education was avoided and private teachers employed for secular studies. During WWI the Jews suffered from hunger and disease. Between the World Wars, economic conditions deteriorated, compounded by anti-J. agitation. While Jews owned five chemical plants and eight sawmills, few Jews were employed there as they persisted in such traditional occupations as peddling and the operation of stalls. The J. Agricultural Association operated a 125-acre farm for agricultural studies which also accommodated pioneer youth preparing for *aliya*. The Zionist movement was fully represented, with wide-ranging cultural activity. By 1931 the J. pop. had fallen to 1,512. Though antisemitism became more virulent in the 1930s, the Jews continued to participate in the town's public life. The Germans arrived on 8 Sept., commencing a regime of persecution and burning down the synagogue in Oct. A *Judenrat* was set up

Jews outside store, Jaslo, Poland

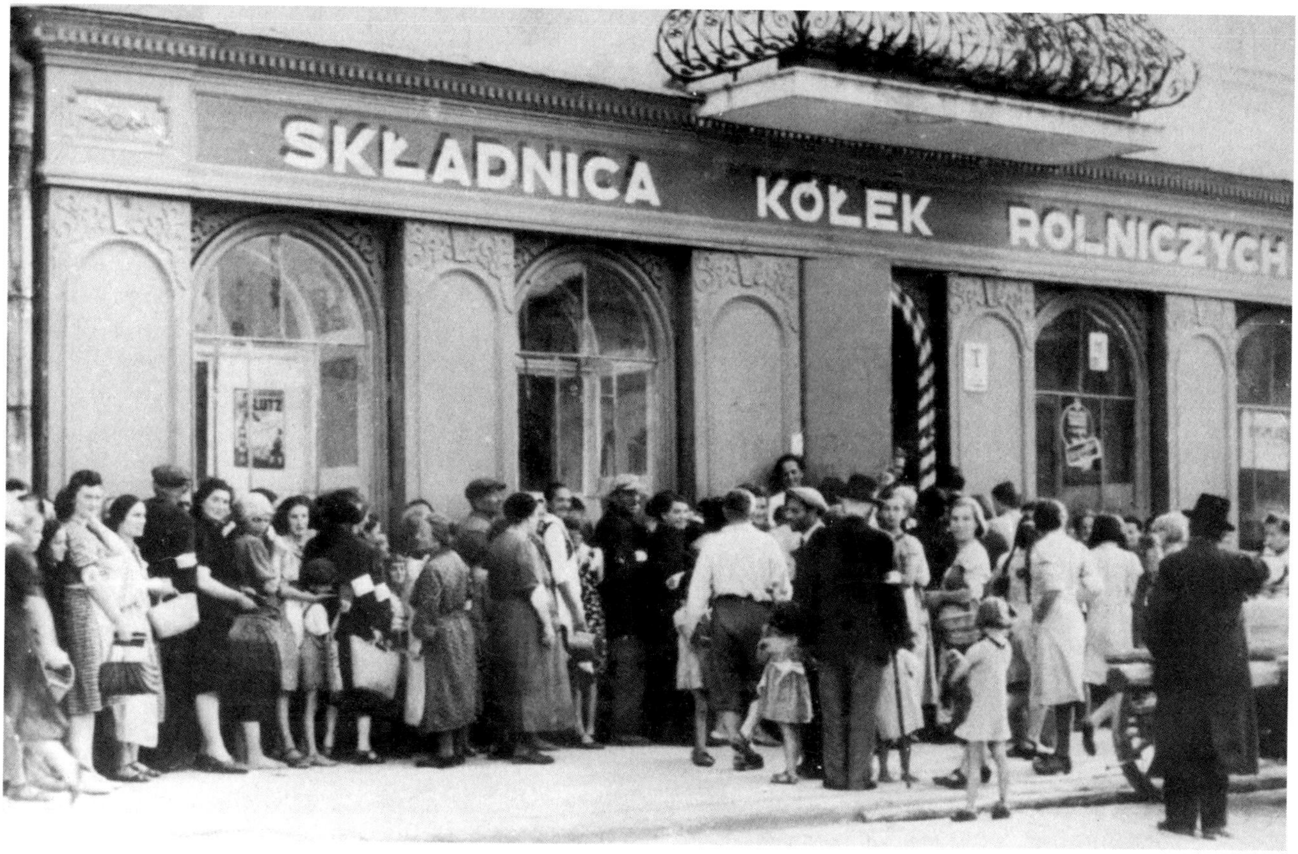
SKŁADNICA KÓŁEK ROLNICZYCH

at the end of the year. To alleviate the general suffering it organized a soup kitchen, orphanage, and hospital, as well as a school for 300 children. At the end of 1941, the Jews were enclosed in a ghetto, swelled by refugees to a pop. of 2,300. In July 1942, 150 Jews, mainly the families of men recently sent to Frysztak on forced labor, were murdered in the forest. In Aug. 500 more Jews from J., Dukla, and Rymanow were murdered in the forest near Barwink. The ghetto was liquidated on 19–20 Aug. when most were deported to the Belzec death camp. The sick and old were taken to the forest and murdered beside freshly dug graves, the crippled being ordered to remove artificial limbs and brought to the graves on blankets. Of the fit, 200 were left to clean the ghetto and were later employed in other work. The entire town was razed by the Germans at the end of 1944.

JASNOGORODKA   Kiev dist., Ukraine. Jews numbered 60 in 1784 and 624 (total 1,614) in 1897. Most were Hasidim. On 15 July 1919, Ukrainian gangs attacked the Jews. In 1926, under the Soviets, ten Jews remained.

JASTROW   (Pol. Jastrowie) Posen–West Prussia, Germany, today Poland. By 1771 there was a J. community with 121 members. The J. pop. grew to 254 individuals in 1788, peaking at 509 in 1849. By 1895, numbers had shrunk to 254. In 1925, there were only 150 Jews living in J. The community maintained a synagogue and a cemetery. After the Nazi assumption of power in 1933, the community's economic situation deteriorated drastically as a result of the boycott measures the Nazis introduced. By 1937 there were still 125 Jews living in J. On *Kristallnacht* (9–10 Nov. 1938), the synagogue was destroyed, J. businesses were demolished, and the men were taken off to the Sachsenhausen concentration camp. The remaining Jews were interned in March 1940 in the Buergergarten camp near Schneidemuehl. They were deported shortly after to the east and most perished.

JASZALSOSZENTGYORGY   Jasz–Nagykun–Szolnok dist., Hungary. Jews arrived c. 1830, building a synagogue in 1840 and numbering 107 in 1880 and 84 in 1930. In 1940, the men were sent to forced labor. In May 1944, the remainder were given a "choice" of two ghettoes, Jaszladany or Szolnok. Most chose the latter. After a short period of time

they were transferred to Jaszbereny and from there to Monor, prior to deportation to Auschwitz on 8 July.

JASZAPATI   Jasz–Nagykun–Szolnok dist., Hungary. Jews settled in the 1830s, numbering 120 in 1880 and 209 in 1931. A synagogue was built in 1854. The rabbi initiated Zionist activity in J. On 8 July 1944, the Jews were deported to Auschwitz via Jaszbereny and Monor.

JASZAROKSZALLAS   Jasz–Nagykun–Szolnok dist., Hungary. Jews settled in the late 19th cent., mostly as grain and fruit merchants. A synagogue was constructed in 1867 and a J. school was opened in 1872. During the White Terror disturbances (1919–20), only the small farmers who had received interest-free loans from the Jews refrained from participating in the violence. The J. pop. grew to 184 by 1930. On 6–8 July 1944, the Jews were deported to Auschwitz via Jaszbereny and Monor.

JASZBERENY   Jasz–Nagykun–Szolnok dist., Hungary. Jews lived in J. under the Turkish occupation in the 16th–17th cents., supplying local farmers with goods and marketing their produce. In the 18th cent., Jews were allowed to enter and trade in J. on certain fixed days. Only in 1850 were they permitted to settle in J., finally obtaining the right to own land in 1860. They prospered as winegrowers. The first rabbi of the community, Jozef Natonek, was forced to vacate his position because he rejected emancipation in favor of emigrating to Eretz Israel. In 1890, a magnificent new synagogue was consecrated. A J. school enrolled 100 children by the end of WWI. In 1910, the Jews numbered 1,017 (3% of the total) and in 1915 there were 110 J. homeowners. By 1941, the pop. dropped to 574. Zionist activity intensified in the 1930s and a pioneer training camp sent a group of youngsters to Palestine in 1942. J. became a camp for dispatching forced labor to the Ukraine and other places in 1942. In 1944, there were more than 10,000 young Jews at the camp, which was commanded by Ivan Zentai, who was later executed for war crimes. After the Germans arrived in spring 1944, the Jews were confined in a ghetto. On 30 June, they were sent to Monor and on 6–8 July deported to Auschwitz. A postwar community of 100 gradually dissolved.

JASZFENYSZARU   Jasz–Nagykun–Szolnok dist., Hungary. A permanent J. settlement existed by the

Interior of synagogue in Jaszbereny, Hungary

early 19th cent., operating a small J. school and building a new synagogue in 1926. The J. pop. was 89 in 1930. The 1938 racial laws sent rich Jews from J. to concentration camps and in 1941 to forced labor in the Ukraine and Germany. In May 1944, the Jews of J. were confined to a ghetto and then transferred to Jaszarokszallas and Monor before deportation to Auschwitz on 6–8 July. Fifteen survivors reestablished the community but most left after 1956.

JASZKARAJENO Pest–Pilis–Solt–Kiskun dist., Hungary. Jews settled in the mid-19th cent. and numbered 142 in 1930. Their economic situation deteriorated after the publication of Hungary's 1938 racial laws, with farms confiscated in 1941–42 and men seized for forced labor in 1942. On 16 May 1944, the Jews were brought to Kecskemet and deported to Auschwitz at the end of June, where the women were used for sterilization experiments and then sent to slave labor.

JASZKISER Jasz–Nagykun–Szolnok dist., Hungary. Jews arrived in 1830, erecting a synagogue in 1860. They played a prominent role in developing the economy of the town and operated a flour mill, brickyard, and sawmill. They numbered 99 in 1880 and 60 in 1930. In May 1944, they were transferred to Jaszapati and then to Monor, and on 6–8 July deported to Auschwitz.

JASZLADANY Jasz–Nagykun–Szolnok dist., Hungary. Jews were only allowed to settle in J. after 1848. They numbered 63 in 1880 and 112 in 1930. On 20 June 1944, they were transferred to Jaszbereny and Monor and then deported on 6–8 July to Auschwitz.

JAUER (Pol. Jawor) Lower Silesia, Germany, today Poland. The first mention of Jews and a synagogue is in 1364 but the modern community was founded only in the 19th cent. The J. pop. was 109 in 1849 and 128 in 1884. The community maintained a synagogue and cemetery. The J. pop. declined to 91 in 1925 and 68 in 1932. Most left during the years of Nazi persecution, 17 remaining in May 1939 and one married to a non-Jew in Oct. 1942. No information exists on the fate of the community in the Nazi era. Presumably those Jews who were unable to emigrate were deported and perished.

JAUNIJELGAVA (Yid. Neyra) Zemgale (Courland) dist., Latvia. J. artisans from the surrounding villages began to settle under Russian rule after 1795. In 1881 the J. pop. reached a peak of 4,128 (total 5,820). Fires in 1863 and 1871 left many homeless. In the late 19th cent. a number of wealthy J. merchants became prominent, dealing in lumber, fur, hides, and bristles. Hovevei Zion became active in the late 19th cent. and the Bund with 100 members engaged in intensive political activity in 1905–06. In 1915, the Jews were expelled from J. by the Russians and during WWI, 453 J. homes were damaged or destroyed. Only 680 returned by 1925 and thereafter the J. pop. declined further as some of the well-to-do and the young left for Riga and other Latvian cities. Despite the community's decline, Jews still dominated trade, owning 52 of the town's 88 business establishments. A Yiddish school founded in WWI had an enrollment of 153 in 1922. Zionist activity exerted a modest influence until the late 1930s. The leading figure in the community was its rabbi and school director, Hayyim Aharon Bezalel Paul, who also served as the town's deputy mayor until 1925. Under Russian rule (1940–41) J. businesses were nationalized and J. public life terminated. The Germans entered the town around the end of June 1941. Latvian "self-defense" forces began killing off Jews, who were thrown out of their homes and herded into a synagogue. In early Aug., a group of young men was executed after digging burial pits in the Serene forest 5 miles outside the town. On 7 Aug. the rest of the community's 167 families were murdered there.

JAWORNIK POLSKI Lwow dist., Poland. Jews engaged mainly in farming in the 19th cent., numbering 89 (10% of the total) in 1880 and 155 in 1921. The Germans arrived on 9 Sept. 1939. A ghetto was set up in 1940–41 and refugees added to the general distress. Some were sent to the Bieshiadka labor camp in 1942; in spring the rest were dispatched to the Rzeszow ghetto.

JAWORNIK RUSKI Lwow dist., Poland, today Ukraine. The J. pop. in 1921 was 105. Its Jews were executed locally or possibly expelled to Przemysl for liquidation in summer–fall 1942.

JAWOROW Lwow dist., Poland, today Ukraine. Jews are mentioned from the mid-16th cent. and by 1629 there was a J. quarter in the town. Most trade was in J. hands also under Austrian rule. Most Jews were Hasidim. Zionist activity was limited until after the WWI, when the J. pop. maintained its late 19th cent. level of around 2,400 (25% of the total) and J. economic life continued unabated with the addition of a professional class. The Soviets ruled the town from 25 Sept. 1939 to 23 June 1941, when the Germans entered and instituted a regime of forced labor. In a two-day *Aktion* commencing on 7 Nov. 1942, 1,300 Jews were deported to the Belzec death camp and about 200 were killed in the streets and in their homes. A ghetto was immediately set up, where 5,000 Jews, including remnants from the neighboring settlements, were crowded into 80 houses. The liquidation of the ghetto commenced on 16 April 1943. Around 4,000 Jews were assembled at the J. cemetery while most houses in the ghetto were set ablaze to ferret out those in hiding. They were consigned to the flames when discovered. All the others were taken to the nearby forest and shot. Another 200 coming out of hiding in the aftermath of the *Aktion* were rounded up and also murdered in the forest. Two groups managed to escape from the local labor camp and form armed bands in the forests, most of whose members were killed in battle.

JAWORZNO Cracow dist., Poland. The J. settlement began to grow only in the mid-19th cent. with the development of modern industry in J. The J. pop. was 684 in 1890 and 1,346 in 1921. The Jews were excluded from industrial employment and found only a limited market for trade among the industrial workers. In 1898 and 1905, anti-J. riots erupted and in Nov. 1918 much J. property was stolen or destroyed in another local rampage. A traditional milieu prevailed, dominated by Chryzanow Hasidism. The Zionists became active in 1895 with Mizrachi taking the lead after WWI. Wide-ranging cultural activities were organized. Agudat Israel also operated a local branch. The Germans entered the town in the first week of Sept. 1939 and immediately murdered a number of Jews. A *Judenrat* was established in Jan. 1940, which organized aid to the many refugees reaching the town and swelling the J. pop. to 2,295 in March 1941. A few months later hundreds of young Jews were sent to labor camps and in May 1942 about 1,000 were dispatched to Chryzanow en route to Auschwitz while the able-bodied were sent to labor camps. The few hundred re-

maining Jews were hunted down and deported to Auschwitz in July. A branch of the Auschwitz camp was established in J. in June 1943, where an average of 3,000–3,500 prisoners were put to work in mines and munitions factories as well as laying railroad track and building power stations; few survived the ordeal.

JAZLOWIEC Tarnopol dist., Poland, today Ukraine.. The J. community dating from the 16th cent. was served by a long line of illustrious rabbis. The Zionist movement became active in the early 20th cent. The pop. declined severely from a peak of 1,642 (over 50% of the total) in 1880 owing to economic hardship and later tribulations under Russian rule in WWI. The J. pop. was 474 in 1921. When the Germans entered the town in July 1941, they gave the Ukrainians a free hand in persecuting the Jews. The community was liquidated in the fall of 1942 when the Jews were expelled to Buczacz and from there deported in two *Aktions* to the Belzec death camp.

JEDLICZE Lwow dist., Poland. The J. community became organized in the early 20th cent, numbering 125 (total 565) in 1900. Rampaging peasants and army deserters burned 14 J. homes and looted J. stores in Nov. 1918. The Germans arrived in Sept. 1939 and instituted a regime of persecution and forced labor as

Two Jewish tombs from the 17th cent., Jazlowiec, Poland

refugees swelled the J. pop. In summer 1942, all were expelled to Krosno, where they shared the fate of the local Jews.

JEDLINSK Kielce dist., Poland. A small J. community attached to Radom was formed in the late 18th cent. By 1921 the Jews numbered 762 (total 1,490). Zionist activity was extensive. After the German occupation of Sept. 1939, Jews were placed under a regime of forced labor. A ghetto holding 1,000 Jews, including refugees, was established in spring 1941. In Aug. 1942, the Jews were deported to the Treblinka death camp after 68, mostly the old and sick, were executed on the spot. Hundreds more were murdered in the local labor camp that operated from Dec. 1942 to Feb. 1944.

JEDWABNE Bialystok dist., Poland. A J. community began to develop in the late 18th cent., growing to 1,941 in 1897 (total 2,505). Jews pioneered the local food and cloth industries as well as producing mead and other alcoholic beverages. Many emigrated at the turn of the cent. In WWI, the Russians expelled the remaining Jews as "disloyal," thus reducing the J. pop. to 757 in 1921. After the war, Zionist groups proliferated. In the late 1930s physical attacks on J. tradesmen increased. After a two-year Soviet occupation, the Germans captured the town on 22 June 1941, burying a number of Jews alive while a Polish mob drowned two J. women with their infants in the local lake. On 10 July 1941, the Poles led 1,000–1,600 Jews to a barn and burned them alive. The remaining 300 were transferred to the Lomza ghetto on 2 Nov. 1942 and perished in Auschwitz.

JEJSE Vilna dist., Poland, today Belarus. Twenty-five J. families settled on village farm land in the mid-19th cent., raising rye, barley, flax, and vegetables. The J. pop. in 1921 was 119. Shortly after their arrival on 27 June 1941, the Germans executed 14 young Jews. On 15 April 1942 the rest were expelled to the Braslaw ghetto. They were murdered near the railway station there on 3 June 1942.

JEKABPILS Zemgale (Courland) dist., Latvia. The few Jews who were present despite a residence ban were expelled in 1739 and only with the annexation to Russia in 1795 did J. merchants begin to settle. An organized community existed from 1810 and in

1830 one of the few *yeshivot* in Courland was founded there. In 1840, 60 Jews emigrated to the Kherson area to settle as farmers. By 1881 the J. pop. reached 2,254 (total 5,512). Jews dealt in lumber, grain, and flax and on the eve of WWI owned two match factories. They also worked as craftsmen. Throughout the 19th cent. an atmosphere of strict Orthodoxy prevailed, with Habad Hasidism also gaining a modest foothold. A Zionist society began to operate in 1902 and the Bund was active from 1905. Most Jews left J. during WWI, when 166 J. homes were destroyed. By 1925, only 806 had returned but the Jews continued to maintain a dominant position in trade, operating 106 of the town's 178 business establishments in 1935. A J. public school existed from the early 1920s and the Zionist youth movements expanded, the biggest being Betar, Hashomer Hatzair, Herzliyya, and Gordonia. Soviet rule in 1940–41 brought J. communal and commercial life to an end. The Germans captured J. on 29 June 1941. The Jews were crowded into the synagogues under a regime of severe persecution and forced labor. In Sept. 1941 they were all marched to the Kokas forest and executed beside four trenches. Stragglers were murdered along the way.

JELENIEWO Bialystok dist., Poland. In 1880 about half the town's 659 inhabitants were Jews. The J. pop. in 1921 was 175 (total 471). All the Jews ultimately perished in the Holocaust after being expelled by the Germans in 1939 to Soviet-held territory.

JELGAVA (Yid. Mitoi) Zemgale (Courland) dist., Latvia. The J. community was one of the oldest in Courland, with a permanent settlement in the late 17th cent. Throughout its history as capital of the Duchy of Courland, the town with its large German pop. secured various expulsion orders against the Jews, generally circumvented. J. trade continued to thrive. In 1784 permission was granted to build a synagogue and in 1799, under Russian rule, when the J. community accounted for 70% of the Jews of Courland, full residence and trade rights were accorded. By 1835 the Jews numbered around 5,000 with nearly half trading in grain, horses, and farm produce and a third engaged as artisans. In 1840, 863 Jews were relocated in the Kherson province as farmers. A typhoid epidemic further diminished the J. pop. The community grew again to 6,295 in 1881 (total 28,530). Thereafter the economic position of the city as a transit point

declined with the creation of a direct rail link between the agricultural heartland and the ports of Libau and Riga. In the 1890s, the world crisis in the grain market and stiff Latvian competition further undermined J. livelihoods, putting 800 J. families on relief. The community came under the influence of Haskala as proponents arrived from Germany and W. Europe. R. Reuven Wunderbar was the first historian of Courland Jewry and R. Shelomo Fucher, who served from 1859 to 1893, initiated the construction of a magnificent synagogue whose churchlike facade aroused the ire of traditional circles. In 1850, the Russian government founded a state J. school for boys — one of five in Courland — and in 1868 the community started a vocational school for girls. In 1880 the community opened a kosher kitchen for J. soldiers in the Russian army. A Hovevei Zion society was founded in 1894 and a Bund group — one of the three largest in Courland — played a leading role in the 1905 revolution. The religious Zionist leader R. Mordekhai Nurock succeeded his father Tzevi Hirsch as government-appointed rabbi of J. in 1913 and followed the community into exile after the Russian expulsion of 1915 despite an invitation to remain. Jews began to return toward the end of WWI, finding 99 of their homes destroyed and suffering a pogrom at the hands of local Germans on the eve of the German withdrawal. Between the World Wars, the J. pop. leveled off at around 2,000 (6–7% of the total). Jews maintained their prominence in trade and operated one of the largest flax-processing plants in Latvia. The community maintained wide-ranging welfare services, including a hospital, orphanage, old age home, and poor house. It operated a *talmud torah*, J. public school (founded in 1920), and Hebrew high school as well as four synagogues. R. Levi Ovchinski, who served the community until the Holocaust, was the historian of Latvian Jewry. Zionist activity was extensive throughout the period. Under Soviet rule in 1940–41, J. community life ceased and J. businesses were nationalized. Many Jews left with the Red Army on the approach of the Germans. The Germans captured J. on 29 Aug. 1941, sending in an *Einsatzkommando 2* unit to execute the Jews. In the space of a week, at least five meticulously planned *Aktions* claiming hundreds of J. lives were carried out with the participation of Latvian police. Some Jews were executed in the forest and others at the local shooting range. In the hospitals, J. women were sterilized, often dying on the operating table. Others were burned alive in the synagogues

or shot at the J. cemetery. Early in Sept. a few hundred mental patients from J. and from Liepaja were also murdered. In fall 1941, the city was declared "free of Jews" (*judenrein*).

JELKA (Hung. Joka) Slovakia, Czechoslovakia, today Republic of Slovakia. Jews arrived in the early 18th cent. In 1843, the community numbered 243, maintaining a synagogue and cemetery. In 1880 the J. pop. rose to a peak of 341 (total 2,297). A modern J. school was opened in the late 1850s. Jews engaged mainly in agriculture and related trading activities. After WWI, 25 settlements were under the jurisdiction of the J. rabbinate. The Zionists and Agudat Israel became active and Jews served on the local council. In 1941, 179 Jews remained. Under the Hungarians, they were seized for forced labor. In May 1944, after the German occupation, they were expelled to the Senec ghetto and on 15 June deported to Auschwitz via Nove Zamky.

JELSAVA Slovakia, Czechoslovakia, today Republic of Slovakia. Jews settled in the mid-19th cent. after residence restrictions were lifted. A synagogue was erected in 1895 and a J. elementary school was opened in 1900 with 47 students as the J. pop. rose to 165 (total 2,603). Under Czechoslovakian rule after WWI, Jews were active in public life. Zionist activity flourished with Mizrachi the leading movement and Betar and Bnei Akiva active among the young. Jews owned 22 business establishments, six workshops, and two factories. In 1941, under Hungarian rule (from Nov. 1938), 184 Jews remained, subjected to persecution and expulsion. Some fled; others were subjected to forced labor; and the rest were deported to Auschwitz on 13 June 1944 after short stays in Plesivec and Miskolc.

JEMNICE Moravia, Czechoslovakia. The community is first mentioned in 1336 in connection with the Armleder massacres of 1336–39. Jews were prominent in the city as merchants and moneylenders. Hungarian soldiers burned down J. homes in 1468 and Jews suffered during the Thirty Years War (1618–48). A J. elementary school was opened in 1812 and the J. pop. rose to 325 in 1830. In 1866, during the Austro-Prussian war, Jews were attacked in riots and many left for Brno, bringing the J. pop. down to 143 in 1869. In 1930, 52 remained (total 3,253), with the Zionists ac-

tive. In May 1942, the Jews were deported to the Theresienstadt ghetto via Trebic. Some were sent on to the Lublin dist. (Poland) in the same month and the others in Oct. to the Treblinka death camp, where they perished.

JENA Thuringia, Germany. Jews lived in J. from the mid-14th century and by 1430 there were at least 15 J. men there. From 1536 to 1790, Jews were not allowed to settle in J. Jews were allowed to enroll at the university from 1790 and from the second half of the 19th cent., there were J. professors on the staff of the Friedrich Schiller University, including the Kantian Otto Liebmann (1840–1912) and the physicist Felix Auerbach (b. 1856). The J. pop. was 64 in 1890 and 277 in 1925. Prayers were held in private homes. According to the Nazi census of June 1933, some four months after the Nazi rise to power, the J. pop. was 111. On *Kristallnacht* (9–10 Nov. 1938), the windows of all J. shops were smashed and the J. men were arrested and deported to the Buchenwald concentration camp, where one perished. In 1941 and 1942 all remaining Jews were deported.

JENDRZEJOW Kielce dist., Poland. Jews first settled after Czar Alexander lifted residence restrictions in 1862. They were active in local industry, operating flour mills, breweries, sawmills, a brickyard and quarry, and a workshop for copper fittings. Others acted as commercial agents for the larger estates. In an atmosphere of general prosperity, Jews purchased land and built homes, their pop. rising to 2,050 (total 5,800) in 1897 and 4,685 in 1921. Public life expanded commensurately as the Zionists and various socialist groups became active in the early 20th cent. In 1918, a J. self-defense group warded of attacks by antisemitic townsmen. After WWI, economic conditions deteriorated under the burden of heavy taxes. Agudat Israel contended fiercely with the Zionists for control of the community, with the latter prevailing in the 1920s. On their arrival in Sept. 1939, the Germans impounded J. business and extorted an exorbitant tribute from the community. In Feb. 1940, a *Judenrat* was established and in June 1940 a ghetto where starvation and disease claimed many lives. On 15 Sept. 1942, 4,556 Jews were marched to the railroad station and deported to the Treblinka death camp where most died on 17 Sept. Of the 230 workers left in the ghetto, 62 were shot in a final *Aktion* on 2 Sept. 1943. The rest were

transferred to the Starzysko-Kamienna labor camp. At the end of the war, there were 80 survivors.

JEREMICHE Nowogrodek dist., Poland, today Belarus. Jews presumably settled in the late 16th cent., their pop. reaching 258 (total 865) in 1897. By 1921 the number had dropped to 113. The Germans confined the Jews to two houses after their arrival on 27 June 1941. On 28 Oct., 20 were executed and on 4 Nov. the rest were murdered in the nearby forest.

JESBERG Hesse–Nassau, Germany. Established in the 18th cent., the community dedicated a synagogue in 1832, maintained an elementary school from 1838 to 1922, and grew to 89 (11% of the total) in 1905. It dwindled to 58 in 1933. The synagogue was desecrated on *Kristallnacht* (9–10 Nov. 1938), and all the Jews left (50 emigrating) by 1939.

JESSNITZ Anhalt, Germany. The first evidence of a J. presence in J. is the establishment of a cemetery in 1680. In 1745 a synagogue was built. During the first half of the 18th cent, the Hebrew printing press, which Moses Benjamin Wulff, banker at the Court of Anhalt, had set up originally in Dessau in 1694, was transferred for several years to J. The local community attained a peak pop. of 153 in 1818, dropping to 81 in 1844. A new synagogue was dedicated in 1865. When the Nazis assumed power in 1933, there were only 28 Jews in J. On *Kristallnacht* (9-10 Nov. 1938), the synagogue was burned down. Most of the 20 Jews who were still in the town in May 1939 were billeted in a "J. house," and later probably deported to the east.

JEVER Oldenburg, Germany. Though tolerated in limited numbers from 1698, Jews were only permitted to establish a religious community in 1779–80. By 1793 there were 17 J. households in the town. They dedicated a synagogue in 1802 and gained civil rights during the Napoleonic era (1807–13). Numbering 140 (4% of the total) in 1814, they employed a rabbi and a teacher. From 1849, Jews served on the town council. A new railroad, commercial development, and the affiliation of Jews in nearby villages (e.g., Fedderwarden, Hooksiel, and Wangerooge) boosted the community's pop. to 219 (4%) in 1882, making it even larger than Oldenburg, the Grand Duchy's capital. Accommodating 300 worshipers, a new synagogue dedicated in 1880 reflected the J. community's growth

and status. As conditions worsened following WWI, the J. pop. declined to 118 (2%) in 1925. The exodus of the young, a shrinking membership, and a local upsurge of Nazism reduced the community to 98 in 1933. Over the next five year, anti-J. boycott measures and propaganda drove Jews out of the cattle trade and forced retailers to sell out and leave. On *Kristallnacht* (9–10 Nov. 1938), Nazis burned the synagogue (which was later demolished), looted J. property, and dispatched 15 local Jews to the Sachsenhausen concentration camp. By Sept. 1939, the last J. enterprises had been "Aryanized" and only 39 Jews, mainly the poor and aged, still remained. Of the 116 Jews who lived in the town between 1933 and 1945, only 29 emigrated. The rest were mostly deported (from Holland as well as Germany) to Auschwitz, Bergen-Belsen, Sobibor, Theresienstadt, and other Nazi camps. At least 63 perished during the Holocaust; only a handful survived. After WWII, about 1,600 J. survivors from Bergen-Belsen were housed at a nearby airfield (1950–51). Most left for Israel or returned to their homelands.

JEVICKO Moravia, Czechoslovakia. Jews are believed to have been present in the 14th cent. and from the mid-17th cent. they lived in a ghetto there. The synagogue was built c. 1666 and a new one in the early 1790s. In 1680, 60 Jews died in the plague and in 1869 most J. homes burned. Subsequently most Jews left for Brno, Prague, and Vienna, causing the J. pop. to drop from a peak of 989 (about 32% of the total) in 1848 to 286 in 1890. In 1930, 86 Jews remained. Under the Nazis, the Jews were deported to the Theresienstadt ghetto in summer 1942.

JEZIERNA (Yid. Azierna) Tarnopol dist., Poland, today Ukraine. The permanent J. settlement began to develop in the second half of the 19th cent. with the purchase of a 3,000-acre estate from a local count by a Jew, Mendel Jampoler, and the operation there of a flour mill and modern distillery. Other parcels of land were purchased as well and Jews were active in farming, trade, and light industry, benefiting from the newly laid railroad and even heading the municipal council. Though the community maintained its economic structure up through WWI, its numbers declined from 1,095 (total 5,843) in 1900 to 700 in 1931. The Germans entered J. on 2 July 1941 and in the following two days staged a pogrom together with the Ukrainians, dragging 180–200 men out of their homes and murdering

them in a courtyard. Anti-J. measures and a regime of forced labor followed. Sporadic torture and murder were the fate of those confined to the town's major labor camp. In an *Aktion* in Aug. 1942, 150 Jews were murdered and another 200 deported to the Belzec death camp. The remainder were expelled to the Zborow ghetto in Oct. 1942. Those in the labor camps were executed by the summer of 1943.

JEZIERNICA Nowogrodek dist., Poland, today Belarus. Jews lived there in the 18th cent. The J. pop. in 1921 was 162 (total 528). The Jews were expelled by the Germans to the Slonim ghetto in March 1942 and apparently murdered in the second *Aktion* there on 29 June 1942.

JEZIERZANKA Tarnopol dist., Poland, today Ukraine. The J. pop. in 1921 was 160. The Jews were possibly expelled to Zborow for liquidation in Oct. 1942.

JEZIERZANY (Yid. Aziran) Tarnopol dist., Poland, today Ukraine. The permanent J. settlement dates from around the end of the 18th cent., constituting a majority of the town's residents from the 1890s when the number of Jews reached 1,823. Known for its horse and cattle market, the town supported many J. traders, who frequented all the fairs in the neighborhood and supplied the Austrian army with horses. J. tailors, furriers, and hatmakers also displayed their wares at the fairs. Jews served as mayors and both Haskala and Zionism got an early start in the town. WWI brought severe tribulations with Russian soldiers, the Petlyura gangs, Bolsheviks, and Polish soldiers all terrorizing the community. By 1921, the J. pop. had dropped to 1,302, but it still constituted a majority. Economic conditions worsened between the World Wars under the pressure of heavy taxes, competition from the Ukrainian and Polish cooperatives, and economic boycotts. J. public and commercial life came to an end with the Soviet annexation of 17 Sept. 1939–8 July 1941. Many Jews were drafted into the Red Army when the Soviet withdrawal commenced. The Hungarian army entered J. on 8 July 1941. The Germans took over in Sept. and in Oct. confined the Jews to a special quarter. Extortion depleted J. resources through the winter of 1941–42 and Jews from the neighboring towns and villages swelled the pop. On 26 Sept. 1942, the J. quarter was surrounded and 700 Jews were rounded

up and deported to the Belzec death camp. In Oct., a final 500 Jews were expelled to other ghettoes. Some remained in the labor camps and as many as 300 may have hidden out in the Dembina forest. Most were hunted down and murdered, leaving about 50 Jews in the town when it was liberated by the Soviets on 6 April 1944.

JEZIEZANY (Ozierany) Volhynia dist., Poland, today Ukraine. Jews were present by 1700 and the only meeting of the Council of the Four Lands in Volhynia was held in J. in 1761. The Jews numbered 1,013 in 1897 and 340 (total 917) in 1921. Presumably they met their end under the Germans after expulsion to the Kowel or some nearby ghetto.

JEZIORNA KROLEWSKA Warsaw dist., Poland. A J. community is known from the 19th cent., numbering 437 (total 824) in 1921. Under the German occupation in WWII the Jews were confined to a ghetto and in Jan. 1941, 612 were sent to the Warsaw ghetto, afterwards perishing in the Treblinka death camp.

JEZIORY Bialystok dist., Poland, today Belarus. J. settlement commenced in the late 17th cent. and was augmented toward the mid-19th cent. by the arrival of many J. artisans. The J. pop. rose to 1,392 (total 3,283) in 1897. J. lumber merchants from Vilna and Warsaw arriving to exploit the forests sometimes settled in the town and Jews opened carpentry shops and at the end of the cent. a sawmill employing dozens of Jews. In summer, Jews also lived off the summer resort trade, renting rooms to J. vacationers. In 1921, the J. pop. was 867. Yiddish and Hebrew schools operated between the World Wars and hundreds joined the Hehalutz movement. After a two-year Soviet occupation, many Jews fled with the Red Army on the approach of the Germans in June 1941. A ghetto was established in Aug. and on 2 Sept. 1942 the Jews were sent to the notorious Kelbasin transit camp near Grodno and from there deported to Auschwitz and Majdanek.

JEZOW Lodz dist., Poland. The J. community developed in the 19th cent. and in 1897 numbered 733 (38% of the total). Antisemitic manifestations were frequent between the World Wars, especially in 1935. On 1 Feb. 1941, the 1,570 Jews of J. (including over 600 refugees) were expelled to the Warsaw gehtto.

JEZOWE Lwow dist., Poland. The Jews numbered 161 (total 4,818) in 1921. The community was apparently expelled to the east to the Soviet zone by the Germans in fall 1939 and met the fate of the local Jews.

JEZUPOL (Yid. Azipoli) Stanislawow dist., Poland, today Ukraine. An organized J. community dates from the mid-18th cent., reaching 494 members (total 3,730) in 1900. It was known for its hasidic court (Stretyn dynasty). The rigors of WWI and particularly the rampaging Petlyura gangs brought the pop. down to 188 in 1921. The community was liquidated by the Germans in fall 1942, most Jews being sent to Stanislawow to be murdered at the Rodolf Flour Mill.

JIBOU (Hung. Zsibo) N. Transylvania dist., Rumania. A J. community was organized here in the 1840s. The J. pop. in 1930 was 640 (18% of the total). The Zionists were active in the 1930s. On 3 May 1944 the community was transferred to the Simleul Silvaiei ghetto and in June deported to Auschwitz.

JICIN Bohemia, Czechoslovakia. A Street of the Jews is mentioned in 1362. The Jews were expelled in 1542 with the rest of the Jews in the state, but began to return in 1549. In the 17th cent., most traded in cloth, apparel, furs, and spices and from 1680 in grain as well. A fire destroyed all houses in the city in 1681 and J. homes and stores were also damaged in riots in the late 19th cent. The J. pop. reached a peak of 358 (4% of the total) in 1880 and then declined steadily to 90 in 1939. Most Jews were deported to the Theresienstadt ghetto in 1942 together with the Jews of Prague and from there to the death camps of Poland.

JIDOVITA (now Rebreanu, formerly Tradam; Hung. Entradam; Yid. Unterdam) N. Transylvania dist., Rumania. Galician Jews settled here in the early 17th cent., making J. one of the earliest J. settlements in the district. It had a constant J. majority: 297 in 1900 (90% of the total) and 137 in 1920 (87%). Jews produced and sold alcohol. In May 1944, the community was transferred to the Bistrita ghetto and then deported to Auschwitz.

JIEZNAS (Yid. Yezne) Alytus dist., Lithuania. Jews first settled here in the beginning of the 19th cent. During WWI the Jews were expelled; most returned after the war. Between the World Wars the community maintained a Hebrew school, library, and social welfare organizations. The J. pop. in 1940 was about 300 (27% of the total). Even before the Germans entered on 25 June 1941, Lithuanian nationalists began abusing and killing Jews. On 3 Sept. 1941, all the remaining Jews (144 in number) were killed in the neighborhood of J. Eighteen succeeded in fleeing; few survived.

JIHLAVA Moravia, Czechoslovakia. Jews are mentioned in 1249 and in 1345 the future Charles IV encouraged them to settle to aid the development of the new cloth industry. Many were moneylenders. Duke Albrecht expelled the Jews in 1425 but they were permitted to settle again in the late 18th cent. The community grew after the 1848 revolution, reaching a pop. of 1,090 in 1869 and 1,497 (6.3% of the total) in 1890. A new synagogue was completed in 1863. The composer Gustav Mahler (1860–1911) lived in J. until he was 17. In 1930, the J. pop. was 1,025, with many arriving from the Sudetenland in fall 1938. The Nazis burned the synagogue and destroyed J. stores and in 1942 deported the Jews to the Theresienstadt ghetto and the death camps of Poland. There were 32 survivors in the town after the war.

JIMBOLIA (Hung. Szombolya) S. Transylvania dist., Rumania. The J. community was founded in 1870. The J. pop. in 1930 was 95 (0.9 % of the total). On 3 July 1941, J. property was confiscated and the J. pop. transferred to Timosoara.

JINDRICHUV HRADEC Bohemia, Czechoslovakia. Jews settled in the late 13th cent. Residence was restricted to four families in the 15th cent. In the 17th cent. Jews traded mainly in cloth, wool, and tobacco. A J. knitting mill opened in 1888 employed 680 workers. The J. pop. was 617 in 1880 and then declined steadily to 234 (total 10,467) in 1930. J. stores were looted in 1919. The Zionists were active after WWI. The Nazis closed the synagogue in Oct. 1941 and in 1942 deported the remaining Jews to the Theresienstadt ghetto and from there to the death camps of Poland.

JODLOWA Cracow dist., Poland. Jews settled in the late 18th cent., with the J. pop. reaching a peak of 301 (total 3,878) in 1921. A spree of looting in 1919 exem-

plified the unremitting hostility of the non-J. pop. while the Polish cooperatives eroded J. livelihoods. The Germans occupied the town in early Sept. 1939 and initiated a reign of terror, with many Jews sent to forced labor. On 10 July 1942, 25 Jews were murdered by German police. On 12 Aug. the remaining 160 were led to the forest in groups, stripped naked, and murdered beside an open grave.

JODY Vilna dist., Poland, today Belarus. Jews apparently arrived only in 1903 owing to a previous residence ban. With recovery from the tribulations of WWI, the Jews opened stores and workshops. Most had auxiliary farms beside their homes. In 1921 the J. pop. was 238 (total 479). Many young people left for want of employment or, in the case of the more prosperous, to study in Vilna. The Zionist youth movements were active in the 1930s. The Germans entered the town on 21 July 1941. In Aug. the local pop. staged a pogrom against the Jews. On 17 Dec., SS machine-gunners and the Lithuanian police massacred 530 Jews from J. and the neighboring villages.

JOEHLINGEN Baden, Germany. The first J. settlers arrived in the first half of the 18th cent. J. homes were attacked in the rioting during the 1848 revolution. The J. pop. reached a peak of 99 (total 2,241) in 1875, then dropped rapidly, numbering 12 in 1933. Four emigrated to the U.S. and one to France in 1933–39. On *Kristallnacht* (9–10 Nov. 1938), the synagogue was vandalized and on 22 Oct. 1940 the last six Jews were deported to the Gurs concentration camp, where all perished.

JOHANNISBURG (Pol. Pisz) East Prussia, Germany, today Poland. Jews settled in J. in the first half of the 19th cent. The J. pop. was 150 in 1843 and 186 in 1880, declining to about 140 in the first decades of the 20th cent. The community established a synagogue in 1855 and a cemetery in 1827 (at the latest). An explosive device went off in front of a J. store in summer 1932. On the eve of the Nazi assumption of power in 1933, about 195 Jews were living in J. Zionist activities were intensified with the establishment of a branch of the German Zionist Organization in Aug.

Jewish blacksmith at work, Jonava, Lithuania

1933. Boycott measures became more acute in 1934–35. By Feb. 1938, the community numbered 59, most of whom needed economic assistance. No information is available on their fate under Nazi rule.

JONAVA Kaunas dist., Lithuania. Jews first settled in the 18th cent. In 1893 a conflagration destroyed the J. community's two synagogues. Many emigrated to America and South Africa. A "modern" *talmud torah* was opened. The J. pop. in 1897 was 3,975 (80% of the total). At the end of the 19th cent. the Zionist Association was founded. In 1912 Avraham Mordekhai Rosenson (Raziel) emigrated to Eretz Israel. His son, David, was a commander of the underground Irgun organization and his daughter, Esther Raziel-Naor, was a Knesset member. During WWI the Jews were expelled by the Russian army. After the war some of the Jews returned. Two-thirds of the municipal council members were Jews, as was the mayor and deputy mayor. In the 1930s Lithuanians boycotted J. businesses. Three J. elementary schools operated: Hebrew secular, Hebrew religious, and Yiddish. Many Jews were Zionists and most of the Zionist parties and youth groups had branches in J. Many young people emigrated to Palestine. There were several social welfare organizations, including a J. hospital. After Poland was occupied by Germany in 1939, many J. refugees arrived in J., including an entire yeshiva from Kleck. The J. pop. in 1940 was 3,000 (60% of the total). On the day of the German invasion, 22 June 1941, the J. deputy mayor was murdered by a Lithuanian. The next day 70 Jews hiding in a cellar were killed by a shell fired from the battlefield. On 26 June all the Jews were rounded up in the marketplace and armed Lithuanians were poised to slaughter them when a mortar landed nearby and everyone scattered. From 29 June, Jews were taken to the Girele grove outside the town and shot. In Aug., first the men and then the women and children were taken to Girele and killed. Altogether 2,108 were shot there.

JONISKELIS (Yid. Yonishkel) Birzai dist., Lithuania. Jews first settled in the 18th cent. The J. pop. in 1897 was 136 (22% of the total). At the end of the 19th cent., many Jews emigrated to America and South Africa. During WWI the Jews were expelled, some returning after the war. In elections for Lithuania's Sejm, most Jews voted for the Zionist list. J.

native Benjamin Miller was among the founders of the American Zionist Federation. The J. pop. in 1940 was 210 (21% of the total). After the German invasion in June 1941, Lithuanian nationalists tortured, robbed, and killed Jews. On 26 Aug. 1941 the Jews were taken to a grove next to Zadeikiai and murdered.

JONISKIS (I) (Yid. Yanishok) Utena dist., Lithuania. Jews first settled here in the 18th cent. The J. pop. in 1923 was 159 (68% of the total). Many Jews emigrated to the west and to other places in Lithuania. The J. pop. in 1940 was 90. All the Jews were shot to death shortly after the German conquest of June 1941.

JONISKIS (II) (Yid. Yanishok) Siauliai dist., Lithuania. Jews first settled in the 18th cent. At the end of the 19th cent. many emigrated to South Africa. Zionist organizations, including Hovevei Zion, were established in J. and many contributed to Zionist funds. The J. pop. in 1897 was 2,272 (48% of the total). Between the World Wars, a J. community council ran the community's affairs. In elections to the Lithuanian Sejm, most Jews voted for the Zionist party. In 1934, two Jews were elected to the nine-member town council and a Jew was elected deputy mayor. In the 1930s many left because of economic conditions, which were aggravated by a boycott of J. businesses. The J. pop. in 1940 was about 600 (10% of the total). After the Germans entered on 24 June 1941, Lithuanian nationalists established a special department for J. affairs, which was behind all the subsequent persecutions. In July 1941, all the Jews were taken to Vilkiausis and killed.

JORDANOW Cracow dist., Poland. An organized J. community existed in the early 19th cent., growing to 238 (total 1,486) in 1921. The cattle market was an important source of J. trade and J. summer camps for schoolchildren from Cracow and elsewhere provided another source of income as well as encouraging the formation of local Zionist youth groups. The Germans took the town on 3 Sept. 1939 and immediately persecuted the Jews, with forced labor for males and females aged 14–60. On 29 Aug 1942, the Germans staged an *Aktion*, murdering many in the town and 70 young children with their mothers in the vicinity before sending about 400 to the Belzec death camp.

JOSEFOW NAD WISLA Lublin dist., Poland.

Jews settled when J. received municipal status in 1765. Their pop. rose to 1,580 (total 1,918) in 1867 but dropped to 736 in 1921 after emigration and wartime flight. Many more fled to nearby towns after the German occupation in Sept. 1939. In May 1942, those remaining were expelled to Demblin-Irena and on 6 May deported to the Sobibor death camp.

JOSVAINIAI (Yid. Yosven) Kedainiai dist., Lithuania. Jews first settled here in the 17th cent. The J. pop. in 1897 was 534 (40% of the total). During WWI the Jews were expelled, most returning after the war. The J. school, which first taught in Yiddish, later taught in Hebrew. The Zionist organizations prepared many young people to emigrate to Palestine. The J. pop. in 1941 was 270. After the German invasion in June 1941, Lithuanians abused, robbed, and killed individual Jews. They then took those still alive and murdered them outside the town.

JOVRA (Hung. Odarma or Darma; Yid. Jure) Carpatho-Russia, Czechoslovakia, today Ukraine. Jews probably settled in the first half of the 18th cent. Four Jews were present in 1768. The J. pop. rose to 193 in 1830 and 325 (total 1,380) in 1880. A few Jews farmed small plots of land and one large farm was also in J. hands. In 1921, under the Czechoslovakians, the J. pop. was 235 and in 1941 it was 241. The Hungarians occupied J. in March 1939 and in 1940–41 drafted a few dozen Jews into labor battalions, sending them to forced labor camps or to the eastern front. In Aug. 1941, a number of J. families without Hungarian citizenship were expelled to the German-occupied Ukraine and murdered. A few hundred were deported to Auschwitz in the second half of May 1944.

JOZEFIN Volhynia dist., Poland, today Ukraine. The J. pop. in 1921 was 322 (total 1,227). Under the Nazis, the community shared the fate of the Jews of neighboring Korzec.

JOZEFOW Lublin dist., Poland. A small J. community existed in the late 17th cent., with Jews engaging in the lumber trade. In the 19th cent., they dominated the trade in alcoholic beverages and opened a number of Hebrew printing presses. A synagogue was erected in 1735. R. Yaakov Yitzhak ha-Levi Horowitz, "the Seer of Lublin," was born in J. in 1745 and R. Shelomo Kluger, "the *Maggid* of Brody" (d. 1869)

officiated there (1815–21). The J. pop. rose from 692 in 1827 to 1,056 (total 1,344) in 1921. After WWI, most Jews lived in straitened economic circumstances. Community life centered around the hasidic *shtiblekh*, with Gur predominating and the Zionists becoming active only in the late 1920s. The German bombardments of Sept. 1939 destroyed most of the town and about 300 Jews fled with the Red Army. The Germans set up a labor camp in J., bringing in Jews from Warsaw and other localities. Many died there because of the particularly harsh conditions. A ghetto was never established at J. In March 1941, the influx of refugees brought the pop. up to 1,300 and to 1,800 in July 1942. After a selection sent 200–400 able-bodied men to labor camps in the Lublin area, 1,200 Jews were executed in the nearby woods by German police on 13 July.

JUDENDORF (from 1940, Chkalovo) Nikolaiev dist., Ukraine. J. was founded as a J. colony in 1871. After their arrival in Aug. 1941, the Germans murdered the few Jews who had neither fled nor been evacuated.

JUECHEN Rhineland, Germany. The first Jew in J. received a letter of protection in 1679. In the 18th cent., the few living there were peddlers and brokers. In the 19th cent., economic conditions improved with Jews trading in grain, livestock, and real estate. The first synagogue was consecrated in 1764 and a new one in 1835. The J. pop. reached a peak of 112 (total 2,328) in 1895 and dwindled to 60 in 1925. On the eve of the Nazi rise to power in 1933, the J. pop. numbered 50. The synagogue was destroyed on *Kristallnacht* (9–10 Nov. 1938). The last nine Jews were deported to the east via Duesseldorf on 9 Dec. 1941. At least 11 Jews perished in the Holocaust.

JUELICH Rhineland, Germany. J. martyrs are mentioned in the 13th cent. The community was destroyed in 1349 during the Black Death persecutions and its property expropriated. A permanent J. settlement existed from the mid-17th cent., growing to about ten families in the 18th cent. and to 137 individuals in 1910. The community maintained an ancient cemetery and in 1816 purchased land for a new one. A synagogue was consecrated in 1861. In 1840, a J. couple were victims of a blood libel. Jews were active in the life of the city, joining local organizations and one Jew even serving on the municipal council in 1903–07. In June 1933,

The old synagogue of Jurbarkas, Lithuania, dating from 1790

the J. pop. was 120. Many Jews, especially the young, emigrated in the 1933–37 period. On *Kristallnacht* (9–10 Nov. 1938), SA troops and local residents burned and looted the synagogue. J. homes were vandalized and 26 J. men were sent to the Sachsenhausen and Buchenwald concentration camps. Of the 52 Jews remaining in March 1939, several still managed to emigrate or find refuge in other German cities by 1941. In March 1941, the last Jews of J. (about 30) and the surrounding villages were dispatched to the Kirchberg assembly camp for deportation to the east. A total of 71 Jews perished in the death camps, including some who had escaped to Holland and Belgium.

JUGENHEIM   Hesse, Germany. Numbering 67 (6% of the total) in 1861, the community fell victim to antisemitism in the 1880s and disbanded in 1927. Most of the few remaining Jews (18 in 1933) left after *Kristallnacht* (9–10 Nov. 1938), when the synagogue was vandalized.

JUODUPE   (Yid. Yodupis) Rokiskis dist., Lithuania.

The J. pop. in 1923 was 194. All the Jews were killed after the German occupation of 1941.

JURBARKAS   (Jurbork) Raseiniai dist., Lithuania. Jews first settled in the 17th cent. In 1790 a magnificent wooden synagogue was built. Haskala influence caused the *talmud torah* (partially supported by Jews from J. living in the U.S.) to teach Hebrew, Russian, and mathematics in addition to religious subjects. One of its teachers, Avraham Mapu (1808–67), was the creator of the modern Hebrew novel. The J. pop. in 1897 was 2,350 (31% of the total). During WWI most of the Jews left, many returning later. Between the World Wars a considerable number emigrated to the west. A majority of J.'s Jews voted for the Zionist list in elections for the Lithuanian Sejm. Jews were elected to the municipal council and one served as its deputy chairman. In the 1930s Jews were pushed out of their businesses and there were violent attacks against Jews and their property. J. economic and communal life suffered under the Soviets in 1940–41. After the German invasion in June 1941, Jews were forced to

Clerks at work in the Jewish People's Bank, Jurbarkas, Lithuania

destroy the ancient wooden synagogue while the rabbi and others were made to burn the town's religious books. In July, 322 Jews were shot in the J. cemetery; 150 elderly Jews were murdered outside the town and 520 women and children were shot in the Smalininkai grove. A few Jews escaped from the town; some formed a guerrilla band that attacked Nazis and Lithuanian nationalists.

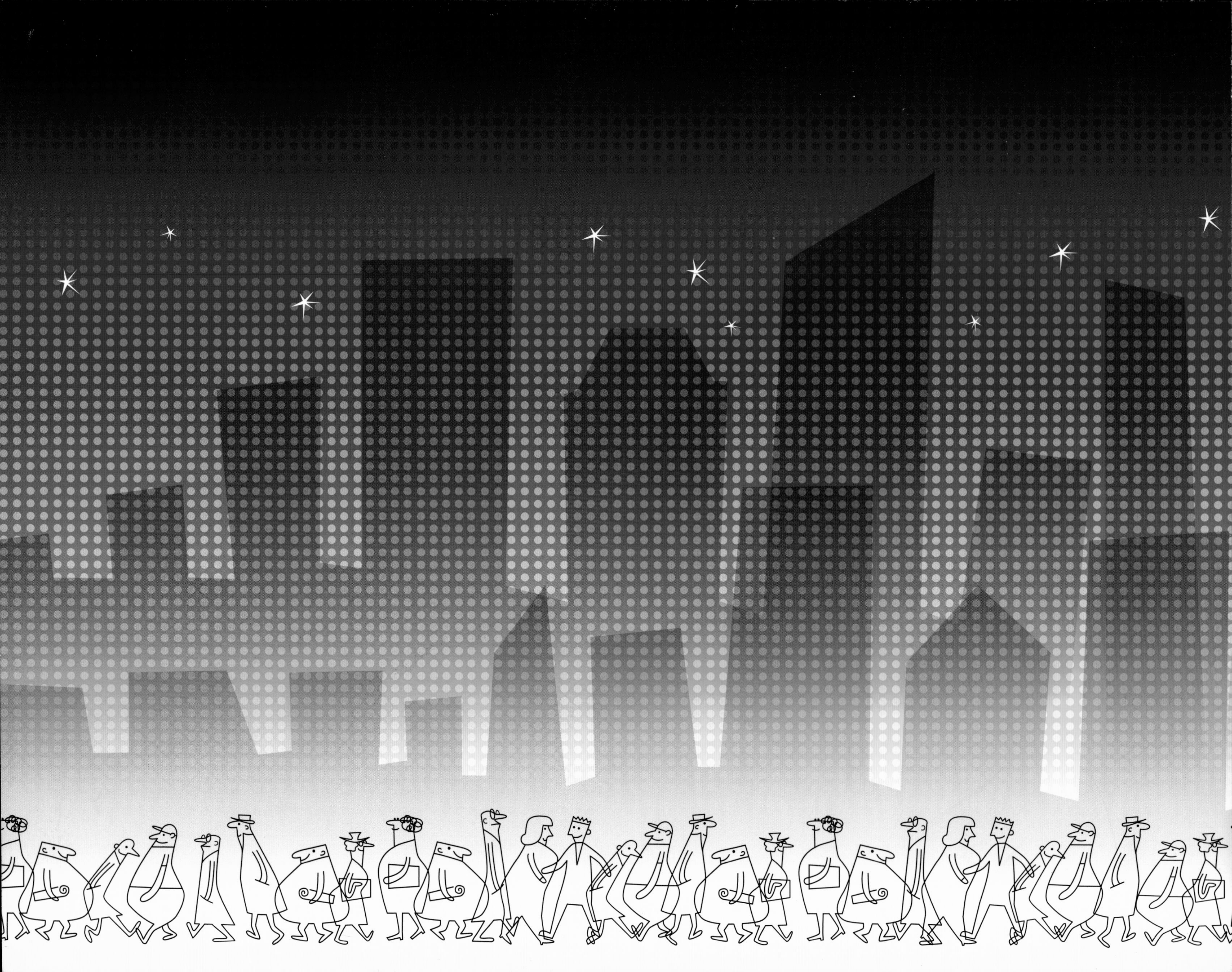

about The Actors Fund

Everyone referred to in this book, from actor to dresser and producer to usher, has been helped by the tireless efforts of a national organization called The Actors Fund.

The Actors Fund's mission is to "help all professionals in performing arts and entertainment.
The Fund is a safety net, providing programs and services for those who are in need, crisis, or transition."

When The Actors Fund was founded in 1882, it was created out of a need to support those in the performing arts: working in entertainment often meant great sacrifices, such as being stranded far from home while on tour, or not being treated with dignity because, at that time, show people were considered to be outcasts from society.

The Actors Fund continues to help the many individuals who dedicate their lives to the arts, and today is a highly-rated, nonprofit human services organization, which provides essential programs to thousands every year— both performers and everyone behind the scenes. The Fund helps people who work in film, theater, television, music, radio, opera, and dance—a group that, even today, makes far less money and has far fewer services (such as health insurance and pensions) than other Americans.

To learn about The Actors Fund, visit online at www.actorsfund.org

*A portion of the proceeds from the sale of this book
will be donated to The Actors Fund.*

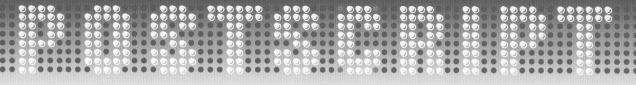

POSTSCRIPT

As I write this
I am inspired by a magnificent thunderstorm
that is raging outside my window—
a noisy collaboration in the sky
that quenches the thirst of the ground.

I smile as I realize
it is not unlike the theatre.

When I am at a show,
I marvel at the complexity and diversity
of individual elements
that somehow all work together
night after night.
I marvel even though I know the secret:

Collaboration.

Like the tiny crystals in a colossal cloud,
it is contact and interaction
that give us the ability to create a thunderbolt,
which can illuminate the heavens
and shake the earth.

Collaboration.

It is the power behind the arts—
behind the book and the music,
the dance and the design.

It is the power
behind those who make the lights shine not only on Broadway,
but all over the world.

—Brian Stokes Mitchell

"All the world's a stage,

And all the men and women merely players:

They have their exits and their entrances;

And one man in his time plays many parts . . ."

—William Shakespeare

Many years ago I found myself completely alone in a theater where I was rehearsing. I walked down to the left front corner of the stage and sat on the edge.

As I looked back and forth between the empty chairs in the audience and the empty stage, I suddenly burst out laughing and thought, *Man, what I do for a living is bizarre!* I show up for work, put on different clothes, put on makeup, and then I step out in front of thousands of people pretending to be someone else.

And yet, I am not alone in this endeavor. I am a member of a company of fellow storytellers who add their own individual ingredients. Writers, lyricists and composers create the words and music that are spoken and sung; set and costume people place us in a specific visual time and space; lighting people add mood and focus; sound people shape the sonic environment; musicians accompany the emotional energy; and a crew maneuvers the physical elements. Choreographers supply a movement language; a director glues it all together; and a producer raises the money so the show can go on.

But why do we storytellers take part in this exercise, day in, day out, year after year?

Because together we get to explore what makes life so interesting. We get to present our discoveries in a captivating and inspiring story. And we get to share it all with you—the audience—in a once-in-a-lifetime-event.

Unlike a movie or television program that is the same no matter where you sit or when you see it, live theater is custom-built for each audience. Every performance is different and every individual in that audience has a unique experience that won't be repeated ever again.

Never exactly the same thing twice.

It's what gives the theater AND life . . . ZING!

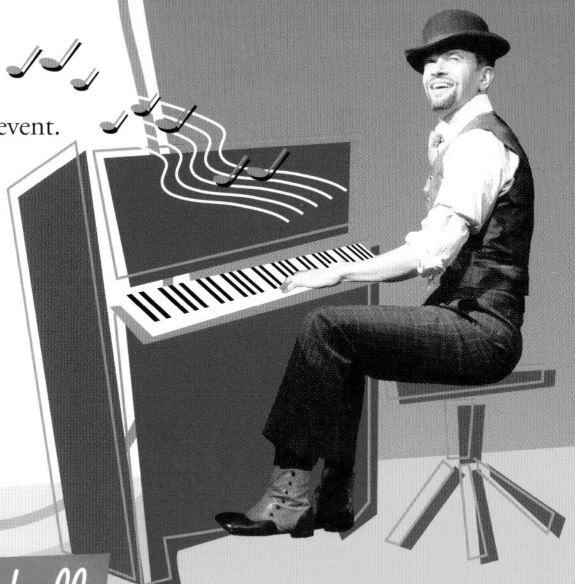

-Brian Stokes Mitchell

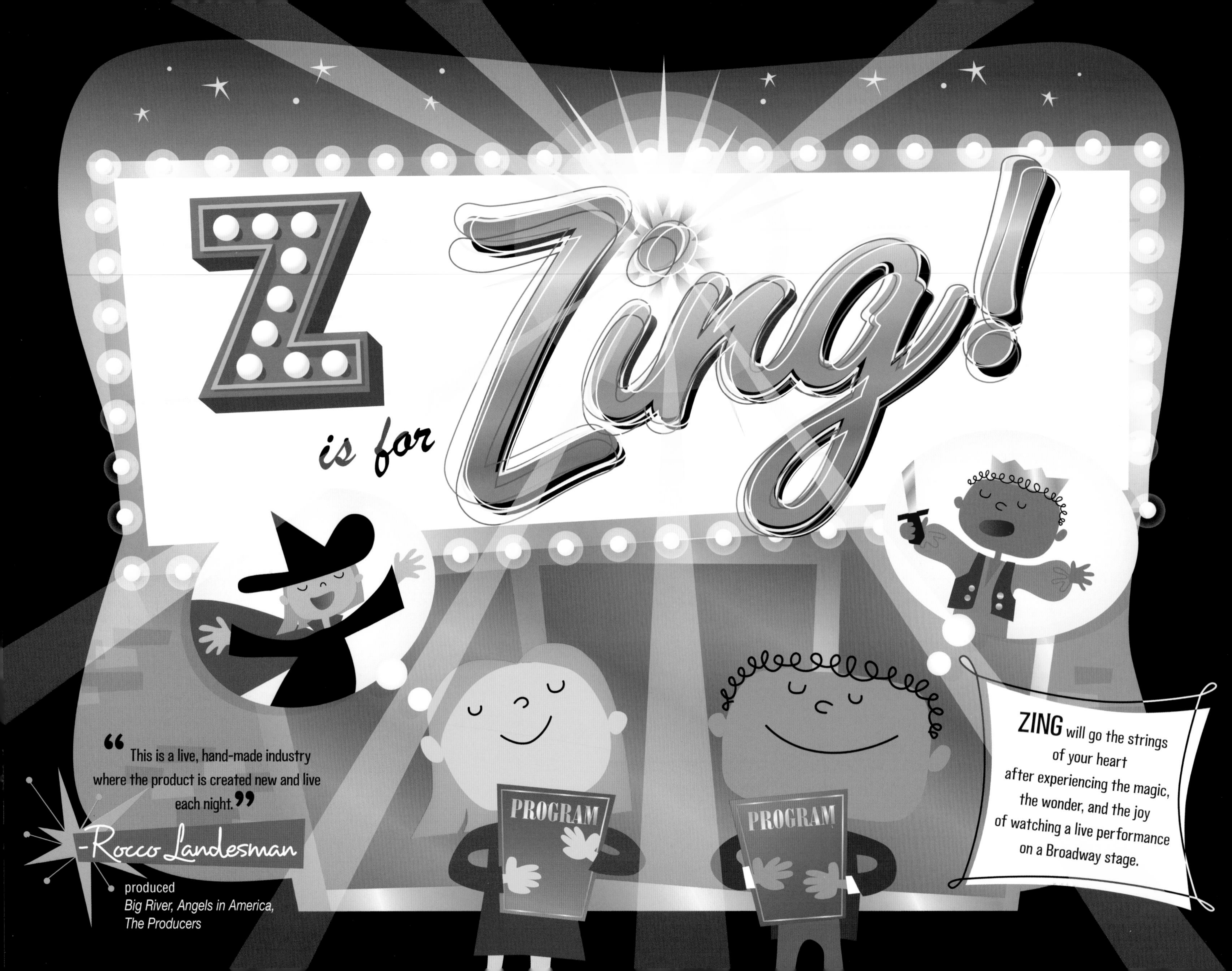

Z is for Zing!
PROGRAM
PROGRAM
"This is a live, hand-made industry where the product is created new and live each night."
-Rocco Landesman
produced *Big River, Angels in America, The Producers*
ZING will go the strings of your heart after experiencing the magic, the wonder, and the joy of watching a live performance on a Broadway stage.

Y is for Young Performers

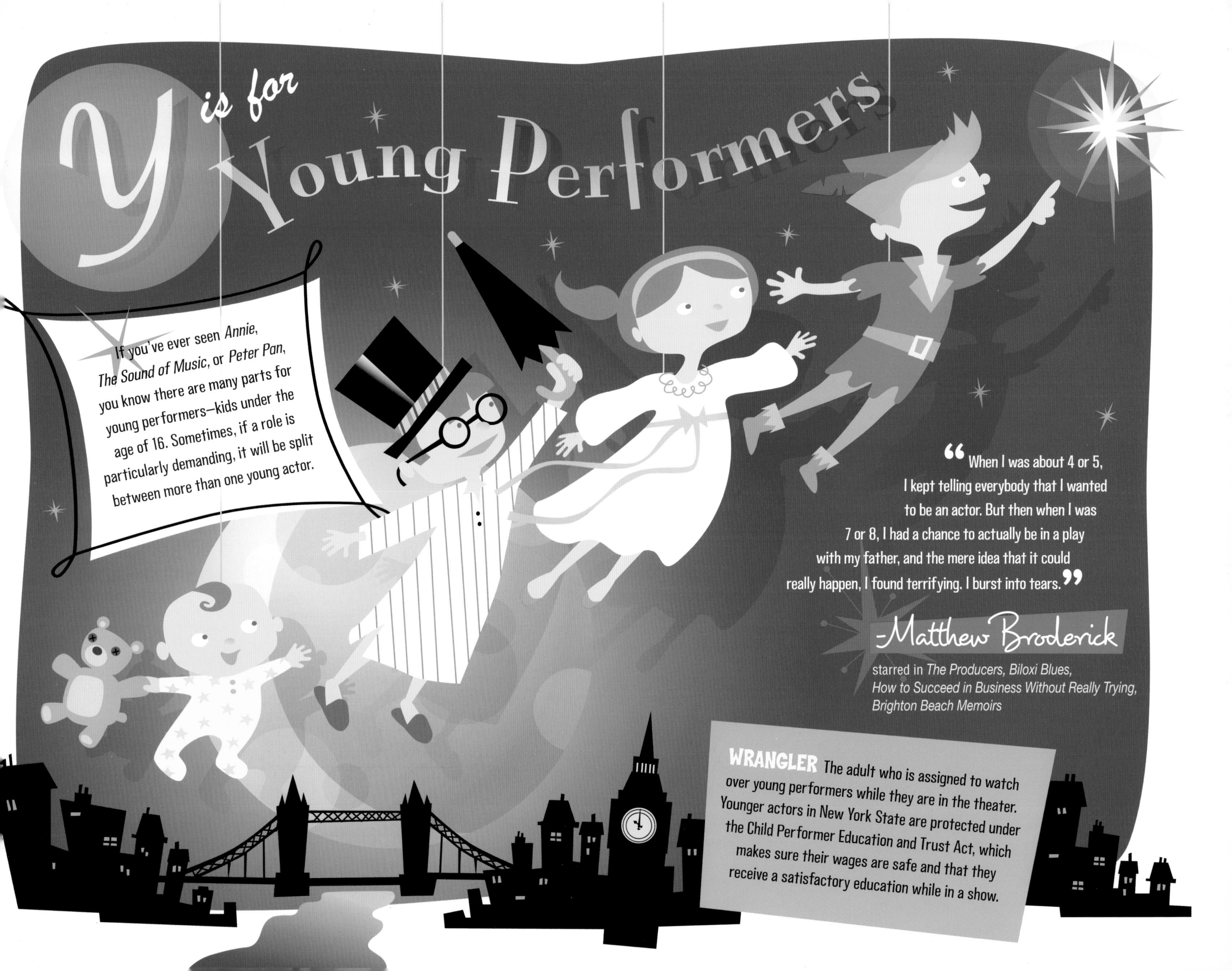

If you've ever seen *Annie*, *The Sound of Music*, or *Peter Pan*, you know there are many parts for young performers—kids under the age of 16. Sometimes, if a role is particularly demanding, it will be split between more than one young actor.

"When I was about 4 or 5, I kept telling everybody that I wanted to be an actor. But then when I was 7 or 8, I had a chance to actually be in a play with my father, and the mere idea that it could really happen, I found terrifying. I burst into tears."

—Matthew Broderick

starred in *The Producers, Biloxi Blues, How to Succeed in Business Without Really Trying, Brighton Beach Memoirs*

WRANGLER The adult who is assigned to watch over young performers while they are in the theater. Younger actors in New York State are protected under the Child Performer Education and Trust Act, which makes sure their wages are safe and that they receive a satisfactory education while in a show.

X is for CROSS

"I work with the director, the designers, the cast, the crew, and even the front-of-house staff. I am responsible for scheduling, making sure that everyone is where they are supposed to be, and doing what they are supposed to do . . . . You name it. I'm sticking my nose into it!"

—Richard Hester

stage managed *Jersey Boys, Titanic, Sweet Smell of Success*

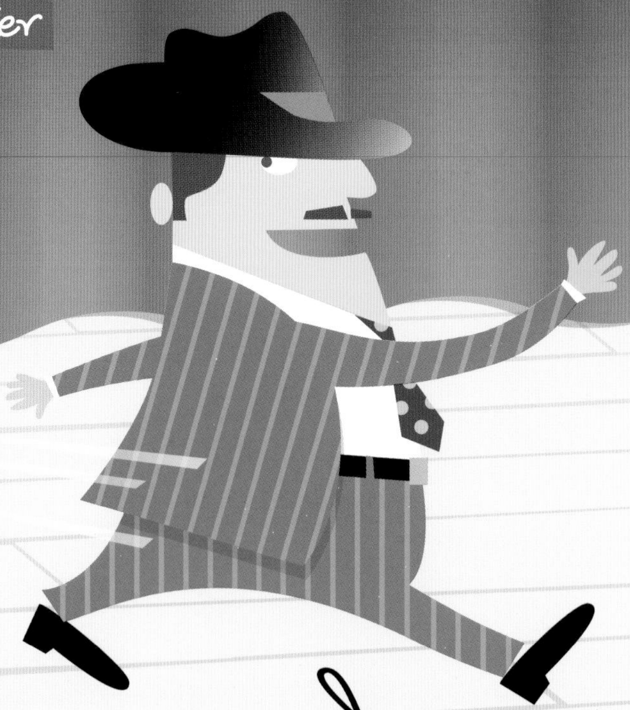

STAGE DIRECTIONS

The playwright's written instructions to the director and actors about when characters enter and exit a scene, how they cross the stage, and how they say their lines. Stage directions also provide details about what happens in the background, what sounds are heard, what the lighting should be, and what the mood of the scene is.

The five main areas of the stage—

upstage
downstage
stage right
stage left
center stage

are also the five basic stage directions given to guide actors' movements.

A notation used by a **stage manager** when an actor crosses the stage. The stage manager keeps a **prompt book**, which has all the notes about actors' movements and positions on the stage (also known as **blocking**), as well as notes about lighting cues, props, and costumes.

PROMPT BOOK 'SECRET CODE'

Stage manager's notation in prompt book:

X DSL to DSC, X US and out SR

What it means:

Cross down stage left to downstage center, cross upstage and exit stage right.

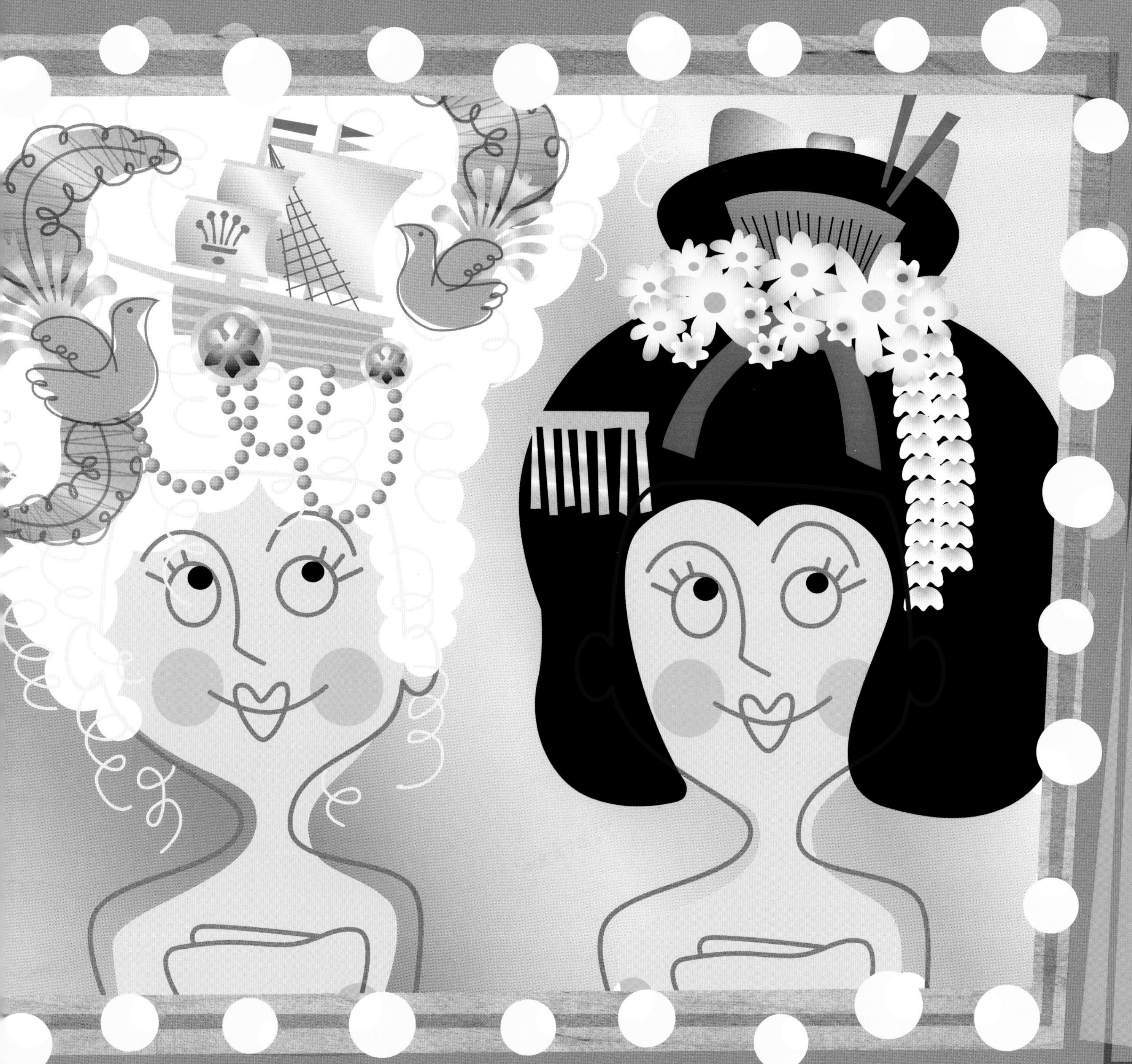

MAKEUP All the cosmetics such as eye shadow, rouge, and lipstick, that are used to transform an actor into a character. In addition to helping an actor 'become' the character, makeup is used to highlight and define an actor's features under the bright lights on stage, which can wash out a performer's face.

BASE The foundation an actor uses to cover his entire face, neck, and ears before he applies the rest of his makeup.

WIG CAP The sheer cap actors put on their heads to cover and flatten their hair so that a wig stays securely in place.

BALD CAP A cap made out of latex that covers up an actor's hair completely, making him appear bald. But some actors shave their heads for a part: Reid Shelton, *Annie*'s Daddy Warbucks, shaved his head daily with an electric razor.

PROSTHETICS The artificial devices, usually made of latex, foam, or gelatin, that change or enhance an actor's appearance. Shrek's horn-like ears, Cyrano de Bergerac's prominent nose, and even wrinkles and warts are different types of prosthetics.

SPIRIT GUM The liquid glue used to make facial hair—beards, moustaches, eyebrows, sideburns, and prosthetics—stick.

W

is for Wigs

The hairpieces (sometimes made of real hair, sometimes artificial hair) that help an actor look like the character he or she is portraying: Little Orphan Annie or Lady Macbeth; Don Quixote or The Artful Dodger.

" Ever since I was probably 11 or 12 I always wanted to do not just makeup, but make characters and creatures and monsters. "

—David Presto

designed prosthetics and did makeup for
Shrek, The Musical

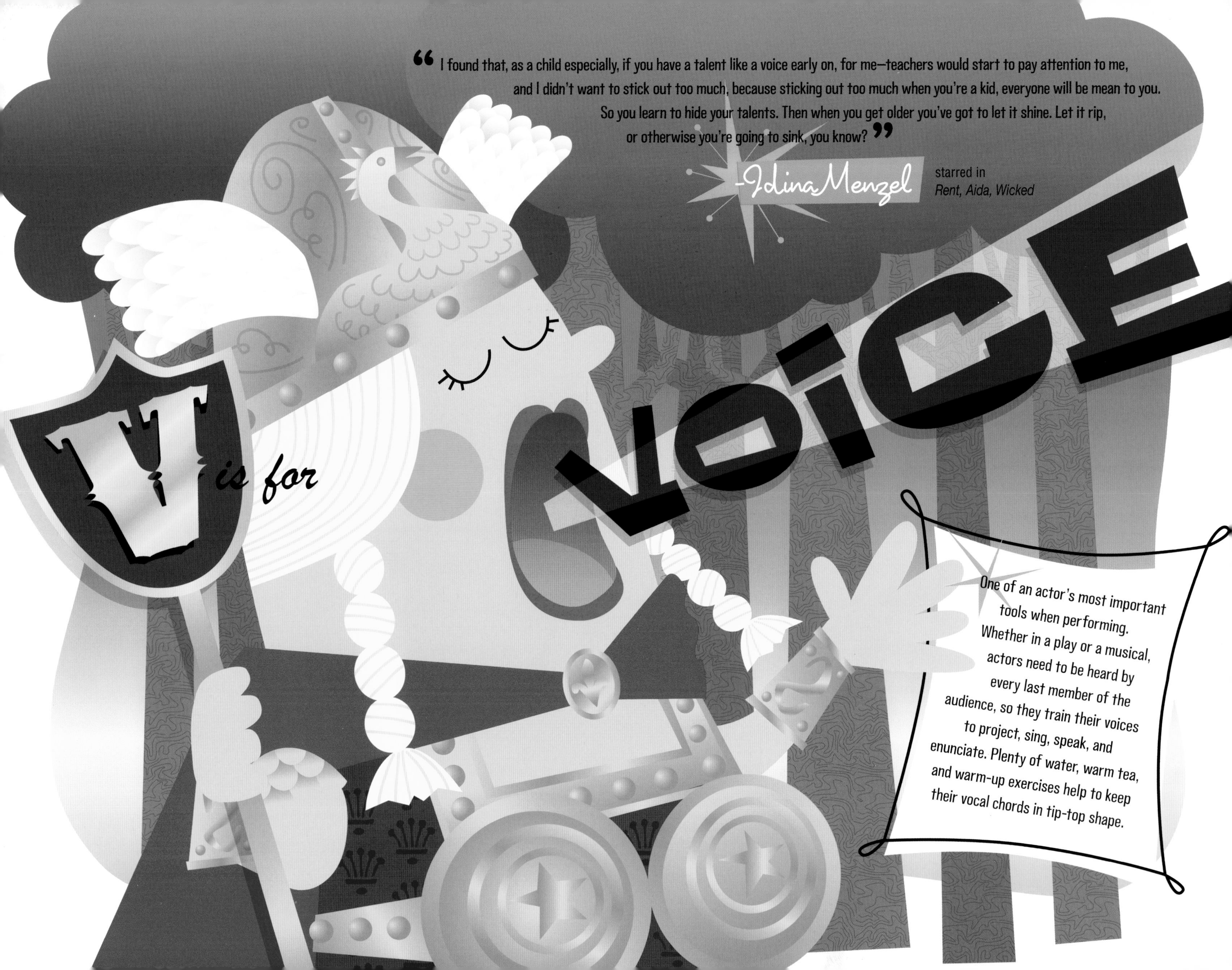

“I found that, as a child especially, if you have a talent like a voice early on, for me—teachers would start to pay attention to me, and I didn't want to stick out too much, because sticking out too much when you're a kid, everyone will be mean to you. So you learn to hide your talents. Then when you get older you've got to let it shine. Let it rip, or otherwise you're going to sink, you know?”

-Idina Menzel starred in *Rent, Aida, Wicked*

V is for VOICE

One of an actor's most important tools when performing. Whether in a play or a musical, actors need to be heard by every last member of the audience, so they train their voices to project, sing, speak, and enunciate. Plenty of water, warm tea, and warm-up exercises help to keep their vocal chords in tip-top shape.

“I was in a panic . . . the Marriott was only a block and a half away, but I hailed a cab and said: ‘You’ve got to take me to the Marriott Marquis. Bernadette Peters is sick, and I’m going on in a Broadway show!’”

–Karyn Quackenbush

understudied for Bernadette Peters in *Annie Get Your Gun*

One of the leads calls in sick! How will the show go on? Who will perform the part? The understudy is an actor in the cast who learns all the lines and blocking of a major role and is able to replace the regular performer at a moment’s notice.

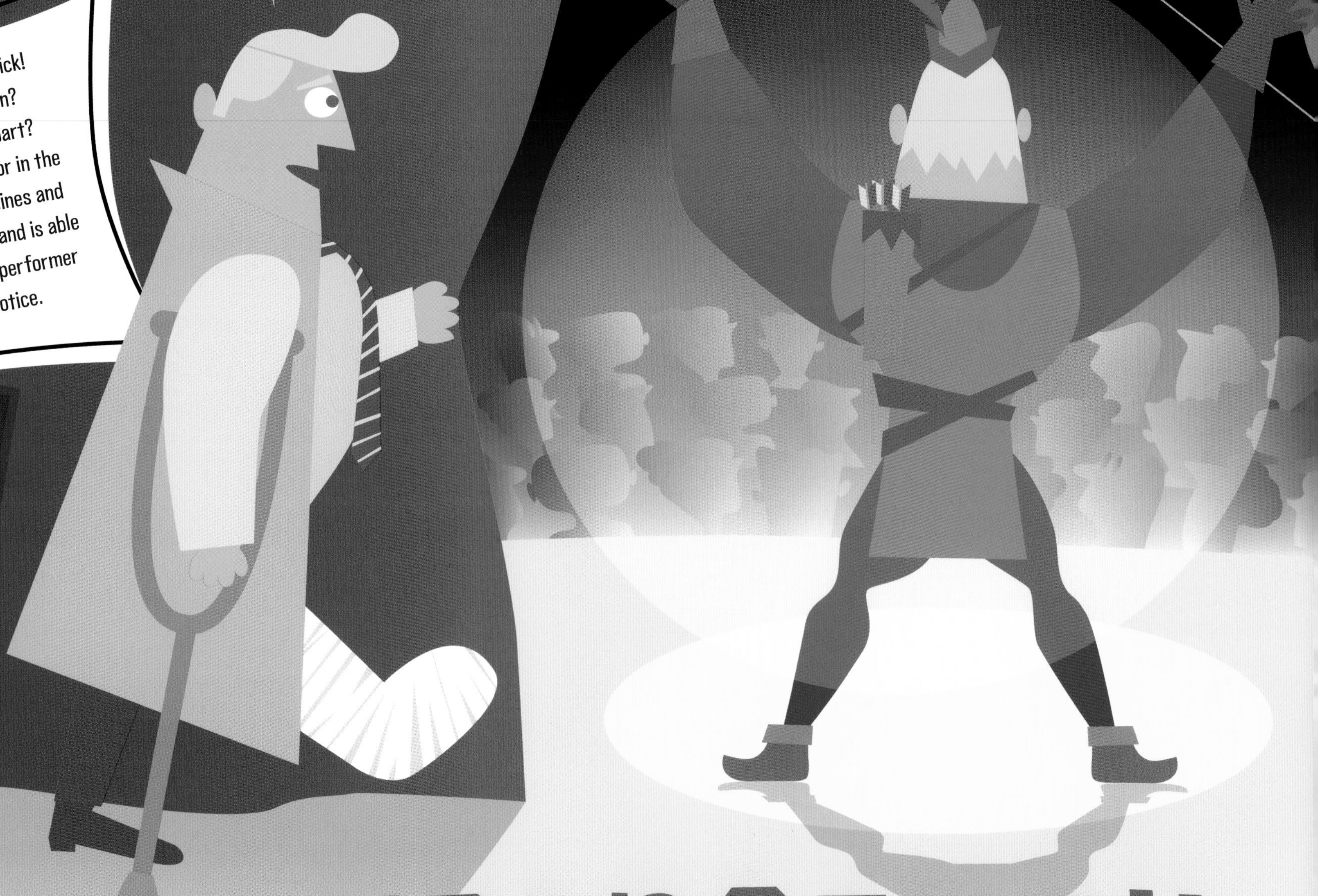

FAMOUS UNDERSTUDIES

Shirley MacLaine
for Carol Haney in *The Pajama Game*

Kevin Spacey
for Harvey Keitel in *Hurlyburly*

Elaine Stritch
for Ethel Merman in *Call Me Madam*

S. Epatha Merkerson
for Lynne Thigpen in *Tintypes*

Lainie Kazan
for Barbra Streisand in *Funny Girl*

U is for UNDERSTUDY

and Tony Award

The Tony Award® recognizes excellence in all areas of theater, including acting, directing, writing, and costume design. The Tony, named for actor, director, and founder of the American Theatre Wing Antoinette Perry, is awarded at an annual ceremony in New York City.

The Tony medallion, designed by Herman Rosse, has the masks of comedy and tragedy—the universal symbols of theater—on one side and the profile of Antoinette Perry on the other.

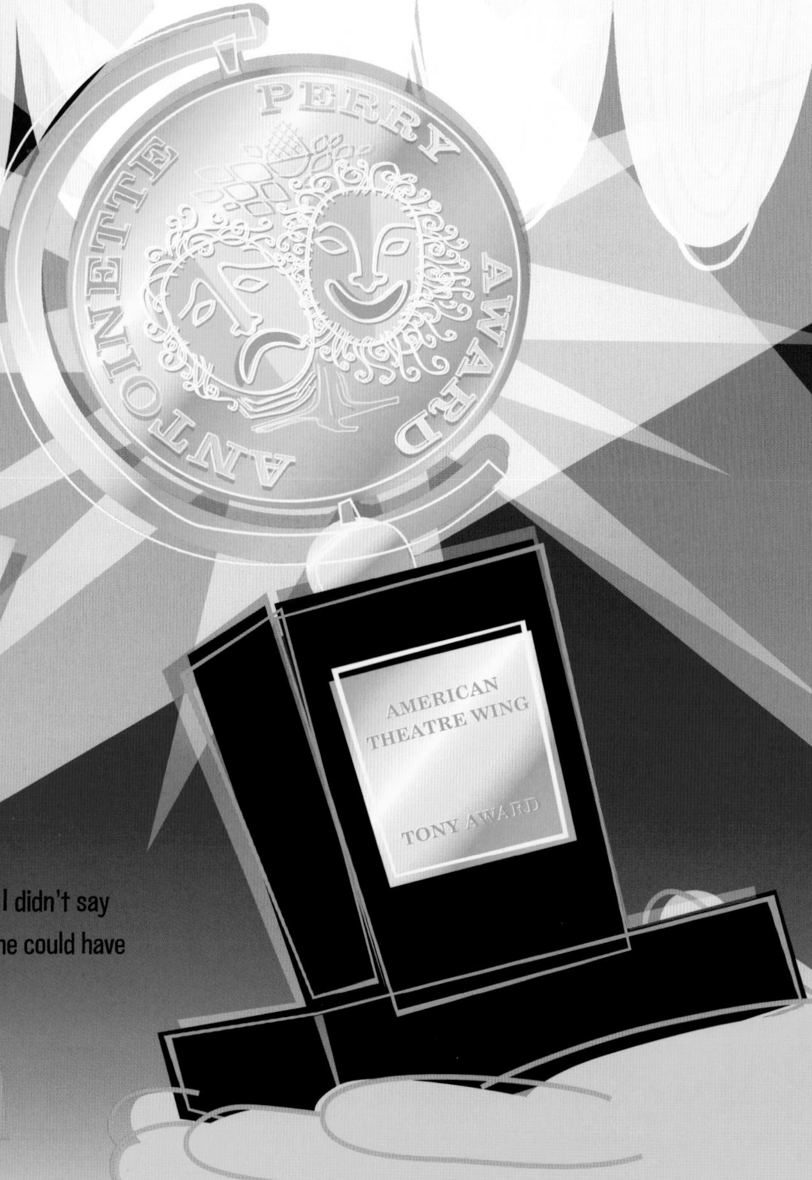
ANTOINETTE PERRY AWARD
AMERICAN THEATRE WING
TONY AWARD

“I wanted to be an actress as soon as I could lisp. I didn't say I was going to become an actress. I felt I was one. No one could have convinced me I wasn't.”

–Antoinette Perry

actress, producer, director, who founded the American Theatre Wing

BOB FOSSE has won eight Tony Awards, more than any other choreographer.

STEPHEN SONDHEIM has won eight Tony Awards, more than any other composer.

HAL PRINCE has won more Tony Awards than any other person, with 21 awards, as a director and producer.

PHYLICIA RASHAD became the first African-American actress to win a Tony for a leading role in a non-musical, in *A Raisin in the Sun*.

FRANKIE MICHAELS, at 10 years old, was the youngest actor ever to win a Tony Award (in 1966, for *Mame*).

DAISY EAGAN, at 11 years old, was the youngest actress ever to win a Tony Award (in 1991, for *The Secret Garden*).

AMANDA PLUMMER is the only winner of a Tony Award whose parents, Christopher Plummer and Tammy Grimes, have both also been awarded Tonys.

JULIE TAYMOR was the first woman to win a Tony Award for directing a musical, *The Lion King*.

T *is for* TICKET

"I've saved every
I've ever seen, even the very first, which was
Beauty and the Beast. The tickets remind me of
how wonderful Broadway is, and how lucky
I am to be able to see great
Broadway shows."

—Trevor Braun

starred in *Beauty and The Beast*, *The Little Mermaid*

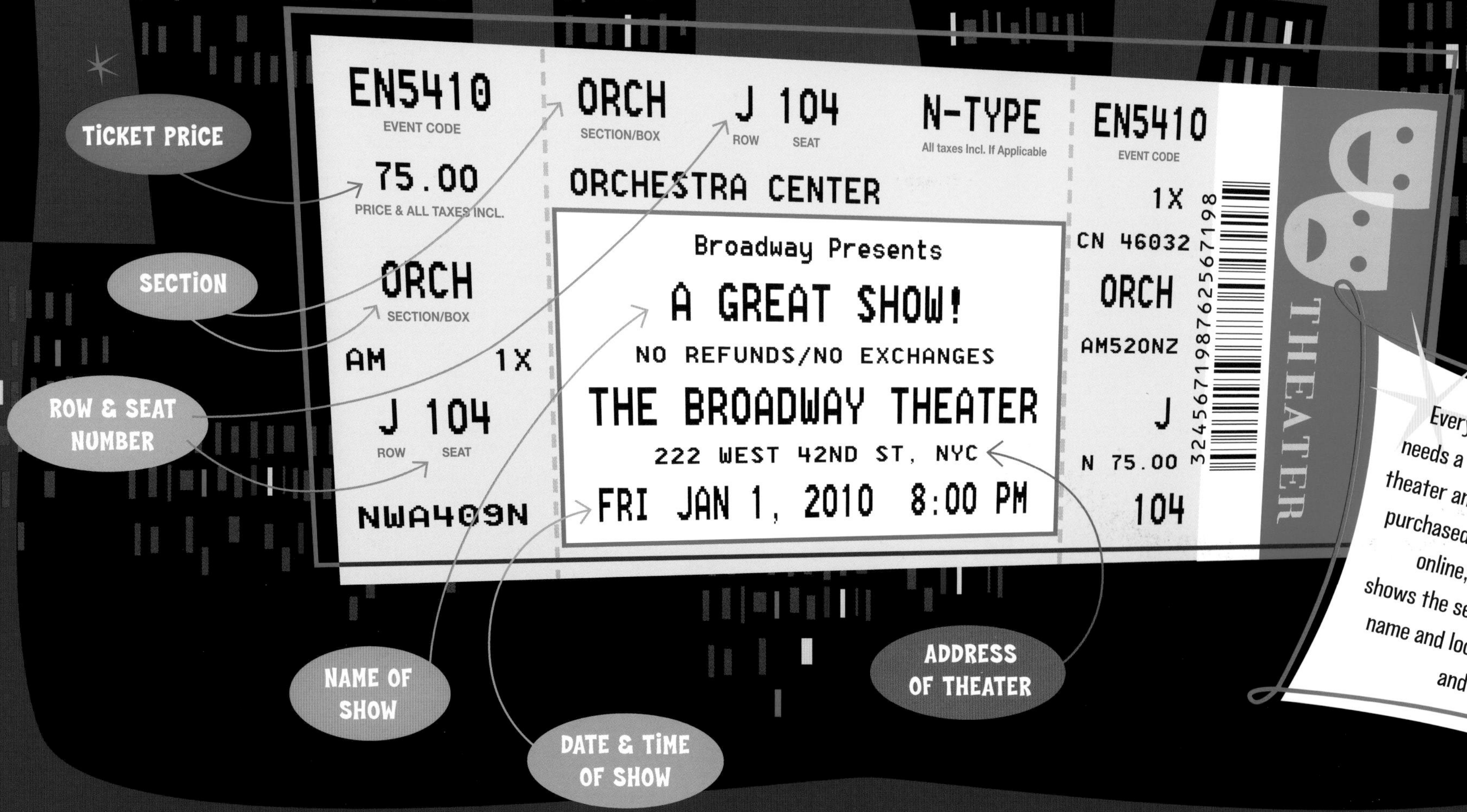
TICKET PRICE
SECTION
ROW & SEAT NUMBER
NAME OF SHOW
DATE & TIME OF SHOW
ADDRESS OF THEATER
EN5410
EVENT CODE
75.00
PRICE & ALL TAXES INCL.
ORCH
SECTION/BOX
AM 1X
J 104
ROW SEAT
NWA409N
ORCH
SECTION/BOX
J 104
ROW SEAT
N-TYPE
All taxes Incl. If Applicable
ORCHESTRA CENTER
Broadway Presents
A GREAT SHOW!
NO REFUNDS/NO EXCHANGES
THE BROADWAY THEATER
222 WEST 42ND ST, NYC
FRI JAN 1, 2010 8:00 PM
EN5410
EVENT CODE
1X
CN 46032
ORCH
AM520NZ
J
N 75.00
104
324567198762567198
THEATER

Every member of the audience needs a ticket in order to enter the theater and see the show. The ticket, purchased either at the box office, online, or over the phone, shows the section and seat number, name and location of the theater, and the price.

and SCENERY and SET

The stage set is the physical setting of the play, designed and created by the **set designer** to express the concept of the show. The scenery is all of the pieces that make up the set, including flats, furniture, and backdrops.

FLAT

A wooden frame with a painted canvas stretched over it; the most basic piece of scenery.

TRAP

An opening in the stage floor that can be used for special effects, or for an actor to enter or exit a scene in a surprising way.

66 When I was in first grade, my parents took me to see Mary Martin in *Peter Pan*—it was trying out in Los Angeles before coming to Broadway. When I came home, I wanted to fly. And I wanted to be a set designer. 99

—*John Lee Beatty*

designed sets for *The Color Purple, The Odd Couple, Footloose, Wonderful Town*

APRON The area at the front edge of the stage.

and Script

The written text of a play, or musical, is called the script. The script also includes the playwright's stage directions—such as when and where a character enters the stage, where he stands, and different scene descriptions. Memorizing lines is one of the hardest jobs an actor has. Whether they are performing Shakespeare's five-act play *Romeo and Juliet*, or learning the songs to Rodgers and Hammerstein's *Oklahoma!*, all actors have to know their lines.

S is for STAGE

The acting area of the theater where a show is performed.

There are different kinds of stages:

PROSCENIUM STAGE
A traditional stage with a frame and curtain separating it from the audience.

THRUST STAGE
A stage that extends out into the audience.

THEATER-IN-THE-ROUND
The audience sits surrounding the stage and is close to the actors and action.

PROSCENIUM
The frame around the stage that creates a boundary between the acting area and the audience. An audience sits facing the stage in a traditional proscenium theater.

CURTAIN
The cloth or drape that separates the stage from the audience.

WINGS
The areas to the left and right of the stage that can't be seen by the audience. Actors stand in the wings, waiting to enter the stage. The wings can also be used to store scenery and props.

"I fell in love with the whole ritual: the lights going down, the curtain going up, telling a story to a large group of people in the dark. It was one of those moments where you think, I can do that."

-Nathan Lane

starred in *Guys and Dolls, The Producers, A Funny Thing Happened on the Way to the Forum*

UPSTAGE
The area of the stage farthest away from the audience.

FLY SPACE
The space high above the stage, out of the audience's view, used for raising, lowering, and storing scenery.

OFFSTAGE
The stage area out of the audience's view.

DOWNSTAGE
The area of the stage nearest to the audience.

STAGE RIGHT
The right side of the stage when facing the audience.

STAGE LEFT
The left side of the stage when facing the audience.

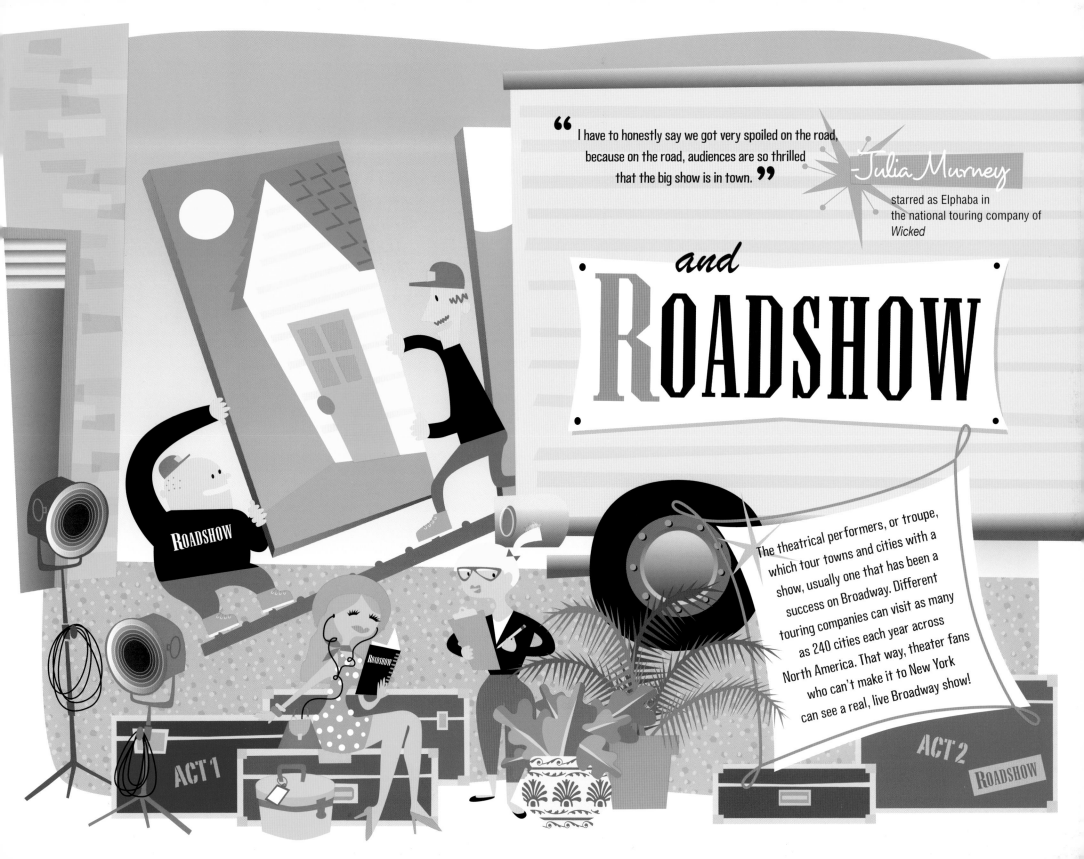

“I have to honestly say we got very spoiled on the road, because on the road, audiences are so thrilled that the big show is in town.”

-Julia Murney

starred as Elphaba in the national touring company of *Wicked*

and ROADSHOW

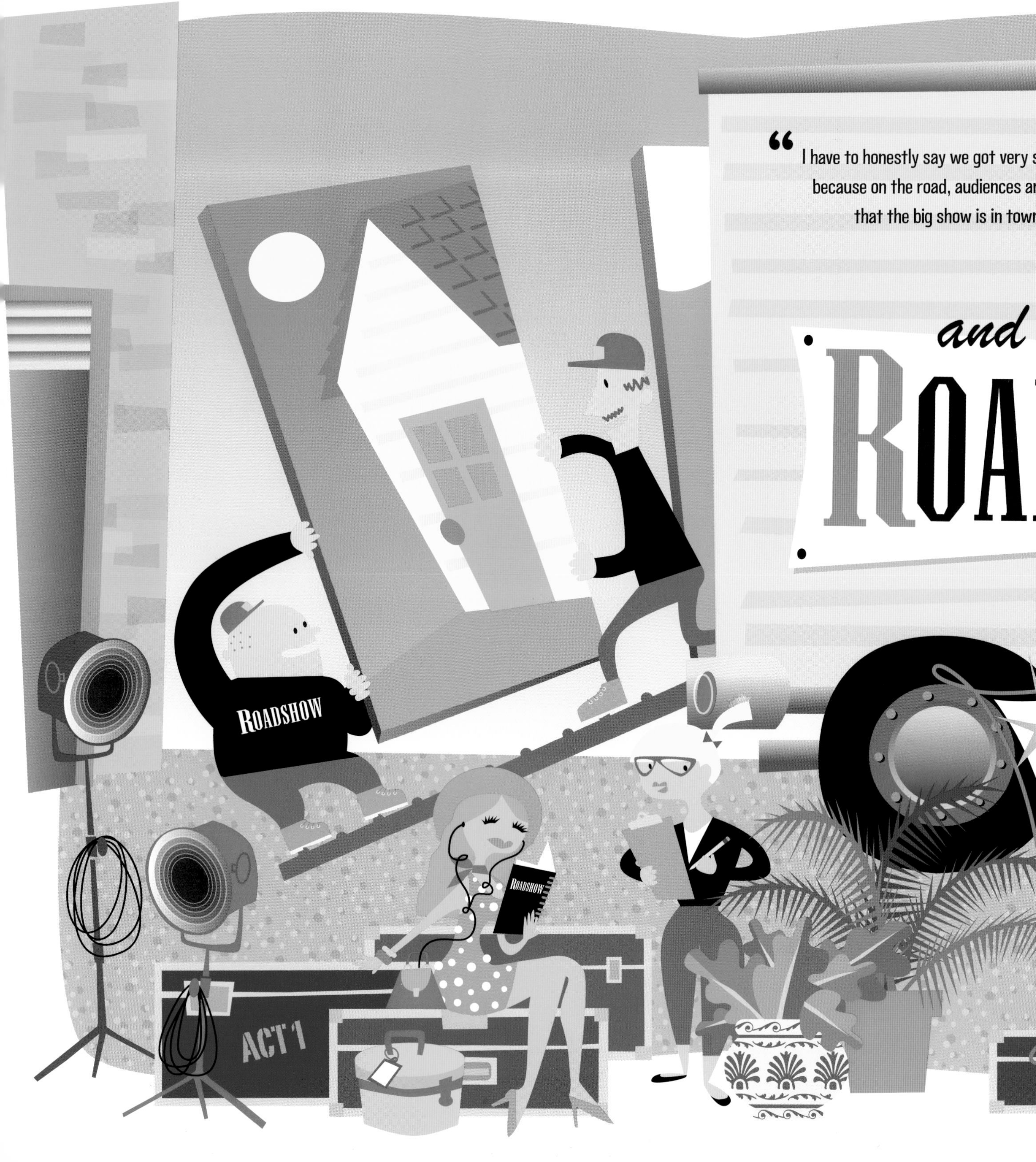

ROADSHOW
ROADSHOW
ACT 1
ACT 2
ROADSHOW

The theatrical performers, or troupe, which tour towns and cities with a show, usually one that has been a success on Broadway. Different touring companies can visit as many as 240 cities each year across North America. That way, theater fans who can't make it to New York can see a real, live Broadway show!

R is for rehearsal

The learning and practicing of a show. The **dress rehearsals** are the last rehearsals—done in full costume, without scripts—before a play opens. **Notes** are delivered by the director to the cast and crew during and at the end of rehearsals. These notes help develop the characters being portrayed and unify the production.

"What looks absolutely fabulous in rehearsal can fall flat in front of an audience. The audience dictates what you do or don't change."

–Harvey Fierstein

starred in *Torch Song Trilogy, Hairspray, Fiddler on the Roof*

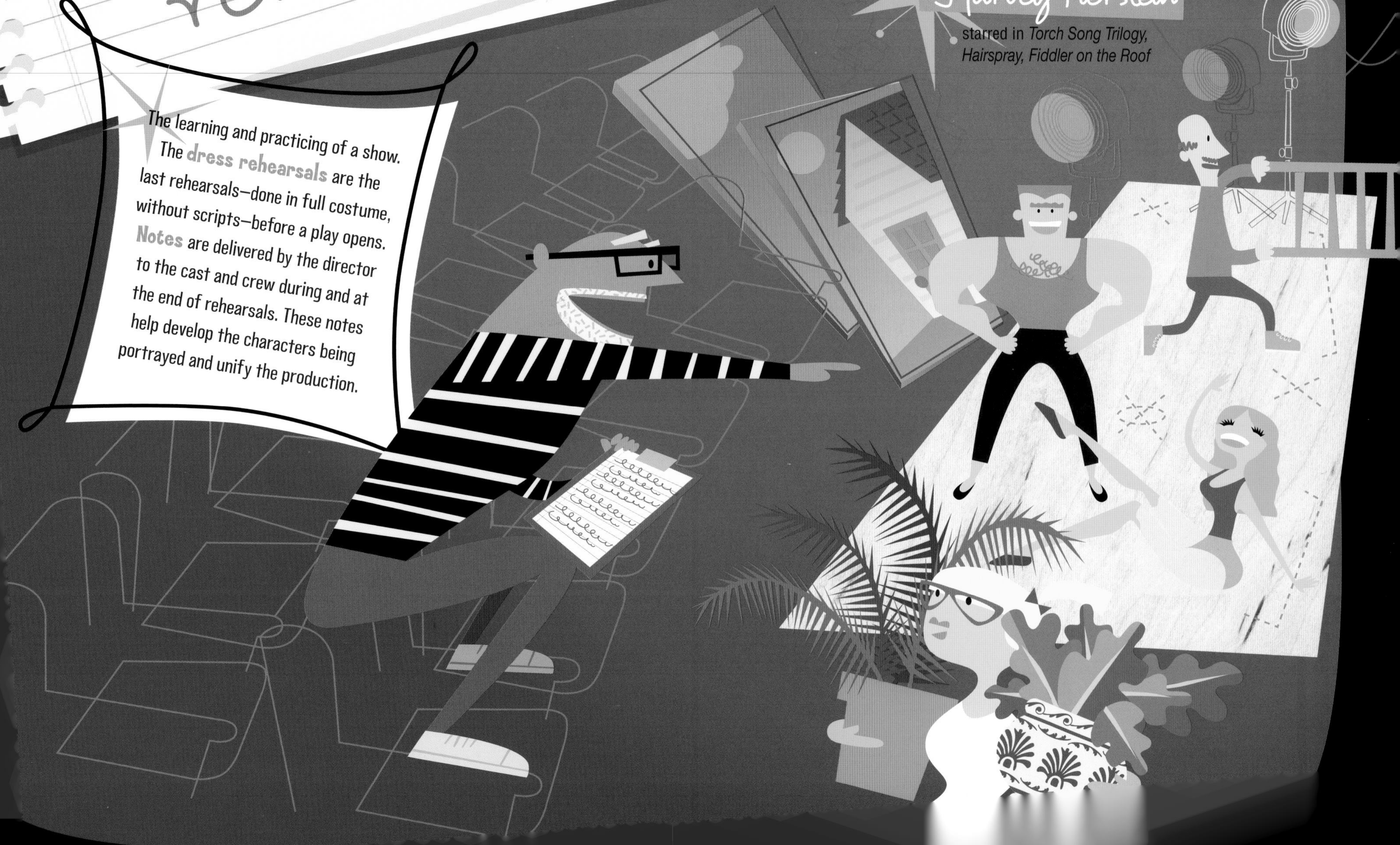

"I love a good quick change. Maybe it's the running offstage into the dark where waiting hands are ready to rip off your clothes and slap new ones on. Maybe it's the rush against time: five seconds to change from the Spy to Mrs. McGarrigle…go! Maybe it's just the pure theatricality of it. The magic of a quick change can only happen live."

-Arnie Burton

starred in *The 39 Steps*, *Amadeus*

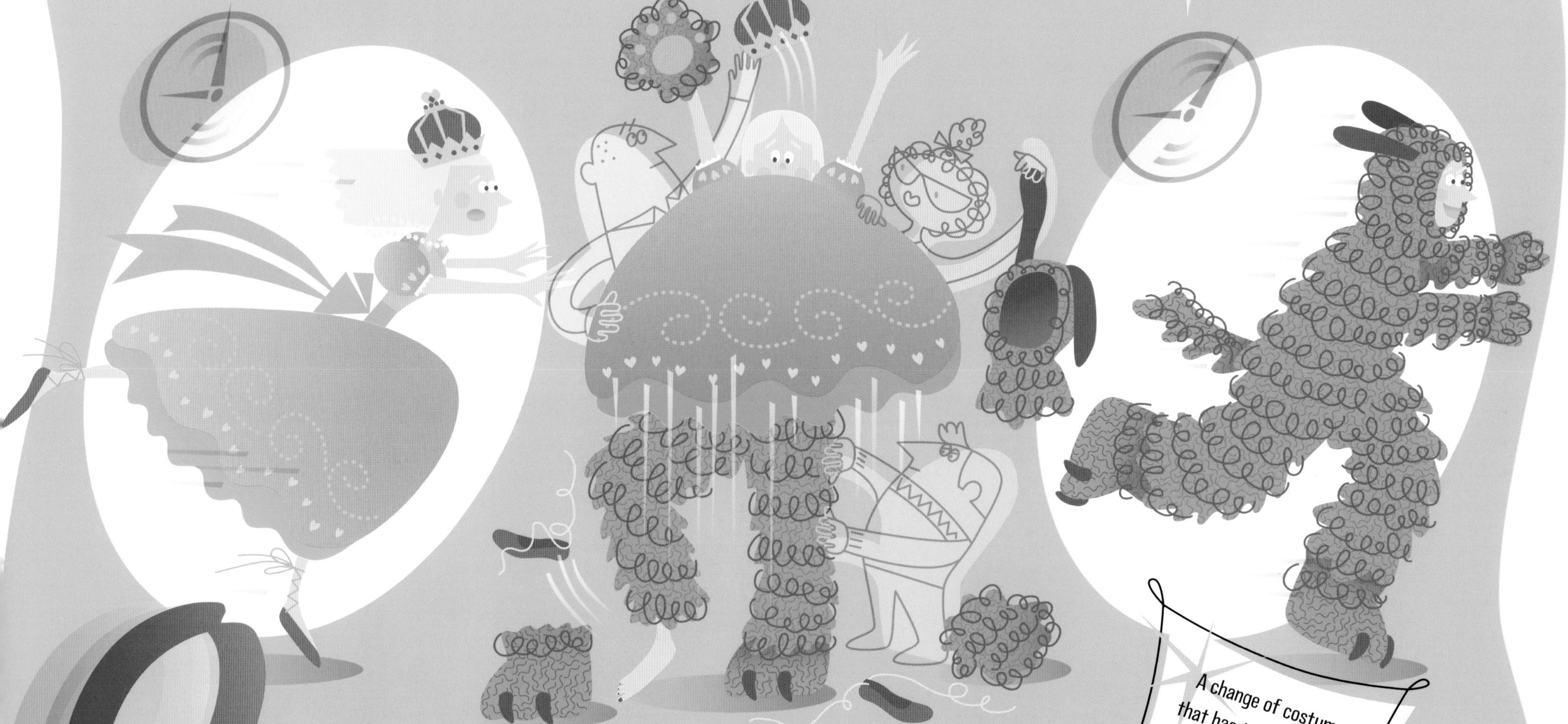

Q is for QUICK CHANGE

A change of costume that has to happen very fast and takes place close to the side of the stage, usually in the wings.

P is for PLAY

The musical, drama, or comedy production that is performed onstage. A **playwright** writes a comedy or a drama, and a **librettist** writes the script (book) for a musical. William Shakespeare, Neil Simon, Eugene O'Neill, August Wilson, Wendy Wasserstein, and Suzan-Lori Parks are some of the best known playwrights.

A **DRAMA** is a serious play, more thoughtful in its theme and subject.

A **COMEDY** is a funny play—the more the audience laughs, the better.

A **MUSICAL** can be either a comedy or a drama, but it uses music and lyrics to tell its story.

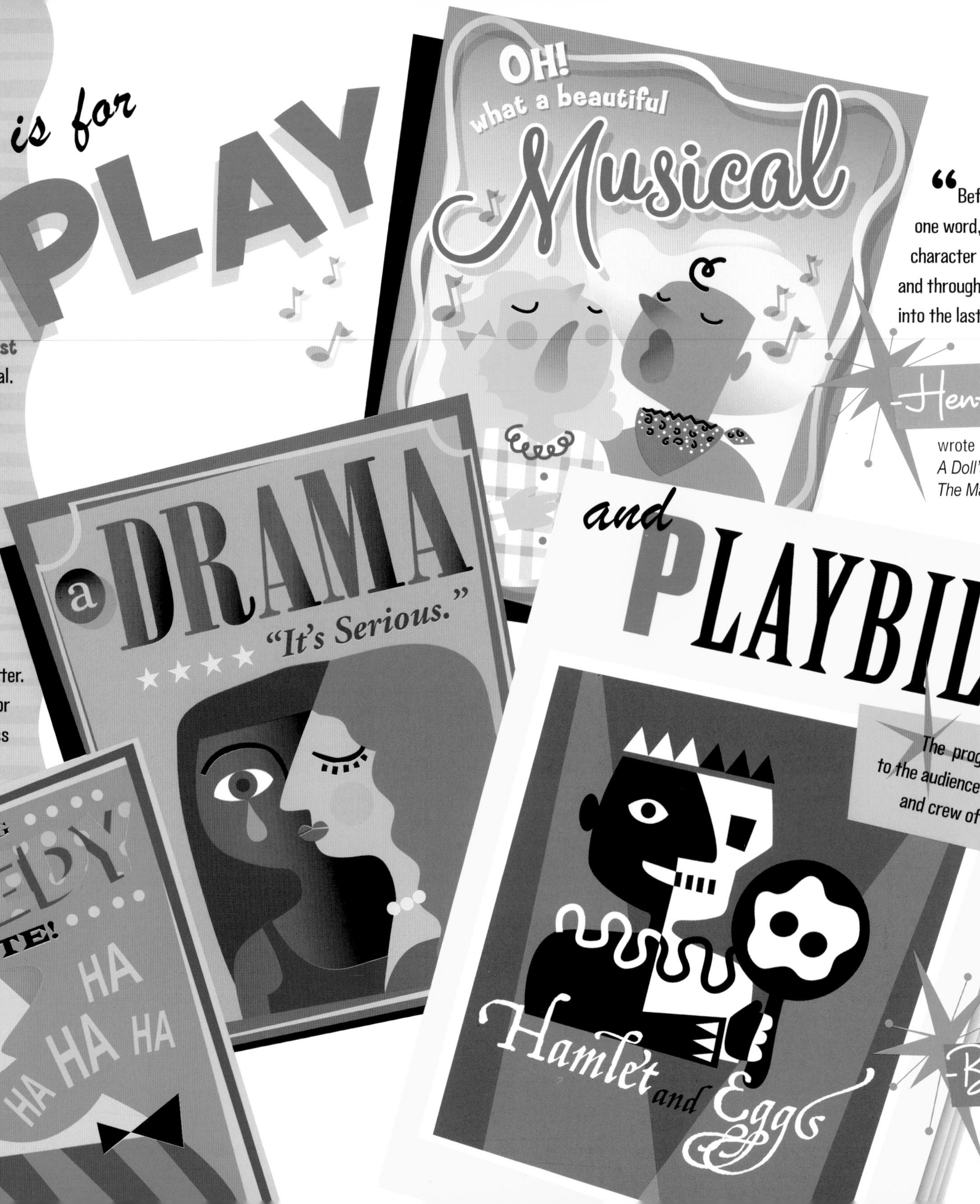

OH! what a beautiful
Musical
a DRAMA
"It's Serious."
Hamlet and Eggs

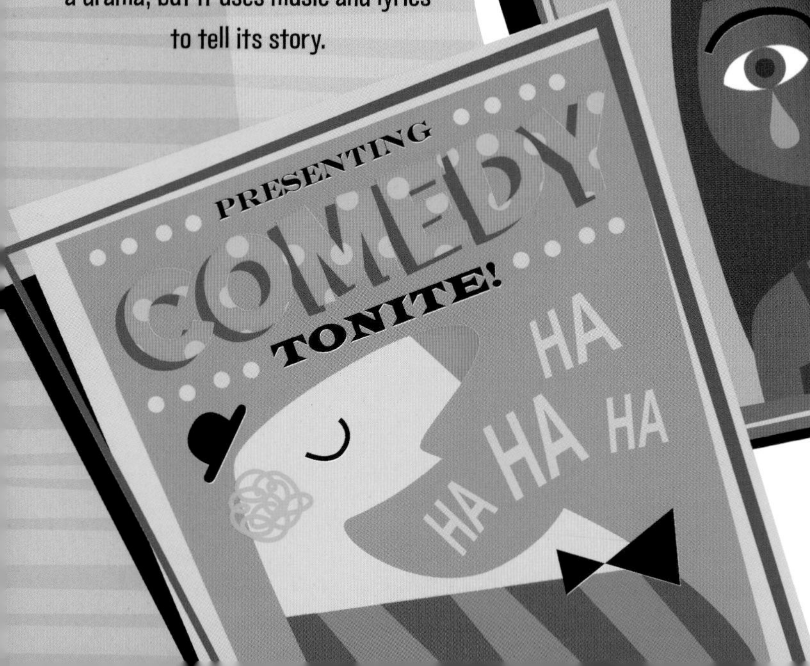

PRESENTING
COMEDY
TONITE!
HA
HA HA HA
HA

"Before I write down one word, I have to have the character in my mind through and through. I must penetrate into the last wrinkle of his soul."

—Henrik Ibsen

wrote *A Doll's House, Hedda Gabler, The Master Builder*

and PLAYBILL®

The program given out to the audience that lists the cast and crew of a production.

"I still have all my *Playbills*. I was starstruck at the theater."

—Billy Crudup

starred in *The Elephant Man, The Coast of Utopia*

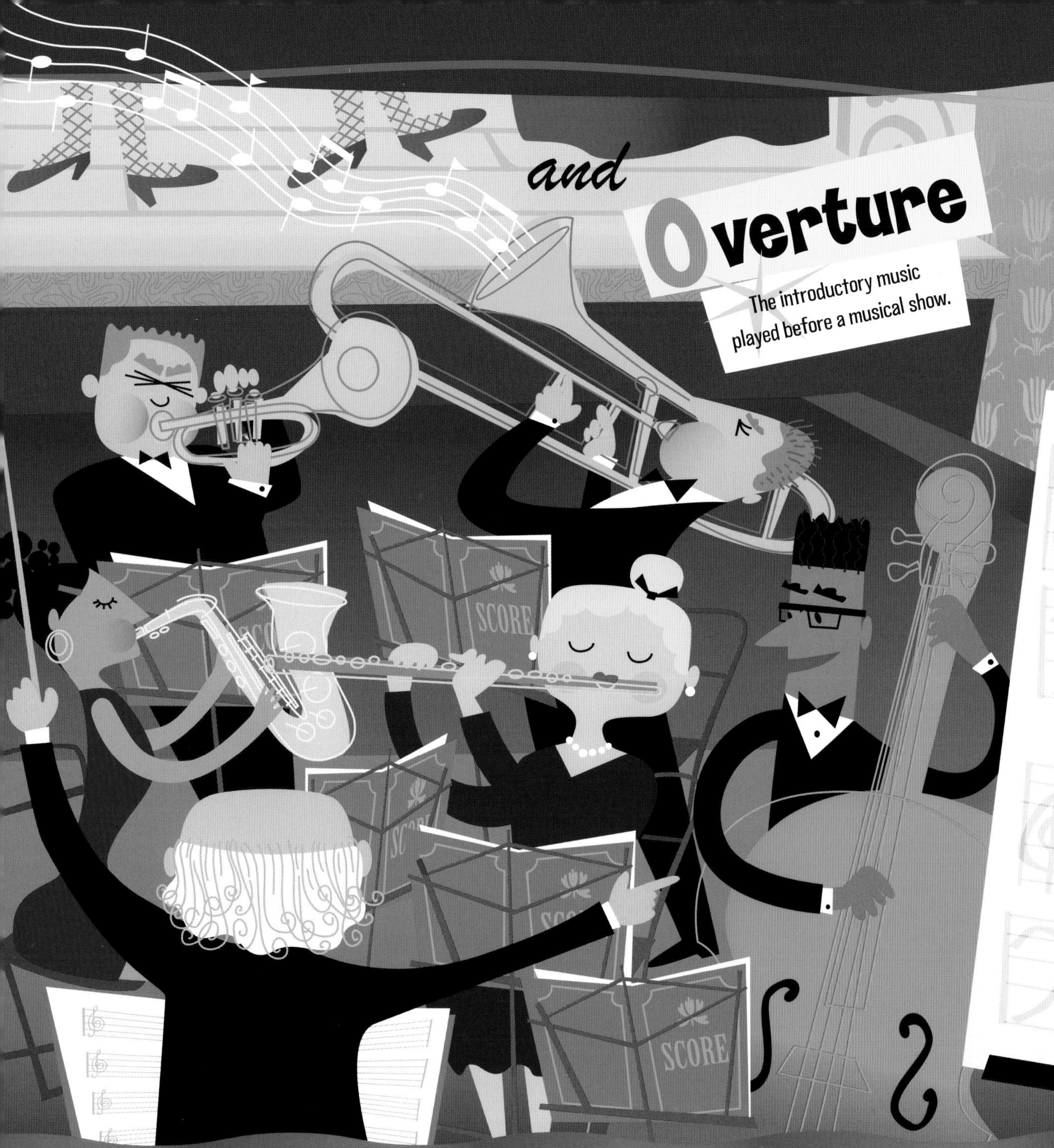
SCORE
SCORE
SCORE

and Overture

The introductory music played before a musical show.

"When the audience heard those first four notes, they immediately began to applaud. It was like those four notes were the four magic notes!"

–Sid Ramin

orchestrated *Gypsy*, with **Red Ginzler**

CONDUCTOR

Responsible for hiring the musicians, running song rehearsals, leading the orchestra during the show; is the connection between the actors and the musicians.

COMPOSER and LYRICIST

In a musical show, the composer writes the music, which is called the **score**, and the lyricist writes the words to the songs. Among the most celebrated musical partnerships are George and Ira Gershwin; Lerner and Lowe; Kander and Ebb; Rodgers and Hammerstein; Andrew Lloyd Webber and Tim Rice; and Lynn Ahrens and Stephen Flaherty.

Does anyone write both music and lyrics? Cole Porter, Stephen Sondheim, Jonathan Larson, and Lin-Manuel Miranda are just a few who have.

"The musicians are confined to the pit for the entire show. I have periods during the show of up to 10 minutes where I have nothing to play . . . . I keep my mind active by reading, studying a language, or doing a crossword puzzle. Then when I play, I approach the music as if I'm doing a practice session. That forces my mind to focus on all the elements of the music."

–Lowell Jay Hershey

played trumpet for *The Phantom of the Opera*

O is for Orchestra

The orchestra is made up of musicians—from pianists to violinists, from drummers to trombonists—who play the music for a show. During a performance they often sit in the **orchestra pit**, which is the lowered area between the stage and the front orchestra seats.

SECTIONS OF THE ORCHESTRA
The orchestra is made up of four sections:

STRINGS
violins, violas, cellos, double bass, harps, and guitars

WIND
piccolos, flutes, oboes, clarinets, bassoons, and saxophones

PERCUSSION
drums, cymbals, triangles, tambourines, piano, and xylophones

BRASS
trumpets, trombones, horns, and tubas

> " I absolutely love it because you're part of this great big machine. Every time you hear the orchestra start, you're setting sail like a big steamship. There are all of these moving parts in it. It just keeps going. "
>
> —Carol Channing

starred in *Hello, Dolly!*, *Gentlemen Prefer Blondes*

SCORE

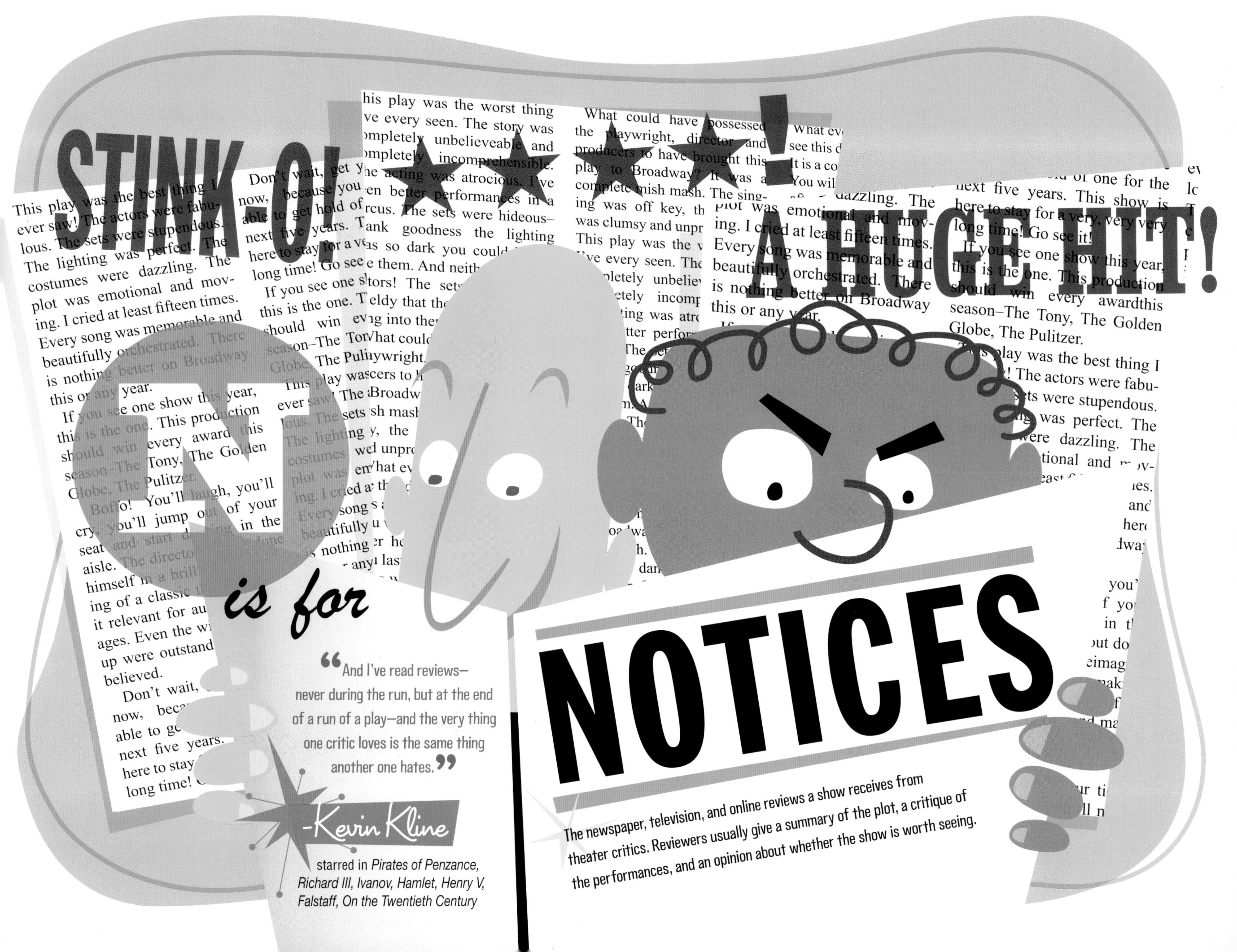
STINK-O!
★★★!
A HUGE HIT!

N is for NOTICES

"And I've read reviews—never during the run, but at the end of a run of a play—and the very thing one critic loves is the same thing another one hates."

-Kevin Kline

starred in *Pirates of Penzance, Richard III, Ivanov, Hamlet, Henry V, Falstaff, On the Twentieth Century*

The newspaper, television, and online reviews a show receives from theater critics. Reviewers usually give a summary of the plot, a critique of the performances, and an opinion about whether the show is worth seeing.

M is for MARQUEE

"Once they put a billboard of your mug in Times Square, it becomes a little surreal. You've just got to focus on what you have to do."

—Cheyenne Jackson

starred in
Altar Boyz, Aida, All Shook Up, Xanadu

STAGE NAME	GIVEN NAME
Rip Torn	Elmore Rual Torn, Jr.
Whoopi Goldberg	Caryn Johnson
Zero Mostel	Sam Mostel
Taye Diggs	Scott Diggs
Elton John	Reginald Dwight

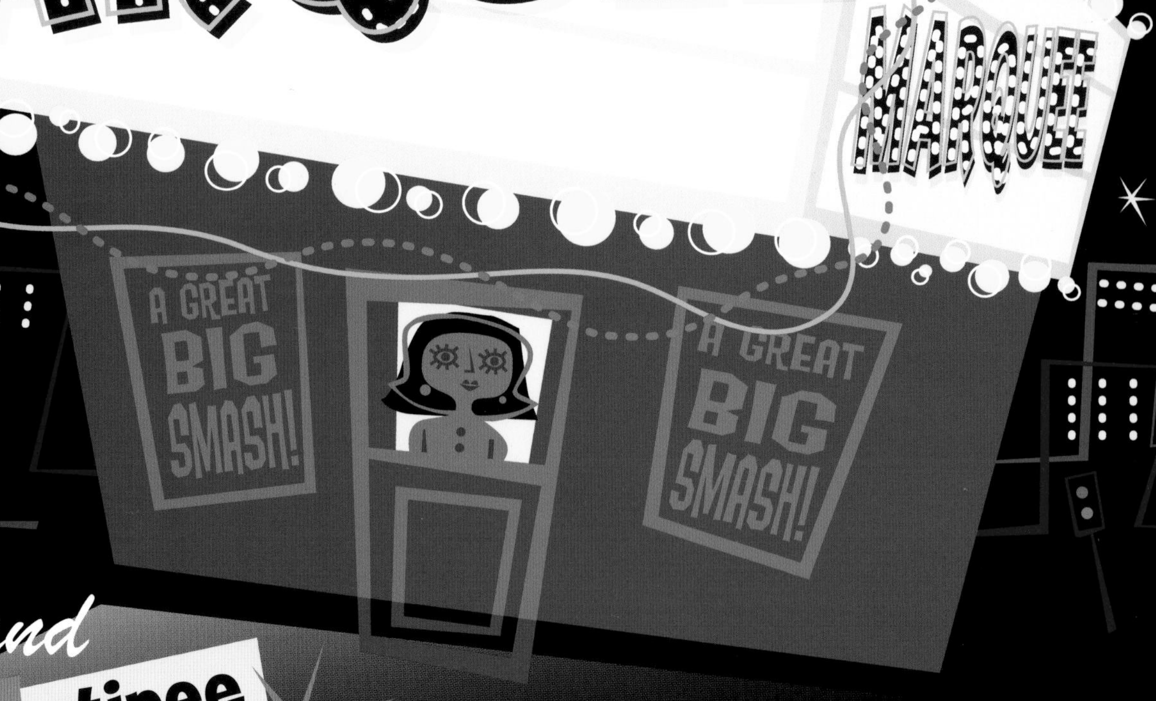
MARQUEE
A GREAT BIG SMASH!
A GREAT BIG SMASH!

A permanent canopy over the entrance of the theater which displays the name of the play being performed. If a performer or director is well known, their name will be displayed as well.

and Matinee

The afternoon performance of a show, usually on Wednesday and Saturday. Sometimes there are two shows in one day—an afternoon and evening performance.

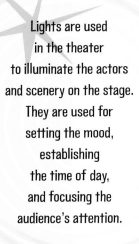

Lights are used
in the theater
to illuminate the actors
and scenery on the stage.
They are used for
setting the mood,
establishing
the time of day,
and focusing the
audience's attention.

LIGHTING DESIGNER

The person who designs the lighting
for a show. He/she plans which
lights are used and when
they are used to help
create a setting.

FOLLOW SPOT

A movable spotlight used by
a member of the lighting crew to
follow and highlight a performer.

GEL

The thin sheets of colored plastic
(in the old days, actually made of gelatin)
placed in front of lights in order to
add color to the beam of light.

" Lights are to drama what music is to the lyrics of a song. The greatest part of my success in the
theatre I attribute to my feeling for colors, translated into effects of light. "

—David Belasco

wrote, directed, or produced more
than 100 Broadway plays, including
*DuBarry, Madame Butterfly,
The Girl of the Golden West*

L *is for* Lights

K is for KICKLINE

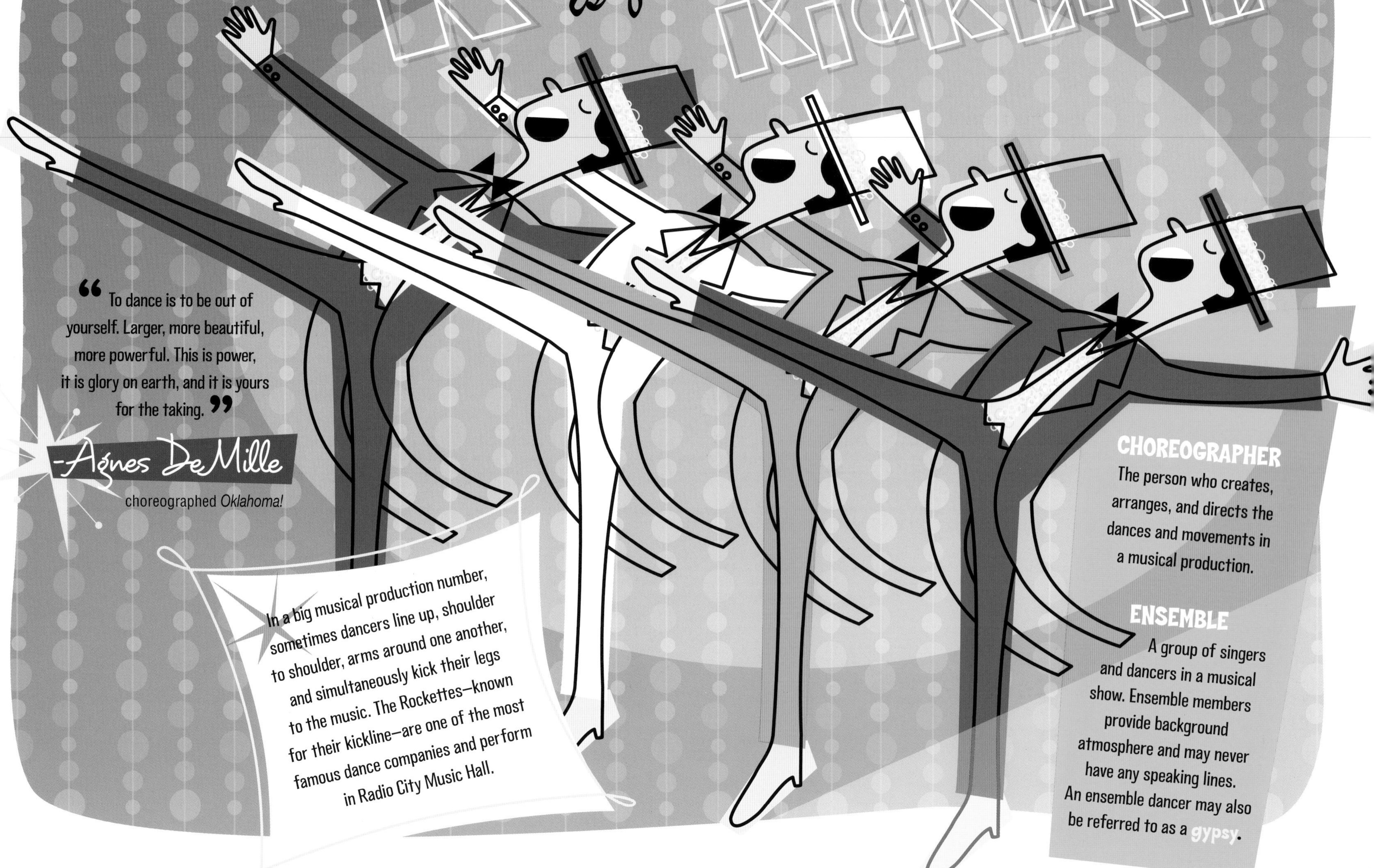

"To dance is to be out of yourself. Larger, more beautiful, more powerful. This is power, it is glory on earth, and it is yours for the taking."

-Agnes DeMille

choreographed *Oklahoma!*

In a big musical production number, sometimes dancers line up, shoulder to shoulder, arms around one another, and simultaneously kick their legs to the music. The Rockettes—known for their kickline—are one of the most famous dance companies and perform in Radio City Music Hall.

CHOREOGRAPHER
The person who creates, arranges, and directs the dances and movements in a musical production.

ENSEMBLE
A group of singers and dancers in a musical show. Ensemble members provide background atmosphere and may never have any speaking lines. An ensemble dancer may also be referred to as a **gypsy**.

J is for JITTERS

"Actually, I'm fortunate because I don't have a 'fear' reaction; I don't panic and then get scared. I think I just get like the good kind of nervous that sort of feeds the adrenaline . . . . But the more I do it, the more comfortable I get with my own nerves."

—Lauren Ambrose
starred in
Awake and Sing!, Exit the King, Romeo and Juliet, Hamlet

"If I'm too relaxed, you kind of know what's gonna happen. I welcome it when there's expectation and excitement. That's when the unexpected can happen."

—Bernadette Peters
starred in *Mack and Mabel, Annie Get Your Gun, Sunday in the Park with George, Gypsy*

The nervousness performers feel before the show begins; also known as "butterflies." When it gets really bad, it's called "stage fright."

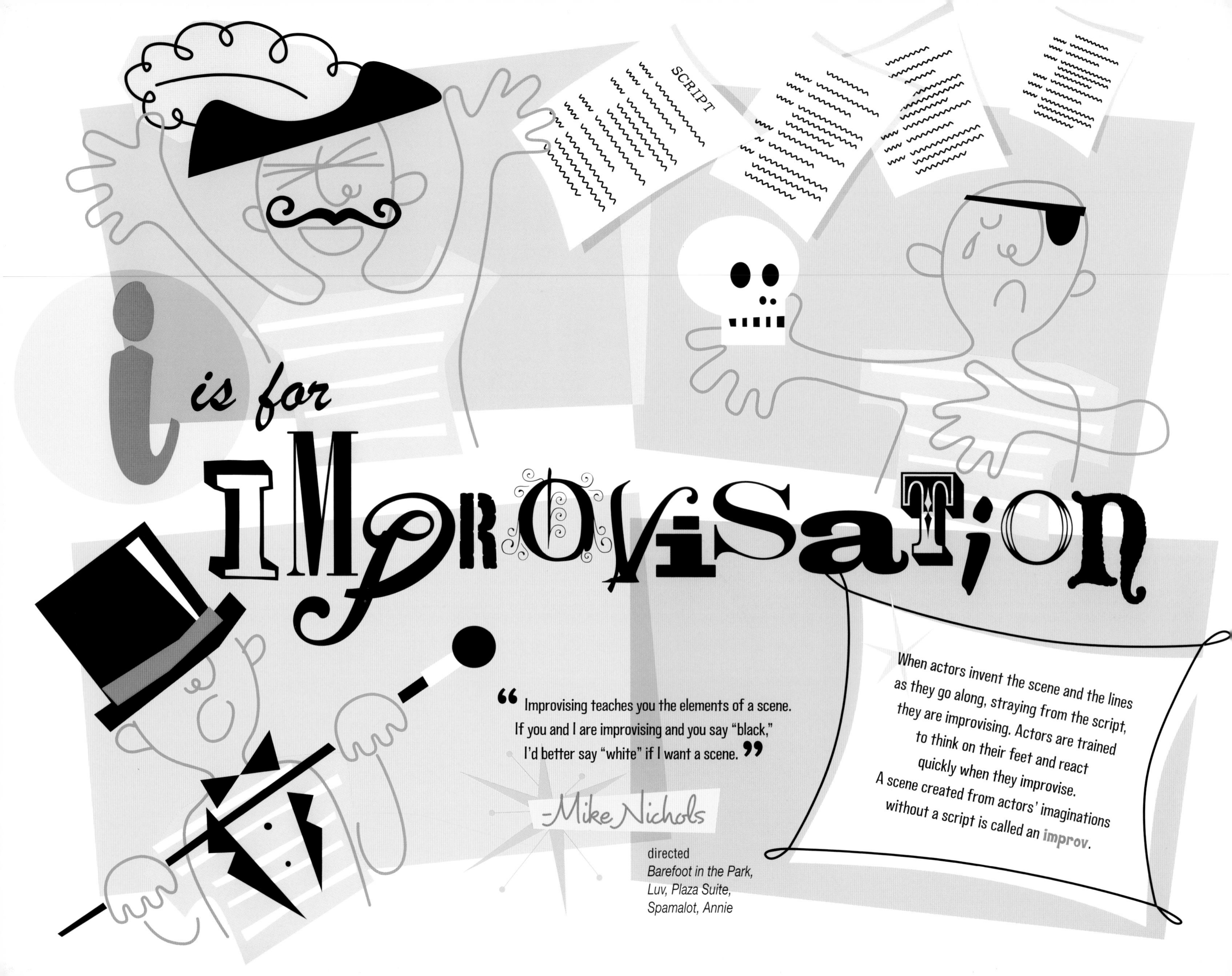
SCRIPT

I is for IMPROVISATION

“Improvising teaches you the elements of a scene. If you and I are improvising and you say “black,” I’d better say “white” if I want a scene.”

-Mike Nichols

directed
Barefoot in the Park, Luv, Plaza Suite, Spamalot, Annie

When actors invent the scene and the lines as they go along, straying from the script, they are improvising. Actors are trained to think on their feet and react quickly when they improvise. A scene created from actors’ imaginations without a script is called an **improv**.

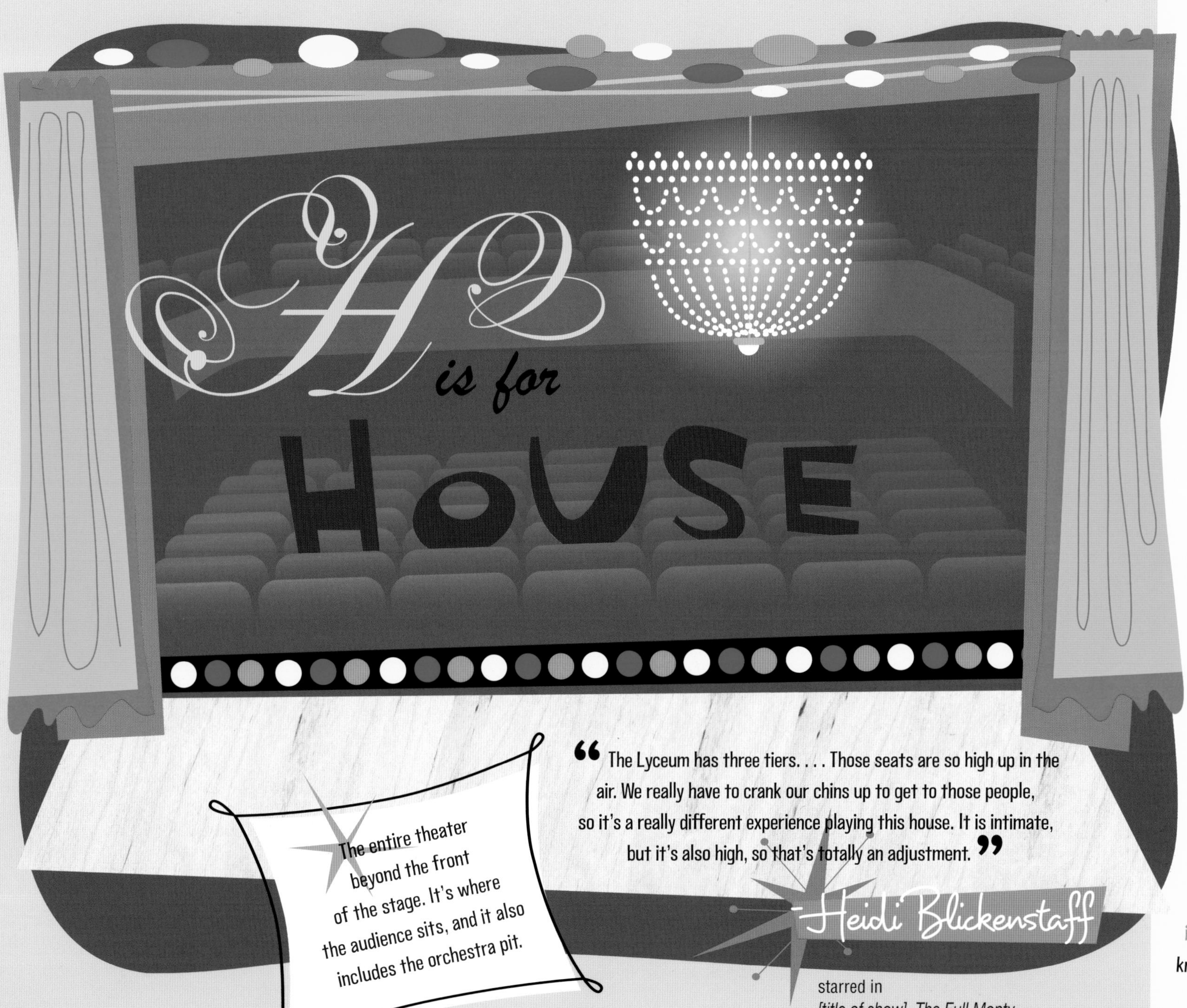

H is for HOUSE

The entire theater beyond the front of the stage. It's where the audience sits, and it also includes the orchestra pit.

“The Lyceum has three tiers. . . . Those seats are so high up in the air. We really have to crank our chins up to get to those people, so it's a really different experience playing this house. It is intimate, but it's also high, so that's totally an adjustment.”

—Heidi Blickenstaff

starred in *[title of show], The Full Monty, The Little Mermaid*

FRONT OF HOUSE

The area in the front of the theater, including the box office, the lobby, and the concession stands, where souvenirs, programs, and refreshments are sold.

HOUSE MANAGER

The house manager is responsible for managing the auditorium, ushers, and anything to do with the audience. Is everyone in their seats? Are the house doors closed and the lights dimmed? Does everyone have a program? The house manager is in charge.

HOUSE SEATING

ORCHESTRA: the main seating area of the auditorium, on the same level as the stage

MEZZANINE: the second level, upstairs in the theater

BALCONY: the uppermost seating area, behind the mezzanine

HOUSE LIGHTS

The lights in the theater where the audience sits, which are turned off during the performance. They are blinked at the end of **intermission** to let the audience know the next act is about to begin.

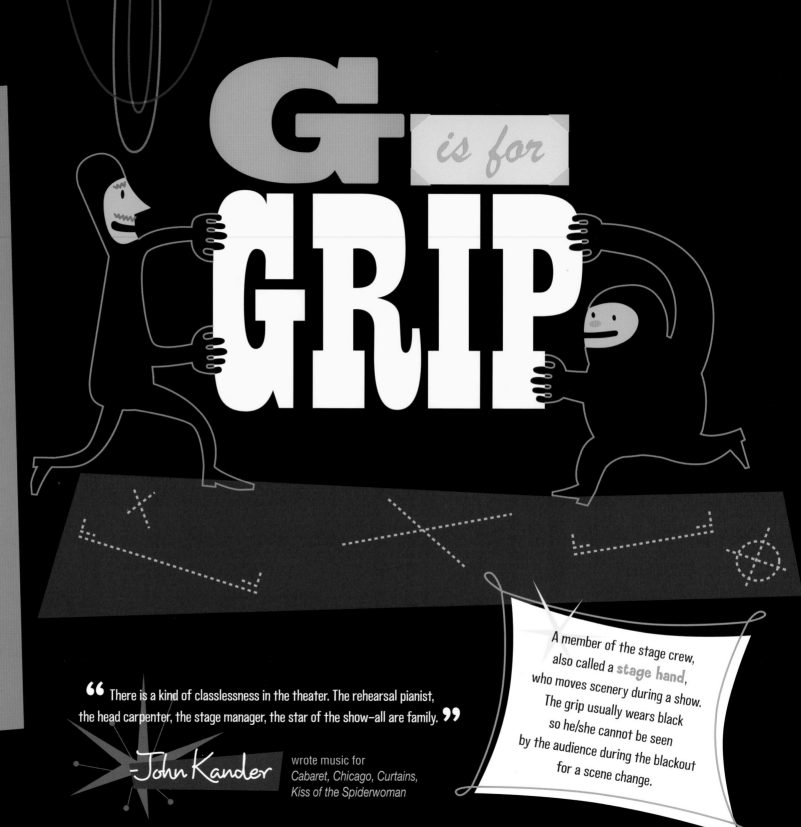

BACKSTAGE

The area out of view of the audience, where dressing rooms, the wardrobe department, scenery and prop rooms, and the crew are located.

CREW

The team of people who work backstage to help put on the production. Technicians, electricians, carpenters, painters, lighting designers, makeup artists, and dressers are just a few of the many people who work behind the scenes.

BLACKOUT

When the lights on the stage are turned off at the end of a scene, both for dramatic effect and to hide the scene change from the audience.

GLOW TAPE

Tape that glows in the dark and is used to mark the stage floor so that actors can locate their places in a blackout.

SCENE CHANGE

When the set is changed between scenes or acts—it may show a new location.

G is for GRIP

66 There is a kind of classlessness in the theater. The rehearsal pianist, the head carpenter, the stage manager, the star of the show—all are family. **99**

—John Kander

wrote music for
Cabaret, Chicago, Curtains, Kiss of the Spiderwoman

A member of the stage crew, also called a **stage hand**, who moves scenery during a show. The grip usually wears black so he/she cannot be seen by the audience during the blackout for a scene change.

F is for FOURTH WALL

"Musicals are by nature theatrical, meaning poetic, meaning having to move the audience's imagination and create a suspension of disbelief, by which I mean there's no fourth wall."

–Stephen Sondheim

wrote music and lyrics for *Company, Into the Woods, Sunday in the Park with George, Sweeney Todd, A Little Night Music*

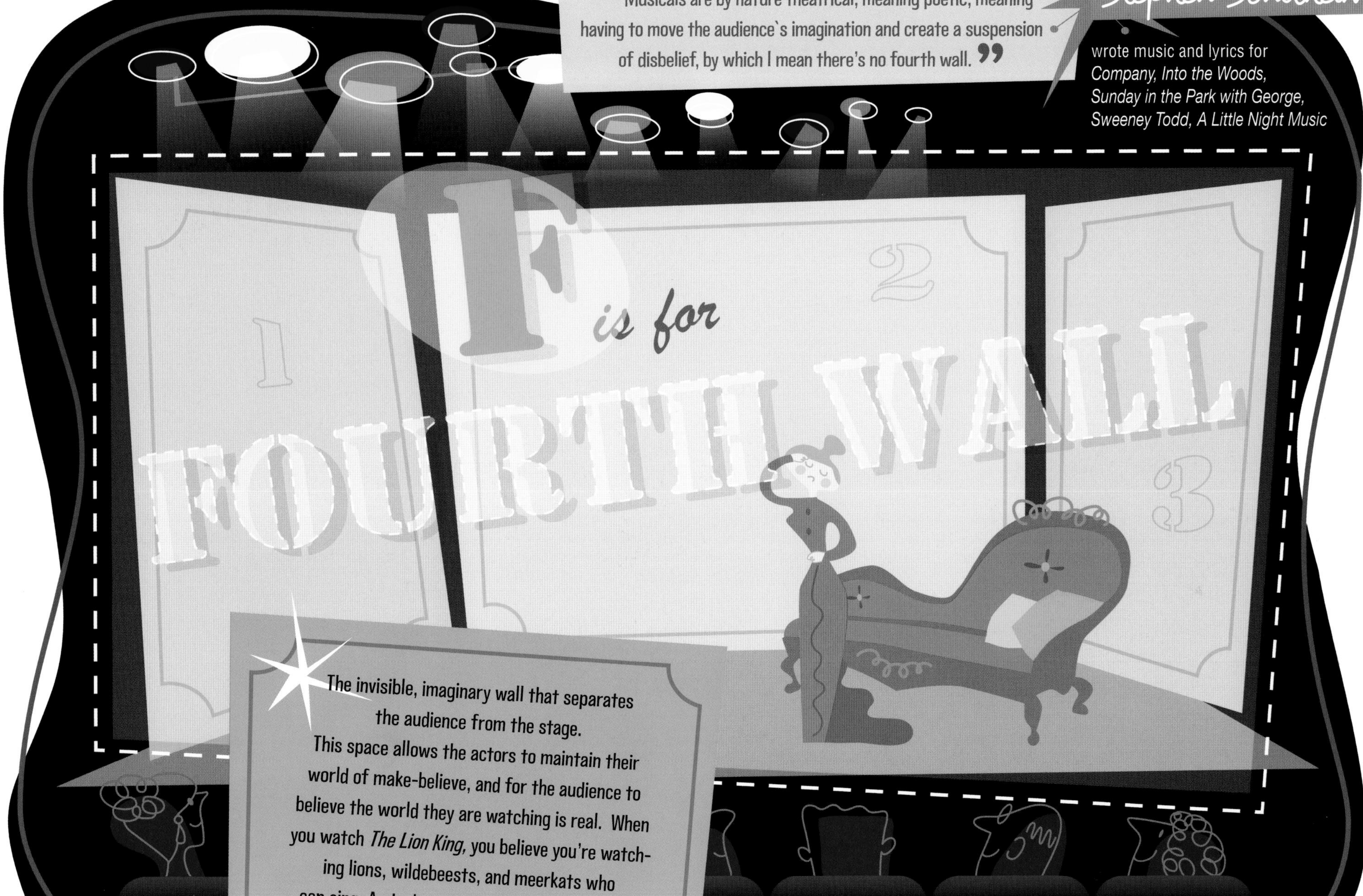

1
2
3

The invisible, imaginary wall that separates the audience from the stage. This space allows the actors to maintain their world of make-believe, and for the audience to believe the world they are watching is real. When you watch *The Lion King*, you believe you're watching lions, wildebeests, and meerkats who can sing. And when you see *Wicked*, you believe you're in the company of a green-faced witch. When a character speaks directly to the audience, he is "**breaking the fourth wall**."

E is for Encore!

When the audience likes a song or dance and would like to see it performed again, they call out "Encore!" (French for "again"). Hearing 'encore' is music to a performer's ears. And if the audience stands up, claps, and cheers, it's known as a **standing ovation**.

"I held a high C note for 16 bars . . . . By the time I'd held that note for four bars, the audience was applauding. They applauded through the whole chorus, and I did several encores. It seemed to do something to them. Not because it was sweet or beautiful, but because it was exciting."

–Ethel Merman

starred in
Call Me Madam, Anything Goes, Annie Get Your Gun, Gypsy

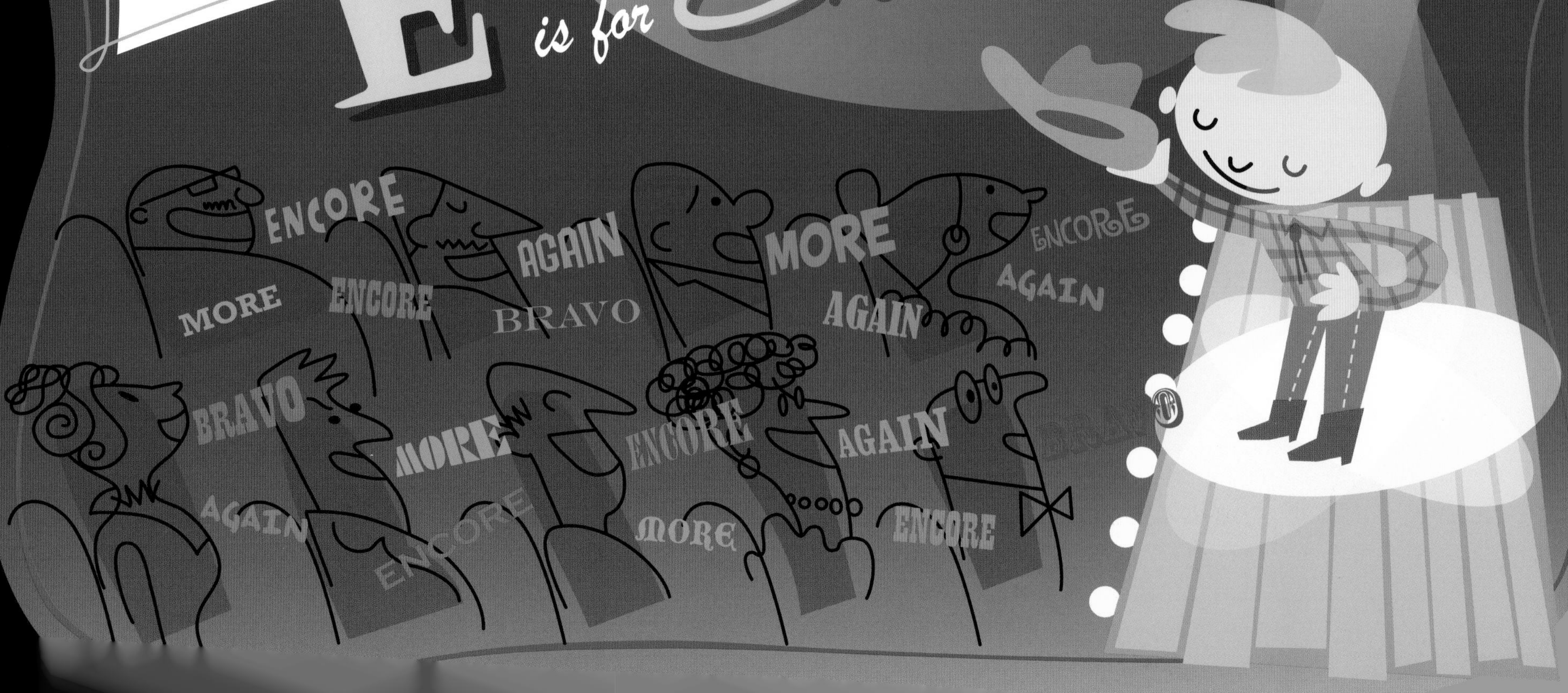
ENCORE
AGAIN
MORE
ENCORE
MORE
ENCORE
BRAVO
AGAIN
AGAIN
BRAVO
MORE
ENCORE
AGAIN
AGAIN
ENCORE
MORE
ENCORE

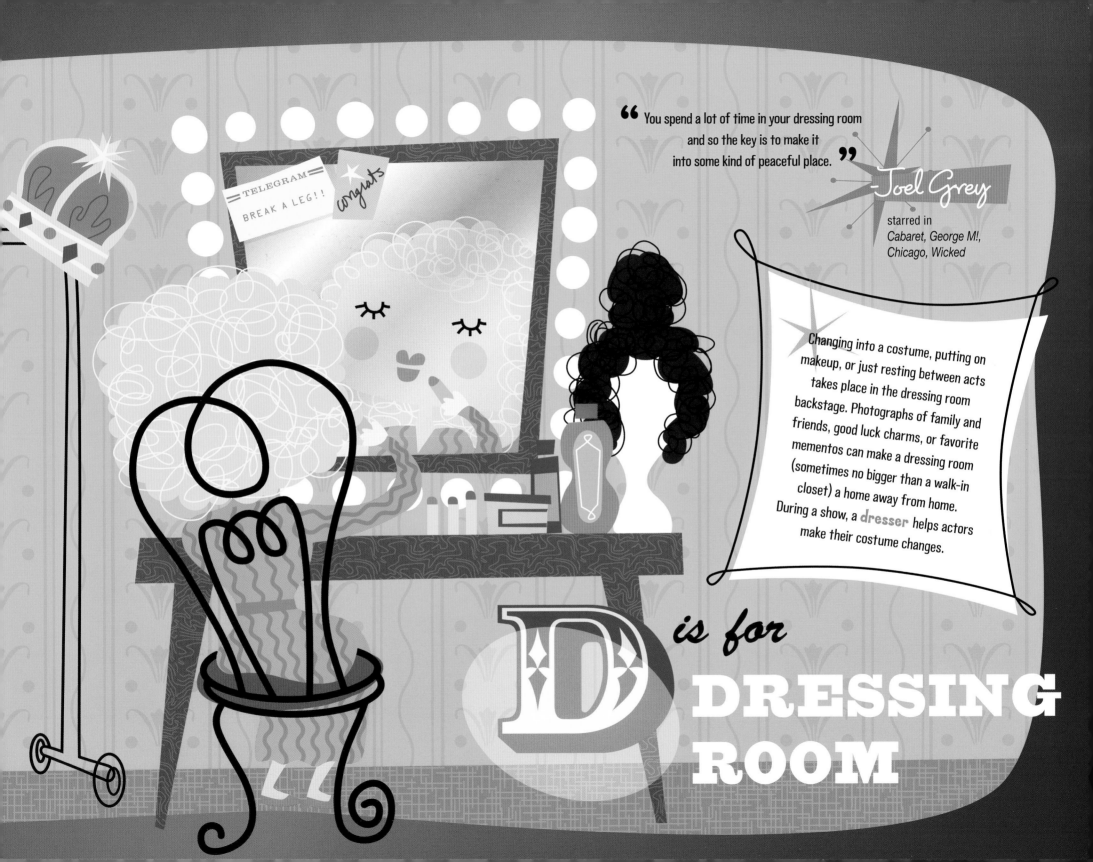

TELEGRAM
BREAK A LEG!!
congrats

" You spend a lot of time in your dressing room and so the key is to make it into some kind of peaceful place. "

—Joel Grey

starred in
*Cabaret, George M!,
Chicago, Wicked*

Changing into a costume, putting on makeup, or just resting between acts takes place in the dressing room backstage. Photographs of family and friends, good luck charms, or favorite mementos can make a dressing room (sometimes no bigger than a walk-in closet) a home away from home. During a show, a **dresser** helps actors make their costume changes.

D *is for* **DRESSING ROOM**

C is for Costumes

The different clothing worn by actors in a performance.

Pirate or princess, Queen of England
or king of the jungle, once an actor
puts on a costume, and wigs, padding,
and makeup, it helps him become the
character he is playing.

COSTUME DESIGNER

The person who imagines, designs, and creates the costumes and is responsible for the total look of the show's characters. The designer has to research the setting, time, and place of a play and determine which colors, fabrics, and accessories will authentically and believably transform an actor into a character.

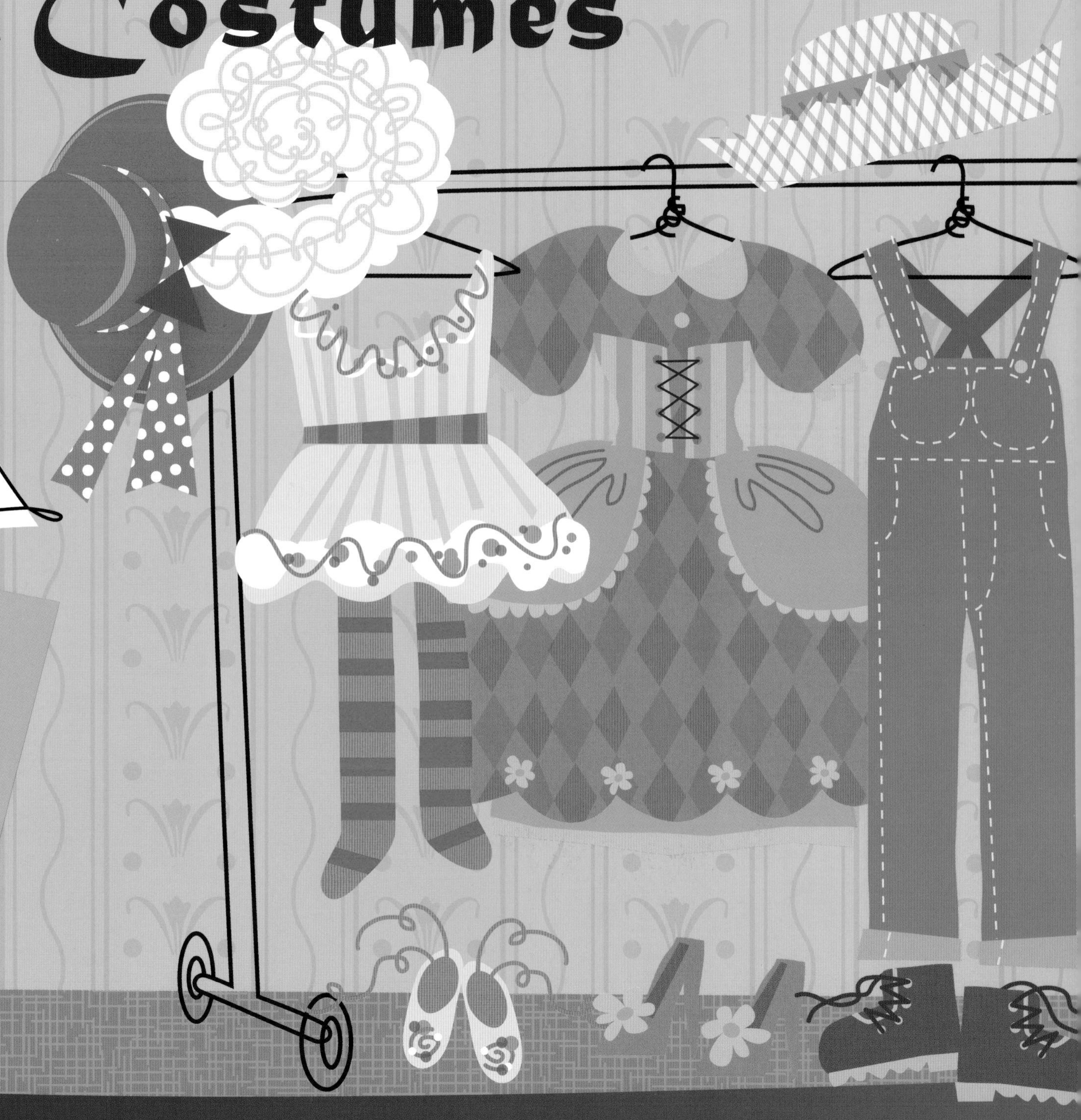

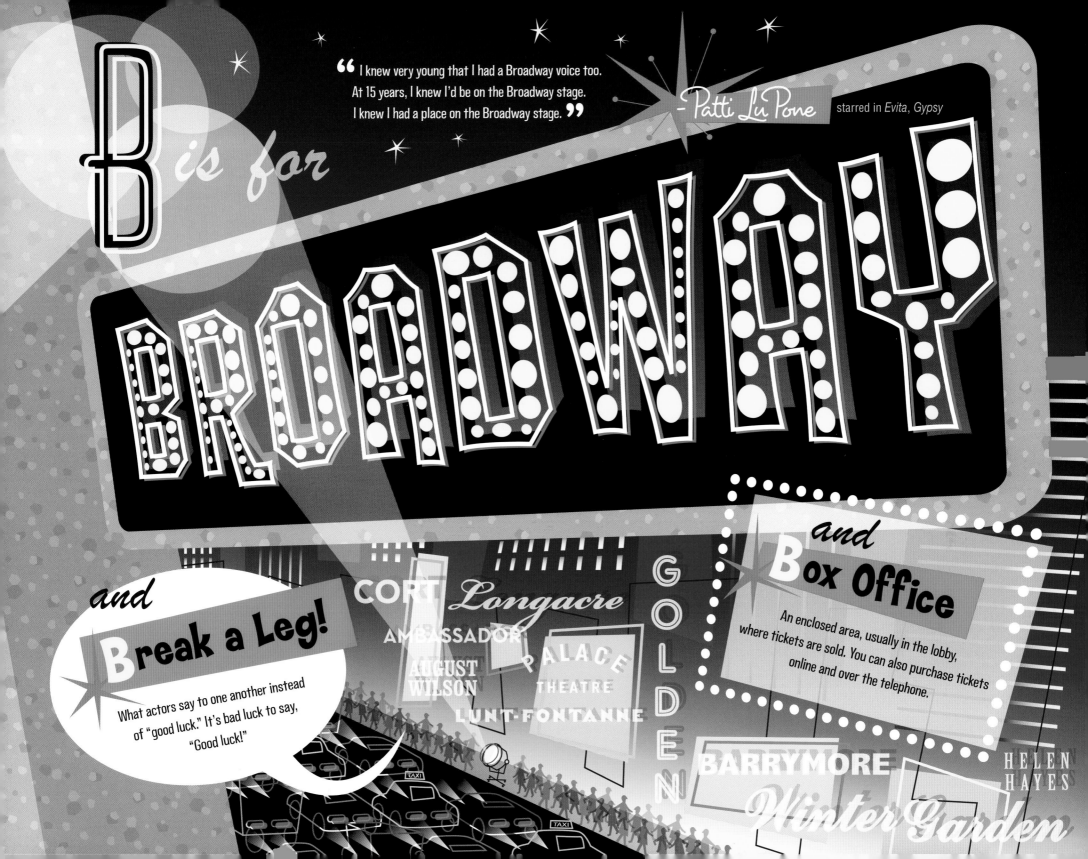

"I knew very young that I had a Broadway voice too. At 15 years, I knew I'd be on the Broadway stage. I knew I had a place on the Broadway stage."

—Patti LuPone starred in *Evita*, *Gypsy*

B is for

BROADWAY

and

Break a Leg!

What actors say to one another instead of "good luck." It's bad luck to say, "Good luck!"

and

Box Office

An enclosed area, usually in the lobby, where tickets are sold. You can also purchase tickets online and over the telephone.

CORT Longacre
AMBASSADOR
AUGUST WILSON
PALACE THEATRE
GOLDEN
LUNT-FONTANNE
BARRYMORE
HELEN HAYES
Winter Garden

“When I was 13, I wanted to be a professional ice skater, right? But my parents took me to see a Broadway show, and it changed my entire life. The show was *Gypsy*, starring Ethel Merman.”

–Liza Minnelli

starred in
Flora the Red Menace,
The Rink

The famous theatrical district in the center of Manhattan in New York City, made up of 40 theaters, where some of the most successful shows in history have been performed. The best actors, singers, and dancers in the world traditionally play eight shows a week (6 evenings and 2 afternoons)—except Mondays, when the theaters are “**dark**.”

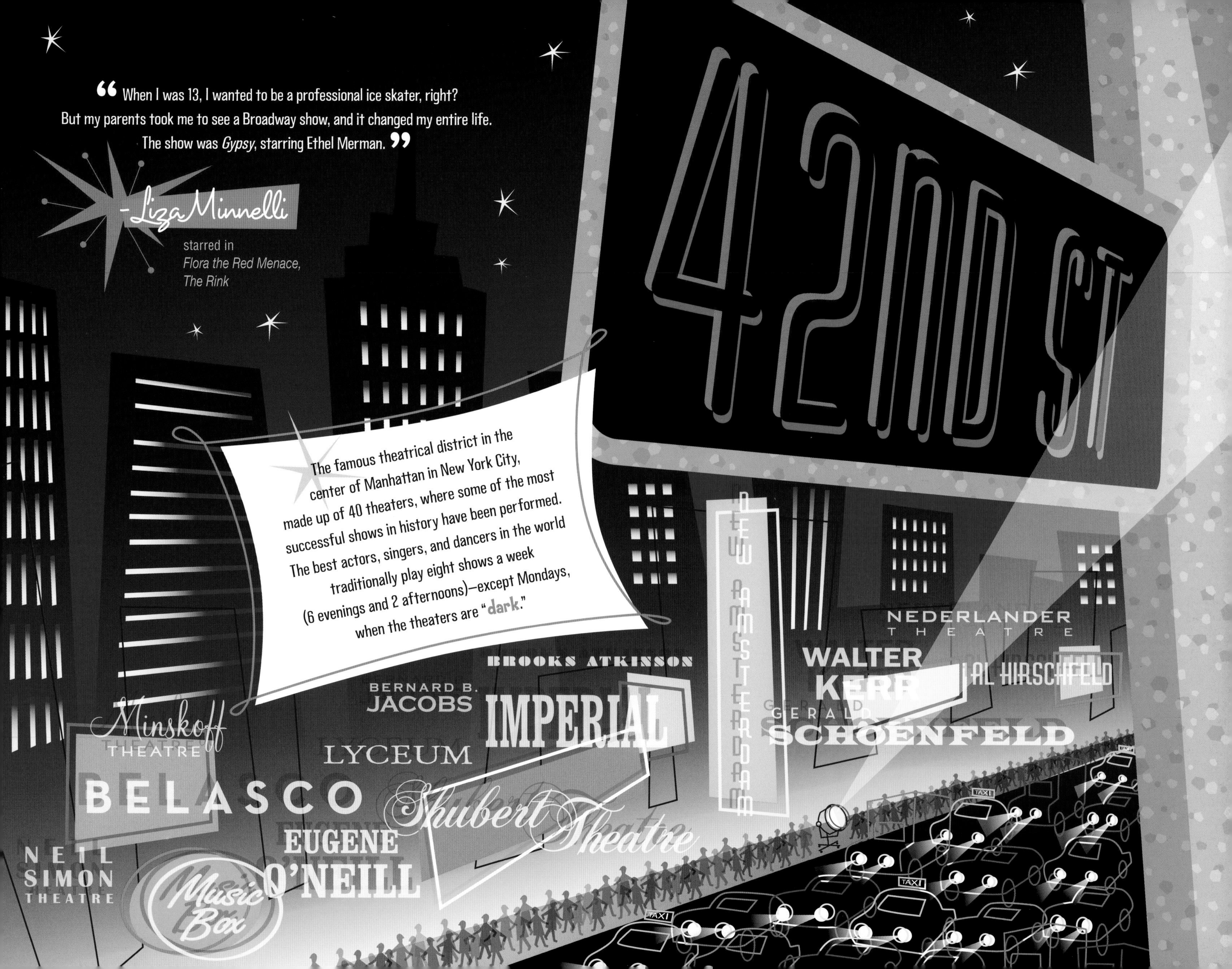

42ND ST
NEW AMSTERDAM
NEDERLANDER THEATRE
WALTER KERR
AL HIRSCHFELD
BROOKS ATKINSON
BERNARD B. JACOBS
IMPERIAL
GERALD SCHOENFELD
Minskoff THEATRE
LYCEUM
BELASCO
Shubert Theatre
EUGENE O'NEILL
NEIL SIMON THEATRE
Music Box
TAXI

"Come on! You know, be an actor because you love to act. Don't be an actor because you think you're going to get famous, because that's luck. But if it's what you want to do with your whole heart and soul, come on. Go everywhere, learn everything."

—Whoopi Goldberg

starred in
A Funny Thing Happened on the Way to the Forum

and

ACTOR

A man or woman who performs a part and plays a character. The part an actor plays can be a lead, featured, or walk-on role; every member of the cast contributes to the success of a show. Many aspiring actors choose to attend acting school, where they learn their craft from A to Z.

"I still believe you have to take your audience somewhere, and don't underestimate how smart they are."

—Hal Prince

produced
West Side Story, Fiddler on the Roof, Cabaret, Company, Follies, A Little Night Music

and Audience and Applause

The audience is made up of people who have purchased tickets to a performance and sit in the area of the theater called the house. The audience will applaud—clap their hands—when they like a song, joke, dance number, or a riveting monologue.

A is for AUDITION

"I showed up at the audition and realized that you have to sing, tap dance, act, and speak with a British accent. I wanted to run away. All the producers and choreographers were seated at a table and were looking at me. I was so nervous."

—David Alvarez
starred in
Billy Elliot

A short performance to show off the talents of an actor, singer, or dancer. The director, producer, the casting director, and the play's creative team watch the audition to decide if the performer is right for the part. Every actor wants to get a **callback**, which means being asked to return after the first audition.

HEADSHOT A photograph that an actor leaves with the director. His resume, with his name and contact information, is attached to the back.

The DIRECTOR Responsible for the overall artistic vision of a production, and also tells the actors what to do on stage.

Headshot

As I soaked in the scene, it struck me that I was gazing into the open arms of one of my impossible dreams: to be an actor on a Broadway stage! I had reached that moment when all those years of training, practice, and dedication—trying, failing, and trying again—would be put to the ultimate test.

However, what I thought might be a kind of final exam turned out to be the beginning of an even greater lesson. The show that brought me to that stage, *Mail*, only lasted a few short weeks, but with those first steps across the threshold of the Music Box Theatre, I had walked into a tradition, a history, and a community of artists and fellow dreamers, which continues to inspire me to this day.

So welcome to my house, my home, my Broadway! As you take this very special tour, perhaps you too will be ignited by the incredible collaborative magic that gives life and light to the theater.

Brian Stokes Mitchell

O*ne* of the most exciting moments I have experienced in my career was the first time I set foot on a Broadway stage—my own Broadway stage. It was the Music Box Theatre on 45th Street, and the company—cast, crew, musicians, creative team, producers— had gathered on the sidewalk to enter the building after months of rehearsals and out-of-town tryouts. I remember walking into the cool of the theater and looking at the old, brick, back wall now freshly illuminated by the reflected sunlight of the street. A sleeping giant stirred . . . .

Suddenly, a journey of many years was ending with a few short steps, and there I was, looking out into the house that would be my new home. It was an empty space waiting to be filled. There were no lights on the trusses, no scenery in the wings, and no players in the pit, only a thousand vacant seats facing the blank stage we now stood upon. Those seats would be filled in a few short weeks with eager audience members waiting to be entertained, to be moved, to be transported to a world that was both different and the same as their own. Our job was as simple as it was complicated: to breathe life into this space, to animate it with our talents, energies, minds, and hearts.

HARRIET ZIEFERT

LIGHTS ON

A Theatrical Tour from A to Z

BROADWAY

with **BRIAN STOKES MITCHELL**

ILLUSTRATED BY

ELLIOT KRELOFF

Blue Apple Books

Text copyright © 2009 by Harriet Ziefert
Illustrations copyright © 2009 by Elliot Kreloff

All rights reserved / CIP Data is available.
Published in the United States 2009 by

❦ Blue Apple Books, 515 Valley Street, Maplewood, N.J. 07040
www.blueapplebooks.com

Distributed in the U.S. by Chronicle Books
First Edition
Printed in China

ISBN: 978-1-934706-68-8

1 2 3 4 5 6 7 8 9 10

Cover, title page, and page 43 photograph of Brian Stokes Mitchell used by permission:
"Sara Krulwich/The New York Times/Redux"

"I Was Here" © 2001 WB MUSIC CORP., PEN AND PERSEVERANCE and HILLSDALE MUSIC, INC. All rights administered by WB MUSIC CORP.

PLAYBILL™ is a registered trademark of Playbill Incorporated, N.Y.C. All rights reserved.

The Tony Award®, the Tony®, the Tony Award® logo and the Tony Award ® medallion are registered trademarks
of American Theatre Wing, Inc. All rights reserved.

4–

LIGHTS ON BROADWAY

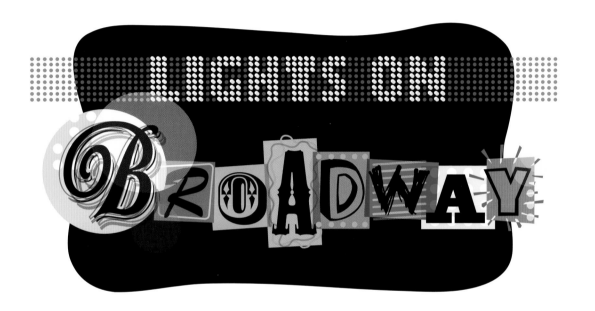

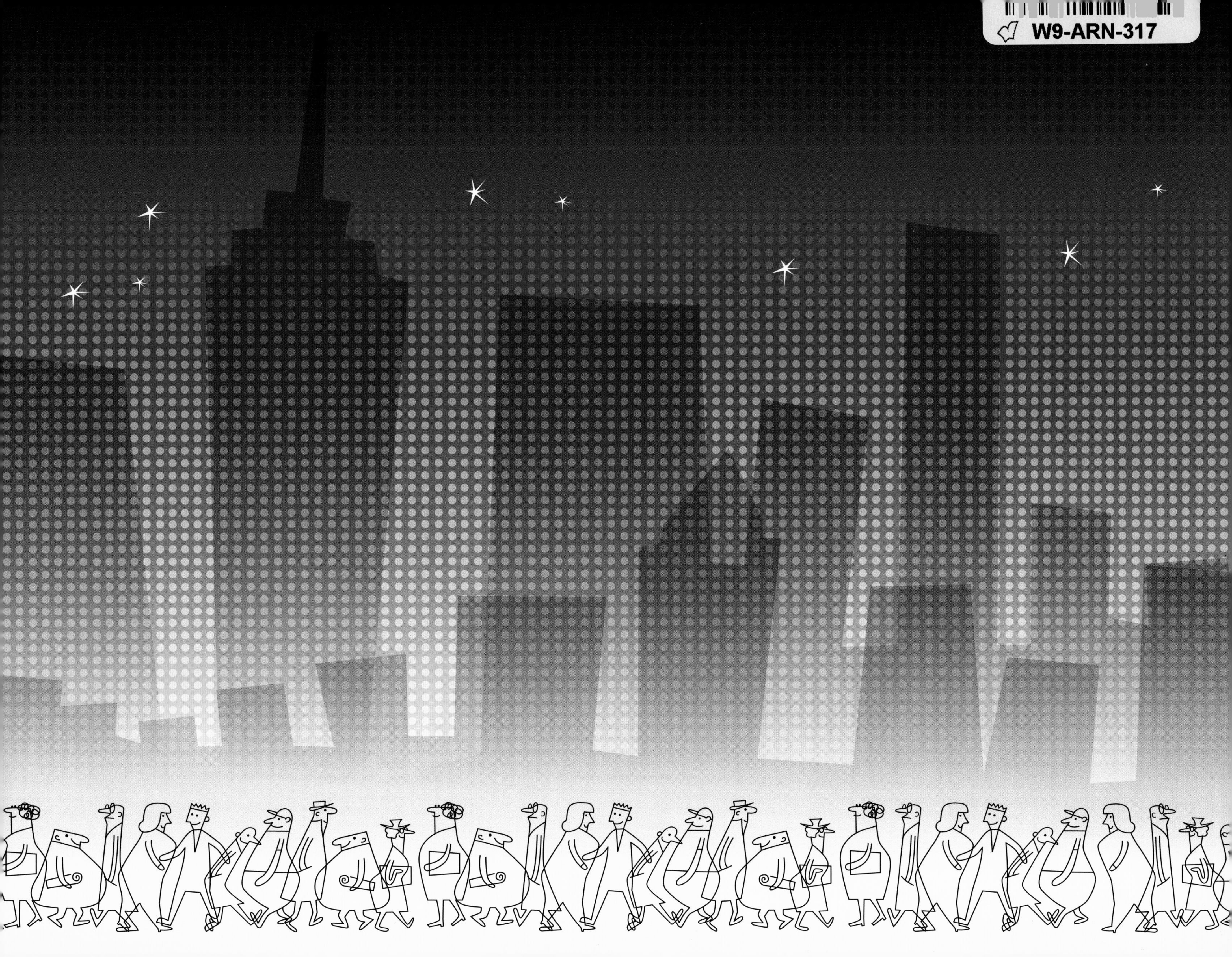

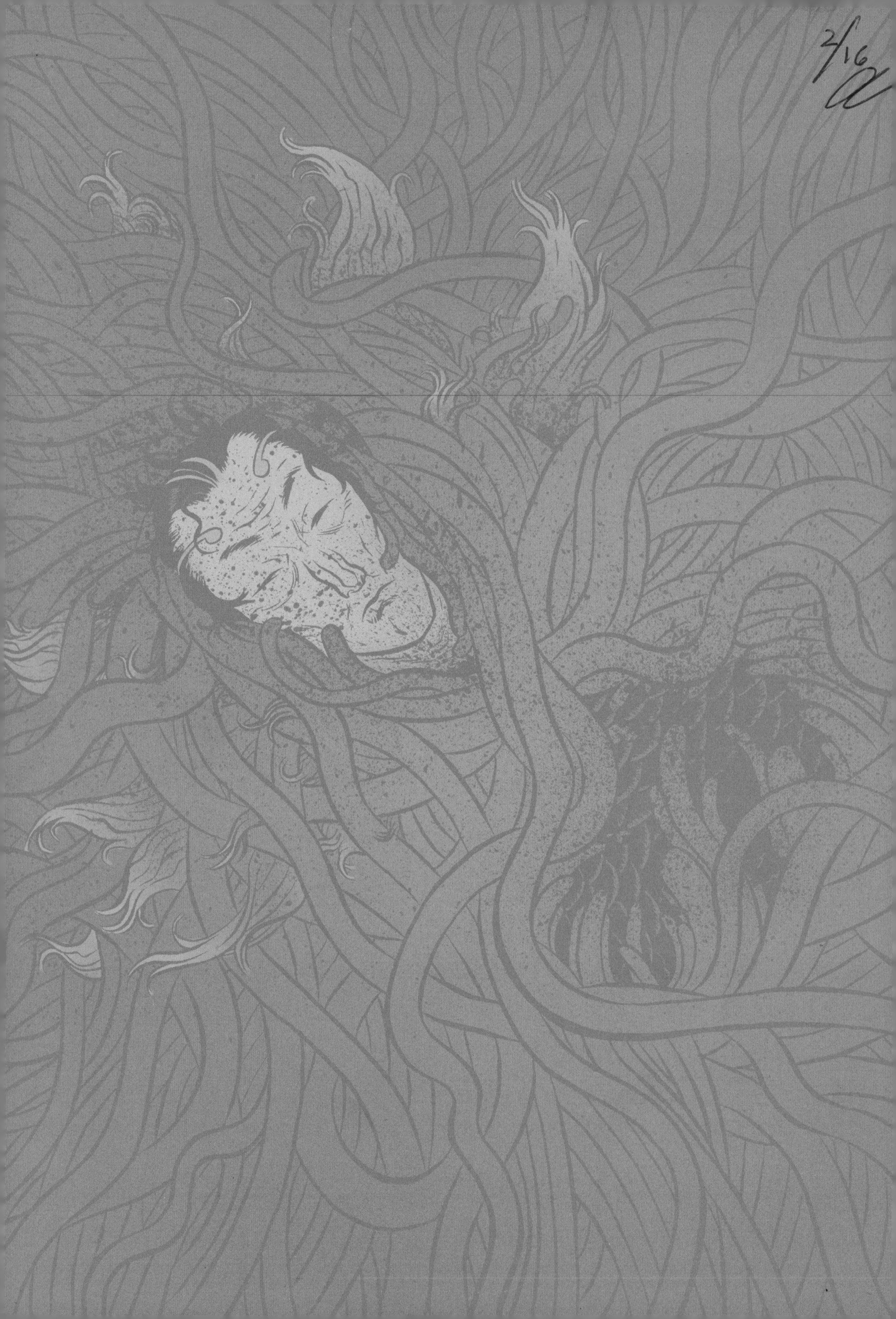